FROM TRIBES
THE MAKING OF FRANCE 500–1799

James B. Collins
Georgetown University

WADSWORTH

THOMSON LEARNING Australia • Canada • Mexico • Singapore • Spain • United Kingdom • United States

WADSWORTH

THOMSON LEARNING™

Executive Editor: David Tatom
Development Editor: Rachel Pilcher
Marketing Manager: Steve Drummond
Project Editor: Rebecca Dodson
   and Cathy Townsend
Production Manager: Lois West
Print/Media Buyer: Lisa Kelley
Permissions Editor: Shirley Webster
Art Designer: Sue Hart

Photo Researcher: Lili Weiner
Copy Editor: Katherine Lincoln
Cover Designer: Sue Hart
Cover Image: Croix, Femmes de Bretagne, 71,
   Peasants Dancing, c. 1630
Cover Printer: Transcontinental Gagne
Compositor: Thompson Type
Printer: Transcontinental Gagne

Printed in Canada
1 2 3 4 5 6 7 640 05 04 03 02 01

For more information about our products,
contact us at:
Thomson Learning Academic Resource Center
1-800-423-0563

For permission to use material from this text,
contact us by:
Phone: 1-800-730-2214
Fax: 1-800-730-2215
Web: http://www.thomsonrights.com

**Library of Congress Cataloging-in-Publication
Data:** 2001099209

ISBN: 0-15-500257-0

Asia
Thomson Learning
60 Albert Street, #15-01
Albert Complex
Singapore 189969

Australia
Nelson Thomson Learning
102 Dodds Street
South Melbourne, Victoria 3205
Australia

Canada
Nelson Thomson Learning
1120 Birchmount Road
Toronto, Ontario M1K 5G4
Canada

Europe/Middle East/Africa
Thomson Learning
Berkshire House
168-173 High Holborn
London WC1 V7AA
United Kingdom

Latin America
Thomson Learning
Seneca, 53
Colonia Polanco
11560 Mexico D.F.
Mexico

Spain
Paraninfo Thomson Learning
Calle/Magallanes, 25
28015 Madrid, Spain

PREFACE

The history of France is an oft-told tale and, like all tales, remade in each telling. My version reflects much of its teller, of his time, and of his contemporaries. A synthetical history relies on the work of countless historians; their ideas, their preconceptions, their problématique, as the French would say, all affect how I have organized, conceived, and written.

I begin with the assumption that France has evolved, and evolves, across time and space. The notion of a single "France," or of a monolithic "French," makes no sense. Fifth-century Gaul contained a confusing mass of tribes—Franks, Burgundians, Goths, etc.—interwoven with the old Gallo-Roman population, themselves primarily Celtic tribes. From that mass of tribes, the people created a modern nation, a process that took over thirteen hundred years. They incorporated, and still incorporate, a steady stream of immigrants. In former times, most of those immigrants came from regions that abutted geographic France. Tens of thousands of French people bear surnames offering witness to the ancient migrations. These names reveal the ties to other modern nations, such as Langlois (the Englishman) or Lallemand (the German), or to groups once subjects of the King of France, but who kept an independent identity, such as Le Breton or Le Flamand (the Fleming). In the early twentieth century, a new wave of immigrants swept in from eastern Europe. Today, the tide comes from the south, across the Mediterranean.

France assimilates these immigrants as it always has, as the ever-evolving synthesis that is "French" identity moves onward. Today, as in the seventh century, when Dagobert I expelled the Jews from his realm, or in the seventeenth, when Louis XIV did the same to the Huguenots, voices call out for exclusion. My tale will show that France may listen for a while to such strident cries, but that the larger, inexorable forces of historical development eventually make them irrelevant. The slogan of today's National Front, "France for the French," calls for an artificially reconstructed "people" to return to a static, isolated place that never existed. The glory of France's history lies in French culture's ability to be energized by the new. The French nation has followed a critical spirit in which the best elements of the past remain vibrant and alive precisely because they are combined with the new. The "French" survive because they do not "preserve" their past by salting it away in a sealed jar kept in the dark cellar of the national house.

French identity evolves slowly, and comprehension of that change, like the Owl of Minerva, flies often at dusk. The documents are silent about a "French" language until 842, when the first text in a language we might call a precursor of French appears. The sureness of speech in the text suggests the language had long been spoken, and doubtless written, too. Three centuries later, people living in what was then called the realm of the King of the Franks abruptly shifted allegiance to a new lord, the King of France, whose title presupposed the existence of France, a place no living person could have easily defined.

Arguments about precise definitions notwithstanding, "France" existed by the twelfth century, and so did its people, the French. Sources still spoke of more tribal identities, like the late-arriving Normans, but texts such as the *Song of Roland* show a clear shift of identity away from terms like "Franks", a tribe, and toward the "franceis," the French, the people of the kingdom of France. In the twelfth or thirteenth century, this loose identity meant little in the face of local and regional identities. The Jewish sources of the period referred always to a northern "kingdom," Sarafeth (France), and a southern one, Provensa.[1] Philip Augustus's enormous expansion of the royal demesne began the process of physical integration of the idealized concept of France, and raised the King of France far above the other princes living in his kingdom.

Culture and politics wove an ever tighter weave. The French language spread to elites in many regions, above all to those in towns. The French state grew in size and strength, developing institutions that gave form to the amorphous mass of desmesnal territories the king had gradually inherited or conquered. Little evidence suggests that ordinary people had much of a conception of France, although the Catholic Church and the state tried to create a sense of unity around the sacerdotal king. Medieval texts all agreed that those living in the valley of the Seine, near Paris, were French, but few could agree on the extent of the term's broader meaning. The war touched off by the English king Henry V's victory at Agincourt (1415) accelerated the move to a different atmosphere: documents of that time speak invariably of "our ancient enemies, the English," whom they contrasted to the "French."

Town elites and the nobility had a clear sense of what they called the commonwealth (*res publica*) of France and of being French by the early fifteenth century. Did the peasants, who made up 80 percent or more of the population, feel the same way? Joan of Arc offers a convenient historical icon for the mythology of Frenchness reaching down to every peasant hut in those times of troubles. Yet the peasants, Joan's story notwithstanding, had very little to do with the commonwealth of France. In most of its representative assemblies, the landlords "represented" the peasantry, which gives us some idea of the structure of society, and of the irrelevance of the concept of "France" to the rural masses.

Joan's story, like many myths, contains a core of truth: national sentiment had developed extensively among the politically active classes, who made of her a convenient example. These men, for they were almost exclusively men, relied on an Aristotelean concept of the "nation": the collectivity of the citizens, who formed the commonwealth of France. The leading citizens, above all the king and adult princes of the royal family, had a responsibility to look after the welfare of this commonwealth. French political discourse always made the critical distinction between a monarch—one man ruling in the interests of the commonwealth—and a tyrant—one man ruling in his own interest. French citizens believed they lived in a monarchy, which was, by definition, a commonwealth.

This commonwealth had a lively political life in the fifteenth and sixteenth centuries. Public political discourse referred again and again to the "public good" (*bien public*), which meant the good of the citizens. To these citizens, France was a nation.

We must be careful about using such a term, however, because most modern Western nations define (or at least claim to define) all native-born or naturalized adults as citizens. The late medieval and early–modern French commonwealth specifically excluded the vast majority of male adults, to say nothing of all adult women. In that sense, "nation" provides an awkward translation for their term commonwealth.

Nor does cultural life provide as much unity as one would like. Local languages and dialects survived all over France well into the nineteenth century. People in western Brittany spoke Breton (Gaelic) and those in the south spoke dialects of Occitan or Provençal, not French. When Louis XIV integrated Alsace into the kingdom, he added a mass of German speakers. Even today, many Alsatian rural dwellers still speak a German dialect as their first language; in fact, the line dividing French and German speakers, which runs just east of Metz, has scarcely budged since the eighth century. The church steeples glimpsed from a train going from Dijon or Paris to Strasbourg make clear the shift in architectural styles from the French to the German. Such boundaries existed even more sharply before the nineteenth century.

The making of the French nation involved far more than politics; thus, this book will integrate social, intellectual, economic, cultural, and political history. A people have a culture, a society, an economic life: all of these elements of their life help to make them a people, and interact endlessly with their political identity. For most of the period discussed here, the social unit was the family; Jean Bodin, the great sixteenth-century political theorist, claimed that the commonwealth consisted of the families, represented by the head of each family.[2] During the Revolution, the family began to give way to the defining unit of modern society, the individual. That shift away from a corporate society—one based on groups (the French used the word *corps*, bodies)—to one based on individualism revolutionized the concept of the nation, by implicitly making every adult French person into a citizen.

I am thus suggesting the path from tribes to nation had four major steps. First, the purely tribal identity (Franks) of the Merovingian and Carolingian empires gave way to a feudal monarchy in the eleventh and twelfth centuries. That monarchy evolved into a political commonwealth by the fourteenth century, a form it kept until the late sixteenth century. The commonwealth shifted form at the end of the sixteenth century, when the king allied with a large group of legal and financial officials to create a monarchy that lay essentially outside the bounds of the old *res publica*. By the middle of the eighteenth century, changes in socioeconomic life made this monarchy a political anachronism, one that the French Revolution would sweep away two generations later.

Much of French history mirrors the history of Europe as a whole. Like the rest of western Europe, France amalgamated elements of Germanic, Classical, and Judao-Christian cultures into a form of European civilization in the tenth and eleventh centuries.[3] That civilization evolved in response to a wide range of influences, from the economic growth of the eleventh through thirteenth centuries, to the demographic crisis of the fourteenth century, and the religious turmoil of the sixteenth. Key political events, such as the governmental crisis of 1346–1358, invariably had direct ties to these non-political factors, such as the Black Death of 1348.

The commonwealth of France provided a mixed form of government in the fifteenth and sixteenth centuries. Economic dislocation, especially after 1570, fed into religious schism and political instability. The great meetings of the Estates General in 1560, 1561, and 1576–1577 sought to create a new form of state, based on the model of a mixed government, much like those taking shape at the same time in England, Holland, and the Polish-Lithuanian Commonwealth. In France, these efforts failed miserably in the cauldron of religious conflict. The commonwealth gave place instead to a new monarchy, often misnamed "absolute," which replaced the "public good" with the "good of the king's service" in its official pronouncements.

This new monarchy rested on an elaborate system of sharing power with ruling elites. The legal class got control of the ever burgeoning state bureaucracy; the nobility kept control of the army; the aristocracy received enormous grants from the Crown, and maintained its stranglehold on key positions in the Church, at Court, and in the army. Just as the demographic and social changes of the early fourteenth century led to the political crisis of 1358, and the religious and cultural upheavals of the middle of the sixteenth century led to the monarchy consolidated by Henry IV, so, too, the social and economic revolution of the early and middle eighteenth century led to the political Revolution of 1789.

That political revolution created the modern nation, but merely embryonic political forms. The modern nation, in its literal sense of the collectivity of all adult citizens (defined automatically by birth in France or by known, legal naturalization procedures), took over a century and a half to emerge fully and completely in France. Women did not become full citizens until 1944, and the Algerian departments of metropolitan France denied the full citizenship of nearly 90 percent of their inhabitants, a situation only resolved when Algeria became independent in 1962.[4]

Politically, our story focuses on the creation of the French monarchy and its demise, and on the rise and fall of the First Republic (1792–1799). From the introduction, which emphasizes the dual creation of "France" and the "French," until the last chapter, which ends with a discussion of issues of culture and identity, this book seeks to synthesize the social, cultural, intellectual, and economic with the political. Relatively little of the book deals with straightforward political narrative, because, like most historians of recent generations, I think the political narrative tells so little of the story of human life. The political does provide a key spine to our story, however, because nations evolve in specific political forms, and usually take shape within the context of political institutional entities, states.

"History" carries multiple meanings: it derives first from the ancient Greek *historein,* meaning to inquire, and so I seek here to inquire about lived life; it derives, too, from the French *histoire,* story, and I seek to tell a story. That story has always a political narrative behind it: battles took place, rulers signed treaties and issued laws. Those political events influenced people's lives and affected every aspect of human life. Yet they tell only a small part of the story, and I simply do not believe, as an historian, that political events respond only to an independent imperative. Politics reflect cultural change, economic evolution, social systems, and demographic reality. The great shifts in politics, like the French Revolution or the events of the 1350s or 1590s, reflect deeper, more fundamental shifts in the basic structures of human life.

My purpose here is to offer readers a small taste of human life in France over thirteen centuries. Their story is one of great historical forces, like mass migration, but of individual genius and its capacity to change society, too. Those great historical forces are composed, as every historian knows, of innumerable individual decisions. Those taking the decision do so for what they believe to be individual reasons; the historian needs to accept their individual reasoning. Yet thousands, often tens of thousands of others reach exactly the same decision at the same time. For the historian, the eternal interplay between the general and the individual offers a perpetual field of inquiry. Studying the great moments of historical change, one is forever struck by the wisdom of W.E.B. Du Bois, who suggested that the sign of a truly great idea is that a lot of people get it at the same time. At key moments in their history, the French people have gotten many such ideas, perhaps most famously on 14 July 1789, when they decided that they were no longer subjects, but citizens, endowed with imprescriptible rights by virtue of their humanity. That day they decided that the "French" were human beings living in "France," a concept so radical that it forever transformed the politics not only of France but of the earth.[5]

Notes

1. No separate "kingdom" existed in the south, which was dominated by regional magnates such as the count of Toulouse. The Jewish community of France had separate chief officials in Rouen, for Sarefath, and in Narbonne, for Provensa.

2. As head of the "family," *paterfamilias,* landlords could thus claim to represent their "dependents." When peasant tenants were serfs, they naturally fit that description, leading to the system in which landlords "represented" peasants. As the peasants obtained their freedom in the late thirteenth and fourteenth centuries, however, the "dependent" justification became harder to sustain. In the end, the third order of the Estates General shifted from being the "communes" (towns) to being the Third Estate, which included all free laic commoners. After 1484, in most parts of France, the peasants thus obtained representation through the Third Estate, not through their landlords in the First and Second Estates (clergy and nobility).

3. Islamic culture, above all in Spain, mediated important elements of Classical civilization into France during the eleventh and twelfth centuries, and added other elements of its own into the European mix, but its influence was not so fundamental as that of the others.

4. This chronology closely follows that of the United States, which granted real citizenship to African-Americans only in the 1960s.

5. As the reference to Du Bois suggests, I do not think the French alone had and acted upon this idea. Throughout the Atlantic World, people had the same idea. They, too, acted upon it, whether in creating new nations in the United States or Haiti, or in trying to revive old ones, as in the United Provinces or the Polish Commonwealth. France's central role in the political system of the time, and its cultural supremacy at the end of the eighteenth century, however, gave events there a resonance that those taking place elsewhere could not match. Newly independent states in nineteenth-century Latin America, like those in twentieth-century Europe

or Africa, often looked, or look to the French tricolor, and not the Stars and Stripes, as their model. Little did most of them know that the French borrowed this idea from the Dutch, who created a tricolor flag for their short-lived republic of 1787.

ACKNOWLEDGMENTS

This book traces a personal journey, as well as the history of France. No work covering so many centuries could possibly rely solely on the author's own research. Instead, it must trace one's intellectual wanderings, following paths cleared by others. My colleagues are legion, and the traces of their labors lay scattered on every page of this text. Yet the text also traces other paths, cleared by different hands. In many parts of France, I have encountered people from all walks of life, of every conceivable background, who have enriched my understanding of France, its history, and its culture. Some of them, like Jean Bart, Bernard Barbiche, or Jean Tanguy, are historians of an earlier generation; others, like Alain Croix, Denis Crouzet, or Robert Descimon, belong to my own; still others, like Ariane Boltanski or Hugues Daussy, belong to the generation to come. Far more of them are not professional historians, but guardians instead of the national memory, which they have generously shared with me.

Special thanks go out here to some in the United States: to colleagues like Andrzej Kaminski, Hisham Sharabi, Jim Shedel, and Bob Weiner, whose support and friendship have meant so much; to the many students and colleagues, too numerous to name, who have read and commented upon parts of this manuscript; to my daughters, mother, sisters, and grandson, who have given me personal sustenance and their love. I would like to thank Georgetown University for several summer research grants and for a sabbatical in 1999–2000 that enabled me to finish the book. At Wadsworth, David Tatom, Rachel Pilcher, Glenna Stanfield, and Cathy Townsend have shown saintly patience, while Lili Weiner did a superb job with the many illustrations and maps. Above all, I want to thank David for assigning Stephen Wasserstein to be my editor. It has been a joy to work with such a true professional. Two Georgetown graduate students, Mériam Belli and Mitra Brewer, deserve thanks for helping me with many of the editorial details, such as the footnotes. Ms. Belli provided invaluable linguistic assistance, checking all translations, and served too as that rarest of colleagues, the good questioner.

If I may, I would offer two dedications. The first is to the people of France, for their years of generosity toward me and my family: may they find here a token of my appreciation. The second is to the countless historians on whose work I have based my text. Like them, I have been inspired by Clio; may she find my labors worthy of her favor.

JIM COLLINS
WASHINGTON, D.C., DECEMBER 2001

Introduction

France made France, and the fatal element of race seems to me secondary. She is the daughter of her freedom. In human progress, the essential part is the living force that we call man. Man is his own Prometheus.

Jules Michelet, *Histoire de France,* preface of 1869[1]

Flying to France from the United States, the traveler often lands at Charles de Gaulle Airport, near the village of Roissy-en-France. How apt a place to begin the history of France, entering an airport named in honor of one of France's leading and most controversial contemporary figures, yet standing hard by a village whose seemingly odd name, Roissy-*en-France,* reminds us of the origins of France. Our story begins here, in the "country" (*pays*) of France, during the dying days of the Western Roman Empire, when Gallo-Romans, Germanic and Gothic tribes, and Huns fought incessantly for control of Gaul. One loose tribal confederation, the Franks, quickly came to dominate the others. The family monarchy created by this tribe maintained a remarkable continuity of control over most of the former Gaul. As Michelet suggests, France made itself out of the conflicting legacies left by Gaul and the Frankish monarchy that succeeded it.

> It was the powerful work of the self on the self, in which France, by its own progress, would transform all of the raw elements. The elements of Roman municipal life, those of the Germanic tribes, of the Celtic clans were abolished, disappeared; in the end, we took away very different, even in large part contrary elements, from all that had preceded them.

From tribes and clans came a nation, the French. I tell here one version of their story of transformation: the long march from Gaul to France.

France offers a superb example of the complex interweaving of the cultural and political fabric of a "nation." At the beginning of the sixth century, the bishops of the former Roman Gaul, almost all of whom were Gallo-Roman aristocrats, deliberately sought to create a legalistic political unity in the regions ruled by the Salian Frank warlord Clovis (d. 511), whom they described as *rex francorum,* King of the Franks.

In 510, the Church Council of Orléans used Roman political thought to vest Clovis with the theoretical stewardship of the political community, or commonwealth. They asked Clovis to add his *auctoritas* to their decisions because he was "such a great king and lord." By asserting that Clovis had *auctoritas,* the supreme power of the commonwealth, the bishops preserved two exceptionally important concepts. First, by insisting that Clovis had *auctoritas,* they necessarily assumed the existence of a commonwealth, in direct inheritance from the Roman commonwealth in Gaul. Second, they kept alive the concept of the individual component of the commonwealth, the citizen. The constant insistence of the learned men of the sixth through twelfth centuries on the existence of such *auctoritas,* and thus of a commonwealth, provided the ultimately unbreakable threads of continuity. One might say that this political tradition served as the weft to the warp of culture.

The Roman commonwealth tradition lived on, in the *auctoritas* of the "King of the Franks." This commonwealth gradually changed names. The few surviving sixth-century documents refer to Gaul, but gradually writers came to use a new term, *Francia,* land of the Franks, which developed into the name for the kingdom ruled by the descendants of the Carolingian Charles the Bald. In 987, the Capetians inherited the title King of the Franks, and the somewhat artificial, yet legally real kingdom attached to the title. Slowly, their *Francia* came to take on a new meaning. By the twelfth century, *Francia* meant France, the land of the *franceis,* the French.

In the twelfth century, no political identification of *Francia* or France with any sort of "nation" could have made sense. The culturally distinct south belonged to the legal commonwealth of France, yet literary sources always made the distinction between "France," essentially north of the Loire, and what the Jewish chronicles called Provensa, in the south. Even cultural France did not necessarily coincide with effective political control. Normandy and eastern Brittany, to cite only the most obvious examples, were French in the cultural sense, but had the same tenuous legal and political connection to the kingdom as the southern principalities.

When did France become a nation? That is our fundamental question. The answer suggested here differs radically from the traditional ones. Adrian Hastings has argued that the English word "nation," carrying its essential modern meaning, existed in the fourteenth century; he extrapolates the logical conclusion that England, the nation, must have existed then, too.[2] I suggest that precisely in the fourteenth and fifteenth centuries France, like England, became a genuinely coherent national commonwealth ruled by a king. I am not suggesting France became a "nation," in the nineteenth-century sense of that word, because a modern nation requires that citizenship be extended to the mass of the population.[3]

What leads me to make such an assertion? During the twelfth century, two new entities came into being: France and the French. By the late twelfth century, the Norman poet Wace could write that "what once was Gaul is today France." Another twelfth-century poet, the anonymous author ("Turoldus") of *The Song of Roland,* reveals the emergence of a new group, the *franceis,* his preferred term for the men of Charlemagne's realm. These two poets bear witness to the emergence of literary French, which paralleled the revival of the concept of political citizenship in the rapidly growing towns.[4] Turoldus's verses make clear that the "French," the collective descendants of the many tribes and clans of the old Frankish lands, existed first as a cultural identity. The political thus emerged from the cultural, which, in turn, had developed within the somewhat artificial, yet legally real commonwealth that became France. The existence of the commonwealth of Francia partly conditioned the creation of the culturally defined *franceis*.

The conquests of Philip Augustus and Louis VIII created the critical central mass necessary for the mental and practical reemergence of a genuine political commonwealth focused on the king. Louis IX's (d. 1270) substitution of trial by inquest for trial by ordeal and his abolition of private war (that is, his assertion of the state's right to a monopoly on organized violence) however ineffective in practice, had profound theoretical implications for the assertion of royal judicial supremacy. His rapid canonization provided an essential spiritual totem for this new French commonwealth. The fourteenth-century meetings of local, regional, and "general" estates, representatives of the citizens of the commonwealth, to deal with a series of issues related to the "public good," makes abundantly clear the broad consensus among elites that a commonwealth of France existed. This commonwealth, which the elites understood to be the collective group of citizens, took political shape in a monarchy, in which the king and the citizens oversaw the common good.

France had three core elements by about 1400:

1. The "nation" of the French, united by a steadily more common culture and sense of identity.

2. A state, to provide form and a means of action for the commonwealth.

3. An imagined unity, constructed around the figure of the King.

France did not have a clearly defined single commonwealth, in that the "general" estates still met in two separate bodies, for north and south, and in that the citizens of the territories ruled by royal princes, such as the duchy of Burgundy, still thought of their lords' lands as their commonwealth. In the fifteenth century, two dramatic developments shifted the structure of the elaborate pentagon of power. First, the "nation"—the population as a whole—slowly *began* to identify itself as a political unit coterminous with a commonwealth. Joan of Arc strikingly illustrates the new broader and deeper sense of being "French," which she tied directly to the King of France. Second, the king effectively asserted his stewardship of a single commonwealth: starting in 1484, general estates met for the entire kingdom.

The second development became obvious only in the sixteenth century, when the king began to share stewardship of the commonwealth with an institutional state. The stunning violence of the Wars of Religion (1562–1628), the massive outbreaks of popular rebellion, and the continuity of popular political participation led French legal elites to ally with the king by means of state institutions. In allying with the king, they rebuffed the provincial nobility's effort to have France follow the path of neighboring polities like England, the Low Countries, and Poland–Lithuania. The nobles wanted the king to share stewardship of the commonwealth with the collective group of citizens, by means of a pyramid of representative assemblies and local courts they would control. The peculiar French solution meant the state—that is the king and his officials—and not the citizens would protect the common good, a phrase they conveniently replaced by the seemingly innocuous yet ultimately sinister "good of the king's service."

Henry IV (1589–1610) served as the mediator of this process, a veritable godfather of the modern state. He and his successors largely returned "France" to the world of culture, where it would remain until the beginning of the eighteenth century. Louis XIV thought of his kingdom and of the French state, not of a French commonwealth. Yet in the depths of despair, driven to the brink of humiliation and defeat in 1709, even he responded with an appeal to something implicitly above the state and the king: "the French," that is, the nation. In the eighteenth century, French political discourse gradually returned to old vocabulary of the common good, yet the commonwealth had now become the "nation," a word whose definition long remained contested, as we shall see.

I am thus suggesting the following chronology in the creation of France:

1. The Gallo-Roman aristocratic bishops identify Clovis as King of the Franks, and assign to him the *auctoritas* of the former Gaul.

2. Gradual transformation of the mixed population of much of the former Gaul into a culturally distinct people, evident in the use of the word "French".[5]

3. Clear emergence in the twelfth century of the idea of a "France," whose inhabitants are the French (*franceis*).

4. Territorial expansion of the royal demesne and institutions of legal unity, between the reigns of Philip Augustus and Philip the Fair, giving centripetal force to the political commonwealth of France; Louis IX provides the moral force in the emergence of a state-centered justice.

5. Regulation of the commonwealth through the use of estates (representatives of the citizens of the commonwealth) by Philip IV and his successors.

6. Some popular identification with "France" in the final stages of the Hundred Years' War (1415–1453).

7. Integration of the nation, the commonwealth, and the state in France during a long struggle (fifteenth to eighteenth century).

The first three chapters concern the evolution from the tribal kingdoms of the Merovingians to the national commonwealth of France. Chapter 4 examines the crucial years of transition to a national state, between the death of Saint Louis and the consolidation of the family monarchy into a personal one (*c.* 1500). Chapters 5–11 deal with the French nation,[6] united in a state that gave political form to their commonwealth, while Chapters 12–15 examine the initial French attempt to turn a national state into a nation–state.

The Making of France

From Gaul to the Land of the Franks (*Francia*)

> [W]e are faced with a hundred, a thousand different Frances of long ago, yester-
> day or today. Let us then accept this truth, this wealth of material, this pressing
> invitation to which it is neither unpleasant nor even very dangerous to succumb.[7]
>
> Fernand Braudel

What is France? We easily locate the clear and seemingly fixed boundaries of contemporary France: north of the Pyrenees and the Mediterranean, west of the Rhine,
northwest of the Alps, east of the Atlantic and the English Channel. Only France's
northern border lacks clarity, having no topographic marker. The Romans called
this area *Gallia* (Gaul), their derogatory adaptation of the Greek word, *Keltoi,* for the
three hundred Celtic tribes of the region. The Latin derivative, *Galatus,* easily led to
gallus (rooster), the bird still used to symbolize France. The Romans left many legacies to France: the roots of the French language, the cultivation of the vine, Christianity, the general boundaries of France—the Ocean, the Rhine, the Alps, and the
Pyrenees. The Roman administrative districts provide the fundamental framework
of France's modern departments: nearly half of today's departmental capitals also
served as the chief administrative town of a Roman *pagus* (*pays*).

In the fourth and fifth centuries, Germanic and Gothic tribes entered into
Roman Gaul: the Ostrogoths in Provence, the Visigoths in the southwest, the Burgundians in the east, the Alamanni in the southern Rhine valley, and the Franks in
the north and northeast. The last four of these tribes gave their names to a region.
Thus, the area near Narbonne became Gothia; east central France became Burgundy;
the Upper Rhineland became Alamannia; and Cologne's hinterland became the first
Francia, named after the so-called Rhenish Franks who settled there.[8]

Fifth-century Roman sources inform us that one Frankish *kuning* (war chief),
Chlodio, captured Arras and Cambrai, which straddle the current Franco–Belgian
border, in the middle of the century.[9] The late sixth-century bishop Gregory of Tours
wrote that "some claim that from his [Chlodio's] line came the king Merovich, of
whom Childeric was the son." The seventh-century chronicler Fredegar suggested
that the wife of this duke Chlodio had a sexual encounter with a "Quinotaur" (sea
monster) while she was swimming: he implies that the son born to this union,
Merovich, gave his name to the Merovingian dynasty.[10] Frankish legend here closely
parallels that of other peoples; the Mongols believed Genghis Khan descended from a
similar union of woman and beast, and many "kings" in Greek mythology descended
from liaisons between a god and a mortal woman. The supernatural union made
royal "blood" special. In Merovingian society, men of royal blood carried an obvious
mark of physical distinction: alone among men, they wore their hair long. Their contemporaries called them "the long-haired kings." People took this sign so seriously
that the simplest way to discredit a potential rival was to cut his hair.

The Quinotaur fable aside, we do have important archeological evidence about
Childeric, supposed son of Merovich, because of the 1653 discovery of his grave at

Late Roman Gaul.

Tournai.[11] The grave included typical Frankish objects: swords, a Frankish axe, gold jewelry. It also held other, Roman objects: a treasure trove of Byzantine coins, a brooch denoting high Roman military office, and a signet ring, inscribed *Childerici Regis* ("by Childeric the king"). On the seal, "King" Childeric wears his hair long, in the fashion of Frankish rulers, sports a Roman military uniform, and bears a lance. Childeric's grave thus provides us with evidence of the extensive interaction of Roman and Frankish elements in fifth-century northern Gaul. Recent excavations have shown that Childeric's retainers followed the common Germanic custom of surrounding a chief's grave with the bodies of warhorses slaughtered for the purpose.[12]

Seal of Childeric I, father of Clovis.

At the time of his death (*c.* 481), the Roman Empire in the West had ceased to exist (476), yet Childeric obviously placed great value on the Roman insignia he had been given. The Byzantine coins alert us to the continued close relationship between the Eastern Roman (Byzantine) Empire and the barbarian rulers of western Europe. As Gundobad, late fifth-century king of the Burgundians, put it: "We admire titles conferred by the Emperor more than our own."[13] He and the other barbarian kings always deferred to the Emperor in Constantinople; indeed, many such kings sought, usually without success, to ally themselves to the Byzantine Emperor by marriage.

Childeric's son, Clovis (d. 511), founded a Frankish tribal kingdom in Roman Gaul.[14] Following in his father's footsteps, he moved south at the end of the fifth century, defeating the last Roman military commander of Soissons, and capturing the small town of Paris (*c.* 486). Just as the lands occupied by the Goths and Burgundians had taken their names, so, too, the lands near Soissons and Paris now adopted the name of their conquerors: *Francia* or "land of the Franks."[15] Thus the villages of Roissy, Puiseaux, Châtenay, Mareil, Bonneuil, and Belloy today carry the suffix "en-France" because they serve as eternal witnesses for the birth of the nation of France.

Clovis, his second wife Clotilde, and the holy woman Geneviève of Paris played the central roles in the foundation of this Francia. Clovis provided three key elements that enabled the Franks to complete the 750-year transformation of most of Roman Gaul into the kingdom of France:

1. A genuine kingship, combining military leadership and the sacerdotal qualities of a Frankish *kuning* with the political authority of a Roman ruler.

2. A strong tie between the Frankish king and Catholicism, which became the official state church under the direct aegis of the king.

3. A coherent principality, Francia, focused on the Paris region.

The Merovingian superiority he created within the Germanic world helped establish the tradition of Frankish cultural and political preeminence that lasted for many centuries. The substitution of the term *irteilen*, the Frankish word for that world's most important rulership function—judgment—for older words used initially by the Bavarians, the Alamanni, and even the Saxons, illustrates this political preeminence.

From the Land of the Franks to France

The Merovingian Kingdoms

> *Once Clovis was dead, his four sons, Theuderic, Chlodomir, Childebert, and Lothaire* [Clothaire], *inherited his kingdom and divided it equally among themselves.*[16]

> Gregory of Tours

Clovis founded a Frankish monarchy on the lands of Roman Gaul. Contemporary documents, like the *Life of Saint Geneviève* (*c.* 520) and letters sent by Theodoric, king of the Ostrogoths (*c.* 507) gave Clovis the title King of the Franks (*rex francorum*).[17] Kings used this official title until the beginning of the thirteenth century. Clovis's four sons divided the Frankish lands at his death and then finished up his conquests. They definitively subdued the Visigoths, conquered Burgundy and Thuringia, and obtained Provence from the Ostrogoths through diplomacy. From the middle of the sixth century until the start of the eighth century, the Merovingians ruled most of the former Roman Gaul as well as some regions beyond the Rhine.[18]

The Merovingians dominated western European politics and culture in the sixth and seventh centuries. The Franks had the best military force; their kings collected taxes, based on written registers, supported local churches and monasteries, and issued laws. Their monasteries produced, by far, the largest portion of the surviving western European manuscripts of this period. This Merovingian empire, made up usually of several kingdoms—the two chief ones called Neustria, centered on Paris; and Austrasia, centered on Reims and Metz—belonged more to a family than to any individual.[19] In the late seventh century, two factors combined to undermine this Merovingian political dominance. First, the gradual decline of the Gallo-Roman aristocratic families undermined institutional solidity because they had provided both the political culture and state administration. Second, Clovis's descendants followed his example in making intra-family murders a major policy tool. Husbands and wives murdered each other; kings and queens, and would-be kings and queens, murdered their own children and grandchildren, to say nothing of stepchildren, nephews and nieces, aunts and uncles, and brothers and sisters. These murders created an absence of adult male leadership, which allowed powerful Germanic aristocrats from the region between the Rhine and the Meuse to usurp state power. The merger of two of the most powerful such families created a new family, first called the Pippinids or Arnulfings, but known to us as the Carolingians. This family used the office of Mayor of the Palace of the kingdom of Austrasia to seize effective power at the end of the seventh century.[20] In 751, Pippin the Short deposed the last Merovingian, Childeric III, and became King of the Franks. In 754, Pope Stephen II came to Saint-Denis in Paris to crown Pippin and his sons, Charles and Carloman. Thus the Carolingian dynasty took royal power with the full sanction of the Church, renewing the alliance begun by Clovis.

The Carolingian Empire

When the Emperor has completed his vengeance, He addressed the bishops of France, And those of Bavaria and Germany.[21]

The Song of Roland

The eighth-century shift from the Merovingians to the Carolingians introduced a temporary shift in the Frankish heartland, from Neustria to Austrasia. Charlemagne (768–814), who brought Frankish supremacy to its widest extent, reasserted the Rhenish roots of the Franks by making Aachen (Aix-la-Chapelle), a town slightly north of Cologne, the old center of the Rhenish Franks, his capital. In that sense, Charlemagne, although a figure of enormous importance in French royal iconography and legend, was more of a European ruler than a French one. In the Middle Ages, German royalty would (rightly) claim his legacy quite as much as would the French.

Charlemagne initially divided up his empire among his three sons, but the death of his eldest son changed those plans. When Charlemagne died (814), he left Italy to Pippin and everything else to Louis, who soon seized Italy from Pippin's son. In 816, Pope Stephen IV crowned Louis "Emperor Augustus, by the grace of divine Providence." French kings later sought to emphasize their close ties to the two Emperors. With the exception of the interlude 1515 to 1610, every King of France from the accession of Charles V in 1364 until the overthrow of Louis-Philippe in the Revolution of 1848 bore the name Charles or Louis.

Emperor Louis the Pious, like his father, and like the Merovingian kings before them, felt obliged to divide his realm among his sons. Louis had three sons by his first wife; he initially gave them each a share. When the Emperor took a second wife, Judith of Welf, and she bore a fourth son (Charles the Bald), civil war soon followed. After Louis's death (840), three of the sons divided the empire at the famous Treaty of Verdun (843). They created three kingdoms. Louis the German received *Francia orientalis,* the land of the East Franks and of the affiliated Germanic tribes, such as the Saxons and the Bavarians. Lothaire, along with the title of Emperor, obtained the family homeland around Metz and a kingdom that stretched from Italy and Provence up through the Franche-Comté and Alsace to the Low Countries. The third son, Charles, became king of *Francia occidentalis,* the land of the West Franks. Within a century, the term Francia had come to refer almost exclusively to this last kingdom, *Francia occidentalis.*[22]

Although the many ninth-century agreements among Carolingian rulers constantly reconfigured the empire, the Treaty of Verdun's geographic legacy eventually endured. The eastern border of the medieval kingdom of France followed the Verdun boundary, running down the line of the four rivers: the Escaut (Scheldt), Meuse, Saône, and Rhône. In 987, when Louis V died without a direct heir, Hugh Capet, duke of the Franks, seized the throne. Hugh's family, like the Merovingian rulers of Neustria, relied on a power base close to Paris and the Seine valley. When Hugh became King of the Franks in 987, contemporaries naturally associated the name *Francia* with his family possessions, in the region immediately around Paris.

The legacy of the Merovingians and Carolingians suggested two additional meanings for *Francia*: the kingdom focused on the valleys of the Seine and Loire rivers, and the much larger area once ruled by Clovis's descendants and then by the great Charlemagne. For centuries, medieval chroniclers, like Richer, tried to tie this larger kingdom directly to Roman Gaul, and to make of "France" the legitimate heir of that ancient territorial unit.[23] Richer's Gaul is limited in the east by the Rhine, in the west by the Pyrenees, in the north by the English Channel, and in the south by the Mediterranean.

By the twelfth century, the "land of the Franks" evolved into "France." Different types of sources all agree on this evolution. Vernacular French had always used the term "France" as a translation for *Francia,* land of the West Franks, but tenth- and eleventh-century texts of all kinds suggest a shift away from the identification with the tribe, the Franks, and toward the primacy of the geographic identification of "France"/*Francia.*[24] The first official document using the term "King of France" (*rex Franciae*), a text drawn up by Louis VI's chancery for the Pope, came only in 1119.

Did this *Francia* or "France" still mean "land of the Franks?" The greatest vernacular French text of the eleventh and twelfth centuries, *The Song of Roland,* provides powerful evidence that it did not. *The Song of Roland* poetically preserves the memory of the 778 annihilation of the Frankish rearguard by Basques (whom the poet turns into Muslims) in the pass at Roncesvalles on the Spanish side of the Pyrenees. Although we have evidence of many early oral versions of the poem, the oldest surviving written version of the main story dates from between 1095 and 1135. Thus, the poem offers a mixture of the myth and history of the intervening three hundred fifty years.[25]

Because the poem interweaves the political and social reality of the eighth through early twelfth centuries, it naturally assigns different meanings to "France." Some parts of the poem use the term to describe Charlemagne's empire (excluding Italy and Saxon lands), with its capital at Aix (Aachen); many verses use the phrase "Aix-en-France," an obvious reference to the eighth-century reality of the Frankish state.[26] Another passage roughly describes a mixture of the kingdom of the West Franks created at Verdun, with its southeastern boundary at Besançon, just east of the Saône river, yet its northeastern one at "Senz" (Xanten, on the Rhine, north of

Cologne), in an area long outside the France of 1100.[27] In the Baligant section, the poet refers to the "men of Lorraine"; in Charlemagne's day, men from this region, and the Emperor *himself* was one of them, would simply have been called Franks.

Elsewhere, the *Song*, both in its description of battle formations and in its listing of members of the council of judgment sitting at the final trial of its villain, Ganelon, suggests that France ends just south of the Loire. The poet implies that the "French" are surrounded by Bretons and Normans on the west, by Poitevins and Auvergnats on the southwest and south, by the Burgundians on the southeast, by the Alamanni in the east, and by the Flemings in the north.

The poet here alerts us to a fundamental political shift of the twelfth and thirteenth centuries. The Loire had long marked a key line of demarcation between the genuinely Frankish area and the more "Roman" south. Jewish sources make quite clear the division between what the 1007 chronicle of Jacob bar Jeqouthiel of Rouen calls "Sarefath" (the Hebrew name for *Francia*), by which they meant the north, and Provensa, the South. They called the south *Provensa*.[28] French sources, like *Roland*, long did the same; as late as the thirteenth century, *The Song of the Narbonnais* tells us: "They came to Orléans and crossed the bridge, At which point they entered France." This definition harks back to the old boundary between the kingdom of Aquitaine and that of the Franks, itself mirroring earlier Roman provincial boundaries.[29]

The seemingly tenuous connections of eleventh-century Aquitaine and Gothia to the King of the Franks should not deceive use. Although the counts of Barcelona or Toulouse, whose lands originally belonged to the Visigothic kingdom, scarcely recognized the king's authority after the dynastic switch of 987, the dukes of Aquitaine and Burgundy were his close personal relatives. Given these close family relations, one can hardly speak of a complete estrangement between the two regions. Rather we can see the Capetians asserting the ancient tribal and familial unities of Clovis's time. Under his overall, rather loose tutelage, his close personal relatives, the dukes of Aquitaine and Burgundy, ruled over their "peoples," who inhabited the areas conquered by Clovis's sons. The Rhenish Franks, in contrast, had shifted allegiance to the German Emperor, now a member of the Saxon royal house.

The first great shift toward the creation of France took place in the twelfth century. I would identify four critical steps. First, as Wace tells us, vernacular language came to associate "France" with what had been "Gaul." Second, vernacular language, such as *The Song of Roland*, began to refer to the inhabitants of the kingdom as the *franceis*. Third, the agreement between Philip I and Pope Paschal II (1106) that gave independence to the "Gallic" Church furthered a strong sense of identity among the main literate group of the time, the French clergy. Fourth, Philip Augustus (1180–1223), by adding the great fiefs, such as Anjou and Normandy, to the royal demesne raised the King of France to a level of power that placed him high above even his greatest vassals. These gains so enlarged the royal demesne that they allowed Philip's grandson, Louis IX, to enforce the idea that his justice extended to all of juridical France, and not merely to the royal demesne. That step marked the definitive resolution of any debates about the nature of "France." The royal expulsions of Jews illustrate the changes: in 1182 Philip Augustus expelled Jews only from his demesne lands; in 1306 Philip the Fair expelled them from the entire kingdom.

From the Kingdom of France to France

It seemed to me that from this work in which, so to speak, each century would tell its own story and speak with its own voice, there must result the true history of France, the history which would never be rewritten, would belong to no individual writer, the history which all would consult as the repository of our national archives.[30]

Augustin Thierry, 1839

The France of history fell together with the French State, which was the growth of centuries.[31]

Lord Acton

Richer's description had tremendous historical staying power: during the French Revolution, Georges Danton and others would pick up the Pyrenees–Mediterranean–Rhine limits as the "natural" boundaries of France. Today's European France, which closely resembles Richer's "Gaul," evolved slowly from the medieval France laid out in the Treaty of Verdun The county of Barcelona slipped away effectively in 987 and legally by 1259. Flanders fell away in the late Middle Ages, although not legally until 1526. In the east, the King of France gradually acquired the Gallic lands of Lothaire's kingdom: Lyon in 1292; Dauphiné, by inheritance in 1349; Provence, also by inheritance, in 1482; the three bishoprics of Metz, Toul, and Verdun in 1559; Bresse and adjacent lands in 1601; the county of Burgundy in 1679; Alsace in the 1680s; and Lorraine in 1765. Two legal parts of the kingdom, the duchies of Burgundy and Brittany, became part of the royal demesne by inheritance (Burgundy in 1477), and by marriage and treaty (Brittany, 1490). Roussillon and Béarn became French between 1589 and 1659, while French Flanders and other northern enclaves rejoined the kingdom a generation later. The mid-nineteenth-century Italian Wars of Liberation added the county of Nice and those parts of Savoy not conquered by Henry IV in 1600–1601.

In recent times, Germany ruled Alsace and part of Lorraine from 1871–1919 and again from 1940–1944/1945. The traveler wandering through the charming villages of Alsace must remind him- or herself that the ubiquitous Monuments to the Dead of World War I, a focal point of all French villages, honor Alsatian soldiers who fought for the German army, not the French one. Certain overseas territories, such as Martinique and Guadeloupe, have become part of metropolitan France; Algeria held such status before it achieved independence in 1962. The reader must remain alert to this shifting geographic France, because the text will focus on the France contemporaneous to the events being described.

The text will also refer implicitly to a second France, the France of the imagination. That France, too, varied over time. Flanders remained part of this imagined France, even after it broke its feudal ties to the kingdom. Other regions, such as Alsace, did not form part of this imagined France until long after they became legally French. Some Romance-speaking areas, such as the Midi, resisted full identification with "France:" well into the twentieth century, country people in the south spoke

Occitan or Provençal, just as those in the Auvergne spoke Auvergnat. Breton peasants spoke Gaelic and Alsatian ones a German dialect as recently as the 1940s.

The litany of territorial accretion partly disguises the fundamental question: when did the kingdom ruled by the King of France become something we might legitimately call "France?" I think that "France" as a meaningful cultural and political entity existed by the 1370s, when Charles V reconquered the provinces lost by his father to the English. Charles V consciously sought to have the leading scholars in Paris, like Nicolas Oresme, translate the great works of Classical antiquity into French. He also added to the existing judicial system the two critical missing elements of a state that could enforce political unity on a national community, a standing army and a fiscal system to pay for it.

Many elements encouraged the growth of a true sentiment of "national" unity, whether among the legal scholars who invented the Salic Law of succession to the throne in the beginning of the fifteenth century, or among ordinary peasants, whose extraordinary voice, Joan of Arc, provided a living embodiment for "national" sentiment in her own time and for centuries to come.[32] The final stages in the creation of a real "France" took place between 1465 and 1527, when the remarkable consolidation of the royal family, which brought the end of the essentially independent states ruled by the family's junior branches, created a unified commonwealth. Yet people thought themselves French long before that; Charles VII's government could appeal for support against "our ancient enemies, the English." If he appealed to the "French," he must have thought they existed. His words raise for us a second crucial question: who are the French?

The Birth of a People: The French

Their eyes are faint and pale, with a glimmer of greyish blue. Their faces are shaven all round, and instead of beards they have thin moustaches which they run through with a comb. . . . in their childhood [they have] a passion for war more normally associated with maturity. If by chance the number of their enemies or the weakness of their position causes their downfall, then only death will defeat them, never fear. They remain in their places, undefeated, and their courage survives, one may say, until they draw their last breath.[33]

Sidonius Apollinaris, fifth-century Gallo-Roman writer,
speaking of the Salian Franks

One cannot find people more dirty or more vile; ignorant of cleanliness, they only wash once or twice a year; in cold water. They never clean their clothes which they put on once forever until they fall apart. They shave their beards which come back each time in an ugly and rude fashion.[34]

Ibrahim ibn Yaqub, tenth-century Jewish merchant

Legal scholars and some royal councilors knew roughly where the medieval kingdom of France lay, but the first map to show a "kingdom of France" appeared only in

1525. People who lived in this kingdom knew that their lord was the King of France, but they also knew that not all of the King of France's subjects lived in his kingdom.[35] If that were so, then what made someone "French," a term virtually everyone in sixteenth-century France would have accepted as describing the group of people who lived in the kingdom.

Here again we must go back to the Romans. Roman Gaul had a population consisting of a broad mix of three hundred mainly Celtic tribes, to which the Romans added another layer of population, especially in the south and in the towns. Second-century Roman Gaul probably had 10 million people in it, most of them Celts. The Romans expanded existing towns like Orléans or Bordeaux and created major cities of their own, such as Lyon and Autun, whose arenas could seat as many as 35,000 spectators. The population fluctuated wildly in the final days of the Roman Empire, both due to the "barbarian" invasions of the fourth and fifth centuries and to the devastating plagues of the sixth century. The best estimates suggest the population declined 75 percent between the second and the late sixth century, with a further decline in the seventh and early eighth centuries, followed by an increase in the late eighth century.

The Franks early-on created legendary ancestors for themselves. As we saw above, Fredegar had Clovis descend from a supernatural union. He suggested the Franks descended from the Trojans, borrowing directly from Virgil. A century later, the anonymous author of the *Liber Historiae Francorum* told a slightly different version of the same story, one that had great staying power in the Middle Ages. This legend made of the Franks a chosen people, like the Romans, and heir to the fallen imperial mantle of their predecessors.[36]

Here the three great traditions whose synthesis formed the basis for European and French civilization each played a role. The basic myths taken from the Romans interacted with Germanic cultural traditions, particularly the special connection of a Germanic war leader (*kuning*) always had to the gods. His band of warriors, taken primarily from his kindred, felt themselves a "chosen," blessed few. The Judao-Christian tradition strengthened such sentiments, through comparisons with the Chosen People of the Old Testament, a model that would remain extremely strong in European political mythology into the seventeenth century. Moreover, chroniclers often made such ties explicit: Fredegar claimed that the Trojan ancestors of the Franks themselves descended from "Cetthin, the grandson of Noah."[37]

Fredegar and Gregory do not seem to make much sense. Roman sources, cited by Gregory, make clear that the Franks lived in the Rhineland, not in Pannonia (modern-day Hungary) during the fourth century. Yet the myths related by Gregory and Fredegar tell a larger truth, if we can bring together the methodologies of history and anthropology. As Joanne Rappaport has written, the Western tradition seeks "chronological or linear narratives," yet other traditions, such as the Germanic one that formed part of the cultural world of Gregory or Fredegar, often are encoded in "entirely non-chronological fashion." Rappaport continues:

> And this also explains the power of the mythic images so frequently encountered in non-Western narrations of the past. It is not that indigenous peoples have no sense of the flow of time, nor that they are unable to dis-

tinguish fact from fiction . . . but that fictive and fantastic images may help them to reflect more fully upon the real. By using mythic or cyclical images to highlight the "holes" in the historical memory, they emphasize more powerfully the importance of the past because it is more readily recognizable. Moreover . . . they link the past to the future, providing a template for understanding where we came from, but also where we are going.[38]

Gregory and Fredegar drew heavily on a key component of the "Western" tradition, its Roman sources, but they also drew upon Germanic myth. Hans J. Hummer offers a nuanced reading of their stories that can help us get a clearer sense of the origins of the Franks, and the French:

> By comparison to what is known of Frankish origins along the Rhine in the third century, the story is preposterous. However, when one considers the movement of central and eastern European groups west towards the Rhine, and the archeological evidence from Childeric's tomb [which contained Danubian jewelry], the Pannonian origin-myth perhaps encapsulates the memory of the complex ethnic and political transformations, which had recently taken place beneath the static Frankish rubric.[39]

If we make a Rappaportian escape from the prison of chronology, then the combined elements tell a beautifully simple story. The initial meaning of "frank" in late antiquity was simply "brave" or "fierce" and had a relation to the *franzisca,* a form of war axe "Franks" carried. The earliest sources suggest that the war bands living in the Rhineland, headed by Frankish "kinglets," as Gregory calls them, were not ethnically homogenous, but heterogeneous. The early myths make of these heterogeneous elements a homogenous one, a traditional function of stories that give unified identity to communities.

As Hummer suggests, Fredegar tells the story in reverse. He begins with the Trojan myth, in which King Frigas, the brother of Aeneas, led a group of Trojans to the Danube valley (Pannonian plain). One part of the band, led by King Turquotus, stayed there; a second band, led by King Francio (hence "Franks") moved to the Rhine. For the period after Francio's death, Fredegar essentially follows Gregory's tale. "Kinglets" ruled over the various bands of Franks, who fought constantly with their neighbors, Roman and Germanic. The Trojan diaspora could thus resolve itself by the reuniting of the three bands: the Roman aristocrats of Gaul (Aeneas's band), the Franks living in the Rhineland (that of Francio), and the Alans and other tribes driven from Pannonia to Gaul by the Huns at the end of the fourth and beginning of the fifth century (Turquotus's group). As Hummer concludes, "The myth indicates not only what Frankishness had come to be in the seventh century, but it also encodes the multiple Frankish pasts up to that point."

Thus the identity of those living in Francia, the Franks, initially had very little to do with ethnicity. The earliest Frankish law code, the *Pactis legis Salicae* of *c.* 506, defined people by their place of origin. With the exception of special groups, such as Jews (subject to Roman law), the law treated someone born in a Salian Frank *pagus* as a Salian Frank, regardless of the individual's parentage. Gregory of Tours, writing in the late sixth century, naturally sought to facilitate the fundamental sociopolitical shift of his own day: the union of Germanic magnates from northern Gaul with the Gallo-Roman aristocrats who dominated the south. Making the Franks into the descendants of the Trojans gave the two groups a common "ancestor." Fredegar took the process one step further, with his inclusion of the Pannonian refugees. This union applied only to the political nation, to what the Romans would have called the citizens. Thus *Frank* came also to mean "free"; only the free people, the Franks, belonged to the reunion of the mystical and mythical ancestors. The other Germanic tribes—such as the Alamanni or the Burgundians—living under Merovingian Frankish rule long preserved a separate legal identity. As late as the ninth century, someone born in a Burgundian *pagus* lived under the Burgundian law code.

Medieval sources allow us to see how the social myth evolved over time. Because of the long accretion of elements in the story and the time of its composition, *The Song of Roland* provides critical evidence of the shift away from the tribal identities of earlier times (Franks) to a new more broadly encompassing identity, the French. Roland and Charlemagne speak often of "sweet France" and of the "Francs" of "France." Charlemagne and Roland love these Franks of France above all other men; the mounted warriors from this region form the cream of the Frankish army. The poem also refers, however, to the *Franceis,* evidence of the shift from "Franks" to "French." Here the two segments of the poem provide evidence of the confusion that twelfth-century people must have felt: the poet of the main section of the *Song* uses *Franceis* 70 percent of the time, whereas the "Baligant" poet uses equally the terms *Francs* and *Franceis.* They use the adjective "French" four times more often than "Frankish."

The *Song of Roland* tells us of the great council summoned by Charlemagne to decide Ganelon's fate, that the Emperor called the inhabitants of his German territories (Alamanni, Saxons, and Bavarians, etc.), the "Poitevins and Normans and Franks," as well as those from the Auvergne. The baron Engeler was a "Gascon [Basque] from Bordeaux," who thus spoke Euskara, a non-Indo-European language. These different groups remind us of the ethnic "melting pot" that was medieval France: Gallo-Romans, Visigoths, Burgundians, Franks, Bretons, Basques, Ligurians, Aquitanians, other Germanic tribes, and the late invaders, the Vikings of Normandy, who settled in the tenth century.[40]

Other groups left only hints of their presence, like the few village names indicating the Saxons in the north, or Ramatuelle, on the Mediterranean, a lingering reminder of the eighth-century Muslim conquest of Gothia. Jewish and Syrian Christian traders had long lived in Gallo-Roman cities. They clustered in the Mediterranean, but Gregory of Tours cites a crowd of Syrians and Jews "carrying their banners before them," who met King Guntram as he entered Orléans in 585.[41] Gregory mentions the synagogue burning at Clermont-Ferrand in the midst of bishop Avitus's campaign to convert the city's Jews. Gregory claims Avitus converted 500 of them (*c.* 576) and that those "who refused to accept baptism left the city and made their way to Marseilles." Other evidence points to important Jewish communities in Paris, Rouen, Burgundy, and, later, in Champagne.[42] Frankish and French kings were divided in their attitude toward the Jewish community. In 629, King

Dagobert issued the first of many edicts that offered the Jews the choice of conversion or expulsion. Kings such as Philip Augustus, Philip the Fair, Charles VI (whose 1396 expulsion edict remained official law until 1789), or Louis XII followed Dagobert's exclusionist mentality, yet others, such as Charlemagne, Louis the Pious, Henry II (1550), or Henry IV took the inclusionist perspective, giving protection to Jews.

In the twelfth and thirteenth centuries, a steady flow of Italians made their way into France, especially Champagne, with its great fairs. In the rural parishes near the fair city of Troyes, later tax rolls showed the most common surname to be Le Lombard (the Italian). Elsewhere in France, people often bear the name Langlois (the Englishman) or Lespagnol (the Spaniard), Lallemand (the German) or Le Flamand (the Fleming), lingering reminders of ancient migrations. Because France provides the easiest land route from the Mediterranean to the northern seas, it always attracted immigration.

The linguistic map of France reflected this ethnic variety, and helps us locate accurately the main region of Frankish settlement. Three linguistic boundaries sprang up in the former Roman Gaul. The most important one, between Germanic and Romance languages, took root in the ninth century and has scarcely moved since. It runs just south and east of the Rhine, through modern-day Belgium, down just east of Metz, along the ridge of the Vosges mountains, and ends just west of Berne, Switzerland. East of the line, Frankish merged with other Germanic dialects, such as those of the Saxons or Alamanni; west of the line, the vastly outnumbered Franks largely adopted the Gallo-Roman language of the conquered peoples.[43] These West Franks shared two other linguistic frontiers: the line between Romance and Gaelic speakers, running from Saint-Brieuc on the English Channel to Vannes on the Bay of Biscay and the barrier, just south of the Loire, between the "Franks" and the "Romans". The linguistic frontier reflects the fact that the Franks rarely moved south of the Seine and never south of the Loire. Romance-speaking France contains three distinct zones: the northern "French" area; the middle area of mixed Franco–Provençal or mountain dialects; and the southern zone, with its western (Occitan) and eastern (Provençal) languages.[44] Educated medieval people wrote in Latin, which remained the primary language of the royal administration until the fourteenth century, and of Languedoc's courts until 1539.

The French are no more a timeless entity than France itself. Just as people had to imagine what "France" was, so, too, they had to imagine who the "French" were. The King of the Franks led a specific tribe, the Franks. The King of France ruled the French, who were not simply the Franks but all those living in "France." The *Roland* poets' use of the two terms, *francs* and *franceis*, in the middle of the twelfth century indicates the shift taking place at that time from "Franks" to "French"; the predominance of the latter term in most of the poem shows us the direction in which things were moving.

Redefining "France," that is, making it mean something other than the territory of the "Franks," went hand-in-hand with creating a new group of people, the "French." Little wonder that the document of 1119, a letter to Pope Calixtus II, came about because of Louis VI's disastrous defeat at the hands of the duke of Normandy. That is, it involved the king's relationship to a group of people who were not Franks, yet who lived within the larger France. In a charter issued that same year for the protection of

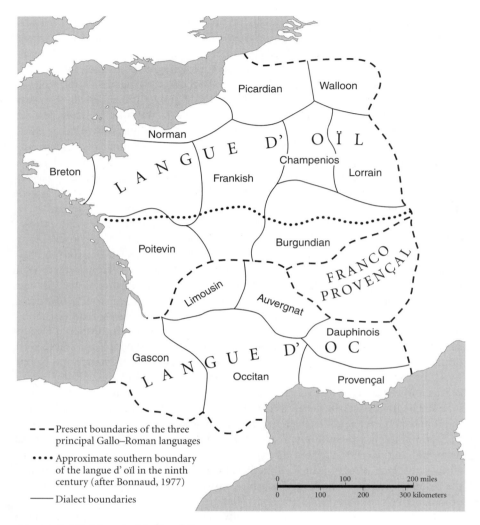

Linguistic Divisions in Medieval France.

Cluniac monasteries in his *regnum* (area of rulership), Louis did not list monasteries in either Normandy or Flanders. He thus excluded two key non-Frankish areas, both of which technically fell within the kingdom of West Francia, but lay outside of the meaning usually attached to "France" in the twelfth century.

∾ A TIMELESS DILEMMA: WHO IS FRENCH?

"France for the French!"

Slogan of the contemporary National Front Party

The group consciousness represented by Fredegar's story of Frankish origins, and Frankish laws' connection of legal identity to geographic location, paved the way for the establishment in the twelfth century of the principle that the "French" are all those living in "France." That principle has remained the basis of membership in the French polity ever since, despite efforts by some, such as the modern-day National Front, to make it otherwise. In the Merovingian kingdoms, men or women could claim to be subject to a given code of laws because they belonged to a specific "nation" (such as the Rhenish Franks, the Burgundians, or those under Roman law). These original laws made an explicit connection between place and legal and "national" identity. Eventually, the two elements—"nation" and location—had to be separated, and law codes had to choose one or the other as the basis of attachment.[45] In German lands, the law chose "nation," or, as later writers called it, race; in French ones, it chose geographic location, but made allowance for "personality." The later monarchy defined a *regnicole* (legal inhabitant of the kingdom) as anyone born in the lands ruled by the King of France. This distinction remains alive: in today's Fifth Republic, all born in France are French; in Germany, only those of German "blood" can be German citizens.[46]

Yet we need to be careful about jumping to modern conclusions based on the ancient distinctions. Rogers Brubaker's useful modern juxtaposition between a "French understanding of nationhood" that is assimilationist, and a German one that is "differentialist" is a shakier proposition when we move back in time.[47] Did "the gradual formation of the nation–state around a single political and cultural center in France" provide "the historical matrix for an assimilationist self-understanding"? I will argue against Brubaker and Lord Acton that it did not. The French nation created a commonwealth, which, in turn, succumbed to a central state in the last quarter of the sixteenth century. If I may borrow Acton's formula about post-partition Poland, the French nation became a soul in search of a body, and sought that body not, as Acton would have it, in the state, but in a commonwealth which possessed a state. The French Revolution reasserted the fundamental identity of the nation and the commonwealth, while redefining them. Yet the Revolutionaries left the definition, and the nation incomplete.

They stumbled over assimilation. They did not assimilate women into citizenship; they excluded Blacks and Mulattos in Saint-Domingue (Haiti) from citizenship; they debated over the extent of male suffrage, that is, full assimilation of all men into citizenship, into the body of the nation.[48] Contemporary France has struggled with assimilation quite as much as its medieval predecessor. Women only became real French citizens in 1944.

The Jews of France offer a remarkable barometer for testing the level of assimilation. Medieval inclusiveness did not extend to them, in part because of the strong union between the Catholic Church and the monarchy, itself both a symbol of unity and a grantor of assimilation. Royal ordinances, beginning with the Merovingians, treated Jews as a separate nation. Louis the Pious (814–843) codified this relationship, issuing charters that treated Jews as foreigners living in the kingdom. In France, as in so many parts of Europe, Jews became the "king's Jews," directly under his jurisdiction and living in the kingdom only on his sufferance. France was a Christian kingdom; Jews could not be members, unless they converted.

This political, religious, and, one might say, cultural exclusion, remained in place for centuries. Charles VI's 1396 expulsion of the Jews, coming during the final stage in the consolidation of a French (Christian) commonwealth, thus reasserted a non-assimilationist definition. Because the nation was the soul of the commonwealth, it had to have spiritual unity; Jews, therefore, had to leave. Jews could not legally live in France again until the 1550s, and even then only if they publicly claimed to have converted.[49] During the French Revolution, the National Constituent Assembly gave Jews the right to become French citizens, provided they renounced their former legal corporate status as Jews. The Assembly extended rights to Jews in two stages. The assimilated communities of Sephardic Jews, in cities such as Bordeaux, obtained full rights in 1789; the less assimilated communities of the east, above all Alsace and Lorraine, had to wait until 1791. Here we see the Revolution creating the nineteenth-century nation, the one Brubaker describes. By removing religion from the soul of the commonwealth, and substituting a spiritual bond with the nation (as represented by its state), the Revolutionaries rendered the "Christian" commonwealth obsolete. That process could only reach fruition, however, in a *République* (the early modern French word for "commonwealth"). The final stage of this process really took place in the 1880s, when the Ferry Laws created mandatory state-run primary education; as the Breton peasant Alain Le Goff told his grandson in the 1920s, the school "is the real seat of the Republic."[50]

This religious element to the definition of "Frenchness" has remained a powerful force throughout French history. The rise of Protestantism in the sixteenth century raised the issue of whether non-Catholic Christians could be "French." The Edict of Nantes (1598), which established limited toleration, meant that they could, but its Revocation (1685) meant they could not. After 1685, only the Lutherans of newly annexed Alsace and nearby territories could be "French" without being Catholic. Louis XVI made the first steps toward civil rights for Protestants in the late 1780s; the Revolutionary government granted full rights to Protestants (1789).

The matter did not end in 1789 or 1791. Even in the secular twentieth century, the connection between Christianity, both as a religion and as a cultural system and "Frenchness" has created problems. In the 1940s, the collaborationist Vichy government stripped naturalized Jews of their French citizenship. The government then deported them to concentration camps or handed them directly over to the Germans. The Vichy government deported far fewer Jews who had actually been born in France.[51]

This issue has arisen again in our own day, with respect to the new Muslim community. Here we can see the old question of inclusion in its modern form. The exclusionists of today implicitly harken back to the old exclusionist view of France that kept medieval Jews from becoming "French." The exclusionists simultaneously deny (or minimize) the Holocaust and demand the expulsion of Muslims living in France: for them, the Vichy deportation of Jews born outside of France and deporting Muslims today amount to much the same thing. The connection is so direct that one of the National Front Senators of the 1970s was the son-in-law of the very man, Vichy Prime Minister Pierre Laval, who signed the orders to deport the Jews.

The argument becomes, as it has been since the twelfth century, one over the definition of France-French. Modern efforts to make the definition based on elements such as language or ethnicity should not confuse us. The "French" have varied sharply by ethnic heritage, by language, and even by geographic location. Some people who thought themselves French have, at many past times, lived outside of what was then "France" in a legal sense. The element of cultural and religious inclusion/exclusion has provided the greatest discontinuity in the definition. In some periods, failure to practice a given religion (Christianity, Catholicism) excluded one from the community; in others, it did not. The elites, especially the nobility, of regions like Flanders or Brittany often felt themselves completely French, when the mass of the population did not. No specific political logic meant that European places culturally not French, such as Brittany or Alsace, to say nothing of Corsica, would be part of France. Many inhabitants of these regions continue to resist, even by violent means (Corsica), the idea that they are French.

French culture often extended outside the literal boundaries of France. Several currents fed into the outpouring of French culture into other regions. Within the kingdom, the ruling elite of the Seine-Loire region imposed its version of French on the elites and, in time, the peasantry of outlying regions. In Upper Normandy, for example, the Viking invaders adopted French quite rapidly. Because of the extensive ties among the nobility of different geographic regions in the eleventh and twelfth centuries, French spread to places like Flanders, where it remained the preserve of the wealthy, but did not become the language of the people. The great Norman conquests of the eleventh century—England, southern Italy, the Holy Land—spread French far from the borders of "France," however defined. Richard the Lion-Hearted spoke French, not Middle English, and so did his knights. The predominance of French speakers among the Crusaders was so great that the people of the Middle East referred to all western European Crusaders as "Franks."

Crises of identity lend themselves to manipulation of history. "France" and the "French" are and always have been evolving entities. In the 1950s, the three Algerian departments practiced rigorous exclusion in defining "Frenchness"—with a few exceptions, only those of European descent could vote in Algeria—at the same time that the European part of France did not make such distinctions. So, too, we see such contradictions in seventeenth-century France, when a Jew could live openly in Metz but had to disguise his or her religion in Nantes or Bordeaux. The legal boundaries of today's France, as set by representation in the National Assembly, are younger than I am. To cite only the most obvious example, Algeria belonged to metropolitan France until 1962 and had elected representatives in the National Assembly.[52] The "France" of today, as its World Cup-winning soccer team demonstrated, includes people of the widest possible ethnic origin. The team had a Breton, a Basque, players of West African, Maghrebian, Italian, and eastern European ancestry, to say nothing of those born in the overseas departments of New Caledonia and Guadeloupe, and even naturalized citizens, born in Argentina and Sénégal.[53] The French are not, nor have they ever been an ethnic group; they are a nation.

The history of "France": it seems so clear what that means to us, what that France is and was. As we trace that history, let us not lose sight of the original France, that "en-France" attached to tiny Roissy. Let us remember, too, that the initial expansion of meaning to "France," as in a kingdom of, was a leap of faith and imagination, and both an offer and threat of inclusion. Just as in Louis VI's day, those on both sides cannot fully agree on the boundaries of inclusion, whether they wish to be included or whether any can be excluded. In France, the boundaries of exclusion often did not revolve around questions of race or ethnicity, but around those of culture. At the start of the twenty-first century, the French commonwealth and its state still demand adherence to their cultural definition of France from all those who would be French. They insist all those who live in France have to choose to be French, that, as Jean-Jacques Rousseau once said, they will have to be forced to be free. Those on the Right who insist on the historic connection of an "ethnicity" to France falsify both French history and what has always been the essence of France. That France is a real place, a community that its inhabitants have imagined, and, in imagining, have transformed.

The French, like France, have an imagined and a real existence. Today's tension about lack of congruity between real and imagined definitions is not new; it is the logical historical outcome of Louis VI's audacious notion that he was the king of a place and a people, and no longer simply the warrior chief of a tribe.

Notes

1. J. Michelet, *Histoire de France,* ed. C. Mettra, vol. 1: *Des origines au XIIe siècle* (Paris: Éditions Rencontre Lausanne, 1965), 49.

2. A. Hastings, *The Construction of Nationhood. Ethnicity, Religion and Nationalism* (Cambridge: Cambridge University Press, 1997), esp. 18–19.

3. Nineteenth-century states extended such rights only to men, so we cannot define nineteenth-century nations in terms of universal adult citizenship. Significant restrictions typically survived into the 1960s in many states, including France.

4. The concept of citizen, tied closely to the Roman *civitas,* or urban community, survived in the towns of southern Gaul, just as it did in the Italian towns. In both places, nobles often lived in towns and participated as citizens.

5. Systematic cultural coopting of southern elites did not take firm root until the late sixteenth century. In many rural areas, peasants became culturally French only in the late nineteenth or even twentieth century. Languedoc's definitive political adherence to the French commonwealth, which took place in the 1420s and 1430s, thus antedated its adherence to the cultural entity called "France."

6. Here emphasizing once again that "nation" in the sixteenth century did not mean the "nation" of the nineteenth century. The term was moving in that direction, and the shifting structure of representation in estates demonstrated such a move, but the sixteenth century nation did not really extend down to all levels of society, as it would be three centuries later.

7. F. Braudel, *The Identity of France,* trans. S. Reynolds (New York: Harper & Row, 1988, 1993), I, 35.

8. Some texts call the Rhenish Franks the Riparian or Ripuarian (riverside) Franks.

9. The word *kuning* led to both the German *könig* and the English "king"; Roman authors usually translated it as *rex* (king). Once in contact with the Romans,

who had a well-developed sense of Imperial power, the Germanic tribal war chiefs began to evolve into something more like what we think of as a king.

10. The Quinotaur, whose name means quintuple bull, was a sort of ultimate male fertility symbol. He may have represented the god Neptune (Poseidon), who had close ties to the bull. In these animal-woman liaisons, the animal form merely disguised a god, as in the many Greek stories about Zeus (or Poseidon) coupling with human women. The tomb of Childeric, supposed son of Merovich, contained a prominent bull's head ornament.

11. The treasure was stolen from a Paris museum in 1831; all we have left are the drawings and catalogue made in 1653 by Jacques Chifflet of Tournai.

12. This custom may have arrived from the Pannonian plains with the Alans and Suevic tribes driven westward by the Huns at the end of the fourth century. See the following text.

13. Cited in K. F. Werner, *Histoire de France: Les origines (avant l'an mil),* v. I, ed. J. Favier (Paris: Fayard, 1984), 292.

14. Clovis's real name was Chlodweg, meaning "famous for his battles." The element "Chlod" ties him directly to Chlodio, because Germanic aristocratic families passed along names in this way to demonstrate descent.

15. Fourth-century Roman sources had given the name "Rhenish Francia" to the lands near Cologne; from the late fifth century onward, "Francia" meant both that region and the new homeland of the Salian Franks, near Paris.

16. Gregory of Tours, *The History of the Franks,* trans. L. Thorpe (London and New York: Penguin, 1974),162 (Book III.1).

17. The two letters of Remy to Clovis merely call him *Chlodoveo regi,* King Clovis, as does a letter from bishop Avit of Vienne (*c.* 499). Although the *Life of Saint Geneviève* refers to Chloderic as *rex francorum,* the document dates from 520. The title King of the Franks, therefore, would seem to date from the first decade of the sixth century.

18. These matters are covered in detail in Chapter 1.

19. Two other units, Aquitaine (chief city Bordeaux), and Burgundy (chief city Autun), maintained some independence; each had its own system of law. Provence, in the far southeast, also belonged loosely to the Merovingian sphere of influence.

20. The Mayor of the Palace, as the title suggests, served as chief official of the king's household and, in some cases, as chief military commander.

21. *The Song of Roland,* trans. G. Burgess (London and New York: Penguin Books, 1990), 156. Verse 297, whose original reads "Quant li empereres ad faite sa venjance, / Sin apelat ses evesques de France, / Cels de Baviere e icels d'Alemaigne." (Burgess, 210). *Alemaigne* here carries the sense of the region of the Alamanni; thus the three words France, Baviere, and Alemaigne refer to regions of a given tribe.

22. The other two kingdoms merged into a new entity, the Holy Roman Empire of the German Nation. One of the five great duchies of that realm, Franconia, preserved

the memory of its Frankish origins. Louis's fourth son, Pippin, received Aquitaine, but his early death left that principality to his son, another Pippin. Charles the Fat eventually usurped Aquitaine from his cousin, who died without heirs. See Chapter 1 for details on these matters.

23. Richer, *Histoire de France,* trans. R. Latouche (Paris: Champion, 1930). Latouche, not Richer, provides this title. Richer was a monk at Reims, writing *c.* 995.

24. The first document in French—the Oath of Strasbourg (842)—contains parallel texts in West Frankish (what would become French), East Frankish (German), and Latin.

25. Scholars have long debated the date of the poem; until quite recently, the prevailing opinion held it to have been written between 1095 and 1100, and tied its composition to the First Crusade (1095). Recent works by Hans Erich Keller and André de Mandach, however, offer strong evidence for the later composition. See especially, by the latter, *Naissance et développement de la chanson de geste en Europe: Chanson de Roland, transferts de mythe dans le monde occidental et oriental* (Geneva, 1993). I have been unable to find any English–language text that offers a summary of this argument. *The Song of Roland* consists of two distinct parts. The second part of the poem, called the Baligant episode because Charlemagne fights a mythic Muslim ruler of that name, likely dates from the time of the Second Crusade (1146–1147).

26. Aachen is in the original Francia, the land of the Rhenish Franks.

27. One verse of the poem places Charlemagne's capital at Laon, in northern France; Laon served as a capital to several Carolingian monarchs in the tenth century. It had no such role in Charlemagne's time, nor did it serve as a capital at the time of the written composition of *The Song of Roland.*

28. Jewish geography reflected Jewish political life. The Jews of these two areas had separate chief officials, one for the north in Rouen, and a second one for the south at Narbonne.

29. Cited in X. de Planhol with P. Claval, *An Historical Geography of France,* trans. J. Lloyd (Cambridge and New York: Cambridge University Press, 1994; French edition, Paris: Fayard, 1988), 97. France thus meant essentially the old Roman provinces of Belgium II and Lyonnais.

30. Cited by C. Crossley, *French Historians and Romanticism. Thierry, Guizot, the Saint-Simonians, Quinet, Michelet* (London and New York: Routledge, 1993), 50.

31. "Nationality," in *Mapping the Nation,* ed. G. Balakrishnan (London, New York: Verso, 1996), 22. Lord Acton's essay appeared in 1862.

32. Again, I would emphasize here that we have very little evidence of such sentiments among fifteenth-century *peasants;* Joan was quite extraordinary in that way.

33. Cited in E. James, *The Franks* (Oxford and New York: Basil Blackwell, 1988), 57, and, after the ellipses, in P. Contamine, *War in the Middle Ages,* trans. M. Jones (London and New York: Basil Blackwell, 1984), 13.

34. Cited in E. Taitz, *The Jews of Medieval France. The Community of Champagne* (Westport, CT: Greenwood Press, 1994), 58.

35. Documents of the time refer to the kingdom and the "other lands of the king's obedience," obvious evidence that the two were not coterminous.

36. Other European peoples had similar myths. The Bretons and English, like the French, tied themselves to the Trojans, while the Polish nobility had a special affection for the so-called Sarmathian Myth, about their ancestors.

37. Sixteenth-century French people still believed the Trojan myth, which political orators invariably cited in their learned speeches. These beliefs fell away in the seventeenth century.

38. J. Rappaport, *The politics of memory. Native historical interpretation in the Colombian Andes* (Cambridge: Cambridge University Press, 1990), 11 and 16.

39. H.J. Hummer, "Franks and Alamanni: a Discontinuous Ethnogenesis," in *Franks and Alamanni in the Merovingian Period. An Ethnographic Perspective,* ed. I. Wood (San Marino: Boydell Press, 1998), 9–21, citation on 13.

40. The phrase "melting pot" comes directly from the magisterial *Histoire de la Population Française. T. 1: Des origines à la Renaissance,* ed. J. Dupâquier (Paris: PUF, 1988).

41. Gregory attributes to Guntram a profound suspicion of these Jews, whose synagogue had recently been burned by the local Christians. Gregory's remarks about Jews place him squarely among the anti-Semites of his time.

42. By the ninth or tenth centuries, Jews, although still a quite small percentage of the population, likely controlled much of Frankish commerce, from their communities in Lyon, Rouen, Troyes, and elsewhere. Frankish aristocrats, the main clients of long-distance commerce, demanded products, such as spices, that came from the eastern Mediterranean. Merchants from that region thus logically dominated Frankish long-distance trade. Some Jews, such as those of Champagne, even owned rural property. The community at Rouen supported not only a synagogue and elementary religious education, but an advanced center of religious learning, which attracted Jewish scholars and students from all over Europe.

43. French is further from its base—Latin—than other Romance languages, but modern French contains relatively few (500) Celtic or Frankish words.

44. Map 3 of E. Weber's *Peasants into Frenchmen* (Stanford: Stanford University Press, 1976), shows that as late as 1865, roughly the southern third of France, the areas east of the Rhône and the Saône, and most of Brittany spoke mainly local languages or dialects or had substantial minorities doing so.

45. The obvious problem involved movement. If your father lived in his original *pagus,* no problem arose. If, however, your father were, say, a Rhenish Frank who had moved to Burgundy, to what law did you belong: that of your father—the law of the Rhenish Franks—or that of your birthplace—the law of the Burgundians? The longer the geographic separation, the more the pressure to associate you with the law of your birthplace. Gender quickly complicated matters. In many areas, the individual took legal status from the mother (see Chapter 2).

46. Thus in Germany, someone of German descent, whose ancestors have lived in Russia since the eighteenth century, can return and claim citizenship; conversely, a child of Turkish descent, even if born in Germany to parents of Turkish descent

themselves born in Germany, is not a German citizen. Citizenship laws are under review today in both France and Germany.

47. R. Brubaker, *Citizenship and Nationhood in France and Germany* (Cambridge, MA: Harvard University Press, 1992), 5.

48. Only citizens who could vote, for example, could belong to the *National* Guard created during the Revolution.

49. Some Jews remained in France in the fifteenth century by outwardly converting to Christianity. Charles VII's personal physician, for example, was a Jew. See Chapters 6 and 7.

50. P.–J. Hélias, *The Horse of Pride. Life in a Breton Village,* trans. J. Guicharnaud (New Haven and London: Yale University Press, 1974), 135.

51. France held between 300,000 and 350,000 Jews in 1940, of whom roughly 195,000 were French citizens and the remainder foreign-born immigrants. All told, some 75,000 of these Jews died in the Holocaust. The mortality rate among the French citizens was about 10 percent, whereas it was over 40 percent for the foreigners. M. Marrus and R. Paxton, *Vichy France and the Jews* (New York: Basic Books, 1982) and S. Zuccotti, *The Holocaust, the French, and the Jews* (New York: Basic Books, 1993), 283–284.

52. Nor is France today legally defined by the entity we think of as France. France has several "overseas departments": Martinique and Guadeloupe, in the Caribbean; Reunion Island, in the Indian Ocean; New Caledonia, in the Pacific; St-Pierre and Miquelon islands off the coast of Canada; Guyana in South America. France also has "overseas territories," such as its Polynesian islands, Tahiti most famous among them.

53. This soccer melting pot began long ago: many top "French" players of the 1950s came from Eastern European families. The greatest star of the 1980s, Michel Platini, came from an Italian one.

BRIEF CONTENTS

CONTENTS

TABLES AND CHARTS

Chapter One

THE LEGACIES: GALLO-ROMANS, MEROVINGIANS, AND CAROLINGIANS

The Germanic societies of the north became more Roman, and the Roman provinces became more Germanic. Through these interactions, the pattern was set for the emergence of the Germanic kingdoms of the early Middle Ages, with their complex intermingling of features from Roman and indigenous societies.[1]

P. Wells, *The Barbarians Speak*

France and the rest of Christian western Europe developed into a distinct civilization in the eleventh and twelfth centuries, building on three powerful cultural foundations: the Germanic, Classical, and Judeo-Christian legacies.

Germanic customs played an important role in Frankish, then French political life. The war band, consisting of a leader, his kindred, and followers, remained a fundamental structure in French life until the seventeenth century. Charlemagne built his initial political system around the annual war raid, leading a substantial army into neighboring lands in search of immediate booty and acknowledgment of Frankish political supremacy, symbolized by payment of an annual tribute. The Germanic insistence on the unique sacred quality of the king also provided an important unifying element in the lands of the King of the Franks, later King of France.

The Classical heritage became diluted during the desperate years of the sixth and seventh centuries. Gallo-Roman aristocrats tried to pass along some semblance of their civilization, above all by means of the "Catholic" Church.[2] The terrible plagues of this period devastated the population, as did the incessant civil wars. In such dire circumstances, civilized life—art, writing, learning—struggled mightily merely to survive. Merovingian France lost contact with much of Classical civilization, but it also preserved other key elements of the ancient heritage. Roman towns continued to be the primary ones of the Frankish territories and Roman law provided the framework for the law codes of the barbarian tribes. The old Roman ways lasted longest in the south. Little wonder that outside observers, such as Princess Anna Comnena of Byzantium, viewed the southern French as far more "civilized" than their northern cousins. Roman Imperial traditions provided an additional, and essential underpinning for political development. Charlemagne even received his crown as Emperor in Rome itself, a fitting testimony to the endurance of the Roman legacy.

1

The Judeo-Christian tradition amplified and modified the sacerdotal kingship of the Germanic tribes. Biblical kings provided important role models for medieval French royalty. The facades of many of the greatest medieval French Catholic shrines, such as the cathedrals of Notre Dame at Paris or Chartres, offer us stunning visual evidence of this connection, with their magnificent galleries of statues of the Kings of Israel, dressed as Kings of France. Christianity spread first to the towns and among the aristocracy. The mixture of Christian and pagan beliefs that became a distinctive western Christianity evolved over six centuries, finally incorporating the mass of the rural population only in the eleventh century.

The non-Christians of France, above all its Jews, provided an essential element in the creation of this western Christianity, because of their close ties to the Muslim world, with its much more developed civilization. Just as Jewish traders brought into the Frankish world eastern Mediterranean spices or silk, so, too, Jewish scholars brought the Franks the superior knowledge of the Muslim world, in which they had an important presence. Because Arab scholars preserved much closer ties to Classical learning than western Europeans, Jewish scholars, moving easily from Muslim Spain into Christian France, helped the Christians become far more familiar with the great thinkers of antiquity. One unfortunate aspect of the elaboration of a distinct western Christianity, accepted by the mass of the population, was increased intolerance of non–Christians. This process culminated in the First Crusade (1090s), whose violence began with assaults on the Jewish communities of Christian Europe.

Chapter 1 focuses on the legacies of the Gallo-Roman world, of the Merovingians, and of the Carolingians. It thus covers chronologically a period running from about 500 to about 1000, during which the tribes of part of Roman Gaul created a confederation of principalities organized around the individual they called the "King of the Franks." Perhaps the most enduring of those legacies was the close interconnection of church and state in the evolving Frankish political and social system, so we will begin with that relationship.

∼ THE FALL OF GAUL

When Eparchius died he was succeeded by Sidonius Apollinaris, one-time Prefect of the City, a man of most noble birth as honours are counted in this world, and one of the leading Senators of Gaul, so noble indeed that he married the daughter of the Emperor Avitus.[3]

Gregory of Tours

CHRONOLOGY	275–481
275	Franks and Alamanni invade Gaul for the first time
355	Second invasion by the Franks

C H R O N O L O G Y	(continued)
418	Visigoths capture Aquitaine
451	Huns invade Gaul; Attila defeated at battle of Châlons-sur-Marne
476	Official end of the Western Roman Empire
481	Death of Childeric

Church and State

Sidonius Apollinaris came from a distinguished Gallo-Roman aristocratic family. As a young man, he served as a Roman prefect; at about age forty, he became a Latin-rite bishop. Sidonius, like many of his fellow bishops, had not been trained in religious orders; in fact, he was a married man, with four children, one of whom succeeded him as bishop and duly canonized his father. This link between powerful aristocratic families and the hierarchy of the Catholic Church, established in the late fifth century, endured until the French Revolution. French landed elites monopolized high church offices, pocketing their income, for thirteen hundred years. The language of church and state alike reveals this remarkable continuity: the Church used the same word, *beneficium*, to describe the income attached to church office that the Romans had used to describe the land attached to Imperial office.

Sidonius's career alerts us to the most important legacy of the late Gallo-Roman and Merovingian periods: the elaborate interweaving of church and central state in the land later to become France. Our modern notions of the separation of church and state serve only to mislead when we examine the history of France. People of the fifth or sixth centuries did not distinguish politically between church and central state: if we consider the "state" to be a set of functions, to be the care and supervision of what the Romans called the *res publica* (commonwealth), we can better understand how the bishops and abbots, and the secular rulers shared that stewardship.

The bishops of late fifth-century Gaul came overwhelmingly from the Gallo-Roman aristocracy. When the Western Empire collapsed, aristocratic Imperial officers sought to preserve their power through Church office: many became bishops, which allowed them to keep secular powers such as judicial rights and substantial landed estates. The Catholic Church received the overwhelming majority (75 percent) of the property it would *ever* own in France during the period 450–650. Roman Imperial officers, such as counts, would have had a particularly strong interest in "donating" lands they held from the Imperial fisc, the property attached to their office for its upkeep. Gallo-Roman aristocratic families would give their landed properties, fisc or private, to the Church; a family member would then become the church officer, such as bishop, who held control of the property in question. The property could now be protected from seizure on the grounds that it belonged to God. One of the largest known such grants came in 679–680, when Nizezius the Aquitainian gave the monastery of Moissac an estate of twenty-two thousand acres. Starting in the late sixth century, Frankish aristocrats used exactly the same techniques, as the will of Bertram of Le Mans demonstrates.

Bertram's will disposed of one hundred thirty-five different estates, containing 714,000 acres, an area roughly the size of Rhode Island. Bertram left most of his property to the bishopric of Le Mans. He owed land everywhere in the former Gaul, from Provence to Lorraine, and from the Pyrenees to Burgundy.[4] Some of it came from his family, but most of it came as gifts from King Clothar II, whom Bertram had supported in the civil wars of the period. Bertram held, and bequeathed, land attached to his bishopric, land granted from the royal fisc, and land purchased with cash given him by the king.

The monarchy, the aristocracy, and the Catholic Church thus early formed an alliance that would last for nearly fifteen hundred years. Royal control over the French church dated from the time of Clovis: archbishop Remy of Reims suggested that appointment to a bishopric took place under the *auctoritas* of the king. In 549, the Council of Orléans, in its tenth canon, stated explicitly that a new bishop, elected by his cathedral chapter and the people and consecrated by his archbishop, had to have the "assent of the king" to take office. From that moment forward, no one could become a bishop in Frankish kingdoms, and later in France, without the approval of the king. Given the enormous prestige, power, and wealth of bishoprics, this right of approval gave the king tremendous leverage over the great aristocratic families who sought these positions. From Clovis onward, even the ruling bodies of the French Church, the episcopal councils, could meet only under the royal aegis. The monopoly of great aristocratic families over the bishoprics and principal abbacies helped entrench their power: in fact, control of church property provided an essential element in the sustained power of these families.

Roman Legacies

> *Attached to this hall is an external appendage on the east side, a piscina [bathing pool] . . . which holds about twenty thousand gallons. . . . A stream is "enticed from the brow" of the mountain, and diverted through conduits which are carried round the outer sides of the swimming-bath; it pours its waters into the pool from six projecting pipes with representations of lions' heads.[5]*
>
> Sidonius Apollinaris, describing his villa in the Auvergne, c. 469

Sidonius's letters reveal a remarkable dual world, in which the remnants of Classical Roman civilization co-existed with the new "barbarous" world of the tribes who had infiltrated Gaul and the rest of the western Roman Empire. His letters speak of tasty dishes and fine wines at banquets given by local notables, although he does comment upon the movement away from the excesses of earlier times, and towards a simpler, healthier diet. Of one such meal, provided by Theodoric, king of the Ostrogoths, he says "the viands attract by their skilful cookery, not by their costliness . . . [and] replenishment of the goblets or wine-bowls comes at such long intervals that there is more reason for the thirsty to complain than for the intoxicated to refrain."[6]

Sidonius makes constant reference to booksellers, evidence of the important written culture that survived in late Roman Gaul. He and members of families such as his long preserved the legacy of written culture, transferring it, at least in part, to the Frankish royal circle. Sidonius despaired of the Empire's weakness in the face of the "barbarian" challenge. His letters suggest that the Gallo-Romans, far from uniting in opposition to the "barbarians," sought alliances with them, sought to use Frankish or Gothic allies against their factional opponents in the dying Empire.

The Gallo-Romans left important practical legacies to their successors. Although the material comforts of Sidonius's world—villas with hot and cold baths, multiple dining rooms, studies, elaborate household staffs—disappeared in the sixth century, the elite continued to have access to some elements of a life of luxury. When Chilperic II granted immunities from tolls to the northern monastery of Corbie in 716, he specifically mentioned exemptions for such goods as pepper, cinnamon, and cloves (all had to be imported from Asia), as well as for dates, figs, olives, almonds, and pistachios (all products of the Mediterranean). Other Roman elements endured. The Gallo-Romans provided the overwhelming majority of the population, so their languages survived, albeit with important Frankish additions in the north. Roman crops—wine, olives, wheat—dominated the landscape, and continue to do so today. Roman political traditions survived, too, not only in the transformation of Frankish war chiefs into kings but in the concept of citizenship, with its attendant civic responsibilities, and privileges. Sidonius writes often of the survival of Roman civic institutions in the towns of southern Gaul: the traditions attached to such institutions long survived in those towns, in the Church, and among part of the aristocracy.

The Romans left medieval France a network of roads, arenas, aqueducts, and bridges that continued in use for centuries: some, like the arena of Nîmes, are still in use today. Roman law (the written law or *droit écrit*) remained the customary law of most of Mediterranean France until the Revolution. Later, Roman Imperial law, taught in law schools such as that of Montpellier, provided a useful starting point for royal pretensions, whether in the time of Philip Augustus or in that of Louis XIV.[7] In popular culture, the legacy of Gallo-Roman times remains strong: writers often use the adjective "Gallic" to describe France; the organizers of the 1998 World Cup even used the rooster (*gallus*) as their official mascot.

THE MEROVINGIAN LEGACY

CHRONOLOGY	486–734
486	Clovis captures Paris and Soissons
492	Marriage of Clotilde and Clovis
496	Clovis defeats the Alamanni
498	Clovis converts to orthodox Latin Christianity
502	Death of (Saint) Geneviève

CHRONOLOGY	(continued)
507	Clovis defeats the Visigoths, slays Alaric II
509	Clovis declared king of Rhenish Franks
511	Death of Clovis; Synod of Orléans
549	Council of Orléans
558–561	Unified Frankish kingdom under Clothaire I
594	Columbanus arrives at Luxeuil
613–638	United Frankish kingdom under Clothar II and Dagobert I
620s–630s	Dagobert founds abbeys of Saint-Denis and Saint-Germain-des-Prés
711	North African Muslims conquer Spain
720–725	Muslim conquests in southern France
c. 732/734	Battle of Tours/Poitiers; Charles Martel defeats the Muslims

Clovis and the Foundations of French Kingship

King Clovis, who believed in the Trinity, crushed the heretics with divine help and extended his dominion to include all the Gauls.[8]

Gregory of Tours

Roman Gaul did not so much collapse as it disintegrated, a process accelerated by the steady infiltration of Germanic tribes and the full-scale invasions by those tribes and others, such as the Huns. The Gallo-Romans allied with Goths and Franks to defeat Attila the Hun in a battle near Châlons-sur-Marne (451), but the Emperor Valentinian soon (454) murdered the victorious Roman general, Aëtius, whose followers murdered Valentinian himself in 455. No real Roman authority ever reestablished itself in Gaul, although outposts, such as Sidonius's Auvergne or the region around Soissons, lasted for another thirty years or so.

Power in the former Gaul passed to the barbarian kings: those of the Ostrogoths in the southeast, of the Visigoths in the southwest, of the Burgundians in east-central Gaul, of the Alamanni and Rhenish Franks in the Rhineland, of the Salian Franks in the north. The last of these groups moved decisively to overcome the others in the first half of the sixth century, under the leadership of Childeric's son, Clovis (d. 511) and his sons.

Clovis, his second wife Clotilde, and the holy woman Geneviève of Paris played the central roles in the foundation of Francia. Clovis followed a determined policy to conquer all of the tribal "kingdoms" of Gaul. He first formed a liaison with a woman from the royal family of the Rhenish Franks and sought an alliance with them. Clovis later repudiated the woman to marry Clotilde (492), the niece of the king of the

Burgundians. Clovis had attained sufficient stature by 494 that the most powerful barbarian ruler, Theodoric the Ostrogoth, king of northern Italy and Provence, demanded in marriage Clovis's sister, Audoflède.

Clotilde, an orthodox Latin-rite Christian, urged Clovis to convert and to become the champion of her co-religionists against the Arians ruling the Burgundian and Visigothic kingdoms.[9] Clovis already had cordial relations with key Catholic figures of northern Gaul, such as the archbishop Remy of Reims, who had congratulated Clovis on following his ancestors in taking over the "administration of Belgium II." He encouraged the king to:

> listen to your bishops and have recourse always to their counsel. Because if you get on well with them, your province can only be consolidated by such action. Give courage to the citizen, relief to the afflicted, favor the widows, nourish the orphans. . . . Joke with the young, deliberate with the old, and if you wish to reign, judge nobly.[10]

Clovis did convert to orthodox Latin-rite Christianity, a process that gave birth to two important legends. First, Gregory of Tours copied the most famous royal conversion story, that of the Emperor Constantine: in his version Clovis converted because of a vow taken in battle against the Alamanni (496).[11] Second, in the late ninth century, Hincmar, archbishop of Reims, invented the story that a dove sent from Heaven had given Saint Remy a Holy Phial filled with oil of chrism, which Remy used to baptize Clovis. Hincmar further claimed that the archbishop of Reims still had this Phial, which God miraculously replenished with oil of chrism for the coronations of the Kings of the Franks. He used oil from the Holy Phial to anoint Charles the Fat as King of the Franks. This oil became the centerpiece of the coronation ceremony and remained so until the end of the monarchy: all but two kings crowned between 987–1824 were anointed with it at Reims.[12]

Clovis's conversion enabled him to ally with the powerful orthodox Latin-rite bishops against the Burgundian, Ostrogothic, and Visigothic kings who supported the Arian heresy.[13] Clovis also allied with another eminent religious figure, Geneviève of Paris. Geneviève, aristocratic daughter of a Romanized Frankish father, had the religious patronage of a dominant ecclesiastical figure of the day, (Saint) Germain of Auxerre.[14] *The Life of Saint Geneviève,* probably composed in 520, tells us that she predicted the invasion of the Huns in 451, and also predicted that the Huns would bypass Paris. Her skeptical fellow citizens at first wanted to assassinate her, but when her prediction came true, they made her into a venerated leader. In the 470s, she led the resistance to Childeric, who failed to capture the town.

Her hagiographer claims Childeric, "King of the Franks" (*rex francorum*), held a great veneration for her, and even spared the lives of prisoners at her request. Clovis, too, listened to her entreaties. She encouraged Parisians to let him into the town (*c.* 486); in turn, he spared the lives of several condemned prisoners. When Clovis converted to the Latin rite, the direct tie between the two grew even stronger: Clovis gave Geneviève permission to build a new church just outside of Paris, which then consisted solely of two islands in the Seine (today's Ile-Saint-Louis and Ile-de-la-Cité), some nearby parts of the river's Left Bank, and a tiny portion of the Right Bank.

The dove bringing the Holy Phial to Saint Remy, so that he could baptize Clovis (9th-century ivory).

SOURCE: J. Marseille, *Nouvelle Histoire de France* (Paris: Perrin, 1999). Illustration is between 192–193. Bibliotheque Nationale

When Geneviève died in 502, Clovis and Clotilde decided to make this church into a basilica, first called the church of the Holy Apostles Peter and Paul and later called Sainte-Geneviève. In a fitting symbol of the remarkable change since Childeric, Clovis received a Christian burial in the basilica. The site now holds the Panthéon, since the Revolution, the official resting place of France's greatest heroes, a stunning example of the historical continuity of certain places of collective memory.

Clovis's newfound religion did not prevent him from shamelessly murdering the leaders of most aristocratic Frankish families in his home region (508–511). Clovis crushed the Alamanni in 506 and defeated and slew Alaric II, king of the Visigoths, in 507. Although Clovis's attack on Alaric had more to do with power politics than with any sort of religious crusade, the triumph of the Franks over the Goths guaranteed that orthodox Latin-rite Christianity, rather than Arianism, would remain the dominant religion of the former Gaul. Clovis's defeat of the Visigoths, however, did not change the underlying demographic and cultural realities of the former Gaul. In the south, where the Goths merged into the existing Gallo-Roman population, Roman ways survived longer and the languages, Occitan and Provençal, stayed closer to Latin. The north, above the Loire, remained the zone of Frankish dominance. The northerners would not definitively conquer southern France until the thirteenth century.

Shifting his focus to the old Rhenish homeland, Clovis convinced Chloderic, son of the king of the Rhenish Franks, Sigibert the Lame, to murder his father; Clovis's men next murdered Chloderic as "punishment." Clovis rode to Cologne to denounce these deeds and to assert he had had no part in them. He successfully urged the Rhenish Franks to submit to his authority (508). Clovis thus left his sons control of all of the former Gaul except the Mediterranean coastline and the Burgundian kingdom.

Not long after Clovis had crushed the Alamanni and Visigoths, the Byzantine Emperor Anastasius named him an honorary Roman "consul." Three years later (510) the Church Council of Orléans, attended by thirty-two bishops from Gaul, asked for Clovis's consent for their actions. They wanted his confirmation of their actions because he was "such a great king and lord"; therefore, the added weight of his *auctoritas* would lead to broader obedience to their decrees. Their use of this Roman legal term, *auctoritas*, shows the special symbiotic relationship developing between the monarchy and the Church.[15]

By asserting that Clovis had *auctoritas*, a word meaning something like our modern term "sovereignty" (the supreme authority in the state, particularly the supreme lawmaking authority), the Council of Orléans vastly increased Clovis's stature. The Council added extra weight to the process already underway in the barbarian kingdoms, by which a *kuning* (war chief) actually became a king. The four most powerful barbarian kings of this time—Theodoric in Italy, Alaric in the Visigoth kingdom, Gundobad in Burgundy, and Clovis—all issued written law codes based on the customary laws of their peoples. The newest member of this royal club, Clovis, thus relied on a combination of Roman Imperial office (inherited from his father), war chieftainship, conquest, marriage, alliance with the Byzantine Emperor, and support from the Catholic Church to make himself into the *rex francorum*, the King of the Franks.

The greater stature of a real king supporting their decrees, and thus orthodox Christianity, against Arianism, in turn buttressed the Council's position.[16] In a letter to Clovis, the Council of Orléans referred to him as "their lord, son of the Catholic Church, the very glorious king Clovis" and praised his efforts to "develop the cult of the Catholic religion." The Council decrees also suggested, by asserting the *auctoritas* of Clovis, that the king was the supreme guardian of the *res publica*, the commonwealth of Gaul. Although such legalistic terminology meant little to ordinary people, the deliberate use of Roman legal terms provided an important framework upon which the few learned men of the time could build some sort of theoretical state edifice. They passed along this theoretical edifice to later writers (all also ecclesiastics), who used it to justify the power of Merovingian, Carolingian, and early Capetian kings.

The Long-Haired Kings

If you have coveted God's possessions, the Lord will quickly remove your king-
dom from you because it is iniquitous that while you should nourish the poor
from your barns, instead it is your barns that are filled with their grain.[17]

Bishop Injuriosus of Tours,
protesting King Clothar's seizure of Church lands

Clovis's family legally ruled the former Gaul from his death until 751, although real power passed to a new family, initially called the Pippinids or Arnulfings, by the late seventh century. For most the Merovingian period, three separate kingdoms existed: Austrasia, in the east, focused on the lands of the Rhenish Franks, with its capital usually at Metz; Burgundy, in east-central Gaul, with a principal city often at Autun; and Neustria, in the north and west, using Paris as its capital. The Merovingians rarely had any real control of Aquitaine; when they did have some authority there, they usually divided the region among their kingdoms.[18]

Clovis himself established the ruthless pattern of family infighting that eventually destroyed the Merovingians:

> One day when he had called a general assembly of his subjects, he is said to have made the following remark about the relatives whom he had destroyed: "How sad a thing it is that I live among strangers like some solitary pilgrim, and that I have none of my own relations left to help me when disaster threatens!" He said this not because he grieved for their deaths, but because in his cunning way he hoped to find some relative still in the land of the living whom he could kill.[19]

His sons followed in his footsteps: when Clovis's son Chlodomer died in battle with the Burgundians (523), the remaining brothers (Theuderic, Clothar, and Childeric) murdered their nephews (aged seven and ten) and divided up Chlodomer's kingdom.[20]

The lines of Theuderic and Childeric soon died out, allowing Clothar to rule a united kingdom. Clothar had five sons, which led to a new division of Francia. One son, Chramn, unsuccessfully revolted against Clothar, whose men strangled Chramn with a handkerchief and burned him, his wife, and daughters in a peasant's hut. The four surviving sons and their wives soon followed the family tradition of dynastic murder. Two of the sons, Sigibert and Chilperic, married the daughters, Brunhild and Galswinth, of the Visigothic king of Spain. When Chilperic's concubine Fredegund convinced him to strangle Galswinth, Brunhild demanded the lands that had been given to her sister at her marriage, touching off a quarrel between the brothers. Sigibert was murdered in 575, probably at Fredegund's behest, and Chilperic in 584, possibly at Brunhild's orders. Fredegund murdered one of her stepsons, drove a second to suicide, and tried to murder her daughter. She and Chilperic even tried an early form of biological warfare, sending his son Clovis to the town of Berny, in the hopes that he would catch the dysentery then raging there. He did not, so Fredegund

From Brunhild to Broom Hilda

Many American newspapers carry the daily comic strip *Broom Hilda,* whose title character is an ugly old witch. The pun in her name preserves the memory of a sixth-century Frankish queen, Brunhild. Gregory of Tours describes this Visigothic princess on her arrival at the court of her husband, Sigibert: "This young woman was elegant in all that she did, lovely to look at, chaste and decorous in her behavior, wise in her generation and of good address."[21] She proved to be a formidable political leader. After the assassination of her husband (575), she married her nephew, Merovich, but his father, King Chilperic, forced them to separate and made Merovich receive the tonsure. Merovich later escaped and sought to rejoin the queen in Austrasia, but he was surrounded by his father's allies and committed suicide.

Brunhild returned to power with her son, Childebert II, and, after his death, with her grandsons, who ruled the kingdoms of Austrasia (Theudebert II) and Burgundy (Theuderic II).[22] Theudebert grew tired of his grandmother's tutelage and expelled her to Burgundy. According to the seventh-century monk Fredegar, she instigated Theuderic against his brother, and convinced him to invade Austrasia. Theuderic defeated his brother, and, at Brunhild's urging, murdered Theudebert and his son. Theuderic then died of dysentery. Never one to give up, Brunhild immediately had his child son, Sigibert, named king and gathered forces. In the end, local aristocratic opposition, led by Arnulf of Metz and Pippin the Old it would seem, combined with her nephew Clothar II's invasion to defeat her. After her capture, she

> was brought before Chlothar who was boiling with fury against her. . . . She was tormented for three days with a diversity of tortures, and then

on his orders was led through the ranks on a camel. Finally she was tied by her hair, one arm and one leg to the tail of an unbroken horse, and she was cut to shreds by its hoofs at the pace it went.[23]

Thus the beautiful, wise princess of Gregory of Tours became the horrid witch of posterity.

Brunhild offers a classic example of a recurring villain of French history: the foreign-born queen. People at first welcome the beautiful foreign princess; if she should seek real political power, however, she becomes an object of hatred and vilification. The list of such queen-villains in French history is long. Among the most famous, whom we will encounter on our journey, are Brunhild, Isabella of Bavaria (fifteenth century), Catherine de Médicis (sixteenth century), and Marie Antoinette (eighteenth century). They form a rogues' gallery of the evildoers of French textbook history, testimony both to xenophobic and misogynist elements in French (and all Western European) culture. Brunhild offers a classic case of the powerful woman resented by men, vilified by them not only because of their fear of her power but because of their fear of the potential power of all women.

Her reputation shows the enormous dangers faced by historians of Merovingian times. Because we have so few written sources, we must often rely on a single narrative of events. The main sixth-century source, Gregory of Tours, got his bishopric due to Brunhild's patronage: he offers an entirely sympathetic view of her life. The main seventh-century source, Fredegar, comes from the camp of Brunhild's enemies, and so places every possible crime at her doorstep.

later had him murdered in a more mundane manner, with a knife. Not to be outdone, Brunhild murdered her grandson and her great-grandson.

The Merovingians reached the peak of their power under King Clothar II. He first ruled (584) a small part of Neustria, but eventually took over a consolidated kingdom in 613. His son Dagobert I ruled jointly with his father starting in 623 and alone (or jointly with a child son) from 629–638. They even asserted some authority over the Saxons and Bavarians, who were ruled by dukes of mixed Merovingian and local ancestry, and who paid tribute to the King of the Franks. Clothar II issued a famous edict (*c.* 613) reforming the kingdom's tax and judicial practices. Dagobert greatly increased the ties to the Church: he founded the abbeys of Saint-Germain-des-Prés and Saint-Denis, near Paris. The latter became the burial site of the French royal family and remained so until the Revolution. Dagobert also provided the model charter for later royal grants: the monastery of Solignac received (632) full immunity from local control, either laic or ecclesiastic. Kings and monasteries could (and did) thus ally against local secular powers such as counts or religious ones, above all, bishops.

The Merovingian Church

See how our wealth has gone to the churches! Only bishops rule nowadays![24]

King Chilperic, complaining of the Church's wealth in 586

Dagobert's generosity to the Church merely reflected larger trends in Merovingian society. Aristocrats used Church property to preserve their family's economic and political power. Such property enabled the royal family and the aristocrats to share in the benefice of land held for the community as a whole. The bishops and abbots got the income from this land, while the commonwealth, as represented by the Church, kept the ownership. The king would later have the same relationship to the royal demesne.

In the seventh century, aristocratic Frankish families strengthened their ties to the Church. First, aristocratic families, and the royal one, offered support to the monastic reforms introduced by the Irish monk Columbanus, and associated with the monastery at Luxeuil in eastern Burgundy. Rich families founded new monasteries and often sent one of their members into the church. By the end of Dagobert's reign, his kingdom, which had had a mere handful of monasteries in the sixth century, had between five hundred and seven hundred of them. The three largest landowners in the Paris basin were the monasteries of Saint-Denis, Saint-Germain-des-Prés, and Sainte-Geneviève: together they owned half of the land within the city's jurisdiction. Even after having some property confiscated in the early eighth century, Saint-Denis still owned about 250,000 acres; Saint-Germain-des-Prés held a bit less, perhaps 160,000 acres. In Normandy, Saint-Wandrille owned 4,000 *manses*; some monasteries, like Saint-Denis, owned twice as many.[25] The wealth created by this property carried with it responsibilities for public welfare: great monasteries, such as Saint-Martin of Tours, had to provide substantial contingents of mounted warriors to the royal army. Bishops and abbeys often let out estates to their "vassals": the vassal would receive the income (benefice) in return for furnishing a mounted warrior, an early example of the later feudal mechanism (see Chapter 2). The church worked its own estates with slaves. Much of this property passed back into the hands of laymen during the civil wars of the late seventh and early eighth centuries.

Women, too, formed religious communities, which were also dominated by the aristocracy. Many of the most important convents dated from the sixth and seventh centuries; they often had royal patronage, such as Chelles, founded by Queen Balthilde, or the convent founded by Queen (Saint) Radegonde at Poitiers. Radegonde's personal example of ascetic piety and bodily mortification established the benchmark of proper behavior for Frankish female religious. Some great aristocratic women, such as Rictrude, sister-in-law of the very powerful Neustrian Mayor of the Palace, Erchinoald, also founded houses.

Aristocratic families publicized the holy lives of one or more of their members, like Rictrude, whom the Church, anxious for powerful support, then cooperatively canonized as official saints. The process of canonization was all the easier for these families because individual bishops, themselves members of the same aristocratic families, had the final decision.[26] These saints provided an institutionalized form of ancestor worship and helped the Catholic Church spread into the countryside, which had been overwhelmingly pagan even in the fifth century. Throughout the Merovingian period, most rural churches were private chapels, often holding relics from "saints" (ancestors) of the family who owned the church. Little evidence survives to suggest that seventh- or eighth-century rural people practiced orthodox Christianity, although some Christian practices began to infiltrate into the countryside.

An eighth-century church council condemned these pagan practices in thirty-one articles. The clergy tried to change burial practices, eliminating the burial of the dead fully clothed, with all the accoutrements of their social status, as well as the pouring of libations and leaving of meals on the tomb site.[27] The council condemned many practices: belief in sacred grottoes; fertility festivals organized around the ancient menhirs; the special powers obtained by eating animal brains; observance of days of rest in honor of Wodin or Thor; pagan festivals at which participants rent their garments in honor of the "gods"; and the murders, blasphemies, and even orgies carried out in the churches.

The royal family itself had an ambiguous attitude toward the Church. Some kings, like Chilperic, detested the clergy. He was not the only one to covet the possessions of the Church: Clothar I confiscated much of the Church's land and redistributed it to his followers. Yet the royal family also had many female saints, such as Clotilde or Radegonde or Queen Balthilde, an Anglo-Saxon slave who married Clovis II in the middle of the seventh century. Balthilde had some unusual accomplishments for a saint: her contemporaries believed her responsible for the murder of the archbishop of Lyon in 658.

The great counselors of the kings often retired from the royal service to become powerful bishops: Médard at Poitiers, Eloi (Noyon), Ouen (Rouen), and Léger (Fécamp). All of these men later became saints, Léger overcoming the disadvantage of having been executed for participating in the murder of King Childeric II. Today, all over France, towns and churches bear the names of these Merovingian "saints." Saint Eloi, son of a metal-working artisan, later ran the royal mint. He remains the patron saint of metal workers. The most famous aristocratic saint was Arnulf, bishop of Metz, co-founder of the Carolingian dynasty. Arnulf, like the others, had lived a full secular life, in his case as a war leader and royal counselor. He "retired" to become bishop of Metz and, at the end of his life, a hermit in the monastery of Remiremont.

❧ THE CAROLINGIAN INTERLUDE

C H R O N O L O G Y	751–987
751	Pippin crowned King of the Franks
768–814	Reign of Charlemagne (sole ruler after 771)
794	Permanent capital at Aachen
802	Major administrative reforms; *missi dominici*
842	Oaths of Strasbourg
843	Treaty of Verdun; Assembly of Coulaines
858	Quierzy agreement of Charles the Bald and his magnates
877	Capitulary of Quierzy; Coronation Oath of Louis the Stammerer
885–887	Siege of Paris by Vikings
887	Charles the Fat deposed as Emperor
888	Charles the Fat dies; Eudes elected King of the Franks
893	Charles III, the Simple, crowned King of the Franks
910	Founding of abbey of Cluny
911	Charles the Simple gives Normandy to Rollo the Viking
918	Richard the Justiciar duke of the Burgundians
922	Election of Robert as King of the West Franks
923	Death of Robert; election of Raoul of Burgundy as King
929	Death of Charles the Simple
936	Return of Carolingian Louis d'Outremer
987	Hugh Capet elected King of the Franks

Carles li reis, nostre emperere magnes

(Charles the king, our great emperor)

First line of the *The Song of Roland*

The Merovingian dynasty began to come apart at the end of the seventh century, as the descendants of Arnulf of Metz and Pippin the Old took center stage. The incessant family murders rarely allowed an adult Merovingian male to remain in power for any length of time. The marriage of Begga, daughter of Pippin, and of Ansegisel, son of Arnulf, merged the two Austrasian families who had played the critical role in defeating Brunhild. Their son, Grimoald, unsuccessfully tried to supplant the Merovingians in the 650s, but his son, Pippin II, Mayor of the Palace of Austrasia, dominated Frankish politics at the end of the seventh century. One of his sons, Grimoald, became Mayor of the Palace of Neustria, while a second son, Drogo, took the title of duke of Champagne. The family fortunes took a bad turn between Drogo's death in 708 and 714, when a Frisian pagan, upset at Grimoald's aggressive support of Christianization, murdered him. Pippin's death a few months later left his widow, Plectrude, acting for Grimoald's son, Theodald, as the leader of the family's forces. In 715, however, the Neustrians rose against her and forced her to surrender part of Pippin II's treasure.

Plectrude had imprisoned her greatest potential family rival, Charles, son of Pippin II and his concubine Alphaïde, but Charles escaped and raised an army of his own. Charles Martel, as he became known, quickly defeated Plectrude, then the Neustrians, and consolidated his power over the kingdoms of Austrasia, Neustria, and Burgundy by 719. At the death of the figurehead Merovingian king of Austrasia, he installed a new one (721). Charles also reconfigured the clergy once again, following the practices used during the civil wars of the seventh century.[28] He made his nephew Hugues bishop of Paris, Rouen, and Bayeux, as well as abbot of Fontenelle and Jumièges, and distributed other bishoprics and abbeys to those who had supported him. Later Carolingian propaganda made out this victory to be foreordained, to be their triumph over the do-nothing Merovingians, but Merovingian power really only disappeared after the death of the Neustrian king Childebert III (694–711).

Charles's military prowess was quickly tested by a new challenge, from the Muslim invaders who had recently (711) conquered Spain. The Muslims moved into the former Gaul, capturing Narbonne and most of Gothia, besieging Toulouse (721), taking Avignon, and sacking Autun (725). Charles solidified his position by leading several successful campaigns against them, beginning with the great victory at Tours/Poitiers, 732/734, and continuing through his victory near Narbonne in 737.[29] In 751, Charles's son Pippin simply dispensed with the last Merovingian, Childeric III, sending him off to a monastery.

Pippin's initial coronation, sanctioned by Pope Zachary, paled in importance to the events of 754, when Pope Stephen II came to Saint-Denis to crown Pippin and his sons, Charles and Carloman:[31]

Good King Dagobert

Every French schoolchild today learns a nursery rhyme that reinforces the Carolingian view of the Merovingians. The song, *The Good King Dagobert,* has as its two main characters the greatest of Merovingian kings, Dagobert I, and his faithful advisor, Saint Éloi. One verse goes as follows:

Good king Dagobert
Was hunting in the plain of Anvers
The great Saint Éloi said to him, "Oh my king!
Your Majesty is really out of breath!"
"It's true," the king responded
"A rabbit was chasing me."[30]

> By the hands of the Pontiff Stephen, in the church of the saint martyrs . . .
> Denis, Rusticus, and Eleutherius . . . he [Pippin], together with his sons
> Charles and Carloman, was anointed and blessed king and father in the
> name of the Holy Trinity. In the same church and on the same day, the
> above said Pontiff blessed . . . Bertrade, wife of the very brilliant king, and,
> at the same time, confirmed his blessing on . . . the principal nobles of the
> Franks and tied them all by . . . law of excommunication never to dare
> henceforth to elect a king issued from another family origin.[31]

The new dynasty, the Carolingians, provided many substantial precedents for
the kingdom of France. First, they reinvigorated the traditional ties of the Frankish
monarchy with the Church. In 753, Pippin III granted the Church the right to tithe
in Frankish lands and approved the Pope's creation of a network of parishes in rural
Frankish lands, a network not fully elaborated until at least two centuries later. In
turn, the Pope sanctified Frankish kingship: first that of Pippin himself, then that of
his son, Charlemagne (768–814), whom Pope Hadrian crowned Holy Roman Emperor on Christmas Day 800.

His larger function, both Emperor and king, made Charlemagne a European,
not simply a French figure. No King of France ever ruled a kingdom remotely the
size of Charlemagne's empire, so we must, at least in politics, treat the Carolingian
period primarily as an interlude. Charlemagne's empire covered much of western
Europe: virtually all of modern-day France, Belgium, the Netherlands, Luxembourg,
the former West Germany, Switzerland, and Austria, Italy from Rome north, and the
county of Barcelona in Spain. The tribes immediately east of this empire—the Slavic
Wends and Sorbs in the northeast (in eastern Germany and Poland), the Avars in the
southeast (in Hungary)—paid tribute to the Emperor. Charlemagne's empire, and
its dependencies, with a few exceptions such as Poland, largely defined the eastern
limits of Western Christianity.[32]

Charlemagne built his empire on military prowess. His grandfather, Charles
Martel, and his father, King Pippin, had created the foundations of a military appa-
ratus built on the exchange of a land grant, often estates confiscated from the
Church, in return for service. They used three major types of grants:

1. Benefices attached to the office of count, which was not hereditary but often
   passed from a man to his son, nephew, or brother.

2. Direct retainers (*fideles*) of the king, who received a small land grant in return for their personal service.

3. Grants of rich abbeys or bishoprics, which owed military service.

Charlemagne had the unquestioned authority to call up all free males (over twelve)
in his empire for military service. Some two thousand men, many of them powerful
lords, had direct ties to him. Some historians suggest that, counting the mounted
warriors of his bishops, counts, and other close retainers, Charlemagne had fifty
thousand horsemen, and even more foot soldiers, at his disposal.

Actual armies in the field rarely exceeded ten thousand men. Each time Charlemagne would fight, he simply called out the men of the nearby sections of his empire, as well as the immediate retainers who followed him everywhere. In 806, for his campaign against the Saxons, Charlemagne ordered the horsemen to turn out with a shield, a lance, a long and a short sword, a bow, and a sheaf of arrows, as well as a cart filled with three months of provisions. His largest armies probably had something like three thousand horsemen and about ten thousand infantry, although little evidence suggests that the catalogue of weapons demanded in 806 could actually be provided by each soldier. (Metal objects were quite scarce in western Europe.)

The Frankish kingdoms, both those of the Merovingians and that of Charlemagne, rested on the exploits of a war chief, who established a tribute-based area of rulership. Charlemagne continuously expanded his tribute area, conquering Italy and the Spanish March (near Barcelona), exacting money from the Saxons, then the Avars and other peoples of central Europe. He began the transition away from this tribute-based empire and toward a more permanent state at the end of the eighth century. He set up a permanent court at Aachen (794) and issued a great reforming ordinance in 802, setting out the lines of ecclesiastical and secular administration. From that point forward, the Franks ceased to be an expansionist group and began to defend what they already had. Charlemagne's initial system, based on successful raids and tribute, paid for itself; his new system, essentially defensive, required new levels of local initiative and substantial local funding. The changed nature of the Carolingian empire made inevitable the diffusion of political power: the Emperors had to rely on an extensive network of counts (about five hundred), bishops (one hundred), and abbots (two hundred major ones).

Carolingian counts provided both military leadership and judicial authority. Like Roman Imperial officers, in return for their service, counts received the benefice (income) of the lands attached to their office, called in Carolingian Latin a *feodum*, a word derived from the Frankish *fĕh-ód* (movable property). Their office and the land did not belong to their families as hereditary property, but were supposed to revert to the king upon their death or dismissal. Most counts were powerful local landowners; in time, they interwove their personal estates and their official ones and sought to change the nature of the benefice, or fief, into personal property, and the countship from office to title, to make both the property and the countship hereditary. Charlemagne himself complained in 806 that "counts and other persons who hold benefices from us treat these as if they were their own allodial possessions."[33] As the Carolingian state weakened, under Charlemagne's successors, the counts gradually succeeded. Shortly after his accession as King of the West Franks, Charles the Bald ratified the accord reached by the great aristocrats of his kingdom at Coulaines (843). The king, the aristocrats, and the administrators of the "commonwealth" promised to respect Church property; the king also promised not to remove anyone from an *honor* (royal office) simply of his own will.

These engagements became more precise in 858, when Charles issued the Cartulary of Quierzy, which reaffirmed the royal promise to the great men of West Francia, in return for their promise of loyalty in Charles's war against Louis the German. This process reached a logical conclusion in 877, when Louis the Stammerer, at the urging of archbishop Hincmar of Reims, took a series of oaths promising to protect the Church and to uphold the laws of the kingdom, before being crowned by Hincmar. Here again we see the mixture of cultural elements: Louis renewed traditional Germanic personal ties between the military leader or king and his retainers; he confirmed those holding royal office, above all counts, whose office had Roman roots; and he participated in a coronation ceremony, including a sworn oath to protect the church and the law, that Hincmar borrowed from the Old Testament.

Official authority in much of West Francia thus passed gradually into individual hands. The Kings of West Francia fought on three levels during the ninth century. First, they sought to maintain the unity of the Christian empire of Charlemagne. Many of the leading clergy of the time strongly supported this combined political and religious unity, and the image remained deeply rooted in western European consciousness for centuries to come. As late as the reign of Louis XIII (1610–1643), the King of France used the phrase the "public good of the Christian commonwealth" in his diplomatic correspondence. Second, these kings had to fight off outside invasions, above all the devastating raids of the Vikings in the valleys of the Loire and Seine. Third, they had to obtain support from powerful magnates in order to fight either their Carolingian rivals or Viking invaders. The need for magnate support led to progressively greater extension of official authority to these men. The individual possession of official authority became the cornerstone of what we call feudalism, a word derived from *fĕh-ód/feodum,* the landed property attached to public authority.[34]

Charles's empire did not long survive him because his heirs followed the Merovingian example of internecine warfare. In 813, with death approaching, the great Emperor made his son Louis the Pious co-ruler. Most of Louis's siblings had died before their father, although Charlemagne had given Italy to his son Pippin.[35] Louis first sought to divide the empire (817) among his three sons: Louis would get Bavaria; Pippin, the Aquitaine; and Lothaire, the core Frankish lands of the Empire and the imperial title. The family wars arrived soon afterward. In 818, Louis's nephew Bernard, king of Italy, rebelled, fearing to lose his independence. Louis crushed the rebellion and blinded Bernard, who lost both life and kingdom in the aftermath. When Louis, become a widower, married Judith, daughter of Welf (a Rhenish aristocrat), and they had a son, his efforts to provide for the boy (Charles) using some of Lothaire's lands led to a rebellion by the three older boys (829). From that point until Louis's death in 840, the children and father fought each other in constantly shifting coalitions. Lothaire originally defeated his father, but then fell out with his brothers, enabling Louis to regain the advantage. Pippin died in 838; his relatives did not install his children as rulers of Aquitaine.

Lothaire, Louis, and Charles fought again after their father died, but they agreed to divide the Empire at the Treaty of Verdun (843). Lothaire became Emperor, with a kingdom centered on the family possessions in Austrasia; Louis the German kept the area east of the Rhine, known as East Francia; Charles got the region to the west of the Meuse, Saône, and Rhône rivers. This region, West Francia, became the core of France. The northern part of the middle kingdom (which later took the name Lotharingia, after its second ruler, Lothaire II) slowly slipped under the authority of the rulers of East Francia. The rulers of East Francia combined their kingdom and most of Lothaire's realm into the Holy Roman Empire of the German Nation (962).

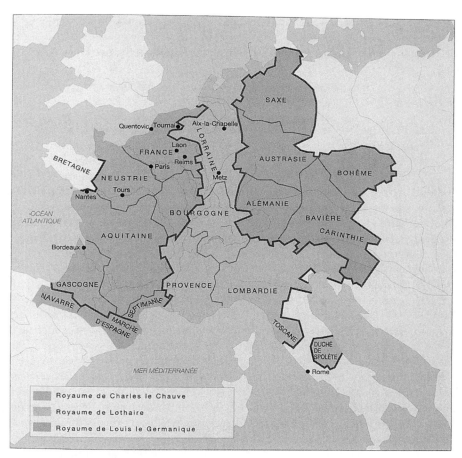

Dividing the Empire: The Treaty of Verdun (843).

They kept both kingdoms throughout the Middle Ages, but many of Lothaire's Gallic provinces, starting with Lyon in 1292 and Dauphiné in 1349, later became parts of the kingdom of France.

The political division of 843 reflected many factors. First, the north–south orientation continued the long-standing tradition by which northern Franks, including abbots and bishops, received territories in the south to provide them with Mediterranean products like wine and oil. Second, the division preserved to a considerable degree the historical geography of Gallo-Roman and Merovingian times. In the north, Lothaire's territories took most of the old Austrasia. The boundary between his kingdom and West Francia also closely followed in that region the old border between the two parts of the Roman province known as *Belgica*.

That boundary had come to reflect as well the linguistic separation between the peoples of East and West Francia. The so-called *Oaths of Strasbourg* (842), an alliance between rulers of East and West Francia, shows the extent to which West

Frankish had become a Romance language, while East Frankish remained a Germanic one. One of its passages—"For the love of God and the salvation of the Christian people and our common salvation"—reads as follows in the two languages:

West Frankish—*Pro deo amur et pro christian poblo et nostro commun salvament*;

East Frankish—*In godes minna ind in thes christanes folches ind unser bedhero gehaltnissi.*[36]

Neither the Treaty of Verdun nor a later (870) agreement between Charles the Bald and the sons of Louis the German to divide Lothaire's kingdom consciously took any real note of language boundaries. The German territorial unit ended up with virtually all of Lothaire's kingdom, including such Romance-speaking areas as the county of Burgundy and Provence. No ninth-century evidence suggests contemporaries viewed these divisions as anything other than temporary arrangements; indeed, the various Carolingians signed a bewildering variety of agreements throughout the ninth century.

The constant civil wars enormously weakened all Frankish kingdoms. Contemporary chroniclers bewailed the terrible loss of trained fighters at the battle of Fontenoy (841): "[the carnage] wrought on that accursed day, which ought no longer to be counted in the year, which should be banished from the memory of men, and be for ever deprived of the light of the sun and of the beams of the morning."[37] All three Carolingian kingdoms failed to protect their inhabitants against the great Viking, Hungarian, and Muslim incursions of the ninth and tenth centuries. West Francia suffered most from the Vikings, who sacked its major towns: Paris and Rouen on the Seine; Nantes, Angers, and Tours on the Loire; Bordeaux and Périgueux in the southwest. It also felt the sting of the Hungarian and Muslim incursions: the Muslims not only conquered Spain and the major islands, but set up raiding bases, such as Freixenetum (near modern-day Saint-Tropez), which they held from the end of the ninth century until 972.

Charles the Bald (843–877) also had constantly to struggle against the dispossessed son of Pippin of Aquitaine, whom he twice imprisoned and finally condemned to death (864) as a "traitor to the fatherland and to Christendom." Charles had less success with the Breton leaders, Nominoé and Erispoë, who permanently attached the counties of Rennes and Nantes to their principality. In the end, after Erispoë's cousin Salomon had him murdered and seized control of the "kingdom," Charles convinced Salomon to swear fidelity (867–868) and accept again the overlordship of the King of the Franks.

Each of the three branches of the Carolingians held the Imperial dignity between 843–875. The kingdom of West Francia passed in rapid succession to Charles the Bald's son and two grandsons, before ending up in the hands of his nephew, Charles the Fat, in 885. This Charles, the last surviving son of Louis the German, briefly reunited the entire empire, from 885–887.[38]

The chaotic situation of the 880s encouraged magnates in outlying regions, with the cooperation of local bishops, to create splinter kingdoms. Many of these efforts failed, but two southern magnates built enduring principalities. Boso of Vienne created a kingdom of Burgundy whose main provinces, Dauphiné, Provence, and the county of Burgundy, long remained outside the kingdom of France.[39] Bernard Plantevelue ("Hairy hands," so-called because of his fox-like cunning), and his son, William the Pious, who took the title "duke of the Aquitanians" in 898, made Aquitaine into a semi-autonomous principality. As a self-styled "prince," William used his princely prerogative to found the abbey of Cluny (910), which became the greatest religious power of eleventh-century western Europe.

Charles the Fat's brief reign in the old empire ended when he could not protect the Frankish heartland against the Viking attack on Paris. His death in 888 led the magnates of the northern part of West Francia to turn to Eudes, count of Paris, rather than the Carolingian child, Charles, youngest grandson of Charles the Bald. In many respects, the northern magnates elected Eudes, who had saved Paris, more to be their *kuning*, or war leader, than any sort of real king. Southern counts seem not to have attended his election and many important bishops, above all the archbishop of Reims, also stayed away. The Carolingian mystique still carried enormous power: when Charles III reached the age of royal majority (fourteen), his followers crowned him king at Reims (893). West Francia thus had two kings until Eudes's death in 898.

Even after Eudes's death, Charles the Simple could not break Robertian power in the Paris region, which passed to Eudes's brother, Robert. Charles further undermined his power in the northwest in 911, when he handed over the county of Rouen and the rest of Normandy to the Viking leader Rollo, in return for support against other Viking bands. The Carolingians had thus lost control of the three richest regions of the western kingdom: the Paris basin and the Loire valley to the Robertians, and Normandy to the Vikings. In the end, these two very rich agricultural regions, the Robertian stronghold in the area between the Seine and Loire and the newly created Normandy, became the effective basis for a powerful and permanent kingdom of France. The Robertians, the Norman ducal house, and the counts of Anjou, who rose to prominence when the Robertians shifted their focus from the Loire valley to Paris, each obtained their initial power in the late ninth and early tenth centuries. They would dominate high politics in this region for the next nine hundred years.

Charles the Simple did not enjoy unalloyed success as king. When he failed to make good his claims on Lorraine (922), the west Frankish barons struck again, naming Eudes's brother, Robert, king. Charles moved quickly against him, defeating Robert and killing him (923). The dissatisfied barons then elected Robert's son-in-law, Raoul of Burgundy, (923–936), as their "king." Charles fell into a trap set by Herbert II of Vermandois (Raoul's brother-in-law); he spent the last six years of his life in prison. Raoul remained sole king from 929–936, when he died, childless.

The pattern of Carolingians and Robertians either ruling in opposition to each other or alternately ended in 936, when the barons called back from England the Carolingian Louis IV, son of Charles the Simple. Louis made a deal with King Robert's son, Hugh the Great. Hugh supported Louis's claim to the throne, in return for which Louis granted Hugh the title, duke of the Franks, raising his family to the same level as those of the dukes of the Aquitainians and Burgundians, who had simply usurped their titles.

The Carolingians and Merovingians provided important legacies for the later French monarchy. The Carolingian legacy, however, might better be termed a European

THE ROBERTIANS

Who was this Eudes and how did he emerge as a potential King of the Franks? The question carries particular importance because Eudes's family, initially known as the Robertians but later as the Capetians, permanently obtained the throne in 987.

The rise to power of his family offers a superb example of the mechanisms of power in the Carolingian empire. They combined the three key elements of success: royal office, church office, and judicious marriage alliances. The royal and church offices surely stemmed from the family's ties to three East Frankish princesses related to the powerful Gerold family: Hildegarde of Gerold, wife of Charlemagne and mother of Louis the Pious; Louis's first wife, Irmengarde; and Ermentrude, wife of Charles the Bald. The Robertians may also have had ties to Judith of Welf, Louis the Pious's second wife.

In 843, when Charles the Bald left Worms with his wife Ermentrude, daughter of Eudes of Orléans and niece of the royal seneschal, Adalard, lay abbot of the great monastery of Saint-Martin of Tours, he apparently took two young clients of the royal couple with him, Robert of Worms and Eudes of Blois, son of William, count of Blois, and a member of the Gerold family. Eudes's name suggests the ties of his father to another great Gerold baron, Eudes, count of Orléans; the elder Eudes and William had moved to the two cities.[40] As for Robert of Worms, he and Eudes of Blois quickly introduced each other's names into their families; moreover, his son, Robert the Strong, inherited all the clients of Eudes of Orléans.[41] Adalard the seneschal's great power in the Loire valley naturally helped his kinsmen receive royal offices there. Robert the Strong held the countship of Tours by the early 850s. The great Gerold barons—Adalard, Robert, and Eudes—plotted with their kinsman Louis the German against King Charles in 858. Robert lost some influence when the plot failed, but further family intrigue enabled him to restore his power by the early 860s, and even briefly to succeed Adalard as lay abbot at Saint-Martin. His death in battle against the Vikings briefly reduced the family fortunes, but his young sons Robert and Eudes regained the family power when they reached adulthood. Eudes, who had become count of Paris in 882, successfully resisted the long Viking siege that started in 885; when the two great power brokers of West Francia (Hugh the Abbot and chancellor Gozlin) died, Eudes became the Seine valley's preeminent baron. Emperor Charles the Fat, now also King of the West Franks, soon invested Eudes with the Neustrian "lands of his father." When Charles the Fat died (888), the archbishop of Sens, a Robertian ally, crowned Eudes king after his election by an assembly of Frankish barons. In time, Robert, too, briefly (922–923) served as king.

The essential role of family ties to women in the rise of the Robertians underscores the centrality of cognatic kinship in the Germanic world. Maternal uncles, men like Adalard, played a critical role in the career of an aristocratic boy. The adoption of names, like Eudes, from the female line bears witness to the importance of cognatic kinship. The Robertians continued the policy of marriage to women of more distinguished families and the adoption of male names from cognatic kin when they took permanent control of the kingship of West Francia (987).

one. The site of Charlemagne's capital, Aachen, in the heartland of the Rhenish Franks, suggests that the Carolingians attempted, and failed, to create a state centered around the great river. The territorial division of the Treaty of Verdun recreated a loose entity, West Francia, that had ties to traditional Merovingian and Roman political geographies. The ongoing struggles within the Carolingian family in the ninth century brought together the three kingdoms of East Francia, Lotharingia, and West Francia in differing combinations, but the shadow of the great empire always lay over Charlemagne's successors. The rebellion of 858, which sought to remove Charles the Bald and make Louis the German king in the west, offers a classic example of the continued integration of the Frankish elite throughout the old empire in the ninth century.

In a political sense, the Merovingian legacy proved decisive to France. Here the Robertians/Capetians and the Merovingians form a continuity; the Carolingians provide a rupture, not continuity. Louis the Pious left his oldest son the family lands in Lorraine and the Rhine valley, not the lands around Paris. The Robertians/Capetians built their new monarchy precisely in the region (Paris, Senlis, Soissons, Orléans) of Clovis's initial strength, not in the old Germanic homeland between Lorraine and the Rhine valley.

The Merovingians also left a legacy of sacred kingship and a tradition of close royal ties to the Church, particularly to powerful abbeys such as Saint-Denis, Saint-Germain-des-Prés, and Saint-Martin of Tours. These ties to abbeys, and the king's right to protect them, proved critical in the spread of royal authority in the twelfth century. In the tenth through twelfth centuries, when early Capetian kings had little real power, the Merovingian legacy of the sacred kingship, that emphasis on royal blood ubiquitous in European mythologies of monarchy, served the monarchy well. The legacy long endured: the Carolingians transformed Clovis into the French Louis, which they quickly claimed as their own. In time the Capetians would usurp the two most prominent names used by the Carolingians, Louis and Charles.

The Carolingian Renascence

This king, who showed himself so great in extending his empire and subduing foreign nations, and was constantly occupied with plans to that end, undertook also very many works calculated to adorn and benefit his kingdom.

Einhard, speaking of Charlemagne

The Carolingians provided a rich cultural legacy for their Capetian successors. Einhard tells us that Charlemagne sought to make many cultural improvements by attracting scholars from all over Europe to his court: he even kidnapped some of them. He built churches, such as the magnificent chapel at Aachen, and tried to rewrite law codes. He ordered scholars to compose "a grammar of his native language" and encouraged their work in other areas. His efforts, and those of his successors, bore much fruit. To Carolingian scholars, we owe the diffusion of modern Western printed script, with lowercase letters, and the use of punctuation. Others created the first western European system for music notation in order to introduce what we know as Gregorian chant into Frankish lands.

The most famous scholar, the Anglo-Saxon Alcuin, was among those who came willingly. Alcuin wrote treatises on grammar (*De grammatica*) and logic (*De dialetica*), thus reviving the study of both. He and other scholars revised existing texts of the Bible, producing a text that, if not completely normative in Charlemagne's Empire, certainly created a much higher level of consistency in biblical texts.[42] The production of a large number of Bibles by the *scriptorium* (general writing room) of the monastery of Saint-Martin of Tours in the 840s—thirteen complete or partial copies survive, as well as almost twenty Gospel sets and a New Testament—helped spread orthodox Christianity. "For the first eight hundred years of the Christian era some eighteen hundred western manuscripts or fragments of manuscripts remain, while over seven thousand survive from the ninth century alone."[43] Even the phrase "Christian era" reminds us of their influence: only from the time of Charlemagne do western European sources provide a date in reference to the birth of Christ: the *anno domini* (A.D.) calendar now ubiquitous in Europeanized cultures.

The Carolingian cultural legacy focused on the written word. Charlemagne ordered all his *missi dominici* to send written reports of their visits to court starting in 802. The first known reference to a *scriptorium* for monks occurs in 820, for the monastery of Saint-Gall; the monastery of Corbie, another key center of manuscript production, had its own parchment maker by 822. Carolingian monasteries had remarkably large libraries: Saint-Gall and Reichenau abbeys had about four hundred manuscripts each (some with multiple works), Saint-Riquier had two hundred fifty-six, with over five hundred titles, and Lorsch's catalogue lists almost six hundred titles. Even Charlemagne's will, as reported to us by Einhard, makes special mention of his library: "He likewise commands that the books which he has collected in his library in great numbers shall be sold for fair prices to such as want them" (see Plate 1).

The Carolingians left a political legacy of close ties between central state and Church, a network of aristocratic local rulers, acting (theoretically) in the king's name, and a tradition of state action, either in inquests or in investigations of actions taken by local authorities. Charlemagne left a network of royal officials, the *missi dominici*, a group of men who oversaw the work of the counts. These officials included many churchmen, so that early on the central state allied with abbeys to fight against powerful local landlords. The *missi dominici*, in a fitting symbol of the decline of the Carolingians, had disappeared by the middle of the tenth century. Some of the records produced by these officials, however, survived into the High Middle Ages. Later kings and their officials had a record of what Charlemagne and *his* advisors had done, which they could use to establish precedents for action. Charlemagne provided the base, the point of reference, for all later state action.[44] Charlemagne even issued a regular coinage, the famous silver pennies. He and Louis minted so many pennies that one ransom paid to a Viking band in the middle of the ninth century included over one million of them.

In a larger context, the Carolingians left an agricultural system of latifundial estates, worked by a combination of slave and free labor, intermixed with peasant holdings. Trade networks tied them both to the Mediterranean and to the north. The largest group of merchants seems to have been the Jews, who had returned to the kingdom after their expulsion by Dagobert I (in 629): Charlemagne confirmed Jewish laws and even employed the Jew Isaac as a translator for his embassy to the Caliph of Baghdad. Louis the Pious gave full protection to the Jews, and weathered harsh criticism from some bishops because of his tolerance. By the ninth or tenth centuries, Jews, although still a quite small percentage of the population, likely controlled much of Frankish commerce, from their communities at Lyon, Rouen, Troyes, and elsewhere.

Charlemagne's Legacy

All the rest of his life he was regarded by everyone with the utmost love and affection, so much so that not the least accusation of unjust rigor was ever made against him.

Einhard

Charlemagne cast a shadow over all medieval European kings. He became a figure of legend, as in *The Song of Roland,* where he is two hundred years old. Many regarded him as a saint, despite the official Church's more reticent position regarding the great king's personal morality. Cults evolved around the Emperor, especially in the fourteenth and fifteenth centuries. The cult became so strong that his name, never before used by the Capetians, was taken by the last of their line, Charles IV, in 1322. From 1364–1498, four of the five French kings bore Charles's name. Many churches had sculptures of him, and the great Gothic structures of Saint-Denis and Chartres each had stained glass windows providing scenes from his life.

Charlemagne left well ensconced in the folk memory an almost mythical tradition of effective government: honest justice, sound money, fair taxation, and military protection against outside threats. He provided a difficult role model for medieval kings, but if they could remind their contemporaries of the great Emperor, they could call upon his moral legacy to strengthen their own rule. Successful French kings did precisely that.

THE CAPETIAN TAKEOVER

Though first among Franks, you are but a serf in the order of kings.[45]

Adalbero, bishop of Laon, writing of King Robert II

Hugh Capet owed his rulership of West Francia, in a literal sense, to an election by its great barons and ecclesiastics, who thereby deposed the last patrilineal descendant of Charlemagne, Charles, duke of Lower Lorraine, uncle of the last Carolingian king, Louis V. The simple assertion that the barons "elected" Hugh king, however, deserves closer scrutiny. Louis V had come to Hugh's estate at Compiègne to sign a treaty with the representatives of the German Emperor, but he died in a hunting accident on 22 May 987. Adalbero, archbishop of Reims, convinced the barons attending the royal court that they needed to reassemble in a few weeks because "all of the princes who, by their wisdom and their devotion, are capable of administering the affairs of the kingdom are not present." He then made the barons swear that they would take no action to choose a king until the electoral meeting.

The meeting took place in June, in Hugh's stronghold of Senlis. As duke of the Franks, Hugh had the right to chair the meeting. The assembly had much the

A CONTEMPORARY DESCRIBES CHARLEMAGNE[46]

Charles was large and strong, and of lofty stature, though not disproportionately tall (his height is well known to have been seven times the length of his foot); the upper part of his head was round, his eyes very large and animated, nose a little long, hair fair, and face laughing and merry. Thus his appearance was always stately and dignified, whether he was standing or sitting; although his neck was thick and somewhat short, and his belly rather prominent. . . . In accordance with the national custom, he took frequent exercise on horseback . . . and often practiced swimming, in which he was such an adept that none could surpass him . . . Charles was temperate in eating, and particularly so in drinking, for he abominated drunkenness in anybody . . . His meals ordinarily consisted of four courses, not counting the roast, which his huntsmen used to bring in on the spit; he was more fond of this than of any other dish. While at table, he listened to reading or music. The subjects of the readings were the stories and deeds of olden time: he was fond, too, of St. Augustine's books, and especially of the one entitled *The City of God*. . . . Charles had a gift of ready and fluent speech . . . He was not satisfied with command of his native language merely, but gave

Charlemagne and a wife: manuscript c. 820, monastery of St. Paul in Carinthia.

SOURCE: F. Herr, Charlemagne and His World (New York: Macmillan Publishing, 1975), 22. Original: Radio Times Hulton Picture Library. © Erich Lessing/Art Resources, NY.

attention to the study of foreign ones, and . . . was such a master of Latin that he could speak it as well as his native tongue; but he could understand Greek better than he could speak it. . . . He also tried to write, and used to keep tablets and blanks in bed under his pillow, that at leisure hours he might accustom his hand to form the letters; however, as he did not begin his efforts in due season, but late in life, they met with ill success.

aura of a family council: the three other dukes within Gaul, those of the Aquitainians (who apparently did not attend), the Normans, and the Burgundians, were Hugh's brothers-in-law and his younger brother; the important counts of Francia—Vermandois, Blois, Troyes, Anjou—were his cousins and vassals. Hugh not only descended from kings Eudes and Robert but, via his grandmother, Beatrice of Vermandois, from Charlemagne. His mother, Hedwige, was the daughter of the German king Henry I.[47] That said, the opposing candidate, Charles, duke of Lower Lor-

The Kingdom of Hugh Capet

raine, had blood ties to most of these barons; he was the son of a Carolingian king, Louis IV.

Hugh had the great good fortune to oppose a man widely disrespected by his peers. Charles had had the temerity to marry the daughter of a simply knight (a vassal of Hugh no less), a fact brought out by archbishop Adalbero of Reims at the election assembly. We get some idea of Charles's reputation from a letter sent to him by bishop Thierry of Metz in 984:

> Bloated, distended by fat, dog . . . you have abandoned the ways of your fathers, denied your creator; remember how many times I have used a finger to close your impudent mouth when, with the hissing of snake, you spread abominable lies about the archbishop of Reims, and even more abominable ones about the queen. You know better than I all that you have done against the bishop of Laon.

Not to be outdone, Charles responded in kind: "Model of hypocrites, public enemy of the State, drunkard . . . you bring disorder to divine and human laws alike."[48]

As this exchange suggests, Charles had particularly bad relations with the bishops of northeastern France: Adalbero of Reims, Adalbero (Ascelin) of Laon, and Thierry of Metz. The first two played the critical roles in Hugh Capet's elevation to the throne. The only surviving account of the electoral assembly gives Adalbero of Reims the central role. His speech, in this account, convinces the barons to support Hugh over Charles.

> Examine the matter closely. . . . Consider the demotion of Charles results more from his own fault than from that of another; wish the happiness of the *Respublica* rather than its misfortune! If you wish its misfortune, raise Charles to the throne; if you wish its good fortune, crown as king the eminent duke Hugh . . . Choose the duke, the most illustrious by his action, his nobility and his military power; you will find in him a defender not only of the State but of your private interests.[49]

Not surprisingly, Hugh's relatives followed Adalbero's advice; the good archbishop finished the job on 3 July 987, when he crowned and anointed Hugh at Noyon.

This brief account of Hugh's election shows that the Church played a critical role in the transferral of the special aura of kingship to the new dynasty. When Adalbero of Reims anointed Hugh with the special chrism oil of coronation held at Reims, he did much to transfer the special attributes of sacred kingship to the new dynasty. Hugh and Adalbero tried to intensify this connection later in 987: at Christmas, the archbishop, in the church of the Holy Cross at Orléans, another of Hugh's strongholds, anointed Hugh's son Robert with the sacred unction. The effective insistence of archbishop Hincmar of Reims in the ninth century that kings had to be anointed with holy oils by a bishop (specifically, the archbishop of Reims), and that the unction gave them special characteristics, here came into play.

Charlemagne's son, Louis, had received a special anointing with holy oils at his coronation (as Emperor) in 816. The Kings of West Francia took up this practice beginning with Charles the Bald. Archbishop Hincmar wrote to Charles that: "It is to your anointing, an episcopal and spiritual act, and to the blessing that flows from it, much more than to your temporal power, that you owe your royal dignity." No one else in Francia received this special anointing from the Church. Hincmar successfully spread the story that Reims held a Sacred Phial, one brought by a dove to Saint Remy at the time of Clovis's baptism. The Sacred Phial held the oil of chrism used only in the coronation of rightful Kings of the Franks (later of France); no human hands replenished it, rather it mysteriously replenished itself through divine intervention. The special aura of divine sanction doubtless helped overcome the obvious difficulties created by starting a new dynasty, one whose royal blood contemporaries openly doubted.[50] Hincmar also introduced the practice of the coronation oath, by which the king promised to protect the rights of the Church and the laws of the commonwealth; Louis the Stammerer, in 877, was the first to take this oath, which became permanent. It provided the basis for a contractual understanding of kingship that undergirded the French political order.

Holy oil or no, Hugh Capet needed four years to make good his effective claim to the throne. Charles raised his standard in the ancient Carolingian capital of Laon, capturing bishop Ascelin. In 989, when Adalbero of Reims died, Hugh foolishly supported a cousin of Charles, Arnoul, as the new archbishop; Arnoul immediately turned the city over to Charles. The great counts of the north—Vermandois, Troyes, Rethel, and Soissons—cousins of both men, now changed sides. The fate of the new dynasty hung precariously in the balance for two years, when Ascelin, restored to his bishopric of Laon in return for sworn promises of loyalty to Charles, carried out the decisive coup. At a banquet on 29 March 991, Charles dipped some bread in a glass of wine which he offered to Ascelin, telling him not to drink it if he were disloyal, lest he be thought a new Judas: Ascelin drained the glass, swearing that "I will keep my faith; if not, let me perish with Judas."[51] The next morning, Ascelin's retainers arrested both Charles and Arnoul, effectively ending the civil war. Three months later, a council of the French church stripped Arnoul of his office, which passed into the hands of Hugh's secretary, Gerbert. The cousins, as might be expected, jumped on the bandwagon again.

Hugh Capet also owed his throne in part to international politics. Adalbero of Reims had very close ties to the court of the child Emperor Otto III of Germany (close enough that he once faced treason charges about them). One can well understand why Otto would want to keep the Carolingian family off the throne of West Francia. Supporting his first cousin, Hugh Capet, for the other great crown of western Europe could only solidify the Ottonian claim to be supreme in Europe. The Ottonians, after 987 in possession of the Imperial throne and that of West Francia (via female line), thus definitely supplanted the Carolingians as the first family of western Europe. The Capetians themselves quickly made clear to all their Ottonian origins: their third king, Henry I (1031–1060), the first one to depart from the traditional male family names (Hugh, Robert or Eudes), took the name of his Ottonian royal ancestor, his great-grandfather, King Henry I of Germany.

Notes

1. P. Wells, *The Barbarians Speak: How the Conquered Peoples Shaped Roman Europe* (Princeton: Princeton University Press, 1999), 225–226.

2. A more accurate term for the orthodox Christian Church in fifth-century western Europe might be the Latin-rite Church, because the term "Catholic" Church suggests both a level of coherence and a continuity with the later Catholic Church that is misleading. Yet the documents of the time, such as the bishops' letter to Clovis, do refer to the "catholic" church and the term has become one of customary usage among historians. Scholars still debate whether a "Catholic" Church, in our modern sense of the term, existed before the Council of Trent (ended 1563) or, for others, before the Fourth Lateran Council decrees (1215). For simplicity's sake, I have generally used the term "Catholic," but readers should be aware of its different meaning in the early chapters of the book.

3. Gregory of Tours, *The History of the Franks*, trans. L. Thorpe (London; New York: Penguin, 1974), 134.

4. Bertram's will of 613 is discussed in I. Wood, *The Merovingian Kingdoms, 450–751* (London; New York: Longman, 1994), 207–211. On donations to the Church in this period, see also J. M. Wallace-Hadrill, *The Frankish Church* (Oxford; New York: The Clarendon Press, Oxford University Press, 1983).

5. Sidonius Apollinaris, *Poems and Letters*, trans. W. B. Anderson (Cambridge, MA: Harvard University Press, 1936), two vols., I, 423–25, book II, letter 2.

6. Sidonius *Poems and Letters*, I, 341, book I, letter 2.

7. In the Middle Ages, French kings had to be wary of law that suggested the Emperor stood above them. French kings, including Louis XIV, often denounced Roman law at the same time that they sought to make use of some of its precepts.

8. Gregory of Tours, *History of the Franks*, 161. The good bishop here refers particularly to Clovis's victories over the Visigothic king Alaric II, who was an Arian. I have modified the Thorpe translation, because the original says "per totas Gallias," an accusative plural form. Robert Latouche's French translation suggests "all the Gauls," which accurately implies a multiplicity of "Gauls" in Clovis's lifetime. The original of Gregory can be found in *Patrologiæ Latinæ* (Paris: Garnier Frères, 1879), t. LXXI, col. 241 (104). See *Histoire des Francs*, trans. R. Latouche (Paris: Société d'édition "Les Belles Lettres," 1963), I, 141.

9. Gregory of Tours suggests she had a special motive to attack her uncle, king Gundobad of Burgundy, because he had murdered her father, Chilperic, and mother, but a contemporary letter from bishop Avit of Vienne mentions Gundobad's profound sorrow at the death of Chilperic. Specialists of the Merovingian period remain divided on this point.

10. The text of the letter is reproduced in M. Ruche, *Clovis* (Paris: Fayard, 1996), 387–388. This letter confirms the location of Francia. Belgium (*Belgica*) II (capital: Reims) took in most of modern-day Belgium and a segment of present-day France to the west of the permanent linguistic boundary between French and German (near Metz), and to the north of the Seine.

11. Gregory here modifies for Clovis one of the greatest Christian stories, the conversion of the Roman Emperor Constantine in 312. Before the battle of the Mulvian Bridge, Constantine supposedly saw a cross in the sky with the words "by

this sign you will conquer." When his army proved victorious, the Emperor (and his co-Emperor Licinius) issued an edict of toleration (Milan, 313), that, for the first time, allowed Christians openly to practice their faith. The Alamanni were another Germanic tribe, whose name is preserved in the modern French word for German: *allemand.*

12. M. Bloch, *The Royal Touch: Monarchy and Miracles in France and England,* trans. J. E. Anderson (New York: Dorset Press, 1961, 1989), 130–133, on the origins of this story.

13. Early Christianity had many sects, which often warred violently against each other. The Council of Nicaea (325) came up with an official Christian creed, one still used by the Catholic Church. The Creed directly attacked the position of Arius, that God the Father created, and was superior to, Jesus and the Holy Spirit. Arian Christians did not accept the Nicene decrees about the equality of the three members of the Christian Trinity; this heresy had particularly strong success among the Goths. Most of the Burgundian royal house (although not most Burgundians) and the Goths subscribed to Arianism; the Gallo-Roman population over whom they ruled remained Catholic. Clotilde, a Burgundian princess, was thus unusual for someone of her house, although other women in the royal family, including the queen, were also Catholic.

14. Her mother, Geroncia, is of uncertain origin. The father, Severus, a Frank, took the unusual step of changing to a Roman name. Geneviève herself bore a Frankish name, *Geno-veifa* ("born of woman's breast"), but was also a Roman citizen.

15. The bishops present at the Council give a clear idea of the limits of Clovis's kingdom: they came from northwestern and central Gaul. The bishops from Rhenish Francia, Burgundy, Aquitaine, and the Mediterranean littoral did not attend.

16. In 507, on the eve of his invasion of the Visigothic kingdom, Clovis sent a letter to the Catholic bishops informing them of his plans and promising that his army would respect Church property (including its slaves). We should not overstress the Catholic-Arian aspect of this battle, because many Catholics, such as Apollinaris, son of Sidonius, himself later a Catholic bishop, fought on the side of Alaric.

17. Gregory of Tours, *History of the Franks,* Book IV, chap. II, my translation. Thorpe has a slightly different version, 197.

18. Clovis's sons conquered Aquitaine themselves; they did not inherit the region. Frankish law treated differently inheritance and acquisitions.

19. Ibid., 158.

20. A third child, Chlodovald, escaped and became a monk; the Church later canonized him as Saint Cloud, now the name of a suburb of Paris.

21. Gregory of Tours, *History of the Franks,* 221. The last phrase might be translated as "agreeable in her conversation."

22. We can see the important continuities between the polity of the Rhenish Franks and the later kingdom of Austrasia in the names of the rulers. Kings of Austrasia

derived their name either from the first Merovingian king of the region, Theuderic, or bore the name of the last Rhenish king, Sigibert.

23. The description comes from Fredegar, cited in P. Geary, *Before France and Germany: The Creation and Transformation of the Merovingian World* (New York: Oxford University Press, 1988), 151. The Latin original of Fredegar is available in *Patrologiæ Latinæ*, LXXI, col. 633.

24. Wallace-Hadrill, *The Frankish Church*, 124, citing Gregory of Tours.

25. A *manse* was a large farm unit; it is discussed in Chapter 2.

26. The Catholic Church did not have a centralized process of canonization until 993 and did not take canonization authority away from bishops until 1234.

27. The standard Roman burial practice had been cremation of a clothed body, buried in an urn with a few objects: a libation vessel, a coin, and a lamp. The Germanic people buried individuals fully clothed: men were fully armed, and graves of both men and women held many objects, such as jewelry, pottery or war-related items like spurs. The Church had little success against the ancient Celtic custom of burial in one's best clothes, which continues to this day in many Christian cultures.

28. At Paris, for example, seven different men sat as bishop between 653–691, as against the three of the first half of the century.

29. This famous battle took place between Tours and Poitiers: the French call it the Battle of Poitiers, but English speakers call it the Battle of Tours. A Christian source from Cordoba dates the battle on 25 October 732 but the most recent English-language scholarship, relying on Arab sources, suggests the battle actually took place in 733 or 734 rather than 732. The inability to locate, either in space or in time, the most important battle of the later Merovingian kingdoms stands as fitting testimony to the unreliability of sources about this period.

30. Geary, *Before France and Germany*, 225, cites two of the verses.

31. Cited in O. Guillot, A. Rigaudière, and Y. Sassier, *Pouvoirs et Institutions dans la France Médiévale. Des origines à l'époque féodale* (Paris: Armand Colin, 1994), I, 108.

32. The eastern limit of Charlemagne's empire has had tremendous long-term resonance: the Iron Curtain of 1945–1989 ran along virtually the same path. The NATO expansion of 1997 took in the regions that paid tribute to Charlemagne, plus Poland.

33. E. James, *The Origins of France: From Clovis to the Capetians, 500–1000* (New York: St. Martin's Press, 1982), 164.

34. The origins of feudalism, which involve Roman, Merovingian, and Carolingian elements, are discussed in detail at the beginning of Chapter 2.

35. Einhard, *The Life of Charlemagne*, trans. S. Turner, ed. S. Painter (Ann Arbor: University of Michigan Press, 1960, 1972), lists thirteen children and we know of a fourteenth; the children had seven different mothers, three of whom were "wives" and four concubines.

36. Cited in P. Wolff, *Western Languages, AD 100–1500,* trans. F. Patridge (New York: McGraw-Hill, 1971), 117. Page 118 contains a facsimile of this section of the oldest extant copy of the *Oaths,* which dates from about the year 1000. During the interview between Louis the German and Charles the Bald in 860, the sources say Louis spoke in "lingua theodisca" (Germanic) and Charles in "lingua romana" (Romance). The *Oaths* are the oldest surviving evidence of any Romance language.

37. The poet Angilbert, cited in *The Cambridge Medieval History, v. III: Germany and the Western Empire,* ed. H. Gwatkin *et alia* (Cambridge: Cambridge University Press, 1922, 1981), 24–25.

38. See list of rulers in the Appendix.

39. Dauphiné joined the kingdom of France in 1349, Provence in 1482, and the county of Burgundy in 1679.

40. Eudes of Blois soon became count of Châteaudun, in the Loire valley; he later became count of Troyes, likely evidence of his ties to Eudes of Orléans and Robert of Worms.

41. Yves Sassier, *Hugues Capet. Naissance d'un dynastie* (Paris: Fayard, 1987), 49–50.

42. All surviving written texts existed only in hand-copied manuscripts; copyists over the centuries had made many, many errors. Even theoretically similar texts, such as the Bible, therefore differed considerably from copy to copy.

43. G. Brown, "Introduction: The Carolingian Renaissance," in *Carolingian culture: Emulation and innovation,* ed. R. McKitterick (New York: Cambridge University Press, 1994), 34. By way of contrast, about three hundred manuscripts or fragments thereof survive from Frankish Gaul for the period 450–750. That number suggests that, at least in the sixth and seventh centuries, Merovingian Gaul was an important cultural center for its time. The surviving evidence strongly suggests that very few manuscripts were produced in this region between 700–740.

44. In the seventeenth century, when the Parlement of Brittany issued an edict about the price of bread, they provided an historical background to justify their policies: they began by stating that in Charlemagne's time, a loaf of wheat bread cost four silver pennies, one of rye bread three silver pennies, and one of oat bread a single penny. Starting with Charlemagne, even if one had to invent the evidence, legitimized state action. In fact, disputants in many medieval lawsuits produced "ancient" charters, often forged.

45. Cited in J. Dunbabin, *France in the Making 843–1180* (Oxford; New York: Oxford University Press, 1983), 133.

46. Einhard, *The Life of Charlemagne,* 50–54.

47. Herbert of Vermandois descended from Charlemagne's son Pippin, king of Italy (d. 811) and from the unfortunate Bernard, blinded and killed in 818. Bernard's son Pippin did not get the Italian kingdom, but kept his father's small holdings in northeastern Francia, Vermandois among them. Hedwig's name, suggests that she, too, descended from Charlemagne. Her brother, Otto, had been crowned Emperor in 962; in 987, her nephew Otto III was Emperor.

48. Cited in Sassier, *Hugues Capet*, 197.

49. Ibid., 198. Sassier here cites Richer, the eleventh-century chronicler, who is widely suspected of having embellished Adalbero's speech.

50. The Capetians here followed the wise precedent set by Conrad I, the first non-Carolingian King of East Francia, who sought and received religious unction for his coronation in 911.

51. Sassier, *Hugues Capet*, 234, following Richer.

Chapter Two

STATE AND SOCIETY IN MEDIEVAL FRANCE

[The king] does not have in the said pays any demesne, where his
men can live and render justice.[1]

Complaint of the villagers of
Is-sur-Tille, Burgundy, 1313

The humble peasants of Is-sur-Tille offered King Philip IV their communal lands, to hold as lord, "as the personal demesne of the king," in order that they might receive the protection of his justice. Living on the frontier of his kingdom, and outside the royal demesne, they felt themselves helpless in the face of evildoers. Their petition illustrates one of the central realities of life in medieval France: the withering away of central state authority and its gradual reconstitution by the Capetian Kings of France. That process developed in two ways: from the center, the king and his men sought to increase their power; from the periphery, ordinary French people sought the protection of the king's justice in an uncertain and violent world.

Socially and economically, medieval France's key rural institutions—serfdom, the village, the seigneury, the manse—took permanent shape in the tenth–twelfth centuries. Village structures varied sharply from region to region, but French peasants overwhelmingly lived in serfdom, under the direct authority of seigneurs who had usually usurped local governing authority. These seigneurs rendered justice, even death, in their own name. Despite their theoretical subordination to the king, in practice, they answered to no higher authority.

In order to examine the four key elements of medieval French society—the Crown, rural institutions, the Church, and the towns—Chapters 2 and 3 treat the same chronological period (987–1270), but focus on different topics. Chapter 2 examines feudalism, which created a synthesis of the rural institutions and the central state. Chapter 3 looks at the Church, at the towns, and at French medieval culture.

Hugh Capet's seizure of power in 987 shifted the core region of royal power from eastern France back to the old Merovingian capital of Paris. The Capetian dynasty passed the throne from father to son from 996 until 1316, when the newborn baby John I died and his uncle became Philip V. Although the "Capetian" dynasty is usually held to have died out in 1328, when the throne passed to a collateral line of the royal family, every king of the Valois (1328–1589) and Bourbon (1589–1792) dynasties was a direct patrilineal descendant of the Capetian Louis IX (d. 1270). After 1792, the French Revolutionaries referred to the deposed Louis XVI as Louis Capet, directly tying him to his tenth-century ancestor.

When the great barons of northern Francia "elected" Hugh Capet, of what precisely was he king? The Francia of the year 1000 was an overwhelmingly rural place, populated by ill-dressed subsistence farmers who lived in simple huts. Hugh and other aristocrats scarcely knew better. The Bayeux Tapestry (c. 1080), embroidered by duchess Mathilda of Normandy to depict the conquest of England by her husband, William, offers clear evidence of the region's relative underdevelopment. William was the most powerful man in northwestern Europe, yet the Tapestry shows he and his barons at table using their fingers to eat spit-roasted meat and fowl, drinking from wooden bowls, and dressed in simple, rough-spun tunics. Francia lay at the outer limits of Mediterranean civilization, its inhabitants barbarians in the eyes of those living in places like Muslim Spain and the Byzantine Empire. In 987, Cordoba and Constantinople housed more people than all of the towns of Francia put together. Within 2 and one half centuries, however, these barbarians had taken both Cordoba (1236) and Constantinople (1203) and had created an advanced civilization of their own.[2]

The dramatic change in monarchical terminology between the election of Hugh Capet and the death of Philip Augustus (1223), makes manifest the political element of that astonishing accomplishment. In 987, Francia held a scattering of villages, organized into local political units headed by members of a large aristocratic clan. These aristocrats led military companies descended from tribal war bands. The chiefs of those war bands, invariably Hugh's relatives, elected him their chief of chiefs. The greatest leaders bore tribal titles: the duke of the Aquitanians, the duke of the Burgundians, the King of the Franks, who was really the *kuning,* war chief, of the most powerful tribe. Yet the other royal legacy, epitomized by Charlemagne, gave Hugh and his descendants the potential to be something far grander than a simple war chief. By the death of Philip Augustus, the first man to adopt officially the title King of France, the Capetians had used these dual legacies to transform the tribal confederation into a kingdom worthy of the name commonwealth.

Before we examine that political process, let us take a look at the collection of villages, for that is where almost everyone lived. The Introduction and Chapter 1 have laid out the legacies that shaped Francia of the year 1000: the close ties between the Church and political authority; the monarchical tradition of the Merovingians and Carolingians; and the linguistic and cultural background. This chapter will take a closer look at medieval society, its economic and social structures—above all, at what we call feudalism. Medieval historians have greatly changed our understanding of this term in the past three decades. Today, specialists of the tenth–thirteenth centuries rarely make the traditional argument that feudalism weakened the monarchy; rather, they believe that the French monarchy used feudalism to strengthen itself. To understand how they have so radically transformed our understanding of feudalism, let us begin our examination of early medieval France in its defining place: the countryside.

MEDIEVAL FRANCE: RURAL SOCIETY

Here below, some pray, others fight, still others work.

Adalbero, Bishop of Laon, *c.* 1030

In 996 or 997, the peasants of Normandy banded together to fight against the emergence of a new society. They formed "parlements," assemblies, and tried to establish "communes," self-governing communities. The twelfth-century poet Wace provides eloquent literary evidence of the memory of their struggle in his *Roman de Rou* (1172).

Wace's testimony, nearly two centuries after the rebellion itself, accurately portrays the typical grievances of medieval French peasants living under the system constructed in the late tenth and eleventh centuries. The eleventh-century chronicler William of Jumièges, in his version of the Norman rebellion, tells of peasants who "desired to live after their own liking" and to manage woods and waters as they had before the "new customs." They formed communes throughout Normandy and demanded all that they believed rightly belonged to them: access to the woods and waters, for hunting and fishing, as well as for pasturage, fuel, and building materials. They complained about labor services, about lawsuits, about "new customs." This last complaint found an echo everywhere: in 994 in Auvergne, in 1000 in Anjou, in 1016 in Burgundy and 1020 in Champagne, the documents speak of the "evil customs," that is, of new customs. The new customs bore on the same matters that so upset the Norman peasants: labor services; taxes paid to landlords; reduced access to woods, streams, and ponds; new jurisdictions. These new customs helped make permanent three elements of the French countryside that would endure until 1789: the seigneurial system, intertwining manors and local courts; the knighthood; and serfdom.

The peasants resisted these impositions with apparent ferocity. The nobility and the knights responded with an even greater ferocity. In Champagne or Berry, in Orléanais or Normandy, the mounted warriors struck the peasants down. William of Jumièges says that duke Richard sent his uncle, Raoul, count of Evreux, to meet with the peasants' negotiators. Raoul arrested them, cut off their hands and feet, and made them crawl back to the assembly.[3] Wace provides a more poetic description, a sort of epitaph to peasant liberty.

The sad fate of the Norman peasants mirrored that of most of their brethren. In southern France, the tide of repression led to the movement of the Peace of God, in which bishops or abbots tried to convince laypeople to swear an oath to respect the property of the church and of the poor. Peasants demanded protection, sometimes with arms in hand. When matters went far enough, an open battle between the peasants and the mounted warriors would take place, as at Châteauneuf-du-Cher. The warriors invariably slaughtered the lightly armed peasants because the warriors had access to two very expensive advantages: horses and metal weapons.

In other regions, the Peace of God movement remained under the control of the Church, particularly of bishops, who used it to try to counteract the rising power of local castellans. They achieved only a mixed success. The writings of these churchmen provide the main evidence about the "evil customs," so that we must carefully

The Norman Peasant Rebellion of 997: Wace's *Roman de Rou*[4]
Part I: The Grievances

There has scarcely ever before reigned
nor scarcely ever been a duke
when there arose such a war
which did (such) great harm to the land.
The *villains* and the peasants,   (*villain*—by Wace's time, a type of serf)
those of the *bocage* and those of the fields,   (*bocage*—area of hedged fields)
no one knew by what enticement
nor who first spread the word,
by twenties, by thirties, by hundreds
they held several parlements.
This word of order came to be counseled,
if they dare put it forward
and say out loud among friends,
"He who is highest is (our) enemy."
Privately, they spoke of it
and several swore (it) among themselves
that never would they admit
to have either a lord or master.
With the lords, no good comes. . . .
Each day passes to great sorrow
in great pains and terrible effort.
Last year was bad, this one worse.
Each day their beasts are taken
for *corvées* and for aids   (*corvée*—forced labor on lord's land)
So many are the complaints and quarrels
and taxes old and new
they cannot have an hour of peace
Each day a new lawsuit
lawsuits for cattle and forests
for sowing and money
for taxes and roads
and lawsuits for the mill,
lawsuits of homage and fealty
of hunting, scuffling or of *corvées* . . .
from the knights we will defend ourselves
Thus we will be able to go into the woods
take the trees at our choice
to the fish ponds to take fish,
in the forest, venison.
Of all that makes up our wishes,
in the woods, waters, meadows.

assess the extent to which the peasants themselves protested such customs (as they did in Normandy), as against the extent to which the "evil customs" merely provided a useful rhetorical device for the Church in its struggle against the castellans and their knightly allies. The Church constantly called into question the premises of lay society's legal system, which then relied on pledges, challenges (such as trial by com-

The Norman Peasant Rebellion of 997: Wace's *Roman de Rou*
Part II: The Reckoning

Either by man, or by sergeant,
either by woman, or by child,
by angry outburst or by drunken bawling,
Richard was quickly informed that
villains were forming communes
and would take away rights
from him as well as from other lords
who have *villains* and tenants
To his uncle, Raoul, Richard
described this agitation . . .
"Sire," he said, "rest at ease
and leave your peasants to me." . . .
Raoul sent his couriers to spy
everywhere in the land
and Raoul found out so much . . .
that he could capture the *villains*
organizing the parlements . . .
Raoul was so enraged
that there was no trial;
all of them were made sad and sorrowful;
several of them had their teeth pulled out
and others were impaled
or their eyes torn out,
hands cut off, limbs roasted,
from which they all must die.
The others were burned alive
or thrown in boiling lead.
Thus they were all taken care of.
It was horrible to look on.
They have not seen in that place since
that which they would recognize well.
The Commune did not go any further
and the *villains* held themselves calm.[5]

bat and private war), and oaths. Canon law, evolving from Roman Imperial law and Christian principles, sought to change the legal basis of society. As Pope Urban II wrote to the count of Flanders in 1092: "Dost thou claim to have done hitherto only what is in conformity with the ancient custom of the land? Thou shouldst know, notwithstanding, thy Creator hath said: My name is Truth. He hath not said: My name is Custom."[6]

At the end of the tenth century, the entire structure of Carolingian society collapsed: the kingship shifted to a new family, the Capetians; the slaves on the great estates achieved their freedom; the mounted fighters or knights (*miles*) started their successful quest for nobility; and in many areas, the peasants lapsed toward or into serfdom. Inheritance shifted away from kin groups and toward patriarchal dynasties.

Between 1000–1100, a new society, a *feudal* society, took shape. That society rested on Adalbero's formula: the three orders of prayers, fighters, and workers. So lasting was this image that as late as 1789 the national representative body of France, the Estates General, met in three estates: clergy, nobility, and third estate, that is, those who worked, be they merchant or lawyer, artisan or farmer.

⌇ RURAL FOUNDATIONS OF FEUDALISM

The Rise of the Seigneury

> *"Moreover, I have your sister as my wife / And by her I have a son, there could be no finer boy. / His name is Baldwin," he says, "and he will become a valiant man. / To him I bequeath my honours and my lands; / Take care of him, I shall never set eyes on him again."*[7]

> Ganelon, speaking to Charlemagne, lines 312–316 of *The Song of Roland*

What was feudalism? Did feudalism actually exist, at least in its pure form? The term comes from the eighteenth century, from the days just before the French Revolution, when French writers coined the word *féodalité* to describe the combination of political, economic, and social power held by the nobility in eighteenth-century France. Some historians have tried to narrow its meaning, to make it a purely political term. They believe feudalism meant the diffusion of public power into many private hands, by means of the lord-vassal system. Other historians prefer to continue the original eighteenth-century meaning: they define feudalism as a socioeconomic system, as well as a political one.

The political aspect of feudalism, like the word for fief (*feodum*) derived from a mixture of Germanic and Roman roots. The Carolingian state borrowed the Roman and Merovingian model of providing the income (*beneficium*) from a grant of public land in recompense for the service given by the holder of an "honor," such as a count. Charlemagne had used the large peasant farm, the manse, as the basis of grants both to holders of "honors" and to his retainers (*fideles*), who owed him military service and counsel. In the second case, the two transactions had no legal tie. An "honor" and its attached land grant were not legally heredity property. In practice, the aristocratic families who monopolized high offices invariably sought to make indistinguishable these public lands and their private ones. Charlemagne complained about this process; his heirs, ruling a much weaker central state, proved helpless to prevent it. A direct tie between military service and landed properties usually became explicit in the late tenth and eleventh centuries, after the properties in question had already become hereditary. Again and again, local rulers sought to claim *auctoritas,* legal authority, to justify their *potestas,* raw power.

The land grants provided the critical connection to the social and economic aspect of feudalism, built around manors and peasant manses. The connection between the two structures, the political one of overlords and lords and the economic one of landlords and their peasants, developed ever more strongly in Carolingian West Francia. Local lords gradually took over most of the state's traditional functions: they dispensed justice, levied taxation, and controlled appointments to Church benefices, even to some bishoprics or abbeys. Some princes, like the dukes of the Aquitanians or the Normans, minted money, one of the ultimate signs of *auctoritas*. In time, political rights such as taxation and justice came to overlap economic rights, such as forced service fees or the obligation to use the lord's mill.

In the tenth century, this top-down structure collided in the countryside with local developments: holders of castles (castellans) systematically extended their authority over nearby peasants. The castellans relied on the armed force provided by their private mounted fighters, knights, to terrorize and subdue the peasants, and to assert their right of jurisdiction. In this respect, ninth-century institutions differed sharply from those of the eleventh century: the old, royally sanctioned local courts, meeting often under the aegis of a count, a bishop or an abbey, had jurisdiction over all *free* men. Their successors, the new castellan courts of the late tenth or eleventh century, had jurisdiction primarily over dependent people. By the year 1000, Francia had three levels of local civil jurisdiction: the comtal courts had authority over free people, above all those of high social status; the castellan's court judged those free, in the sense of not slaves, but dependent, and thus not fully free; and the master ruled over his or her slaves.

In the tenth and eleventh centuries, the castellans played the pivotal role in the emerging economic and political system. The two core elements of rural life, the manor and the seigneury, often overlapped in their hands. Many holders of manors tried to associate seigneurial authority with their manors, but only castellans could claim their seigneurial authority derived legally from the king, often through the intermediary of a count. Legally the situation remained clear: the landlord had certain rights attached to the manor itself and to its extended demesne, but had no rights over the surrounding population. When castellans owned manors, however, the separate functions of seigneur and landlord tended to become obscured.

The overlapping authority of the manor and the seigneury undermined the integrity of private property, as did the violent creation of seigneurial authority over holders of peasant allods. The seigneury, existing at the intersection of all elements of social life, negated two of the basic principles of civil society, handed down from the Romans through the Carolingian monarchy: public sovereignty and private property. Public sovereignty now belonged to private individuals who had little real oversight from their "official" superiors (i.e., the king); independent private property could not exist when the seigneur and the village community effectually had rights of eminent domain.

The unfortunate peasants suffered the consequences. In the late Carolingian period, landlords increasingly turned to nonslaves for the cultivation of their demesnes. The "free" peasants who replaced the slaves on the great estates, however, retained certain legal dependencies on their lords. They often had to become serfs. Some peasants voluntarily did so: a peasant gave land to a lord, who would give it back to the serf as hereditary property. The serf got protection; the lord got labor services. The peasant, his or her family, and their livestock could seek shelter from raiders, either Vikings (in the early tenth century) or the armed bands of other castellans (after 950). The lord also agreed to feed the peasant family in case of famine, as in 1031–1033.[8]

Although some peasants voluntarily opted for such an arrangement, the evidence suggests that many more of them had little choice in the matter: the local lord simply forced them to give up free title to their land.

Simple arrangements—labor service for the right to land—quickly became more complex. The enormous economic disequilibrium between landlord and peasant greatly facilitated the emergence of dependency. Once they had broken the power of the peasant community, as in the Norman rebellion, the landlords alone had the resources to build a mill or a wine press. A landlord could then make an agreement with the peasants that, in return for his substantial investment in constructing the mill, they would all grind their grain there. They would pay a fee for this service; most mills charged $^1/_{16}$th of the grain. This practice would soon become custom; in the Middle Ages custom became law. Now all the peasants *had* to grind their grain at the lord's mill, a complaint Wace's Norman peasants specifically mention. In the case of landlords who held seigneurial rights, lawsuits about the mill would often go to the court of its owner.[9] Early twelfth-century iconography, such as the capitals of Saint-Lazare at Autun, still shows peasants grinding grain by hand, but landlords gradually, inexorably enforced the milling monopoly in later years. They kept this monopoly until the French Revolution. In wine-growing regions, the same procedure held true of the wine press. These monopolies became one of the most important sources of revenue for noble landlords.

One can easily understand the confusion in the minds of peasants about manorial and seigneurial obligations. Serfs owed labor services on the demesne in return for hereditary use of their tenures. Landlords obviously needed to extend their jurisdiction over the *person* of the serf, not merely over his land (his tenure), in order to be assured of a labor force. After all, a serf could move away. The serf's children might marry in another village, reducing the future labor force. Landlords expanded the conception of the manor to include the persons of its tenants; they became the bondsmen (the *hommes de corps*) of their landlord. Landlords now required serfs to obtain permission before moving; the landlord also restricted the serf's choice of marriage partner to his other serfs (the right of *formariage*).[10]

In ideal feudalism, the landlord would also be the seigneur. He could then combine those obligations owed to him as landlord—labor service, *formariage,* inheritance taxes, milling rights—with those belonging to the seigneur. The seigneur, having taken possession of a share of the public power, now demanded some of its benefits. He wanted taxation, such as war taxes. He wanted all peasants to settle their legal disputes in his court. He could also claim, as lord of the manor and as seigneur, proprietary rights over "unowned" lands such as woods, meadows, ponds, and streams. Once he had established his rights in these areas, he would try to create monopolies, such as those on hunting, fishing, and timber gathering. In a heavily feudal region such as Normandy, in which manorial and seigneurial rights often overlapped, we should not be surprised that the peasants, as in the complaints of 996–997, lumped them both together.

Not content with those restrictions, landlords sought more. They established the "custom" (another of the "bad customs") that heirs had to reside physically with those from whom they inherited. This restriction prevented complicated cases of mixed jurisdiction. They established inheritance taxes: heirs of male peasants often had to give the lord the best animal, heirs of female peasants had to render their best garment. Landlords also sought to prevent morselization of the tenures, and the concomitant impoverishment of their labor force, by restricting all forms of land transfer. Anyone selling land had to pay a transfer tax to his feudal overlord; even powerful nobles had to pay this tax to their overlords, often to the king himself, starting in the reign of Philip Augustus. Families of vassals dying childless usually had to give back a portion of the deceased's property to the overlord.

In time, people began to distinguish between two sorts of seigneurial justice: high justice, which including the right to condemn people to death, and low justice, which tended to be an outgrowth of the manor and to hear cases about the manor or disputes between its serfs.[11] High justice represented the devolution of state power into the hands of an individual; low justice represented the spread of the *paterfamilias*'s rights from members of the households to residents of the manor. In most of ninth-century northern and western France, *free* peasants paid a head tax, the *chevage,* to the seigneur to whose justice they belonged. After slavery disappeared, the *chevage* became a sign of *serfdom.* Thus a payment that began as proof that a free man or woman had a protector ended up as evidence of lack of freedom.

The Manor

> *A manor was first and foremost an estate (terre)—there was scarcely any other word for it in spoken French—but an estate inhabited by the lord's subjects.*[12]
>
> Marc Bloch

Many historians distinguish between the seigneury, building block of the political and judicial system (seigneuralism), and the manor, building block of the economic system (manorialism). The peasants, as the testimony of both William of Jumièges and Wace makes clear, often did not. Just as the seigneury evolved from the decentralization of the larger state, the manor emerged from the wreckage of the great estates of Carolingian (and earlier) times. Carolingian manors had two distinct forms. Aristocratic families owned manors with large fields, often worked by a slave labor force. These manors sometimes included limited rights over nearby peasants on free farms (allods); the documents speak of the lordship (*dominium*) over such people. Free peasants had the right to attend, give evidence in, and be judged by the comtal court, meeting under the authority of the king, to whom they owed an oath of allegiance. Simple landlords owned the second type of manor, which consisted of free possession of land, often scattered throughout a village or across several villages. In time, the manor developed two distinct elements: the actual residence of the landlord with the land attached to that residence, the demesne, and the extended rights held over the land worked by the free peasants.

Noble or knight, bishop or abbey, the landlord owned one or several manors. The manor itself had a physical form quite similar to that of many hamlets in contemporary France's open fields areas. Its buildings formed a fortified perimeter; outlying peasant farms also used this pattern to protect both people and animals from wanderers. Crop yields on large estates tended to be low (2 to 1 or 3 to 1), so the landlord

Carolingian cavalry and infantry. Ninth-century Psalter of the monastery of Saint-Gall.

SOURCE: St-Gall, Stifsbibliothek, Codex 22.

Eleventh-century knights. This panel from the Bayeux Tapestry shows the importance of the individual leader: William the Conqueror raises his helmet to disprove rumors he has been killed at Hastings.

SOURCE: © Giraudon/Art Resource.

needed a substantial estate in order to extract a sufficient income.[13] This income supported two critical activities: the writing and praying of monasteries and the fighting of the lay upper classes. Praying and singing mobilized many monks, seeking divine protection for the entire Christian commonwealth or for specific, usually aristocratic, benefactors. These prayers required buildings, such as churches and dormitories, and constant upkeep. Writing required money, not only to support the

Thirteenth-century knights in single combat.

Source: © Corbis.

copyists, but to pay for the materials: medieval manuscripts used expensive parchment (animal, especially sheep skin) and inks often made from imported dyestuffs.

The lords and their knights had to have a horse and metal weapons. The horse could not be a runty nag, uncoupled from its plough: it had to be a *destrier,* war horse, an animal so valuable that some early law codes levied higher fines for killing a *destrier* than for killing a man. Metal weapons—armor, swords, and an array of other lethal paraphernalia—cost dearly. The local castellans and counts also faced important construction costs for the erection and maintenance of their castles. Early "castles" were little more than a wooden palisade surrounded by a muddy ditch, but, in the eleventh century, when stone replaced wood as the building material, expenses rose precipitously. The upper class also used their estates to provide themselves with the good life. Their desire for imported luxury goods, such as Asian spices, motivated much of Francia's international trade.

The landlord obtained income from two distinct types of land: the direct demesne and the extended estate. On the direct demesne, the landlord used either slaves or free tenant farmers, who performed labor service in return for their tenures. On some estates, peasants paid rent for the tenancies and owed minimal labor service: one to three weeks per year. The extensive intermingling of slaves and free people enabled the landlord to extend his rights as *paterfamilias,* incontestable with respect to slaves, to the free peasants on his estate. In southern France, although landlords generally worked their latifundial estates only with slaves, most landlords held estates that did not encompass broad grain fields; they relied on free peasants working small plots cut from the woodlands or on mixed agricultural usage.

Tenth- and eleventh-century scribes struggled to translate the reality of everyday life, known to all by vernacular words, into Latin. They used a bewildering variety of terms to describe peasants: *mancipia* meant "slave," but how did one distinguish among *servus* (which meant "slave" in the eighth or ninth century but "serf" in the eleventh), *villain* (originally meaning "free" but later meaning "serf"), *collibertus* (a former slave freed by a dying master), *colonus* (a free man given a tenancy but bound not to leave it), and the various other terms used in different localities? *Coloni* were free, not slaves, yet unfree: they did not take the freeman's oath of fealty to the king. In time, the essence of their condition, the inability to leave one's tenure, on pain of forfeiture, became the sign of serfdom; it remained so in the duchy of Burgundy until 1789.

The free peasants of northern France cultivated their own tenures; in some cases they held freeholds, but in others they had to make a payment to the landlord holding the rights of extended demesne. They could provide him a share of their crop or, and increasingly landlords encouraged such an arrangement, they could provide the landlord with labor for the direct demesne. In return for working every week on the lord's direct demesne (a common deal was three days per week, plus seasonal supplements), the peasants obtained a hereditary tenure. In southern France, free peasants usually held their farms as allods, although some tenancies required payment of a small share of the crop to the lord. The free tenant farmers of the south typically paid rent rather than labor service to the estate owner.

The labor force for the direct demesnes of these manors changed from slave to free in the tenth and early eleventh century. The catalogue of the surviving royal acts of the period 814–1108 shows us the chronology of change (Table II-1). Other evidence points to the steady decline of slavery in the tenth century and to its virtual elimination, except for female household slaves, between 1000–1030. Slavery disappeared first in the south, where references to slaves became rare by the early tenth century. Landlords, like the abbey of Saint-Germain-des-Prés near Paris, replaced the slaves with *coloni*, semi-free peasants, who received a grant of land, but became dependents of their landlord. While slaves outnumbered free people 18 to 1 in the seventh-century will of Bertram of Le Mans, *coloni* households outnumbered those of slaves by the same margin in the ninth-century cartularies of Saint-Germain. This contrast overstates somewhat the rate of change. As late as 999, a great aristocrat like Gérard of Aurillac (Pope Sylvester II) could free one hundred slaves and be criticized because he failed to free others—but the move to freedom was unmistakable.

Recent scholarship strongly stresses the extreme localism of developments in the condition of the peasantry, but much of it implies that the former slaves joined the free peasantry. The Carolingian countryside thus resembled a patchwork quilt: small peasant farms, held by free people owing either little or no service or fees to any landlord, interspersed with latifundial estates owned by great lords and farmed by slave labor. In the ninth and tenth centuries, these extremes—the slaves on the large estates and the free peasants on small farms—stood at the ends of a broad spectrum of mixed systems of tenure and personal status.

In many parts of Francia, a three-stage process took place: the collapse of slavery, followed by the amalgamation of slaves into the free, albeit often dependent population, and then the final forced subjection of this larger free but dependent

TABLE II-1: Royal Acts Mentioning Slaves (*Mancipia*), 814–1108	
Dates	**Percentage of Acts Mentioning *Mancipia***
814–935	40.0
935–1030	20.0
1031–1108	1.5

peasantry by the landlords. Recent work on the core lands of the monarchy, in the middle Loire and Seine valleys, reinforces the old theory that some of that region had a fully developed seigneurial and feudal system before the year 1000. Many of the other regions of Francia evolved such systems between 1000–1100.

The slaves freed themselves by running away and clearing new land (assarting); in isolated areas, the local lord gladly granted favorable terms in order to attract a labor force. Northern and southern France seem to have diverged significantly in the immediate response to the rapid emancipation of slaves in the tenth century and early eleventh century. In the north, seigneurs tried to undermine the independence of the free peasants. French law codified these two different systems: that of "no land without lord," in the northern region of customary law, and that of "no lord without title," in the southern region of written law. In the north, the legal burden of proof thus fell on the peasant, whereas the lord had to bear it in the south.

Peasant Farms

In the course of the tenth, eleventh, and twelfth centuries, this system [of large demesnes, worked by serfs] gradually ceded to a completely different organization. . . . The portions of the demesne the tenants formerly cultivated for the lord they now attached to their own holdings.[14]

Marc Bloch

Carolingian peasants lived, in theory, on a manse, or full-sized family farm. Such farms ranged, even in Charlemagne's time, from 5 to 30 hectares; the Emperor judged a minimum farm of 16.5 hectares necessary for the upkeep of each parish church. At its origin, the word likely revolved around the term for a house. By the sixteenth century, the derivative French word *masure* had restored the old meaning: a house and the small plot on which it sat. The manse provided a useful unit for the authorities, because the count or king or landlord could set taxes or labor obligations in terms of so much money or so many days per manse. Those holding the various pieces of the manse could work out the division on their own. Kings and counts also granted fiefs in terms of a given number of manses, whose income enabled the fief holder to support himself and his household, including his knights.

This neat little correlation quickly ran afoul of the tendency of peasants to divide their lands for inheritance or to sell parts of their manses: already in 864, King Charles the Bald issued an edict futilely decrying the latter practice. By the eleventh century, in the open-field areas, the manses had become so subdivided as to have ceased to exist. Yet in the *bocage* or mountain areas, they became hamlets that have lasted to the present day: Verdinas and Roudersas in today's department of the Creuse preserve manses that existed already in 626! Open-field, *bocage,* or mountain village, the general process described by Bloch moved forward everywhere. The great Carolingian demesnes, which had existed side-by-side with small peasant tenures, began to break up. The forced labor (*corvée*) of traditional serfdom steadily gave way to a system in which the serfs paid the lord a share of the crop from their tenure, rather than working three days a week in his demesne fields. Eleventh- and twelfth-century lords shifted rapidly to the new system because it produced higher returns: crop yields appear to have been much higher on small peasant tenures than on large demesnes.

Idyllic images of rough-and-ready egalitarianism in medieval peasant villages ignore the substantial social stratification within the peasantry. Ideally, the peasants should all have had tenancies sufficient to support a family; in practice, population growth made that less and less the case. Francia held at most 5 million people in 1000; France held 15 or 16 million by 1300. The steady growth of population after 1100 led peasant families to divide and subdivide their tenancies. Eventually, a given peasant would inherit parcels from all over the village: a peasant "farm" did not consist of a contiguous segment of land, but of small strips of cultivable land from different fields. Landlords here ran up against one of the defining characteristics of customary law regarding commoners: partible inheritance. All male heirs had rights, often equal rights, to the inheritance, except in Normandy, which practiced primogeniture, and in the Roman law south, where the father could will his property as he saw fit. In some regions, such as Brittany and Anjou, female heirs enjoyed equal rights.

The peasant tenure usually consisted of three parts: the inner garden, the grain fields, and the outlying land. Women tended the heavily fertilized inner gardens, in which they grew vegetables, flax, and hemp; workshops of women converted this flax and the wool of sheep pastured on the outlying lands into linen and cloth. Men, aided by women in periods of peak labor demand, tended the grain fields. The peasants used the outlying lands for grazing, for scrounging wild plants and firewood, and, on occasion, for irregular planting. As the population of Francia expanded after 950, peasants responded by clearing new areas. Soon, these new fields became subdivided among heirs. This pattern of strip cultivation, universal in the open fields of northern France, gave way in some areas, such as Brittany or Lower Normandy, to fields permanently enclosed by hedges, the *bocages,* in which consolidated fields alternated with the tiny strips so familiar elsewhere.

The peasants greatly raised productivity between the ninth and twelfth centuries: yields seem to have increased from 2 to 1 or 3 to 1 to perhaps 4 to 1. The great medieval warming of northern Europe, which lasted from about 1000–1300, probably played the greatest role. Production also went up because the larger population farmed more land and because peasants made several technological improvements. They developed better harness systems for horses and oxen, and the use of the wheeled plough, which allowed them to cut more deeply into the soil and, with the addition of the mouldboard, to turn and aerate the soil. This new wheeled plough made the greatest difference in the north, because of the heavier soils there.

*Rural Life: Haying. Notice that women
and men shared the work (c. 1400).*

SOURCE: © Giraudon/Art Resource.

Northern France also changed its system of field rotation. Following Gallo-Roman practice, the Franks had relied on a two-field rotation: each field received seed every other year, thus lying fallow one year in two. By the eleventh century, northern farmers often practiced a three-field system (Chart 1). The three-field system provided an ingenious solution to the problem of soil depletion. It allowed each field to give two crops every three years, yet also to rest half of the time. The oats could be used for human consumption, as in Celtic areas, or, more commonly, for animal fodder. More fodder meant more animals; more animals meant more manure; more manure meant more fertilizer; more fertilizer meant higher yields.[15] In the south, however, two-field rotation remained standard because the lack of summer rainfall made sowing a spring grain like oats impossible.

The three-field rotation fitted in neatly with the idea of collective property rights. In Chart 1, the first field would have belonged to a specific peasant from the start of Year I until July. That peasant usually established temporary barriers around the field, to keep out wandering animals. From July of Year I until the spring of Year II, the field became the possession of the community as a whole: all members of the community could pasture their animals in this field, which now lay open. They got access to more pasture, the field "owner" got more manure for the soil. From the

---

CHART 1: Three-Field Crop Rotation

	Field A	Field B	Field C
Year I	Harvest wheat (July)	Sow oats (spring)	Fallow to fall
	Fallow to spring	Harvest oats (fall)	Plant wheat (fall)
Year II	Sow oats (spring)	Fallow until fall	Harvest wheat (July)
	Harvest oats (fall)	Plant wheat (fall)	Fallow to spring
Year III	Fallow to fall	Harvest wheat (July)	Sow oats (spring)
	Plant wheat (fall)	Fallow to spring	Harvest oats (fall)

---

spring of Year II until its fall, the field would once again be enclosed by temporary barriers, and its possession would revert to the peasant. The field then returned to community usage from the fall of Year II to the fall of Year III. Even immediately after the harvest, the field became part of the community's patrimony: the poor of the village had rights to the gleanings of everyone's fields. The constant rotation of the property status of fields, from private to communal and back again, gave the village community enormous power over its constituent individuals. The community as a whole often fought its seigneur(s) for control of collective property such as common pastures and woods at the edge of the village.

The Village Community

Early societies were made up of groups rather than individuals. A man on his own counted for very little. To earn his bread and protect himself he needed the association of other men.[16]

Marc Bloch

Village communities took a wide variety of forms, from the peasant oligarchies of the isolated mountain regions, such as the Auvergne, to the clustered houses of the open field areas like the Beauce. In the Auvergne, a village patriarch or a small group of elders ran the village, allocating the fields, which belonged collectively to the clan or clans living there: some of the Auvergnat mountain peasant dynasties lasted for a thousand years. Other areas, particularly in the eleventh century, had "brotherhood" farms (*frèrèches*) to divide up labor and risk.

In many parts of western France, peasants established villages of relatively isolated individual farms. In the *bocages* of Lower Normandy, Brittany, and Poitou, peasants built up high hedges to enclose their fields and prevent soil erosion. These fields often went hand-in-hand with large, untilled commons, used to pasture cattle. In the south, many hilltops held a tightly knit group of houses, gathered together for protection. Wherever possible, landlords built castles on higher elevations, in a manner to dominate physically the villages below them.

Northern and eastern France had many open-field villages, clustered in a central core near the parish church (after 1000 or 1050). The outlying manses formed the nuclei of individual hamlets, loosely attached to the village and to its parish church. By the twelfth or thirteenth century, these hamlets might include two to four substantial family farms, along with the subordinate population needed to work on them. Riding French trains even today, one can see the survivals of many of these early medieval hamlets. You look out the window and see a rectangle of buildings: two or three houses, a barn or two, with a central courtyard and only one entry point. The obvious defensive advantages of such an arrangement provided its key justification in medieval times.

Local variations make it almost impossible to generalize about medieval villages, particularly since the social and economic structures did not remain static. If we looked at a given village in 1000, we would likely find a small number of peasant farms, probably worked by people free yet dependent. These people would have had access to woods and open lands because of the low population density. By 1100, that same village would have had a few more people. Its landlord would probably have enforced serfdom on the peasants, who thereby lost free access to the woods and gained labor services on the lord's demesne lands. By 1200, this village would have had many more people, with progressively smaller individual holdings and less common land. Lordship rights might have become confused over time, with two, three or more landlords sharing authority in the one village. By 1300, the village would be packed: it would have a clear social hierarchy among its peasants, with large numbers of day laborers. The lords might be increasingly uneasy about their feudal rights, given that the King of France himself had recently freed his serfs. Lords, short of cash, might also seek to commute certain dues into fixed money payments. A new force, the central state, demanded taxes from the village. An old force, the Church, continued to play a key role.[17]

The Church organized peasants into spiritual communities, parishes. In theory, a parish and a village covered the same territory; in practice, they often did not. Although Pippin III granted (753) the Pope the right to establish parishes throughout Frankish lands, the spread of Christianity to rural areas took centuries. The tenth-century rural Church still consisted primarily of private chapels and the great monasteries and convents. The world's "new raiment of churches" (Raoul Glauber) appeared only in the eleventh century, as the archeological evidence makes clear. The new rural churches brought a much more numerous secular clergy into the countryside, genuinely introducing Christianity for the first time in many areas.

Medieval rural Christianity compromised with pre-existing fertility cults. The Christian calendar fitted neatly into pre-existing ones: four of its main medieval holidays—Christmas, Easter, Saint John the Baptist's Day (24 June), and Michaelmas (29 September)—corresponded roughly to seasonal changes. The Church had other holidays for the mid-seasons: Candlemas (2 February), Pentecost, the Assumption (15 August), and All Saints' Day (1 November).[18] The peasants simply Christianized many of their earlier beliefs, often creating cults of local "saints," who were sometimes recognized by a local bishop. In the twelfth century, the Church even began to enforce Pope Gregory VII's prohibition of priestly marriage: many priests continued to have "concubines" (common-law wives), but their children no longer had any inheritance rights. In northern France, the Church also successfully reinstituted the tithe: a percentage (ideally 10 percent) of the net crop used to maintain the parish priest. Local lords continued to name parish priests, just as aristocrats continued to name bishops, but the earlier corruption of the Church lessened significantly.

The village churches, however, were the small fry of the Christian world. In the countryside, the big fish were the monasteries and convents, which often owned massive estates. These monasteries traditionally had strong ties to the monarchy, which had many times provided the initial land grant. The Carolingians preferred to leave monasteries under the authority of counts, in part because houses such as Saint-Martin of Tours supplied a substantial portion of the Frankish army. Income from church lands thus provided a critical element in the rise of the political system we call feudalism.

◜ THE BIRTH OF FEUDALISM

A commonwealth, according to Plutarch, is a certain body which is endowed with life by the benefit of divine favor, which acts at the prompting of the highest equity, and is ruled by what may be called the moderating power of reason.[19]

John of Salisbury, *Policraticus*, c. 1160

C H R O N O L O G Y	987–1127
987	Hugh Capet elected King of the Franks
996	Robert II succeeds Hugh
1002	Burgundian civil war; Robert II seizes the duchy
1031	Independent Capetian duchy of Burgundy
1031–1033	Great famine in Francia
1037	William the Bastard inherits Normandy
1066	William, duke of Normandy, conquers England; becomes its king
1095	Urban II preaches the First Crusade at Clermont
1099	Crusaders take Jerusalem
1106	Count of Anjou again does homage to King of France
1107	Concordat between King Philip I and Pope Paschal II on investiture of bishops
1108	Louis VI crowned at Orléans
1127	Count of Flanders again does homage to King of France

The Capetian kings inherited the unique sacred aura of kingship from the Germanic, Judeo-Christian, and Classical traditions. Rather than descending from gods, like Germanic kings, the Capetians, like the kings of Israel in the Old Testament, received special anointing from the servants of the "true" God, in their case by means of the miraculous oil of the Sacred Phial. Shortly after his succession, Robert II began to apply the royal touch: he began to heal by laying on of hands, a power his contemporaries believed he received from the holy unction at the coronation. The king could thus call upon sacerdotal powers in his struggles with the counts or even with his own castellans. These powers did not make the kings any stronger in direct military confrontations with vassals, but gave them an inestimable long-term advantage: they reasserted the principle that legitimate authority, sanctioned by God, passed only through the medium of the king. The combination of such divine sanction and the very real powers of the feudal overlord undergirded the construction of the Capetian state.

The Capetians received a wide range of theoretical and practical powers from their Carolingian predecessors. The king maintained his special position as defender of the realm. He kept nomination rights over certain abbeys and bishoprics and, at least in theory, the right of approval of most episcopal appointments in his kingdom. He had incontestable direct rights over his immediate subordinates, the counts, stemming from their initial status as a royal official, who owed service to the king. Frankish counts kept, too, the traditional Roman comtal obligation to an abstract entity, the commonwealth (*res publica*).

The Early Capetian Kingdom

The clearest legacy of feudalism to modern societies is the emphasis placed on the notion of the political contract. The reciprocity of obligations which united lord and vassal and caused with every grave dereliction by the superior the release of the inferior in the eyes of the law was transferred in the thirteenth century to the state.[20]

Marc Bloch

The early Capetians solidified their power by marriage and inheritance, which made up for their martial ineptitude. They had direct ties to virtually every major noble family of the former Gaul: to the four dukes—of the Burgundians, Normans, Aquitanians, and of Upper Lorraine; to many northern counts—Flanders, Ponthieu, Hainaut, Vermandois, Blois, Anjou, Troyes, and Nevers; and to the royal houses of nearby kingdoms—Burgundy, Italy, and Germany. Henry I capped this process by his marriage to Anna of Kiev, a woman descended, via her mother, from the Byzantine Emperors. Anachronistic focus on individual kings and on purely paternal descent obscures a deeper reality: throughout the eleventh century, male and female lines of the Capetian family ruled the duchies of Burgundy, Aquitaine, and Normandy, and the county of Flanders.

The early Capetian kings performed several notable services to their line. They maintained, however tenuously, the principle of royal government. Their remarkable dynastic continuity had much to do with their success: son succeeded father without interruption for more than three hundred years. The kings also had long reigns, always an advantage in a society built on personal relationships. Hugh Capet himself ruled only for nine years (987–996) but his son Robert II ruled for thirty-five, Henry I for twenty-nine, and Philip I for another forty-eight. Three kings in more than a century: that continuity did much to establish the dynasty.

Capetian propaganda intimated that the family owed its throne to election. Clergymen, accustomed to the election of bishops and Popes, drew parallels between that process and the one by which Hugh Capet became king. They pointed out that the great Charlemagne had followed this principle, when he elevated his son Louis to joint rulership (813). As Einhard tells us:

> he [Charlemagne] summoned Louis . . . and gathered all the chief men of the whole kingdom of the Franks in a solemn assembly. He appointed Louis, with their unanimous consent, to rule with himself over the whole kingdom.

The chronicler Richer claimed that at Hugh's election bishop Adalbero suggested that true kingship did not come from hereditary right, but had to devolve upon he who "distinguishes himself not only by the nobility of his body but even more by the wisdom of his soul."

Hugh immediately sought an affirmation or election of his son Robert as his successor: Adalbero crowned Robert on Christmas Day 987. Thereafter, until the succession of Philip Augustus (1223), the Capetians followed this same election-affirmation process for the king's oldest son during the lifetime of the ruling king. The "election" of the king's oldest son became little more than a formality but at its origin it did much to establish the legitimacy of the kingship among the aristocrats who participated. The memory of this process long lingered: the coronation ceremony of the kings of France always preserved an acclamation by the great nobles of the kingdom, as well as by the people, assembled outside the cathedral. When the direct line ran out in 1328 and again, in the view of some, in 1590, the French ruling elite had no doubts as to how to choose a new king: election.

The Capetian dynasty lacked the panache of the Carolingians. At the outer reaches of the kingdom of West Francia, especially in the south, the royal authority quickly dissipated. No French king sent a charter of any kind to a church in the south from 987 until the early twelfth century. Both the counts of Toulouse and of Barcelona stopped sending their charters to the royal court for affirmation in 987. The count of Barcelona, angry that Hugh Capet had not sent aid against a Muslim attack in 987, even stopped using Frankish regnal years to date his charters.

The Capetians made up for their lack of pedigree by intermarrying with the princely families of West Francia. The family tentacles extended from Aquitaine to Flanders. As we have seen, the northern barons who elected Hugh Capet king in 987 were almost all cousins or relatives by marriage. The two greatest barons of southern France were William V, duke of the Aquitainians and Hugh's brother-in-law, and Henry, duke of the Burgundians and Hugh's younger brother. When duke Henry died (1002), King Robert II seized the duchy. After confiscating the archbishopric of Sens for the Crown,[21] the king passed the duchy to his son Robert. Duke Robert solidified the Capetian network in southern France by marrying his daughter, Audeart, to Guy Geoffrey of Aquitaine. Relatives often played important roles in the royal government. In 1060, when the minor Philip I became king, duke Guy Geoffrey of Aquitaine, husband of his first cousin, led the coronation procession. Philip's uncle, count Baldwin V of Flanders, acted as his guardian until he reached legal majority. The count of Flanders, not coincidentally, provided the Capetian king with his largest single contingent of mounted fighters.

ELEVENTH-CENTURY CAPETIAN MARRIAGES TO PRINCELY HOUSES

Aquitaine	Audeart, d. of Robert (Capet) of Burgundy, m. duke Guy Geoffrey
Flanders	Adela, sister of King Henry I, m. count Baldwin V
Normandy	Emma Capet, sister of Hugh Capet, m. duke Richard II
	Matilda, d. of Adela and Baldwin V, m. William the Conqueror

---

The Diffusion of Authority: Vassals and Fideles

> *For his lord a vassal must suffer great hardship / And endure both great heat and great cold; / He must also part with flesh and blood. / Strike with your lance and I with Durendal, / My good sword, which was a gift from the king. / If I die here, the man who owns it next can say / That it belonged to a noble vassal.*
>
> Roland, speaking to Oliver, lines 1117–1123 of *The Song of Roland*

Political feudalism, at its highest level, combined the personal loyalty the king's vassals owed to him with the professional obligation their "honors" carried. Latin documents used two words to describe these men: they were the king's faithful retainers (*fideles*) or, less often, his vassals. These terms evolved greatly in meaning between the seventh and thirteenth centuries. The late seventh-century formulary of Marculf, giving him the power of a count, notes that he should "act and reign" in his county

> in such a way that all the people who live there, be they Franks, Romans, Burgundians or those of other nations, will live there in a regulated manner under your regime and governing . . . and that you appear as the greatest defender of widows and orphans, and that the crimes of thieves and evildoers will be very severely punished by you, so that the people will live well, will be happy under your regime, and will live united in calm.[22]

Marculf thus had to reign, meaning rule like a king, in the territory under his power. He owed personal loyalty to his king.

Under the Carolingians, the tie between public office and personal loyalty to the king became far tighter. The king's faithful retainers had long sworn personal loyalty, but some grants from the eighth century speak directly of vassalage. When Tassilo, duke of the Bavarians, visited king Pippin III in 757, he offered him homage:

> recommending himself by his hands in vassalage, as duke of the Bavarians, he swore multiple and countless oaths, putting his hands on the relics of saints, and promised fidelity to king Pippin and his above said sons, the seigneur Charles and Carloman, as a vassal of upright spirit and firm devotion, as a vassal justly must be toward his seigneurs.[23]

Becoming a knight: the dubbing of young Roland (thirteenth-century manuscript).
Source: Contamine, Histoire Militaire.

Tassilo thus acted (or rather, was said by a royalist source to act) in a manner that would become associated with the classic tradition of vassalage, placing his hands between those of his lord as he knelt before him to pledge his fealty. Tassilo also received full investiture as duke, thus tying directly his obligations as public official (duke) and as faithful retainer (vassal).[24] Frankish kings tried, but failed to keep the countships or marquisates and benefices from becoming hereditary, but, in practice, the counts often passed their "honor" to their sons, brothers, or nephews. After a few generations, the family came to regard the countship as its property, which it sought to make indistinguishable from family estates.

The same process occurred at the next level down. The counts granted castles to castellans, who sought to make that position hereditary. They, too, succeeded. The castellans relied on armed mounted fighters, knights, to hold their castles and keep peace in the region around their castle. The knights, too, sought land grants, which they tried to turn into hereditary property. The tangled web of such connections has come down to us as the feudal pyramid, with the hierarchy king-count-castellan at its heart and a large group of knights at its base. Alas, life was not so simple: the king's vassals, such as the counts, invariably believed that *their* vassals did *not* owe allegiance to the king, but only to them.

The use of the term *feudalism* to describe the society of the tenth century makes little sense because the famous pyramid of king-count-castellan, based on fiefs and homage, had very little to do with the reality of political life. The most recent survey of French medieval institutions rightly calls the eleventh century the "age of the seigneury" and the twelfth century the beginning of a "feudal epoch." Two key elements provided the route to power, and explain the political system of the time. First, the remnants of imperial authority created the real political framework, in conjunction with the simple power of local strongmen. Second, family ties everywhere proved critical to success. Feudalism focuses heavily on ties of man to man; in reality, the ties of man to woman explain much more satisfactorily the rise of certain families, like the Capetians or the Angevins, and the nature of their power.

Castles, Knights, and Local Authority

The unanimous adoption of this vocabulary [of customs] at the approach of the eleventh century proves that, from that point, essentially regalian powers were no longer founded on an express delegation of sovereignty but on habits and on the testimony of the collective memory; it also proves that public power and private power had become absolutely confused.[25]

Georges Duby, describing castellan courts in the Mâconnais

The king would give a share of his authority to a count; the count would sometimes do the same to the holder of one of his castles. In the late tenth and eleventh centuries, these castellans firmly established what Georges Duby calls their *seigneurie banale,* a combination of elements of state authority, of lordship rights attached to land, and of paterfamilial authority of lords over their slaves.[26] From the old state courts, the castellany courts took over blood justice, guardianship of the peace, and the minor criminal and civil cases once heard in vicarial courts. Just as the bishops, counts, and dukes stopped coming to the royal court by the 1020s, so, too, the castellans stopped going to comtal courts in the early eleventh century.

Here we see the creation of what we have traditionally called the feudal system, with its pivotal figures, the castellans, in the center of a three-pronged offensive. First, they asserted their authority over the surrounding countryside and its peasant inhabitants. Second, they assured themselves of a loyal supply of knights by means of cash payments, extracted from those suppressed in step one or taken as booty during raids against peasants of other castellans. Third, they obtained a legal justification of their *de facto* seizure of power by offering to hold their castles as fiefs of their overlord. This justification helped to legitimize their seizure of judicial authority over the population of the surrounding countryside. Magnate castellans, that is, those from old aristocratic families, had long held this authority, often in direct grant from the king; in the early eleventh century, *all* castellans seized such authority.

The general pattern of the tenth century, contrary to what the old historiography would have us believe, was for people to *refuse* to do homage. Sometimes a powerful aristocrat, like the count of Angoulême, would only promise "friendship" instead of fidelity to his overlord (the count of Poitou/duke of Aquitaine). More often, the most powerful vassals simply stopped swearing fidelity, as happened in Burgundy, where the count-bishop of Langres and the count of Mâcon ceased to swear fidelity to the duke by 960. Historians often point to Normandy as an exception, but tenth-century Normandy provides a prototypical example of the rise of a kinship group rather than of a feudal principality based on vassalage. As late as 1040, the chronicler Raoul Glaber thought Normandy as united as "one family."

At the local level, the castellans relied on their knights as the strike force of the offensive against the peasantry. These bands of knights varied from five to fifty, and their payment could be a piece of land, as in Forez, or just cash and upkeep, as in Normandy, Flanders, or much of the south. Knights remained single, unless they could marry a landed heiress who would enable them to move up in the social hierarchy by joining the ranks of the lords. Dissatisfied with their money payments, knights progressively demanded land in the form of a fief, for which they promised aid and counsel. What better source of land than the holdings of the previously free yet dependent peasantry?

In the north and east, castellans freely granted such lands to their knights, spreading the system of fiefs into almost all landed property. Just as Charlemagne had given out peasant manses to royal officials such as counts, so northern castellans gave manses to their knights in return for promises of military service and an oath of fealty. The castellans thus changed the purely personal tie of earlier times into the feudal relationship based on homage. Yet these small knightly fiefs, unlike the ones held by aristocrats, rarely had any judicial rights: in early thirteenth-century Champagne, 75 percent of the fiefs had no rights of justice. Many twelfth-century knights still received a simple money fief, in return for guard service at castles. In Champagne, the virtual disappearance of such arrangements reduced the total number of fiefs by 40 percent between 1200–1250.

Prior to the year 1000, the documents illustrate the highly localized society of Francia. In some regions, such as the county of Vendôme in the Loire valley, scribes attached the term *knight* (*miles*) to nobles as early as the tenth century. In this region, the earlier word *vassal* disappeared, to be replaced by *knight* by 1060: in both cases, the term referred to a social status. Scribes in many other regions, such as the Mâconnais or parts of the north, used *knight* to describe an occupation, that of mounted fighter. For them, a knight was *not* a noble. Richer's comment that the barons rejected Charles of Lorraine's candidacy for the throne in 987 because "he had married a wife who, being of the knightly class, was not his equal," reveals the social ambiguity of the knights.[27] Aristocrats did not yet accept the principle that a knight was a nobleman, but knightly families were making their way up in the social hierarchy: the daughter of a knight married a Carolingian duke. Charles of Lorraine's wife showed the way of the future: by the second half of the eleventh century, the Loire Valley practice, equating knight and noble, became normative. The knights, their prestige raised by possession of the defining property of the aristocracy, land, demanded greater social standing as well. In the twelfth century, even aristocratics styled themselves *miles*. By the middle of the thirteenth century, the aristocrats and the knights had merged to form a nobility.

Toward a Feudal Order: The Rise of Homage

If he wishes to appear worthy, he [the vassal] must faithfully furnish aid and counsel to his lord.[28]

Fulcher of Chartres, c. 1020

In the second half of the eleventh and first half of the twelfth century, the greater courts began to revive and overlords systematically forced their vassals to do homage. In the principalities, the rulers got stronger and their administration developed rapidly. Princely courts became more intrusive; officials even began to produce systematic documents, such as tax rolls, and to preserve them. The King of the Franks summoned his leading aristocrats to special councils in 1049, 1077, and in 1094, this last to hear a critical case about the succession to the duchy of Normandy. The claimants were the sons of King Philip's first cousin Mathilda. Just as the count of Anjou demanded that his castellans do homage to him, so the King of France demanded that the count of Anjou do homage for his fief. The count insisted that the knightly vassals of his castellans held their fiefs ultimately from him. The Kings of France insisted that all people in the feudal pyramid owed their ultimate loyalty to the king, as the suzerain, the human apex of that pyramid.

In the eleventh century, knights had ties to castellans; castellans had ties to counts; counts had ties to the king. These ties, however, rarely had any connection to each other. All that changed in the twelfth century: feudalism, the integrated hierarchy of a pyramid of homages, far from being a force weakening royal power, served to create a more cohesive kingdom. This process took a very long time. A broad schematization of it might look like this:

Twelfth century: Major vassals of the king again do homage to him.

Twelfth and thirteenth centuries: King establishes principle that vassals of his vassals hold ultimately from him.

Late twelfth and thirteenth centuries: King creates network of bailiffs in his demesne (1190) and in the entire kingdom (1254).

Fourteenth century: King establishes his right to tax all inhabitants of the kingdom, based on consent of the landlords and towns.

Fifteenth century: King effectively asserts (1445) his unique right to tax within the kingdom.

Early sixteenth century: King enforces the principle that he has ultimate judicial authority over all those living in the kingdom.

Late sixteenth century: King asserts his absolute right to make law.

Duty to the King: The Trial of Ganelon

The Song of Roland tells the story of the massacre of Charlemagne's rearguard at Roncesvalles in 778. Only one contemporary source mentions the event, in which the Wascones (Basques) slaughtered the rearguard of the Frankish army, which included the count of the Breton marches, Hrolandus. The tale quickly became the stuff of legend; the first written version, dating from the early twelfth century, contains elements of ninth-, tenth-, and eleventh-century songs. *Roland* shows the contradictory nature of a count's ties to the king. The villain of the story, count Ganelon, betrays count Roland and the rearguard of Charlemagne's army. Ganelon claims he did so for private revenge, and thus acted legitimately; he even warns Roland in front of Charlemagne and the royal council that he will seek revenge. At first, the Frankish barons, afraid of Ganelon's mighty champion, Pinabel, are willing to let him go, but the young Thierry of Anjou springs forward to be Charlemagne's champion. He tells the king:

Whatever Roland may have done to Ganelon,
The act of serving you should have protected him.
Ganelon is a traitor in that he betrayed him;
He committed perjury against you and wronged you.
For this I judge that he be hanged and put to death

The poet does not allow any doubt about the reason for Thierry's triumph: at the outset of their combat, Charlemagne cries out, "O God, make justice [*dreit*, or 'right'] shine forth." When the slender Thierry slays the behemoth Pinabel, "The Franks shout out: 'God has performed a miracle. It is right for Ganelon to be hanged. And his kinsmen who upheld his suit.'" Ganelon and his thirty clansmen are executed.

The poem shows us the ambiguity of the relationship between the king and the aristocracy at the end of the eleventh century. The poem highly praises the "marvelous vassals," Roland and his bosom friend, Oliver. Roland

The first stage of the process involved recognition by all of their obligations to the king, and of the king's unique status. The greatest epic poem of the age, *The Song of Roland,* offers remarkable testimony to the complexity of this process.

The revival of homage helped the Capetians create a stronger, feudal monarchy. Capetian prestige reached its nadir under the much reviled Philip I (d. 1108), who requested that he be buried at the abbey of Fleury rather than the royal necropolis at Saint-Denis. Suger, abbot of Saint-Denis, claimed Philip so acted because "no one would consider his tomb important among so many noble kings."[29] Philip did sign an important concordat with Pope Paschal II (1107) that regulated the investiture of bishops, a key element of royal power. The compromise satisfied all parties. The cathedral chapters kept their right to elect, and their tradition of independence; the Pope maintained his primacy of ecclesiastical investiture and obtained an ally in his struggle with the Emperor; and the king obtained the satisfaction of both advanced consultation with the chapter about the election and the investiture of the secular rights.

Philip's heir, Louis VI, suffered the humiliation of being crowned at Orléans, by the archbishop of Sens, who used ordinary sacramental oil, rather than the holy oil of Reims: Louis was one of only two kings after 987 not crowned at Reims. Louis the Fat, whose body was so "weighted down . . . by burdensome folds of flesh," that "no one else . . . would have . . . been able to ride a horse when hampered with such a

(CONTINUED)

does not wish to bring shame on his own name, on that of his kinsmen, or on that of "fair France." When Thierry accuses Ganelon at the end, he describes the crime as "felony," betrayal of one's feudal lord.

The poem highlights the dual nature of the king's power and of his relationship to the other great lords of the realm. On the one hand, the king has a special place as king. In the poem Charlemagne communicates directly with God and the angels, and God intervenes twice to save the king's cause. On the other hand, the poem also celebrates Charlemagne as suzerain, as the feudal lord of Roland, Oliver, and Ganelon. Here we can see that at the end of the eleventh century people now confused the count's obligation to the king because of his office, his "honor," and the count's obligation to the king because of his personal tie to him. French kings sought to solidify both types of bond, insisting on royal rights derived from their *auctoritas,* that is,

from their position as sovereign, and on feudal rights, that is, from their position as suzerain. At late as the sixteenth century, the nobility invariably referred to the king as their "sovereign seigneur" in their appeals to him, a fitting testimony to the dual heritage that created the French monarchy and its state.

As for Ganelon and Roland, they had different fates. By 1100, the name Ganelon had disappeared from Western Europe, so great was the shame attached to it. Roland became one of the greatest medieval heroes. Legend has it that a poet sang a version of Roland's song to William the Conqueror's troops on the eve of the battle of Hastings. In the fourteenth century, chroniclers made Roland and Charlemagne two of the Nine Worthies (peerless knights) of all history. Even in the sixteenth century, Bernal Diaz, companion of Cortez in the conquest of Mexico, compared the *conquistadores* to "the paladin Roland" and his men.

dangerously large body," proved to be an effective king, despite his inability as a military leader. Louis VI greatly enhanced the feudal nature of the kingship. The dukes of Normandy, Burgundy, and Aquitaine refused to do homage at Louis's coronation, but the king gradually used favorable diplomatic situations to get them to change their minds. Succession crises in Normandy (1120) and Flanders (1127) led to their rulers again doing homage to Louis.

In 1127, Louis claimed the right to name the new count of Flanders, but the representatives of the Flemish towns radically disagreed:

> the election and installation of the counts of Flanders is nothing to do with the king of France, whether the previous count has died with or without an heir. The peers of Flanders and the citizens have the power to nominate the individual most closely related, and the right to raise him to the office of count.[30]

Here we see the remarkable mix of the new—the principle of election of rulers— and the old—the Carolingian legacy that the countship was an "office."

According to Suger, Louis had also convinced the great vassals of one of the most important principles that would soon underlay the expanded authority of his grandson (Philip Augustus). Suger tells us that William X, duke of Aquitaine said to the king:

> May your royal highness see fit to receive the service of the duke of Aquitaine and preserve him in his right. For even as justice demands the service of a vassal, so it also demands a just lordship. The count holds the Auvergne from me, which I in turn hold from you. And if he has done anything wrong, I must deliver him to your court for trial when you command it.[31]

Suger suggested to Louis that the king no longer do homage for fiefs he held of others; instead, Louis became the liege man of Saint Denis (the saint, not the monastery), whose holy banner, the *oriflamme,* henceforth accompanied the royal host in battle. No immediate evidence suggests that Louis got his vassals to agree to Suger's interpretation, but the logic of their own positions eventually forced them to go along. They, too, had subvassals (that is, the vassals of their vassals) and they, too, demanded that subvassals admit their ultimate dependence on them. They could hardly claim that their subvassals owed them homage but then deny that their own vassals, as subvassals of the king, did not hold of him.

French kings took the offensive throughout the twelfth century. Louis VI issued four times as many charters as his father, issued them for a broader area, including the county of Toulouse, an area with no prior Capetian charters, and even began to promulgate direct royal orders (mandates) and judgments. The monarchy carefully, steadily, ceaselessly expanded its authority and power. Where Louis VII acted above all to guarantee settlements reached by the parties before they came to his court, Philip Augustus, through his baronial court, proposed the terms of the agreements.

Louis VI and Louis VII took seriously the legal limits of their kingdom and sought to expand their effective power within that imagined legal entity. Louis VI extended his protection to all bishoprics lacking a specific patron, such as Clermont and Arras. When Louis VII married Eleanor of Aquitaine, he went to Bordeaux, took an oath as duke of Aquitaine, and issued charters for the entire region (albeit as duke, not king). The king even got his brother-in-law, Raymond, count of Toulouse, to do homage. Louis VII thus received homage from virtually every important baron in the old kingdom of West Francia, from Flanders to Toulouse, creating a feudalized kingdom of France to leave to his son. That both Louis VI and Louis VII deliberately sought to do so seems little in doubt; in one telling passage of his *Deeds of Louis the Fat,* Suger calls him "the king of Gaul," an obvious effort by the earnest royal counselor to suggest that Louis ruled the territory of ancient Gaul, rather than simply the more ambiguous, and much smaller, Francia.

Starting in 1119, following in the footsteps of the great dukes, Louis VI also claimed a new title: King of France. The old, essentially tribal titles gave way to pro-tonational ones, based on a geographic region. Official documents usually kept the old title until the time of Philip Augustus (d. 1223), but the monastic chronicles, especially the royalist one of Saint-Denis, invariably used the new one. When Philip Augustus took the throne in 1180, he directly ruled a tiny amalgamation of territories focused increasingly around Paris, but as King of France he also had recognized, albeit ill-defined authority over a much wider area, ranging from the west bank of the Rhône river to the Atlantic and from the Mediterranean to Flanders. Philip faced a critical question: could he use the combination of traditional royal rights, which his monastic allies sought always to emphasize and glorify in their texts, and the new techniques of "feudalism" to create a more powerful state?

Principalities and the State

In order to enlarge the area of his authority, the king, conforming to feudal law, required the counsel of his vassals, dukes or counts: he submitted his ordinance to this "court of barons," demanded that they adhere to it and swear to respect it. In this manner, the "establishment" was applicable not only in the royal demesne but also in those of the barons who accepted the ordinance; it was not applicable, however, on the lands of those who refused to attend the court or who did not subscribe to it.[32]

Jean Bart

The answer to this question could be found in the principalities, where the castellans had rapidly lost power to their overlords, the counts and dukes. Hard at work creating the basic structures of a regional state in the twelfth or thirteenth century, the princes paved the way for the creation of the kingdom of France. The enormous differences in wealth and military strength between the princes and the castellans explain why these local principalities gained so much greater power: where a castellan might have a group of ten knights, the duke of Normandy or the counts of Flanders or Champagne each had fifteen hundred knights who owed them military service. As King of England, Henry II had the theoretical right to over five thousand knights' services; the Kings of France had an even larger feudal host.

Normandy, Anjou, and Flanders provide the best examples of the emerging power of the regional units. The duke of Normandy had a unique range of powers within his duchy: the exclusive right to try serious crimes; a universal right of appeal of all Normans to his justice; and ownership of all Norman castles, whose castellans and viscounts distributed justice only in the duke's name. The duke also held regalian rights: only he could mint coinage, levy tolls, and establish customs (such as weights). Starting with William the Conqueror in 1037, the dukes of Normandy refused to do homage to the King of France.

Effective rulers, like William the Conqueror or Fulk Nerra and Geoffrey Martel of Anjou, regained control over their castellans, convinced feudal lords to do them homage, established new castles in disputed regions, allied themselves with powerful monasteries, and named relatives to important bishoprics. When William of Normandy conquered England, he brought this system with him, establishing a complete hierarchical system of fiefs throughout the country. His work in England shows the extent to which French feudalism enhanced royal power: William introduced the hierarchy of fiefs to solidify his power, not to reduce it. He further established other clearly royalist policies, such as a uniform system of weights and measures. To cement his control over the church, he made his maternal half-brother, bishop Odo of Bayeux, archbishop of Canterbury.

Counts and dukes set up their own chanceries, often collected taxes (sometimes to defend the "kingdom"), and tried to establish their right to judicial overlordship. Government strengthened first at this level, creating a patchwork of powerful regional states in France. By the second half of the twelfth century, the regional princes used their superior force to make the castellans do homage for their castles, to define them as fiefs held directly of the count or duke. By 1172 in Champagne, 47 percent of the nineteen hundred fiefs owed the count homage; at the beginning of the thirteenth century, that figure had risen to 78 percent.[33] In Normandy, Anjou, or Flanders, the local rulers had long since established the principle that every castellan held of them and that the feudal pyramid extended directly from the humblest knight to the prince. The King of France, of course, sought to get these counts and dukes to recognize the same principle with respect to his authority within the kingdom. As Jean Bart has noted, the king invariably took these steps with the approval of the key barons; even in the late fourteenth century, when the king sought to establish royal taxation on the peasants of feudal lords, he had to obtain their permission, often by granting them a share of the proceeds.

We have long been accustomed to speak of "feudalism" as a decentralizing system that relied on four key factors: division of public authority; lack of private property; a dependent peasantry; and a system of vassalage centered on the fief. In fact, rather than being a system of local autonomy set against centralizing authority, twelfth-century feudalism enhanced, indeed made possible, state organization. Just as Louis VI and Louis VII successfully sought to enhance royal power, often through "feudal" means (like the collection of relief in Flanders in 1127), so, too, the princes sought to use these same principles to organize more efficiently their states. Philip Augustus became King of France at a moment by which these regional rulers had largely succeeded in their goal of making themselves unquestioned rulers, supreme guarantors of the peace, in their principalities. If Philip could get his hands on their holdings, he could expand the royal state simply by amalgamating the existing local administration into the royal one.

Champagne or the royal demesne, Normandy or Flanders, the same changes were afoot. The rulers used the system of fiefs and homage to tie directly to themselves the aristocrats and the knights of their territories. Comtal, ducal or royal officials began to interfere more directly in the affairs of everyday life, particularly in matters of common defense. Princes tried to establish the principle that their justice stood above all others. Counts Baldwin VII (d. 1119) and Charles the Good (d. 1127) of Flanders accomplished the pacification through highly personal means: Baldwin once ordered a knight who stole a peasant woman's cow to be boiled in oil; Charles supervised the hanging of ten men who had violated his peace. Charles forced each man to hang one of his fellows and then placed the rope around the neck of the last victim himself.[34] Charles's successor, Thierry, even established the principle that all death sentences in the county had to be approved by the comtal court. In France as a whole, the king could not effectively enforce this principle until the sixteenth century.

Kings, dukes, and counts began to use bailiffs (called seneschals in southern France and in Brittany) to insinuate their administration into local affairs. These officials differed radically from the older provosts, whose primary duty consisted of collecting revenue. Whether it is the King of France's *Census* of 1202, the *Gros Brief* of the count of Flanders (1187) or the Norman roll of 1198, the accounts show the great rulers of the time receiving chickens, peas, oats, wheat, wood, and the widest possible array of agricultural produce from their serfs. Provosts sold this produce, collected fees at fairs and tolls, and, in time, levied judicial fines.[35] Many times the local provosts simply leased out the collection rights to sub officials, who provided a cash equivalent of in-kind dues.

The bailiffs had much broader powers related to justice, state finance, and the maintenance of public order. They were the first in a long line of officials sent to the provinces by the Kings of France to enforce their will and to mediate between the interests of local elites and the central state. Philip Augustus here followed the example of the far superior organization of Normandy and Flanders. When (1190) Philip created a board of audit at Paris, he copied an institution that had existed in Flanders for more than a century and in both England and Normandy for over three generations. Everywhere officials introduced proper record keeping, holding inquests that provided written evidence of all obligations owed to the ruler. Philip Augustus instituted (1190) permanent monthly meetings of the bailiff's assize courts in his demesne lands; his grandson, Louis IX, made that policy standard for the entire kingdom. Lest we get carried away by the majesty of this state institution, we do well to remember that even the Norman assizes sometimes sat in open fields for lack of a proper building.

The great ordinance of 1190 also established tri-annual meetings of the royal court (*curia regis*), which likely took place at the newly mandated rendering of accounts made by the bailiffs and provosts: on All Saints' Day (1 November), Candlemas (2 February), and Ascension Thursday (in May/June, date varying with Easter). The king kept his budget surplus with the Templars, whose house at Paris often served as a deposit bank for the wealthy. That the king required the services of a third party merely to store his cash gives us some idea of how primitive royal administration remained.

The princes had additional sources of irregular income. They could manipulate coinage or levy fines on "outsiders," such as the Jews. Unlike his father, who treated the Jews with respect, Philip Augustus, a confirmed anti-Semite, exploited the Jews for financial gain. He expelled the Jews from his demesne lands and expropriated much of their property in return for allowing them to return. An English chronicler speaks of more than 30,000 *l.p.,* which would have been about a third of his annual revenue at that time.[36] Throughout the thirteenth and fourteenth centuries, in between expulsions, French kings periodically levied fines on the Jewish community, as in 1227, 1254, or 1268 (the latter two aimed specifically at moneylenders).

Feudal overlords also collected "relief" for inheritance of fiefs held directly of them. The King of France took a cash payment for the transferral of the county of Flanders in 1127, 1192, and 1212, but insisted on land in other cases. A great lord could also levy special taxes, such as the classic feudal *tailles* (tallages): for the marriage of the lord's eldest daughter, for the knighting of the lord's eldest son, for ransom, and for going on Crusade. Philip Augustus and Richard the Lion-Hearted each levied a tallage for the Third Crusade. Philip also collected emergency military taxes, such as the levy for "sergeants" (infantry) in 1202.

Better administration, the addition of Artois and Vermandois (from inheritance/relief settlements), and more rigorous use of "special" taxes enabled Philip Augustus to increase revenue from the royal demesne by 80 percent between 1180–1202. The conquest of the Angevin Empire and other fiefs raised his revenues by another 80 percent before his death. Because Philip left his son a state that combined the resources of three of the richest principalities in western Europe (Normandy, Anjou, and the royal demesne), the King of France henceforth had an income that dwarfed that of his barons: Philip had roughly 200,000 *l.p.* to the mere 12,000 of the count of Forez. Such figures exclude special wartime taxes or such levies as Philip's fines on the Jews. Philip thus took the kingdom from a situation in which the king constantly had a vassal (Henry II of England) whose revenue roughly equaled his, to one in which the king had revenue vastly larger than that of any other prince.[37]

Inheritance and Power: The Critical Role of Women

> *They take the pagans up to the baptistery; / If there is anyone who withstands Charles, / He has him hanged or burned or put to death. / More than a hundred thousand are baptized / True Christians, with the exception of the queen. / She will be taken as a captive to fair France; / The king wishes her to become a convert through love.*
>
> *The Song of Roland,* lines 3668–3674

The marriages of Louis VII and Philip Augustus, and their children, played a critical role in their long-term strategies of creating a larger royal demesne and a more unified kingdom. Each married a woman from a powerful northern family: Louis married Adela of Champagne, whose family's great counties of Champagne and Blois surrounded the royal demesne; Philip wedded Isabelle of Hainaut, niece of the childless count of Flanders, the greatest baron of the north. Isabelle, whose inheritance rights provided Philip with important territorial gains when her uncle died, illustrates again the fundamental role of women in creating and consolidating family power, which depended on both agnatic and cognatic lines of alliance. Until the eleventh century, families gave more importance to the family status of the woman bearing the child than to "legitimacy." Aside from churchmen, few western Europeans thought much about the concept of "legitimate" birth. The Church had so little to do with marriage in the ninth or tenth century that the Frankish church did not even have a marriage liturgy.

In some areas, people inherited status solely from their mothers, because of the obvious ambiguity over the paternal identity. All that changed in the eleventh century.[38] Throughout France, strict patrilineal lines of inheritance became recognized in law for the nobility. Oldest sons came to have special rights; younger sons and, especially, daughters, lost property rights. Daughters, who had retained rights to family property after marriage, now began to receive their dowries in lieu of (and not in addition to) an inheritance. In most parts of France, equal division of property after death soon became *prima facie* evidence of commoner status: only nobles practiced primogeniture.[39] These rules did not change one vital element of inheritance laws: lacking a male heir, the land could pass to a woman. Given the appalling death rate among young male nobles in the eleventh and twelfth centuries, women inherited many, many fiefs.

Marriage to such an heiress provided an important means of social mobility for three groups of men: knights seeking to move into the nobility; the now disinherited younger sons of noble families; and aristocrats hoping to obtain a principality or even a kingdom. Although the French Crown passed from father to oldest son from 996–1316, most of the leading principalities fell to female heirs: Aquitaine in 927 and in 1137; Burgundy in 956; Brittany in the tenth, eleventh, and twelfth centuries; Vermandois and Gascony in the eleventh century; Flanders and Normandy in the twelfth. The rulers of all the great principalities had intermarried to such an extent that when any given male branch of the family ran out, another one stood to gain new titles and territories. The importance of female branches of the family can readily be seen in the ongoing practice of taking names from more prestigious cognatic ancestors. It was an old game: when the Carolingians adopted as their own the greatest Merovingian name, Clovis, "modernized" to Louis, the dynasty's apologists spread the word that it descended from Blitilde, an imaginary sister of the great Merovingian king, Dagobert I.

The counts of Anjou offer the best example of a family ascent through marriage to powerful women. Over the course of three centuries, judicious marriages raised the family of the simple warrior Tortulfus to the hereditary countship of Anjou (third generation) and, in the end, to the Crown of England. (See "The Rise of the Angevins" chart in the accompanying box, *The Names of Kings and Queens*.) The Angevins demonstrate the key mechanisms for obtaining power in tenth- and eleventh-century Francia: marriage into the right families, personal ties to powerful individuals, royal offices, and control of church property. The Angevins had key bishops and abbots in every generation. These included bishops at Angers, Soissons, and Le Puy; an archbishop at Tours; the lay abbacy of Saint-Martin; and by personal patronage, ties to the greatest abbey of the tenth century, Cluny.[40] The church properties provided substantial revenues, and, in the case of Saint-Martin, a network of knights, who owed service to the abbey.

Women did not merely pass along property; they played important roles in the politics of their day, just as Brunhild or Fredegond had done before them. Aristocratic women often received the same education as their male relatives. Einhard tells us that Charlemagne had "both the boys and the girls [his children] instructed in the liberal arts." Dhuoda, wife of the duke of the Aquitanians, wrote a handbook of conduct for noblewomen and men, the *Liber Manuelis*, in the middle of the ninth century. The *Liber* can also be read as a detailed political analysis of her society, particularly of the intricate relationship among the three fathers of patriarchy: God, the king, and the male head of household. Queens and duchesses from Leutegarde of Normandy (942)

The Names of Kings and Queens

"You're truly Odysseus' son?" . . . And young Telemachus cautiously replied. /"I'll try, my friend, to give you a frank answer. / Mother has always told me I'm his son, it's true, / but I am not so certain. Who, on his own, / has ever really known who gave him life?"

The Odyssey, lines 240–251 (Fagles translation)

The naming practices of aristocratic clans in tenth- through twelfth-century northwestern Europe demonstrate the intricate pattern connecting the giant clan and the critical role of women in transferring status. Social climbers, like the Capetians, invariably took names from more prestigious cognatic ancestors. Capetian kings took on Henry, through his royal German mother (Hedwige), then Philip, through his mother, Anna of Kiev, and even Louis, the Merovingian name stolen by the Carolingians. Capetian dukes of Burgundy kept the Robertian names: every duke from Hugh I (1076) to Hugh III (d. 1191) was a Hugh or a Eudes. Beatrice of Vermandois (mother of Hugh the Great), great-great-granddaughter of Charlemagne, brought with her the family female names—Adela/Adelaide, Gisele, and Beatrice—which soon became "Capetian." Capetian princesses, like Matilda of Flanders (daughter of Henry I of France), later passed the names Robert, Eudes, Emma, Matilda, and Adela into the families of the counts of Flanders and Champagne, and the dukes of Normandy. Matilda's marriage to William the Conqueror moved "Henry" into the English royal family. Her namesake granddaughter later married Geoffry Plantagenet, count of Anjou. In 1154, their son became Henry II of England.

Philip I's choice of the Carolingian name Louis for his heir offers a dramatic example of this effort to enhance the prestige of his family, which thus moved beyond the many Henrys and Roberts around them. Counts and dukes, once intermarried into the Capetian family, took over the traditional Capetian names Robert and Eudes, and the English royal family that of Henry (not royal again in France until 1547). This name, Henry, was used for the son born *after* William had be-

CHRONOLOGY	1137–1217
1137	Louis VII marries Eleanor of Aquitaine
1147	Louis VII goes on the Second Crusade; fails to take Damascus
1152	Eleanor and Louis divorce; Eleanor marries Henry Plantagenet
1169	Plantagenets do homage for Normandy, Anjou, Maine, and Poitou
1180	Accession of Philip Augustus
1183	Death of the young Henry Plantagenet
1186	Death of duke Geoffrey of Brittany
1189	Death of Henry II of England; Richard I, king of England
1190	Richard I and Philip Augustus leave on Third Crusade

(CONTINUED)

come king of England. Alone among the great barons, count Charles the Good of Flanders, who was the son of King Cnut IV of Denmark, bore a kingly name. Only sons or grandsons of kings, it seems, could take one of the recognized royal names.

Nobles began to take family names, and eleventh-century customary laws banned "bastards" from the inheritance. Normandy, which first passed to an "illegitimate" son in 942 (after a civil war), was the last major principality to be inherited by such an heir, when duke Robert died without legitimate heir in 1037. The new duke, known to his contemporaries as William the Bastard, is known to us by the more edifying William the Conqueror. The Church demanded, and got, the right to bless marriages, which consolidated this new system of relations.[41]

The Rise of the Angevins

Tortulfus, "soldier"	m. Petronilla, niece of Hugh the Abbot, chief counselor of King Charles the Bald; Tortulfus became viscount of Anjou
Ingelgarius (s), count	m. Adelais, niece of archbishop of Tours and of bishop of Angers
Fulk the Red (s), count	m. Roscilla, granddaughter of Adalhard the seneschal, uncle of Empress Irmentrude, chief counselor of Emperor Louis the Pious, and probable relative of Robert the Strong; lay abbot of Saint-Martin of Tours; countship becomes heredity
Geoffrey Greymantle (gs)	m. Adela of Vermandois, daughter of Herbert, count of Vermandois, niece of Hugh Capet, descendant of Charlemagne
Geoffrey Plantagenet (gs)	m. Mathilda of England, daughter of King Henry I of England
Henry II (s)	from his father, inherited county of Anjou; from his mother inherited duchy of Normandy, county of Maine, kingdom of England m. Eleanor of Aquitaine
(s) = Son	(gs) = Grandson

to dowager Queen Constance (1030s) to Eleanor of Aquitaine fought civil wars against stepsons, sons, and even husbands. Women like Eleanor not only wielded enormous political power, but provided critical patronage of the arts. Eleanor mediated the transferral of the cultural achievements of southern Francia to the north.

The tremendous strengthening of the principalities, and the tight network of intermarriages that united them, combined to create the foundations for the triumph of Philip Augustus. His father and grandfather had carefully established the obligation of the princes to do homage and had insisted that the vassals of royal vassals also owed the king homage. They had also used regalian rights over the Church, above all the bishoprics, to enhance their power. Philip would pull all these elements together into the coup that created a real kingdom of France.

∿ CREATING THE KINGDOM OF FRANCE

> *Luck is the residue of design.*
>
> Branch Rickey

Philip II Augustus (1180-1223) was the luckiest of men: his enemies died young. His greatest foe, Richard the Lion-Hearted of England, died in 1199, felled by a stray arrow at a minor siege. Count Philip of Flanders, and the brother counts Thibaut of Blois (royal seneschal) and Henry of Troyes, died at the siege of Acre (1191). Philip Augustus's own health suffered terribly in the Levant. Disease caused his hair and nails to fall out, but he returned alive, leaving "the barons of his father's generation buried in the Syrian sands."[42]

Historians often stress Philip's discomfort in the shadow of his more illustrious co-Crusader, Richard the Lion-Hearted, as the primary reason for the king's departure after the capture of Acre (July 1191), but the June 1191 death of Philip of Flanders, without issue, surely provided a powerful incentive to return to France and claim a share of the inheritance. When he got back to Paris, Philip recognized Baldwin of Hainaut as the new count, but obtained for his wife (Isabelle of Hainaut) both the immediate possession of Artois and recognition of inheritance rights to the counties of Vermandois, which he had already seized, and Valois.

Luck, or design? The serendipitous death of Philip of Flanders and survival of Philip of France at Acre easily lead us astray from the larger, carefully designed policies of the heirs of Hugh Capet. The great families of northern France—the rulers of the house of Blois-Champagne, the dukes of Normandy/kings of England, the counts of Anjou, the counts of Flanders, the counts of Vermandois, the kings of France, the dukes of Burgundy—cousins all, were enmeshed in family web so tight as to preclude the overall family's loss of power, whatever might happen to an individual patrilineal branch. The patrilineal line of the kings of France happened not to run out between 996–1316, so the matter of collateral inheritance did not arise for the crown itself, but we would be much mistaken to assume that had the male line run out, descendants of female lines would not have inherited. The history of every other principality of the region suggests precisely the opposite. Moreover, when Louis X

The seal of Philip Augustus, seated on the throne of Dagobert I.

died without a son, in 1316, his youngest brother, Charles, unsuccessfully supported the right of his niece, Jeanne, to the throne.

Philip Augustus expanded the relatively tiny royal demesne partly by means of family inheritance, as in Artois, Vermandois, and Valois, and partly by means of rights he claimed as feudal overlord, as in Normandy, Anjou, and Maine. The long pattern of intermarriages and the careful construction of a feudal pyramid went hand-in-hand in the creation of the kingdom of France: we might call it the marriage of luck and design.

The roots of the decisive struggle of Philip with the Angevin rulers of England and Normandy lay in the middle of the twelfth century. Louis VII had married Eleanor of Aquitaine, heir of duke William X (d. 1137), but, after having a daughter (Marie), they divorced in 1152. Some chroniclers speak of Eleanor's reputed affair with her uncle, Raymond of Antioch, during the Second Crusade (1147), as the cause. Eleanor quickly remarried, to Henry Plantagenet. In 1154, Henry II inherited England and Normandy (through his mother), to add to his father's Angevin lands, giving the couple control of the entirety of western France, as well as England. Henry later forced duke Conan of Brittany to marry his daughter and heir, Constance, to Henry and Eleanor's son Geoffrey (1166).

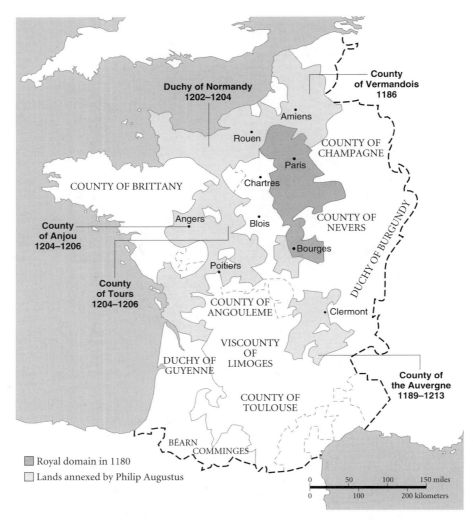

Philip Augustus's additions to the royal demesne.

Louis VII and Henry II tried to use the familiar marriage strategy to head off conflict: Louis's daughters, Marguerite and Alice, became engaged to Henry's sons, Henry and Richard. The first marriage ended abruptly in 1183, when young Henry died of dysentery. After his son's death, Henry II refused to return Margaret's dowry, the critical Vexin region laying between Paris and Normandy. Philip agreed to transfer the Vexin to his sister Alice, but, in the end, Richard refused to marry her, perhaps because of her rumored "affair" with his father.[44] Henry II and Eleanor had divided their lands among their three oldest sons: Henry was to get his father's lands, Normandy, Anjou,

ELEANOR OF AQUITAINE AND CHIVALRY

Few women had so close a relationship to so many kings as Eleanor of Aquitaine. She married two of them—Louis VII of France and Henry II of England—and three of her sons received the title (young Henry only shared it with his father, whom he predeceased). She has long provided a further example of female agency in medieval society, following along lines laid out by Brunhild and Constance of Arles. Eleanor initially administered much of Richard's land when he went on Crusade and she personally brought his ransom to the Emperor and freed him.

Her important political career notwithstanding, Eleanor played an even more critical role in mediating the cultural achievement of southern Francia for the "barbarous" northerners. Eleanor's grandfather, duke William IX of Aquitaine, a renowned poet, often is called the first of the troubadours; her father, William X sponsored the most cultured "French" court of his time. By mediating the transmission of Occitan culture to northern France, Eleanor helped create a second, enduring element of chivalry. Northern French poets had long since created a male chivalric literature, best represented by the *chansons de geste,* literally the songs of deeds. *The Song of Roland* is merely the most famous example of a broad literature whose heroes included Roland, his companion archbishop Turpin, Charlemagne, Godfrey of Bouillon, and other famous chivalric champions. This tradition glorified the warlike deeds of men. The knight demonstrated his "chivalrous" qualities on the battlefield: bravery, loyalty, prowess. Women played little part in many of the stories, as in *The Song of Roland,* in which there are only two named female characters and only Bramimunde, the Muslim queen, speaks.

Eleanor, like her father and grandfather, provided patronage to the leading poets of her age, who wrote in Occitan, not French. Occitan poets did not primarily focus on military deeds, or on nonreligious subjects; they wrote about that most profane of subjects: love. The troubadours sang the praises of courtly love, of mutual affection and respect. The proper male noble no longer defined himself purely through bravery and prowess, but by means of his refinement and elevated sensibility. Bernard de Ventadour, a poet known to have had Eleanor's patronage, once wrote: "In accord and in assent / is the love of two noble lovers. / Nothing can be of profit in it / if the will thereto is not mutual." (En agradar et en voler / Es l'amors de dos fis amans. / Nula res no.i pot pro tener / Si.lh voluntatz non es egaus.)

This love of equals (*egaus*) did not necessarily lead to marriage; indeed, rare was the case of the husband as lover. Noble women and men married for reasons of family politics, not for affection. The young men who lived as knights in the great aristocratic households became the devoted servants of their lady. Many romances focused on a sort of platonic love between such a knight and the lady of his house, but other works, like Chrétien de Troyes' *Knight of the Cart,* involved sexual liaisons. Chrétien retells the ancient Celtic legends of the peerless knight Lancelot and his lady, Queen Guinevere, wife of Lancelot's lord, King Arthur.

The troubadour poets inspired northern imitators, the greatest of whom were Chrétien de Troyes and Guillaume de Lorris. Chrétien, author of *Tristan and Iseult* (see Plate 2), *Yvain,* and several Arthurian legends, had direct ties to the world of Eleanor. His patroness, to whom he dedicated the *Knight of the Cart,* was Marie of Champagne, Eleanor's daughter. The greatest known woman writer of the time, Marie de France, wrote in Norman French, and also had obvious ties to the court of Eleanor and Henry. Her *lais* show the influence of Eleanor's Occitan poets on the Norman court to which she moved in mid-century.

Marie de France and the other courtly romantics provided a second current of chivalric behavior, one to place beside the male one so evident in the *chansons de geste.* They

---

emphasized mutual respect, the knight serving his lady, and the subordination of the military virtues to those of *courteoisie*—the behavior expected of a courtly gentleman. Even the word *gentil*, meaning noble and courteous, became more prominent in this time. In the most direct manifestation of this subordination, Guinevere, in the *Knight of the Cart,* makes Lancelot deliberately fight poorly at a tournament, thus humiliating himself in public, merely to demonstrate his service to her. (She later lets him redeem himself, but her point is made.) This victory of the female notion of chivalry over the initial male (martial) one has modern linguistic traces in both English and French: the English "chivalric" now refers invariably to politeness, especially toward women, while the French *gentil,* once the word for noble, refers as well to social graces.

The most famous example of this courtly poetry came from the pen of Guillaume de Lorris: the *Roman de la Rose.* Lorris wrote in the early thirteenth century, perhaps in the 1220s. His work inspired Jean de Meun, in the 1260s, to write a "completion" of the great allegory. The version we have today consists of these two distinct elements. Guillaume de Lorris, like Chrétien de Troyes or Marie de France, speaks the language of courtly love between equals, of male respect for the female lover. Love tells the poem's male protagonist:

"First of all," said Love, "I wish and command that, if you do not want to commit a wrong against me, you must abandon villainy forever" . . . "Next, take care not to utter dirty words or anything bawdy. You should never open your mouth to name anything base. I do not consider any man courteous who names anything that is filthy or ugly. . . . Honor all women and exert yourself to serve them. If you hear any slanderer who goes around detracting women, take him to task and tell him to be quiet. If you can, do something that is pleasing to ladies and girls, so that they will hear good reports told and retold about you. By this means you can rise in people's esteem."

The poet also provides his readers/listeners with a portrait of ideal beauty:

Her flesh was as tender as dew; she was simple as a bride and white as the fleur-de-lis (lily). Her face was clear and smooth, straight and somewhat thin. It was not rouged or painted, for she had no need to adorn or decorate herself. She had long, blond hair that reached to her heels.

The poem proceeds on multiple levels, both an allegory of erotic love, with the rose an allegory for female genitalia, and one of a higher, more spiritual love. Jean de Meun, too, would continue the dual allegory, but he would present a very different picture of women, as we shall see in Chapter 4.[43]

---

and England; Richard, like a typical second son, got his mother's fiefs, Aquitaine. Geoffrey received Brittany, from his wife. When Geoffrey died in a joust, in 1186, he left Brittany to his infant son, Arthur. Henry and Eleanor's fourth son, John, initially got nothing: his contemporaries called him Jean *sans Terre* (John Lackland). When Richard refused to give up his mother's lands to John, he created a serious rift between the two brothers. Philip consistently used John's resentment against Richard to advantage.

In the 1180s, Philip strengthened himself by taking Arras and Vermandois by means of inheritance rights, but the key events took place in the 1190s. The great quarrel remained on hold while Philip and Richard went on the Third Crusade (1190). Richard left John as his regent; the embittered younger brother cut a deal

The Royal Loser: Jean sans Terre

Richard's death was Philip's greatest stroke of luck. The new head of the Angevin Empire, John Lackland, was a miserable excuse for a king, ridiculed in his own day as he is in ours. The figure of popular culture—whether the conniving schemer of the 1930s *Adventures of Robin Hood* or the toad-like butt of coarse humor in the 1990s *Robin Hood, Men in Tights*—bears some relation to the real man. Throughout his early life, John schemed against his father and his brother, humiliating himself on his knees before them on more than one occasion, as he begged forgiveness. Once ruler of the Angevin empire, he displayed a notable lack of honor. Perhaps John's most heinous deed was the murder of his nephew, the teenaged duke Arthur of Brittany: some chronicles suggest he did the deed with his own hands. Revulsion at the murder turned many Loire valley nobles against John in his great contest with Philip.

with Philip when the king returned from the Holy Land in 1192. In January 1194, John did homage for Normandy and Anjou and even signed over Normandy north of the Seine to the king. Richard, whose return had been delayed because he was held for ransom by the Emperor (Philip's ally), got back in May 1194. He humiliated John and routed Philip at Fréteval, near Gisors, site of the great oak, traditional meeting place of the kings of France and England:

> The bridge over the Epte was broken by the impact of French knights in full retreat. The king fell into the river and twenty of his knights were drowned; I [Richard] unhorsed Matthew of Montmorency, Alan of Roucy, and Fulk of Guilleval with my lance.[45]

Richard even captured Philip's archives, which had been traveling with the king. Philip responded by setting up a permanent archival depository in Paris, a major step in the creation of a more centralized government. Richard shortly thereafter constructed the massive Château Gaillard, the ruins of which (well worth a day trip from Paris) still dominate the Seine near Les Andelys. Philip gained only Gisors: he cut down the great oak.

Petty fighting continued for another five years, until Richard's death, which brought John to power. Philip acted quickly, using John's failure to appear (1204) at the court of barons for a lawsuit as grounds for seizure of his fiefs: Anjou, Normandy, Touraine, Maine, and Aquitaine. Philip's troops immediately overran Normandy, Touraine, Maine, and Anjou north of the Loire; Philip incorporated these well-administered rich fiefs into the royal demesne, either coopting existing local officials or replacing them with his own men. The final military decision came in 1214. Facing a coalition that included John, the Emperor Otto of Brunswick (John's nephew), Ferrand, count of Flanders, and Renaud of Dammartin, count of Boulogne, Philip fielded two armies. He marched north to Flanders to meet Otto and the northern counts, while crown prince Louis set out for the Loire valley to settle with John. Otto and the counts forced Philip to retreat, and then compelled him to fight at Bouvines on Sunday, 27 July 1214.

In one of the rare battles as decisive politically as it was militarily, Philip routed his enemies and captured many nobles, among them the two counts. He paraded Ferrand in a cart on the road back to Paris. Dogs barked at him; serfs spat on him; fishwives reviled and insulted him. At Paris, the celebrations rang through the streets for a week. Ferrand spent many years in prison; when the king released him, Renaud, hearing the news, committed suicide in his cell. In the Loire, Louis drove the cowardly John out of Anjou, never to return. John's failure led directly to a baronial revolt in England, and to the issuance of the Magna Carta (1215), foundation of English and American liberties. Louis mounted France's last invasion of England; he failed at Lincoln (1217). Becoming king in 1223, he turned his attention away from England to the south of France, where dramatic events were taking place.

The Albigensian Crusade: Northern France Conquers the South

Forward, soldiers of Christ! Forward, volunteers of the army of God! Go forth with the church's cry of anguish ringing in your ears. Fill your souls with godly rage to avenge the insult done to the Lord.[46]

Pope Innocent III, 1208

CHRONOLOGY	1208–1271
1208	Murder of Peter of Castelnau, papal legate, at Avignon
1209	Start of Albigensian Crusade
1212	Pedro of Aragon defeats Muslims at Las Navas del Tolosa
1213	Simon of Montfort defeats and slays Pedro of Aragon at Muret
1215	End of Fourth Lateran Council
1226	Louis VIII heads a new Albigensian Crusade
1228	Death of Louis VIII; Blanche of Castile Regent
1229	Raymond of Toulouse does public penance at Notre Dame of Paris
1243	Mass burnings at Montségur
1248–1254	Louis IX on Crusade
1254	Louis IX issues great reforming ordinance; first surviving *Olim* (records of the Parlement of Paris)
1271	Death of Alphonse of Poitiers; Poitou and Toulouse revert to the Crown

These momentous events in the north had striking parallels in the south. France shook with religious fervor at the end of the twelfth century. Some went to the Holy Land on Crusade but others followed a different religious impulse: they attacked the orthodoxy of their time and sought a more perfect religion, calling their leaders the *Cathari,* the "perfect." The southern French town of Albi, which lay in a region of heavy Catharism, gave its name to the repression: the Albigensian Crusade.

The south of France rang with heretical teachings from the middle of the twelfth century on. In much of the area, the Waldensians, a sect who preached the virtues of poverty and condemned the material wealth of the Church, flourished openly. The Cathars took the teachings of the Waldensians much further. They preached a Manichaean heresy: that two gods existed, one of good and one of evil, one of the spirit and one of the material world. The Cathars found many converts among the peasantry, who knew little of Catholic doctrine, but also among the merchants and the local nobility. The Church tried its usual techniques against both the Waldensians and the Cathars. In the north, the authorities burned Waldensians. In the south, Cistercian monks set out to convert the Cathar peasants.

They failed miserably. Southern peasants deeply resented new Church innovations, notably a payment similar to the tithe imposed elsewhere in Europe, but unknown in southern France before 1150. In 1179, the Pope held a council at the Lateran Palace; the Council denounced the heretics and demanded that the nobility of southern France, above all the count of Toulouse, extirpate the heresy. Little happened. At the beginning of the thirteenth century, a new, more activist Pope, Innocent III (1198–1215), intervened in France. He placed the entire kingdom under the interdict (banning all Church ceremonies) because of Philip Augustus's unlawful second marriage. He also called for a crusade against the Cathars, starting in 1204. When Innocent's legate, Peter of Castelnau, was assassinated near Avignon in 1208, the Pope excommunicated the count of Toulouse, one of whose servants did the deed, and actively organized a crusade.

Philip, then fighting John, did not want to go, and feared the military impact of allowing his knights to do so. In the end, he gave in: the Capetian duke of Burgundy, Odo III, the count of Nevers, and various bishops mustered an army at Lyon. Raymond of Toulouse sought to forestall an invasion of his lands by doing public penance for his past misdeeds and by taking the Crusader's cross. The invading army thus had to focus on the lands of the other great southern baron, Raymond-Roger of Trencavel, count of Carcassonne, who was suspected of harboring heretics. The Crusaders stormed Béziers, putting its inhabitants to the sword, and marched to the great fortress of Carcassonne, which surrendered, thus avoiding a massacre, but not a thorough looting. The Crusading army then left, leaving behind about thirty knights, under the leadership of Simon de Montfort, whom they had chosen as the new count of Carcassonne.

For the next fifteen years, the fighting would wax and wane; one atrocity led to another. Montfort burned one hundred forty Cathars on a giant pyre at Minerve (1211); later, the northerners conducted an even larger mass burning, at Montségur (1243). The convoluted politics of early thirteenth-century southern France involved the royal houses of the Spanish Christian kingdoms (Castile, Navarre, and Aragon), as well as England and France. Pedro II of Aragon ruled Montpellier and its region, and had close family ties to the houses of Toulouse and Carcassonne. From 1212 to 1213, Pedro briefly made himself master of the situation by routing a massive Spanish Muslim army at Las Navas de Tolosa (1212) but his foolish disposition of troops enabled Montfort's tiny band of knights to annihilate the Aragonese army at Muret (1213). Pedro himself was among the slain. Montfort had little time to celebrate: he died in battle not long afterward.

The intermittent struggle took a more decisive turn in the 1220s, when King Louis VIII led a large army south to besiege Avignon (1226) and to force Raymond of Toulouse again to give way. Louis's death (1228) gave the southerners false hope of a reprieve, because his widow, Blanche of Castile, proved to be a formidable regent. By 1229, Raymond had to do public penance at Notre Dame of Paris and to betroth his daughter and heir, Jeanne, to the king's brother, Alphonse of Poitiers. When the couple died without heirs in 1271, all of their possessions, from Toulouse to Poitou, reverted to the crown of France. Together with the earlier confiscation of the region of Carcassonne, this inheritance gave the King of France effective legal control of the south of France.

Saint Louis

I never, on any single occasion, heard him speak evil of any man.

Joinville, speaking of Louis IX

King Louis IX, Saint Louis, although a man unwilling to speak "evil of any man" did not extend that policy to those not Christian. He had no indulgence for the enemies of his faith. As his biographer and friend Jean de Joinville recounted, the king once remarked, on hearing a story about a knight who had beaten a Jew with a crutch,

> no one, unless he is an expert theologian, should venture to argue with these people. But a layman, whenever he hears the Christian religion abused, should not attempt to defend its tenets, except with his sword, and that he should thrust into the scoundrel's belly, and as far as it will enter.

Louis lived a life of the most rigorous piety. Joinville tells us that Louis used to dispense justice while sitting under an oak tree in the forest at Vincennes (near Paris) and that he led a life of unimpeachable simplicity, decency, and justice:

> He was so temperate in his appetite that I never heard him, on any day of my life, order a special dish for himself, as many men of wealth and standing do.[47]

Louis IX towered over his contemporaries: rulers far and wide sought Louis's mediation, so certain were they of his justice. Joinville cites Louis's instructions to his son to be "always following what is just, and upholding the cause of the poor till the truth be made clear." In truth, Louis IX's reign marked, in many ways, the apogee of French medieval society. He had constructed one of the jewels of Gothic architecture, the Sainte Chapelle, and the University of Paris provided one of the dominant centers of Western intellectual life.

Louis's mother, Blanche of Castile, initially acted as regent for her fourteen-year-old son. Some of the barons chaffed at a woman's rule: she put down three initial rebellions, the most serious of which involved Henry III of England and the count of Brittany. Her remarkable ability left a stable kingdom to the young king, who also put down several minor rebellions, and kept Henry III from expanding his French holdings beyond the hinterlands of Bordeaux. For most of Louis's reign, the kingdom and its people prospered peacefully. Domestic stability encouraged Louis to look abroad: in 1248, he set out to reconquer the Holy Land. The practical results in the Levant were little but Louis inestimably increased his prestige and moral standing. The Crusade also took its usual toll on the baronage, weakening their resistance when the king returned home.

In France itself, Louis had a fundamental impact on the evolution of the monarchy. Philip Augustus had placed the central government on an entirely new footing. Louis made universal the bailiff system created by his grandfather for the royal demesne. In the 1250s and early 1260s many barons grumbled about the ability of the king to interfere in their relationship with their "subjects" (their serfs). The king's absence after 1248 had accelerated the turnover among the bailiffs that began the year before. His great ordinance of 1254 reformed the existing group of bailiffs, replacing many of them, and began the centuries-long process of establishing administrative norms. Under Louis the *curia regis* continued its evolution into a permanent, fixed body, the Parlement of Paris. In his reign, the evolution away from a court dominated by great vassals and towards one dominated by professional lawyers quickened, but a

Blanche of Castile nurses her son, Saint Louis, back to health. Women handled most health care in medieval and early modern France.

SOURCE: Corpus Christi College, Cambridge.

professional court with established rules of procedure did not emerge fully until the reign of Louis's grandson, Philip IV.[48] Louis failed to develop mechanisms to replace the earlier, household-based administration abolished by Philip Augustus. The great Crown office of seneschal, abolished by Philip, was not reinstated, yet Louis did not create an effective central administration to take its place. Had he done so, the dichotomy between household and state administration (especially in finance) might have been resolved earlier. As it was, the King of France did not create a clear distinction between the two until 1523.

Louis managed to enforce most of his rules: the reports of his investigative commissioners suggest that the bailiffs (and other officials) did not take bribes and generally managed their offices with efficiency and honesty. These bailiffs usually came from the core regions around Paris; they thus provided both a greater sense of unity and a common grievance for the barons, who disliked royal interference in their affairs. They particularly disliked Louis's 1261 ordinance that abolished the judicial duel, and made everyone subject to the new form of trial, based on evidence. One song of the time proclaimed that:

> Men of France, you are much astonished / I say to all those born to hold fiefs: / Thus God aids me! You are no longer free (*francs*) / They have greatly distanced you from freedom / because you are judged by inquest.[49]

Louis continued to seek the approval of the great barons for his important ordinances, but he had a strong sense of his rights as king. Joinville tells the story of Louis ordering two of his sons to sit close to him, only to have the boys refuse on the grounds of politeness. When the king ordered Joinville to sit next to him, Joinville did so without delay. The king then rebuked his sons: "You have acted very wrongly, seeing you are my sons, in not doing as I commanded the moment I told you. I beg you to see this does not happen again." Louis's envoys and his bailiffs brooked little interference, and the king stood behind them, so long as he believed their claims on his behalf to be well founded.

Although Louis shared many of the attitudes of the chivalric knights of his day, he did not underestimate the value of his townspeople. He detested "usury" (the word then used for moneylending): he exiled Jewish, then Christian "usurers," and seized their property. These moves put something of a damper on commerce in his lands, but he never lost sight of the economic source of his power. He wrote to his son:

> Above all maintain the good cities and communes of your realm in the same condition and with the same privileges as they enjoyed under your predecessors. . . . keep them in your favor and your love. For because of the wealth and power of your great cities not only your own subjects, and especially your great lords and barons, but also the people of other countries will fear to undertake anything against you.[50]

Here we have the king explicitly recognizing the centrality of the urban contribution to his ability to overawe the nobility and establish the supremacy of the royal government.

Much as he did so, Louis (and his father, Louis VIII), also established the basis for a problem soon to bedevil the monarchy: apanages. Louis IX's brother, Alphonse, received a large apanage, but Alphonse's death without heirs brought it back to the royal demesne. Two other brothers, Robert of Artois and Charles of Anjou, produced heirs, and took their lands out of the main line of the royal family; neither province returned to the Crown for over two hundred years. Charles proved a formidable figure in his own right: he married the heiress of the county of Provence, successfully invaded and conquered southern Italy and Sicily, and then Achaia (in Greece). The Sicilian Vespers (1282) undermined his authority there but the Angevins kept both their eponymous apanage and Provence until 1482.

Louis IX greatly exacerbated the apanage problem because he and his wife, Marguerite of Provence, had eleven children, eight of whom lived into adulthood. In classic Capetian fashion, he married the oldest daughter, Isabelle, to the count of Champagne, paving the way for the Capetian inheritance of that county. Other daughters married the duke of Burgundy, the count of Brabant, and the king of Castile. His oldest son, Louis, predeceased him (in 1260), so the second, Philip, got the throne. Jean-Tristan received the county of Valois, Pierre that of Alençon. The youngest, Robert, count of Clermont, soon took the family name of Bourbon: in 1589, his descendant, Henry of Navarre, inherited the Crown. All of these apanages greatly weakened the royal treasury, because the prince holding the apanage obtained all its revenues, with its other officials answering to him, as well. In the fourteenth and fifteenth centuries, the constant quarreling among the apanage princes would plunge France into near constant civil war.

Saint Louis was, in many ways, a contradictory ruler. He strengthened the central monarchy by improving its administration, but weakened it by creating apanages for his sons. He took great pride in his personal management of the kingdom, yet twice left on Crusade: the first of these absences lasted six years. He sympathized with the poor and downtrodden, and prided himself on his piety, justice, and simplicity of manner. He was that rare individual who practices his religious faith: he took seriously the Christian message of justice. Because he cared so deeply about his faith, however, he often persecuted Jews in France. His expulsions focused on "usurers" (Christian ones, too), but he banned the Talmud, forbade the construction of new synagogues, and actively, and somewhat coercively, tried to convert France's Jews to Christianity. Conversely, recognizing that his edicts against Jews in the 1240s had led to riots against them, later in his reign he went out of his way to protect them from the violence of others. Saint Louis is a towering figure among French kings, but few men have so amply demonstrated Homer's ancient truth that our greatest strengths are also our greatest weaknesses.

Notes

1. Cited in G. Leyte, *Domaine et domanialité publique dans la France médiévale (XIIe–XVe siècles)* (Strasbourg: Presses Universitaires de Strasbourg, 1996), 94.

2. Spanish knights, with some French help, took Cordoba; the knights of the Fourth Crusade, most of them French, took Constantinople.

3. The words of William of Jumièges are cited in E. Searle, *Predatory Kinship and the Creation of Norman Power, 840–1066* (Berkeley: University of California Press, 1988), 111.

4. The relevant passage in the *Roman de Rou* can be found in George Duby's *The Rural Economy and Country Life in the Medieval West,* trans. C. Postan (Columbia, SC: 1968), 73; I have used my translation of Duby's original French edition: *L'Économic rurale et la vie des campagnes dans l'Occident médiéval* (Paris: Aubier, 1966 and 1970).

5. The word *villain* offers a glimpse into the tricky vocabulary of the Middle Ages. At first, it meant a free inhabitant of the *villa* (large estate). By the twelfth century, however, the meaning had evolved to that of unfree person, that is, serf. Our modern world villain thus derives from the social prejudices of our ancestors.

6. Cited in M. Bloch, *Feudal Society,* trans. L. Manyon (Chicago: University of Chicago Press, 1961), two vols., I, 113.

7. I am using throughout the splendid translation of Glyn Burgess, *The Song of Roland* (London, New York: Penguin, 1990).

8. The date of this great famine, 1031–1033, correlates closely with the onset of widespread serfdom, a coincidence which suggests to some historians that many peasants may have placed their land in feudal arrangements at precisely that moment to avoid starvation.

9. In some regions, such as Brittany, such a case would go to the court of the overlord of the lord owning the seigneurial rights.

10. As noted above, the legal promise not to move dated from the earliest agreements between the free peasants, *coloni,* who accepted tenures from landlords with that restriction. This stricture, originally applied to free people, came to be a sign of being unfree once slavery ceased to be a common condition of holding a tenure.

11. Some documents refer to a third, "middle" justice, as in the phrase "high, middle, and low justice," but I know of no cases of anyone owning only a "middle justice." The only reliable study of local justice in monarchical France emphasizes precisely the dichotomy high and low.

12. Bloch, *Feudal Society,* 241.

13. A crop yield of 2 to 1 means the farmer gets two seeds for every one planted; at such a yield, the farmer would have to put away half the harvest for the next year's seed. Modern crop yields, which are much higher, are listed in bushels/acre.

14. M. Bloch, "De la grande exploitation domaniale à la rente du sol: Un problème et projet d'enquête," in *Mélanges historiques* (Paris: Serge Fleury, Éditions de l'École des Hautes Études en Sciences Sociales, 1963, 1983), two vols., II, 671.

15. The old system, with a crop yield of 2 to 1, would yield two bushels of grain for every bushel sown, and would do so on half the total arable land: on a twenty-acre farm, that would be twenty bushels, if one sowed a bushel an acre. With greater fertilizer use raising crop yield to 4 to 1, that same farm would produce 29.3 bushels of rye or wheat: 4 bushels/acre on 7.33 acres. The oat fields would have added a roughly equal amount of that crop.

16. M. Bloch, *French Rural History. An Essay on its Basic Characteristics,* trans. J. Sondheimer (Berkeley: University of California Press, 1966; French edition, 1931).

17. The Church is discussed in detail in Chapter 3.

18. The dates of Easter and Pentecost vary each year.

19. J. Kirshner and K. Morrison, *Medieval Europe* (Chicago: University of Chicago Press, 1986), 213. John taught at the cathedral school of Chartres.

20. M. Bloch, "European Feudalism," in *Mélanges historiques* , I, 188.

21. Sens had particular importance for the Paris region because the archbishop of Sens was the ecclesiastical superior of the bishop of Paris.

22. Cited in O. Guillot and Y. Sassier, *Pouvoirs et Institutions dans la France Médiévale. Des origines à l'époque féodale* (Paris: Armand Colin, 1994, 1995), two vols., I, 78–79.

23. Ibid., I, 124.

24. The titles "duke," "count," and "marquis" at first had very different meanings. A duke meant the ruler of a tribe; a count held authority over a specific *pagus,* or local district. A marquis stood between the two: he had the authority over a frontier region (march), which encompassed several counties. Usually himself the count of one unit, he had military authority over other counts in his march.

25. G. Duby, *La société aux XIe et XIIe siècles dans la région mâconnaise* (Paris: EHESS, 1982), 174.

26. The adjective *banale* derives from the medieval word *ban,* meaning authority. Modern French preserves this ancient meaning in the word *banlieue,* or "suburbs," which derives from the area (*lieu*) in which the town government's authority (*ban*) held good.

27. Cited in J. Nelson, "Kingship and empire in the Carolingian world," in *Carolingian culture: Emulation and innovation,* ed. R. McKitterick (Cambridge; New York: Cambridge University Press, 1994), 76.

28. Cited in Guillot and Sassier, *Pouvoirs et institutions,* I, 200.

29. Suger, Abbot of Saint-Denis, *The Deeds of Louis the Fat,* trans. R. Cusimano and J. Moorhead (Washington, DC: Catholic University of America Press, 1992), 62.

30. G. Duby, *France in the Middle Ages, 987–1460: From Hugh Capet to Joan of Arc,* trans. J. Vale (Oxford; Cambridge, MA: Basil Blackwell, 1991), 150, citing the chronicle of the notary Galbert of Bruges.

31. Suger, *Deeds of Louis the Fat,* 137; the expedition took place in 1127.

32. Jean Bart, *Histoire du droit privé: De la chute de l'Empire romain au XIXe siècle* (Paris: Ed. Montchrestion, 1998), 145.

33. T. Evergates, *Feudal Society in the Bailliage of Troyes under the Counts of Champagne, 1152–1284* (Baltimore: Johns Hopkins University Press, 1975).

34. J. Dunbabin, *France in the Making, 843–1180* (Oxford; New York: Oxford University Press, 1985), 319.

35. The king (like counts or dukes) also collected money for other reasons. He had the right to the revenues of bishoprics in the interval between the death of a

bishop and the installation of his successor. In 1202, this source provided five percent of total royal income.

36. Medieval France had many different monies of account; in the kingdom, the two most common were the pound of Paris (the *livre parisis,* or *l.p.*) and the pound of Tours (*livre tournois,* or *l.t.*). Prior to Saint Louis, sixty-eight pence of Tours equalled one hundred of Paris; from his time forward, five *livres* of Paris equalled four of Tours.

37. Figures and details of Philip's administrative changes come from J. Baldwin, *The Government of Philip Augustus: Foundations of French Royal Power in the Middle Ages* (Berkeley: University of California Press, 1986). Henry II was Philip's vassal as duke of Normandy, count of Anjou, and prince of various other territories.

38. The customs of Champagne derived status from the mother until the fourteenth century.

39. In Normandy, however, even commoners practiced primogeniture.

40. The great abbot Odo of Cluny, who turned that monastery into the mother house of the greatest monastic order in Western Europe, began his monastic life at Saint-Martin of Tours, where he received the patronage of Fulk the Red.

41. The Church only declared marriage a sacrament in the thirteenth century. Ordinary people did not consider the church liturgy to be the marriage ceremony until after 1600. The Church did play a fundamental role in outlawing incest; it created and enforced draconian consanguity rules for prospective marriage partners.

42. Baldwin, *The Government of Philip Augustus,* 80.

43. I am using the prose translation of C. Dahlberg, *The Romance of the Rose,* by Guillaume de Lorris and Jean de Meun (Princeton: Princeton University Press, 1971). The first citation comes from 2077–2079, then 2109–2124, and finally 991–995. The original reads:

Vilenie premierement, / ce dist Amors, voel et conment / que tu gerpisses sanz reprendre / se tu ne velz vers moi mesprendre. . . . Aprés gardes que tu ne dies/ ces orz moz ne ces ribaudies: / ja por nomer vilainne chose/ ne doit ta bouche estre desclouse. / Je ne tien pas a cortois home / qui orde chose et laide nome. / Toutes fames ser et honore, / et aus servir poine et labeure; / et se tu oz nul mesdisanz / qui aille fame despisant, / blasme le et di qu'il se taise. / Fai, se tu puez, chose qui plaise / as dames et as demoiseilles, / si qu'eus oient bones noveles / de toi dire et raconter: / par ce porras em pris monter. Using here the French edition of F. Lecoy, *Le Roman de la Rose* (Paris: Librairie Honoré Champion, 1983), v. 1, lines 2074 *a–d* and 2097–2112.

44. Here following Baldwin, *The Government of Philip Augustus,* 269, who suggests Henry II raped her. Other historians view the relationship as more consensual; still others believe the rumors to be false.

45. Duby, *France in the Middle Ages,* 217.

46. Cited in J. Sumption, *The Albigensian Crusade* (London; Boston: Faber, 1978), 77.

47. Joinville & Villehardouin. *Chronicles of the Crusades,* trans. M. Shaw (Baltimore: Penguin Books, 1963), 167–168. Most historians believe the oak tree story to be apocryphal.

48. Many works on this period suggest that the Parlement became a permanent court at Paris beginning in 1254, because the first set of records of their decisions (called the *Olim*), begins in that year. W. Jordan, *Louis IX and the Challenge of the Crusade: A study in rulership* (Princeton: Princeton University Press, 1979), 143, rightly challenges that view, noting that the beginning date for the *Olim* is fortuitous.

49. Cited in J. Richard, *Saint Louis: Roi d'une France féodale* (Paris: Fayard, 1983), 310.

50. Joinville, 348.

Chapter Three

THE ORIGINS OF FRANCE AND
OF WESTERN CIVILIZATION, 1095–1270

*Compared with the safety of my sons, my brother and our women,
the loss of the rest meant little to me, except for my books. There had
been four thousand fine volumes on board, and their destruction has
been a cruel loss to me for the rest of my life.*[1]

Usama ibn Munqidh, amir of Shaizar, *c.* 1130

One imagines with difficulty anyone living in France, or in Christian Western
Europe, echoing Usama's lament about the loss of such a library: the amir likely had
more books than existed in King Philip's entire demesne in 1095. Yet this cultural
backwater, the often frightened, defensive, inward-looking society of tenth- and early
eleventh-century Francia, had begun to grow in confidence and to develop its own
intellectual and cultural life. When Pope Urban II, a native Frenchman, made the
call for a Crusade to liberate the Holy Land, Francia and its Christian neighbors responded enthusiastically. Urban, and other lay and church leaders, sought some way
to harness the enormous energy of an entire society: of its growing peasantry, of its
emerging towns, of its restive warriors, of its reformed church.

The energy of the people of Christian Western Europe created in these centuries
a new civilization, what we call Western Civilization. They combined elements of the
heritages they had received from Classical (Greco-Roman) civilization, from
Judaism and Christianity, and from Germanic tribes into a social, economic, political, and cultural system whose greatest strength would be its ability to synthesize. As
at any birth, much blood was spilt. The Norman warriors, who cut the umbilical
cord to the Classical mother when they attacked Byzantium in 1081, and their Crusading successors saw to that.

The First Crusade galvanized French, indeed European Christian society like no
other event. Tens of thousands of people, from humble peasants to counts and dukes,
set off to liberate the Holy Land. The initial Crusading army that besieged Nicaea in
1097 had some seven thousand knights and between fifty and seventy thousand men,
by far the largest western army of the Middle Ages. The First Crusade also attracted
women (and some children); later, thousands of western Europeans would migrate
to the kingdom of Jerusalem. The Crusaders came overwhelmingly from French-
speaking areas: from a swath that ran from Limoges to Angers, then across to Paris;

A Moorish lady plays chess with her Christian visitor, as they listen to a lute player. This illustration allows us to see that women participated in many of the same leisure activities as men, whether it be hunting or the more cerebral pastime of chess. The interaction of the Muslim and the Christian here reminds us that chess was one other importation from the Islamic to the Christian world.

from Normandy north to Boulogne and Flanders; then southeast to Burgundy. French-speaking knights from Lorraine, Provençals, and Norman adventurers from southern Italy joined them. The French barons who led the Crusade, above all Godfrey of Bouillon, first Christian ruler of Jerusalem, became legendary heroes whose renown lasted throughout the Middle Ages.

The First Crusade was not, however, an isolated case of French or Christian expansion. Norman knights had already conquered southern Italy, from the Byzantines (1071), and Sicily, from the Muslims (1061–1091). The duke of Normandy himself had recently (1066) subdued England; Spanish and French knights had taken the great Islamic city of Toledo (1085). The First Crusade pushed forward the attack against Islam. The Crusade and its related expeditions conquered Jerusalem and the coastal regions from Gaza to modern-day Turkey. The Fourth Crusade (1202), whose initial goal was Jerusalem's reconquest, inadvertently created a second French empire in the east. The Crusaders stormed Constantinople (1204), creating the Latin Empire of Byzantium (1204–1261) and a series of Frankish states in the Aegean. In 1204, virtually the entire coast of the eastern Mediterranean, from Acre to Athens, was in the hands of French barons; by 1311, virtually all of these regions had been lost.

The Crusades were merely one part of the great European enterprise of the twelfth and thirteenth centuries. The French clergy, above all its monks, sponsored the creation of medieval Europe's two dominant architectural styles, Romanesque and Gothic, helped to organize revivals of law and learning (revivals that originated in Italy), educated unprecedented numbers of people, and created many relief organizations for the sick and the poor. The working people adopted and popularized a dazzling array of technological improvements—water mills, the horizontal loom, new harnesses, better metallurgy—that provided the material prosperity undergirding the creation of a new civilization.

Catholic Europe's collision with the two great civilizations known to it, those of Islam and of Byzantium, enormously speeded up its emergence from backwardness. The first great wave of expansion ended around 1270. Europe's population boom slowed and stopped; Europeans' successful offensive against the two great civilizations sputtered out. The Mongols dominated the Eurasian land mass in the late thirteenth and early fourteenth centuries, sweeping all before them in a conquest as complete as it was rapid. In many ways, the French, like other western Europeans, became again inward looking and defensive between about 1270–1450. At the end of this period, however, Western Civilization would burst forth again, this time both to expand its conception of the known world and to dominate it.

THE CRUSADES AND THE "FIRST FRENCH EMPIRE"

Wherefore, I exhort with earnest prayer—not I, but God—that, as heralds of Christ, you urge men by frequent exhortation, men of all ranks, knights as well as foot-soldiers, rich as well as poor, to hasten to exterminate this vile race from the lands of your brethren, and to aid the Christians in time. I speak to those present; I proclaim it to those absent; moreover, Christ commands it.[2]

> Pope Urban II, preaching the First Crusade at
> Clermont (Auvergne), 27 November 1095

CHRONOLOGY	1071–1270
1071	Norman Conquest of Southern Italy
1085	Christians capture Toledo; Robert Guiscard dies in Greece
1061–1091	Norman Conquest of Sicily
1095	Urban II preaches the First Crusade
1096–1099	First Crusade; Christians take Jerusalem, 15 July 1099
1147	Second Crusade fails at Damascus
1187	Saladin routs Christians at Springs of Cresson and at Hattin; takes Jerusalem

C H R O N O L O G Y	(continued)
1191	Third Crusade. Acre retaken; Jerusalem not taken
1202–1204	Fourth Crusade. Crusaders sack Constantinople, 1204, and establish the Latin Empire of Byzantium
1248–1254	Louis IX on Crusade; defeated at Mansurah (1250)
1261	End of Latin Empire of Byzantium
1270	Louis IX dies at Tunis

The real center of the early medieval Christian world lay in the east, at Constantinople.[3] Saint Sophia dwarfed any church in the west, just as Constantinople and its Emperor stood far above any western counterparts. The eastern Christian churches—Syrian, Armenian, Coptic, Greek—had long coexisted uneasily with the western, Latin church within the overall framework of Christianity. As the West grew more self-assured, the two main churches, Greek and Latin, began to quarrel more systematically about their doctrinal differences. In 1054, the split became an open one. In hindsight, this division marks the creation of the Eastern Orthodox and Western Catholic churches, but the permanent division did not seem so clear to medieval people.[4]

Pope Gregory VII called for an expedition to help the Byzantines in the aftermath of their terrible defeat by the Seljuk Turks at Manzikert (1071). Open conflict, however, between his key ally, the Normans of southern Italy, and Byzantium led to a further breach between 1078–1081, when Gregory excommunicated successive Byzantine Emperors. He lifted the excommunication of the second of these Emperors, Alexius Comnenus, in 1089. Alexius then sent a conciliatory mission to the Western Church Council of Piacenza (1095), seeking aid against the Muslims. He wanted to reconquer Anatolia, lost in the aftermath of Manzikert, but he couched his appeal in terms of freeing the Holy Places, above all Jerusalem. Islam, like Eastern Christianity, contained a multiplicity of sects, who detested each other almost as much as they disliked the surrounding infidels. Everywhere in the Eastern Mediterranean, Arabs, Turks, Persians, Armenians, Bulgars, Normans, Byzantines, and various tribal groups engaged each other in endemic warfare throughout the eleventh century. Jerusalem actually changed hands from one Muslim ruler to another (1098) while the First Crusade was in progress.

Two key elements stand out as background to the Western decision to set out on Crusade to the Holy Land. First, the split with the Eastern church, and the regular warfare between the Normans of southern Italy and the Byzantines, created profound mutual suspicions between the two churches. The Crusaders wanted to regain the Holy Land for "Christianity" but to them that meant Western Catholicism. As one later Crusader wrote: "Constantinople is arrogant in her wealth, treacherous in her practices, corrupt in her faith." Anna Comnena, daughter of the Emperor Alexius, reveals the parallel Byzantine suspicions of the Westerners:

> He [Alexius] dreaded their arrival, knowing as he did their uncontrollable
> passion, their erratic character and their irresolution, not to mention the
> other peculiar traits of the Kelt ... their greed for money, ... which always
> led them, it seemed, to break their own agreements without scruple ... in
> order to fulfil their dream of taking Constantinople they adopted a com-
> mon policy ... to all appearances they were on pilgrimage to Jerusalem; in
> reality they planned to dethrone Alexius and seize the capital.[5]

Second, Western Christians had been on the attack against Islam for much of
the eleventh century. Norman adventurers, led by the many sons of the Norman
knight, Tancred de Hauteville, above all Robert and Roger *Guiscard* ("wily"), eventually subdued the whole of southern Italy and Sicily. Islamic and Byzantine sources
describe these western warriors as savages. Simple armed bands, not unlike the
Viking raiders of the ninth century, often carried out the great European, Christian,
French offensive of the late eleventh and early twelfth centuries.

The Normans took the marauding spirit of their Viking ancestors and combined it with the armor, weaponry, and tactics of the Frankish cavalry to create a formidable new military force. Their bands could be quite small: Anna Comnena claims
Robert Guiscard initially left Normandy with only five knights and thirty foot soldiers; his brother Roger invaded Sicily in 1061 with a mere one hundred sixty-five
knights. Even the Norman state, in duke William's invasion of England (1066), could
muster an army of only seven thousand, perhaps half of them cavalry. Many Norman soldiers did not have full armor.

Their numbers aside, the Normans and other French struck terror into the
hearts of the civilized worlds of Constantinople, Cordoba, and Damascus. Anna
Comnena, in a mixture of awe and condescension, offers unforgettable portraits of
many of the "barbarians" from the West. She tells us of the broad-shouldered, flaxen-
haired giant Robert Guiscard (whom she was too young to have met), with "eyes
[that] all but emitted sparks of fire" and a voice that "put thousands to flight."[6] Guiscard's death (1085), due to illness while on campaign in Greece, may well have saved
the Byzantine Empire from Norman conquest. Anna was a teenager when the Crusaders arrived in Constantinople. She found Hugh of Vermandois, brother of King
Philip of France, a self-impressed snob, but Raymond of Saint-Gilles, count of
Toulouse, from the more civilized south of France, to be a man of "superior intellect" and "untarnished reputation."

Hugh, Raymond, and their fellow Crusaders posed a real threat to Byzantium.
Anna recognized that most Westerners had noble motives—"the simpler-minded
were urged on by the real desire of worshiping at our Lord's Sepulchre, and visiting
the holy places"—but she and her father greatly feared Bohemund of Taranto, dispossessed son of Robert Guiscard, whom they (rightly) suspected of wanting to create a state for himself to rule. Bohemund did exactly that at Antioch. Later, he
unsuccessfully sought to overthrow Alexius and conquer the Empire.

Alexius sought limited help from Urban II. Instead, he found "the whole of the
West and all of the barbarian tribes between the further side of the Adriatic and the
pillars of Hercules, had all migrated in a body and were marching into Asia." (Anna

A Byzantine Princess. Empress Irene, sister-in-law of Anna Comnena, c. 1120.

Source: © Chris Hellier/Corbis.

Comnena). The Crusaders were a motley crew. Agitation for the Crusade had begun among ordinary people, above all in northern France and the adjacent German lands; the army of the poor, many of them French peasants, led by the messianic preacher Peter the Hermit, arrived first at Constantinople. The Byzantines helped them across the Bosporus, thence to Asia Minor, where they were slaughtered like sheep, and the survivors sold into slavery. This popular agitation stands as background to the appeal made by Urban II, at the Church Council meeting in November 1095, at Clermont, in the Auvergne.

Urban made his appeal at Clermont for two reasons: (1) Clermont, although in Francia, was not under King Philip I's effective control; and (2) he needed French knights to provide the strike force of his Crusade. He knew that Catholicism's assault on Islam, from Iberia to Italy, relied on these knights. Philip could not lead them because Urban had excommunicated him in response to the king's doubly adulterous

THE PRINCESS AND THE BARBARIAN:
ANNA COMNENA DESCRIBES BOHEMUND

Anna Comnena bears witness, in her description of the great Crusader, Bohemund, to the Byzantine wonderment at the bearing, audacity, and customs of the Western barbarians.

> Bohemund took after his father in all things, in audacity, bodily strength, bravery, and untamable temper . . . he was . . . like the pungent smoke which precedes a fire. . . . These two, father and son, might rightly be termed "the caterpillar and the locust"; for what escaped Robert, that his son Bohemund took to him and devoured.
>
> [H]e was a marvel for the eyes to behold and his reputation was terrifying. . . . / His stature was such that he towered almost a full cubit over the tallest men. He was slender of waist and flanks, with broad shoulders and chest, strong in the arms. . . . His eyes were light blue and gave some hint of the man's spirit and dignity. . . . He had about him a certain charm, but it was somewhat dimmed by the alarm inspired by his person as a whole; there was a hard, savage quality in his aspect—owing, I suppose, to his great stature and to his eyes: even his laugh sounded like a threat to others.

Taken from: *The Alexiad of Princess Anna Comnena*, trans. E. Dawes (New York: AMS Press, 1978, reprint of 1928 London edition), 37–38 and 347. In the section after the "/" I have used the translation of J. Norwich, *Byzantium, The Decline and Fall* (New York: Knopf, 1996), 37–38, which I find reads a little more smoothly.

marriage to his cousin. Urban had to forbid Philip's participation. Urban pulled out all the rhetorical stops to convince his listeners to take the cross:

> And if those who set out thither should lose their lives on the way by land, or in crossing the sea, or in fighting the pagans, their sins shall be remitted. This I grant to all who go, through the power vested in me by God. Oh, what a disgrace, if a race so despised, base, and the instrument of demons, should so overcome a people endowed with faith in the all-powerful God, and resplendent with the name of Christ! . . . Let those who . . . have been robbers now become soldiers of Christ. Let those who once fought against brothers and relatives now fight against barbarians, as they ought. Let those who have been hirelings at low wages now labor for an eternal reward. . . . when the winter has ended and spring has come, let them zealously undertake the journey under the guidance of the Lord.[7]

His appeal succeeded beyond his wildest dreams. His tour of Europe, preaching the Crusade, prompted tens of thousands of people to sign up.

German knights (and a few French ones) began their march to "glory" by attacking the Jews in the Rhineland, killing thousands of them at Mainz, Cologne, Worms, and elsewhere. Norman knights drove out Rouen's Jews in 1096. Guibert de Nogent wrote of these massacres:

"We want, after having crossed great distances, to attack the enemies of God in the East, while the Jews, who, of all peoples are the worst enemies of God, can be found right before our eyes. That . . . is the equivalent of accomplishing our task in reverse." Having thus spoken, and taking up their arms, they forcibly brought the Jews to a certain place of worship, pushing them thence by force or trickery—I do not know by what means—and without distinction for age or sex they used their arms such that only those who submitted to Christian laws escaped from the sword blows that threatened them.[8]

Worse was yet to come: when the Crusaders stormed Jerusalem (1099), they burned most of its Jewish residents in a synagogue and slaughtered everyone else. Fulcher of Chartres, an eyewitness, tells us that "(i)f you had been there, your feet would have been stained up to the ankles with the blood of the slain. . . . Not one of them was allowed to live. They did not spare the women and children."[9]

The initial leaders of the Crusade came primarily from French-speaking nobility: Godfrey of Bouillon, who led knights from Flanders, Lorraine, and parts of Germany; Hugh of Vermandois, with a tiny band, whom Alexius "detained . . . and left . . . not without supervision, but certainly free."[10] Soon Bohemund arrived with his Normans from Italy, then Raymond of Toulouse, with a large contingent of knights from Burgundy and Provence. The next wave included some of France's greatest barons: count Robert of Flanders; duke Robert of Normandy, who had mortgaged the duchy to his brother to pay for his expedition; and count Stephen of Blois, Robert's brother-in-law. After some initial fighting, the Byzantines and Crusaders reached an agreement and together they captured the key city of Nicaea. The Crusaders then twice routed the Turks, enabling Alexius to regain much of Anatolia, his most important goal.

The Westerners marveled at Constantinople, a city of 400,000 people. The clash of cultures could not have been more stark. Fulcher highlighted its wonders:

Oh, what an excellent and beautiful city! How many monasteries, and how many palaces there are in it, of wonderful work skilfully fashioned! How many marvelous works are to be seen in the streets and districts of the town! It is a great nuisance to recite what an opulence of all kinds of goods are found there; of gold, of silver . . . and of holy relics. In every season, merchants . . . bring to that place everything that man might need.[11]

How could largely illiterate Western barbarians, who lived in drafty rural manors, who ate with their fingers and dressed in simple tunics, fail to be overwhelmed by a city such as Constantinople, or even Antioch, whose houses had running water, or the great towns of Islamic Spain, like Cordoba or Toledo, with their lighted streets and stunning markets? Although the Westerners stood in awe of the riches and buildings of a Constantinople, they had a sense of being morally superior to the Orthodox and the Muslims, both of whom lived in a comparative lap of luxury. Their lifestyles rebuked the austere piety of the monks then so powerful in the West. As Odo of Deuil, a member of the Second Crusade (1147), put it: "In every respect she [Constantinople]

The Crusaders bombard Muslim defenders of Nicaea with the heads of their captured comrades. In fact, many of the defenders were Christians.

Source: Bibliothèque Nationale.

exceeds moderation; for, just as she surpasses other cities in wealth, so, too, does she surpass them in vice."[12]

The events of the Crusades touch but lightly on our story here. The First Crusade suffered horrible losses (70–90 percent of those who participated died), above all to disease, but it managed to capture much of the Levantine coast, finally taking Jerusalem itself on 15 July 1099. That goal accomplished, most of the great lords who had survived went home. The counts of Flanders and Toulouse and the duke of Normandy left, leaving Godfrey, his brother Baldwin, and Bohemund to divide up the spoils.

The Crusader states offer a fascinating glimpse at the idealized polity of Western Christians *circa* 1100, because the Crusaders got to organize four states from scratch. They claimed they created an ideal feudal order, based largely on the Norman model of knights' fees (fiefs), a world in which, Usama wrote, "the knights have a monopoly of the positions of honor and importance. . . . They are the men who give counsel, pass judgment and command the armies. . . . Once the knights have given their judgment neither the King nor any other commander can alter or annul it, so great an influence do their knights have in their society."[13] The reality looked somewhat different. The Western Christian settlers, most of whom had not been actual Crusaders, settled particularly in regions that had large Eastern Christian populations, above all near Jerusalem and along the coast from Acre to Caesarea, and may have avoided those with substantial Muslim majorities. The merchants and artisans seem to have come overwhelmingly from southern France and, in the case of port city merchants, from Italy, so it is not surprising that this new society resembled southern France far more than it did Normandy.[14] Male immigrants substantially outnumbered female ones (4 to 1), which led to intermarriage with Eastern Christian women.

The kingdom of Jerusalem had only six hundred fifty knights in its heyday (*c.* 1135); it came to rely on the new Crusading orders, above all the Templars and the Hospitallers, for its defense. The Templars developed important ties to French kings, who used the Paris headquarters of the Templars (on today's rue du Temple) to store their treasure. The Templars owed their monastic rule to the French monk Bernard of Clairvaux, the greatest Christian leader of twelfth-century Europe, which helps explain the overwhelming predominance of French possessions in the order's holdings. The Templar houses could be found, above all, in the south of France and in Provence, and in northeastern France (Flanders and Champagne) and Lorraine.[15] The Muslims greatly feared the Templars and Hospitallers as warriors, sufficiently so that Saladin himself purchased the Templar and Hospitaller captives taken at the great Muslim victory of Hattin (1187). The Arab historian Baha' ad-Din explains why: "At the Sultan's command the King and a few of the most distinguished prisoners were sent to Damascus, while the Templars and Hospitallers were rounded up to be killed . . . [and] were decapitated at his command. He had these particular men killed because they were the fiercest of all the Frankish warriors, and in this way he rid the Muslim people of them."[16]

Saladin's victories at the Springs of Cresson and Hattin (1187), and his capture of Jerusalem and Acre, touched off an instant response in Europe: the kings of France and England took the cross and set sail for the Holy Land. The Third Crusade recaptured Acre and some other fortresses, and Richard the Lion-Hearted did get Saladin to provide access to the Holy Places for Christian pilgrims, but Jerusalem remained a Muslim city. The Christians hung on to some coastal territory for another century. In 1291, an Egyptian force retook Acre, put its Templar garrison to the sword, and ended the adventure of the Crusades.

The Holy Land played a significant role in French politics from the middle of the twelfth century until 1270. In addition to Philip, two other French kings led Crusades. King Louis VII and Conrad of Germany led the unsuccessful Second Crusade (1147), preached by the preeminent moral figure of the day, Bernard of Clairvaux, at Vézelay (Easter 1146). The two kings lost most of their force on the march across Anatolia, "where the flowers of France withered before they could bear fruit in Damascus," as Odo of Deuil put it. Things did not go much better at Damascus, where the siege lasted only five days. Despite his failure at Damascus, Louis restored much prestige to the Capetian family by taking up the cross.

The failure to retake Jerusalem in 1191 hardly dampened the Crusading spirit of the French. In 1202, count Baldwin of Flanders led a massive army toward the Holy Land, by way of Constantinople. The Fourth Crusade (1202–1204) brought the premonitions of Alexius Comnenus to fruition: the Crusaders got involved in Byzantine politics and finally stormed the city (1204), installing Baldwin as "Emperor." The French chronicler Villhardouin, who was there, called it the richest pillage in history. The French took not only gold and silver, but holy "relics." A certain abbot Martin "filled the folds of his gown with the holy booty" of a church, including such items as an arm of Saint James, a piece of the True Cross, much of Saint John's body, Saint Cosmas's foot, a trace of the Lord's blood, and parts of thirty-six other saints.[17] The Crusaders set up a kingdom of Thessalonica, a duchy of Athens, and a principality of Achaia.

Neither Baldwin nor the states lasted too long: the "Emperor" disappeared in battle against the Bulgars in 1205; successors held a significant territory only until the 1220s, when a rival Byzantine house (ruling from Nicaea) retook most of Asia Minor and even the outskirts of Constantinople. The Latin Emperors (1204–1261) lived in progressively greater poverty, gradually pawning many of Constantinople's greatest treasures.[18] The most famous of them, Christ's Crown of Thorns, ended up in the hands of Louis IX of France, who built the Sainte Chapelle to house it. French barons dominated Greek politics for most of the thirteenth century, but in 1311 Athens fell to a company of Catalan adventurers. Achaia, although ruled in theory by the Angevin princes of southern Italy until 1464, drifted out of the French orbit long before.

The Greek adventure did not destroy French interest in the Levant. The famously pious Louis IX, canonized shortly after his death, an inveterate crusader, led one army into Egypt (1248–1254), where it suffered a catastrophic defeat at Mansurah (1250). The Egyptians captured Louis himself: he paid a ransom of 200,000 *livres*. After his release from prison, Louis had more success in the Holy Land, rebuilding several key castles and restoring order among the squabbling Christian barons and Crusading orders. When he left in 1254, however, they quickly resumed their quarrels. Louis decided to launch another Crusade in 1267. At the last minute, to the stupefaction of his army, he stopped at Tunis on the way to Egypt. His death beneath its walls in 1270 marked a fitting end to the quixotic Crusading enterprise in the Near East.

The failure in the Latin East notwithstanding, the Christian West did succeed, in part by means of its struggle against Islam and Byzantium, in creating a functioning, thriving civilization of its own. The French share in that creation forms the rest of our story in this chapter. Let us begin with the greatest cultural force of the age: the Church.

THE NEW CHURCH

What a fine thing it would be to be archbishop of Rheims, if only one did not have to sing mass![19]

Remark attributed to archbishop Manasses, *c.* 1080

At the end of the eleventh century, the French Catholic Church had changed dramatically from its Carolingian predecessor. First, the Church kept a clear hierarchical structure running from archbishops, to bishops, to parish clergy, but this network, through the framework of rural parishes, now covered most of the kingdom.[20] Second, the monastic orders had risen to a position of complete preeminence in the Church. The Cluniac wing of the Benedictines provided the dominant ecclesiastical voice of the times. The new patronage of these monasteries, combining aristocratic and royal abbeys, bore witness to the changed political order. Third, the Church had established itself as sole arbiter in religious matters. It sanctified kings, in the coronation ceremony; it extirpated heresy; it administered to the spiritual needs of virtually the entire population of the French kingdom. One unpleasant offshoot of this rise of religious orthodoxy struck hard at a French minority: the new orthodoxy led to persecution of Jews, both in France and in the Holy Land, where the French knights of the First Crusade massacred the Jews of Jerusalem.

Bishops, who often came from aristocratic families, struggled against the rising power of the monastic orders and against the emerging power of the castellans. The most extreme example of the battle between castellans and bishops came in the South, where the bishops spearheaded the movements for the Peace of God and the Truce of God. The Peace of God protected the property of churches from marauding bands, as well as the persons of churchmen and, remarkably, poor peasants. The Truce of God forbade all Christians, on pain of excommunication, from fighting other Christians between Wednesday evening and Monday morning, and during certain holy seasons and on holy days. The movements broke out in southern Francia, where the authority of the king could no longer enforce a royal peace. The aristocratic bishops reacted against the rising power of the castellans and their mounted thugs, the knights.

The great abbeys of northern Francia had dominated the religious life of the kingdom in Charlemagne's time, but their influence waned between 850–950. That period's invaders, especially the Vikings, headed straight to the monasteries because they held much of the wealth of Frankish society. Abbeys lost their lands to laymen, as they had in the civil wars of the late seventh century. The monastic revival began in the early tenth century; William, duke of the Aquitanians, took what proved to be the decisive step in 910, the founding of the abbey of Cluny. The new abbey received the unusual privilege of exemption from the authority of its local bishop; instead, the monks answered only to the Pope. The Cluniac order spread slowly at first, but by the early eleventh century, several hundred monasteries all over Europe owed allegiance to Cluny, with all of them sharing the mother house's exemption from episcopal jurisdiction. Starting with Gregory VII, five successive Popes were monks, a fitting symbol of their new dominance.

The French Church established in these years its firm independence from the Papacy, an independence codified in the 1106 agreement between Philip I and Pope Paschal II. Throughout the Middle Ages, as in the 1106 agreement, the French Church balanced the interests of the bishops (aristocrats), the Pope, and the King. The Church and its property formed just as important a part of the *res publica* (commonwealth) as did the state. The king and the aristocracy had charge of the former, just as much as the latter. The Church provided many of the commonwealth's services, such as poor relief and education. The Church and the lay rulers, the king and the princes, although they often quarreled about the precise division of authority and power, essentially agreed about the unity of this new, Christian commonwealth.

Abélard and the New Theology

Nothing is less in our power than our heart [animus], which we are forced to obey rather than able to command.[21]

Héloïse to Abélard

The knight Berengar and his wife Lucia, who lived in the border castle of Le Pallet between Brittany and Francia, named one of their sons Dagobert, for the most famous Merovingian king. To their oldest son, however, they gave one of the new Christian names: Peter. This family planned for Peter Abélard to follow his father's military career, but Peter preferred the "conflict of disputations to the trophies of battle," and so set off to study with the great teachers of his time. He studied with Roscelin, the leading logician of the 1090s, and with William of Champeaux, the preeminent teacher of philosophy in early twelfth-century Paris.

Paris in 1100 had begun its remarkable growth, above all the merchants' community on the Right Bank, but it was merely one among a number of important towns in northern Francia. The King of the Franks, its leading resident, was a vagabond estate owner, moving from manor to manor, living from the produce grown by his serfs rather than from tax revenues paid by his "subjects." Parisian intellectual life did not shine forth. Indeed, many northern towns, such as Chartres, site of a Platonist revival at its cathedral school, or monasteries, like Le Bec Hallouin in Normandy, home both to Lanfranc and his famous pupil, Anselm, had greater reputations as centers of learning. The environs of Paris held several important monasteries, like Sainte-Geneviève, Saint-Germain-des-Prés, and Saint-Denis, but the city remained quite tiny in comparison with the giant it would soon become, both physically and intellectually.

In Paris, Abélard effectively challenged his master, William of Champeaux, for intellectual supremacy. Abélard's lectures drew large crowds: many of his surviving works are known to us by means of his notes for those lectures.[22] Abélard had two careers as a scholar; the first one focused on logic and the second on theology. Abélard provided new methods of examining the few available texts of Classical logic. Scholars of his day remained within the boundaries of two short works by Aristotle, the *Isagoge* of Porphyry, and the works of the early Christian scholar Boethius. Abélard's *Dialectica,* probably written around 1117, prodded French scholars to a more serious consideration of the logic of statements, especially the syllogisms so central to medieval thought. Here Abélard built on the work of scholars such as Anselm, who had tried to prove the existence of God by means of syllogistic reasoning.[23]

Abélard sought to establish a method by which the absolute truth of a statement could be determined. As he wrote in his manual for students, *Sic et Non* (*Yes and No*): "For through doubting we come to inquiry and through inquiry we discover the truth." His work accelerated Western advances in philosophical methodology and made French (and other Christian) scholars better able to understand the wealth of Classical learning transmitted to them by Jewish, Byzantine, and Arab scholars in the twelfth and thirteenth centuries.

Abélard has two other claims to fame: the condemnation of his theology by Church councils in 1121 (Soissons) and 1140 (Sens) and his relationship with one of his students, Héloïse. The two Councils rejected Abélard's request that he be allowed to defend his ideas in person, to rebut his critics face-to-face, as no one living in twelfth-century France wanted to face the greatest debater of the age. Abélard's first condemnation had much to do with Court and Church politics. The Council of Soissons ended with Abélard renouncing his views and himself casting his great work, *Theologia Summi Boni,* into the flames. Abélard quickly recommitted his ideas to parchment and created a new great work of theology during the 1130s. This treatise, the *Theologia Scholarium,* ran afoul of several of Abélard's rivals in the Paris region, notably Hugh of Saint-Victor and William of Saint-Thierry. The latter introduced into the controversy Abélard's greatest opponent, the most influential person of twelfth-century Western Europe, Bernard of Clairvaux, the driving force behind Cistercian monasticism.

Once Bernard, with his towering moral authority, had condemned Abélard's work, the work of the Council of Sens was a foregone conclusion: full condemnation on all nineteen counts. The key principle at issue in both 1121 and 1140 was that Abélard wanted to use the techniques of dialectics to examine religious issues, whereas Bernard and his supporters viewed with great suspicion the fusion of rational philosophy and faith. As Bernard wrote,

> There is nothing in heaven above nor in the earth below which he deigns to confess ignorance of: he raises his eyes to heaven and searches the deep things of God and . . . brings back unspeakable words which it is not lawful for a man to utter. He is ready to give a reason for everything, even for those things that are above reason.[24]

Abélard's end, and his apparent conversion to the Christianity of contemplation and spiritual union with God, left the field open to his great adversary, Bernard of Clairvaux. In some ways, their conflict pitted the advocates of the new learning, like Abélard, against the mystical religion of Bernard's Cistercian Order. It likewise pitted the town against the country, the worldly monk (Abélard's superior, Suger of Saint-Denis) with the otherworldly ascetic, Bernard. In the universities, there could be no question of the victor; shortly after Abélard's death, another master at Paris, Peter Lombard, published four volumes of *Sentences* (1159), a book that followed Abélard's method of juxtaposing the opinions of conflicting authorities on key theological matters. Lombard's text became the foundation of the dominant medieval Christian methodology, known as Scholasticism.

The Star-Crossed Lovers: Héloïse and Abélard

Abélard's personal life both aided his notoriety and undermined his moral standing. Héloïse and Abélard's affair is one of the most famous love stories of European civilization. In 1115–1116, he obtained a position as personal tutor to the young Héloïse, niece of Fulbert, one of the canons of Notre Dame of Paris. In his autobiographical letter, he writes of her:

> In looks she did not rank lowest, while in the extent of her learning she stood supreme. A gift for letters is so rare in women that it added greatly to her charm and had won her renown throughout the realm. I considered all the usual attractions for a lover and decided she was the one to bring to my bed. . . . so with our lessons as a pretext we abandoned ourselves entirely to love . . . with our books open before us, more words of love than of our reading passed between us, and more kissing than teaching. . . . In short, our desires left no stage of love-making untried.[25]

Abélard and Héloïse, fourteenth-century manuscript of the Roman de la Rose. *Note that Abelard has his leg crossed in a lascivious manner.*

Source: © Giraudon/Art Resource.

Héloïse became pregnant and gave birth to a son, Astrolabus. At Abélard's insistence, and over her strenuous objection, they married, but immediately separated and sought to keep the marriage a secret. Fulbert reacted violently: he bribed one of Abélard's servants to let his thugs into the master's house, where, in 1117, they castrated Abélard. Abélard tells us that the civil authorities later captured, blinded, and castrated the evil servant and one of the thugs.

The story of Héloïse and Abélard lived on because of a series of letters they exchanged in the 1130s. Their story of unbridled passion followed by platonic love and devotion to the love of God became, as one Abélardian scholar put it, "an integral part of the cultural inheritance of France."[26] As early as the thirteenth century, the *Roman de la Rose,* one of the most popular love poems of the Middle Ages, provided a summary of the story of the star-crossed lovers. Abélard, in one letter, wrote "by how just a judgment of God was I stricken in that portion of my body wherein I had sinned," but Héloïse took a different view. She gloried in their love, because she felt the purity of their affection preserved the purity of the deeds: "Wholly guilty though I am, I am also, as you know, wholly innocent. It is not the deed but the intention of the doer which makes the crime, and justice should weigh not the crime but the spirit in which it is done."

In the 1130s, when he had not written to her for many years, she chided him: "When in time past you sought me out for sinful pleasures your letters came to me thick and fast, and your many songs put your Héloïse on everyone's lips, so that every street and house echoed with my name. Is it not far better now to summon me to God than it was then to satisfy our lust?" In the end, they reconciled, Abélard offering constructive advice on a rule for nuns at Héloïse's nunnery. Abélard ended his days at the greatest monastery in Western Europe, Cluny, living the life of the penitent monk: "Master Peter, who was reputed throughout nearly all the world for his unique mastery of learning, and was known everywhere, ended his days as the pupil of him who said, 'Learn from me, because I am meek and humble in heart.'"

∼ THE NEW CHURCH—BERNARD AND SUGER

> *The church sparkles and gleams on all sides, while its poor huddle in need; its stones are gilded, while its children go unclad; they make use of the goods of the poor to embellish the view of the rich. Art lovers find in it enough to satisfy their curiosity, while the poor find nothing there to relieve their misery.*[27]

Bernard of Clairvaux, writing about the abbey church of Saint-Denis

The Romanesque Moment

> *Hic facit Gislebertus. (This Gilbert made.)*

Inscription on the tympanum of Saint-Lazare of Autun, early twelfth century. Gislebert was the first Western sculptor since Classical times to sign his work.

Church institutions had suffered enormously in the invasions of the late ninth and tenth centuries, and the moral standing of the clergy declined in most areas. Only some of the monks avoided this moral decline, though they steadily rose in influence around the year 1000. In the late tenth and eleventh centuries, the dominant monks came from the Cluniac wing of the Benedictine order, headquartered in southern France. In the twelfth century, two distinct wings of monasticism developed in France: the traditional Cluniacs, now best represented by Abbot Suger of Saint-Denis, near Paris; and the new Cistercians (also Benedictines), led by Bernard of Clairvaux. The great Romanesque churches of the twelfth century, with few exceptions (such as Saint-Lazare), were those of the Cluniac order. In the south of France, the third church of Cluny (begun in 1086) and Vézelay, the monastic church of Mary Magdelaine, bore witness to the order's supremacy. Cluny, the largest church in Western Christendom until the completion of Saint Peter's in sixteenth-century Rome, had a nave (built 1088–1118) almost one hundred feet high and, in the main church alone, over four hundred feet long.[28] Lacking the technical expertise of the later Gothic builders, the architect–builder constructed walls nearly eight feet thick to support the enormous edifice. Yet the walls notwithstanding, Cluny moved French churches away from the so-called Lombard style, with its tiny windows and massive walls, and toward lighter interiors.[29] Romanesque quickly covered much of Mediterranean Europe, from Castile across to Sicily. These churches stand as living monuments to the domination of Cluny in the spiritual and artistic life of Catholic Europe.

Vézelay, with its magnificent tympanum and its remarkable capitals, represented the pinnacle of the Romanesque achievement. Vézelay's nave is roughly half the length and height of Cluny's and uses a different pattern (two stories rather than three), but many of its capitals are direct copies of those of the mother church. Vézelay also revealed a newly confident French Christianity, one willing to move away from the dominant Byzantine models of earlier times. Charlemagne's chapel at Aachen, for example, relied overwhelmingly on Byzantine models. Even some Romanesque churches, such as Moissac or Saint-Sernin of Toulouse, bore striking resemblance to traditional Byzantine models. Although showing a gradual shift toward the longer nave and shorter transept typical of later Western building, these churches preserved the central dome derived from Byzantine models. Cluny and Vézelay dispensed altogether with the dome and emphasized the long nave soon to be copied by Gothic architects.

Vézelay's decoration similarly showed the sharp break at the end of the eleventh century. Late eleventh-century churches, such as the Abbaye aux Hommes and the

Great Mosque of Cordoba, c. 785. The great mosques of the Islamic world, such as those of Cordoba, Cairo, or Baghdad, provided important models for eleventh- and twelfth-century Christian churches in Western Europe.

Source: © Alinari/Art Resource.

Nave of Vézelay, c. 1130. One notices at once the influence of Islamic models on Christian architecture. Both derived key principles from Byzantine architecture, yet Vézelay especially has moved away from the central dome.

SOURCE: © Paul Almasy/Corbis.

Abbaye aux Dames of Caen, had a stark front, with a near vertical wall confronting the worshiper. Vézelay, and other early twelfth-century churches like Saint-Lazare, in contrast, had a magnificent tympanum of Christ in majesty, rendering the Last Judgment. Near Vézelay, a rather different church revealed the architectural and theological ideals of the Cistercians. The abbey of Fontenay, designed by Bernard himself, relied on a simplicity of design and lack of ornamentation so central to the quasi-mystical austerity of the Cistercians. In the Burgundian countryside, the traveler of today can visit in a single day these two special places of memory that speak eloquently to us of the twelfth-century world.

VÉZELAY: PLACE OF MEMORY

Western culture has long privileged the written source: our notion of history relies upon its existence and our analysis of it. French historian Pierre Nora and his collaborators have recently produced a remarkable new history of France, *Les Lieux de Mémoire,* that begins with a reconceptualization of history itself.[30] They sought to consider the impact of geographic places, and places of the collective imagination, on our historical notion of "France." Some sites, like the Eiffel Tower, have an association with historical events (in its case, the Paris World's Fair), that makes their physical remains the places of memory for an historical moment.

Christ in Majesty, tympanum of Vézelay, c. 1130.

SOURCE: © Giraudon/Art Resource.

Vézelay is such a privileged place of memory, marking that seminal moment in the creation of Western Civilization when western Europeans emerged from the figurative and literal darkness of the tenth century into the light: the light of critical thinking, personified by Abélard; the spiritual light of God, represented by Bernard of Clairvaux; and the physical light of the new churches, like Cluny, where Abélard went to die, and Vézelay, where Bernard preached the Second Crusade.

Peter the Venerable, the early twelfth-century abbot of Cluny who harbored the dying Abélard, offered a description of the great abbey church of Mary Magdelaine at Vézelay that captures the exhilaration one feels, especially when arriving via the road from Clamecy, when the church appears suddenly, after rounding a curve, glistening like what, to a medieval French Catholic, must have seemed God's own shimmering palace on the hill:

> This monastery, raised on an arid mountain darkened by shadows—he [abbot Alberic] has made it so fertile in good works and so resplendent in the éclat of a just renown; . . . in all of our pays, Cluny excepted, Vézelay knows no rival in all of the houses of our order, and one can say, with the Psalmist (67, 16–17): Here is the fertile mountain, a mountain filled with abundance, a mountain where God is pleased to reside.

Peter was not alone in his sense that God was pleased to reside at Vézelay; his contemporaries, too, believe the site to have special, holy significance. The abbey had a storied past, beginning with the foundation of a convent on the site by Gérard de Roussillon (legendary hero of a *chanson de geste*) in 860. By the early tenth century, the nuns had made way for Benedictine monks, who allied with Cluny starting in 1027, and soon claimed to possess the relics of Mary Magdelaine. Construction on the church began in 1104, its cost doubtless a factor in the rebellion of the local townsmen against the abbot Arnaud, whom they murdered in 1106. Further disturbances from 1125–1128 led to the appointment of the Alberic cited by Peter the Venerable, who clapped "almost all of the brothers . . . into irons, exiled [them] to Provence, Italy, Germany, Lorraine, France, England" and introduced "strangers" into the abbey. The next abbot, Pons de Montboissier, brother of Peter the Venerable, oversaw the completion of the great nave (1138). Who knew that it would be the swan song of Romanesque, that a mere two years later abbot Suger of Saint-Denis would begin the first Gothic church, marking the end of the Romanesque ascendancy?

(CONTINUED)

The crowning moment of Vézelay's existence came in 1146, when Bernard of Clairvaux, in the presence of the Pope Eugene III and of King Louis VII of France, preached the Second Crusade. This event marks out Vézelay as the place of memory for the Crusades and their special role in the creation of France. The king did not have rights over the abbey, but he did hold them over the bishopric in which it sat. Vézelay lay at the boundaries of Francia, Provensa, and Burgundy: no one in 1146 would have said that the king had much sway there, even though it legally lay within his kingdom. Yet King Louis VII came to Vézelay to hear the "heavenly instrument," as Odo of Deuil called Bernard's voice, preach the Second Crusade. Little wonder that royal apologists claimed that King Louis VII had initiated the idea of the Second Crusade, and that Bernard of Clairvaux had preached at Vézelay, not directly under the king's authority but a potential "royal" abbey in a border region of great importance, at the king's wish, rather than that of the Pope. (In fact, we know the Pope and Bernard jointly planned the event.)

Bernard's presence drew so large a throng that organizers set up a platform in an open field nearby, so that "the dew of the divine word" could be drunk by all. Bernard, always quick to reprimand, perhaps asked them to "Consider the hollow pit of your piety, sinners, and stand amazed at it" or demanded "Why do you delay, servants of the cross? Why do you dissimulate, you have bodily strength and material substance? Take up the sign of the cross. . . . Take up the gift which has been offered to you."[31] Odo of Deuil, Louis VII's chaplain, says that demand for crusading crosses was so great that Bernard rent his own garments to make additional ones, after the initial supply ran out. Bernard then set out to preach the Crusade everywhere in France.[32]

> I opened my mouth, I spoke, and soon the numbers of crusaders multiplied. Villages and towns are empty. You would have difficulty in finding one man for seven women. One sees only widows whose husbands are yet living.

Vézelay retained its close connection to Crusading throughout the twelfth century: in 1190, Richard the Lion-Hearted and Philip Augustus met at Vézelay to take their crosses, hear Mass, and start their journeys to the Holy Land for the Third Crusade. Kings and Popes alike stood in awe beneath Vézelay's tympanum, whose Christ in Majesty has been called by the eminent French medievalist Georges Duby "the most majestic figure of the living God that Christianity has ever conceived."[33] Today's visitor can follow in the footsteps of Bernard or Richard, walk the narrow streets of the little town, marvel at its tympanum (restored in the nineteenth century), its capitals, and its famous arched nave. Gazing down from the heights to the fields below where cows still graze, one can imagine Bernard on his platform, perhaps standing on the site in the little village of Saint-Père-sous-Vézelay that today holds a country inn, *L'Espérance,* which many believe to be the world's finest restaurant.

Gothic France

One looks back on it [Gothic art] all as a picture; a symbol of unity; an assertion of God and Man in a bolder, stronger, closer union than ever was expressed by other art.

Henry Adams, *Mont-Saint-Michel and Chartres*

In the north, the Cluniacs at Saint-Denis spearheaded the creation of an entirely new architectural style: Gothic. Abbot Suger, in the opulent tradition of Cluny, wanted a magnificent church, one that would humble all those before it.

> Let every man think as he may. Personally I declare that what appears most just to me is this: everything that is most precious should be used above all to celebrate the Holy Mass. . . . We maintain that the sacred vessels should be enhanced by outward adornment, and nowhere more than in serving the Holy Sacrifice, where inwardly all should be pure and outwardly all should be noble.[34]

Suger received aid from what, to a Christian monk, would have seemed the unlikeliest of quarters: Islam. Eleventh-century Christian Europe was an intellectual backwater. When Christians captured the great Islamic city of Toledo, they greatly accelerated the already ongoing process of the transferral of Roman and Greek texts (as well as Arabic ones) to the West. Some of these texts, such as many of the writings of Aristotle, became available to Western scholars (monks) for the first time. Islamic and Jewish scholars introduced Christians to Classical mathematics, especially Euclid, as well as to the works of Arab mathematicians such as Al-Khwarizimi. Such knowledge diffused slowly, but became available to a significant number of people by the mid-twelfth century.

The builders of the Romanesque churches along the routes of the great pilgrimage to Santiago de Compostela, supposed burial site of the apostle James the Greater, relied exclusively on empirical knowledge because they knew nothing of geometry; they had no theory behind their practice of construction. The early twelfth-century spread of Greek geometry to Christian Western Europe allowed Abbot Suger's builders to rely on *theory* before they built. They redistributed the weight of the wall into columns by means of ribbed vaults and ogival arches. The new system allowed the architects to remove mass from the walls and to replace stone with windows, to let in light. By the standards of earlier times, these Gothic cathedrals were palaces of light.

The windows also allowed the patrons of the cathedral, such as guilds or town governments, to endow religious scenes they found appropriate. Guilds would often sponsor a set of stained-glass windows in honor of the patron saint of their guild. These stained-glass windows often provide us with some of our best images of the daily life of medieval craftspeople. The bishops, too, took advantage of the opportunity, allowing the stained-glass panels to tell important stories from the Bible. Many of these churches, unlike those of the early twelfth century dedicated to saints, bore the name of *Notre Dame* (*Our Lady*), in honor of Mary. They bore witness to the Marian cult that spread through much of Europe in the twelfth and thirteenth centuries. In northern France especially, the great towns, responding to the call of their bishops or archbishops, built magnificent Gothic cathedrals.

The new architecture style, begun at the basilica of Saint-Denis outside of Paris, spread rapidly after 1140. New cathedrals sprang up first in or near the Ile-de-France and Picardy: Laon, Soissons, Paris, Sens, Noyon, Senlis, Troyes. Next, they appeared

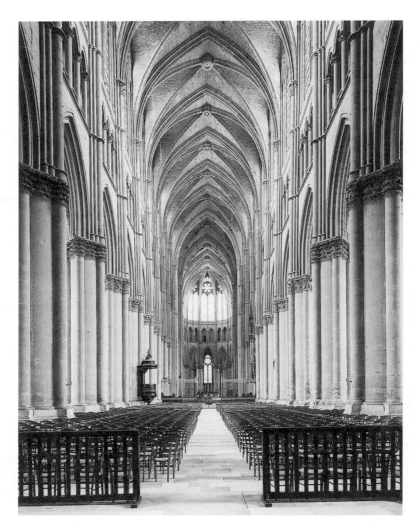

Nave of Notre Dame of Reims, thirteenth century. Here we see the use of the Gothic arch in place of the rounded Romanesque arch.

SOURCE: © Foto Marburg/Art Resource.

in the Loire valley (Angers, Tours, Orléans, Bourges, and, most famous of all, Chartres), Champagne (Reims and Châlons), and Normandy (Rouen, Bayeux, Caen, Evreux). Gothic expanded from France into England and the rest of Europe, from Salisbury to Vienna. Gothic spread slowly in the south of France, still faithful throughout the twelfth century to Romanesque, but eventually towns such as Lyon, Limoges, and even Narbonne would have their Gothic cathedrals, too.

Fittingly, the greatest surviving example of this art form can be found at the heartland of Gothic art: in the royal chapel, the Sainte-Chapelle, on the Ile de la Cité of Paris, built in the middle of the thirteenth century. (See Plate 3.) Saint Louis had constructed a small jewel of a church to serve as a massive reliquary for the greatest of all medieval relics, Christ's Crown of Thorns. In the upper chamber of the Sainte-Chapelle, the visitor can still see the astounding play of color, especially that unforgettable blue that was the glory of the stained-glass craftsmen, in what may be the most beautiful room ever created by Western Civilization.[35]

Gothic cathedrals also contained vast arrays of statuary. Some, like Laon, still have amusing collections of fanciful and everyday creatures, including the oxen whose labors made possible the transportation of the stone. Others, like Reims, contain holy figures such as the enigmatic smiling angel next to three figures of the Annunciation on the cathedral's west facade. These mid-thirteenth-century figures point the way to a more realistic style of sculpture, and away from the elongated statuary typical even of early Gothic cathedrals, such as the kings and queens of Israel/France on the west facade of Chartres (mid-twelfth century).[36] These Gothic cathedrals, following up the philosophical traditions started in places like Chartres's cathedral school, emphasized the new relationship of man to God. God had created man in His own image, and had made the universe for man's use, to be understood by man's singularly divine attribute: his reason.[37]

The statuary and stained glass of Gothic churches, like the capitals and paintings of Romanesque ones, provided an easily understood, visible text of a living Christianity. (See Plate 4.) Church iconography told lay people, almost all of them illiterate, about the great stories of the Christian religion. This iconography evolved over time, in response to social and cultural changes. Twelfth-century churches had more scenes from the Old Testament—Daniel in the lion's den, the three "Hebrews" in the furnace, Adam and Eve, Cain, the sacrifice of Isaac, and Noah's ark were quite popular—than the New, but the hanging of Judas was a common theme, too. Thirteenth-century iconography focused more on the New Testament, but even so the Old Testament stories could play a predominate role in a given church, as they do in the Sainte-Chapelle. Gothic cathedrals usually stressed the cult of Mary, so popular in the thirteenth century. Here, too, iconography changed over time. Early Gothic cathedrals, as at Laon or Le Mans, often contained stories taken from popular religious mythology, such as the tale of the two midwives who bore witness to the Virgin Birth. Real midwives invariably served as legal witnesses to legitimate birth, so the popular mythology simply made Christ's birth conform to what ordinary people knew of birth legality. This story appears only in apocryphal gospels, not in the New Testament,[38] and later Gothic churches do not present it. They focus instead on traditional, Scriptural episodes—the Annunciation, the Visitation, the Assumption—or on the most popular of all Marian images, the Holy Mother and Child or Madonna.[39] Cathedrals could also provide visual support for other beliefs. The frequent presentation of the replacement of the Synagogue by the Church as the repository of God's authority (visually presented as occurring at the moment of crucifixion) surely buttressed anti-Jewish sentiments, especially in the reign of a confirmed anti-Semite like Philip Augustus.

Romanesque and Gothic Statuary: The Visitation at Moissac (l) and at Reims (r): Here we see the spiritual emphasis of Romanesque, as against the more naturalistic quality of Gothic.

Source: © Ronald Sheridan/Ancient Art & Architecture Collection.

The cathedrals also bear witness to a dramatic shift in the power structure of the Church, which reflected the rising economic and political power of the towns. Cathedrals had episcopal, not monastic sponsors. Power in the French Church shifted sharply in the twelfth century, away from the monks and toward the secular clergy, above all the bishops. These bishops drew their power in part from the greater importance of the towns in which they lived and in part from the vastly expanded secular church they headed. Everywhere in France, the network of rural parishes expanded, becoming denser and more effectively organized. The monks had led the re-

SOURCE: Archives Photographiques.

form movement of the eleventh and early twelfth centuries, a movement that sought successfully to make the secular clergy more like the monks themselves: celibate holy men. At the height of the reforms, one monk succeeded another as Pope. That changed in the twelfth century. At the level of bishoprics, if Auxerre is any indicator, the same thing happened in the late twelfth century, as the three bishops of Auxerre from 1115–1167 all had previously been abbots. The three bishops who served from 1167–1220, however, all had prior experience as cathedral canons, not as monks.

The two dominant religious figures of twelfth-century France, Abbot Suger and Bernard of Claivaux, were both monks. Indeed, Bernard turned down the Papacy, preferring to remain a simple monk. We can see his influence in the fact that he, not the Pope, preached the Second Crusade at Vézelay in 1146. By the end of the century, however, the episcopacy dominated the French Church. Pope Innocent III led these bishops toward a more structured Christianity. They set out to define more clearly the doctrines of the Church, which they laid out in the papers of the Fourth Lateran Council (1215). The Council followed Innocent's lead in denouncing the Cathar heresy and gave official sanction to a wide variety of practices hitherto debated within the Church: belief in Purgatory (and thus in the efficacy of prayers for the dead), indulgences, and the seven sacraments.[40] The general councils, and the Popes, gradually enforced the idea that archbishops should hold synods every year and they encouraged national synods as well. The "nation" of France included the archbishoprics of Sens, Reims, Rouen, Tours, and Bourges (which gives us some idea of what "France" meant at this time). These general councils, however, also quarreled with Popes. The controversy over supremacy in the Church—whether the Pope or a general Council of the Church held supreme authority—gave rise to an enormous literature defending each position. Later, laymen seeking justification for royal or parliamentary power would use these medieval antecedents to justify their positions.

The Church thus played a central role in the evolution of political philosophy; it also spearheaded the general intellectual explosion of the twelfth century. At the beginning of the century, Church theologians teaching in Paris started to develop a more rigorous critique of Church doctrines. They relied on logic, not on faith alone, to justify their theology. Like the architects who built Saint-Denis and the Gothic cathedrals, these scholars benefitted enormously from exposure to some of the great minds of antiquity, notably Aristotle's treatises on logic, and of the Islamic tradition. Abélard himself merely started this process: many key texts became available only after his death. Other scholars, such as his late rival Alberic, repudiated some of Abélard's key ideas, but did so by means of the methodology he had helped establish. Although Bernard succeeded at Soissons and Sens, he and others like him, such as Pope Gregory IX, who vainly banned the teaching of Aristotle in 1228, failed to stem the tide. Bernard's mystical attachment to God certainly impressed his contemporaries but it could not stem the long-term attraction of a logical inquisition into the nature of God and the universe, which spread outward from the university at Paris. Pope Gregory notwithstanding, Aristotle became the normative philosopher of medieval Europe and, by the late thirteenth century, the writings of the greatest of the Scholastics, Thomas Aquinas, who taught for a time at Paris, became the new orthodoxy.

Abélard's old haunts, the streets of Paris, gave birth to a new institution, a new center of learning: a university. By 1200, Paris had a distinct university, today called the Sorbonne (after the mid-thirteenth-century rector, Robert de Sorbon), and a special student neighborhood, the Latin Quarter, situated where it can be found today, on the Left Bank. Those living in the quarter benefitted from special privileges and rights; all those who received a bachelor's degree obtained lifelong exemption from taxes (!) and students had the right to be tried in church rather than secular courts after 1200. The remnants of these real privileges in the formulaic phrase still appear on American university diplomas. A Columbia degree, for example, admits one to "all the rights privileges and immunities thereunto appertaining." Today, such phrases are an amusing anachronism; in the thirteenth century, they carried a literal meaning.

Academic Freedom, Parisian Style

Papal Regulations for the University, Issued 1231

But because, where there is no order, horror easily creeps in, we have conceded to you [the university rectors] the function of making due constitutions or ordinances as to the method and hour of lectures and disputations, as to the costume to be worn . . .

We order, moreover, that the bishop of Paris so punish the excesses of delinquents that the honor of the scholars is preserved and crimes do not remain unpunished . . .

Students partying. No matter what the rules said, students found a way to celebrate life in their own way.

Source: Bibliothéque de la Faculté de Médecine de Montpellier.

Furthermore, the summer vacation shall henceforth not exceed a month . . .

Moreover, we expressly enjoin that scholars shall not go about town armed . . . and those who pretend to be scholars but do not attend classes or have any master shall by no means enjoy the privileges of scholars.

We, with the general need and utility of the church in view, will order that henceforth the privileges shall be shown to the masters and scholars by our dearest son in Christ, the illustrious king of France, and fines inflicted on their malefactors, so that they may lawfully study at Paris without any further delay or return of infamy or irregularity of notation. To no man then be it licit to infringe or with rash daring to contradict this page of our provision. . . . If anyone shall presume to attempt this, let him know that he will incur the wrath of almighty God and of the blessed apostles Peter and Paul.

Source: J. Kirshner and K. Morrison, *Readings in Western Civilization: Medieval Europe* (Chicago: University of Chicago Press, 1986), 339–342.

Universities expanded in the thirteenth century, above all in Italy, but France, too, had important centers of higher learning: Paris, Montpellier, and later Orléans and Caen, among others. The rise of the university paralleled the rise of the towns in which they were located. Greater rural surplus helped create greater trade, more trade led to more specialized production in towns and to larger markets for goods; all of these factors led to urbanization. The larger towns of the twelfth and thirteenth centuries created new social groups and gave great impetus to movements for codified laws, and thus for lawyers, trained in the new schools of law at Montpellier and Orléans. Greater trade created demand for legal contracts, for those who could draw them up, and for those who could read them. Here French contacts with Italian and Arab traders—whose methods were far more sophisticated than those of the French—spearheaded the advance.[41] Let us turn to these great engines of medieval expansion, the towns, for, as the great Arab medieval scholar Al-Farabi wrote: "the most excellent and sovereign good and the most elevated perfection is obtained first in the city, and not in minor and more imperfect societies."

∼ THE RISE OF TOWNS

It is a commonwealth of men who live magically outside of Nature's order.[42]

Cellorigo, a sixteenth-century lawyer of Vallodolid, speaking of the town

Early eleventh-century Francia had few towns worthy of the name. The old Roman cities remained the most important urban centers; the Mediterranean region contained far more of them than the overwhelmingly rural north. Here and there an important town—a Paris, Rouen or Troyes in the north, a Narbonne in the south—broke the monotony of the vast countryside. The important towns invariably housed a bishop or archbishop whose court, by attracting the wealthy of the district, provided a market for the wares of merchants. Nobles sought out spices and other exotic imported goods. In many towns, such as Narbonne, where the Jewish quarter covered a third of the city, Jewish merchants dominated the international trade, limited though it was, that provided such products. Many of the larger towns had a *rue de giourie* (Troyes, Paris) or a *rue aux Juifs* (Rouen). Rouen, as well as Narbonne and several other southern towns, had Rabbinical schools that drew students from all over western Europe.

These filiations with currents of international trade aside, the urban community of Francia played a limited role in social, economic, and political life. The rapid surge in population after 1000, however, began to change the situation. Small towns—called *bourgs* in the Loire valley, *Villeneuves* (new towns) around Paris or in parts of the Midi—sprang up everywhere, especially in the twelfth century. The existing towns grew quickly, bursting out of their tiny traditional walled centers. Whether it was Bordeaux in the southwest, Tours in the Loire valley, Paris on the Seine or Lyon on the Rhône, the town authorities constantly extended their boundaries from the middle of the eleventh century onward. At Tours, the successive town walls increased its size from about twenty acres (eleventh century) to over one hundred forty acres (mid-fourteenth century): the vastly larger population within those walls required fifteen parishes by 1217, as against the four of 1079. Paris built new walls in the late twelfth century (the so-called wall of Philip Augustus, parts of which are still visible today), primarily to protect the huge merchant and working community that had sprung up on the Right Bank of the Seine.

Towns grew in every conceivable manner. Seigneurs encouraged the creation of bourgs near their castles: in most cases, the sources indicate a foundation date between 1050–1100. Many of these bourgs sprouted up near an existing town. In time, the larger cities, a Paris or a Bordeaux, simply swallowed up the bourg into the overall agglomeration. In the southwest, lay and ecclesiastical lords combined to found dozens of *bastides* (quadrangular, planned towns) in the thirteenth century. Many of these *bastides,* situated on hilltops, constructed defensive walls in the fourteenth century. The river valleys of the Dordogne and the Garonne still hold beautifully preserved *bastides,* like Cordes (near Albi), that provide us with a sense of the intimacy of the medieval small town.

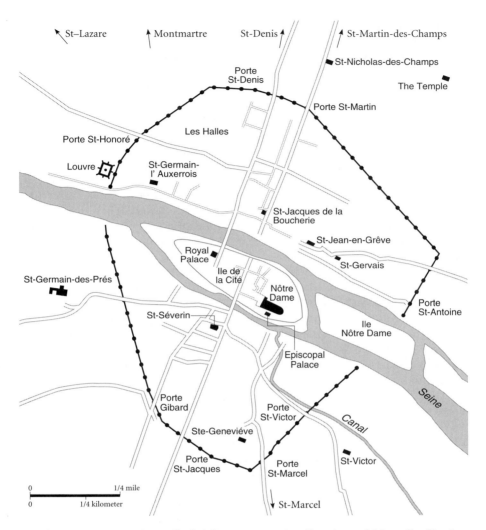

Twelfth-century Paris: the Wall of Philip Augustus. Small sections of this wall still exist near the old Porte Saint-Antoine, next to the current Lycée Charlemagne, and near the Panthéon.

Lewis Mumford, in his masterpiece *The City in History* (1961), argued that medieval towns sprang up "organically," that their narrow winding streets and seemingly chaotic disorganization responded to the logical needs of medieval times.

In organic planning, one thing leads to another, and what began as the seizure of an accidental advantage may prompt a strong element in a design, which an a priori plan could not anticipate. . . . Those who dismiss organic plans as unworthy of the name of plan confuse mere formalism and regularity with purposefulness, and irregularity with intellectual confusion or technical incompetence. The towns of the Middle Ages confute this formalistic illusion. For all their variety, they embody a universal pattern; and their very departures and irregularities are usually not merely sound, but often subtle, in their blending of practical need and aesthetic insight.[43]

The surviving streets, whether in Albi or Dijon, in Rouen or Paris, in Carcassonne or Rennes, bear witness to a purposeful "plan" of settlement.[44] The old quarters of these cities often have streets whose names bear modern witness to their medieval purpose: Bakers' Street, Butchers' Street, Tanners' Street, Parchment Maker's Street. Many trades, such as tanners, had to concentrate in a given area (in their case, near water); the organization of the local quarter responded to their needs, not to those of itinerant passersby. Until the 1860s, the main thoroughfares into Paris simply ended in a jumbled mass of tangled, narrow streets, now visible only in small parts of the city, such as the Marais or the Latin Quarter.

Large or small, new or old, most medieval French towns shared certain characteristics. Virtually all of the larger towns had Gallo-Roman antecedents on the same site. The main towns that had not been Roman sites were Montpellier, first mentioned in 985, Caen (1025), Lille (1063), La Rochelle (1130), and Montauban (1144).[45] Montpellier, which did not join the kingdom of France until the fourteenth century, had perhaps 12,000 people by 1100 and nearly 40,000 by the early fourteenth century. Lille, which gradually agglomerated a castle town, a bourg, and a suburb, put up a wall around 1200, covering an area of 200 acres (just slightly smaller than Paris). By the fourteenth century, it had perhaps 30,000 inhabitants, most of them textile workers.

The textile industry provided the driving motor of economic and demographic expansion. Twelfth-century Champagne had substantial manufactures at Troyes, Provins, Bar-sur-Aube, Châlons-sur-Marne, and Reims. The first three of these towns, together with Lagny, established fairs to market these wares. The six fairs (two each at Troyes and Provins) lasted throughout the year. After 1130, these fairs grew to be the preeminent center of northwestern European commerce, providing a useful midway point between the great textile centers of Flanders and the leading towns of Italy. Merchants came from German towns, Italy, Iberia, England, France, and the Low Countries. The count of Champagne provided duty exemptions for the fairs and safe conduct for all merchants and their goods. Merchants of territories that violated the safe conduct, jointly issued by the count and by the king of France, faced expulsion from the fairs. Their great renown bears a faint echo in our own day: jewelers still weigh gold in Troy ounces, which get their name from Troyes, site of the largest Champagne fair.

France's economy soared in the twelfth century. Agricultural productivity increased; trade expanded; population grew rapidly. Between the years 1000 and 1328 (the first official hearth count) the population of the kingdom of France rose from perhaps 6 million to nearly 16 million people. The rural population reached levels it would not exceed until the nineteenth century.[46] Hearth counts from such regions as the county of Vendôme, where the rural parishes had a population 15 percent larger in the 1250s than in the 1660s, and Normandy, whose thirteenth-century records suggest it had a higher population density then than 22 of France's departments had in 1836, give us some idea of how full rural France had become by 1270.[47]

These overall figures disguise enormous local and regional differences. The Paris basin, Normandy, indeed the north and northwest in general, had dense populations, ranging from 10–23 hearths/km^2. The regions around Bordeaux and Toulouse, or the provinces of Champagne and Burgundy, had lower densities, but averaged between 8–10 hearths/ km^2. The mountains and the interior heaths, far from urban centers and water-borne transportation, had far fewer people, often only 5 or 6 hearths/ km^2. Thus the very rich *pays de France,* near Senlis, had 22.2 hearths/ km^2, whereas the poor countryside of the chastellany of Chevreuse, southeast of the city, had a mere 5.8 hearths/ km^2.

The available figures suggest that the population stopped growing around 1270. Population estimates from this period are notoriously fragile, in part because the figures vary so much from one year to the next, but the overall trends are unmistakable. Between 1100–1300, towns grew to sizes unknown since Roman times. Paris, which had been a relatively small town focused on the Ile de la Cité, expanded most rapidly of all. By the middle of the thirteenth century, it had perhaps 160,000 people. Indeed, the 1328 hearth count suggests 200,000–220,000 residents, making Paris the largest city of western Europe.

Paris existed on a scale apart from all other French towns, but the kingdom had many "great towns" of 10,000 or more people. One estimate of 1270 places Rouen at 50,000, which is perhaps a bit high. Five cities in the traditionally urban south had between 25,000–40,000 inhabitants: Lyon, Bordeaux, Montpellier, Toulouse, and Narbonne. The region had many other towns of eight or ten thousand people—Carcassonne, Albi, Rodez, Périgueux. The Loire valley had two towns of 25,000 or more—Tours and Orléans—and many of eight or ten thousand: Bourges, Angers, Chartres, Nantes, Poitiers. By 1300, Flanders and Artois held large industrial towns such as Ghent (56,000), Bruges, Arras, Saint-Omer, and Lille (30,000 people each), Tournai, Douai, and Ypres (10,000 each). In Champagne, Reims and Troyes had fifteen or twenty thousand, while Burgundy's capital, Dijon, held perhaps 10,000.[48] The smaller towns, too, expanded in the twelfth and thirteenth centuries.

The rapid urban growth of the larger towns rarely followed a fixed plan, although, as Mumford suggested, it did follow an overall logic. Individuals moved to the outskirts of town, the suburbs, and sought work or set up shop. Migrants came, above all, from the surrounding countryside, but port towns drew from larger geographic regions because of the relative ease of travel by water. Rivers provided an essential transportation for all towns. Large towns always lay on substantial rivers or on the seacoast, because bulk goods, like grain, had to come primarily by water. Medieval people used relatively small streams, which could support a middling town or provide the first stage of transport for goods moving to a large town. Thus the Seine had Rouen, Paris, and Troyes; the Loire ran through Nantes, Angers, Tours, and Orléans; the Gironde served Bordeaux and Toulouse; and the Rhône flowed by Marseille, Avignon, Arles, and Lyon. The lesser rivers, too, often had a large town, such as Reims on the Vesle or Dijon on the Ouche. Many of the great French cities lay at the intersection of a major river and a smaller tributary, or at the first point at which a major river could be bridged. For example, Paris sits at the juncture of the Marne, the Bièvre, and the Seine, just as Nantes, the first point at which one can bridge the Loire, also lies at the Loire's confluence with the Erdre and the Sèvre. River-borne transport was so important that the first recorded commercial corporation at Paris was that of the "merchants of water-borne trade," which dated from the beginning of the twelfth century. The city seal still bears a ship in recognition of their importance. The Loire towns, too, had a special guild of "merchants frequenting the Loire," who had exclusive rights to large-scale river commerce.

Rivers provided two other necessities of urban growth: power and water. Towns required drinking water and a means of sanitation; rivers played a key role in both activities (although towns preferred to take water from wells, if possible). Rivers and their feeding tributary streams, like the Bièvre at Paris, infamous for the stench created by the tanners who lined its banks, also provided the power to turn the wheels of the mills and the mechanism by which to get rid of industrial wastes, especially those of the tanners and dyers. The mills provided the power that drove the urban economy.

The Urban Economy

The civilization of country people is inferior to that of city dwellers; . . . above all, the manual arts do not exist there.[49]

Ibn Khaldun, fourteenth-century Arab historian

Three sectors dominated the urban economy: food and drink, housing, and clothing. Some medieval tax rolls, such as that for 1421 in Paris, list occupations: on that list we find twenty-three different food trades, ranging from the obvious—bakers, butchers, tavern keepers, grocers, fishmongers—to the surprisingly exotic—herb seller, pastry maker, *rôtisseur,* and tripe maker. The roll includes members of eighteen clothing trades, nine each from building and leather, eight from metalworking, and a wide variety of others: jewelers, potters, painters, and money changers. The Parisian tax rolls of 1296, 1297, and 1300 paint a similar picture, one that complements the famous *Book of Crafts* of 1268, which listed one hundred one different crafts at Paris, even though it left out some known ones such as butchers, the oldest craft guild in the city!

The towns initially provided services to the rich and powerful, to the lord of the castle near the bourg or to the bishop, and thus attracted both skilled craftspeople, who produced specialized, quality goods for the rich merchants who sold the rare commodities like silks or spices only the rich could afford. The rising population of the town or bourg, however, soon developed needs of its own. As Cellorigo suggested in the sixteenth century, townspeople lived magically outside of Nature's order. They ate the finest produce of the land, yet many did not grow their own food. The extensive gardens and fields within medieval towns often produced specialized goods for the market, rather than standard produce for one's own table.

The presence of such a population, one that required others to produce its food, and used specialized workers to build its houses and produce its cloth, provided an enormous spur to the urban and rural economies. In most towns, providing sustenance, clothing, and housing for the local people provided employment to the mass of the population. Only in the great textile towns of Flanders and Artois did a majority of people work in the export trades. In the suburbs and the nearby countryside of the towns, peasants began to specialize, to produce for the consumption of others. From the eleventh century through the twentieth, ties to the market largely dictated the economic fate of the different regions of France.

A medium-sized town such as Vendôme did not have the level of specialization of a Paris or a Ghent, but evidence from the eleventh through early fourteenth centuries reveals the standard groups: weavers, fullers, construction trades, jewelers, money changers, saddle makers, shoemakers, tailors, tavern keepers, bakers, butchers—in short, all those trades necessary for medieval urban life. The town held flour mills as early as the eleventh century; their number rose considerably thereafter. The count leased out a fulling mill, as well as multiple ovens subject to his *ban*.[50]

The mills of Vendôme give some inkling of France's vast network of these early industrial powerhouses. Roman Gaul and Carolingian Francia had had water mills, but their use exploded from the eleventh to the thirteenth century. Historians estimate that France had 20,000 water mills by 1100 and 40,000 (more than one per parish) by the late thirteenth century. These mills, as at Vendôme, performed many functions: grinding flour, fulling cloth, tanning, and, in the fourteenth century, making paper. In the most advanced regions, the density of mill placement along running streams reached two per mile. Windmills, although they existed, did not spread widely until later.

Urban dwellers obtained raw materials, including wool, hemp, and linen for cloth; grain and meat; wine, perry, cider or beer from their surrounding countryside. Documents from Charlemagne's time list many of these products, telling millers to keep flocks of geese and chickens; encouraging others to keep partridges, pheasants, peacocks (much prized by aristocratic eaters), pigeons, and ducks; making provision for fish ponds; and laying out regulations about sheep, cattle, oxen, and horses. These regulations discuss, among other products, butter, vinegar, honey, cheese, herbs, soap, wax, shoes, sausages and smoked meats, all manner of beverages, different types of cloth (wool, linen), dyestuffs (woad, madder), oil, tallow, and metal goods. Early legislation directed that royal stewards see to the proper production of all these commodities on their manors. By the eleventh or twelfth centuries, production of many such commodities, particularly of the best crafted ones, had shifted from manorial workshops to urban ateliers. Medieval toll lists provide us with clear evidence about the most frequently trafficked goods: wine, grain, and cloth. As time went on, the listings for cloth became more complex, because the skilled weavers of the cities created so many new varieties.

France's many vineyards animated a lively wine commerce. The remarkable growth of the Parisian region in the twelfth and thirteenth centuries owed much to its wines, and towns as far north as Soissons had vineyards. One church at Soissons bore the name Saint John of the Vines.[51] Parisians, including the king himself, owned vineyards in neighboring villages, such as Montmartre, Vanves, la Montagne-Sainte-Geneviève, and Clignancourt (all today within the city limits). Most of these vineyards produced white wine, enjoyed even by the king, as one thirteenth-century ditty recounted:

> The good king, Philip by name
> Who happily wets his gullet
> With good white wine.[52]

The king, like most medieval drinkers, preferred his wine young (within a year of harvest), pressed from grapes harvested much earlier than in modern times, and so of low alcohol content. Around the end of the thirteenth century, however, somewhat stronger wines started to enter into vogue. Medieval drinkers, above all northern ones, also liked adulterated wines, flavored with spices and/or sugar, and sometimes fortified with additional alcohol.

The rise of stronger wines, and of red wines, in the thirteenth century created great prosperity in some regions. Bordeaux exported virtually no wine to England in 1200, yet by the early fourteenth century, its wine exports to England peaked at 90 million liters a year. The royal court led the way: Henry III placed an order of only 90,000 liters in 1255, while Edward II demanded ten times that much for his coronation celebration in 1307. Bordeaux's wines also had (and would keep) an important market in the duchy of Brittany, above all its western, non-wine producing region. The economic connection to England had important political ramifications: the Bordeaux wine regions remained personal possessions of the king of England throughout the thirteenth, fourteenth, and early fifteenth centuries.

The wine trade gave work to many individuals: coopers, to make the barrels; distillers, to create brandy and adulterated wines; carters; shippers; merchants, both retail and wholesale; tavern keepers. Existing tax rolls, as at Toulouse in the thirteenth century or Paris in the early fifteen century, indicate women ran some of these taverns, but rarely list them in other wine-related occupations. They played a greater role in other food trades, such as grocer (*épicière*, literally, "spice seller") or baker. Many a widow ran her former husband's bakery after his death. The woman fishmonger became a figure of colorful legend in France, just as in England. Existing iconographic evidence shows women shopping at open-air markets, often buying from women sellers. By way of contrast, the tax rolls virtually never indicate a woman butcher. Tax rolls also indicate women clothiers: drapers, mercers, old clothes sellers.

Virtually all guilds required masters to be married. In many shops, the woman sold the goods made by the man. Visitors to contemporary France are familiar with this arrangement: the neighborhood *boulangerie* almost always has a woman out front, selling the bread, and a male baker in the back. Women ran the household as well as the business. They typically controlled the urban family's money, because the main family expense, food, lay in the domain of the woman. Female control of the money of daily life, both of consumption and, in many cases, of production, carried an important social implication. The shop-holding widows, once past the age of thirty-five or so, had little incentive to remarry because they could hire a journeyman to do the work. Shop-owning widowers, in contrast, desperately needed to remarry, because only a member of the family could be trusted with the money.

Women merchants and artisans practiced their crafts much as men did, but they did not have the same legal or political rights as their male counterparts. Most guilds forbade women from voting in their elections and banned women officers. Some

*Parisian street scene, fifteenth century. The woman and man
work together in the cloth shop on our left.*

SOURCE: © Giraudon/Art Resource, NY.

women did get such political rights—those in lace-making guilds, flower sellers, and
some fishwives—but most had to settle for the simple right to a shop or market stall.
Nor did these independent businesswomen constitute a small portion of the urban
population. The available records suggest that women headed about one urban
household in eight in the north and perhaps one in twelve in the south, where Roman
law, which sharply discriminated against women's property rights, prevailed.[53]

The food trades began in a simple way—a miller, a baker, and, in the larger
towns, a butcher. In time, food production became more complex. The baker continued his or her work, yet the pastry maker appeared, along with the professional
caterer. Some of these trades, notably the butchers and the related tanners, created

little enclaves for themselves where others feared to tread. A nineteenth-century Bordeaux merchant, describing the medieval section of Limoges that still housed the butchers in his day, wrote:

> I suddenly found myself in a street forming a horseshoe, humid, and closed tightly by relatively tall houses . . . There I found only the exhalations of sweat and blood, a chaos of buildings, of muffled animal groans, and the hoarse moos of cattle; in the somber interior of the shops, nothing but ropes, hooks, and the dank smell of dead flesh . . . This was the rue de la Boucherie.[54]

At Paris, they dominated several streets near the Châtelet, one of them called Middle Massacre Street. Their parish came to be called Saint-Jacques-de-la-Boucherie: a lonely and haunting sentinel, the Tour Saint-Jacques, legendary starting place of the Milky Way (the pilgrimage route to Santiago de Compostela in Spain), is all that remains of their parish church today. One estimate of 1293 suggested the Parisian butchers slaughtered nearly 250,000 head of livestock a year, while another, of 1434, offered similar figures.[55] The royal court issued an ordinance in 1366 requiring Paris's butchers henceforth to slaughter the animals outside of the city limits, alongside a stream. The tanners, who used acid to treat the hides, had an even lower reputation than butchers: many guilds forbade members to marry a tanner's daughter. The numbers of butchers and bakers expanded with the population, and these trades tried to set up monopolies within their towns. Following the example of the workers in the textile industries, they formed guilds to protect their interests.

These organizations often fought each other. One can easily imagine the quarrels between pastry makers and bakers or between pork and beef butchers. Street vendors, who often quarreled with guilds, sold goods familiar to us only in song, like the four-and-twenty blackbirds baked in the pie. (Medieval people really did eat

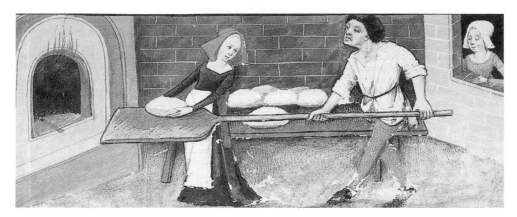

The medieval bakery, like the modern one, relied on the cooperation of the woman, running the shop, and the man, baking the bread. Most of the customers, too, were probably women.

Jean, duke of Berry at table, c. 1400. We can compare the duke's sumptuous table with that of Odo of Bayeux, half-brother of William the Conqueror in the following photo.

SOURCE: © Reunion des Musees Nationaux/Art Resource, NY.

blackbirds baked into pies!) The wealthy ate peacocks, swans, and a wide range of songbirds, often flavored with herbs not commonly consumed today, like hyssop. Fancy chefs sometimes "set before the king" or another lord pies containing live birds, added to the baked pie and covered with a crust, allowing the birds "to sing,"

Odo of Bayeux giving a banquet for William the Conqueror and his knights. Bayeux Tapestry, c. 1080.

Source: © Gianni Dagli Orti/Corbis.

and fly out, when "the pie was opened." Such chefs would cook the swan or peacock and then sew the finished product back into its origin skin, feathers and all: it must have made for a stunning presentation. The wealthy added large doses of more exotic spices, above all pepper, cinnamon, and cloves. Meat and fish dishes on rich tables came in a sauce called verjuice, made from the juice of unripe grapes or crab apples, often thickened by adding breadcrumbs. The surviving medieval recipes (and even those from slightly later periods) suggest that people liked their food heavily flavored, to an extent that would sicken our more fragile palates.

Peasants ate a simpler diet, one more focused on bread and boiled root vegetables; they naturally poached game and fish whenever possible. These peasants participated in the manufacturing process, particularly its earliest stages (like spinning), but we have far less evidence of the earlier rural workshops, attached to a lord's manor, in which peasants produced cloth. The existing documentation for the ninth or tenth centuries suggests that women did almost all of this rural textile work. In time, as a town grew up around the manor or a monastery, the number of textile workers expanded and their skills became more specialized. Technical progress in the late eleventh century enabled workers to produce far more cloth; the ever-expanding cities provided them with new markets. Artisans themselves, and other local residents, often bought the cheaper cloth, but certain cities, above all in Flanders, produced expensive, specialized cloth for export or for consumption by local elites.

The clothing trades employed large numbers of women and men. Women did all of the preparation work: they cleaned the raw wool, often carded it, and spun it into thread. Peasant women did much of this low-paying work, in addition to their farm tasks. The rapid spread of the spinning wheel in the twelfth century greatly accelerated the ability of Europe to produce cloth. Another stage in the process, the fulling, also relied on technological innovation. Europeans combined the techniques of the water grain mill and the cam shaft to create fulling mills: the first known such mill in France appeared in 1086. Again, the innovation spread rapidly in the twelfth century, especially in northern France.

Better textiles required greater specialization. In addition to spinners and fullers, cloth production required a wide range of other craftspeople. The main textile artisans, of course, were the weavers, who worked on the new horizontal loom. Here the move to the town seems to have led to a dramatic change. The descriptions of rural textile workshops invariably refer to the "workshops of women." In the towns, men now replaced women as weavers. The master weavers played the dominant role in many cities, notably the great textile centers such as Ghent, Bruges or Saint-Omer. At Ghent, the four main cloth guilds (weavers, dyers, fullers, croppers) constituted more than half of the population in 1357; the other cloth towns looked much the same. These towns obtained rights of self-jurisdiction from their overlords (counts, bishops, or abbots) by the middle of the twelfth century, a sure sign of their rising power. Their guilds demanded, and got, a share of municipal authority.

The towns of Artois and Flanders imported the wool for their looms from England. Cloth from Ypres, Lille, Ghent, Bruges, and the other towns soon appeared on markets as far away as Novgorod (Russia), Constantinople, Morocco, and Tabriz. Flemish cloth spread rapidly in the Mediterranean, in large measure due to the Italian merchants who purchased it at the Champagne fairs. The towns of Artois and Flanders quickly developed specialized workers for all production processes. Cloth needed to be dyed, which required access to flowing water and meant the importation, often from distant lands, of dyestuffs and of alum for setting the colors. In time, even more specialized work evolved, to handle the finishing of garments destined for elite customers: fine lace work and embroidery, both done by women; and the use of gold and silver threads. Tailors, glove makers, hatters, furriers, and a wide range of other craftspeople soon created a demand for their services as well.

The craftspeople, organized into guilds, also directly subsidized specific parts of the churches, such as stained-glass windows devoted to the life of their patron saint or statues on the portals of members of particularly important guilds, like the dye merchants of Amiens, neatly ensconced in one of cathedral's towers. Right next to the side chapel built for duke Jean of Berry, the cathedral at Bourges has small side chapels built in the late fourteenth or early fifteenth century specifically for local guilds, with a particularly fine surviving collection of stained-glass portrayals. The towns used churches, especially cathedrals, as a form of municipal competition. For some years, cathedrals competed to see which would have the highest nave. Beauvais won, but the roof later collapsed. Although peasant contributions played a critical role in financing cathedrals, the townspeople themselves also paid heavily and, at times, unwillingly. In Reims, for example, sales taxes on wine and other goods led to a rebellion that delayed construction on the cathedral.

The weavers and other textiles workers needed housing, which provided work for the third large group of craftspeople. Building construction occupied 10 percent or so of a town's population, in trades ranging from carpenter and mason to joiner and roofer. Unlike the food and clothing trades, the building industry employed a largely male labor force, although there is a little evidence about some female construction workers. Town governments often hired substantial work gangs, building the walls that protected them from outsiders. Once constructed, the walls required constant repair and supervision, and provided an early form of public works employment.

The many different occupations organized to protect their economic and political interests. Most important towns had four substantial economic groups: merchants, artisans working for export trade, artisans supplying local demand, and day laborers. In addition, the gradual spread of the rule of law in the twelfth and thirteenth centuries meant that a legal system, complete with lawyers, judges, and many subordinate personnel (like clerks), emerged in urban centers. The great towns invariably had two other important political and economic powers: the nobility and the clergy. Paris housed thousands of secular and regular clergy, who provided an important market for many producers of luxury goods. The specialized producers included clothiers, for vestments; goldsmiths, for ornaments such as chalices; glaziers, for stained-glass and clear windows; expert builders, such as carpenters and stone masons; and wine merchants. The richest clergymen—the bishops, abbots, and cathedral canons—often kept the fanciest tables in town. In many French towns, as at Nantes or Paris, the finest white bread was called "chapter bread," after its primary customer, the rich canons of the cathedral chapter. Nobles, too, maintained urban residences, especially in the south: in Languedoc or Provence, as in Italy, the nobility continued to play an important role in urban politics and to hold municipal office.

Merchants or butchers, bakers or weavers, people created organizations to regulate their segment of the economy. After an initial period of experimentation, French towns gradually developed corporations for groups of producers, such as butchers, or merchants. The French called these groups "corps de métier," literally, the "craft body," a term we render in English as "guild." Guilds oversaw the quality and quantity of production and limited access to their trades. Merchant guilds tried to create monopolies on the sale of certain goods, such as cloth. In both the craft guilds and the merchants ones, only the masters had full membership in the guild. The masters oversaw the production of their journeymen, the skilled workers who helped them make the goods, and their apprentices, the young shop assistants. Apprentices learned the basic skills of a trade while doing simple tasks in the shop: their families often paid the master to take them in. Although the guilds had legal jurisdiction over the journeymen and the apprentices, neither group actually belonged to the guild. Journeymen probably had their own clandestine organizations, but firm evidence of these brotherhoods (*compagnonnages*) dates only from the sixteenth century.

GUILD STATUTES NORTH AND SOUTH

TOULOUSE, THIRTEENTH-CENTURY WEAVERS

All weavers may work wherever they wish, day or night, in the city and suburbs.

All apprentices who live with a master may work with other men and women who work on cloths, in their workshops or elsewhere, wherever it may please them, on the sole condition that they work well and honestly.

All men and women who produce cloths and have them made in their houses are authorized to hire and keep weavers, without anyone being able to oppose them, so long as they have a contract with these weavers, the other weavers cannot oppose it.

Each year four wardens (*prud'hommes*), two from the city and two from the suburbs, will be made guards of the entire craft of wool. The day of the election of the consuls [municipal officers] or the following day, they will be installed by the consuls.[56]

ARRAS, THE SHEARERS' GUILD, 1236

1. Whoever would engage in the trade of a shearer shall be in the Confraternity of St. Julien, and shall pay all the dues, and observe the decrees made by the brethren.

6. And no one may be a master of this trade of shearer if he has not lived a year and a day in the town, in order that it may be known whether or not he comes from a good place.

16. . . . . And when a master does not work hard he pays 5 shillings [fine] and a journeyman 2 shillings [to the Fraternity].

22. And no one who is not a shearer may be a master . . .

25. And each master ought to have his arms when he is summoned. And if he has not he should pay 20 shillings.

32. And if a master does not give a journeyman such wage as is his due, then he shall pay 5 shillings.

34. And whatever brother of this Fraternity shall betray his confrère for others shall not work at the trade for a year and a day.[57]

From the thirteenth century until 1791, in every part of France, in almost all sectors of the economy, guilds monopolized and regulated every facet of urban production, with most guilds allowing each master only one shop. In addition, they set production limits for all masters; they fixed prices and wages (in theory); they checked for quality of work; and they restricted access to the given profession. Only registered guild masters could run a shop. Only a member of the bakers' guild, for example, could bake and sell bread within a given town. Some guilds got the right to regulate themselves through elected wardens, but other guilds operated under the direct authority of the municipal government. In theory, French towns adopted one system or the other; in practice, the municipal government always interfered with guild management, as the thirteenth-century clothmaking statutes for Toulouse demonstrate.

The guilds played an important role in personal life as well. Guilds, like the shearers of Arras, invariably organized confraternities—lay religious organizations that held festivals for the guild's patron saint, celebrated marriages and births, paid for funerals, and provided relief for widows and orphans. The butchers of Limoges claimed their confraternity dated from 932, perhaps an exaggeration, but one that provides some sense of the early origin of these manifestations of collective spiritual life.

Town Government: The New Political Force

A city is said to exist for the liberty of its citizens.

John of Viterbo, *c.* 1240

I shall . . . agree to have the right judgment of the aldermen enforced against anyone, myself included. I also grant to the aldermen liberties as extensive as any which other aldermen in my land may have.[58]

William Clito, count of Flanders,
confirming the liberties of Saint-Omer, 1127

Even before we have evidence of guilds, we can see that the urban dwellers demanded political rights. The artisans would combine with the merchants to oppose the main political authority of their town. Such opposition took place first in the larger towns: a bishop often provided the target. In northern France, the movement to create urban political entities, "communes," began at Le Mans in 1070, where the bishop and clergy combined with the townspeople to demand a commune from the count. The next recorded commune, at Noyon (1108), had the bishop's permission, but the residents of nearby Laon set up their commune in direct opposition to their bishop, buying a charter from the King for 400 *livres.* When bishop Gaudry paid the king 700 *livres* to abolish the commune, the arrival of the letters of abolition led to a riot and to his murder.

Many urban communities obtained the support of the local bishop in their effort to obtain the immunities offered by a commune against surrounding landlords. The general pattern everywhere was for the violence of the twelfth century to turn into a peaceful, lawful settlement in the thirteenth. By the early thirteenth century, a new municipal officer appeared everywhere: the juridical counselor, or town lawyer (often known later as the *procureur syndic*). Many such officers had even received specialized training in the new law universities.

The main issue involved urban identity. The towns needed to have a separate, legal identity if they were to establish any independence. Merchants in particular needed legal protection for their trade, so that nobles could no longer pillage merchants' wares. In the course of the twelfth century, towns all over France began to establish such identities. The commune movement provided the first stage of a longer process. Towns soon obtained charters from the king, giving them specific rights and privileges, usually in return for money payments to the king. Many towns adopted seals, like noble families. They built bell towers, to symbolize their independence, and town halls.

Politically, northern and southern French towns moved to self-government by different means. In southern France, towns formed consulates, town councils, in imitation of Italian models. The consulate format moved from Italy westward in the twelfth century, from Avignon (1129), to Arles (1131), and then to Béziers (1131), and to Narbonne (1132), Carcassonne, and many other towns. By 1200, virtually every town in Provence and Languedoc had a consulate. Northern towns preferred to form communes: Le Mans, Cambrai, Beauvais, and Noyon by 1109; Laon, Amiens, Soissons, Bruges, Lille, and Saint-Omer by 1127. In some cases, as at Laon (see box), the commune involved a violent seizure of power. In other cases, such as the charters granted to the Flemish towns by the new count, William Clito (1127), the towns ne-

THE COMMUNE OF LAON, 1116

The violation of the clauses of the said commune caused such a furor, such a stupor in the hearts of the bourgeois, that all of the officers deserted their offices, all the shoemakers and repairers closed their shops, and the tavern keepers and cabaret owners removed all their wares from sale because they knew nothing would be left, the lords (seigneurs) looting everywhere . . . The next day (Holy Saturday), when the bishop followed his clergy in the procession, he ordered his men and all knights to march behind him, carrying swords under their coats. During this procession, when a minor disorder began, as sometimes happens in crowds, one of the bourgeois came out of his cellar and, thinking that the execution of the murder plot had started, cried, "Commune! Commune!" . . . The bishop, unable to turn back the assaults of the commoners, put on the clothing of one of his serfs and fled to the cellar of the church, where he hid in a small wine barrel. . . . A certain Teudegaud stopped in front of the barrel in which the bishop was hiding and, having taken off the hoops, asked the bishop several times who he was. The bishop, with difficulty moving his lips frozen in fear, murmured: "a wretch". . . . Gaudri who, although a sinner, was nonetheless the anointed of the Lord, was brutally torn from the barrel and pulled out by his hair; he was beaten with multiple blows and brought with great commotion through the streets. . . . Teudegaud, seeing the ring of office on the finger of the dead bishop and unable easily to pull it off, cut off the finger of the dead man and removed the ring.[59]

gotiated for power. In still others, the bishop or lord encouraged the townspeople to establish a communal government under his or her aegis.

These northern towns initially had aldermen and usually a chief seigneurial official, called the provost (revenue collector), selected by the town's overlord. In time, the appointed aldermen turned into elected councils, often headed by an elected mayor. These elections could involve corporations, the normal procedure by the thirteenth century, and often left to the overlord the final selection of mayor. He or she could choose either of the top two vote getters. The communes of northern towns initially involved compromises between the artisan guilds and the merchants; in time, a third group, the men of the law, also became an important faction. The largest towns often had multiple councils. The town council of aldermen might answer to a council consisting of former aldermen, which, in turn, answered either to a general assembly of the male citizens or to a large council that included the officers of the town militia (that is, the leaders of each neighborhood). In the south, the consulates typically had only a few places, with each ranked consul representing a specific constituency, such as the nobillity or the merchants. Everywhere in France, as in Italy, town politics involved a conflict between those who wanted a broader suffrage and those who wanted only the most important men of the town to have a say. In the textile towns, this dispute invariably pitted the artisans against the merchants.

The urban resident differed fundamentally from his or her rural counterparts, as he or she was free. French urban dwellers, like German ones, liked to believe in the old proverb that "town air makes free." Twelfth-century charters, like that of Lorris (1155), stated explicitly that "anyone who shall dwell a year and a day in the parish of Lorris, without any claim having pursued him there, and without having refused to lay his case before us or our provost, shall abide there freely and without molestation."[60]

Peasants liked to believe that such clauses meant they were no longer subject to re-enserfment by their lord, but landlords rarely respected such clauses and royal courts upheld lords' control over runaway serfs (even in Paris!) as late as the eighteenth century. Town jurisdiction often did not even apply to the whole town. Paris provides the most notorious example: by the fourteenth century, in addition to the king, twenty-four different lords held judicial rights within the city, covering areas ranging from the one hundred five streets subject to the bishop to the five streets under the canons of Saint-Honoré. By the end of the Middle Ages, Paris had a thicket of jurisdictions so dense that it nearly defies description.

Southern France's consulates often represented specific oligarchic groups within the town's population; the first consul in most towns had to be a noble. Southern towns thus had a fifth political group, the nobility, in addition to the four customary ones: clergy, merchants, artisans, and legal men. The great manufacturing towns, above all those of Flanders, developed severe economic and political conflicts between the merchants and the artisans over control of labor. In the late thirteenth century, struggles between the kings of England and France caught Flanders in the middle. Flemish towns relied on English wool for the raw material of their cloth production, yet Flanders lay within the kingdom of France. When King Edward I of England first taxed and then restricted wool exports to Flanders, it led to widespread unemployment and civic unrest in the great towns.

In 1302, fed up with the unruly weavers, an army of French knights marched north to teach them a lesson. They caught up with the urban militias at Courtrai. The battle proved to be a harbinger of things to come, as the militias routed the knights. Not caring much for the niceties of chivalric warfare, they slaughtered the defeated. They killed so many knights that the melted down spurs produced enough metal for a new town bell at Courtrai. The bell survives today, although it rings the hour in Dijon, not Courtrai. How it got there is a tale for Chapter 4.

Notes

1. *Arab Historians of the Crusades,* trans. F. Gabrieli, E. J. Costello (Berkeley: University of California Press, 1969), 75–76.

2. Using here the translation of J. Kirshner and K. Morrison, eds., *Readings in Western Civilization. V. 4: Medieval Europe* (Chicago: University of Chicago Press, 1986), 163. The entire chronicle is available in an English translation: Foucher de Chartres, *Chronicle of the First Crusade,* trans. M. McGinty (Philadelphia: University of Pennsylvania Press, 1941); this passage appears on p. 16.

3. Medieval Christians believed Jerusalem was the literal center of the world. The oldest surviving European map of the world, which dates from the fourteenth century, bears witness to this belief, as do medieval books such as the *Travels of Sir John Mandeville.*

4. The critical issue at the time was a verse interpolated into the Apostle's Creed by Visigothic scholars, but made normative in the West by those working for

Charlemagne. This verse, called the *filioque,* made the Holy Spirit emanate from Christ as well as God the Father in the Christian Trinity. The Orthodox stuck with the original version, which suggested the Holy Spirit emanated only from God the Father. Other differences included marriage of priests, liturgical variations, and attitudes toward the Roman Pontiff.

5. Cited in P. Geary, ed., *Readings in Medieval History* (Peterborough, Ont.; Lewiston: Broadview Press, 1989, 1991), 448–449. The Western Crusader is Odo of Deuil, an official of King Louis VII of France: Odo participated in the Second Crusade (1147). Odo of Deuil, "De profectione Ludovici VII in orientem," in *The Journey of Louis VII to the East,* ed. and trans. V. G. Berry (New York: Norton, 1965), 86 (Latin original) and 87 (English translation).

6. Anna Comnena, *The Alexiad of Princess Anna Comnena,* trans. E. Dawes (New York: AMS Press, 1978, reprint of 1928 London edition), 27 (book I, ch. 10).

7. Again, I have preferred the translation of Kirshner and Morrison, *Medieval Europe,* 163, to that of McGinty, 16–17. Fulcher likely was in the audience but the four surviving versions of Urban's speech agree only on the sermon's main points.

8. Text reproduced in N. Golb, *Les Juifs de Rouen au Moyen Age: Portrait d'une culture oubliée* (Rouen: Publications de l'Université de Rouen, 1985), 95. Guibert was one of the Crusaders. The Crusaders of 1096 thus followed the precedent of those who marched across southern France to fight the Muslims of Spain in 1065; they, too, attacked Jewish communities en route.

9. McGinty, trans., Fulcher of Chartres, *Chronicle of the First Crusade,* 69.

10. Anna Comnena, *The Alexiad,* 254. Alexius demanded that the Crusaders promise to return to his Empire any of its previous territories they conquered and that they do homage to him. Initially, most of them refused but through a combination of force and denial of provisions he forced them to acquiesce.

11. Fulcher of Chartres, *Chronicle,* 28.

12. E. Berley, trans., Odo of Deuil, *De profectione Ludovici VII in orientem,* 64–65.

13. Gabrieli, *Arab Historians of the Crusades,* 73–74.

14. R. Ellenblum, *Frankish Rural Settlement in the Latin Kingdom of Jerusalem* (Cambridge, New York: Cambridge University Press, 1998), especially Map 1, offers a detailed look at these questions. Some scholars have questioned his findings, believing Western Christian settlement to be more widespread than he suggests.

15. The maps provided by M. Barber, *The New Knighthood: A History of the Order of the Temple* (Cambridge, New York: Cambridge University Press, 1994), 22 and 252–253, make this situation strikingly clear.

16. The massacre of captured prisoners was standard practice in this Christian–Muslim fighting; as early as the siege of Antioch (1097–98), the two sides regularly beheaded prisoners and threw the heads into the enemy camp. Gabrieli, *Arab Historians of the Crusades,* 124–125.

17. H. Mayer, *The Crusades,* trans. J. Gillingham (Oxford, New York: Oxford University Press, 1988), 203.

18. A series of "Emperors" and "Empresses" without empires used the title until 1382. Many French ecclesiastics also claimed to possess "bishoprics" in the former Latin Empire.

19. A papal legate shortly thereafter stripped Manasses of his see. Bloch, *Feudal Society,* II, 347.

20. Church geography often repeated that of the Romans: many a bishopric covered the territory of an ancient Roman *pagus.*

21. Héloïse to Abélard, letter six of their exchange. I have used the edition edited by E. Hicks, *La vie et les epistres Pierres Abaelart et Heloys sa fame* (Paris; Geneva: Champion-Slatkine, 1991). He reproduces the original Latin text of the municipal library of Troyes (ms. 802), which dates from around 1300, and a French translation attributed to Jean de Meun (early thirteenth century), of which the sole surviving copy is in the BN, Ms. Fr. 920, and dates from the fourteenth century. The Latin text uses the word "animus," which Jean de Meun has rendered as "coraige." B. Radice's translation, *The Letters of Abelard and Heloise* (London, New York: Penguin Books, 1974), in which this letter is number five, notes that Héloïse here uses an idea from Boethius's translation of a work of Aristotle, yet I must admit to being a little troubled by the translation "heart" for the Latin "animus," which usually means spirit or even soul. In that same paragraph Héloïse cites Matthew's gospel and uses the traditional "cor" for heart. In my view, the use of "animus" strongly suggests a spiritual element to her lament.

22. Our main source of knowledge of Abélard's remarkable career is his own (often self-serving) autobiographical letter, but its general claims can be verified by independent sources.

23. Anselm argued that men, themselves imperfect and living in an imperfect world, had a conception of perfection, embodied in God. Because their cognition of the perfect could not come from the imperfect, that cognition presupposed the existence of perfection, that is, of God. Anselm's ontological proof of God, while it provided an important point of debate for theologians, was not widely accepted by his contemporaries.

24. This citation from Bernard's *Patrologia latina* and the earlier one from Abélard's *Sic et Non,* are provided on p. 223 of the textbook *The Mainstream of Civilization,* 4th ed. (San Diego: Harcourt Brace Jovanovich, 1984), by the great medievalist Joseph Strayer and Hans Gatzke.

25. Radice, ed. and trans., *Letters of Abelard and Heloise,* 67–68.

26. The view of Hubert Silvestre, as cited by J. Marenbon, *The Philosophy of Peter Abélard* (Cambridge; New York: Cambridge University Press, 1997), 83. The quotation from Peter the Venerable appears on p. 35.

27. Cited by G. Duby, *The Age of the Cathedrals: Art and Society,* 980–1420, trans. E. Levieux and B. Thompson (Chicago: University of Chicago Press, 1981), 123, and in *Histoire de la France religieuse. T. I: Des dieux de la Gaule à la papauté d'Avignon,* ed. J. Le Goff and R. Rémond (Paris: Seuil, 1988), 347. The third clause of the first sentence appears only in the second source.

28. It remained the largest church in Western Christendom until the completion of the new Saint Peter's Basilica in Rome, in the sixteenth century.

29. Although we rarely can see traces of it today, painting covered the walls of most of these churches. Faint traces can be seen in places such as the abbey of Saint-Michel in Thiérarche; the best remaining examples survive outside of France, in Italy and Spain: one of the latter is currently housed at the Cloisters Museum in New York. Prof. Pierre Boulle informs me that the church of St-Savin-sur-Gartemps is the best surviving example in France.

30. P. Nora, et al., *Les Lieux de Mémoire* (Paris: Gallimard, 1986), 3 volumes. Now available in English translation: *Realms of Memory: Rethinking the French Past,* trans. A. Goldhammer (New York: Columbia University Press, 1996), 3 vols.

31. These phrases come from Bernard's letter to King Wladislaus of Bohemia, in which he asked the king to take the cross. Cited in P. Cole, *The Preaching of the Crusades to the Holy Land,* 1095–1270 (Cambridge, MA: Medieval Academy of America, 1991), 48–49.

32. Bernard's letter to Eugene III, cited in Cole, *The Preaching of the Crusades,* 43.

33. G. Duby, *The Age of the Cathedrals,* trans. A. Goldhammer (Chicago: University of Chicago Press, 1981), 88.

34. Cited in Duby, *Age of the Cathedrals,* 98.

35. Most of the great stained-glass collections have been destroyed by wars and revolutions. Notre Dame of Paris has only one rose window surviving from its originals and Reims, bombed during World War I, has nothing left. The great cathedrals of more favored towns—Chartres, whose rose window is the Gothic rejoinder to Vézelay's tympanum, or Bourges, whose windows span several centuries of craftsmanship—survive still, offering us some indication of the glories of earlier times.

36. E. Panofsky, *Renaissance and Renascences in Western Art* (New York: Harper and Row, 1972; original edition 1960), demonstrates that these Gothic statues often directly copied earlier Roman models, such as figures on Roman sarcophygi.

37. Although many medieval (and later) texts used the word "man" to mean humankind, in this case "man" meant man. Medieval (male) authorities, following Ancient philosophers such as Aristotle or Patristic writers like Paul or Jerome, invariably denied that women had this higher level of reason.

38. Jerome, whose fourth-century Latin translation of the Christian Bible, the Vulgate, was the official Catholic text of Scriptures throughout the Middle Ages, denounced this story.

39. That Jerome should deny women such an important role is not surprising; his other writings demonstrate his profound misogyny. Joseph, Mary's husband, rarely appears in medieval iconography, except in the stories of the flight into Egypt and the adoration of the Magi, themes common in both Romanesque and Gothic art. The later Holy Family theme, so popular in Renaissance art, did not exist at all in medieval art.

40. Christianity initially presented the dichotomy between Heaven and Hell, follow-ing standard practice of most Mediterranean religions. In part because of the enormous demand among the laity for prayers for the dead, the Church gradu-ally promulgated the existence of Purgatory, a sort of holding area for those not quite worthy enough to enter into Heaven at the moment of death. Those pray-ing for the dead sought to release them from Purgatory. In Catholic doctrine, all those in Purgatory on the Day of Judgment would go to Heaven.

41. Some Italian merchants adopted Arabic numerals in the thirteenth century; they did not spread widely in France until four hundred years later.

42. Cited in G. Huppert, *After the Black Death: A Social History of Early Modern Europe* (Bloomington, IN: Indiana University Press, 1986), 14.

43. D. Miller, ed., *The Lewis Mumford Reader* (New York: Pantheon, 1986), 115.

44. The "plan" was economic rationality, rather than some specific urban blueprint. Readers might contrast the relative chaos of lower Manhattan, which followed economic needs, with the extremely planned layout of Washington, DC, created from Pierre L'Enfant's blueprint.

45. Contemporary continental France has 37 urban agglomerations with 100,000 or more people. Twenty-four of them were the capital of a Roman *pagus*. Four others were a Roman military town (*castrum*), and nine have no known Roman roots.

46. Some historians estimate as many as 21 million people lived within the bound-aries of today's European France, but that seems a bit high. These estimates rely on a 1328 investigation of hearths that lists about 2.47 million hearths in the kingdom of France, but has some omissions. Extrapolating from overall figures to today's France on a proportional basis makes little sense, because some of the areas thus included (such as the Alps) had very small populations. A figure of 18 million within today's European France seems a reasonable estimate.

47. D. Barthélemy, *La société dans le comté de Vendôme de l'an mil au XIVᵉ siècle* (Paris: Fayard, 1993), 225, for the figures on that region; Dupaquier, *Histoire de la population française,* for the others. These Norman figures suggest total popu-lation densities of 50–65 people/km^2; by way of contrast, the department of the Creuse had only 39 people/km^2 in 1801, and that of the Indre a mere 30.

48. In addition, several cities then outside of France, but now part of it, had large populations: Strasbourg (25,000), Metz (25,000), Marseille (12,000–15,000), and Avignon (15,000).

49. This passage, and the earlier one from al-Farabi, are cited in C. Mazzoli-Guintard, *Villes d'al-Andalus: L'Espagne et le Portugal à l'époque musulmane (VIIᵉ-XVᵉ siècles)* (Rennes: Presses Universitaires de Rennes, 1996), 29, 81.

50. Those living in the area covered by the *ban* (area of authority) would have been required to do their baking in the oven owned by the count.

51. The Paris and Soissons areas no longer produce much wine, due to climate changes after 1580.

52. The French verse is, alas, not well suited to translation: *Bon roi qui ot non Phelippe / Qui volentiers moilloit sa pipe / Du bon vin qui estoit du blanc.* Cited in R. Dion, *Histoire de la vigne et du vin en France des origins au XIXe siècle* (Paris: Dion, 1959; Flammarion, 1977), 240.

53. The figures from Paris come from the published tax rolls, J. Favier, *Les Contribuables Parisiens à la fin de la guerre de Cent Ans* (Geneva, Paris: Droz, 1970); those from Toulouse are taken from J. Mundy, *Men and Women at Toulouse in the Age of the Cathars* (Toronto: Pontifical Institute of Medieval Studies, 1990), 34, n. 72. This relationship—roughly 50 percent more women headed households in northern as against southern France—remained true at least until the seventeenth century.

54. J. Merriman, *Red City: Limoges and the French Nineteenth Century* (New York and Oxford: Oxford University Press, 1985), 12. Another observer of the time wrote of the butchers themselves: "They delight in the most excessive filth. Under no circumstances will they change their clothes" (Merriman, 13).

55. The comparative figures for different types of animals are: sheep—188,522 (1293) as against 208,000 (4,000/week, in 1433), oxen—30,346 as against 12,500, calves—19,604 versus 26,000, pigs—30,784 compared to 31,200 ($^1/_3$ of them salted). The figures from 1433 are rough weekly estimates, that of 1293 purports to be an accurate annual figure. Guillebert de Metz, the source for 1433, suggests that the city's inhabitants drank 700 tons of wine a day. His figures all sound a bit high, given the decline the in city's population between 1348–1433.

56. G. Duby, ed., *Histoire de la France urbaine*. T. 2: A. Chédeville, J. Le Goff, and J. Rossiaud, *La Ville Médiévale* (Paris: Seuil, 1980), 284–285.

57. Kirshner and Morrison, eds., *Medieval Europe*, 97–99. I am here using "shilling" for *solidi* (which became *sol*, then *sou*, in French): $^1/_{20}$th of a pound.

58. The two texts appear in Kirshner and Morrison, *Medieval Europe*, 102 and 90–91.

59. A. Chédeville *et alia*, *La Ville Médiévale*, 168–169, taken from Guibert de Nogent.

60. Kirshner and Morrison, *Medieval Europe, 97.*

Chapter Four

The Dark Interlude:
The Black Death and the End
of Medieval France, c. 1270–c. 1492

The thriving, vibrant civilization in place by the year 1100 produced two centuries of extraordinary demographic, economic, cultural, and political growth. Toward the end of the thirteenth century, however, the great expansion began to slow. Demographic growth ended. The Great Famine of 1315 ushered in a period of scarcity, high prices, and malnutrition. When the Black Death reached France in the spring of 1348, it encountered a population debilitated by more than a generation of undernourishment. The Grim Reaper took a terrible harvest: between a quarter and a third of the French population died in a single year.

In the two centuries from the death of Saint Louis (1270) until the European "discovery" of the Americas, medieval France died a slow, agonizing death. The population, which doubled between 1050 and 1250, declined by nearly 50 percent between 1348 and 1450. Plague and war disrupted the economy and transformed society. France became a new, free society. Saint Louis died in the midst of an important wave of emancipations of serfs, but for most of the thirteenth century the majority of France's rural population lived in servitude. By the end of the fifteenth century, except in the duchy of Burgundy, virtually all French peasants were free people. The massive population loss helped the survivors to achieve important economic gains. Individual farms became larger, often in the wake of remarriages by those who had lost a spouse to the dreaded disease. Low-paid workers, above all women and male day laborers, received important pay increases, due to the labor shortage. The available statistics suggest for many areas that women's wage levels reached 80 percent of those of men by 1450, a ratio reached again in France only at the start of the third millennium.

Late medieval France left a mixed cultural legacy. Many of the leading European intellectuals lived and worked in France, but cultural supremacy had certainly shifted to Italy by the late fourteenth century. French architecture evolved slowly, remaining strongly Gothic in flavor well into the sixteenth century. French painting, save for the remarkable miniatures in illuminated manuscripts, could not compare with that of Italy or, in the fifteenth century, of the Low Countries. The leading "French" painters and sculptors of the fifteenth century did not work in Paris, but in the outskirts of the French political sphere, in Flanders and Burgundy. The relative position of France in European culture in the medieval centuries can be grasped by the origins and patterns of the great artistic trends. The two great styles of the twelfth and thirteenth centuries, Romanesque and Gothic, both emanated out from France to the rest of Europe. The great artistic trend of the fourteenth and early fifteenth centuries, Renaissance art, came to France, not from it.

War with England dominated French politics from the late thirteenth century until the middle of the fifteenth century. The fifteenth-century conflict overlapped with a civil war between members of the French royal family. The civil war really ended only with the death of Charles the Rash of Burgundy in 1477. His daughter, Mary of Burgundy, grandmother of the Habsburg Emperor Charles V, essentially transmitted the quarrel across international borders.

The period from 1270 to about 1450 marked a transition from medieval to Renaissance France. In the larger Eurasian context, the thirteenth-century surge of the Mongols transformed the political system and created new patterns of trade. The Turkish defeat of the western, largely French Crusaders at Nicopolis (1396) helped seal the fate of the Byzantine Empire, which disappeared with the fall of Constantinople in 1453. For at least one hundred years before the city's fall, however, knowledge flowed steadily from East to West, helping provide Western Europeans with their first real knowledge of ancient scholars such as Archimedes, and with a fuller range of the writings of Plato, Aristotle, and others. This knowledge helped fuel the Italian Renaissance, which provided an intellectual foundation for the renewed European offensive of the late fifteenth century.

The period 1348–1450 stands out for its special demographic characteristics. The constant revival of the plagues and the steady decline in France's (and Europe's) population marks a dramatic contrast to the steady population growth of the tenth through thirteenth centuries and to the period after 1450. Let us begin with the calamity of 1348, for, as John Bell Henneman has written: "For Philip VI, the Black Death was the crowning misfortune of a far from happy reign."[1]

∼ The Plague

> *And no bells tolled and nobody wept no matter his loss because almost everyone expected death . . . And people said and believed, "This is the end of the world."*[2]
>
> Anonymous chronicler of Siena

In the late autumn of 1347 a strange new disease appeared in Mediterranean Europe, brought there on ships from the Levant. Mediterranean France, like Italy, quickly fell under its terrible blow. This disease, called then the Black Death because of the purplish-black pustules that formed on the skin of its victims, devastated Europe like nothing before or since. In 1348, something like one-third of the population of Western Europe died of this disease. Georges Duby estimates that four to five million people died in the north of France alone.

Victims caught the disease, showed the dreaded pustules, and, writhing in agony, died within two or three days of the first infection. Entire towns virtually disappeared: Albi lost 75 percent of its population. Certain religious communities, like the Franciscan houses of Marseille or Carcassonne, lost every friar. Everywhere, people recoiled in terror from this hecatomb. As so often happens, the massive suffering led to a search for scapegoats. In southern France and in Flanders and Brabant, as in the Rhineland, Christians turned against Jews, whom they massacred by the thousands.

How can one imagine the impact of so vast, so overwhelming a disaster? To put the epidemic in modern American terms, one hundred million people would have to die of the same, hitherto unknown disease in the next six months. People of the time had no idea how to fight the disease. Many of those who tried to assist the sick caught the disease and died.

The plague exacerbated social tensions, because many of the rich sought relief on rural estates in order to escape from the crowded, unsanitary conditions of the towns. The poor stayed put and died by the millions. Even so, some of the rich and powerful succumbed: the Queen, the Crown Princess, and the chancellor of France were among the victims. For part of 1348, King Philip VI simply wandered through the kingdom, his council dismissed, without a chancellor to oversee his administration. Notaries, whose trade brought them into close contact with the families of the recently deceased, died in astounding numbers. Those who survived, often fled. Local government, which often relied on royal officials who came from the ranks of notaries, fell rapidly into chaos. The sudden deaths of tax collectors, for example, meant that the government could not get accurate accounting for levies.

The plague remained a central part of French life from 1348 to 1721, when the last outbreak occurred in southern France. It would go away, only to return to take its usual massive quota of victims, above all the young, the old, the poor, and women.

The Dance of Death, Parish Church of La Ferte-Loupiere, fifteenth century. After the plague of 1348, French (and European) art frequently presented images of death and suffering.

The later plagues tended to be more localized, in part because authorities enforced ruthless quarantines on all infected areas. We now know that rat fleas spread the disease, but medieval Europeans had little sense of that connection. They focused on quarantine—on preventing people *and* goods from leaving infested regions. Despite such efforts, the plague remained virulent from the 1350s until 1420. The population somewhat recovered from the initial assault by means of a sharp upsurge in births. The fact that the plague disproportionately struck children and the aged helped the population recover. Major epidemics returned in 1353–1357, 1378–1380, 1403, and 1418. The cumulative effect of the plagues of the period of 1348–1418 drove the population living in France (2000 European borders) from 18 million down to as few as 10 million. Paris, which had been a city of 200,000, declined to 75,000.

The plague alone did not sap the vitality of Paris. The constant warfare of the 1410s and 1420s made commerce difficult and exacerbated famines. An unknown bourgeois lamented the fate of the poor in the hard winter of 1420–1421, when groups of twenty or thirty children cried out through the city, "I am dying of this hunger!" as they lay "dying of hunger and of cold on the rubbish heaps." He spoke of the wolves "who were so hungry at this time that they came into the good towns at night and did a very great deal of damage, often swimming across the Seine . . . [to] dig up and eat newly buried corpses . . . and in several places they ate women and children." Three years later, he wrote that Paris had 24,000 empty houses.

In the countryside, the massive decline in population had fundamental consequences. Peasants abandoned the cultivation of the poorer soils. More than 20 percent of the land under cultivation in the early 1340s no longer felt the plough by the 1380s. Entire villages ceased to exist, never to reappear. The shortage of labor led to immediate changes in the social and economic conditions of the peasantry. Average holdings increased dramatically in size. The constant deaths and remarriages enabled the new peasant households to amass holdings large enough to feed a family. In some outlying areas, such as the hills of the Massif Central, peasants returned to the system of communal households (*frérêches*). The partners were supposed to share the holding "like brothers (*frères*)." These *frérêches* lasted for centuries in certain regions, like the Morvan and the Auvergne.

The dramatic shortage of labor obviously drove up wages, despite the efforts of town and central governments to fix wage rates. King John vainly sought to impress upon the deputies to the Estates General of 1356 his intentions in this matter:

> As for the shortage of workers and laborers, we have made certain statutes and ordinances . . . [and] we wish them to be kept, point by point, as to penalties and fines, and so have accorded and given leave to high justiciars, each in his land, to inflict the said penalties and levy the said fines . . . and to judge those who disobey, and in cases in which they refuse to act or are negligent, we or our men will levy them in their place, and the giver will pay the same fine as the taker.[3]

The constant reiteration of such ordinances bears witness to their lack of success. Day laborers received better wages, better food, and better wine to drink. Peasants obtained better terms from their landlords. In most parts of France, the remaining serfs obtained their freedom in the second half of the fourteenth century.

The great peasant rebellions in France, the Jacquerie (1358), and England, Wat Tyler's Rebellion (1381), played a key role in enfranchisement, but serfdom collapsed in both places primarily because freeing the peasants made economic sense. Yields on large estates had long been well below those on peasant farms; landlords increasingly turned to using paid farmers, often sharecroppers in France, to work their estates. No longer needing a large labor force for the demesne, landlords found commutation of serfdom to be an economically intelligent solution. In the middle of the fifteenth century (1439), the state even usurped the traditional seigneurial right to levy *taille* (direct tax).

War, Plague, and Social Mobility

The image offered by the peasantry after 1360 is not that of a simple reduction (by half) of the earlier image; it is that of a vigorous society, more dynamic, in some ways tempered by the trial it had undergone.[5]

Guy Bois, describing the peasantry of Normandy

The Black Death disrupted families at all levels of society, accelerating the process of social reorganization already evident in the early fourteenth century. The deaths of so many people made for advantageous conditions for social climbers. Consolidation of property followed multiple deaths, leaving survivors with considerable resources.

The 1311 and 1355 lists of fief holders in the county of Vendôme reveal the patterns familiar all over France. The list of 1311 includes such commoners as Jean de l'Espine, but the vast majority of the one hundred fifty-eight fiefs listed still belonged to a noble. In 1355, however, one reads constantly of men (or women) like Colin de Bois-Raoul, *bourgeois* of the town of Vendôme or Raoul Germain, a simple carpenter. Jean de l'Espine, a *bourgeois* of Vendôme, had become the second most important fief holder in the county.

This purchase of noble rural property by the richer people of the towns (merchants, rent holders, and lawyers), although theoretically illegal, had long been accepted practice. Those summoning feudal armies instituted a special tax, the *francs fiefs,* collected on commoners owning fiefs to pay for the knightly service originally attached to the fief. The example of Vendôme shows how important it had become by the mid-fourteenth century, but the slaughter of nobles in the Hundred Years' War—seventy-five hundred of them died at Crécy (1347), Poitiers (1356), and Agincourt (1415) alone—vastly accelerated the process.

Many seventeenth-century French noble families traced their lineage back to precisely this era (late fourteenth century); they represented only the tip of the iceberg. The statistics compiled in the seventeenth century by François Godet de Soude, recently reworked by American historian Ellery Schalk, demonstrate the extent to which new families entered the nobility in the second half of the fourteenth century. Almost one-third (916) of the 2,826 families ennobled between 1345 and 1660 crossed that threshold between 1350 and 1409. The average of 153 per decade (peaking at 216 in the 1370s) was more than double that of most ensuing decades. The murderous slaughters of Courtrai or Crécy, coupled with the effects of the plague, necessitated a massive influx of new blood. Fifteenth-century sources do not speak much about noble "blood," in sharp contrast to those of the late sixteenth century, for whom it became an obsession.

The plague and the Hundred Years' War combined to redefine the "French." The constant warfare brought many soldiers into France: men from Spain, England, Brabant, the Swiss cantons, Germany, and elsewhere. Given that ordinary people began to adopt surnames at this time, we should not wonder that so many of them took on a geographic name. These still-common surnames included Langlois (the Englishman), Lallemand (the German), or Lespagnol (the Spaniard). The widespread use of such names in modern France demonstrates the important waves of immigrants, mostly men, from surrounding regions. The surname Le Breton suggests, too, that late medieval French people still viewed the kingdom's Celtic residents as foreigners.

The fifteenth-century war with England enhanced people's sense of being "French" by giving them a contrasting entity, the "English," against whom to identify themselves. The English moved out of the French cultural orbit, as works such as Chaucer's *Canterbury Tales* attest. The Francophone Edward III claimed to be king of France through his mother, daughter of Philip IV, of whom Edward was the only surviving grandson. Henry V knew scarcely any French at all and had a dubious claim to the throne of England, let alone that of France. The two men accurately reflected the cultural formation of their peers.

This heightened awareness of being "French" adversely affected the Jews of France. Philip IV had persecuted them for financial reasons. Charles VI expelled them from the kingdom in 1396; they would not legally return until the 1550s, when Henry II allowed Iberian *Conversos* to enter certain French port cities. Moreover, when the king of France inherited regions with Jewish populations, such as Provence, he soon expelled (1501) them, too. Many of these Jews fled into the eastern Mediterranean; they found the Islamic rulers of the Ottoman Empire and of North African principalities to be far more tolerant than the Christians of western Europe.

The expulsions of Jews had adverse economic effects, above all in Provence, where they had very large communities and often dominated the trade of major towns. Although the plague and the Hundred Years' War, by encouraging the creation of a climate hostile to Jews, had something to do with this economic change, their larger economic effects were much more direct. The plague often helped individuals to become wealthier, due to consolidation of multiple family properties, but France as a whole did not prosper in the late fourteenth and early fifteenth centuries. Trade fluctuated wildly, but the general trend worked against several important regions of France. Champagne's fairs lost their critical role in western European trade, in part due to the political conflicts between the kings of France and England and the ongoing tensions between the Flemish cloth towns and the King of France. Italian merchants set up factors in Bruges and shipped their goods by sea. The relative economic decline of Troyes and Provins in subsequent years had one interesting side effect: many of their medieval buildings still survive, making Troyes and Provins today the ideal places to visit for a taste of medieval French life.

Flanders underwent a roller coaster ride of development. The kings of England continuously used wool exports as a weapon. Cutting supplies of wool to Flemish looms created social and economic chaos, destabilizing a key region of the kingdom of France. The Flemish weavers often allied with the English, as first Jacques van Artevelde and then his son Philip would do during their revolts (1340s and 1380s). In the long run, Flanders had to find other, more reliable sources of wool (above all, Spain), as England began to shift to cloth rather than wool exports, which declined by almost 80 percent between 1300 and 1450.

Economic instability plagued many French towns. The constant royal policy of currency manipulation did not help matters. Whenever they had trouble collecting taxes, kings reminted or revalued the coins in circulation to raise money, which undercut the French economy.[6] Throughout most of the fifteenth century, France seems to have suffered, like much of western Europe, from a bullion shortage. This shortage, too, sapped economic strength. Arbitrary revaluation cut off trade: no one wanted to trade products for super-valued currency. Heavily alloyed coins, like the "red" silver coins of which the bourgeois journal keeper of Paris complained around 1420, had so little silver that merchants refused to accept them.

Despite these difficult conditions, France made major economic progress in certain industries, often due to technological change. The spinning wheel and the fulling mill spread (mainly in the north), as did the water-driven bellows, which permitted the construction of the first blast furnaces (after 1380). The higher temperatures achieved by such techniques allowed more advanced metallurgy—a technology that focused, for the most part, on war materials, such as the vastly superior armor of the final stages of the Hundred Years' War.[7] The spread of paper-making technology increased rapidly in the second half of the fourteenth century, so that early fifteenth-century scribes could rely on a steady supply of rag-based paper, rather than on the much more expensive parchment. The widespread existence of paper, and the improvements in metallurgy, eventually paved the way for the invention of printing in the 1440s in Rhineland Germany. This fundamental transformation, one of the three great changes in the history of human communication, spread more slowly to France than to some other areas, such as Italy. Printing took root in France only in the late fifteenth century.

In what must rank as one of most little known, yet supremely important changes of the fourteenth century, Charles V changed time itself. Medieval Frenchmen lived according to canonical and seasonal hours. Each day had twelve hours of light and twelve of darkness, so the hours varied in length from forty to eighty minutes. Church bells rang seven times a day, for the canonical hours. Charles V, following the example of several northern Italian cities, introduced (1370) in Paris a modern clock, striking the hour every sixty minutes. He then ordered all church towers to ring their bells for the hours in time with his clocks. In short, Charles V introduced the modern notion of time into France. His innovation rapidly spread into provincial towns, whose earliest clocks, like the famous one still present today on Rouen's *rue du grand horloge,* initially had but a single hand, for the hours.

Charles V introduced many other innovations. He encouraged scholars to translate the great works of antiquity into French, created the first permanent royal library, and issued ordinances on all aspects of state activity. He, more than any other king, laid the legal foundation for the early modern French state, with his great ordinances of 1372, 1373, and 1379. Let us turn now to the forging of that state, hardened by the fires of the great War.

⌁ Creating the Central State, from Philip the Fair to Louis XI

> He [the prince] must singularly love the good and profit of his country and people, and this, rather than his private profit, ought to occupy all of his attention.
>
> Christine de Pisan, *The Book of the Body Politic* (*c.* 1407)

As human communities grow, so, too does their conception of the commonwealth or public good. Small, isolated rural communities often have a quite specific concept of the "commons," one that survives in modern English as the word to describe the meadow shared by the animals of all. Medieval and early modern French villagers used that precise word, commons, to describe those parts of the parish's land, not only meadows, but woods and waters, they shared. The rapid growth of population and the increasingly interdependent economy of the twelfth and thirteenth centuries, however, helped create a larger sense of the "commonwealth." The public good, even at the village level, had always involved more than just lands held in common; everyone understood that the village itself had collective needs to assure its survival, and thus the survival of its members. Someone had to feed the poor, to employ the landless, to tend for the sick, to see to the broad education of the children, to offer protection. Above all, someone had to dispense justice.

Medieval society evolved different institutions to share these responsibilities. The Church everywhere provided much of the stewardship of the commonwealth: feeding the poor, caring for the sick, and creating the literate. Lay people, too, participated in these activities. Landlords, often acting from an ethos derived from the old responsibilities of the *paterfamilias,* provided work for the landless and relief to the poor. They sought, often for reasons of enlightened self-interest, to preserve some of the resources of the community, above all its wood. The king and the seigneurs provided order, through their courts and their collective military force. In some cases, above all in towns but in some villages, too, the inhabitants themselves created institutions, like town councils, to oversee their collective good. Town councils quickly took up precisely the traditional public matters: food supply, poor relief, protection, justice. The guilds also shared in this stewardship of the "public good," a phrase their statutes use again and again to justify the listed rules. They offered stewardship by means of regulating all facets of production, as well as by providing relief and education to members, their families, and all those who wanted to participate in their sector of the economy.

The king and the regional princes claimed collective responsibility for the "public good" or commonwealth. The emergence of Aristotle as "The Philosopher" led political writers and their masters to adopt Aristotle's terminology and assumptions. They took his definitions of tyranny—"tyranny is just that arbitrary power of an individual which is responsible to no one, and governs all alike, whether equals or betters, with a view to its own advantage, not to that of its subjects"—and justice, which was the highest good of political organization. Aristotle argued that "governments which have a regard to the common interest are constituted in accordance with strict principles of justice, and are therefore true forms; but those which regard only the interest of the rulers are all defective and perverted forms, for they are despotic, whereas a state is a community of freemen." Fourteenth-century French people understood Aristotle's maxim that the state "aims at the highest good," which was not merely the preservation of society and its members but the attainment of the "good life," a condition both moral and material.[9] His ideas fitted well with traditional Christian precepts about the moral superiority of the proper state.

As far back as the time of Clovis, the bishops sought to vest him with the *auctoritas,* or overarching authority of the commonwealth. That one-to-one correlation between the commonwealth and the king (or, in some cases, Pope) as its steward hardly prevailed in the Middle Ages, but some theorists sought to make it so. The dominant perspectives of the thirteenth through fifteenth centuries, that is, the period of the creation of the central state, were those of the king as the father of his subjects and of the king and the great individuals of the kingdom sharing the stewardship of the commonwealth. The familial nature of the kingship enhanced this second perspective.

Public political discourse in France focused on the "public good" or the "commonwealth." When representative bodies (estates) began to appear in the early fourteenth century, documents drawn up for their meetings invariably mentioned the public good, and so did the princes who called the meetings.[10] The deputies of the Estates of Burgundy of 1460 wrote to duke Philip the Good that:

> we are all together, those of the Clergy, the Nobles, and of the Good Towns, representing the people of all the estates of the duchy of Burgundy and the county of Charolais, assembled in this town of Dijon, for the good and the commonwealth of the said *pays.*[11]

Estates quickly established three bedrock principles of consultation: (1) that what touches all must be deliberated upon by all; (2) when the cause ceases, the effect ceases; and (3), that the three orders had to agree unanimously to important decisions, such as a new tax. These principles meant that all of the powerful men (men only) of the community had to participate in decisions that affected the commonwealth and that such assemblies would have to be called on a regular basis, because the "cause" of a given meeting gave rise only to a temporary remedy.[12] In practice, this second principle provided protection from taxation without representation, because the end of a given war led immediately to the cessation of the taxes levied to pay for it. The response of the Burgundian deputies, cited above, also alerts us to the composition of these early assemblies: deputies from the clergy, nobility, and the towns. In fourteenth- and fifteenth-century assemblies, ecclesiastical and noble landlords represented the countryside; the town deputies represented only town dwellers. Following along lines laid out by Aristotle, as well as long-standing practice both in Germanic and Roman cultures, nonfree people (i.e., serfs) had no right to participation, because they were not citizens. Free peasants constituted an anomalous group. As the "subjects" of the landlords, they did not have to be consulted, because their lord would look after their interests. Such "representation" offends our modern sensibilities, which view peasants and landlords as opponents, but on the key issue debated by most assemblies, taxation, the landlords and peasants did make common cause against the townsmen. The unanimity clause—"that the voice of the two estates may not conclude for the third," as King John put it in 1355—meant that levies had to take into account urban and rural interests.

Citizens, those men who held a certain property and standing in the community, alone had a right to be heard. These early fourteenth-century representative bodies, in France as elsewhere in Europe, thus evolved from a combination of the traditional feudal obligation of lords to ask the counsel of their vassals and from the Classical traditions of a mixed constitution, as laid out above all in the writings of Aristotle. As Marc Bloch eloquently put it:

> The originality of the latter system [feudalism] consisted in the emphasis it placed on the idea of an agreement capable of binding the rulers; and in this way, oppressive as it may have been to the poor, it has in truth bequeathed to our Western civilization something with which we still desire to live.[13]

On all fronts, French society marched toward an ever larger view of the commonwealth. Fourteenth-century legislation invariably differentiated free peasants from serfs in matters such as taxation or jurisdiction. No longer serfs, these peasants thus had a different relationship with the central state, embodied in the king or, in some cases, an apanaged prince. In the fourteenth century, the king had limited ties to peasants living outside his demesne; the subjects of high justiciars, in reality, answered to their lords. Nobles and townsmen were citizens, with ties both to the commonwealth and to the king as an individual. Peasants were subjects, tied to their lord and, more loosely, to the lord of lords, the king. By the end of the fifteenth century, however, the king had direct ties to all of his subjects. He levied taxes on all commoners, and all were subject to his justice, at least on appeal.

The administrative apparatus of this state emerged slowly in the centuries after Louis IX's death. In the early fourteenth century, the Parlement became permanent at Paris, and King Philip IV created another specialized central court, the Chamber of Accounts, which audited the books of all royal financial officials. Philip made the transition from royal finance based on lordship to finance based on sovereignty; the King of France slowly came to be the head of a state, not simply the lord of an exceptionally large demesne.[14] By the time of Philip's death (1314), France had had nearly a generation of broad-based state taxation, of extensive royal court oversight of local affairs, and of ongoing military activity. At the local level, the bailiffs coordinated all three of these governmental activities: French bailiffs thus shared a combination of judicial, legislative, and executive powers. This combination of powers in the hands of officials would remain a defining characteristic of the monarchy until its demise in the eighteenth century.

Philip's expenditures on military matters far exceeded those of his predecessors. He spent more than 2.1 million *livres* from 1294 to1295 on the Gascony campaign alone. Normal royal revenues could not hope to pay for such an expedition, so Philip sought additional sources of money. Not content with the normal annual tallage paid by the Jews (15,000 *l.p.*), he extorted 215,000 *l.p.*, from them for the 1294 campaign. Twelve years later, he expelled Jews from the entire kingdom and confiscated their property, worth over a million *livres,* according to some contemporary estimates. France had a large Jewish community at this time, between 100,000 and 150,000 people. Most of them lived along the Mediterranean or in Champagne or Paris, although many French towns, like Dijon, had small Jewish quarters.

Philip did not stop with dispossessing the Jews. He regularly debased his currency, making large profits in 1296 and again in 1298–1299 (1.2 million *l.*). Public protest forced Philip to call an assembly of clergy, nobles, and town deputies, soon named the Estates General, to discuss reminting a sound coinage (1303). Italian sources suggest that Philip's need for bullion to carry out the reminting led to another of his confiscations: the seizure of the treasure of the Templars at Paris, in 1307. Philip also seized all Temple properties throughout France, and under threat of a similar action, the Hospitallers agreed to pay the king a huge fine. Although the evidence indicates that Philip actually believed accounts of the Jews and the Templars profaning the host and carrying out other "impious" activities, nonetheless, his financial needs certainly dictated these unscrupulous activities. Moreover, Philip acted in a faithless and illegal manner toward other groups, too: he levied taxation on church property without consent (1294) and essentially reneged on the repayment of the great loan of that year (800,000 *l.*), owed primarily to the burghers of his walled towns.

Philip's financial chicanery gave great impetus to the development of permanent governmental structures, operating by fixed and known rules. Philip wanted to obtain regular revenue; his subjects wanted him to stick to known legal action. The need for a mutually agreeable solution to the financial problem drove Philip to convene assemblies of leading members of the three orders—clergy, nobles, and townsmen—to discuss taxes and other important matters, such as coinage reform. French political society created a pyramid of assemblies, starting at the bailiwick level, moving up to provincial estates, and to the supra-regional bodies, somewhat misleadingly called

The Persecutions of the Jews. This late thirteenth-century manuscript shows one of the many pogroms carried out against France's medieval Jews.

SOURCE: The Granger Collection, New York.

the Estates General, which met for two broad areas: the Estates General of Langue d'Oïl (north) and of Langue d'Oc (south).

These Estates Generals did not actually vote the taxes or take definitive actions. In fact, at no time did anyone suggest that they had legislative authority. Medieval political theory believed the king discovered the law, not that he made it. To fourteenth-century assemblies, the right to dispense justice formed the essence of rulership. The king wanted to preserve his role as the supreme judge in the kingdom, who alone could "discover" new law; the deputies wanted their local assemblies to maintain ultimate authority over local customs and taxes. Deputies to the Estates General would listen to the proposals of the king and his men, but their assent, although it served a vital political purpose, was not binding on anyone. They had to return to their home provinces to seek approval from local assemblies, which alone had the authority to authorize collection of local taxes. This cumbersome procedure remained in force throughout the fourteenth century and, with some modifications, in the fifteenth as well. Even the Estates General of 1560 insisted on ratification of new taxes by bailiwick assemblies. Although nineteenth- and twentieth-century historians have often accused later French kings of fiscal absolutism, in fact they believed themselves bound by the agreements reached with estates in the fourteenth and fifteenth centuries. The ransom taxes voted in 1363, for example, were never collected in provinces that had not been represented at the meeting.

Philip the Fair laicized governmental administration by appointing the first nonclerical chancellor, by removing the royal treasure from the Templars, and by institutionalizing state control of the Church. Philip won a complete victory in his conflict with the Papacy about royal supremacy over the French Church. In 1298, Philip and Pope Boniface VIII began a quarrel about a new tax, and about their respective rights over the clergy. In 1302, Boniface issued the most extreme statement of papal supremacy, *Unam Sanctam,* which asserted that all seeking salvation had to get it through the Roman Pontiff, and that all kings had to be subject to the Pope. Philip called an assembly of the French clergy at Paris (1303), which stated the basis of the doctrine known as Gallicanism: that the French Church had control of itself, through Church councils, under the aegis of the King. Philip demanded that Boniface submit to the judgment of such a council, and sent one of his henchmen, Guillaume de Nogaret, to so inform Boniface. Nogaret instead seized the Pope and his retinue at Anagni (in central Italy), roughed them up a bit, and then released the aging Pontiff. Boniface died less than a month later.

The new Pope, Benedict XI, lasted only a few months; his successor, Clement V (Bernard de Got, archbishop of Bordeaux), spent most of his Papacy wandering around southern France, often staying at the papal castle in Avignon. The next Pope, John XXII, settled in Avignon, where all Popes resided until 1378. The Avignon Popes proved a very tractable ally of the king of France. In 1311, for example, Clement V went along with Philip's destruction of the Templars. Leaders of the Temple, accused of homosexuality, of blasphemy, and of many other "crimes," went to the stake in 1314. French kings used the papal alliance to remove from cathedral chapters their independent right to elect bishops, which passed effectively to the King. In 1378, the Papacy, badly damaged by the "Babylonian Captivity" at Avignon, suffered a further blow: assemblies of cardinals elected two Popes, one each in Rome and Avignon, a situation that lasted until 1423. Philip IV's conflict with Boniface profoundly destabilized the Catholic Church and did much to undermine the moral authority of both the Pope and the Church.

A Death in the Family: The Hundred Years' War, 1337–1380

> *Because the frauds, malice, and new actions of our enemies have greatly burdened and damaged our kingdom—its churches are violated, our subjects robbed and pillaged, suffering great damages, with the aid of God, to obviate the evil will and hold of our enemies, who daily still do worse, who, with their allies, invade and damage our kingdom, we have called together and assembled the good men of all the three estates of our kingdom of Languedoïl and the lands of customary law.*[15]

King John, December 1355

CHRONOLOGY	1328–1380
1328	Philip VI of Valois chosen king of France; battle of Cassel
1329	Edward III does homage for Guyenne
1337	Philip VI confiscates Guyenne from Edward III of England; war starts
1340	Breton Civil War starts
1346	English rout the French at battle of Crécy
1348	Black Death arrives in France
1349	Death of Humbert of Dauphiné; province passes to French royal family; purchase of Montpellier
1356	English destroy French army at Poitiers; King John captured
1358	Jacquerie
1359	Peace of Brétigny
1360	Estates General of Langue d'Oil creates long-term taxation to pay John II's ransom
1363	Estates Generals create standing army and taxes to pay for it
1367–1374	Du Guesclin defeats the English; France regains lost provinces
1378	Battle of Roosebeke: French defeat Flemish militias
1378–1382	Rebellions at Paris, Rouen, and in rural south (Tuchins)
1380	Death of Charles V; "abolition" of taxes

The First Death of Chivalry: Crécy and Poitiers

"Who there knocks at this hour?"

Robert de Grandcamp, castellan of la Broye

"Open, open, castellan, it is the unfortunate king of France."

Philip VI, seeking refuge in the aftermath of Crécy

Philip IV's quarrels with Edward I of England over Guyenne and the county of Flanders proved to be the harbingers of problems to come. Philip's oldest son, Louis X, reigned only two years. His death in 1316 left the kingdom to his pregnant (second) wife and a seven-year-old daughter, Jeanne of France, born of his first wife, Margaret of Burgundy. The princes of the royal blood set up a Regency to wait for the birth of the child, who, if male, would be the obvious heir. Baby John lived only five days. The obvious question now became, who would rule France? The logical choice for most principalities would be the daughter. That a woman could inherit the throne, however, seemed far less clear because no woman had ever done so. Jeanne had two other strikes against her: her age and a terrible scandal involving her mother. Late in the reign of Philip IV, two of his daughters-in-law, Margaret of Burgundy and Blanche of Burgundy, were accused of adultery with two knights at Court. Philip executed the two knights and sentenced the two princesses to life imprisonment in convents. Jeanne of France thus faced suspicion that she was not Louis's child.

One of her uncles, Charles, supported her cause, as did many of the barons, but her senior uncle, Philip, seized power and had himself crowned king in 1317. He even despoiled Jeanne of the county of Champagne, which she inherited from her father's mother. Philip called a special assembly of barons, prelates, and teachers from the Sorbonne, who issued an ordinance claiming that the Crown of France, like the position of Emperor, could only be held by a man. Philip V ruled for only six years. He, too, left only daughters. Charles, who had championed the rights of Jeanne in 1316, now followed his brother's precedent, setting aside claims of all of his nieces and taking the throne. He, too, died without male issue.

The royal transitions of 1314 and 1316, taking place at the precise moment of a great famine, led to tremendous social and political upheaval. The nobility, upset at Philip IV's transgressions of its traditional rights and powers, created leagues against Louis X and Philip V. The nobility of Champagne demanded that Jeanne of France, the rightful heir to the county of Champagne, be given her inheritance; that is, they wanted to get out from under the direct rule of the King of France. In Normandy, the nobility extracted a clear statement of rights and privileges called the Norman Charter (1315), that gave Normans the right to consent to all taxation levied. The Charter thus gave legal foundation to the necessity of the assemblies of the Estates of Normandy, which alone had the right to vote its taxes. Other provinces tried to extract similar concessions, although generally with less success than the Normans.

Charles IV's death (1328) raised an even more thorny succession question than the deaths of his brothers. The precedents of 1316 and 1322, and the declaration of the assembly of 1317, established clearly the inability of a woman to inherit, but did little to solve the riddle posed in 1328. When Louis X and Philip V died, they had a living brother to inherit. Charles IV's closest male relative was his first cousin, Edward III of England, son of Philip IV's daughter, Isabelle. Jeanne of France had married Philip of Evreux, grandson of King Philip III; combined they provided another highly plausible royal couple. Should they have a son (as they did, in 1332), he would have had a strong legal claim, as grandson of Louis X. The assembly called by the senior prince of the royal blood, Philip, count of Valois, decided to go back to the descendants of sons of King Philip III, despite the fact that Philip IV had one living direct male descendant, his grandson, Edward III of England. The assembly decided that Valois, grandson of Philip III, should take the throne as Philip VI.

In the middle of the fourteenth century, royal lawyers invented a famous *ex post facto* justification for the actions of 1316, 1322, and 1328. They claimed the Salic Law, which stated that the oldest male in line of direct male issue became king, governed inheritance of the French throne. No document from 1328 makes any such claim. Indeed, as late as the sixteenth century, chancellor Michel de l'Hôpital would tell an Estates General (1561) that the highest duty of the Estates had been carried out by the meeting of 1328: the election of a new king.[16] The available evidence suggests that the assembly of 1328 believed that direct male heirs having run out, the throne passed to a new royal house. Ever after, chroniclers referred to the shift to the Valois dynasty in 1328, even though Philip VI was just as much a Capetian as Philip IV. The latter was Saint Louis's grandson, and the former his great-grandson.

Isabelle and Jeanne may have grumbled a bit but we have no evidence of any major objections to the legality of what transpired in 1328. Isabelle was in no position to act decisively on behalf of her son (then only sixteen), because she and her lover, the earl of Mortimer, had just invaded England, overthrowing, imprisoning, and murdering her husband. In 1328, she sought to make Edward King of England, not of France. The next year the young Edward did homage to Philip VI for Guyenne and Ponthieu, an homage he declared to be liege homage in 1331. The kings of France and of England had quarreled persistently over their respective rights in southwest France throughout the thirteenth and early fourteenth centuries. Edward III's declaration gave the King of France a strong legal weapon to use against his English vassal.

Phillip's agents intensified their activities in his Gascon lands: the king declared Edward a felonious vassal in May 1337, and confiscated the duchy of Guyenne. Yet Edward was no longer the callow youth of 1331. He had imprisoned his mother and murdered Mortimer. Firmly in control in England, he invaded Scotland, a traditional French ally. As part of his political response to Philip's action of 1337, Edward wrote to the Pope, claiming that Philip had unlawfully deprived him of the throne of France.

The term "Hundred Years' War" provides a neatness and a determinacy to the political and military events of the period 1337–1453 that bears little relation to reality. The various stages of the War had little to do with some sort of national conflict between "France" and "England." Each of the three major stages of the war reflected internal politics, above all in France, where the fighting took place. The first stage lasted from 1337 to 1359. During these years, England decisively defeated France at the battles of Crécy and Poitiers and forced King John of France to surrender nearly a third of his kingdom in the Peace of Brétigny (1359). The second stage, 1363–1380, reversed this verdict. Led by constable Bertrand du Guesclin, the French harassed the English out of all but Guyenne and the Calais enclave. The third stage began as a civil war in France between the Burgundian and Orléans branches of the royal family. The Burgundians allied with Henry V of England, who invaded Normandy, hoping to regain the duchy. Henry V's easy triumph at Agincourt (1415) encouraged him to seek a fatter prize: the throne of France. In the end, the French finally drove the English (1453) from the Continent, save for Calais.

This last stage of the Hundred Years' War was not some sort of precursor of great national conflicts of later times; it was a straightforward dynastic quarrel within the broad French royal family. That said, the long conflict between the two kings did encourage the development of national feeling. Kings encouraged such sentiments: fifteenth- and sixteenth-century French royal documents invariably used the phrase "our ancient enemies, the English." The documents from the fourteenth century differ considerably from those of the fifteenth. The great war of the 1340s and 1350s elicited relatively little "national" feeling, in part because kings Philip VI and John II faced opponents of direct recent French descent—grandsons of a French king—who claimed, by right of inheritance, to be King of France. The documents of the Agincourt (1415) war, however, place much more emphasis on the French–English dichotomy. Henry V, his propaganda notwithstanding, had no right to the throne of France; indeed, his father had usurped that of England. Henry really wanted Normandy, not so much because of some dubious ancient legal claim, but because it was one of the richest provinces in Europe. Little wonder that Henry's French contemporaries consistently used nationalist appeals, such as the fictitious Salic Law, to oppose him. The great heroine of the French resistance to the English, Joan of Arc, provides a living embodiment of such sentiments.

The War took place in fits and starts. Philip IV had fought several times with Edward I over Flanders. Philip captured the county, but his officials so infuriated the local population that an uprising at Bruges (1302) led to a massacre of its French garrison and a general revolt. At Courtrai, the weavers of the great textile cities massacred the French army sent to restore order, in the process redefining medieval warfare. Not only did an army consisting almost completely of infantry defeat the mounted knights, but the weavers refused to follow the customs of knightly fighting. When the knights tried to surrender, the weavers gave them the treatment usually reserved for infantry, death on the spot. Medieval battles had usually involved few knightly casualties—fewer than ten knights died at Bouvines, for example—because the winning side "courteously" held the knightly prisoners for ransom.[17] Knights could thus fight courageously, confident that, even if they lost, they would not die. The weavers of Bruges changed all that. In the great fourteenth-century battles, like Crécy (1346) and Poitiers (1356), the knights of the losing (French) side were slaughtered, not held for ransom. War became even more murderous in the fifteenth century, with the serious advent of artillery.

The discontent among in the Flemish towns spread to the peasantry. The villages held assemblies, elected captains, demanded an end to certain royal and comtal taxes, and refused to pay their tithes, especially to the enormously wealthy monasteries. Soon, they went beyond simple fiscal demands: some peasants wanted an end to the elaborate system of feudal seigneurialism and the expulsion of all lords from the countryside. The towns took up their cause. In 1325, a rebellion in Courtrai captured the count himself. Charles IV decided to put an end to this "plague of insurrection" by marching his great host to Flanders, but he died before he could leave.

Philip VI took up his predecessor's project, invading Flanders to restore its count and put down the peasant rebels. His force included some four thousand knights, one of the largest armies of the period. They encountered the peasants at Cassel (1328). After a bitter struggle, in which the peasants nearly prevailed, the knights feinted a retreat; when the peasant pikemen broke ranks to chase down the "retreating" cavalry, the latter wheeled their horses and annihilated the infantry. More than three thousand of them died on the field and thousands more in the reprisals that followed. Every village captain whom the French could capture, they decapitated or broke on the wheel.

The first part of the Hundred Years' War evolved directly out of the Flemish civil war. In the late 1330s, the weavers of Ghent, led by the rich cloth merchant Jacques van Artevelde, revolted again. When the count allied with Philip VI, the great towns turned to Edward. In January 1340, on the main square of Ghent, Edward received homage from the Gantois as King of France. At the naval battle of the Zwin, only twenty-four of the one hundred ninety French ships survived, and corpses floated up along the shore for days afterward. This triumph proved short-lived. In 1345, an uprising in Ghent murdered van Artevelde and put an end to English predominance in Flanders.

The English and French used proxies to fight in the early 1340s. In Brittany, the death of the childless duke John III (1341) allowed Philip VI to support the claim of John's niece, Jeanne de Penthièvre, wife of Philip's nephew, Charles of Blois. Most Bretons supported John III's half-brother, John of Montfort, married to Jeanne of Flanders. Montfort naturally turned to England for help. The "War of the Two Jeannes," who took up the cudgels for their prisoner husbands, finally ended in 1364, when Montfort became duke.[18]

Edward III decided to take matters into his own hands in 1346 by invading Normandy. He quickly captured many fortresses. Philip brought his entire feudal host in pursuit, so Edward retreated north, wishing to avoid battle with an army much larger than his own. On 26 August 1346, Philip forced Edward to fight at Crécy. Philip's experienced leaders opposed an attack on three grounds: (1) that their men needed a rest after a long march; (2) that the hard rain had turned the field into a quagmire, inappropriate for a cavalry charge; and (3) the rain had rendered the cords of the Genoese crossbowmen too slack to discharge their bolts. Philip foolishly ignored their advice: the French cavalry suffered one of the greatest defeats of the Middle Ages. Froissart has left us dramatic testimony of the deaths of some of the leaders.[19]

> The valiant and noble king of Bohemia . . . [who] was blind . . . said to his men . . . , "Lords, you are my men, my friends, and my companions; today I ask . . . that you lead me forward so that I can get in a sword blow. And those who were close to him, and who loved his honor and his reputation, accorded him this wish. . . . to carry out their promise and to be sure not to lose him in the crowd, they tied their horses reins together, putting their lord in front, to better accomplish his wish; and thus they rode at their enemies. . . . The good king . . . fought most valiantly; . . . they were found the next morning, with all their horses attached. . . .
>
> "The count Louis of Blois and the duke of Lorraine, his brother-in-law, with their men and their banners, fought . . . valiantly and were surrounded by a troop of English and Welsh, who took no prisoners. There they carried many great exploits of arms, for they were valiant knights and good warriors; but nonetheless, their prowess was worth nothing to them. . . .
>
> "The king [Edward] took counsel and ordered that the battlefield be searched to find out which lords lay among the dead. Two very valiant knights were ordered to go out to the field, accompanied by three heralds to

recognize the arms of the dead, and by two clerks to write down and register the name of those they found. . . . In the evening, the two above-mentioned knights returned to the king, who was about to dine, and made their report of what they had seen and found. They said eleven princes lay there, eighty bannerets, and twelve hundred knights with crested shields, and about thirty thousand other men."[20]

Philip wanted to fight on, but his companion Jean de Hainaut grabbed his reins and scolded him, "Sire, it's time to get out of here. Do not lose yourself so easily. If you have lost this time, you will win on another." Philip wisely followed his advice. The victorious Edward marched north, massacring a force of infantry from Rouen on his way. He went to Calais, which he captured after a siege lasting nearly a year. Edward brought in English settlers to replace the original inhabitants; Calais remained English until the 1558.

Philip's catastrophic defeat had some positive consequences. The dire situation encouraged the Estates General of Langue d'Oïl, meeting in the fall of 1347, to create an entirely new system of taxation. They established a hearth tax (*fouage*) apportioned by region, to be used to pay for an army, also apportioned among the regions. Philip had tried various expedients to raise money, including fines for failure to appear for military service, a sales tax, a tax on salt (*gabelle*), special wartime direct subsidies, and manipulating the currency. The Crécy disaster had the merit of convincing everyone of the gravity of the situation and encouraging a positive response to the king's demands. Philip seemed on the verge of establishing the sort of permanent revenue base that would enable him to build the state. At that moment, the Black Death scuttled all plans for governmental reform, derailed the war effort, and fundamentally restructured French society.

The Crisis, 1348–1358

In the first part of this book . . . we depicted the aforementioned prince or princes as the head of the body politic . . . and [in the second] knights, which are the arms and the hands. In this part, with God's help, let us continue with . . . the whole of the people in common, described as the belly, legs, and feet, so that the whole be formed and joined in one whole living body, perfect and healthy.[21]

Christine de Pisan, *c.* 1407

The Black Death brought the Hundred Years' War to a screaming halt. Not only did the Queen, crown princess, and chancellor succumb to it, but so did many local officials. Those local leaders who themselves did not die of the plague focused all attention on the silent killer. Some of these leaders earned the respect of their constituents by their valiant efforts; others, bishops notable among them, earned opprobrium by fleeing to the relative safety of their rural estates. The plague vastly increased social and political tensions in France.

THE BURGHERS OF CALAIS

The surrender of Calais involved a remarkable set of gestures. Edward sent an emissary, Gautier de Mauny, into the city to demand its final surrender. He authorized de Mauny to agree to spare the city from massacre only if six of its leading citizens would walk barefoot to his camp, dressed in nightshirts, their heads bare, their necks in nooses, the keys to the city in their hands: "I will do as I wish with them, and I will grant mercy to the rest," Edward said. When the captain of the city called an assembly on the market square, tearfully announcing the terms, Eustache de Saint-Pierre, one of the richest men in the city, stepped forward, "For myself, I have such great hopes to obtain grace and pardon from Our Lord, if I die to save this people, that I

The Burghers of Calais, Auguste Rodin.
SOURCE: © Foto Marburg/Art Resource.

wish to be the first." The crowd rushed to him, throwing itself at his feet. Soon, others joined— Jean d'Aire, Jacques and Pierre de Wissant, and two others. Walking to Edward's camp, they presented themselves to the king, asking only that he save their fellow citizens and have pity on them. The king, much annoyed at the long siege, refused; he ordered their heads cut off at once.

De Mauny sprang to their defense:

> Ah! Genteel sire, please rein in your fierce courage; you have the name and reputation of sovereign gentility and nobility; thus, you should not wish to do something by which it would be reduced, nor which would allow others to speak of you committing any villainy. If you have no pity on these men, all other men will say that it would be great cruelty if you are so hard as to make die these honest bourgeois, who of their own will threw themselves on your mercy to save the others.

Edward responded: "Shut up. . . . Call the executioner." His pregnant wife, Philippine of Hainaut, intervened: "Since I have crossed the sea at great peril, . . . I have asked you for nothing; but I beg you humbly and request in simple gift, for the Son of blessed Mary, and for love of me, that you would have pity on these six men." The king relented, and exiled them to Picardy.

The great nineteenth-century French sculptor Auguste Rodin immortalized this scene in one of his most stunning monuments, *The Burghers of Calais,* which depicts the barefooted town aldermen, nooses around their necks, keys in hand, unforgettable expressions of agony and despair etched on their faces. Visitors to Paris can see it at the Musée Rodin, but a casting sits as well in the Hirschorn Garden in Washington, D.C., where lunching government workers and countless tourists have long marveled at the embodiment of suffering, etched on the faces of men whose story they know not.[22]

Philip VI's son John inherited a dismal situation in 1350. French forces had been routed on land and at sea, and internal disputes simmered in French politics. The eighteen-year-old Charles of Navarre, son of Jeanne of France, sought everywhere to undermine the new Valois dynasty in hopes of himself becoming King of France.[23] To expand his personal possessions, Charles "the Bad," as contemporaries called him, allied himself effectively with Edward III. John had to face a four-fold threat in the early 1350s: (1) renewed hostilities with England; (2) the potential claim to the throne of Charles of Navarre; (3) the material aftermath of the plague; and (4) rising social tensions.

John handled these matters poorly. He wrongfully deprived Charles the Bad of Angoumois, then sought amends by marrying his daughter to him. When John reneged on the dowry, Charles allied with Edward III and then murdered John's favorite, the young constable Charles of Spain. Too weak to exact revenge, John signed over to Charles the Cotentin peninsula, which, together with the county of Evreux, gave him control over vital Normandy, an area that provided about 20 percent of total French tax revenue.

The loss of Norman tax revenues made John financially unable to continue the war with Edward, so he offered him most of southwestern France, in full sovereignty. John quickly changed his mind and called an Estates General of Langue d'Oïl to get subsidies. These Estates, meeting in November 1355, began the process by which France would get both permanent state taxation and a state financial bureaucracy. Acting "for the profit of the commonwealth," they voted sales (3.33 percent) and salt taxes and created a system of elected local and national oversight and collecting officials.[24] The Estates agreed to provide John with money, but he had to accept their control of subsidies.

Problems collecting the taxes, perhaps because local assemblies argued that the central Estates did not have the power to vote them, led to a new Estates General in March 1356. This body voted direct taxes, based on income, with a sliding, gradually reducing scale.[25] A new Estates even increased the upper-level rates in May. These maneuvers set the merchants of the towns, who favored the income taxes, against the nobles, who preferred indirect levies. In the midst of this political turmoil in Paris, King John suddenly seized Charles of Navarre while he was dining with the heir to the throne, Charles, duke of Normandy (April 1356). Full-scale war followed immediately.

Two small English raiding parties ravaged France, one in Normandy and the other, under Edward, the Prince of Wales, in the southwest. King John marched his army in pursuit of the latter party, catching up with them outside of Poitiers in September 1356. The king, ever chivalrous, listened to the pleadings of the Papal legate that he postpone the fight, so as not to break the Truce of God by fighting on a Sunday. Given a full day to entrench themselves, the English archers once again decimated the French knights. Many of the French fought bravely, with more than two thousand nobles dying on the field, but others fled or surrendered after a brief struggle. The Prince of Wales, known and pathologically feared in France as the Black Prince, captured eighteen titled men, twenty-one barons, and another two thousand men-at-arms. The ultimate disaster befell the losers: the English took King John and his fourteen-year-old son Philip prisoner.

Courtrai, Crécy, and Poitiers marked the first death of knightly warfare. The weapons of the foot soldiers, the bows and pikes, had become too effective against mounted knights, insufficiently protected against their penetrating power. Chivalric excesses like the famous Combat of the Thirty, soon moved out of warfare itself and into the realm of mock warfare, the tournaments. The French victories of 1367–1374 came not in battles pitting rows of knights against each other, but in petty combats and ambushes organized by the master of delay, constable du Guesclin. The catastrophic defeats encouraged the non-nobles to reconsider the political structure of society. Led by the merchants of Paris, the townsmen sought, and briefly obtained, control of the French government. Froissart tells us "those knights and squires who returned from the battle were so blamed and detested by the commons that they were reluctant to go into the big towns." The "Complaint on the battle of Poitiers," a poem entered into the registers of Notre Dame of Paris in 1359, summarizes the feelings of most, calling on God to "confound the traitors, who by their great fear have betrayed their lord, to whom they owed faith."[26]

The Poitiers disaster initiated one of the turning points of French political history. Crown Prince Charles, acting as lieutenant in his father's absence, called an Estates General of Langue d'Oïl in Paris, which met two months after the great defeat. Some deputies believed the Estates should name six men from each order "by whom Charles would be governed. These words seemed to the young prince not to give him any help but to impose law on him and to give to the seditious and to those who like novelties a very powerful, bold, and audacious leader." Charles put them off, claiming he daily awaited word from his father. He later suggested to some deputies that some of the members of the Estates had "the intention and desire, by personal ambition, to themselves govern all the affairs of the kingdom in all assemblies, and that they colored their requests in the paint of the public good."

The wily Charles temporized, but found he had to give considerable power to the merchants of Paris, led by their provost, Étienne Marcel. Marcel, whose statue today looks out over the Seine, next to the Paris Town Hall, dominated the 1356 Estates and the ones that succeeded them in the spring of 1357. By early 1358, he and his collaborators had complete control of Crown Prince Charles: they released Navarre from prison, forced the removal of unpopular royal councillors, and demanded new taxes. The Estates were to meet regularly henceforth, and to do so only in Paris. In February, a crowd in Paris, egged on by Marcel, murdered several of Crown Prince Charles' noble supporters in his own bedroom.

Events moved rapidly in the spring of 1358. First, Charles assumed the title of Regent; he then fled Paris. In May, he called a rival Estates General, dominated by the nobles, at Compiègne. They overturned the ordinances carried out by the merchant-dominated Estates, and reinstated the noble exemption from taxes, which had been rescinded by the meetings of 1355–1358.[27] At precisely this moment, the peasantry of the Ile-de-France, Vermandois, and the Beauvaisis rose up in the largest peasant rebellion in French history, the Jacquerie.

Marcel and his allies in Paris wavered at first but then decided to support the peasants. Charles of Navarre took the opposite approach—allying with his fellow nobles, even though it meant aiding the Regent. After some initial success, the Jacques suffered a predictable defeat: one chronicle says twenty thousand died.

Marcel vainly tried to save his position by allying with Charles of Navarre. A week after Navarre entered Paris, amid general chaos, a group of discontented Parisians murdered Marcel. The Regent returned to a chastened Paris: the revolution was over.

THE JACQUERIE OF 1358: THE REBELLION

Jean Froissart, a contemporary (albeit a young one) of the events, tells the story of the Jacquerie, relying in part on the chronicle of Jean le Bel and in part on his own interrogation of witnesses. Froissart wrote his chronicles for a noble audience, and so reflects faithfully their view of the Jacques.

The Jacquerie—the Peasant Offensive, from a fifteenth-century manuscript of Froissart's Chronicles.

SOURCE: Bibliothèque Nationale

> There were strange and terrible happenings in several parts of the kingdom. . . . They began when some of the men from the country towns came together in the Beauvais region. They had no leaders and at first they numbered scarcely a hundred. One of them got up and said that the nobility of France . . . were disgracing and betraying the realm, and that it would be a good thing if they were all destroyed. At this they all shouted: "He's right! He's right!" They banded together and went . . . to the house of knight who lived nearby. . . . They killed the wife, who was pregnant, and the daughter and all the other children, and finally put the knight to death with great cruelty and burned and razed the castle. . . . Their ranks swelled to six thousand. . . . And those evil men, who had come together without leaders or arms, pillaged and burned everything and violated and killed all the ladies and girls without mercy, like mad dogs. Their barbarous acts were worse than anything that ever took place between Christians and Saracens. . . . Among other brutal excesses, they killed a knight, put him on a spit, and turned him at the fire and roasted him before the lady and her children. After about a dozen of them had violated the lady, they tried to force her and the children to eat the knight's flesh before putting them cruelly to death. . . . Those evil men burned more than sixty big houses and castles in the Beauvais region. . . . Other wicked men behaved in just the same way between Paris and Noyon and between Paris and Soissons . . . and destroyed more than one hundred castles and houses belonging to knights and squires.

The abortive revolution of 1358 had profound consequences on the long-term development of the French state. The monarchy remained suspicious of the Parisian merchants and of townsmen in general, especially after the Parisians tried to make an alliance with the ever-rebellious Flemish towns. The nobles emerged victorious on all fronts. They defeated Marcel and the merchants in Paris and they crushed the peasants in the countryside. As a result, the northern nobility were able effectively to claim an exemption from taxation that they kept until the end of the seventeenth century and, for most taxes, until 1789. The Regent Charles took a new look at the institution of the Estates, particularly at the demand of the Estates to supervise the collection of the subsidies at the national level. He would soon act to see that he would not have to put up with such interference again.

THE JACQUERIE OF 1358: THE PEASANTS' DEFEAT

Froissart, in his usual colorful language, recounts the end of the rebellion:

> When the gentry of the Beauvais and of the other districts . . . saw their houses destroyed and their friends killed, they sent to their friends in Flanders, Hainaut, Brabant and Hesbaye to ask for help. . . . The foreign noblemen joined forces with those of the country who guided and led them, and they began to kill those evil men and to cut them to pieces without mercy. Sometimes they hanged them on the trees under which they found them. . . . There were fully nine thousand of them altogether, all filled with the most evil intentions. . . . [the people of the town] let them in . . . [and] all the streets were filled with them as far as the market place. . . . When those evil men saw them [the knights] drawn up in this warlike order—although their numbers were comparatively small—they became less resolute

The Jacquerie—the Nobles' Revenge at Meaux, from a fifteenth-century manuscript of Froissart's Chronicles.
SOURCE: Bibliothèque Nationale.

> than before. The foremost began to fall back and the noblemen to come after them. . . . Those who felt the blows, or feared to feel them, turned back in such panic that they fell over each other. The men-at-arms . . . mowed them down in heaps and slaughtered them like cattle. . . . They went on killing until they were all stiff and weary. . . . In all, they exterminated more than seven thousand [Jacques] on that day [and] they set fire to the mutinous town of Meaux and burnt it to ashes . . . . After that rout at Meaux, there were no more assemblies of the Jacques, for the young Lord de Coucy . . . placed himself at the head of a large company of knights and squires who wiped them out wherever they found them, without pity or mercy.[28]

Poitiers led to the catastrophic peace of Brétigny (1359), which gave England most of southwestern France. The debacle also had remarkable, unintended long-term consequences. In theory, the monarchy could now institute, of its own authority, the taxes necessary to pay the ransom of the king (a feudal right): three million crowns. The amount was so great that the king had obtained the *de facto* right to long-term taxation. John called the Estates Generals of Langue d'Oïl and of Langue d'Oc to ratify the taxes. These taxes lasted until the French Revolution.[29]

Charles V and the Revival of France, 1363–1379

> *"I know of only one pleasure in kingship." [Pray tell us what it is.]*
> *"Certainly it is in the power to do good for others."*[30]

Remarks attributed to Charles V by Christine de Pisan, in
The Book of the Deeds and Good Character of King Charles V the Wise

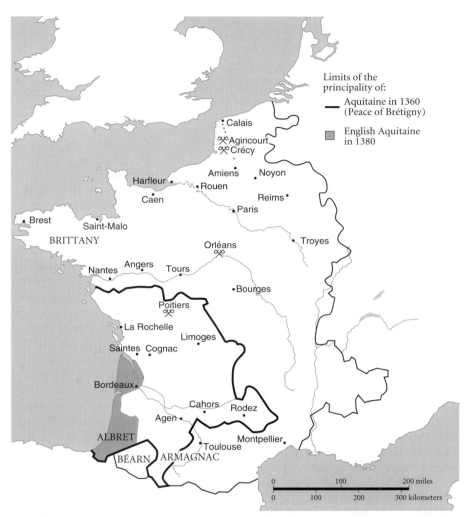

Limits of the
principality of:

— Aquitaine in 1360
(Peace of Brétigny)

◼ English Aquitaine
in 1380

The Peace of Brétigny and the French Reconquest.

The next stage of the Hundred Years' War gradually undermined the English position. The pieces fell into place rapidly after the death of King John. When his son Louis (who had taken John's place as a hostage) fled his captivity at Calais in 1364, John voluntarily returned to captivity in England to take Louis's place. He died a few months later. The Crown Prince now became King Charles V. He quickly resolved his major problems.

First, Charles V gave his younger brother Philip the inheritance of the duke of Burgundy. That provoked a war with Charles of Navarre, who had the best claim to the duchy. Constable du Guesclin defeated Navarre, reclaiming both the Cotentin peninsula and the approaches to Paris for the king. Philip married Margaret of Flanders, ruler of the county of Burgundy (now called Franche-Comté), and sole heir of the count of Flanders. Charles gave the young couple the county of Artois as a marriage gift, in recognition of his joy that Margaret turned down a much more dangerous suitor: Edmund, duke of York, son of Edward III of England.

Charles V set out to reform every aspect of French government; in the long run, he succeeded, even though the new institutions struggled to survive under his son, Charles VI (1380–1423). Charles VII (1423–1461) either revived the lapsed institutions of his grandfather, as in the case of the army reforms, or he simply reinvigorated them, as in the case of the financial ones. The institutions created by Charles V blended carefully together. In the military, he established a system of regional apportionment of men-at-arms, using important local nobles as commanders of standing companies of mounted knights. He simultaneously reintroduced a hearth tax (*fouage*) to pay for local troops. Local officers, selected by local estates, supervised the raising and spending of money, and powerful local barons recruited local nobles to serve as men-at-arms in the new companies. With the assistance of local, regional, and supra-regional estates, Charles thus put in place the full system of taxation that would last until 1790: the sales taxes (*aides*) and salt taxes (*gabelles*) voted to pay the ransom of his father and the hearth tax levied to pay for the royal army. Charles also created the core of royal officers: the *élus,* who supervised the collection of local taxes and acted as judges in the first instance in tax cases; the *grenetier*s, who ran the salt warehouses of the state monopoly and also acted as judges; and various receivers and controllers. All of these offices lasted until the French Revolution. One measure of the effectiveness of his tax reforms was his reminting of the currency, at full value, an act that demonstrated one of the principles of royal fiscal policy. When the king had sufficient tax revenue, he maintained a sound currency; when tax revenues flagged, he debased the currency to raise money. The devaluations provided short-term cash relief, but at considerable cost to French commerce.

The hard lessons of the 1350s convinced Charles he needed more control over these men than the system of the 1360s would allow him. He first made the overall supervisors into royal councilors, which meant that he, not the Estates General, had the right to name them. In 1373, in the guise of reforming a system become corrupt, Charles fired the local officials and reappointed new ones on his own authority, making all of the tax collectors into royal officials. Those among them who handled money had henceforth to render their accounts not to local estates, but to the royal Chamber of Accounts in Paris. Charles reaffirmed these principles in a great ordinance issued in 1379, a year before his death.

Charles V's reforms gave the King of France the three basic elements of an early modern state. First, he had a judicial system, represented by the bailiffs at the local level and by the Parlement of Paris at the center. Second, he had a permanent army, paid for by the grants of 1363. Third, he had a tax system, based on the taxes of 1360 (for the ransom of King John) and 1363, and a group of royal financial officials, an-

The Reluctant Constable: Bertrand du Guesclin

Charles V's greatest commander was the unlikeliest of heroes, the Breton constable Bertrand du Guesclin. Du Guesclin was a short, unprepossessing knight; his contemporaries held his ugliness to be proverbial. He had the alarming habit of not merely losing battles, but being captured (four times) and held for ransom. Du Guesclin, however, had many admirable qualities. He was a master of minor sieges and of campaigns of harassment. Oddly enough, even his worst defeat, at Najera in Spain (1367), proved a victory of sorts. A large company of mercenaries, the dreaded *routiers,* had followed him to Spain; their deaths at Najera relieved the French countryside of their depredations.

Froissart claims that Charles held a council of his greatest barons in 1370 to name a new constable; they "unanimously elected sir Bertrand du Guesclin as the most valiant, the best informed, the most virtuous and fortunate in conducting affairs for the crown of France of all those who were bearing arms in its defence." Summoned to Paris, du Guesclin "modestly and sagely excused himself, saying, 'he was not worthy of it: that he was a poor knight and simple bachelor, in comparison with the great lords and valorous men of France.'" The king insisted, but du Guesclin demurred a second time: "I cannot, I dare not, whatever I may wish, oppose what may be your good pleasure: but in truth I am too poor a

man, and of low extraction, for the office of constable, which is so grand and noble . . . Here are my lords your brothers, your nephews and your cousins, who will have different commands in your armies . . . and how shall I dare to order them?" The king would not accept no for an answer, insisting that no one, "neither brother, nephew, cousin, count or baron in my realm" would refuse du Guesclin's orders. "And should any one act otherwise, he would so anger me that he should soon feel the effects of it."[31]

Du Guesclin continued the Fabian tactics that had proved so successful in earlier campaigns. When a large English army invaded in 1370, he allowed them to pillage the Loire valley while he conquered the southwest. The success of the combined French and Castilian navies at La Rochelle (June 1372) destroyed another English invasion. By 1374, du Guesclin had reconquered all the lands lost at Brétigny: only the region surrounding Bordeaux, and Calais, remained in English hands. When the deaths of the Prince of Wales and of Edward III left England in the hands of the child king Richard II, du Guesclin struck again, conquering Charles of Navarre's Norman possessions. The great constable died, aged eighty, soon afterwards. Recognizing his enormous debt to this simple Breton knight, Charles V had him buried in the royal crypt at Saint-Denis, the first person outside the royal family accorded that honor.

swerable only to him and to other royal officials. On his deathbed, Charles V undermined this accomplishment by revoking the "taxes." Contemporaries divided as to whether he abolished all taxes (the position taken by the ordinary people) or merely the hearth tax (the opinion of the royal government). The sales and salt taxes continued to be levied, but the hearth tax ceased, not to return permanently until the 1440s.

Charles died in 1380, leaving his child–successor, Charles VI, to the tender mercies of his uncles, the dukes of Anjou, Berry, and Burgundy. In Flanders, discontent had again led to rebellion, led by Philip van Artevelde, son of the leader of the rebellion of the 1340s. The count had little choice but to call in his son-in-law, Philip of Valois, duke of Burgundy, uncle of the child king of France. Philip marched an army to Flanders and butchered the weavers at Roosebeke (1382): the chronicles claimed that van Artevelde and twenty-six thousand companions met their deaths, whereas only forty-three of the French had died. The figures exaggerate, of course, but they give an accurate sense of the slaughter. Philip took the most galling symbol of urban independence, the town bell of Courtrai, back to Dijon with him. The Jacquemart, as it is known, still rings every hour; the good burghers of Dijon later gave him a "wife," who rings the half hour, and a "child," who rings the quarter hours.

Social unrest appeared in other regions, such as rural Languedoc, site of the Tuchins uprising. The situation turned bad even in the heartland of the kingdom because the word of Charles V's deathbed abolition of "all taxes" spread like wildfire. In fact, Charles had abolished only the hearth taxes, but that did not stop the Maillotins in Paris, the Harelle of Rouen, and other urban rebels from trying to prevent the collection of the indirect taxes. Roosebeke allowed the royal princes to put down the urban rebels who allied with the Flemings. The Crown confiscated the office of provost of the merchants of Paris, hanged the leaders of the rebellion, and levied large fines on Paris and Rouen.

Charles VI had little to fear from England, where Richard II had problems enough of his own, such as Wat Tyler's Rebellion.[32] France's international position did suffer a hard blow just before the new king took power: the last of the Avignon Popes, Gregory XI, died at Rome in 1378. The College of Cardinals elected an Italian Pope, Urban VI, but some of cardinals, unhappy at the choice, withdrew to Naples and chose the Frenchman Clement VII, who quickly fled to Avignon. From 1378 until 1423, the Church had two Popes, a deadly blow to its moral authority and a particularly harmful loss for the King of France, who had dominated the French Popes of the Avignon years.

Charles VI's uncles looted the kingdom for eight years, before he took effective control. The path of the new king took a bizarre turn on a quiet road near Le Mans, where Charles had marched a small army to discipline Pierre de Craon, who had tried to murder the Constable, Olivier de Clisson. On 5 August 1392, a madman rushed from the brush, warning Charles of traitors. A little later, when two squires created a sudden loud noise, the King had a seizure and began striking, and killing, the members of his escort. His knights subdued him with difficulty. For the remainder of his life, Charles VI suffered intermittent bouts of madness.

Fortunately for France, England, too, continued to have internal problems, which led eventually to the dethroning of Richard II by his cousin, Henry of Lancaster (Henry IV). The relative lull in Anglo–French hostilities allowed the French nobility to look outside the kingdom for potential battles. In 1396, a large segment of the nobility joined a Crusade against the Turks then surrounding Constantinople. Marching through the Balkans, the western knights quarreled with local Christians and then among themselves. As was so often the case, prideful knights refused to listen to reason—to those who had fought the Turks before—and charged into a catastrophic defeat at Nicopolis (12 September 1396) in which virtually all of the French knights were either killed or captured. Nicopolis marked the end of western Crusading in the eastern Mediterranean, as well as the low point of chivalric military foolishness.

THE CIVIL WAR: THE HUNDRED YEARS' WAR, 1392–1453

CHRONOLOGY	1392–1453
1392	Onset of madness of Charles VI
1396	Disaster at Nicopolis
1407	John of Burgundy has Louis of Orléans murdered
1413	Cabochien rising at Paris
1415	Agincourt: Henry V annihilates French army
1419	Entourage of the Dauphin Charles murders John of Burgundy
1422–1423	Deaths of Henry V and Charles VI
1428–1429	Joan of Arc; Charles VII crowned at Reims
1435	Charles VII and Philip of Burgundy make peace
1436	Charles regains Paris
1445	Charles regains Normandy
1449–1453	Charles conquers Guyenne; end of Hundred Year's War

"And gentlemen in England now a-bed / Shall think themselves accurs'd they were not here, / And hold their manhoods cheap whiles any speaks / That fought with us upon Saint Crispin's day."

Shakespeare, *Henry V,* act IV, scene 3

The illness of Charles VI allowed his uncles to dismiss the ruling councilors, known as the Marmosets, and to put their greedy hands into the royal till. The dukes of Anjou, Berry, and Burgundy consolidated their positions. Louis of Anjou held that county, and, through Louis's marriage, the county of Provence, then not part of France. The duke of Berry's apanage covered much of central France; he maintained control over Languedoc as the king's lieutenant. Philip of Burgundy had inherited Flanders, the county of Burgundy, the duchies of Nevers and Rethel, and Artois. His son, John, soon inherited Brabant, Hainaut, Holland, and Zeeland. The king's younger brother, Louis of Orléans, held that region and a wide variety of others. In these apanages, the prince, not the King, collected the taxes and dominated the administration.

Sooner or later, the royal princes were bound to quarrel. In 1407, John the Fearless, duke of Burgundy, hired thugs to murder Louis of Orléans. John fled to Lille, and civil war began. In 1413, after a preliminary rapprochement between the two sides, Burgundians and Armagnacs, had failed, the king had called Estates in Paris.[33] John the Fearless, ever popular in the city, fomented a rebellion led by a butcher, Simon Caboche. They massacred the Armagnacs, took control of the royal household and issued a famous reforming ordinance, the *ordonnance cabochienne,* The ordinance

THE EVIL QUEEN?

Charles VI married Isabella of Bavaria, who never learned to speak French. Her reputation has led an even more tortured existence than the queen herself. Fifteenth-century sources show a remarkable lack of consistency about her. No source in her lifetime accuses her of infidelity, yet late fifteenth-century sources (above all Burgundian ones) suggest she had an affair with Louis, duke of Orléans, the king's brother. One poem even suggests that John the Fearless murdered Louis because of the adultery. In the sixteenth century, prominent writers such as Brantôme picked up the story, which became an integral part of French mythology.

Although some Parisian sources contemporary to her claimed Isabella had a frivolous court and squandered money, even those ill disposed toward her do not suggest she was an adulteress. She did swear in 1420 that her youngest son, Charles, was illegitimate, but she did so only under duress from the king. Surely rumors floated about, because Charles later pointedly asked Joan of Arc for reassurance of his legitimate birth, which she provided.

Why has this story had so long a life? Isabella provides the most convenient of all villains: the foreign queen. We have seen earlier the case of Brunhilde and the discontent over Blanche of Castile's regency. In the sixteenth century, Catherine de Médicis would have an even darker reputation than Isabella. All offered the ultimate outsider as scapegoat: a woman interfering in politics; a foreigner betraying France. Isabella lived at a critical dual moment with respect to both of these elements. First, royal lawyers actively promulgated the Salic Law theory, insisting as never before on the primacy of male inheritance, through the male line only. Second, the fifteenth-century fighting brought in, as the war of the mid-fourteenth century had not, the elements of a national conflict. Joan of Arc bears witness to this rising tide of identification with "France." Salic Law theorists, and those establishing the on-again, off-again regency to look after the intermittently mad king wanted to exclude women. The many powerful adult male princes of the royal blood, through their apologists, wanted to exclude Isabella from any important role in the government, so that they could loot the treasury. Apologists for an emerging French nationalism naturally wanted to find a foreign scapegoat for the obvious mess into which the kingdom had fallen. Isabella's evil image thus became a sort of place of memory for the birth of France.

tried to fire corrupt officials and to streamline the administrations of taxes and justice; it failed. John the Fearless fled Paris a few months later.

Fallen from royal grace, John of Burgundy turned to the English, with whom he hoped to divide up the kingdom. Their new king, Henry V, marched a small army into Normandy, capturing Harfleur. Henry V claimed to be King of France, but his main interests lay in clear-cut recognition of his sovereignty in Aquitaine and in the conquest of Normandy. Even the weakened Armagnac party refused to dismember the kingdom. After taking Harfleur, Henry marched north to Calais; the French army cut him off at Agincourt. Once again, English archers annihilated the French knights, killing over fifteen hundred barons, if the English chroniclers can be believed. They captured several royal cousins. In short order, the two oldest sons of the King of France died, leaving Charles as Dauphin.[34]

The French Court, chaotic in the extreme, turned one way and then the other. The rival powers—Isabella of Bavaria, the new Dauphin, the royal princes—could not agree on any policy. John the Fearless offered peace just as Henry V began his conquest of Normandy, taking Rouen in January 1419. John and the Dauphin arranged a meeting on the bridge at Montereau, southeast of Paris, in September 1419. After some heated verbal exchanges, Charles' entourage murdered John. Now the English had an implacable ally in John's son, Philip the Good.

Philip and Isabella convinced the old king to agree to the Treaty of Troyes (1420), which disinherited the Dauphin, denouncing him as a bastard: Isabella grudgingly swore an oath admitting to her own infidelity. Charles VI's daughter, Catherine, married Henry V, whom Charles recognized as his heir. When Henry V and Charles VI died within the year, Catherine's son by Henry became Henry VI of England and, some claimed, King of France. In reality, the English had carried out the plan of 1415, dividing France with the duke of Burgundy. They got Normandy and the southwest, while the Burgundians held Paris and much of north central France. The Dauphin, for such people still called him because he had not been crowned king, set up his capital in Bourges, from which he took his derogatory sobriquet, the "king of Bourges."

Joan of Arc and the Revival of France

> *I believe Jeanne was sent by God, and that her deeds in the war were the fruit of divine inspiration rather than of human agency.*
>
> Jean, count of Dunois, bastard of Orléans,
> commander of the French army in 1429

Fighting broke out again: the key stages of this war took place in the late 1420s and early 1430s, and the late 1440s. The English pressed Charles so hard in the 1420s that he barely kept himself and his cause alive. In 1429, a young woman turned the tide in his favor; she has been the national heroine of France ever since: Jeanne d'Arc, Joan of Arc, known to her contemporaries simply as *La Pucelle,* The Maid. This young peasant woman from the village of Domrémy on the borderlands between Champagne and Lorraine began to hear voices telling her to go to the rightful king, Charles VII, and lead him to a proper coronation, at Reims.

In 1429, after convincing the local castellan of the legitimacy of her visions, she set out for the Court. Her earliest days at Court gave rise to many legends, all amply presented in the chronicles of the time. Joan cut her hair short and dressed as a man, believing she would have to fight for her king. When offered various swords, she refused, so the chronicles tell us, because she knew that her sword would be found behind the altar of Sainte-Cathérine-de-Fierbois; miraculously, a party of searchers found the sword just as she described it. Later, when brought to Charles VII's court, she easily found him out in a large crowd, although he dressed in a disguise. Her ability to pick him out of the crowd, the "miracle" of Sainte-Cathérine, and Joan's private reassurances to Charles that God had told her that the "Dauphin" was his father's son, convinced Charles to allow her to join his main army. Despite being wounded, she led his army in a relief of the siege of Orléans. She then conducted Charles to Reims, to be crowned.

La Pucelle

History offers few characters as improbable or as remarkable as Joan of Arc, who has remained for more than five centuries the symbol of France. Born in the village of Domrémy, straddling the boundary of the duchy of Lorraine and the kingdom of France, she came from a family of well-off peasants. Like most women of that social background, she could neither read nor write. The testimony at her trials, both the one sponsored by the English to prove her a witch, and that conducted in the same city (Rouen) by the French, to rehabilitate her, tells us that she began to hear voices in the fields near her home. The speakers identified themselves as saints: above all, Saint Catherine (patron saint of Fierbois, where Joan found her sword) and Saint Michael the Archangel, one of the patron saints of the kingdom. Joan testified that she heard Saint Michael's voice from 1425 to 1428, and that he informed her of the terrible situation in France. She sought guidance by praying in front of his statue in her village church. Later, she put his image on her banner; in the hour of her death, she called out his name.[35]

Like Dunois, Joan's French contemporaries took her to be an emissary from Heaven. Christine de Pisan composed a poem in Joan's honor, whose verses testify to her divine agency:

Through such a miracle, indeed, / That if the facts were not well-known / And evident in every way, / There's none who would put faith in them? / Indeed this is a thing quite worth / Remembering, that God had wished / To grant such mercy unto France / (Yes, truly!) through a tender maid. / Oh, what an honor to the crown / Of France, this proof divinely sent, / For by the blessings He bestows / It's clear He approves of France.[36]

Her presence electrified the troops; Dunois further testified that: "I swear that the English, two hundred of whom had previously been sufficient to rout eight hundred or a thousand of the royal army, from that moment became so powerless that four or five hundred soldiers and men at arms could fight against what seemed to be the whole force of England." She tried, with some success, to introduce moral order into her army and revived its fighting spirit. She herself led the assault on the forts the English army had built outside the city. After she received an arrow wound and withdrew from the assault, the French attack lacked the necessary *élan*. Late in the evening, Dunois says at eight o'clock, she led another charge. The French forces stormed the walls and broke the English siege. Her victory a month later at Patay, which cost the English four thousand men, led them to retire to Normandy.

In 1430, the Burgundians captured Joan at a siege in eastern France; they turned her over to the English, who tried and executed her as a witch (Rouen, 1431). Despite the enormous moral loss of Joan's capture and execution as a minion of the Devil, Charles VII gained inestimable prestige from his coronation. His generals, notably Dunois, gained several lessons in "good sense" from the simple peasant girl. They learned from Patay that they could defeat the English if they could attack *before* the English archers set up a proper defense. The French modified their tactics accordingly, going back to the wisdom of the simple Breton knight, du Guesclin, who had led them to victory in Charles V's time.

In the mid 1430s, Charles VII finally reconciled with Philip of Burgundy. Philip's brothers-in-law, the dukes of Bourbon and Richmond, convinced him to accept Charles's apology and extensive offer of expiation for the murder of John the Fear-

(CONTINUED)

Joan next convinced Charles to march to Reims, there to receive legitimate coronation; he was crowned or rather anointed (the literal crown then being held by the Burgundians in Paris) on 18 July 1429. The coronation played a critical role in Charles's eventual success; Joan herself referred to Charles as the "Dauphin" until the ceremony at Reims. In this usage, she mirrored popular opinion, which believed the king became king only when properly crowned and anointed by the Holy Oils.

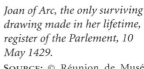

At her trial in Rouen, directed by bishop Pierre Cauchon of Beauvais, the doctors of the Sorbonne condemned her: "The said women is apostate, both because, with evil intention, she had cut that hair which God gave her for a veil and because she set aside women's clothes and wore the habit of a man, in a design no less evil." The inquisitors tortured the poor girl, who briefly "confessed," but then recanted. The English burned her at the stake and flung her ashes into the Seine on 30 May 1431. As Michelet said, the originality of Joan of Arc was perhaps "not so much her valor or her visions, it was her good sense." Happily for Charles VII, its example lived on after her.

Modern-day visitors to France can recapture some of her spirit in Rouen, where a statue honors the reputed spot at which the English threw her ashes into the Seine. Perhaps more touching still is another site, less known, rarely remarked: on a dark side street running alongside the great Gothic cathedral, one of the side chapels bears a small plaque, noting that in 1451 an ecclesiastical court cleared Joan of the charges of witchcraft and attested that her voices were indeed those of Saints Catherine and Michael. This remarkable young woman had to wait another four hundred fifty years for full justification. After a heavily politicized campaign in the 1880s and 1890s, the Pope made Joan a saint.

Joan of Arc, the only surviving drawing made in her lifetime, register of the Parlement, 10 May 1429.

SOURCE: © Réunion de Musées Nationaux/Art Resource, NY.

less.[37] Their reconciliation meant the death knell for English interference in most of France. When Charles marched into Paris in April 1436, the English held only Normandy and Guyenne.

Going back to the ways of his grandfather, Charles VII re-instituting the system of a standing army paid by means of a direct tax. He solidified the royal administration by various reforms. In almost all cases, these reforms merely restored the proper workings of the system established in the 1370s. He established a new Parlement, in Toulouse, to hear legal cases in the south, with its Roman law. He continued to call Estates, both national and local, to vote the taxes he needed. The great ordinances of the period 1439–1452 established one after another the principles that would rule France for more than three centuries. Charles also established himself as the only person in France with the right to levy taxes; he abolished seigneurial *tailles* and stated the principle that only the king could levy direct taxation.[38] In practice, powerful lords continued to levy *tailles, but* they now did so illegally. The king, relying on the legality of the decision of 1439, eventually would be able to establish the principle that only he could authorize any tax levied in France.

On the field of battle, little happened from 1436 until 1449, when Charles invaded Normandy. His artillery demolished the first castle he besieged; the remaining castles surrendered in a matter of months. Two years later, Charles turned to Guyenne, which his forces also captured. From 1452 to 1453, in the last gasp of the war, the Gascons threw out the French and called in an English army led by marshal Talbot (then over eighty). The French defeated and killed Talbot, ending the Hundred Years' War. For the first time since the marriage of Eleanor of Aquitaine and Henry II, southwestern France belonged in reality to the King of France.

The main armies of the 1430s and 1440s did relatively little damage, but the mercenary companies, called *Écorcheurs* ("skinners"), pillaged friend and foe alike. All of the sources speak eloquently of their thefts from the peasants, and of the peasants abandoning their fields rather than having to face a year's toil on behalf of these companies of brigands. Jean Juvenal des Ursins, bishop of Beauvais, and later chancellor of France, wrote of them in 1433:

> [some claiming to fight for the king] take men, women, and little children, without respect for age or sex, force the women and girls . . . kill the husbands and fathers in the presence of the women and girls, take the nursemaids, leaving the nursing children to die, lacking sustenance, take pregnant women, spread them out, leave their "fruit" there to die without baptism [or throw the babies in the river]. . . take priests, monks, and clergy, ploughmen, and spread them out violently and torment them in other manners, called "*singes,*" [literally, apes] and these people thus spreadeagled, they beat them, mutilating some and causing others to become crazy and lose their sense[39]

Charles VII's reforms allowed peace to return to town and village alike and helped pave the way for economic recovery.

The King of France now held legal authority over an area much more like the France with which we are familiar. He did not, however, have immediate power in many of these regions. Duke Philip the Good, his greatest rival, inherited both the duchy and county of Burgundy, most of the Low Countries, Charolais, the duchies of Nevers and Rethel, most of Picardy, and the regions of Auxerre and Macon. The Orléans family held much of central France, the Bourbons a large territory in the southeast, and the house of Anjou that province and Provence. Far to the west, the duke of Brittany was an independent ruler in all but name. All of these men, with the exception of the duke of Brittany, were members of the royal family. Their apanages, lacking a male heir, would revert to the Crown. Amazingly, all of them did revert, in a process we will examine in the next chapter.[40] Here, let us turn back to the middle of the fourteenth century, to consider more closely France's social and cultural development.

The Transition

The Autumn of the Middle Ages[41]

> *To the world when it was half a thousand years younger, the outlines of all things seemed more clearly marked than to us. The contrast between suffering and joy, between adversity and happiness, appeared more striking. . . . Every event, every action, was still embodied in expressive and solemn forms, which raised them to the dignity of a ritual.*
>
> Johan Huizinga

French towns declined sharply in population after 1348 and did not begin to recover fully until the late fifteenth century. Their overall economies suffered, but one can point to progress in metallurgy, clocks, paper making, and the broader diffusion of textile techniques. Some magnificent monuments date from this period, such as the jewel-like church of Saint-Maclou of Rouen, whose Flamboyant Gothic stands in vivid contrast to the nearby high Gothic splendor of Rouen's cathedral. Flamboyant Gothic enabled builders to provide still more light to buildings, and encouraged them to create a lighter pattern of exterior decoration and design. Many fine examples of late Gothic secular architecture survive, from the luxurious house of the royal banker, Jacques Coeur, in Bourges, to the town halls of northern textile towns. In the country-side, the end of the Hundred Years' War encouraged the creation of the château, the lightly fortified country house that emphasized material comfort at the expense of military defense. These châteaux blossomed above all in the Loire valley, where French kings spent much of the late fifteenth century.

Fifteenth-century elites vied with each other in setting forth magnificent displays; this urge to make a brilliant appearance helped create a more amenable style of life for many. Aristocrats retained many of the simpler mores of earlier times: at the great banquets, diners still ate off of trenchers (slices of hard wheat bread), rather than plates; a distinguished guest would be given four slices. The guest would take his or her own slices of meat from the roast, and would share liquid dishes (soups, stews) with his or her neighbor, using a small bowl called an *écuelle*. The duke of Burgundy led the way toward a new sensibility when he introduced trenchers made of silver; porcelain plates came one hundred fifty years later. Diners relied on knives, spoons, and fingers. The privileged few, like the duke of Burgundy, had the occasional fork: he used his only to eat mulberries.[42]

Household furnishings, too, improved, both for aristocrats and for rich merchants. The latter built magnificent urban houses for themselves. These people took great pride in their wealth, in their ability to display it, in its social and political implications. Thus Jacques Coeur had a mason carve into one of his door mantels: "Jacques Coeur does what he wishes, the king does what he can."[43] His great house, today a museum in Bourges, which used large stones from the town wall for its foundations, presented a new floor plan, one that had no place for the typical boutique on the street level. Coeur planned to receive guests in the style of a country house;

Taillevent and the Medieval Banquet

Late medieval banquet menus revolved around meat. Just as Charlemagne's favorite dish was the roast, so, too, fourteenth-century diners made it their culinary centerpiece. The Householder of Paris (c. 1392) tells us one menu for a festive dinner:

first course: fish-liver turnovers; a meat stew with a sharp cinnamon sauce; ox-marrow fritters; eel stew; loach (fish) in broth with a green sage sauce; a large piece of meat; and ocean fish

second course: roast, the best available, and freshwater fish; a piece of meat, larded and boiled; a spiced chopped meat dish garnished with crayfish tails; capon pasties and crisp pancakes; bream pasties; eels; and blancmange

third course: frumenty [wheat berries boiled in broth]; venison; lamprey with a hot sauce; *lechefrites;* roast breams and turnovers; sturgeon in aspic

Other menus indicate that courses mixed every conceivable food—meats and fish, both meats and fish, and sweets—and a wide variety of sauces, often relying on Asian spices (cinnamon, cloves, pepper).

Several short cooking treatises survive from around the year 1300, but the most famous medieval cookbook is the *Viandier* of Guillaume Tirel, known as Taillevent, of which manuscripts survive from about 1400. Taillevent began work as a kitchen boy for the king by 1326. He rose steadily in the ranks and became chief royal chef (by 1373), a position that led to ennoblement: his shield bore three cooking pots. Taillevent's work shows the importance of outside influences, such as Arabic cooking, but maintains the primacy of French sensibility. His elaborate creations often involve such ingredients as gold or silver leaf, to say nothing of sugar and Asian spices. He explains how one roasts a swan and then serves it in its plumage, or how one disguises a meat dish by reforming the finished product into the shape of a fish (such disguise was a staple of great banquets).

Most medieval recipes created dishes of extreme flavors, ones that we would find disgusting. Some recipes, however, survive virtually intact. Below we have one of each.

For the brave, Barbara Ketcham Wheaton offers a modern version of *Hypocras,* as well as an up-to-date rendition of *blancmange,* which remains a staple dish of French cooking.

Hypocras (spiced wine), from the *Viandier* of Taillevent, c. 1400

a pint of wine, powdered spices (three measures cinnamon, one or two of ginger, two of whole cloves), six ounces of sugar: blend together and let settle.

Blancmange, recommended for a sick person, from the *Viandier* of Sion, c. 1302

poach breasts of capon (2 1/2 lbs) till done; cut and grind them, beat in a cup of ground almonds and some spices (cardamon and ginger), using the cooking liquid to make the right consistency (moist but stiff); insert six almond slivers in one half of the blancmange and pomegranate seeds in the other, which should be dusted with sugar

Recipes and menu from B. K. Wheaton, *Savoring the Past.*

his contemporaries called the new house an "urban château." The haughty Coeur never had a chance to live in his house. Disgraced for peculation in 1451, he escaped from prison in 1454 and fled to Rome. He died in Italy, in 1456. His name became a synonym for mercantile pretension: contemporaries claimed he, like the duke of Burgundy, fed his guests on silver plates.

France's late medieval artistic monuments bear witness to the interregnal quality of the civilization. While Italy broke free in the first stages of the Renaissance,

France remained wedded to the Gothic tradition. Architecturally, revised Classical forms spread rapidly in Italy; in France, the new architectural style, a more delicate and light-filled one to be sure, was a variation on Gothic forms. The artistic dominance of the cadet branches of the royal family bears witness to the decline of the Court of France in the early fifteenth century. In sculpture, the greatest "French" artist of the fourteenth and fifteenth centuries was a Dutchman, Claus Sluter, who worked for the dukes of Burgundy. Sluter worked first with Jean de Marville, on the burial crypt for the ducal family. Sluter's *Well of Moses,* at the Charterhouse of Dijon, and the *Tombs of Philip the Bold and Margaret of Flanders* he completed with the assistance of his nephew, Claus de Werve, are among the finest examples of medieval European sculpture.[44]

Claus Sluter, Moses, the Well of Moses,
early fifteenth century.

Source: © Giraudon/Art Resource.

Artistic innovations from Italy spread more to the duke of Burgundy's territories than to those ruled by the King of France. Here the direct economic connections of northern Italy with Bruges, connections that no longer included a French overland route, surely had much to do with Italian innovations skipping over France and moving directly to Flanders. Paris, long the cultural center of northern Europe, lost much of its luster in the fifteenth century. Paris has no fifteenth-century monument to compare to the glorious sculptures of Dijon or to the church of Saint-Maclou in Rouen. In painting, the sole French master of any lasting importance from this period was Jean Fouquet, the great miniaturist of the middle of the fifteenth century (see Plate 5). Fouquet worked in the tradition of the Limbourg brothers, the peerless manuscript illuminators of the late fourteenth and early fifteenth centuries.[45] The Limbourgs carried out their most famous work, *The Very Rich Hours of Jean, duke of Berry,* as its name suggests, not for the king but for his uncle. Berry also employed other great artists, such as those who illuminated some of the stained-glass windows in his chapel at the cathedral of Bourges.

The major painters of the time worked for the dukes of Burgundy. Here again, Burgundian ties to Italy meant that styles moved rapidly from northern Italy to Flanders. Even the great illuminators, like the Limbourg brothers, came from areas not now (although then) part of France. The Limbourgs learned from Jacquemart de Hesdin, who produced masterful illuminations for other manuscripts ordered by Berry in the 1380s. Hesdin and the Limbourgs relied heavily on models from late fourteenth-century Italian painting. The great painters of the fifteenth century all came from the north, above all from the region of Tournai, in Flanders.

The line of these painters began with Robert Campin, known as the Master of Flémalle (see Plate 6), and ran through his apprentice, Rogier van der Weyden. A second group of painters, of whom the most famous was Jan van Eyck (see Plate 7), who came from the region of Maastricht (in the modern Netherlands), flourished in Bruges. These painters worked both for the Burgundian ducal house, for the burghers of Ghent and Bruges, and even those of London. They introduced northern Europeans to the innovations of Renaissance Italian painting, such as perspective.

French literature had a somewhat happier existence than French painting. Relatively few major "literary" writers have come down to us: Christine de Pisan, Charles of Orléans, Alain Chartier, and François Villon are the most famous among them. In addition, several important chroniclers wrote in this period. Jean Froissart's chronicles of the first half of the Hundred Years' War established the parameters of the genre. His successors included Georges Chastellan, chronicler of the dukes of Burgundy, and Philippe de Commynes, who worked both for the dukes of Burgundy and for the kings of France.

Two other political writers deserve special mention. Philippe de Mézières's late fourteenth-century texts, including his letter of King Richard II of England, provide a clear exposition of practical political thought in late medieval times. Thomas Basin, author of the *History of Charles VII* and the *History of Louis XI,* provides an entirely new voice, one that moves away from the chivalric chronicle tradition of Froissart and Chastellan and faces toward the more modern historiographic tradition then taking root in Italy. The contrast between the bourgeois Basin, with his precise reporting on the details of government, and the aristocratic Chastellan, obsessed with the details of every banquet and tournament, brings out in startling clarity the dynamic tensions of a world undergoing massive social and cultural change.

Christine de Pisan, active at the end of the fourteenth and beginning of the fifteenth centuries, offered a spirited defense of women's status in society. Born in Venice (*c.* 1364), she spent her adult life at the Court of France, where her father was Charles V's physician. In her *Letter to the God of Love* and her *Letter in Response to the Roman de la Rose,* she denounced the doctrines put forward by Jean de Meun in the *Roman de la Rose,* the classic medieval love poem. Jean de Meun, writing in the late thirteenth century, had greatly modified the tone of Guillaume de Lorris's first segment of the poem.[46]

MEDIEVAL MISOGYNY: JEAN DE MEUN

Si sunt eles voir pres que toutes	But yes, they are nearly all
covoiteuses de prendre, et gloutes	covetous to take, and greedy
de ravir et de devorer,	to ravish and devour,
si qu'il ne puist riens demorer	until nothing can remain
a ceux qui plus por leur se claiment	to those who most seek them
et qui plus leaument les aiment	and who most loyally love them

---

Jean de Meun dredges up every available nasty remark or story about women, often relying on the Roman poet Ovid, who frequently speaks ill of women.

Christine de Pisan, in attacking Jean de Meun, initiated one of the dominant themes of French intellectual life of the period 1400–1800: the *querelle des femmes* ("the woman question"). De Pisan stressed the deceitful character of men. In what has become her most famous work, *The Book of the City of Ladies,* she laid out a case for the capacities of women in every aspect of life, from the arts to justice. In one of her most famous passages, she discusses with Lady Rectitude the works of male authors, like Jean de Meun or Ovid, who claimed that women were deceitful. These authors had argued that they informed men of the deceitfulness of women in order to serve the "public good." Lady Rectitude replied that Christine de Pisan had already discredited the deceitfulness charges in her earlier books. As for the claim of the male authors that they served the common good, Lady Rectitude stated that "the common good of a city or land or any community of people is nothing other than the profit or general good in which all members, women as well as men, participate and take part."[47]

Arguments such as this one—that women and men share equally in the public good—set forth the dominant themes of the *querelle des femmes.* Christine de Pisan's books, among them most prominently *The City of Ladies,* would be printed shortly after the introduction of that new technology to France. The *querelle des femmes* would develop through the writings of Marguerite d'Angoulême and Louise Labbé in the sixteenth century, those of Marie de Gournay and François Poullain de la Barre in the seventeenth, and, in a modified form, into many works of the Enlightenment. Christine de Pisan provided the foundation for this fundamental topic of French intellectual inquiry.

In her own day, de Pisan had greater fame for other works, such as *The Deeds of Charles V* and her poetry. How remarkable that Philip the Bold, duke of Burgundy, commissioned a *woman* to write the history of his brother's deeds. His patronage reconfirms the central role of Christine de Pisan in the intellectual culture of her time. She wrote a well-respected political treatise, *The Book of the Body Politic* (a title taken from John of Salisbury), whose later fate reconfirms what we know about the profoundly patriarchal nature of late medieval and early modern French society. Publishers brought out early editions of her poetry and *City of Ladies;* after all, a woman could write about love. They ignored her political text, which did not see the light of day until 1743: politics was men's business; a woman had no right to meddle in it.

In her poetry, Christine de Pisan sets out themes that would recur again in French literature of the sixteenth through eighteenth centuries. Speaking of the perfect love for one's lady, she writes:

> But to serve her with loyal and perfect heart
> Her alone, and to keep her from blame . . .
> There lies love

Her lovers speak of equality, of chastity (on both sides), of the spiritual dimension of love.

Charles of Orléans and François Villon, in contrast, each in their own way, speak to the misery of their century. Orléans, cousin of Charles VII, spent more than twenty-five years in an English prison, after his capture at Agincourt. There he wrote poetry, often love poems for his second wife, Bonne d'Armagnac. Writing in the tradition reaffirmed by Christine de Pisan, rather than in the misogynist vein of Jean de Meun, he speaks often of his faithfulness to his distant wife:

> Beauty whom I hold for friend
> Think, no matter where I am,
> That never will I forget you

He tells her of his desire, both spiritual and physical, for her:

> Ardent desire to see my mistress
> Has again assaulted the stronghold
> Of my poor heart, which languishes in sadness,
> And therein put all aflame[48]

As one might expect of someone separated from his love, his family, his country, and his responsibilities for so many years, Charles of Orléans fills his poems with longing and sadness. His Bonne died during Charles' confinement—"Alas, Death, who was so bold / To take the noble Princess / Who is my comfort, my life." Charles returned

Epitapse dudit Billon
freces humains qui apres no⁹ viues
Napez les cueurs contre no⁹ endurcis
Car se pitie de no⁹ pouures auez
Dieu en aura plustost de bous mercis
Dous nous boies cy ataches cinq six
Quãt de la char q trop auõs nourrie
Elleft pieca deuouree et pourrie
et no⁹ les os deuends cēdres a pouldre
De nostre mal personne ne sen rie
Mais pries dieu que tous nous Bueil
se absouldre   g iii.

The gibbet of Monfaucon in Paris, fron-
tispiece of volume of poetry published by
Francois Villon, after c. 1485.

SOURCE: Frontispiece of volume of poetry published by François Villon, after *c.* 1485.

to France, there to help reconcile the king and the duke of Burgundy. He married a third time, to Mary of Cleves; their son, Louis, became King of France in 1498.

François Villon came from a rather different social background, that of a petty ecclesiastic sprung from the Parisian middle class. Villon spoke, and wrote, the language of the people, of the streets of Paris. He lived a hard life—as thief and murderer. Spared from the gallows by the king himself, Villon returned to his hard living ways. A second conviction for murder could not be pardoned; the court exiled Villon from

Paris. Although there are some who suggest that Villon lived the remainder of his days in Poitou, enlivening the local cultural scene, in fact we cannot establish with certainty any part of his life in exile.

Villon leads French poetry away from the allegory-filled romance of Alain Chartier, whose long poetic work *La belle dame sans merci* had a profound impact on noble culture and its ideals of love, and from Charles of Orléans. Chartier represents the height of the male chivalric ideal of love and knightly conduct, much as Christine de Pisan carries forth its female ideals. Chartier could write, in his *Ballad of Fougères,* "Lying and treason are detestable / To God and men / For that reason the image of Jason / Is not placed at the table of worthies" (Jason lied to get the Golden Fleece). Villon moves away from the chivalrous. He offers frequent puns, often quite crude, and integrates the traditions of high culture with those of popular culture. He borrows from the latter its distrust, often its contempt, for the rich and powerful. In his *Legacy,* Villon leaves humorous gifts to some fellow Parisians. The Carmelite monks get special mention:

> *Item* I leave to the Mendicants
> The Holy Ones and the Beguines
> Many nice tidbits and relishes
> Custards, capons, and fat hens
> Then let them preach the Fifteen Signs
> And knock down bread with both hands
> Carmelites mount our neighbors' wives
> But actually that's the least of it.

In the opening stanzas of his *Testament,* he denounced the miserly bishop of Orléans, Thibault d'Aussigny, renowned pursuer of lawsuits:

> In Thibault d'Aussigny's clutches
> Bishop he may be as he signs the cross
> Through the streets, but I deny he is mine
> . . . .
> He fed me on a small loaf
> And cold water a whole summer long
> Open-handed or mean he was stingy with me
> God be to him as he's been to me

Villon makes fun of love and lovers: the beautiful helmet seller laments her blond hair, full pink cheeks, and hard body of thirty years before. Now she sees gray hair, pale cheeks, and thighs reduced to "sticks / Speckled all over like sausages." Villon, as is his style, also offers comments on more intimate physical details, blending a combination of reference to high culture—borrowing the image of the garden from Jean de Meun—and to popular culture—slang terms for breasts and genitalia. Later Villon tells us of love, that everyone is willing to accept "For one joy, a thousand sorrows" and that "Foolish love makes beasts of us all." He makes of these contrasting images, borrowed from chivalric poetry and popular songs, a synthesis that moves French letters into the world of Rabelais.

The relative decline of Paris in the late fourteenth and fifteenth centuries did not mean a complete absence of important intellectuals. Although the earlier pre-eminence, built on the reputation of an Abélard or an Aquinas, certainly disappeared; nonetheless some of the towering figures of the day lived and worked in Paris. Saint Louis had granted land in Paris to Robert de Sorbon (and his colleagues William of Chartres and William of Mémont) to build a college, now known as the Sorbonne. In the late thirteenth century, the dominant influence on Paris was the Italian Thomas Aquinas, who taught at the University from 1252 to 1259 and again from 1269 to 1272; his reconciliation of Aristotle's teachings with those of the Church helped make Aristotle the preeminent philosophical influence on fourteenth-century Europe. William of Ockham, too, taught at Paris. Indeed, his departure in 1328 marked Paris's loss of supremacy in many ways.

The revival in Paris came less in the Sorbonne and more in the new colleges. In 1305, Jeanne de Navarre, wife of King Philip IV, left her private residence to the University, creating the College of Navarre. Its masters helped revive the study of rhetoric in the fourteenth century (again, following an Italian example). One of its students, Jean Gerson, became chancellor of the University (1399) and developed into an important spokesman for the conciliarist position in the Church. Gerson fought tirelessly for the proposition that a General Council of the Church could put an end to the Great Schism. He played a leading role in the Council of Constance (ended 1418); his influence in the French Church helped pave the way for the consolidation of 1423, which ended the Schism.

The reign of Charles V (1364–1380), despite the terrible effects of plague within the city, marked an important cultural landmark in the history of Paris. Charles was a passionate collector of books; he put his exceptionally large collection at the disposition of the scholars of his day. At this death, his collection became the basis for the royal library, which would later be open to all scholars and others showing legitimate cause. Today's Bibliothèque Nationale traces its origins directly back to the great library of Charles V. Charles sought to make the knowledge contained in his Classical treatises available to more people. Christine de Pisan wrote of his sponsorship of more than thirty translations of great Latin works into French: "and it was a noble and perfect action to have [them] translated from Latin into French to attract the hearts of the French people to high morals by good example."[49] The translator of Augustine of Hippo's City of God, Raoul de Presles, noted the king's desire to act on behalf of the good "and utility of your kingdom, of your people, and of all Christianity."

The most important translator was Nicolas of Oresme (another graduate of the College of Navarre), who worked on the great texts of Aristotle: the *Ethics,* the *Politics,* and *On the Heavens.* Those around Charles V, such as Christine de Pisan, cultivated the image of Paris as a new Athens, in which scholars like Nicolas of Oresme were translating (and thus making available to a new audience) the wisdom of Athens' greatest philosophers. Oresme baldly stated in his prologue to the texts that Greek had given way to Latin as the language of learning, and that Latin was now giving way to French. Oresme, in his own writing, applied the learning of the Classical authors to problems of his own day. His most famous work of the 1350s, *On Money,* offered a clear statement of mid-fourteenth century political ideals in Paris. Oresme denounced royal debasement of currency, arguing that the king had no right to debase because the coinage was the property of the entire community, and not of the king. Oresme argued that only a representative body could regulate the coinage. Just as in the later writings of Gerson on behalf of the conciliar approach to Church reform, Oresme's text emphasizes the Classical ideal of a *res publica,* commonwealth, whose leading citizens collectively looked out for its best interests.

The ideal of a *res publica* affected every aspect of fourteenth- and fifteenth-century French life. Many of the later legal attributes of the French monarchy date from this period. Charles V's lawyers came up with the Salic Law, just as legists of his period emphasized the inalienability of the royal demesne. By the early fifteenth century, everyone in French political society accepted the idea that the Crown (the immaterial king), not the living, individual king owned the royal demesne. The living king had only the use of the demesne, whose purpose was the support of the commonwealth.[50] In this sense, the royal demesne became the benefice attached to the Crown. Moreover, the king could not remove Crown officers, such as the constable or the chancellor; they held their positions for life.

Whether we look at Nicolas of Oresme's writings in the 1350s, at the arguments of deputies to provincial or general assemblies in the 1350s, 1360s or even 1440s, at the writings of Christine de Pisan in the early 1400s or at the *ordonnance cabochienne* of the rebels of 1413, the same overwhelming concern with a mixed polity comes through. No one questioned the need for a monarchy, yet the monarchy had to be tempered. The leading citizens of society—the great nobles and ecclesiastics and the leaders of the important towns—shared with the king the responsibility for the commonwealth. In 1465, a group of important princes, led by the dukes of Burgundy and Brittany, and the king's own brother (Charles, duke of Berry), even rebelled against King Louis XI in the name of the "Public Good." In his public manifesto, the duke of Berry claimed:

> those of the royal blood and other noble men and counselors of our late, very dear father the king, may God absolve him, have duly alerted and informed us by remonstrances of the great calamity in which the public good of this kingdom can be found, through the actions of certain enemies of the same surrounding my lord the king; their appetite has enormously wounded and trampled justice. . . . The clergy are oppressed, molested, and removed from their estates and benefices, and even worse made to perform marriages against the wishes, will, and consent of fathers and mothers and other relatives, which things are against all order of rightness, dishonor and bring vituperation on the kingdom, and bring confusion to the public good.[51]

Here, too, we see the influence of Italian humanism, and the revival of Classical notions of citizenship. The French, with their strong central monarchy, never went the way of the Italian city–states, with their constitutional governments and occasional republicanism, but French elites, like Italian ones, identified the *res publica* not with a form of government, one juxtaposed to monarchy, but with the common good. Following the translations of Oresme, French elites could read of Aristotle's three forms of legitimate government and see in their government what they believed to be Aristotle's best form, monarchy.[52]

The War of the Public Good ushered in a struggle among French elites to define the nature of monarchy's relationship to the commonwealth. The royal government argued that the king alone held its stewardship; elites suggested that a mixed form of government provided the best polity. This same conflict emerged throughout the Western world in the sixteenth century. Three remarkable changes gave it unprecedented urgency. First, Renaissance ideas, above all Humanistic culture, spread from Italy to western and central Europe. Second, the longstanding unity of Western Christianity shattered in the aftermath of Martin Luther's defiance of the Pope in 1517. Third, the voyages of discovery opened up both a new route to Asia and an entirely new world view, one that had to reflect the existence of a "New World." Well might people living in late fifteenth- or early sixteenth-century France say, along with Villon, "Where are the snows of times gone by?"[53]

Notes

1. J. B. Henneman, *Royal Taxation in Fourteenth Century France. The Development of War Financing, 1322–1356* (Princeton: Princeton University Press, 1971), 237.
2. Cited in B. Tuchman, *A Distant Mirror. The Calamitous 14th Century* (New York: Alfred A. Knopf, 1978), 99.
3. BN, Mss Fr 16,248, fol. 29v.
4. *A Parisian Journal, 1405–1449,* ed. and trans. J. Shirley (Oxford: Clarendon Press, 1968), 131. The estimate of fifty thousand dead, of course, is a considerable exaggeration.
5. G. Bois, *Crise du féodalisme* (Paris: Presses de la Fondation Nationale des Sciences Politiques, 1976, 1981), 275.
6. The king could revalue coins because the official money of account, the *livre,* did not correspond to an actual coin. A given coin thus had a legal value expressed in *livres* (or parts thereof), a value set simply by royal edict.
7. German metallurgy far surpassed that of France, which imported many metal goods, above all weapons and armor, from the Rhineland.
8. Here I would follow the insight of one of my Columbia mentors, Eugene Rice, who has suggested that the three great technological changes in human written communication have been the invention of writing, the invention of printing, and the computer.
9. Here I am using the translation of B. Jowett, as edited by S. Everson, Aristotle, *The Politics* (Cambridge; New York: Cambridge University Press, 1988).
10. The general evolution of western and central European society created the demand for such bodies; whether Parliament in England, Estates in France or Germany, Cortes in Iberia, Diets in central Europe, representative bodies sprang up everywhere by the early fourteenth century.

11. *Recueil des édits, déclarations, lettres-patentes . . . concernant l'Administration des Etats de Bourgogne* (Dijon: By order of the Estates, 1784), 125, 131, 133. I have translated the phrase *chose publique* by commonwealth because *chose publique* (literally "public thing") was itself a translation for the Latin term *res publica* or "commonwealth."

12. Documents of the time referred to the "better" part of the inhabitants or to the "weightier" part of the inhabitants, for example, those with more goods. This distinction, too, harkened back to Aristotle's ideas about who should be a citizen.

13. M. Bloch, *Feudal Society,* trans. L. A. Manyon (Chicago: University of Chicago Press, 1961), v. 2, 452.

14. J. Strayer, *The Reign of Philip the Fair* (Princeton: Princeton University Press, 1980), 147.

15. Bibliothèque Nationale, Mss. Fr. 16, 248, fol. 8.

16. Charles V's lawyers made some use of this doctrine in the 1350s but it became part of normative French political discourse only in the beginning on the fifteenth century, when Henry V of England claimed the French throne.

17. Courtesy meant, at that time, behavior appropriate to a noble. Froissart often uses this adjective, and explicitly does so to describe the practice of holding a prisoner for ransom. The winning army often massacred the other side's infantry, who were not nobles; at Bouvines, the French thus slaughtered the Emperor's Brabantine footmen to the last man.

18. Charles of Blois died, and became a saint. Montfort passed the duchy to his son, who did homage to Charles V of France.

19. Le duc de Lévis-Mirepoix, *La guerre de cent ans* (Paris: Albin Michel 1973), offers Froissart's version of the first English invasion. The story of Crécy appears on pp. 173–194. Citations from 186 and 192–193.

20. The English actually did make such a register, which survives to this day. A banneret was a knight who had the right to lead others into battle, under his banner. The figure for "other men" is, of course, a wild exaggeration. The number "thirty thousand" simply means a great many. The relative unconcern about such casualties reveals much about social attitudes.

21. C. de Pisan, *The Book of the Body Politic,* ed. and trans. K. L. Forhan (Cambridge; New York: Cambridge University Press, 1994), 90.

22. Lévis-Mirepoix, *La guerre de cent ans,* 223–28, reproduces the relevant sections of Froissart's Chronicle, from which the above narrative is taken. Citations from 227–228.

23. Charles of Navarre's mother, Jeanne of France, daughter of Louis X, died of plague in 1349. On his father's side, Charles descended from Charles of Evreux, making him the great-grandson of Philip III.

24. They called the local supervisors the *élus* (elected ones), a name they would keep until 1789, and the national ones the *élus généraux,* later shortened to *généraux.* This name, too, survived until 1789.

25. The first 10 *livres* of income paid 10 percent, but the rate then declined to 5 percent (40 *livres* and up), and 2 percent (over 100 *livres* to a maximum assessable amount of 1,000 *livres,* for commoners, and 5,000 *livres,* for nobles).

26. Reproduced in Lévis-Mirepoix, *La guerre de cent ans,* 365–367.

27. The Estates continued the exemption for nobles actually fighting in the king's army, but removed it from those who, though able, did not serve.
28. Both selections from Froissart come from the translation of P. Geary, ed., *Readings in Medieval History* (Peterborough, 1991), 746–747.
29. In a fitting example of fourteenth-century particularism, the Estates General of Langue d'Oc changed the form of the taxes there to a hearth tax; in 1363, they then voted a sales tax and a *gabelle* to pay for the men-at-arms. The north and south thus had the same package of taxes, but collected them for the opposite reasons.
30. C. C. Willard, ed., *The Writings of Christine de Pizan* (New York: Persea Books, 1994), 242.
31. *Chronicles of England, France, Spain, and the Adjoining Countries, by Sir John Froissart,* trans. T. Johnes (New York: New World Press, n.d.), 201.
32. Social unrest appeared in many areas of Europe at the end of the fourteenth century. The rebels of Wat Tyler's Rebellion (1381) marched on London, seized the king, and very nearly succeeded. The inevitable repression slaughtered thousands, especially in Kent.
33. The Orléans family forces took the name Armagnacs because of the key role of Bernard of Armagnac, husband of an Orléans princess, after Louis's death.
34. The last ruler of Dauphiné, Humbert, died without issue in 1349. He left his principality to the King of France, with the stipulation that the King's oldest son would bear the title of Dauphin. That arrangement lasted until the end of the monarchy.
35. Colette Beaune, *Naissance de la nation France* (Paris, 1985), offers a nuanced reading of Joan as a symbol of emergent French national sentiment in the fifteenth century. This fine book is now available in English translation, *The Birth of an Ideology: Myths and Symbols of Nation in Late-Medieval France,* trans. S. R. Huston; ed. F. L. Chayette (Berkeley: University of California Press, 1991).
36. The translation is that of C. Willard, *The Writings of Christine de Pizan,* 354 and ff.
37. Charles did not fulfill his promises about the expiatory actions to be carried out for forgiveness of the sin.
38. Many towns and seigneurs continued to have the right to levy tolls on goods passing through their lands. Towns also levied indirect taxes, but only with the king's permission.
39. Letter to deputies called for Estates General of 1433; BN, Mss Dupuy 519, fol. 5v. Elsewhere he speaks of the rapes of girls, prostitution of married women, profanations of holy places, thefts, larcenies, murders; he claims some people have committed suicide to escape from the deeds of the soldiers. One French phrase bothers me in the translation I offer. Juvenal des Ursins uses the phrase *mettoient en seps* twice: I have taken it to mean "spreadeagling on a post" (*sep*) but it may well mean "put in irons" (*ceps*—"irons"). Neither sounds very pleasant.
40. The Orléans holdings became Crown property because the family inherited the throne in 1498.
41. The phrase is taken from the classic book by Johan Huizinga, newly released in a complete English translation, which uses this title, rather than the earlier one, *The Waning of the Middle Ages,* which also deleted certain sections of the original.

42. The best description of medieval cookery and eating appears in B. Ketcham Wheaton, *Savoring the Past. The French Kitchen and Table from 1300 to 1789* (Philadelphia: University of Pennsylvania Press, 1983).

43. J. Heers, *Jacques Coeur* (Paris: Librairie Académique Perrin, 1997), 166. "Jacques Coeur fait ce qu'il veut, Et le Roy ce qu'il peut."

44. The tombs are at Dijon's Musée des Beaux-Arts. *The Well of Moses* sits in what must be one of the most unprepossessing sites for any of the great masterpieces of Western art, a courtyard in an administrative complex on the site of the former Charterhouse.

45. The "Limbourg" brothers took that name because of their Netherlandish origins. Their real names were Pol, Herman, and Jehanequin Maelweel; they apparently came from Guelders (just east of Utrecht in the modern-day Netherlands) rather than Limbourg.

46. Lecoy, ed., *Le Roman de la Rose,* lines 8251–8256.

47. C. de Pisan, *The Book of the City of Ladies,* trans. E. Richards (New York: Persea Books, 1982), 187.

48. E. McLeod, *Charles of Orleans, Prince and Poet* (New York: Viking Press, 1970), 168–169.

49. Cited in C. Richter Sherman, *Imaging Aristotle: Verbal and Visual Representation in Fourteenth-Century France* (Berkeley: University of California Press, 1995), 7.

50. A king could give part of the royal demesne to a royal prince as an apanage, but any sale or exchange of Crown land was subject to perpetual repurchase.

51. BN, Mss Dupuy 539, fol. 19.

52. Modern readers of *The Politics* can easily see that Aristotle does not say monarchy is the best form of government, yet writers of the fifteenth century, such as Christine de Pisan (in her *Book of the Body Politic*) routinely cite him as saying just that.

53. Except for this one sentence, which I have translated, I used the convenient translation of G. Kinnell, *The Poems of François Villon* (Hanover: University Press of New England, 1982). This edition contains parallel texts in Villon's French and in English.

Chapter Five

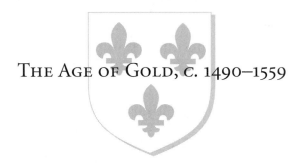

The Age of Gold, c. 1490–1559

*In the fields as well, we know well the abundance of people, because
many places and great countries that had been uncultivated or lying
fallow or wooded, are now all cultivated and occupied by villages
and houses.*[1]

Claude de Seyssel, *La Grande Monarchie de France*, 1519

Sixteenth-century Europeans had to redefine themselves in every aspect of their humanity. Explorers proved to Europeans the existence of vast, heavily populated, hitherto unknown continents. Humanists undermined the accepted meaning of fundamental texts and writers by subjecting the sources of Classical times and of early Christianity to rigorous, scholarly analysis. Scientists would soon revise people's view of the heavens, and of Earth's place in the Universe, to say nothing of the laws of motion and the understanding of the human body itself. Religious reformers destroyed the seemingly immemorial unity of the European Christian community. Virtually no important institution or fundamental belief of the European world of 1450 survived intact in 1650.

In the fifteenth century, the cold plains of northern Europe felt the first warm winds of intellectual and moral change from Renaissance Italy. We see evidence of early Humanistic influences in the Paris of Charles V (1363–1380), but the kingdom's periphery, above all Flanders, absorbed the artistic and cultural revolution in the early fifteenth century well before its capital. The spread of printing from Rhineland Germany into other parts of Europe after 1450/1460 further accelerated the spread of new cultural norms. Just as artistic change moved first from Italy to an outlying region of the kingdom of France, Flanders, so, too, printing set in first at Lyon, on the southeastern frontier. Paris, long the uncontested center of French cultural life, lost that position briefly in the fifteenth century: the Renaissance, like printing, got to Bruges or Lyon well before it got to Paris.

The French invasion of Italy in 1494 accelerated the acceptance of Renaissance ideas in France, but in many cultural forms, such as architecture, the medieval traditions carried out a spirited rear-guard action. Continued architectural conservatism aside, however, by the time Francis I became king (1515), the French aristocracy had

185

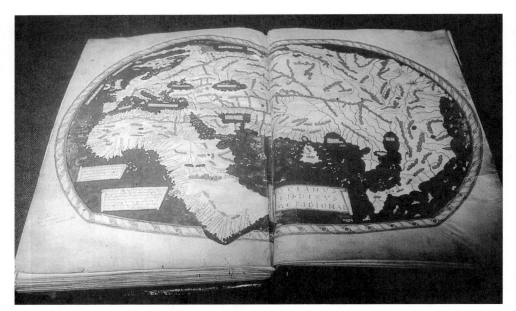

World Map, Juan de la Cosa, c. *1450/1460. Note the absence of the Western Hemisphere.*

SOURCE: © Ronald Sheridan/Ancient Art & Architecture Collection.

turned openly to Italian models of dress, of comportment, and of taste. French intellectuals, many of whom had had contacts with Italian Humanists as far back as the fourteenth century, now followed those Humanists in their pursuit of Classical wisdom. Classical ideas fundamentally modified French political thought and French literature, indeed all of French culture.

Shortly after digesting the dramatic new philosophies that came from Italy, France had to deal with unprecedented religious change. The outbreak of the Reformation (1517–1520) in the Holy Roman Empire touched France immediately. By the 1520s, France had several groups of "Reformers," most notably those grouped around bishop Guillaume Briçonnet of Meaux. These "Reformers" benefitted from the protection of one of the most powerful people in France, Marguerite d'Angoulême, the king's sister. She shielded them from the more conservative forces in the French church, such as the Sorbonne professors, who had the temerity briefly to ban a book she had written. Marguerite, although she remained a Catholic, played a critical role in the survival of Reformist ideas in France.

The great age of religious change lay slightly in the future, when the sudden explosion of Calvinism led to the outbreak of the Wars of Religion. At the very moment of the initial Protestant explosion (1550s), France also accommodated Jews for the first time since the expulsion of 1396. Although the King of France had driven out (1501) the important Jewish community of Provence shortly after he inherited that province, he allowed the Jews of Metz to remain when that city passed into his hands (1559). Moreover, Henry II (1547–1559) also permitted Iberian Jews, driven out by the stepped-up Inquisition in Portugal, to settle in Bordeaux.[2]

World Map, Battista Agnese, c. 1543. North America remains a little hazy, especially its Pacific coast, but the larger presence of the "New World" is clear.

SOURCE: The Granger Collection, New York.

Finally, the intellectual and material worlds both required new thinking after the voyages of Columbus and of Vasco de Gama. Columbus's voyages to the New World made public the existence of the Americas. Although Breton and Basque fishermen might well have been fishing in the Grand Banks at the end of the fifteenth century, Columbus's voyages, followed shortly thereafter by those of other explorers such as the French-sponsored cartographer Giovanni Verranzano or Jacques Cartier, bore witness to the existence of hitherto unimagined regions of the world. In a material sense, the Spanish conquest of Mexico in the early 1520s led to a striking increase in Spain's power and, in the long run, to a fundamental restructuring of the European economy.

The Portuguese voyages around Africa to Asia similarly revolutionized world trade. By the 1520s, even the Venetians, who had held a virtual monopoly on the pepper trade scarcely a generation before, bought spices in Lisbon. These two events—the ocean-borne connections of Europe to Asia and of the Americas to Europe and Asia—marked the death knell of the Mediterranean as the center of European life. France, the only country with one foot in the Mediterranean and the other in the north Atlantic, the new locus of power, would play a critical role in the transition from one system to the other. Henceforth, French people lived in an economic world system, the first genuinely global market. That market evolved slowly at first, but in the eighteenth century it would trample all pre-existing economic relations and drive the creation of the modern world.

The early sixteenth century does not fit neatly into any of the traditional chronological periods constructed by historians to explain European history. Clearly, the Middle Ages had died in an agony of upheaval, disease, and warfare. Yet medieval modes of thought and comportment survived everywhere: some survive still. Early modern times had not really begun, because the great changes of the late fifteenth and early sixteenth centuries—the invention of printing, the Renaissance, the integration of the Eastern and Western Hemispheres, the Reformation—had to take place before a genuinely early modern society could be in place. Perhaps we do best to think of the "happy sixteenth century" as the "foundation of early modern" France, to borrow the apt phrases of the historians Bernard Quilliet and Eugene Rice.[3]

CREATING THE FRENCH COMMONWEALTH: THE DEATH OF PRINCIPALITIES

> *No one can deny that the king was constituted by God to administer justice to all his subjects.*[4]
>
> Crown attorney Bourdin, speaking to the Parlement of Paris, 1562

France, real and imagined, underwent dramatic changes at the end of the fifteenth and beginning of the sixteenth centuries. France, as its elites would imagine it, took shape during the Italian wars. Catholic France, so central to the country's identity even today, had to face its greatest challenge, Protestantism. The village of French memory, the village of *la France profonde,* faded from existence, not to return until the nineteenth century. Even France's place in the world had to be reconsidered, because of the voyages of discovery. Frenchmen such as Jacques Cartier brought back tales of a New World, forever transforming the Old one.

Before France could take on all of these challenges, however, the political nation had to construct a coherent commonwealth of France. Charles VIII's 1494 invasion of Italy completed the dramatic reconfiguration of that commonwealth between 1445 and 1491. During this period, the kingdom of France absorbed many of the semi-independent principalities within its legal borders, beginning with the expulsion of the English from France (except for Calais) and ending with the marriage of Charles VIII and the last independent ruler of Brittany, the duchess Anne. The three major steps in this process were the French victory in the last stage of the Hundred Years' War, the crisis initiated by the War of the Public Good (1465), and the resolution of the Breton and Burgundian successions between 1488 and 1493.

The French victory in the Hundred Years' War (1337–1453) drove the English out of France (Calais excepted) for the first time since the twelfth century. Normandy returned to the royal demesne and Guyenne, the area near Bordeaux, became for the first time a real part of the kingdom. The solution to the crisis related to the War of Public Good effectively determined that the Crown, and the state, would have guardianship of the French commonwealth. The War of the Public Good and its after-shocks marked a definitive shift toward the new, more centralized state, unified around a king effectively claiming to be the sole protector of the commonwealth. The Breton and Burgundian marriage settlements of 1488–1493 became the basis for lasting polit-ical divisions, and for interminable international conflict. Those settlements, the suc-cession of the two branches of the house of Orléans to the Crown in 1498 and 1515, and the confiscation of the great Bourbon enclave in 1527 completed the transforma-tion of France from a family-run collection of principalities into an effective single kingdom. Little wonder that state institutions and the definition of kingship under-went fundamental transformation at the same time, above all in the reign of Francis I.

The passage of the great principalities of Burgundy, Brittany, and Orléans into the royal demesne formed the most important part of the dramatic reconfiguration of the kingdom of France between 1453 and 1527. Historians have long misrepre-sented this reconfiguration because they have focused on specific individual rulers rather than on the royal family. At the start of the fifteenth century, the French royal family, *taken as a whole,* ruled modern-day France (except Alsace) and the Low Countries; by marriage, they had claims to the Kingdom of the Two Sicilies and to the duchy of Milan. Three distinct elements existed simultaneously within this mas-sive family corporation: (1) the specific individuals, such as the King of France; (2) the Crown of France; and (3) the family corporation. The royal family thus closely resembled the family of a rich peasant, who looked out for his individual interest within the larger context of his family's holdings. In both cases, the family worked together against outsiders, yet also fought internal battles over control of the family resources. Neither peasant nor duke blanched at seeking outside help to win the family battles. Both sides in the French civil wars of the early fifteenth century ap-proached Henry V of England for help.

The Crown of France, and its corollary, the French state, won the family con-flict because an imagined entity did not have the temporal limitations of real people. The king died, but the kingship did not. The fifteenth-century kingdom of France included many principalities in which the king had only vague rights as overlord and/or as sovereign. Documents of the time, and even in the sixteenth century, make clear the overlap of these two roles: the Estates General of France invariably addressed the king as their "sovereign seigneur," a term that strikes us as an oxy-moron. A sovereign has authority over all, above all the ultimate rights of judgment and lawmaking; a seigneur is merely the lord of his vassals. A seigneur, by defini-tion, is not a sovereign, yet fifteenth-century people were quite right to use the term "sovereign seigneur" because the king, although he did have vaguely defined legal rights as sovereign over the entire kingdom, in fact ruled important parts of it merely as the personal overlord of his great vassals. Louis XI quite explicitly stated the limits of his power in the appanage granted to his brother Charles. The king re-served for himself only "fealty and liege homage, and sovereignty and court juris-diction, with the guardianship of cathedrals and other churches of royal foundation and of privileges such that they cannot or must not be separated from the Crown of France." In 1465, Louis even granted the judges of his sister Jeanne and her hus-band, Jean of Bourbon, rights of sovereign justice, without appeal to any royal court in their appanages.[5]

The dukes of Bourbon, Brittany, Burgundy, and Orléans, the counts of Armagnac, Saint-Pol, and Alençon, and other lesser vassals of the king ruled essentially independent states. Many of these rulers, such as those of Burgundy or Brittany, issued
their own coins, had their own armies, promulgated laws, authorized courts, and
collected taxes. The King of France collected not a single penny in taxes from Brittany or Burgundy or these other principalities. In the appanages in which officials
did levy royal taxes, the holder of the appanage, not the king, got the money. That
said, the rulers owed him homage, which meant they held their lands in fief from the
King of France, that is, the Crown. In many cases, such as that of the duchy of Burgundy, they held their lands as members of the royal family corporation. An appanage reverted to the Crown when direct male heirs ran out, just like a noble fief
would, under some local customary laws, return to the male heirs if a man had had
no male children.

The great princes strongly believed that they and the king collectively had cus-
tody of the French commonwealth, of what they called the "public good" (*bien pub-
lic*). In 1465, the great princes of the kingdom—the king's brother, Charles, duke of
Berry; duke Philip of Burgundy and his son Charles; duke Francis II of Brittany;
Jean, duke of Bourbon; Jean, duke of Calabria; Pierre of Bourbon; Charles, count of
Albret; Jacques, duke of Nemours; Jean, count of Armagnac; and Louis, count of
Saint-Pol, among others—rebelled against him, calling themselves the League of the
Public Good. One of their manifestos made clear their understanding of how the
kingdom should be governed:

> for the great and principal affairs of the king and the kingdom the king can
> and is held to employ the princes and lords of royal blood, as the principal
> members of the Crown, by the counsel of whom, and not that of others, he
> should give order to the state, police, and governance of the kingdom.[6]

The aged Philip the Good, duke of Burgundy, who was too infirm to take part in
the military confrontation, spoke eloquently to the Estates of Burgundy, whom he
called in April 1465 to vote a subsidy for the upcoming war.

> His subjects of his said land (*pays*) have always been true, good, and obedient
> [to him] as their seigneur and head of the commonwealth (*chose publique*)
> of his said land, and how for that reason he has so loved them that for their
> ease and tranquility he has many times exposed his body and his goods for
> them, without holding anything back, how he has by arms defended them
> against his enemies and those of his said lands, how by justice he has main-
> tained them in good union and by his clemency, kindness, and pity he has
> been as benign and gracious as any prince has ever been to subjects . . .[7]

Philip, like the other great feudatories, accepted as a given that he was the "head of
the commonwealth" for his lands, so that he and the other feudatories shared with
the king the stewardship of the commonwealth of the kingdom as a whole. He, like the
duke of Berry, believed the princes of the royal blood, who held most of the great

principalities, were the most important "members" (which carries in French the sense of parts of the body) of the Crown of France. The king, of course, had other ideas.

The rebels forced the king to agree to the treaty of Saint-Maur-des-Fossés (29 October 1465) that gave in to almost all of their demands. Charles received the duchy of Normandy, in place of the much poorer one of Berry. Other rebels received back lands the king had earlier seized from them. Contemporary observers focused on these purely selfish gains, yet the agreement spoke as well to the needs of the commonwealth. The king promised not to call nobles to do military service "except for the defense and evident good of the kingdom." He further agreed to see to the complaints and grievances "of the said lords and of many subjects of the king of diverse estates about certain disorders and faults in the matters of the church, of justice, and of many exactions and vexations come about, to the great crushing and damage of the people and of the public good of the kingdom." He promised to appoint a commission of thirty-six "notable" men (twelve clergy, twelve nobles, twelve judges) to seek remedies. They were to meet in December 1465. Louis agreed that ordinances issued by the commission should take full effect, "as if the king himself had made them," and promised to issue letters patent to that purpose within fifteen days of receiving their report. These letters were to be published in all royal courts; local royal judges (bailiffs and seneschals) had to swear an oath to uphold forever the new rules. The great lords promised to do the same, and to have their officers take a similar oath. The Parlement of Paris even registered the agreement in November.

This astonishing document, which forced the king to share effective sovereignty with a sort of legislative commission drawn from the three estates of the realm, never took effect. Louis, the "universal spider," cleverly spun his webs, buying off first one prince and then another. Remarkably, one conspirator after another died in the 1470s and 1480s: Charles, dead of natural causes in 1472; Jean d'Armagnac, assassinated in 1473; Louis, count of Saint-Pol, the king's brother-in-law, executed for treason in 1475; Charles of Burgundy, dead at Nancy (1477); Jacques of Nemours, executed for treason in 1477; René, duke of Anjou, count of Provence, and "king" of Sicily, dead of natural causes in 1480; Francis II of Brittany, dead of natural causes in 1488.[8] The death of these great princes, and the reversion of their principalities to the Crown (either due to lack of male heirs for an appanage, as in Burgundy or Anjou, or as escheat in a case of treason, as for Saint-Pol), effectively demolished the central premise of the Leaguers. If they had held the stewardship of the commonwealth in their lands, their heir, the king, naturally took over that stewardship when he inherited their principalities.

The great conflict of the fifteenth century over stewardship of the commonwealth of France came about because the French royal family had split into so many branches in the fourteenth and early fifteenth centuries. The conflict resolved itself primarily because they died out: Jean, duke of Berry, had no direct heirs; the last duke of Burgundy died in 1477 and the duke of Anjou in 1480. The king's own branch of the royal family expired in 1498, so the house of Orléans, which had two branches by then, inherited the throne. When the elder branch of that family ran out of male heirs, in 1514, the cadet branch took the throne (Francis I).[9]

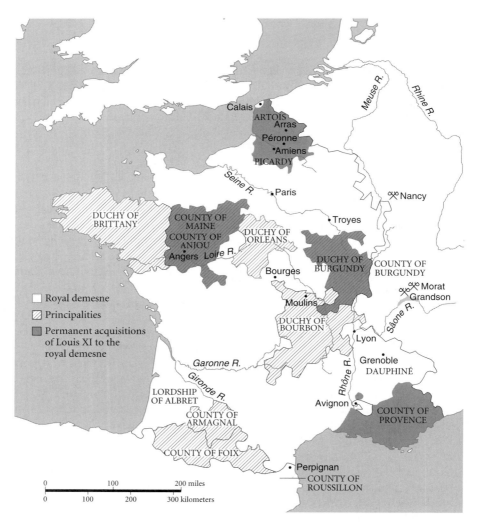

Death of the apanages.

This remarkable conquest, often called the destruction of the great feudatories, had almost nothing to do with military success. The extinction of five lines of the royal family provided France with a remarkable opportunity to create a single commonwealth near the end of the fifteenth century. The long-standing ability of princes holding appanages to siphon off royal revenues into their own pockets, and to run their appanages as all-but-independent states, stopped. The tax collectors in Burgundy now paid the money to the king, not to the duke. The king recognized the special situation of these provinces by allowing some of them—Brittany, Burgundy,

Provence—to maintain local institutions, such as Estates. Each of these provinces soon had a chief royal court, a Parlement, which often merely replaced a pre-existing local court. They also kept their individual tax systems: the king never collected any of the regular French taxes in Provence or Brittany; he simply continued the taxes initially voted by local estates to the count of Provence or the duke of Brittany.

Like the companies in any modern conglomerate, the branches of the French royal family corporation naturally coveted wholly owned subsidiaries. This tendency of the constituent "companies" of the corporation to obtain subsidiaries outside of France lay at the root of the Italian Wars. When René of Anjou died in 1480, he left the Crown not only his duchy of Anjou and the county of Provence (which had never been part of the kingdom of France), but a claim to the kingdom of Sicily. The Orléans branch, by means of marriage with the Viscontis of Milan, claimed that duchy, first in 1494, as part of Charles's invasion of Italy, and then, after 1498, when the Orléans branch itself took the throne in the person of Louis XII.

The Burgundian inheritance provided the most intractable problem, particularly after it became intertwined with the succession of Brittany. Louis XI spent much of the 1460s and 1470s fighting with duke Charles the Rash of Burgundy. Louis's armies had little success, but the pikemen of his Swiss allies routed the chivalric Burgundian cavalry at Grandson, Murat, and Nancy (1477), where scavengers looting the corpses of the dead Burgundians found Charles lying face down in the mud. His sole heir, Mary of Burgundy, inherited an enormous and fabulously rich agglomeration of semi-independent principalities: the duchy and county of Burgundy, almost all of the Low Countries, Artois, most of Picardy, and several smaller feudal entities, such as the county of Charolais.[10] Louis XI discovered the news of Charles's death before Mary because of improvements he had made to the royal postal system; ever the gentleman, the king immediately sent troops to confiscate the duchy of Burgundy from his cousin Mary. Louis justified his action by French law, which mandated that an appanage reverted to the Crown in the absence of a direct male heir.[11] Louis tried, but failed to seize other French-speaking territories, such as Artois and the county of Burgundy (Franche-Comté).[12]

Mary naturally detested Louis. She believed her family had inherited Burgundy from the last Capetian duke, who had died without issue, so that Louis had no right to seize the duchy. This personal quarrel proved to have momentous long-term consequences: Mary married Maximilian of Habsburg, a German prince with holdings in nearby Alsace. His wife's fabulous wealth raised Maximilian to the upper ranks of European politics, a position solidified by his election as Holy Roman Emperor (1491). Mary died in 1482, after falling from her horse, but the couple had two children: Philip of Habsburg and Margaret of Austria (b. 1480). Mary's death thus left her nonappanage lands, *some of which lay in juridical France,* in the hands of a foreign prince. When Maximilian became Emperor, he faced the legally bizarre situation of owing homage to the King of France, as count of Flanders.

Mary had passed her visceral hatred of Louis XI to her husband and son, but high politics enmeshed Maximilian ever more deeply in French politics. Soon after Mary's death, the families sought reconciliation by arranging a marriage between Charles (b. 1469), son of Louis XI, and Margaret of Austria. Margaret, still a small child, went to live at the French Court; Louis XI obtained immediate legal rights to her dowry, Artois and the Franche-Comté.

Louis XI's death (1483) made Charles VIII king, although Charles's sister, Anne of Beaujeu, ran the country during his minority. Charles and Margaret had still not married, due to her age, when the death of duke Francis II of Brittany (1488) dramatically reopened the old wounds and set in motion a series of events that created the fundamental political and diplomatic structure of European politics for the next two hundred fifty years. Shortly before Francis's death, Maximilian had carried out a proxy marriage to the twelve-year-old Anne of Brittany, heir to the duchy. Charles, not wanting one of the richest provinces in Europe to fall into Maximilian's hands, marched an army into Brittany and forced Anne to renounce her proxy marriage. He reneged on his promise to marry Margaret and married Anne (1491). Maximilian understandably demanded that Charles return both Margaret and her dowry. Charles refused, so war broke out.[13]

Charles VIII's duplicity did him little good. He died in 1498, without issue, which meant that Brittany again became an independent principality. The new king, Louis XII (1498–1514), could take no chances: he repudiated his wife, Jeanne of France (sister of Charles VIII), and married the widowed Anne of Brittany. They had no son, but their daughter, Claude of Brittany, married Louis XII's successor, Francis I (1515–1547), and thus brought the duchy of Brittany permanently into the French royal family.

The Burgundian and Flemish legacies, however, were not so neatly resolved. Mary of Burgundy had left more than a few territories. Her heirs also inherited a profound sense of grievance for the loss of her French fiefs, above all the duchy of Burgundy. Philip passed along to his son, Emperor Charles V, that grievance and the intense sense of dishonor his father had suffered from the broken marriage promises of the 1480s.[14] This personal quarrel took on even broader European dimensions because Philip married Juana the Mad, daughter of Ferdinand and Isabella of Spain in 1496. When Juana's siblings later died without issue, she got the kingdoms of her mother (Castille) and father (Aragon). Juana and Philip's oldest son, Charles V, thus inherited the largest territory ruled by any European prince since Charlemagne. From his mother, he obtained the kingdom of Spain; from his grandmother Mary, he received the Low Countries and the Franche-Comté; from the Habsburgs he got German lands and, in time, a claim to the Imperial title. The seven Electors chose him as Holy Roman Empire in 1519.[15]

Time and again, the county of Flanders, so much a part of the imagined France of the country's elite, yet so tentatively part of the legal kingdom, haunted the commonwealth. The King of France ever sought to bring the region under his control; he failed at every turn. These efforts continued long after the death of Mary of Burgundy; French armies fought to conquer Flanders in the sixteenth, seventeenth, and eighteenth centuries. Whatever the outcome of the individual battles, the end results of the wars were always the same: France could never again make Flanders, an integral part of the France of the imagination, into a part of the real France.

Charles VIII's agreement with Maximilian shifted French focus in a new direction. The death of the last Aragonese King of Sicily gave him the opportunity to claim Naples, as heir to René of Anjou.[16] He invaded the peninsula in 1494. Once the French nobility had seen Renaissance Italy, France would never be the same.

Effigy of Anne of Brittany, 1514. Anne was one of the great art patrons of her time; in addition to this work, she commissioned the splendid funeral monument of her father, duke Francis II, at Nantes.

SOURCE: Cathédrale Basilique Saint-Denis, Tombeau Renaissance, Anne de Bretagne, 1514.

THE ITALIAN WARS AND THE CREATION OF MODERN FRENCH CULTURE

Where are the heroes of yesterday?

François Villon

Early modern France had few heroes to compare to Pierre du Terrail, lord of Bayard, the "knight without fear and without reproach," whose statue graces the main square of today's Grenoble. Bayard and his contemporaries proved their worth in the Italian wars of their masters, which began in 1494, with Charles VIII's invasion of the kingdom of Naples. This invasion provided an opportunity for the nobility to demonstrate its prowess in fighting far from France. Moreover, the advent of printing allowed people to read about these exploits in books such as the one written about Bayard by the Lyonnais physician Symphorien Champier: *The Worthy Deeds of the Life of the Courageous Knight Bayard,* published in 1525. Bayard became the stuff both of legend and of the knightly curriculum. Every French sword noble sought to model his conduct on the life of the peerless Bayard.

French nobles brought back from Italy a taste for the peninsula's more refined lifestyle and manners. Throughout the sixteenth century, one of the best-selling books in France would be a translation of Baltasare Castiglione's *Book of the Courtier,* a manual for the proper behavior of ladies and gentlemen infused with the Humanistic values of Renaissance Italy. Francis I had a personal copy of the earliest (unauthorized) edition of the *Courtier* as early as 1514; as soon as Castiglione came out with a corrected edition, Francis ordered it translated into French in 1537.

The French invasion of Italy followed closely on Charles VIII's and Maximilian's agreeing to the Peace of Senlis (May 1493), which gave some satisfaction to both sides. Charles recognized Maximilian's claims to Artois and the Franche Comté and returned Margaret to her father. These losses, although considerable, should not mask the advantages France obtained. Charles received full recognition of his hold over Picardy and the Somme towns, as well as *de facto* recognition of his rights over the duchy of Burgundy. Maximilian later even did homage for Artois and Flanders.

The long series of wars, which took place intermittently from 1494 to 1559, ran concurrently with a constantly shifting set of negotiations that centered around marriage alliances between the different royal families. Charles started the wars by waltzing an army down the Italian peninsula, stopping at many large cities. At the news of their approach, the King of Naples, Alphonso, abdicated in favor of his son Ferdinand II. Local resistance quickly crumbled in the face of the French army, and Charles had possession of Naples by late February 1495.

The French proceeded to loot southern Italy. French nobles grabbed all the important positions in the kingdom; some of them married rich Neapolitan heiresses. Local nobles turned against the French, much as their ancestors had done two centuries before, when the Neapolitans had massacred the Angevin French and driven them from the kingdom. Charles's success immediately alarmed his former enemies, who created a new alliance, the League of Venice (March 1495) to counteract the French.[17] The new alliance included Venice, the duke of Milan (France's original ally in Italy), the Pope, Maximilian, and Ferdinand and Isabella of Spain. Charles VIII left Naples within weeks of his official "entry" into the city. The inconclusive fighting between Charles and the League of Venice in northern Italy did not prevent the loss of Naples in 1496.

In the short term, politics went on as usual. Charles VIII died in 1498; his cousin successor, Louis XII, immediately restarted the Italian wars. Louis had returned Milan to the Sforza in 1496 as part of the peace settlement but, as soon as he became king, he reclaimed the duchy and invaded. He first took, then lost, then retook the Milanais. In 1502, he signed an agreement with Ferdinand of Aragon to divide the kingdom of Naples, but the French rapidly lost control of their area, their army wasting away in the Neapolitan swamps. Shortly after the end of the Naples debacle, Louis XII and Maximilian had another rapprochement. They engaged Maximilian's grandson, Charles V, to Claude of France, infant daughter of Louis XII and of Anne of Brittany. Louis promised Claude a dowry including Burgundy, Blois, Brittany, Genoa, and Milan; the young couple were to receive as well the kingdom of Naples.

This diplomatic chicanery, known as the treaty of Blois, never took effect. One can seriously doubt whether Louis ever intended to put it into place. He used it to obtain a respite in the fighting, at a moment when hostilities had turned sharply against his forces. Indeed, scarcely three years later, on the dubious pretext that a special assembly of "Estates" meeting at Tours demanded the marriage of Francis d'Angoulême, heir presumptive of France, and of Claude, Louis reneged on the marriage and allowed her to marry his presumed male successor.[18]

Years of diplomatic maneuvers followed, along with many famous battles. The French won many of the battles, led by their redoutable knights, but lost far more of them. These knights included in their number fighters legendary for centuries thereafter, among them the incomparable Bayard, the "knight without fear and without reproach." The "final" great victory, in which Bayard played a critical role, came in 1512, when the French army under Gaston of Foix routed the Venetians at Ravenna. Bayard exhorted his chosen band of five hundred men-at-arms: "Friends, crush these bourgeois Venetians!" Despite their deeds, Bayard and his companions found it a hollow victory; Gaston of Foix had fallen and his loss meant that "if the king has gained the battle, the poor gentlemen have surely lost it." Bayard might well have said that the king, too, lost the battle, for Gaston of Foix's successor could not match his exploits. A year later, at Novara, the Swiss demolished the French army and reconquered the Milanais for the Sforza family. They even marched on Dijon, laying siege to it and forcing its commander, La Trémoïlle, to pay a substantial ransom and to make, in Louis XII's name, important territorial concessions. Louis, of course, reneged on these "unauthorized" promises.

These wars, inane as they seem to our eyes, had a profound political and cultural impact. Politically, Spain replaced France as the dominant outside power in Italy, a position it would hold until the eighteenth century. Machiavelli long ago chastised the French for their unskillful diplomacy in these years; he rightly suggested that Louis XII foolishly sought alliances with Pope Julius II, a man certain to be unreliable. He also condemned as folly Louis's call to Ferdinand against the kingdom of Naples. Surely his criticisms ring true these (nearly) five centuries later. That said, Louis played the diplomatic game in much the same way as other rulers of his time. He and Maximilian would quarrel, fight, make up, quarrel again; one could say as much about Louis and Ferdinand or, indeed, of Ferdinand and Maximilian. In hindsight, we see that the ties between Maximilian and Ferdinand, through the marriage of their children, would become more lasting, yet the proposed marriages of various members of the Habsburg, Valois, and Spanish families could well have produced very different results.[19]

The wars began anew with the accession of Francis I (1515). Francis led an army into Italy, using Alpine defiles previously considered inaccessible to troops. Facing a massive army of Swiss mercenaries at Marignano, in a two-day battle the French and

The Knight without Fear and without Reproach

Pierre du Terrail, sieur de Bayard belonged to an old noble family of Dauphiné. Through the influence of his maternal uncle, the bishop of Grenoble, he became a page of duke Charles of Savoy. While in the duke's service, Bayard's horsemanship so impressed Charles VIII that he requested this young page from the duke. Bayard spent the rest of his life in the service of France. He made his early name in the company of the great French captain Louis Dars, whose exploits in southern Italy inspired poets and chroniclers. As a young man, Bayard fought a famous duel with the Spanish nobleman Alonso of Sotto Mayor. Bayard had captured Alonso during a battle. When Alonso returned to the Spanish army, he claimed Bayard had mistreated him, leading Bayard to demand satisfaction. Bayard, sick with fever, killed Alonso in front of the two armies and cried out:

> O all-powerful God! That I have made die my Christian brother, who was such a noble and chivalrous man! O damned hour, when I took you prisoner, noble Alonso.... O sovereign God, by your mercy have pity on me, and make me able to be consoled, because I never fought with him with the intention to make him lose his life, but it was only my intention to save my honor! But there is no remedy for it, so I beg you, redeemer of the world, to be willing to have mercy on the soul of this noble knight and to allow him to be led to the kingdom of the living.[20]

Bayard carried through countless other deeds of bravery, some of them foolhardy and tactically ill-advised. His reputation grew to the extent that, rather than flee in the face of advancing Imperial troops near Thérouanne (in Flanders), he willingly surrendered—to the Emperor Maximilian in person.

As Champier recounts the story, Maximilian recognizes Bayard at once and soon introduces him to his ally, King Henry VII of England:

> My brother, do you recognize this Frenchman?
> No, replied Henry, by my faith.
> Certainly, said the Emperor, you have often heard him spoken about; among the Spanish, he is the most famous, feared, and hated Frenchman who has ever lived.
> Aha, replied the king, . . . it must be Bayard.

Later, after the battle of Marignano, Francis I will give Bayard the ultimate compliment; he asks that Bayard dub him a knight: "Bayard, my friend, I wish today to become a knight by your hands, because you are the battle-hardened knight among all others who is held and reputed to be the most worthy knight." Bayard at first declines, out of modesty, but the king insists. Bayard calls upon the names of great French knights of the past—on Roland and Oliver, on Godefroy of Bouillon and King Baudouin of Jerusalem (leaders of the First Crusade)—to bear witness to this king who has proved himself, at Marignano, also to be a worthy knight. Bayard dominated the French memory of these wars for generations; his deeds far overshadowed the actual military events, which proved so pointless in the end. He, and his peers, like Louis Dars or la Trémoille, left a mighty legacy to the imagined France of the nobility.

their Venetian allies, who arrived the morning of the second day, to turn the tide, effected an enormous slaughter. The battle seemed to decide the fate of northern Italy, with France in control of Lombardy and with Venice and Savoy firmly in its orbit. This arrangement lasted only six years, until the next great war between Francis I and Charles V.

Francis wanted to keep the Milanais; Charles, his feudal overlord for Milan, wanted to eject him. Charles also harbored deep grudges for the wrongs done to his grandmother, Mary of Burgundy. He believed that the duchy of Burgundy and other

French lands rightly belonged to him. Francis, for his part, wanted Charles to do homage for Flanders and Artois, as his father Philip had done. The two rulers first competed to see which would become Holy Roman Emperor; both bribed the seven Electors. Charles won.

Francis's allies took Luxemburg and Navarre in spring 1521, but lost them almost immediately. Charles then helped to create the Italian league that drove the French from the Milanais (1521–1522). His allies invaded northern France, there to be held off by Bayard, who defended Mézières against all odds and prevented an invasion of France proper. The following year, Francis sent an army into Italy; he intended to lead it himself, but had to remain in France when the commander-in-chief of the French army, the constable Charles of Bourbon, turned traitor and went over to the side of the Emperor.[21]

Francis's army disintegrated in Italy. The renegade Bourbon, who commanded the Imperial forces in the region, invaded southern France, unsuccessfully besieging Marseilles in August 1524. Francis then marched into Italy. At Pavia (1525), the Spanish army inflicted the greatest French defeat since Agincourt, capturing Francis himself. Many of his close friends, like Admiral Bonnivet, died on the field and others were taken prisoner. The king remained in Spain until March 1526, when he bought his freedom only by promising to give Charles back the duchy of Burgundy. Francis sent his two oldest sons to Spain as hostages and asked for the hand of Eleanor of Portugal, sister of Charles, in marriage. Charles accepted these conditions, over the strenuous objections of his chief advisor, Mercurino di Gattinara.

Francis repudiated the Treaty of Madrid as soon he got back to France. On the pretext that the Estates and Parlement of Burgundy refused to ratify the Treaty, the king refused to relinquish Burgundy. After three more years of intermittent and utterly futile warfare, the two sides agreed to a new settlement: Charles received 2 million crowns and a release from obligations to do homage for Flanders and Artois. He did not get Burgundy. Upon full payment of the first installment of the ransom (1.2 million crowns in gold), Charles agreed to release the two princes and Eleanor.

The Peace of Cambrai marked a definitive change between medieval and modern France because it reconfigured juridical France. Francis I's abandonment of suzerainty over Flanders and Artois ended a connection more than half a millennium old. France remained obsessed with the conquest of Flanders and Artois, but its rulers could no longer claim a legal right to them. The final incorporation of Brittany, in an edict of 1532, completed the integration of the traditional kingdom, minus the "lost" provinces of Flanders and Artois.

The remaining wars between Francis I, his son Henry II (1547–1559), and Charles V, decided nothing new but they had an important element distinguishing them from the earlier fighting: the role of religion. By the 1530s, Charles V faced substantial opposition within the Holy Roman Empire from Protestant princes, especially those of northern Germany. Throughout the sixteenth and seventeenth centuries, Catholic France consistently made the political choice to support those Protestant German princes against France's sworn Catholic enemy, the Habsburg Emperor. Important forces within France opposed this policy on the grounds that Catholics should unite to extirpate Protestantism. In the sixteenth century, the Guise family, which came from the Imperial province of Lorraine, headed the pro-Catholic faction; as late as 1630, the debate over siding with Protestants against Catholics raged on in the royal council.

The fighting of the 1540s and 1550s favored first one side, then the other, not only in the Valois–Habsburg conflict but in that between Charles V and the Protestant princes. In 1557, however, the perennially inept constable, Anne de Montmorency, lost the catastrophic battle of Saint-Quentin to the Spanish. At the battle and later capture of the town, the Spanish captured the constable, the admiral of France, and the colonel–general of the French infantry, as well as the dukes of Montpensier and Longueville, and more than three hundred other nobles. Fortunately for France, the Spanish frittered away their advantage. The campaigning the following year led to a signal French victory: the duke of Guise captured Calais, which had been held by the English since the fourteenth century. Henceforth, Calais would be a French city.

The peace of Cateau-Cambrésis primarily codified settlements reached in earlier treaties. France made one significant territorial gain: the Emperor recognized France's temporary overlordship of the bishoprics of Toul, Metz, and Verdun, a harbinger of French territorial ambitions to come. In return, France made a decisive territorial concession: Henry II renounced all rights over Italian territory. Many historians suggest that Henry's willingness to give up his claims, for which the French nobility had so long fought on behalf of the "king's just cause," undermined support for the king among the nobility. That support declined even further in the aftermath of a dreadful accident: at the tournament celebrating the treaty and a pair of royal marriages (Henry's daughter, Elisabeth, married Philip II of Spain; and Henry's sister married the duke of Savoy). The tip of the lance of captain Montgomery glanced off the king's shield and through the eye slit in his helmet. Henry died ten days later, after having forgiven Montgomery, whom he ordered not to be harmed. He left his sickly fourteen-year-old son, Francis II, as king.[22]

The early sixteenth-century wars determined that France would not dominate Italy, an outcome obvious in Charles VIII's time and merely reconfirmed by later events. Although the connection did not take place in a political sense, in a cultural sense the two regions had an enormous impact on each other. Above all, the Italians fundamentally changed French culture.

∾ The Cultural Revolution

> *I write in my mother tongue / And try to value it / In order to make it eternal / As the ancients did with theirs / And I maintain that it is great unhappiness / To undervalue one's own possession / To favor that of another. / If the Greeks are so very famous / If the Romans are as well / Why not do as they did / To be, like them, eternal?*

Jacques Peletier, 1545, introduction to the
French translation of the *Poetics* of Horace

Many French male nobles spent a considerable portion of their lives in Italy between 1494 and 1559. Thousands died there. Those who returned came back with new tastes, their perspectives revolutionized by what they saw. During the 1494 march to Naples, French nobles stayed at Italian villas, so different from the drafty, cavernous castles of France. Contemporary accounts suggest they found the new Charterhouse of Pavia (completed in 1491) to be a particular source of inspiration, with its Classical, balanced design. They encountered a culture of refinement, one whose values created a new image for the nobleman: that of the courtier. Many French nobles, like the hundred-plus young men seen by Montaigne at Padua in 1580, studied fencing, dancing, and riding at Italian schools specially set up for them.

We know much of the ethos of those times through the remarkable work of Baltasare Castiglione, *The Book of the Courtier,* a manual for the would-be gentleman (or woman). Castiglione describes for us the court of Urbino, an Italian city–state ruled by duke Guidobaldo da Montefeltro. The duchess, Elisabetta Gonzaga, from the ruling family of Mantua, set the tone for the Court. She provided an example for all ladies to follow:

> everyone endeavoured to imitate her personal way of behaviour, deriving as it were a model of fine manners from the presence of so great and talented a woman . . . [who had] prudence and a courageous spirit and all those virtues very rarely found even in the staunchest of men.[23]

The gentlemen of the Court paid homage to her, in a sort of ritual dance. The final flowering of the Courtly love tradition had taken place at the Burgundian court in the middle of the fifteenth century, so French nobles well knew the conventions and rituals of an elegant life, but Castiglione sketched for them the true Renaissance courtier. He was honest with his prince, faithful to his friends, modest in his demeanor, learned (but not pedantic), fluent in his orations, stylish—not modish—in his dress, graceful in his movements, whether in sport (including fighting) or dancing. Alas for the mass of humanity, most of Castiglione's courtiers agreed that grace is usually a natural quality, not an acquired one, an idea that fitted well with the prejudices of the nobility in all countries.[24]

Italian Court life differed fundamentally from traditional French Court life. The level of magnificence, on a *daily* basis, far exceeded that of earlier times. The level of comfort, too, was much different. Italian nobles lived in towns but kept rural villas. These villas, like Italian urban architecture, relied on Classical models. They made great use of windows, of columns, and courtyards; they emphasized exterior design for ornamentation, not merely for defense. Building wings now had balconies on top, not the steeply pitched roofs so typical of fifteenth-century construction. The change came so rapidly that some chateaux, like Fontaine-Henry in Normandy, show an amalgamation of the two styles, side by side.

The changes can best be seen in the chateau of Blois, to which both Louis XII (1498–1515) and Francis I (1515–1547) added. The wing added by Louis XII demonstrates some of the mixed elements of Italian architecture, with its covered promenade and large windows, yet it remains fundamentally Gothic in conception. By contrast, the famous façade of the Francis I wing demonstrates the full conquest of Renaissance architecture. One sees the Classical elements everywhere: the elaborate decoration of the corniches, the emphasis on light and columns in an outside wall, the double loggia design, unique among French châteaux. Only the sharply pitched roof remains of the traditional French château.

Francis's love of the Loire valley, with its pleasant climate and its magnificent forest hunting, kept him there much of his life. His nobles and his non-noble courtiers built châteaux there, where they remain a mecca for tourists. In some cases, such as the château of Lude or at Verger, built for the French marshal, Pierre de Rohan, a powerful noble sponsored the new dwelling. In many other cases, the patrons came from the royal government. Louis XII's chief minister, Cardinal George d'Amboise, had built one of the best examples of the new château, at Gaillon in Normandy (1505–1510), while the intermarried financier families of Berthelot and Bouhier paid for two of the loveliest examples, Azay-le-Rideau and Chenonceaux. Chenonceaux, in particular, with its world-famous gallery straddling the Cher river, mixes lingering elements of Flamboyant Gothic with Italian Renaissance motifs.

French kings ameliorated existing châteaux (Charles VIII at Amboise) or built new ones (Francis I at Chambord). Chambord shows the process at its most extreme, with its perfect rectangular shape, its fantastical roof, its cupolas, the central one crowning (at a height of 130 feet) the famed double staircase. On this twin spiraling staircase, one could either choose the ascending or descending stairs and never encounter a person headed in the other direction. The staircase provides a fitting symbol to the more elaborate Italianized Court etiquette introduced under Francis I, while the roof, with its bizarre mixture of Italian Renaissance and traditional French ornamentation, shows the limits of the new style's influence.

Francis I invited many of the greatest Italian artists to come to France. Leonardo da Vinci, who spent his final years at Amboise, provided the greatest luster early in the reign, but the great sculptor Benvenuto Cellini passed a tumultuous time at the French Court twenty-five years later. The royal masterpiece of the 1520s through the 1540s, the château at Fontainebleau, combined French elements with Italian ones. The French elements shown through in the work of the architect Jacques Androuet du Cerceau, who designed the courtyard, with its lovely Renaissance details, such as the Golden Door (1528). The Italian elements appear in many places, such as the interior decoration of the Francis I wing (1530s). This wing contains a magnificent gallery with splendid frescoes by the Italian artist Giovanni Battista di Jacopo de' Rossi (known as Rosso Fiorentino), and the royal bedchambers, superbly decorated by Francesco Primaticcio (called Primatice). Rosso relied heavily on Classical themes and produced a series of fresco allegories highlighting themes important to the French monarchy, such as the *Unity of the State* or *Ignorance Expulsed,* much in keeping with the times (see Plate 8). He also created some canvases, such as the nude figures of Venus and Bacchus, that had less political and more cultural resonance.

The Henry II wing of the Louvre, finished in 1556, shows the extent to which the work of Italian painters such as Rosso or architects such as Serlio, designer of the Cardinal of Ferrara's palace at Fontainebleau and of the château of Ancy-le-Franc, had been studied by their French counterparts. Henry II made the stunning decision to award the contract for the royal palace not to Serlio but to a French architect, Pierre Lescot. Here we see Renaissance style in full French flower, with splendid

Royal Fancy: Chambord, 1519–c. 1535. This wildly fanciful château incorporates a bewildering mix of French and Italian influences in its famous roof, and contains a magnificent dual central staircase, in which those descending and ascending are continuously shielded from each other's view.

SOURCE: Photo courtesy of Liz Collins.

sculptures by the great French artist Jean Goujon. Goujon also produced the Classic perfection of the tomb of Louis de Brézé (Rouen cathedral), the organ columns of the Flamboyant Gothic church of Saint-Maclou (Rouen), and, most famously, the Fountain of the Innocents in Paris (*c.* 1550). Many of these monuments, such as the Fountain of the Innocents, have been partially destroyed, but others, such as Fontainebleau or Lescot's wing of the Louvre, survive to this day, reminding us of the new *douceur de vivre*—sweetness of life—of the mid-sixteenth-century elite.

Louvre, Pierre Lescot, wing of the Louvre Palace, begun 1546. Lescot shows here the influence of Italian Renaissance architecture in France.

Source: © Ronald Sheridan/Ancient Art & Architecture Collection.

Lest we get carried away, we should remember that etiquette remained relatively primitive. People ate with their fingers; French nobles would use utensils, other than knives, only in the seventeenth century. All manner of physical functions took place in public; the corners of palace rooms, like those of village churches, often stank of urine. Guests of the king at Fontainebleau complained constantly of the stench of its dark corners. Nobles belched, farted, scratched themselves in every conceivable orifice, spat, and threw unwanted food on the floor: all of these behaviors only in time became scandalous. French elites borrowed from the Italians the use of porcelain plates and of glassware, which permitted the creation of a clearly defined individual space at table. Soon municipal governments (or even the royal administration) would begin to enact and to enforce with much greater rigor ordinances protecting public hygiene and public morality. Even in the sixteenth century, cleanliness was next to Godliness.

The food itself began to change in the middle of the sixteenth century. Nobles ate more special vegetables, a trend that would accelerate in the seventeenth century. Demand for these exotic foods would provide a considerable economic stimulus to the market gardeners near the larger towns, especially Paris. Wealthy households, both noble and commoner, began to eat differently, abandoning birds such as peacocks for the more delicate partridge. Cooks spiced the food less violently, often using local herbs, such as thyme. Much of the demand for more refined and lighter food came from those with experience in Italy, so that French elite cuisine emerged from the amalgam of regional cooking, traditional bourgeois and noble tastes, and the newly introduced Italian subtlety. These three cooking traditions would, in the seventeenth and eighteenth centuries, create the foundations of French *haute cuisine,* one of the defining characteristics of French civilization.

No figure more neatly summarizes the boundless confusion of French culture in the time of Francis I than François Rabelais, whose name has come down to us, in English as in French, as an adjective for, as *The American Heritage Dictionary* tells us, "coarse humor, exuberant learning, or bold caricature." One does not usually associate learning and coarse humor, yet Rabelais's work interweaves both to an astonishing degree. He moves back and forth between traditions of popular culture and learned debate. One minute Gargantua, the giant, "undid his fine codpiece and, brandishing his tool in the air, he bepissed them so ferociously that he thereby drowned

A monk and his mistress are placed in the stocks. These two illustrations of monks offer typical examples of the widespread perception of monastic moral decline at the end of the Middle Ages.

A monk drinking sacramental wine.

260,418 of them, not counting the women and children." The next minute, we listen to a theological debate about the most arcane matters or to a discussion of an obscure Classical author. Rabelais constantly makes reference to figures such as Timotheus, the Greek musician who used to make his students forget everything they "had been taught under other musicians" or Cato, whose advice about separating "the water from diluted wine" Gargantua learns to follow. Rabelais shifts from learned references to Classical authors—Pliny, Plato, Virgil, Theophrastus, Galen (Rabelais had been trained as a doctor)—to references to Scholastic literature and the Patristics, to the most extreme vulgarities.

Rabelais brings us back to another of our cultural icons, Bayard. Side by side with the heterogeneous intellectual life springing from Rabelais and his contemporaries, we can see a new cultural and political perspective arising among the upper classes. Bayard and his fellow warriors demonstrate this shift, so critical to the political development of the nation in the sixteenth and seventeenth centuries.

Rabelais's patroness, Marguerite d'Angoulême, shows clearly the connection in her collection of stories, *The Heptameron,* based, of course, on an Italian model: Bocaccio's *Decameron.* In the fortieth of her stories, she tells us of the count of Josselin, a member of the Rohan family, murdering his sister's husband because he was not of sufficiently high birth to merit such a match. In the long dispute about the justice of Rohan's action, one of the storytellers, Dagoucin, sums up the matter by telling us that:

> in order to maintain peace in the state, consideration is given only to the rank of families, the seniority of individuals and the provisions of the law, and not to men's love and virtue, in order that the monarchy should not be undermined.

In response, Parlamente (usually identified as the voice of Marguerite herself) argues that "if people submit to the will of God, they are concerned neither with glory, greed, nor sensual enjoyment, but only to live in the state of matrimony as God and Nature ordain, loving one another virtuously and accepting their parents' wishes."

Those around Francis I provided the patronage necessary for a remarkable flourishing of French letters. In addition to Marguerite d'Angoulême, François, cardinal Tournon; and Charles de Guise, cardinal of Lorraine, both extraordinarily rich from ecclesiastical properties and closely tied to King Henry II (Tournon was his chief minister; Guise's niece, Mary of Scotland, had married Henry's heir, Francis), provided important patronage. The new schools of Paris—places like the Collège de Coqueret, led by Jean Dorat, or the Collège de Presles, founded by Pierre de la Ramée (known in his own day by his Latin name, Petrus Ramus)—gave shelter to an intellectual revival based on the French language.

Scholars violently debated the worth of vernacular as against Latin literature. The Parisian upstarts, like Ramus or his students Pierre Ronsard, Pierre Belon, and Joachim du Bellay, challenged the intellectual superiority of Latin and insisted that both great literature and learned works should be written in French. Du Bellay published the most famous statement of their principles in 1549: *The Defense and Illus-*

THE ABBEY OF THÉLÈME

Rabelais lampooned the Church, from the Scholastic buffoon Janotus to the monk Jean des Entommeures, "a real monk if ever there was one since the monking world first monked in monkery." Brother John worries that the vineyards of his monastery will be destroyed by passing troops. "But the wine service, let's see to it that it is not disturbed; for you yourself, My Lord Prior, love to drink of the best. So does every good man; never does a noble man hate good wine: that's a monastic precept."

Rabelais offers some of his harshest criticism of society and the Church in the inscription placed over the gate of the abbey of Thélème, founded for our Brother John:

> Here enter not, shysters athirst for fees,
> Clerks, lawyers, who devour the common folk,
> Bishops' officials, scribes and pharisees,
> Doddering judges, binding at your ease
> God-fearing people to a common yoke;
> . . .
> Here enter too, all you who preach and teach
> The Gospel live and true, though many hound;

> You'll find a refuge here beyond their reach
> Against the hostile error you impeach,
> Whose false style spreads its poison all around;
> Enter, we'll found herein a faith profound,
> And then confound, aloud or penned unheard,
> The foemen who oppose the Holy Word.
> The Word of grace
> We'll not efface
> From this God's shrine;
> Let each entwine
> In close embrace
> The word of grace.

The rules of Thélème had only one clause: Do what you will. Rabelais explained Gargantua's rationale:

> people who are free, well born, well bred, moving in honorable social circles, have by nature an instinct and goad which always impels them to virtuous deeds and holds them back from vice, which they called honor. These people, when by vile subjection and constraint they are oppressed and enslaved, turn aside this noble affection by which they freely tended toward virtue, to throw off and infringe this yoke of servitude[25]

tration of the French Language. Another of the students of the day, Étienne Pasquier, later a famous historian, wrote in 1552:

> You believe that it is a waste of time and a waste of good paper to write in the vernacular. You think that our language is too common to express noble ideas. If we have anything beautiful to say, you maintain, we should say it in Latin. Now, as for me, I shall always belong to the party of those who have confidence in the vernacular. I believe that we shall recreate the Golden Age once we abandon this degenerate affectation of favoring foreign things.[26]

These Humanists thus differed greatly from most of their predecessors of the generation of the 1520s through the 1540s, who had given primacy to the ancient languages. They shared with those predecessors, however, a common enemy: the ossified Sorbonne, the theology faculty of the University of Paris. From Clément Marot, the great poet of the 1530s and 1540s, through Ronsard and his companions in the Pléiade (the seven great poets of the mid-century), everyone attacked the impenetrable ignorance of the Sorbonne fathers.[27] Marot wrote of them in 1542:

Francis of Angoulême (later King Francis I) and his sister Marguerite playing chess. Marguerite had an outstanding education for a woman of her time. She wrote one of the premier literary works of the middle of the sixteenth century, the Heptameron, and championed the cause of religious reform.

SOURCE: Miniature from the *Livre des echecs amoreux* by Jacques Le Grant.

> Oh poor men, of such limited knowledge!
> They prove true the common proverb:
> Science has no greater haters than the ignorant.

Marot makes reference here to the Sorbonne's long fight against the spread of learning of Greek and Hebrew (even of Latin!), enterprises that had been supported by

Francis I himself in creating the Collège de France. Marot's conflict with the theology faculty of the Sorbonne fit into a much broader context. The Sorbonne lumped together the works of the great Reformers—Luther, Calvin, Melancthon, Zwingli—and those of French humanists—Dolet, Marot, Rabelais—in their list of works condemned in 1544. Marot, who actually was a Protestant, fled the country to avoid a fate similar to what would befall Dolet two years later on the place Maubert.

The religious element introduced by Marot and the circle around Marguerite d'Angoulême makes a critical connection to the royalist argument of Dagoucin. Nobles fought in the wars of Francis I or Henry II "for the profit of the king and the kingdom, and to acquire honor in their position." Many, like the French army who pillaged Brescia, thought first about material gain, even looting monasteries. Bayard, the knight beyond reproach, took no part in such pillaging, but we can get a sense of normal behavior by the reaction of the family with whom he stayed while wounded. The mother and two "very beautiful daughters . . . came to him in tears and knelt before him." The mother asked him to take all their goods but to leave the daughters alone; Bayard, of course, told her all would be well. Later, addressing the master of the house, he told him:

> have no fear of me or my men, as I did not become a man-at-arms to enrich myself or die rich; because it is very difficult while in arms to follow the Christian law and die rich; it is sufficient to live according to God and to have enough. That is why you, lord, and you, noble lady, can sleep at your ease, because I have taken great care to guard your house and the goods within; and there is no man among mine so foolhardy as to give you displeasure.

Earlier, Bayard did warn the noble lady that she had to be on guard against others, even though he had given orders that no one should trouble this house. The lord, astonished at such treatment, offered Bayard all that he might wish from his belongings, even the hand of a daughter in marriage; the noble chevalier declined.

Bayard, in this seemingly innocuous passage, alerts us to the gathering storm within French noble elites. He emphasizes his service to God, to Christian law, as a guide to his conduct. His biographer, in the dedicatory preface to the bishop of Grenoble, tells the bishop that "his [Bayard's] story declares sufficiently the affection that he always had for the public good of the nation of France." The death of the son of Bayard's contemporary, Louis de la Trémoille, makes plain the potential conflicts. His biographer (who calls him, in imitation of Bayard, "the knight without reproach") tells us that la Trémoille always wanted to die in a "bed of honor, that is, in the service of his king in a just war." The funeral oration for la Trémoille's son summarizes all the elements of the perfect noble death:

> Consider, Madame, that . . . your son did not die of any of those evil accidents, but as a man of virtue, in the company of worthy men; not among beasts, but with men; not among brigands and pirates, but in a just war; not bitten by woodland beasts, but by warlike thrust; not by cannon, but by lance; not cowardly, but bravely; not alone, but in the company of his father; not in the service of tyrants, but in that of his King; not in reproach,

but honestly, covered with honor, enveloped by his good name and by the
love and grace of God.[28]

De la Trémoille himself wrote to his wife that their son died in an act of virtue, fighting for the "public good and in a just quarrel."

Here we have our multiple complications in French civil society. Nobles died
happily in the service of their king, in a just war, with God on their side. They fought
for their king, for their own honor (and, often, profit), for the public good, and for
God. What would happen if the king and God stood on different sides? What would
happen if the public good meant opposing the king? What would happen if the king's
quarrel were not just?

These questions moved beyond the realm of idle speculation immediately after
the death of Henry II. Many nobles felt betrayed by the Peace of Cateau-Cambrésis
(1559), in which the king seemed to admit his quarrel had not been just. Other nobles, led by the daughter of Marguerite d'Angoulême, Jeanne d'Albret, and by some
members of the Coligny and Bourbon families, had begun to turn to Protestantism.
In the religious wars of the second half of the century, the Huguenot nobles would
return precisely to this issue of the distinction between the "public good" and the
king. These religious wars contained conflicts among all four of the self-defining elements of noble service: to God, to the public good, to one's personal honor, and to
the king. In the second half of the sixteenth century, the conflict of the first three elements with service to the king created a civil war that lasted, with only one substantial respite, from 1562 until 1628. Before examining the origins of the religious split
that touched off that war, let us examine the fundamental social and economic
changes of the early sixteenth century.

❧ Social and Economic Change

> The most striking fact about the sixteenth century between 1500 and 1570 was
> the great boom in population.[29]
>
> Emmanuel Le Roy Ladurie

For centuries after his death, French people referred to King Louis XII (1498–1514)
as the "father of the people." His reign remained forever a Golden Age. Frenchmen
living at the end of the sixteenth century, whether noble deputies to the Estates General or peasant rebels, invariably demanded that taxes be reduced to their level at the
time of the good king Louis. In the duchy of Brittany, people still think of the days of
Louis's wife, duchess Anne, as their Golden Age. They have preserved her memory in
the name of countless hotels, restaurants, and boutiques. For a while, it seemed as if
God had indeed answered people's incessant prayer to spare them from "plague,
famine, and war." The population of France, which had declined steadily for a century after the Black Death, began to rise in the third quarter of the fifteenth century
and moved up sharply after 1475. The population of 9 or 10 million (*circa* 1450)
reached perhaps 16 million by 1525, still well below the 18 to 20 million people of

the early fourteenth century.[30] One 1520s observer in Languedoc thought the peasants there as numerous as "mice in a barn," although, in truth, severe rural overcrowding set in only after 1600.[31] With the exception of short-term disasters, such as 1626–1631 or 1693–1694, the population of France grew steadily from 1450 until the late eighteenth century, when a new demographic pattern began to emerge.

Many historians have argued that the wild population fluctuations of the fifteenth century led to a crisis of feudalism as an economic and political system. In Germany, this crisis, so the argument goes, led to the Peasants' War of 1525, in which tens of thousands of peasants in southwestern Germany, which then included Alsace, rose up against their landlords. They demanded an end to serfdom, the abolition of death taxes, and access to common property, such as woods and waters. At first successful, they lost several pitched battles, the key one near Saverne (in Alsace). The repression probably cost 80,000 peasants their lives. In the end, however, they did receive some satisfaction; serfdom soon died out in southwestern Germany.

In France, the situation was more complex. Serfdom itself had already died out in most regions, except the duchy of Burgundy. Can we therefore continue to speak of feudalism? Throughout the second half of the fifteenth century, French peasants enjoyed a period of remarkable prosperity, so long as they did not live in an area (like Picardy) regularly ravaged by war. Land rents declined, because there were fewer farmers; serfdom largely disappeared, in part because landlords had to offer better terms to tenants in order to make them stay put. Laborers, too, profited from the situation; their wages reached a pre-modern peak in the third quarter of the fifteenth century. Women also benefitted from the shortage of labor; in many regions of France, women's wages reached 80 percent of those paid to men.

The rapid population increase of the century between 1470 and 1570 put an end to the golden age of the laborer. Wages dropped steadily, in real terms, against the inflation of the sixteenth century. Women suffered most of all; their wages declined to between one-quarter and one-third of what men received by 1600. Day laborers paid primarily in wheat and good wine in 1480, received a wheat–rye mixture and plonk in 1580. Rents jumped rapidly in the sixteenth century. Indeed, they started upward at the end of the fifteenth, as landlords took advantage of the increased demand for arable land among the far more numerous population. After a long period of deflation in the fifteenth century, complete with a comparative shortage of bullion coinage, the sixteenth century began with a steady long-term inflation fueled by rising demand and by new sources of bullion: silver in central Europe, gold from the Americas. In the second half of the sixteenth century, the massive influx of silver from Mexico and Peru would touch off an even more rapid period of inflation.

The peasants of early sixteenth-century France lived in a world far different from that of the fifteenth century. North and south, villages held relatively egalitarian populations in the late fifteenth century. Many peasants held a tenancy large enough to support their family; in the mountain regions, the shortage of labor forced families to live together, in the so-called brotherhoods (*frèrêches*). The rapid population increase in the period between 1470 and 1520 changed the structure of village land holdings. The medium-sized holdings of the peasants had to be cut into smaller pieces for the larger number of heirs. Two or three generations repeated this procedure, setting in motion the process that would create the highly stratified villages of the seventeenth and eighteenth centuries, in which a handful of tenant farmers would lease 70 or 80 percent of the land, leaving only tiny morsels for the rest.

The village of the fifteenth century, or perhaps the early sixteenth century, was the France of the imagination for its people. Throughout the sixteenth and seventeenth centuries, peasant rebels would demand a return to the days of good king Louis XII, the "father of the people." They wanted more than his low tax rates: they also rightly remembered his time as one in which many peasants had a farm of their own large enough to support their family. The egalitarian village so central to peasant conceptions of "their" France had existed in the fifteenth century. Thus Louis XII's time became also a place, the place of memory for the Land of Cocaigne, the earthly paradise.

Sixteenth-century peasants lived instead in villages with an emerging and hardening class division within the peasantry. Most villages had three or four groups of peasants. The richest, the ploughmen (called in most areas, *laboureurs*), owned or rented a plough team; they leased substantial farms and often owned plots of their own. They also paid the bulk of the village's taxes. The middling group, the cottagers (*manouvriers*), owned a cottage and a tiny plot next to it. They rented a farm too small to support a family, so they had to supplement the family income by selling their labor or its products. The third group, the day laborers (*journaliers*), sold their labor, typically to the ploughmen.[32] The fourth group often overlapped with the cottagers and day laborers: village artisans. Some artisans could make a living entirely from their craft, but most of them combined their artisanal work with farm labor.

These village artisans take us into the world occupied by a large portion—perhaps a majority—of the French population: the life of *bricolage* or "putting together."[33] People assembled their economic lives from odd pieces of this and that: the typical village family tended a small farm, itself requiring a wide range of economic activities, but also engaged in several other "jobs" to make ends meet. The man might work as a part-time artisan—roofer, carpenter, mason—or as a carter or day laborer on large farms. The woman would spin, weave cloth, make lace, pick fruit, or hire herself out as a field laborer during peak periods, such as the harvest. Women and children gleaned the village fields; men, women, and children scavenged the woods for firewood, wild fruits, small game, and herbs. Children and old people (women, if they were widows), might beg part of the year. This pattern of multiple economic activities, each making a small contribution to household viability, remained the basic pattern of life for most French peasants until the late nineteenth or even the twentieth century.[34]

The land, although divided into ever smaller strips as the sixteenth century wore on, had the same functional divisions we saw in medieval France. On the outskirts of the village, lay the "waste"—often grazing land, sometimes scraggly woods. At an intermediate distance, one found the arable land, while closer in, the houses were surrounded by their gardens. The sexual division of labor remained the same: men took primary (although by no means sole) responsibility for the outer (grain) fields, and women supervised and tended the inner fields and gardens. The product of male labor, grain, paid the rent and provided a substantial portion of the family's food; the products of female labor—eggs, poultry, cheese, cloth, lace, vegetables, flax, hemp—provided the cash needed to buy tools and pay taxes, as well as what little variety their diet possessed.

These villages did not much resemble those of the France of contemporary imagination. Just as France has specific geographic places of memory, so, too, it has spaces of memory. One of the most important is the peasant village. This village of memory contains a fairly egalitarian population, one deeply rooted in the soil of its *pays*. Families remain for generations. Such families did, of course, exist; at Alligny-en-Morvan, fifteen families found on the tax roll of 1475 still lived in the village at the beginning of the eighteenth century. The local political elite of 1994 contained a member of the Regnault family, one of the fifteen families of 1475. Several other such families still live in the village or nearby.

Yet this "immobile France" existed side by side and interwoven with a mobile, unstable France. The process of morselization, in which family farms grew smaller and smaller, meant that many people simply had to leave their native villages. They moved to nearby villages and, above all, to towns. The villagers who remained did not live among equals; they lived in a world profoundly stratified by age, gender, and economic condition. In the sixteenth and early seventeenth centuries, these economic divisions became ever more pronounced, affecting every aspect of human life. Early in the sixteenth century, we can see clear evidence of one of the most fundamental changes, one unique in human societies: the postponement of marriage, practiced in France as elsewhere in Christian western Europe. (Jews living in western Europe still practiced marriage at puberty for girls.)

Virtually all known human societies have practiced marriage at puberty for young women. In sixteenth-century France, as elsewhere in Europe, puberty arrived later than it does today in France, in part because of poorer diet. We have only fragmentary evidence about age at marriage in medieval France, although that evidence suggests that people married at a younger age in the troubled fifteenth century than they had before the plagues. In the sixteenth century, improved local records enable us to know with certainty that age at marriage began to rise; it continued to do so for the next two centuries. Early sixteenth-century French women married in their early twenties, already late by world standards. Soon French women married, on average, at twenty-four, then twenty-six. Median male age at marriage rose to twenty-seven or twenty-eight.

Why did this pattern of late marriage evolve in France, and in western Europe as a whole? Two factors played a critical role: (1) economic viability required late marriage; and (2) late marriage helped slow down population increase. Much historical research shows that people often married shortly after the death of one of the fathers of the couple. His death opened up a tenancy in the village, which the new couple could then take over. The fixed number of tenancies made any other arrangement unthinkable. Here we understand the economic equation. The father typically dies at age fifty-five to sixty. As the father married at twenty-seven, his oldest son is likely twenty-five to thirty at the father's death, and thus a legal adult (twenty-five). The heir can now marry, at age twenty-six or twenty-seven and begin the cycle again.

The later age at marriage also reduced births: a woman marrying at twenty-five instead of seventeen would have, on average, two–three fewer children. A family with six births could expect to see two or three of them live to adulthood; society could absorb that survival rate, particularly given the unusually high rate of celibacy in the French population. Society could not provide for a population in which four or five children survived in each family.

Late marriage created social tensions, especially among young men. The sexual and social frustrations of these young men manifested themselves in several ways. In the towns, the municipal governments sponsored brothels, so that young men would not molest the wives and daughters of the good burghers of the town. This solution, widely popular in southern France, lost its attraction after 1520, in large measure because of the spread of syphilis. This dreaded sexual disease, introduced into Europe around 1500, spread rapidly among the promiscuous nobility; Francis I suffered from it, as did Henry VIII of England. The disease then entered the social mainstream, in part because of prostitution. Syphilis had no real cure until the twentieth century; early modern people treated it with mercury poured directly on the sores or with folk remedies.

The unruly young men of early modern France formed distinctive social groupings based on age. These youth organizations could be found in most villages or in quarters of towns. Workers, journeymen, also organized themselves into groups known as *compagnonnages,* although their heyday would come a bit later. These young men tried to enforce a sociosexual police on their communities. In villages, a young woman engaged to a man from outside the village might be raped in an assault involving many of the young men of their village. The young woman's honor would be ruined, jeopardizing the marriage; more importantly, from the perspective of the young men, the other young women of the village would hesitate to marry outside it. The brides of remarrying widowers often faced similar threats. We can understand this behavior only if we realize that a young man who failed to marry was doomed to economic and social marginality. The loss of a young woman, either to an outsider or to a widower (who had already had his chance), meant one more young man in the village would never become a member in full standing of the community.

Women held the key to entry into the community. Men (and women) had to marry. Landowners would not rent to single men; in town, guilds would not allow unmarried men to join. Landlords understood that the rural farm required a female and a male adult to be a viable economic unit. Guilds, too, knew that the wife invariably ran the front of the shop, while the man produced its goods. Both in town and in the country a two-adult household provided the basic unit of society. The control of the marriage market legally belonged to the male heads of households but social reality far more often placed it in the hands of the village or neighborhood women, which gave women enormous social power. They often arranged marriages at the *veillées,* the evening gatherings for handicraft work that broke up the monotony of rural winters. The role of women as social police extended into the towns as well, where women dominated many of the public areas, such as markets. Men resented this power, as the ancient stereotype of the "gossipy old woman" implies. Women did not trade idle tittle-tattle; they traded information about the work habits, the morality, and the material well-being of the marriageable young people of the village (or, in the town, of the local quarter). In the sixteenth century, men would organize against these older women, some of whom they would call witches (see Chapter 6).

Women formed an integral part of the fabric of village life. On most farms, the woman and the man each produced an important share of the economic output. Young women, aged fifteen to twenty-five or so, supervised the children and some of the animals (poultry, cows), learning as apprentice housewives the trade they would later practice.[35] Some farms, five to ten percent (moving from the former to the later between 1500 and 1670), had women tenants: widows. These widows had to hire men to do the field work, thus playing a critical role on the village labor market. In so doing, of course, they created a situation of women on top, a reversal much resented in early modern society. Even at the manor house, the seigneur's wife acted more as manager. When he was off at war, a frequent occurrence in the sixteenth century, she supervised the defense of the castle, when necessary.

The farm couples struggled to make ends meet in the sixteenth century. As plots became smaller, people had to seek out additional forms of income. In parts of France, especially in the north, villagers turned to textiles. Women increased their spinning production for the looms of the towns; they also took over looms themselves, as did many rural men, in what historians call the putting-out system. Faced with rising labor costs due to guilds, urban merchants tried to put out their textile orders into the countryside, with its cheaper labor force. The lighter, cheaper textiles in particular utilized this form of production. The two most important regions of such textile production were Flanders, where it competed with the production of the old draperies in the great towns, and Brittany, which specialized in linen cloth, exported to England and Spain.

The wages paid to these workers formed part of the constant flow of money between town and country. The increased rents flowed into the towns, where many landowners lived; this money helped increase conspicuous consumption. The money wages paid to rural workers enabled them to buy more manufactured goods. Manufactured production, led by textiles, jumped sharply at the turn of the sixteenth century. Everywhere in France, towns grew rapidly in size. Paris, which had shrunk to perhaps 50,000 people by 1450, began to grow again. By the early sixteenth century, it had well over 100,000 people once more and it would double that figure by the 1550s. The other "good towns" of the king—the Loire cities like Tours and Angers, the ports like Rouen and Bordeaux, the southern cities like Marseilles or Toulouse— also expanded. The fastest rising star of all, however, lay in the southeast, on the Rhône river: Lyon.

Lyon received its key favor from Louis XI, who granted it four annual fairs. Lyon then lay right on the French border with lands ruled by the duke of Savoy and by the Habsburgs, as heirs to the dukes of Burgundy.[36] In the middle of the fifteenth century, Lyon served as an important outpost of royal power in the southeast. Dauphiné remained quasi-independent, Provence did not belong to France; the border of the kingdom in the southeast lay on the Rhône river. Even in the sixteenth century, the proximity of the Franche-Comté, in which many citizens of Lyon owned rural property, meant that the city provided a first line of defense in the southeast.

Lyon provided a key entry point for goods coming from Italy into France. Goods moved up the Rhône to Lyon, there to be moved by water or by land and water into the northern reaches of the kingdom. Italian and German merchants flocked to the city after the creation of the free fairs, bringing with them a rapid increase in the total population. Lyon now produced silken cloth, a technique introduced from Italy; silk workers teemed on the east bank of the Saône. The city's fairs allowed it to become a center of banking as well, although its bankers came from outside of France: the Bonvisi and their compatriots from Lucca; the German and Swiss syndicates. Lyon, not Paris, served as France's economic focus during the sixteenth century.

Everywhere, cities replenished the populations lost to the century of epidemics. In the Loire valley, Tours, like Lyon, developed silk manufacture. Breton ships dominated the coastal trade of the west, plying the waters between Bordeaux and the Low Countries; the populations of Rennes and Nantes increased accordingly. Wine from Bordeaux flowed into Flanders, Brabant, and Holland; textiles made the return trip. Salt from the western marshes similarly was transported up the coast to the mouth of the Scheldt and, in many cases, through the Sound to the Baltic. The English, too, bought French products, whether wine from Bordeaux (although far less than in the early fourteenth century, the apex of that commerce) or linens from Brittany. The Bretons also exported a wide range of goods to Spain; above all, they sent grain, linen, much of it produced in nearby Maine, and paper. France imported large quantities of luxury products: Italian silks; Asian spices, by way of Italy and of Portugal; Spanish and German metal goods, especially weapons; and high-grade Flemish woolens and tapestries.

The thriving commerce within Europe naturally led the French to seek further markets in the climate of world expansion. Portuguese sources indicate extensive French merchant contact with West Africa in the late fifteenth century: French pirates captured Portuguese gold ships in 1492 and 1495.[37] In the early sixteenth century, the French followed the Portuguese to Brazil. The first known French presence came in 1504, but the captain of this ship, Paulmier de Gonneville, testified that "for several years" ships had been going to Brazil from Normandy and Brittany. By the 1530s the Atlantic ports—above all the Norman ones—sent convoys of merchant ships to Brazil for dyewoods. In 1550, during the entry of King Henry II into Rouen, the city put on a "Brazilian" festival. They used fifty Brazilian Indians and two hundred fifty sailors painted black and red "completely nude, haltered, and curried, without in any way covering the parts that nature commands" to create the festive atmosphere. The city fathers made use of a wide variety of parrots, borrowed from the collections of the good bourgeois of Rouen, to further impress their royal visitors.[38]

The Normans and Bretons sought out the entire American coast. Jacques Cartier, of Saint-Malo, made two voyages to North America (1534, 1535–1536), focused on the bay of the Saint Lawrence River. When he stayed through the winter of 1535–1536, the staggering cold and disease ravaged his small expedition. Twenty-five of its one hundred men died of scurvy and the others brought back terrifying tales of the Canadian winter. Later expeditions in 1541 (one by Cartier and the other by Jean-François Roberval) had little more luck: Cartier headed home in spring 1542 and Roberval gave up his efforts to set up a colony in Newfoundland in the fall. The French would not return to the Saint Lawrence as colonists until the beginning of the next century, but they continued to fish extensively in the Grand Banks—the fleet grew to over five hundred ships by 1580—and to trade for furs with the Indians of the Saint Lawrence valley.

Religious conflict gave considerable stimulus to missionary zeal and led, in France as in England, to quests for religious refuges in the New World. The Protestant leader Admiral Coligny did much to encourage French efforts to establish colonies in the New World, first in the bay of Guanabara (bay of Rio de Janeiro) and then in "Florida," a region running from near Saint Augustine up to Charleston, South Carolina. In 1555, an expedition of six hundred people left for Guanabara, for what they called "Antarctic France," where they set up a fort. The Calvinists preachers invited by the fort commander gave the Portuguese an excuse to wipe out the "nest of heretics" near their own Brazilian colony (March 1560). France would not reestablish a permanent base in South America until 1612.

The next effort took place further north, where Coligny sponsored the creation of "Charlesfort" (just outside the current Charleston), as a Huguenot refuge. This colony, too, failed.[39] In 1564, another expedition set out for "Florida," this time settling on the Saint John's River. A follow-up expedition brought the number of colonists to about nine hundred, almost all of them Huguenots. Philip II sent (1565) a large military force to wipe out the French, "not as Frenchmen, but as heretic enemies of God." He created a Spanish colony, Saint Augustine, the oldest permanent European settlement in the current United States.

The relative lack of success in the Americas may have reflected a greater emphasis on Mediterranean expansion. The French signed commercial accords with the Mamelukes of Egypt in 1511 and with the Ottoman Empire in 1528: these accords ("capitulations") allowed the French to trade freely in the Ottoman Empire and Egypt and to have significant legal protection rarely accorded to foreigners. They soon developed a monopoly on the coral fishery off North Africa and set up the Bastion of France, a seaside fort near the present boundary of Algeria and Tunisia, in 1560. The coral trade between North Africa and the Levant illustrates a central element of French Mediterranean trade: French merchants often carried goods within the eastern Mediterranean, as well as trade between the Levant and Marseilles. This trade would flourish even more strongly in the second half of the sixteenth century.

The Mediterranean success aside, the French fell dramatically behind other Europeans in the overseas expansion of the sixteenth century. Real French colonial expansion had to wait for the seventeenth century and a more systematic pursuit of overseas commerce, but the early sixteenth-century voyages fundamentally altered people's understanding of the world. Jacques Cartier published an account of his second voyage in 1545 and French elites had access to the many accounts written by those from other countries. In the second half of the century, such narratives multiplied, as did synthetical works such as those of André Thevet that sought to describe large regions of the Americas.

The traditional French economy flourished in the early sixteenth century. Production, both agricultural and manufactured, increased steadily. Prices rose continuously, albeit slowly: the price of grain in Paris roughly doubled between 1500 and 1550. Wages did not keep up with prices; they increased far more slowly, although the gap between wages and prices shifted dramatically only after 1570. Nonetheless, in periods of high grain prices, urban workers often protested violently. These protests typically pitted the artisans, those who sold goods they made themselves, against the wealthier merchants, who sold goods made by others.

These protests contained political and social elements, as well as economic ones. One of the most important, the Grande Rebeyne of Lyon (25–27 April 1529), demonstrated this combination of motives. It took the form of the customary grain riot: some two thousand women, men, and children marched against the high price of bread. They moved from the usual immediate expedient—looting bakers' shops— to the higher level of retaking a political initiative lost to them in the early sixteenth century. They marched to the site of the municipal assemblies, whose power had largely passed to the permanent Consulate; there, they decided to force open the municipal granaries and the grain cellars of the richer members of the town's population. These actions followed precisely the methods formerly used by the town assembly during famines. In this case, however, the town's population acted on its own, in direct conflict with the Consulate. Later, after the disturbances had died down, the Consulate rounded up and executed several of the ringleaders. The artisans did not demand any specific political changes during the Grande Rebeyne. The municipal assemblies still existed in 1529. They merely sought to express, by their actions, their sense that the new order of things, the overwhelming dominance of the merchants forming the Consulate, did not work.

These events can only be understood within the context of the wider changes in European urban politics at the end of the fifteenth and beginning of the sixteenth centuries. Conflicts between artisans and merchants took place everywhere in Europe. This conflict became evident in Flanders by the late thirteenth century and appeared again in the late fourteenth and fifteenth centuries. In Italy, many towns had social and political disorders at the end of the fourteenth century, while in German towns the dispute raged most violently in the fifteenth century. Town councils, traditionally a mixture of representatives of guilds and of merchants, shifted toward the preponderance of the latter. Everywhere in France, as in Lyon, the guilds lost their political rights, either *de facto,* as at Lyon or Nantes (in the 1580s), or *de iure,* in a wide range of French towns, from Provence up to Flanders. Again and again, town oligarchies established networks of councils, with the smaller, cooptive central council taking all real power. In some cases, they restricted voting rights in general assemblies. By the middle of the sixteenth century, in almost all French towns, the merchants had defeated the artisans and taken complete control of the town government.

In addition to the obvious differences between artisans and merchants, towns might be divided by geographic quarter (as at Marseilles), by occupation (as at Dijon, where the winegrowers formed a key interest group), or by ancient clientage ties that cut across the other boundaries. These internal conflicts took on another, more insidious characteristic toward the middle of the century: religious diversity. In town after town, interest groups split along religious lines. In some cases, the journeymen became Protestants, while the merchants remained Catholic. In Dijon, the winegrowers remained staunchly Catholic, but some of the artisans, once the winegrowers' allies against the merchants, turned Protestant. Unlike the urban conflicts of the first half of the sixteenth century, which led to almost no loss of life, those of the second half of the century, exacerbated by religious fervor, led to widespread massacres.

The artisans organized themselves in many ways: within trades, they created guilds, many of which dated back to the thirteenth or fourteenth century. Most of the guilds only allowed men to be full-fledged members, but some of them, such as the weavers guild of some towns or the mercers guild of others, had female members. Women even had their own guilds, such as the famous fishmongers of Paris, or the flower sellers or lace makers of other towns. Most guilds allowed widows to keep open their former husband's shop: in many French cities, widows owned 20 or 25 percent of the bakers' shops or of other guild enterprises. Such women rarely had full-scale rights within the guild. Municipal archives suggest that widows owning guild shops did not vote on admitting new members to the guild.

The guilds had three groups: masters, journeymen, and apprentices. The masters owned the shops; only they truly belonged to the guild, in the sense that they voted in its assemblies. Journeymen, typically men in their twenties, helped the master produce the goods, learning the trade so that, in theory, they, too could become masters. Apprentices, boys in their teens, did the little tasks around the shop and learned basic skills; in time, they would become journeymen. In many trades, the would-be or fledgling journeyman would set out on the Tour of France, moving from city to city to learn how his trade was practiced in different places.

The guild regulated production: each shop could produce only a limited amount of goods and no master could own more than one shop. Guilds also watched over the morality of their members. Guild masters (and their spouses) usually had to be of legitimate birth; masters had to be married. Later, some guilds would insist that members had to be Catholic. Guilds provided relief to orphans and widows, although their attitude toward the latter depended heavily on local connections. The guilds regulated relationships between masters and journeymen, although they represented solely the interests of the former. Guilds theoretically fixed wages and tried to allocate workers among the various shops in each town. They prevented journeymen from starting workshops of their own, at least within the town and its contiguous area (the *banlieue* or area of the town's authority). Merchants constantly sought to evade these guild rules by hiring workers from outside the town to do the work. In the sixteenth century, this technique spread quite rapidly in Flanders. The journeymen, too, tried to organize themselves against their employers. The organizations, the *compagnonnages,* existed in many trades, but we know little about them before the seventeenth century. The main conflict between the masters and journeymen involved control of labor. Masters claimed the exclusive right to place journeymen in shops, but the journeymen claimed for themselves the right to place workers. In the sixteenth and seventeenth centuries, the sketchy available evidence suggests that the journeymen usually won this battle or, at the least, achieved a workable compromise with local masters.

Apprentices, young boys (rarely girls), went to work for a master, to learn the basics of a trade. Regulation of apprentices provided a key weapon in the hands of the guild; in the sixteenth century, many guilds passed rules forbidding widows of masters from hiring new apprentices. When the contracts of the remaining apprentices ran out, after the master's death, the widow would be forced to sell the business or to marry another master. Widows often found ways around such rules; they might marry a man from another profession, who then joined the guild as a "master" but who really left the work to the woman. In Breton towns, widows who had relatives among the other guild masters of their craft had no trouble keeping open the shop of their husband. Widows who had no relatives in the guild, however, found the legal restrictions, such as the prohibition to take on new apprentices, enforced against them. One of the great paradoxes of French urban development from the sixteenth to the eighteenth centuries is that legal restrictions against female economic participation became consistently more stringent, yet actual female economic participation rose steadily.

The guilds had spiritual offshoots, the confraternities. The lay religious organizations allowed people with common interests—guild members, urban parishioners, villagers—to join in prayer and burial societies. The confraternities also had important festive functions; in many carnivals and parades, people joined or marched with their confraternity. Political authorities, however, took a dim view of such activities. They felt confraternities allowed artisans an opportunity for political organization. Thus, in many towns, authorities banned all confraternities. Church authorities often took a similar view after 1520, criticizing the drunkenness and debauchery of confraternity banquets. In 1539, the king banned trade confraternities. These bans did not prove successful; even rich merchants joined confraternities of their own, because they offered such a convenient means to associate with one's peers. At Nantes, the four hundred thirty-five members of the confraternity of Our Lady at the Carmelite convent included almost all the members of the city's mercantile elite, such as Michel Le Lou. In the ensuing fifty years, families such as the Le Lou would take over most of the important local offices (mayor, alderman, and high offices in the Chamber of Accounts) and would heavily intermarry. The confraternity of Our Lady at the Carmelites provided them with one more means for social interaction, just as similar organizations cemented ties among journeymen or guild masters or neighbors.

Most confraternities included people from a wide range of social groups, as well as both men and women. The phenomenon spread rapidly in the fifteenth century. The archbishop of Rouen approved the creation of more than twelve hundred of them in his diocese between 1430 and 1550: of this twelve hundred, over five hundred of them appeared in the period between 1480–1519. French towns of more than ten thousand people usually had twenty or more confraternities within their walls; Rouen had over one hundred, while Paris had more than three hundred fifty.

∾ Catholicism under Siege

"Catholic" France in 1500

> *The true religion and love of God bring with them all love and concord and they conserve the integrity of all kingdoms and monarchies, and are the nursing mother of peace and friendship among men.*[40]

> Cahier of the Nobility, Estates General of 1560

Many artisans left their confraternities to become Protestants after 1540 but, before we turn to the conflict within the French Christian community, let us examine the nature of that community. Fifteenth-century French Catholicism encompassed many different strains and movements. The largest mass of Catholics, the peasants, believed in an amalgam of ancient fertility rites and nominal Catholicism. Their Catholicism focused on mystery and ritual, elements equally rooted in ancient pagan practices.

The village Catholics practiced a religion not entirely in accordance with official doctrine. Village priests took into consideration the beliefs of their parishioners, lest they forfeit their allegiance. We must close our eyes and imagine a different sort of religion than the one we know today as Catholicism; indeed, it bore little resemblance, in many respects, to the Catholicism of the towns of 1500. The village church itself often had distinct, socially created divisions. Peasants entered through one door, the seigneur through another. His door bore the family's seigneurial arms on top, symbol of his patronage of the church. He sat in a seigneurial banc; the peasants usually stood. The priest on the altar was a dim and distant presence, hiding behind a rood screen. This carved wooden screen, typically four to five feet high, obscured the altar for all but the privileged few in the front rows. Behind the screen, the priest said the Mass in Latin, with his back to the congregation through most of the ceremony.[41] The priest alone took the Eucharist, save at Easter, when the entire congregation did its annual communion.

This ritualized, mysterious practice aptly suited the needs of the peasantry. The complaints of the Reformers (both Protestant and Catholic) for more lay involvement in the Mass resonated less deeply among the sixteenth-century rural faithful, who looked for powerful ritual symbols in their Mass. They placed strong belief in the ritual powers of the priest and of his greatest "magical" achievement: the host. Peasants in England or Italy, just as in France, believed in the healing powers of consecrated hosts. The peasants also treated the priest like a magician. He performed a wide range of blessings and superstitious ceremonies. Churches had to ring their bells during thunderstorms, a practice that led to periodic electrocutions of bell ringers, widespread even in nineteenth-century France. Priests had to purify recent mothers, who had to skulk to the back door of the church after giving birth. They could not enter the sanctuary itself until the priest had purified them. This practice, known as churching, directly violated the orders of the hierarchical Church, yet it lasted until the twentieth century.[42]

The Church still had no control over such fundamental activities as marriage. Although canon law stipulated that a couple had to be married in order to live together, peasant practice dictated otherwise. Couples would get betrothed in the spring, by means of an exchange of promises and gifts before witnesses; they would then start to live together, as man and wife in the eyes of their neighbors. The marriage, in a church, would come later: perhaps in the fall, perhaps after the couple had proved their suitability by a pregnancy. Church authorities fulminated against such practices throughout the sixteenth and seventeenth centuries; only toward the end of the seventeenth century, however, did peasants widely begin to practice church marriage before living together and "frequenting each other in a familiar manner," as one rector put it. As late as the end of the seventeenth century, episcopal visitors in the countryside near Nantes issued ordinances denouncing the profanation of the cemeteries: "it is forbidden to play *boules* or to sell grain or to pasture animals or do other profane things in the cemetery." Peasants all over France held markets in their village cemetery, just as peasant women used the space to dry their laundry.

The Church wisely followed a pagan, agricultural calendar. The Church held its major festivals around the two solstices (Christmas and St. John's Day, 24 June) and the two equinoxes (Easter and St. Michael's Day, 29 September), as well as at the four midpoints (Candlemas, 2 February; Pentecost; Assumption, 15 August; and All Saints' Day, 1 November). The Church set the calendar in rural areas; peasants gave the date according to a saint's day or in reference to a major holiday. Virtually all rural leases, for example, began on St. Michael's Day, and peasants paid their rents on All Saints' Day, on Easter, Pentecost, and St. John's Day. In most parts of France, the New Year itself began on Easter Sunday.

For the peasants, religious ritual often focused on fertility. Priests had to bless marital beds and brides' wombs, as part of protection against the dreaded *aiguillette* (noose). French peasants universally believed in the widespread existence of this ritual castration. According to the most common version, a wise woman (*sage femme*) tied a knot in a string and threw a piece of money on the ground.[43] If the money disappeared, the marriage would be sterile. The wise woman here followed the practice of pig castraters, who tied string around the testicles to make them fall off.

Peasants tried to fight off the *aiguillette* by seeking a special blessing for the marriage bed. The most common prayer came from Pope Paul V himself:

> Lord, our God, bless this bed and its occupants. May they live in your peace, persevere and grow old in the obedience of your will; may they multiply themselves all their days and come to the kingdom of heaven.

Priests also had to perform incantations over sexual organs of infertile couples, to say nothing of those of various animals. They blessed fields, houses, stables, barns, beehives, chicken coups—in short, everything related to rural life. In many areas, animals received holy salt water once a year; the blessed water warded off illness and even, in some cases, protected poultry from thieves! Priests blessed the candles brought by village women to the bedsides of the sick and dying. They blessed, too, the fires of St. John's Day. All over Europe, villages lit massive fires of purification (an ancient pagan ritual denounced by the hierarchical Church) on the eve of the 24th of June. Indeed, in some regions (Burgundy, the Rhine valley), people still practice this ritual, now often supervised by the local fire department. In the Rhineland, both its German and Alsatian sides, every hilltop seems to have a fire on St. John's evening.

Parishioners demanded that priests excommunicate rats and insects, which the priests did not fail to do. In the Alps, the inhabitants of Chamonix begged their bishop to bless the local glacier. When he had done so, the leading inhabitants of the parish signed an attestation that the glacier then receded a half a league from the parish and ceased ravaging their lands. The peasants prayed often to saints, not merely to those recognized by the Church but also to local "saints," something like a Christianized version of ancestor veneration. Saints had specialized functions. One prayed to Saint Roch to avoid the plague, to Saint Macrou to avoid scrofula. The most widespread cult, of course, centered on the Virgin Mary, who had shrines everywhere. Pilgrims voyaged to her shrines, many of which had special significance for given illnesses or causes; pilgrims also flocked to the shrines of saints, like Mont

Saint-Michel in Normandy or to the relics of countless saints held in monasteries throughout France. The King possessed particularly potent relics, such as a piece of the True Cross and the Crown of Thorns, housed in the greatest of all reliquaries, the Sainte-Chapelle at Paris.

Townspeople practiced a Christianity more familiar to the hierarchical church. Indeed, the towns sent forth emissaries to "convert" the countryside. In the second half of the fifteenth century, the French rural church changed rapidly. Rural priests became more literate: available statistics suggest that most could read and write by 1500. These priests often kept records—of births, marriages, and deaths—even before being required to do so by the Church authorities or the state. They belonged to a great liturgical revival sweeping France in the fifteenth century. Just as the number of confraternities grew, so, too, did religious communities of friars. Between 1250 and 1550, French people created more than eight hundred new communities of Franciscan or Dominican friars.[44] In Brittany, the three hundred mendicant friars of 1350 had become seven hundred by 1450 and more than nine hundred by 1500, when the rapid increase of the previous century tapered off. Brittany held twenty-three Franciscan houses by 1520, as well as an equal number of other mendicant houses.

The monks, in contrast to friars, encountered considerable difficulties in the fifteenth and early sixteenth centuries. Their numbers tended to decline on the eve of the Reformation; they also received fewer and fewer grants of land from testators. The great house of Cluny, which held three hundred monks in 1300, housed only sixty by 1450. Rural monasteries could not keep pace with the attraction of the urban friars, whose devotional style and interaction with the laity gave them enormous recruiting advantages. Lay people, men in the friaries and women in the *béguinages* (associations of lay women living together in a religious community), created lay spiritual communities. The largest such group, the Brethren of the Common Life, expanded rapidly in the Low Countries. The most famous northern Humanist, Desidarius Erasmus, grew up in such a community. These communities had an enormous influence on urban piety at the end of the fifteenth century, both by encouraging people to demonstrate their piety through charitable works and by associating lay people with religious functions.

Women religious, too, had difficulties. Fewer women could belong to the *béguinages* after the Church and lay authorities began to disapprove of them in the fifteenth century. Women from wealthy families, above all the nobility, found their way into convents: it saved money and protected family heritages. Again, as with men, mendicant orders, like the Clarisses, maintained their numbers, whereas the traditional, contemplative houses had more difficulty. Women religious continued to provide important services to early modern French society, most notably in its hospitals. The great age of female religious revival, however, would come in the seventeenth century.

The French Church of the early sixteenth century still had profound medieval roots, yet it also bore witness to the many aspects of Christian revival evident in other areas, such as Italy and the Low Countries. The intolerant element of the medieval heritage reappeared at the end of the fifteenth century. After fully incorporating Dauphiné into the royal demesne, Louis XI expelled its Jews (1466). Louis XII did the same in Provence in 1501, driving the Jews from the more than fifty Provençal towns they then inhabited and in which they had flourished. Their loss severely damaged the Provençal economy. Some of them fled to the nearby Papal enclave of the Comtat Venaissin (near Avignon), where their community survived. After this expulsion, Jews could not legally live in any part of France until the 1550s, when two distinct Jewish communities entered the French commonwealth. Henry II allowed Portuguese Jews, fleeing the stepped-up Inquisition, to settle in Bordeaux and Montpellier. These Jews could not openly practice Judaism; they had to pretend to be "New Christians." In contrast, the second Jewish community, that of the great episcopal city of Metz, which legally became part of the kingdom of France in 1559, could practice its religion.[45]

France and the Early Reformation

True Articles on the horrible, great, and insupportable abuses of the papal Mass, invented directly contrary to the Last Supper of Jesus Christ.[46]

Title of the placards posted throughout Paris on 17 October 1534 by
Zwinglians

In the broader Christian community, the end of the fifteenth century ushered in a multitude of reform movements. Much of the impulse for reform came from Humanists, who had gone back to the ancient texts in their original languages, above all, Greek and Hebrew. The spread of printing allowed scholars to reconstruct accurate renditions of early Christian, as well as Classical texts. Erasmus reconstructed the New Testament based on early Greek and Latin manuscripts, calling into question many of the passages in the fourth-century Vulgate, the official Biblical text of the Church.[47] French Humanists joined in the reconstruction of Scripture and in its propagation. In 1523, Jacques Lefèvre d'Etaples took the greatest step forward in this reformist revolution: he published the first translation of the *New Testament* in French.

The French religious climate of the 1520s seethed with possibilities. The critical reforming group, centered around Briçonnet and Lefèvre d'Etaples at Meaux, questioned many of the Church's dogmas. They echoed, as did Erasmus himself, many of Luther's criticisms in that they denounced indulgences, recommended the diffusion of the Word of God to the faithful, questioned transubstantiation, and generally spoke up against abuses. Briçonnet tried to reform his bishopric by making sure the parish priests could read and write, knew their Scripture, performed their duties, and lived celibate lives.

Some of these reforms belonged well within the tradition of Catholic discourse. Different Catholic theologians had long held opinions similar to those of Luther. Once Luther codified those opinions into a loose-knit system, and once the hierarchical Church condemned them as heresy, reformers suddenly faced a double assault. On the one side, some demanded full-scale reform, on the model of Luther or of the Zwinglians of Zurich. On the other side, the hierarchical Church demanded an end to reforms. The Parlement of Paris, a staunch voice of conservatism in religious matters, first forbade the reading or possession of French translations of the Scripture, and then condemned the reformers of Meaux in 1526:

> [they] read books of holy Scripture, translated from Latin into French, invent several heresies, form conventicles, dispute and question the Catholic faith, condemn the commandments and ministers of the Church, separate themselves from the common line of true faithful as to the sacraments, preaching, and service of the Church, and spread great errors, from which come and might further come many scandals.[48]

Full-scale repression lay close at hand. The Reformers benefitted at first from the support of important individuals, especially that of Marguerite d'Angoulême, the king's sister. She intervened constantly with Francis to prevent the arrest and even the execution of some reformers. She protected Lefèvre d'Étaples and his friends; under her patronage, they issued a new Latin edition of the Bible, a French translation of the Old Testament, and a poetic (French) rendering of the Psalms, by Clément Marot, valet of the princess's bedchamber. Francis had long fancied himself as a patron of Humanism; in 1519, he had invited Erasmus to head a new college for the study of ancient languages in Paris. He intermittently encouraged the study of Greek and Hebrew, eventually founding two permanent professorships in each in 1530: the origins of the Collège de France. He added a third Hebrew professor and a mathematician the following year. These professors stood in stark contrast to the ossified theological faculty of the hide-bound Sorbonne.

The Sorbonne allied itself with the most antireform elements in the French clergy. As the dominant European voice in theological matters, the Sorbonne carried enormous weight in Church discussions. Its faculty discouraged the study of ancient languages—in 1523 they condemned all editions of Scripture in Hebrew and Greek—and Classical philosophy and sought constantly to condemn any doctrines that varied from Scholasticism. They sought to prosecute those who disagreed with them. They cast their net too widely in the early 1520s when they tried to condemn Lefèvre d'Étaples and Erasmus, protegés of Francis I. Their persistence could pay off, however, as in the famous case of Louis de Berquin, the young French Humanist whom they had arrested as early as 1523. Francis I intervened to get him released. During the king's captivity in Spain, the Sorbonne and the Parlement arrested Berquin again and condemned him, but the king released him upon his return. In the end, the Sorbonne got their man; taking advantage of the king's weak bargaining position in 1528 (due to military failure in Italy), they condemned Berquin to life in prison. Berquin appealed to the Parlement, which proved to be a bad move: they changed his sentence to the death penalty, and had it carried out two days later.

In the 1530s, the king's attitude hardened against the reformers. His new enthusiasm against heresy had several causes. First, he reacted strongly to the affront of the Day of the Placards (17–18 October 1534), when some Zwinglians nailed posters denouncing the Catholic doctrine of transubstantiation to sites in Paris and some other cities. Contemporary accounts suggest they even nailed one to the king's bedchamber door. The Parlement took the lead in the repression, burning several "heretics" in

November and then considerably more in January, after a second incident. The king himself participated in a massive expiatory procession (21 January 1535) through the streets of Paris, walking bareheaded and carrying a torch behind the bishop of Paris holding aloft a monstrance bearing the Host.

Second, Francis faced a much changed religious situation. In the 1520s, the definitive split within Christianity did not seem apparent. Many people believed that a general council of the Church might restore Christian unity. Many reformers in France did not, in fact, become Protestants. Marguerite remained one of these Evangelicals; Erasmus and Lefèvre d'Étaples died Catholics. In the 1530s, however, positions hardened. On the eastern borders of France, Strasbourg forbade Catholic mass (1529) and Geneva turned to Protestantism (1534).

Third, the conservatives stepped up their efforts at repression. Francis needed the support of both the Sorbonne and the Parlement of Paris for his political agenda. He also needed the support of the Pope in his efforts to counteract the political successes of Charles V. The conservatives forced the king's hand by means of the Council of Sens (1529), which specifically defined as heresy a wide range of "Lutheran" doctrines and also laid out clearly official Catholic doctrine on subjects such as transubstantiation, justification by works, and the efficacy of the sacraments. Once the Church council had spoken authoritatively, the grounds for argument within the Church (a traditional defense of Evangelicals) became much smaller. In 1533, after a meeting with the king, Pope Clement VII issued a bull against French "Lutherans," which again reduced the freedom of action of reformers and king alike.

The division within French Christianity deepened and widened in the next twenty-five years. Certain dissidents within the population, such as the artisans of some towns, went over wholesale to Protestantism. Geneva, led by the Frenchman John Calvin, who studied briefly at the Collège de Montaigu in Paris, became the center of international Protestantism. The city sent trained preachers by the thousands into France to seek converts. They spread out in the Midi, helping to create large Protestant communities in such cities as Montauban and La Rochelle and important minorities in Lyon, Nîmes, and even northern towns such as Rouen. These Protestants remained hidden, to the extent possible.

The king and other authorities, notably the Parlement of Paris, stepped up persecution of Protestants. Francis gave the Parlements jurisdiction over heresy cases in 1540; they and the subordinate courts immediately used these powers to arrest "Lutherans." The seneschalsy of La Rochelle, for example, rounded up one hundred eighteen people and sentenced twenty-five of them to death. In 1542, the Sorbonne drew up the first French Index, or list of forbidden books. The Parlement of Paris backed up the Index by threatening death to those found with banned books in their homes or shops. The court particularly sought out printers, prosecuting six in Paris and burning two of them at the stake. In 1546, Etienne Dolet, famed publisher and author, several times arrested and released (with a royal pardon), went to the stake in Paris.

Those who openly practiced different rites risked persecution. In 1545, Jean Meynier, baron d'Oppède, First President of the Parlement of Provence, offered a sample of the violence to come. Acting on the king's orders, d'Oppède led troops into the valleys of the Vaud, where the peasants had for centuries practiced a variant of the thirteenth-century Waldensian heresy. Oppède's troops burned ten villages, massacred several thousand Vaudois, and committed mass rape on the women of the region, most of whom had gathered at the church of Mérindol, whence they were dragged out and assaulted.[49] The massacre of the harmless Vaudois gave an evil harbinger of the bloodshed to come in the Wars of Religion.

Notes

1. Cited in H. Neveux, J. Jacquart and E. Le Roy Ladurie, *L'Age classique des paysans, de 1340 à 1789,* vol. II of the *Histoire rurale de la France* (Paris, 1975), 86.

2. Spain expelled its very large Jewish community in 1492.

3. E. Rice, *Foundations of Early-Modern Europe, 1460–1559* (New York: Norton, 1969); B. Quilliet, *La France du Beau XVIe Siècle: 1490–1560* (Paris: Fayard, 1998).

4. BN, Mss. Fr. 16, 517, fol. 177.

5. BN, Mss Dupuy 539, fol. 5 for letters to Charles, fol. 206 for letters to Jeanne and Jean of Bourbon. The agreement covered such important provinces as the counties of Forez and Beaujolais; the duke already had such rights in the Bourbonnais and the Auvergne. This Bourbon mini-state lasted until 1527, when the king confiscated it as part of the judgment for treason against Charles, constable of Bourbon.

6. Ibid., fol. 106, letter of Charles, count of Charolais, later duke of Burgundy.

7. Ibid., fol. 71.

8. René claimed to be King of Sicily, but his subjects there disagreed; he never actually held the throne. Charles VIII invaded Naples in 1494, pushing his claim as René's heir.

9. This branch, too, ran out in the male line in 1589. At that time, the last remaining branch, the Bourbon descendants of Robert of Clermont, youngest son of Louis IX (d. 1270), claimed the throne.

10. Mary's mother, Jeanne of Bourbon, belonged to a collateral branch of the French royal family.

11. Mary's grandmother, Margaret of Flanders, had received the Somme towns, such as Amiens, as an incentive for marrying the duke of Burgundy instead of the duke of York; Mary believed them to be hers by right of simple inheritance. Louis seized them, too. Artois and Picardy posed a special problem because so many people (including the King of France) could make claims to parts of these areas, based on the various marriage settlements dating from the time of Philip Augustus!

12. The final solution to the problem of Mary's inheritance demonstrates the remarkable tenacity of the law. The King of France obtained back precisely those areas—the duchy of Burgundy and the Somme towns—to which he had a genuine legal right. He did not obtain those areas—like Flanders or the county of Burgundy—to which he had no real legal rights.

13. Margaret eventually came back. She later married the duke of Savoy, and the Habsburgs maintained control of Artois and the Franche-Comté after some desultory fighting.

14. The surviving contemporary accounts all stress Charles V's intense personal desire to right the "wrong" done to his grandmother in Burgundy.

15. Seven German princes elected the Holy Roman Emperor: the Electors of Saxony, Brandenburg, and the Rhineland Palatinate; the archbishops of Cologne, Trier, and Mainz; and the King of Bohemia.

16. The Angevins ruled Naples in the thirteenth century, until the revolt of the Sicilian Vespers. When the last member of the Aragonese house, the legitimized bastard Ferdinand I, died in 1494, Charles VIII claimed Naples by means of legitimate descent from the Angevin line and invaded Italy to enforce his claim. Ferdinand of Aragon, king of Spain, likewise put forth a claim, as collateral heir of Ferdinand I of Naples.

17. The most lasting effect of the League of Venice was the marriage of Philip of Habsburg and Juana the Mad.

18. The marriage did not actually take place until 1514, after the death of Anne of Brittany, Claude's mother, who opposed the union.

19. Two critical examples will suffice. If Francis II of Brittany had lived another few years, Anne of Brittany might have carried out her proxy marriage to Maximilian of Austria. If the son born to Ferdinand of Aragon's second wife, Germaine of Foix, niece of Louis XII, had lived, he, not Juana, and then Charles V, would have inherited the kingdom of Aragon.

20. D. Crouzet, ed., *La vie de Bayard* (Paris: Imprimerie Nationale, 1992), 144. My translation. The initial title of this work was *Les gestes ensemble de la vie du preux chevalier Bayard*.

21. Bourbon ruled a massive feudal state in central France, one that he had jointly inherited with his cousin–wife, Suzanne. When she died without heirs in 1521, Louise of Savoy, Suzanne's aunt, claimed the duchies of Bourbonnais and the Auvergne and the counties of Clermont, Forez, Beaujolais, and La Marche. Despairing of defeating the king's mother in a lawsuit in front of the Parlement of Paris, Bourbon defected to Charles V. Francis had the Parlement declare Bourbon guilty of treason, and seized his lands. When the constable died at the sack of Rome in 1527, the absence of a direct heir eliminated any legal confusion about the seizure of the last great feudal enclave within France. Several small enclaves, such as the viscounty of Turenne, survived into the eighteenth century.

22. Henry's wife, Catherine de Médicis, was not so forgiving. She wanted to execute Montgomery, but could not after the king's order. Catherine bided her time. Montgomery later converted to Protestantism and fought against royal forces. When he was captured in 1574, Catherine had him tried for treason by the Parlement of Paris. The Parlement found him guilty, ordered his execution, and stripped his family of its nobility.

23. B. Castiglione, *The Book of the Courtier,* trans. (Hammandsworth; New York: Penguin Books, 1976).

24. The discussants disagreed on this point. All agreed that the proper upbringing could help one obtain grace; some argued further that anyone could obtain grace, but the consensus held that the most graceful were those of proper upbringing combined with good family background. French nobles would certainly have taken the latter meaning from the text.

25. Quotations from Rabelais are taken from: *The Complete Works of François Rabelais,* trans. D. Frame (Berkeley: University of California Press, 1991).

26. Letter to Adrien Turnèbe, cited in G. Huppert, *The Style of Paris: Renaissance Origins of the French Enlightenment* (Bloomington: Indiana University Press, 1999), 4.

27. The name Pléiade comes from the constellation containing seven stars. The original seven poets were Ronsard, Joachim du Bellay, Pontus de Tyard, Jean-Antoine de Baïf, Etienne Jodelle, Jacques Peletier, and Dorat.

28. Jean Boucher, *Le Panegyric du chevalier sans reproche, ou Mémoires de la Trémoïlle* (Paris: Foucault, 1820), which is volume 14 of the *Collection complète des mémoires relatifs à l'histoire de France,* series one. Original edition of 1527 at Poitiers. Funeral oration on p. 509.

29. Cited in E. Le Roy Ladurie, *The Peasants of Languedoc,* trans. J. Day (Urbana, Chicago, London: University of Illinois Press, 1974, 1980), 51.

30. Here using the 2000 boundaries of continental France, not the widely different boundaries of the years in question.

31. Le Roy Ladurie, *The Peasants of Languedoc,* 51; the original, unabridged French edition, *Les Paysans de Languedoc* (Paris: S.E.V.P.E.N., 1966), 2 vols., contains much more extensive details on these matters. I have translated the French word *grange* as the more common English "barn," rather than "grange," used by Day.

32. The three words derive from the verb *labourer,* meaning to till with a plough, from hand (*main*) worker (*ouvrier*), and from day (*jour*) worker.

33. The French word *bricolage* refers to what a handyman does around the house. The great French anthropologist Claude Lévi-Strauss initiated scholarly use of it.

34. This pattern existed in most other European countries and in North America. It persists today in parts of America, such as some sections of the rural South.

35. The modern term "housewife" has misleading connotations, of an individual primarily concerned with the care of the house itself and with raising children. Early modern housewives should be thought of as managers, directing a small (sometimes large) enterprise. They supervised the money, made most of the purchases, and sold most of the goods, except grain. In towns, they usually kept the books of the business. They spent very little time tending a house and their role with respect to children was often a supervisory one, overseeing a young girl minding the children.

36. The traditional border between the kingdom of France and the Holy Roman Empire ran down the Saône and the Rhône rivers, which meet at Lyon. The ecclesiastical principality of Lyon did not become part of the kingdom of France until the early fourteenth century.

37. Most of the gold in late medieval Western Europe came from the west coast of Africa, from the area known as the Gold Coast (modern-day Ghana). It originally passed through the desert, overland to the north coast of Africa, but the Portuguese developed an extensive ocean-bound trade with this region by the fifteenth century.

38. P. Haudrère, *L'Empire des Rois, 1500–1789* (Paris: Denail, 1997), 28.

39. After the Revocation of the Edict of Nantes (1685), many Huguenots moved to the English colony created at Charleston. They became important members of the city's ruling elite and created enduring ties between South Carolina and France. A number of important French companies, such as Michelin, have invested heavily in contemporary South Carolina.

40. BN, Mss. Fr. 15,494, fol. 49v. Text forms part of a work by Jacques de Montigny, a sixteenth-century jurist.

41. In many places, such as the United States, priests continued to say the Mass in Latin, with their back to the congregation, until the reforms of Vatican II (1962).

42. Pierre-Jakez Hélias, in his delightful memoirs of growing up in a Breton village in the 1920s, *The Horse of Pride: Life in a Breton Village,* trans. J. Guicharnaud (New Haven: Yale University Press, 1974), offers a touching description of his mother's churching.

43. The French term *sage femme* means both wise woman and midwife. Midwives, who supervised all births, were powerful figures in French villages. Many of them also acted as herbalists. In time, people accused these "wise women" of being witches.

44. Friars did not have property. They lived by means of charitable donations. Monasteries held property, often large blocks of land.

45. Metz had a large and thriving Jewish community. Perhaps the economic dislocation that followed the Provençal expulsions led to the willingness to allow the Jews to stay in 1559. One might also point to the greater respect accorded to the Hebrew *Old Testament*—Francis I created a professorship in Hebrew at Paris—by the mid-sixteenth century.

46. Huldreich Zwingli led the Protestant Reformation at Zurich. He and Luther broke over the issue of communion, with Zwingli arguing the purely spiritual nature of the communion. Zwingli's position on this issue later became that of the followers of John Calvin.

47. Among other discoveries, Erasmus found that Saint Jerome had added the only Biblical reference to the Trinity; early manuscripts did not contain the passage. Luther used the Vulgate as the basis of his German Bible, thereby evading the problem of lack of Scriptural evidence for the Trinity.

48. *Histoire de la France religieuse,* ed. J. Le Goff and R. Rémond (Paris: Seuil, 1988, 4 vols.), II, 226.

49. Most estimates put the Vaudois at about six thousand people; casualty estimates for the massacres range from a few hundred to eight thousand. Male Vaudois captured during the repression ended up as galley rowers.

Chapter Six

THE AGE OF IRON, NEW IDENTITIES, AND THE FAILURE OF ORDER

In former times men lived in an Age of Gold; we live in an Age of Iron.

The duke of Alba, Spanish governor of the Low Countries, *c.*1566

The Reformation disrupted European societies in a way so fundamental, so central to human existence that we understand with difficulty its passions. Living in a culture suffused by a rationalist conceit, conflicts of emotion pose particular problems for us. In our own day, those problems can be ethnic (the Balkans or Rwanda), religious (Yugoslavia, Algeria) or racial. In the sixteenth century, as now, passions alone do not lay behind the terrible deeds; they become intertwined with more traditional personal and political motives: territorial ambitions, *realpolitik*, and simple human greed.

The Catholic self-definition of France and western Europe became markedly more restrictive in the fourteenth and fifteenth centuries. States expelled their non-Christian populations, although many Jews in southern France and, later, in Provence, chose to "convert," so that sixteenth-century France, like Spain, had communities of *Conversos* and *Marranos*.[1] The legal prohibition against Jews lasted until 1550, when stepped-up persecutions in Portugal led Henry II to accept Portuguese *Marranos* into French southern and western ports. When Philip II of Spain inherited Portugal's throne in 1580, he initiated a renewed wave of persecution; many Jews fled to the Muslim world or to the great Atlantic ports of the north, like Amsterdam and Hamburg. Smaller numbers moved to France. Some of these sought out *Marrano* communities in cities such as Montpellier, whose famous medical school attracted Jewish doctors and pharmacists, but others resettled in ports such as Nantes or Bordeaux, where, as at Montpellier, Jewish doctors joined the medical faculties and Jewish merchants became involved in international and local trade.

These Jews formed a small current in the migratory flood of the sixteenth-century: French Protestants fled to Geneva to escape persecution, but Catholics in England or Protestant parts of the Low Countries emigrated to France. Economic factors pushed or pulled even more people, from the flocks of Auvergnats who migrated to Spain in search of work to the Flemish peasants or burghers seeking relief in France from the brutal civil war in the Low Countries. The constant fighting of the Wars of Religion brought tens of thousands of foreign soldiers—Germans above all, but Swiss, Irish, Scots, Italians, and Walloons, too—into France, where many of them settled.

These migrations added fuel to the fire of emergent national feeling. The proselytizing of Genevan Protestants and the preeminence of Italian bankers at the royal Court provided French Catholics and Protestants with convenient targets for expressing the profound popular hostility toward "foreigners." The Estates General of 1561, who generally recommended a policy of tolerance as a way to prevent civil war, took a harder line toward some "outsiders," such as Gypsies. The king responded with an ordinance ordering bailiffs to "command all those who call themselves Bohemians and Egyptians, their wives and children and others of their households, to leave the kingdom . . . within two months, on pain of corporal punishment and imprisonment as galley rowers." Violators, even women and children, were to have their heads shaven clean. Although the deputies recommended that Protestants simply be "admonished by double exhortations rather than . . . molested for reason of religion," they would not tolerate those whose beliefs "were similar to those of atheists, Anabaptists, Arians, Epicureans, and libertines."[2]

These struggles about inclusion and exclusion naturally paralleled discussions of the essence of "Frenchness." Sixteenth-century French nobles believed a Trojan myth of their origins, most famously stated in the opening lines of Pierre de Ronsard's epic poem, *La Franciade* (1572):

> Muse, honor of the summits of Parnassus,
> Guide my tongue and sing to me of the race
> Of the Kings of France, issued from Francion,
> Child of Hector, Trojan by nation,[3]

This myth united the French nobility in its self-definition, yet excluded commoners from the mythological unity. Obsession with "blood" or descent underlay the distinctive noble ideology of the late sixteenth and early seventeenth centuries, but the state could not afford to exclude non-nobles from the definition of the "French" nation. The government sought to focus attention on the French Trinity: one faith, one king, one law.

The intrusion of schism into a world so militantly conscious of its religious unity, indeed, into a society that defined religion largely in terms of communal unity, led to frenzied violence in the Holy Roman Empire, the Low Countries, the British Isles, and France. Western Europe's discovery of a vast new world across the Atlantic, particularly the heavily populated Aztec Empire, added insecurities about the European place in the world to those of mounting religious fears. The Atlantic encounter, and closer contact with Africa and Asia, often reinforced the old Crusading impulses, which encouraged religiously justified violence in the conquest of the Amerindian empires. Bernal Diaz, companion of Cortez, repeatedly compared the *conquistadores* to the brave knights of the *Reconquista* of Spain from the Muslims and even to "the paladin Roland" and his men. The ongoing struggle with the Ottoman Empire in the Mediterranean encouraged similar views; later, slave traders would use the Christian "just war" theory to excuse their foul commerce. France initially played a supporting role in the events outside of Europe, but its own religious civil war blended seamlessly with those of its neighbors to the north and east. Religiously justified violence thus permeated the Atlantic world, from the slaving raids in western Africa to the conquest of Mexico and back across to the Wars of Religion in France or the civil war in the Low Countries.

Many early modern French people could not imagine a world of religious diversity; for them, Catholic France meant France as the "eldest daughter" of the Church. It meant the King of France's unique, papally sanctioned title as the Most Christian King, and it meant France had to be pure—a Christian kingdom on earth. We need only look across the border to Geneva to understand that most others in early modern Europe had similar ideas. The Burgundian town deputies to the Estates General of 1560 expressed the nearly universal opinion of their day:

> . . . this kingdom, which from time immemorial has been Christian, finds itself divided into several sects, which always brings with it division and sedition, as has happened in Germany, England, and Scotland, and of which we see the beginnings even in this kingdom. Such division is the cause of subversion and mutation of kingdoms and the depopulation of all states.[4]

In the Empire, the Reformation helped incite the greatest European peasant rebellion, the Peasants' War of 1525. Eighty thousand peasants lost their lives. Elites all over Europe shuddered at this example of ordinary people making their own religious decisions. They later cheered the ruthless extermination of the Anabaptist radicals who had captured Münster (1534). German Protestant princes soon began a war with the Catholic Charles V; Protestants in the Low Countries rebelled against his son, Philip II, in the 1560s. These religious wars ended only with the Peace of Westphalia (1648). Catholic France allied in both places with the Protestant forces against the old Habsburg enemy, champion of Catholicism or no. These cross-religious alliances indicated the complex intermingling of family interests, state politics, and religion. France still coveted the "lost" province of Flanders, so the French government usually looked with favor on the Netherlandish rebels, who attacked France's old Habsburg foe. When France's own Protestant rebels allied with the Dutch ones, however, the French government developed profound misgivings about Protestants rebelling against a Catholic king.

In the France of the imagination, one part of France has always imagined itself wholly, *purely* Catholic; the other part of France has imagined itself a diverse and glorious mixture of ingredients. As late as 1973, one could predict the voting behavior of parishes near Vitré in eastern Brittany by determining whether the given parish had supported the Protestant Henry IV or the Catholic League during the 1590 siege of the city.[5] For four centuries, this region, like so many others, demonstrated a continuity among those who gave primacy to the imagined religious unity of France and among those who gave precedence to the secular idea of "France."

The political and religious events of the last four decades of the sixteenth century laid the foundations for the development of the modern European political system. The Protestant rebellion in the Low Countries and the consolidation of the Protestant ascendancy in England created a powerful Reformed redoubt in northwestern

Europe, precisely the area of emerging economic supremacy. In retrospect, we can see how extraordinary, how fundamental for the development of France, were the years between the Estates General of Orléans, which began in December 1560, and those of Blois, which ended in March 1577. France underwent a virtual religious revolution after 1557: Protestantism spread like wildfire, undermining both political and religious unity. The Calvinists made enormous inroads in the late 1550s, culminating with the Psalm singing at the Pré-aux-Clercs near Paris (1558). Some 40 percent of the nobility in Normandy or Guyenne had converted; Protestantism surged, too, among urban artisans and the middle class. Politically, the national representative assembly, the Estates General, seemed ready to join comparable institutions in nearby countries, but then failed to take root.

The French Wars of Religion combined three major problems: first, Protestants fought Catholics; second, the Crown sought to create a new form of state; and third, France became embroiled in semipermanent international conflict. These three strands wove a second Gordian Knot, which Henry IV cut only by repeated deft strokes between 1589 and 1598. Disorder seemed to threaten every element of French life. France reacted to this disorder by creating a much more highly ordered society. This new order extended everywhere: politics, religion, cultural life. To understand why the problem of order came to dominate French life in the way that it did, we must first look at the time of disorder, which began in earnest with the accidental death of Henry II in 1559.

ꙮ The Civil War: Religion, Politics, and State-Building

C H R O N O L O G Y	1559–1589
1559	Death of Henry II; Francis II king at fourteen
1560	Tumult of Amboise (February); death of Francis II (12/5); Estates General of Orléans opens (12/13); Jeanne d'Albret declares for Protestantism (12/25)
1561	Estates General of Pontoise (August); Colloquy of Poissy (September)
1562	Edict of Saint-Germain (March); Massacre of Wassy (3/1); Protestants seize major towns (March–April); Catholics take Rouen (10/26); death of Antoine de Bourbon (11/17); battle of Dreux (12/19)
1563	Assassination of François de Guise (February); peace of Amboise (3/19)
1564	Edict of Paris: first day of the year set as 1 January, not Easter; Charles IX and Catherine de Médicis begin their two-year trip around France
1566	Ordinance of Moulins (February); iconoclasm in the Low Countries

CHRONOLOGY	(continued)
1567	Attempted seizure of Meaux by Condé (9/26); *Michelade* at Nîmes (9/30); Second War of Religion begins; battle of Saint-Denis (11/10), deaths of Anne de Montmorency and marshal Saint-André
1568	Peace of Longjumeau (3/23); Alba executes counts Egmont and Hoorn (6/5); de l'Hôpital removed from royal council (June); Third War of Religion starts (8/1)
1569	Battle of Jarnac (3/13), death of Condé; Parlement of Paris condemns Coligny to death (9/13)
1570	Peace of Saint-Germain
1571	Coligny returns to the Court (September); Gastines riot (12/20)
1572	Dutch "Sea Beggars" take Brill (4/1); death of Jeanne d'Albret (6/9); marriage of Henry of Navarre and Marguerite de Valois (8/18); attempted assassination of Coligny (8/22); Saint Bartholomew's Day Massacre (8/24); massacres of Protestants at Orléans (8/26), Lyon (8/31), Rouen (9/17), Toulouse (10/3); siege of La Rochelle begins
1573	Henry of Valois elected King of Poland–Lithuania (May); failure to take La Rochelle, peace of Boulogne (July)
1574	Fifth War of Religion starts (March); death of Charles IX (5/30); Henry III leaves Cracow (6/18), reaches Lyon (9/6); death of cardinal of Lorraine (12/26)
1575	Henry III crowned (2/13) and married to Louise of Vaudemont (2/15); duke of Alençon flees the Court (9/15)
1576	First organization of the Holy League (January); Henry of Navarre flees the Court (2/2); Edict of Beaulieu/ Peace of Monsieur (May); opening of Estates General (12/6), Henry III calls for the extirpation of Protestants
1577	Start of Sixth War of Religion (January); Estates General endorses toleration (February); Peace of Bergerac (9/14) and Edict of Poitiers (9/17)
1579	Union of Utrecht creates United Provinces of the Netherlands (1/23); start of Seventh War of Religion (November)
1580	Peace of Fleix
1583	White penitent movement begins (March): Assembly of Notables at Saint-Germain-en-Laye (November)
1584	Death of duke of Anjou/ Alençon (6/10); assassination of William of Orange (7/10); Holy League reconstituted (fall)

C H R O N O L O G Y	(continued)
1585	Pope bars Henry of Navarre and prince of Condé from throne of France (9/9)
1587	Navarre routs royal army at Coutras (10/20); duke of Guise destroys German mercenary armies (October–November)
1588	Guise enters Paris (5/9); Day of the Barricades (5/12), Henry III flees Paris; Edict of Union declares Protestantism to be treason (7/15); Invincible Armada destroyed off England (summer); Estates General at Blois (10/16); Henry III declares Edict of Union a fundamental law (10/18); assassinations of duke of Guise (12/23) and cardinal of Guise (12/24)
1589	Death of Catherine de Médicis (1/5); antiroyal riots in Paris (January); alliance of Henry of Navarre and Henry III (4/3); Pope Sixtus V excommunicates Henry III (5/26); Jacques Clement stabs Henry III (8/1); death of Henry III, Henry of Navarre (Henry IV), King of France (8/2)

Abuses in the Catholic Church: How Much Reform?

> . . . all the laws made by the Popes or others concerning the Christian religion cannot subject Christians to follow any rule or doctrine other than that found in the Bible . . . God is perfect and His doctrine is as well, needing no gloss or augmentation.[6]

> Anne du Bourg, former clerical councilor of the Parlement of Paris,
> at his heresy trial in 1559

Anne du Bourg laid out the simple difference between Protestants and Catholics. The famous doctrinal controversies (see Chapter 5) touched relatively few people in the 1550s; the French laity focused instead on the many abuses they saw in the organized Church. The *cahiers* of 1560–1561 demonstrate a seemingly naive faith in the ability of a Church council, either national or general, to resolve matters of doctrine by reforming abuses. These documents drip the venom of hostility, indeed contempt toward the clergy. When the spokesman of the clergy, Jean Quentin, doctor of theology at the Sorbonne, proclaimed that the Protestants were "heretics and Arians" who had to be rooted out by fire and sword, the nobility demanded that he apologize for his "invective against the honor of God and the supplicants [i.e., in this case, the nobility]" and accused him of blasphemy. The nobility of the viscounty of Paris put the blame squarely on Quintin's colleagues: "most of them [the clergy] live so dissolute a life that all of the troubles we currently have in religion proceed only from them."[7]

The reforming sentiment created paralyzing doubt in people's minds: the Reformers denounced abuses detested by nearly all lay believers, but did their objections to more fundamental doctrines make sense, too? Laymen rightly sensed that

Protestants and Catholics shared the most important doctrines: the Trinity, the belief in Christ's divinity, salvation through Christ. Alas, they also shared the utopian view that a unified Christianity could be rebuilt on that basis, expressed in a naive faith in the ability of a national or general Church council to reform abuses and thus resolve doctrinal conflicts.

In the late summer of 1560, Francis II, still uncertain which religious policy to follow, consulted "various men well versed in doctrine." They offered the following advice:

> The question of religion is of such importance that one must proceed with the greatest possible deliberation, without being transported by any private affection, but conducted solely by a holy desire for the honor of God, the salvation of men, and the public tranquility. . . . One must use such gentleness [*douceur*] and benignity that those who are in error may receive instruction, to which there is nothing so bad and so contrary as force and violence, according to the saying of Saint Augustine.

The good doctors went on to note that the Protestants accepted the doctrines of the early councils, were not Manicheans or Arians, accepted the Trinity, believed that salvation came through Christ, and had shown an "admirable constancy, and a superhuman faith, by which they overcome the terrors and apprehensions of death, even singing in the midst of the flames, invoking at the top of their lungs the name of Our Lord Jesus Christ." These "wise men" then pointed out that the Protestants had so expanded in the kingdom, and included so many notable personages, that it would be impossible to "tear out something with such deep roots." They worried about the economic effects of Protestant emigration and insisted that the Protestants had not become seditious. In short, they recommended gentleness as the best policy, "both for the repose of the consciences of the king's subjects and for the good of his service."[8]

To the laity, religion meant communal unity, not a set of abstruse doctrines. They had no illusions about the naked self-interest of the clergy—the deputies demanding a national council in 1561 insisted that the king, queen, and princes of the blood be present, so that the clergy would not be "judge in their own case," nor did their demands for church reform change much from 1560 to 1577. They feared the interference of religious leaders in national politics: the general *cahier* of the nobility at Orléans went so far as to suggest that all members of the clergy, save princes of the blood, be excluded from the royal council.[9]

The immemorial link between the Church and the French monarchy created two potentially divisive loyalties, as the deputies of the nobility of Burgundy unwittingly made clear in their *cahier* for the 1560 meeting. They began with seemingly ringing endorsements of the Catholic church and of the monarchy:

> First, the said gentlemen wish and desire to live and die in the observance of the commandments of God and of our mother the holy Roman Catholic church, according to the constitutions and sanctions of them contained in the holy decrees and councils. The said gentlemen also wish and desire to

live and die in the obedience of His Majesty and the Crown of France, offering to expose their lives and those of their children, their families and
goods for his service.[10]

Those formalities out of the way, the deputies launched into a stinging critique
of the Church. Like the full body of the Estates General, they asked the king to convene a national church council or to plead with the Pope, "to assemble a holy, legitimate, and free general council as soon as possible to proceed with a reformation of
all that will be found" wrong and in "need of reform in the Church of God and with
his ministers."[11] All laymen seem to have agreed on the abuses in the Church: they
wanted benefice holders to be adult "men of knowledge, being well versed in letters, of
good life and morals and integrity, and that they actually serve as priests, singing and
celebrating the mass." They demanded that all bishops and archbishops, abbots
and priors, and vicars actually reside in their bishoprics, monastery, prior, or parish,
and that each of them hold only one benefice. They insisted that no woman be accepted into a convent, unless she had reached the legal age of consent, and that, once
accepted, all nuns remain cloistered at all times.[12] They castigated the parish clergy
for demanding money from villagers for admission of the sacraments and for burials. They even insisted on their right to elect the clergy, from parish priests all the
way to archbishops. Both lay orders demanded that the king and Queen Mother act
with gentleness and eschew violence.[13]

Many Catholic laypeople agreed with the Protestants that the Church's interest
in secular matters undermined its spiritual mission. The nobility of the Paris region
offered a general explanation as to why the Church had lapsed into so many evil
practices:

> The goods of the Church have grown so much and have augmented avarice
> and ambition, nursing mother of all evil, that . . . there is not a single one, or
> very few [clergy] . . . who will preach and announce to the people the word
> of God, which is his Scripture, nor to instruct what is belief, and is necessary
> for salvation. Thus through lack of instruction, both by word and by example
> of clean living, your poor people remains in such ignorance that it has lost
> all knowledge of God and abandoned all of his commandments.[14]

The Estates Generals of 1560 and 1561 recommended removal of the Church from
all temporal matters, including elimination of all lay jurisdiction from Church
courts; royal intervention in life rental contracts granted on Church property; a ban
on ecclesiastics holding royal offices, including membership in the king's council;
and, most radically, stripping the Church of its property. At the 1561 meeting at Pontoise, the Third Estate proposed a remarkable scheme, which involved seizing virtually all of the Church's landed revenues, which they estimated at 4 million *livres*, and
selling the property for thirty times its revenue.[15] The clergy reacted with suitable
outrage. They used the principle of unanimity to prevent any sort of legal move toward religious accommodation. After the king declined the Third Estate's request to
sell the lands of the clergy, on the grounds that it would violate the property rights

of his subjects, the clergy's assembly at Poissy came up with an immediate subsidy of 1.6 million *livres* a year for six years and allowed the king to sell annuities guaranteed by Church revenues. The clergy continued its grant at its 1567 assembly and renewed its support ever afterward. This ready money enabled the Church to buy off the threats of confiscation and gave it enormous leverage over the royal government.

The clergy forever emphasized the importance of a single faith, of the French trinity of one faith, one king, one law, knowing that most people focused on the necessity of religious unity for civil peace. Even Catholic moderates, like chancellor Michel de l'Hôpital, feared the logical outcome of the priesthood of all believers: "if it is preferable for each to take a new religion at his whim, you must be watchful lest there be as many ways and manners of religion as there are families or leaders of men. You say your religion is better. I defend mine. Which is more reasonable, that I follow your opinion or that you follow mine?" At the Estates General of 1560, de l'Hôpital begged his countrymen to settle the religious question by gentleness (*douceur*, literally sweetness)—"the knife is worth little against the spirit"—but he knew well that "there is no other opinion as profound in the hearts of men as that of religion" and that "religion, good or bad, gives men their greatest passion." Sooner or later, he argued that December morning, religious division would lead to fighting. He didn't have long to wait.

A Family Affair

> *This [unity of religion] is the firmest bond of union, friendship, and obedience owed, which, if lacking, produces nothing but contention, rancor, and division. One could not say that God resides there.*
>
> The Parlement of Paris, objecting to the Edict of Saint-Germain, 1562

The religious background to the outbreak of civil war thus had two key elements. First, French laypeople demanded reform of the Catholic Church's abuses. Second, some of those who demanded reforms believed that the institutional Church would have to be destroyed in order to carry out those reforms. In the late 1550s the rapid upsurge in Protestant activity in France, best symbolized by the participation of members of the extended royal family at the Psalm singing outside Paris (1558), coincided with dramatic political changes. France and Spain signed the Peace of Cateau-Cambresis (1559), ending more than a half century of intermittent warfare. At the tournament held to celebrate the dual royal marriages arranged to cement the new friendship, Henry II died from an accidental wound suffered in a joust. His death left the kingdom to a boy of fourteen, Francis II, and added political instability to the religious turmoil. Throughout the Wars of Religion, politics and religion would remain inseparable.

The internal political side of the civil war that broke out in 1562 had its roots in the break-up of the great feudal states at the end of the fifteenth century. Most modern historians simply assume these states stood in the way of the inevitable triumph of the French nation state, and further assume that the Crown actively sought to

eliminate them. Such is only partly the case. French kings certainly wanted to eliminate the powerful dukes of Burgundy or the essentially independent Breton state,
but they had no interest in the disappearance of the great nobility. These aristocrats
enabled the state to act; without their dominating presence in a given region, the
king's power suffered, too. The demise of those states encouraged the King of France
to create royal governors in the major provinces of the kingdom; at first, these positions went primarily to members of the extended royal family. At the start of Francis
I's reign (1515), six of the seven governorships belonged to members of the extended
royal family: four in male lines and two in female ones. When Henry II took the
throne (1547), only one of the eleven governors, Antoine de Bourbon, governor of
Picardy, represented a male line of the royal family.

Historians have long focused on the feuds among the three great aristocratic
families of middle- and late-sixteenth-century France—Bourbon, Guise, and Montmorency—as a driving force in the Wars of Religion, yet to do so somewhat misrepresents both the Wars and early modern French society. Defining clans such as the
Guises or Bourbons solely in patrilineal terms ignores the reality that aristocratic
families intermarried at least every second or third generation; children as often inherited great estates from their mother's family as from that of their father. Such alliances among cousins meant that families who fought political battles at Court, also
fought legal ones, over inheritance rights, in court. Although French law barred
women from the throne, it also guaranteed that aristocratic heiresses, including those
from the royal family, would have substantial inheritance rights over the landed
property that underlay family power in early modern society. Aristocratic women
did more than pass along landed estates: their husbands often obtained key provincial offices, such as governorships, that had belonged to men in their families. Thus,
Charles of Bourbon inherited not only his mother's (Marie of Luxembourg) great
Picard estates, but also the governorship of Picardy, a post long held by her family.
Marie, as was usual, passed her estates to her younger son, Louis, who took his title,
prince of Condé, from a Luxembourg family estate. Older brother Antoine gave up
his post as governor of Picardy to Louis and moved to the southwest, where his wife,
Jeanne d'Albret had her estates. Following in the footsteps of Jeanne's father, he became governor of Guyenne.

If the survival of multiple sons could divide a family into separate branches, the
equally frequent absence of surviving sons meant that daughters often inherited the
family lands. Between 1450 and 1550 a staggering number of high aristocratic families died out in the male line. The broad royal family followed a bewildering pace of
family intermarriage in those years. These intermarriages paralleled the steady extinction of one male line after another, until, by 1527, only three males lines survived: the
king himself and the houses of Bourbon-Vendôme and Bourbon-Montpensier.[16]
The extinction of so many ducal lines meant that Francis I desperately needed to expand the peak of the sociopolitical pyramid of French society—the duke–peers, who
provided most of the provincial governors. In 1527, therefore, he made Claude de
Guise, husband of Antoinette de Bourbon-Vendôme, the first nonroyal duke. Twelve
years later, Marguerite de Bourbon, niece of Antoinette, brought a ducal title to her
husband, François de Clèves, who became duke of Nevers. Henry II elevated a simple

baronial family, the Montmorency, to a duchy in 1551; once again, the new duke had a Bourbon connection. His wife, Madeleine of Savoy, was the granddaughter of a Bourbon.[17] Although only a single governor of 1547 descended from a male line of the royal family, seven of the eleven men had close family ties (marriage or descent) to a female branch of the royal family.[18]

Francis I and Henry II showered the Guise and Montmorency families with high offices: Claude de Guise became royal chamberlain, master of the royal hunt, and governor of Champagne (1524). Henry II made his bosom companion François de Guise (son of Claude) governor of Dauphiné and soon raised four other Guise family estates—Aumale, Mayenne, Joinville, and Elbeuf—to the status of duchy, giving the Guise family the astounding total of *five* duchies in a single family. All five of these duchies belonged to sons or grandsons of Antoinette de Bourbon; their connection to the royal family thus derived from the female line.[19] The Guise family held governorships in Burgundy, Champagne, and Dauphiné, to say nothing of offices as Grand Master of the King's Household, royal chamberlain, master of the hunt, and commander of the king's galleys. Their sister, Marie, married King James V of Scotland. In 1558, her daughter Mary, Queen of Scots, completed the Guise family's meteoric rise: she married Henry II's eldest son and heir, Francis II.

The Montmorency family had almost as much success. Anne de Montmorency became governor of Languedoc (1526), Grand Master of the King's Household, and, in 1536, Constable. Anne's son, Henry de Montmorency-Damville, succeeded him as governor of Languedoc and, in time, as Constable. A second son, François, became governor of the Ile-de-France in 1538, an office he held, save for the six-year (1551–1557) rule of his cousin, until his death in 1579. Anne's nephews, Gaspard de Coligny and Henri d'Andelot, became Admiral of France and colonel–general of the infantry, which gave the three men virtually complete control over promotions in the French army in the 1550s. Coligny briefly held the governorship of Picardy.

The Bourbon and Guise families dominated the Church hierarchy, too. Royal favor enabled Claude de Guise's brother Jean to become a cardinal, just as it obtained red hats for Claude's sons, Charles and Louis. Charles, as cardinal of Lorraine, archbishop of Reims, was endowed with a benefice which enabled him to become the richest private man in France, with an income of 300,000 *livres* a year. Louis, cardinal of Guise, archbishop of Sens, held religious jurisdiction over Paris.[20] As for the Bourbons, Antoine's brother Charles became cardinal of Bourbon, as well as archbishop of Rouen and abbot of Saint-Germain-des-Prés in Paris. The cardinal's income did not quite match his brother's 225,000 a year, but we need shed no tears for him.

The Montmorency were minor players in the Church, save for Anne's third nephew, Odet de Coligny, count–bishop of Beauvais, who became a cardinal at sixteen! Anne de Montmorency more than made up for this shortcoming through his remarkable accumulation of landed property. Although Bernard Quilliet calls Anne de Montmorency the "zero among zeroes" for his combination of military ineptitude, most famously demonstrated at the catastrophic battle of Saint-Quentin (1557), and gratuitous cruelty, shown in his ruthless suppression of a salt tax revolt in the Southwest, the Constable's legendary cupidity bore stunning results.[21] He created, virtually from scratch, the third largest family property in France. Contemporaries estimated that he owned the astonishing total of six hundred seigneuries, in thirteen different provinces, including seven châteaux, as well as four townhouses in Paris, altogether capital assets of 3 million *livres*, producing an income of 200,000 *livres* a year.[22]

Henry II kept the Guise and Montmorency families in relative balance, but the accession of the fourteen-year-old Francis II quickly shifted the balance to the Guise. Legally an adult king, Francis quickly fell under the control of the uncles of his eighteen-year-old wife, Mary, Queen of Scots: Charles, cardinal of Lorraine, and François, duke of Guise. The young king, crowned by his cardinal–uncle in September 1559, soon gave the reins of the royal household to his uncle François. The Guise and Montmorency each had control of substantial parts of the kingdom. In 1559, the Montmorency held the governorships of Languedoc, the Ile-de-France, and Picardy. François and Claude de Guise held those of Burgundy and Dauphiné. Claude's brother-in-law, the duke of Bouillon, was governor of Normandy (where the Guise had two duchies, Elbeuf and Aumale). The duke of Nevers, father-in-law of François de Guise's son Henry, held Champagne, the heartland of the Guise influence.

❧ THE WARS OF RELIGION, 1562–1589

The license of war so long continued has stifled true piety and the honor of God in the hearts of men, and in consequence removed from their spirit the respect and the veneration due to the majesty of Kings, which is the bond of civil society.[23]

Guillaume du Vair, Keeper of the Seals,
addressing the Parlement of Toulouse, 1621

The political readjustment of 1559 came at a singularly inopportune moment in the struggles of the gigantic aristocratic clan—the Colignys—under the influence of their mother, Jeanne de Montmorency, had just converted to Calvinism. Schism racked the Bourbon family, too: Antoine de Bourbon flirted briefly with Reform in the late 1550s, inviting Calvinist preachers to his private quarters, and his brother Louis, prince of Condé, converted.[24] Although Antoine eventually remained a conviction-free Catholic, his wife, Jeanne d'Albret, strongly favored the Reformed: on Christmas Day 1560, she publicly declared herself a Protestant. The Guise family remained ardent Catholics and supported rigorous persecution of Protestants.

Seeking to remove Francis from the control of his uncles and his mother, Catherine de Médicis, Condé, and the Protestant nobles plotted to seize the king at Amboise (February 1560). The Tumult of Amboise failed utterly: Guise forces surprised and slaughtered hundreds of the rebels. Condé, called before the king's council, denied involvement and challenged to a duel anyone who would dare accuse him of such treason. When no one accepted, he quickly fled the Court. Despite Condé's failed coup, moderate forces, led by Catherine and chancellor de l'Hôpital, remained powerful at the royal Court. In August, at a special assembly held at Fontainebleau, the Council considered five options for Protestants:

Execution of Conspirators of Amboise; the child king, Francis II, watches from the battlements.

SOURCE: Châteaux of the Loire.

1. "Extermination by fire and sword."

2. Banishment.

3. Leaving "everyone in liberty of conscience and of religion, to assemble and pray to God."

4. Waiting for the rulings of a general Church council.

5. Calling a national Church Council.

The Council decided to call for a meeting of the Estates General of France, which had not met since 1483–1484; they set the opening session for early December 1560, at Orléans.

While the Council debated, intermittent fighting between Catholics and Huguenots broke out, especially in the Protestant parts of the Midi and in those northern towns with large Protestant minorities. Francis II blamed Bourbon and Condé for the disorders and commanded them to answer for their actions at Court. When they arrived at Orléans, the king had them arrested. The Guise convinced Francis to empanel a special tribunal to try Condé for *lèse-majesté*. Some members balked at a guilty verdict, fearing the dramatic change in the air of November 1560. The tribunal finally voted for the death penalty in late November, but it was too late.

The young king, always a sickly youth, had taken ill. On 5 December 1560, he died. His death made his nine-year-old brother, Charles IX, king; because Charles was under fourteen, the kingdom would now have to be ruled by a regent.

The Estates General opened on the thirteenth; the chancellor praised the willingness of all members of the royal house to obey the king and his mother, "in which is demonstrated the virtue of the king of Navarre [Bourbon], who, as first prince of the blood, was the first to show the path to others and to give an example of obedience."[25] These Estates had a dubious legal status. Because Francis II had summoned them, they had no mandates to ratify the Queen Mother's claim to be Regent and provide her with advice about constituting the royal council that would assist her. French law required them to return home to their bailiwick assemblies and get new mandates. Many deputies suggested that the meeting had to be adjourned at once; some left without attending any sessions. The government set the new meeting for August 1561, at Pontoise, a town near Saint-Germain-en-Laye, where the king would then be staying.[26] At Pontoise, after some hesitation by supporters of Antoine de Navarre, who as senior prince of the blood had a strong claim to be regent, the deputies voted to ratify the private agreement reached by Catherine and Antoine, by which she obtained full powers.[27] Antoine got the somewhat empty title of Lieutenant-General of the kingdom and his brother Louis, prince of Condé, regained the family's traditional governorship of Picardy (September 1561).

The Estates hoped that a special meeting of the clergy, the Colloquy of Poissy (September 1561), would solve the religious issues: it failed. At Poissy, the French clergy listened to a doctrinal debate. Theodore Beza, one of the leading Protestant preachers of Geneva, clearly laid out the doctrinal differences between the two sides, focusing especially on the communion controversy: "the body and blood of Christ is as far from bread and wine as the highest sky is from the earth." The cardinal of Lorraine, seeking to set a trap for the Protestants, asked them to move away from their Calvinist theology and to accept the compromise Lutheran position on communion; Beza responded by asking that the cardinal himself first sign the Lutheran "Augsburg Confession." Lorraine refused. So ended the French clergy's only open colloquy.

Despite this failure, Catherine and the chancellor, like the lay deputies to the Estates General, supported a policy of reconciliation. The tolerance even reached the royal palaces, where Huguenots such as Condé and Coligny invited Protestant ministers to preach to them in their private apartments. Her policy of accommodation led to the remarkable Edict of Saint-Germain (January 1562), which, for the first time, allowed certain liberties of conscience to Protestants, although banning the construction of their "temples" and limiting their services to daytime meetings to be held outside of any towns. The Parlement of Paris held up its registration for two months. Relying on the classic political metaphors of their day they argued: "Laws both sacred and profane insist that the woman is in holy bond to her husband and children in holy bond to their father . . . the entire family is of the same religion as the father of the family."[28] In France, whose Catholic king was the father of his people, that meant everyone had to be Catholic.

The Calvinists profited from the respite by proselytizing rigorously in all areas of the kingdom, and by 1562 perhaps one French person in five practiced Protestantism. Catholics responded vigorously to what they viewed as an incendiary provocation; the Guise furnished the spark needed to start a conflagration. After holding a meeting on doctrinal differences with the Lutheran duke of Württemburg, they promised "not to seek the least evil toward the Reformed, either in public or secretly." The promises barely survived their journey home: when Protestants gathered for services at the small town of Wassy, within one of his estates, the duke of Guise massacred twenty-three of them.[29] Condé and several thousand Huguenot noble horsemen retaliated by thundering into Orléans. Huguenot armed forces captured sixteen other major towns, including France's second and third largest cities, Rouen and Lyon.[30] Huguenot militants carried out iconoclastic riots in Rouen and Orléans, which fueled a vigorous Catholic response. Anne de Montmorency and Antoine de Bourbon had remained Catholic. Thus, they allied with the Guise against their own relatives in support of the old-time religion.[31] Armies led by the two princes, François de Guise, and marshal Saint-André quickly retook many of the lost towns, massacred local Protestants, and successfully laid siege to Rouen and Orléans.

These successes carried a high price. Wounded during the siege, Antoine de Bourbon died at Rouen, passing the leadership of the Bourbon family to two Protestants, Condé and Bourbon's widow, Jeanne d'Albret. Although Guise captured Condé at the battle of Dreux, which was fought just after the capture of Rouen, the Protestants captured Anne de Montmorency and killed marshal Saint-André. Guise himself fell to a Huguenot assassin, Jean Poltrot de Meré, at Orléans. Before being drawn and quartered on the place de Grève in Paris, Poltrot de Meré, under torture, implicated Admiral Coligny in Guise's murder. This "confession" created a permanent enmity between the Guise family and the Admiral.

In early March, Catherine de Médicis got Condé to agree to terms; she promulgated the Edict of Amboise, ending the war. The Edict gave Protestants the right to worship privately in the homes of nobles; in the suburbs of one town in every bailiwick, except that of Paris; and in temples that had already existed on 7 March 1562. Catherine tried to divide the Protestants, giving them the rights to hold rural services in private (essentially noble) households, but denying them the right to proselytize in most towns. Mindful of the lessons of the spring of 1562, Catherine sought, above all, to prevent a repetition of the Protestant success at taking over towns, and the extreme violence to which it led, as at Rouen, Tours, and Lyon. Protestant leaders, such as Coligny and even Jean Calvin, rebuked the prince of Condé for signing the agreement.

So began the seemingly interminable cycle of war, truce, and more war between Catholics and Protestants. The Edict of Amboise led to four years of official peace, followed by two brief wars, lasting from September 1567 to March 1568, and from August 1568 until August 1570. Events during the apparently peaceful interval between 1562 and 1567, however, had a greater long-term influence than the wars themselves. Four important changes took place between 1562 and 1567. First, the dominant political figures of the 1550s all died by violence: Bourbon (1562) and Montmorency (1567) in battle; Saint-André (1562), Guise (1562) and Condé (1567) by murder.[32] Their successors, above all Admiral Coligny and Henry de Guise, naturally held strong personal grudges: Guise blamed Coligny for the murder of his father; Coligny suspected Catherine de Médicis of poisoning his brother, d'Andelot, who died in 1567.[33]

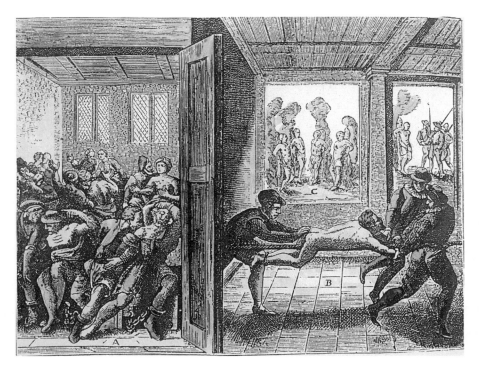

Catholic propaganda against the Protestants, from the Theater of the Heretics' Cruelties, printed at Antwerp in 1587. We see the Protestants disemboweling people, slaughtering babies, and impaling one poor soul. Protestant propaganda showed Catholics doing the same to them.

SOURCE: © Ronald Sheridan/Ancient Art & Architecture Collection.

Second, the two sides hardened attitudes and stepped up proselytizing efforts. In some towns, such as Lyon, the moderates gradually withdrew from the municipal government, leaving their places to more militant leaders. The violent events of the spring of 1563 were not soon forgotten. At Bar-sur-Seine, a crowd of Catholics cut out the heart of a murdered Huguenot and passed it among themselves, each taking a bite. Urban militants of each party threw the bodies of victims to the dogs or sold pieces of their flesh in the markets. Women victims suffered public humiliation, gang rape, and ritualized murder.

At Troyes, even after the peace, public authorities flogged a school teacher who dared to instruct his students in the "Genevan pestilence." The edicts of Saint-Germain and Amboise had reawakened Catholics all over France. They responded by ritualized violence and by creating new organizations, often confraternities, for the preservation of the faith. Official tolerance bred public intolerance, hatred, and a desire on the part of both sides to learn from their mistakes of 1562, in order to win the coming struggle. When war broke out again in September 1567, opposing forces

J.-L. David, The Oath of Horatii (1785). David's painting well illustrates the rising cult of the nation, here made manifest in the famous Roman story of the sons of Horatio. The remarkable physical thrust of the bodies of Horatio's sons particularly struck the critics of the Salon of 1785; they made David's painting a sensation.

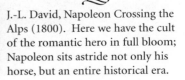

J.-L. David, Napoleon Crossing the Alps (1800). Here we have the cult of the romantic hero in full bloom; Napoleon sits astride not only his horse, but an entire historical era.

Adam and Eve. Bible of Charles the Bald, produced at St-Martin of Tours, c. 846.

The courtly couple (Tristan and Iseult), Breton marriage chest, 12th century. Here we see the new courtly behavior that nobles were expected to learn.

Sainte-Chapelle, Paris, c. 1240. The stained
glass tells many stories from the Bible, above
all the Old Testament and the Life of Jesus.

Rose window at Chartres, c. 1200. Gothic
cathedrals had large circular windows, often
in the shape of a budding rose, over their main
entrance. Chartres offers what is probably the
finest surviving example of a great rose
window.

Elizabeth Vigee-Le Brun, Marie Antoinette and her children, (1787). Vigee-Le Brun's prominence as a painter is amply demonstrated by this extremely important commission, a remarkable coup for a female artist in the 18th century.

Francois Boucher, Mme de Pompadour. Boucher painted several portraits of this important royal mistress, who was arguably the most important patron of the arts in her day. As in most of these paintings, she holds a book, this time reading in her garden.

Louis XIV, aged 15, dressed to play the role of the
Sun in The Ballet of the Night, 1653. Here we have
the image of the Sun King in its earliest form, the
rays of the adolescent king, whose age, and
implicitly, precocious ability bode so well for the
future. The cult of personality around the king led
to major problems in the late 18th century, at the
end of Louis XV's life and in the reign of the
ineffectual Louis XVI.

The Glory
of Versailles

ry day is one long round of dances,
ts, comedies, music of all kinds,
omenades, hunts and other
tainments" wrote Jean-
ste Colbert about Ver-
s. Colbert, the king's finance
ster, was not proclaiming its
ures, but rather was protesting the
expenditures for the palace and
festyle of its inhabitants, saying
racted from the king's glory.
he monarch, a master of
e rebutions, knew other
Versailles, a glittering
l with a palace large
gh to house
ands, and
with glass, tapes-
marble, and lace beyond
ure, would enhance both
nd France's prestige in
pe. Soon, heads of state were
ing from all over to marvel
most dazzling court in the most beau-
place on the Continent.
ance's peasants shouldered the burden of
g for such splendor, and Louis destroyed
nancial records to avoid a furor over his
vagance. But it was noted that the estate's
fountains used more water than the city
rs and that upon command, garden-
ould replace flower beds so that Louis
d not see the same view twice.

'Love conquers al
medieval-style bu
against ladies. Ver
fetes amazed the

Louis XIV dances
the role of the
sun god Apollo in
a ballet. Fond of
performing, he
was instrumental
in popularizing
classical dance.

The king p
of hunting
the palace

Near the e
bound k
by the Ap
C

Jean Jouvenet, The Triumph of Justice, late 17th century. This painting adorned the main chamber
of the Parlement of Brittany; its theme, the importance of justice in the well-ordered state, played an
important role in early-modern French political discouse. Stylistically, the figures at the bottom fore-
shadow developments of the eighteenth century.

Jean Fouquet, Virgin and Child, also known as The Lady of Beauty, c.1450. This painting is believed to be a portrait of the king's mistress, Agnes Sorel.

Robert Campin (Master of Flemalle), Merode Triptych, c. 1426. The Annunciation. Campin offers one of the earliest French examples of the use of perspective, which spread from Italy. Campin, like van Eyck and van der Weyden, came from the north, from the lands belonging to the duke of Burgundy, even though in the legal kingdom of France.

Rosso Fiorentino, Fontainebleau, "The Unity of the State," c. 1573. This painting provides visual evidence of a theme dear to the heart of the royal government from the sixteenth to the eighteenth centuries.

The courtly couple (Tristan and Iseult), Breton marriage chest, 12th century. Here we see the new courtly behavior that nobles were expected to learn.

Nicolas Poussin, The Assumption, 1631. Poussin had an important influence in his own day, but his reputation later waned. In the twentieth century, he became again the most admired French painter of his time.

carried out new massacres, such the *Michelade* of Nîmes, in which Protestants slaughtered eighty Catholics, mainly clerics, in the bishop's own courtyard.

Third, international events clouded the situation. In 1566, (Protestant) iconoclastic riots spread throughout the Low Countries, prompting Philip II of Spain to send an army to quell the insurrection. Philip's commander, the duke of Alba, adopted policies like those favored by the hardline Guise. He decapitated the leaders of the Netherlandish opposition, the counts of Egmont and Horn, and vigorously repressed Protestantism. Alba achieved momentary success, but in the spring of 1572, the "Sea Beggars," the irregular navy of the Dutch rebels, seized the port of Brill and started a new uprising. Religious tensions on the border exacerbated the French situation, because the different factions at the French Court suggested different policies to adopt toward the Low Countries.

Fourth, the attitude of the young king, Charles IX, shifted dramatically in the aftermath of Condé's 1567 attempt to kidnap Charles during his stay at the town of Meaux. Henceforth Charles placed much more credence in theories of Protestant conspiracy. François de la Noue, an important Protestant military commander, chastised Condé for his shortsighted coup, and warned that, because of it, "they [the Huguenots] aroused the indignation and hatred of the King against themselves, because they made him rapidly and fearfully retire into Paris; so that ever since he has always kept ulterior motives toward them."[34]

The Saint Bartholomew's Day Massacre

Everyone agrees in praising the prudence and magnanimity of the king, who, after by his kindness and indulgence having so to speak fattened up the heretics like cattle, suddenly had their throats cut by his soldiers.[35]

> Joachim Opser de Wyl, Swiss student at the Jesuit collège of
> Clermont in Paris, in a letter of 26 August 1572

The peace of Saint-Germain (1570) ended the Third Religious War. It limited Protestant worship to fewer towns, but also guaranteed them four armed places of surety: La Rochelle, La Charité, Cognac, and Montauban. Rising passions on both sides and events in the Low Countries constantly endangered the peace. Coligny tried to convince Charles IX that an alliance with the Dutch rebels and with Elizabeth of England against Philip II of Spain would enable France to regain Flanders. The Guise wanted to ally with Philip and wipe out Protestantism. In the summer of 1572, Coligny tried and failed to convince the royal council to intervene in the Low Countries.

Considerations of high politics aside, popular passions ran high on religious issues. Parisians particularly detested Coligny, whom the Parlement condemned to death *in absentia* in 1569; Parisians hung his dummy corpse in the place de Grève for almost a year. Parisians regularly assaulted local Protestants, killing several of them in the Gastines riot (January 1569). The Parlement hanged the Gastines brothers, owners of the house sacked by the mob, on the grounds that they had allowed Protestant services in their house, and further ordered that the civil authorities raze the house and erect a stone cross on its site. This cross became a symbol of Catholic faith to the people of Paris. When the king ordered it moved to the cemetery of the Holy Innocents, in 1571, local officials refused, fearing a riot. The forced removal of the cross in December bore out their prediction.

In this climate of deep-seated hatred, Jeanne d'Albret and Catherine de Médicis sought to bring together the leading families of the two parties. They set up two marriages: Henry, prince of Condé, was to marry his first cousin, Marie de Clèves, whose sister, Catherine, was married to Henry, duke of Guise.[36] Jeanne d'Albret's son, Henry of Navarre, was to marry the king's sister, Marguerite of Valois. Condé and Marie de Clèves married on 10 August, Henry and Marguerite eight days later. The hard-line Catholics, above all the Guise family, looked askance at these marriages, because both young princes were Protestants. Henry de Guise also had a personal grudge: he and Marguerite had been in love and had entertained, as recently as 1570, hopes of a marriage. Charles IX and Catherine had strongly rebuked Marguerite for writing love notes to Guise, who had had to marry (1570) Catherine de Clèves, daughter of the duke of Nevers, to get back in their good graces.

All of the leading nobles of the kingdom had come to Paris to witness the weddings. Four days after the marriage of Henry and Marguerite, an assassin wounded Coligny as the Admiral walked home from a meeting with the King.[37] The next day, Charles IX and his council—led by Catherine, the Guises, and the duke of Nevers—sent Guise to finish off the Admiral. In this action, we see the bitter legacy of Condé's attempted seizure of Charles IX at Meaux in 1567. The king later claimed he feared a *coup d'état* by the Protestants, although we have no evidence to suggest one was planned.[38]

According to tradition, the bells of the little church of Saint-Germain l'Auxerrois, just across the present rue du Louvre from the palace, on a square today bearing the macabre name of the Place de Coligny, rang the tocsin, sounding the start of the massacre. Catholic nobles and royal troops sought out the leading Protestant nobles and murdered them. The people of Paris, roused by the noise, or perhaps organized to contribute to the murders—historians disagree about which—lent a hand. Organized armed groups ran through the streets, murdering Protestants, like the luckless Mme. de Gestines. Protestant sources claim she was murdered in front of her two little boys, who screamed until "blood came out of their noses and mouths." Her little niece, such sources say, suffered worse. The mob dipped her in the blood of her murdered parents, warning that she would suffer a similar fate if she did not convert.

Catholics in many quarters rejoiced as the Pope issued a special medallion to commemorate the assassination of Coligny. Joachim Opser de Wyl, a Catholic Swiss student in Paris, like many others, cited the blooming of the "dead" hawthorne tree in the cemetery of the Holy Innocents just after the massacre as proof of God's approval.

The Parisian massacre emboldened those in the provinces who longed to do the same. In a dozen cities—Bordeaux, Toulouse, Angers, Saumur, Orléans, Rouen, and Lyon among them—Catholics turned on the Protestants. At Orléans (26–27 August), crowds marched singing through the streets of the city, accompanied by lutes and guitars, as they massacred their Protestant neighbors. The Catholic town government of Lyon rounded up all Protestants in the city, on the pretext of communicating special royal letters to them: instead, they massacred seven hundred of them (28 August–

The Massacre of Saint Bartholomew's Day, 1572. This eyewitness drawing offers a somewhat stylized view of the massacre, but does show the extent to which large numbers of ordinary Parisian citizens participated in the murders.

SOURCE: The Granger Collection, New York.

2 September). Rouen authorities, hearing of the Paris massacre, placed hundreds of Huguenots in protective custody, but radical Catholics seized the prisons and massacred three hundred to four hundred Protestants: "The rich [Protestants] escaped by a bridge of silver, and the poor were put to death."[39] At Toulouse, a crowd stormed (3 October) the prisons in which the Parlement and town council had placed the local Protestants in protective custody. All told, some five thousand Protestants lost their lives in the massacres. Most of them came from the upper classes, from the nobility above all, but also from the judges and richer merchants of the towns.

Many Protestant merchants and artisans from Lyon resettled in nearby Geneva, giving an enormous boost to Genevan printing, silk making, and banking.[40] The Rouen Protestant community, who numbered sixteen thousand in the mid-1560s, soon dropped to two thousand. North of the Loire, France reverted to a single faith, with isolated, frightened Protestant communities only in a few large towns. South of the Loire, solidly Huguenot regions blamed Charles IX for the massacres; they rejected the legitimacy of royal authority and took up arms.

The war–truce pattern of the Wars of Religion resumed after the Saint Bartholomew's Day Massacre. Events moved rapidly between Charles IX's premature death (May 1574) and the meeting of the Estates General at Blois (December 1576). At the time of Charles's death, his brother, Henry III, was in Poland, where he had been elected king.[41] Henry snuck out of Poland in the dead of night (18 June) and reached Lyon in September 1574. Henry III initially maintained his alliance with the

THE MASS OR DEATH

The night of 23–24 August 1572 set slowly in motion one of the decisive events of French history, one vehemently disputed by historians even today. The initial failed assassination of Coligny (22 August) led to a meeting of the royal council on Saturday, 23 August, at which the assembled members agreed to kill Coligny and the many Huguenot gentlemen then lodging in or near the Louvre. The council settled on the Swiss and the personal guards of Henry, duke of Anjou (the king's brother), then a close Guise ally, to do the deed.

Guise and his personal escort went to the chambers of the wounded Coligny, recruiting the very guards protecting him. The pastor Merlin, who was present, gave this account:

> [Merlin] "My Lord, it is God who is calling you to himself. They have broken into the house, and there is no way left to resist.
>
> [Coligny] "For a long time, I have prepared myself to die . . . save yourselves, if it is possible, for you cannot protect my life. I recommend my soul to the mercy of God."

Coligny's retainers left through a window in the roof; Guise's men finished off the Admiral. One of them cut off Coligny's head, to bring to Catherine and Charles. They had it embalmed and shipped to Rome, for display to the Pope and the cardinal of Lorraine. A Parisian crowd claimed Coligny's body, which they ritualistically dismembered, cutting off the hands and genitals, dragged through the streets, burned, dumped in the Seine and then fished out, and finally turned over to the Parlement, which ordered him hanged, upside-down, at the royal gibbet at Montfaucon, there "to be meat and carrion for maggots and crows." After the royal family had visited this macabre site, a group of Huguenots secretly cut the body down and buried it.[42]

Generations of historians have argued, and still argue, over the "blame" for the massacre, or even for the initial attempt against Coligny. Little evidence suggests that the king *directly* sanctioned the wider massacre. The duke of Nevers wrote Charles in September 1572 that God "made you his minister for exterminat-

Guises: he even married their cousin Louise of Vaudemont (Lorraine) two days after his coronation (February 1575).[44]

The initial Guise success quickly faded and the political position of the hardline Catholics weakened steadily. In December 1574, their leader, the cardinal of Lorraine, died; in September 1575, the king's brother and heir, the duke of Alençon, fled the Court. He allied with Montmorency-Damville, rebel governor of Languedoc and Condé, once again the military leader of the Protestants. In February 1576, Henry of Navarre also fled the Court, and renounced his conversion.[45] Three months later the overwhelming military power of the combined princes forced Henry III to issue the Edict of Beaulieu, usually known as the Peace of Monsieur (that is, of Alençon). The Edict threw the Catholics a few bones—renewing the Paris ban, forcing Protestant towns to allow Catholic services, and officially designating Calvinism by a derogatory name, the "So-called Reformed Religion"—but gave the Huguenots unprecedented concessions. These concessions included freedom of worship everywhere but Paris; eight garrisoned towns, paid for the king; and a new network of courts, of mixed Protestant and Catholic judges, to hear interfaith disputes. Henry III, responding to a demand made by Alençon when he left the Court, agreed to call an Estates General within six months.[46]

ing them, not with your powerful forces, but by low, unarmed people of the cities, using only their little knives, to make known that He alone was the cause of this deed and not the force of men of this world."[43] Charles would scarcely have needed such a reminder if he had ordered the massacre. Guise's Parisian clientage networks, which had an important role in the militia, supervised much of the killing, yet Guise himself saved the lives of several Protestants, and even harbored three Protestant children.

Charles IX did summon Jean Le Charron, merchant's provost (*de facto* mayor and a Guise client), at midnight on the twenty-third and ordered him to close the city's gates and arm the militia to defend the king against a pending Huguenot attack. The king gave Le Charron other, unspecified "instructions." Were they orders to carry out a general massacre? No one can say, but Parisians hardly needed a direct order to kill, given their intense hostility toward the Huguenots. Ordering the closure of all means of escape (or of

succor from outside), arming a militia known to be clients of the duke of Guise, and telling Parisians that the royal family were in danger from Protestants: these three steps, in the Paris of August 1572, amounted to a license to kill, direct order or no. Charles IX surely must have suspected as much and Catherine, wily politician that she was, can have had no doubts about what was going to happen.

Soldiers had arrested Navarre and Condé and massacred their friends. One report claims Charles spared the princes because someone remarked to him that these two young men "had scarcely any religion other than women and amusements." Another suggests that Charles had harsh words with Condé—offering him the choice of "the Mass or death"—and drew his dagger when Condé replied he would take the latter. The two princes ended up in the Bastille; they "converted" to Catholicism. Condé soon escaped to Germany and renounced his conversion, and Henry of Navarre remained a prisoner at Court until February 1576.

Catholic militants reacted violently to the agreement. Led by the marquis d'Humières, lieutenant general of Picardy, and the duke of Guise they formed the Holy League, a society devoted to the extirpation of Protestantism in France. Henry III tried to emasculate the League by issuing an edict naming himself as its leader, but this charade fooled no one. In this tense atmosphere, the Estates General opened at Blois, in December 1576. The deputies, many of them partisans of the Guise family, initially demanded that the king repudiate the Peace of Beaulieu and wipe out the Protestants, but their debates gradually strengthened the hands of the moderates among the nobility and the Third Estate. (The Estates General are discussed in detail in a later section.)

The End of the Valois, 1577–1589

I would prefer to die in this flower of my age, my reign, and my life . . . rather than to grow old amidst the calamities of my subjects, without being able to remedy them, so that my reign would forever stay in the memory of posterity as an unhappy one.

Henry III, addressing the Estates General of Blois, 6 December 1576

MEMORY'S VICTIM: HENRY III

Henry III's bad reputation goes beyond the obvious failures of his government. In recent years, in part because of the evolution of social attitudes toward sexual preference, Henry has gotten better press. Henry III, Henry of Valois as he is known in Poland, had a decisive impact on the political and institutional development of two of the greatest European states of his day: France and the Polish–Lithuanian Commonwealth. In the former, developments in Henry's reign paved the way for an alliance between the rising legal group and the government by means of governmental institutions (see below). In the latter, the Henrician Articles (1574) became the foundation of a constitutional government that vested enormous power in a representative body, the Sejm, dominated by the landed nobility.

Between 1576 and 1583, Henry consulted with a broader array of representative institutions than any French king since the Middle Ages: the Estates General of 1576; frequent meetings of provincial estates; and the Assembly of Notables of 1583.[47] He had the treasurers of France create a monumental set of reports on finances and administration for this last meeting; these reports collectively provide the most comprehensive look at the state of the kingdom gathered before the time of Louis XIV. The king issued wide-reaching reform ordinances at Blois (1579) in response to the recommendations of the Estates General, and in the mid 1580s, in response to the Assembly of Notables. Yet he ultimately accomplished nothing, in part because of the tumultuous events of 1584. The desperate need for money made him quickly forget his promises to abolish useless offices (made in 1576 and 1583); in 1585, he created more venal offices than any of his predecessors had ever done.

Henry III also faced opposition on personal grounds. His contemporaries perceived Henry as a weak, vacillating individual, one much given to physical pleasures and to the whims of his favorites. His "handsome" young male favorites, or *mignons*, competed with the older high-ranking nobles for leading positions; when Henry gave the *mignons* important responsibilities and raised them to ducal rank, he alienated the grandees.

Henry's image further suffered from his profligate spending and "decadent" lifestyle. He and his *mignons* sometimes dressed in women's clothes when in the king's private quarters. The great feasts of spring 1577 left a bitter taste in many mouths; some reported that Henry spent 60,000 *livres* on the green silk for the feast of 15 May 1577, at which he appeared dressed as a woman, bejewelled, heavily made up, his hair elaborately done. Opponents of the king ac-

Henry III did not get his wish, as posterity has judged his reign as a time of unremitting misery, and the king himself as a failure. Yet France had few kings more intelligent, more cultivated, and better intentioned than Henry III. Institutional historians point to his reign as a decisive moment in the evolution of the state, and cultural historians contrast the brilliance of his Court with the dowdiness of that of his successor. His good qualities, however, cannot hide his shortcomings: the inability to end the religious wars; the assassination of the Guise brothers; the failure of the many reforms he attempted; the ill-timed excesses of his personal life.

Henry had to deal quickly with the Sixth (January–September 1577) and Seventh (January 1579–November 1580) Wars of Religion. They repeated the usual pattern of military stalemate, often due to financial exhaustion, followed by religious compromise. The Peace of Bergerac (1577) essentially repeated all the clauses of the Peace of Monsieur, except that it limited urban Protestantism to one town in each bailiwick.

(CONTINUED)

cused Henry and the *mignons* of seducing young pages and of raping nuns.

Henry's contemporaries believed him to be bisexual. Although Ronsard wrote private verses attacking the king's homosexual behavior, noble elites generally tolerated discreet bisexuality. The king's failure to produce an heir, however, raised for his contemporaries significant doubts about his masculinity, doubts confirmed by the stories emanating from his Court.[48] Quite aside from the fact that male lovers could compete for important royal posts (such as military commands), Henry's contemporaries associated effeminacy with weakness.[49] Long after Henry III's death, government spokesmen took great pains to emphasize the masculinity of the king. Guillaume du Vair, Keeper of the Seals, had this to say about the twenty-year-old Louis XIII in 1621:

> [the fine qualities of the king] are a necessary consequence when one's childhood is spent being nourished in the fear of God, when youth is passed in male and generous exercises, and when his affections are ruled by the laws of modest decency and of chastity. Moreover the way of life that has always pleased him, in the exercises of the hunt and other military actions, demonstrates nothing of softness and effeminacy, which must never enter into this male and martial soul.[50]

Du Vair wished his listeners to associate Louis XIII with his father, the essence of traditional masculinity and martialness, rather than the "effeminate" Henry III. The speech is all the more revealing in that Louis XIII was a bisexual, who, at the time of the speech, was deeply and publicly in love with his male favorite, the duke of Luynes, whom he had made Constable.[51]

The image of the weak, effeminate king—ever changing sides, ever revoking his previous ordinances (and Henry III did both)—did much to undermine the monarchy in the 1580s, and have permanently marked the historical memory of his reign. Henry III and Henry IV have, for generations of historians and for the French folk memory, stood as the tokens of memory for the "bad" monarch, given to profligate waste and "decadent" sexuality, and the "good" monarch, the hardened soldier, beloved of his subjects for restoring order and for giving them a "real man" for a king. Henry III certainly ruled at a time inauspicious for a man of his mixture of weaknesses and strengths, yet centuries of bias related to his sexual preferences have done their fair share to tarnish his memory.

Everyone accepted the necessity for reform of Church and state alike, but Catholics and Protestants drew different conclusions from the need to reform, just as the Second and Third Estates differed on the right direction for the state. The Protestants believed that doctrine itself had been corrupted and that the "true church" had to be restored to its original purity. The Catholics focused on reform of the institutional Church and on the spiritual renewal of each individual within the framework of the traditional beliefs, which they viewed not as corrupt in themselves but rather as corrupted by the weakness of human nature. The Catholic response to the Protestants thus took multiple forms, not simply violent confrontation, but also a genuine spiritual reform of the Church and of individual Catholics.

In 1583, in the midst of a famine, a massive Catholic penitential movement began in Lorraine and Champagne, heartland of the Guise. Thousands of peasants marched in orderly religious processions, wearing white linen sheets and intoning holy chants. These processions sought the intercession of the Virgin Mary, a special focus of Catholic, anti-Protestant piety. In the summer and early fall of 1583, more than 72,000 pilgrims participated in such marches at Reims, where Louis, cardinal of Guise, served as archbishop. The white penitents movement spread to the Ile-de-France and north toward the Soissonais and Picardy. Thousands of people descended on holy sites in Soissons, in Laon, in Amiens, and in the surrounding countryside. In most cases, the penitents sought out churches associated with Mary, to offer special prayers in churches like Notre Dame of Reims.[52]

The penitents showed the profound sense of religious dislocation among many northern French peasants, yet also demonstrated the critical role of the ecclesiastical hierarchy in organizing the movements. A mere two months before the start of the procession movement, the archbishop of Reims had convoked an archdiocesan synod to accept the decrees of the Council of Trent, which only the bishop of Boulogne failed to attend. When the penitent movement began, marches took place in every bishopric within the jurisdiction of Reims, except in Boulogne—strong evidence that the penitents acted where they could expect to find a favorable official response.

Elites, too, took action in 1583 and 1584. During this period, the Guise and their allies revived the Holy League. The League created a daunting new challenge to the king, given that Guise cousins held the governorships of Brittany (Mercoeur), Burgundy (Mayenne), Normandy (Joyeuse), and Champagne (Guise), and that Henry of Navarre and his allies controlled most of the south.[53] The League took on truly sinister dimensions in 1584 because the heir to the throne of France, Hercule-François, duke of Anjou, brother of the childless Henry III, died on 10 June. A month later, the Spanish assassinated William of Orange, leader of the Dutch revolt. Anjou's death made Henry of Navarre, a Protestant, heir presumptive, while Orange's murder created visions of a massive Catholic offensive led by Philip II. On 31 December 1584, the Guises signed an alliance with Philip. Three months later they took up arms against Henry III, seeking, above all, to bar Navarre from the succession. Philip made plans to stamp out heresy in the Low Countries and prepared to send the Invincible Armada against England (1588).

Constitutional crisis loomed in 1585, when Pope Sixtus V declared Henry of Navarre and Condé to be disqualified from inheritance of the throne of France, because they had become Protestants. Who, then, would be the heir? Navarre and Condé had an uncle, Charles, cardinal of Bourbon. Although a sufficiently ardent Catholic to sign the treaty of Joinville with the Guises and Philip II, Charles had two major disadvantages: he was sixty-three years old and, as a cardinal, sworn to celibacy. The scion of the male line of the Bourbon-Montpensier, François de Bourbon-Montpensier, supported Henry of Navarre.[54] The Guise position suffered constantly from this fundamental weakness: they had no obvious candidate to succeed Henry III.

The War of the Three Henrys (1585–1589) created uneasy alliances first between Henry III and Henry of Navarre and then between Henry de Guise and Henry III. When the king shifted to a Guise alliance, Henry of Navarre allied with Montmorency-Damville and the *Politiques*. After Henry of Navarre routed the royal army at Coutras (1587), killing its commander, the duke of Joyeuse, Henry III sought a new rapprochement with Navarre, outraging the Guises. Unable to prevent Henry de Guise from entering Paris, the king had to flee his capital on the Day of the Barricades (12 May 1588). Guise soon forced the king to sign the Edict of Union, outlawing Protestantism and making all Protestants guilty of treason. Henry III also called an Estates General for Blois, a meeting completely under the control of the League. Fed up with the Guise ascendancy, the king had the duke murdered in the royal apartments at Blois (23 December 1588). Some said the king himself wielded one of the daggers. The next day, royal assassins killed Louis, cardinal of Guise.

Paris exploded with rage and grief when word reached the city. Massive crowds demolished symbols representing the royal family. The Catholic hierarchy responded vigorously. The theology faculty of the University of Paris ruled that the French people no longer owed obedience to their tyrant king; the Pope excommunicated Henry III. The League seized control of many of the major cities of the kingdom, including Rouen, Lyon, Toulouse, Nantes, and Dijon. In many parts of France, Henry III was now king in name only. He allied again with Navarre, and their joint force laid siege to the capital. On 1 August 1589, at the army headquarters in Saint-Cloud, the monk Jacques Clément stabbed Henry III; the king died the next day. A Protestant, Henry of Navarre, was now Henry IV, King of France. Or was he? That is a question for Chapter 7. Let us turn now to the rapid changes taking place in other aspects of French life in the second half of the sixteenth century, because, they too, drove France in the direction of a new system of order.

French Society: Readjustment or Collapse?

Religion and Economic Life

> There were a great, not to say infinite, number of beautiful cities, large towns and villages, and especially, countless chateaux and beautiful houses which stood resplendent in the midst of countryside better tilled than any other.[55]

> Guillaume du Vair, describing France on the eve of the Wars of Religion

The dramatic changes of the century before 1560 had disrupted many aspects of French life, in both positive and negative ways. The Wars of Religion exacerbated many of the negative effects, and undermined many of the accomplishments. Du Vair's description of the happy state of the French economy *circa* 1560 can certainly be contrasted to the unending tales of woe spread by those writing a generation later. The Wars of Religion disrupted almost all sectors of the French economy, from the western coastal trade, often interrupted by Protestant pirates from La Rochelle, to the manufacturing and banking of Lyon, which had been largely in Protestant hands before 1562. When Lyon's Protestants fled persecution or expulsion in the 1560s and early 1570s, they went to Geneva, which became the new center of banking in that region. The fairs of Lyon never recovered from the combined effects of the royal bankruptcy of 1557 and the religious fighting of the 1560s.

The slow, healthy price rise that began in 1480 gave way to rampant inflation after 1560. Three factors contributed to the skyrocketing prices:

1. The massive influx of silver from the New World.

2. The dislocation created by war.

    3. Henry III's switch of the money of account from the fictional *livre tournois* to the *écu*, a real coin, which coincided with a sharp devaluation of French currency.

The devaluation increased prices but helped relieve debt for French borrowers, of whom, of course, the most prominent was the king. Henry here merely followed the unwise example of his immediate predecessors: the *livre tournois's* silver content declined by about 50 percent between 1550 and 1577.

    Economic dislocation followed war, so that certain regions suffered enormous losses. In much of Burgundy, village populations declined by 30 to 50 percent between 1575 and 1595. Some of these people merely moved, but the cumulative effect devastated the Burgundian economy. Brittany, little touched by the fighting of the 1570s and 1580s, prospered throughout those decades. When full-scale war arrived in 1589, the Breton economy collapsed, with sea-going trade at Nantes and other Breton ports declining by 40 to 60 percent.

    Soldiers ravaged villages in Languedoc, in Poitou, in Burgundy, and in Dauphiné, yet other villages in Normandy or some of the Loire regions suffered little, if at all. Rouen and its hinterlands suffered through two sieges, yet the fighting spared Caen. The disruption of commerce strangled some regions, but only on a temporary basis. The climate contributed its share to the economic dislocation. A series of extremely harsh winters, part of the "Little Ice Age," led to crop failures throughout the 1580s and 1590s. Large vineyards permanently disappeared from many parts of northern France, such as the Paris region. Tens of thousands starved to death in the famine of 1597, which affected all of northwest Europe.

    Noble deputies to representative assemblies voiced not only their own complaints, but those of their peasant tenants. They complained of losses due to troop depredations, debased currency, and higher taxes. They claimed peasants stopped paying their rents because direct taxes had risen so high. In fact, adjusted for inflation, direct taxes remained fairly stable, *except* in those regions that had to pay for the upkeep of troops.[56] At the Estates Generals of 1560–1561, 1576, 1588, and 1614, and at annual meetings of provincial Estates, nobles complained that "this charge comes in direct diminution of their farm rents"; they (unsuccessfully) demanded that their tenants be exempt from the *taille*.[57]

New Identities: Nobility, Social Mobility, and National Sentiments

None can deny that the greatest and principal force of this kingdom, from which you must have the greatest hope, is your nobility, which alone first put the crown on the head of the kings your ancestors . . . [and that] if you are united with your nobility, you are invincible.[58]

           Noble deputies of the Estates General of 1576, addressing Henry III

Many historians, relying on the ample documentation provided by the economic and social complaints of the nobility, have suggested the nobility went through a crisis in the late sixteenth century. The available evidence does not support that conclusion.

Economically, some nobles lost out, as they had to sell off lands because of the demands of fighting, either outfitting themselves or paying ransoms if captured. Others, however, profited from the steady increase in rents. Those receiving rents in kind, especially in grain, even kept pace with the rampant inflation that ruined wage earners.

Social ascent into the nobility proved unusually easy in the second half of the sixteenth century. Many historians have argued that most new nobles were rural landowners who simply insinuated themselves into the nobility. These historians claim that such men bought noble estates, called themselves "*sieur*" (lord), demanded that the local priest inscribe their title as *écuyer* (squire) on the village birth and marriage register, and then paid off the locals to agree to their tax exemption (due to noble status). In the anarchic climate of the Wars of Religion, so the argument goes, such assimilated nobility was easier to achieve than in more peaceful times. The noble deputies to the Estates Generals from 1560 to 1614 complained constantly about such social climbers. Yet the assimilationist model of ennoblement fundamentally makes very little sense. It is unlikely that any parish would have allowed its richest taxpayer to obtain tax exemption, forcing the remaining villagers to come up with his contribution. The court records suggest village communities fought tooth-and-nail against those seeking exemption, for whatever reason.

Far more people obtained noble status by means of official royal letters. With the exception of the late fourteenth century, when the nobility had been decimated by the plague and by losses in the fighting of the Hundred Years' War, the second half of the sixteenth century had more official ennoblements than any period between the fourteenth century and 1789. Some of these people obtained the king's grace through military deeds, but others, such as the Breton peddler Gilles Ruellan (on whom, see Chapter 7), simply became so rich that the king had little choice but to ennoble them. Moreover, the old nobility, however much it looked down on men like Ruellan, had no problems assimilating his family into its ranks. Indeed, Ruellan's daughters married a duke, three marquis, and a baron, and his son bought a judge-ship in the snobby Parlement of Brittany, bastion of the landed nobility.

The change had actually begun at the top, in the 1520s and 1530s, with Francis I's efforts to expand the number of duke–peers in the aftermath of the extinction of several patrilineal ducal families. Henry II kept up this policy. His sons, too, tried to swell the ranks of the upper aristocracy. Henry III created a new royal order, the knights of the Holy Spirit, to set off the highest nobility. At more modest social stations, well-to-do lawyers could buy royal offices that led to eventual nobility. In Brittany, the legal elite of Nantes bought petty royal office, and then moved to the Chamber of Accounts. From the Chamber of Accounts, one-third of the sixteenth-century families passed into the Parlement of Brittany, there to mingle with the old noble families of the province. Even merchant families, especially the Spanish immigrants, moved in one generation from commerce into ennobling royal office, like master of accounts or Parlementaire. This rapid ascension became virtually impossible in seventeenth-century Brittany.[59]

What was true in Brittany applied elsewhere. Merchants sent their sons to the new municipal *collèges*, established in major towns starting in the 1560s. These sons became lawyers and, in some cases, minor court judges. Their sons bought offices in higher courts, such as the Chambers of Accounts or Parlements. Rich merchant families also bought offices in the financial bureaucracy. These royal officers provided an important, but gradual influx of new nobles.[60] Certain town governments, such as that of Angers, created the so-called nobility of the bell tower (*noblesse de cloche*): the mayor and aldermen of these towns obtained hereditary nobility from their offices. The old nobility had particular contempt for such "nobles."

Sixteenth-century society had a remarkable degree of social mobility, which strengthened rather than weakened the nobility. Ensuring the survival of family power by preventing splintering of the family's landed power base encouraged small families. This practice, however, made those same families highly vulnerable to extinction of their male line in a time of such violent warfare. The French social and political system required a given number of nobles to function. Given the extinctions of growing numbers of families, the system had to ennoble new families to take their place. Moreover, allowing the growth of a competing elite, one outside the traditional sociopolitical hierarchy constructed around nobility, would have destroyed the system.

This social mobility accentuated a remarkable *prise de conscience* by the nobility. They sought every means possible to prevent the creation of new nobles. In 1576, the Second Estate demanded that the king forbid commoners from purchasing fiefs and even insisted that he force commoners then owning fiefs to sell them to real nobles. They wanted governorships of all towns and fortresses, and places in the royal cavalry reserved to *French* nobles.[61] Nobles became more sensitive to issues of precedence and blood, emphasizing in one meeting after another the importance of ancestry in true nobility. The nearly universal acceptance of the myth of the Trojan origins of the Franks, and thus the French nobility, strongly reinforced the "racial" theory of nobility. This renewed emphasis on blood, which by no means replaced other defining characteristics of nobility, like valor or virtue, peaked at the Estates General of 1614, when the Second Estate refused to allow legally noble Parlementaires to sit with them. The social crisis of the second half of the sixteenth century created a much more exclusionist mentality among the French nobility, and indeed among French people in general.

Deputies to the Estates Generals of 1560–1561 and 1576 harped incessantly on "foreign" influence in the state. The nobility of 1576 suggested that foreigners seeking information about the king's "estate and affairs be recognized as disturbers and reasonless enemies of all nations, kingdoms, and commonwealths." They harshly denounced Italian financiers as bloodsuckers. The prince of Condé's letter to these Estates asked them to relieve the people from the "unsupportable tributes invented by the Italians," so that the "French" could be delivered from "the infinite and tyrannical servitude to which they have been reduced."

The deputies of 1576 had an almost paranoid obsession with the Spanish. Condé suggested that the Spaniards had paid off "evil" royal advisors and had subverted some of the deputies to the Estates General. One deputy from the Third Estate called them "ingrate and villainous," and blamed them for imposing so many calamities on France. He had harsh words, too, for the English, "enemies of this state, favoring the weaker party" to make sure the civil war continued. For this deputy, the Religious War was a foreign plot: "Foreigners, in all times enemies of the king and of his state, and holding nothing more odious than his state's power, did not lose this occasion, which they have, with reason, forever desired." The nobility demanded that the king remove all foreigners from any official position, because "they could not bring a natural affection for the country (*pays*) and for its good."

The noble deputy Pierre de Blanchefort and some colleagues sent a special petition to the king asking him to seek peace, suggesting that

> . . . it is to be feared that our neighbors are joyous spectators of the miseries of this poor kingdom (which defeats itself by its own hands and means) . . . some of them . . . embrace one of the parties to ruin them both, as happened in the Empire of Constantinople, and in your France . . . between the houses of Orléans and Burgundy, when the English intervened. . . . These neighbors laugh when we cry and cry when we laugh in France.[62]

Debates about inclusion and exclusion, about foreigners and French people, helped to revive discussion of the society of orders model. Everyone had his or her place; they had merely to accept it for all to do well. As chancellor de l'Hôpital told the Estates General of 1560: "if each estate contents itself with its fortune and its goods . . . [and] . . . submits itself to the obedience of its prince and his laws and ordinances, we will live in peace and repose." Such rhetoric should not hide from us the reality of enormous social mobility in those years. Many of great ministerial and noble families of the seventeenth and eighteenth centuries began their meteoric ascent precisely in the last chaotic days of the sixteenth century.

THE LIFE OF THE MIND

There is no desire more natural than the desire for understanding. We try by all means we can to get to it. When reason fails us, we employ experience to achieve it.[63]

Montaigne, *Essays*, "Of experience"

Chancellor de l'Hôpital's wish that France live in peace and repose never made it to God's ear: France lived amid fire and sword. The chaos tremendously affected French intellectual life, and the new identity issues raised by individualism and Protestantism helped transform everthing from French political theory to literature. Political ideologies, like religious ones, spread by means of the printed word, often paid for by the princes and dukes engaged in factional conflict. These paid writers included many of the great poets of the age, such as Pierre de Ronsard, whose contributions to the French language made the second half of the sixteenth century one of the most important periods in its development.

The clarion call of the new literature came in 1549, when a then-obscure poet, Joachim du Bellay, issued *The defense and illustration of the French language*. Du Bellay denounced earlier French poetry as insipid. Doubtless influenced by the appearance of the first French translation of Horace's *Art of Poetry* in 1542, du Bellay demanded that French poets look to worthy Ancient models, such as Homer, Pindar, and Horace. Yet du Bellay insisted above all on writing poetry in *French*, not in the Latin so beloved of the early sixteenth-century erudites. He launched a critical new movement in French letters, the so-called Pléiade. Du Bellay himself was one of its great poets, but he took second place to Ronsard, who issued his first poetry in 1550.

Ronsard provided a wide range of themes, from celebrations of the great heroes of France—among them Roland, Charlemagne, and Bayard—to odes of love, both requited and unrequited ("unhappy is he who falls in love"), to pastorals in praise of nature. Du Bellay wrote on these themes—love, nature—in terms similar to those of his friend. Both of them relied heavily on aristocratic vocabulary and sensibility; both lapsed, on occasion, into obscurantist pedantry, as one might expect of poets striving to imitate Horace or Ovid. Yet Ronsard hardly abandoned the traditions of Villon and Rabelais: he, too, spoke of his beloved in erotic terms ("kiss me, with a mouth filled with love").

Du Bellay and Ronsard, like Rabelais also wrote satires. Where Rabelais satirized the Church or the Sorbonne, Ronsard attacked hypocrisy or, in unpublished work, the morality and sexuality of Henry III. Du Bellay lampooned the courtiers, "those old apes of the Court, who know how to do nothing" except imitate the prince.

> If they see someone receive the king's good look
> They go to caress him, even as they tremble with rage:
> If he receives ill, they ridicule him.[64]

The Pléiade's rivals, the school of Lyon, led by Maurice Scève (1500–1564), friend of Clément Marot, followed closely Petrarch's theories of poetics. Like many sixteenth-century intellectuals, Scève also demonstrated the influence of Platonism in his love poetry. The woman sometimes becomes a distant object of desire, yet, Scève, like Ronsard, does not forget her physical reality. One of his followers, Louise Labé, the leading French woman poet of the sixteenth century, also wrote of love, although she wrote more of the combination of the physical and the emotional. She moved away from the distinction so typical of the work of Scève, and introduced an element of female eroticism. She had great renown in her own time—intellectuals passing through Lyon invariably stopped at her salon, and many, like the great Huguenot historian Agrippa d'Aubigné, called her the "Sappho of her time."[65]

She also provided a different social voice. Unlike Ronsard or du Bellay, who came from noble families, Labé came from the urban middle class, and her work took its language from daily life. She also expressed clearly women's sexual, as well as emotional desires:

Baise m'encor, rebaise moy, et baise:	Kiss me again, kiss me once more, and kiss:
Donne m'en un de tes plus savoreux,	Give me one of thy most savory ones,
Donne m'en un de tes plus amoureus:	Give me one of thy most loving ones,
Je t'en rendray quatre plus chaus que braise.	I will give thee four, hotter than a fiery brand.[66]

Labé's sensual imagery subverted the dominant poetic style of her day, which was based on the models of the Italian poet Petrarch, who focused "on the lonely suffer-

"Sweet Liberty"

Pierre de Ronsard, born in 1524 at a chateau in the Loire Valley region, had close ties to the royal Court and to the intellectual world of Paris, where he studied Latin and Greek. In 1545, while at Court, he fell in love with Cassandra Salviati, who married another the following year. Mademoiselle Salviati inspired Ronsard to his first major book of poems, *Loves for Cassandra.* Ronsard took Pindar and Horace as his models, reviving such genres as the sonnet.

Œil, qui des miens à ton vouloir disposes,	Eye, which takes advantage of mine at thy will,
Comme un Soleil, le Dieu de ma clairté;	Like a Sun, the God of my light;
Ris, qui, forçant ma douce liberté,	Laugh, which, overcoming my sweet liberty,
Me transformas en cent metamorfoses;	Transforms me in a hundred metamorphoses;
Larme d'argent, qui mes flammes arroses,	Silver tear, which waters my flames,
Lors que tu feins de me voir mal traité;	When thou thinkst to see me mistreated;
Main, qui mon cœur captives arresté,	Hand, which holds my heart captive,
Emprisonné d'une chaisne de roses;	Emprisoned by a chain of roses;
Je suis tant vostre, et tant l'affection	I am so much yours, and affection has so
M'a peint au sang vostre perfection,	Deep in my blood imprinted your perfection,
Que ny le temps, ny la mort, tant soit forte,	That neither time, nor death, strong though they are,
N'empescheront qu'au profond de mon sein,	Can prevent that, at the core of my being,
Tousjours gravez en l'ame je ne porte	Forever graven in my soul, I carry
Une œil, un ris, une larme, une main.	An eye, a laugh, a tear, a hand.

ing of a poetic speaker consigned to love an absent, inaccessible beloved."[67] In her poetry, a woman can love spiritually, emotionally, physically, sexually: in short, she can love as a complete human being. For many of her male contemporaries, if Labé was right, if a woman was a complete human being, then one of the cornerstones of their society, the patriarchal family, had to be reformulated. Threatened in this way, as in so many others, men responded with a ferocious legal assault on women.

Mothers, Fathers, and Witches

> *I am going to tell you my advice on the utility that women may get from the excellence of such learning: it is that I have almost always seen it to be useless to young ladies of modest condition, like you, as the least happy have more often abused than used it: the others found this labor useless, finding out what they commonly say, that when the nightingale has young it no longer sings.*
>
> Agrippa d'Aubigné

D'Aubigné's letter to his daughters about learned women of the sixteenth century dramatically demonstrates the ambiguous attitude of men toward women, particularly toward their education. Early in the letter, d'Aubigné tells them that it is "too dangerous" for women to show their learning to their husbands, and recommends instead that they follow the rules of "*bienséance*" (polite behavior). Yet the same letter tells them that d'Aubigné's mother knew Greek and Latin, and praises many learned women of the times, especially Elizabeth of England, who "so well employed her ethics and politics, that she held steady the ship of her kingdom for forty years on a very troubled sea and in a tempestuous century: her name and memory will be blessed forever." Moreover, he included a Latin poem for the young girls to read, obvious evidence that they had received an advanced education.

D'Aubigné's letter details one of the important intellectual debates of the sixteenth century, what the French called the "querelle des femmes"—the woman question. Christine de Pisan (*c.* 1400) had rekindled this debate with her attack on Jehan de Meun, misogynist author of the revised version of the most influential medieval love poem, *Le Roman de la Rose.* Many sixteenth-century male authors, following a tradition dating back to Aristotle, depicted women as inferior men. In their view, men were superior to women, just as nobles were superior to peasants. Marguerite d'Angoulême attacked such views in her *Heptaméron*, a collection of stories supposedly told by a group of noble narrators amusing themselves while trapped at a remote abbey.

Some of the male characters, notably Hircan (usually felt to be Henry d'Albret, Marguerite's husband), argue that women exist essentially for the pleasure of men. Hircan believes that a man, having once made known his "love" for a woman, must consummate that love or lose his honor. In response to one of the stories, one likely based on Admiral Bonnivet's actual attempted rape of Marguerite, Hircan suggests that the male protagonist should have murdered the woman's maidservant, so that she could not cry out, and then demonstrated his strength of his "love" by forcing the princess of his affections to have sex. Where Hircan and some other male tale tellers stress invariably the unfaithfulness of women, and the dangers in letting female emotionalism escape its proper bounds, the female participants, like Oisille and Parlamente (usually identified as Marguerite herself), argue that women have honor, reason, and perfections of their own.

The "querelle des femmes" had broad repercussions for French women, because it created an intellectual climate of concern about the status of women in society. The Renaissance and, in another way, the Reformation, emphasized the individual at the expense of the group. Even though early Protestant worship in France tended to be overwhelmingly oriented toward the group, the central tenet of Protestantism—justification by faith—created a strong bond between the individual and God. Similarly, Humanism emphasized the individual at the expense of the group. This rising tide of individualism created a new threat to society: the individual woman. Many women, both Protestant and Catholic, used the newly fluid religious situation to create positions of power for themselves. Moreover, the central role of mothers in providing the first stages of moral education for their children gave women a particularly important new role in mid-century France, as most of the major male Protestant leaders got their religious convictions from their mothers, not their fathers.

In the *Heptaméron* story discussed in Chapter 5, the response of Dagoucin, that allowing individual nobles to choose their spouses would undermine the monarchy, amply reflects the attitude held by French jurists and kings alike. Henry II's 1556 edict forced never-married children to obtain parental (patriarchal) consent for marriage, and raised the age of majority for men from twenty-five to thirty and for women from seventeeen to twenty-five. The edict also outlawed clandestine marriages (those contracted without parental permission), a special personal concern of Henry II, who wanted François de Montmorency to break off a clandestine marriage and wed Henry's illegitimate daughter. (He did.) Henry II here responded to widespread demands from jurists, such as Jean de Coras, Parlementaire of Toulouse, who called clandestine marriages "polluted conjunctions" that "disturbed the public good."[68] Many great aristocratic houses died out in the male line during the sixteenth century, so their property passed to female heirs. Men did not want to allow such women to choose their own husbands, and thus the potential possessors of the family's property. Noble *cahiers* in both 1560 and 1576 expressed special concern that commoners sought clandestine marriages with noble heiresses as a means of social and economic advancement. Jean de la Guesle, the king's attorney at the Parlement of Paris, speaking on Henry III's behalf to the Estates General of 1576, took a hard line on these issues. He insisted that all noble widows with children, if they remarried to a "low person, unworthy of their dignity, or to their valets or other persons who had served their husbands," should lose all rights over their property, and that the king should forbid them to sell, or others to buy, such goods.

To judge from the evidence in northern France, clandestine marriages had formed a considerable percentage of weddings in the fifteenth and early sixteenth century. Henry III's 1579 edict added to the property exclusion mandated in 1556; it defined a clandestine marriage involving a minor (i.e., a woman under twenty-five) as *rapt* (abduction), a capital offense. It made no allowance for alleviation of the penalties in cases in which parents later ratified the marriage. The edict also banned the formerly widespread custom of a binding civil exchange of vows; henceforth, binding vows had to be taken in front of a priest. The king, and the churches, sought to end the custom of people promising marriage to each other, and then living together as a married couple prior to the church wedding. In rural areas, that custom remained deeply rooted: parish visitation records continued to denounce it even in the 1660s.

Henry III extended the rights of parents and guardians over children, even requiring widows under twenty-five to seek parental consent to remarriage. Louis XIII would take the final step in 1639, when he mandated that *all* women, widows or no, of whatever age, had to obtain the permission of a male guardian before marriage (or remarriage). The children of "clandestine" marriages lost inheritance rights over the goods of the two families, further evidence of the overwhelming familial concerns of the aristocracy about property falling into the hands of men of insufficient station. Royal ordinances restricted the rights of women to dispose of property in cases of second marriage, and cut down on the rights of women in guilds, barring many of them from hiring new apprentices.

Although some women ended up imprisoned in convents by their families, other women effectively resisted these efforts, as the constant reiteration of royal prohibitions suggests. Despite progressively greater legal restrictions on marriage choice, women increasingly chose their own husbands, especially *after* the 1639 royal edict. Economic restrictions also failed: the economic role of women *increased* in the seventeenth and eighteenth centuries. In the Parisian book trade, books published by female printers rose from two hundred sixteen in the first decade of the seventeenth century to seven hundred forty-four in the 1640s, and by the eighteenth century, 20 to 25 percent of the printers of Paris were women. Royal edicts likely demonstrate less the king's efforts to forestall change, than royal reaction to a threatening situation.

The monarchy consistently stressed the special authority of fathers at precisely the moment when it stressed the special authority of the monarch. The king would have supreme authority in his kingdom, just as the father would have supreme authority in his family. Both authorities came from, and were modeled on, the supreme authority of God the Father. Leading jurists, like chancellor de l'Hôpital or the great French political philosopher, Jean Bodin, particularly favored the metaphor of the king as the father of his people. The people owed obedience to their king as a family owed obedience to its father. Thus, the king, as the sieur de Bauffremont told the eleven-year-old Charles IX at the Estates General of 1561, "must comport himself towards his subjects as the father of the family towards his children." Again and again, Frenchmen referred to the three fathers: God the Father; the king, father of his people; the father of the family. The kingdom itself was merely the amalgamation of the families headed by French fathers. These philosophies flourished in a political climate in which women played an unusually important role. Such women showed precisely what a threat a woman could be to a male power structure. Even the deputies who praised Catherine de Médicis in 1561, and who insisted that she should have the reins of government, at the same time insisted that she and the princes of the blood swear a new oath to uphold the Salic Law, forever banning women from the Crown, or even from the possibility of transferring the right to wear it.

The plight of women in the second half of the sixteenth century demonstrates the extent to which the expansion of monarchical power came about because the monarchy had powerful social and political allies. The king offered real benefits, increased power, to certain elements in society, in return for their support for his efforts to expand royal authority. He reached out to male heads of households in this way. Lawyers trained in Roman Imperial law naturally used its strong emphasis on the rights of male heads of households to support this attack on women. Male aristocrats, too, supported such strictures because of the property and political implications of marriages by women from their houses. The succession of royal ordinances against women remind us that the state did not arise from simple pitting of one class (however defined) against another, but that it used privileged groups of all kinds to help it more thoroughly dominate all. They also remind us that such efforts did not fully succeed because the target groups offered effective resistance. Moreover, the strong central state offered women protection, too.

The most (in)famous example of the combined elements was the witch trials. Medieval Frenchmen conducted a few witch trials—Joan of Arc, after all, was legally burned as a witch—but the witch craze did not begin until 1550. The climate of religious conflict contributed greatly to the increase; in a world obsessed with doctrinal unity, aberrant behavior easily became "heresy." The most common manual used by witch hunters, the *Malleus Maleficarum* (*Hammer of Evil*, written in the late fifteenth century by two Dominican monks), simply assumed women were more likely to be guilty. The monks posed the question "why superstition is chiefly found in women?" Women could take little comfort in their answer: "what else is woman but a foe to friendship, an unescapable punishment, a necessary evil, a natural temptation, a desirable calamity, a domestic danger, a delectable detriment, an evil of nature, painted with fair colours!"

The first French-language book on witchcraft appeared in 1564, just before the great wave of witch hunts. In legal France, the persecutions, although considerable, did not take on the fervor seen in nearby Francophone or border regions, such as Lorraine and the Franche-Comté, where witch hunts burned thousands of women. In the Basque country too, straddling three kingdoms, hundreds of innocent women went to the stake. Here we can see how a strong central state could protect women, as well as seek to take away their rights. As was true in most of Continental Europe, French witch hunters primarily (80 percent or more) targeted women.

The witch hunters did not focus on younger women, but rather went after the weakest members of the most powerful female group: widows. The widow of fifty-five or sixty often had substantial economic resources at her control. Five to ten percent of all farms lay in the hands of widows, who thus had control of a significant portion of the labor market. The woman on top—that nightmare of all nightmares for the sixteenth-century man—was the outcome of the widow farmer and her hired male help.[69] Witch hunters did not burn such women, who had too much power and often had strong ties to family members elsewhere in the village. Instead, they persecuted the isolated, poor older widow. Her fate served as an example to her more powerful sisters, that they not lose sight of their "place" in society. In many cases (a majority in some jurisdictions), witch hunters targeted the village wise woman or herbal healer. This woman also acted, in many cases, as the midwife, a powerful figure in charge of one of the most important of human activities: birth. French used the same term, *sage femme*, for both occupations.

Elites divided in their opinions on witchcraft. Some, like Bodin (who wrote a treatise about it), believed in witchcraft. Others, like the judges of the Parlement of Paris, tended to be skeptical: they rarely upheld a death sentence against a witch, unless she was guilty of another capital crime. In a sop to public opinion, however, the Parlement published "official" condemnations of witches, complete with death sentences. Only in their secret registers did they reveal their leniency. Ordinary people sometimes demanded action. The 1576 *cahier* of Saint-Loup asked that the king search out and punish "atheists, Epicureans, sorcerers, and magicians," a request that speaks more to their suspicions of the educated than of fear of elderly widows. The surviving evidence indicates that peasants suspected "witches" of evil deeds, such as a spell cast on a child or an animal; only elites took seriously the stories of Devil worship and Sabbats, with their inverted religious ceremonies.

Religious schism played a critical role in the witch craze, as did elite efforts to take control of popular culture, but the overwhelming misogyny of the trials can only be understood in the context of the concerted male effort to suppress the collective individuality of women. Just as d'Aubigné gave conflicting advice to his daughters, and Ronsard placed "honor, virtue, grace, and knowledge" before "beauty" among his true love's qualities, so, too, individual men respected, and often defended individual women. Yet, whether we look at royal ordinances on marriage, at official harangues about the family and the state, at the treatises of Bodin, or at guild rules, from top to bottom in society, French men worked together to overcome the renewed threat of women on top. As we shall see, this male alliance against women formed one of the foundation stones of the Bourbon monarchy, descendants of that Henry d'Albret who provided the model for the proto-rapist Hircan of the *Heptameron*.

The Estates General and the Death of the Mixed Constitution

> *The conservation of all Commonwealths and monarchies depends on the will and power of immortal God, on the observance of his commandments, and on the ancient laws and customs of each kingdom.*

Cahier of the Third Estate, Pontoise, 1561

> *[We want] one God to love, you our King to serve, one law to keep, and France to inhabit . . . [we seek] the glory of God, the grandeur of Your Majesty, and public Tranquility.*[70]

Cahier of the nobility of Nivernais, Estates General of Blois, 1576

The French monarchy ruled by "Hircan's" grandson, Henry IV, developed in a different way than the polities of several nearby states, such as England, the United Provinces of the Netherlands, or the Polish–Lithuanian Commonwealth. The medieval mixed constitutions of those states evolved into mixed constitutional monarchies in the late sixteenth century; their monarchs consulted regularly with a representative body. By looking at the meetings of the Estates General of France at Orléans (1560), Pontoise (1561), and Blois (1576), we can see how France moved in its own constitutional direction during this critical quarter century, following a distinct path. The representative bodies of other states voted taxes and loans, brought abuses to the monarch's attention, requested remedies for those abuses, and, in time, came to share lawmaking authority with the monarch. In France, none of that transpired, a fact that shaped fundamentally France's political destiny until 1789.[71] Why?

Four critical factors combined to prevent the creation of fixed meetings and to destroy the Estates General as an effective institution in France: (1) divisions among the three orders; (2) the intractability of the religious conflict; (3) money; and (4) the decision of the French urban elite, above all those in the legal professions, to obtain a share of political power not through representative institutions, but through the state administration itself.

A key procedural decision of the deputies to the meeting at Orléans created the structural foundation for the first problem. The deputies decided that each order should meet separately, thus breaking with the practice of the previous Estates

General, held at Tours in 1484 when the three orders had debated in common.[72] All subsequent meetings of the Estates General followed the Orléans precedent. Because the immemorial custom of the French Estates General required that all three orders, if meeting separately, had to agree for a measure to pass, dividing the assembly into orders effectively gave each order veto power over decisions.

The Estates Generals of 1560 and 1561 divided sharply along lay–ecclesiastical lines. The decision to meet as separate orders, however, gave the clergy the ability to prevent the two lay orders from enacting their agenda of desecularization of the Church. The lay orders did manage to enact a general *cahier* at Pontoise that demanded that the king respect liberty of conscience and foreswear the use of force in matters of religion, except in cases of punishment of "seditious, libertines, Anabaptists and atheists, enemies of God and of the public tranquility."[73]

The Estates General of 1576 brought forth the main currents of public opinion about both religious and political issues. Henry of Navarre, Condé, and Montmorency-Damville suspected the legitimacy of these Estates, whom they felt had been suborned by the Guise; they refused to come. *Cahiers* at every level, like that of the nobility of Nivernais, did seem to follow the Guise position on religion, yet they expressed, too, a profound popular desire for religious unity. The parishioners of Saint-Loup, near Chartres, wrote that "it would be a thing both worthy and very holy to observe and guard the constitutions of our holy mother church . . . and to extirpate heresies and new doctrines that pullulate [in France] and also to punish those guilty of them."[74]

At first, the apparent dominance of the Guise, Catholic position made it appear that the Estates General would unite on religious issues. The king took a hard line against the Protestants in his opening remarks (6 December): he wondered at "the strange change that one sees everywhere since the times of the kings of praiseworthy memory, his father and grandfather." He sought to bring the only possible remedy to the situation, peace.

> For these reasons, I pray and foreswear you all, by the faith and loyalty you have for me, by the affection you hold for me, by the love and charity you have for your fatherland, for the salvation of you, your wives, children, and posterity, for the conservation of your goods, that in this assembly all passions be put behind you . . . to aid me in assuring this so necessary tranquility, extirpate as much as possible the roots and seeds of divisions, reform the abuses, restore justice in its integrity, in short purge the bad humors of this kingdom to restore it to its health, vigor, and former disposition.[75]

Two weeks later, the deputies denounced the recent edict of pacification as "extorted from the king by force of arms, against the coronation oath, which His Majesty cannot violate," and insisted on "one single Catholic, apostolic, and Roman religion, and the sole exercise of the same." They were willing to allow the Protestants liberty of conscience in private, but forbade them any public worship. A small number of noble deputies objected; more critically, the Third Estate refused to vote the new taxes needed for war.

Here again the necessity of unanimity among the three orders effectively prevented decisive action. By February, under the pressure of revived fighting and responding to emissaries from Navarre and Montmorency-Damville, the Estates shifted to a new consensus about religion.[76] Louis of Bourbon, duke of Montpensier, the king's emissary to his kinsman Navarre, made the critical points on behalf of toleration. Citing the "calamities such as those which I saw on my journey here, of poor people immersed in poverty without hope of ever being able to raise themselves from that state, except by means of peace," Montpensier felt "constrained to advise their Majesties to make peace."

The shift to accommodation fitted neatly with what might be called the "Protestant" demands of even the most ardent Catholics, like the peasants of the Chartrain. Parishes wanted to *elect* worthy men, "properly trained and capable both in literature and in honesty," to parish cures, so that the sacraments could be administered in a holy way and so that there "would not arrive in the future any scandal from the ill life of the said ecclesiastics." Deputies at all levels demanded schools, with bishops footing the bill. In parish after parish, the peasants spoke out against ecclesiastical abuses: against priests playing dice or cards in taverns or wearing costly vestments, against charges for the sacraments and for burials, against uneducated clerics. They bewailed an epidemic of blasphemy, "which is now so common that women and children of seven or eight do it every day," in terms that would have warmed the hearts of the Genevan Consistory.[77] These demands illustrate the degree to which Protestantism voiced concerns—election of priests and bishops, access to literacy, an improved clergy—that had broad public support.[78]

Protestantism loomed large as well in the political fate of the Estates General, because of the existence of elected Protestants assemblies: leaders in each community, a general Council of twenty-four to direct their affairs, and a Council of one hundred to debate major issues. Given the association of Protestantism with representative bodies in England and the Low Countries, and with rebellion in the latter, similar developments in France encouraged the royal government to associate representative bodies with a dual threat to Catholicism and to monarchical power. De l'Hôpital spelled out the government's view of Estates in 1560. He stated that "the king communicates with his subjects about his greatest affairs, to take their advice and counsel, also to hear their complaints and sufferings, and acts upon them as reason allows." The king acted on this advice *only if he wished to do so*: "even though the king is not required to take the counsel of his men, nonetheless, it is good and honest that he do things by council."[79]

The deputies had other ideas: from the *cahiers* of Estates General of Orléans, to grievances of parishes, bailiwicks, provincial estates, and the Estates General of 1576, everyone wanted a permanent national representative body so that "all could be heard freely in their complaints and demands" (Saint-Loup, 1576). At Pontoise (1561), the nobility suggested a remarkably radical plan:

> that every year on the fifteenth of October in each bailiwick or seneschalsy
> the inhabitants can hold their local estates with a royal commission or letters,

in order that they can better see to apportionment and levy of the king's taxes, to the things related to his service and the public utility, and that they might take action on those things that might be in conflict with respect to the rights of ecclesiastics, nobles, and the third estate . . . that the grandeur and authority of the king could not in any way be diminished by it, if it pleases him to communicate often with his subjects, and to that end, desire and request that it be ordered that the Estates General of his kingdom be held every two years in His Majesty's presence.[80]

Later assemblies and local *cahiers* changed the interval for the Estates General to five years, but kept the insistence on annual meetings of bailiwick assemblies, which were to provide detailed local reports to the royal council.

While the Orléans and Pontoise meetings divided mainly along lay–ecclesiastical lines, that of Blois split between nobles and commoners. In 1560–1561, the strong insistence of the nobles and Third Estate on reform of the Church, including the seizure of its property, had no chance of receiving the clergy's support. In 1576, *cahiers* at all levels repeated demands for reform of the Church, but the fundamental divide lay between the nobility and the Third Estate. The roots of that divide could be seen at Orléans and Pontoise, where the nobles demanded that high justiciars have sole right of initial justice over all their "subjects" and suggested that royal judges and sergeants be severely restricted in their access to lands under the authority of high justiciars. (In northern France, that would have meant virtually everywhere outside of the towns.) At Blois, the nobility nuanced this demand, suggesting that cases tried in seigneurial courts no longer be appealable to royal courts, "in all cases whether civil or criminal."[81] Local nobles were to elect the royal bailiffs, who were to be noblemen, serving three-year terms. In short, the nobility had a clear agenda to establish a state in which they would have virtually complete control of local society, and in which the central state would have no real local presence, other than they themselves.

The deputies of the Third Estate, taken overwhelmingly from the world of royal courts, naturally opposed such measures; they turned ever more strongly to the state apparatus itself for a share of political power. Royal courts increasingly enabled them to rule local society, in the king's name. The nobles and clergy even sent a delegation to the Third to remind them "if they [the Third Estate] persist our intention is to address ourselves and make an agreement with the real third estate, which is the people of the countryside, while they are only a body of officers and men of justice."

The clergy's vote of a large sum of money in 1561, renewed in 1567 and regularly thereafter, shifted the focus of the third major issue, money. The government shifted its quest for more money to the lay taxpayers. In 1576, the Second and Third Estates fell out over taxation. When the nobility proposed a graduated direct tax on commoners, the Third Estate called it a "Capitulation of the Turkish fashion, which could bring about a change in the state itself in such tumultuous times." The Third Estate insisted that nobles contribute to taxation; the nobles claimed they paid taxes twice: first, through the feudal levy (*arrière-ban*) and second, through the payments of their tenants. They insisted that the latter payments violated their privileges, and demanded at the Estates Generals of 1560, 1561, 1576, 1588, and 1614 that their tenants, farmers, and millers benefit from the nobles' own tax exemption. The king refused.

The endless wrangling about money, and the fundamental dispute about how to create a more effective local system of governance, crippled the Estates. These problems can easily obscure the wide degree of agreement among the deputies. The meetings at Orléans and Pontoise, and the royal ordinance issued in response to the suggestions of the later meeting, provide us with a long list of reforms agreed to by all three Estates.[82] In addition to reform of the usual clerical abuses, they wanted the hiring of a doctor of theology for every cathedral or collegial church and of an instructor for the youth in all such churches. All agreed, too, on a hard line against a supposed decline in public morality: harsh prohibitions against blasphemers; bans on fairs, markets, tavern keeping, bowling, and plays during Sunday Mass; bans on publication of almanacs and other works containing "prognostication based on astrology, against the expressed commandment of God"; outlawing bordellos; and mandating punishment of all adulterers. These efforts had their usual success!

The Estates General suggested civil reforms, too, such as a uniform system of weights and measures.[83] The royal ordinance supported that idea, but it, like so many others, broke on the rock of privilege. Local lords or towns owned the right to set the local measure, as private property; their privileges/property rights prevented the use of any single royal measure. The same problem confronted the king in his efforts to reform justice. The lay orders demanded that the king abolish ecclesiastical courts, on the grounds that the clergy had no right to be involved in the administration of civil justice. The king refused on the grounds that he had no right to strip any of his subjects of their property and ancient privileges.

The king's response demonstrates the bizarre interaction of French legal principles and political practice. Precisely because the king could not intervene in matters of custom and property, everyone used the privilege/property argument to defend their interests. Unable to combine control over property regulation and lawmaking authority in a representative, later legislative assembly, France's growing urban elites sought a share of power instead in the royal administration, whose offices themselves were part of the intricate web of property.

This ever-growing royal bureaucracy gave the urban legal elite a mechanism for seizing control over part of the political system.[84] The bureaucracy essentially defeated the only alternative mechanism, representative bodies. Such bodies had hardly had an important role in the French state prior to 1560, but, had the king responded to the demands for regular meetings of the Estates General, coupled with annual meetings of local estates, they could have developed into a powerful political institution, where urban elites, like those of the Netherlands or England, could share political power with traditional rural landlords. In France, because the landed nobility dominated the representative bodies, and because, alone among these three states, France had a large government administration, urban elites seized control of the state itself. They obtained their share of political power by means of governmental institutions rather than representative bodies. Little wonder that these men created the prototype of the modern European state apparatus, while their brothers in England and Holland created modern political culture.

CONSTITUTIONALISM AND THE BIRTH OF MODERN POLITICS

*The first mark of the sovereign prince is the power to give law to all in general,
and to each in particular.*

Jean Bodin, *Six Books of the Commonwealth*, 1576

These practical debates about lawmaking, taxation, and religion had profound theoretical consequences: out of them sprang our modern, Western notion of the state.
France provided an ideal location for this critical debate because of the variety of its
institutions and the vibrancy of its intellectual life. Michel de Montaigne's *Essays*
show that critica! spirit, that skepticism so familiar a part of French civilization.
Montaigne, like so many of his contemporaries, feared change, respected the ancient
laws, and called for the maintenance of order.

> In all things—except quite simply for those which are evil—change is to be
> feared, including changes of seasons, winds, diets and humours; and no
> laws are truly respected except those to which God has vouchsafed so long a
> continuance that no one knows how they were born or that they had ever
> been different.

Once Henry of Navarre became heir apparent (1584), he offered many such people
the worst possible choice: become king, he violated the sanctity of the established religion; denying him the throne, they violated the ancient Salic Law of inheritance of
the crown. The dilemma presented itself to all between 1589, when Henry did become king, and 1593, when he abjured Protestantism.

The political debates of 1560–1598 shaped the destiny of European state development. The struggle between Henry III and various representative bodies directly
overlapped the struggle among various political philosophies, in part because the
most important political philosopher, Jean Bodin, served as chief spokesman of the
Third Estate in 1576. Bodin, already well known for his *Method for the Easy Comprehension of History*, published his greatest work, *The Six Books of the Commonwealth*
(*Les Six Livres de la République*) in that year.

Bodin built on the work of his famous predecessors, who included the constitutionalists like Claude de Seyssel and Étienne Pasquier, who placed "bridles"—religion, justice, the *police,* state institutions (above all, Parlements)—on the king and
the absolutists like Barthélemy Chasseneuz, who argued that the king had unlimited
power. Chasseneuz promulgated the ideas that the king could tax at will, and that
because the "will of the prince is law," the king was not bound by his own laws. De
l'Hôpital, in some ways a constitutionalist, agreed with Chasseneuz on this last point
during his speech to the Estates General of Orléans: "the subjects . . . [owe the king]
true obedience, which is to guard his . . . laws, edicts, and ordinances, . . . to which all
must obey, and to which they are subject, *except the king alone.*"

Bodin created a powerful synthesis of these arguments, setting out the first coherent definition of sovereignty known in western Europe since Roman times: "the
first mark of the sovereign prince is the power to give law to all in general, and to

each in particular." Bodin here fundamentally altered the nature of rulership, following in the direction laid out by the actions of Francis I and by the words of de l'Hôpital. The medieval habit of addressing the king as "sovereign seigneur" disappeared in the late sixteenth century. Yet, while the principle of divided stewardship of the commonwealth evaporated, the attributes of sovereign power remained divided. Local lords levied tolls, established weights and measures, and judged most cases. The most powerful lords, the high justiciars, held the right to condemn people to death, subject to review by a Parlement.

Bodin rejected the idea of divided sovereignty: for Bodin, sovereignty was perpetual, inalienable, and indivisible. Virtually all modern political philosophers, such as Thomas Hobbes and John Locke, accepted Bodin's central premises about sovereignty.[85] Bodin argued that the prince held absolute, but limited power. The king's power was "absolute" because he held inalienable sovereignty, which gave him an absolute right to make positive law. His power was limited because the king was not above *all* laws. The laws of men, made by the king alone, could not, as the de l'Hôpital put it, "change or silence the laws of nature."

Bodin wrote that "the absolute power of Princes and sovereign seigneuries does not extend in any way to the laws of God and of nature. . . . all the Princes of the Earth are subject to the laws of God and of nature, and to many human laws common to all people." Here Bodin made the critical distinction between public law and private law or contract. The king had unlimited right to make public law. He had no right to violate contracts or to change property rights, because natural law, the laws common to all nations, and Divine Law protected both contracts and property. Thus, for Bodin, taxation without consent was not one of the attributes of royal sovereignty, because it violated Divine Law. This principal had immediate practical consequence for Bodin, who unsuccessfully asserted it in his role as chief spokesman for the Third Estate at Blois.

French society, like all early modern European societies, made strong distinctions between right (*droit*), which the king could not change, and law (*loi*), which he could. One of the king's emissaries to the Estates General of 1576, Marshal Brissac, offered an intriguing argument for Henry III's intention to violate the Peace of Monsieur:

> in truth there is no greater treasure and guarantee than the faith and word of a king, but it is also true that it is so only to the degree in which it is for the good of his subjects, it would be a thing of too dangerous a consequence if he could give his faith in prejudice of all his state and against the ancient and praiseworthy customs of the kingdom . . . that there is a difference between laws of the king and laws of the kingdom . . . in as much as the latter can only be made in general assemblies of the kingdom . . . with the common accord and consent of the three estates.[86]

Brissac's arguments did not carry the day; the Assembly, rejecting a position it had taken in December, held Henry III bound by his word.

Bodin's claim that the king held an inalienable sovereignty came under immediate attack from Protestant theorists. The most influential treatise, the *Vindiciae, Contra Tyrannos*, probably came from the pens of Philippe du Plessis Mornay and Hubert

Languet, two Huguenot noblemen. Presaging the arguments of Locke, they held that if the king derived his power from the "people," and if sovereignty were inalienable, then the people must still retain ultimate sovereignty.[87] The people could delegate sovereign authority, but never sovereignty itself. Moreover, the *Vindiciae* specifically argued that the people had the right to rebel against a tyrant (a king ruling for his own, not the public's benefit). A king not following the "true path" (a phrase used by Jeanne d'Albret), urging his people to worship God in the wrong way, was by definition, a tyrant. Other Huguenot theorists, such as François Hotman, author of *Francogallia*, asserted (rightly) that the king had originally been elected. They claimed that a real king had to consult popular assemblies, such as periodic meetings of the Estates General. Royalists, of course, took a different view. As chancellor de l'Hôpital put it in 1560: ". . . Every time one of them wishes to leave his place . . . evil comes . . . that is what has happened and will always happen when the subject wishes to exceed himself and to command rather than to obey."

When Henry III murdered the duke and cardinal of Guise, he unleashed the full fury of the radical Catholics. Their poets rendered homage to duke Henry de Guise and cried out for struggle and revenge: "Our cause is holy and just, We must not have fear, Fighting for our faith, For the public, for the Church, For our good and freedom, Against a *heretic* King." The *heretic* (emphasis added) king was a king to whom the people did not owe allegiance. Both the theology faculty of the University of Paris and the Pope, who excommunicated the king, publicly supported this proposition. Henry III was, by definition, a tyrant, worthy of God's vengeance. Eight months after the deaths of the Guise, the monk Jacques Clément carried out that vengeance, assassinating the king. At his execution on the place de Grève, Clément shouted that he offered up "this sacrifice of my body, my soul and my life" in order to act as God's avenger.

Protestants writing in the immediate aftermath of the Saint Bartholomew's Day Massacre had naturally attacked royal tyranny. Once Henry IV, a Protestant, became king, Huguenot writers switched to the argument that all should rally behind the king, to salvage order. They took up Stoicist traditions to justify the status quo; they argued that "above all the Creator finds obedience agreeable, and that he is displeased by rebellion."[88] Mornay, a close friend of Henry IV, waxed prolific on the importance and uniqueness of royal power. Catholic radicals now took up the old Huguenot line, arguing that Catholics had an obligation to resist the "tyrant," and that the people had the right to elect the king.[89] Radical Catholic pamphleteers went even further, suggesting that regicide was a legitimate act against the Protestant tyrant.

Political philosophy in France did not take a constitutionalist track; it followed the "absolutist" consensus developed by Bodin. These debates took place not simply in learned treatises, but in public fora, such as the Estates General. Henry of Navarre, later to become king, suggested to that assembly that "equity, public utility, and the common salvation" served as "public law to all kingdoms and commonwealths." Few debated these principles, yet few could agree precisely on how to implement them, particularly in the matter of religion.

The disorder of the times and the rapid growth of the royal government called for a new political philosophy. This philosophy focused on law making authority, making that authority into the entity known as sovereignty. In creating the idea of unified, inalienable sovereignty, and in juxtaposing that creation with the rise of a larger, more powerful government, the people of late sixteenth-century France left to the modern world one of its defining intellectual and practical characteristics: the sovereign state.

Notes

1. *Marranos* made a public conversion to Christianity, but maintained some Jewish practices, such as dietary restrictions. *Conversos* gave up the practice of Judaism. French *Marrano* Louis Saporta was Court physician to Charles VII. His grandson, Antoine, Rector of the Medical School at Montpellier in the 1550s, converted to Calvinism. Many Iberian and Provençal Jews fled to the Papal States or Avignon, but the 1553 massacre of the Jews of Ancona, Italy, by the Papal Inquisition ended such migration.

2. BN, Mss. Fr. 16,249, fol. 166v.

3. P. de Ronsard, *Œuvres complètes*, ed. G. Cohen (Paris: Gallimard, 1950), I, 614. Muse, l'honneur des sommets de Parnesse, / Guide ma langue et me chante la race / Des ROIS FRANÇOIS yssus de Francion, / Enfant de Hector, Troyen de nation. The Trojan myth of Frankish origins could be traced back to Fredegar, a seventh-century chronicler.

4. AD Côte d'Or, C 3469, Third Estate *cahiers* for the Estates General of 1560, deputies of the duchy of Burgundy, meeting in Dijon, November 1560.

5. Those parishes who sided with the Catholic League voted for the Right.

6. Cited in A. Croix and J. Quéniart, *Histoire Culturelle de la France, vol. 2. De la Renaissance à l'Aube des Lumières.* (Paris: Seuil, 1997), 95. Du Bourg was executed.

7. BN, Mss. Fr. 16,249, fols. 103v–104.

8. BN, Mss. Fr. 15,494, fols. 20–26v.

9. This demand had obvious political motivation: The policy would have eliminated the two Guise cardinals from the council, but allowed the cardinal de Bourbon, as a prince of the royal blood, to stay on.

10. AD Côte d'Or, C 3469.

11. French public opinion did not accept the legitimacy of the Council of Trent, although the king's spokesman informed the deputies that no council could be held until the king had been informed of what had transpired there. The Gallican Church did not fully accept the decrees promulgated at Trent (1562) until 1615.

12. The king actually issued an edict setting that age at twenty for nuns and twenty-six for monks.

13. Some deputies in each of the lay orders, particularly among the nobility, supported a violent solution, but they were a distinct minority.

14. BN, Mss. Fr. 16,249, fol. 102v.

15. The projected 120 million *livres* would be divided between the state (72 million) and the clergy. The clergy would take its 48 million and loan it out at interest (8.33 percent), which would provide them with the same 4 million *livres* of revenue as before, and simultaneously provide the citizens of France with much needed capital for productive investment. This action did not involve seizure of tithe income.

16. See the Appendix for a sixteenth-century genealogy of the royal family, the Guises, and the Montmorencys.

17. Madeleine was also the niece of Louise of Savoy, Francis I's mother.

18. Claude de Guise (Burgundy), married to a Bourbon; François de Cleves (Champagne), duke of Nevers, married to a Bourbon; François de Guise (Dauphiné), son of a Bourbon; Henri d'Albret (Guyenne), married to Francis I's sister; François de Montmorency (Ile-de-France), great-grandson of a Bourbon; Anne de Montmorency, husband of a Bourbon descendant; Claude of Savoy, from bastard line of Savoy ducal house (married with Bourbons).

19. The Guise, like other members of the Lorraine family, claimed to be descended from Charlemagne. Others took that claim with a grain of salt.

20. If we can trust the estimate of the Estates General of 1561, Charles of Lorraine, all by himself, thus collected 7.5 percent of the landed revenue of the French clergy. This amount would not have included revenues from tithes.

21. Quilliet, *La France du Beau XVIᵉ Siècle*, 104.

22. To be fair, he was also a remarkable patron of the arts, employing the best architects of his day to rebuild his châteaux at Chantilly and Ecouen in the new Renaissance style, creating a famous study in his Parisian hôtel on the rue Sainte-Avoye, and decorating his residences with frescoes by Italian painters, such as Nicolo Dell'Abate. See: B. Bedos-Rezak, *Anne de Montmorency: seigneur de la Renaissance* (Paris: Editions Publiard, 1990), and M. Greengrass, "Property and Politics in Sixteenth-Century France: The landed fortune of Constable Anne de Montmorency," *French History* (1988): 371–398.

23. BN, Mss. Fr. 16,517, fol.16. Du Vair was also bishop of Lisieux. "He had the reputation of having the most integrity of any man of his time, and of being its most eloquent magistrate and one of its best writers." M. Popoff, *Prosopographie des gens du Parlement de Paris (1266–1753)* (Saint Nazaire le Désert: Références, 1996), entry 2407.

24. Gaspard and Henri converted by 1558; Odet de Coligny converted to Protestantism in 1561 and married soon afterward. Showing a good ecumenical spirit, however, he continued to collect the revenues from his Catholic benefices!

25. French customary law in almost all provinces divided the oversight between the mother of the child and the senior male member of the deceased father's lineage. The male guardian had obligations to look after the child's property; in this case, of course, that would be the kingdom itself.

26. The two meetings of the Estates General are discussed in the text that follows, in a special section on that institution.

27. Catherine herself belonged to the same branch of the Bourbon family as Antoine: her maternal grandmother was Jeanne de Bourbon-Vendôme.

28. Cited in M. Holt, *The French Wars of Religion, 1562–1629* (Cambridge and New York: Cambridge University Press, 1995), 48.

29. Given the solemn promises made by the Guise to the duke, no wonder Michelet wrote that "the personal and natural element of the cardinal of Lorraine was the lie." J. Michelet, *Histoire de France, Le Seizième Siècle*, v. VII, ed. C. Mettra (Lausanne: Editions Rencontre, 1966), 28.

30. Tours, Blois, Sens, Angers, Poitiers, Bourges, Vienne, Grenoble, Nîmes, Montpellier, Orange, Beaucaire, Béziers, and Le Havre.

31. The 1561 alliance of Montmorency, Guise, and marshal Saint-André, the "triumvirs," called for Catholic forces to "obliterate completely the name of the family and race of the Bourbons." The phrase offers interesting insights into sixteenth-century noble definitions of "family" and "race." The triumvirs defined the two terms solely in terms of male descent, given that François de Guise's mother was a Bourbon and so was Anne de Montmorency's wife. They politely dropped this demand when Antoine de Bourbon joined their coalition.

32. Unhorsed at the battle of Dreux, Saint-André tried to surrender, but a Huguenot noble whose estates he had seized rode up, drew out his pistol, and shot the marshal. Condé fell wounded at the battle of Jarnac; when he tried to surrender, a Catholic captain deliberately murdered him.

33. The three Coligny brothers all fell violently ill in 1567; d'Andelot died, the two others recovered. Contemporaries universally believed they had been poisoned and held Catherine de Médicis responsible. We have no direct proof of her involvement.

34. *Mémoires du sieur François de la Noue*, in *Collection complète des mémoires relatifs à l'histoire de France*, v. XXXIV, ed. M. Petitot (Paris: Foucault, 1823), 193–194.

35. Cited in B. Diefendorf, *Beneath the Cross: Catholics and Huguenots in Sixteenth-Century Paris* (New York: Oxford University Press, 1991), 105.

36. Jeanne d'Albret died (9 June) before the marriages actually took place.

37. Responsibility for this deed is much debated; traditional French historiography held Catherine to be guilty. In recent years, however, scholars have looked more toward the Guise, seeking revenge for the murder of François de Guise. The assassin fired his shot from a house owned by the duke of Guise.

38. The duke of Nevers's letters to the king suggest that the duke believed the rumors. Moreover, Coligny's brother-in-law had an army of four thousand men in the outskirts of Paris.

39. Words of a contemporary chronicler, cited in P. Benedict, *Rouen during the Wars of Religion* (Cambridge: Cambridge University Press, 1981), 128.

40. The Protestant bankers of Geneva would play a critical role in the development of the French monarchy in the late seventeenth and eighteenth centuries, as we shall see.

41. Henry consolidated the mixed Polish constitution. The Sejm (Diet) forced him to sign a set of articles delimiting royal powers and firmly establishing a mixed constitution. All subsequent Polish kings had to swear to uphold the Henrician Articles.

42. R. Kingdon, *Myths about the Saint Bartholomew's Day Massacre* (Cambridge, MA: Harvard University Press, 1988), 30. Merlin's story comes from the collection of Protestant documents amassed by Simon Groulart and published in 1576; this collection provided the basis for much of the later Protestant martyrology of Coligny and for their collective memory of the massacre itself. See also, Diefendorf, *Beneath the Cross*, 103.

43. Ariane Boltanski provided me with this citation, which comes from her important dissertation in progress on the duke of Nevers. The letter can be found in BN, Mss. Fr. 3950, fols. 112–113. Denis Crouzet has also discussed this memoir, in his provocative recent book on the massacre, *La nuit de la Saint-Barthélemy*.

44. Louise's mother belonged to the Montpensier branch of the Bourbons.

45. François de Montmorency, who had been imprisoned in May 1574, at the urging of the duke of Guise, was also released in the late fall of 1575.

46. Alençon did not forget his private interest: he had the king grant him the new title of duke of Anjou, with vast estates in the Loire Valley and a pension of 300,000 *livres*.

47. The Estates Generals of 1576 and 1588 were the only two meetings of that body between 1480 and 1788 to take place in the presence of a fully adult king. The meetings of 1560 and 1614–1615 took place when the king was just fourteen, those of 1483–1484 and 1561 during royal minorities.

48. The surviving evidence about sixteenth-century attitudes toward homosexuality is ambiguous. The documents from the Estates General and provincial estates, for example, universally denounce adultery and prostitution; some attack the loose morals of women at Court. They do not mention homosexual behavior. The pamphlet literature of the time, however, used Henry III's bisexuality as a grounds for political attack. Its use of such themes suggests that *some* contemporaries condemned homosexual behavior (which was illegal), but the preponderance of material implies that a much more tolerant attitude toward people's private sexuality prevailed among educated elites.

49. Here one must recognize their distinction between femininity—a woman behaving like a woman—and effeminacy—a man behaving like a "woman." Sixteenth-century writers focused on effeminacy, which they defined as "unnatural," hence as reprehensible.

50. BN, Mss. Fr. 16,157, fol. 24v.

51. Louis XIII had both female and male favorites. His private physician, Jean Hérouard, whose diary of Louis's daily life is one of the richest sources of French history, called Louis's affection for his favorite the duke of Luynes "shameful," but neither Hérouard nor any other reliable source specifically suggests Louis

had intercourse either with his male favorites, like Luynes, or female ones, like Louise de la Fayette.

52. D. Crouzet, *Les guerriers de Dieu: la violence au temps des troubles de la réligion, vers 1525–vers 1610* (Seyssel: Champ Vallon, 1990), II, 306, offers a fine description.

53. Henry III had married Louise of Vaudemont, half-sister of Mercoeur, and of Marguerite of Lorraine, wife of Joyeuse. The Lorraine family were cousins of the Guises.

54. Montpensier's male line ran out in 1608; the heiress married Navarre's son, Gaston.

55. Cited in R. Mandrou, *Introduction to modern France, 1500–1640. An essay in historical psychology*, trans. R. E. Hallmark (New York: Harper & Row, 1975, 1977).

56. Direct taxes, *excluding* military levies in the field, roughly tripled between the 1520s and the 1580s. Grain prices at Paris increased four fold in that period; at Toulouse, they went up 350 percent. In areas of military campaigning, the situation was rather different: Dauphiné paid over one million *livres* in military taxes in some years during the 1580s and 1590s, more than ten times the standard levies of the 1550s.

57. Had he accepted, the king would have lost 75 percent of his direct tax revenue.

58. BN, Mss. Fr. 16,250, fol. 297, journal of the noble deputy Pierre de Blanchefort.

59. In the seventeenth century, only 4 percent of the families entering the Chamber of Accounts later made their way to the Parlement.

60. Many offices made the individual owner a noble; however, the family became noble only after several generations of office holding. The rules on such matters became looser in the seventeenth century, often in return for payments from the officers in question.

61. A constant stream of "foreign" nobles entered the French nobility; some, like the Guise family, came from Lorraine; others, like the Nevers family, came from Italy.

62. BN, Mss. Fr. 16,250, fols. 369–369v.

63. *The Complete Works of Montaigne. Essays. Travel Journal. Letters.*, trans. D. Frame (Stanford: Stanford University Press, 1958, 1967), provides the standard English translation. This passage appears on page 815; I have provided my own translation here and in the other quotations from Montaigne that follow.

64. Si quelqu'un devant eux reçoit un bon visage / Ils le vont caresser, bien qu'ils crèvent de rage / S'il le reçoit mauvais, ils le montrent au doy.

65. Agrippa d'Aubigné, in a letter to his daughters about learned women. *Œuvres Complètes de Thédore Agrippa d'Aubigné*, I (Geneva: Slatkine Reprints, 1967), 446.

66. Sonnet 18. Louise Labé, *Œuvres complètes*, ed. E. Guidici (Geneva: Droz, 1981). Guidici points out that du Bellay, too, used this metaphor of the kisses hotter than a *braize*.

67. D. Lesko Baker, *The Subject of Desire. Petrarchan Poetics and the Female Voice in Louise Labé* (West Lafayette, IN: Purdue University Press, 1996), 155.

68. Moviegoers may recognize the name Jean de Coras: he was the presiding magistrate in the trial in *The Return of Martin Guerre*. They might also remember that Coras died for his Protestant faith during the Saint Bartholomew's Day massacre at Toulouse. His case demonstrates the extent to which the defense of patriarchal authority united Protestant and Catholic men. I am indebted to Professor Sarah Hanley for this reference to Coras's attitudes.

69. Sixteenth-century preachers fulminated against sexual intercourse in the female superior position. They considered any intercourse in which the man was not on top to be sinful. See the path-breaking article by N. Z. Davis, "Women on Top," included in her collection of essays, *Society and Culture in Early Modern France* (Stanford: Stanford University Press, 1975).

70. Taken from the journal of Pierre de Blanchefort, one of the noble deputies who drew up the *cahier*. A seventeenth-century copy of Blanchefort's journal can be found in BN, Mss. Fr. 16,250. This citation comes from fols. 13v–14.

71. France continued to have provincial estates. The successful ones—Brittany, Burgundy, and Languedoc above all—furnished the king with money; they, like bodies elsewhere in Europe that provided rulers with money, flourished. Although the government had tacitly accepted—in the 1561 Edict of Orléans—the right of the Estates General to vote all new taxes, it acted consistently as if it did not need permission to levy taxation anywhere, save in the provinces whose provincial estates retained the right to approve all local taxation. Alone among the orders, the clergy continued to meet in regular assemblies. Every five years from 1567 until the end of the monarchy, the clergy of France met in a national assembly, which voted a "free gift" to the king. The clergy then collected tenths (*décimes*) from its members to raise the money.

72. The three orders met separately in most local jurisdictions, too. The 1560 Estates were also the first ones for which many peasants had met in parish assemblies and in which, for most areas, the deputies of the Third Estate represented both the countryside and the towns.

73. BN, Mss. Dupuy 646, fols. 122v–123.

74. The *cahiers* for the parishes around Chartres are found in BN, Mss. Fr. 26,324; the bailiwick of Saint-Loup's *cahier* begins on fol. 21.

75. BN, Mss. Fr. 16,250, fols. 83v–84, Blanchefort's journal. The word "humors" refers to the "humors" of the body (dry, wet, etc.), which people then felt controlled human health. A healthy person had balanced humors.

76. This interpretation comes from Blanchefort's journal, which I find more convincing than the argument of the journal kept by the duke of Nevers, which denies such influence. Nevers, a hard-line Catholic, had obvious reasons for belittling such effects.

77. The Consistory oversaw the morality of the population of Geneva and strictly enforced what we in America would call Puritanism.

78. In 1561, the lay orders convinced the royal government to include in the king's ordinance their most radical religious request, election of bishops by local

assemblies of twelve members from each of the three estates. The clergy, which included key members of the Regency council, successfully convinced the Parlement of Paris to remove that clause during its registration process.

79. Quotations from de l'Hôpital come from the very convenient edition of several of his speeches edited by Robert Descimon, *Discours pour la majorité de Charles IX et trois autres discours* (Paris: Imprimerie Nationale, 1993).

80. BN, Mss. Fr. 15,494, fol. 88.

81. They allowed three exceptions: bearing arms in a group exceeding ten people; counterfeiting money; and secular treason.

82. Although the Estates accomplished no fundamental changes, the king issued an important reforming ordinance (Blois, 1579) based on their suggestions about specific abuses.

83. The Estates also demanded governmental reform: lower taxes, reduced spending, payment of debts, abolition of venal offices, and punishment of pillaging troops. The government responded with a wide array of promises, most of them unkept.

84. In order to give readers a better sense of long-term developments of state institutions, their evolution from 1450 to 1634 is treated in a single section, in Chapter 7.

85. Bodin's work appeared in an English translation in 1601.

86. BN, Mss. Fr. 16, 250, fols. 325v–327. Interestingly, Brissac made his argument about the power of the Estates General using the specific case of religion. He claimed that Clovis had consulted an Estates General to institute Catholicism as the official religion of France, and that Charlemagne had done the same in creating the framework of parishes.

87. Bodin agreed with the first half of this formulation, that the king derived his authority from the people; he disagreed only with the second idea, that, in given circumstances, the people could take it back. In this respect, Bodin did not support a theory of Divine Right monarchy.

88. It should be noted that those favoring parliamentary government also took up Stoicist principles, above all those of Cicero.

89. Historians often take lightly this proposal, yet chancellor de l'Hôpital himself, in his opening speech to the Estates of Orléans in 1560, had specifically stated that: "And there [in the Estates] sat and presided the kings, except at those Estates, at which were decided the most noble cause ever (that is, to whom did the kingdom of France belong, after the death of Charles IV, to Philip of Valois, his cousin, or to Edward of England)."

Chapter Seven

THE NEW ORDER

At last, after so many years / Here is the happy season, / In which our endless miseries / Are going to have their cure.[1]

François de Malherbe,
"To Henry the Great, on taking Marseille" (1596)

The death of Henry III created political chaos; many French people refused to accept the apparent legal heir, Henry IV (Henry of Navarre), as king, because he was a Protestant. Moreover, the full range of authority rejected Henry IV's claim: the Pope (1585), the Parlement of Paris (1588), and the Estates General (1588). The Salic Law may have pointed to Navarre but, for most Catholics, God's law did not. The intensely Catholic Estates of Burgundy went so far as to swear an oath on their principles: "We swear to live and die in the holy Roman Catholic faith and religion, not to recognize any heretic . . . as king."

The civil war that followed Henry IV's accession brought fire and sword to many regions of France, particularly because it coincided with reinvigorated fighting between Protestants and Catholics in the Low Countries. Several times between 1589 and 1597 Spanish armies descended into France to help the Catholic League in its struggle against the Protestant "tyrant." Henry eventually determined that he could not be king without converting to Catholicism. Legend has him saying that "Paris is worth a mass." He abjured Protestantism on 25 July 1593, at Saint-Denis, burial place of the kings of France.

Six months later, the archbishop of Chartres, taking the place of the Leaguer archbishop of Reims (the cardinal of Guise), crowned Henry as king in the great cathedral, making Henry IV the only French king after 1108 not to receive his crown at Reims. The final, critical step came in September 1595, when the Pope absolved Henry of his past sins and accepted the legitimacy of his conversion. Henry, for his part, agreed to raise his nephew and heir, the infant prince of Condé, as a Catholic, and to raise any future children in the Church.

These events traumatized the French more than words can express. Many years spent in the French archives dealing with this period, reading the thoughts of the widest possible range of people—peasants and artisans, merchants, lawyers, royal officials, aristocrats, the king himself—have perpetually reinforced the absolute horror with which ordinary French people remembered the dark years at the end of the six-teenth century. Henry IV, invariably called Henry the Great after his death, remains the most popular French king. If his name comes up in any conversation, someone will mention his legendary wish that every peasant in his kingdom should have "la poule au pot" (a chicken in the pot) every Sunday. In Revolutionary Paris, the first wave of crowds ripping down the statues of French kings initially spared only that of Henry IV, astride his horse, overlooking the Pont Neuf, although they soon pulled him down, too.[2] Why should this man enjoy such extraordinary popularity, nearly four centuries after his death? His personality aside, Henry's popularity rests on his association with the ascent from the French Slough of Despond of the terrible 1590s.

Henry IV brought order and prosperity. Much as people liked to use an old vo-cabulary to describe this order, saying that Henry had "restored" the French monar-chy, in fact the king and his collaborators created a completely new order. They seem to have feared, above all, the dangerous implications of individualism, associated with Humanism and with religious choice. Henry tried to maintain an order based precisely on allowing individual choice in religion, but not in politics; his successors refused to separate the two. They demanded absolute obedience in civil matters and, in time, religious ones, too.

He became king at a critical moment in the evolution of the French nation–state. The strong sense of a specifically French commonwealth that emerged from the final stages of the Hundred Years' War took on a decidedly new context in the sixteenth cen-tury. The enormous increase in state power and presence between 1461 and 1589 cre-ated a framework for a merger of the state and the commonwealth. The initial meaning of commonwealth, the collective group of citizens, became effaced, as the royal gov-ernment sought to establish the principle that the king alone had stewardship of the commonwealth. He shared this stewardship not with the leading citizens (i.e., the no-bility and some urban leaders) but with his officers. The great royal administrators often came from the ranks of Parlementaire families; they shared with the judges a perspective that made the Parlements and the high royal administration the king's chief collaborators in the direction and preservation of the common interest.

Henry IV's synthesis took in hand three critical elements of the development of the nation–state:

1. He consolidated the identification with a specifically French nation and commonwealth.

2. He transferred identification with the commonwealth (the public good) to the Crown (the good of the king's service).

3. He revitalized existing state institutions to create a more effective government.

At the time of his death (1610), France had a distinctive monarchical commonwealth, in which the king shared his power with the important elites whose members consti-tuted the citizenry. The nobility shared power through the military and related estab-lishments, such as governorships of provinces and towns; the legal men shared power through the court system; and the financial elite shared power through the tax and state finance system. Henry maintained limited mechanisms of consultation, such as the provincial estates of Brittany or Languedoc, but primarily compromised with elites through the mechanism of government itself. This French synthesis of nation, commonwealth, and state created a model of monarchical government that had far-reaching influence throughout Continental Europe in early modern times. This monarchical nation–state served as an important transition mechanism between the commonwealth-centered polity of the fifteenth century and the popular nation–state of the nineteenth century. It sought unsuccessfully to remove the concept of citizen from political life, a failure that became evident in the eighteenth century. In the long run, however, that effort created a fundamental confusion between the citizen as a member of government (state official) and the citizen as a political actor outside and above the government, a confusion that exists to this day in France.[3]

The two great institutions, the Catholic Church and the state, worked tirelessly to stamp out ambiguity. The distinction made by President Brulart, between the king and the commonwealth, could no longer be tolerated: all had seen where this dangerous bifurcation could lead. Henceforth, royal proclamations and, more insidiously, requests sent to the king, abandoned the old vocabulary of the "public good" and substituted instead the phrase dear to the hearts of Henry III's royal secretaries, "the good of the king's service." Petitioners ceased to be "very faithful and loyal servants" and became instead "very humble and obedient servants."

Political theorists of the time accurately reflected this new mindset. They invariably praised the king's "absolute" power and abandoned the political discourse common to Europe since early medieval times, a discourse based on Classical models of Greece and Rome. Seventeenth-century theorists, men such as Cardin Le Bret or Bossuet in France or Hobbes and Filmer in England, spoke of order. In England, Poland–Lithuania, or the United Provinces of the Netherlands, opposition voices, inspired often by the arguments of sixteenth-century French constitutionalists, reached back again to the old models: the Ancient Constitution, as the English called it. In France, however, few such voices could be heard. The state progressively stifled political dissent, tying it always to religious diversity and hence to the collective memory of the dreaded 1590s. The old rallying cry voiced by chancellor de l'Hôpital and other sixteenth-century jurists—one faith, one king, one law—took on a sinister new meaning.

The Catholic Church and the state struggled mightily in the early seventeenth century to implement their visions of the world. In the larger context, they worked together to stifle individualism and impose conformity, but they often opposed each other in specific matters. Their efforts bore some fruit in the second half of the century, but the undercurrents of individualism never ceased to flow. Indeed, both Church and state, in their own way, encouraged them. Those currents would emerge again in the eighteenth century, brandishing the same weapons—reason, humanistic values—that had failed in the sixteenth.

These efforts by the Church and the state had substantial popular support, not only among the elites but among common people. Elites did not simply use the two institutions to impose their value systems on others: people at all levels of society sought to use their social institutions to create a new social and moral consensus to replace the old one shattered by the Renaissance and Reformation. Humanist questing for truth did not immediately create definable limits of inquiry, either in terms of subject or in terms of those inquiring. Sixteenth-century elites certainly agreed that only some people should engage in such independent thinking, but once people got started on the path of inquiry, stopping them could prove impossible. Those who were not "supposed" to think for themselves, like women, once given access to education and to a range of literature, proved remarkably able to think for themselves. The Reformation, with its emphasis on Bible reading and individual relationships to God, similarly broke down the old barriers. Disputes about the nature of communion aside, one of the great revolutions of sixteenth-century Christianity was the democratization of the communion. In medieval Europe, except on Easter, only the priest took communion; in seventeenth-century Europe, even many Catholic theologians supported frequent communion.

The discovery of the New World and the much greater contact with Africa and Asia similarly destroyed old certainties. A text like John Mandeville's *Travels* (fourteenth century), which fifteenth-century Europeans took as a serious work of geography (Columbus carried a copy with him on his voyage, to use as a guide), became now a humorous work of fables. A new generation of authors created a new generation of fables, to be sure, but Europeans suddenly knew much more about the world around them. The great Amerindian empires forced them to reconsider their ideas of how societies functioned, just as the encounters with the Indians of North America shaped emerging ideas about the "state of nature." Educated people could have access to maps that presented a far more accurate view of the earth; kings now examined local maps that enabled them to establish clear and fixed boundaries where none had existed before.

Early seventeenth-century France and its European neighbors faced a remarkable challenge: the creation of a new social, moral, and philosophical consensus on which to base society. Historians are wont to focus on specific aspects of that enterprise, such as the creation of the modern state, but to ignore the larger process. The internalization of the new value system, a system that would replace the medieval one, lay at the core of that process. Much like the Franks of sixth-century Gaul, who also had to create a new system of shared values, seventeenth-century French people made the moral authors of this process into saints.

∾ The Birth of the Modern State

Henry IV and the League

The favor of a great Prince is the soul of a good heart.

Ronsard, "Les Mascarades"

CHRONOLOGY	1589–1610
1589	Henry IV becomes king (8/2); Henry defeats Mayenne at Arques (9/21)
1590	Henry defeats Mayenne at Ivry (3/14); death of Charles, cardinal of Bourbon, "Charles X" (5/14)

CHRONOLOGY	(continued)
1593	Estates General meet to elect a "king"; Henry abjures Protestantism (7/25)
1594	Henry crowned at Chartres (2/27); Brissac sells Paris to the king (September)
1595	Pope Clement VIII accepts Henry's conversion (9/17); Mayenne agrees to terms
1596	Assembly of Notables at Rouen (December)
1597	Spanish seize Amiens (February); Henry retakes Amiens (9/19)
1598	Mercoeur surrenders in Brittany, Edict of Nantes (April); France and Spain sign Peace of Vervins (5/2)
1600–1601	War with Savoy; France gains Bresse and surrounding area; execution of Biron
1610	Assassination of Henry IV by Ravaillac (5/10)

Henry IV, a profligate and unrepentant sinner if ever there was one, hardly qualified as a saint. That the offensive of the Devout began during his reign is surely one of the greater ironies of French history. Henry was a man of the old stamp: he enjoyed Carnival, gambling, indeed virtually everything the Devouts opposed. Yet his reign marked the defining moment in the creation of the modern state that ultimately would carry through the Devout agenda. His chief collaborator in that enterprise, Maximilien de Béthune, duke of Sully, a confirmed Calvinist, shared with the Catholic Devouts a visceral dislike of "immoral" behavior. Sully disapproved strongly of the king's womanizing and gambling, often rebuking the king for payments to his favorites or those who had taken advantage of him at the tables.

That Henry would lay the foundations of a powerful French state seemed preposterous in August 1589. The assassination of Henry III placed Catholics in a terrible quandary. Many, following the logic applied by Marshal Brissac in his speech of 1577 (Chapter 6), did not accept the legitimacy of a Protestant king. They also feared that Henry would undermine their Church. Historians have long focused on this group, the Leaguers, and on their decision to place the "honor of God" above the law of France. Yet such a perspective overlooks the substantial number of Catholics who supported Henry because the fundamental law of France said he was king. Henry immediately reached out to these Catholics, issuing the declaration of Saint-Cloud promising to preserve the Catholic religion in all its privileges and calling for a national religious council to help instruct him in matters of faith.

These steps did not mollify all Catholics. The Parlement of Paris, like Paris itself, remained staunchly Leaguer; only a small segment of the court moved to Tours and swore loyalty to the king. The Parlements of Bordeaux and Grenoble, in regions dominated by Protestant nobles, sided with Henry. The Parlement of Brittany, in a province devotedly Catholic, held for Henry, and did so precisely on legalistic

THE MAN WHO WOULD BE KING

Henry IV cheated constantly on both of his wives, the first of whom, Marguerite de Valois, he unceremoniously dumped after twenty-five years of (mutually unhappy) marriage because she failed to produce an heir. His mistresses are well known to all French schoolchildren. Among the most famous were Gabrielle d'Estrées and Henriette d'Entragues. The first bore him four children, including César de Vendôme, and the latter was involved with her relatives in more than one plot to overthrow him. Legend has Henry sleeping with peasant women (even dressing as a peasant himself, in order to court them *incognito*), burghers' wives and daughters, various courtesans, and a wide assortment of noble ladies. His account books constantly mention the presents given to his mistresses.

His lovers even interfered with Henry's political judgment. His contemporaries believed Henry besieged Chartres instead of Rouen in February 1591 because he wanted to restore Gabrielle d'Estrée's uncle to his governorship there. As always, however the king had political reasons, too. Because of its symbolic value as a center of the Marian cult and French Catholicism, one imagines with difficulty a cathedral other than Chartres which Henry

could have substituted for Reims. From 1609–1610, his infatuation with the fifteen-year-old Charlotte de Montmorency helped precipitate the European diplomatic crisis that led to his assassination. To keep Charlotte at Court, Henry forced his ineffectual nineteen-year-old cousin, Henry II of Condé, to marry her. Condé ran off to Brussels with his bride, there to seek Spanish protection. Henry was still incensed at this behavior in 1610, when he gathered an army to invade the Rhineland, in a dispute with the Spanish about the election of a new ruler in a minor German principality (Julich-Cleves). The Spaniards' role in harboring Charlotte made Henry more intransigent in his demands over Julich-Cleves.

Henry also gambled (and lost) to excess, leading to frequent admonitions from the dour Sully. Yet these vices did not anger his subjects; in fact, they provided one of the principal sources of his popularity. After Henry III, a king noted for his refined tastes, his scandalous Court, his sterility, his vacillation, a rough-and-ready Gascon like Henry IV was just what many people wanted. Henry IV's womanizing reassured those among his subjects who had objected to Henry III's bisexuality. When Henry IV and his second wife, Marie

grounds. The other provincial Parlements—Aix, Dijon, Rouen, Toulouse—sided with the League, but small, rump royalist courts sprang up.

The leader of the League—the murdered Guises' brother, Charles, duke of Mayenne—quickly sought to take advantage of Henry's weak position. Mayenne twice gave battle to the king, at Arques (21 September 1589) and Ivry (14 March 1590). Badly outnumbered both times (5 to 1 at Arques), Henry won the day with his superior disposition of infantry, artillery, and cavalry. In both victories, Henry, a real general and military leader (unlike so many royal "commanders"), himself led the decisive cavalry charges. After each victory, Henry tried to follow up, but Spanish armies relieved the siege of Paris (1590) and that of Rouen (1591).

Stalemate played into Henry's hands in one way. The League's "king," Henry's uncle, Charles, cardinal of Bourbon, whom the king held prisoner, died. The League now had no obvious candidate for the throne. Salic Law made Henry's infant Protestant cousin, Henry (II) of Condé, next in line, but the Pope had declared the prince

(CONTINUED)

de Médicis, produced a son (1601), they set off universal, genuine rejoicing in France: Louis was the first Dauphin born since 1545. Even Henry's gambling marked him as an ordinary gentleman of his time; his friends, too, lost large sums of money at the tables.

Henry had much of the soldier about him. He had spent many years campaigning, and living in dismal conditions. He also grew up as a noble (although titular king of Navarre), not as the heir to the throne of France, which gave him a very different frame of reference than his son would have. Indeed, when he once rebuked Louis that "he [Henry] had never behaved in so haughty a manner when a young boy," the young prince replied, "but you were not raised to be a King of France." Henry maintained a strong bond with many of the nobles who had supported him during the years in the wilderness, yet he also held out the hand of friendship and reconciliation to the defeated Leaguers. Brissac, the man who surrendered Paris to Henry in 1594, became a highly trusted lieutenant, and Henry gave governorships to members of the Guise family and the duke of Nevers. The only serious noble revolts against Henry came from among his old friends, like the duke of Bouillon, whose prin-

cipality of Sedan Henry captured in 1606. Bouillon suffered the humiliation of being dragged off to Paris, yet Henry put him back in charge of Sedan little more than two years later.

Henry's combination of personal style and genuine accomplishments endeared him to his subjects. In a country fed up with the preciousness of the Valois Court, his rough edged style found many admirers. In 1603, when he and the Court examined the unfinished Pont Neuf, Henry leapt across the unfinished section, despite a warning that several people had thus gone to their deaths. Henry replied that, "they were not a king, like he was." His subjects reveled to hear that the stuffy Spanish ambassador found the king on his knees, playing with the royal children. Henry raised his natural and legitimate children together and, scandal of scandal, even let them call him "papa." His restoration of order allowed a wide range of economic benefits: increased trade; reduced direct taxes; lower military spending. Henry even forgave all tax arrears dating from before 1598. Little wonder his subjects called him "good king Henry."

---

of Condé (Henry I) ineligible for the throne at the same time he excluded Henry of Navarre.[4] The other members of the Condé line—Francis, prince of Conti; and Charles, cardinal of Vendôme (after 1590 of Bourbon)—supported Henry IV, even though they held to the Catholic faith. The last survivor of the Montpensier line, Henry, duke of Montpensier, also supported the king.

When Mayenne, as lieutenant–general of the kingdom, convoked an Estates General in 1593 to elect a Catholic king, he faced the difficulty of finding a candidate acceptable to public opinion, which strongly opposed election of a foreigner. The response of chancellor Cheverny, a long-time client of the Guise family, illustrated their fundamental problem:

> [I received] every day very great offers of authority and friendship from M. de Mayenne and from all those of his party, to attract me to their side, with the obligation that I have to the house of Lorraine [Guise], all of whose

princes have always given me the honor of liking me, above all the great Cardinal of Lorraine, who brought me into the royal palace, and honored me with the main establishments I obtained after I came to the Court; but, despite all these things, my conscience, my honor, and my oath to the true interest and conservation of this monarchy, brought and obliged me to the best resolution, which was to serve the king whom God had given me for master by true and legitimate succession.[5]

Mayenne's chief ally, Philip II of Spain, wanted the Estates to elect Mayenne's nephew, Charles, duke of Guise, so that Philip's daughter Isabelle (granddaughter of Henry II), could marry him. Mayenne harbored royal ambitions, so he initially opposed the Spanish plan. The delay played into Henry's hands. When eight of Henry's supporters met with a committee from the Estates in April 1593, they dropped a bombshell: he was ready to convert again to Catholicism. Three months later, Henry abjured Protestantism, at the richly symbolic basilica of Saint-Denis.

The governors of the main League towns decided to take advantage of this opportunity to change sides—for a price, of course. The king purchased the surrender of Lyon, Amiens, Tours, Orléans, Rouen, and, in March 1594, of Paris itself, sold by the duke of Brissac for 500,000 *livres*. Henry soon bought off his major noble opponents, promising millions to Mayenne, Mercoeur (who surrendered Brittany in 1598), Nevers, and others. Henry understood that these massive bribes, expensive though they were, were much cheaper than fighting. Paying the money slowly kept the former Leaguer chiefs beholden to him. Nevers received nearly 80,000 *livres* per year and Mayenne even more, until his death in 1611.

Henry IV had taken over a state in disrepair. Although its institutions functioned remarkably well in the 1590s, given the political circumstances, the need for reform was beyond question. The Assembly of Notables he convened at Rouen in 1596 disagreed somewhat with him about the precise measures to enact, but they agreed on the problems: marauding troops, unpaid royal debts and officers, tyrannical governors. Henry followed much of their advice. He reduced the size of the army, particularly after the surrender of Brittany and the Peace of Vervins (1598), ending hostilities with Spain. In Brittany alone, between 1597 and 1599, military spending dropped from 1.9 million to under 100,000 *livres*. Henry rearranged the governors, moving Guise from Champagne to Provence and shifting Condé from Picardy to Burgundy, once again carefully following the old strategy of decoupling the institutional authority of great aristocrats from their landed power base. The 1601 treason trial and execution of his old comrade-in-arms, Marshal Biron, served as an example to others that Henry would brook no further disobedience. Henry brought the grandees sufficiently to heel that when he died in 1610, the country did not collapse into civil war.

Henry achieved three remarkable goals in the spring of 1598: he signed the Treaty of Vervins with Spain; he ended the civil war; and he issued the Edict of Nantes. The Edict legalized the practice of Protestantism but kept some of the usual restrictions, such as banning Protestantism from Paris. Henry showed tolerance to others as well. Following the practice of Henry III, he allowed Jews to settle again in

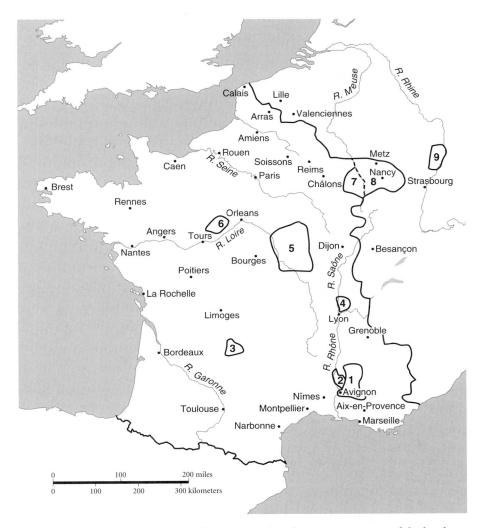

*Early seventeenth-century France. The numbered enclaves were not part of the legal
kingdom of France; number 1 (Avignon and the Comtat), for example, belonged to
the Pope.*

France. The immigrant Portuguese *Marrano* community in France increased rapidly
after the Portuguese Inquisition revived in 1579. From Montpellier, Bayonne, and
Saint-Jean-de-Luz, up north to Nantes, Rouen, and Paris, new Sephardic Jewish communities sprang up. In eastern France, Henry regularized the situation of the thriving community of Jews at Metz in 1595; henceforth, they could openly practice
Judaism. By the end of the seventeenth century Glückel of Hameln would write of
Metz's large Jewish suburb, of its synagogue and cemetery. Truly, Henry IV practiced
a toleration rare in his time.

The "Portuguese" of Nantes

In the early 1590s, a new wave of immigrants entered into the upper part of the suburb of Nantes known as the Fosse. The tax roll of 1592–1593, for the parish of Saint-Nicolas, offers the first indication of their presence. The roll listed Anthoinne Diaz, Anthoinne Rodriguez, Francisco Henri, and Manuel Mendez, all noted as "Portuguese." Their next-door neighbors included Manuel Mello, a doctor; Marie de Mirande; Simon de Victoria; and Pierre Rodriguez and his mother-in-law—all of them "Portuguese," although the roll does not mark them as such. A few streets away lived Manuel Rodriguez, "Portuguese," Anthoinne de Mirande, and the widow of Alonso de Aragon. Another Iberian concentration included Sebastien de Laringaga (from Bilbao), the widow of Jan de Villesquez, and Pedro de Gastara, assessed for the considerable sum of 20 *écus*.

These isolated names provide tantalizing evidence of the Jewish presence at Nantes in 1592. Many of these "Portuguese" sought naturalization in France beginning in the late 1590s. Manuel Mello, the doctor, informed the royal court that he taught at the University of Nantes, and that he came from "Villanicose" in Portugal. Pierre Rodriguez, his wife and niece; Gabriel Rodriguez, and his wife (surnamed Lopez); Manuel Rodriguez d'Espinoze; and Francisco Lopez and his wife all claimed to have come from Lisbon and to have lived in Nantes for between three and eight years (this in 1597 or 1598): the Chamber of Accounts duly registered their letters, and those of ten families in all, making them French citizens.

The community of Jews continued to grow; a steady trickle of "Portuguese" sought naturalization: Emmanuel Mendez d'Acosta, from Lisbon, in 1599; Balthazar Peires Voure and his wife, in 1600; Durot d'Aranjo and his wife (1606); Francisque Dalmeide and his wife (1607); Gaspard Gomez, doctor at the faculty of medicine of the University of Nantes, and his wife, Helenne Mendez (1608); André Botello, his wife Felipes Rodriguez, and their son, Emmanuel; along with Diego Lopes de Ivas, his wife Agnes; and Jan Rodriguez and his wife and daughter (Lienor), all in 1610. Every one of these people told the Chamberthat they lived in Nantes. This Jewish community created their own little quarter; they even suffered an anti-Jewish riot in 1636, which they seemed to have quelled by themselves, in part by stretching a giant chain across their main street, to prevent crowds from marching through.[6]

The Origins of the State Bureaucracy

Royal virtue seems most to consist of justice.

Montaigne, "Of Coaches"

Henry IV and Sully took over a desperate situation, but the underlying strength of the state apparatus should not be underestimated. French kings had gradually constructed the model early modern European state. They built on medieval foundations, but the changes of the sixteenth century produced an institutional structure that bore little resemblance to its ancient forebears. The great change took root primarily in the second half of the fifteenth century.

Royal apologists working for kings from Louis XI onward increasingly tried to argue that the public good, a phrase traditionally connected to legitimate government, and the king's good meant essentially the same thing. Kings and their officials sought to redefine kingship along the lines spelled out by theorists such as Jean Bodin. He maintained that the sovereign king made the law, rather than being a judge who *discovered* law made by God. That said, the king could only make *public* law; as the government admitted to the Estates General of 1561, "the king cannot justly infringe on the conventions of men that conform to customary law (*droit*)." In matters of private property, the king's judges "discovered" the application of such customary laws and then enforced what was, in essence, the community's decision.

In some cases, such as inheritance or property, customary law had clear jurisdiction, but the lines were not always so well drawn. Relying on an ordinance issued by Charles VII in 1452, Francis I sought to clear up that ambiguity by creating a commission of royal officials and local notables to codify and write down each bailiwick's customary laws.[7] Armed with the knowledge of the gaps in such law, Francis issued more laws than all of his predecessors combined. He provided a visual affirmation of the king's new, higher status when he altered the immemorial order of procession in royal entry ceremonies. He decreed that henceforth, the pageants would end with the progression "France," the king, God, rather than with "France" interposed between its king and the divinity. For the next two hundred seventy years, the king and his supporters would try to get French people to accept the new hierarchy of God–King–France.

Francis I modified heavily two of the three main elements of his state: the judiciary and the financial system. He greatly expanded the power of the seven royal Parlements, which had to register all edicts and ordinances before they could become law.[8] This network of Parlements gave the king an important tool for the expansion of royal power and authority; their judges provided him with an essential ally in provincial politics, yet also offered local elites protection of their interest. Because it could take a month or more for a letter to go from Paris to a distant provincial court, remonstrances could (and did) delay implementation of royal edicts for years on end. Judges would often send remonstrances to the king, suggesting modification of an edict, or even its rescission.[9] If the king insisted on the original edict, he would send back *lettres de jussion*, ordering the Parlement to end its opposition and register the edict. The Parlements often responded with still more remonstrances, leading to further delays. The king could circumvent this process for about 40 percent of France by going himself to the Parlement of Paris, in a ceremony known as a *lit de justice* (bed of justice). Because its authority emanated from the king, in his presence the Parlement had no right to oppose his will. The need to promulgate financial edicts of dubious legality led Francis I to conduct several *lits de justice* to force registration of unpopular decisions. Those registrations, however, had force only in the jurisdiction of the Parlement of Paris; in the jurisdiction of the other parlements, only registration in that court made the edict legal.

The extremely important edict of Villers-Cotteret (1539) removed many cases from ecclesiastical courts, ordered review of all death sentences by a parlement, and mandated the use of the vernacular (in theory, French), rather than Latin (as at the Parlement of Toulouse) in royal courts. The king could even change the calendar (as he did in 1564), making the first day of the year January 1st, rather than Easter. Fittingly, local governments did not always go along. The town council of Poitiers kept their old system, in which 25 March was the first day of the year, long after the king's edict. In 1582, Henry III adopted Pope Gregory XIII's new calendar, but he failed to impress Montaigne:

> Two or three years ago, they cut ten days from the year in France. How many changes should have followed that reform! It was properly to remake at a stroke the skies and the earth. Yet nonetheless, nothing moved from its place: my neighbors found the time for their sowing, their harvests, the right days for their markets, the harmful and proper days at precisely the same points to which they had been assigned from time immemorial.[10]

The king similarly tried to introduce order and regularity into his finances. Francis I created (1523) a distinction between the king's personal income, handled through the new private treasurer, and the income of the state, handled by a newly created Central Treasurer.[11] Francis stopped the practice of referring to tax revenue as "extraordinary" income and issued annuities guaranteed by the tax revenues of the city of Paris, the *rentes sur l'Hôtel de Ville de Paris*, which remained a central credit mechanism of the monarchy for the next two hundred seventy-five years. He institutionalized the hitherto anarchic sale of royal offices. Henceforth, with rare exceptions (such as First Presidents of Parlements), the king sold all royal judicial and financial offices. This "villainous" practice elicited universal opprobrium, yet it paralleled the long-standing relationship between public authority and private property that went back to Clovis's time. Everyone recognized that public officials needed protection from arbitrary interference, especially interference from the state itself. Sixteenth-century French society knew no better way to preserve such independence than property rights, whose protection lay in the realm of inalterable custom. Sale of offices also enabled the king to get ready access to the cash of his richer urban subjects.

The second major shift occurred in the 1540s and early 1550s, when the king firmly established the permanent regional administration based on the *généralités* (regional financial districts), and *élections* (local districts) that lasted until the Revolution.[12] Brittany, Burgundy, Dauphiné, most of Guyenne and the Pyrenees, Languedoc, and Provence had provincial estates that voted, apportioned, and collected taxes, while Normandy had both provincial estates and *élections*. This patchwork of different tax systems made a great deal of sense, because the king always needed the cooperation of local elites to obtain money. Elites cared particularly about the form of taxation. Provinces with estates, dominated by rural landlords, preferred indirect taxes, such as the Breton wine taxes or the Burgundian salt duties, rather than direct taxes, paid more heavily by the peasantry. Local conditions even dictated the choice of taxable product: Bretons had no tax on salt, which they produced, and heavy duties on wine, which they did not.[13] To the extent possible, the royal government sought to tailor the tax system to local sensibilities, to make collection easier.

Henry III carried out the third major change when he sold staggering quantities of royal financial offices in the mid 1580s. Henry created new jurisdictional units, at both the regional and local levels, and sold thousands of offices in existing jurisdictions. France had fewer than twenty-five treasurers-general to oversee tax collections

The Tree of State, 1579. This "tree" shows the theoretical lines of authority within the French state. Its virtually impenetrable labyrinth accurately reflects contemporary views of the needless complexity of the emerging state administration.

in 1500, but nearly two hundred of them by 1586; Louis XIII would have more than six hundred fifty. The *élus*, chief local tax oversight officials and tax court judges, increased from about one hundred under Francis I to more than one thousand by 1589. Why? Well, Henry III made 2.5 million *livres* selling offices of *élu* in 1586.

The unprecedented increase in the size of the royal administration created a qualitatively different state. Francis I, for all his legislative activity, had a tiny administrative apparatus; entire provinces of the kingdom could have fewer than a dozen royal officials. Henry III permanently altered that situation; after the 1580s, the king had ten, twenty or more financial and judicial officials in every substantial town.[14] Moreover, the government's heavy forced loans on royal officials in the 1570s gave them a powerful personal incentive in the financial well-being of the state. Given the widespread purchase of tax-collecting offices by mercantile families, the new borrowing techniques, combined with the traditional annuities guaranteed by the municipalities of Paris, Rouen, and Lyon, made the ruling elites of the towns staunch partisans of the state: the merchants dominated the tax system, the lawyers the judicial one.

The Estates Generals of 1561 and 1576, and the Assembly of Notables at Moulins in 1566 all unsuccessfully supported an end to venality and a reduction in the number of officers to the level of Louis XII's time. Although the royal government did not (or could not) act on that piece of advice, it did follow other recommendations. The king issued great reforming ordinances at Orléans (1561), Moulins (1566), and Blois (1579), which recodified a wide range of administrative practices, in both legal and financial matters. In addition to codifying the Parlements' right of remonstrance, the Edict of Moulins removed legal civil jurisdiction from town councils and gave it to local royal courts. This change formed part of a royal effort to establish clearer lines of authority in the provinces.

This royal offensive against local courts explains the primordial concern demonstrated by the nobility at the Estates Generals of 1560, 1561, and 1576 to protect the integrity of seigneurial courts and to limit severely the ability of royal officials, both judges and sergeants, to interfere in the lands under the jurisdiction of a high justiciar. Yet the Crown also created new local institutions. Many towns, like Nantes (1565) got an elected town council and mayor, and merchants received special courts to try commercial cases involving one merchant against another. An ordinance even spelled out the conditions of use of traveling investigators, taken from the masters of requests of the king's household. These investigators later evolved into the most important officials of the provincial administration, the intendants. France's reputation as a statist country, the phenomenon the French call *dirigisme*, has its origin in this late sixteenth-century expansion of the state and in the creation of strong congruencies between the interests of the state and those of the mercantile elite.[15]

The Godfathers: Henry IV and Sully

Your best privilege is to be in the good graces of your king.

> Henry IV to the town government of Châlons-sur-Marne,
> requesting renewal of their privileges in 1595

Henry IV and his able group of ministers, led by chancellor Pomponne de Bellièvre, superintendent of finances Sully, and the longtime royal counselors Pierre Jeannin and Nicolas de Villeroy, thus inherited the framework for a more interventionist state. The wonders of peace, and the strong direction of Henry and his ministers, enabled this state to bring a remarkable degree of order to France in an astonishingly short time. Peasants who had refused to pay their direct taxes in the 1590s—shortfalls remained at 15–20 percent even in 1597 or 1598—began to pay. Henry generously forgave all arrears for years prior to 1598, which helped make collection of current taxes much easier. Governmental administration became a matter of routine, a situation unthinkable in the France of the Wars of Religion.

The two most powerful figures in Henry's administration, Bellièvre and Sully, stood for different interpretations of how to use this state. Bellièvre believed in moderation and in the sort of judicial state justified by chancellor de l'Hôpital forty years before, but Sully stood for something rather different. Like Henry, he was a soldier who liked discipline, regularity, simplicity, and directness. Henry placed Sully in charge of a wide range of governmental activities, which included royal buildings, the artillery, roads and bridges, and, most importantly, finances. Sully became proverbial for the economy and effectiveness of his administration. Revenues quickly rose to about 30 million *livres*. Miracle of miracles, for the only time in its history, the royal government ran a surplus. He managed to accumulate a treasure of 15 million *livres* in the Bastille, 5 million of it in bullion.

Sully did not innovate; one searches in vain for new ideas in his efforts to balance the books. He created the usual *Chambre de Justice* (investigating commission), which checked into the peculations of royal officials and tax farmers, scaring many financial officers into relative honesty. He re-leased the main tax farms, creating (or re-creating) general farms for the salt tax monopolies, the royal demesne, the transit duties, and the sales and production taxes. In a sharp departure from earlier practice, he leased these farms to *French* financiers, not Italians. The financial center of France thus shifted from Lyon to Paris, a development of fundamental importance in the evolution of the country. This shift paralleled the move of the economic center of Europe from the Mediterranean to the North Sea. Indirect tax revenues climbed steadily under Sully, allowing the state to cut direct taxes. Lower direct taxes reduced capital outflow from agriculture, and increased investment in agriculture helped to produce a much healthier economy.

Sully provides an early archetype of the effective officials of the seventeenth-century state. He, like Louis XIV's minister Jean-Baptiste Colbert, took concerted action on given problems because he held multiple offices. As superintendent of finances, Sully provided himself, as supervisor of roads, with the necessary funds to improve roads and bridges. He spent more money on the main roads and bridges than any other minister prior to the mid eighteenth century. He also approved money for new artillery and restoration of dilapidated fortresses, both of which he oversaw as grand master.

Sully put the state's finances on the soundest foundation they would ever have. He started with an efficient bankruptcy, which repudiated some dubious debts and cut the interest rates on others. Royal officers held most of this debt. Sully and Henry, over the strenuous objection of Bellièvre, concocted a scheme to mollify them, the infamous *paulette*, an annual payment of 1/60th of the value of a venal office that guaranteed the office's status as hereditary property.[16] The government got a steady income of close to 2 million *livres* from the annual payments, and obtained an even greater financial bonus from the reduced rate of interest it paid to borrow money by means of sale of new offices.[17] People clamored to buy offices, now a secure investment, with the result that prices often doubled or tripled in the next twenty years. Bellièvre rightly warned that, while the king would receive new income, he would also lose control of his officials, who would become "officers of their purses" rather than officers of the king. Sully's triumph proved a decisive step in the triumph of the financial state over the judicial one. In the 1640s, however, Bellièvre's premonitions about loss of control over officers proved to be right.

Sully streamlined the state in every direction. He and Henry cut expenses of the royal Court by 60 percent. They reduced the pensions of the nobility, paid off Henry's foreign debts, and even carried out large-scale repurchases of alienated royal demesnes and tax revenues. Sully shunted off royal expenses onto the budgets of the major towns or provincial estates, a practice amplified greatly in the late seventeenth and throughout the eighteenth century. He and Henry made no efforts to reform the basic structure of government. Henry breathed life into dormant existing institutions and relied on precisely the same governing elites who had long run the country. Many great nobles served Henry with loyalty and effectiveness. High-ranking Protestants like Sully and marshal Lesdiguières allayed Huguenot suspicions of the lapsed king.

THE BLUEPRINT: BRISSAC'S EULOGY FOR HENRY IV

Sixteenth-century *collèges* took great pains to teach their students the core elements of a Classical education, not only Latin but grammar, rhetoric, and eloquence. Certain families prided themselves on a tradition of public speaking. The Brissac family obtained such a reputation at the Estates Generals of 1576–1577, when Artus de Brissac, marshal of France, gave a noted speech on behalf of Henry III. Artus's nephew, Charles de Cossé-Brissac, himself marshal of France, gave a famous eulogy for Henry IV, delivered to the 1610 meeting of the Estates of Brittany. Brissac laid out a remarkably clear statement of what the government wanted people to think, and where France should go:

> For if the Great Henry is dead, if the King, if the Father, if the liberator of France has been taken from us, if my good Master and yours is kidnapped from us, where are the words that can complain of it, where are the tears worthy of being shed before his tomb, where are the signs of mourning sufficient to express the bitterness of our misfortune.
>
> The Lightning Bolt of Rebels, the Salvation of the French, the Terror and the Admiration of Foreigners, the mirror of generosity and clem-

ency, the tamer of nations in France and even in the Alps. . . . The moderator of Europe has disappeared from among us. Is it not thus for us now to act? . . . We must serve the King and France. We must stifle at their birth these monstrous Harpies, these abominable worms who wish to gnaw on the entrails of this State and with a complete inhumanity act against the child and the Mother, having nothing in their heart but to destroy the Patrie . . . [the sovereign justice of the king] gives the means to Pastors to tend to their flocks, to judges to keep the balance of rightness and equity, to Gentlemen to live with authority over their vassals and to attain honors . . . by means of the rewards of their Princes, to cities to embellish and police themselves, and to the People to enrich themselves, in short for each to achieve his salvation and success in his affairs without any fear.

> The duty and the good of France are the only limits to the will of their Majesties [Louis XIII and Marie de Médicis]. It is reasonable that you have the same ones, and that your zeal, ardent in fidelity, comfort their right intention. They live and act only for this Kingdom and for you, you are obliged to live and to breathe only for them and for the State.[18]

On 14 May 1610, François Ravaillac, a fanatic Catholic, stabbed the king as he traveled through a narrow Parisian street in his coach. No one has ever been able to prove the existence of a conspiracy behind the deed, despite the suspicions against certain powerful nobles. All over France, people reacted with anguish at the loss of the beloved king.

MARIE DE MÉDICIS AND LOUIS XIII

. . . my first opinion is to have the said princess [Marie] served and assisted by ladies and servants of our nation, both for my relief and contentment and because I can assure myself that she will be bettered served.[19]

Henry IV, 1601

CHRONOLOGY	1614–1632
1614	Estates General meets in Paris (October)
1615	Marriage of Louis XIII and Anne of Austria
1617	Assassination of Concini; war breaks out with Protestants
1620	Marie de Médicis defeated; Catholicism restored in Béarn
1621–1622	Failed siege of Montauban; Montpellier taken
1624	Richelieu rejoins the royal council
1626	Assembly of Notables leads to reforms, notably Code Michau (1629); Chalais conspiracy; Michel de Marillac given the Seals
1627–1628	Siege and capture of La Rochelle
1629	Grace of Alès eliminates Protestant right to fortified towns (June)
1629–1630	Mantuan War
1630	Day of the Dupes (10–11 November)
1632	Deaths of Michel and Louis de Marillac and of d'Effiat

Henry's death led to a Regency headed by his wife, Marie de Médicis. After firing Sully, with whom she had long had an acrimonious relationship, Marie kept the other ministers and continued to follow Henry's basic policies until 1614. Relying on the sound revenue base and large treasure created by Sully, Marie bought off potential opponents. Pensions jumped from 3.74 million *livres* in 1609 to an average of 6.5 million a year between 1611 and 1614. Marie also spent the 5 million *livres* in cash that Sully had stored away. The great aristocrats elbowed their way to the trough, with Condé (300,000 in cash) and Marguerite de Valois (250,000) at the front of the line.

WOMEN AND POWER: THE "EVIL" FOREIGN QUEENS

Henry II and Henry IV each married women from the Medici family of Florence. Catherine de Médicis differed from her distant cousin, Marie, in that she had a French mother and a grandmother who belonged to the Bourbon branch of the royal family. The two women both acted as Regents, Catherine from 1560–1564 and Marie from 1610–1614, and each essentially ran the French government on behalf of teenaged sons. Marie's daughter-in-law, Anne of Austria, would play a similar role in the 1640s and 1650s. In the deceptive light of hindsight, these Regencies seem natural, but at the time that Catherine became Regent, as one deputy put it, the principle had long been established that "as women are incapable of the Crown of France by the Salic Law, so too are they incapable of having the government of France, and . . . that ever since Saint Louis renewed the Salic Law they had never received the king's mother to administer the kingdom," as Saint Louis's own mother, Blanche of Castile, had done starting in 1228.[20]

Chancellor de l'Hôpital offered a clear summary of male thinking about female Regents in his testament, when discussing Catherine's seizure of power in 1560–1561:

> The faction that dominated the government during the reign of Francis could not stand the fact that others would be managing the state affairs. . . . they provoked the king of Navarre and other princes (who complained that their power and authority were diminished by that of a mere mother) to take up arms under the pretext of religion.[21]

The attitude here attributed to Antoine de Bourbon and other nobles perhaps reflected their frustration at the considerable impor-

tance of women in the politics of their day. Most observers felt that Catherine dominated the royal government throughout the 1560s and most of the 1570s; they similarly believed Jeanne d'Albret, Antoine's wife, to be the real brains behind the Huguenot forces.

Catherine de Médicis and, to a lesser degree, Marie de Médicis provide classic examples of the "evil" foreign Queen. Catherine had to overcome opposition to the idea of a woman running the state. Her supporters cited the fine qualities and virtues of "this excellent princess, joined to a prudence that surpasses human capacity," and suggested that Henry II himself had left her "the government of his kingdom and of all the affairs of state [because he] knows better than any other her capacity and sufficiency." Yet even the pro-Catherine forces had to address the underlying misogynist bias of their contemporaries. They suggested that God had given her "invincible virtues that by the order of nature the Divine Majesty is accustomed to refuse to this weak feminine sex." Others felt Catherine would take better care of her son's interest than anyone else, because she was his mother, an interesting example of empowerment through gender stereotype.

The same arguments resurfaced in 1610. Marie, like Catherine, had to face charges of Italian Machiavellianism and of female incapacity, and like Catherine, Marie benefitted from the dead king's publicly expressed desire to leave her in control. Marie had an even stronger case than Catherine in this regard, because just days before his assassination Henry publicly named her as acting Regent during his projected absence on military campaign. Marie also faced fewer sexual innuendoes than her predecessor. Contemporary

Two factors created a dangerous situation in 1614. First, the tap ran dry: pensions and gifts dropped from 6.7 million in 1614 to 3.9 million *livres* in 1615. Second, Marie announced a dual marriage for Louis XIII and his sister Elisabeth. He would marry Anne of Austria, oldest daughter of the King of Spain, and she would

---

(CONTINUED)

accounts accused Catherine of using attractive women to seduce, spy on, and even poison her political opponents.

Marie de Médicis had her disadvantages. Unlike Catherine, she did not speak or write French properly. The shock of Henry IV's death gave Marie a short respite, as did the exceptionally strong state Henry had left her. Although long-standing criticism of Marie's dilapidation of Sully's treasure has some merit, she had little choice but to buy loyalty. Moreover, she spent large sums paying off France's foreign allies, such as the Dutch (500,000) and James I of England (300,000), to preserve France's international position.

Historical memory has treated the two queens in quite different ways. Protestant accounts of the Saint Bartholomew's Day Massacre invariably made Catherine its mastermind; even the great *History of France*, edited by Ernst Lavisse, repeats the charge that she ordered the murder of Coligny. She becomes in his text, and in generations of French schoolbooks (one of which Lavisse himself wrote), the wily, sneaky Italian, the perennial evil foreign queen. Marie gets some criticism for squandering Sully's treasure and for her inveterate scheming, but her legacy as a patroness of the arts defines her place in the collective memory.

Marie patronized the leading architect of her time, Salomon de Brosse, who built her the Luxembourg Palace, which today houses the French Senate. Generations of Parisian children have spent their Sundays sailing little rented boats on the waters of its reflecting pool. Nor is that happy association the only one that Marie left behind. She commissioned Peter Paul Rubens to execute a stunning series

of portraits telling the history of her life. In what is France's most remarkable room dedicated to the image of one person, today they provide visitors to the Louvre with an overwhelming iconographic image of a queen perpetually surrounded by the Virtues, saving France from the clutches of anarchy. Marie's political shenanigans are now long forgotten, but the towering earthly goddess created by Rubens remains forever a part of the collective memory of art lovers the world over.

P. P. Rubens, c. 1614. Henry IV leaves the governance of France to Marie de Médicis. Marie sought to use this painting, and the others in the series Rubens created, to create effective propaganda for her rule, and to leave posterity a positive image of her efforts.

SOURCE: © Archivo Iconografico, S.A./Corbis.

---

marry the *infante*, Philip, heir to the Spanish throne. The prince of Condé, senior Prince of the Blood, Louis's half-brother, César de Vendôme, and other aristocrats, violently opposed these marriages.[22] They demanded a larger share of power in the government and insisted that Marie call an Estates General. Marie, a far shrewder politician than the young Condé, turned the princes' demand for an Estates General into a personal triumph. At the assembly, she outmaneuvered them and obtained support for many of her policies. The marriages took place in 1615, after an emotional parting between Louis and his beloved sister Elisabeth at the Bidossa river (on the Spanish frontier). The marriage provided the fourteen-year-old couple with an immediate trauma; Louis found himself impotent on the wedding night and refused to try again for four more years. This personal problem placed severe strains on Franco–Spanish relations.

Marie's government stumbled along for three more years, becoming steadily more embroiled in a sort of low-grade civil war against the high nobility, led by Condé and some of the Protestants. Much as Henry IV had feared, everyone detested Marie's Italian favorites—Concino Concini (Marshal d'Ancre) and his wife, Leonora Galigai, Marie's childhood friend. The situation turned from bad to worse in 1616, when in September, Marie arrested Condé, whose noble allies fled to their provincial strongholds. In 1616, she dismissed Henry IV's old counselors, Villeroy and Jeannin, disgraced chancellor Brulart, and called into the royal council some new men, most prominent among them (in hindsight, although not at the time) Armand du Plessis, bishop of Luçon, later cardinal of Richelieu, her strong ally in the Devout faction.

Concini seemed triumphant, but he had made a dangerous enemy: Louis XIII. The king detested the "Italian upstart," whom he felt had insulted his honor, once even having the temerity to keep his hat on in the king's presence. The king, like his subjects, grew progressively unhappier with his mother's friends. A large Parisian crowd stormed Concini's private residence, destroying paintings of he and his wife and throwing a portrait of Marie into the street. They did not harm a picture of the young king, who, when informed of the riot, told his companions, "Didn't you hear clearly what I told you?"[23]

The king and a small group of friends plotted Concini's fall. On 24 April 1617, acting with Louis's acquiescence, the captain of the king's guard, Louis de l'Hôpital de Vitry, assassinated Concini in the courtyard of the Louvre. Louis immediately dismissed the new ministers, and brought back Villeroy, Jeannin, and Brulart. Vitry replaced Concini as a marshal of France, while Charles d'Albert, another of the plotters and Louis's favorite, became duke of Luynes and, later, constable. Parisians stormed the church holding Concini's body, tore it to pieces, and fed the pieces to the dogs. The Parlement of Paris condemned his wife to death for witchcraft and had her beheaded on the place de Grève in July.

Marie went into exile at the château of Blois. The next ten years brought renewed civil war and governmental instability. Louis could not find the ministers he wanted, and the old councillors (Villeroy, Jeannin) gradually died off. The noble rebels of 1617 gave up their arms as soon as they heard the news of Concini's fall, but the Huguenots continued to resist the government. Louis had problems, too, with his own mother; in February 1619, Marie squeezed her ample frame through a narrow window at Blois and bravely clambered down a swaying ladder to freedom. She escaped to Angoulême and raised an army to rescue her son from his favorite Luynes. Louis slowly marched an army toward her. He gladly accepted her offer of a truce, yet it lasted only a few months. This time Louis marched in earnest, routing the rebels in Normandy and defeating Marie's army at Ponts-de-Cé in Anjou.

The Last War of Religion, 1617–1629

For three years I have put up with this contempt. But I see that my presence is needed in Béarn, and I will set out to assure the repose of the province.[24]

Louis XIII, 1620

Once Louis had defeated his mother and her allies, he could turn to a more pressing problem: the Huguenots. He had several times commanded the provincial authorities of Protestant Béarn, which he ruled as king of Navarre, to allow once again the practice of Catholicism. They had temporized for years, claiming to be impotent in the face of local resistance. Louis expected his subjects to obey him. Taking advantage of the little army he had in Anjou, he marched directly to Béarn in order, as he wrote to the governor and the Parlement, "to firm up your weakness." He marched into the capital, Pau; reestablished Catholic worship in its cathedral; seized the key fortress of Navarreins; replaced wavering local officials, often with Catholics; and left.

This incident touched off the last of the full-scale Wars of Religion, though sporadic hostilities had begun in 1617, with the resumption of piracy by the Protestants of La Rochelle. After the conquest of Béarn, the Huguenots assembled in La Rochelle, seeking redress of grievances from the king. They created eight Huguenot regions, each under the orders of what was, in essence, a military governor. In the summer of 1621, Louis marched an army into the Protestant heartland. His troops cowed many cities into surrender; those that resisted, they stormed, putting the inhabitants to the sword. The army came up short only against the great fortress of Montauban. As was usually the case in long sieges (this one lasted more than three months), the besieging army fell victim to disease, which carried off the Keeper of the Seals, Guillaume du Vair, and Luynes.

The 1622 peace left the Protestant towns in possession of only two big citadels, La Rochelle and Montauban, and some minor towns in the Cévennes. Fighting resumed again in 1625, when the Huguenot leaders, the brother dukes of Rohan and Soubise, began to rearm the southwestern towns. In 1627, Louis laid siege to La Rochelle to put an end to Protestant independence once and for all. The Rochelais received reinforcements from England in July 1627, but Louis's forces defeated the English, led by the duke of Buckingham, whom Louis personally detested because of Buckingham's efforts to woo Anne of Austria. After a brutal siege lasting more than a year, the town surrendered, its starving population yielding unconditionally to their king. Richelieu himself said the Mass of reconsecration in the cathedral, but Louis allowed Protestant worship to continue.

The Grace of Alès (1629) allowed Huguenots freedom of worship in traditional areas, but permanently removed their right to fortifications. Henceforth, French Protestants would be completely at the mercy of their king. The Protestants could no longer pose a political threat to the monarchy, because they had lost their strongholds. The capture of La Rochelle made it impossible for Protestant powers, such as England, to interfere in internal French affairs. Louis XIII opened the way for the state to enforce religious uniformity in France, although he himself did not do so. His son, as we shall see, took a different approach.

Good Frenchmen and Devouts

Let your actions henceforth make known to all that I have well judged your virtues and well augured your merits, and you will acquire an immortal glory, you will acquire the graces and favors of this great King who illuminates you now with the splendor of his face, and whom the Heavens have destined for the felicity of our century.[25]

Guillaume du Vair, Keeper of the Seals, speaking to the Parlement of
Toulouse, 1621

The siege of La Rochelle had the united support of Louis XIII's ministers; earlier in the 1620s such unanimity had been sadly lacking. Luynes's death at Montauban in 1621 had exacerbated factional fighting in the king's council. Louis XIII liked to make his own final decisions, but he preferred to have others do the groundwork and make his choice as simple as possible. In the early 1620s, he listened to a wide range of advisors, ranging from his mother and the prince of Condé, to new council members such as Claude Bullion and Henri de Schomberg, to revived old hands like chancellor Sillery de Brulart and his son, Pierre Brulart, marquis of Puisieux, now the foreign minister. Schomberg and Condé lost royal confidence in 1622: the former due to his fiscal incompetence, a dangerous characteristic in the superintendent of finances, the latter because Louis disagreed with his militant anti-Huguenot policy.

Between 1622 and 1626, Louis regularly restructured his council. In 1624, following his mother's advice, Louis brought back one of the disgraced ministers of 1617, her old ally Armand du Plessis, cardinal of Richelieu since 1622. The king also brought in two other key figures—Michel de Marillac, to whom he gave the Seals in 1626; and Antoine Coiffier de Ruzé, marquis d'Effiat, who took over direction of finances when Marillac got the Seals.

Louis now had a strong team of advisors, led by Richelieu, Marillac, and Marie de Médicis, all of them apparently deeply attached to the Devout party. The ministry of the years from 1624–1630 often gets subsumed into the later personal dominance of Richelieu, but the Cardinal by no means acted alone in these early years. Marie still had great influence over her son, and Marillac and d'Effiat were exceptionally capable men. D'Effiat managed the Assembly of Notables of 1626, which called for financial and judicial reforms in the state. D'Effiat, acting in a climate that required desperate measures, took them. He sold ever more new offices; stepped up the sale of liens on tax revenues (sold to royal officers), which doubled the direct tax burden; raised the salt tax; and created new indirect taxes.[26] In the early 1630s, experienced officials, growing increasingly suspicious of these dubious procedures, began to sell off their offices in record numbers. Their prescience saved their purses. In 1634, the king converted the liens sold to officers into ordinary annuities, cutting his interest bill by 10 million *livres* a year. He saved money, but alienated many of his officers, which helped lead to the collapse of effective administration in the late 1630s.

The urgent need for money came from two directions. First, the king needed money to fight the Protestants: the siege of La Rochelle alone cost at least 40 million *livres*. Second, the king needed money for the impending conflict with Spain. This second conflict divided Louis's council into two factions, which contemporaries and historians ever after have called the Good Frenchmen and the Devouts. Cardinal Richelieu headed the first faction, Marie de Médicis, his original patroness, the second. The two sides agreed on the La Rochelle campaign, as both parties wanted to crush the Huguenots for religious reasons. The Good Frenchmen also had political motivations. The council acted with a firm consensus until the fall of La Rochelle (October 1628).

In December 1628, the French duke of Nevers inherited the Italian duchy of Mantua. The King of Spain, his cousin the Holy Roman Emperor, and the duke of Savoy all opposed Nevers' claim; they sent troops to besiege his main fortress, Casale. Louis led an army into Savoy (in winter, a most unusual move in that period), storming the Savoyard positions at the Susa pass and forcing the Spaniards to withdraw from Casale. Louis's brother, Gaston, then intervened in a singular manner; he announced his plans to marry Nevers' daughter, Louise-Marie de Gonzague. Marie de Médicis, acting as Regent in Louis's absence, locked up the poor princess at Vincennes.

Gaston had merely roiled the already troubled waters of international diplomacy. The events of 1629 led to a second, open conflict between France and Spain over the duchy of Mantua. Louis's forces seized the great fortress of Pignerolo and he led an army toward Savoy. When the fighting bogged down into sieges, a papal envoy, Giulio Mazarini, negotiated a compromise that left Nevers with Mantua, and kept Pignerolo for France, but banned foreign troops from Mantua. Richelieu was much taken with this young Italian, whom he brought into his service. Mazarini subsequently became a cardinal himself; when he moved permanently to France, he adopted the French form of his name: Cardinal Jules Mazarin.

The fighting in Italy deeply divided Louis's advisors. The Devouts, led by Marie de Médicis and Michel de Marillac, believed that France and Spain should ally with the Holy Roman Emperor, to stamp out Protestantism. The Good Frenchmen, led by Richelieu, ably seconded by d'Effiat, argued against an alliance with the Habsburgs. They wanted to maintain a political balance in Europe and perceived Spain as France's main rival. Louis XIII essentially subscribed to this viewpoint, in large measure because he identified the Spaniards as his father's enemies. In the final crisis in the council, Louis finally supported "Richelieu's" position, but we do well to remember that it was, for the most part, his position as well.

The Day of the Dupes, 10–11 November 1630

Why yes! We were indeed speaking of you and saying that you were the most ungrateful and wickedest of men.

Marie de Médicis, to Richelieu, in the presence of Louis XIII

The Day of the Dupes (10–11 November 1630) stands as one of the defining moments in French history. When a French publishing house decided to do a series called "The Thirty Days that Made France," they selected the Day of the Dupes as one of the charmed thirty. Its melodramatic *dénouement* makes it a wonderful candidate, but we should try to see it in a broader context. The Day of the Dupes merely stands out in a continuum of rapid change taking place between 1627 and 1634. First, as we have seen, the king destroyed the power of the Huguenots. Second, he stepped up the fiscal pressure on his subjects. French taxation roughly doubled between 1625 and 1634. Third, the king changed the governor of almost every province, rupturing clientage networks and allowing the government to implant networks that had direct ties to Richelieu. Fourth, the king reformed the royal administration. Michel de Marillac spearheaded a revision of the administrative codes, creating the Code Michau of 1629, in response to the demands of the Assembly of Notables of 1626. The Code laid down the administrative guidelines the state would try to follow for the next generation: revising court jurisdictions, establishing village tax collection rules, and streamlining accounting methods.

As part of the program of reform, Marillac, Richelieu, and d'Effiat expanded the powers of the treasurers general and tried to extend the system of *élections* into Languedoc, Burgundy, Provence, and Dauphiné. This effort led to riots everywhere, most famously at Dijon. In the end, the government settled for massive fines—7 million *livres* from Provence, Burgundy, and Dauphiné and a similar amount from the Estates of Languedoc, who had to buy the king's pardon for supporting Montmorency's 1632 revolt as well as pay for the abolition of the dreaded *élections*—and restored the Estates. Shortly thereafter, however, Provence and Dauphiné lost their Estates.

Only the Bretons, Burgundians, and Languedocians kept their estates, in large measure because those bodies proved so effective at raising money. The Bretons decided after the death of their serving governor in 1629 that "it is fitting to cast eyes on one of the *grands* of this Kingdom, in the power, affection and good offices of whom the said province can be assured to be protected." Thus, they had the foresight to ask Richelieu (1630) to become their new governor. That allowed them to provide the Cardinal, his clients, and relatives with about 150,000 *livres* in legal "gratifications" at every session. Given that Richelieu created *élections* in all of the other *pays d'États* (1630) and sent an intendant into every *généralité* except Brittany (1634), he came cheap at the price.

Louis XIII became so ill that he received the last rites on 29 September 1630. When his internal infection burst, he recovered rapidly, under the watchful eye of his mother, whose influence seemed to be on the rise. Allying with Gaston, Marie tried to use her renewed closeness to force out Richelieu, their mutual enemy. On 10 November, Louis tried to reconcile Gaston and Richelieu; Gaston reluctantly went along. That evening, the king and his council named Louis de Marillac, brother of Marie's ally Michel de Marillac, as new commander of the army in Italy. After the meeting, Marie confronted Richelieu, calling him a deceiver, a traitor, and an ingrate.

The next day, when he returned to the Luxembourg Palace, Richelieu could not obtain entry. Acting with the assistance of a spy he had in Marie's household, he snuck into her private chapel. Thence, by means of a secret door, he proceeded to her private apartments, where Marie and Louis were engaged in a vehement argument about

The Peddler and the Cardinal

Cardinal Richelieu made use of many clients in his efforts to manipulate provincial elites. One of the most unusual was Gilles Ruellan, a semiliterate former peddler. Ruellan, a native of the small Breton town of Antrain, began his remarkable career transporting linen for a local merchant. He decided to borrow some money from a widow of Saint-Malo and become a wine tax farmer, "because he knew, right down to the pint, how much they drank in every village." He began by leasing local tax farms but soon moved up to larger regional ones; in time, he became the chief tax farmer in Brittany, leasing the royal wine tax and that levied by the Estates of Brittany. He also sold weapons to Henry IV during the League War.

Like any self-respecting parvenu in early modern France, he bought landed estates, above all in the area around his home town. Soon he had created seigneuries at Rocher-Portail, Tiercent (made a barony in 1611), and Ballue, which the king made into a marquisat in 1622. Our simple peddler had come a long way: first *sieur*, then baron, finally marquis. His son, Gilles, bought a judgeship in the snobby Parlement of Brittany. Cardinal Richelieu could not help but notice such a man, and he quickly made Ruellan into an important client in Brittany. When Ruellan died, in 1627, Richelieu expressed to his cousin, de la Meilleraye, lieutenant–general of Brittany, his profound regret: "the poor M. du Rocher Portail has let himself die, from which I am much put out." Richelieu's comments, as one might suspect knowing him, had less to do with sentimental attachment than with family business, which brings us to Ruellan's daughters.

They married into the highest echelons of the Breton elite: to the First President of the Chamber of Accounts, Jacques Barrin, to the marquis of Goulaine, and the marquis of Coëtlogon. Barrin and Goulaine were important clients of Richelieu, but the cardinal had a much greater interest in the marriages of the other two Ruellan daughters, Jeanne and Guyonne. Jeanne married the most powerful nobleman of the Antrain region, Thomas de Guémadeuc, governor of the great fortress town of Fougères. Not long after their marriage, Guémadeuc, caught up in one of the inevitable quarrels over precedence at the Estates of Brittany, murdered the baron of Nevet in the streets of Nantes. Louis XIII condemned Guémadeuc to death, but as a special favor to Jeanne Ruellan's family, did not confiscate his possessions.

As the last member of his line, Guémadeuc left vast estates to his and Jeanne's daughter, Marie-Françoise; the young girl also obtained enormous resources from her mother, whose dowry had included 300,000 *livres* in cash. A short time after Guémadeuc's execution, the very man who had arrested him, François de Cossé-Brissac, married Jeanne's sister, Guyonne, who brought a dowry that included 400,000 *livres* in cash. Cossé-Brissac came from the highest nobility of France: his father, Charles, the man who surrendered Paris to Henry IV, was a marshal of France and lieutenant–general for the king in Brittany. The young couple had a daughter, named, like her cousin, Marie-Françoise.

What special interest did Richelieu have in these two cousins? Just before Ruellan's death, Richelieu had arranged for the marriage of his favorite nephew, François de Vignerod, marquis of Pontcorlay (to whose son the Cardinal bequeathed his coat of arms and title of duke of Richelieu), to none other than the supremely rich heiress Marie-Françoise de Guémadeuc, Ruellan's granddaughter. Moreover, in the 1630s, the Cardinal managed to arrange the marriage of her cousin, Marie-Françoise de Cossé-Brissac to *another* relative, his cousin the duke of la Meilleraye. The Cardinal was so happy that he personally gave the couple 200,000 *livres* in gold coins. He even took a shine to his "*bonne cousine*," whom he visited frequently in Paris. Thus the Cardinal's family made off with a major portion of the old peddler's fortune.

him. She denounced the Cardinal to his face and even accused her son of preferring this "lackey" to her. Richelieu fell on his knees, sobbing; Marie, too, unleashed her tears. Louis ordered Richelieu to leave and, moments later, in full view of everyone at the Palace, snubbed the minister in the courtyard.

Was this the fall of the hated Cardinal? Everyone in Paris thought so. Gaston and Marie rejoiced; Richelieu contemplated flight to Le Havre, where he was governor. Louis duped them all. Staying in a private house, Louis reflected on the policy implications of what he was about to do, and decided on continuity. He disgraced the Marillac brothers. The poor Louis de Marillac received letters appointing him commander of the army in Italy at the same time that he received orders of his arrest on charges of treason! The king exiled his mother to Compiègne. Shortly afterward, Marie fled to the Spanish Netherlands and never returned. Michel de Marillac died (1632) in forced exile at Châteaudun, while his brother Louis perished to the executioner's ax on the place de Grève. Richelieu engineered the poor marshal's death, with a handpicked court specially impaneled for the purpose.[27]

D'Effiat, too, died in 1632, although of natural causes. His death left Richelieu searching for worthy collaborators on the council. He pushed forward several of his clients, his "creatures" as they were called. This coherent ministry continued the program of reform started in 1626. Although Richelieu allowed several provinces to buy off the *élections*, he did not abandon the idea of reform in the structure of French administration. The government regularized the use of the intendants, investigating commissioners who had been used since the time of Henry II. The intendants, drawn overwhelmingly from the masters of requests of the king's household, who invariably came from Parlementaire families, now moved into each of the *généralités*, except Brittany. The king had long used intendants in his armies, to check on the logistical situation and on the political reliability of his generals. In the early seventeenth century, the king sometimes sent intendants into the governorships, where they had broader powers of oversight. The shift of 1634, from a military jurisdiction to a financial one, indicates the changed nature of the position. The king also responded in these years to another request of the 1626 Assembly of Notables: he reduced the power of the grandees by reshuffling the provincial governors, ten of whom he replaced between 1625 and 1635.

Louis took two other decisive steps against the great nobility in these years. First, he decided not to name a successor to Lesdiguières when the constable died in 1626. Louis did not abolish this Crown office, he simply refused to name a new constable, for fear of the great power it provided over the army. Second, a new rebellion by the hapless Gaston involved the greatest baron of France, the duke of Montmorency. Not only was Montmorency one of Louis's closest childhood friends, he was the uncle of Louis of Condé, who appeared, in 1632, to be a likely heir to the Crown. Captured by the king's troops at Castelnaudary, Montmorency went to the block for treason, despite the desperate pleas of the entire great aristocracy and of the queen. In this way, Louis gave the signal to all that any grandee, no matter how high his status, would be held accountable for his actions.

The intendants became critical officials in the long-term evolution of French government. In the short run, however, they were more of a reaction to the February 1634 decision to default on the interest owed to officers for their liens, which necessitated the use of a special device to oversee the everyday collection of the taxes. The king and Richelieu decided on the use of intendants, who had long proved so effective in such matters in certain provinces, such as Languedoc. The intendants quickly became embroiled in conflicts with the local tax officials. When they sought to go directly to the king's council for disciplinary measures against these officers, the officers responded by appealing to the Parlements. These courts naturally resented the impingement of their jurisdiction by the royal council, so they supported the tax officials. This conflict gradually ground the wheels of government to a halt in the late 1630s and early 1640s, under the crushing fiscal pressure of French participation in the final grand struggle against the Habsburgs, which began when France entered the Thirty Years' War, in 1635.

The Generation of the Saints

> *Like bees who never put anything but honey in their tiny mouths, so too your tongue will be always honeyed with God, and will have no greater sweetness than to feel running between your lips the praises and benedictions of his name, just as they say of Saint Francis [of Assisi] that when he pronounced the name of God he sucked and licked his lips, in order thus to take from it the greatest sweetness in the world.[28]*

> François de Sales, *Introduction to the Devout Life*

Henry IV's political solution to religious problems, and the devout Catholicism of Marie de Médicis and Louis XIII, enabled the French Catholic Church to intensify its remarkable efforts at renewal. The tide swept forward in the second half of the sixteenth century, accelerated by the momentous events in Italy. The Council of Trent (1545–1565) finished its work just as the Wars of Religion broke out in France. The French Church had little opportunity to accept formally the decrees promulgated at Trent, although individual bishops and archbishops did so. Trent defined orthodox Catholicism, establishing its basis for centuries to come. This sharp definition both reduced diversity within the Church and clarified its differences with the various Protestant churches. After the Council of Trent had spoken, compromise between Catholics and Protestants became impossible.

The Council laid out important doctrinal differences between Catholicism and Protestantism: transubstantiation; continued emphasis on the combination of grace *and* works; acceptance of free will; belief in saints; the importance of Mary; the maintenance of seven sacraments; and the legitimacy of the Church's magisterium. Some of the less important doctrinal matters, such as the reassertion of the existence of Purgatory, had profound practical consequences. If Purgatory existed, then prayers for the dead, a very lucrative source of income for many priests, still made sense.[29]

The Council also made many practical suggestions for the reform of the Church. It mandated archdiocesan councils and diocesan synods, to introduce the decrees of Trent to the widest possible range of clergy. Eight of the fourteen French archbishops convened such councils in the 1580s. In the seventeenth century, the metropolitan councils fell into disuse but bishops frequently convened diocesan synods. The Clergy of France itself met every five years, to discuss religious matters and, most importantly, to vote the king his quinquennial "free gift."

The Jesuit Order, allowed into France in 1561, helped to spread the Catholic counteroffensive. The Jesuits focused on the education of elites, through their *collèges*, where the teenaged sons of nobles and judges received their training. The order, banned from France in the late sixteenth century, returned in 1604. They quickly moved to take over the existing municipal *collèges* or to establish competing *collèges* in some towns. Where sixteenth-century French urban elites received their education at a secular school, in the seventeenth or eighteenth century those same elites invariably attended a Jesuit *collège*. Although the Jesuits placed considerable emphasis on certain Classical authors (like Cicero), they taught the legacy of the Ancient World in a far different manner than did the civil *collèges*. Whereas sixteenth-century French humanists had often corresponded, and even collaborated across doctrinal lines, such comity largely ceased in the seventeenth century.

Some of these young men went on to the priesthood, even to the episcopacy; they helped spearhead the great offensive of the early seventeenth century. Henry IV's marriage to Marie de Médicis further strengthened this movement, because of her devout Catholicism. She encouraged the spread of the reformed Italian Catholicism best represented by (Saint) Charles Borromeo, archbishop of Milan. Borromeo introduced rigorous standards for his priests, regularly made episcopal visits to his parishes, and led a life of moral rectitude.

Catholicism was on the march everywhere in Europe at the beginning of the seventeenth century. The Jesuits provided the Catholic Church with its "warriors of Christ." Jesuit confessors became normative for European Catholic kings. In France, Henry III had a Jesuit confessor, but the trend really started with Pierre Coton, confessor of Henry IV and Louis XIII, and continued into the eighteenth century. In the Holy Roman Empire, the Jesuit-educated archduke Ferdinand of Styria gave his subjects the choice of conversion, exile or death. In 1618, when Ferdinand became Holy Roman Emperor, he touched off the Thirty Years' War. All over Europe, Catholics dreamed of the dual Crusade. First, they would stamp out Protestantism; then, they would recover the Holy Land from the Turks. The duke of Nevers, a Leaguer in the 1590s, a princely rebel in 1611, 1614, and 1617, co-founded a new Crusading order, the Christian Militia, to unite European Christians in an assault against the Turks. The reestablishment of France's North American colonies, starting at Acadia and Québec between 1603 and 1608, led to efforts to Christianize the "savages" of the New World.

Catholic fervor and desire for disputation did not stop with the dream of a new Crusade or of converting the heathen. Religious writers in France published treatises on every conceivable doctrinal issue. From 1598 to 1610, more than one hundred such titles appeared each year, a figure that jumped to one hundred fifty a year in the next decade. After the 1620s, when again one hundred titles appeared each year, publication rates dropped dramatically, to forty to sixty titles a year for the next half century. This chronology, of course, follows the political fate of the French churches. Publications jumped after the Edict of Nantes and declined sharply after the siege of La Rochelle (1627–1628), where the Protestant threat died.

The Catholics went far beyond the war of words; they sent their foot soldiers out into the lands of the enemy. These missionaries, for such they called them, took the word of the "true" Church to the poor "misled heretics" of Protestant regions.[30] The Protestants proved notably unwilling to receive instruction from their visitors: conversion rates in Huguenot areas remained abysmally low. Later in the century, the Catholic Church sent missionaries into supposedly Catholic areas. There they encountered "pagan savages," the peasant Catholics whose religious beliefs bore little relation to the doctrines of the hierarchical Church. The most famous of these missions, that of Julien Maunoir, brought official Catholicism to the Celtic-speaking Bretons. Maunoir learned Breton and wrote a catechism in the language; the royal government even used his good offices to help subvert the rebellion of 1675 in western Brittany.

The primary direction of the Church, however, remained inward. It focused on the reform of the clergy and on the revival of inner spirituality. The Jesuits educated many of these great reformers, among them Pierre de Bérulle, François de Sales, and Maunoir. De Sales, titular bishop of Geneva, wrote the most influential French treatise on spirituality, *The Introduction to the Devout Life* (1609), which went through more than forty French editions in his lifetime. His works countered Protestantism's appeal to the "priesthood of all believers" by offering a new emphasis on the piety of lay people. He borrowed the emphasis of (Saint) Teresa of Avila, the great Spanish mystic, on the spirituality and the humanity of Christ. Teresa of Avila's influence on de Sales can be seen clearly in the target of his pastoral work: women.

One of the legacies of the *querelle des femmes* was the explosion of female piety in early seventeenth-century France. Upper-class, educated women chafed against the restrictions placed upon them, yet they lacked the mechanisms to attack directly those restrictions. Religion offered them an escape, particularly in light of the example of Teresa of Avila. Her biography, translated into French at the beginning of the century, inspired female and male religious reformers alike. Through the good offices of Bérulle, Barbe Acarie, wife of a prominent Parisian judge, obtained royal permission to bring seven reformed Carmelites to France from Spain. Mme Acarie, visited by visions of Teresa, spearheaded a movement to spread Teresan Carmelites throughout the kingdom. With the help of Bérulle and others, she succeeded. Between 1604 and 1668, the order established sixty-two houses in France. She also revived the former habit of pious women visiting hospitals. She and Michel de Marillac (the royal minister) tried in 1620 to convince the Ursuline convent of Paris to serve the community around them, rather than retiring to the clausura; they failed.

This decision reversed the original purpose of the Ursulines, founded in Italy in 1544. They had lived in private homes, ministered to the sick, and instructed women and girls in religion. Borromeo convinced the Ursulines in his bishopric to congregate in one house. The earliest French Ursulines, often women of modest social station, had followed the Italian traditions, but the French male hierarchy, always suspicious of women religious outside the cloister, eventually enforced clausura. They did not, however, eliminate one of the most important innovations of the Ursulines: schools for girls. This order, like the Reformed Carmelites, enjoyed enormous success: by 1700, France had more than three hundred Ursuline houses, with over ten thousand sisters.

François de Sales and (Saint) Jeanne de Chantal jointly founded the Visitation order, a religious community in which women could come together to express their spirituality, but would not be, as all nuns *had* to be, cloistered. The four original Visitation sisters of the village of Annecy lived a simple life, but not one of mortification of the flesh or extreme demonstrations of piety. They prayed and did charitable works, such as visiting the sick and the poor. The second Visitation house, at Lyon, did the same, but soon fell afoul of the archbishop, who demanded clausura. De Sales offered a remarkable defense of the role of women in religion:

> Woman . . . no less than man, enjoys the favour of having been made in the image of God; the honour is done equally to both sexes; their virtues are equal; to each of them is offered an equal reward, and if they sin, a similar damnation. I would not want woman to say: I am frail, my condition is weak. This weakness is of the flesh, but virtue which is strong and powerful is seated in the soul.[31]

The archbishop remained unmoved: the sisters of the Visitation became ordinary nuns, and the order prospered. By 1700, it had nearly one hundred fifty houses and about sixty-five hundred nuns.

Jeanne de Chantal and Barbe Acarie paved the way for later reformers, who would get women out of the cloister and into the community, where they ran hospitals and schools (for girls). The Sisters of the Infant Jesus, founded at Reims in the 1670s, experimented with the great pedagogical innovation of the seventeenth century: simultaneous instruction.[32] They modified similar techniques used by the Jesuits in their *collèges* for use with younger girls. Later, their second patron, Jean-Baptiste de la Salle, founded a male teaching order, the Christian Brothers, who made simultaneous instruction the normative mode of teaching boys. Both orders focused on children from middle and lower class families. Many of the Church reformers focused on women because they agreed with the assessment of François de Salignac de la Mothe Fénelon, who wrote that women "ruin or sustain houses . . . and, who, in consequence, decide on those things which most closely touch upon the entire human experience."[33] Given this extraordinary power of women, men could hardly let them exercise it without male direction.

Pierre de Bérulle took the spirituality of Teresa of Avila and transformed it into a model of Christian piety for all. He founded the Oratory, a training school for preachers, and led the Devout party in the 1620s. At first an ally of Cardinal Richelieu, he fell out of favor in the late 1620s, when they split over treatment of the defeated Huguenots and relations with Spain. Bérulle placed great emphasis on the Eucharist and, more fundamentally, on Christ, who became the mechanism by which man, unworthy though he was, could attain salvation.[34]

The generation of saints—Bérulle, de Chantal, de Paul, de Sales, to mention only the most famous—created an atmosphere of religious fervor in early seventeenth-century France. To understand the hatred inspired by Cardinal Richelieu, we must understand the sense of betrayal felt by his former allies in the Devout party. Oddly enough, one of the key figures of the Devout party, François Le Clerc du Tremblay, universally known as Père Joseph, remained with Richelieu. Père Joseph and the duke of Nevers co-founded the Christian Militia, which worked ceaselessly for a Crusade against the Turks. He agreed with Richelieu, however, about the overmighty Habsburgs, and served as the cardinal's key diplomatic agent from the late 1620s until his death in 1638. He belonged to one of the new male orders, the Capuchins, a group devoted, like so many of the new female orders, to the poor and downtrodden. The Capuchins, at their origin, lived the simple life, preaching to the less fortunate of their world. Père Joseph always wore their simple habit, yet he pined for success among the powerful of the world: his fondest wish was to become a cardinal.[35]

Converting the Heathen

Puritanism is the suspicion that someone, somewhere is having fun.

H. L. Mencken

Catholic fervor increased sharply in the seventeenth century, as part of the double Catholic Reformation taking place in France. The Jesuits spearheaded a movement toward elaborate churches, Catholic militancy, and intolerance of Protestants. The Jansenists, although opponents of the Jesuits, in some ways provided a second wave of Catholic militancy, one focused on personal piety and internalization of a new, more rigorous morality. Some great religious figures, such as Vincent de Paul, straddled both movements: his male order sent priests into the "wild, pagan" countryside to "convert" rural Catholics to a more genuine Catholicism.

This religious ferment deeply marked French politics and society. The effort to get the lower classes to "behave themselves" invariably came clothed in the language of religion. Everywhere, civil and religious authorities tried to clamp down on popular culture. Royal ordinances forbade artisans from demanding "any money from newlyweds, nor from their families" or from making "any cries or clamors, nor to offer any dishonest words, to sing illicit or defamatory songs in front of the doors of newlyweds." They prohibited journeymen's banquets "on pretext of confraternities" as well as "public, scandalous or dissolute dancing." Town authorities at Nantes condemned the "artisans and craftspeople of the town and suburbs [who] pass the greater part of working days in taverns, gambling and getting drunk, rather than everyone sticking to his work to gain his living and serve the public." Upper-class descriptions of the endemic popular disturbances invariably claimed that the rioters insulted "God, the king, and justice."

The problem for ordinary people was that the state, by means of the royal officers, began to criminalize ordinary, daily behavior. These royal officers, like Barbe Acarie's friend Michel de Marillac, themselves participated in religious revivalism through their Devout politics. Many religious reformers, like Mme Acarie or Bérulle, whose father was a judge in the Parlement of Paris, came from high judicial circles. Later in the century, the Jansenist movement (see Chapter 8) would receive its strongest impetus from the Parlementaire Arnauld family. These people brought their legalistic mentality to bear on morality.

Peasants dancing, c. 1630. Throughout the sixteenth and seventeenth centuries religious and state authorities tried to stamp out such activities, which were in their view tied too closely to the little devil at the end of the dance line. Happily, such efforts had only a mixed success.

Source: Croix, Femmes de Bretagne.

Many important Church officials, such as cathedral canons, came from the same legal families as the judges. These canons, Vincent de Paul and his "missionaries," and the other clergy had plenty of paganism to combat. When bishops sent a canon to make the obligatory parish visitations, they compiled reports on the abuses they saw, which the bishop then used as the basis for reforming edicts. The investigator at Saint-Saturnin of Nantes found in 1638 that the church's latrine bordered on the altar, "which throws much humidity on the said altar, which is an indecent thing." Thirty-one years later, the visitation records of the rural parishes near Nantes provide a telling contrast between popular attitudes toward the Church and the view of the authorities as to the "proper" attitude. The canon discovered a deplorable lack of respect for the hallowed ground of cemeteries. At Drefféac parishioners used it for a market; at Pihiriac they played games in it; and at Mesquen they held a bowling tournament. Inhabitants of several parishes dried their laundry in their cemeteries.

The canon tried to ban night-time assemblies in Saint-Nazaire, and to eliminate the immemorial custom of *veillées* in Couëron or Pontchâteau. The *veillées*, at which parishioners got together during the long winter nights, the women to discuss local affairs (above all potential marriages) and to sew, and the men to drink and talk (after 1650, to smoke), provided one of the most important venues of village sociability. That the hierarchical Church would seek to eliminate them shows its profound distrust of popular culture. This worthy Catholic canon evinced a Puritanism that would make any New England Calvinist proud: he banned small children from Mass (they made too much noise), objected to the nearly universal practice of men placing their hats on the altar during services, and tried (just like English Puritans) to eliminate popular holidays, like the night before All Saint's Day (what we call Halloween) or the ubiquitous bonfires lit on the eve of Saint John the Baptist's Day (24

June), which the Church (rightly) viewed as a holdover from ancient Druid ceremonies welcoming the summer sun. These efforts had mixed success. Cohabitation before Church marriage declined sharply, but many hillsides in Catholic areas have bonfires on Saint John's Eve to this day.

This criminalization touched virtually all classes, with the possible exception of the judges themselves. The nobles, those inveterate profligates, had to stop one of their favorite pastimes: dueling. Richelieu and Louis XIII both detested it; Richelieu for personal reasons (his older brother Henri died in a duel), Louis because he thought it violated his royal dignity. In the most famous case, Louis ordered the death penalty for the best known duelist in France, François de Montmorency-Bouteville, despite the desperate pleas of Charlotte de Montmorency and the great nobles of the Court. Bouteville had the temerity to duel in the Place Royale (now Place des Vosges). Louis took personal affront and demanded Bouteville's execution. This signal from the King began the rapid decline of dueling, a custom that died down after 1660.

For ordinary people, the king, town governments (now often dominated by royal officers and lawyers), and the Church issued legislation against a wide range of what people considered to be normal behavior. Ordinances condemned charivaris and confraternity banquets, cohabitation before Church marriage, elopements, tavern keeping on Sunday mornings, wearing masks in public (a traditional part of Carnival), and, increasingly, swearing. Swearing, or blasphemy, had long been "illegal" but had also long been tolerated by authorities. In the sixteenth and seventeenth centuries, however, authorities all over the North Atlantic world severely stepped up prosecution of this "offense." In short, in France as in Puritan England, sin became crime. As in England, sin, as crime, now became liable to civil, rather than ecclesiastical justice.

The generation of saints accelerated a fundamental reorientation of French culture, one that had started with the Humanists and religious reformers of the sixteenth century. The saints stepped up efforts at public repression of "sinners/criminals" at the same time that they reemphasized the inner spirituality of the individual. They tried, with limited success at first, to get people to internalize the values that led the saints to criminalize so much of ordinary behavior. In the long run, they largely (although not completely) succeeded. They created that society of the "gens de bien" (the worthy people), of "honnêteté" (respectability) that would come to dominate France. How appropriate that France would be led, during this generation of saints, by two cardinals: Richelieu and Mazarin. They, too, like the Devouts, had a firm commitment to the new morality and the new sociability. Whatever one might say about these two cardinals, however, one could never accuse them of being saints.

People and Politics

Recovery

> (A)round this town [Nîmes] and the whole province of Languedoc is a pleasant flat country, full of vines and olive trees and fruit enough and to spare.[36]

> Arnold von Harff, 1499

THE SWORD OF JUSTICE

Sixteenth-century authorities did not enforce justice with a mild hand. Felix Platter, a young Swiss medical student who attended the University of Montpellier in the 1550s, left unforgettable descriptions of individuals punished for a wide array of offenses, ranging from heresy to murder and infanticide. When he neared Montpellier, "we crossed the bridge near the inn at Castelnau, and afterwards passed the place of execution, which is in the fields in front of the town. Pieces of human flesh hung from the olive trees, and this sight gave me a curious sensation." In May 1553, his friends witnessed the burning of five Protestants, newly returned from studying in Lausanne. Two months later, Platter himself witnessed an execution:

> The executioner bandaged the young man's eyes, and then laid him down on his stomach, with his neck bare across the block. He then drew out a great sword, which he had kept hidden beneath his cloak, and struck the condemned man two blows on the neck. The severed head rolled across the floor. Afterwards the executioner cut off both legs and both arms, and arranged them on the scaffold with the head in the middle, and left them there all night. In the morning he hung them on an olive tree outside the town and there they were left to rot.

About a year later, Platter witnessed another execution, this one for an accomplice in a murder. The poor fellow had to recount "in rhyme the crime he had committed, and at the end he added: 'Pray to Holy Mary that she may intercede with her Son to take me to Paradise.'" This time the executioner broke the man on the wheel: tying the victim to two hollowed out trunks in the shape of a cross, the executioner used a sharpened metal bar systematically to break one limb after another. "The last blow was struck on the chest, and this killed the victim."

Platter recounts as well the gruesome hanging of the servant girl Beatrice, who had once worked in the household where he boarded. Beatrice left to serve a priest, in whose house

> She became pregnant, and when her child was born, she threw it into the latrine, where it was found dead. Beatrice's body was taken to the anatomy theatre, and it remained several days in the College. The womb was still swollen, for the birth of the child had occurred no more than eight days before. Afterwards the hangman came to collect the pieces, wrapped them in a sheet, and hung them on a gibbet outside the town.

Popular justice, it must be said, was not much more lenient: Platter recounts the tale of the musician Petrus Fontanus, caught *in flagrante delicto* by a jealous "doctor of law named Bigottas. The husband, with several masked students, surprised the young man in bed with the wife. They strangled him with a cord, and after cutting off his genitals and his nose, threw him thus mutilated into the street." Amazingly, Fontanus survived; Bigot (the husband) obtained acquittal; his wife disappeared from Montpellier.[37]

No one traveling in France in 1600 would have recognized the place Arnold von Harff described a century before. The fighting of the Wars of Religion laid town and country to waste. Soldiers burned down barns and cottages; besieged urban dwellers leveled nearby suburbs to remove the cover of their attackers; Protestant privateers sank Catholic merchant ships; and Catholic ones returned the favor. Breton peasants from one village claimed that their parish had dropped from six hundred hearths to twenty-five (following the ancient Celtic custom of exaggerating for effect) and begged the Estates for tax relief, complaining (1603) that they were "so poor and ne-cessitous and so afflicted that, as soon as they step out of their houses, they are eaten by the wolves with which the entire region is filled."

The wolf was at everyone's door in 1600, but Henry IV's restoration of order drove it back to its lair. The French economy boomed in the first decades of the seventeenth century, yet most of the growth merely made good the appalling losses of the last two decades of the sixteenth century. Whether one looks at Brittany in western France or Burgundy in the east, village hearth counts dropped severely between 1580 and 1595 or 1600. As late as 1610, many parts of Burgundy had scores of empty or ruined houses. The Estates of Burgundy conducted an official hearth investigation from 1610–1611 that turned into a census of the housing stock of the entire province. Parishes near Dijon still showed the terrible effects of the wars: roughly a quarter of their houses remained uninhabited. Twenty miles away, whether to the north (Saulx-le-Duc) or south (Gevrey), only seven percent of the houses were unoccupied. (See Table VII-1.)

TABLE VII-1: Housing Stock in Bailiwick of Dijon, 1610

Parish	Total Houses	Owned	Rented	Uninhabited	Ruined	Distance to Dijon (dir.)
Parishes close to Dijon						
Fontaines	132	65	67	48	—	5km N
Quétigny*	39	23	11	4	—	5 E
Chenôve*	42	15	18	4	5	5 S
Plombières	140	114	26	62	—	10 W
Hauteville	31	5	26	7	—	5 NW
Parishes 20 km away						
Notre Dame de Saulx-le-Duc	14	12	2	2	1	
Saulx-le-Duc	86	78	8	1	—	25 N
Gevrey	100	59	41	7	—	25 S

*Owners unknown for nine houses in Chenôve and five in Quétigny.

Many villages recouped their losses by 1610 or 1615 and began anew the long cycle of population growth that had started in the final quarter of the fifteenth century. Between 1600 and 1650, the population of "France" (using today's Continental French boundaries) grew from about 19 million to 20.5 million; in the second half of the century, it rose to 22.4 million. During the first half of the century, only the combined pestilence and famine of the late 1620s and early 1630s (both particularly virulent in western France) interrupted the steady march forward.

General population figures do not tell us much about local situations. Some towns, like Orléans, lost 20 percent or more of their population during the Wars of

Religion; others, like Saint-Malo, scarcely suffered at all. Paris's population dropped sharply in the early 1590s due to the two sieges: eyewitnesses reported that bakers cut their flour with the ground-up bones of the dead during the worst days of 1590. By the end of that three-month siege, rich and poor alike ate horses, donkeys, and mules. Chancellor Cheverny claimed that the dead lined the streets, and that the final tally counted 30,000 of them.

The wounded Paris of 1594 recovered rapidly. Henry IV and Sully actively supported urban renewal, first on Ile de la Cité, in the place Dauphine, where private builders created a new, more open urban space. The king and Sully then turned to a planned royal square, which we know as the place des Vosges. The lovely arcaded square attracted members of the highest nobility, who helped make the local district, known as the Marais (Swamp) into Paris's most chic address. Sully himself constructed a magnificent hôtel nearby.[38] Their initiative helped the city regain its vitality; by the middle of the century, its population had reached between 250,000 and 300,000 people.

France's second and third largest towns, Rouen and Lyon, did not fare so well. Neither fully recovered from the Wars of Religion, although Rouen did better than Lyon. The latter's fairs had lost their luster after 1560, and many leading bankers (who were often Italian or German) had moved from Lyon to Geneva. The other major cities generally began a steady increase, although port towns, such as Nantes or Bordeaux, would soon begin to outpace administrative, landlocked rivals such as Rennes or Toulouse. That trend accelerated in the late seventeenth and eighteenth centuries, as we shall see.

The return of peace and order allowed the reestablishment of the rhythms of everyday life. Peasants sowed their fields; artisans returned to their loom, or hammer, or needle; merchants began once again to trade, both in France and abroad. Western France, in particular, began to develop much stronger ties with Holland and, through Holland, to more distant regions, such as Asia or Eastern and Central Europe. Shipment of French wine to Holland, often through the Baltic, rose steadily into the 1620s and then took off. The Thirty Years' War naturally disrupted that commerce, leading to some troubled times on the Atlantic seaboard in the 1640s. French salt, too, made the long voyage north and east. In return, the Dutch shipped grain (in famine years only), cheese, colonial goods (cloves, pepper), and naval stores. Breton looms hummed throughout the early and mid-seventeenth century, producing linen for export, above all to England. Northern textile towns, in contrast, began a steady and devastating decline in the late 1620s. The constant fighting on the French northern border in the late 1630s and 1640s struck hard blows at the already beleaguered textile towns like Amiens.

Material Life

Hunger and cold, these were the two outstanding material factors of human life at that period. It is fortunate that only exceptionally did they coincide, for then they resulted in disaster and annihilation.[39]

Robert Mandrou

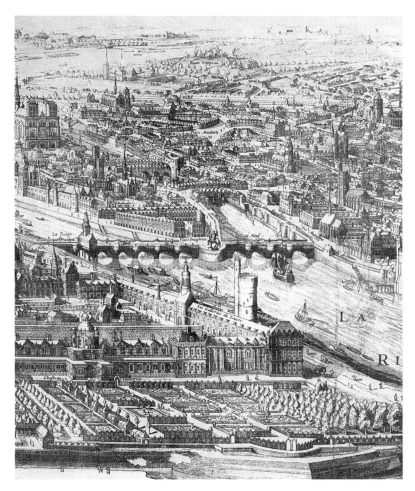

General view of Paris, focusing on the Louvre Palace, 1615. Henry IV's statue, on Pont Neuf, dominates the center of the picture.

Looking back at early modern French people's lives, as Mandrou reminds us, we must never forget three simple elements of almost everyone's existence: they were hungry and cold, and it was dark. Local records tell us much about how hungry and not a little about how cold and how dark. The Burgundian investigation of 1610 tells us who owned their house and, in many cases, the occupations of both renter and owner. A parish like Quétigny, right at the city's doorstep, had many houses owned by the Dijon middle classes or its religious houses (eleven of twenty-three). The owners included a barrister, two officers of the Chamber of Accounts, a merchant, and a tennis court proprietor. Wine-growing villages, like Gevrey-Chambertin (then called Gevrey-en-Montagne), had far more owners: forty-seven of its seventy-three vintners owned their own houses. At both Fontaines and Plombières, forty or so locally owned houses lay uninhabited, while Saulx-le-Duc, a small town, had only a single uninhabited house. The little town also had a remarkably high level of owner–occupiers (91 percent).

Who lived in a small town such as Saulx-le-Duc? It showed the typical mix of town and country in such places. On the urban side, there were five textile artisans, eleven other artisans (masons, a blacksmith, etc.), two lawyers, a notary, two royal officials, a royal sergeant, three rentiers, and a school teacher (who rented his house); on the rural side, twenty ploughmen, sixteen cottagers, eight vintners, a cowherd, and a shepherd. Most French towns, even quite large ones, had similar population distributions; Saulx-le-Duc stood out only because of the absence of artisans in the food trades, such as bakers, butchers, and tavern keepers. Gevrey, of about the same size, had one of each, although its rural population consisted almost exclusively of wine growers. All four parishes with eighty or more hearths had a school master: everywhere, he rented.

The Estates of Burgundy conducted these investigations about once a decade. Although no other commissioner followed the practice of the 1610 census, they did provide us with descriptions of thousands of peasant homes. Virtually all of them looked the same: a simple earthen cottage with a thatched roof. The commissioners always made note of a tiled roof, a sure sign of the wealth of the inhabitant. Except for the wartime investigations of the late 1630s and 1640s (Imperial troops laid Burgundy to waste in 1636), they usually found the houses "in a quite good condition," but "poorly furnished." In parish after parish, only some ten percent of the houses would be noted as "passably furnished."

The houses in question rarely had rooms: they consisted of four walls, enclosing a single common space. The usual furnishings were a large bed, in which nearly everyone slept. Notarial contracts suggest the cottagers rarely had more than one bed in their home, while ploughmen (who admittedly had larger households) often had a second one. Families did not yet have the large, long table so familiar from nineteenth-century paintings of peasant households. Rather, they had a small table, a few stools, and perhaps a bench. Peasant women brought small dowries, which invariably included all of the household's linens. A middling peasant family might start off with a bedcover, a few sheets, a large cloth, and a half-dozen small ones. The woman also had to furnish a trunk; the poorest provided only a wooden one, but most had an oaken trunk with a metal lock.

The giant room focused around the fireplace: little wonder that peasants thought of the house, little more than an expanded kitchen, as "female space." The chimney gave off what little warmth one could find. A cold draft came in as the chimney carried up most of the hot air, to say nothing of the sparks that caused the inevitable roof fires: "no farm without a fire," as the German proverb had it. The hearth provided much of the light; only a few tallow candles created an isolated dim circle or two of light in the dingy gloom of these often windowless huts. In many parts of France, in the winter, the animals moved in, too, separated from their human companions only by a rudimentary wooden bar. Long since inured to farm smells, the peasants appreciated the added warmth the animals brought to the house.

Slightly richer brides simply provided more of the same goods, but ploughmen's daughters usually added a few animals—a ewe and a few lambs, sometimes a cow, on truly rare occasions a bull or a horse—or a tiny morsel of land. These young women also brought cash, perhaps 50 to 100 *livres*, invariably paid in installments over several years, to make sure the marriage worked out (i.e., that the couple had children and both survived). The Boire sisters, Jeanne and Françoise, who married the brothers Vivand and Jean Gauthard, agreed to set up a single household, and to hold all goods in common. The sisters brought two bulls, a pig, a sow, two furnished beds, the usual linens, two strongboxes, and 130 *livres* in cash; Françoise even got a wedding dress.[40]

As one moved up the social scale, of course, household goods became more elaborate, as did dowries. A rural merchant's daughter, like Adrienne Bailly, might provide a fully furnished bed, a strong box, a cow and her calves, a half-dozen ewes, a wedding dress "appropriate to her standing," 200 *livres* of silver goods, and 100 *livres* in cash (half on the wedding day, half a year later). One step higher still, Claudine de la Porte, daughter of the local notary, provided her lucky husband with 1,500 *livres* from her father and 1,100 more from her uncle. She and her husband had the right to live with her family for a year, at the family's expense. These households might have better light—real beeswax candles; those of rural merchants or notaries could have stone walls, even stone floors, and two or more rooms.

Urban dowries started at a few pounds, for the poorest artisans, moved up to a few hundred or even a thousand for artisan masters, then to a few thousand for merchants and lawyers. The richest merchant and legal families could provide 10,000 *livres* or more; among the richest of all, the financiers involved in royal tax collection, dowries typically ran from 10,000 up to 150,000 *livres*.[41] The truly rich, like Ruellan (see box, "The Peddler and the Cardinal"), gave their daughters astronomical sums: Guyonne Ruellan obtained 400,000 for her dowry, and her father paid off a debt of 50,000 owed by her fiancé.

Unlike rural houses, urban ones changed dramatically at the beginning of the seventeenth century. In Paris, concerns about fire fueled a switch from wood to stone, the material used in virtually every house built in Paris after 1600. Most houses were fairly simple: many had a workshop on the ground floor, topped by a series of apartments in the second, third, and even fourth storeys. The upper floor held simple garrets, very often occupied by poor widows. A typical artisan's house might cost only 1,000 *livres*, more elaborate ones five times as much. The houses of the truly wealthy—merchants, legal men, nobles—cost far more. Dijon contains an unusually rich collection of such houses, which show the evolution from the fortress-like merchant–banker's home of the mid-sixteenth century to the famous House of the Cariatides, with its sculptured false pillars. Aristocratic houses, such as those of presidents of the Parlements of Dijon or Rennes, were even more elaborate. (See Chapter 8.)

Artisans had much more elaborate furnishings than farmers: their houses might have 1,000 or 1,500 *livres* worth of goods: beds, tables, perhaps a chair or two, metal goods, tools, merchandise and raw materials, linens, some cheap tapestries hung on the walls to cut down on the cold. Merchant families had the same sorts of objects, albeit more finely made. They might also have a few books (most often religious) and, in some cases, a cheap painting, often on copper. In the seventeenth century, merchants, followed by artisans, began to have finer household goods, such as glassware, perhaps some porcelain plates; by the end of the century, they might even have a fork or two.

The great transition in urban eating habits lay just ahead. For ordinary people, the daily menu varied little: watery soups and gruels, bread (wheat in the towns, usually rye in the country), a few vegetables, above all beans and peas, cheap wine, or, in some areas, beer (north and east) or cider (Brittany and Normandy). Peasants hunted small game—often illegally—and poached fish whenever they could, but their diet had a very low animal protein content. Fairy tales tell us all we need to know about peasants and food. Like the man who had three wishes, many a peasant's fondest dream was a fat sausage or a larded slice of game. France's many localized climates encouraged enormous dietary variations. People in the south lived amid vineyards and olive trees; those in the west had dairy cows pasturing under apple and pear trees; peasants in the Parisian basin had fields of wheat, and those in regions of poorer soil made do with rye or buckwheat (Brittany) or millet (south). In the Cévennes mountains, peasants mixed chestnut flour into their bread, one of the reasons for widespread goiter problems there.

Dietary deficiencies and unsanitary conditions led to a bewildering array of diseases. Eating bread made from diseased rye could lead to ergotism. Bad water could carry any number of diseases, dysentery most lethal among them (far more soldiers died of it than of battle wounds). Ubiquitous cuts could become infected. People carried an infinite variety of internal and external guests: tapeworms, fleas, ticks, lice, "vermin" of every kind. The poor battled gamely on against their implacable enemies, but the rich fared little better. Few people took baths. Indeed, doctors advised strongly against them, for health reasons. Most of the rest of medical advice was little better; in fact, the overwhelming majority of the population relied on "Doctor Mom," as she is known today. A housewife had to have a wide array of recipes for potions and salves to use for every conceivable illness or injury. Householders' manuals, whether that of Olivier de Serres in France or Gervaise Markham in England, contained scores of "recipes" for medicines treating every condition. In really serious cases, rural people visited the local "wise woman," who whipped up a magic potion and chanted secret chants, or perhaps the village priest, who sprinkled holy water, gave communion (only in the gravest cases), and made special incantations of his own. Urban people did not disdain wise women, but the better-off among them might call in a doctor or a barber–surgeon, who invariably prescribed a good bleeding or an enema. Many of the wealthy, like Louis XIII himself, received regular purges. All in all, the herbal potions of the wise women, based as they were on generations of experience, were probably a safer, more effective form of treatment.

Daily life meant a constant struggle to keep one's head above water. Rural people worked in the fields, foraged in the woods (for wood and fuel), tried their hand at one trade or another. Many a tax roll lists a villager as a roof thatcher one year, a day laborer the next, and warehouseman the third. Women, like men, spent their lives in a multiplicity of tasks: spinning, harvesting, overseeing cows and poultry, healing, nursing, preparing the dead for burial, or helping a neighbor give birth. Tens of thousands of these people, especially widows from poor households, spent part of their lives, or even part of every year, begging. Rare is the village tax roll that fails to list the "poor beggars" at the end, assessed for a penny or two. In many ways, the beggar–widow's life depended on that simple penny, because her listing on the village tax roll gave her the right to use the community's property—to take fuel from the community's woods or to glean in the fields of her neighbors.

Poor and rich alike sought relief from daily concerns. Men went to the local tavern or to a fellow villager's cellar. Urban police records are filled with complaints about artisans and workmen crowding into illegally open taverns during High Mass on Sundays, "as if it were an ordinary work day." Elites vainly sought to enforce laws that forbade householders from going into taverns. How could these men have passed up the main locus of community life? In these taverns workmen hired themselves out; people worked out business deals, and drank on the bargain; tavern keepers provided tables for card games and dice, and alleyways for bowling or quoits. On Sunday afternoons or on feast days, at the tavern or at a fair, whole families would come, to dance to the tunes of local musicians.

Alcohol and violence, then as now, went hand in hand. Authorities in port cities like Saint-Malo worried about the many "seamen, who are ordinarily very rude," among whom "little contestations can lead to disorder and to blows." They feared meetings of journeymen could lead to strikes, like that of the tailors of Nantes, who met at the tavern of the White Cross to plan their work stoppage. Even worse, among men who feared "neither God, nor the king, nor justice" (as they always put it, emphasizing rejection of the French Trinity of one faith, one king, one law), people could plot riots or rebellions. Every town dweller, from the poorest worker to the royal seneschal, believed that the people did have certain legitimate rights, above all the right to affordable bread. When grain prices drove bread beyond their reach, people rioted. Towns had no real police force, only judges, a few sergeants, and, in large cities, some garrison troops. They relied instead on a militia, often consisting of the same people who rioted.

Popular Political Action

God will look over our enterprise and by this means make justice upheld against blasphemers, thieves, and tyrants, which will be a perpetual reminder to us. God wish it by his holy grace.[42]

The Tard-Avisés, peasant rebels of Limousin, 1594

The political events of the period from 1589 through 1635 had a decisive influence on the course of the French monarchy. Certain traditions well established in the sixteenth century fell into disuse; a new political discourse replaced the vocabulary that had dominated discussions in the fifteenth and sixteenth centuries. In the midst of the miseries of the Wars of Religion, ordinary people increasingly took action, rebelling against urban authorities, against local landlords, and against the competing armies. They organized to take over city governments, as in Paris, or to create assemblies that would petition the king for his support, as in the southwest. The much larger provincial estate meetings of the end of the sixteenth and beginning of the seventeenth centuries were also part of this trend toward greater public participation in politics.

Grain riots and other civil disturbances formed part of ordinary people's political participation. Local officials, like the town council of Poitiers, invariably described the rioters as beggars and do-nothings, as "outsiders and unknown persons." Discussing a 1630 grain riot, the town council wrote:

> The mayor remonstrated that at the end of the council meeting the populace who had gathered this morning at town hall on the subject of the famine and high cost of grain joined with a large number of people cut from the same cloth, making together some four or five thousand people, almost all of them beggars and do-nothings.[43]

In fact, local artisans, masters and journeymen alike, as well as shopkeepers and laborers, made up the crowds. Royal officials naturally wanted to convince their superiors that they had not lost control of their population, but had been overwhelmed by nefarious outside forces. Those familiar with modern urban disturbances know contemporary authorities like to use the phrase "outside agitators" for the same reason. Everyone understood this little charade; everyone knew that civil order ultimately depended on the artisan masters of the towns and the ploughmen of the countryside. These people often lacked political representation, but they did not shy away from direct political action. They had a clear sense of their rights, of society's obligations to them, of what they considered to be "just." When the authorities did not give them justice, they took matters into their own hands.

The French people had a long tradition of such direct political action, especially in the towns. They did not suddenly jump into politics in the 1590s. The famous Sixteen at Paris—the citizens who ran the city from 1590 until 1594—did not materialize from thin air. They merely accelerated a development apparent in the 1560s and 1570s, when local leaders like Claude Marcel, merchant's provost of Paris, and receiver general of the Clergy of France, created extensive clientage networks in its neighborhoods. Ordinary people became heavily involved in politics for three reasons. First, they cared deeply about the defining political issue of the time, religion. Second, the succession of weak or ineffectual kings left a power vacuum at the center, debilitating the overall structure of authority. Third, the country suffered from a variety of ills—inflation, economic dislocation, widespread violence and insecurity—about which the traditional ruling classes seemed unable to do anything.

In such a situation, people began to take matters into their own hands. The provincial estates took the extraordinary step in the late 1570s of corresponding with each other, of bypassing the normal channels of communication through the king. Other local people took similar action, to combat the immediate problems around them. Rampaging troops provided the most widespread cause for common action. In the Vivarais, in Dauphiné, and in other regions, peasant villages banded together in an attempt to battle the troops, from the 1570s through the 1590s. In the 1630s, these regions again burst into rebellion, furious at tax increases that struck peasant and artisan alike. The boatmen of the Charente, particularly hard hit by the transit tax increase of the mid 1630s, led the first of the large rebellions, which self-consciously revived the name of the rebels of the 1590s, the Croquants.

Peasant militias often fought pitched battles with entire regiments; the peasants obtained more than one victory in this incessant guerrilla warfare. In larger battles, involving several thousand combatants on each side, professional troops invariably broke down the discipline of the militias, leading to massive slaughter in the aftermath of the "battle." The peasants long remembered these encounters; even in the twentieth century, Breton peasants frightened their children by using the name of the sieur de la Fontenelle, a rogue Leaguer who slaughtered more than fifteen hundred peasants in a single day.

The resistance to the forces of order reached its broadest dimension in the Midi. From Dauphiné in the east, through the Midi proper, and into Guyenne, peasants and townspeople rose up against their tormentors. In Dauphiné, peasant militias formed armies and laid siege to the castles of noble bandits. In the late 1570s and early 1580s, the town of Romans had a steadily more acute factional warfare, pitting the artisans of the town against its burghers. The artisans staged mock Carnival parades. When the rich adopted the rooster for a symbol, the artisans paraded behind a flag bearing the image of a capon (a neutered rooster). The artisans chanted slogans about eating human flesh at six *deniers* the pound and, according to bourgeois witnesses, threatened to kill the rich men and marry their wives and daughters. Eventually, the rich murdered the leader of the artisans and conducted reprisals that mirrored simultaneous retribution against the peasantry.

Across the river in the Vivarais, the situation looked much the same. Peasant complaints in a special petition to Henry III (1579) give some idea of their general situation:

> Their heads had been bound with ropes and tightened until their eyes spurted from their sockets; they had been buried alive in heaps of manure, thrown in wells and ditches and left to die, howling like dogs; . . . they had been stretched in front of fires, their feet fricasseed in grease; their women had been raped and those who were pregnant had been aborted; their children had been kidnapped and ransomed, or even roasted alive before the parents.[44]

Landlords suffered from the inability of oppressed peasants to pay rent; many petty nobles supported these rebellions, at least until the rebels seemed to threaten the social order. Further west, the constant restiveness of the peasantry finally broke loose between 1593 and 1595. The peasants of Périgord, of Rouergue, of Limousin, and of nearby regions created armies numbering in the thousands. They struck out at the soldiers, but also at the nobles and clergy. They convened large assemblies, with representatives from rural parishes, meeting in a form similar to provincial estates. These assemblies appealed to Henry IV for protection, claiming that they supported his cause and opposed only the oppression of lawless soldiers and of rapacious landlords. Henry, in no position to do much of anything about the Limousin in 1593 or 1595,

temporized; he wrote sympathetically to the peasant assemblies. In time, the Croquants created a unified elite opposition to social chaos. They, like all peasant rebels,
faced defeat in the field; at Pousses in the Limousin, fifteen hundred peasants died.

At Nantes, Dijon, and other cities, political parties began to form in the 1560s
and 1570s. One side, such as the winegrowers of Dijon or the merchants trading
with Spain at Nantes, would favor radical Catholicism. Senior royal judges, like Jean
de Charette, seneschal of Nantes, often led the *Politique* faction. At Nantes the Leaguer merchant families allied in a dense social and political network. Within the
boundaries of this network they served together as aldermen or as judges of the merchants' court. They intermarried, stood as godparents to each others' children, and
bought and sold royal offices only with each other. Nor did these party affiliations
die down quickly. In Brittany, some reconciliation could be seen in Henry IV's lifetime, but the old Leaguer and *Politique* families only fully buried the hatchet in the
1630s. Some wounds took even longer to heal: Jean de Charette's grandson fought
with the descendants of Leaguer families in the 1650s.

The situation in Paris looked much the same. The confraternity movement of
the middle of the century led, in time, to the later leagues and to the League itself. The
political networks of men such as Marcel enabled them to put together street demonstrations or, some would argue, to bring Parisians into the streets to massacre Protestants on Saint Bartholomew's Day. The politics of these cities involved three
substantial groups: royal officers, legal men, and merchants. In some cases, like Dijon,
artisans played a role in the voting (not in holding office), but most large cities, like
Paris or Lyon, effectively eliminated artisan participation in the late fifteenth or early
sixteenth century because local elections became steadily more tumultuous.

The struggle for control of the cities played itself out in the 1580s and 1590s.
Nantes provides an excellent case study. Between 1565 and 1589, Nantes had nineteen
mayors: five lawyers, six royal officials, and eight merchants. The royal officials tended
to belong to the *Politique* faction, the merchants to that of the League. In the 1590s,
when the League controlled Nantes, *Politique* royal officials left town, with two-thirds
of the masters of accounts and presidents of the Chamber of Accounts joining a loyalist Chamber in Rennes. The more recent officers, who still had ties to the mercantile
world, stayed in Nantes. Nantes continued to have merchant mayors, the last of whom
served in 1595–1596. When Henry IV regained control of Nantes in 1598, he overturned the results of the mayoral election and appointed a loyalist royal officer as
mayor. Every mayor of Nantes from 1599 to the Fronde was a royal officer.

Paris demonstrated a similar pattern. The main local officials had come from
the royal officers, from lawyers, and from merchants in the sixteenth century. During
the days of the Sixteen (1588–1594), the situation changed in favor of the merchants
and legal men, who provided more than 80 percent of the local councillors in 1589.
The captains of the local militia also came more often from the traditional urban
groups. Royal officers dropped from 15 to 10 percent between 1589 and 1591, but
their numbers tripled when Henry IV returned (1594) and reached nearly 40 percent by 1619. By way of contrast, the numbers of lawyers, merchants, and artisans
increased to 60 percent during the League, but then declined back to 40 percent.

Here again we see the great jump in broader popular participation in governance in the 1590s, and the strong reaction spearheaded by the king after 1594.

Widespread popular participation in politics created the illusion of what we might call "parties." The democratization of politics followed lines that would be quite similar to the situation of the 1780s and 1790s. Democratization did *not* mean the participation of the mass of the city's population: far from it. The artisans who took part in the running of the city, as its militia captains, came from among the richest masters in the city. Poor masters, journeymen, day laborers: these groups had no direct input. Even the crowds so useful to the factions came overwhelmingly from among those with a stake in the situation, such as guild masters. That is, they originated from precisely the *opposite* group on whom the authorities blamed the problem. The same patterns would recur in 1789 in Paris.

The steady upsurge of popular political participation continued into the seventeenth century. Seventeenth-century civic life paled beside that of the sixteenth century, but local elites still had important mechanisms for communicating with the king. The provincial estates, which attracted hundreds of deputies by the 1620s or early 1630s (as against the few dozen who had attended in the 1570s or before), offered especially important sites for sounding public (that is, elite) opinion. The state also used these *pays d'Etats* to conduct experiments of various kinds, including new systems of taxation; in fact, France as a whole would, in the next generation, adopt a tax revenue model very similar to that constructed in Brittany in the 1620s and 1630s. The king and his ministers continued to make every effort to provide public justification for their policies, such as the war with Spain that broke out in 1635. Louis went so far as to send a herald riding to Brussels to make an official declaration of hostilities. The herald publicly posted the king's grievances to the sounds of a trumpet and then he and his escort rode off.

Such concerns with the niceties of feudal right aside, the royal government went out of its way to assure that political discourse would be conducted solely on its terms. The wide-open pamphlet campaigns of the 1570s and 1590s had, in the eyes of the government, greatly exacerbated existing tensions. The revival of the pamphlet wars in 1614 reminded everyone of how dangerous open debate could be. Richelieu always employed many writers to get out his version of events; in the 1630s, he even sponsored the creation of the Académie Française, to which he wanted to assign guardianship of the French language. (See Chapter 9.)

The events of 1625–1635 created a newly restive public. The war against La Rochelle cost everyone lots of money and eliminated the strongest, most independent voice against the Crown. In the late 1620s and early 1630s, plague spread rapidly through western France, killing hundreds of thousands of people. The plague outbreak of 1626–1627 was soon followed by terrible famines, especially in 1630–1631, so that the people of western France had nonpolitical reasons to be restive. In 1628, a wave of violent confrontations between royal troops and peasants broke out in Brittany. In one case, a troop of peasants assembled from nine parishes killed the captain of the troops and routed his forces, prompting his widow to file a lawsuit against the leaders, asking for damages. The Estates of Brittany intervened in the case, on the side of the peasants, fearful that the taxes would not be paid if all peasant leaders had to go into hiding. They did issue a stern warning, however, that "it is forbidden to the populace henceforth to take up arms and rise up without the order of the King"!

The continued military build-up of the 1630s led to more spending, to higher taxes, to more selling of offices, and, eventually, to the partial bankruptcy of 1634. The 1634 attack on royal officers, especially financial ones, alienated those who had to carry out government policy. When open participation in the Thirty Years' War (1635) touched off a new round of tax increases, the recalcitrant royal officers, burned by the bankruptcy of 1634, proved reticent to enforce the new edicts. These equivocations helped start a new round of rebellions in the southwest and in Normandy in the late 1630s.

The French folk memory has long remembered these terrible years of the 1630s and 1640s. Few people have been so vilified as Cardinal Richelieu, the individual most associated with the policies of those times. Moreover, the Cardinal gets more odious as time goes on; from the evil schemer of Alexandre Dumas's mid-nineteenth-century *The Three Musketeers* we have arrived at the epitome of evil presented in the new American movie (and cartoon!) versions of the tale. These new versions even have Richelieu scheming to marry Anne of Austria and proclaim himself king (one wonders what Dumas, let alone Louis XIII, would have made of such things). Why has the Cardinal so long endured as the very embodiment of evil? Surely it goes beyond the simple increase of the tax burden associated with him and reaches back to a profound public sense of a government that had stifled the voices of its people.

In the short run, Richelieu's efforts failed; in the long run, his failed policies would be successfully revived a generation later, just as Henry IV successfully revived many of the failed initiatives of Henry III. Richelieu stands for the great enterprise of those days, for the marriage of Church and State that sought to make people the same, without making them equal. When people resisted, the State and the Church struck back harshly, whether it meant quelling a peasant rebellion or an urban revolt or vigorously prosecuting the new moral offenses. Church and State worked together to get people to absorb the new norms of behavior, of what they liked to call civility. In short, they sacrificed civic society in order to create a civil one. Louis XIV would soon show where that path led.

Notes

1. François de Malherbe, *Œuvres*, ed. A. Adam (Paris: Gallimard, 1971), 29. Enfin, après tant d'années / Voici l'heureuse saison, / Où nos misères bornées / Vont avoir leur guérison.

2. The current statue is not the original one, which was melted down later in the Revolution to make cannons.

3. The Hegelian idea of the state as mediator of conflicting interests, and state officials as the mechanism of such integration, owes much to the French model.

The eighteenth-century definition of citizen eventually came to differ markedly from earlier ones, as we will see.

4. Henry I, prince of Condé, died in 1588. His wife, Catherine de la Trémoïlle, produced a son shortly after his death. Contemporaries universally believed the boy to be illegitimate and further believed (with little evidence) that Catherine had poisoned Henry to cover up her infidelity. Henry IV took the boy in, but imprisoned the mother for years. Shortly after he became king, Henry IV recognized the boy, Henry II of Condé, as legitimate and thus as heir to the throne. He remained heir apparent until the birth of Henry IV's son, Louis, in 1601.

5. *Mémoires de Messire Philippe Hurault, comte de Cheverny, Chancelier de France*, in *Collection complète des Mémoires relatifs à l'Histoire de France*, v. XXXVI, ed. M. Petitot (Paris: Foucault, 1819), 166–167.

6. The naturalization papers are found in the AD of the Loire-Atlantique, series B. Mello, for example, can be found in B 65, fol. 298v.

7. The Estates Generals of 1560–1561 complained that this important work had not yet been completed in many bailiwicks. Most published customs came out in the 1570s and 1580s.

8. Toulouse (*c.* 1420), Grenoble, Bordeaux (both 1453–1454), Dijon (1477), Rouen (1499), Aix (1501), and Paris. Henry II raised the long-standing chief local court of Brittany to the status of a Parlement in 1553–1554.

9. The Edict of Moulins (1566) specifically codified the Parlements's right of remonstrance before registration of edicts.

10. *Essais*, "On lameness." The standard English translation of Montaigne is that of Donald Frame, originally done for *The Complete Works of Montaigne. Essays. Travel Journal. Letters* (Stanford: Stanford University Press, 1957). All translations used here are my own.

11. Money obtained by sale of offices went to the new treasurer of the *parties casuelles*.

12. Brittany and Languedoc used dioceses as local districts, Dauphiné the bailiwick.

13. In the middle of the sixteenth century, many parts of Brittany had vineyards, and the Estates voted a mixed package of taxes. When climate change destroyed the vineyards, save those in the bishopric of Nantes, the Estates moved quickly to increase duties on wine.

14. I would emphasize again that the royal administration was tiny by modern standards, in which state governments can employ ten percent or more of a labor force. By the standards of European governments in 1589, however, it was unusually large. It consisted of about ten thousand officers, many of whom served part-time and pursued other business interests and/or administered large estates.

15. The word *dirigisme*, which has no precise English translation, derives from the verb *diriger*, meaning to lead. *Dirigisme* means the replacement of private by state initiative. Modern *dirigisme* involves the state's interference in many economic decisions, as well as the pivotal role played by the central government in most aspects of French life. That sort of *dirigisme* took firm root much later, but

we must not ignore the fundamental attitudinal shift that took place in response to developments between the reigns of Henry II and Henry III.

16. Most French officials owned their offices; they could sell the office to whomever they chose provided they survived the transfer by forty days. Charles Paulet came up with a simple solution to overcome their fears. Each officer would make the annual payment in return for the right to sell the office (or bequeath it) to whomever he chose, without fear of the forty-day clause.

17. This complicated matter is discussed in greater detail in J. Collins, *The State in Early Modern France* (Cambridge: Cambridge University Press, 1995).

18. Cited in *Marie de Médicis et le Palais du Luxembourg*, ed. M.-N. Baudouin-Matuszek (Paris: Fondation Septentrion, 1991), 125.

19. BN, Mss. Fr. 16,517, fol. 162–170. This volume is a collection of famous speeches delivered between 1564 and 1648, of which President Harlay of the Parlement of Paris had copies made for his library.

20. The deputy here could only be referring to child kings, because Francis I left his mother in charge of France when he was captured and held prisoner in 1525.

21. The emphasis comes from the chancellor's original. Cited in Seong-Hak Kim, *Michel de l'Hôpital. The Vision of a Reformist Chancellor during the French Religious Wars* (Kirksville, MO: Sixteenth Century Journal Publishers, 1997), 60–61.

22. Condé had selfish reasons for such opposition. So long as Louis XIII and Gaston did not produce children, Condé stood to inherit the throne.

23. L. Moote, *Louis XIII. The Just* (Berkeley and Los Angeles: University of California Press, 1989), 90–97.

24. Moote, *Louis XIII*, 122.

25. BN, Mss. Fr. 16,517, fol. 33v. Du Vair, who was on the point of dying, told the Parlement that his final days would be happy ones if the "final accents of my voice can make so lively an impression on your spirits" as to inspire them to the desired action.

26. The king sold a percentage surtax to a given tax (usually the *taille*) either to an existing officer, like the local receiver, or to a newly created one, such as the keeper of the petty seal of each *élection*. The officer paid ten times the annual value of the surtax: thus a receiver in a district that paid 200,000 *livres* in taxes would pay 50,000 *livres* in cash for a surtax of 2.5 percent. The receiver bought the right to collect 5,000 *livres* each year, forever. D'Effiat and his predecessors added 140 million *livres* of liens on the direct taxes between 1620 and 1634.

27. The weakness of the evidence against Louis de Marillac can be judged by the fact that even this court of stooges voted the death penalty only by 13–10.

28. François de Sales, *Introduction à la vie dévote* (Montreal: Fides, 1947), 17. Cited in K. Taylor,"La Maison Royale de Saint-Cyr," Ph.D. diss., 2000, Georgetown University, chap. 1.

29. Catholics believed that those guilty of minor sins, that is to say, virtually everyone, did not go to Hell but only to a sort of holding area, known as Purgatory.

After spending a certain time in Purgatory, these souls would ascend into Heaven. Protestants believed only in Heaven and Hell. On the other doctrinal matters, mainstream Protestantism rejected transubstantiation, the cult of the saints and of Mary, and free will. It also reduced the number of sacraments (agreeing only on baptism, although some churches counted communion) and rejected the magisterium of the Church. Protestants also relied solely on Scripture for guiding authority in spiritual matters. Lastly, Protestants believed people were saved by grace alone, not by works.

30. Protestants, of course, similarly viewed Catholics as misguided heretics.

31. Cited in E. Rapley, *The Dévotes. Women and Church in Seventeenth-Century France* (Montreal: McGill-Queen's University Press, 1990), 37.

32. At this time, teachers taught young students one at a time. The rest of the class sat unattended during the individualized instruction.

33. Cited in Taylor, "Introduction."

34. The use of the male pronoun here is intentional, reflecting Bérulle's emphasis on "man" ("l'homme"). The term means, in French as well as in English, all human beings, yet its use, in place of a more gender neutral term, reemphasized the primacy of man over woman. The emphasis was, I would argue, intentional.

35. Through Richelieu's support, Père Joseph got his wish; his cardinal's hat arrived at his deathbed just before he passed away.

36. *The Pilgrimage of Arnold von Harff*, ed. and trans. M. Letts (Wiesbaden: Hakluyt Society, 1946, 1967), 260. Von Harff often comments on the fine French towns of the period.

37. *Beloved Son Felix. The Journal of Felix Platter a medical student in Montpellier in the Sixteenth Century*, trans. S. Jennett (London: Frederick Muller Limited, 1961), quotations from pp. 43, 64, 83, 128, and 93. See also note 45. E. Le Roy Ladurie, *The Beggar and the Professor: A Sixteenth-Century Family Saga*, trans. A. Goldhammer (Chicago and London: University of Chicago Press, 1997), provides many fascinating details on the Platter family.

38. The place Dauphine, the place des Vosges, and the hôtel de Sully all survive today, as do many old houses throughout the Marais and the adjacent district closer to the Hôtel de Ville.

39. Mandrou, *Introduction to modern France*, 32.

40. This double marriage followed by two weeks the wedding of Claude Boire and Edmée Gauthard, sister of the two grooms. The Church strictly forbade marriage of in-laws, so they would have had to get a dispensation. Holding goods in common was unusual in seventeenth-century France; the custom persisted in this village (Alligny-en-Morvan) because its inhabitants were serfs. Feudal law required that the heir of a serf's property live in the same house as the serf; otherwise, the family forfeited the property to the lord. Rich peasants got around this legal disability by living in large, communal households. These records can be found in AD Côte d'Or, 4 E 49 12.

41. Detailed study of one hundred twenty-four such dowries by Françoise Bayard showed that 37 percent gave their daughters between 10,000 and 50,000, and another 46 percent from 50,000 to 150,000. F. Bayard, *Le monde des financiers au XVIIᵉ siècle* (Paris: Flammarion, 1988), 442.

42. Y-M. Bercé, *Histoire des Croquants. Étude des soulèvements populaires au XVIIᵉ sièce dans le Sud-Ouest de la France* (Geneva: Droz, 1974), 2 vols., 702.

43. Bercé, *Histoire des Croquants,* v. 2, 712. The town council of Dijon used virtually the same words to describe the 1630 rebels there.

44. Cited in J. H. M. Salmon, "Peasant Revolt in Vivarais, 1575–1580," *French Historical Studies* XI, 1 (1979): 1–28, citation on p. 13.

Chapter Eight

WAR TO THE DEATH:
SPAIN AND FRANCE

The King has made sufficiently known by all his actions from the beginning of his reign until now, the passionate desire he has had to conserve the peace for his peoples, and also to maintain peace with his neighbors, having taken particular care to turn away the ancient envy and the ill will of the Spanish against France.

Louis XIII defending his decision to declare war
on Spain to the Parlement of Brittany, 1635

In the early 1630s, France began its decisive and successful struggle with Spain for dominance in European power politics. France's victory made it the preeminent European power, around which Continental alliance systems revolved for two hundred years. Spain had dominated European politics in the second half of the sixteenth century and stood preeminent among the powers in the early seventeenth. Its supremacy rested on three key factors:

1. The riches produced by its colonial empire in the New World.

2. The superiority of the Spanish army, the massive blocs of pikemen, known as the *tercios.*

3. The weakness of France, caused by the long religious wars.

Between 1600 and 1660, all three of these advantages disappeared: economic hegemony in Europe shifted decisively to its northwest corner, Holland, England, and northern France. The Dutch, the Swedes, and the French developed new tactics, based on massed firepower, that made the *tercios* an anachronism; and France emerged united from the Wars of Religion, ready to assume a dominant place in European politics.

The great war with Spain took place in two distinct stages. First, France marshaled every resource to defeat Spain and the Empire in the Thirty Years' War. The massive financial requirements of the war forced the French state to change its fundamental structures of governance and administration. The initial effort to enact such change failed miserably. By the late 1640s, the strains of the war effort and the institutional revolution, combined with a royal minority, led France into the second stage of the conflict, marked by a series of civil wars, known collectively as the *Fronde*. Louis XIV's coming of age and his coronation (1654) marked the effective end of the revolts and launched France toward the final victory over Spain (1659).

Louis XIV had the good fortune to be king in the midst of a remarkable flowering of French culture that had begun in his father's time. That cultural renascence took place within a Europe adapting to the first genuine world economic system and to the Scientific Revolution. France, which had abandoned colonial ventures in the New World in the middle of the sixteenth century, substantially stepped up its efforts in the West Indies and in Canada after 1650 and reached out extensively to parts of Africa and Asia, too. The Scientific Revolution drove French intellectual life in one new direction, while other currents encouraged the Golden Age of French theater and a revival of French painting and architecture. Politics interacted constantly with these intellectual developments. Indeed, the French Court often provided patronage for the great playwrights. In contrast to the second half of the century, however, when Louis XIV offered royal patronage, royal ministers such as Richelieu, Mazarin, and Fouquet employed the leading playwrights, writers, architects, landscape designers, musicians, and painters of the 1630s through the 1650s.

Politics and religion continued their elaborate *pas de deux*: the Court took the part of the Jesuits in their quarrel with the Jansenists (a dissident Catholic group) and added its weight to the forces of Catholic intolerance of Huguenots. From the 1650s onward, local authorities, fully supported by the Crown, stepped up harassment of Protestants. By the 1670s, Louis XIV actively sought to suppress Calvinism, a policy brought fully to fruition by the Revocation of the Edict of Nantes (1685), which banned Protestantism from most parts of France.[1]

The next two chapters have followed historiographical tradition in adopting Louis XIV's assumption of personal power in 1661 as one of the chronological markers of French history. They move away from that tradition by emphasizing the continuties before and after 1661. Louis's successes invariably resulted from his implementation of reforms unsuccessfully attempted by Richelieu and Mazarin. Richelieu's efforts to reform the state, to create an apparatus less dependent on the venal officers, ultimately failed in his lifetime, but the process he started bore fruit a generation later. Mazarin barely held onto power during the Fronde, when Louis XIV was a child, but he managed to survive the series of civil wars and, once the king had attained legal adulthood, to reinstitute permanently many of Richelieu's old policies. Mazarin provided Louis with his political education, just as the king took fundamental lessons in attitudes and deportment from his mother and from the viscount of Turenne, held to be the model gentleman of their time.

Continuities remained strong in all areas. Coopting an effort to create a standard French language begun by the poet Malherbe and his circle at the start of the seventeenth century, Richelieu initiated the Académie Française in the 1630s. Louis XIV made himself its chief patron in 1672 and created or institutionalized Academies of Science, Architecture, Music, and Fine Arts. Where Richelieu gave support to Corneille in the 1630s, Louis XIV provided it for Racine in the 1670s. Royal ministers—whether Richelieu in the 1630s or Fouquet in the 1650s or Colbert in the 1670s—actively collected great works of art. Colbert's collection included works by Veronese, Titian, Raphael, and by leading French painters, such as Charles Le Brun or Philippe de Champagne. They collected books as well: Colbert once wrote that "the pleasure of forming my library is practically the only one I have in my work." Much of his extraordinary collection ended up in the royal library. The massive state patronage of Louis XIV's time had its roots in the patronage provided initially by the great royal ministers, whom Louis deliberately sought to outdo. For the most famous example of his emulation of excess, Versailles, he enlisted many of the team of architects, landscape designers, and artists who had built the magnificent palace of Vaux-le-Vicomte for finance minister Nicolas Fouquet.

Richelieu passed to Mazarin and to Colbert a profound respect for the printed word and for its utility—and potential threat—to those in power. Richelieu took exception to the political writings of the Dutch bishop Cornelius Jansenius (or Jansen), which criticized French policy in the 1630s; ever after, he viewed Jansenism, a Catholic movement centered on Jansenius's religious ideas, as essentially political and antimonarchical. Mazarin, Louis XIV, and Louis XV would all share this view: to them, the Jansenist religious dissent was, by definition, political dissent. From the 1650s until the 1760s, government policy toward the Jansenists played a central role in French internal politics, binding together religious and political issues.

Richelieu strongly supported increased foreign commerce, overseeing the founding of the Morbihan Company (1626) for monopoly trade with the Western Hemisphere and encouraging trade with the Levant. Louis XIV's government, led by controller general Jean-Baptiste Colbert, gave similar support to monopoly companies in the New World, in the Baltic Sea, in Africa, and in Asia. The new economic realities—the steadily increasing importance of these distant markets—led to a major shift in political alignments, beginning in the 1660s, when it became obvious that the new rivals to France would be the states of northwestern rather than Mediterranean Europe. Where Richelieu focused on the Spanish, Colbert feared and envied the Dutch; his successors, in turn, obsessed about the English.

France moved steadily forward in the middle decades of the seventeenth century, despite such problems as the deadly epidemics and famines of the late 1620s and early 1630s or the political instability of the Fronde. In the long term, population rose from the 1630s into the early 1690s. Many regions, such as Provence or parts of Brittany, thrived economically, while others, such as the textile towns north of Paris, suffered severe recessions. This emerging socioeconomic structure encouraged the construction of a new state edifice. As in the economic sphere, so, too, in the institutional one, such changes developed in earnest in the 1630s. Here France was the pacesetter, yet its state development did not proceed evenly and rationally, but erratically, shifting wildly under the force of events. Time and time again, French administrators made it up as they went along. Many of these policies failed dismally, but others succeeded. More importantly, the constant press of events led the administrators to develop more effective structures, to create the bureaucratic system that would become normative for almost all Continental European states.

↬ THE DUEL WITH SPAIN, 1635–1659

His Majesty maketh known to you his resolution to have recourse to arms to obtain satisfaction for this offence which importeth each and every prince of Christendom.

Louis XIII's declaration of war against the King of Spain, made by the royal herald on the public square of Brussels, 1635

CHRONOLOGY	1635–1661
1635	France enters the Thirty Years' War
1635–1640	Endemic rebellions of the Croquants in the Southwest
1636	"Miracle" of Corbie; Spanish invasion stopped
1639	Nu-Pieds rebellion in Normandy
1642	Death of Richelieu (12/4)
1643	Death of Louis XIII (5/14); victory at Rocroi (5/19)
1648	Peace of Westphalia
1648–1649	Parlementaire Fronde
1649–1653	Fronde of the Princes
1654	Louis XIV crowned (6/7)
1658	Victory of the Dunes (6/14)
1659	Peace of the Pyrenees (11/9)
1661	Death of Mazarin (3/9); Louis XIV assumes personal power

Louis XIII had crushed internal opposition to his rule by 1632. He had conquered La Rochelle, forced the Protestants of Languedoc to lay down their arms, and humbled the great nobility. Gaston of Orléans's pitiful uprising of 1632 led to the execution of the first baron of France, François de Montmorency. Despite desperate pleading from virtually every powerful person in the kingdom, including Anne of Austria, Louis held firm: Montmorency went to the scaffold. The dynasty still had great uncertainty. Neither Louis nor Gaston had a male heir, nor did it seem likely either would produce one. In contrast, however, the internal political situation had calmed completely. Louis faced no more serious rebellions from his nobles. The prince of Condé, next in line for the throne after Gaston, became a faithful client of Cardinal Richelieu. Condé also produced a male heir, providing some assurance of continuity.

Outside of France, however, Louis faced a grimmer situation. France had tried to stay out of the direct fighting in the Thirty Years' War, paying first Denmark and then Sweden to do the dirty work. Christian of Denmark proved to be a disaster but Gustavus Adolphus of Sweden, the "Lion of the North," gave the Imperial troops bloody lessons in the new warfare at Breitenfeld and the Lech (1631). Gustavus defeated the Imperial army again at Lutzen (1632), but died himself on the field; he left an infant daughter as his successor. When a combined Spanish and Austrian force annihilated the Swedes at Nordlingen (1634), the two major German Protestant powers, Saxony and Brandenburg, sued for peace, leaving France with no alternative but to enter the fray itself. Thus began a generation of war with Spain (1635–1659) and with the Austrian Habsburgs (1636–1648).

Louis took great pains, in his letter to the Parlement of Brittany (a letter likely sent to the other Parlements as well), to explain the long history of Franco–Spanish wars. He castigated Emperor Charles V, accusing him of deliberately introducing "the evil doctrine" (Protestantism) into France in order to destabilize the country. Louis noted that his predecessors had allied with "the wisest of the Protestants . . . in the interest of public liberty" to prevent Spanish and Habsburg domination in the Holy Roman Empire. The latest outrage, the king went on, was the arrest of the Archbishop of Triers, "a sacred person, a prince and Elector of the Empire," a violation of "all divine and human law." By this act, the princes and Electors of the Empire had received "such an offense that in our days no one has viewed its like." The king had also learned by "certain proofs" that the perfidious Spanish intended to capture the best towns of Champagne, Picardy, and Languedoc, as part of their designs on France. The king assured the Parlement that he hoped for a speedy peace, so that he could relieve his poor subjects

> of the charges that he has had to impose on them for their preservation, which is as dear to him as his own life, which he has often exposed and will always voluntarily continue to expose on all occasions when it is a question of the honor of his divine Majesty, of the peace of this state, and of the conservation of his good neighbors and allies.

The "rightness" of Louis's cause notwithstanding, the Spanish army quickly marched into France and threatened Paris. Hundreds of the leading Parisian families fled the city, their carriages "covering the road" to Orléans; the entire royal council wanted to abandon the city. Louis XIII, showing the physical courage for which the French Bourbons were justly famous, refused to do so; he and Richelieu then openly moved about the city, with small escorts, to reassure the citizens. The nation rallied behind its king. Parisian artisans sent a delegation promising soldiers and money. Nobles from all over the kingdom rode to Paris to answer the king's summons, enabling him to amass 30,000 men in a matter of weeks. The Spanish offensive stalled north of Paris, at the fortress of Corbie. By the end of the year, Louis drove that army beyond the borders, just as his troops (and a well-timed flood of the Saône river) drove off an Imperial force that had invaded and devastated Burgundy.

The war dragged on: in the Low Countries, in Germany, in Italy, along the Franco–Spanish border, and along that between France and the Holy Roman Empire. The French eventually gained the upper hand, especially after the stunning demolition of the main Spanish army by the young prince of Condé at Rocroi (1643).[2] The old *tercios* who formed the core of the Spanish army had not lost a field battle in over a century. Condé's victory, achieved through a judicious mix of artillery fire and cavalry charges, transformed the mental climate in which the war was fought, and raised enormously the prestige of the French army. Rocroi came too late for either Richelieu or Louis XIII; the former died in December 1642, while the king passed away just five days before the battle.

Most of the other battles were not so glorious; in fact, the war usually bogged down into sieges of one fortress or another. The French and their allies had the best of the fighting, Condé obtaining another notable success at Lens (August 1648). One stage of the war had already ended in early 1648, when the United Provinces reached an agreement with Spain. Lens helped convince the Emperor to sign agreements with France (Münster) and Sweden (Ösnabruck), together called the Peace of Westphalia. In these agreements, the Emperor had to reconfirm the rights of the Protestant German princes. As a private individual, he also granted France some territorial gains in Alsace and certain vague jurisdictional rights over ten of its towns. Sweden and, to a lesser degree, Brandenburg received important rewards: the Swedes got extensive territorial gains in northern Germany, while Brandenburg, which had reallied with France at the end of the war, obtained the lands of the bishopric of Halberstadt and the inheritance rights of the archbishopric of Magdeburg. The Peace of Westphalia thus raised the Elector of Brandenburg well above the other German princes and solidified Sweden's position as the preeminent power of northern Europe.

The war between Spain and France, however, did not end at Westphalia. They continued the fight until the Peace of the Pyrenees, in 1659. Their war ended for three reasons:

1. French military success.

2. Diplomatic pressure from other states.

3. Financial exhaustion.

France won most of the major battles, especially toward the end, when Henri de la Tour d'Auvergne, viscount of Turenne, led them to success in the Low Countries, culminating in his victory at the Battle of the Dunes (1658). Here diplomacy took a hand: the Dutch, now more fearful of France than of Spain, strongly opposed further French gains on their southern frontier. Neither the Dutch nor the English had any desire to see France obtain Flanders, Brabant, and Hainaut. For the Dutch merchants, their worst nightmare was Antwerp in French hands.[3]

Diplomatic complications aside, France and Spain each needed peace for domestic reasons. The relative domestic balance, which had somewhat favored Spain in the early 1650s, shifted sharply in favor of France. The French internal disorders known collectively as the Fronde (1648–1653, see below) had crippled French war efforts and even led to Condé's desertion to the Spanish. Mazarin's wiliness and Louis XIV's coming of age restored internal peace in France and partly eased the financial crisis caused by the bankruptcy of 1648–1653. The Spanish, by way of contrast, had failed to put down a rebellion in Portugal (which regained independence), had barely regained control of rebellious Catalonia, and were in much worse financial shape than the

French. At the Peace of the Pyrenees, Spain ceded Cerdagne and Roussillon, creating in the Pyrenees mountains the oldest land boundary existing in today's Europe; they also gave up some of Artois and a portion of Flanders. Philip IV agreed to marry his daughter, Maria-Theresa, to Louis XIV—her double first cousin—with a dowry of 500,000 crowns.[4] In return, the French agreed to accept the rebellious Condé back into all his honors and offices and to cease their support for the Portuguese rebellion.

THE PRICE OF GLORY

The assembled communities protest that they are most humble subjects and obedient servants of the King, and that they wish to employ their goods and life for the conservation of his state and crown. That their uprisings, the taking up of arms, they carried out for the conservation of their liberty and to redeem themselves from the manifest oppressions with which they are daily worked over and afflicted, given that it is certain that [these oppressions] are done by those underneath the King and against the intention of His Majesty.[5]

Complaint of the Communities of Périgord, 1630s

The relentless pursuit of glory came at a high price. Much of the internal political development of France between the 1630s and the 1680s directly reflected the enormous strains placed on French society first by the titanic struggle with Spain for dominance in Europe and then by Louis XIV's efforts to achieve European hegemony. The contest with Spain began at an inauspicious moment: western France had just recovered from a devastating attack of the plague (mid and late 1620s) and from the great famine of 1629–1631. Taxes had risen sharply in the late 1620s to pay for the La Rochelle war; they continued to rise precipitously in the 1630s. In 1634, the king conducted a partial bankruptcy at the expense of his officers. The following year, he attempted to raise direct taxes 60 percent and asked those same officers to collect the money. Little wonder that peasants, like the communes of Périgord, refused to pay, resisting either by armed rebellion or through tax strikes. Little wonder that some of the aggrieved officers abetted local tax strikes or rebellions. Others, more cautious, merely performed less assiduously.

The rapid increase in direct tax rates paralleled the imposition of a wide range of new indirect taxes. The higher salt tax and increased transit taxes led to open rebellion in many parts of the kingdom. In the southwest, a new generation of Croquants rose against the increased transit taxes levied on the Charente river. What began as a boatmen's revolt against a single transit tax became a widespread peasant rebellion against all taxes; the focus soon shifted to the direct taxes. The peasants requested (later demanded) the abolition of the new surtaxes levied along with the direct taxes, as well as the new indirect taxes. When they did not get satisfaction, they marched on local towns, capturing Bergerac but failing to take Périgueux. The governor of Guyenne responded by routing five thousand peasants at La Sauvetat, killing more than one thousand of them.

Jacques Callot, Soldiers loot a farm. *1633. This scene would have been all-too-familiar to French peasants, especially those living on the northern, eastern, and southern borders. The looting soldiers were as often in the French army as in those of France's enemies.*

SOURCE: Histoire Militaire de la France, vol. I.

No sooner had the royal army pacified the southwest than rebellion broke out in Normandy. The *Nu-Pieds* (Bare Feet) revolt followed several years of unrest in southern Normandy. Urban workers had risen against new indirect taxes; the Norman peasants of the Cotentin peninsula, believing they would soon have to pay the salt tax, went on a rampage in 1639, murdering the usual collection of minor tax officials and clerks and raising an army.[6] The king had to withdraw eight regiments from the army in Flanders, who slaughtered the peasants in a battle near Avranches. The king then punished the entire province, suspending its regular courts, levying massive fines on its cities, and ordering reprisals.

These "armies of suffering," as the Nu-Pieds called themselves, quickly learned that passive resistance was much more effective than armed action. Tax strikes spread from region to region. Villages outside of the reach of the royal army or other armed forces rarely paid their taxes; only those unfortunate enough to live on the line of march or near a garrison had to put up their money. In practice, this meant that regions such as those around Paris or Rouen paid heavy assessments, while places such as the Midi escaped royal authority. In the *élection* of Coutances, where the Nu-Pieds rebellion took place, more than half of the villages had not paid any of their taxes and only one of the 163 parishes had paid even *one-third* of its assessment a year after the military defeat. In the mountains of the Midi, the regional districts of Moulins and Limoges owed the king millions of *livres* in back due taxes. Eastern France, scene of so much fighting and of constant movement of royal troops, often paid its assessments in kind, to troops on the march, so that the regular tax collectors received nothing.

These popular rebellions and tax strikes took place in an atmosphere of institutional chaos brought on by the widespread introduction of the intendants in 1634. The intendants would become the defining institution of the *Ancien Régime,* but they began inauspiciously. They quickly ran afoul of the authority of the old finan-

Jacques Callot, The Peasants' Revenge. *1633. Peasants often took matters into their own hands, either by attacking isolated bands of soldiers or by full-scale rebellions. The latter invariably ended in defeat and massacre.*

SOURCE: Histoire Militaire de la France, vol. I.

cial officers, who found ready allies in the Parlements, jealous of the judicial authority of intendants. Intendants, in turn, sought to evade the jurisdiction of the Parlements by appealing to the king's council. The Parlements fought violently against the intendants, yet these officials usually came from Parlementaire families. Nicolas Fouquet, intendant to Dauphiné in 1643 (he was nearly lynched) and later superintendent of finances, was a typical case: his father and several uncles served in the courts at Paris and Rennes. In the government's view, intendants had greater freedom of action because they did not own their office as intendant; they held instead a commission, which limited their tenure and could be revoked at any time. Officers believed that the dependence of the intendants on the king's arbitrary will made them a threat to the "freedom" of all Frenchmen. Venal officers, who owned their office and could not be removed, saw in the intendants pernicious threats to their power and to their often considerable investments in their offices, yet virtually all intendants (more than 90 percent) themselves owned the (very expensive) venal office of master of requests of the king's household.

The series of rebellions in the late 1630s testified to the dissatisfaction of the regular officers and to the government's inability to run the country without them. The government, ever more desperate for money to prosecute the war, resorted to progressively more dubious fiscal expedients, such as mortgaging future tax revenues to financiers. By the end of 1641, the government had already spent all of its revenues for 1642 *and* 1643. Unable to rely on the traditional officers, the government gave the intendants still more power: in 1642, they began to apportion the direct taxes of the parishes without even consulting the officers. Soon they took the unprecedented step of leasing out the recovery of the direct taxes to private contractors, who paid in advance a percentage of the amount to be levied. By the late 1640s, financiers often paid only half the projected amount because they discounted in advance the expected arrears. Wise, well-connected investors advanced money in return for the right to collect taxes in secure areas like Upper Normandy; unsuspecting speculators ended up with trouble spots like the Midi. Such *ad-hoc* methods naturally lent themselves to corruption, particularly because Richelieu relied on another time-honored method of governance: the clientage network. He built up an impressive array of loyal "creatures" and made sure that his relatives and close allies obtained many important positions in the military, judicial, and financial administrations. The shake-up of governors around 1630 placed Richelieu's men everywhere: even those, like the old prince of Condé, who had once had independent networks of their own, now became full-fledged clients of the cardinal. In Brittany, Richelieu himself held the governorship; his cousins de la Meilleraye and Cambout held the posts of lieutenants general. He also stacked the royal council with his men. By 1636, he had two "creatures," Bouillon and Bouthillier, running the king's finances, Bouthillier's son in the foreign office, and loyal clients Pierre Séguier (chancellor in 1635) and François Sublet de Noyers, the secretary of war (1636).[7]

This jerry-built system managed somehow to support the French armies in the field, but its shortcomings hamstrung the military effort at key junctures. Many great French victories, such as Rocroi or Lens, could not be effectively followed up because the armies lacked money. Unpaid soldiers melted away, leaving victorious generals unable to savor the fruits of their triumphs. Inside France, the use of Richelieu's system of clientage undermined respect for the government. That system began *within* the framework of traditional government, and worked quite well in that context. Once the cardinal went outside the traditional system, by relying so heavily on the intendants, however, he alienated large segments of the existing officer class.

Richelieu's death revealed the weakness of his *ad hoc* system of government. His carefully constructed clientage network immediately collapsed. The clients fought over the spoils; those at the top sought to disgrace their rivals and to take the cardinal's place as the king's chief advisor. Sublet de Noyers, whom Louis XIII replaced with Michel Le Tellier, was an early loser in the game. Richelieu's place as first minister fell to another cardinal, Jules Mazarin, the Italian diplomat who had first worked for the French during the Mantuan crisis.

The death of Louis XIII left the kingdom to a child of four, Louis XIV. That a direct heir existed was something of a miracle. Louis XIII and Anne of Austria had been estranged for much of their married life but their relations became a little less glacial in the mid 1630s. On 5 December 1637, so the story goes, the king, caught in a driving rainstorm, was unable to return to the hunting chateau of Versailles, where he had been lodging.[8] He went instead to the Louvre, but his bedroom had no furniture; the captain of his guards had the happy suggestion that the king spend the night with the queen, in her apartments. This night of connubial bliss produced a boy nine months later—Louis XIV, whom all France called the "God-given." Encouraged, the royal couple tried again and produced a second son, Philip.

Anticipating the usual problems of a royal minority, before he died Louis XIII tried to create a Regency Council, consisting of Anne of Austria, Gaston of Orléans, the elder prince of Condé, Mazarin, chancellor Séguier, superintendent of finances Bouthillier, and state secretary Chavigny. When the king died, Anne acted quickly to overturn this arrangement, convincing the Parlement of Paris to throw out the king's will and name her as Regent.[9] Gaston became lieutenant–general of the kingdom.

Anne and Gaston had hated Richelieu, so it is little wonder that they set about dismantling his clientage network. The shortcomings of the personal governing system revealed themselves immediately. Many of Richelieu's clients lost favor: Schomberg lost his post as governor of Languedoc to Gaston; Richelieu's cousin, the duke of La Meilleraye, lost control of Brittany to Anne, who declared herself its governor. Bernard de la Valette, disgraced under Richelieu and condemned to death *in absentia* (for treason) by the Parlement of Paris, regained his post as governor of Guyenne and conducted a veritable purge. The intendant wrote to Mazarin that la Valette, even though a loyal client of the cardinal, "lived only for vengeance" against Richelieu's local supporters. When the Fronde broke out, Guyenne proved to be one of the most hardened centers of resistance to Mazarin.

The Frondes, 1648–1653

> *Nothing is more sad or more shameful in our history than these four years of war without honor for anyone, if not for a few officers of the old regiments, whose firm loyalty saved the king and France.*[10]

E. Lavisse (1906)

The Revolt of the Judges, 1648–1649[11]

> *One does not destroy the authority of kings in combating it in its excesses; on the contrary, one upholds it in resisting him.*

Pierre Broussel, 1648

Mazarin, an Italian, and Anne of Austria, a Spaniard, labored under the enormous disadvantage of being foreigners. Their chief financial officer, Particelli d'Hémery, also came from "Italy."[12] They turned to ever more desperate financial policies throughout the early 1640s. Urban unrest spread everywhere, from Nîmes in the south to Angers in the Loire Valley. By the winter of 1647–1648, the government had all but lost control of the country. The unrest then spread from the provinces to Paris, where the Regency tried to put new pressure on the royal officials. This time the clever policy manipulators went too far; they threatened to abolish the *paulette* and with it the security of venal offices. Particelli d'Hémery combined this provocation with a reduction in payments for *gages* and annuities. These provocations, and demands for new taxes, above all excise levies in Paris, further angered the officers. The infelicitous combination of taxes that alienated the general population and measures that alienated the most important royal officials led to a rebellion.

The central breakdown began, oddly enough, with the masters of requests, the corporate recruiting ground of the very intendants who had provoked so much opposition. Particelli d'Hémery's efforts to eliminate the *paulette* in December 1647–January 1648 led to a work slowdown by the seventy-two masters of requests, who refused to bring forward cases to the king's council.[13] They turned to the Great Chamber of the Parlement, where the four senior masters sat *ex officio,* for support. Anne and Mazarin reacted harshly, bringing the boy king to the Parlement for a *lit de justice* on 15 January 1648. After a stirring speech by the king's own attorney (Omer Talon) attacking the government, the Parlement sullenly registered six edicts designed to raise money by means of new offices and new excise taxes.

This tactic raised obvious constitutional questions. Could an uncrowned boy king conduct a *lit de justice*? What precise powers did the Regent have over the Parlement, given that the Parlement itself had defined her powers in 1643? The miscalculation of d'Hémery and Mazarin, attacking the security of royal offices, which represented a third or more of the capital of most Parlementaires, provoked progressively greater militancy from the judges.

The context of these events is easily forgotten in most descriptions of the outbreak of the Fronde. The Frondes, for they were really several separate rebellions, did not really start in Paris and spread to the provinces; rather they began with the breakdown of order in the provinces and spread to the capital. Open rebellions had died down, but millions of ordinary French people refused to pay their taxes. Vast segments of the royal administration felt alienated from the government and (rightly) worried about the security of their investments in offices, annuities, surtaxes, and forced "loans." The international context was even more troubling. On the Continent, civil war had broken out in Naples, in the revolt led by the fisherman Masaniello. After his death, the rebels declared Naples a republic. France sent a fleet to help put down the rebellion.

More troubling, and more clearly fixed in the minds of all French elites, were the events in England. The Puritan New Model Army had routed Royalist forces in the Civil War of the 1640s. In 1648, Charles I was a prisoner in Puritan hands. His wife, Henrietta-Marie, daughter of Henry IV of France, aunt of Louis XIV, fled to France, where she received a tumultuous welcome. Provincial estates from Brittany to Languedoc voted her large gifts to help her through her time of troubles. In 1648 and 1649, the Puritan-dominated Parliament made a Revolution. They abolished feudal laws, the House of Lords, the established Church, and the monarchy itself. On 31 January 1649, they executed Charles I. Mme de Motteville, Anne of Austria's lady-in-waiting, voiced the sentiments of most at the French Court when she called it "the most criminal action that men have ever committed."[14]

The specter of English republicanism haunted the French events of 1648 to 1654. Anne of Austria did not hesitate to accuse the Parlement of Paris of "wanting to make a republic" in the spring of 1648. Nothing like what happened in England in the late 1640s had ever happened before. As Mme de Motteville wrote, "this tale will cause amazement to coming races; and it was surely an evil omen for our queen [Anne]." The English events conditioned every response taken by Mazarin and Anne and limited the freedom of action of Mazarin's Parlementaire opposition, terrified lest they be tarred with the brush of "republicanism." Throughout the crisis of 1648–1649, most Parlementaires, even while attacking the policies of the government, strongly supported monarchical "absolutism," that is, the king's unrestricted right to make positive law. They sought to defend themselves within the realm of contract, of private and "fundamental" laws. Nonetheless, some Parlementaires, like the king's attorney Omer Talon, bruited about ideas of a form of mixed sovereignties shared among the king, the Parlement, and the "people" (an entity left undefined, to be sure). Talon and others claimed to act in the name of the "public good," defending the child king against evil foreign ministers. Talon did not pull any punches in his speech to Anne at the infamous *lit de justice* of 15 January:

> These great and illustrious personages who formerly occupied our positions were never deprived of their suffrages in matters important to the State; when Kings came to the Parlement to confer with them about the utility or the Justice of new establishments of offices, which today ruin families, they always let them contradict them and speak with liberty. . . . But today by a disorder in morals and an illusion in politics, they bring us fully completed edicts, of which they are assured of the verification. . . . They [the ministers] levy taxes on everything one can imagine. Nothing remains to your subjects except their souls, the which, if they were venal, would have long ago been put up for sale. . . . Who does not know that there is no state in Europe where the royal authority is as absolute as in France? And that Your Majesty is only accountable for his actions to God alone, and to his conscience; but sire, you are also King of the French. Such a despotic and sovereign government that does not admit limits, and is not tempered by any gentleness, would be good among Scythians, Barbarians, and peoples far away and northern who have only the face of humans. But in France, which has always been the best policed state in the World, where the people have always held themselves to be born free and to live as true Frenchmen, such a thing is found completely strange and insupportable. Nonetheless, they are treated like Slaves or galley rowers. . . . There are many who are obliged to show respect on the exterior, but who curse under their breath. . . . Madame [Anne] make it such that kindness, gentleness, and humanity can henceforth have letters of naturalization in the Louvre.[15]

In part as a sop to such forces, Anne issued letters calling an Estates General to meet in 1649. Preliminary meetings did take place in some provinces, which actually drew up *cahiers,* but the Estates themselves never met, because of the chaos in Paris.

France suffered through four rebellions between 1648–1653:

1. The Parlementary Fronde from 1648–1649.

2. The princely Fronde, an amorphous collection of rebellions caused by personal feuds among the ruling elite.

3. The religious Fronde, pitting the Jansenists and their ally Cardinal de Retz against Mazarin, the Jesuits, and the Church hierarchy.

4. The endemic rebellions in the provinces, which often dovetailed with the first or second problems.

THE CHANCELLOR AND THE "ROMAN"

The leader of the Parlement in this rejection, Pierre Broussel, a former soldier then in his seventies, was a councillor, not one of the presidents. Broussel lived in relative poverty, was known to be incorruptible, and had a special reputation as an implacable enemy of tax farmers and of tax increases on the Parisian population. He enjoyed enormous popularity in his own district of the city because of the simplicity of his lifestyle; throughout the city, he had the reputation as the protector of its interests. He was, in short, the worst possible opponent for an administration riddled with corruption. Mazarin and his cronies had a well-deserved reputation as avaricious opportunists. When he died, Mazarin, a man of extremely modest means when he began royal service, left the largest private fortune ever amassed in France.

Little wonder that public opinion in Paris favored the saintly Broussel over the cupidious cardinal. After temporizing for much of August, the royal council, acting in the aftermath of Condé's victory over the Spaniards at Lens, decided to crack down. On 26 August, the very day of the great *Te Deum* mass in Notre Dame to celebrate the Lens victory, the council arrested Broussel. This clumsy, oafish manuever led to insurrection. The inhabitants of Broussel's quarter near the place de Grève, roused by the screams of his old maidservant and by the tocsin bell of the local church, turned out en masse, erecting barricades of cobblestones, overturned carts, and whatever else lay at hand. Talon estimated that more than twelve hundred barricades appeared in a single day. Mme de Motteville summarized the Court's view of this man:

> He [Broussel], counselor of parliament, who had constantly raised the standard against the king and opened all the discussions that tended to destroy the royal authority; he had made himself the mouthpiece of the people, showing on every occasion the spirit of a man born in a republic, and affecting the sentiments of a veritable Roman.

Anne of Austria sent chancellor Séguier to the Parlement at 5 A.M. the next day; his brother, bishop of Meaux, and his daughter, the duchess of Sully, accompanied him. They all soon had reason to regret their rash behavior:

The Parlementary Fronde involved tortuous negotiations between Mazarin and Particelli d'Hémery, and the royal officers. Government intransigence even forced the Parlement of Paris to make unprecedented common cause with the other Parisian Sovereign Courts and with important financial officers. The representatives of these courts formed an assembly called the Chamber of Saint-Louis (13 May 1648) and declared themselves a "union." The king's council, not surprisingly, summoned the chief judges and announced a royal edict rescinding the Act of Union. Unknown Parisians responded by placarding the city with copies of Concini's death sentence, a clear warning to the "evil Italian" ministers (Mazarin and d'Hémery), and a foreign queen, once more leading a child king astray.

The government alternated between the carrot and the stick. The council accepted actions taken by the Chamber of Saint-Louis (which it had declared illegal!), yet also tried intimidation, arresting some of the leaders of the treasurers of France. The Parlement reacted by demanding the abolition of the intendants. The Chamber and the king's council debated a seven-point reform package:

(CONTINUED)

Parisians accosted the carriage at every turn and the barricades prevented them from escaping. The trio abandoned their carriage at the duke de Luynes's hôtel, fleeing into the house to escape the threatening crowd. Mme de Motteville gives this account of their adventure:

> He was received by a good old woman who, seeing the chancellor asking for help, took him by the hand and led him to a little closet made of pine boards at the end of a hall. He had no sooner entered, he and his party, than the *canaille* [mob] arrived with furious shouts, demanding to know where he was, and declaring, with many oaths, that they meant to have him. Some said: "Prisoner for prisoner; we will exchange him for our dear protector [Broussel]." Others, more malignant, said he ought to be killed and quartered, and the pieces hung in the public squares to show their resentment by their vengeance. They came at last to the little closet in search of him, but as the place looked deserted they contented themselves with giving a few kicks against the planks and listening if they could hear any sound; after which they went to seek him elsewhere. It is to be supposed that the chancellor while this was going on was not at his ease, and that he felt himself human. While in that closet he confessed to his brother, the bishop of Meaux, and prepared himself to die.[17]

The duke of la Meilleraye luckily arrived with two companies of Swiss guards to bring Séguier's party back to the safety of the Palais-Royal.

As for Broussel, he remained in custody, so the crowds turned uglier and uglier. When Parlement itself returned on foot from a failed attempt to get Anne to release him, the Parisians refused to let them pass and sent them back with a warning that they would all be killed, should they return without Broussel. Under threat of physical violence, they returned to the palace and agreed to Anne's terms. The next day, Broussel returned home to a hero's welcome: "never was the triumph of king or Roman Emperor greater than that of this poor little man, who had nothing to recommend him but his obstinacy for the public good and his hatred of taxes." The people wanted to celebrate a *Te Deum* in his honor, but "the man himself, ashamed of the uproar, escaped from their hands, and getting out by a small door of the church fled to his house."

1. Revocation of intendants.

2. Return of direct tax collection to proper officers.

3. Reduction of the *tailles* by one-eighth (later by one-fourth).

4. Forgiveness of *taille* arrears.

5. Limitation of arbitrary arrest to twenty-four hours.

6. Payment of *gages*.

7. Payment of annuities.[16]

Soon Parlement revoked, *on its own authority,* the commissions of all intendants who had not registered their letters with the appropriate Parlement.

Smelling blood, the sharks circled their victims. Anne tried to mollify them by forcing Particelli d'Hémery to resign. The judges howled his poor son, a president of the Parlement, out of the court. On 31 July, at a *lit de justice,* Anne had chancellor Séguier announce a virtual capitulation: Anne renewed the *paulette* on the traditional basis for all officers and reduced the *tailles* by one-eighth in the current year and by one-quarter in each of the next two years. She promised to pay annuities and *gages,* eliminated some new taxes, agreed to register all edicts for new taxes in the Parlements, and went along with limits to arbitrary arrest. The declaration also ordered the Chamber of Saint-Louis to cease its meetings, and demanded that Parlement stop its political discussions and get back to work on legal cases. Anne created a special tribunal to look into tax farming fraud. Parlement initially applauded her proposals but, a week later, decided to remonstrate against these last two elements, violating all precedents of *lits de justice,* in which the king ordered registration of an edict without dissent and without further remonstrance.

The quarrel continued throughout the summer and into January of 1649, when Anne, Mazarin, and the boy king fled Paris. Condé laid siege to the city in the king's name, causing a famine of terrifying proportions: the price of bread reached its seventeenth-century high in February 1649. Although Anne and Mazarin won the siege in a military sense, the international situation (Spanish military successes in the north) led them to compromise with the Parlement in the form of abolition of intendants, payment of annuities and *gages,* renewal of the *paulette,* and amnesty for all rebels. In return, the officers agreed to stop the joint meetings among the different courts and to return to their judicial functions (*Peace of Rueil,* March 1649).

The Parlementary Fronde appeared to some as a constitutional crisis: many historians have treated it as such. The Parlement stood up to the Regent and effectively made her accountable for her actions to them. The judges made plain their belief that they acted to preserve the king's authority: as Broussel said, "sometimes the best way to serve a prince is to disobey him." The Parlement took seriously its responsibilities to make the Regency conform to the ancient ordinances (notably those of Orléans, Moulins, and Blois), using language not entirely different from that of the defenders of England's "Ancient Constitution" in the 1680s. Yet two decisive factors should not be forgotten:

1. Broussel made his remarks about a *child* king (Louis was only 9); the Parlement demanded accountability in a way that would have been unthinkable had the king been an adult.

2. The Parlement claimed to defend *French* interests against two rulers of France who were not French: Anne of Austria and Mazarin.[18]

The Parlementary Fronde did lead to a decisive constitutional outcome. In the mid 1650s, Mazarin, in the name of a now adult king, established the principle that the Parlements served a primarily judicial function, not a legislative one. Louis XIV would make that principle into the cornerstone of his policy. In his *Memoirs* he would even insist that the Parlements and other courts "having recently taken the name sovereign courts" [a false accusation] had begun to "regard themselves as separate and independent sovereignties," which he would not tolerate. Louis accepted

Bodin's idea of sovereignty—that whoever made the law was sovereign—and so demanded that the Parlements and other high courts be judicial, not legislative bodies.[19] As for its practical importance, Parlements and local royal courts continued to make law even in the heart of Louis XIV's reign; they lost authority only over decisions taken by the king's council.

The Parlement of Paris never suggested that its authority sprang from any source but the king himself. The Parlementary Fronde began as a defensive action: Mazarin threatened the stability of the judges' investments; they acted to defend them. The judges got what they wanted most:

1. Security of their investments (renewal of the *paulette* and at least partial payment of *gages* and annuities).

2. A drastic reduction in the number of cases evoked from the Parlements to the king's council.

The King got what he wanted: Parlements that acted as law courts, not as political bodies. By the mid-1650s, this compromise was already clear; in 1673, Louis XIV only codified what had been agreed to fifteen years before.

The Princely Fronde, 1649–1653

France was torn up by people who did not have a single noble idea, a single generous sentiment.

Ernst Lavisse, writing of the princely Fronde

Widespread disorder in the provinces accompanied the revolts in Paris. Tax collections, already far in arrears, simply ceased in broad sections of the country: the rumor spread that the king had rescinded the *tailles* for 1649. In the Loire valley, the town government of Angers sponsored a fleet of ships to bring duty-free salt to the city. When the salt tax farmers and their armed guards tried to collect the *gabelle,* the guards hired by the town and some members of the local nobility defeated them in a pitched battle involving hundreds of combatants. In Provence, Mazarin's efforts to create a second session of the Parlement led to open rebellion in early 1648. The Parlementaires masterminded the assassination of poor Philippe Guiedon, the first purchaser of such an office, and soon arrested the intendant and the governor. The government did not regain control of the province until the summer of 1649.

This success paralleled positive developments elsewhere. The government obtained substantial grants from the estates of Brittany and Languedoc, pacified vital Normandy (key source of hard currency), and even calmed a rebellion in Guyenne. Yet these successes should not hide the difficulties of the situation; provincial cooperation with royal officials remained sporadic. The Rueil agreement may have put an end to the revolt of the Parlement of Paris, which had had the support of some of the princes, such as Conti and Beaufort, but it did not end the cycle of revolts. Opposition now shifted to members of the princely elite: the prince of Condé; his brother, the prince of Conti; their sister, the duchess of Longueville and her husband; the brother dukes of Vendôme and Beaufort (grandsons of Henry IV); the viscount of Turenne; Gaston and his daughter; and Cardinal Retz. The schemers also included an assortment of lesser figures, such as the duchess of Chevreuse, an eternal conspirator who had played a role in the plots of the 1620s.

The victorious quartet of the spring of 1649—Anne, Mazarin, the young Condé, and Gaston—fell out over the spoils in the fall. They hired pamphleteerists to proclaim the sincerity of their devotion to the public good; in reality, they fought for intensely personal reasons. Again and again, the memoirs of the period emphasize the role of women heading the factions: the princess of Condé (Charlotte of Montmorency), the duchess of Montbazon (Rohan), her daughter-in-law the duchess of Chevreuse, the duchess of Longueville (daughter of the princess of Condé), and Anne-Marie-Louise d'Orléans-Montpensier (the Grande Mademoiselle), daughter of Gaston. Their quarrels could be intensely personal, as in the 1645 controversy created by the princess of Condé and her daughter-in-law sitting next to the Grande Mademoiselle during services at Notre Dame cathedral. Soon afterward, Anne had to move the marriage of Marie of Mantua to the king of Poland out of Notre Dame and into a private chapel because Gaston would not permit the prince of Condé to share in his private kneeler during the ceremony.[20] Later, the duchess of Longueville, Anne of Austria, and the other great ladies of the Court fell out over who should receive the right to a stool in the queen's presence.

Despite the desertion of Turenne, Anne and Mazarin's forces triumphed everywhere in 1650: they led the boy king on a triumphant march that pacified Normandy, restored order in Bordeaux, and returned royal authority even in the heart of Condé's power base, Burgundy. Yet these successes only created a new coalition against Mazarin: the coadjutor bishop of Paris, Retz, the duchess of Chevreuse, and the duke of Beaufort. Mazarin himself rode to Le Havre to deliver the edict releasing Condé and Conti from prison. Condé returned to Paris, where he immediately alienated everyone again; he fled to Bordeaux. Mazarin, who had fled to Germany, came back, then left again, when Paris gave Condé a hero's welcome. The prince once more bungled the situation, leading to the return of Anne and the young Louis (October 1652) and even of Mazarin, in January 1653. The long cycle of double-crossing eventually led to marriages between Mazarin's nieces, and Conti and Vendôme. Condé fled to Spain, for whom he commanded armies for the next six years.

In the provinces, the last holdout, Bordeaux, did not receive royalist forces until August. There, the internal political forces of the city had created a chaotic situation. The Parlement sometimes allied with Condé, but sometimes not. The citizenry, mainly the artisans, took matters into their own hands, creating a party known as the Ormée (named after the elms under which they met). The Ormée issued by far the most radical manifestos of the Fronde; some elements even extolled the virtues of republican government and sought to ally with Oliver Cromwell: he wanted nothing to do with this "rabble." In the end, the Parlement broke the leader of the radical faction on the wheel, and the city meekly surrendered to royal forces.

What can we make of the princely Fronde? Many have presented it as a sort of last stand of the "feudal" nobility against the "absolutist" state. That characterization

Politics and "Beauty"

The princely cabals formed and re-formed based more on personal feelings—the ever-shifting combinations of lovers—than on substantive difference. Anne-Geneviève de Bourbon, duchess of Longueville, sister of the young prince of Condé, dominated the events at several moments; her contemporaries attributed her power to the great beauty she had inherited from her mother, Charlotte of Montmorency, who, as a fifteen-year-old had so dazzled Henry IV in 1609. What did they mean by "beauty?" Mme de Motteville offers this description of the duchess of Longueville, in explaining why the viscount of Turenne, like so many courtiers, became infatuated with this "angel":

Charlotte of Montmorency. Henry IV had a crush on this princess when she was fifteen; he forced his cousin Condé to marry her, to make sure she would have to live at Court.

The duchess of Longueville, daughter of Charlotte of Montmorency, sister of the Grand Condé. Many of the great nobles of mid-century France, such as marshal Turenne or the duke of La Rochefoucauld, fell in love with the duchess. She and la Rochefoucauld had a son beloved of them both.

> Her ideas, her intellect, and the opinion formed of her discernment made her the admired of all men; they were convinced that her esteem alone was enough to give them reputation. . . . The very air of her person had a charm, the spell of which extended even to her own sex. It was impossible to see her without liking her, and wishing to please her. . . . Her eyes were not large, but beautiful, soft and brilliant, and the blue was wonderful, like that of the turquoise. Poets could only compare to lilies and roses the tones of her face; and the silvery fair hair that accompanied such marvels made her resemble an angel—such as the weakness of our nature makes us imagine them—much more than a woman.[21]

The description focuses on physical appearance, yet it begins with praise for the duchess' intellect and the manner in which she carried herself. We see the same attributes praised so long before, by the *Roman de la Rose*—the blond hair, the blue eyes. In the late sixteenth century, Ronsard even wrote poetry telling his brown-eyed mistress that "She had so lighted me with thy flame, That another green eye could never vanquish" her "beautiful brown eye, which I feel in the soul." Ronsard aside, the blond hair–blue eyes syndrome continued, and continues to carry almost mystical power in French, and Western culture.[22]

makes little sense. Each prince wanted control of the state for private gain. Condé followed in the time-honored path of his ancestors. Members of the Condé family, as leading adult Princes of the Blood, led rebellions against Regency governments in 1560, 1614, and 1650. The princely Fronde centered around the personal, selfish conflicts within France's highest aristocracy. Not one of these people supported any significant change in the nature of the French monarchy.

ᴗ A New Day: The Coup of 1661

> *... in these sorts of things it is not in the power of kings, because they are men, and have to deal with men, to attain all the perfection that they propose to reach, too distant for our weakness; but this impossibility is a bad reason not to do what one can, and this distance never to advance ourselves, which would not be without utility and without glory.*
>
> Louis XIV, describing to his son his state
> of mind on the eve of his 1661 reforms

Once the tragic farce of the princely Fronde had whimpered to a halt in the summer of 1653, the government could get back to the business of running the kingdom. One of its first acts was among the most symbolically powerful: the coronation of Louis XIV. Whatever the legists might say, popular opinion still had a strong sense that the king was truly king only after his coronation. Louis received the sacred anointing on 7 June 1654, in the presence of all the great nobles of France, save the rebel Condé. Louis made all of the requisite promises, binding himself to the kingdom (like a husband to a wife, as the oath said), to his nobility, to the Church. Louis promised to temper justice with mercy and to preserve order in his kingdom.

The king's reception in various cities at the end of the Fronde amply demonstrates the extent to which ordinary people and elites alike wanted a return to order. Mazarin recounts the story of how the Frondeur garrison inside the fortress of Bellegarde responded to the child king's presence with wild shouts of "Vive le Roi!" and surrendered shortly after he arrived. Once the fiction of the child king duped by evil (foreign) advisors no longer could be maintained, meaningful opposition to royal authority sharply decreased. Relying on the authority of an *adult, crowned* king, Mazarin could re-establish his control and his clientage networks in those areas in which he had lost it.

Intendants returned to the provinces by 1653, albeit often with different titles. Mazarin's new superintendent of finances, Nicolas Fouquet, had impeccable Parlementaire credentials: king's attorney at the Parlement of Paris, son and nephew of Parlementaires from Paris and Rennes. The secretary of state for War, Michel Le Tellier, a loyal client of the cardinal, reaffirmed his authority over the army. Here the key person was Turenne, who, happily for Mazarin, had developed a strong sense of personal loyalty to the king. Mazarin also had the unshakable support of his godson, Louis XIV. Much as the teachings of the Church would have it, the godfather (Mazarin) replaced the deceased father (Louis XIII).

Mazarin did not neglect his own interests. Although he lost virtually all of his fortune during the Fronde, between 1653 and his death in 1661 the cardinal recovered all of that and more. When he died, he left a fortune estimated at 38 million *livres,* by far the largest private inheritance in French monarchical history (the previous record, of 22 million *livres,* belonged to Richelieu). Mazarin possessed 9 million *livres* of cash, an inconceivable sum in a country chronically short of specie.[23] These massive holdings came about because of fraud and corruption, of that there can be little doubt. Mazarin's collaborators knew all; would they tell all? The two chief fiscal collaborators were the superintendant of finances, Fouquet, and Mazarin's personal intendant, Jean-Baptiste Colbert. In the months after Mazarin's death, Colbert defeated Fouquet in their contest for the king's confidence because, while Louis recognized Fouquet's "intelligence and a great knowledge of the interior workings of the State," the superintendent lacked Colbert's "great work effort . . . and probity."

Fouquet did not help his cause with the fabulous ball he gave in the king's honor at the château of Vaux-le-Vicomte on 17 August 1661. The king was outraged that his superintendent of finances could live in such luxury, when the royal finances were in such difficult straits. Only the vigorous objections of Anne of Austria—who told Louis, ever mindful of his manners, that he could not be so impolite a guest as to arrest his host—prevented Fouquet's arrest on the spot. In his *Memoirs*, Louis XIV singled out Fouquet's audacious conduct:

> The sight of the vast establishments that that man had built, and the insolent acquisitions that he had made, could only convince me of the unbounded level of his ambition; and the general calamity of all my people solicited constantly my justice against him.

Louis had Fouquet arrested at Nantes scarcely more than two weeks later, on 5 September. His contemporaries did not yet realize it, but the era of first ministers—of a Richelieu or a Mazarin—was over. Louis did more than fire Fouquet; he abolished the position of superintendent of finances and, what is more, he abolished, too, the informal system of a first minister:

> I resolved above all to never take a first minister; and if you listen to me, my son, you and all your successors after you, the name of first minister will be forever abolished in France, nothing being more unworthy than seeing on one side all the functions of a ruler and, on the other, the sole title of King.

Later, Louis would add this cautionary note:

> . . . do not confound two very different things: I would say that to govern by oneself, without listening to any council, would be another extreme as dangerous as that of being governed by another. The cleverest individuals take advice from others in their little affairs. What should be the case of kings, who have in hand the public interest, and whose decisions make the bad or good of all the earth?[24]

The great French institutional historian Roland Mousnier called Louis's actions in 1661 a revolution in government. That is a bit excessive, but they did mark a significant step forward on a path begun in the 1620s. The main Crown officers—the constable, the admiral, the chancellor, the superintendent of finances, and the colonel–general of the infantry—had traditionally wielded its greatest powers. Louis XIII and Louis XIV abolished all of these offices, except that of chancellor. Louis XIV significantly reduced the political power of the chancellor by excluding him from the highest royal council. The constable, admiral, and colonel–general of the infantry had named virtually all officers in the French military; under Louis XIV, that power passed definitively to the king.

∼ A Golden Age of French Culture

Make our century illustrious, in letters as in arms.[25]

Jean Desmarets, "Discourse on poetry,"
written to Cardinal Richelieu in 1633

The decades between the 1630s and the 1690s have long been known as the Golden Age of French theatre because France's three defining playwrights—Corneille, Molière, and Racine—composed then their greatest works. In the broader realm of culture, too, one can say that Desmarets got his wish. The list of important, indeed pathbreaking writers extends to virtually every genre: France's great philosopher, René Descartes, wrote in the 1630s and 1640s, and his scarcely less distinguished contemporary, Blaise Pascal, published from the 1640s to the 1660s; Mme de Lafayette published the first modern French novel, *The Princess of Cleves,* in 1678; her close friend, Mme de Sévigné, became the model for French letter writers. Another friend, the duke de la Rochefoucauld, left a justly famous book of *Maxims* and his contemporary Jean de La Fontaine's *Fables* remain beloved by children the world over. From painting to architecture, from music and dance to landscape gardening, France enjoyed a rarely paralleled epoch of genius in the final eight decades of the seventeenth century. Contemporaries often compared themselves to those living in ancient Athens during its Golden Age.

René Descartes laid the intellectual foundation for much of this intellectual flowering in his revolutionary book, *The Discourse on Method* (1637), which he wrote in French, not in the Latin of the Humanists, so that a broader audience could approach his text. *The Discourse* provides so fundamental a foundation to our intellectual universe that few Westerners can analyze the world in terms other than those he laid down. Descartes used mathematics to combine pure empiricism and the abstract rationalism of the Scholastics to create a "scientific method" based on "the long chains of reasoning, so simple and easy, which enabled the geometricians to reach the most difficult demonstrations." Science would henceforth, in this view, create truths whose certainty would match those of mathematics. These scientific truths would replace the previously accepted "truths" provided by revealed religion. The old "truths" became superstitions, belief in them an incontestable sign of cultural backwardness. As Descartes himself said, the method embedded in these geometric chains of reasoning

> made me wonder whether all things knowable to men might not fall into a similar logical sequence. If so, we need only refrain from accepting as true that which is not true, and carefully follow the order necessary to deduce each one from the others, and there cannot be any propositions so abstruse that we cannot prove them.

Descartes moved onto extraordinarily dangerous ground. For him, as for countless generations of Europeans before him, the two most abstruse propositions that needed proof were obvious: the proofs of the "existence of God and of the human soul," as he entitled Chapter 4 of the *Discourse*. The title, with its traditional ordering of God, then human, promised little in the way of a revolution; the chapter itself belied its title.

Descartes proved the existence of the human *before* he proved the existence of God. Even though Descartes himself was a sincere believer in God, the radical step of proving the existence of humans *without reference to God* opened the door to a dramatic shift in philosophy.[26] In a certain sense, one could say that it made possible all modern philosophy, because it definitively separated the study of philosophy from the study of God. Although some philosophers would still make reference to God, the linkage between philosophy and theology would never be the same after Descartes.

Descartes wrote, "I think, therefore I am." He argued that even if he doubted the truth of this statement, he could not doubt that someone doubted; the existence of this doubt, proved the existence of the doubter. His argument about the existence of God relied heavily on Anselm's ontological proof. Man could conceive perfection, yet was himself imperfect; therefore, some perfect being must exist, to allow of the conception of perfection. Descartes pushed this analysis one step further, arguing that mind and matter consisted of different elements.

In a later work, *Meditations* (written in Latin, published in 1641), Descartes posited another radical idea. When discussing the human capacity to think, he mused:

> But how do I know that there is not some entity, of a different nature from what I have just judged uncertain, of which there cannot be the least doubt? Is there not some God or some other power who gives me these thoughts? But I need not think this to be true, for possibly I am able to produce them myself.[27]

Descartes himself did not subscribe to the idea that the human mind operated independently from the Divinity, but others soon made that connection. His great contemporary, Blaise Pascal, would specifically chastise Descartes: "I cannot pardon Descartes. In all his philosophy, he has wanted to be able to dispense with God." The duke of Luynes soon funded the translation of the *Meditations* into French. The *Meditations* achieved a far greater diffusion in France than the *Discourse*.

Although the *Meditations* touched more closely on the subject most deeply of interest to Descartes's contemporaries—the existence of God—the *Discourse*, together with the works of the great English philosopher Francis Bacon, had the greater long-term impact, because these works created a new intellectual world. Bacon and Descartes laid down the principles of scientific method, principles that have come down to our times virtually unchanged. As Descartes put it,

> The first rule was never to accept anything as true unless I recognized it to be evidently such. . . . (T)he second was to divide each of the difficulties which I encountered into as many parts as possible. . . . (T)he third was to think in an orderly fashion . . . even treating, as though ordered, materials

COGITO: THE BIRTH OF SCIENTIFIC METHOD

René Descartes offers a classic example of the intellectual preeminence of the rising legal elite of early–modern France. His father, Joachim Descartes, held the office of president of the Parlement of Brittany; one of his sons succeeded him as a judge. René began on the typical path for a young man of his social standing. He attended the Jesuit *collège* at La Fleche, where he studied Aristotle, literature, and mathematics. He then went on to the law school at the university of nearby Poitiers, from which he graduated in 1616. After his studies, René, like many male members of the seventeenth-century European elite, decided to travel. He headed for the Netherlands, where he encountered many of the leading mathematicians and scientists of the age, and soon joined the Dutch army, led by Maurice of Nassau, the most innovative general of his day. When he left military service, he traveled further: Poland, Germany, and, in 1625, Italy. The following year, he returned to Paris, for a time joining the intellectual circle around Father Marin Mersenne.

Descartes had long corresponded with Mersenne and with other leading humanists and scientists of Europe. His three years in Paris (1626–1628) established his international reputation as a physicist and mathematician. (All schoolchildren know his invention, analytical geometry, with its Cartesian coordinates, to say nothing of his system of superscript notation of magnitudes.) In these years, Descartes encouraged his colleagues to abandon the old Aristotelian methods, which relied on authority to establish proof, and to substitute the rigorous application of reasoned analysis to experience. Except in optics, where he formulated the law of refraction, Descartes' own scientific contributions—which rarely followed his proclaimed method—were minimal. In fact, his erroneous theories on physics, botany, and anatomy led many eighteenth-century French philosophers to discredit his work altogether.

which were not necessarily so. . . . The last was always to make enumerations so complete, and reviews so general, that I would be certain that nothing was omitted.[28]

Descartes placed rationalism at the center of human activity. His emphasis on scientific method, on a rational explanation for everything, and on the importance of using reason to rule over human passion, transformed French elite culture, which remains today permeated by the mythology of Cartesian rationalism. No longer did a significant section of educated, elite society look to revelation for explanations. They demanded rational explanations. That attitude led them to question natural phenomena, to abandon superstitious or religious explanations for natural events. It led them to question religion itself; finally, in the eighteenth century, it led them to question the political system under which they lived. The French Revolutionaries consciously applied Descartes's doctrines to politics. In their eyes, received authority ("tradition") provided no justification for political structures; only the application of reason to determine universal principles (liberty, equality), and the creation of a society and a state based on those principles, could be legitimate. When the Revolu-

(CONTINUED)

These eighteenth-century philosophers, like Voltaire, turned away from Descartes's rationalism, which differed importantly from the ideas of his English contemporaries, like Francis Bacon, whose *Novum Organum* (1620) outlined the experimental method of scientific inquiry. Where Descartes relied on inductive reasoning—on the presumption of innate consciousness, as reflected in the mind–matter duality—Bacon and the English empiricists who followed him, like Thomas Hobbes (who had been Bacon's private secretary) or John Locke, relied solely on deductive reasoning. They held that all knowledge derived from sensory perception. They applied scientific reason—what Hobbes called sapience—to experience, whether in Bacon's experiments, or Hobbes's analysis of social organization (*Leviathan* [1651]). Humans had no innate ideas; they were, in Locke's famous phrase, a blank slate.[29] Descartes's principles led eventually to the more idealist strain of modern philosophy, based heavily on the work of the eighteenth-century German philosopher Immanuel Kant. Conversely, Bacon's principles led to the realist strain, based on the work of the great eighteenth-century Scottish philosopher, David Hume.

His failed forays into physical science notwithstanding, Descartes's principles helped destroy the preeminence of Aristotle in European scientific thinking. As the eighteenth-century editor of the *Encyclopédie,* d'Alembert, put it: "his method alone would have sufficed to make him immortal." In one field of human endeavor after another, people rejected the premise of relying on authority—on the Bible, on Aristotle—to establish the truth or falsehood of an assertion. Descartes and the other early leaders of the Scientific Revolution—Galileo in Italy, Bacon in England, Kepler in Germany, Brahe in Denmark, Copernicus in Poland—laid the foundation for the work of scientists such as Newton or Leibniz and, in the process, fundamentally restructured the Western world's conception of knowledge itself.

tionaries discussed burial of Descartes's ashes in the new Panthéon they had instituted for the great men of France, they praised him above all for being

> the one who, by breaking the shackles on the human spirit, laid the early groundwork for the permanent destruction of political servitude . . . Descartes's genius gave its general impetus to the human mind, the original source of a revolution in the destiny of the human race, to the felicitous epoch of pure and total social liberty. . . . [with Descartes] the human spirit was not yet free, but it knew that it was made to be free.[30]

Descartes did not create his revolution in a vacuum; he lived in the age of the Scientific Revolution. He and Blaise Pascal, the great mathematician, were the two most important French contributors to this movement, although one could cite others, such as the most famous mathematician of their day, Pierre de Fermat, one of whose theorems bedeviled those seeking to prove it for more than three hundred years.[31] Pascal, like Descartes, came from a legal family: his father held a position as president at the Court of Aids of Clermont. Pascal belonged more directly to French society than did

Descartes; he participated in Mersenne's meetings in Paris and had close personal ties to high Parisian society. In the 1650s, Pascal even read aloud his *Provincial Letters* (attacks on the Jesuits, see below) at the salon of Mme du Plessis-Guénégaud.

This society included many important intellectual figures. Parisian elites, particularly those associated with the Parlement, had met for intellectual evenings (*soirées*) since at least the time of Henry IV. One group met at the house of the Parlementaire amateur historian Jacques-Auguste de Thou, who had a magnificent library that he allowed other Parisian scholars to use. De Thou left his library to his relatives, the Dupuy brothers, who followed his practice of opening it to scholars. In the late afternoons, they would welcome a wide range of the leading intellectuals of the time to discuss their work and larger issues of philosophy.[32]

Paris hosted other gatherings as well, the most famous of which took place at the house of Mersenne, well-known as a mathematician and astronomer. Mersenne invited his colleagues to his house on the place Royale (today, place des Vosges) to discuss their experiments, theories, and correspondence with scientists elsewhere in Europe. He himself maintained what was probably France's second widest range of epistolary contact with scholars. The little circle of Mersenne grew to include more than one hundred people: judges, clerics, doctors, even a handful of sword nobles. Some of them ranked among the great scientists of Europe: Étienne Pascal and, later, his son Blaise; Pierre Gassendi; and, during his stays in Paris, Descartes.

Lest we be blinded by the Parisian sun, however, we should remember that Mersenne had only the *second* largest correspondence among French men of letters: he had to cede the place of honor to Nicolas Peiresc, of Aix-en-Provence. Peiresc had state-of-the-art telescopes and the most renowned collection of curiosities in Europe. He corresponded regularly with more than five hundred people, in places as far away as Damascus or Goa. Peiresc kept an open house for all interested in intellectual inquiry; Jean-Jacques Bouchard described it in 1630:

> A man who has no equal in Europe for courtesy and humanity, as well as for wisdom, curiosity about beautiful things and informed opinions about all that goes on in the world: there is no kingdom, land or well-known city where he does not have correspondence and of which he does not know and have all that it is remarkable and rare, either by men of merit and knowledge with whom he corresponds, or by men whom he keeps on his expense there for that purpose.[33]

Peiresc had less famous counterparts in other cities, notably those with a Parlement. At Dijon, Jean Bouhier and Jean-Baptiste Lantin, both presidents in the Parlement, led a circle of erudites. Their in-town mansions remain as visual symbols of the power, wealth, and artistic patronage of the Parlementaire elite of the seventeenth century. Toulouse had a similar gathering; Rennes had its erudites, like Parlementaire Charles d'Argentré, who revised his father's *History of Brittany* for presentation to the provincial Estates (1618).

Paris, because of its size, had more gatherings. These salons could even specialize in one area. Mersenne's focused on science. Others, led by women, met to discuss literature. Cathérine de Vivonne, marquise of Rambouillet, held the most famous, and aristocratic of these salons at her *hôtel* every Wednesday from 1617 until 1665. Her guest lists read like a who's who of seventeenth-century France. In her early days, she hosted Richelieu; somewhat later one could find the great theologian Bossuet or the prince of Condé, to say nothing of such writers as Mme de Lafayette or Mme de Sévigné. Corneille once read his play *Polyeucte* to her salon before allowing it to be staged. In time, others, such as Mme du Plessis-Guénégaud, Mlle de Scudéry, the duchess of Montpensier, and a wide range of women from the high nobility and the legal elite, imitated her. These salons helped bring about a dramatic change in taste and behavior. Women set the tone for these changes and so became the arbiters of French taste.

Not all men accepted female ascendancy in such matters. Cardinal Richelieu found the role of the salons, such as that of the *hôtel* de Rambouillet, to be intolerable. Some of the salons had been meeting places of people hostile to the regime: the duchess of Montpensier, daughter of Richelieu's archenemy, Gaston of Orléans; and Mme des Loges. Mme des Loges received a pension from Gaston and had the temerity to invite many Huguenots to her salon. Attendance at these salons did little for one's reputation at Court.

Richelieu had first made a name for himself as a speaker for the First Estate at the Estates General of 1614—that is, as a writer and orator. He later wrote plays and collaborated with others on *Memoirs* and a *Political Testament*. Deeply aware of the power of the written word, he subsidized writers of every sort, from common pamphleteerists to historians and professional journalists. One of his clients, Théophraste Renaudot, founded a weekly newspaper, the *Gazette de France,* in 1631. Renaudot received most of his information from Richelieu's clients, so the *Gazette* became a semi-official government organ and provided the government with an invaluable propaganda tool in its efforts to woo public opinion.[34]

Given his interest in literary matters, Richelieu unsurprisingly set out to undermine the literary salons by creating one under his indirect control. Following the initiative begun in the time of Henry IV by the poet Nicolas Maleherbe and his circle, Valentin Conrart, a royal secretary, had started (1629) to host an all-male club of writers each week. As the reputation of Conrart's group spread, prominent writers and intellectuals such as Nicolas Faret, the poet Claude Malleville, the literary critic Jean Chapelain, François Mainard, and Jean Desmarets joined them.[35] Malleville recruited François Boisrobert, a devoted client of Richelieu. The group consciously sought to continue Malherbe's efforts to unify the French language, with fixed rules of orthography and grammar. The Cardinal, seeing the utility of such a group, coopted it by authorizing official meetings at Desmarets's house and making Desmarets their official secretary. Richelieu obtained royal letters patent to make the group official "under the name of the Académie Française." On 5 February 1635, the king issued the chartering letters:

> Our well beloved and dear cousin Cardinal Richelieu has represented to Us that one of the glorious marks of the felicity of a State is that the sciences and the arts flourish there and that letters as well as arms are held in honor, because letters are one of the principal instruments of virtue . . . and he judges that we cannot begin better than by the most noble of all the arts,

which is that of Eloquence; that the French language, which until now has felt only too much the negligence of those who could have rendered it the most perfect of modern languages, is more capable than ever of becoming so, given the number of persons who have a singular knowledge of the advantages that it possesses . . .

Not one to take chances, the Cardinal placed two key royal officials—chancellor Pierre Séguier and Abel Servien, secretary of state for foreign affairs—among the "forty immortals," as the group would come to be known, and insisted that article one spell out his control: "no one shall be received who is not agreeable to Monsieur the Protector" (Richelieu). The Académie of these forty men became one of the defining institutions of French intellectual life, which, with a brief interlude during the Revolution, has kept jurisdiction over France's most precious cultural object, its language.[36] Article 26 left no doubts on that score:

> The principal function of the Academy will be to work with all the care and diligence possible to provide sure rules to our language and to make it pure, eloquent, and capable of treating the arts and the sciences. . . . A dictionary, a Grammar, a Rhetoric, and a Poetic shall be composed based on the observations of the Academy.[37]

After Richelieu's death, the Académie moved to Séguier's hôtel in Paris; when he died, in 1672, Louis XIV named himself as the official patron and moved the Académie to the Louvre. The dictionary appeared in full only in the 1690s, but Richelieu got precisely what he wanted: henceforth, a body sanctioned by the government would have theoretical control over language itself. His successors also continued the practice of ministerial involvement in the Académie: Colbert had himself elected in 1667, and Cardinal Fleury, chief minister of Louis XV, followed that example in 1717.[38] Words would now have an official meaning, whatever meaning local dialects might choose to invest them with. Three centuries after its first dictionary, the Académie Française remains the *official* arbiter of French language, although then, as now, private dictionaries remain the primary mechanisms for disseminating ideas about word meaning to the broader public.[39]

In many ways, Richelieu established the legitimacy of the Académie in 1636, when he asked it to rule on the suitability of a shocking new tragedy, *Le Cid,* by Pierre Corneille, hitherto best known for mediocre comedies and as one of Richelieu's stable of paid writers. Corneille, like Descartes, came from a legal family, received his secondary education from the Jesuits, and went to the law faculty of the university. He had imbibed many of the Stoicist ideas modified by Descartes in his philosophical writings. Corneille, though himself a commoner, wrote most effectively about the passions of the nobility; his plays, many of them historical tragedies based in Republican Rome, focused on the noble virtues of loyalty, courage, and honor. In contrast to earlier writings about the nobility, however, Corneille's plays understated physical violence and treated love as one emotion among many driving human behavior. Corneille's heroes are often torn by indecision, haunted by inner demons.[40]

In *Le Cid,* his most famous play, Corneille had the temerity to present a Spanish hero, right after the outbreak of open war between France and Spain. The play revolved around a duel in which its hero (Don Roderigo) kills the father of his beloved. Given that Richelieu and Louis XIII had just finished their crackdown on duels, Corneille's glorification of noble honor justified in blood seemed certain to provoke the cardinal's wrath. Yet scarcely a month after the opening performance, Richelieu approved the ennoblement of Corneille's family. The Académie commission, under the pen of Chapelain, offered a balanced assessment that mixed praise and judicious criticism and thus helped give the fledgling body a little credibility. (Corneille took the assessment as a vicious attack and retired to Rouen for three years.)

Le Cid tells us much about the evolving culture of the French nobility in the 1630s. Throughout the play, the main characters seem obsessed with honor: as Don Gomes, father of the Cid's fiancée says when justifying his slap of the face of Don Diego (the Cid's father), "I have a heart above the proudest disgraces / And one can reduce me to living without happiness, / But not resolve me to living without honor." The play praises the courage and honor of the nobility, and regularly suggests the human qualities of the king, who can "err like other men" and who has "less power than you have merit" when he seeks to reward *Le Cid* for his bravery against the Moors.

Again and again, Corneille's plays return to these themes, so dear to the hearts of the traditional nobility. In them, we can see the influence of Classical philosophy and historians—Seneca, Cicero, Tacitus, Polybius—on the ideology of seventeenth-century French elites. Corneille's succeeding tragedies often went back to Classical antiquity for their themes—*Horace* (1640), *Cinna* (1642), *Polyeucte* (1643)—but he worked, as well, on Christian themes. Dominant in the theatre of the 1640s, he fell into disfavor in the 1650s, returned briefly to eminence in the early 1660s, but then ceded definitively his preeminence to Jean Racine and Molière. Elected to the Académie in 1647, he continued to play an important role in French letters into the 1670s, but he himself recognized that he did not fit into the world of Louis XIV. In his poem celebrating the Peace of Nijmijgen (1678), he lamented that "this happy century has arrived so late for me, that I can pretend to little or no part in it."

Reason, Spirit, and Visual Arts

We must not judge by our senses alone but by reason.

Nicolas Poussin to his patron, Paul Fréart de Chantelou

The visual arts occupied a central place in French culture because of the tenuous literacy of so many members of the elite, who swam in an ocean of illiterates. Some of these artists, like the great Breton sculptors of the parish closes of Léon, remain anonymous. We can see in their sculptures the influence of Renaissance high culture, yet we see as well their determined peasant realism. Many rural churches in France still preserve artistic monuments from the seventeenth century. Gilded altarpieces, such as that of Lampaul-Guimiliau in Brittany, with its panel of fallen angels based on a painting by Rubens, show the ways in which peasants could have access to high culture. While some high culture artists, like the Le Nain brothers, painted idealized peasants, other artists, like Claude Lorrain, provided more realistic representations. Jacques Callot made no pretense of idealization: his vivid drawings of peasants suffering during the Thirty Years' War bring to life the misery of everyday life. High culture rarely reflected such unpleasantries, yet their reality and an art accessible to all that gave voice to common suffering surely played a role in the collective consciousness of the time.

Buildings, too, presented a public face for art.[41] The great Parisian projects included the Place Royale (today, Place des Vosges), with its symmetrical, colonnaded pathways; the Palais Cardinal (today Palais Royal) or the Sorbonne chapel, both built for Richelieu by Jacques Lemercier; and many townhouses (*hôtels*) constructed for the rich and powerful members of the robe, sword, and financial elites. The richest members of the elite hired architects such as François Mansart (best known to us for the sharply angled roof that bears his name) to redesign or build new country châteaux, as he did for Gaston of Orléans at the château of Blois. Mansart's work includes several sites in Paris, such as the current *hôtel* of the Bank of France. His work pointed the way to the Classicism that would dominate French architecture in the second half of the century.

Provincial France bears witness to the orgy of ornamental building. Salomon de Brosse, who created the Luxembourg Palace, also designed the magnificent Palace of the Parlement in Rennes. The interiors received the attention of the leading artists, such as Noël Coypel, who carried out the *France Protecting Justice*, or Jean Jouvenet, who would later execute the *Triumph of Justice* (See Plate.) at the Parlement of Brittany, as well as the painting of the Holy Spirit at the royal chapel of Versailles.[42] In Dijon, one can still see the *hôtels* constructed by Bouhier, Lantin, Des Brosses, and others. Bouhier's house, on the present rue Chabot-Charny, contains all the classic elements of the type: outer gate with porch; inner courtyards; Classical simplicity; large windows, allowing the entry of air and light; separation of private and public space within the home. When urban rioters turned against their masters, as in the Lanterlu rebellion at Dijon in 1630, they invariably headed straight for one of these new houses and destroyed the physical, visual evidence of wealth and taste: they looted the treasures of the house, usually to burn them.

The interior layouts now had a mixture of public and private rooms. Bedrooms had long fallen into the former category, but now became private refuges. Even the placement of the bed betokened the new mores: it moved from the center of the room to one of its edges. These new buildings, with their dramatically different internal design, emphasizing personal space, helped fuel greater demand for art objects such as paintings and sculptures. As Orest Ranum has pointed out:

> . . . architects created new private spaces in the homes of the well-to-do, or, rather, they increased the amount of private space by transforming into rooms what had previously been mere objects of furniture. In the various languages of Europe, words such as study, *cabinet*, *bibliothèque* (shelf or library), and *écritoire* (writing desk or writing room) may still refer to items of furniture, but they also designate rooms serving a particular, often private, function. . . . From here it was but a short step to the nineteenth-

century bourgeois home, with its accumulation of objets d'art, papers, books, and curiosities . . . [43]

Seventeenth-century urban *hôtels*, whether in Paris or a provincial capital such as Rennes or Dijon, invariably had the new private rooms: a study or a library, above all in the houses of the Parlementaires or government officials. These rooms often housed collections of art objects, not simply paintings but statuary, "curiosities," many of them archeological, and, in some cases, scientific instruments. Both such instruments and the books shelved in the library served a dual function as tools of learning and as objets d'art. Even France's kings had heard of important provincial collections; we know of many cases of the king making a special visit to private homes to see renowned "curiosities."

Inventories after death suggest these houses held a wide range of paintings. Many people hung up galleries of ancestor "portraits"; virtually all of them had religious paintings, done on canvas, wood, or even copper. French customers differed somewhat from contemporary Dutch ones in that they bought far fewer landscape paintings. While Dutch Calvinists had to avoid representations of Jesus, and so bought Old Testament subjects, the Catholic French reveled in them. The extraordinary catalogue (100+) of paintings offered for sale by the Dutch merchant Pierre Le Brun to the elite of Brittany, gathered for its Estates in 1632, offers some sense of the larger French art market. "Histories"—paintings of Classical or Biblical subjects—dominated his stock: he featured such works as *Our Lord Carrying the Cross* (150 *livres*), Nativity scenes, paintings of Mary and of Mary Magdelaine. Most portraits were cheap (8 *livres*) little pictures of prominent people of the time, like Richelieu or members of the royal family, but he did offer one of *The King Dressed as Mars* for 90 *livres*. Classical subjects—Bacchus, Atalante, Prometheus, and the like—sold for a much higher average price than other themes, an obvious indicator of the higher level of wealth associated with those who had received a Classical education.[44]

The remarkable element of Le Brun's catalogue of pictures is the extent to which the themes he offers mirror those of the great painters of the time. In one case, Le Brun offered a painting of an unusual theme, a blind man playing a viola, that matches one of the great master Georges de la Tour's works. Moreover, that very picture belonged to a family from Nantes (and now hangs in the city's Fine Arts Museum!). Just as de Brosses brought the most up-to-date architecture style to Rennes with his Palais de Justice for the Parlement, so, too, provincial elites could have access either to the finest new art or to copies of it by lesser artists.

As in the literary arts, so, too, change ocurred in the visual ones. French style shifted from the exuberant Baroque style of the early seventeenth century to more regulated Classicism between the late 1620s and the late 1650s. Important French painters, such as Simon Vouet, the preeminent master in France in the 1630s and 1640s, visited Italy and came back with a new appreciation of the work of such masters as Caravaggio. Vouet and his studio carried out many commissions in the second quarter of the century: he worked for the king, for Richelieu, chancellor Séguier, superintendent of finances Bullion. His Mannerist style brought to French painting the most avant-garde Italian methods, and had profound influence on those who followed him.

Other artists, such as Philippe de Champaigne, Nicolas Poussin, Georges de la Tour, and Claude Lorrain moved French painting in dramatically new directions in the waning days of Vouet's ascendency at Court. Champaigne and Poussin worked briefly together on the decoration of the Louvre (in the 1620s) but their careers diverged sharply thereafter. Champaigne's main voyages outside of France took him to Brussels, where he learned much of the styles of van Dyck and Rubens; in contrast, Poussin spent virtually his entire adult life in Rome. Champaigne is famous for his portraits, such as the 1629 portrait of Louis XIII, the remarkable three-sided study of Richelieu, or his renderings of the Parlementaire elite (like Omer Talon or chancellor Séguier). He also painted Mère Angélique Arnault, leader of the Port-Royal nuns (and member of a powerful Parlementaire family) and Colbert (in 1655, well before his rise to power). Champaigne demonstrates well the close interaction of larger cultural currents and painting. Converted to Jansenism in the early 1640s, his palette gradually became more somber, with an overwhelming emphasis on black and white.

Nor was Champaigne the only painter to reflect accurately the intellectual currents of his time; other great painters of the seventeenth century had important ties to such movements. The Le Nain brothers visually presented two distinct elements of intellectual and cultural change. Intellectually, their emphasis on humble subjects, such as Louis Le Nain's *Peasant Family,* gave visual weight to the idea of human equality. Their peasants appear not merely as appendages to rural scenes, but as the focus of the painting. In a cultural sense, these paintings of rural dwellers re-emphasized the pastoral, a conscious praise of the simplicity of rural life. Le Nain's famous peasant family, with its wily father, its well-fed children, its robust mother (and withered grandmother), enjoyed the simple pleasures of life: bread and wine. That few peasant families would have drunk wine from a glass is of little moment; Le Nain wants to present the purity and simplicity of the rural. The pastoral theme returned in literature as well; indeed, the tales of the peasants themselves became part of high culture at the end of the seventeenth century, with Charles Perrault's edition of folk tales, *The Stories of Mother Goose.*

The interests for ordinary subjects of the Le Nain brothers did not point the way to the immediate future (indeed, quite the opposite). One had to look abroad, to Rome, to the work of another great French painter, Nicolas Poussin. He traveled to Venice and then to Rome in 1624; like most painters of the time, he quickly fell under the influence of Caravaggio. Poussin spent the rest of the 1620s and much of the 1630s studying with major Italian painters and building up his expertise of Classical forms and motifs. He wandered throughout Rome, sketching and copying both Classical and Renaissance models; unlike most painters of his day, he also passionately studied Classical literature (above all the Roman love poet Ovid) and philosophy. Well established in reputation after the success of *The Death of Germanicus* (1626–1628), the first Western painting to depict a hero on his deathbed, by the early 1630s, Poussin received commissions for a wide range of religious and Classical paintings. Many of the paintings, such as his first *Arcadian Shepherds* (1628), followed a Venetian style reminiscent of Titian. Others, such as the *Assumption of the Virgin* (1631), gave evidence of Poussin's interest in a new palette of colors—the astounding blue of Mary's cape, her pink dress, the multihued sky. (See Plate 9.) This painting shows as well Poussin's life-long obsession with Classical architectural forms: Mary ascends to Heaven between two columns.

Poussin moved away from this Venetian, Baroque style and toward active emulation of Raphael and his followers in the early 1630s, a shift evident in the great bacchanals painted for Cardinal Richelieu between 1635–1636 (such as the wild orgy of *The Triumph of Pan*) and, perhaps most clearly in his second version of the *Arcadian Shepherds* (1638–1640). The 1628 *Arcadian Shepherds* shows him much influenced by a romanticized understanding of Classical motifs, a theme that continued in such works as *Echo and Narcissus* (1629–1630) or *Diana and Endymion* (1630). The shepherds of 1638, their muscles scaled down to human size, their body language a somber rejoinder to the romanticized stylization of the 1628 version, reflect the important influence of Stoicism on Poussin's mature work. In that sense, Poussin's intellectual evolution paralleled that of European political elites: seventeenth-century political theorists everywhere reached back to neo-Stoicist arguments.

The Poussin of the late 1630s, 1640s, and 1650s dealt with an astounding variety of themes, and presented works in a wide range of styles. The haunting *Eucharist* of 1638–1640, with its eerie lighting, reminds one of de la Tour's work of the same period. Poussin moved in a different direction, however, after his disastrous stay in Paris (1641–1642). He first devoted himself to his second set of *Seven Sacraments* and then moved decisively into landscape painting. He continued both religious—*Eliezer and Rebecca*, the *Judgment of Solomon*, the *Holy Family on the Steps*, the *Ecstacy of Saint Paul*—and Classical themes. The Classical themes included several canvasses on the Greek hero Phocion and a famous landscape with Diogenes. These landscapes, whatever their theme, continued to present Classical architecture in their background. Poussin's paintings thus mirrored the architectural themes of his day—the Classicism of architects such as Mansart—yet their austerity also bears witness of the asceticism that drove religious leaders from Vincent de Paul to Mère Angélique.

Where inner spirituality has a limited influence on Poussin's overall output, it dominates the paintings of his contemporary, Georges de la Tour, whose work provides a visual reaffirmation of many of the ideas of Blaise Pascal and of the great religious revival. Like Champaigne, de la Tour moved to a darker palette in the 1630s and 1640s; he also shifted subjects. In the 1620s and early 1630s, he painted many scenes from daily life: the *Fortune Teller* (c. 1621), the *Beggars's Brawl* (c. 1629), the *Hurdy-gurdy Player* (c. 1631). Although he continued to paint similar subjects in his later years (such as the famous *Dice Players* of 1650), he focused more often on religious subjects, above all on Mary Magdelaine.

In his *Thoughts* (*Pensées*), Pascal gives us some insights into the new mental universe of de la Tour and his contemporaries:

> Faith is different from proof. One is human, and the other is a gift from God. . . . this faith is in the heart and makes one say, I believe, not, I know. Nothing conforms so much to reason as this disavowal of reason [faith]. Faith often says what the senses do not say, but not the opposite of what they see; it is above them, and not against them.

Georges de la Tour, The Repentant Magdelaine. *De la Tour's work here demonstrates the inner light so central to the thinking of Pascal and the Jansensists.*

SOURCE: © Giraudon/Art Resource.

This inner spiritualism bore tangible, physical fruit in such works as de la Tour's *Repentant Magdelan* paintings of the late 1630s or the *Newborn Child* (1646). He often uses a candle (typically hidden) as the only source of light. This inner, hidden light, as in the *Newborn,* illuminates the features of the subjects of the painting—the newborn, her mother, and the nurse—but their outer selves blend into the darkness behind. De la Tour offers stunning visual evidence of the representative quality of Pascal's spiritualism. As Pascal himself wrote, "The heart has its reasons that reason knows not; one knows it in a thousand things."[45] The spiritualism associated with Pascal or de la Tour, like the rationalism associated with Descartes, remains an integral element in French intellectual life. Indeed, one might trace this duality back even further, to the twelfth-century debates of Bernard and Abélard, in their own way precursors of Pascal and Descartes.

The Kingdoms of Heaven and Earth

> *Men distrust religion. They hate it and fear that it is true. To heal that distrust we must begin by showing that religion is not contrary to reason.*
>
> Blaise Pascal, *Thoughts*

Pascal takes us to the heart of a fundamental conflict in mid-seventeenth-century French society: the nature of faith. This seemingly philosophical question had profound political applications, because the two leading groups within French Catholicism, the Jansenists and the Jesuits, constantly intertwined politics and religion. France had just undergone one of its greatest religious revivals. New monastic orders for both men and women had sprung up like wildfire during the generation of the saints. One did not have to go far to see the physical evidence of such change. By 1661, Paris alone had forty convents, sixty-five monasteries, and sixty *collèges*—many of them recently founded. All told, the city had over three hundred churches and chapels.

The religious conflict played itself out most clearly in two ways: in the religious Fronde and in the gradual escalation of the persecution of the Huguenots (on the latter, see Chapter 9). In many ways, the religious Fronde had the most enduring impact of any of the Frondes. Two distinct traditions came into play during this conflict. First, religious opponents of the Jesuit order revived the longstanding hostility toward it. In so doing, they could reach back to the works of a prominent Parisian attorney, Antoine Arnauld, who had written a violent attack on the Jesuits on behalf of the Sorbonne in the 1590s.[46] Arnauld's son, also an Antoine (called the "great" Arnauld), became one of the leading theologians of the 1640s, composing most famously his attack *On Frequent Communion,* which, like his father's works, assaulted the Jesuits, who had been preaching it. His 1655 work, *Letter to a Person of Rank,* led to his expulsion from the Sorbonne faculty and to the unprecedented step of his name being removed from the list of Sorbonne graduates.

Arnauld retired to live near the Cistercian convent of Port-Royal des Champs, outside of Paris, where his sister, Jacquelin-Marie-Angélique, best known by her religious name of Mother Angélique, had been abbess for many years. An ally of Devouts like François de Sales and bishop Sébastien Zamet of Langres, she sought to bring reform to each convent she headed.[47] Through her brothers, she had ties to another key Devout figure, Jean Duvergier de Hauranne, abbot of Saint-Cyran and a distinguished theologian. Saint-Cyran had studied at the University of Louvain and become good friends with a fellow student, the Dutchman Cornelius Jansen. They studied together for five years (beginning in 1604), not only in Louvain, but at Paris and later at Camp-de-Prats, near Bayonne, where Saint-Cyran had obtained a cure.

Their work focused on the Fathers of the early church, notably Augustine, whose doctrines of "efficacious grace" they sought to elaborate.[48]

The defeat of the Devout party at the French Court (the Day of the Dupes, 1630) did not mean its dissolution. With Bérulle dead (1629) and the secular leaders of the Devout party either dead (Marillac) or in exile (Marie de Médicis), Saint-Cyran became its intellectual guiding force. The French declaration of open war against Spain in 1635 naturally offended the Devouts: in France itself, the king's own confessor told him his policies were "sinful," which earned the good father a one-way trip to Brittany. In the Spanish Netherlands, Saint-Cyran's old friend Jansen, now rector of the University of Louvain, published an anti-French diatribe, *Mars gallicus,* denouncing the French alliance with the heretic Protestants against the Catholic Spanish. Richelieu, who had once acted as Saint-Cyran's patron, now viewed him with progessively greater suspicion. Finally, in May 1638, Richelieu had Saint-Cyran arrested and thrown in the royal dungeon of Vincennes because of his association with Jansen's Devout interpretation of French policy.

Jansen died that same year; two years later, his monumental *Augustinus,* a complete elaboration of Augustine's theology, tied the theological ever more closely to the political. Richelieu immediately connected these theological doctrines with the Devout resistance to his policies and with Jansen's political tract, *Mars gallicus.* For the Cardinal, as for the leaders of every French government for the next one hundred years, Jansenism meant political dissent masquerading as theology. Richelieu's death eased matters somewhat: Saint-Cyran even got out of Vincennes, although his health, broken by the long, arduous captivity, soon gave out. Antoine Arnauld took his place as the head of the Devout group.

Arnauld, Mother Angélique, and Port-Royal managed to stay out of the early Fronde, despite their close ties to the Parlement of Paris. Both Arnaulds believed strongly in loyalty to the king, so they rejected overtures from both the judges and the princes. The religious Fronde, however, broke down their isolation and made Port-Royal into the very symbol of religious dissent in seventeenth-century France. The overtly political religious fracture came in 1652, after the arrest of the coadjutor archbishop of Paris, the cardinal de Retz, one of Mazarin's chief political rivals. After his arrest, Retz had difficulties carrying out his episcopal duties. When Retz's uncle died in 1654, making Retz sole archbishop of Paris, the government refused to recognize his authority. He threatened an interdict in the diocese.[49] Retz escaped from his prison at Nantes and fled to Rome. The parish priests supported their bishop, leading to a tense showdown in the late 1650s. In the end, faced with the implacable hatred of Mazarin and, after Mazarin's death, of Louis XIV, Retz gave up his see in 1661. The political and ecclesiastical ramifications of the conflict, however, went beyond his personal case.

Retz relied for support on those opposed to the royal government and to its allies, the Jesuits. In religious matters, that meant the Jansenists, among whose numbers were many members of the parish clergy of Paris and, of course, the Arnauld family, with their ancient anti-Jesuit pedigree.[50] The Paris clergy had private (financial) grievances against the Jesuits, who urged parishioners to seek the sacraments from easygoing Jesuit priests, rather than from rigorous parish clergy. The priests allied with Retz to attack the Jesuits; the assembly they formed lobbied, unsuccess-fully, for greater power for the lower clergy in the church hierarchy.

The religious Fronde helped touch off a spirited pamphlet war between the Je-suits and Jansenists. In 1653, Pope Innocent X, egged on by Mazarin and the Jesuits, issued a bull, *Cum occasione,* condemning the basic teachings of Jansen about grace. The propaganda war again dragged in the Arnauld family when the Sorbonne con-demned Antoine Arnauld's *Letters to a Person of Rank* and expelled him from the ranks of doctors.

Their action brought the intervention of Blaise Pascal, whose *Provincial Letters* rapidly turned the tide of public opinion against the Jesuits. Lampooning the situa-tion ethics of the Jesuits and ridiculing the Sorbonne, Pascal created a masterpiece, of which the great nineteenth-century French historian Lavisse wrote: "There is not, in all our literature, a book more French than the *Provincial Letters*." Louis XIV took a somewhat different view: in 1660, he condemned the book and had it publicly burned in Paris. The following year, a general Assembly of the French Clergy, under royal urging, mandated that all priests sign an oath condemning the five "Jansenist" propo-sitions supposedly found in Jansen's *Augustinus* (his supporters denied the proposi-tions existed there).

Royal orders aside, Pascal's arguments had particularly strong resonance among the Parisian robe elite. They sided with his interpretation of the dispute with the Jesuits. In his "twelfth letter," the great Jansenist stated his view of the situation quite succinctly:

> The insults that you say to me do not clarify our disagreements, and the threats that you make against me in so many ways will not stop me from defending myself. You believe that you have force and impunity, but I be-lieve I have the truth of innocence.[51]

These lines echo those of the great politico–religious quarrels of the sixteenth cen-tury, with their emphasis on moral rightness in the face of royal arbitrary action. Even though the Jansenist controversy died down in the late 1650s, the ideological conflict sustained a mental environment of enormous staying power. For more than a century, the king would remain the bulwark of the Jesuit position, and *part* of the Parlement would maintain the Jansenist one. The Jansenists believed, like Pascal and like the religious polemicists of the sixteenth century before them, that they held the right, the moral high ground. They thus sustained their political position from the very "reasons of the heart" identified by Pascal in his *Thoughts.*

Pascal's *Thoughts* also reveal some of the dangerous political propositions inher-ent in certain ideas associated with Jansenism. He suggested that the king's power rested more on the "madness" of the people than on their reason. Where judges and doctors dressed themselves in elaborate costumes to hide the fact that they did not have "true justice" or "the real art of healing," kings did not have to disguise them-selves: "They do not have the [special] clothing; they have only force." Pascal, like most contemporaries, detested disorder. For him, tyranny itself lay in it: "tyranny consists in the desire to dominate, universally and outside of its order." Louis XIV shared Pascal's obsession with order, although not his views on government. He had his own ideas about the state, whose power he wanted to use to establish order in things both large and small. He succeeded beyond anything Pascal could have imagined.

═══════════════ *Notes* **═══════════════**

1. The Edict of Fontainebleau, the Revocation's official title, did not ban Lutheranism in the newly added province of Alsace or in nearby territories.

2. The Spanish army of 27,000 men sustained 8,000 killed and 7,000 prisoners; Condé lost 2,000 dead in his force of some 23,000. In 1643, because the prince's father was still alive, Condé bore the official title of duke of Enghien, but I have used prince of Condé throughout because he is universally known by that name, as the Great Condé.

3. Antwerp, the greatest north European port in the sixteenth century, had been blockaded by the Dutch navy since the 1580s. Its commerce (and its merchants) went to Amsterdam, which took over preeminence. The Amsterdam merchants feared, above all else, the revival of Antwerp as a rival. Their main foreign policy goal after 1655 or so was keeping Antwerp out of French hands, because that would have meant its reopening.

4. This marriage greatly troubled the Spanish, because only Philip's sickly two-year-old son stood between Maria-Theresa and the throne of Spain; that son would become king as Charles II. When he died without an heir, Spanish fears came to fruition: Maria-Theresa's grandson, Philip, became king of Spain (1701).

5. Y.-M. Bercé, *Histoire des Croquants* (Geneva: Droz, 1974), v. 2, p. 751, my translation.

6. The Cotentin region had the special privilege of boiling sea water to make its own salt; the king received one-fourth of the salt they produced in lieu of salt taxes. The salters worked barefoot, hence the name of the rebellion.

7. Louis XIII's other two state secretaries, Loménie de Brienne and Louis Phélypeaux de la Vrillière (in charge of relations with the Huguenots), were the only two people in the central government who did not belong overtly to Richelieu's clientele, and Brienne was sufficiently reliable that the cardinal allowed him to be the state secretary with responsibility for Brittany.

8. Lloyd Moote, in his excellent biography, *Louis XIII, the Just* (Berkeley: University of California Press, 1989), notes this story's inconsistencies. Other evidence shows that the king and queen also had sexual relations in late November; thus the 5 December episode was far from the isolated, chance encounter the rainstorm story implies. Nonetheless, we can understand why the monarchy wanted to propagate a story that suggested divine intervention.

9. In return, Anne permitted the councillors of the Parlement of Paris to achieve permanent nobility after twenty years in office, a dramatic change from the existing rule that required three generations of the family to hold the office to obtain full nobility.

10. E. Lavisse, *Histoire de France*, t. VII, part 1: *Louis XIV. La Fronde. Le Roi. Colbert (1643–1685)* (Paris: Hachette, 1906), 44.

11. In homage to Lloyd Moote's fine book, *The Revolt of the Judges* (Princeton: Princeton University Press, 1968).

12. Particelli d'Hemery's family had lived in France for three generations, but his opponents universally identified him with the "Italians."

13. The masters of requests sorted through the background information and presented a possible course of action to the royal council; they often prepared the necessary edict. Without anyone to do this essential preliminary work, the council could not act.

14. Françoise Bertaud (Mme de Motteville), *Memoirs of Madame de Motteville on Anne of Austria and her Court*, ed. C.-A. Saint-Beuve, trans. K. Prescott Wormeley (Boston: Hardy, Pratt & Co., 1901), 3 vols., II, 84.

15. Speech of Omer Talon, 15 January 1648, reproduced in BN, Mss. Fr. 16,517, fols. 256 and ff.

16. O. Ranum, *The Fronde; A French Revolution* (New York: Norton, 1993), 134–135.

17. *Memoirs of Mme de Motteville*, I, 313; 322–323.

18. Although some pamphlets asserted Anne's incapacity for rule as a woman, the gender issue rarely came up. Critics focused far more often on her "foreign" origins.

19. This principle lasted for over a century. Louis XV explicitly reiterated it in 1766, but it lost its theoretical power once Montesquieu published his *Spirit of the Laws* (1748). See Chapters 11 and 12.

20. Marie Gonzaga de Nevers married King Ladislas III by proxy, as he was still in Poland. He died shortly thereafter; Marie then married his heir (and brother) Jean-Casimir.

21. Mme de Motteville, *Memoirs*, I, 188.

22. The perfect "shade" for these blue eyes could vary: green, as in Ronsard, or even grey, quite popular in Victorian England.

23. Mazarin left the cash, and his 6 million *livres* of treasury paper to the king. These papers, part of a massive system of fraud, consisted of old royal debts, bought up for a fraction of their face value. Only a person with close connections at Court could hope to get them redeemed, hence Mazarin's affection for them.

24. All citations are from Louis XIV's *Mémoires pour l'instruction du dauphin*. I have used the edition of P. Goubert (Paris: Imprimerie Nationale, 1992), my translation. A fine English translation with an introduction has been done by Paul Sonnino; alas, it is not available in paperback.

25. H. Hall, *Richelieu's Desmarets and the Century of Louis XIV* (Oxford: Clarendon Press, 1990), 83.

26. His contemporaries recognized this potential at once: Voët, the rector of the University of Utrecht, filed a lawsuit against Descartes, accusing him of atheism. Only the intervention of the French government prevented the suit from going forward.

27. R. Descartes, *Discourse on Method and Meditations*, trans. L. Lafleur (Indianapolis: Bobbs Merrill, 1960), 81–82.

28. Descartes, *Discourse*, 15.

29. Hobbes distinguished between knowledge based on simple experience and prudence, and knowledge based on scientific analysis of that experience, which he termed "sapience." The broader distinction between rationalists (idealists) and empiricists still follows the old geography: Continental philosophers have tended to be idealist, Anglo-Americans to be empiricists.

30. Cited in F. Azouvi, "Descartes," in P. Nora, ed., *Realms of Memory*, v. III, *Symbols*, trans. A. Goldhammer (New York: Columbia University Press, 1998), 492.

31. Fermat's Theorem posits that
$$x^n + y^n = z^n$$
if
$$n > 2$$
and *n, x, y,* and *z* are whole numbers
Professor Andrew Wiles provided definitive proof that Fermat was right in 1993.

32. The Dupuy brothers expanded the collection, adding a wide range of manuscripts, as well as books, medals, and other precious objects. The Manuscrits Dupuy collection today forms one of the most important subseries in the Bibliothèque Nationale de France.

33. Cited in R. Mandrou, *Des humanistes aux hommes de science (XVIe et XVIIe siècles)*, vol. 3 of *Histoire de la pensée européene* (Paris: Seuil, 1973), 147.

34. Renaudot, a slippery character if ever there was one, survived Richelieu's death and maintained his monopoly into the 1650s. During the Fronde, taking no chances, he published two papers. He himself fled Paris with Mazarin and wrote for the government; his sons published the main newspaper of the Frondeurs.

35. Many of these men also attended salons, such as that of the hôtel de Rambouillet.

36. No women belonged to the Académie prior to the 1970s.

37. Articles reproduced in R. and S. Pillorget, *France Baroque, France Classique, 1589–1715*, vol. II, *Dictionnaire* (Paris: R. Laffont, 1995), 10.

38. The great ministers also made sure family members belonged to the Académie. Armaud du Cambout, duke of Coislin, son of Richelieu's first cousin, became a member in 1652—his seat remained in the family until 1733. Colbert's son, Jacques-Nicolas, archbishop of Rouen, got his chair in 1678. Another member, the duke of Beauvillier (elected 1663), married his son to Colbert's daughter.

39. Very few historians turn to the Académie's dictionary to look up the seventeenth-century meaning of a word; they instead use the dictionary of Antoine Furetière, published in 1690, a year after his death, because of Furetière's insistence on tying his definitions to actual daily French practice. That said, it must be noted that Furetière himself was a member of the Académie from 1662 onward.

40. This inner conflict fitted well with the age of Louis XIII; indeed, one of the king's biographers, P. Chevalier, titled his work: *Louis XIII: Roi Cornélien* (Paris: Fayard, 1979).

41. The habitat of ordinary French people is discussed in Chapter 10.

42. The Palace of the Parlement at Rennes, alas, suffered a tragic fire in February 1994; some of its great inner decoration was destroyed and the famous oak roof went up in flames.

43. O. Ranum, "The Refuges of Intimacy," in R. Chartier, ed., *A History of Private Life. III. Passions of the Renaissance*, trans. A. Goldhammer (Cambridge, MA and London: Belknap Press of Harvard University Press, 1989), 210–211.

44. Mythological subjects cost, on average, 62 *livres*; religious ones could be had for about 25 *livres*, portraits and still lifes for a mere 12. See J. Collins and A. Croix, "Le marchand de luxe: inventaire de Pierre Le Brun, marchand "flamand" aux États de Bretagne (1632)," in *Église, Éducation, Lumières . . . Histoires Culturelles de la France (1500–1830)*, ed. A. Croix, A. Lespagnol, and G. Provost (Rennes: Presses Universitaires de Rennes, 1999).

45. All selections come from B. Pascal, *Thoughts*. I have used the *Œuvres Complètes*, ed. L. Lafuma (Paris: Editions du Seuil, 1963). The *Pensées* appear on pp. 493–641. My translations.

46. These works, little studied today, had an enormous long-term impact on European intellectual history. Arnauld's arguments became the foundation of anti-Jesuit writings during the Enlightenment, during the German *Kulturkampf* of the 1870s and 1880s, and into the twentieth century. I am indebted to Dr. Roìsin Healy for bringing the German connection to my attention.

47. Here again we see the strong post-Tridentine Italian influence: Zamet's father had been the chief Italian financier of Henry IV and de Sales had close ties to the great Italian reformer Charles Borromeo.

48. "Efficacious grace" allowed the few chosen to avoid sin, through the grace of God, and could be withdrawn by God at any time (thus leading even the chosen to sin). The Jesuits argued on behalf of "sufficient" grace, which allowed mankind to choose to resist temptation. The Jansenist position thus resembled the Calvinist one, in that God chose the predestined few for reasons unrelated to their own worth.

49. An interdict forbade clergy to perform their ecclesiastical functions. Thus no masses could be said in the diocese. Priests also could not perform other sacraments, such as baptism or extreme unction.

50. Retz himself was certainly not a Jansenist, being a man well known for his luxurious tastes and high living.

51. Pascal, *Lettres Provinciales*, letter 12, p. 429 of the Lafuma edition. My translation.

Chapter Nine

THE AGE OF LOUIS XIV

Thus revered by his subjects, feared by his enemies, admired in all the earth, he seemed to have nothing to do but enjoy in peace a glory so firmly established, when Holland presented him with new occasions on which to distinguish himself, and paved the way for actions which would never be erased from the memory of man.[1]

Jean Racine, *Short History of the Campaigns of Louis XIV*

I would praise you more, if you had praised me less.

Louis XIV, to Racine

When Louis XIV announced that he would be his own first minister, no one believed him. Contemporaries took his pronouncement as the bravado of a young man feeling his oats; they had no doubt that one so devoted to the pleasures of life (see Plate 10) would soon tire of the work of kingship. Louis did not give up his pleasures—far from it—but neither did he shirk his duties as king. He regularly attended the royal councils throughout his long life and carefully balanced the authority of each of his great ministers against that of the others. Louis detested disorder: he sought to make sure everything around him followed a known and invariable rhythm and valued especially those subordinates who, like him, had an obsession with detail and order.

Historians customarily break Louis's long personal reign (1661–1715) into two parts. In the first stage, lasting until the early 1680s, France dominated Europe as no power had for centuries. States everywhere worried about French hegemony; societies sought to emulate French culture, which also achieved preeminence by the 1660s. When Louis XIV built his fabulous palace at Versailles, other European rulers, such as Emperor Leopold I, immediately mimicked him by building their own elaborate palaces, such as the Schönbrunn in Vienna. Louis's enormous military, and the state apparatus needed to keep it running, led to institutional emulation, too. His initial military successes reflected the far superior organization of the French army; the more mixed results of the 1690s and after demonstrated the degree to which other states, in order to compete with France, adopted its state-building model.

Three decisive actions in the early 1680s combined to change drastically European attitudes toward Louis XIV: the move to Versailles (1682), the failure to join the other Christian powers at the Turkish siege of Vienna (1683), and the Revocation of the Edict of Nantes (1685). Versailles became the symbol of royal absolutism, of a king removed from his people, and of a man bent on dominating the European world just as he dominated the miniature world he had created at his palace. The French seizure of Luxembourg during the siege of Vienna called into question Louis's commitment to the Christian commonwealth, and the Revocation made Louis into the anti-Christ of European Protestants. English, Dutch, and German pamphleteers and political writers, even English tourists, now portrayed France as the Evil Empire of Catholic absolutism, led by the brutal tyrant, Louis XIV.

This dual image of Louis—the good king of the brilliant 1660s and 1670s and the old despot of the 1680s and after—has come down to us virtually unaltered. This image comes, above all, from the memoirs of the duke of Saint-Simon, one of the members of Louis's Court. Saint-Simon wrote of 1688: "here finished the apogee of this reign, and this height of glory and prosperity. The great captains, the great ministers within and without were no more; there remained only the pupils."[2] Although it has the virtue of simplicity, Saint-Simon's view grossly misstates the complex realities of Louis's exceptionally long reign. Historians have followed Saint-Simon in defining Louis's collaborators of the early period, above all the marquis of Louvois and Jean-Baptiste Colbert, as his "great" ministers, while reserving scorn for the "non-entities" of his final twenty-five years.[3] Every French school child knows about Colbert. Few, if any of them have heard of his successors, Pontchartrain and Desmarets. The "great man" obsession unfortunately gives a misleading impression of Louis's reign. Current research suggests that the greatest institutional changes came after 1695; what is more, those changes became the essence of the new bureaucratic state of the Ancien Régime. The process of transition from the dominance of the individual minister to the pre-eminence of the *ministry* took place in the last twenty-five years of Louis's life.

The good Louis–bad Louis dichotomy has roots that go beyond Saint-Simon. In the wars fought between 1667 and 1684, Louis's forces always won and France constantly expanded its borders. The War of the Spanish Succession (1702–1713) was a desperate affair; France barely averted total defeat and just managed to keep most of its earlier gains. Culturally, the magnificent achievements of the 1660s, 1670s, and 1680s dwarf the output of the end of the reign. Louis himself took less interest in cultural display as he got older: he stopped dancing in the ballets at Versailles, just as he stopped accompanying his troops in the field, and drastically cut back on the palace's great festivals. The pomp and circumstance of Court daily life became more and more ponderous; cultural leadership shifted decisively back to Paris and away from Versailles at the beginning of the eighteenth century.

Louis's odious religious policies damaged his reputation, both at the time and for posterity. Protestant writers pummeled him unmercifully throughout the eighteenth and nineteenth centuries, not only for the Revocation of the Edict of Nantes but for the brutal campaign against the Protestant villages in the Cévennes mountains at the beginning of the eighteenth century. Huguenot refugees spread tales of Louis the evil tyrant wherever they went: England, Holland, Prussia, or the New

World. The terrible famines of 1693 and 1709 became, in the eyes of Protestant commentators, God's just punishment of the evil deeds of the king. Contemporaries and modern historians alike have highlighted the economic effects of the expulsions, which removed Protestant capital and skilled labor from France.

The hard-and-fast division in the 1680s, however, misrepresents matters more than a little. Louis essentially fought all of Europe to a standstill in his final two wars, a remarkable achievement. He kept the throne of Spain for his grandson Philip, maintained French gains in the north and east, and left his successor the best army in Europe. The final years of his reign provided essential staging time for eighteenth-century expansion in the economy, in cultural life, and in state institutional development. Although deeper historical forces certainly had more to do with the economic and cultural trends than anything he did, Louis stood astride his time as a Colossus. Historians incessantly debate the "greatness" of Louis XIV; his contemporaries had no doubt that they lived in the Age of Louis XIV.

THE CULTURE OF THE SUN

Eight days after it [Tartuffe] *was banned, a company put on for the Court a play entitled,* Scaramouche ermite [a licentious comedy] *and the King, on leaving the theater, said to the prince of Condé what I want to say: "I would like to know why those who are so scandalized by the comedy of Molière say nothing about* Scaramouche?" *To which the Prince replied, "The reason is that* Scaramouche *makes fun of Heaven and of religion, neither of which these people care about one bit; but that of Molière makes fun of they themselves; that's what they cannot suffer."*

Final words of Molière's preface to the first edition of his play *Le Tartuffe*

Pierre Corneille's tragedies dominated the French stage for a generation, but, in the early 1660s, comedy became the rage, and Molière its master. Jean-Baptiste Poquelin, for such was his given name, traveled the provinces with his theater company in the 1650s. They returned to Paris in 1658, playing a comedy to some success at the Louvre. After a brief failure putting on tragedies in 1659, Molière returned to what he did best, with his first great play, *Les Précieuses ridicules*. In it, he ridiculed two self-impressed "learned women" *(précieuses)*, Magdelon and Cathos, as provincials, lacking genuine taste. The poor father, Gorgibus, himself a worthy bourgeois, and satisfied to be one, rebuked his daughter (Magdelon) and niece (Cathos) for their excessive expenses on "egg whites, virgin milk, and a thousand other worthless trifles that I do not know. They've consumed, since we've been here, the lard of a dozen pigs, at least, and four valets live daily from the sheep's trotters they use." When the young women wished to be called by names they believed taken from Classical sources—Polyxène and Aminte (in fact, taken from two contemporary novels)—Gorgibus told them that "I do not intend that you have names other than those given to you by your godfathers and godmothers." In the end, he denounced the foolishness borne from "idle minds" weaned on poetry and novels.

This play, with its condemnation of social climbing and reinforcement of social order, found immediate approval among the theater-going noble public, including Louis XIV. In his next play, the *School for Wives,* Molière took a different approach. He ridiculed Arnolphe, who wished to have a wife who "knows how to pray to God, to love me, stitch, and sew." He had a young woman in mind, one whose father had committed her to Arnolphe's care: "In a little convent, far from all practical life / I had her raised according to my system / That is, ordering whatever care was necessary / To make her an idiot, as much as one could."

Arnolphe had all the bad qualities of the "précieuses ridicules": he changed his name to Monsieur de la Souche (Lord of the Stump) because "La Souche pleases my ears more than Arnolphe." His friend Chrysalde ridiculed Arnolphe's pretension: "What devil advised you thus / At forty-two years of age to unbaptise yourself." Chrysalde argued that one must find a wife with intelligence and education, someone who will choose the good, not simply follow the counsel of others. In the end, of course, Arnolphe's beloved, Agnes, ran off with a young man, Horace. In this play and in others, such as the *School for Husbands,* Molière advanced the idea that people should marry for love. The plays illustrated the dramatic tension about gender roles and marriage that played so critical a role in early modern society.

Molière exposed the phony social climber not only in the *Bourgeois Gentilhomme* but also in *Le Tartuffe,* his attack on the piety of the Jansenists and other devouts, another subject sure to win royal favor. He and his company presented the play for the first time at the end of the "Pleasures of the Enchanted Isle" festival, a two-week long extravaganza put on by Louis XIV at his hunting chateau of Versailles in May 1664. In the play, poor Orgon, a good bougeois, was taken in by Tartuffe, a hypocritically devout swindler. Orgon's family was unable to convince him of Tartuffe's character until the decisive scene in the play, when Orgon hid under a table, listening to his wife, Elmire, and Tartuffe discuss adultery. When Elmire said, "But the laws of Heaven give us so much fear," Tartuffe replied,

> I can dissipate those ridiculous fears for you,
> Madame, and I know the art of removing scruples.
> Heaven forbids, it's true, certain contentments;
>   ["It's a criminal speaking," Orgon]
> But one can make accommodations with it;
> It's a science, when needs be,
> To extinguish the bonds of our conscience,
> And to rectify the evil of an action
> With the purity of our intention.

A few lines later, Orgon emerged from under the table, his illusions shattered, his eyes opened to the hypocrisy of this "religious" zealot.

Molière had great success with the play, but it provoked violent opposition from the clergy and the devout party at Court. He published the play, with a short preface, not long after it opened at Paris. His preface tells us that his earlier victims—nobles,

THE TAILOR AND THE "GENTLEMAN"

Molière returned again and again to these broad themes. In the *Bourgeois Gentilhomme,* we find the title character, Monsieur Jourdain, trying to learn how to dance, to fence, to write, to dress, to speak like a gentleman. He hires various masters to teach him these skills. He and his tailors have the following exchange:

Journeyman tailor: My gentleman, give some drinking money to the journeymen, if you please.

M. Jourdain: What did you call me?

Journeyman: My gentleman.

Jourdain: "My gentleman!" You see what happens when you dress like a person of quality. When you dress as a bourgeois dresses, no one ever calls you "my gentle-man." Take this for "my gentleman." [Hands tailor money.]

Journeyman: Monseigneur, we are much obliged to you.

Jourdain: "Monseigneur" Oh my! "Monseigneur!" Wait my friend: "Monseigneur" merits something; it is not a little word that "Monseigneur." Here, here is what Monseigneur gives you. [Hands over more money.]

Journeyman: Monseigneur, we will all drink to the health of Your Grandeur.

Jourdain: "Your Grandeur!" Oh my, oh my! Wait, don't go yet. To me, "Your Grandeur!" My faith, if he goes all the way to Highness, he will get all the purse. Take this for "My Grandeur." [Still more money.][4]

précieuses, cuckolds, doctors—have all suffered in silence and laughed along with everyone else at his gentle mockery of them, but that "these Hypocrites have never been made fun of; they have reacted violently from the start, and have found it strange that I had the boldness to make fun of their grimacing, and to wish to decry a craft which so many respectable people practice. . . . Following their praiseworthy custom, they have hidden their own interests beneath the cause of God; in their mouths, *Le Tartuffe* is a play that offends piety." The devouts managed to get the play suppressed for three years, but Molière won in the end: even the dictionary of the Académie Française defined *tartuffe* as a synonym for hypocrite.[5]

Molière's company initially played for great aristocrats—the playwright himself had been one of the writers of the entertainment for Fouquet's ill-fated ball of 1661—and for the Court. In time, he sought to set up a permanent base in Paris, which the king allowed. Later, after Molière's death, the king merged his company and another Parisian troupe into the Comédie Française, which remains to this day the national theater company of France.

Molière's own company gave Jean Racine his first break in 1664; unable to perform *Le Tartuffe* because of the interdiction, the company put on Racine's *La Thébaïde.* Racine had his first great success the next year, with *Alexander the Great,* which he dedicated to Louis XIV: "Here is a second enterprise that is no less bold than the first. I did not content myself with putting the name of Alexander in my title; I also added that of Your Majesty, that is, I put together the greatest things that previous centuries and our own can produce." Two years later, Racine produced *Andromaque,* a Classic tragedy of love unrequited; his success rivaled that of Corneille's *Le Cid.*

Oui, puisque je retrouve un ami si fidèle,	Yes, because I find again so faithful a friend,
Ma fortune va prendre une face nouvelle: . . .	My fortune will take on a new face: . . .
Hélas! Qui peut savoir le destin qui m'amène?	Alas, who can know the destiny that brings me here?
L'amour me fait ici chercher une inhumaine;	Love makes me look here for an inhuman one;
Mais qui sait qu'il doit ordonner de mon sort,	But who knows how it will rule my fate,
Et si je viens chercher ou la vie ou la mort?	And if I come to find life or death?

The other tragedies—such as *Brittanicus* or *Phèdre*—repeated similar themes of love lost, their main characters, like Phèdre, expiring as she tells Thésée of the innocence of her son (himself dead) and of Phèdre's own guilt. These characters, such as Hippolyte in *Phèdre*, expressed noble sentiments, born into them:

Ami, qu'ose-tu dire?	Friend, what dost thou dare say?
Toi, qui connais mon cœur depuis que je respire,	Thou, who hast known my heart since I first breathed,
Des sentiments d'un cœur si fier, si dédaingeux,	The sentiments of so proud, so disdainful a heart,
Peux-tu me demander le désaveu honteux?	Can thou demandest of me a shameful denial?
C'est peu qu'avec son lait une mère amazone	Forgetting that with her milk an Amazon mother
M'ait fait sucer cet orgueil qui t'étonne	Had made me suck that pride that astonishest thou

These plays served as vehicles for ballets, such as the elaborate Turkish dance at the end of the *Bourgeois Gentilhomme*. The ballet master, Jean-Baptiste Lully (born in Florence as Giovanni Battista Lulli), revived Court dancing and created a new age of French music. Lully emigrated from Italy at the age of eleven, and received almost all of his musical education in France. In the early 1660s, he stood for a distinctly French music, against the traditional dominance of Italians, such as Mazarin's favorite, Cavelli. Lully's ballets greatly pleased Louis XIV, who danced himself in most of them. (See Plate.) Beginning in 1665, Lully combined with Molière on spectacles that combined dance and a comedic play; in the 1670s, the age of Racine's tragedies, Lully wrote the first French operas. He dominated French music at Court throughout the end of the seventeenth century. His greatest contemporary rival, Marc Antoine Charpentier, could not break through Lully's monopoly at Court but wrote successfully for Molière's troupe and later, for its successor, the Comédie Française.

The combination of talents accessible to Louis XIV, and his willingness to patronize them, made the French Court the center of European high culture. From the Court, this new culture spread to Paris and to the provinces. By other paths, it spread also to the great Courts of Europe. Louis XIV spent much of the 1660s and 1670s as the brilliant patron of much of what was best in European high society. Learning from Richelieu and Mazarin, he employed a stable of writers (and artists) to publicize such an image throughout Europe. In 1677, Racine retired from the theater to become the king's official historian.

French letters also flourished outside of the theater. The duke of la Rochefoucauld published his *Maxims* in 1665, La Fontane's *Fables* appeared three years later, and Mme de Lafayette published the first modern French novel, *The Princess of Cleves,* in 1678. The culture of the sun was, above all, a noble culture. Mme de Lafayette set *The Princess of Cleves* at the Court of Henry II. La Rochefoucauld's maxims often concerned such traditional noble topics as pride, honor, and love. The duke, famous for his courtly manners, emphasized the importance of one's demeanor: "Good graces are to the body what good sense is to the mind."

Graceful movement extended to one's daily life: table manners, vocabulary, gestures, home decoration. People had to learn to follow the manners laid out at Court, and then in Paris, by authors such as Antoine de Courtin (*New Treatise on Civility Practiced by Decent People,* 1675). Courtin's *Treatise* went through more than twenty French and foreign-language editions in the next seventy-five years. He offered counsel on the basics of modern civility, a civility accessible to all, provided they practiced it in a manner appropriate to their station. One had to use one's utensils, each for its proper purpose; one could not spit on the floor; one had to perform one's physical functions in private and to blow one's nose into a handkerchief; a gentleman had to take off his hat when inside. All these rules, most of which we today take for granted, were radical departures from traditional behavior in the seventeenth century. One's vocabulary, too, had to conform to the rules of good society (*bienséance*): the Académie Française's official dictionary (1691–1694) informed all decent (i.e., educated and wealthy) people of proper usage. The obsession with personal delicacy helped create a sense of privacy, of individual space. The houses of aristocrats, and then those of wealthy merchants, lawyers, and officials, took on a new configuration: they had dining rooms, studies, and private bedrooms. More people used their study or library to read in solitary silence, rather than in the customary manner, in a group, aloud.

The Académie Française provided the prototype for state intervention in cultural life. Louis XIV soon took over or founded a series of royal academies: the Academy of Sciences (founded by Colbert) in 1666; the Academy of Fine Arts, chartered in 1648 but really active only from 1664, when Charles Le Brun became its director; the French Academy of Rome (1666), which subsidized twelve French artists to study there; the Academy of Architecture (1671); and the Royal Academy of Music (1672). These academies sought to provide assistance to artists, architects, musicians, and scientists. They did help many, but at the cost of providing a limited elite around the king with too great a power in the establishment of artistic standards. The academies tended to stifle artistic creativity in a direct sense, but the great French artists of the seventeenth and eighteenth centuries often achieved their highest levels of creativity by fighting against the standards established by a given academy.

Louis XIV funded many important buildings in Paris: the Invalides, a hospital for wounded veterans; new wings of the Louvre and the Tuileries Palace; the *collège* of the Four Nations; and several royal squares, the place des Victoires and today's place Vendôme chief among them. He employed the leading architects of the day, such as Jules Hardouin-Mansart and Louis Le Vau, to carry out these commissions. These architects developed and amplified the Classicism begun by Mansart, in such commissions as the Val-de-Grâce, funded by Anne of Austria. The church combines a double Classical temple front, somewhat awkwardly matched with a domed central altar. In its day, it was the largest dome in Paris. Inside, the church contained lovely side chapels and two mid-century masterpieces—the dome fresco of Heaven, and the altarpiece, by Michel Fouguier—which inspired Molière to write: "Well seasoned with the salt of our Antique graces, And not the insipid taste of Gothic ornaments, Those odious monsters of ignorant centuries." Molière did not have far to go to see even quite new Gothic ornaments: the parish church of Saint Eustache, near Les Halles, built in a late Gothic style, dated only from the late sixteenth and early seventeenth century.

The Val de Grace, then the largest dome in Paris, begun by Jules Hardouin-Mansart, 1663.

The Val-de-Grâce, although not a Jesuit church, has close affinities with the new Jesuit constructions in Paris and the provinces. The Jesuit church at Rennes, like so many others, closely models the order's great church in Rome. In the late seventeenth century, the order built a number of new churches, such as Saint Paul in Paris, in the new Classical style. Inside, these churches often had close ties to the Baroque and, later, Rococo excesses we associate with Italian and south German churches (such as Weis) of the time. This stylistic element, far more than Classicism, spread to the provinces. The local churches in many regions, such as Brittany, constructed stunning gilded altarpieces, such as that of Lampaul-Guimiliau.

Hardouin-Mansart and Le Vau developed French Classicism into the leading architectural style of late seventeenth-century Europe. Le Vau first developed its principles for Fouquet's château of Vaux-le-Vicomte, which features an enormous domed round ballroom as its centerpiece. Louis XIV, when he cashiered Fouquet, immediately took over the stable of artists—Le Vau, the landscape architect; André Le Nôtre, the painter; Charles Le Brun—who had produced this jewel. He set them to work on the small hunting chateau of Versailles that had been such a favorite of his father. Le Vau and his nephew, François d'Orbay, developed long symmetrical wings for the chateau in the new Classical style; Le Nôtre laid out the famous gardens. Le Brun and other leading artists of the time, such as Jean Jouvenal and Antoine Coypel, painted appropriate scenes on the walls and ceilings. Their greatest triumph, the Hall of Mirrors, combines the innovative use of a mirrored wall to double the light of the windows, creating an image of an elongated, profoundly lighted space, with frescoes cataloguing Louis XIV's great "triumphs." Memoirs of the time suggest that foreign visitors took deep offense at the presentation of these events, especially at the one that portrayed Louis "giving" peace to the Dutch and their allies in 1678.

The Birth of French Cuisine

Du beurre; toujours du beurre.[6]

Fernand Point

Louis XIV's Court revolutionized many aspects of French and European life. Louis's style of living certainly lay beyond the means of other people, but the basic elements of that lifestyle—its food, its clothing, its courtesy, its manners—provided one of the key foundations of modern European sensibilities. Louis could claim some responsibility for such changes, but only as an accelerator of broader social and cultural trends. Changes in Court life paralleled those in urban life. In the early stages of Louis's reign, when he split time between Paris and several chateaux in the vicinity of the city, the Court provided the guiding light to others. After the king moved to Versailles (1682), however, he became more isolated from his dynamic capital city. By the early eighteenth century, Paris rather than Versailles set most of the trends. The democratization of these trends took a long time. By the middle of the eighteenth century, however, wealthy urban dwellers had adapted their clothing or their

THE PALACE OF THE SUN

Louis XIII had loved the little hunting château at Versailles; his son decided to transform his father's favorite hideaway into a palace that would astonish the world. He offered a stunning series of entertainments there in the spring of 1664, the Feast of the Enchanted Isle. Louis's Queen, Maria-Theresa of Spain, had little taste for such ostentation. In the eyes of contemporaries, she lacked Louis's physical attractiveness and grandeur of carriage. She did not like to participate in the ballets, so Louis turned to other partners, first to Louise de la Vallière (1661–1667), then to Françoise-Athénais de Rochechouart-Mortemart, known as the marquise of Montespan (1667–1681).[7] Louis finally tired of Mme de Montespan's haughty demeanor; he replaced her with a quiet, devout woman, Françoise d'Aubigné, better known as Mme de Maintenon. She had served as governess to Louis's natural children. After the death of the queen, Louis took the extraordinary step of marrying Mme de Maintenon, although he did so in secret and never publicly acknowledged the union. Louis became more devout as he aged; historians have perennially debated the impact of Mme de Maintenon on the change.

Louis liked to play the noble. Like any good noble, he enjoyed certain leisures: the dance, the theater, the hunt, polite society. Louis did all that he could to encourage these activities. He brought musicians and playwrights to his Court; he himself often danced in the Court ballets. He hunted constantly, as a way to escape from the cares of his office. He created a large Court around himself. When the existing royal palaces proved inadequate for this Court, he had constructed a new one: Versailles.

Louis liked elaborate balls, centered around magnificent ballets commissioned specifically for the occasion; many courtiers participated in minor roles. These displays also involved expensive and elaborate stage machinery. In this manner, Louis imitated Richelieu, who had recruited artists such as the great Italian sculptor

Bernini to produce stage machinery for the productions at the Palais Cardinal. Louis spared no expense for the great festival of 1664. The opening night began with a procession of nobles, Louis among them, dressed as medieval knights—Roland and his companions, among other famous heroes—leading the carriage of Apollo. The knights fought mock combats—the king, of course, distinguished himself—and dedicated their triumphs to the ladies, such as Louise de la Vallière. Guests marvelled at the two hundred wax torches and the chandeliers that made night into day. The next night, Molière and Lully put on a play, followed by a massive costume drama, complete with sea monsters. The festivities continued for a week: feasting, dancing, and jousting.

Louis would repeat these impressive events on several occasions: in 1668, several times in the 1670s, again in 1684. After that they became less common, but the Court could rouse itself for a single great occasion. The duke of Saint-Simon claimed he and his wife spent 20,000 *livres* for their clothes for one such ball early in the eighteenth century. Versailles provided a setting for such magnificent displays. Louis had moved from palace to palace in the 1660s. He spent time at the Louvre and the Tuileries in Paris, at Saint-Cloud and Saint-Germain in its outskirts, and at the palace of Versailles, during its construction throughout the 1670s. He finally moved the Court permanently from Saint-Cloud to Versailles in 1682. Here, on the site of the famous events of 1664, Louis built the greatest palace in western Europe, employing 25,000 workers year-round in its construction, for years on end.

He began with the theme of Apollo, the Sun God, special patron of the Sun King (*Roi Soleil*) Louis XIV. The new palace had a series of magnificent rooms, such as the Salon of Apollo, where scenes of the Sun God predominated; elsewhere in the palace, one often encountered representations (paintings, statues) of Apollo or Mars or great Classical rulers, such as Alex-

Aerial view of the Palace of Versailles; main sections completed by 1683.
Source: © Ronald Sheridan/Ancient Art & Architecture Collection.

ander the Great. Hardouin-Mansart designed Versailles's greatest room, the Hall of Mirrors (75 meters long and 10 meters wide), where a wall of mirrors "opposite the real ones [windows], multiplies a million fold that Gallery, which seems to have no end at all." Le Brun decorated it with paintings of Louis as Apollo and as Hercules, allegorically showing him taking personal charge of his kingdom or crossing the Rhine. Louis took such pride in his creation, for he viewed himself as its moving spirit and constantly intervened himself in the details of construction, that he personally drew up a guide for those who would tour his gardens.

Building continued at Versailles long after Louis became a permanent resident. The king added new stables, outbuildings for the government officials, new adornments of the palace such as the Grand Trianon, in the royal park, completed in 1688. By 1710, the king could visit the finished royal chapel, painted by Antoine Coypel and Jean Jouvenet. Ceilings and walls everywhere bore paintings. The chapel had appropriate religious subjects; elsewhere the painters detailed the king's many triumphs, as well as his favorite Classical themes. Saint-Simon went so far as to claim that all of Europe was offended by the portrayals of Louis's triumphs.

The magnificence of the palace, much of which survives relatively intact, can easily mislead us as to what life was like within its walls. Courtiers complained, rightly, of their tiny apartments; the more prominent among them

kept hôtels in Paris. The long drafty corridors could not be heated, so courtiers froze in the winters, especially the dreadful one of 1709. The squadrons of servants could not keep up with all demands; those on portable latrine duty were not always available, and many a courtier—to judge from complaints about the stink—relieved himself in the darkened corners.

In the final decades of his life, Louis tired of this numbing Court ritual and of the pressures of being permanently on display. He would run away to his small château at Marly (built by Mansart-Hardouin between 1679 and 1686), taking a few friends with him. There people sat where he wished them to, not according to the rigid protocol always followed at Versailles. Invitations to Marley were among the most highly sought prizes of the Court. The king used his invaluable valet, Alexandre Bontemps, to distribute the invitations the night before the departure. Bontemps usually handed the invitations to a woman, the king addressing his wishes always to the wife, never the husband. The king always invited his family and, often, the officers of his Household. He gave Racine a permanent apartment at Marly, a unique mark of favor, and handed out invitations to the wives of officials whom he wanted to reward in a special way: Controller General Desmaret's wife got an invitation and a royally guided tour of Marly's gardens in 1709, much to the astonishment of the Court, and the chagrin of many aristocratic ladies who had never had the privilege.

diet to the trends begun at Court in the middle of the seventeenth century and amplified at Paris, and in other cities, in the succeeding century.

A fundamental marker in the evolution of French cooking appeared in 1651, when the cook of the marquis d'Huxelles, François Pierre de la Varenne, published the first new cookbook to appear in France in nearly a century: *The French Cook* (*Le Cuisinier Français*). In the next forty years, another dozen major cookbooks appeared, as well as some seventy-five subsequent editions of the most successful ones. They sold nearly 100,000 copies. La Varenne and his successors, especially François Massialot (published 1691), revolutionized French cooking by creating the foundations of the haute cuisine renowned the world over.

Medieval cooks rarely committed their knowledge to paper; in their trade, as in most others, masters guarded trade secrets with their lives. Two short cookbooks survive from the early fourteenth century; they both suggest a cuisine based on local products, using French herbs (sage, parsley) and a few vegetables (onions, fava beans). These early cookbooks make virtually no mention of sugar. How different is the famous *Viandier* of Guillaume Tavel, known to posterity by his nickname, Taillevent.[8] Taillevent made extensive use of Middle Eastern/Asian spices—above all

The Hall of Mirrors, Versailles, finished in 1686. This room has been the site of many great events of European history, including the signing of the Peace of Versailles in 1919. Paintings glorifying the greatness of Louis XIV line its walls between the seventeen mirrors that reflect the light of the parallel number of windows.

cloves, cinnamon, and pepper—and of sugar, also obtained from the Arabs. The upper-class cuisine of the late fourteenth century, which remained dominant until the seventeenth, employed these spices (and sugar) to mask food flavors. Cooks boiled or roasted, the latter a practice particularly common among the rich, who could afford meat. Wealthy households rarely ate "butcher's meat"; they preferred game or whole roasted mutton or pork. Ordinary people could not eat such expensive foods; for them, sugar was a medicine, not a cooking ingredient.

The great art of the medieval or sixteenth-century chef consisted in altering the taste of the food being consumed. The chef would sculpt the food into odd shapes, disguising its flavor with sugar and spices, in order to make it seem what it was not. Ordinary people, of course, did not eat in such a manner. They consumed coarse bread, soupy stew, and cheap wine or *piquette.* In France, custom dictated that one adulterated one's wine with water, even at the higher levels of society. The wine, in virtually all cases, was quite young; we should not project back before the eighteenth century the existence of the deep, complex French wines with which we are familiar. This young wine had a lower alcohol content than does modern wine, thus allowing remarkable levels of wine consumption: seventeenth-century Parisians consumed between one hundred fifty and two hundred twenty liters a year. If we consider how many of these people were children, and that women drank far less than men, we realize that an adult man probably drank between one and two liters of wine a day. Consumption levels of wine varied little between the sixteenth and eighteenth centuries. Urban dwellers drank much more than peasants, at least in non-wine-growing regions. In some areas, people drank a regional or local beverage: in Normandy or in much of Brittany (after 1600), people drank mildly alcoholic cider; in Artois or in Alsace, they drank beer.

La Varenne and his contemporaries dramatically changed upper-class eating habits, although they had little short-term effect on the diet of the peasants. Taillevent rarely used butter: only 1 percent of his recipes called for it. By way of contrast, the recipes of La Varenne, Massialot, and the anonymous author of the *Art of Good Catering* (1674) relied heavily on butter. In the *Art of Good Catering,* 55 percent of the recipes contain butter, and 80 percent of the sauces have it.[9] Here we have the foundation of modern French cooking: butter. This cooking also reverses traditional medieval practice; modern French cooking stresses the emphasis of real flavors, rather than their disguise. La Varenne offers a recipe for a *roux* of pork fat and floor; *roux* soon replaced bread crumbs as the binding and thickening agent of most sauces.[10] He also discusses the creation of stocks, thus offering the beginning of the "modular" system of cooking, in which the cook prepares a series of elements that can be combined in different ways to make sauces appropriate to a given dish.

In Massialot's recipes, in particular, one can find the fundamental ideas behind the sauces so critical to French haute cuisine. He continued the trend toward butter and toward the creation of what he called "essences," those deeply intensified sauce bases so central to modern French cooking. Massialot's cookbook could also give greater place to recipes for vegetables, because the gradual introduction of products from the New World had so dramatically increased the range of fruits and vegetables available in Europe. The most important short-term change in France probably came from the new beans, among them the green bean so readily associated today with

---

Seventeenth-Century Nouvelle Cuisine:
Recipes from la Varenne and Massialot

Mushrooms Olivier, from la Varenne

4 cups mushrooms; a small onion; butter; parsley and chives; cream or *blancmange*

Wash and quarter the mushrooms; cook them slowly until they give off their liquid; press them between two plates to remove all juice; take fresh butter, chives, and parsley and fricassee the mixture, then simmer them until well cooked; you can add butter or *blancmange*, and serve.

Meatloaf, from Massialot

1 1/4 lbs. thinly sliced veal; 1 lb. bacon; 1/4 cup diced, blanched bacon; 1/4 cup beef suet, diced; 1 1/4 lbs. lean ground veal; 1/2 cup cooked (Virginia) ham, ground; 2 tbsp. finely chopped fine herbs; 1 cup raw, diced chicken breast; 1 1/2 cups diced mushrooms (and truffles); 1 tsp. spice mixture (to make the mixture, combine the following ingredients: 7 2/3 tbsp pepper; 3 2/3 tbsp ground ginger; 2 tsp ground cloves; 1 ground nutmeg; 2 1/2 tsp cinnamon; 3 cups and 3 tbsp salt); 1/4 cup cream

Pound the veal cutlets (to soften); line a round oven casserole with the bacon; then cover with the veal cutlets, reserving one; grind the blanched bacon and suet, adding the other ingredients as you grind, to make a smooth mixture; place this mixture on top of the veal strips; fold over the veal strips, using the reserved strip to cover the hole in the center; cover and cook for two hours in a 350 oven. Remove and let stand for 30 minutes. Drain off the liquid, invert the "loaf" onto a serving dish, and serve.[11]

Barbara Wheaton wisely recommends a single teaspoon of the potent spice mixture, but seventeenth-century cooks would have used far more, because diners liked their food much more heavily spiced than we do. She also suggests adding a clove of garlic to the ground mixture.

France, although the long-term effect of corn and potatoes would prove more dramatic after 1800. The greatest single change from New World products came from beverages, notably coffee and chocolate, and, of course, from sugar. Other vegetables came from the Middle East, usually by way of Italy.

New foods went hand-in-hand with new ways of cooking and with new ways of eating. In the kitchen itself, the French introduced the *potager,* a niche next to the main chimney. This first stove allowed slow cooking and the preparation of elaborate sauces. In most families, everyone ate in the kitchen, but in the sixteenth- or seventeenth-century upper-class household people might eat in a large hall specially set up with long tables or even in their private rooms. The increased importance of dining led aristocrats to a significant change in household architecture: the dining room. In the eighteenth century, this innovation spread to the houses of the bourgeoisie in towns such as Paris.

Diners themselves had new manners. In the sixteenth century, eating habits resembled those of Rabelais' Gargantua: boisterous, lewd, and uncouth. People ate with their fingers, spitting unwanted morsels directly onto the floor, throwing bones and unfinished food under the table, and tossing the cups and plates out the window. Even King Charles IX himself engaged in food fights at the royal table. In one famous case, the entourage of the king's brother demolished the banquet hall of the bishop of Angers, under the pretext of a food fight gotten out of hand.[12] A generation later, Henry IV used to amuse himself by filling the water glasses of unsuspecting young ladies with white wine. Belching and passing wind at table—as Rabelais shows us—provided a source of general amusement, although some (particularly women) sought to create a more genteel atmosphere. Attitudes toward physical functions were such that gentlemen sitting on their "pierced chairs" regularly received guests. The last great aristocrat to follow this practice, the duke of Vendôme, one of Louis XIV's leading generals, horrified his guests: "He produced a great deal; when the basin was completely full, they took it away and passed it beneath everyone's nose, often more than once. On days when he was shaved, he used the same basin in which he had relieved himself as a shaving bowl."[13]

How different was the world of the seventeenth century. At the table, among the upper classes, food fights would have been unthinkable. Nobles and rich bourgeois began to use forks. Once in use, utensils quickly diversified: by the middle of the eighteenth century, a place setting might have a bewildering array of cutlery designed for specific courses. People kept their physical functions to themselves; men even removed their hats indoors. The wealthy began to eat from porcelain plates, which arrived from Italy in the late sixteenth century, and drink from glasses. Pewter cups, too, gave way to glasses, in the homes of the wealthy. Ordinary people continued to use

Dinner in honor of Louis XIV's recovery from an illness, Hotel de Ville of Paris, 1688. We notice that many diners still use their fingers, and even those using forks, like the woman on our center right, do so awkwardly.

SOURCE: Musée des Art décoratifs.

the more primitive pewter and wooden plates, cups, and bowls of their medieval ancestors. In many cases, as in taverns, the common pewter plate came to the center of the table and the diners placed their share on a trencher of bread.

The innovations in upper-class eating habits—types of food, utensils, dishes—gradually made their way down the social scale. In the memoirs of Jacques Ménétra, an eighteenth-century Parisian glazier, we read of dishes that would have been unknown to men of his social origins a century before. Elements of personal hygiene also spread slowly down the social ladder. Very few French people followed habits of personal hygiene in the sixteenth or early seventeenth century (their medieval ancestors were much cleaner). Gradually, habits of washing, of cleaning, and of basic hygiene took root. Among the rich peasant farmers of the Ile-de-France, for example, households began to possess mirrors and copper washbasins only after 1650.[14] In paintings of rich peasants, one sees wine-filled glasses on the tables.

Louis XIV led the way in these changes. He laid an elaborate table for his guests each night. His chefs, such as Massialot, created the recipes that would spread to the tables of others. Louis himself loved to eat; Saint-Simon and other diarists of the time noted that the king never lacked appetite. Louis's sister-in-law, Liselotte von der Pfalz, described a typical meal:

> More than once, I watched the king eat four plates of different soups, a whole pheasant, a grouse, a large, full plate of salad, mutton served with its own juice and with garlic, two large hunks of ham, a full plate of pastries, and fruit and candy.[15]

Louis's friends shared his affection for good eating. Superintendant Fouquet employed the most famous *maître d'hôtel* of the day, Vatel, who switched to the service of the prince of Condé after the fall of his first master. Vatel is known to every French school child as the epitome of the proud chef; when informed (incorrectly as it turned out) that sufficient fish had failed to arrive for an evening banquet in honor of the king, poor Vatel committed suicide rather than lose his honor. Mme de Sévigné, who relates the original version of the tale, tells her daughter:

> They rushed to Monsieur le Prince, who was terribly upset. Monsieur le Duc wept, for the whole of his trip to Burgundy depended on Vatel. Monsieur le Prince told the King very sadly, explaining it was a matter of honor as he saw it; he [Vatel] was greatly praised.[16]

More than a century later, the great chef Antonin Carême, in many ways the founder of nineteenth-century gastronomy, praised Vatel's devotion to his craft.[17]

Background to the Enlightenment

> *One never sees in them* [Persians] *that liberty of spirit and that contented air that one sees here* [Paris] *in people of all estates and conditions.*
>
> Montesquieu, *Persian Letters,* "Uzbek" to "Ibben," letter 34

Louis XIV had more on his mind than the pleasures of the table, although he never failed to eat well. These meals also provided occasions on which to implement the rules of Court etiquette, which played so great a role in establishing the sort of order Louis wanted. He constantly stressed to his son the importance of ceremony and of its impact on others. In between meals, Louis had to tend to the business rather than ceremonial end of kingship. His style of kingship had much to do with the cultural output of the final years of his reign.

Versailles was not a static achievement of the 1670s; rather it remained a work in progress. Although the main palace was sufficiently finished for Louis to move to it in 1682, work continued on such artistic masterpieces as the royal chapel or the Grand Trianon, both finished in the early eighteenth century. In literature, too, the end of Louis's reign had its stars: Jean de La Bruyère, who offered biting caricatures of the social types of the age; Charles Perrault, author of one of the enduring classics of world literature, the *Stories of Mother Goose,* and famed partisan of the Moderns against the primacy of Classical models; and Bernard de Fontenelle, who provided summaries of recent scientific developments in language accessible to laypeople. The Académie Française published its two-volume *Dictionary of the French Language* (1691–1694).

Three authors stand out among those writing in the waning years of Louis XIV: Jacques-Bénigne Bossuet, François de Selignac de La Mothe-Fénelon, and Pierre Bayle. Bayle began as a spokesman for religious toleration, attacking the government's policy of persecution of Huguenots (of whom he was one). Bayle published in Holland, to avoid the French censors. His *Critical and Historical Dictionary,* published in 1696, summarized his views about complete civil toleration of religion, but it went far beyond that simple religious theme. Bayle patiently and clearly explained the meaning of scientific research, notably the work of Newton, to a lay audience. In the *Critical Dictionary,* Bayle set out to demolish myths of all kinds. He called into question the accuracy of Classical authors, such as Herodotus, and applied the same critical scrutiny to the most sacred of texts, the Christian Bible. The great figures of the Enlightenment obtained much of their modern skepticism from Bayle. Indeed, we can see in Bayle one of the great founders of French Republicanism, not because of his explicitly political ideas, but because his reasoned skepticism and his irreverent attack on sacred texts led the way to the secular Republican tradition that would dominate much of French life under the Third Republic (1875–1940).[18]

Bossuet, like Bayle, wrote about religion, but did so in a broad context. Bossuet served as bishop of Meaux but his responsibilities at Court far exceeded that humble title. He spearheaded the movement for the Gallican Articles of 1681 (see below). In the 1690s, he again could be found in the forefront of controversy, attacking the mysticism of Mme Jeanne Guyon, then much in vogue at Court among the Devout party headed by Mme de Maintenon and Fénelon. Bossuet's *Instruction on the states of prayer* (1696) established the intellectualist, anti-mystical mainstream philosophy of the French Catholic hierarchy. In the eighteenth century, this anti-mystical emphasis would allow a schismatic movement, Jansenism, to develop close ties to mystical movements. Bossuet also published the strongest French defense of religiously justified absolutism, his *Politics taken from the Holy Scripture* (1679), which made God the judge of the prince. Even Bossuet, however, enjoined the prince (i.e., the king) to honor God's laws, a fundamental check on royal power in a society built upon contracts, and thus on the sixth commandment. Bossuet's *Discourse on Universal History* offered a superb compendium of traditionalist arguments on behalf of Catholicism and on behalf of respect for Classical authors. Perrault and others assaulted the defense of immovable Classicism, launching the so-called quarrel of the Ancients and the Moderns that dominated French intellectual life at the end of the seventeenth century. In the long run, the Moderns won, defending the thesis that the writers of their own time, building on the useful model of the Ancients, should set off in their own direction, based on the progress of their own times.

Fénelon provided Bossuet with his greatest opponent. Fénelon's abilities (and his connections) landed him an important Court position: preceptor of the duke of Burgundy, Louis XIV's grandson (and likely heir).[19] In the mysticism controversy, the Pope sided with Bossuet, forcing Fénelon to recant his views. Similarly, in the early eighteenth-century debate about Jansenism, Bossuet's justification of persecution found a ready disciple in Louis XIV; Fénelon's pleas for toleration fell on stony ground. Fénelon propagated many of his educational ideas in one of his most influential works, *Telemachus,* which laid out the ideas of the traditional provincial nobility about the functioning of French society.

Fénelon's ties with Mme Guyon led to his exile from Court, and to his archbishopric of Cambrai. Fénelon's pen, however, did not suffer from the exile. He offers us one of the most paradoxical of writers. Most of his ideas were profoundly conservative, reflective of the views of the provincial nobility of the sword about social structure. Although his description of France's problems shared much with the cutting-edge reformers, he suggested sharply different solutions than did members of the administrative elite. Yet his work, seemingly supportive of the Ancients in his praise of traditional virtues, implicitly supported the Moderns, because he demanded change, believing, as did Perrault and Bayle, in progress. He first opposed the arguments of the theologian Nicolas Malebranche, who insisted on the necessity of a rational basis for religion, but later came suspiciously close to the Malebranche–Bayle skepticism. Fénelon, too, would argue that reason enabled people to obtain true understanding of theology. Fénelon, like Bayle, argued on behalf of religious toleration.

In two of his most famous works, a letter to Louis XIV on the state of the kingdom and his letter to the Académie Française (1713) about the quarrel of the Ancients and the Moderns, he placed himself firmly on the side of change. In the former, he denounced the king's administration of the kingdom and posited the idea (admittedly an ancient one) that the king's function consisted in making his subjects prosperous. He described the horrible poverty, the oppressive taxation, and the general disorder in French society *circa* 1707 in terms Louis XIV had not heard before. The letter to the Académie posited two basic criteria for writers: truth and utility. We might call those three words the official program of the Enlightenment.

The Creation of Modern France, 1667–1713

CHRONOLOGY	1667–1684
1667–1668	War of Devolution; France seizes Franche-Comté, Artois, part of Flanders
1668	Peace of Aix-la-Chapelle; France returns Franche-Comté to Spain; keeps major towns of Artois, such as Lille
1672–1678	Dutch War
1672–1673	Unsuccessful siege of Amsterdam; capture of Maastricht; annexation of Franche-Comté
1674	English withdraw from French alliance; Emperor allies with Dutch
1675	Death of Turenne; retirement of Condé
1678	Capture of Ghent
1679	Treaty of Nijmegen; France keeps Franche-Comté; gives up Flanders
1681	Louis XIV seizes Strasbourg; Four Gallican Articles
1683	Turkish army defeated by Christian coalition at Vienna
1684	France takes Luxembourg; Truce of Regensburg

The Wars of Expansion, 1667–1684

King Louis the Great, in making the Peace of Nijmegen, had reached the summit of human glory. After having on a thousand occasions proven himself by the conduct of his armies and by his personal bravery, he disarmed himself, in the midst of his victories, and content with his conquests, gave peace to Europe on conditions which it pleased him to make.[20]

Abbé Choisy, writing of Louis XIV

The cultural achievements of Louis's reign paralleled in some ways its political evolution. Louis had great military success until the mid-1680s. The later wars seem less glorious because of the lack of conquest and several stunning battlefield defeats, yet the preservation of most of the early gains, in the face of nearly universal European opposition, should be recognized as a remarkable feat. Similarly, historians have long focused on the more effective government introduced by the great ministers Colbert and Louvois in the 1660s and 1670s, yet the real institutional changes took place between 1690 and 1715.

The international political order underwent fundamental change in the 1660s. France's longtime ally, the Netherlands, replaced Spain as its chief enemy. Louis's first two wars formed part of a lengthy process extending from the Peace of Westphalia (1648) to the Truce of Regensburg (1684). Although France made some small territorial gains in the north at the Peace of the Pyrenees (1659), its northern and eastern borders remained extremely vulnerable. Louis and his advisors had four key goals after 1659:

1. Obtain as much of the southern Netherlands as they could.

2. Alsace.

3. The Franche-Comté.

4. Lorraine.

France had a traditional claim to Flanders but the Franche-Comté, although Francophone, had never been part of the kingdom. As for Alsace, France had no historic ties to this German-speaking part of the Holy Roman Empire, except for the connection of the region to the Frankish kingdoms of the sixth century and its earlier attachment to Roman Gaul. Lorraine's dukes had been a thorn in France's side for almost two centuries: absorbing the duchy would put an end to their meddling.

The marriage of Louis XIV with Maria-Theresa of Spain created a major problem in the southern Netherlands because Spain, immersed in bankruptcy, could not pay her substantial dowry. She and Louis XIV had made the customary renunciation of rights against her father's estate in return for the dowry (peasant couples followed the same procedure). Philip IV's failure to pay opened up (as it would in any peasant marriage) the possibility of a lawsuit against his estate. When Charles II, the sickly child of Philip IV's second marriage, inherited the Spanish empire, Louis did not waste time with a lawsuit. Basing his claims for dowry compensation on the clause of "devolution" (in Brabant, the father's property "devolved" on the children of his first marriage), Louis sent 70,000 men into Artois and Flanders, where they captured most of the important towns and poised themselves to take Brussels and Ghent as soon as the spring 1668 campaigning season began. The prince of Condé waltzed an army through the Franche-Comté, encountering virtually no resistance.

Brabant, Flanders, and the Franche-Comté were all in Louis XIV's hands! That daunting prospect jarred the other European powers into action. England and Holland, who had been at war with each other again, signed a peace; they immediately pressured Louis to settle with Spain. The Emperor Leopold I, poised like a vulture over the apparent carcass of the Spanish empire, signed an agreement with Louis in January 1668, giving France the southern Netherlands, the Franche-Comté, Sicily, Naples, the Philippines, and Navarre. Leopold would get Spain, the New World empire, and the northern Italian lands. This agreement, predicated on the assumed imminent death of Charles II of Spain, might have transformed European power politics. As it was, the sickly Spaniard survived for more than thirty years, when his death without a direct heir touched off a European war.

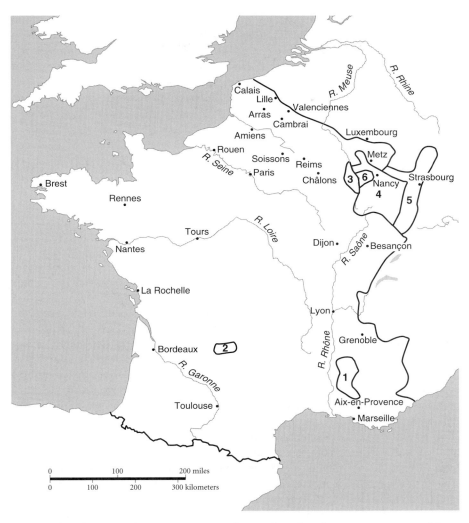

France after the gains of Louis XIV, 1715. The numbered enclaves were not part of the legal kingdom of France; number 1 (Avignon and the Comtat), for example, belonged to the Pope.

The prospect of England, Holland, and Sweden joining Spain against him led Louis XIV to agree to terms, particularly since he expected shortly to get everything he wanted anyway. France kept the key towns Turenne had captured in Brabant; Sébastien Le Prestre, better known as marshal Vauban, constructed a state-of-the-art fortress line anchored by Lille, Tournai, Douai, and Courtrai. The new fortifications made Paris much less vulnerable to attack from the north.

Louis knew what he wanted, and Lille was only part of it. His expectations of a share of the Spanish empire faded in the late 1660s, so he turned his attentions to the obvious enemy: the Netherlands. This dramatic shift, away from viewing Spain as the great enemy and toward such a perception of Holland, transformed European diplomacy, because France and Holland had been allies against Spain from the 1560s until the 1640s.[21] The change reflected three key new elements of French thinking on foreign policy:

1. The decline of Spain.

2. Louis XIV's desire for personal glory, best achieved by bringing "back" into the kingdom the "lost" northern provinces of Flanders and Artois.

3. French desire to break what many Frenchmen, such as Colbert, perceived as the Dutch stranglehold on European trade and French dependence on imported Dutch goods, especially manufactured ones.

The Dutch War, like the wars between England and the Netherlands in the 1650s and 1660s, formed part of a contest for political and economic supremacy in the new seat of hegemony.

As he had done in the run-up to the successful campaign of 1667, the ever-wily foreign minister Hugues de Lionne spun his spidery webs everywhere: an alliance with England (1670), neutrality of the wavering League of the Rhine (the small German states of that region), alliances with the ecclesiastical electorates in the Rhine, and neutrality of the Emperor. When Lionne died in September 1671, he left Louis a clear field for his attack on the Dutch. The king conducted a sort of seventeenth-century *blitzkrieg*. Turenne and Condé raced through the Dutch defenses, overrunning most of the country. Condé urged Louis to send cavalry to Amsterdam, to capture the defenseless city; Louis, in a decision that would haunt the rest of his life, declined. Louis also rejected the Dutch offers of peace in June 1672 because they could not offer him what he wanted: Flanders, Brabant, and Hainaut, all legally part of the Spanish Netherlands.

At this moment, supporters of William III murdered the de Witt brothers, then in charge of the Dutch government, whom they suspected of insufficient vigor in prosecution of the war, and turned over power to William.[22] William, Louis's greatest adversary, stood for war to the death. He immediately ordered the dikes to be cut, flooding the province of Holland and isolating the French army. Louis had no choice but to retreat.

The French did quite well in the rest of the fighting; the king himself supervised the capture of the great Dutch fortress of Maastricht (1673) and commissioned a famous tapestry to commemorate his glory, but no tapestry could hide the fact that France could not defeat the Dutch. Lionne's death had left French diplomatic affairs in the hands of Simon Nicolas Arnauld, marquis of Pomponne, who, though a capable man, could not extricate Louis XIV from the mess he had created. The diplomatic failure quickly led to a more diffuse war. England and Cologne withdrew (1674). The Emperor, the king of Spain, and many small German states allied with the Dutch; Louis had only Sweden, an ally that did nothing but lose battles.

French efforts shifted to the east, where Condé retook the Franche-Comté and Turenne helped consolidate French claims to parts of Alsace. Turenne died on the field (July 1675); the aged Condé retired to his estates. Their successors, notably marshal Luxembourg, continued the tradition of military excellence. Luxembourg and the king captured Ghent in 1678: as Mme de Sévigné wrote, "What do you say of the taking of Ghent? It's been a long time, my cousin, since we have seen a King of France there. In truth, our king is admirable." Even the French navy, long the butt of jokes, became a serious fighting force under the stewardship of Colbert.

Louis compromised at the Peace of Nijmegen (1679) as he had at Aix-la-Chapelle (1668): France did not get to keep everything of which it then had possession, but it did make its greatest territorial gains of the period between 1500–1789. These gains included the Franche-Comté, recognition of extensive rights in Alsace, and consolidation of gains in the north, even control of two fortresses on the far bank of the Rhine (Kehl and Freiburg). Louis claimed in his *Memoirs* that he could have had more, but gave it up so that his defeated ally, Sweden, could get back the territories it had lost (which it did). Yet Louis was more than a bit disingenuous, both in his *Memoirs* and in the fresco celebrating the peace "given" by Louis to his enemies, that adorned part of the ceiling of the Hall of Mirrors. A continued war against a European coalition made little sense, and none of the other major powers—the Emperor, England, Holland—was willing to let him keep Flanders and Brabant.

French policy during the wars from 1667–1713 revolved constantly around the fate of the Spanish empire, to which, absent Charles II producing an heir, the French royal family had the strongest claim.[23] However enfeebled the home country might be, Spain controlled very rich territories in Europe—the southern Netherlands and Milan, to name only two—as well as a massive colonial empire. The Austrian Habsburgs had collateral claims to the vast inheritance, claims that Louis XIV was willing to recognize, as in the arrangement of 1668. England worried more about trade to the Spanish New World. Holland wanted to protect its southern border and to preserve the monopolistic hold of Amsterdam on European transit trade. Areas controlled by Spain dominated each of these concerns; little wonder that the powers in question fought three major wars about those areas in the period from 1672 to 1713.

The peace of Nijmegen offered Europe only a temporary respite. War in eastern Europe provided Louis XIV with the diversion he needed to act in the Rhine valley. In 1681, he suddenly marched 30,000 men to Strasbourg and demanded that the city accept French sovereignty. The city fathers surrendered without a fight. Two years later, with all of Europe engaged in a sort of crusade against the Turks, then besieging Vienna, Louis struck again, this time seizing Luxembourg. Public opinion throughout Europe denounced this action: only France, among the major Continental powers, did not send troops to help defeat the Turks. That Louis chose this moment to use his troops to conquer disputed lands elsewhere in the Empire marked him, to many, as a traitor to the Christian commonwealth.[24]

The Truce of Regensburg (1684) marked the high water mark of Louis's territorial expansion; it recognized for twenty years all territorial acquisitions made by all parties in the Rhine region, leaving to some future date the legal adjudication of the sovereignty of these regions. One wonders if Louis considered the prospect of later trading these new acquisitions, neither of which had ever belonged to France, in negotiations over the southern Netherlands. Perhaps he envisioned the Emperor accepting a deal in which German Alsace and polyglot Luxembourg returned to the Empire, while France obtained Imperial acquiescence for its control of, say, Flanders, Brabant, and Hainaut? Such considerations were surely not far from Louis's mind, because the inheritance of the childless Charles II remained in the balance.

These matters, at once dynastic and national, had momentous long-term consequences for France. The settlement with the Burgundians at the end of the fifteenth century had removed Artois and Flanders from France, that France of the imagination that Louis XIV had learned as a child. The Burgundian inheritance included other French-speaking areas French speaking although traditionally part of the Empire, places like Hainaut, Namur, and Liège, as well as the Franche-Comté in the east. In the end, Louis failed to capture Flanders and Hainaut and he soon lost Luxembourg, but he kept his other gains; in time, Lorraine did fall into French hands. In effect, Louis's policies and wars added Artois, Alsace, the Franche-Comté, and Lorraine to France—about 12 percent of its total land mass.

This France, a France that extended to the Rhine and crossed over the Meuse in the northeast, differed sharply from the medieval one. The northern and eastern borders of the France of traditional imagination ran along the Meuse, the Sâone, and the Rhône. Louis XIV defined "France" for modern times. This new "France" would not include Flanders, one of its traditional elements, yet it would include the Franche-Comté, which had never belonged to France, and even Alsace, both culturally and politically German. The configuration Louis XIV bequeathed to his heirs had no special internal logic; in some regions, like Alsace, it defied historical logic. Louis created, quite unwittingly of course, what has ever after been France. In time, this creation became, too, a new France of the imagination. Louis remade the map of Europe, and gave his nation a far more secure frontier than it had ever enjoyed before. France's "natural" eastern boundary, its imagined limit, became and has ever after remained the Rhine.

Revocation and Religion

Nothing has a greater effect in less time than the reputation of a prince.

Louis XIV, to his son

C H R O N O L O G Y	1685–1715
1685	Revocation of the Edict of Nantes (Edict of Fontainebleau); death of Elector of the Palatinate
1688	Death of Archbishop–Elector of Cologne; French troops pillage the Rhineland; English depose James II and call in William and Mary
1689–1696	War of the League of Augsburg

CHRONOLOGY	(continued)
1692	French Navy destroyed at La Hougue
1693–1694	French victory at Neerwinden; capture of Namur; famine kills 1.3 million French people
1697	Peace of Ryswick; Louis relinquishes Luxembourg
1701	Death of Charles II of Spain; Philip of Anjou (Philip V), King of Spain
1702–1713	War of the Spanish Succession
1704–1705	French routed at Blenheim and Ramilies
1709–1710	Famine kills 600,000 French people; winter freeze destroys olive trees and vines of all of southern France; battle of Malplaquet
1711	Death of the Dauphin
1712	Villars's victory at Denain; deaths of duke of Burgundy and his oldest son
1713–1714	Treaties of Utrecht and Rastatt
1715	Death of Louis XIV; five-year-old Louis XV is king; Philip d'Orléans is Regent

Few events in French history so starkly mark a contrast as the Edict of Fontainebleau, better known as the Revocation of the Edict of Nantes. The Revocation marks, for many, the transition from the good Louis to the bad Louis, yet his decision to ban most forms of Protestantism in most of France did not come suddenly. The king and many of his officials had conducted a steady campaign of persecution since the 1650s. The Revocation merely formed part of Louis's larger religious policy; some of his advisors thought it would help the king restore good relations with the Pope, who had quarreled openly with Louis since the 1670s.

Louis had alienated the Pope in a series of disputes that intensified steadily. The first dispute involved money, the *régale:* who, king or Pope, would keep the revenues of bishoprics in southern France between the death of the serving bishop and the consecration of the new one? In 1681, a special assembly of the French Church, led by Bishop Jacques-Bénigne Bossuet of Meaux, rejected Pope Innocent XI's claims of supreme authority by promulgating the Four Gallican Articles:

1. The Pope has authority only over ecclesiastical matters.

2. Ecumenical Councils have authority superior to that of the Pope.

3. The Pope could not overturn the special rules of the French (Gallican) Church.

4. The Pope held supreme authority in matters of faith, *unless* overruled by a Council.

Innocent XI violently rejected the Articles and refused to confirm bishops named by Louis XIV (Bossuet among them). In 1687, Innocent sided with the Emperor in the dispute about the succession to the archbishopric of Cologne that underlay the War of the League of Augsburg.

Louis's disputes with the Pope certainly affected his decision to revoke his grandfather's Edict of Nantes, which had guaranteed the Huguenots fairly broad religious toleration. Their situation had changed steadily under Louis XIII, especially after the fall of La Rochelle. The Grace of Alès (1629) removed the military security attached to the Edict, but Louis XIII did not overturn its other clauses. The steady drumbeat of governmental and Church pressure did lead to an ongoing decline in the number of Protestants in the kingdom, especially outside of the heavily Huguenot parts of the Midi. By the middle of the seventeenth century, the Huguenots numbered as few as 700,000. In the 1660s, Louis, a firm believer in the political importance of doctrinal unity in his kingdom, stepped up pressure on the Protestants. He feared the "republicanism" of the Calvinists, a tag with which they were perpetually stuck after the English Revolution. In 1668, under intense pressure from the king, Turenne converted to Catholicism, a clear indicator that Louis had lost all tolerance for religious diversity. After 1678, the ascendancy of Louis's morganatic second wife, Françoise d'Aubigné (Madame de Maintenon), only made the king more fervent in his religious beliefs. She came from a very prominent Protestant family—her grandfather had been one of the leading Huguenot intellectuals of Henry IV's time—but she had been forcibly converted to Catholicism after her father's death. Her ardent religious beliefs strengthened the hand of religious hardliners at Court.

The king's own feelings aside, the Revocation responded to the desires of many of his subjects. The Estates of Languedoc, an area with many Protestants, turned progressively more hostile to them after 1640. They even banned Protestants from all participation in the province's estate process. They constantly urged the king to take sterner measures, an attitude mirrored by the militantly anti-Huguenot Parlement of Toulouse. Ordinary Catholics launched violent attacks on Huguenots, burning their temples at Nîmes and Montpellier.

Catholic fervor increased sharply in the seventeenth century, as part of the double Counter-Reformation taking place in France. The Jesuits spearheaded a movement toward elaborate churches, Catholic militancy, and intolerance of Protestants. The Jansenists, although opponents of the Jesuits, provided a second wave of Catholic militancy focused on personal piety and internalization of a new, more rigorous morality. Catholic orders sent "missionaries" into the "wild, pagan" countryside to "convert" rural Catholics to a more genuine Catholicism. In Brittany, Julien Maunoir reached out to these "misguided" Christians, organizing massive pageants at which costumed children asked questions of the "dead:"[25]

> . . . the living interrogated the damned: every one of the listeners were moved by their requests, which interested all; but the lugubrious voices, which expressed the cries of the damned, coming from under the theater, as from the bottom of the abyss, so frightened that grand mass of people, more than four thousand, that everyone pounded their chest, and formed new resolutions to do penance and to avoid sin.

When Louis signed the Edict of Fontainebleau (17 October 1685), he sent companies of dragoons into Protestant regions to enforce the new law. Protestant ministers could choose exile or death; laypeople had either to convert or to die for their faith. Many merchants and artisans fled to Holland, England, Prussia, and the New World. In the 1690s, the combination of a ban on trade with England, high war costs, and famine led to severe economic dislocation; the loss of Huguenot economic skills and capital exacerbated the problems.

This episode also did more than any other to undermine Louis XIV's reputation, both in his time and for posterity. Beginning with the War of the League of Augsburg, the Protestants of Europe began to treat their conflict with Louis as a sort of Crusade. He had been the very epitome of good taste and of cultural refinement, but the Revocation created the image of Louis the evil, absolutist tyrant. His enemies, above all the Huguenot refugees, lost no time in promulgating such an image. It gave religious, and hence emotional meaning to a conflict that really had very little to do with religion. The echoes of this emotional rupture poisoned Franco–British relations (not merely diplomatic but more broadly cultural); the lingering effects remain evident today, in popular attitudes on both sides of the Channel.

Moreover, Louis exacerbated his poor image by ordering more *dragonnades* in the early eighteenth century. He quartered troops throughout Huguenot villages in the Midi and persistently prosecuted those who participated in clandestine services. In January 1702, the authorities hanged Françoise Brès, a poor servant girl of Pont-de-Montvert: "She walked firmly to the place of her death, refusing with a firm but modest gentleness the missionary who walked with her and was urging her to change her religion."

Not all of the Protestants were so resigned to their fate. A large crowd of them gathered in Pont-de-Montvert in July 1702 and murdered the Catholic "missionary," Abbé du Chayla. Louis sent troops to track down the leaders, one of whom, Esprit Séguier, responded to the incomplete severing of his hand by chewing off the remaining skin and telling his captors, about to burn him alive, that his soul was "a garden full of shade and fountains."[26] The dragoons carried out brutal "conversion" campaigns in the Cévennes mountains, massacring Protestants and burning four hundred villages to the ground, driving thousands of peasants into penniless exile. French Protestants ever after called these the "Years of the Desert."

The Desperate Hours, 1688–1715

> *A minister who signed such a treaty would be lost in his own time and dishonored before history.*
>
> Foreign Minister Torcy, speaking of Louis XIV's 1709 offer
> to the Dutch, which he nevertheless presented to them

The decisive diplomatic event of Louis XIV's reign occurred in England, at the turn of the year 1688–1689. English Protestants had long detested their Catholic king, James II. The first effort to expel him, the Monmouth Rising, failed in 1681. In 1685, James and his second wife had a son, whom they baptized a Catholic. James's high-handed manner, coupled with the prospect of a Catholic succession, proved to be too much: the Glorious Revolution of 1688–1689 removed James and called in his Protestant daughter, Mary, and her husband, William III of Holland. James II fled to France, seeking Louis XIV's help to restore his throne.

Louis already had problems on the Continent, where the disputes over the inheritance of the Elector of the Palatinate and over the election of the archbishop of Cologne led to war between France and the Emperor. William III, once in charge of England, only too gladly allied with Emperor Leopold II against his hated French enemy. Thus began the War of the League of Augsburg, which pitted France against virtually all of Europe. Even traditional French allies, like Bavaria, turned against Louis because his troops pillaged the Rhineland, carrying out a ruthless campaign of atrocities viscerally remembered even today.[27] France's Huguenot exiles, many of whom had fled to England, Holland, and Prussia, helped fan Protestant hatred of Louis. Some of the exiles of 1685, such as marshal Schomberg, brought French military expertise to the Allied armies: Schomberg assisted William III in the key Battle of the Boyne (10 July 1690) that decided the fate of James II of England. The substitution of the Protestants William and Mary for the Catholic James II did more than anything else to undermine Louis's achievements. He had steadfastly clung to an alliance with England but the co-accession of William III, and the distinctly religious overtones of the deed, pushed Louis ever more deeply into an isolated corner. Louis and James, who lived at Louis's Court when in exile, became the dual personifications of Catholic absolutism and tyranny.

Things went better on the Continent. The well-trained and ably led French army defeated the allies in Italy, overrunning Savoy and the county of Nice, in Spain, where they captured Barcelona, and in the Low Countries. At sea, the French navy, rebuilt under the direction of Colbert and his son, the marquis of Seignelay, initially took the measure of the Dutch and the English. French privateers, such as Jean Bart and Duguay-Trouin, ravaged European and Caribbean commerce. The naval tide turned in 1692: the French, at first successful in an action against the joint English and Dutch fleets, ended up trapped in shallow waters off Barfleur and La Hougue and suffered a catastrophic defeat. On land, Louis himself undermined the Flanders campaign of 1693, by dispersing his troops massed there into other sectors. Marshal Luxembourg reportedly got down on his knees and cried, begging the king not to break up the armies. When Luxembourg won the great victory of Neerwinden and captured the key fortress of Namur, lack of reserves—the very men sent away by Louis—and the invariable ineptitude of marshal Villeroy, the king's childhood friend, undid the gains.

By 1697, everyone involved in the conflict suffered from exhaustion. The Peace of Ryswick made Louis give up Luxembourg, the Rhenish bridgeheads, the Savoyard fortress of Pignerolo, and a few northern towns. The Dutch and English also received the satisfaction of reduced French tariffs on their goods and ships. Louis got full recognition of his 1681 seizure of Strasbourg and his control over Alsace; William III got recognition as King of England.

The clauses related to England and the Holy Roman Empire proved to be more long-lasting than many suspected, but everyone involved in these negotiations understood that the decisions related to the southern Netherlands had little meaning because King Charles II of Spain had no children. The major powers wasted little time getting down to the real diplomatic business at hand: division of the Spanish empire after the death of Charles II. The four powers—England, France, Holland, and Austria—carried out secret (and not-so-secret) negotiations with each other. William III and Louis XIV reached two separate agreements. The first collapsed when the prospective heir to Spain, Joseph Ferdinand of Bavaria, died. The Emperor, whose brother Charles had a claim as a cousin of Charles II of Spain, and Charles II himself objected to the second. In the end, Charles II left his entire empire to one person, his nephew and closest heir: Philip of Bourbon, grandson of Louis XIV. Thus began the greatest and most terrible of Louis XIV's wars, the War of the Spanish Succession (1702–1713).

Spain's massive empire spanned most of the globe. The King of Spain held the southern Netherlands (modern-day Belgium and Luxembourg), the Milanais, the Kingdom of Naples, and other small Italian states; he also ruled much of the New World, with the great mines of Mexico and Peru, and parts of Asia, notably the Philippines. The War of the Spanish Succession took place on a worldwide scale, enhancing the trend begun by the Anglo–Dutch wars of the 1650s and 1660s and the War of the League of Augsburg, with its North American fighting.

France now had allies; Spain, of course, but Bavaria and Cologne, too, rejoined their traditional friend. Savoy and Portugal briefly sided with France, but then shifted to the other side. The core of the Grand Alliance—Austria, the Holy Roman Empire, England, and Holland—remained intact. As in the War of the League of Augsburg, French armies swept to victory at the outset of hostilities, both in the Rhineland and in Italy. The three capable French generals—Catinat, Vendôme, and Villars—seemed everywhere to have the measure of the Allies. Unfortunately for France, Louis disgraced Villars and gave important commands to three blunderers: the ubiquitous Villeroy, marshal Tallard, and La Feuillade.

Villeroy performed his usual magic, losing contact with the Anglo–Dutch army led by the duke of Marlborough. Marlborough joined up with the Austrians, led by Prince Eugene of Savoy. Together they annihilated the Franco–Bavarian army led by Tallard and Marsin at Blenheim (1704), killing or capturing 30,000 of the 50,000-man army. The mystique of the French army, universally feared and invariably successful for almost two full generations, died as well at Blenheim. In Italy, Catinat's death and the recall of Vendôme left the able corps commander La Feuillade in charge of an entire army. He was not up to the challenge, and the allies drove his army from Italy. The next year, Marlborough crushed Villeroy at Ramilies, leaving the French and Spanish in an extremely precarious position.

Few campaigns offer a better illustration of the fundamental weakness of Louis XIV's monarchy. "Absolutism," although never a systematic form of government, did leave enormous leeway to the king's whims. Just as Louis could decide to transform a small hunting chateau near some swampy ground into the greatest palace in western Europe, cost what it might, so, too, he allowed personal prejudice to interfere with governance. The three men most to blame for the Blenheim disaster—Villeroy, for letting Marlborough get away; Tallard, for laying out the foolish troop placements; and the count of Blanzac, who surrendered the large force under his command without sufficient reason—all escaped scot-free. Villeroy, as the king's friend, always received exoneration. Tallard, who had been captured during the battle, became a marshal of France. Blanzac escaped blame due to family connections. Tallard's co-commander, Marsin, whose command successfully held off Eugene's troops and who preserved what little of the French army survived the battle, got nothing.

Villars and Vendôme, back from disgrace, consolidated Franco–Spanish control of the main Flemish cities in 1707, but Eugene of Savoy and Marlborough routed the French at Oudenarde and swept forward, capturing Ghent, Bruges, and Lille. In 1709, France again had to deal with tremendous famine, which killed perhaps 600,000 people. Desperate, Louis offered to give up almost all of his gains—such as Strasbourg, and even Toul and Verdun (French since 1559)—and to recognize archduke Charles of Austria as King of Spain. When the Dutch insisted that Louis send troops against his grandson Philip, however, he balked.

Louis responded with one of the most remarkable gestures of his reign. He sent a letter to the French public, appealing for their support. Parish priests read this touching message from their pulpits:

> I share all the evils that war has made such faithful subjects suffer. . . . [but] I am persuaded that they would themselves oppose the acceptance of conditions equally contrary to justice and to the honor of the name French.

Public opinion supported the king's decision. He soon outfitted a new army, using confiscated Spanish bullion from the New World; under marshal Villars, this army inflicted crushing casualties on Marlborough's troops at Malplaquet, although the English "won" the battle.

Happily for Louis, international events began to break his way. In England, the antiwar Tories captured Parliament and demanded an immediate peace. On the Continent, Emperor Joseph I died and left the Holy Roman Empire to his brother Charles, who thus became to the other Great Powers a far less attractive King of Spain. Villars managed one last victory, at Denain, enabling France to retake Douai and other important forts. The Peace of Utrecht (1713) essentially restored France's territorial integrity. Philip got Spain and the New World empire, but he had to give the Southern Netherlands, Milan, and the Kingdom of Naples (treaty of Rastatt, 1714) to Emperor Charles and his family. The duke of Savoy obtained Sicily, as well as the return of lost territories, like Nice. England received Gibraltar, Minorca, Newfoundland, and the all-important *asiento,* exclusive rights to sell slaves in the Spanish empire.

On 1 September 1715, Louis XIV died, not much mourned by his subjects, who had grown tired of the old king's quest for glory. Contemporaries speak of drinking in the taverns and bonfires in the street. Louis XIV's succession had seemed assured as late as 1710; at that time, his son, oldest grandson, and great grandsons appeared in fine health. In 1711, however, the Dauphin died; the following year, his son, the duke of Burgundy, and Burgundy's older son, succumbed within weeks of each other to the measles. When Louis XIV died, therefore, the French succession devolved upon a five-year-old child, Louis XIV's great-grandson, whom the population quickly dubbed Louis the Well-Beloved. Louis stipulated in his will that a Regency Council should be formed, dominated by the princes of royal blood. In a parallel to the situation of 1643, the acting Regent, Louis's nephew, Philip of Orléans, had the Parlement of Paris overturn the dead king's will. Philip became sole Regent; the Parlement received back its right of pre-registration remonstrance.

The Transformation of the Modern State

I am going but the state remains forever.

Louis XIV, on his deathbed

Everyone knows the famous saying attributed to Louis XIV: "L'État, c'est moi" ("I am the state"). Specialists of Louis's reign have known this story to be apocryphal since the late 1940s, yet modern textbooks repeat it to this day. Why has so obviously false a statement remained part of textbook European history? Does it matter that Louis did not say precisely these words: did he not believe them to be true? As his dying words suggest, he did not believe he was the state; in fact, Louis did more than any other person to establish the French state as an independent entity, one above individuals, including the king. When Louis took personal power, the administration of the kingdom relied overwhelmingly on individuals, often on royal favorites; by the time of his death, he and his subordinates had created a state that relied far more extensively on institutions. The immediate reaction to Louis's death by the great aristocrats provides telling proof of the change. When his father died (1643), leaving a child as king, the great nobility responded with open military rebellion; when Louis XIV left a child heir, the great nobility allied with the Regent to take over the ministries, by means of a new series of councils. They failed. Long before Louis XV came of age, the old ministries and council had been restored, because the kingdom could be governed in no other way.

Why? What had become of the state since the middle of the seventeenth century that made it so strong and, in a way, so independent? In the late sixteenth and early seventeenth centuries, Louis XIV's predecessors had gradually marginalized the Classical meaning of the "state," the collective group of its citizens.[28] They had so separated this concept from the meaning of "state" that seventeenth-century commentators no longer associated the Roman phrase, *res publica,* or its modern equivalents (republic or commonwealth) with monarchy. Whereas the sixteenth-century theorist Bodin spent most of his work *The Six Books of the Commonwealth* (*Les Six Livres de la République*) discussing monarchies, seventeenth-century theorists took monarchy to be the antonym for "republic."

The disorder created by the Wars of Religion demonstrated the problems inherent in the contrast between the public good (that of all citizens) and the good of the state, as represented by the king. French kings gradually convinced their subjects to identify the good of the state with the "good of the king's service" and eventually substituted that good for the more dangerous one of the "public good."[29] By the time Louis XIV claimed personal power, the king and his magistrates had long been the official guardians of the public good, pushing aside the claims both of the mass of the citizens and of the high aristocracy. In the late sixteenth century, France had chosen a different path from the one followed by England or Holland. The urban elites of those countries had allied with the landed gentry to create a representative body to balance the power of the monarch; in France, the urban elites rejected a coalition with the landed gentry in representative bodies, and sought to share power through the state apparatus. As we have seen in Chapter 6, the decoupling of the landed power base and the institutional power of the high aristocracy after 1527 created a special situation in France, one in which they, too, sought to share power by means of the central government. The provincial landed gentry, a critical element in the representative bodies of England, Holland, and Poland, were a voice in the wilderness in France, and never more so than under Louis XIV. Fénelon's letter to Louis, discussed above, offers us a rare example of the public expression of their criticisms of Louis's state.

Louis XIV's state still had the three basic medieval elements—the military, the judicial system, and the financial system—but it had begun to take on *some* of the other responsibilities of the *res publica,* such as poor relief and education. Despite the greater central state role in such activities, the Church provided most of them. Formal education usually meant a school run by the Catholic Church; vocational education meant apprenticeship, whether in guild trades, on farms, or in households. Even local protection usually meant a local court, run by the seigneurial judge, and some sort of local militia. Early modern people would not have recognized the *central* state's obligations for education or public welfare, only the obligations of those institutions—including the Church, the guilds, town councils, seigneurial courts and lords—for specific aspects of the *res publica.* The governments of Louis XIV, Philip of Orléans, and Louis XV began the slow evolution from the old idea of the state as the mere provider of protection, of order, to the state as the protector of society in a larger sense.

Louis XIV intervened directly in famine relief, in 1661, again in 1693, and, especially, in 1709. This relief flowed mainly to northern France, when it helped to alleviate suffering in many cities (above all Paris). Louis also acted to assist other poor people. He built the Invalides, for wounded old soldiers; he reformed the hospital system of Paris, an example followed in many provincial towns. Outside of Paris, the state itself rarely took on such responsibilities, but, increasingly, the functionaries of the state, mainly its judges, acting as private individuals, took control of urban hospitals from the Church.

Such activity, as Michel Foucault has suggested, formed part of a larger process of domestication of the mass of the population. Elites, through the mechanisms of control—increasingly the state more than the Church—sought to create a disciplined people, and to do so on a wide range of levels. The ultimate goal, according to Foucault, was the creation of a self-disciplined population that would essentially regulate itself according to norms promulgated—he might say imposed (I would prefer insinuated)—by the elites. This model takes insufficient account of the effective means of popular resistance, and of the complex interplay of the powerful and the "powerless." Ordinary French people adopted some of these "imposed" elite norms, but invariably modified them to conform to their own needs. That said, research by historians such as Robert Schwartz demonstrates the extent to which the state did succeed in changing attitudes in some regions. Schwartz's work shows the extent to which people in Normandy, and in some other regions, accepted the new mechanisms of repression, such as the prison, as a manifestation of their own desires. As Foucault rightly suggests, that process continued unabated, and intensified in new and more complex ways, in the nineteenth and twentieth centuries.

The central state became more involved in activities such as poor relief in part because of the vast scale of disasters such as the famine of 1693. The population of France had risen steadily in most of the sixteenth and seventeenth centuries, except for a brief interruption in the late 1620s and early 1630s, due to plague and famine in western France. Climatological disasters, Europe's mini Ice Age, led to crises in 1693 and 1709. In 1693–1694, 1.3 million people died of starvation or malnutrition-related disease; the Midi suffered most of all, losing perhaps a quarter of its population. Thousands begged in the streets of Rouen, Paris, and other northern towns: the good bourgeois of these towns expected the state to do something about such suffering.

The crisis of 1709 occurred during the darkest days of the War of the Spanish Succession. In this instance, a poor harvest preceded the most severe winter of the Ancien Régime. The temperature remained in the single or low double digits (Fahrenheit) for weeks on end: the duke of Saint-Simon claimed in his memoirs that wine carried through the palace of Versailles froze in its decanters. The Midi again suffered enormously, its vital olive and fruit trees all split by the cold and its vines damaged. In village after village, once prosperous peasants, unable to pay their rents, took to the roads to beg. Once again, the king intervened rigorously in certain areas, notably the large towns. Overall casualties likely reached "only" 600,000. Yet the population of France quickly recovered from these disasters. The total population, perhaps 22 million (2000 European boundaries) in 1690, declined to 20.7 million by 1694, but reached 22 million again by 1705 or so. France made good the 1709 losses even faster.

The king's laudable efforts at poor relief notwithstanding, such expenses took up precious little of the central state's resources, which went overwhelmingly to the traditional purpose: war. For this purpose, Louis needed to raise a larger army, to levy heavier taxes, and to sell more venal officers. Louis kept France on this merry-go-round for nearly half a century. This never-ending quest for greater resources forced the king and his advisors to reinvent royal government, a process that took his entire reign.

Louis began in 1661, when he abolished the positions of first minister and superintendent of finances. In place of these dominant offices, Louis instituted an interlocking system of three *royal* councils: the Royal Council of Finances, which he created ten days after the disgrace of superintendent of finances Nicolas Fouquet; the Council of Dispatches; and the Council of State (*conseil d'en haut*).[30] As the word *royal* suggests, the new councils included the king himself as a permanent member. The Council of State included only those invited by the king: these people alone had the right to the title "royal minister." Louis always kept the Council of State quite small; during his reign, its membership varied from three to five ministers. Starting in 1691, Louis also invited his thirty-year-old son to join, and in 1702, he extended the privilege to his eldest grandson, the duke of Burgundy, then twenty. This Council made all the important decisions, especially those related to foreign policy.

Unlike many kings, Louis XIV took great enjoyment in the close supervision of his affairs. He regularly attended all three royal councils, spending most mornings and many afternoons on state business. Louis usually held the Council of State from 9:30 to 12:30 on Sundays, on alternate Mondays, and on Wednesdays and Thursdays. He met with the Council of Dispatches on alternate Mondays, and with the Royal Financial Council on Tuesdays and Saturdays. He dealt with religious matters on Fridays. After attending Mass and eating lunch with members of his extended family, the king sometimes went for walks, rode, or hunted. In the late afternoons, he again returned to business, meeting individually with the secretaries of state and the controller general. In the evenings, three times a week, starting at 7 P.M., the king officially received guests, often playing billiards. In the 1680s, a judge from the Parlement of Paris, Michel Chamillart, reputed to be one of the greatest billiard players in France, received a special invitation to join the king for the evening game. Chamillart soon became a royal minister, many said due to his billiard skills! After the billiard game, the king returned to the company of the ladies of the Court, usually offering a small ball until midnight. While the young Louis XIV spent his evening hours with his mistresses or in Court festivities, at the end of his life, on evenings when he did not receive, he spent time privately with Mme de Maintenon.

The three royal councils sat atop a pyramid of institutions that served much the same purpose that the Parisian "Grandes Écoles" serve today. They formed an elite leadership cadre to run the state. This cadre drew its members almost exclusively from the judicial families at the Parlements and other important courts. The young man would first serve as a master of requests in the king's household—Louis increased their number from seventy-two (1661) to eighty (1674) and then eighty-eight (1689). As in the time of Louis XIII, the king chose the intendants from their ranks. The masters did all of the preliminary work for the royal councils, preparing the dossiers from which ministers acted. At the end of his career, a successful master would become a royal councilor of state.[31] One or two of these men often sat in on the meetings of the Royal Council of Finances and the Council of Dispatches, to present dossiers prepared by their subordinates.

Six people stood at the apex of the pyramid of state: the chancellor, the four secretaries of state, and the controller general. The chancellor, a Crown officer, supervised the judicial system, relying heavily on the First Presidents of the Parlements, on the king's attorneys in those courts, and on the lieutenants–general of the bailiwicks.[32] Louis believed that the chancellor had enormous power within the royal judiciary, so he steadfastly tried to keep political power out of the chancellor's hands, often refusing even to make his chancellors into royal ministers.[33] Even the great judicial reforming commission of the 1660s, which did so much to establish clearer jurisdictional guidelines and change the criminal code, sat under the chairmanship of a royal councilor of state, Henri Pussort, uncle of Controller General Jean-Baptiste Colbert. (See Plate.)

The four Secretaries of State had two sets of functions, supervision of a group of provinces and jurisdiction over a specific functional category: War; Foreign Relations; Religious Affairs; and the combined Marine (and Colonies), King's Household, and Paris ministry. Side by side with this official state apparatus, a small group of extremely powerful aristocrats (in conjunction with the Secretary of State for the King's Household) directed Louis's enormous Court. Positions such as Grand Master of the

King's Household, First Gentlemen of the King's Bedchamber, or Grand Equerry carried enormous prestige, as well as extensive patronage powers. Every noble family wanted its sons appointed as pages in the king's stables or in the household. These great household officers had daily, protracted personal contact with the king, a source of inestimable advantage in the search for royal favor. The Court had no official governing function, but it provided a fundamental alternative center of power.

Louis thus developed three competing loci of power—the king's council, the ministries, and the king's household—all of which evolved out of the medieval *Curia Regis* (royal household). In his time, the members of the judicial elite dominated the first two, while the great nobility held sway in the third.[34] The first two elements of this power structure legally excluded women, who could not hold these offices, but the third one created a more gender-neutral power center. Because women played so central a role in the power politics of the Court, heading two of the three Court factions in the 1690s, they obliquely affected the work of the two exclusively male power networks.

Women wielded power, which was personal, rather than authority, which was legal. Yet individual men often wielded their power by personal means. The chancellor, as an individual, could provide the king with a critical conduit to the Parlements, as was the case of Louis Phélypeaux, count of Pontchartrain, chancellor from 1699 to 1714. Pontchartrain had been First President of the Parlement of Brittany in the 1670s and 1680s, so he knew firsthand the best methods for managing the courts. He and his wife, Marie de Maupeou, had countless relatives on the Parisian courts. When Pontchartrain's son, Jérôme, became Secretary of State for the Navy and the King's Household, his wife, Eléonore de la Rochefoucauld-Roye, who came from a ducal family, used her personal connections with the other great aristocrats to smooth her boorish husband's relations with the great officers of the King's Household. Everywhere one looked personal connections had a fundamental impact on the functioning of government.

That said, Louis both increased the range of state activity and the bureaucratization of its institutions. He insinuated the state into new areas, mandating (1667) the maintenance of civil registers *for the state*[35] and setting up a detailed legal code for French forests (1669, a code largely still in effect). He took famous "absolutist" steps, such as the 1673 removal of the right of pre-registration remonstrance from the Parlements. He also stripped them (and all other high courts) of the title "sovereign court"; they became instead "superior courts." This apparent attack on the Parlements masked a far more fundamental agreement with them. In practice, Louis strengthened the legal role of the Parlements. Although he virtually eliminated their ability to interfere in political matters, he also stopped removing cases from their jurisdiction, to be heard in his council. He relied on Parlementaires for three decisive elements of effective rulership:

1. Because the king could not rely on thirty-five or forty intendants to rule a kingdom of 20 million people, the Parlements and other royal law courts provided the main local mechanism for implementing and supervising royal policies.

2. Because the titled nobility, the only group who could balance against them in terms of prestige and wealth, had moved to Court, Parlementaires provided the highest ranks of the royal bureaucracy and the leadership of local society as well.

3. Parlementaire families provided almost all of the masters of requests.

Louis XIV and his ministers fundamentally altered the three basic aspects of monarchical government: justice, finance, and the military. The absence of the titled nobility (who had moved to Court or to Paris) left rural justice in the hands of royal officials. In many cases, the richest officers of the provincial Parlements, such as the *présidents à mortier,* bought the local seigneurial courts. Seigneurial court judges came from the ranks of lawyers or even minor judges of the royal courts. These petty judicial officials developed an ironclad control of local societies during Louis's reign. For example, they often manipulated local land markets through their inside knowledge of upcoming probate cases. While some regions, like parts of Brittany or the Auvergne, kept powerful seigneurial courts dominated by the old nobility, in many other regions such courts lost their caseload. The contrasts could be remarkable. At Pont-Saint-Pierre (near Rouen), the seigneurial court heard over fifteen hundred cases in 1580 but only three hundred seventy by 1700. Yet in Burgundy, even at the end of the eighteenth century, local seigneurial courts thrived, offering an effective system of local justice to the peasantry.[36] During the reign of Louis XIV, many ordinary French peasants came increasingly, and often for the first time, under the immediate jurisdiction of a royal court. In those regions, the state envisioned by royal officials and the Crown had triumphed decisively over the state proposed by the provincial nobility at the Estates Generals of Orléans and Blois. Yet the nobility essentially preserved the alternative system in places such as Burgundy or Brittany, with their powerful provincial estates and strong seigneurial court systems.

The second leg of the state trinity, the army, remained firmly in the hands of the nobility. Louis campaigned with his armies until 1693, so he knew firsthand the perils of warfare and had considerable personal expertise on military questions. Louis built up the largest, best-trained army in Europe, which peaked at some 360,000 men during the War of the Spanish Succession. Louis created a force of such magnitude that it demanded qualitative as well as quantitative change, both in France and in enemy states.[37] Completing the work of his father, Louis XIV definitively eliminated the two greatest military positions, colonel–general of the infantry and constable.[38] Louis insisted that anyone serving as captain or higher had to be presented to him at Court. The king could not, however, name whomever he pleased: Louis himself once reminded Minister of War Louvois that failing to replace a certain regimental commander with the man's son would lead to the resignation of the regiment's entire officer corps, who were all relatives of the family in question. Louis understood that he could not attack such family monopolies without destroying the unity of his army.

The great commanders of Louis's army often came from the extended royal family—Condé, Vendôme—or the high aristocracy—Turenne, Luxembourg—but some men of lesser nobility, like marshals Villars or Vauban also rose to the top. The War

Ministers—three generations of Le Telliers (Michel Le Tellier, Louvois, and Bar-bezieux), Chamillart, and Daniel Voysin[39]—and their aides, above all the marquis of Chamlay, introduced many innovations. The French army wore uniforms, obtained standardized weapons, and even learned to march in step, under the direction of In-spector General Martinet, whose name became an English noun describing his meth-ods. They created much better networks of supply, especially in peacetime. Relations with the French population improved: very little documentation of conflict between soldiers and civilians survives, a stark contrast to the flood of complaints of the 1630s or 1640s. The changes took place partly on paper—weapons were not fully stan-dardized, by any means—but they did represent real progress. The French army often defeated its foes in the early wars of Louis XIV simply because it had better organi-zation. The losers learned their lessons: they quickly copied the French model.

Louis, urged on by Colbert and his son, the marquis of Seignelay, also built a real navy in the late 1680s and early 1690s, but the defeat at La Hougue (1692) damp-ened Louis's maritime ardor. Louis's beloved army got the resources. Its constant losses (dead, wounded, desertions) meant constant recruitment: royal sergeants rounded up some 250,000 poor souls during the War of the Spanish Succession alone. The dreadful losses of the last two wars had a long-term impact on French de-mography and social life. For a generation after Utrecht, people commented on the absence of men in the demographic cohort that fought the Spanish war. The nobil-ity, too, suffered grievously. Louis encouraged noble participation in the fighting. Many families, including his own, responded. The male line of many such families expired at Blenheim or Malplaquet. When the war ended, Louis immediately re-duced the size of his army, to a peacetime level of 140,000 men. This reduction en-abled him to furlough many newly created officers, almost all of them commoners. Thus began the long eighteenth-century purge of non-noble officers in the French army, which would have momentous consequences in 1789.

Louis always relied extensively on a small group of ministers. He kept these of-fices in the hands of a few families, above all Le Tellier, Colbert, and Phélypeaux. In the 1660s, he relied on four men: Michel Le Tellier and his son, François, marquis of Louvois, Jean-Baptiste Colbert, and Hugues de Lionne. Louvois and Colbert, both of them somewhat imperious and habitually harsh on their subordinates, demanded accurate information. They did not like vague comments. They wanted to know how many—how many taxpayers, how many ploughs, how many guns, how many troops? Their quest for information, easily seen as the motivation for the requirement that local priests turn over the civil authorities copies of their registers of births, mar-riages, and deaths, led France in the direction of modern government. Such govern-ments act, and need information to do so. The state envisioned by Colbert and Louvois collected such information to an extent inconceivable to their predecessors. In the eighteenth century, the ministries collected even more information; they did so in a systematic and permanent manner.

Louis and his ministers reformed the internal administration of France, intro-ducing a level of order and central control achieved only sporadically in earlier times. To say as much, however, is to say nothing about "absolutism." Louis XIV faced mam-moth logistical difficulties in carrying out his will; he also faced (and accepted) legal and theoretical limits to his power, which closely resembled what the English called the royal prerogative. French elites remained firmly protected from arbitrary royal behavior behind their wall of contracts, codified in customary law. Respecting such limits meant testing them. Because he had authority over the most important internal matters, such as the financial system, Colbert, more than any other minister, carried out the tests.

Colbert's family remained firmly entrenched at the top of the royal administration after his death, despite a few worries in the 1680s. Colbert's son, Seignelay, succeeded him as Secretary of State for the Navy, although that position passed to Pontchartrain when Seignelay died. Charles Colbert de Croissy, the controller general's brother, kept his post as Secretary of State for Foreign Affairs from 1679 until his death in 1696; his son, the marquis of Torcy, succeeded him, but only became a minister in 1700. Colbert's son-in-law, the duke of Beauvillier, joined the Council of State as a minister without portfolio in 1691, and most contemporaries believed a second son-in-law, the duke of Chevreuse, acted as a kind of "secret minister," as Saint-Simon called him. Even the financial system, of which they lost control in 1683, returned to their network in 1702, when Colbert's nephew, Nicolas Desmarets, became second-in-command (and *de facto* head) of finances. Louis named him Controller General in 1708.[40] The second dominant family of Louis's later years were the Phélypeaux. Louis, marquis of Pontchartrain, held the offices of Controller General and Secretary of State for the Navy in the 1690s; when he became chancellor, Louis passed the latter office to his son Jérôme. Their cousins, the La Vrillière family, kept the office of Secretary of State for Religious Affairs into the reign of Louis XV.

Louis XIV's reliance on a small group of ministers often left him—and the French government—very much at their mercy. The ministers, and their immediate subordinates, controlled most of the information that reached the king, by which means they could limit his options. Yet the pattern began to shift during the last years of Louis XIV. Rarely did a family member of the minister become a chief clerk at a ministry; Desmarets was one of the last exceptions. More and more, the minister stayed at Versailles, and had staff there, but the ministry, with most of the subordinate personnel, remained in Paris. High-level permanent bureaucrats, like the six intendants of finance, took more and more control of the real workings of government. They were the state that Louis XIV left behind.

The intendants of finances belonged to a dense network of financiers who completely controlled state finances. Colbert again demonstrated the complex interweaving of traditionalism and "rational" reform. He streamlined and centralized financial administration, combining all the tax farms into one General Tax Farm in 1668, but he leased it to a syndicate of his cronies, institutionalizing the insidious personal connection between the controller general and the tax farmers who provided roughly half of the government's revenue. Colbert moved toward a tax mix more similar to that of other advanced states, like Holland and England, in which indirect taxes provided about 60 percent of the money. Yet the inherently corrupt system he created stimulated abuse. When Colbert died in 1683, his successor, Claude Le Peletier, abolished the General Tax Farm and investigated the corruption of Colbert's collaborators. In that way, Le Peletier could introduce his own cronies into the

COLBERT: TRADITIONAL MODERNIZER

Colbert's career superbly illustrates the combination of new and old methods in Louis XIV's evolving system of government. Colbert progressively took control of more and more of the elements of the state, yet he did so overwhelmingly by means of accumulating traditional offices. Originally one of the two intendants of finance, Colbert became unofficial head of finances in 1661 and then began the steady accumulation of royal officers from which he obtained different rights and responsibilities: superintendent of royal buildings (1664); Controller General (1665); treasurer of the royal chivalric orders of Saint Michael and the Holy Spirit (1665); superintendent of commerce (1665); president and director of the French East India Company (1665); member of the Académie Française (1667); Secretary of State for the Navy and Colonies, for the Clergy, and for the King's Household (1669); and grand master of mines (1670). These offices did not come cheaply: Colbert paid 242,500 *livres* to be superintendent of buildings, 700,000 for his office of Secretary of State, 400,000 more to be treasurer of the chivalric orders, and a stunning 1.3 million *livres* for his office as Controller General.

Colbert used the comprehensive package of responsibilities created by these offices to develop new synergies in royal administration

The chief financial officer (Controller General) had obvious interests in colonial commerce (Secretary of State for the Navy and Colonies and director of the East India Company), in general commerce (superintendent of commerce) and in mining (grand master of mines). Colbert's responsibility for royal buildings fitted neatly with his duties overseeing the King's Household. The other positions, too, gave Colbert important rights: as treasurer of the royal chivalric orders, he had the right to sit at the king's dinner table; as member of the Académie Française, he could oversee France's cultural direction.

Colbert used the combination of authority from his wide range of offices to integrate royal policy in many fields: finances, colonies, trade, manufacturing, transportation, and economic development. Colbertism, as the French call mercantilism, posited the integration of financial and economic policy, which casts the state itself in the role of merchant. His many offices made Colbert into something like a joint Minister of the Interior and Finance Minister, but because the offices split up after his death (1683), many of his initiatives—for example, his efforts to improve French roads and canals—lapsed due to later jurisdictional conflicts.

lucrative tax farms; in fact, he soon reinstituted the General Tax Farm. In the eighteenth century, the Farmers General, as its directors were known, became some of the most powerful and richest men in France, famous for their patronage of the arts as well as for their unshakable power over royal finances.

Their system ran from a group of about fifty major financiers—the controller general; six intendants of finance; the central treasurer; the receiver general of the clergy; about ten of the seventy receivers general (those from the largest districts, like Paris and Rouen); the treasurers of the great provincial estates, like those of Brittany and Languedoc; and the Farmers General—down through local (*élection*) receivers and holders of sub-sub-subleases of tax farms, and even to the elected village collectors of the humblest village in France.[41] The fifty men controlled everything: the direct tax system, the General Tax Farm, and the monopoly trading companies. French law made it illegal for those involved in tax farms to be royal officials, either in the administration of the direct taxes or in the judiciary. In practice, however, officers such as receivers general or local judges violated these restrictions all the time, creating a dense interconnected, if unofficial network of control.

These financiers pushed for greater power for the intendants, who remained under control of the head of the financial syndicate, that is, the Controller General. Colbert's shift to a greater role for the intendants in local tax collection, including supervision of individual parish tax rolls, created a permanent new element in the French state. The primacy of financial interest has led some historians to call this a "financial state," that is, one in which the interests of the financiers conditioned the very manner in which the state operated. The drive for financial viability moved the state into ever more areas of new responsibility. Interested in tax returns, the state took more interest in manufactures, in agricultural production, in regulation of the poor, in international trade. The syndicates of financiers fought for control of the apparatus headed by the Controller General; their conflicts helped drive French internal politics and foreign policy.

Colbert and his network did give the state a much more reliable and effective financial system. Overall revenue increased to about 120 million *livres*. Arrears of direct taxes disappeared because Colbert reduced direct taxes to tolerable levels, and undertaxed areas, like the *pays d'Etats,* contributed more.[42] Colbert also restored fiscal credibility by drastically cutting extraordinary, off-budget expenses (down from 88 million to 7 million *livres* from 1659 to 1663) and reliance on dubious loans ("extraordinary" affairs), which declined from 57 million *livres* in 1657 to scarcely a tenth of that in the 1660s. Colbert stayed away from currency manipulation and from the sale of offices, but his successors, facing much more desperate times, practiced both. The wars of the League of Augsburg and the Spanish Succession devastated French finances, leading the king to invent and sell vast quantities of offices (royal, municipal, guild, provincial), and even, in 1695, to the supremely radical innovation: the *capitation,* a tax, based on a classification system, levied on everyone in the kingdom. The clergy managed to buy an exemption, but the king had established the radical principle that all lay people were subject to taxation. The king, keeping his word, abolished the capitation when peace came, but re-established it as soon as the Spanish war began. Louis also issued new forms of annuities, most notably the lifetime annuity, carrying double the interest of the traditional perpetual annuity, with rates reaching 9 or 10 percent.[43] Ruinous borrowing practices, constant currency fluctuations, and manipulation of government paper financial instruments undermined the financial stability of the monarchy, leading to a virtual bankruptcy by 1709. Desmarets's clever creation of the Legendre Bank, which guaranteed government paper by the collective personal credit of the chief receivers general, got Louis through that crisis, but, by 1713 the government owed something like 1 billion *livres.*

The extraordinary measures required by the War of the Spanish Succession had a mixed success at the time. Philip of Orléans tried and failed to change the system; he found that he had no choice but to return to the old system in the 1720s. The financial failures of the early eighteenth century should not obscure the fundamental structural change of those years: the intendants of finance, with their permanent of-

VIVE LE ROI, FI DES ÉLUS

Few officials of early–modern France engendered the hatred focused on the *élus,* the overseers of local direct tax collection. Peasant rebels invariably chanted, "Long Live the King, Down with the *élus,*" and urban rioters often took up the refrain. Colbert's correspondence demonstrates his inveterate hostility to the old financial apparatus. He wrote constantly to the intendants that they must be wary of the treasurers of France (regional overseers) and of the *élus.* He reminded the intendants that the just apportionment and full collection of the *tailles* was their "most important" job. He viewed the *élus* as the single greatest obstacle to fairness. Because Colbert's correspondence has long been in print, and his letters imply that the old officials lost power to the intendants, historians have traditionally parroted his claim that he broke the power of the local officials.

In fact, out in the field, the intendants made extensive use of local officers. They often got into conflicts with one faction of the local officer elite, but they could not possibly carry out their tasks without the cooperation of other officers. In a ritual dance that would be repeated until the end of the Ancien Régime (and, truth be told, long after that), these rabid reformers from the center could make little headway against the inertia of the provincials. The provincials profoundly suspected the process of reform, the imposition of an outside will, even if (as was not always the case) they approved of the reform itself.

To help allay such suspicions, intendants formed alliances with local officers. In purely practical terms, how could thirty-five or forty men supervise the tax collection of 30,000 parishes? Intendants quickly created local assistants, whom they called sub-delegates; they naturally chose sub-delegates from the local officer elite, who had the most knowledge of the situation. Colbert inveighed constantly, yet uselessly, against this practice. Shortly after his death, the royal government recognized the necessity for the use of sub-delegates; in the eighteenth century, the government even officially divided intendancies into districts called sub-delegations.

The old officers did not simply disappear. The *élus,* quite apart from their continued role in the levying of taxation, kept their substantial judicial powers. The *élus* heard virtually all tax cases because only about one-quarter of taxpayers had an assessment superior to the amount judged in the first instance in the court of the *élus.* What is more, the amount paid by more than half of all French taxpayers entitled them to a hearing only in front of the *élus,* with no hope of appeal. Such authority, needless to say, gave the *élus* enormous local power—power Colbert may not have liked, but power which he could do little to undermine. In fact, we should read his correspondence in that way: he complained so much about the power of the *élus* precisely because he could do so little about it.

---

fices in Paris, now met collectively to determine the nuts and bolts of government financial policy. In the first half of the eighteenth century, the six offices remained in the hands of a few families and provided a remarkable degree of stability to the high fiscal administration of France.[44]

The decisive shift came during the 1690s and 1700s, when the policies and practices of new ministers—Louis and Jerome Phélypeaux, Colbert de Torcy, and Desmarets—dramatically modernized the French state. New ministers in the eighteenth century came increasingly from the corps of men prepared by service as masters of requests and as intendants. The shift from one narrow set of families to a broader group recruited from a specifically central formation "school" underlay the gradual evolution of the French government toward a more professional bureaucracy. In time, the alliance between certain Court factions, such as the aristocracy, and certain ministries, such as the War Ministry, became institutionalized. Court intrigue thus had a profound impact even on decisions taken within the ministries based in Paris. The painfully inept General Villeroy offers a perfect example. Quite apart from his personal friendship with Louis XIV, he had close ties to Mme de Maintenon, head of one of the main Court factions. Her faction included Colbert's two sons-in-law, who gave her a means of influencing the Council of State. Marshals Villars and Vauban lost commands because she detested them; Villeroy, despite his appalling record of ineptitude, consistently received command of important armies because of her support, and Louis's friendship.

Mme de Maintenon offers an excellent example of how elite French women of the end of Louis XIV's reign influenced events. At Court, the great aristocrats influenced patronage appointments of all kinds. Mme de Maintenon and her friends, through Saint-Cyr (a school for provincial noble girls) and other projects, created an amalgamation of Devout religious principles and the traditional ideology of the middling provincial French nobility that profoundly marked education of girls not only in France but throughout Europe.[45] This educational philosophy was one of the most powerful of French cultural exports in the eighteenth century. In Paris, wives and daughters of the great administrative elite, including the Farmers General, sponsored a thriving salon culture that both transformed the standards of behavior in polite society and offered a venue to the emerging ideas of the early Enlightenment.

❧ Mercantilism and Colonial Expansion

> [The French] *should discover in those lands and countries of New France, called Canada, some habitation capable of sustaining colonies, for the purpose of attempting, with divine assistance, to bring the people who inhabit them to the knowledge of the true God, to civilize them and to instruct them in the faith and Apostolic, Catholic and Roman religion.*[46]
>
> Louis XIII, letters establishing the Company of Morbihan, 1626

Court intrigues spilt into every facet of French life. Women's salons led the way in Parisian cultural life, and in the creation of demand for new fashions. Those fashions often involved new fabrics, above all cotton. The Farmers General, the men who dominated the monopoly trading companies that imported cotton, often were married to the women running the leading salons and setting the fashion trends. The complex intertwining of financial and mercantile activities has only come to light in the past twenty years, above all through the research of the French historian Daniel Dessert. His work demonstrates clearly that Colbertism, the French version of mercantilism, was a financial rather than an economic system.

The Netherlands offered the ideal mercantilist state, in which the state itself seeks to operate as a merchant, making sure that exports exceed imports, which produces a "profit." Colbert worried particularly about the loss of bullion, exported to pay for "useless" luxury goods, such as silks or Asian spices. He wanted to discourage imports of such goods, to encourage, where possible, the substitution of French production (such as silk), and to expand French export markets. As part of this policy of expanding French trade, Colbert encouraged development of colonies with the specific intent of enriching the mother country. He convinced the king to issue monopoly trading privileges to chartered companies. He also invested money in road and bridge improvement, and supported the greatest Ancien Régime public works project, the Canal du Midi, linking the Atlantic and the Mediterranean.

Mercantilism provided Colbert and his financial allies with a theoretical justification for their domination of government finances. French merchants overwhelmingly opposed the monopolies, often writing memoranda to Colbert praising the "liberty of commerce."[47] The Farmers General and other tax financiers provided virtually all of the money for Colbert's monopoly companies: East Indies, West Indies, Northern trade, African trade. Merchants provided virtually none of it. As for the public works projects, spending on them paled in comparison to the expenditure on Versailles and other palaces.

Colbert's vaunted efforts to support manufacture, particularly by means of royal monopoly, had mixed success. His local agents complained constantly of the petty, narrow-minded provincials with whom they had to deal; they contrasted these backward business people with the enlightened Paris investors. Local people naturally distrusted the motives of the controller general's clients. Colbert succeeded with a few development projects—such as the famous Gobelins tapestry works, whose primary client was the king himself—but overall his mercantilism was more talk than action. After Colbert's death, the state continued to follow many of his policies, with mixed results. The royally funded textile workshops of Languedoc, for example, never succeeded on their own, but they did help spark a splendid manufacturing revival in the eighteenth century. Above all, Colbert's systematic use of manufacturing inspectors spread and took root in the late seventeenth century and became one of the defining aspects of eighteenth-century French industry. In that sense, "Colbertism," the intricate and close relationship of the state to manufacturing that persists to this day in France, can be traced back to his policies.

The Dutch drew their economic sustenance from the entire world: they traded extensively and profitably in Asia; they benefitted more than anyone from the bullion of Spanish America; they dominated trade to the Baltic; and they carried the lion's share of European coastal trade. Colbert, like the English, sought to engage them on every front, not simply in Europe itself. To that end, he gave encouragement to the fledgling colonial enterprises started in the beginning of the century. The French colonists in Canada, who had reestablished permanent settlements there under Samuel de Champlain in the first two decades of the century, remained a tiny and hardy band as late as the 1660s; the census of 1665 counted only 3,215 Europeans in the colony. Twenty years later, Canada had 12,000 people. It reached 25,000 by 1713.

Despite the rapid growth, Canada remained demographically a tiny settlement in comparison to the nearby English colonies along the Atlantic coast, which had more than 250,000 people by 1713. Canada's small population focused on servicing the export of raw materials. Those inland, near the main towns of Québec and Montréal, traded with the Indians for furs or trapped furs on their own.

These intrepid trappers, called *courreurs du bois* (runners of the woods), and the redoubtable Jesuit missionaries explored much of the interior of North America. Louis Jollier and Fr. Jacques Marquette explored the western Great Lakes and found the upper Mississippi River (1671–1672). Their "discoveries" led to the subsequent voyage of Robert de La Salle, who sailed down the Mississippi to the Gulf of Mexico in 1682. A later mission that sailed from France to Louisiana—named, of course, for the king—failed miserably, but the French returned to the mouth of the Mississippi in 1699 under the sieur d'Iberville and his brother, the sieur de Bienville. In time, these two men would found settlements at Mobile and New Orleans, where the main streets of the French Quarter still preserve their names and Lake Pontchartrain that of their master, the Secretary of State for the Navy and foreign commerce.

The coastal settlements in Canada serviced the enormous fishing industry on the Grand Banks. The annual cod fleet from France brought some 12,000 sailors a year to Newfoundland, a group that, prior to 1690, outnumbered the entire French population of Canada. Far more French settlers made their way to the West Indies than to Canada. French naval expeditions claimed the Windward Islands of the Caribbean one after another: Saint Christopher, Guadeloupe, Martinique, Nevis, Dominica, Sainte-Croix, Saint-Martin, Grenada, Tobago, the famous pirate den at Tortuga, and Saint-Domingue (now called Haiti), an illegal settlement on the Spanish island of Hispaniola.[48] These colonies developed very slowly prior to Colbert—a few thousand settlers, most of them indentured servants living in dismal conditions. They focused on producing tobacco, which enjoyed a great boom in mid-seventeenth-century Europe. Virtually unknown in France prior to 1640, it became so popular that by 1675 peasant rebels in western Brittany demanded that "the money of the traditional hearth taxes should be employed in buying tobacco, which will be distributed with the blessed bread at the parish Masses, for the satisfaction of the parishioners." The French government, seeing in tobacco a commodity easily taxed, instead created substantial excise taxes on its sale. In the 1670s, Colbert established a government monopoly on tobacco that has lasted to the present day.

Rapid increases in tobacco production severely cut prices and profits: both French and English tobacco colonies suffered severe economic dislocations by the 1660s. The French islands began to shift their chief crop from tobacco to sugar, introduced in the mid 1650s. This shift fundamentally altered the nature of West Indian societies. Most tobacco plantations relied on indentured servants, tilling relatively small plots; sugar plantations preferred to use African slave labor on their much larger fields. Islands like Martinique and Guadeloupe, which had white majorities in the 1650s, developed black majorities by the 1670s.[49] By the middle of he eighteenth century, 90 percent of their populations came from Africa.

Sugar-producing techniques came to the French West Indies in the 1650s, brought by the Dutch planters expelled from Brazil. Those planters provided a haven for the

Georges de la Tour, The Smokers Den. *Here we see the new vogue for tobacco, which spread rapidly in the middle of the seventeenth century. The French government established a tobacco monopoly, which lasted until contemporary times. The presence of a black man reminds us of the ties between colonial commerce and the early modern African diaspora.*

Source: © Réunion des Musées Nationaux/Art Resource, New York.

Portuguese Jewish sugar technicians driven from Brazil at the same time. Colbert initially sought to use a monopoly company, the West India Company (created 1664), to drive out the Dutch. He required that French planters buy only French goods, that they ship their raw sugar only to France, and that they send their goods only in the ships of the Company. The colonists rejected this policy, preferring the cheaper, more efficient Dutch; on Saint-Domingue and Martinique crowds pillaged the storehouses of the West India Company. The monopoly quickly collapsed (1674), but private French shippers soon developed a lively competition for the Dutch. Aided by the government's policy to limit trading to French ships, they gradually supplanted their northern rivals, although smuggling remained endemic throughout the Caribbean.

The colonists laid the foundations for eighteenth-century prosperity in the last quarter of the seventeenth century. On Martinique and Guadeloupe, sugar plantations increased from about seventy in 1660 to between two hundred and two hundred fifty in 1700; sugar now took up 70 percent of the tilled area. Planters initially shipped crude sugar, called muscovado, to the Netherlands, where refineries made it into the finished product, but Colbert demanded that they use French refineries. The great

duty controversy created by the 1667 tariffs had a dramatic effect on sugar production. Within five years, thirty-six refineries sprang up in metropolitan France and a
like number closed in Holland. Little wonder the two sides were ready for war by 1672.

The planters disliked the reduced profits created by monopoly refining, so they
sought to refine sugar on the islands themselves in order to cut shipping costs.[50] The
government, which introduced a royal administration structure in the 1670s and
1680s, enforced a ban on island-based refineries, in order to protect home-based industries. Planters did increase their profits by sending processed "clayed" sugar to
France, but sugar refining became and remained a monopoly of metropolitan
France, above all the cities of Bordeaux and Orléans.

The West Indies formed a second leg of the infamous triangle trade—northwest
Europe–Caribbean–Africa—that would become so prominent in the eighteenth century. The French mounted a military expedition to the west coast of Africa in 1651,
when they established Saint-Louis at the mouth of the Senegal River. They later built
Fort Saint-Joseph further inland and captured Gorée Island from the English in
1677. These forts enabled them to dominate much of the Senegambian coast, except
for the Gambia River itself, controlled by the English. These seventeenth-century
forts created long-lasting colonial relationships. Senegal would become a full-fledged
French colony and remain a French possession until its independence, just as Gambia fell to England.

A French participant in the trade explained its principles in 1682:

> In exchange for these negroes we trade cotton baft, copper, tin, iron, spirits
> and a few glass trinkets. From such trading we make a profit of 800 percent.
> Hides, ivory, and gum go to France. As for the slaves, they are sent to the
> French islands in America to work on sugar plantations. Good quality slaves
> can be had for ten francs apiece, to be resold for over a hundred écus [more
> than 400 francs]. Often enough, you can get a pretty good slave for four or
> five jars of alcohol. So one spends less on purchases than on transport, since
> outfitting the ships costs a great deal.[51]

This trade developed slowly in the last quarter of the seventeenth century: French
planters bought a few thousand slaves each year, initially from Dutch slavers but increasingly, after the mid 1670s, from French merchants. By the end of the century,
French slavers sold about three thousand Africans a year to West Indian plantations.[52]

Just as in the Americas or in Africa, the French sought to rival the Dutch, Portuguese, and English in other areas of the world. French merchants sought to establish fortified trading posts in India and encouraged the government to develop
diplomatic relations with Siam (Thailand). The need for a base at the midway point
of the long voyage to India led to the failed effort to create a colony on the island of
Madagascar, off southeastern Africa. The French had been there since Richelieu's
time, but made their first major effort to consolidate Fort Dauphin in 1665; it failed
completely. They then moved to a tiny island east of Madagascar, which they named
Isle Bourbon, and created a small colony (five hundred people).[53]

In India, the efforts of the late 1660s and early 1670s led to the creation of major
French entrepots (an intermediary center of trade) at Surat, on the west coast, at

Pondicherry, in the southeast, and at Masulipatam in the east, as well as at a number of smaller posts. Pondicherry quickly became France's main Indian center; by 1690, it had a population of more than 20,000 people, most of them from the Subcontinent. The French East India Company, in league with the government, ran these outposts and maintained its monopoly hold on French Asian commerce. They shipped the usual products—silk, pepper, cotton—the last of which, often in the form of dyed cloth, helped create a momentous change in French attitudes toward clothing. European efforts to copy Indian cotton cloths lay at the root of the later Industrial Revolution, which began as the application of mechanized production to cotton spinning.

In the eastern Mediterranean, French merchant colonies could be found scattered throughout the Ottoman Empire's great ports: Istanbul (Constantinople), Izmir (Smyrna), Aleppo, and Cairo. Colbert tried to encourage these developments with a monopoly company, but the dominance of merchants from Marseilles could not be challenged. Even here, however, the government managed to convert its local representative in the Ottoman ports, called a consul, from an officer into a *commissaire,* by the 1690s. French merchants in these ports, as well as in those of the North African coast, made many of their profits in local trade, rather than in shipping goods back to France. Unlike French merchants in other overseas territories, those living in the lands of the Ottoman Empire or in North Africa remained under local political jurisdiction. Their communities negotiated special agreements with local officials, had an official assembly of all merchants, and even funded community projects, such as special translators (dragomen), and language programs for young French merchants trying to learn Ottoman and Arabic.

The basic lines of the new world trading network—routes, products, partners—had been established by 1700. The immediate cultural impact of such trade within France had also begun in earnest, whether in the audacity of the wife of the first president of Parlement of Brittany, who promenaded dressed "in Indian fashion" or in the rise of fashionable cafés in Paris, such as that of the Italian "Procope" Coltelli, where elite society would soon gather to discuss politics.[54] The War of the Spanish Succession severely disrupted colonial trade, but the Peace of Utrecht provided French merchants, manufacturers, and agricultural exporters with an opportunity to make an economic and social revolution, building on the changes wrought in the last quarter of the seventeenth century.

Notes

1. *Racine. Œuvres completes,* ed. L. Estang (Paris: Seuil, 1962), 387.

2. *Mémoires de Saint-Simon,* ed. Y. Coirault (Paris, 1983), v. 5, 474.

3. Despite his criticism of the ministers of the final years, Saint-Simon singles out one of them, Louis Phélypeaux de Pontchartrain, as a man of exceptional abilities and intelligence.

4. The successive titles indicate higher levels of nobility. People used Monseigneur only for dukes or bishops, Your Highness for those of royal blood (except the king).

5. Molière's play *George Dandin,* about a yeoman farmer who tries to become a noble, similarly provided the French language with new words. A *dandin* is a dolt, while the verb *se dandiner* means to move one's body in a ridiculous fashion.

6. "Butter; always butter." Fernand Point was the most important French chef of the middle of the twentieth century; many of today's senior stars trained under him.

7. In addition to these "official" mistresses, Louis had other, briefer liaisons. He had a strict sense of the place of such women in the Court hierarchy, and of his obligations to certain outward appearances of propriety. By all accounts, he returned each evening to the queen's bedroom and he kept many of his temporary liaisons so secret that we do not know with certainty the precise nature of his relations with some women. In a household of arranged marriage, a certain liberality with respect to personal feeling could be allowed. Louise de la Vallière got along very well with the queen, although the marquise de Montespan, who had a haughty personality, did not.

8. A three-star Parisian restaurant today bears his name.

9. J.-R. Pitte, *Gastronomie française. Histoire et géographie d'une passion* (Paris: Fayard, 1991), 130.

10. Butter gradually replaced pork fat as the basis for the *roux* in the eighteenth century.

11. Recipes adapted from B. Wheaton, *Savoring the Past. The French Kitchen and Table from 1300 to 1789* (New York: Simon & Schuster, 1983), 252–256.

12. In fact, the "food fight" had been staged; the entourage objected to the social temerity of the bishop, a mere commoner, in his treatment of the prince. Nonetheless, the fact that they staged the destruction in the guise of a food fight demonstrates that society accepted such behavior as within the range of normal comportment for young male nobles.

13. The story comes from the memoirs of Saint-Simon, cited in R. Muchembled, *L'invention de l'homme moderne* (Paris: Fayard, 1988), 51.

14. This matter is covered in much greater detail in Chapter 11.

15. Cited in J.-R. Pitte, *Gastronomie française,* 127–128.

16. Mme de Sévigné, *Selected Letters,* ed. L. Tancock (London and New York: Penguin, 1982), 98–99, letter of 26 April 1671 to Mme de Grignan. Mme de Sévigné later notes that while some praised Vatel, others blamed him (for what she does not say).

17. Vatel, it should be noted, was not himself a cook. Be that as it may, he is one of the patron saints of French cooking. Restaurants bear his name, just as they bear those of La Varenne and of Carême (the latter two at one time famous Parisian tables, to say nothing of provincial namesakes). Gerard Depardieu has recently starred in the film *Vatel.*

18. In the nineteenth century, middle class supporters of the French Republic developed an almost religious belief in Republicanism. They used the public school system—universalized in the 1880s—to propagate a secular Republican ideology that directly attacked the traditions of French Catholicism. Intellectually, these people reached back to a tradition founded by Malebranche and Bayle.

19. Louis XIV had one son, also Louis, known simply as the Dauphin, who was heir to the throne until his death in 1711. At that moment, the duke of Burgundy, the Dauphin's oldest son, became himself the Dauphin, that is, heir to the throne. Burgundy died of measles in 1712.

20. Cited in F. Bluche, *Louis XIV* (Paris, 1986), 385.

21. Dutch concerns about French expansionism in the late 1640s led to their separate peace with Spain in 1648, an action directly in violation of the alliance agreement with France.

22. The assassination of Jan de Witt, leader of the Estates General, shifted power back to the office of Stadhouder, the titular head of government and the armed forces. William III, who had been a child when the Estates effectively abolished the office in 1650, thus reclaimed power.

23. Louis XIII of France married Anne of Austria, eldest daughter of King Philip III of Spain. Her brother, later Philip IV of Spain, married Louis XIII's sister, Elisabeth. The children of these two marriages, Louis XIV of France and Maria-Theresa of Spain, also married. Louis XIV himself was thus the grandson of Philip III. His son, the Dauphin, was the only surviving grandson of Philip IV and thus the closest heir to Charles II. The Dauphin passed his claim on to his son, Philip, who eventually became King of Spain, as we shall see.

24. France had long had a sort of informal anti-Habsburg alliance with the Ottoman Empire, a fact that encouraged Louis's contemporaries to view him as a traitor to Christian civilization.

25. L. Châtellier, *La religion des pauvres. Les sources du christianisme moderne, XVIe– XIXe siècles* (Paris: Aubier, 1993), 64.

26. P. Higgonet, *Pont-de-Montvert. Social Structure and Politics in a French Village, 1700–1914* (Cambridge, MA: Harvard University Press, 1971), 38 and 32.

27. In each of my visits to this region, local people have brought up the devastation, frequently pointing out local castles ravaged by Louis's troops.

28. Western political theorists took this definition from Aristotle's *Politics*.

29. As noted in Chapter 6, loyalty to the public good could lead subjects to rebel against their king, for instance if he followed a religion they believed to be false. Protestant rebels in the 1570s and Catholic ones in the 1590s had used precisely that argument in France.

30. The Council of Dispatches dealt with internal matters; its seven members included the four Secretaries of State, the Controller General, the chancellor, and the king. Over the course of Louis's reign, its meetings declined from two per week (1660s) to one per month (1715). Recent research by John Rule, however, suggests that this Council did its business in ways other than official meetings and that it kept important responsibilities. Louis had a fourth royal council, the Council of Commerce, from 1664 to 1676. At the end of his reign, Louis created another Council of Commerce, which he did not attend.

31. One must distinguish between the purely honorific title, royal councilor (*conseiller du roi*), attached to several thousand offices, and the functional title, royal

councilor of state (*conseiller du roi en ses Conseils d'État et privé*), which gave its bearer the right to participate in the work of the king's council. Louis had no more than thirty of the latter at any one time.

32. As a Crown officer, the chancellor could not be removed. If the king lost faith in the chancellor, he could remove the royal seals and create a special official, the Keeper of the Seals, who could be removed at will. Louis XIV used this office only once, after the death of chancellor Séguier (1672); he named a new chancellor in 1674. By way of contrast, Louis XV used this tactic six times, covering twenty-nine of the years between 1722 and 1774.

33. He did name some ministers, such as Pontchartrain, as chancellor.

34. Many great judicial families had close ties to people in high finance. Chancellor Louis Phélypeaux de Pontchartrain (1699), a man whose family had long held the highest judicial offices, descended from a central treasurer of the 1620s. Fouquet, superintendent of finances in the 1650s, descended from two generations of Parlementaires.

35. Registers had been mandatory for the *Church* since the Council of Trent.

36. Peasant *cahiers* in 1789 often praised seigneurial courts for their regulation of local disputes between peasants, yet they offered strong criticism of such courts adjudicating disputes between the seigneur and the peasants. I am indebted to Dr. Jeremy Hayhoe's recently defended Ph.D. thesis for this information.

37. Henry IV had an army scarcely one-tenth this size; Louis XIII had one less than half as big, even during the height of the Thirty Years' War.

38. Even Louis XIV's boundless admiration for Turenne never made him give in to the marshal's request to be named constable; Turenne had to be content with the new, purely honorary title, *generalissimo* of the king's armies.

39. In Louis XIV's day, these ministers sparred constantly with the high aristocracy: the battles of Louvois and Turenne were legendary. Later, the high aristocracy adopted a different tactic. They took over the War Ministry. See Chapter 12.

40. The Le Tellier fared less well. When Louvois died (1691), his son, the marquis of Barbezieux, succeeded him as Secretary of State, but did not become a royal minister; Barbezieux's death (1701) removed the family from affairs of state.

41. The government spent about 7.5 percent of the money at the local (*élection*) level and another 15 to 20 percent at the regional (*généralité*) level; all such spending had to be approved by the Royal Financial Council. The General Tax Farm consisted of thousands of subleases and sub-subleases held by local people, who often formed syndicates to come up with money.

42. Only 20 percent of this money actually came to Paris as cash; the rest circulated as government financial instruments, which provided a sort of large denomination paper currency. The doubling of the Breton contribution contributed to a massive rebellion in 1675.

43. The king paid only the interest on the annuity; he never reimbursed the principle. The person buying the annuity did not have to list his or her *own* life as the

one applicable to the annuity; enterprising financiers often listed the life of a young girl on the annuity.

44. Desmarets's chief secretary, Philibert Orry, would later himself become Controller General, and hold the post for fifteen years, providing still further stability.

45. Catherine the Great of Russia modeled her school for noble girls, Smol'ny, on Saint-Cyr. Fénelon's ideas on the education of girls also affected Rousseau. In Rousseau's treatise on education, *Emile,* the favorite book of the hero's prospective bride, Sophie, is none other than Fénelon's *Telemachus.* Mme de Maintenon's own grandfather, d'Aubigné, had a powerful impact on the political ideas of Fénelon and, later, those of Rousseau. Karen Taylor's dissertation on Saint-Cyr and two forthcoming articles provide details on the connection.

46. Cited in A. Pagden, *Lords of All the World* (New Haven and London: Yale University Press, 1995), 34. Pagden notes his unusual translation of "les faire policer" as "civilize them"; it more literally meands to bring order to them or to administer them in an orderly way.

47. "Liberty of commerce" did not mean free trade; merchants demanded an end to monopoly companies, but supported the continuation of special privileges for themselves.

48. Spain recognized the legitimacy of France's claim to the western third of Hispaniola at the end of the seventeenth century. France also set up a colony in Guyana in 1612.

49. The French, like the Spanish and English, largely exterminated the small indigenous populations of these islands. Many of these Caribs died because of their lack of resistance to European diseases, such as smallpox.

50. It took two hundred twenty-five pounds of muscovado to make one hundred pounds of refined sugar.

51. Cited in B. Barry, *Senegambia and the Atlantic slave trade,* trans. A. Armah (Cambridge: Cambridge University Press, 1998), 49.

52. The slave trade is discussed in greater detail in the next chapter.

53. Now called Réunion Island, it, like Martinique and Guadeloupe, forms a legal part of metropolitan France.

54. P. Haudrière, *L'Empire des Rois, 1500–1789* (Paris, 1997), 153, mentions the story about the First President's wife, but does not identify her (or the precise date). Internal evidence suggests the story comes from the early 1690s, which would make her Françoise Ferrand, wife of René Le Feuvre. Moreover, it cannot be a coincidence that Le Feuvre's predecessor was none other than Louis Phélypeaux, who was, by 1690, both Controller General and Secretary of State for the Navy and overseas trade!

Chapter Ten

THE SOCIAL AND ECONOMIC REVOLUTION

*Is there a need to add, in that spirit, that I reject the narrow concep-
tion of a 'society of orders,' to the extent that this notion, certainly
interesting and useful and very often exact, claims to explain absolutely everything? I refuse as well the notion of a 'society of classes,'
in its intransigent formalism, even though it, too, is useful and partly
accurate. But what I accept even less is to be caught in a dilemma, to
be able to choose only between these scholasticisms, which is the
negation of the greatest and dearest of liberties, that of the spirit, as
well as of historical research itself.[1]*

Pierre Goubert

Louis XIV's death ushered in an era of relative peace and prosperity. The Peace of
Utrecht allowed French merchants, manufacturers, and agricultural exporters to
take advantage of the economic revolution they had begun in the last quarter of the
seventeenth century because trade opened up again with French colonies and trading outposts worldwide. This external commerce grew by leaps and bounds between
1715 and 1754, when massive colonial war broke out between France and England.[2]

The new king, Louis XV, was only five when his great-grandfather died, so a regency had to take the reins of power. As in 1643, the chief power broker—in this case
Louis XIV's nephew, Philip, duke of Orléans—allied with the Parlement of Paris to
overturn the dead king's will. Once again, the Parlement agreed to name a single
regent (Philip) rather than setting up a Regency Council. Once again, the new regent gave important concessions to the Parlement: Philip restored their right of pre-
registration remonstrance, laying the groundwork for a struggle that would dominate
French politics later in the century. For decades, that conflict focused around another
critical act of the end of Louis XIV's reign, the issuance of the Papal bull *Unigenitus*
condemning Jansenism. Louis XIV, Philip, and Louis XV all insisted, against violent
opposition from the Parlements, that *Unigenitus* be treated as a constitutional law
of France.

Philip and his aristocratic allies began their assault on Louis XIV's legacy by
attacking his ministerial system. The Regent abolished the ministries and created a

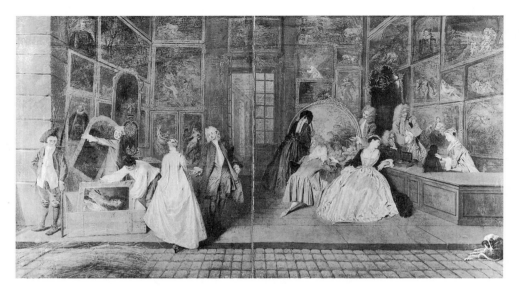

J.-A. Watteau, The Shop of the Art Merchant Gersaint *(1719). The portraits of Louis XIV are being put into storage; his death, little mourned by his subjects, immediately rendered them out of style.*

SOURCE: © Foto Marburg/Art Resource.

broad group of councils, the Polysynody, headed by leading aristocrats. He fired the Controller General and brought in new financiers. This new system lasted three years, when the Regent had to restore the secretaries of State and even the hated position of Controller General. The high aristocracy, who had chafed for years under the tutelage of ministers with lesser pedigrees, had failed completely in its effort to run the government. Philip thus unwittingly ensconced a permanent ministerial system of government. He had abolished the ministers without abolishing the ministries, whose work enabled the government to function. From the early 1720s until the early 1750s, the restored ministerial system maintained a high level of stability and quietly hardened into something like a modern bureaucracy.

The quiet progress of the central state stands in sharp contrast to the dramatic reconfiguration of the French economy and society, which had already begun in the last quarter of the seventeenth century. In the dominant agricultural sector, the climatological pattern from about 1650 to about 1750 led to some long strings of good grain harvests: the late 1660s, the 1670s, 1683–1691, 1700–1707, 1716–1720, much of the 1720s through the 1740s. These good harvests meant that grain prices remained virtually stable for close to a century.[3]

The solid agricultural foundation enabled the colonial and international sector to drive rapid economic development and fundamental social change. People began to change their everyday habits. In towns, they wore different clothes, ate different foods, drank new beverages, and read more often. In town and country alike, people began to migrate more often and to marry people from outside their home parish. Women, in particular, became substantially more mobile; legions of young, single rural women moved to towns, to take on jobs as servants. In the first half of the eighteenth century, most of these women moved back to their home village after amassing some savings. When they returned, they brought back not only money, but many of the new practices and customs they had seen in the town. In the second half of the century, these women far more often remained in the town, marrying an artisan, shopkeeper or servant.

Everywhere, especially in northern France, more people could read and write. Many more men than women could read and write, but, by the 1780s, more than a third of women in northern France possessed basic literacy. Women increasingly ran businesses, which required them to learn fundamental skills, such as elementary bookkeeping and reading, so that they could understand the many contracts they now had to sign. Even in rural areas, landlords demanded that both wife and husband sign the lease for the farm. In the most economically advanced regions of France, such as Normandy, the wife often put down her name, rather than the traditional cross.

In the towns, the higher rates of literacy among the ordinary people created a new reading public. Literacy rates climbed steadily after 1650, with a particular leap after 1710. The primary schools of the Christian Brothers played a critical role in the expansion of literacy. In Normandy, around Paris, in areas of Champagne, male literacy achieved rates of 70 to 95 percent by 1785. Female literacy always lagged behind, yet more women in these regions than men in southern or western France could read. Artisans led the way, with their need to read contracts and conduct business. In Lyon, by mid-century, more than 70 percent of the bakers and 60 percent of the bakers' wives could read.

Eighteenth-century France thus had a new mass of readers. These artisans, and some wealthy peasants, did not buy works of high philosophy, insofar as we can judge by their after-death inventories. They knew something about such authors, however, just as people today have vague conceptions of authors like Locke or Marx or Freud, whom they have not read. In the eighteenth century, artisans and others could hear discussions of the works of the *philosophes* in the cafés. Servants overheard debates at the salons of their masters, and carried the tales into their taverns and into the street. Those who could not read listened to others who could. These new ideas interacted with long-standing popular political traditions, with the eternal dreams of equality and the Land of Cocaigne. Sailors, artisans, and laborers of all kinds developed their own political discourse, one that paralleled that of the elites. They did so in part in response to changing economic conditions, which required workers to think anew their place in society.

From the 1660s to the 1750s, France transformed itself into an early capitalist society. Although this process did not magically make medieval remnants disappear or transform France into an industrialized country, it fundamentally altered French social relations, French culture, and, in the end, French political life. More and more people worked in manufacturing (most of them part of the year); more and more people lived in large cities, above all in Paris; and more and more people worked for a larger enterprise, one in which they did not have the traditional contact with the owner. Broader literacy led to demands for more published material. This information led to an increasingly lively public debate about social, cultural, religious, and

political life, which, in turn, led to the demand for yet more information, especially
that possessed by the state.

The majority of French people, especially women, remained illiterate; they had
little interest in the debates that raged among intellectuals. Most of them still farmed,
went to church on Sunday, dressed in the dark clothes and sabots of their ancestors,
and ate the traditional gruels, soupy stews, and rye or wheaten bread, perhaps washed
down with a vinegary local wine, cut with brackish water. They lived in dark, dank,
musty, miserable huts. Yet they, too, slowly began to change. Urban capital returned
to villages with homebound servant girls or itinerant masons. More parish schools
popped up, and more peasant households had a book, invariably a religious one. In
Lower Normandy, at the end of the seventeenth century, the registers of those moving from parish to parish contain fascinating evidence of the changes. In case after
case, when father-and-son teams moved, the father made a cross but the son signed
his name. By the 1780s, in this region of Normandy, 90 percent of the men could do
so. Other rural areas lagged far behind prosperous Normandy, but the trend everywhere moved in the same direction.[4]

The contrast from place to place, from the lush fields of Normandy to the barren wastes of the Midi, from the lively port towns like Nantes to the sleepy backwa-
ters like Châteaudun, scarcely a hundred miles away, has led many historians to speak
of two Frances evolving in the eighteenth century. The first one, along much of the
seacoast and the river valleys, drew ever closer to international markets. Its inhabitants ate the new foods, wore the new clothes, drank the new drinks, learned to read,
and took on new jobs. The second France had much lower literacy, and had much
less contact with the new economy. Its economy stagnated and fell rapidly behind
that of the new France.

All these changes did take place, yet no simple geographic formula explains why a
particular place would align more rapidly with the evolving France of the thriving international market. Nor did the two Frances exist in separate worlds; they had a close
symbiotic relationship. The towns, those nests of silent killers, took a terrible toll on
their people, especially the children. Without constant immigration, no eighteenth-
century French city would have kept a stable population, let alone a growing one. This
new migration went both ways: many of the rural immigrants returned to their home
villages each year or after several years in the city. Women, in particular, followed the
second pattern. Their villages did not immediately adopt the new ways. Far from
being reticent rustics, frightened of innovation, these villagers knew how to calculate
risk and gain. They lived on the margins of subsistence, so that a miscalculation could
lead to starvation. Those areas, particularly regions close to Paris or another large city,
in which innovation posed the least risk, witnessed the greatest changes.

Eighteenth-century France offers a textbook case of one of the most remarkable elements of modern capitalist societies: the creation of demand. New products
flooded the market, making necessities of previously unknown products such as coffee,
sugar, and even cotton underwear. Luxury products, like mirrors or clocks, became
commonplace. New luxury products, like fine wines and exotic vegetables, provided
the new means of social differentiation. This new material world helped create a demand for new ideas, too. Society's needs changed, as did its demands on its institutions, such as the church and the state. One easily underestimates the impact of

material change on mass consumption of ideas, yet who among us has not experienced the dramatically different conversations typical of a group drinking beer in a bar and of that same group sipping coffee in a café? The elites of eighteenth-century Europe—above all England, Holland, and France—invented the Western European café. For them, it was a place of polite conversation among the well-educated and the better-off. The café encouraged discussion about politics; its existence encouraged another new phenomenon, the newspaper, which created ever-greater demand for information.

Capitalism created demand for coffee, for the newspaper, for all the trappings of "modern" life not simply among elites, but among all those who would emulate them. In time, artisans, too, would frequent cafés as well as taverns. Wealthy women, largely excluded from such public places, hosted salons, where they could have access to the new debates. Economic theorists after the mid-century would stress a new principle of business related to this ever-expanding, created demand. They urged business to maximize sales and total profits and argued that the fastest way to success was not high profit per sale, but high volumes of sale. Democratization of consumption thus paved the way to economic success.

This democratization had three dramatic and largely unintended consequences. First, it carried with it social and, in time, political democratization. Second, it encouraged the development of new ideas and the greater diffusion of all ideas. Third, it drove a mania for mass production at lower costs. This third consequence produced one of the most shameful episodes in European (and French) history: the exponential growth of slavery in the New World. This chapter will focus on these three socioeconomic and cultural developments during the course of the eighteenth century (to 1787) and provide a brief summary of political and institutional events. Chapter 11 will deal more with political life and cultural changes on the eve of the Revolution. Let us begin with a description of the social and economic bases of this rapidly evolving France.

Toward a Modern Economy ⤳

The variations that come up daily in commerce demanding a continuous surveillance, it has seemed necessary to us to order trained individuals to oversee everything that might affect the commerce and manufacture of fabrics in their jurisdictions.[5]

Royal instructions to the inspectors of manufactures, 1781

La France Profonde

Nicolas Géhenaut and Claudine Le Maire, who lived in the village of Gonesse, about five kilometers from where the Charles de Gaulle Airport now sits, rented the lands of the abbey of Maubuisson at the beginning of the eighteenth century. Géhenaut's family had held these lands since at least 1459. Here, in the *pays de France,* to use that term in its original sense, we find the heart of France. Géhenaut and Le Maire and their fellow merchant–farmers of the region have been one of the building blocks of French society for centuries. These people dominated the countryside; many of the families gradually worked their way into the upper ranks of urban society. In the *pays de France,* of course, educated young people gravitated to Paris, the traditional market for their families' produce. The early eighteenth century, however, did not treat kindly many of these families. Géhenaut and Le Maire lost the lease on the abbey's property in the aftermath of the terrible winter of 1709. In the farmlands of the Ile-de-France, as in so many sectors of the French economy, the shakeout of the early eighteenth century destroyed old, established businesses, paving the way for larger, more consolidated ones.

Géhenaut and Le Maire take us into the world of what the French still call *la France profonde* (deep, or perhaps inner France). Foreigners often underestimate the remarkable resilience of the hold of this mystical place over the French imagination. Even at the start of the twenty-first century, this seemingly quaint, even archaic place of memory remains the idealized home of many French people. In contemporary France, politicians who have spent their entire life in Paris seek to become the mayor of some small village, so that they can claim to represent their own little corner of *la France profonde.* Even in death, as President François Mitterand showed, a politician who spent virtually his entire life in Paris will choose to be buried in "his" little village. The entire country agrees that the continuation of the family farm, that essential building block of *la France profonde,* is a matter of national social policy, because a country built on family farms possesses a sounder *moral* foundation.

The rural place of memory goes back to the late eighteenth century, to the Romantic image of the idyllic countryside propagated by painters and writers after 1750. Prior to the middle of the eighteenth century, writers and painters (with rare exceptions, such as Le Nain) did not treat kindly the French rural population. Did something happen in rural France in the early eighteenth century, something that might help account for such a change in sensibilities? Did changes in French urban life accelerate this shift in sensibilities and help create the need for a rural place of memory?

These questions take us back to the demographic expansion of the sixteenth and early seventeenth centuries, which had disrupted the socioeconomic equilibrium of many villages. The village of relatively equal peasants—a majority of them with tenancies sufficient to support a family (that is, the mythical village of *la France profonde*)—gave way to a village with a few ploughmen leasing large holdings and a mass of peasants leasing tiny plots. Everywhere in France, this process of morselization grew more pronounced in the seventeenth century. The Norman village of Aubermesnil, near Dieppe, stands as a typical case. In 1695, the village had twenty-five taxpayers, of whom three—two ploughmen and one bourgeois of Dieppe farming his own land—paid 54 percent of the taxes; yet this burden *underestimated* their share of the village's land because they controlled 75 percent of the arable land. Moreover, two citizens of Dieppe listed on the roll as farming their own lands (sixty-eight acres combined) and outsiders or those exempt, like the seigneur of Aubermesnil, owned all but five of the village's four hundred fourteen acres of arable land.

The merchant–farmers of the Ile-de-France provide further evidence of the top-heavy socioeconomic structure of these villages. The generations who lived in the *pays de France* in the time of Henry IV and Louis XIII held substantial farms, typically 60–75 hectares and two plough teams; they usually increased slightly the size of

J.-B. Greuze, The Village Betrothal *(1761). Here we see visual evidence of the striking change in marriage customs. The well-off young couple, clearly in love, get the warm approval of the woman's father. The notary writes down the legal niceties; the young man receives the first installment of the woman's dowry (a bit unusual at the betrothal). This painting was the greatest success of the Salon of 1761, bringing the astounding price of 35,000* livres, *nearly nine times the usual going tariff for a Boucher, who was the leading painter of the day.*

SOURCE: © Alinari/Art Resource.

their holding between their marriage date and the death of the husband. By the 1680s, successful merchant–farmers rented 120–150 hectares. In the early eighteenth century, the typical newlywed husband held four plough teams and 126 hectares. At his death, he left an estate of six plough teams and 200 hectares. Little wonder that by 1758, the one thousand richest taxpayers of the *élection* of Paris, representing, at most, 2 percent of the taxpayers, paid nearly 37 percent of its taxes.[6]

In the region south of Paris, this same process took place a generation later, between 1720 and 1750. The massive discrepancies of scale, the merchant–farmers with their 200 hectares and the cottagers with their five or six, made the transition from cottager to merchant–farmer, formerly difficult, impossible. Nor could one marry into this caste: 97 percent of the children of merchant–farmers in the *pays de France* married the child of another merchant–farmer. The concentration of most of the village's arable land in the hands of four or five large-scale farmers left the other villagers out in the cold.[7]

SELLING THE FARM

Land sales often involved debts to a third party, like poor Claude Labbé, forced to sell his meadow to the ploughman François Boisloup, for 160 *livres:* Labbé immediately had to pay 72 *livres* to a Mademoiselle Beneteau of the nearby town of Saulieu and a further 46 *livres* to his seigneur, the dame of Alligny. Things were even worse for Pierre Boedot, who sold his tiny meadow for 10 *livres,* paid immediately to a M. Rolland of Dijon, or for the widow Janne Regnault, who owed the dame of Alligny more money in feudal arrears than the sale of her tiny field produced. Many debts had been contracted to buy land. Edmé Barbotte, a ploughman, borrowed 200 *livres* from Dimanche Perruchet, another ploughman, and from Gabriel Guillaume, a royal secretary in Dijon, to buy a meadow, for which he paid 240 *livres.*

These transactions often involved remarkably complex scenarios. François Bourgeois exchanged his small meadow for one three times its size owned by François Collenot. In return, Bourgeois paid 110 *livres* to Nicolas Champeault, a merchant of Saulieu, and a further 40 *livres* to Pierrette Collenot, daughter of François, for the amount still due on her dowry. This transaction did not stand alone. The same day, Collenot and his brothers, with whom he lived in community of goods (they were serfs), sold the new meadow to François Beugnon for 110 *livres.* Once again, Champeault ended up with the money. Nor did Beugnon put up his own cash; he borrowed it from Claude Donel. Transactions involved goods, too. Dimanche Germaine bought three *journaux* of arable land from Philibert Choreault for 9 *livres* in cash, a mare (valued at 20 *l.*), a bushel of wheat (11 *l.*), and the promise to pay 40 *livres* in a year.[8] These endless petty transactions consistently demonstrate the peasantry's relative lack of access to cash. They invariably had to have access to a merchant or notary from a nearby town or to the credit of their seigneur, such as the dame of Alligny, who appears constantly in the land sales, both buying and selling. Moreover, she used her ability to sell small fields, meadows, house lots, and buildings to maintain her effective clientage ties with the villagers.

The same process held true, on a smaller scale, in most parts of rural France tied to larger markets. Peasants progressively lost their share of arable land: in the Vannes region of Brittany, by 1700, peasants owned less than 10 percent of it. Again and again, they had to sell their tiny plots to pay family debts. On the other side of France, in the isolated Morvan region, the same process proceeded steadily. Notarial contracts demonstrate that virtually all land sales involved an indebted peasant (often a widow) selling a tiny plot to a member of the urban elite or to one of the richer peasants of the village.

These villages had precious little to do with our image of a group of self-sufficient farmers, living off the land. Each parish had a few large-scale farmers, most of whom rented rather than owned land; in some regions, such as Burgundy, these large-scale farmers even rented their plough teams.[9] The ten to fifteen percent of the population who held these large farms cultivated 75 percent or more of the tillable land. The vast majority of the rural population, therefore, could not possibly subsist on the crops from their tiny plots. The *manoeuvriers* (cottagers), usually married couples, had a small plot of two or three hectares and a cottage. The *journaliers* (day laborers) often were young and unmarried. The teenagers of the village hired themselves out as ser-

RURAL SOCIAL STRUCTURE: THE CAPITATION OF 1695

Louis XIV introduced a radical new tax in 1695: the capitation or head tax. The government devised a system of twenty-two "classes" to describe the contributors. Almost all of the descriptions applied to royal offices, but the administrators also put ordinary people into the categories they thought appropriate. Assessments ranged from 2,000 *livres,* for a handful of princes and some of the great officers of state, down to a single *livre* for shepherds, farm servants, and apprentices. Non-noble civilians did not appear until the tenth class (100 *livres*), which included wholesale merchants and exchange bankers.

Rural society appeared only in the fifteenth class (40 *livres*), which included farmers whose lease price exceeded 3,000 *livres* and millers whose lease topped 2,000 *livres*. In the next class (30 *livres*), one found "some of the farmers and ploughmen," others of whom appeared in the seventeenth (20 *livres*) or eighteenth (10 *livres*) classes; the latter also included some winegrowers. Farmers and ploughmen appeared again in the twentieth class (3 *livres*), along with millers holding leases of under 2,000 *livres,* winegrowers, small town artisans, and assorted servants. "Simple cottagers and day laborers" appeared only in the last class, assessed for a single *livre*. The 20 to 1 ratio between ploughmen and day laborers matched that between the poorest nobles (having "neither fief nor chateau"), assessed at six *livres* (class nineteen) and the lords of parishes, who paid 120 (class ten).

The surviving rolls suggest that 40 percent of the nobility belonged to the lowest group and that another 40–50 percent of them belonged to class fifteen, nobles owning fiefs and chateaux (paying 40 *livres*). The peasants, too, had a similar configuration: scarcely 20 percent of them were in their top classes (sixteen to eighteen) and half of peasant taxpayers or more certainly belonged to class twenty-two. Yet that gloomy statistic is a bit misleading. The ploughmen and richer cottagers had much larger households than day laborers, who were often single. Although ploughmen constituted only about 15 percent of the taxpayers, their households contained a third or more of the total population of the countryside. These rich peasants carried an assessment five times higher than that of the poorest nobles, who constituted 40 percent of their order.

vants; girls, in particular, might work on one of the large farms of the parish, perhaps in the household of a relative. In the eighteenth century, more and more of these girls sought employment as servants in towns.

These rural parishes concealed an extremely complex social and economic system. By the middle of the eighteenth century, the local seigneurs had usually moved to a city. With the exception of a few regions such as Brittany, the only nobles left in the countryside were those of the poorest "classes" and many of them lived far more modest lives than the neighboring ploughmen. The landlords' agents, local lawyers and notaries, oversaw rural society. These agents themselves bought up land and tried to constitute rural estates. The ploughmen (or merchant–farmers in the most advanced regions), like the Géhenaut family, dominated local life: contemporaries called them the *coqs du village* (cocks of the walk). Because they controlled two-thirds, three-quarters or even nine-tenths of the land, the other middling and poor inhabitants of the parish had to work for them in order to survive. Like their sixteenth-century ancestors, an eighteenth-century cottager couple had to *bricoler* (cobble together) their life.

The poorer peasants farmed their few hectares. They had no plough team, so they had to rely on the good offices of one of the richer farmers to get their fields ploughed. The poorer among them simply used hoes. The grain they grew helped feed their family, but it could not provide enough bread in and of itself. A family of five people would have needed something like 10 hectares, far more than the two or three of a typical cottager, to feed itself. The man of the house worked as a field hand for one of the big farmers; he tried his hand at a craft, such as carpentry or roofing. The woman worked as a spinner or as a lace maker, produced marketable goods in the garden, oversaw the poultry yard and sold its eggs and chickens, hired herself out as a wetnurse, and sold her labor to the neighboring large farm at harvest time and other periods of peak demand. The children helped as best they could, the older ones watching the younger, joining the harvest crews, and hiring out as servants or day laborers.

These struggling peasants sometimes bore the same surname as the rich farmers. The well-off farmers typically had far more children. Their children survived more often, so many inhabitants of hamlets in rural France shared a surname. Although the richer farmers sought individual gain, they did not lose sight of the family as a whole. The survival of the collectivity mattered just as much as individual success, and families followed strategies to guarantee both outcomes. The law codified the importance of family, not only through inheritance customs, which usually specified equal inheritance for male commoners, but also through social mores. Except in western France, women did not get specific legal protection for their equal rights to inheritance, yet testamentary practice dictated that women get a full share. French social mores provide clear evidence of the rights of women to the family goods. Women did not change their name at marriage, but kept their original family name. The preservation of the surname offered clear evidence to all of the woman's right to some of the inheritance of her family.

The division of French villages into strata of large farmers, cottagers, and day laborers was more complex than it might seem. Many rural people hoped for a progression of their status over time. Most day laborers were under thirty (even twenty-five) and unmarried. Cottagers tended to be between twenty-five and forty and to be married. Marriage often symbolized the transition from day laborer to cottager: landlords virtually never rented to unmarried men. Marriage, for both men and women, meant acceptance into civil society. Many peasants remained cottagers, or even day laborers, throughout their lives, but others rose through the ranks. At the top of the scale, ploughmen usually were over thirty-five or forty and had a relatively large household. The possibility of upward mobility from cottager to ploughman had long provided a key safety valve of the social system. As such mobility became more difficult in the eighteenth century, rural society developed greater social tensions.

The demographic web supporting this socioeconomic system unraveled in the eighteenth century, exacerbating those tensions. The old system operated on some simple assumptions. People would marry, on average, at age twenty-five to twenty-eight. Those who lived to adulthood (roughly half of those born), would survive until their late fifties or early sixties. The limited number of tenancies in a parish thus could pass from generation to generation.[10] One study of the marriages

Eighteenth-century ploughing. *The peasant uses a team of horses, effectively yoked, and a wheeled plough. Notice that the engraving shows the woman of the family hard at work in the grain fields, too.*

Source: The Granger Collection, New York.

in southwestern France in the seventeenth century found that well over half of all couples tied the knot within six months of the death of the father of either bride or groom. In the eighteenth century, this simple yet delicate mechanism came apart because people began to live longer. Demographic studies of regions such as the Beauvaisis, north of Paris, indicate more people lived past seventy in the late eighteenth century than had survived to be sixty in the seventeenth century. In one rural parish after another, 60 percent of adults reached the age of sixty and two-thirds of that group reached seventy or more. Even popular attitudes toward age shifted markedly. In the seventeenth century, detailed comparisons of parish registers and court testimony indicate that older people could only approximate their age, whereas eighteenth-century people far more often provided an exact figure.[11]

This simple increase in life expectancy of adults had profound consequences for the socioeconomic system. What would society do about the old? Would the aging farmer keep his lease, thus depriving his son of the chance of obtaining a tenancy? Would the aged agree to live in a corner of the house? Notarial records provide many examples of agreements between widows and their children about such living arrangements, but one rarely encounters an elderly man becoming a dependent in the household of one of his children. If the old farmer refused to give up the lease, the young prospective farmer had more trouble getting married. Who would want to marry a man who would not have a farm? The police records suggest more and more old people, especially men, took to the roads in the eighteenth century. In Brittany, in Normandy, the great lock-up of vagrants in the 1720s incarcerated men sixty and over. The massive increase in the number of wandering poor in the late eighteenth century surely had much to do with changing demographics.

Two other factors contributed to change in the French countryside: specialization, especially in luxury products, and the impact of rural manufacturing. Farmers near large towns had long been able to specialize, producing products for the tables of the urban well-to-do. Other areas had local products—wine, olive oil, dairy items, fruits—that dominated their agriculture even in medieval times. The eighteenth-century shift came in the direction of more refined products, produced for the upper echelons of the market. In the Champagne and Bordeaux regions, for example, wine-making procedures underwent fundamental change. In the 1730s, the region near Reims and Épernay began to shift production to the sparkling wine for which Champagne is famous. The procedure took firm root in the second quarter of the eighteenth century. This shift to Champagne required the region to produce far less wine, but to charge much more for it.[12] In Bordeaux, the emphasis on quality meant that wine exports from Bordeaux tripled in value between the 1720s and the 1780s, even though the quantity exported went up only 50 percent. The great Parlementaire families of Bordeaux, such as the owners of the château of Haut-Brion, created the *grand cru* wines internationally renowned ever since. These wines, among the first to be aged, commanded spectacular prices, often 20 times the cost of an ordinary Bordeaux.

As with wine, so with vegetables, fruits, and cheeses. The new vegetables, such as artichokes, began to appear on sophisticated tables. These same consumers who demanded beaver hats (furs from Canada), coffee (from Martinique), sugar (from Saint-Domingue), wanted to drink château Haut-Brion with their artichoke hearts and their Roquefort, the "king of cheeses," whose strict production rules date from 1671. The shift in recipes toward the use of butter gave a considerable boost to dairy producers who could reach urban markets, especially Paris. Farmers near Bordeaux exported large quantities of prunes, the justly famous *pruneaux d'Agen*. People called the little market gardeners around Beauvais *haricotiers* (green bean growers), because of their specialty crop, widely sold in Paris. These different crop systems, to say nothing of widespread variation in livestock, led to agricultural systems quite different from those of grain regions like the *pays de France*.

The greater concentration of land into fewer hands, like the demographic shift, disrupted rural life. As the gap between the richer farmers and the others grew progressively larger in the eighteenth century, more and more rural dwellers took the traditional path of social mobility; they moved. They moved to nearby villages, in search of a vacant tenancy; they moved to small towns, in search of work; they moved to the suburbs of the bigger towns, where they could work in a combination of rural and new urban jobs. Rural industry provided a particularly important new means of social mobility in the eighteenth century. Peasants did not have to move to a town to get a job in the textile industry; such jobs, particularly in the cotton industry, came to them. They could use the wages from these jobs to help pay for a small plot of land or to buy animals. In the cotton-spinning regions of Normandy, for example, livestock herds expanded rapidly after 1720. Cottagers living close to towns could use their new capital to change their product mix, focusing more heavily on a specialized product for an urban market. That practice had long been followed, of course, in the wine-growing villages. Those villages, unlike others, had many small and medium-scale farmers who could support a family on 5 hectares.[13]

The world of rural France had traditionally held two forces: the centripetal ploughmen, monopolizing the land and settled for centuries in their home village; and the centrifugal day laborers, wandering desperately in search of a plot of land to call their own. The cottagers had one foot in each camp, living as they did one step from penury, yet, at least until the late seventeenth century, always hoping that industry and luck would help them obtain a viable tenancy. They usually had to move to a nearby village to make this step. People moved far more often prior to 1750 than we have believed, but the rate of migration increased markedly in the second quarter of the eighteenth century.

Alligny offers an apparently clear case of what French historians often call the "immobile village." Yet matters were not so clear. Many people came and went in the village; some of them stayed on, and became successful. All over France, villages maintained a core of families dominating the possession of tillable land, yet these same villages included many transients. The poor, of course, moved constantly, but even the middling and well-off tended to displace themselves. The surviving records suggest that 75,000 to 100,000 middling or well-off farmer families moved each year. In addition, another 200,000 to 250,000 poor taxpayers decamped for what they hoped would be greener pastures.[14]

In the eighteenth century, this two-tiered village came under dramatic new stresses. The regions that offered new access to markets, either by means of specialized agricultural products (wine, vegetables, flax) or through manufacturing employment (usually textiles), offered some hope to their inhabitants. The poor and middling peasants might not have any immediate prospect of taking over a large farm, but they could make a living by means of the new mixture of employment and small-scale farming. In the regions that did not enjoy access to markets in such a way, however, the poor and middling could become desperate, because they had no realistic chance of getting one of the newly expanded greater farms and traditional agriculture could not sustain them. The result in France as a whole was a curious combination of greater prosperity and increased immiseration. Successful peasants could afford a wide range of new products, whereas unsuccessful ones took increasingly to the road to beg. In the 1770s and 1780s, nearly 20 percent of the French population received relief for part of each year and as much as 50 percent of it had obtained relief at some time in their lives.

THE TWO BOISSEAU: PLOUGHMAN AND COTTAGER

Fétigny, the richest hamlet of the Burgundian parish of Alligny-en-Morvan, lay in the northern part of the parish, closest to the dominant local town, Saulieu. Its peasants were serfs of the cathedral chapter of Saint-Lazare in Autun. In other ways, Alligny was a fairly typical French parish. An elite group of twenty-five families (defined by surnames) controlled more than 70 percent of the land, from the fifteenth century into the middle of the eighteenth. The neighbors who did not share such a surname tended to move in and out of the village: of the twenty-eight surnames held by a single taxpayer in 1551, only eight remained in 1611. In 1682, the families who had been in Alligny since 1551 (50 percent of the taxpayers) paid 72 percent of the village's taxes, and the families who had been there for a single generation (12.2 percent) paid only 6 percent of the taxes.

The land survey of 1757 demonstrates that Fétigny, like most villages, consisted of hundreds of tiny plots; individual farmers held a piece here and a piece there, rather than a contiguous farm. With luck and perseverance, however, one could put together some relatively coherent chunks. The first two men on the survey, Dominique Boisseau, ploughman, and Pierre Boisseau, cottager, shared a surname that could be traced back at least to 1475 in the village and which can be found on the village Monument to the Dead of World War I. Like most other villagers, they were serfs (*mainmortables*), subject to full justice and to feudal dues, most important

among them escheat. Dominique Boisseau worked his holdings with unnamed "partners," whose presence is explained by his liability to escheat: unless the heirs lived with the testator, the seigneur confiscated all of the dying serf's possessions. Peasants like Dominique Boisseau thus lived in large, communal houses, in which everyone held a share of all goods; in that way, the seigneur did not obtain the land.

Dominique Boisseau held forty-one different parcels of the village; Pierre Boisseau held only four. Dominique succeeded in amassing some contiguous holdings (hash-marked area). Parcel 163, at the center of the hamlet, contained his house, just as it had contained that of the rich ploughmen Pierre and François Regnaud in 1676 and that of Guyot Girard, one of the two richest men in the village in 1543. A large farmhouse still stands there today, bearing the name Regnault on the mailbox! One of the Regnault family members, in the late 1980s, sat as the local deputy to the National Assembly.

Pierre Boisseau possessed only three tiny parcels of meadow, one minuscule field (0.2 hectares), and a house. His house, that of a substantial cottager, sat in the middle of the hamlet of La Sarrée; in 1676, a man of virtually the same status, Dimanche Beugnon, the shoemaker, lived on the lot, which today holds a modest home. Beugnon, like Pierre Boisseau, held little land—four parcels adding up to about 0.25 hectares and a share in a tiny copse nearby.[15]

The greater wealth of merchant–farmers led to more possessions. As they became wealthier, they left more cash, greater stocks of silver plate (always favored because it could be melted down and coined, if necessary). Beyond their greater wealth, however, they also developed new sensibilities in the 1740s and 1750s. Those changed sensibilities provide clear evidence of a dramatic cultural rupture in the middle of the eighteenth century. Several generations of literacy helped pave the way for the adoption of many of the other elements of urban civilization.

Few merchant–farmers had fancy, specialized goods prior to 1730. In the late seventeenth century, the inventories suggest a slow movement toward a greater

(CONTINUED)

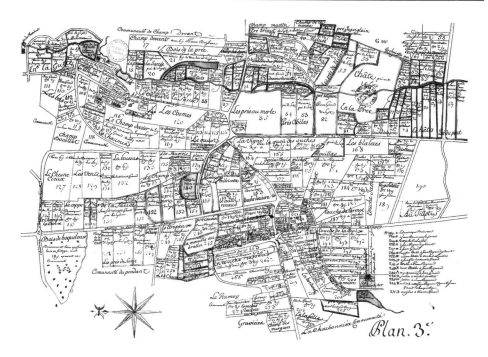

The hamlet of Fétigny, parish of Alligny-en-Morvan, land distribution of 1757 in the center of the hamlet. Dominique Boisseau created one fairly large contiguous area in the center-left of the image, but his "farm" remained, like most farms of the time, highly diffuse. He held over 40 separate parcels.

SOURCE: Archives départementales de la Côte d'Or.

sense of self. Households began to have copper washbasins and mirrors. We imagine with difficulty the seismic shift from a world in which one viewed oneself only through the eyes of others, to a world in which one could see oneself every day and form one's own opinion. We must also force ourselves to remember that for centuries only the wealthy could have a firm idea of themselves, in purely physical terms.[16] The mirrors and washbasins presaged a cultural revolution in the middle of the eighteenth century. Jean-Marc Moriceau's study of these merchant–farmers provides startling figures on their cultural transformation between 1710 and 1750.

THE VILLAGE COW: AUBERMESNIL, 1695–1789

In 1966 I recall having read in the newspapers that a young boy from . . . the Corrèze had just been killed by a freight train [while trying] to save one of his cows . . . People even said that a cow wasn't worth risking one's life for. Perhaps. I should merely like to pay homage to the conscience of a little cowhand who was at most twelve, in remembrance of my own adolescence, when a cow—just one single cow—was our most valuable possession. . . . I'm prepared to swear that more than one of us, at age twelve, would have been perfectly capable of facing death to save his one and only cow.[17]

Pierre-Jakez Hélias

Elsewhere in his memoirs of growing up in a Breton village in the early twentieth century, Hélias relates how his aged grandfather, Alain Le Goff, "throbbed with emotion as he thought of his happy fate on this earth. It's really something to own a black cow!" Nor was Hélias simply overwhelmed by nostalgic reminiscences of his youth: the tax records of eighteenth-century French villages suggest that ownership of a single cow provided a level of security unlike anything else. To see why, let us take a look at the Norman village of Aubermesnil, near Dieppe.

Aubermesnil offers a remarkable illustration of larger patterns in eighteenth-century village life.[18] The parish increased in population over the century, rising from twenty-five taxpayers (and one "fugitive") in 1695 to thirty-three taxpayers (five of them beggars) in 1758, and to thirty-two taxpayers and three "fugitives" in 1789. Not all of the these people really headed a household. In 1695, five people simply rented a room; a similar number did the same in 1758 or 1789.

The sieur of Aubermesnil owned much of the village; he leased an an enormous farm of 160 Norman acres (36 percent of the arable land of the village) to a ploughman in 1695; his descendants leased it out to the widow Blondel and her son in 1789. Although renting only

---

TABLE X-1:   The New Consumers—Household Possessions of Merchant Farmers in the *pays de France,* 1690–1709; 1750–1759

	1690–1709	1750–1759
Quality wines	0	14
Coffee and sugar	1	14
Tobacco	0	8
Large clocks	2	22
Watches	4	13
Quality tapestry	1	9
Dressers	0	11
Card tables	1	17
Religious paintings	1	15
Books	7	22
Dresses in exotic fabrics	1	15
Mirrors	6	24
Total number of inventories	26	28

SOURCE: *J.-M. Moriceau, Les fermiers de l'Ile-de-France Xve XVIIIe siècle (Paris: Fayard, 1994). Adapted from Table 81.*

(CONTINUED)

---

100 acres, she paid almost half of all the rents owed by the thirty-two villagers and controlled 47 percent of the arable land listed on the tax roll. In 1695, 1758, or 1789, seven or eight villagers held 90 percent or more of the farmland, a situation quite typical in most of France.

The villagers of 1695 took their living almost entirely from the land; only one person called himself a weaver (of linen). In 1758, by way of contrast, the village had four weavers and three tailors (five and three in 1789), most of whom also rented a small farm. The villagers of 1695 had overwhelmingly owned their own houses (fifteen of nineteen living in a house). Those of 1758 or 1789, however, tended to rent. In 1758, fourteen of the seventeen people living in a rented house; in 1789, twenty of the twenty-two living in a house did so. One of the two owners descended from an owner of 1758.

This series of documents thus confirms much of what we know about larger patterns. People far more often considered themselves to be textile workers after 1730 or 1740: only one of twenty-five in 1695, but seven of twenty-five in 1758 and eight of thirty-two in 1789. Individuals not on the tax roll owned virtually all of the arable land, and a handful of ploughmen rented almost all of it. Only these four or five people had a plough or horses or any large animals, other than cows. Most cottagers or artisans had a house and garden—which they often owned at the start of the eighteenth century but rarely did after 1740—and a cow.

The records imply greater stability in the village after 1758: only four of the twenty-three surnames of 1695 reappear in 1758, whereas sixteen out of the twenty-two names of 1758 are still there in 1789. Moreover, five of the six surnames that disappeared came from among the nine poorest families. Only one family that owned a cow—that of the weaver Duchiron—had its name disappear from the village in that forty-year period. Little wonder that rural people attached such enormous importance to the possession of this humble yet essential animal.

Let us consider for a moment the meaning of some of these objects. Clocks and watches: why did peasants need to know the time? Rural people traditionally had little reason to know precise hours and minutes: they lived by the clock of the day and the seasons. Dawn, noon, dusk: those were the meeting times. The Church gave names to the days, thus June 24th was universally known as St. John the Baptist's Day, and the days around it listed in reference to this great holiday. Even in the towns, the shift to precise time took root slowly. People did not work from 9 to 5; they worked a full day, which often had "hours" (6 A.M. to 7 P.M., in the summer, was typical), but rarely enforced them. The world of business—of the market, as we know all too well—changed that forever. Business people had fixed appointments, at given hours. Merchant–farmers had clients to meet, so they needed to know the time. Even when they did not need to know it, they needed to show others, by the presence of the physical objects of time, that they had such a need. The existence of the need created social preeminence.

Religious paintings and books demonstrate the penetration of the new piety into the countryside.[19] Just as urban elites began to turn away from organized religion, rural elites became more closely wedded to the Tridentine church. They moved away from the "superstitious" religion traditional in the countryside, and toward the new faith approved by the Church hierarchy. Many children of such families became religious, either priests or nuns (less often monks). The one dissonant note in this renewed piety was the card table, perhaps symbolic of the different cultural impulses coming from Paris.

Coffee mills and sugar rasps, unknown in the inventories before 1710 and extremely rare until the 1750s, take us into the larger world. French farmers now drank a beverage based on beans grown in the West Indies, produced by the labor of African slaves, and flavored with another West Indian product, also grown by African slaves. The small amounts of coffee and sugar consumed in the countryside, however, paled beside the massive increase in urban demand. In Paris, Nantes, Rouen, Lyon or Marseilles, to say nothing of smaller towns, the middle and, soon, artisan classes sat down to daily cups of sugared coffee. They began the large-scale process of those in the most economically advanced countries consuming previously rare products. These products were now cheaply produced in the far corners of the globe by those receiving wages far below those paid in the consuming countries (in the case of slaves, no wages at all).

"The Manner in which slaves are moved." This late eighteenth-century engraving shows the slaves yoked at the neck, as they are marched off to their terrible fate.

Source: © Réunion de Musées Nationaux/Art Resource, New York.

Other farmers, less well-off than their brethren in the Ile-de-France, made these cultural steps more slowly; in many cases, the objects in question appeared only in the middle of the nineteenth century (in the most isolated areas, often in the decades around 1900). Yet the same processes can be seen at work. Slowly, inexorably, more and more people throughout France learned to read and write. By the 1780s, in northern France, roughly half of all men could sign their name, as could a third of the women. In the most advanced regions, such as the Ile-de-France or Normandy, the proportion of literate men reached 90 percent and of literate women 60 or 70 percent. Book production mirrored this literacy: Lorraine and Normandy, regions of high literacy, produced over a million reprinted books between 1778 and 1789. Nearly two-thirds of these books were religious in nature, most of them liturgies, books of devotion or books of hours. Here we can see the stark contrast between northern, literate France, and southern, illiterate regions. All of southern France combined produced just over 10 percent of the provincially printed books. Literate southerners also had different tastes: fewer than half of their books had a religious content.

One could find endless variations on these basic structures. Rich wheat lands like the Ile-de-France or the Beauce had one system; poor heaths like central Brittany had another. The wine-growing regions always stood apart, both for their extensive peasant ownership of land and for the viability of the small plots. Mountain villages in regions such as the Auvergne often formed little peasant oligarchies, with a patriarch running the entire hamlet with an iron hand. Certain villages of that region had remained in the same clan since the ninth century. Seigneurs could play an important role, as they did in western Brittany or in parts of the Auvergne and Limousin, or they could be enfeebled, as they were in Lower Normandy. The Catholic Church could be a powerful presence, or it could be effaced.

One study of the later department of the Yonne demonstrates the astonishing variety of the countryside in a small area.[20] In the area around the town of Sens, the peasants owned over half of the land (the Church 13 percent). These better-off peasants could sign their names—64 percent of the men, 35 percent of the women. About 25 miles south, around Auxerre (classic wine-growing country), peasant smallholders possessed 75 percent of the land. These peasants, too, were literate and wanted their children to be so. Indeed, 87 percent of the villages had a school. Fifteen miles west, however, in the *pays* of Puisaye, around the town of Saint-Fargeau, the poor land lent itself to large landowners and landless, illiterate peasants. Eighty-one percent of the men and 90 percent of the women could not sign their marriage contracts. Thus we have three tiny *pays,* all within a radius of fifty miles, with profoundly different social, economic, and cultural structures. The wheat lands have considerable peasant property (albeit mostly in small plots, one would imagine) and high literacy; the vineyards have landowning, literate peasants; and the forests and bocages have illiterate, landless peasants toiling as sharecroppers for rich absentee landlords.[21] As this amazing variety in so small an area suggests, *la France profonde,* to the extent that it existed as a coherent entity, existed primarily as a place of imagination and of memory.

❧ Towns, Manufacturing, and Commerce

I have read all of the rulings [on manufactures]; I think we must eliminate them all. I have seen nothing better than liberty.[22]

Roland de La Platière, inspector of manufactures

The first, most fundamental change in the manufacturing and commercial economy came with respect to the scale of enterprises, which expanded rapidly in sector after sector. Maritime commerce led the way. At Le Havre, the portion of the total tonnage in ships over one hundred fifty tons nearly doubled between 1664 and 1686. At Bordeaux, average capacity of ships nearly tripled in the eighteenth century. At Nantes, by 1790, the port held fourteen ships that displaced more than six hundred tons, that is, ten times the average ship of the late seventeenth century and nearly double the size of the largest ship of the 1720s. The amount of capital necessary for outfitting these enormous ships dwarfed the capacities of individuals; merchants in Nantes or Bordeaux or La Rochelle formed societies jointly to sponsor the colonial trade ventures. These rich individuals, formerly called merchants, took on new names, *négociants* or, for those in the colonial trade, *armateurs*. Even nobles, banned in most of France from trade of any kind, could participate in this commerce.[23]

Colonial Trade

I went straight to a master who had a big shipment of window panes to cut for the Isles.[24]

Jacques Ménétra, journeyman glazier, on arriving in Nantes, 1759

The first great period of expansion of the colonial trade came between the Peace of Utrecht (1713) and the start of open hostilities between France and England in the War of the Austrian Succession (1744). This colonial expansion created fundamental change not only in France but in Europe as a whole. The creation of a new world economy permanently altered the economic, social, and, eventually, political systems of the major European countries. French, Dutch, Portuguese, and English slave traders also fundamentally altered the demographic structures of three other continents: Africa, North and South America. These Europeans shipped more than 10 million Africans across the Atlantic between the fifteenth and nineteenth centuries; roughly ten to thirteen percent of them (1 to 1.3 million people) died on the voyages.

This shameful episode in human history reached its nadir in the eighteenth century, when approximately 6 million African slaves crossed the Atlantic. French ships made three thousand slaving voyages between 1713 and 1793, carrying 1.2 million Africans to the New World. They began on the West Coast of Africa. The French took their slaves from four locations: the mouth of the Congo River (by far the most common), the Gold Coast running west from Benin, the mouth of the Senegal River, and Angola.[25] Important French outposts sprung up along the coast, above all between the Gambia and Senegal Rivers. The largest of these ports, Saint-Louis at the mouth of the Senegal, held about three thousand people by mid-century, and shipped something like two thousand slaves each year. Despite their presence in Senegal, the French preferred slaves from Congo, whom the planters claimed were "less likely to revolt" than those from Senegambia and "harder workers" than those from the Gold Coast.

Most of these slaves ended up in the French West Indies, especially in Saint-Domingue (Haiti) and Martinique: 95 percent of French slave ships landed on these two islands. The limited number of slave shipments of the late seventeenth century grew to an annual average of twenty-three between 1713–1736 and then rose sharply, averaging fifty-three voyages a year between 1737–1743 and again after the Seven Years' War. The wars of the American Revolution interrupted the trade but French slavers redoubled their efforts after 1783, averaging one hundred ten voyages a year from 1783–1791 (350,000 slaves).

In return, the planters shipped ever greater quantities of sugar—an annual average of 59 million pounds (worth about 12 million *livres*) in the 1730s—indigo, and coffee (worth 3.5 and 2.0 million *livres* each by 1742). Here, too, volume exploded in the second half of the century: exports of sugar to France reached 187 million pounds by 1790 (worth about 75 million *livres*). France, in contrast to England (which ate 75 percent of the sugar it imported from its colonies), re-exported 60 to 70 percent of this sugar to northern Europe. Re-exports grew from about 35 million pounds in the 1730s to 125 million pounds in 1790. Even so, consumers in large cities such as Paris or Marseilles easily ate ten or fifteen pounds of sugar a year by the 1780s, spearheading an important internal market.[26]

The colonial trade had a larger impact on the total French economy than these figures suggest. Capital investment in the West Indies likely had reached two billion *livres* by the 1780s and the combined elements related to colonial commerce—shipments of goods to France, shipments of goods to the colonies, re-export of colonial products—could well have amounted to 500 million *livres* of business a year in the 1780s. All of this commerce depended, in the end, on the shameful commerce in human beings.

Slaving ships carried an average of three hundred slaves, crammed usually in the hold. The voyages began inauspiciously:

> the moment one has completed one's trade and loaded the Negroes on the ship, one must set sail [because] . . . the slaves have such a great love for their land that they despair to see that they are leaving it forever, and they die from sadness. I have heard merchants who participate in this commerce affirm that more Negroes die before leaving port than during the voyage. Some throw themselves into the sea and others knock their heads against the ship; some hold their breath until they suffocate and others starve themselves.[27]

Once the voyage actually began, things got progressively worse; records of the time suggest that about 13 percent of the slaves, and of the crew members, died en route.[28] Crews routinely flogged any African who resisted and meted out severe punishments to those engaged in open revolt. One such revolt, in 1738, led to the spreadeagling of the ringleaders, who were flogged front and back, their wounds rubbed with a burning mixture of gunpowder, lemon juice, and pepper brine.

French ships, like English ones, stank; the remarkable Olaudah Equiano left an unforgettable description of the hold of the ship that carried him to the New World:

> I was soon put down under the decks, and there I received such a salutation in my nostrils as I never experienced in my life ... I became so sick ... that I was not able to eat ... now that the whole ship's cargo were confined together, it [the stench] became almost pestilential. .... the deplorable situation was again aggravated ... [by] the filth of the necessary tubs, into which the children often fell, and were almost suffocated. The shrieks of the women, and the groans of the dying, rendered it a scene of horror almost inconceivable.[29]

The ships came overwhelmingly from the great Atlantic coast ports, especially Nantes (fourteen hundred slave ships during the century), Bordeaux (four hundred fifty), La Rochelle, and Le Havre (four hundred each). The merchants made most of their profits on the slaves: the 1723 account books of the West India Company show that 1.36 million of its 1.8 million *livres* profit came from that source, as against much smaller sums for rawhides, wax, gold, gum, and ivory. The French also sold cloth, alcohol, and guns to their African trading partners. Those partners then used the guns on the slaving raids that produced the slaves for export.

In the New World, slaves died in large numbers, some of them worked to death but most of them succumbing to local diseases for which they had no antibodies. The tiny seventeenth-century African populations of Guadeloupe and Martinique, perhaps three thousamd slaves each, became overwhelming majorities. Each island had 70,000 or more African slaves by the 1770s. Saint-Domingue, not really developed until the eighteenth century, dwarfed these figures: its African population reached 450,000 by the end of the century. The catastrophic losses among slave populations, likely between 2.5 and 4.0 percent per year net declines, mandated the continued importation of 8,000 slaves a year into Saint-Domingue alone. French merchants and planters tied up massive amounts of capital in slaves. Most estimates "valued" slaves at 1,000–1,800 *livres* each, even though auction prices in the 1740s tended to be closer to 600. The slave trade thus engaged some 50 million *livres* per year; the slave populations of the islands represented investments of close to 1 billion *livres* by the late eighteenth century. Relatively few French people spoke out against the moral outrage of this commerce, although some prominent figures, such as Jean-Jacques Rousseau, were exceptions.

The slave trade produced uneven margins of profit. Money from the blood of slaves built the prosperity of Nantes, notably the Ile Feydeau quarter and the Royal Theater district. Nantes originally had a balanced profit from slaves and sugar, maintaining its place as the top importer of the latter until the War of the Austrian Succession. In the second half of the eighteenth century, however, slave profits tended to dominate. Bordeaux replaced Nantes as the dominant port of the Atlantic trade by the 1740s, particularly in terms of the export leg of the triangle trade. Bordeaux exported wine, grain, and other foodstuffs to Africa and the New World. Nantes exported some wine and grain, as well as cloth, paper, and other goods, but in lesser quantities than Bordeaux. Nantes also specialized in direct trade with Saint-Domingue, whereas Bordeaux had strong ties to Martinique, from which it obtained coffee as well as sugar. In time, the Bordelais shifted significant resources to Saint-Domingue. Bordeaux's merchants thus received the largest share of their profits from sugar, coffee and French exports, in contrast to the profits at Nantes, which came from slaves and sugar.

The Loire valley benefitted from Nantes's role in the sugar trade, accepting a significant portion of the raw sugar imported into the city. Orléans, in particular, had a massive sugar refining industry, the leading one in France, turning out 13 million pounds of sugar by 1790. Bordeaux re-exported a larger share of its raw sugar than did Nantes; the rest of the sugar remained in the city itself, which stood second to Orléans among the refining centers, producing 7 million pounds in 1790.

Workers and Workshops

Every year a prodigious quantity of people from most of these parishes abandon their native land, from which misery chases them . . . to become mercenaries in countries of abundance, Spain, for example, takes many from us; others are masons, roofers, lumberjacks everywhere in the various provinces of the kingdom.[30]

Inhabitants of Saint-Pardoux to the intendant of Limousin, 1762

The other sectors of the economy showed the same tendencies toward concentration and specialization as did the colonial trade. In the textile manufacture, individual enterprises grew larger. Workshops that had employed a master with only one or two journeymen became rarer. By the 1720s, in their place, one found workshops of five to ten journeymen, which grew sometimes to fifteen or twenty in the 1750s and after. These new workshops often existed outside of traditional textile centers. Seeking to avoid guild regulations, merchants established manufacturing workshops in rural areas or in suburbs.[31] These workshops gave employment, often temporary and seasonal, to large numbers of rural inhabitants. In the Rouen region of Normandy, cloth production, now focused in the countryside rather than in the city itself, rose 700 percent between 1715 and 1743.

Slowly at first, but then inexorably faster and faster, France moved in two directions. In the favored regions, tied into international, above all Atlantic trade, the economy boomed. Nantes and Bordeaux doubled in population in the eighteenth century, to 80,000 and 100,000, respectively. Paris, too, grew rapidly, moving steadily past the half million mark in the 1740s and reaching more than 650,000 by the 1780s. Overall urban population, however, remained relatively stable, because the small and medium-sized towns tended to lose people.

In the north, textiles flourished in parts of Artois, Picardy, Champagne, and Normandy. In Brittany, the traditionally wealthy Léon region languished but the

Saint-Brieuc area boomed, the population of all its towns doubling or trebling. The Loire valley showed stark contrasts. At the mouth of the river, Nantes made its fortune in the slave and sugar trade; a mere 60 kilometers upstream, the town of Angers and its environs languished. In the east, isolated manufactures sprung up in parts of Alsace or the Franche-Comté, and the axis running down from Lyon to Marseille flourished as a result of trade with the Levant and, increasingly, with the Americas. Marseille's export of textiles, mainly from Languedoc, grew sharply in the first half of the century. Local manufactures provided other products for the growing international trade: shoes, playing cards, and hats. Yet the largest local manufacture, of soap, produced essentially for the French home market.

The new commercial economy led to a new occupational distribution among the population. In the areas tied to international trade, the poor increasingly came to be textile workers. In many Norman villages, by 1750, a quarter or more of the population worked in textiles. These people also worked, seasonally, in agriculture: planting, harvesting, winnowing. France came to have four basic population distributions:

1. The heavy reliance on one manufacture for employment—in most cases (Normandy, Languedoc, the Saint-Brieuc region, Reims) that meant textiles, often cotton textiles, but in others, such as Marseilles, it could mean a product such as soap.

2. Artisanal diversity associated with the major port cities, such as Nantes or Bordeaux (these cities exported many goods made by other areas, but their local populations often provided a wide range of goods to round out cargoes intended for Africa or the Americas).

3. Isolated regions, whether rural or urban, whose population structure remained what it had been, (a pattern shown in local studies of Châteaudun and Vannes).

4. Administrative towns, such as Rennes, Toulouse, or Aix-en-Provence, that possessed flocks of lawyers, clerks, and servants (who formed 16 percent of the population of Aix at mid-century), as well as the many traditional artisans needed to serve the local market.

Paris must stand as a case apart, amalgamating several different characteristics: luxury trades producing for export; thousands of local market artisans; rising numbers of manufactories; hordes of servants (50,000 of them); ubiquitous lawyers, government officials, and clerical workers.

Young rural women often moved to cities: the servants in Toulouse or Aix came overwhelmingly from the countryside. Urban artisan or shopkeeper households took on a single (invariably female) servant, who played a critical role as household assistant and in overseeing the children. The artisan woman invariably had an important economic function. Those who have visited France know that nearly every French bakery has a woman running the shop, selling the bread, made in the back of the

J.-S. Chardin, The Return from Market *(1739). The market basket shows us the range of goods needed for a meal in a well-off household: meat, wine (on the floor), and the enormous loaves of bread.*

SOURCE: © Foto Marburg/Art Resource.

shop by her husband. The shops ran in much the same way in 1720. These women often needed help with household responsibilities, particularly if the shop expanded in size. The intermediary size, larger than a two-person operation but too small for a foreman, doubtless put the greatest strain on the adult woman. Her critical economic role to the household as a unit of production made the use of a servant an economically sound decision. The pressures of social emulation, each social group trying to imitate the lifestyle of the group above them, also played a significant role in the desire for a servant.

The young woman could save up enough money for a dowry, as well as put aside the basic elements of the trousseau (sheets, other household goods). She became a much sought-after partner. In the first half of the eighteenth century, such women often returned to their home village; most servants married rural men. In the second half of the eighteenth century, however, that pattern changed, with servants tending increasingly to marry within the artisan class. These women also spoke forthrightly about their *right* to choose their own marriage partner. The economic independence created by the presence of a self-earned dowry gave practical punch to female emancipation in this matter. No longer dependent on her parents (especially her father) for a dowry, a young woman could now ignore his wishes when choosing a spouse. In short, she could marry for love. Where surviving sixteenth-century requests for Church dispensation from consanguity invariably claimed that everyone living in the village was related or that the marriage would end a family quarrel, in the eighteenth century, such requests showed an entirely different mentality. The couples emphasized their suitability, attraction for each other, their love. These records primarily concern those of relatively modest social status, but the same problem obviously occurred at the highest rungs of society.

The individual grew ever stronger at the expense of groups in eighteenth-century France. Women, like men, began to assert themselves as individuals. Perhaps because men felt themselves in a precarious position as individuals, they deeply resented the individuality of women. Upper-class men used *lettres de cachet* (arbitrary letters of arrest) to imprison in convents daughters who refused to marry the person designated by their family/father or who sought to marry a person the woman herself had chosen. The rise of individualism, however, opened new opportunities for women, which they quickly seized. The evidence suggests that progressively more women headed households as the seventeenth century wore on, and that, despite the government's efforts to curtail their economic rights, women also ran more and more businesses. In the realm of high culture, women orchestrated the salons of Paris, which established standards of appropriate social behavior and determined acceptance of new ideas. These salons, as Richelieu foresaw, became an alternative source of legitimacy for new modes of behavior and new ideas; in that way, they directly threatened the government's (and thus the Court's) monopoly in such matters. Female empowerment and male resentment of it both expanded in the eighteenth century, leading to a tragic *dénouement* during the Revolution, as we shall see.

Economic, social, intellectual, and cultural change went hand-in-hand in early eighteenth-century France. The new economy emphasized large units of production, be they farms, ships or workshops. It relied on a more mobile population and a shift of the day laboring population into a more mixed occupational structure, one involving more manufacturing work, especially in textiles. The booming sectors of the economy tended to have connections either to the colonial trade or to the burgeoning consumer sector. These new elements coexisted with old ones. Most French people still made their living in agriculture and many towns and villages witnessed little change in patterns of production or consumption. Even allowing for such continuity, however, the structural changes of the French economy between 1680–1750 underlay fundamental new patterns in social relations, in intellectual currents, and in cultural trends.

THE NEW STATE

I wish to follow in all things the example of the late King, my great-grandfather.[32]

Louis XV, in 1726

The rapidly evolving socioeconomic structure called forth demands for a more responsive government. The spread of ideas rooted in the Scientific Revolution gave impetus to progressively stronger calls for greater rationality in government. The state did not stand aloof from this process; indeed, many of its own officials led the way in reform programs. The process began with Philip of Orléans and his rapid rejection of his uncle's policies. The Regent tried to institute a new structure of government that would take power away from the entrenched families of the high administration and return it to its "rightful" possessors, the great nobility. Philip's efforts failed utterly, most bitterly in his financial schemes, which ended up in one of the great fiascoes in French fiscal history, the so-called John Law Bubble.

International Relations

[the political system should consist] in keeping in Europe the equilibrium established by the Peace of Westphalia, in protecting the body of German liberties . . . tying by perpetual treaty Turkey, Poland, Sweden, and Prussia, under the mediation . . . of France, and, finally, in separating by this means the house of Austria and Russia, throwing the latter back into its vast deserts and relegating it outside the limits of Europe.[33]

The prince of Conti, foreign affairs counselor of Louis XV, 1745

Philip inherited the political system established by the Treaties of Utrecht (1713), Rastatt, and Baden (both 1714), which recognized the national and dynastic needs of all of the Great Powers. In England, the succession passed, in 1715, to the Hanoverian line. The death without heirs of Queen Anne (Protestant daughter of James II's first marriage) meant that the descendants of her great aunt, Elizabeth (and wife of Frederick, count of the Palatinate), had to inherit the throne, to keep it out of the hands of the Catholic Stuarts.[34] This Elector of Hanover became George I of England; he did not speak English. Supporters of the Stuart dynasty rose up briefly in Scotland, and the failed Pretender, James III Stuart, sought refuge in France.

The French supported George I because of the happy confluence of personal and national interests of Philip of Orléans. The death of the child Louis XV would have meant, in *French* law, that the next heir was Philip V of Spain (second son of Louis XIV's only son); Louis XIV's will explicitly reaffirmed this principle. The Peace of Utrecht, however, specifically barred Philip V from the throne of France. With Philip V and his line excluded, the succession would pass to the house of Orléans, in the person of the Regent. Little wonder that Orléans strongly supported a treaty with England that would guarantee the succession rights laid down for both kingdoms in the Peace of Utrecht! In 1716, his chief minister, the abbé Dubois, signed such a treaty, the Triple Alliance, with England and Holland. When the Habsburg family fell out over the disposition of Italian territories in 1717, the Emperor joined the three new allies to create the Quadruple Alliance, which primarily sought to guarantee the rights of succession laid down by the Peace of Utrecht. France thus recognized George I and expelled James III Stuart to Rome, over the strenuous objections of French public opinion, which sympathized with James.

England agreed to bar Philip V of Spain and his descendants from the French throne, to the advantage of Philip of Orléans' house. To be fair to Orléans, one must admit that he and Dubois also believed (rightly) that France could not go back to war in 1715. The country remained exhausted—financially, demographically, psychologically—from the debacle of the War of the Spanish Succession. France needed peace; the Triple Alliance with England and Holland guaranteed that peace.

After the expulsion of James Stuart from France, the key barrier to peace remained the Spanish refusal to accept the situation imposed on it by France and the Emperor with respect to Italy. The Triple Alliance tried to mediate between the Emperor and Spain by proposing a new division of territories in Italy. The 1714 Rastatt agreement had given the kingdom of Naples and the duchy of Milan to the Emperor; Savoy had received Sicily. In 1715, after the death of his first wife (Mary Louise of Savoy) Philip V of Spain had muddied Italian waters by marrying Elizabeth Farnese, daughter of the duke of Parma. Philip and Mary Louise had had two sons, who stood to inherit Spain, so Elizabeth Farnese, as soon as she had sons of her own, sought to find them principalities in Italy.

This combination led to a brief war between the Quadruple Alliance and Spain (1718–1720). France, now allied with its enemies of the war of 1702–1713, invaded its erstwhile Spanish ally with a small army, while the Emperor and the Spaniards fought over Italy. On the mainland, the Spaniards made little progress, but their naval superiority allowed them to control Sardinia and Sicily. In 1721, Spain and France signed an alliance, cemented by promised marriage between Louis XV and the three-year-old Spanish princess, Marie-Anne-Victoire of Spain, and between the heir to Spain and Philip of Orléans's daughter.[35]

These arcane diplomatic dealings ushered in twenty years of relative peace for France. Louis renounced his Spanish princess in 1724, on the pretext that he wanted to marry and have heirs right away. Unable to find a suitable princess from a great family, Louis made the bizarre decision to marry Maria Leszczynska, daughter of Stanislas Leszczynski, the deposed king of Poland. The marriage of the most powerful king in Europe with so humble a princess startled contemporaries. Perhaps the most likely explanation is that factional politics at Court made it impossible to agree upon a different alliance.[36]

Ties to Leszczynski brought France to war in 1733. The death of Augustus II of Poland, the man who had deposed Leszczynski, led to the latter's re-election (September 1733). A few days later, a Russian-backed dissident Electoral Diet chose Augustus III, son of Augustus II. A Russian army marched into Poland, touching off the War of the Polish Succession (1733–1734). The French declared war on Austria, whom they held responsible for the Russian coup. Fighting in Italy produced two important results:

1. France recognized the Pragmatic Sanction, by which Charles VI's daughter, Maria Theresa, would inherit his lands.

2. Archduke Francis of Lorraine, Maria-Theresa's husband, very reluctantly agreed to give Lorraine to Leszczysnki, in return for possession of the grand duchy of Tuscany.[37]

On Leszczynski's death, the duchy would pass to the King of France. This little episode rounded out the borders of modern European France, save in the extreme southeast. Amazingly, even the adjustments there, which took place in 1859, had been presaged by promises made by duke of Savoy in 1733.[38]

The key element in the peace of western Europe remained good relations between France and England. Abbé Dubois stressed this connection and his eventual successor as chief minister, Cardinal Hercule Fleury, followed a similar policy. Fleury held virtually unopposed sway in the king's councils until the early 1740s. Fleury lost out in the debate about the Polish War, but otherwise maintained the diplomatic system enshrined at Utrecht and Rastatt. This relatively peaceful era might have allowed the government to reform the state itself, but despite some changes enacted in the early 1720s, needed reforms did not take place.

Despite the Pragmatic Sanction, Joseph I's death touched off a feeding frenzy among the European powers. Frederick the Great of Prussia, relying on a dubious sixteenth-century agreement, successfully seized Silesia from Maria-Theresa in December 1740. Maria-Theresa's half-sisters, daughters of Joseph I's first marriage, quickly contested the Pragmatic Sanction. France allied with Charles, Duke-Elector of Bavaria, son-in-law of Joseph I. French troops captured Prague in 1742, enabling Charles to obtained election as Emperor, but they had to abandon the city at the end of the year. Frederick withdrew from the alliance, which shifted the focus of the war to the contest between Austria and France. By 1744, England had joined in. In France, Fleury's death in January 1743 had greatly weakened the peace party. Marshal Belle-Isle, the hawkish Minister of War; and the violently anti-Austrian Foreign Minister, the marquis d'Argenson, now made foreign policy.

In 1745, the diplomatic situation changed dramatically once again. Frederick of Prussia reentered the war, and Charles VII of Bavaria died, re-opening the question of who should be the Emperor. Augustus III of Poland, husband of Joseph I's remaining daughter, declined to seek the office. Maria-Theresa's husband, Francis of Lorraine, became the new Emperor. The French army, commanded by marshal Maurice de Saxe, accompanied by Louis XV himself, defeated the English at Fontenoy. Louis XV prided himself for the rest of his life for this military exploit. French troops quickly captured Ghent and Bruges, and in a brilliant surprise march, even Brussels (1/1746). France held firm possession of the Austrian Netherlands and even several Dutch fortresses at the beginning of the peace negotiations (spring 1748).

Those negotiations led to the Peace of Aix-la-Chapelle (Aachen), which restored, for France and England, the pre-war status quo. The marquis d'Argenson had suffered disgrace in 1747, so the peace party, less hostile to Austria, obtained the king's ear. The population wanted peace, both to obtain relief from the heavy taxation imposed to pay for the war (a new *dixième,* or tenth on income, followed by surtaxes on all direct levies) and to reopen the previously thriving colonial commerce. France's European victories had been balanced by colonial defeats, above all the loss of Louisbourg, at the mouth of the Saint Lawrence River. Despite the population's clamor for peace, the actual terms of the settlement shocked public opinion; France, after all, held the Austrian Netherlands. Surely, after all the unsuccessful efforts to take Flanders, now that France had it in hand, it would keep it. That Louis XV so meekly gave back the "lost" territories gained by Maurice de Saxe greatly undermined public support for his government.

Internal Reforms

Councils, work with the ministers, hunting, and suppers in the cabinets every other day, such are practically all of the amusements and occupations of His Majesty.[39]

The duke of Luynes, 1743

The end of the War of the Austrian Succession marked as well the end of an important period of institutional consolidation in the French government. Philip of Orléans's Regency had begun with ideas of dramatic reform, based on the principles of aristocrats such as the dukes of Beauvillier and Saint-Simon. Philip wanted to do something about the state's chronic shortfall of money, so he turned first to the time-honored device of disgracing the Controller General and prosecuting his financier friends, levying fines of 220 million *livres,* of which the state actually collected about one-fourth. Philip then turned the financial system over to self-promoting Scottish "financier," John Law, who promised to solve all the state's problems. Law started with a small bank, but soon got control of the state's financial system and all of the monopoly colonial companies. He sold shares in his syndicate, backed by the profits of the companies, especially the Mississippi Company (for African and New World trade), and by tax revenues. The certificates proved at first a great success, but Law got greedy, and the system unraveled.

Law issued about 150 million *livres* worth of certificates in 1718 and slightly more in the first six months of 1719. In a classic pyramid scheme, he used the sales of new certificates to maintain payments to those who bought the earliest ones. The cycle quickly spun out of control. In the first five months of 1720, he had to issue 1.7 billion *livres* of certificates to keep up. The flood of certificates led to a bankruptcy. Clever borrowers quickly repaid their loans, using the devalued certificates, still legal tender. Law left the state with an unfunded debt of 2.5 billion *livres.* His System discredited the idea of a central bank, and the use of paper money. The absence of these two items severely undercut the French economy, and the French state, in the eighteenth century, because England had a much more advanced system of credit, based on the Bank of England, established in 1694. The English state enjoyed a powerful wartime advantage because of its access to cheaper, and broader, credit.

Philip had little choice but to turn back to the traditional financiers. Desmarets had died, but his ministerial co-workers lived on. In short order, Desmarets's old subordinates took over supervision of the collection of direct taxes and of salt taxes, as intendants of finance. Other subordinates became dean of the royal councils, Keeper of the Seals, and, in 1730, even Controller General (Philibert Orry). Orry and the others had close ties to the world of the Parlement (such as the two Lefèbvre clans) and to the dominant financiers, the Pâris brothers, through whom they could tap Genevan capital markets. These disciples of Colbert quickly restored some of his policies, most notably the stable *livre*. It would undergo no further manipulation until 1785.

They administered a system that differed in fundamental ways from the one of Colbert. The General Tax Farm was more powerful than ever, but direct taxes now often included the capitation, a tenth (created in 1710, abolished in 1721, levied thereafter during wars), and, after 1749, a twentieth. These new taxes hit most laypeople, although some provinces (such as Brittany) bought exemptions. Overall resources rose to about 200 million *livres* a year: 91 million from the General Tax Farm, 41 million from the old direct taxes, 33 million from the capitation, and the rest from a broad range of taxes and grants. Expenses, in peacetime, ran about the same, with the military getting the largest share, officially estimated at 55 million (too low an estimate), followed by interest (45 million) and the royal household (30 million).

Wars obviously disrupted the equilibrium. The military budget doubled during the War of the Polish Succession; the War of the Austrian Succession cost over a billion *livres*. Total debt rose by about 200 million *livres*. In the midst of this war, the king dismissed Orry, because he had fallen out with the king's all-powerful mistress, Mme de Pompadour. Given her close ties to the Pâris brothers and the Farmers General, Orry's fall certainly reflected their loss of confidence in him. His successor, Machault d'Arnouville, came from the same Colbert–Desmarets system. Machault introduced the twentieth on landed revenue of all owners. He had close ties to all the right circles, but he, too, fell afoul of Mme de Pompadour in 1757.[40] His removal as Controller General touched off two generations of constant instability in that most important of offices. Indeed, few contrasts are starker than that between the stability of Louis XV's early government and the chaos into which it descended after 1750.

The stable administration of the second quarter of the eighteenth century institutionalized practices that had long been current, above all the recruitment policies for high royal offices. In theory, royal councilors could move up from the lower social ranks: Superintendent Fouquet's grandfather had been a draper, the grandfather of long-time councilor Pierre Jeannin, a tanner. French society, even at the top level, relied on a constant replenishment of capable newcomers. Like the peasants discussed in the previous section, however, the highest ranks of society also contained core elements that maintained staggering levels of continuity. The existence of such people allowed society to perpetuate, promulgate, and believe the myth of stability, yet also allowed the necessary flexibility to change with the times.

Government officials provide an excellent example of the dual nature of the system. On the one hand, certain families, like the Phélypeaux, who served every Bourbon king as councilors of state, stayed on top forever. Jérôme-Frédéric Phélypeaux, count of Maurepas, disgraced by Louis XV in 1749, returned in his old age to become Louis XVI's chief counselor in 1774. (See Chapter 11.) Other families from the Parlement–master of requests nexus had similar longevity in office. The Le Fèvre de Caumartin family had five generations involved with the Royal Council as masters of requests (from 1585 until 1748); four of these men became councilors of state (the fifth died young); three of them sat on the *Grand Conseil,* one as its president. The unrelated Lefèvre d'Ormesson family had more than ten masters of requests in the late seventeenth and eighteenth centuries, in addition to seven members of the Parlement of Paris (four of them among the ten masters).

The functions of the masters of requests had not changed much from Louis XIV's time. They did the work for the lesser councils, in which the king himself did not participate, and passed along their recommendations to the royal councils. These councils needed reliable local and regional agents to carry out their orders; they used the provincial (and army) intendants for that purpose. In the eighteenth century, as in the seventeenth, intendants came almost exclusively from the masters of requests. In one study of ninety-four eighteenth-century intendants, ninety had been masters of requests before becoming intendants and two of the others became masters after gaining an intendancy. Many of them came from families with long-standing ties to the central administration and the highest royal courts. Of the eighty-eight men whose grandfathers could be traced, twenty had been judges on a sovereign court and twenty-one had sat on the Royal Council. Their fathers (ninety-two in the sample) included twenty-six judges and thirty-seven members of the Royal Council. About 10 percent of the families had worked for the Royal Council for three or more generations. One-third of the ninety-four masters became councilors of state at the end of their careers. Eighteen of them ended up as presidents of one of the Sovereign Courts. These great families of administrators lasted for generations at the top of the hierarchy.

In the eighteenth century, the ranks just below minister had great stability. At the ministerial level, however, Louis XV introduced a very high level of instability after 1750. We might think of the modern American comparison of the permanent high-level bureaucracy in Washington, to which a sitting president adds a small number of political appointees at the very top, such as secretary of state or of defense. Ancien Régime France increasingly followed similar practices in the eighteenth century. By the middle of the century, such policies had led Louis XV to alter fundamentally the structure of the Council of State and the ministries by introducing members of the sword nobility to each.

Out in the provinces, the two elites had moved in very different directions after 1650. The great provincial administrative families often stayed in the provinces, whereas the titled nobility moved to Paris and Versailles, abandoning for good the provinces in the second half of the seventeenth century. An entire province, such as Berry, might have only three titled nobles. Most provinces had two or three dozen titled nobles, but these people tended to live at Court, to judge from the capitation rolls of the 1690s and early 1700s. Even the untitled seigneurs of parishes had left the land. In the *élections* of Pont Audemer, Eu, and Neufchâtel (near Rouen), only 11 percent of the nobility on the capitation rolls could claim lordship of a parish, and only six had a title. In five of the bailiwicks of Burgundy, the situation looked the same: only six old nobles among the one hundred fifty-eight fief holders. Brittany provided a rare exception to the pattern.

The missing sword nobility had given way to a new provincial elite: the robe nobility, who provided the administrators and judges. These people avidly sought titles.[41] Presidents of provincial Parlements sought out lesser titles, such as baron or viscount, in the middle of the seventeenth century. Later, they received the title of marquis, or, in the eighteenth century, count. These people now had the largest provincial households, although they were much smaller than the vast establishments of titled nobles in the early seventeenth century. In the early eighteenth century, a First President might have a dozen servants, including a cook, a coachman, and even a Swiss guard at his door. A typical *président à mortier* usually had a coachman, a cook, and two or three other servants; a lowly auditor of accounts, holder of a non-ennobling office, would have had only a female servant, little different from a master artisan's household.

In the first half of the eighteenth century, the royal judges established their firm primacy in local society. Many of the presidents purchased seigneuries, complete with courts, often administered by lawyers who practiced in front of the Parlements. These judges provided the leadership for the group of medium and large-scale landowners who dominated French society, a domination that lasted well into the twentieth century in most regions.

French society remained strongly in the hands of the administrative elites until the 1770s. The overwhelming dominance of the judges and royal administrators in the provinces provided a new context for the restoration of the old power of pre-registration remonstrance to the Parlements. In earlier times, the local titled nobility provided an effective counterweight to the judicial and administrative elite; few people in sixteenth- or seventeenth-century France questioned the social supremacy of the old nobility. In the eighteenth century, however, the traditional nobility had moved to Paris or other large cities, leaving the Parlementaires and high-level royal administrators, invariably from Parlementaire families, without an effective rival for power. When the king had a conflict with his Parlements, he no longer had any important allies in the provinces. The administrative elite thus developed a stranglehold on most levers of power—political, cultural, social, often economic—in provincial France.

THE EARLY ENLIGHTENMENT

> *There is another magician . . . who is called the Pope. Sometimes he makes people believe that three are only one, that the bread one eats is not bread, that the wine one drinks is not wine, and a thousand other things of that sort.*
>
> Montesquieu, *Persian Letters* 24

The deaths of Bayle, Bossuet, and Fénelon (1706, 1713, 1715) paved the way for a new generation of intellectual leadership, dominated by two authors: Charles de Secondat (baron de Montesquieu), and François-Marie Arouet, known to us by his pen name, Voltaire. These men and their intellectual allies began the movement known as the Enlightenment, which sought to democratize the ideas of the Scientific Revolution and to apply them to all aspects of human life, including political organization. Early eighteenth-century writers often focused their political writings on one of two issues: the controversy over the Papal bull *Unigenitus* and reform of the system of government. One early proposal for reform came from a seemingly unlikely source, Marshal Vauban, the king's chief military engineer. Vauban's *Project for a Royal Tithe* recommended abolition of the existing tax system and the creation of a single 10 percent tax on all income, including that of privileged individuals. Royal agents seized every existing copy of the book, even those from the house in which Vauban lay dying, but the project soon became public knowledge.[42]

The anything-goes climate of the Regency encouraged ever-more radical attacks on French government and on the Church. Montesquieu had fired the first salvo with his *Persian Letters,* in which Persian visitors describe incredulously the French society they encounter at Court. Montesquieu played on French ideas about "Oriental despots" to suggest that the French themselves lived under such a ruler.

> The King of France is old. . . . They say he possesses to a great degree the talent of making himself obeyed . . . People have often said of him that of all the governments in the World, that of the Turks or that of our August sultan pleases him the most, so much does he set great store in an Oriental policy. [43]

Versailles created a world in which form mattered more than substance and in which mindless tradition denied the possibility of appeal to reason. Like many French writers of the early part of the century, Montesquieu soon looked across the Channel for inspiration.

Montesquieu and Voltaire both spent time in England in the late 1720s and early 1730s, bringing back to France a profound admiration for their great political rival. Voltaire published his *Letters on the English* in 1733. He sharply contrasted the two societies, in terms of the fairness of their judicial and tax systems, in terms of religious toleration, and in terms of respect for property. His book condemned by the royal censor, Voltaire went into exile and turned to writing about science. He later became an official royal historian and published his *Century of Louis XIV* in 1751, establishing the main lines of historical interpretation of that reign that have lasted until the present. His criticisms turned away from the state and toward the Church, which he satirized ruthlessly in works such as his comic masterpiece *Candide* (1758).

Montesquieu followed a different path. As a judge at the Parlement of Bordeaux, he had a strong connection to the law itself. He, like many Parlementaires, took a great interest in Roman history; he even published (1734) a book on the grandeur and collapse of Rome. His masterpiece focused on a subject closer to hand: the law.

In 1748, he published the most important book to appear in the first half of the French Enlightenment: *The Spirit of the Laws.*

The publication of *The Spirit of the Laws* marked the intellectual end of the Ancien Régime. Montesquieu argued on behalf of two fundamental changes. First, he presented the doctrine of the separation of powers. Montesquieu believed that an effective government had to divide judicial, executive, and legislative powers. The three branches of government should be established in such a way as to prevent abuses of power by any one branch. This system of checks and balances would offer the best protection for civil society, above all for property. We can see easily the influence of Montesquieu's time in England, just as we know that his doctrine of checks and balances provides one of the foundation stones of the American Constitution.

The second major change also reflected the influence of the English example. Montesquieu argued that the French Parlements, like their English namesake, constituted the *legislative* branch of government. In France, in Montesquieu's time, the king made the law. He issued an edict, but it became legally binding only when registered by the Parlements and duly inscribed in their registers. As we have seen, Parlements could suggest emendations by means of written remonstrances. The king, however, maintained the prerogative of peremptory implementation of the law by means of a *lit de justice*—his personal presence in the Parlement, requiring registration without dissent. Montesquieu argued that because Parlementary registration made a law the law, Parlement must have the real authority to make law. Law had to be consonant with natural law, a determination made by the reason of the judges. Montesquieu believed *man,* not God, made the law, and that man determined the right laws through his powers of reason. If we may go back to the words of Fénelon, the judges determined the empirical truth of the law and, above all, its utility.

Montesquieu's book thus provided the last of the three invaluable markers for the destruction of the Ancien Régime as a viable intellectual construct. Descartes's *Discourse on Method* (1637) had established the primacy of reason over tradition, the method of applying reason, and the universality of reason.[44] Once elites had accepted these Cartesian principles, they could no longer rely solely on tradition as a justification for law, for the social system or for ideas. Pierre Bayle's *Historical and Critical Dictionary* (1697) demonstrated some two generations later the results one could obtain through the application of Cartesian scientific method to traditional texts of all kinds, including the Christian Bible. Montesquieu's *The Spirit of the Laws* completed the revolution by removing God from questions about human society, making human reason the final arbiter of its regulation. Montesquieu spoke to the deepest fears of French elites, because he offered them a model that would protect their property, even as the system that hitherto had done so collapsed.

The legacy of Descartes, Bayle, and Montesquieu called everything into question. Such an intellectual tradition made abundant sense in a society in which all of the basic structures either had collapsed or were on the verge of doing so. Demographically, people moved in unprecedented numbers, undermining the geographic stability so essential to the Ancien Régime. Economically, new goods, new commercial currents, new techniques, and new relations of production had definitively overturned the old system, although remnants of traditional production hung on in many sectors and even in entire regions outside of the new system of distribution. Culturally, significant portions of the elites turned to science and reason, and away from religion, for explanations. Because so many more people could read, ideas circulated more rapidly and to a much broader audience. The state struggled to maintain control of the diffusion of such ideas, but rapidly became merely one voice (or rather several, because the different Court factions all published their own versions of events) among many.

These political debates, like the wider range of intellectual output, reached an eager audience in Paris and in the provinces. These people created provincial organisms that paralleled those of the capital. In intellectual life, for example, provincial urban elites founded local Academies of Arts and Sciences: thirteen of them between 1650 and 1715, twenty-one more by 1760. These Academies allowed members of the three orders—clergy, nobles, commoners—to come together on grounds of relative equality, rather like the salons of Paris. The commoners, and no small number of the nobles, in fact came overwhelmingly from the world of the royal administration, especially the judicial administration. Of the roughly six thousand known members of such societies, only three hundred or so were merchants. The Academies had members whose libraries evolved slowly between the late seventeenth and early eighteenth centuries. In contrast to the merchants, who owned few, or sometimes no books in Louis XIV's time, the administrative elite possessed considerable libraries. Even as late as 1750, the after-death inventory of a judge was twice as likely to have a library as the inventory of a merchant.

The judges possessed the sort of books one might expect: above all, their libraries contained works of jurisprudence and Classical texts. Forty percent of the books of the travelling library (seventy-seven books) of one late seventeenth-century intendant of Agen, Claude Pellot, dealt with law or politics. Pellot had such works as the philosophy of Francis Bacon, *The Prince of Machiavelli* (in Italian), as well as recent literature. Men like Pellot grew up reading the works of Cicero or Virgil at school (booksellers' inventories show dozens of copies of such schoolboy texts) and moved on to more contemporary authors: Bossuet, or, later, Voltaire or Montesquieu. During the eighteenth century, however, the libraries of the legal elite underwent dramatic change: one might say they became feminized. The rapid increase in real literacy, especially among upper and upper-middle class women, created a new market for literature. In 1700, the libraries of judicial officers contained an average of 5 percent literary works, whereas by 1790, the figure had risen to 30 percent. Moreover, such figures underestimate the increased influence of literary works, because eighteenth-century libraries contained so many books left over from their seventeenth-century origins. Those older books, overwhelmingly religious, often gathered dust on the shelves.

Although men, too, read the novels of Rousseau, Mme de Lafayette or Diderot, women provided the primary audience for literary works. The trend since the late seventeenth century had been away from works of piety—invariably written in French, for a female audience—and toward modern letters. Upper-class women became progressively more secular in their reading. Having learned to read through works of piety (the overwhelming majority of books in the libraries of girls' schools), they used their skills in ways perhaps unintended by their nun teachers. Already in the late seventeenth century, cities such as Paris or the provincial seats of Parlements had a strong market for literary works. One inventory of a bookseller of Bordeaux in 1672 indicated sixty copies of Molière's play *The Misanthrope,* selling for a mere 5 shillings apiece. By the 1750s or 1760s, sales of novels, such as Rousseau's *The New Heloise,* would dwarf such figures, as tens of thousands of copies flooded the market.

Smaller provincial towns gradually began to mimic the great cities in the first quarter of the eighteenth century. The rich peasants increasingly bought a book or two by 1750. Lower class readers, such as artisans or servants (30 percent of whose inventories in Paris in 1700 contained books), tended to own religious books: a Christian Bible, a book of hours, an *Imitation of Christ* or the life of a saint. Book-sellers's shelves were jammed with such items, hundreds of copies, selling for very modest sums. Even these sales, however, paled in comparison to the tens of thousands of copies of simple catechisms that an important book dealer in a city such as Rouen might have on hand by the 1760s.

The revolution in reading tastes that had begun in Paris in the second half of the seventeenth century and spread to the larger cities in the first half of the century accelerated after 1760. Indeed, one might say that the complete break between traditional reading tastes and practices provides one of the clearest signs of the end of the Ancien Régime and the beginning of a transitional society in France in the years between 1750 and 1770. French society laid the foundation for that change in the years between 1690 and 1750. The volume of books published increased steadily, rising from about three hundred titles a year in Paris at the end of the seventeenth century to more than five hundred a year after 1730. This increase presaged the explosion of the late eighteenth century, when the annual average of titles varied between fifteen hundred and four thousand. Similarly, the number of newspapers exploded: nine hundred different newspapers appeared in France at some time in the eighteenth century (pre-Revolution). Most of these newspapers had to receive royal permission, and thus promulgated the official government line about the issues of the day, but clandestine ones also persisted. The most famous subversive newspaper was the *Nouvelles ecclésiastiques* (*Ecclesiastical News*) published weekly by the Jansenists throughout the eighteenth century, despite the strenuous efforts by the royal government to stamp it out.[45] Authors of works condemned by royal censors had an easy remedy: they could publish their books (or newspapers) in the nearby French-speaking territories, such as Liège or Neufchâtel (in Switzerland). Rousseau, for example, published his writings in Neufchâtel. The Jesuits, too, published a journal that did not have full official permission; they called it the *Journal of Trévoux,* implying that it came out in the tiny town of that name in the independent principality of Dombes, near Lyon, and thus could escape the royal censors.

This society presents us with striking cultural contradictions. In the realm of religion, the Catholic Church simultaneously grew stronger and weaker. The strength developed above all in the late seventeenth and early eighteenth centuries. Louis XIV appointed better bishops: following in the footsteps of his father, he virtually eliminated the practice of underage appointments and usually turned to mature clerics in their forties. These bishops had a generally higher level of education than their predecessors of the early seventeenth or sixteenth centuries. They also demonstrated, in most cases, a sincere piety. They took their pastoral duties far more seriously than had been the case, as the episcopal visitation records demonstrate. Most importantly, they oversaw the creation of an effective system of seminaries for the training of priests. By the early eighteenth century, virtually every parish priest in France had been to a seminary. Unlike their sixteenth-century predecessors, they were universally literate, trained in the basic doctrines of the Church, and assiduous in their catechismal duties.

In the century between 1620 and 1720, the French clergy waged an often violent campaign against the "paganism" of French laics, especially rural ones. We saw in earlier chapters that the episcopal visitation records spoke of one abuse after another: "pre-marital" cohabitation, vulgarities in the church itself, drunken clergy, pagan superstitions, and total ignorance of basic Church doctrine. The seminary-educated clergy struggled long and hard against these problems. They did inculcate a much clearer understanding of Church doctrine by means of universal catechism classes. These classes, conducted orally, drilled into every French person (female and male), especially those in rural areas, the fundamentals of Catholic belief.[46] The church building became less subject to indignities; "pre-marital" cohabitation virtually disappeared; the clergy's morals improved (both in terms of drinking and sexual habits).[47] One can sense the changed mood of the laity in parish *cahiers* from the Estates General of 1614 and those of 1789. In the former, some peasants complained that the local priest should be required to have a concubine, who would make him leave their wives and daughters alone. In the latter, peasants complained if the priest had a concubine. The one area of fairly broad failure concerned pagan practices; the Church had little success against those practices, as they persisted into the nineteenth (and even twentieth) century.

The tremendous success of the Catholic Church, notably in rural areas, went hand-in-hand with a steady de-Christianization of some elements of the population. Among elites, the purchase of religious books declined throughout the eighteenth century. Even among Parisian priests, the percentage of religious books in libraries declined from 38 percent of the titles in 1710 to 29 percent by 1765. In the provinces, the same decline took place, but the level of religious reading remained high. In the cities of western France, religious works dropped from 4/5 to 2/3 of the listed books. From 1723–1727, some 35 percent of the books seeking publication permission in Paris had a religious content, a figure that dropped to 25 percent from 1750–1754, and to a mere 9.5 percent in the 1780s. In the provinces, however, we find a different story: almost two-thirds of the books reprinted in the eighteenth century were devotional works. Books of Hours alone accounted for a fifth of all books.

Here we see a profound division between elites, particularly certain segments of the elites, and ordinary people. Most poor people who possessed books, owned religious ones. Among elites, the old nobility still kept to more traditional reading habits, while judges and administrators turned increasingly to history and, especially, to literature. Ordinations of priests rose steadily until the 1740s and then began a long decline in many dioceses. The number of monks also began to decline in the 1740s, although the great collapse took place a generation later. The social origin of priests, monks, and nuns began to shift in the first half of the century, becoming progressively less urban and more rural. Fewer monks and nuns came from the urban middle classes (their share dropped from about half in 1700 to only a third by the 1730s). More and more priests came from rich peasant families, a trend intensified in the nineteenth century.

This split between a progressively more de-Christianized urban France and a more Christian (read *Catholic*) rural France foretold profound social and political cleavages to come. During the Revolution, the religious split helped to fuel a civil war; in the nineteenth century, it would provide the fundamental schism of French politics. Yet the Church still had an enormous presence in the towns. Most towns had many churches and, often, convents or monasteries. Angers had twenty-eight abbeys and convents and sixty-nine churches, including a cathedral; Paris had hundreds of religious establishments. The Church thus played an important role in the economy of the town, and in some cases, the clergy interfered effectively in urban politics. Artisans in some trades did turn against the organized Church. Some guilds, such as those of textile workers and printers, were notorious for their antiestablishment attitudes, but even these artisans often turned less against God than against the rigid ecclesiastical hierarchies they found oppressive. Other guilds, such as the butchers, remained deeply devout.

Two issues dominated eighteenth-century religious debates: toleration for non-Catholics and the internal split within Catholicism between the Jansenists and the Jesuits. Some leading writers, such as Voltaire, took up the cudgels for the Protestant and Jewish minorities.[48] The Protestant communities, as in the time of Louis XIV, had to put up with periodic rounds of persecution and intimidation. The Sephardic Jews of Bordeaux, Montpellier, and the other port cities lived in relative security, as did the large Jewish community at Metz. The Ashkenazic Jews of the small Alsatian towns, however, faced more serious physical threats, and the Jewish community of Paris, re-established in the early seventeenth century by immigrants from the east, lived in some insecurity.

The split between Jansenists and Jesuits continued to focus on the papal bull *Unigenitus,* which had declared Jansenists to be heretics. Cardinal Fleury and Louis XV, like Louis XIV, insisted the bull be declared a fundamental law of France. Most career judges, even chancellors Pontchartrain or d'Aguesseau, found it an illegal assault on the French monarchy.[49] The endless dispute between the government and the Parlements over the bull peaked in the 1730s, in a dispute that crystallized in the parish church of Saint-Médard in Paris, and in the 1750s, in the affair of the refusal of communion.

In the 1730s, people took the Jansenist deacon of Saint-Médard, François de Pâris, to be a saint. After his death, people came from all over to visit his grave, seeking his miraculous intervention. The faithful took to trembling with religious fervor at this holy shrine. The crowds grew so large that the authorities closed the cemetery, leading to civil disturbances. In the 1750s, the rabidly anti-Jansenist archbishop of Paris commanded priests to refuse extreme unction to those religious who had not taken the oath in support of *Unigenitus.* Several well-publicized Parisian cases of priests dying without benefit of the sacraments outraged public opinion, including the Parlement, which intervened to order extreme unction given to all of the faithful. The issue petered out after the attempted assassination of Louis XV by the madman Jacques Damiens in 1754, but the Jansenist controversy provided one of the most powerful stimuli for the abandonment of traditional Catholicism by important elements of the French elite. It also offered a unifying issue to those seeking reform of the "arbitrary" element of state governance.

Despite the rapid changes in so many elements of life, the Ancien Régime continued on in two important ways. First, the state remained a monarchy in which the king made the law; Louis XV brooked no interference in his theoretical prerogative to do so. Second, the legal and social remnants of the society of orders remained in place. Nobles demanded social preference and legal privileges. Guilds tried to protect their monopolies. The economy often chafed at such interference, just as the middle classes grew increasingly restive about the social and legal pretensions of the nobility, the clergy, and the monarchy.

At the time of the publication of *The Spirit of the Laws*, France lived in the most dangerous of situations: its political system had failed to evolve with its social, economic, and cultural life. France spent most of the next one hundred twenty-five years searching for a political system that would fit together with its socioeconomic realities. Time after time, the political system would change, and sometimes survive for fifteen or twenty years, but it would change in a manner insufficiently flexible for growth and adaptation in an age of such radical transformation. The first failed effort to create an adapted political system took place between the 1750s and the 1780s. Its failure led to the greatest political event of French, and, arguably, European history, the French Revolution. Let us turn now to the momentous years of the second half of the eighteenth century, that period between the death of the Ancien Régime as a social and economic system (by 1750 at the latest), and its political death (in 1789).

Notes

1. P. Goubert and D. Roche, *Les Français et l'Ancien Régime* (Paris: Armand Colin, 1984), I, 31.

2. In Europe, the great mid-century conflict, the Seven Years' War, began in 1756 and ended in 1763; however, the colonial fighting, known to the English colonists (and American schoolchildren) as the French and Indian War, began in 1754.

3. The unusually cold winters of several years between 1690 and 1715, however, also precipitated massive mortalities, above all in 1693–1694 and 1709–1710 (on which, see Chapter 9).

4. Literacy maps not surprisingly demonstrate that those areas in which the population did not speak French—areas such as western Brittany (Breton), parts of the Midi (Auvergnat, Occitan) or the Basque region—had the lowest literacy rates.

5. Cited in P. Minard, *La fortune du colbertisme. État et industrie dans la France des Lumières* (Paris: Fayard, 1998), 196.

6. The *élection* (local financial district) of Paris did not include the city or its suburbs. Information on this social group comes from J.-M. Moriceau, *Les fermiers de l'Ile-de-France XVe–XVIIIe siècle* (Paris: Fayard, 1994). Table X-1 is adapted from his Table 81.

7. These merchant–farmers rented the land in question, which invariably belonged to people, such as nobles and citizens of Paris, not subject to the *tailles*.

8. These examples all come from the records of the rural notary Claude Coujard, a sample of sales taking place in April and May 1658. AD Côte d'Or, 4E 49 12.

9. The ploughmen often owned small farms, which they rented to other peasants.

10. A man marrying at age twenty-eight would be fifty-seven to sixty years old when his eldest son (or, barring surviving sons, daughter) reached age twenty-eight. His death at age sixty or so would open up his tenancy, paving the way for a new household to take its place in village society.

11. Those testifying in court had to give their name and age before answering other questions. The comparison of these documents with parish birth registers gives us an indicator of how accurate their answers were. In the seventeenth century, any older person most often answered "about sixty"; in the eighteenth century, older witnesses far more often gave a specific (and accurate) answer.

12. In many agricultural sectors, such as the wines of Bordeaux or Champagne, quality substituted for quantity, precisely the opposite procedure from what happened in manufacturing. Sparkling wine required a lighter pressing of the grapes, which extracted less wine; bottling of such wine, rather than leaving it in barrels, also substantially increased storage loss. T. Brennan's prize-winning *Burgundy to Champagne. The Wine Trade in Early Modern France* (Baltimore and London: Johns Hopkins University Press, 1997), provides all the details.

13. The capitation "classes" of 1695 reflected this reality; winegrowers appeared as early as class twenty.

14. Taxpayers had to report their move to the local tax office (*élection*) to receive a certificate of tax payment for their old parish, which exempted them from taxation in their new residence for the current year. The records, which list only well-off and middling taxpayers, suggest the figure of 75,000–100,000 families. The tax rolls themselves demonstrate that 3 to 5 percent of all taxpayers changed residence each year.

15. All of the families mentioned here—Boisseau, Beugnon, Regnault, Girard—had lived in Fétigny since at least 1475; all of them could be found in Alligny in the twentieth century.

16. The poor could, of course, see their images reflected in ponds, sharpened knives, and the like, but such glimpses did not form part of everyday experience. The rapid diffusion of the mirror paralleled the rise of philosophical individualism.

17. P.-J. Hélias, *The Horse of Pride. Life in a Breton Village,* trans. J. Guicharnaud (New Haven and London: Yale University Press, 1978, translation of the French edition of 1975), 230.

18. It differed from other parishes in that its landlord, the sieur of Aubermesnil, periodically lived in the village, held intact a larger share of its land than was normal, and sporadically farmed his own land, thereby removing it from the tax roll (the farm was on the roll in 1695 and 1789 but off in 1758).

19. In the nearly one hundred ten inventories from the period of 1650–1750 Moriceau examined, he found only seven households with nonreligious paintings, as against thirteen with religious ones. Although nonreligious paintings became more common, too, in terms of the number of paintings, religious subjects dominated far more than the ratio 15 to 9 of inventories would suggest.

20. As we shall see, during the French Revolution, the National Assembly abolished the jurisdictions of the Ancien Régime and created new local districts, called departments. The department of the Yonne, which takes its name from a local river, sat at the conjunction of the three Ancien Régime *généralités* of Paris, Châlons-sur-Marne, and Burgundy.

21. S. Desan, *Reclaiming the Sacred. Lay Religion and Popular Politics in Revolutionary France* (Ithaca, NY: Cornell University Press, 1990), 32–36.

22. Cited in Minard, *La fortune du colbertisme,* 257.

23. Except in Brittany, French nobles faced derogation, loss of nobility, if they participated in trade. Breton nobles could not participate in retail trade, but could be involved in wholesale, sea-going commerce. Brittany also had the curious system of "sleeping nobility," in which a noble family that suffered derogation due to its participation in trade could reclaim noble status if it renounced its commercial occupation.

24. J. Ménétra, *Journal of My Life,* intro. D. Roche, trans. A. Goldhammer (New York: Columbia University Press, 1986), 48.

25. Plantation censuses show that "Congos" made up half or more of the African slaves; however, by the second half of the eighteenth century, the largest group of slaves were "Creoles," those of mixed ancestry.

26. Rural consumers ate far less sugar; total French per capita consumption of sugar, about one pound a year in the middle of the century, doubled by the 1780s.

27. The observations of Jacques Savary, author of the principal commercial treatise of the time, *Le Parfait Négociant,* as quoted by R. Stein, *The French Slave Trade in the Eighteenth Century* (Madison, WI: University of Wisconsin Press, 1979), 97.

28. Stein points out that most of the European crew members probably died while the ship was near the African or West Indian coasts, due to local diseases; most of the slaves died during the voyage itself. (Stein, *French Slave Trade,* 99.) Stein's figures also suggest that the state-run West India Company had a much lower mortality rate (7 percent) than did private shippers.

29. O. Equiano, "The Interesting Life of Olaudah Equiano," in *Classic Slave Narratives,* ed. H. L. Gates (New York: Mentor, 1987), 33–35. Equiano crossed the Atlantic on a British ship; as noted by Savary, conditions were similar in French ones, for which we lack quite so eloquent a description.

30. Cited in A. Poitrineau, *Ils travaillaient la France. Métiers et mentalités du XVIe au XIXᵉ siècle* (Paris: Armand Colin, 1992), 147.

31. Guilds regulated most aspects of production. They set production limits, established prices and wages (the latter more theoretical than real, as we shall see), and mediated disputes between masters. They excluded from towns all production not controlled by the guild. Historians often call this shift of production to rural areas the "putting-out system."

32. M. Antoine, *Louis XV* (Paris: Fayard, 1989), 435. Louis uttered these words when he disgraced his cousin, the duke of Bourbon, and removed him from the royal council, which he had dominated for several years.

33. Antoine, *Louis XV,* 645.

34. Parlement had specifically barred Catholics from the English throne in 1689, as part of the Glorious Revolution. They also forbade the monarch to marry a Catholic.

35. In the new arrangements, Elizabeth Farnese's children managed to get the rights to Tuscany and Parma.

36. Europe did have a dearth of eligible princesses at that time. Louis had already rejected the King of Spain's daughter and been rejected in turn by an English princess. Louis considered a Russian princess—a clear sign of changing European power politics—as well as several Frenchwomen. The former seemed still a bit "barbarous," as one advisor put it; the latter posed problems because of the consequent elevation of either the House of Orléans (mother of the princess of Lorraine) or that of Bourbon.

37. The Pragmatic Sanction recognized Maria Theresa as heir to the Habsburg dominions. Charles's older brother, the Emperor Joseph I, had had daughters, so that, lacking a male heir, the lands should, by law, have passed to them. Charles spent the later years of his life getting the other European powers to agree to the despoiling of his nieces.

38. The duke promised to give Savoy to France, if the latter helped him take the Milanais—precisely the bargain struck in 1859, when Napoleon III helped the Italians drive the Austrians from the peninsula and create a united Italy.

39. Antoine, *Louis XV,* 445.

40. Machault gave up his position as Controller General in 1754 to become Secretary of State for the Navy.

41. Some courts, such as the Parlement of Brittany, became progressively more restrictive in their entrance requirements. The Bretons demanded nobility from Parlementaires after the 1660s. In the eighteenth century, based on the prices

people were willing to pay for these offices, the judgeships became much less highly prized, especially after 1750.

42. A few years later, Louis enacted a modified version of this tax, which he called the *dixième*. It lasted only during wartime and did not levy anything like a ten percent tax on landed income; Louis did not abolish other taxes when he created it. In 1749, the government finally introduced a similar tax, the twentieth (*vingtième*). Initially, all had to pay it, but the clergy and several of the *pays d'États* soon bought exemptions.

43. *Persian Letter* number 37.

44. Descartes himself did not specifically address the issue of whether women had reason. One of his earliest disciples, François Poullain de la Barre, applied the master's principles and declared that women, like men, have reason, and therefore that women and men were equal.

45. The *Histoire de la France religieuse,* vol. III, 37, contains a wonderful diagram of how those responsible for the *Nouvelles Ecclésiastiques* distributed it with the minimum of risk to all involved.

46. Those who remember even twentieth-century catechism lessons will recall the essentially oral technique of question and response built into the Baltimore Catechism used in the United States in the 1950s and 1960s.

47. I have use quotation marks around "pre-marital" because only the clergy, at first, viewed these unions as pre-marital. Village people believed a couple to be married once they had made promises to each other and exchanged gifts. These couples often waited several months, for a more convenient season, to hold the church wedding and the party. The Church insisted that only the church wedding made the marriage legitimate. During the seventeenth century, the Church successfully changed popular opinion on this question.

48. Here again we see the contradictions so common to Enlightenment thinkers. Voltaire fought strongly for religious tolerance, yet was himself an anti-Semite.

49. Pontchartrain took the startling step of resigning his office as chancellor while still in good health rather than have to take the edict to the Parlement for registration.

Chapter Eleven

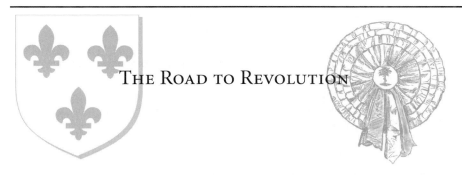

THE ROAD TO REVOLUTION

Our Father, who art in Versailles. Abhorred be Thy name. Thy kingdom is shaken. Thy will is no longer done on earth or in heaven. Give us back this day our daily bread, which Thou hast taken from us. Forgive Thy parlements who have upheld Thy interests, as Thou forgiveth those ministers who have sold them. Be not led into temptation by du Barry. But deliver us from that devil of a chancellor. Amen![1]

Louis XV reigned for fifty-nine years; ironically, just as the measles brought him to the throne by killing his father and older brother in 1712, so smallpox ended his life in 1774. France greeted Louis the once "Well-Beloved's" death with as much joy as his accession, because he had long lost the respect of his subjects, as the parody of the *Our Father* attests. His death placed his feckless grandson on the throne as Louis XVI, and made an Austrian princess, Marie Antoinette, France's queen. This unlucky pair would lose their thrones, and their heads, in a Revolution made inevitable by Louis XV's failure to reform successfully the French political system.

Louis XV had a deserved reputation as a lecher, a man easily misled by his seemingly boundless sexual appetite. The du Barry of the "prayer" is Jeanne Bécu, a Parisian prostitute whom Louis XV made his official mistress, giving her the title of countess of Barry. That a woman of such low social status could become a dominant figure in a Court at which one needed four generations of noble ancestry merely to be presented, gives us some idea of the extent of Louis's depravity. Eighteenth-century opinion held that du Barry owed her success to her ability to overcome the king's impotence. Sexual innuendo aside, the "prayer" also shows people directly tied the moral issue to the political one, to the "devil of a chancellor," seeking massive judicial and governmental reform.

The desacralization of the monarchy evident in the *Our Father* parody destabilized the French monarchy because the political order rested on the premise that the king, although unlimited (absolute) in his ability to make human law, was bound to God's law. The privileged of Ancien Régime France protected themselves and their property from the king precisely under "God's law," by means of contracts. Any weakening of the religious aura surrounding the monarchy, therefore, deeply threatened their position. The government had long preached the value of the king's unlimited authority to make law; when God's law checked such authority, elites could tolerate his claim. Spreading secularization among urban elites undermined one part of that political consensus. Louis's blatant flouting of God's commandments, and the public rebukes he received for it from his own confessor starting on Easter 1739, completed the job. Elites began to look for a new way to protect their property and position, a search that led directly to the French Revolution.

Louis XV and Louis XVI ruled over a kingdom undergoing rapid transformation in basic demographic structures, in economic organization, and in social and cultural life. During Louis XV's lifetime, French adults began to live longer: life expectancies for those who reached twenty moved past sixty years of age. In the last third of the century, another dramatic demographic shift took place: more children survived. Infant mortality, which had been 50 percent in the period before 1750, dropped to 40 percent, anticipating the improvement in child survival in the nineteenth century. In the countryside, mortality of those aged one through nine dropped from about one in six to one in seven; in towns, the rate dropped from one in four to one in five. The greater life expectancy of adults and, to a much lesser extent, the decline in infant mortality, led to a sharp increase in the French population, which rose to more than 26 million. At the end of the century, the birth rate dropped slightly, perhaps in reaction to changing infant mortality, presaging the massive decrease in the birth rate in the nineteenth century.

Chapter 10 provided details on the French economy in the eighteenth century, with special emphasis on changing rural structures. Those changes, however, could not be fully effective because of the lingering legal and political impediments to economic liberty. Despite the modernization of many economic sectors, the old state structures remained in place; indeed, in many sectors the Crown amplified the structure of privilege. Virtually all commercial transactions theoretically involved a royal official, collecting a fee, or an individual, such as guild warden or a wine broker, who had paid a fee to the Crown in order to supervise a given activity and pocket the transaction fee. Although almost all economic activity should have come under such supervision, in fact, public annoyance at such interference encouraged an enormous black market sector, which, alas for historians, has left relatively few records.

Much of that activity took place inside the great agents of change: the towns and their suburbs. Paris stood far above any other French city, its population more than 600,000 by the time of the Revolution, so it deserves a description of its own. Rouen, Nantes, Bordeaux, Marseille, and Lyon, although only about a sixth (or less) the size of Paris, dominated their hinterlands and expanded rapidly after 1720. The middling towns, those of 20,000–50,000 population, followed widely different trajectories, while most smaller towns (10,000 or less) actually declined in population. The total urban population of France remained remarkably stable in the eighteenth century, but its distribution shifted markedly toward the larger cities.

∾ The New Urbanism

Paris

> *Paris is the only city of the kingdom where sensations are at their most vivid, where the spirit and the heart acquire their maximum energy.*[2]

> Parisian bookseller Nicolas Ruault, to his brother
> (living in Evreux), August 1786

In the spring of 1757, the young Parisian Jacques-Louis Ménétra set out, like so many thousands of craftsmen before him, on his Tour de France. Ménétra traveled by way of Versailles to Orléans, thence through the Loire valley to other large towns such as Tours and Angers. After a brief stint with the Royal Navy at Saint-Malo, he ended up at Nantes. From Nantes, he visited the major southwestern towns: Poitiers, La Rochelle, and, of course, Bordeaux. Crossing France, he passed by way of Toulouse, through the great towns of Languedoc, like Montpellier, Narbonne, and Béziers, and up the Rhône valley, through Arles, Valence, and Lyon. He finished his great circle by way of Dijon and Auxerre, arriving back in Paris in 1763. He revisited this last leg of the route a year later, but then settled in Paris.

This intrepid wanderer left us a journal of his trip, one filled with countless details of everyday life. Ménétra borrows tales from others (taking on himself the role of hero); he exaggerates his own importance at every turn; he maltreats women and brags constantly about his successes as a lover. Despite his many flaws, Ménétra offers a penetrating look at popular attitudes toward many subjects: work, leisure, politics, and family life among them.

What did it look like, this France of 1757, as seen through the eyes of a young apprentice, later journeyman glazier? We can see elements of continuity. Ménétra often works for clergymen (churches, after all, had lots of glass) and for nobles. Again and again, he encounters aristocratic clients such as the abbess of Beaumont-lès-Tours, Henriette de Bourbon-Condé. As a journeyman, "he" has dealings with the major political figures of Bordeaux—intendant, First President of the Parlement, and governor of Guyenne—during a crisis involving recruitment of journeymen for the militia there in 1758.[3] The journeymen had a clear conception of the political rivalry among these men, using the First President against the intendant to achieve their goal. Later, back in Paris, we see him crossing paths with various Parlementaires and even, as a court tennis player, with the duke of Orléans and the prince of Condé. His work takes him to the palace at Versailles, where he sees the royal children.

Ménétra follows the normal life of a young artisan from Paris. As a young man, he takes his Tour de France, living fast and loose. Coming back from the Tour, he obtains work in Paris and soon settles down, getting married and starting his own shop. He raises two children and even, as a member of the fire brigade, becomes himself a member of the forces of order. As a guild master in a building trade, he lived through good times from the 1760s through the 1780s, because Paris expanded its habitat so rapidly in those years. Louis-Sébastien Mercier, writing in the 1780s, felt that a third of the city's buildings had been constructed since 1760. The duke of Orléans, who owned the largest forests near the city, became the richest man in France selling wood for this building boom.

Ménétra violates many of the rules of his own guild. He subcontracts work for others. He fights constantly with the guild wardens, accusing them of seeking to monopolize the trade of the city to their own benefit. At the fireworks for the marriage of the future Louis XVI and Marie Antoinette, his wife nearly becomes one of the scores trampled to death by the panicked crowd. In the chic café de la Régence, in what is now the Palais-Royal, he claims to have played checkers with a certain M. Rousseau: "We played I lost." The glazier informs us that "Both of us had the same clothes but not at all the same (breadth of knowledge) Between us (the difference) was like night and day."[4]

Ménétra's Paris changed dramatically, both in terms of the social distribution of the population and in terms of geographic size. The city of Louis XIV encompassed perhaps 1,000 hectares; that of Louis XVI included more than 3,400 hectares. As we can see from the city plan (see map, below), Paris engulfed such former suburbs (*faubourgs*) as Saint-Germain, Saint-Jacques, Saint-Honoré, and Saint-Martin. Places such as Montmartre that had been distinct villages in the seventeenth century became faubourgs in the eighteenth. Even so, Paris had a much tighter circumference than it does today. When the government erected the customs wall around the city in the 1780s, it established barrier posts at such sites as the current place Denfert-Rochereau, the place de la Nation, and the place Stalingrad. The sixteenth through twentieth *arrondissements* of today's Paris were then independent villages like Montmartre. Areas now in the heart of the city, such as the Invalides, only began to be integrated into Paris in the eighteenth century.

Starting from the Left Bank, we would find in late eighteenth-century Paris a poor workers' district near the place Maubert and the rue Saint-Jacques, extending out to the faubourg Saint-Marcel. At the center of the Left Bank lay the Latin Quarter, dominated by the Sorbonne and the students. Further west, the enclave of Saint-German-des-Prés, owned by the monks of that abbey, did not form a legal part of the city. Beyond this district, Paris expanded rapidly, particularly in the section near the Luxembourg Palace. Continuing along the river, the Invalides quarter and the Faubourg Saint-Germain had many new aristocratic homes.

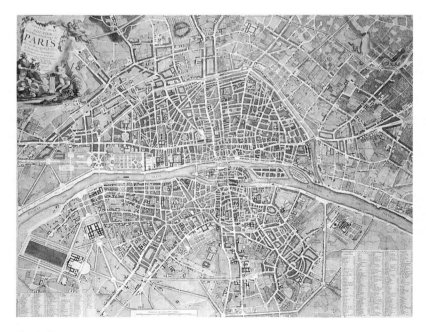

Paris in 1767.

*Rousseau at the Café de la Régence in 1771. Menétra may or may not have played
checkers with Rousseau, but he could well have seen him at the Café de la Régence.*

SOURCE: Musée du Petit Palais.

Crossing the river to the Right Bank, the Marais, the center of elite society in the
early seventeenth century, fell out of fashion: immigrant Jews from Alsace settled
there. The most chic elements of Parisian society gathered in the Faubourg Saint-
Honoré, near what is now the place de l'Opéra, and around the Champs-Elysées,
where the government created the place Louis XV, known to us as the place de la
Concorde. These sections of the city had relatively low population densities, as few
as fifty or even twenty-five people per square hectare.

The Louvre and the Tuileries dominated the river bank down to the Pont Neuf,
but just across from the palace one found a teeming popular quarter leading to les
Halles. France's greatest market had thousands of merchants and shop owners, and
tens of thousands of carters, porters, and day laborers, to say nothing of those working
in the food trades: butchers, bakers, vegetable sellers, wine merchants, and countless
others. People lived cheek by jowl in old parishes like Saint-Germain-l'Auxerrois or
Saint-Jacques-de-la-Boucherie. The old center of the city became progressively more

The interior of the Café of Manouri. Most of the clients are men, some of whom also smoke.

SOURCE: Bibliothèque Nationale, Cabinet d'Estampes.

overcrowded with the poor: densities reached $1,300/ha^2$ (square hectares) and never fell below $500/ha^2$.

The east end of the city included the parish of Saint-Antoine and the Faubourg Saint-Antoine, quarter of artisans and immigrants. More than 60 percent of its metal, wood, and construction workers came from outside Paris, as did almost 80 percent of those in its food trades. Much of the economic activity in these suburbs escaped official supervision; Ménétra, although a sworn master of the glaziers' guild, illegally subcontracted work in the suburbs and collected his money under the table. The Bastille, looking down on the working populations of Faubourg Saint-Antoine, dominated the eastern end of the city. The profound social divisions within the city had important political consequences from the Revolution until the expulsion of many of the poor from Paris in the "urban renewal" after World War II.

Some elements of eighteenth-century Paris survive in the contemporary city. One gets a sense of the crowded, narrow streets in sections like the Marais or the rue Mouffetard. Many of the great aristocratic hôtels, such as the Musée Rodin (built for the financier Peyrenc in the 1720s) survive throughout the city; the monumental buildings dot its landscape. The eighteenth-century churches—Sainte-Geneviève (the Panthéon), Saint-Roch, the Madeleine, and Saint-Sulpice—can still be seen, in their Classical splendor. In a certain way, contemporary Paris, despite its many churches, substantially understates the remarkable number of ecclesiastical buildings the city once held: parish churches, convents, and abbeys. The interiors of many of the parish churches bear witness to artistic embellishments of the eighteenth century, particularly in the ornate preaching pulpits, made usually of carved wood but, on occasion, as at Saint-Roch, of marble. Among the secular monuments, perhaps the two most enduring are the Hôtel de Ville, built to replace the town hall gutted by fire in 1772, and the place Louis XV/place de la Concorde.[5] The place de l'Hôtel de Ville, like the place de la Concorde, shows a greater emphasis given to open space, air, and light, in comparison with earlier conceptions of the city. One easily compares the place de la Concorde, with its vast open spaces and its broad array of avenues branching out in many directions, with the place des Vosges (built under Henry IV and Louis XIII), with its colonnaded sides and its tight enclosure, or even with the tightly enclosed place Vendôme, finished in 1697.

Eighteenth-century Parisians lived in a world in transition, one to which we would have difficulty adapting. Their city had limited, albeit much improved access to water; they lived in poorly heated and ventilated rooms, in houses known only to the initiated, on streets often without signs. In the late eighteenth century, the central and city governments fought to put numbers on the buildings and tried, with less success, to make all corner building owners put up a street sign so that people did not have to rely simply on the forest of shop, tavern, and merchant ensigns festooned on every building. The city government introduced a better police force, one with substations throughout the city and nearly three times as many men as under Louis XIV. The city fire company also took root; at first, people did not like this innovation, but they soon came to accept the obvious benefits of fire brigades. They and other Parisians demanded better lighting; in the 1760s, the city introduced the reflecting street lamp, greatly improving illumination.

Despite better lighting, improved sewage disposal, numbered houses, named streets, fire brigades, and a larger, more efficient police force, Paris remained a premodern city. Houses had better insulation—the poor less often hung cheap tapestries on their walls for warmth—but still could not provide amenities we would take for granted. Quite apart from the obvious lack of ready water, which had to be carried to upper floors by hand, most dwellings afforded little privacy: people performed bodily functions in hallway enclaves, in full view of passing neighbors. Families lived in single rooms, surrounding a fireplace, although after 1750 stoves slowly began to replace the hopelessly inefficient open hearth fireplaces. Many workers lived in holes-in-the-wall, using the public facilities around them as part of their "private" space. Thus artisans often ate in taverns or obtained meals from professional food preparers. The poorer elements of the population could not receive someone into their home, but rather met with others at the local tavern to share a meal or a drink. However much the police might call such taverns public space, and consequently demand the right to oversee them, neighborhood inhabitants viewed them as private space, as an extension of their homes. People lived in intimate connection, bound together by smell, sound, and sight. The German novelist Patrick Süskind has captured the essence of this world in a brilliant description of eighteenth-century Paris:

> there reigned in the cities a stench barely conceivable to us. . . . The streets
> stank of manure, the courtyards of urine, the stairwells stank of moldering

wood and rat droppings, the kitchens of spoiled cabbage and mutton fat; the unaired parlors stank of stale dust, the bedrooms of greasy sheets, damp featherbeds, and the pungently sweet aroma of chamber pots. The stench of sulfur rose from the chimneys, the stench of caustic lyes from the tanneries, and from the slaughterhouses came the stench of congealed blood. People stank of sweat and unwashed clothes; from their mouths came the stench of rotting teeth.... The rivers stank, the marketplaces stank, the churches stank.[6]

Our eighteenth-century Parisian rarely bathed, often bought prepared food or ate in a tavern (the latter more typical of men), and lived in a world of pungent aromas, with few modern creature comforts. Yet these people, above all the women, founded mass consumer society. The same consumer objects that suddenly appeared in households of rural notables in the middle of the century began to spread rapidly among the Parisian lower classes in the second half of the century. Women bought hand-held face mirrors and changed the style of their clothing. Previously, people had typically owned brown, black, and grey woollen clothing. In the days just before the Revolution, however, women bought blue, green, or yellow garments, often made of cotton. Women owned leather shoes, even multiple pairs! They wore silk or cotton stockings; some adopted cotton undergarments.

Men more slowly adopted these habits, but Ménétra's *Journal* bears ample witness to the changes. He has many of the old habits: he lives a violent life as a young man, constantly on the lookout for the police. Time and again, one of his friends dies in a fight, drowns, or is severely injured at work; he himself breaks a leg. He suffers from syphilis and takes mysterious powders, which he sells to others, for a cure. He drinks heavily, in taverns, where he goes to seek work and companionship. Yet he also participates in the emerging modern lifestyle. He eats meat all the time, sometimes orders "salad," drinks coffee, and, most notably of all, writes well enough to keep a journal. He provides an ideal example of the lower middle class of the towns, who provided the mass market so critical to the spread of the products of eighteenth-century manufacture and colonial trade.

Provincial Towns

[Saacken] *said, "Now we'll burn Paris!"*—*"Do nothing of the sort; France will die of that alone!" Blücher replied, indicating the great ulcer gaping below them in fire and fume in the valley of the Seine.*[7]

Balzac, *Colonel Chabert,* reproducing the supposed
conversation of the Prussian generals in 1814

What about other French cities? One of the enduring elements of French culture is the contrast, often hostility, between the capital and provincial cities. Parisians have long looked down their noses at "backward provincials"; those living in provincial cities have long agreed with Blücher, viewing with disdain the "moral swamp" of Paris. Such surface hostilities aside, Paris has also provided a cultural model for

The new professions: a pastrymaker shows his wares in an eighteenth-century version of advertising.

SOURCE: © Ronald Sheridan/Ancient Art & Architecture Collection.

provincial elites. Fashions spread out from Paris to Nantes or Dijon or Marseille in the eighteenth century, just as in the twentieth. In the eighteenth century, the royal government encouraged such developments. Architects who found royal favor in Paris obtained important commissions in the provinces. One royal architect, Jacques Gabriel, father of Ange Gabriel, designer of the place de la Concorde, developed the baroque place Royale in Bordeaux, while another, Victor Louis, created the new royal theaters of Bordeaux and Nantes. The wealthy merchants of Bordeaux put up a new Chamber of Commerce building; they and their peers at Nantes built new houses in

Fishwives and launderesses. Women dominated certain professions, such as these two, or lace-making (and selling); they ran many shops in other trades.

Source: © Giraudon/Art Resource, New York.

previously undeveloped quarters of their cities, such as the Ile Feydeau at Nantes. Where the Ile Feydeau section relies on streets only slightly wider than the traditional narrow ones, the later place Royale allows a half dozen broader thoroughfares to come together in an open, airy circle. These newer buildings, like the theaters, demonstrate the shift away from the Rococo style of the early eighteenth century, toward the neo-Classical style of its second half, but many of the mid-century developments remained Rococo.

Perhaps the most magnificent example of this airy, open square appeared in Nancy, the capital of Lorraine. The last duke of Lorraine, Stanislas Leszczynski, had constructed a central place; its focal point, as in similar new *places* at Nantes or Bordeaux, was a statue of Louis XV. The place Stanislas is one of the glories of European Rococo, bearing ample witness to the importance of eighteenth-century French provincial cities as cultural centers in their own right, yet it clearly demonstrates as well the dominance of Paris, in that a royal architect designed and executed it.

Today, one of the buildings of the place Stanislas houses a luxury hotel. In the eighteenth century, a similar establishment could be found on the place Royale of Nantes: the hotel Henri IV, a prototype of a new level of amenity for travelers. The Englishman Arthur Young, who traveled through France in the 1780s, cited the Henri IV as one of the finest hostelries in Europe. He contrasted it sharply with the ubiquitous traditional inns, somewhat rough-and-ready for the sophisticated traveler–tourist of the late eighteenth century, which he castigated as dirty, poorly managed, overpriced,

*The great stairway of the Opera House of Bordeaux, created by the
royal architect Louis Henry in the 1780s. Henry built a similar structure
at Nantes, one that also illustrates neo-Classical architecture reaching
the provinces.*

SOURCE: © Giraudon/Art Resource, New York.

and distinctly inferior to their English counterparts. Here again, we see one of the beginnings of consumer culture: better-off people traveled in Italy and France for leisure and education, taking what some already called the Grand Tour of Europe.

The growing provincial cities, like Rouen or Bordeaux, mirrored developments in Paris. Bordeaux ripped out its old housing, but kept the narrow medieval streets; Rouen's city center kept buildings and all, as the city's rabbit warren of narrow streets today charmingly attests, and built around it. Caen created wider, airier spaces by building up: 10 percent of its windows could be found on the third story of a building, as against the 0.3 percent of a nearby small town like Bayeux. At Nantes as in Paris, the government tore down the houses on bridges, to improve traffic circulation. Many towns tore down their walls, evidence of internal security and of the greater need for freedom of movement.

These provincial cities followed widely divergent paths in the eighteenth century. Nantes and Bordeaux, doubling their populations, form something of an exception, both in terms of their demographic growth and in terms of the rapid expansion of their wealth. Other large cities, such as Caen or Lille, expanded due to the growth of manufacturing, usually located in the suburbs. Towns that relied on domination of a largely agricultural heartland, like Vannes or Châteaudun, or on their roles as administrative centers, like Rennes or Aix, tended to stagnate. Their economies remained strongly traditional, with fewer dynamic elements of new trade or new manufacture. France developed profound social, economic, and political rifts. One France expanded in population, diversified and prospered in its economy, and evolved a new society. The second France sent its children to the first, seemed to stick to its old ways, and, in many ways, absorbed changes, such as increased popular piety, that had taken root in the first France a century earlier. Yet many of these children came back to their villages, acting as agents of cultural change in rural France. They brought with them new cultural objects and ideas, which penetrated even into mountain valleys. The contrast between the "two Frances" should not obscure their fundamentally symbiotic relationship.

The great provincial cities provided a kind of halfway house for the transition to the more modern society and economy. Ménétra's *Journal* offers extensive descriptions of many of the great towns and of an even larger number of small ones. He encounters many of the same socioeconomic upheavals common in Paris. At Nantes, the journeymen are on strike against the masters. In the Loire Valley towns, the two main groups of journeymen fight a pitched battle over hiring rights. In Bordeaux, call-ups for the militia (during the Seven Years' War) lead to massive demonstrations and to conflict between visiting journeymen and those from Bordeaux itself. In Nîmes, Ménétra nearly marries a Protestant widow; nearby, in the Papal enclave of the Venaissin, he finds the papal legate maltreating Jews. He recounts tales of murderous innkeepers, of unsafe roads, yet also of widespread companionship and sociability. He finds himself welcome everywhere—his nickname on the Tour is the Welcome Parisian—and spreads his tales of life in Paris. He and others like him spread ideas and cultural norms into every corner of France. His journal provides clear evidence that the great conflicts over control of labor that took place in Paris and in other modernizing cities, took place as well in small provincial towns. The pace of change may have varied, but not its ubiquity.

Urban tax rolls provide direct insight into the pace of change. The surviving rolls for the Breton towns of Morlaix and Lannion (each holding between eight thousand and ten thousand people), which lay about twenty miles apart, show how change created new identities and new professions. Morlaix had close ties to the international market, especially England and Ireland, as the center for export of linen textiles from western Brittany. In the 1720s, its tax rolls offer listings for such professions as bookseller, café owner, coffee merchant, pastry maker, caterer (*traiteur*), and lemonade seller. The rolls of Lannion, a town not directly connected to international markets, do not indicate a single person following any of these trades in the 1720s. By the 1750s, however, Lannion, too, had cafés and pastry specialists and caterers.

Kingship and the State

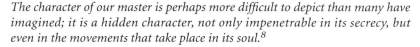

Louis XV: from the Bien-Aimé to the Old Roué

The character of our master is perhaps more difficult to depict than many have imagined; it is a hidden character, not only impenetrable in its secrecy, but even in the movements that take place in its soul.[8]

The duke of Luynes, speaking of Louis XV in 1743

The ruler of this rapidly changing France, Louis XV, had a tempestuous relationship with his subjects. The peace and prosperity of the 1720s and most of the 1730s gave way to the war and economic dislocation of the 1740s and 1750s. The entire country rejoiced when Louis and his wife, Maria Leszczynska, produced a son in 1729, and again in 1744, when he recovered from a dangerous illness. Yet Louis's reputation had started to decline in 1739, when he faced the extraordinary personal humiliation of being denied the sacraments. His confessor refused to give the king Easter communion because Louis's persistent infidelities demonstrated his lack of contrition. The king, refused communion, suffered the public humiliation of being unable to perform the ancient ritual of the king's touch.[9] His reputation in Paris suffered considerable damage from this lapse, although the evidence from the countryside suggests that the king remained popular there.

In the 1740s, Louis also assaulted the social sensibilities of his courtiers by choosing a commoner, Jeanne-Antoinette Poisson, as his "mistress in title," a position traditionally reserved for an aristocrat. Louis soon made her marquise of Pompadour. Mme de Pompadour came from a family associated with the General Tax Farm. She brought Farmers General socially into the highest echelons of Court life. Many in the old nobility resented it, and Louis had great difficulty getting someone officially to present her at Court.[10]

Popular opinion reviled Mme de Pompadour. Singers on the Pont Neuf denounced the "emptying of the king's treasury for buildings, for frivolous expenses; the State falls into decadence and the king gives order to nothing, nothing, nothing."[11] Unlike previous royal mistresses, Mme de Pompadour had an important say in government policy. She conducted business with ministers: the king once forced chancellor Lamoignon to discuss a decision with her and the surviving correspondence of many eighteenth-century ministers shows that they wrote directly to her about government affairs. She made and unmade royal ministers, such as the count of Maurepas, whom she forced out as minister of the Navy in 1749, or Machault d'Arnouville, whom she first raised to the highest positions and then discarded. Louis even admitted to Machault in the letter demanding his resignation that personality conflicts between Machault and Pompadour led him to dismiss a minister whom he felt to be supremely capable.

Most of the literature about Mme de Pompadour and later mistresses focuses on the scandalous and salacious, rather than on the important political role of the Court.

Given that courtiers often wrote or sponsored the street songs of Paris, the massive outpouring of abuse on Pompadour likely originated with unhappy courtiers and dismissed ministers.[12] Personal vendettas aside, Pompadour served as the representative of the Farmers General, who wanted control over the key royal oversight officials: the controller general, the minister of the Navy, and the Keeper of the Seals. Louis XV claimed that he fired (1745) Controller General Philibert Orry, a man of uncontested capacities, because Orry had "insulted" Mme de Pompadour. Orry's fall, however, surely stemmed more from the resentment of his former allies the Farmers General at his close supervision of their financial network than from an insult to their protector.

Pompadour's death hardly ended the connection between the royal mistress and the king's ministers. Louis XV's continued personal debauchery, and his choice of Mme du Barry as his final official mistress, exacerbated the government's problems. She allied with the ministers Terray and Maupeou to overthrow (1770) Pompadour's favorite, the duke of Choiseul. Well after his death, Louis XV's sexual escapades fascinated his former subjects. The *Anecdotes on Mme the countess of Barry* (1775) was one of the best-selling forbidden books of the last decades of the Ancient Régime. This salacious inside look at palace intrigue painted a picture of an old king devastated by his loss of virility. According to the anonymous author:

> Thanks to her apprenticeship with Mme Gourdon [a Parisian procuress], she [Mme du Barry] picked up tricks that would help arouse the feeble libido of the aging Louis XV, that would confound her competitors at court . . . In short, prostitution was the secret of her success. The duc de Noailles had said it all when the king expressed his amazement at the unprecedented pleasures he had experienced with his new mistress. "Sire," the duke replied, "this is because you have never been to a whorehouse."[13]

Talk of prostitution at the Court did much to sap the prestige of the monarchy. The reputation of Louis the malevolent and often pitiful roué tarnished the entire Court. Louis XV's personal conduct, combined with broader political, social, and cultural developments, delegitimized the government and desacralized the monarchy. After a brief interlude in the 1770s, the vitriol heaped upon Louis XV and Mme du Barry found a new target: the "Austrian"—Queen Marie Antoinette. Assaults on her moral turpitude provided a leitmotif of political discourse throughout the 1780s and into the early days of the Revolution.

The Fatal Wound: The Seven Years' War and the Death of the Old Regime

The country certainly suffered . . . from a deficiency in military direction, and in political and ministerial leadership . . . a deficiency all the more astonishing in that intellectual, manufacturing, and commercial cadres manifested an astonishing prowess.[14]

E. Le Roy Ladurie, describing France
at the moment of the Seven Years' War

CHRONOLOGY	1754–1787

1754	Start of French and Indian War in North America
1756	Start of Seven Years' War in Europe
1757	French routed at Rossbach; French victories in North America
1759	British forces drive French from North America (Plains of Abraham); British Navy annihilates French at Quiberon Bay
1763	Peace of Paris; France loses Canada, Louisiana, and Sénégal
1772	First Partition of Poland
1778	French ally with the United States of America in War of American Revolution; Russian war with Ottoman Empire
1781	French Navy defeats British at Yorktown and in India
1783	Peace of Paris; United States becomes independent; French regain Senegal; Russia seizes the Crimea
1787	Prussians invade the Netherlands, suppress republican uprising; Russia attacks Ottoman Empire

Intrigue at the Court of Louis XV destabilized his state, but the French defeat in the Seven Years' War struck the fatal blow to the political Ancien Régime. The Peace of Aix-la-Chapelle (1748), ending the War of the Austrian Succession, did little to restore relations between Austria and Prussia. In the New World, British and French colonists harbored deep-seated animosity, which burst into war again in 1753. A minor encounter in the wilds of Pennsylvania, in which a young Virginia colonel named George Washington surrendered the aptly named Fort Necessity to superior French forces, led a year later to a full-scale British invasion of the disputed region near today's Pittsburgh. General James Braddock marched two crack British regiments and a large contingent of Virginian militia into the wilderness. The small French force fled at first volley, but France's Indian allies took to the woods and slaughtered the cream of the British army.

Braddock's Defeat touched off the French and Indian War. In 1757, a combined French and Indian force drove south from Canada and captured the British forts on Lakes Ticonderoga and George, events immortalized in James Fenimore Cooper's *The Last of the Mohicans.* The tide turned decisively in 1758 and 1759, when Britain mounted three expeditions: one force turned Fort Duquesne into Fort Pitt; a second drove the French from the Hudson Valley; the third sailed up the Saint Lawrence River to Québec, capital of Canada. Trapped below the city, the English found a hidden trail up the cliffs, forcing the French to do battle on the Plains of Abraham, outside the city. On 13 September 1759, the famous opponents, Wolfe and Montcalm, met their deaths in the battle that made Canada an English colony.

The European fighting began in 1756, after the "diplomatic revolution." Since the late fifteenth century, the European system of alliances had revolved around the quarrel between the Habsburgs and the ruling family of France.[15] The Austrians played on the French desire to preserve the status quo in Europe, as the prince of Conti had successfully argued to Louis XV in a famous memorandum of 1747. Austria suggested that the two states had a common enemy, Prussia, because a third major land power, dominating central Germany, upset the balance of power. Frederick II, hearing of these negotiations, abandoned his French ally for an English one, in the Treaty of Westmister (January 1756). This new alliance system, France and Austria against Prussia and England, did not go over well in France, particularly among the army officers, who detested the Austrians.

The Seven Years' War produced a complete stalemate in Europe. One battle deserves special mention for its long-term impact on France: the catastrophic defeat of Rossbach (1757). Frederick the Great, outnumbered 54,000 to 21,000, routed a Franco-Imperial army, capturing 7,500 officers and men at a cost to his army of only 165 killed. French military commentators alternately blamed the troops, the large number of non-noble officers, and bad training. Non-military commentators blamed the noble officers, particularly the many who surrendered without a fight. The real culprit, the incompetent prince of Soubise, got a promotion.

The Peace of Paris (1763) restored the status quo in Europe, but it changed the map of much of the rest of the world. The decisive English victory in North America, and the Royal Navy's annihilation of its French rival at Quiberon Bay (1759), led to great French losses. The Treaty of Paris gave Canada and Florida to England, Louisiana to Spain (a French ally, in recompense for the loss of Florida), and stripped France of many other colonial enclaves, such as Sénégal, several Caribbean islands, and almost all its possessions in India. Economically, the return of peace demonstrated the economic benefits preserved by the skillful French negotiators. They managed to keep Saint-Domingue, Martinique, Guadeloupe, and the tiny islands of Miquelon and Saint-Pierre, off Canada, used by French mariners to work the Grand Banks, the world's richest fishing grounds.

France emerged from the war with virtually no navy, with a tattered army, with its finances ruined by debt, and with a fundamental conflict between the king and his most important judicial and political institution, the Parlement of Paris, over the nature and practice of government. The dismal failures of 1753–1764—in religious policy (1753–1757), in prosecution of the war (1758–1761), and in fiscal reform (1760–1764)—obliterated any chance that the status quo could continue and created a climate for fundamental, all-encompassing reform. In keeping with the evolving ministerial system of government, the state sought to enact such changes purely within the realm of administrative reform. Those outside the government, however, had begun to question the legitimacy of the state itself. During the initial phase of the dispute, in the 1760s, the opposition focused on strengthening traditional checks on the monarchy, above all the Parlements. By the 1780s, however, public opinion had come to reject both the ministerial system and the Parlements as means to reform the state.

How did this momentous change come to pass? What precisely did "institutional reform" mean in the France of the 1760s? Louis XV's state superficially resembled that of his predecessor, but the French government increasingly fell under the aegis of the royal ministers, rather than that of the king. People took to calling them the six kings: the king himself, plus the "kings" of Paris, finances, the army, the navy, and foreign affairs. This system, which contemporaries called "ministerial despotism," differed markedly from the monarchical government practiced between about 1660–1750. It lacked central direction, either provided by a Louis XIV or by a king working with a key minister, as during Cardinal Fleury's ascendancy in the 1730s. By the 1780s, the ministers of war or of the Navy would make substantial financial commitments without checking with the controller general to see if he had the money; individual ministers conducted what amounted to private foreign policies.

Louis XV exacerbated the problem of ministerial infighting by a dramatic policy shift in the middle of the 1750s. Under Louis XIV and during the first half of the eighteenth century, the French state kept the key state positions in the hands of two distinct groups. The great nobility monopolized military commands and the important positions at Court, such as the first gentlemen of the king's bedchamber. Court positions did not carry any policymaking attributions, yet they gave their occupants daily access to the king. The king rotated the two positions of first gentleman every year, in recognition of their extraordinary importance to a noble family's ambitions.[16]

The leaders of the ministerial bureaucracy came from a different milieu, that of the highest families of the administrative and Parlementaire elite. Louis XV abruptly changed this division in the 1750s, inviting marshal Belle-Isle to be minister of war; he later appointed nobles to the Navy and foreign affairs ministries.[17] Under Louis XVI, the ministers of war and of the Navy remained titled sword nobles, while the old administrative and judicial elite kept the remaining ministerial positions. The two elites did not get along; indeed the marriage patterns of their leading members indicate profound social hostility.[18]

The entry of titled nobles into the Council of State had the unintended, and unpleasant, side effect of dragging Court intrigues ever more deeply into the already Byzantine struggles played out in the Council. The close connections of the ministers with lobbying interests exacerbated the problem. Here the split between the old noble families in charge of the ministries of war and the Navy, and the robe nobility families serving as controller general and chancellor (or Keeper of the Seals) abetted permanent ministerial infighting and governmental instability. With the exception of Jacques Necker, all of those running government finance from 1763–1787 came from the Parlement—l'Averdy, Terray, Joly de Fleury, d'Ormesson, and Calonne—or members of robe dynasties who had made a life in the high administration, like Turgot. In the 1760s, Controller General Terray and Chancellor Maupeou, both Parlementaires, fought the dukes of Choiseul and Praslin, ministers of war and of the Navy, just as in the 1780s Ségur and Castries, sword noble ministers of war, fought the career diplomat Vergennes (Foreign Minister) and the Parlementaire Miromesnil (Keeper of the Seals).[19]

These quarrels represented more than personal infighting. The most powerful groups in French society—the sword nobility, the Parlementaires, the financiers, and the bankers—all had, or sought, representatives within the Council of State and control of individual ministries. Like the key elements of modern American government, ministries represented both their own institutional needs and the desires of powerful interest groups. The controller general usually answered to the financiers, just as the minister of war represented the interests of the military complex.[20] The sword nobility favored an aggressive foreign policy because war was good business for them: more commissions, more chances for promotion, massive military spending. Little wonder that the duke of Choiseul plotted constantly for renewed war against England in the 1760s or that the duke of Castries pushed an active military solution to the Dutch crisis of 1786.

The state consisted of several interlocking elements, running down from the Council of State to the village tax collectors. The ministers and their staffs stood at the top, yet the central bureaucracy had scarcely four hundred full-time employees in 1750, and perhaps twice as many in the 1780s. They relied on a network of about forty provincial intendants, drawn from the masters of requests of the King's Household; the intendants had a local staff of about five hundred subdelegates, assisted by clerks. The army, the General Tax Farm, and the venal officers dwarfed these tiny nascent bureaucracies. The peacetime army had about 140,000 men, complete with a bureaucracy attached to the Ministry of War. The General Tax Farm employed platoons of inspectors, accountants, clerks, and "archers" (armed guards); it had so many long-term employees that it became the first French business to offer a retirement plan to its workers in the 1780s. The venal officers, who ranged from the proud presidents of the Parlements down to the humble collectors of taxes on tanned hides, numbered about 70,000; they provided the physical mass necessary for governance.[21] Historians who portray eighteenth-century French government as a struggle between these venal officers and the intendants ignore two fundamental realities:

1. Intendants all owned a venal office—master of requests.

2. Forty men could hardly administer a country of 26 million people.

The intendants increasingly interfered with every conceivable aspect of local life, and they did become the symbols of royal absolutism in the countryside, but their subdelegates, to cite only one example, invariably came from the ranks of the venal officers. Moreover, the old administrative system, built around the financial system of élections and the judicial one of bailiwicks and seneschalsies, still provided the government's first line of contact with most French people.

The royal courts, in particular, fleshed out the first line of government in the provinces. On a daily basis, the regular judicial pyramid (bailiwick/seneschalsy/provosty; presidials; Parlements) did more than any other institution to administer the kingdom. The many specialized courts, from the sovereign Chambers of Accounts, Courts of Aids (chief tax courts), and Currency Courts, down to ecclesiastical courts, Waters and Woods courts, courts of the constabulary, merchants' courts, and, of course, seigneurial courts, to which at least two-thirds of French people were still subject, handled the civil litigation that wove the fabric of everyday life. The Parlements, above all that of Paris, which had jurisdiction over about 40 percent of France, stood at the apex of this system.[22]

Royal officials had both judicial and executive functions; some of them, such as the Parlements, had *de facto* legislative ones. Our modern ideas of the separation of powers, although they date back to precisely this period (and in large measure to a specific eighteenth-century Parlementaire, the baron of Montesquieu), did not apply to eighteenth-century French government. The combination of executive, judicial, and *de facto* legislative power made judges the essential mediator between the government and civil society.

Nor should we ignore the largest number of government employees: the village tax collectors. The peasants themselves elected four to six collectors in each parish, about 160,000 men per year. These men served for a year, receiving a percentage of the money collected as their "salary." Yet even "permanent" royal officials usually had other interests and other jobs. Royal office provided relatively little direct financial return, but it offered the opportunity to share power and thus to obtain money in other ways. Tax officials could offer assessment breaks to their friends and relatives; guild wardens, acting on behalf of the state, could use their position to drive rivals out of business.[23] Royal judges could use their knowledge of upcoming property settlements to manipulate land markets.

The government failed so utterly during the Seven Years' War that reform of every aspect of state administration dominated the political agenda of the 1760s. The War demonstrated France's economic reliance on its empire, and so spurred reinvestment and reform in the Navy. The duke of Choiseul and his cousin, the duke of Praslin, overhauled everything, from ship construction to procurement, recruitment, and training. The humiliation at Rossbach spurred similar changes in the army: the troops received more training, better weapons, better sutlering, and improved permanent barracks. Regimental commanders lost control of recruitment and, to some degree, of responsibility for discipline, which began to be more systematic (and thus, in theory, more equitable). The government established a naval college, a training facility for civil engineers, the Royal Military Academy at Saint-Cyr, and the school of military equitation at Saumur. The corps of trained engineers helped greatly improve the road system of eighteenth-century France, cutting travel and postal times between Paris and other major cities: by 1765, couriers could ride from Paris to Lyon or Bordeaux in under a week.

These positive steps to reform the military included one fundamental mistake. The reforms eliminated many superfluous officers and created a relatively streamlined force, but, starting in the 1740s, the army's officer corps grew increasingly distant from the larger nation, due more stringent rules against commoners becoming officers.[24] The elite French Guards, 40 percent of whose officer corps of the early 1740s came from the families of financiers and judicial nobles, instituted (1745) rules requiring four and then five (1781) generations of nobility in the male line for new officers. The rule worked: only five of the five hundred men received as officers after 1745 got an exception.

The rules got tougher everywhere after the Seven Years' War. By the 1770s, the Royal Bodyguard demanded three hundred years of proven nobility for its officers. In 1781, the infamous Ségur Law mandated that all officers in the infantry, cavalry, and dragoons demonstrate four generations of male nobility in their families. The Ségur Law accurately reflected the intense quarrel between the administrative elite and the military one, although it also reflected the concerns of the reformers about the professionalization of the army. Nonetheless, the sharp split between the noble officers and their men had momentous consequences in June 1789.

The hue and cry for reform exacerbated Louis XV's post-1750 penchant for government by whim. His constant shuffling of ministers created permanent turmoil in the central administration. He changed controller general in 1754, 1756, 1757, 1759 (twice), 1763, 1768, and 1769. The often innovative reforms of a l'Averdy (1763–1768) or a Turgot (1774–1776) invariably failed due to a combination of resistance from entrenched interest groups, of Court intrigue, and of royal vacillation. The nonfinancial elements of the controller general's responsibilities offer an ideal example of the terrible effects of inconsistent policies. The government created a free market in grain in 1763, restored price controls in 1768, a free market in 1774, and finally went back to price controls for good in 1776.

Louis created instability in French foreign policy by conducting private diplomacy, known as the "Secret of the King." Louis first used his cousin, the prince of Conti, as a conduit for secret negotiations in Poland. When Conti fell into disgrace for plotting against the king, Louis took over this private network, without bothering to tell his own foreign minister about the parallel negotiations. When the chief clerk of the Ministry, who had handled both sets of correspondence, lost his ministry job in 1759, the "Secret of the King" lost its only connection to official channels. Two-track diplomacy hamstrung foreign policy.

The supercharged political climate of the 1750s, with its violent dispute about religious and jurisdictional matters, encouraged people to discuss reform, but the Seven Years' War brought such discussions to a halt. The dismal end to the war brought financial, political, and philosophical issues together again, and encouraged a flood of reformist pamphlets. In this climate of total reform, many legists even began to take up Montesquieu's ideas and to question the nature of sovereignty in France. Louis XV supported many of the ministerial reforms, but he explicitly rejected these ideas. In a dramatic shift in the French political landscape, his leading subjects, above all the Parlements refused to back down.

The Sovereignty Question and the End of Legitimacy

The sovereign power resides in my person only.

Louis XV, 1766

The quarrel over sovereignty at first remained hidden behind an ancient religious dispute: the dying embers of the feud between the Jansenists and the Jesuits. The Parlement of Paris, Gallican to the core, had long supported the Jansenists and objected to *Unigenitus* on the grounds of the public good: the king simply could not give away his rights over the French Church because he did not possess them.[25] They claimed to defend the right of the French kingship, an eternal entity and public office instituted to protect the common good, against the whims of a living individual, the actual person reigning as king. That person, although the living embodiment of the kingship, did not *own* anything related to the commonwealth, he merely had use and stewardship of it. The king could not act in as an individual to limit the powers and authority of his public office because he lacked the right to do so.[26]

The opponents of *Unigenitus* thus argued that an individual king, Louis XIV or Louis XV, could not accept a Papal bull that would limit the authority of the kingship. The royal government, supported by much of the Church hierarchy and, above all, by the Jesuits, continued to press for the interpretation that *Unigenitus* was a constitutional law of France. When the Parlements seized on the occasion of a civil lawsuit to confiscate the property of the Jesuits in France and then to expel them (1762), the king first sought to defend his old allies; two years later, he had to give in and sign the order for their expulsion. Without the Jesuits, Jansenism became irrelevant, so the debate turned to a purely secular issue that had lain at the root of the quarrel all along: who held the sovereignty?

By the 1760s, a state bureaucracy had essentially taken over the stewardship of the commonwealth from the king. The debate in the evolving public sphere thus sought to redefine the *res publica* (commonwealth) as the preserve of the nation; in time, that argument led to a rejection of both the king and the Parlements. Increasingly unsatisfied with a system in which the king alone made law, elites demanded that they have a hand in making the law. The most vocal proponents of such a view, precisely because they had an institutional venue, were the Parlements, notably that of Paris, and the lawyers who practiced before them.[27] These legal men focused on the authority to make law, which they situated in the nation, not the king. Steeped in two centuries of political theory that enshrined lawmaking as the defining mark of sovereignty, the Parlements now claimed, on behalf of the nation, to share that authority with the king.

The conflict became evident in a series of quarrels lasting from 1764–1771. The Brittany Affair, a dispute both jurisdictional and personal between the Parlement of Brittany, led by the king's attorney, Louis de La Chalotais, and the royal government, in the person of the duke d'Aiguillon, governor of Brittany, laid out the fundamental conflict. The intersecting lines of principle, personality, and politics created a chaotic situation.[28] Louis arrested La Chalotais and sought to break a strike by the Parlement by suspending the court and threatening to create a new one. The Parlements of Rouen and Paris leapt to the defense of their colleagues, insisting that the king had a responsibility to the "nation," represented by all of the Parlements, who together formed a "union of classes," a phrase they took from the sixteenth-century chancellor Michel de l'Hôpital.

The king and the Bretons eventually compromised, in large measure because Louis needed the cooperation of the Estates of Brittany to borrow money. Louis restored the Parlement and withdrew d'Aiguillon. The locus of conflict now shifted to Paris. The Parlement of Paris, taking up Montesquieu's argument in *The Spirit of the Laws* (1748), argued that the nation was the source of all sovereignty and that the Parlement itself, together with the king, represented the nation.[29] On March 3, 1766, Louis XV unexpectedly appeared at the Parlement, to hold a *lit de justice* and address the issue. The famous Seance of the Scourging left no doubts in anyone's mind about the king's position:

... the sovereign power resides in my person only ... my courts derive their
existence and their authority from me alone ... to me alone belongs the
legislative power ... the rights and interests of the nation, which some dare
to regard as a separate body from the monarch, are necessarily united with
my rights and interests, and repose only in my hands.

Four years later, the Parlement of Paris, trying the disgraced d'Aiguillon, explicitly
stated that the nation held the sovereignty. The king responded quickly: he dismissed
all charges against the duke and, in a final insult to the Parlement, even named him
as Foreign Minister.

Louis XV sought to mollify the Parlement by bringing two of its key members
into the government. First president of the Parlement of Paris, René de Maupeou,
became chancellor, while a councilor, the Abbé Terray, became controller general. In
1770–1771, these two men masterminded another royal attempt at reform. Terray
reduced payments on some forms of royal debt and rescheduled others, cut expenses,
and streamlined parts of the financial administration; he carefully avoided tamper-
ing with the Paris annuities, the form of royal debt most owned by Parlementaires.
Terray sought as well to reform the new land tax, the *vingtième,* which heretofore
had relied on declarations of landowners as the basis of assessment.[30] He did not
fully succeed. He and his cronies also practiced extensive corruption; shares in the
General Tax Farm suddenly found their way into the hands of Mme du Barry, to
members of Terray's family, to his notary, and to the king and two of his daughters.

Parlementaire opposition to some of Terray's financial edicts, coupled with existing conflicts between the king and the courts, led to a showdown in the winter of
1770–1771. The Parlement had accepted the debt rescheduling but balked at regis-
tering an edict that enunciated the absolutist principles of the Seance of the Scourging. The court declared a cessation of activities. Maupeou responded by suspending
the Parlement of Paris and the Court of Aids. Soon, the suspension spread to other
Parlements, which Maupeou abolished, setting up alternative courts in their place.
This new court system functioned for three years, rendering justice in the king's
name, and instituting much-needed reforms, such as the abolition of special fees
(*épices*) paid to judges by all litigants. Maupeou's Revolution, as his contemporaries
called it, alerts us to the differing opinions among French elites as to how to enact
reform. As first president of the Parlement, Maupeou served its interest, but as the
king's chancellor, this same man masterminded the abolition of the Parlements.

Louis XV's death derailed the Maupeou Revolution. The new king, Louis XV's
grandson, Louis XVI, and his queen, Marie Antoinette, detested Maupeou, Terray,
and their protector, Mme du Barry. Louis XVI quickly dismissed the two ministers,
locked du Barry in a convent, and brought back the old Parlements, which provoked
universal rejoicing. Parisian crowds stoned the carriages of the disgraced ministers
and burned them in effigy, while the welcome-back ceremonies for the Parlements
in cities such as Bordeaux lasted for days. Louis XVI recalled the 76-year-old count
of Maurepas, disgraced by Pompadour in 1749, to be his chief minister, and began
anew the game of musical chairs with the seats of his Council of State. The young

king turned to Anne-Robert-Jacques Turgot, former intendant of Limoges and well-known Physiocrat, to be his new controller general.

Financial Woes

The government needs money; that says it all.[31]

Nicolas Ruault, January 1787

Turgot offers a particularly interesting example of a minister seeking reform, because of his close ties to the Physiocrats. Turgot and the Physiocrats represented a step in the direction of modern government and modern economics, although they remained also firmly rooted in the past. The Physiocrats denounced government interference in the economy, and sponsored free market ideas.[32] These ideas had some currency in France in the 1760s: the government briefly created a free market in grain and abolished the state monopoly West India Company in 1769. The free market in grain led to riots on behalf of fixed prices and against the so-called Famine Pact. The latter belief, quite popular in the 1760s, held that Louis XV had made a pact with the grain producers to help them increase prices; he and his corrupt courtiers, of course, would get their share of the increased profits. Louis responded by firing the minister who proposed the free market and by reinstituting controls.

Turgot restored the free market as part of a broad program of reform. Once again, a minister set out on an ambitious search for progressive change; once again, the powerful vested interests of the kingdom defeated him. Turgot's deregulation of the grain trade, enacted on the eve of a widespread grain shortage, led to riots so severe they are known as the Flour War. He also attacked other forms of interference with the free market, such as guilds. His attack on these privileges, in the Six Acts of 1776, led to his dismissal. Louis XVI henceforth followed his grandfather's dangerous example, constantly changing controllers general.

Turgot's failure alerts us to the remarkably charged atmosphere of the 1770s. The dramatic economic growth of the eighteenth century had spun the French economy out of control. Old mechanisms of control, such as the guilds, could no longer function in the same manner. The massive change in relations of production, market conditions, and capitalization in some sectors of the economy far outstripped the capacity of existing authorities to deal with the situation. Guild masters and journeymen fought tooth and nail for control over human labor; guild masters fought each other for control of market segments; masters and merchant–manufacturers fought for control of markets. The government did not follow a consistent economic and tax policy. Reformers such as Turgot or Silhouette wanted to unleash free market forces, but because the government had sold massive amounts of its debt to guilds—by means of offices and annuities—and other corporations, it could not afford to alienate them. The same forces had been at work in the Brittany Affair of the 1760s. Louis XV may have wanted to override the Estates of Brittany and humble its Parlement, but he needed them to borrow money.

The practice of borrowing money through corporations—provincial estates, the Church, town governments, guilds, royal officers—made the government dependent on those corporations. Most government reforms of the late eighteenth century, however, targeted the privileges of one or more of these corporations. Rousseau, in the *Social Contract,* provides us with a clear contemporary view of the danger of these corporations to the public good. He defines three wills—individual, corporate, and general—held by people in civil society. Modern commentators invariably focus on the conflict between the individual and general wills, but Rousseau singled out the corporate will as the most damaging to the social peace. He accurately reflected the opinion of his time that the great corporations stood in the way of any serious effort to reform state or society. Most reformers wanted to free individuals to choose their own actions. The abolition of the West India Company monopoly, the debates about the grain trade, the abolition of the guilds, the rise of the Physiocrats: all of these symptoms were evidence of the increased pressure to recognize individual rights. The government often supported such efforts, in theory, but found itself hamstrung in practice because of its financial dependence on the corporations.

Shortly after the fall of Turgot, political and diplomatic events combined to exacerbate the financial difficulties. France offered clandestine aid to the rebel British Colonies of North America in their fight for independence. Beginning in 1778, France joined the war. This time, with a reformed army and navy and an American ally, France won. The French Navy, in particular, acquitted itself admirably, both in American waters—where it played the determining role in the successful siege of Yorktown (1781)—and in the Indian Ocean. This military success came at a staggering financial price: the government sold more than 650 million *livres* of annuities to cover its costs, which ran to more than a billion *livres.* This debt, combined with the 1.5 billion *livres* borrowed during the Seven Years' War, left the government on the verge of bankruptcy. Moreover, the government's financial difficulties became matters of public discussion when Necker, head of finances after 1778 and disgraced in 1781, published what he claimed was an accurate picture of royal finances, the *Accounting to the King* (1781). The book was a runaway best-seller.

The government's finances, long a secret matter known only to the king and his ministers, had become the subject of open public debate. Necker's figures for pensions paid to the great nobility scandalized the public, and annoyed those courtiers who felt themselves underappreciated. Six years later, another controller general, Calonne, published his version of the budget (a more accurate one), showing receipts of about 475 million *livres,* but expenses of 600 million, half of it for interest. Despite the greater accuracy of Calonne's figures, public opinion tended to accept Necker's version of the story; Parisians made of this Swiss banker their prospective financial savior and, indeed, the savior of the nation.

French government finances required four immediate reforms: administrative stability; reduction of privileged exemptions (both full and partial); public control of public finance (i.e., an end to the General Tax Farm); and rational debt service policies. Very powerful forces opposed these reforms. The Farmers General and their financier allies wanted to keep control of state indirect taxation and to continue the ruinous debt service structure, from which they profited, and many of the powerful privileged, such as the nobility and the Church, wanted to keep their fiscal privileges. At the highest levels of government, the financiers demanded one set of policies, with full control to remain in the hands of the receivers general and the Farmers General. The bankers demanded different policies. Little wonder that reform proved so elusive.

The Death Rattle, 1781–1786

> . . . the discontent of the wise and settled people, of the true people, of magis-
> trates, even of nobles, that's what the Court must fear, inasmuch as this sedi-
> tion is one of the spirit and is practically universal. It is not those who break
> windows, throw fruit at noses, who flog police informers, who are to be feared,
> but those who reason, who reflect.[33]

Nicolas Ruault, August 1787

The government stumbled from reform to reform throughout the late 1770s and early 1780s. Ministers such as Necker and Calonne tried a wide range of administrative changes. Necker went the furthest, cutting down the number of disbursement treasurers in the military from twenty-seven to two and even abolishing the most powerful position in the royal direct tax system, the receivers general. His first disgrace, in 1781, led to the restoration of the receivers general and to the revival of the old financial mafia running the government's finances. The receivers general and the Farmers General retained an ever more iron-clad grip on the government's money: between 1781 and 1788, the share of money siphoned off by the tax farmers and the royal tax officials rose from 43 to 55 percent. The bankers, upset at the fall of Necker, were mollified by an increase in interest paid on life annuities, which rose to 10 percent in 1782.[34] The central government's expense for interest rose from 160 million *livres* a year in the late 1770s to more than 300 million *livres* by 1787. Available figures from town governments and provincial estates suggest that their interest expenses for forced government loans also nearly doubled in the final decade of the Ancien Régime.

The heart of the Ancien Régime's terminal political crisis was very simple. It could not raise enough taxes to pay interest on its loans. Moreover, by the late 1780s, the government had exhausted its credit. Potential creditors were very wary of lending more money, no matter what the rate of interest. When the king asked the clergy for a special grant of money in 1788, their official spokesman, the archbishop of Narbonne replied:

> You demand 80 millions from us. . . . Your Majesty knows that we will have to borrow it, that one cannot borrow without being assured of the public confidence, that the public confidence can only be acquired by a legal registration [of the edict], that the nation is accustomed to view as legal only a registration in the Parlement, that at this moment there is no Parlement, that the clergy cannot thus count on a registration, that there will therefore be no registration, and [therefore] the clergy cannot pay the 80 millions demanded.[35]

Moneyed elites wanted guarantees that they would actually get paid the interest on the annuities they bought. A key difference between the French monarchy of the seventeenth century and that of the late eighteenth century was that the moneyed elites would no longer tolerate a partial bankruptcy. Creditors, whether in France or Geneva or Amsterdam, no longer trusted the government; they wanted better assurances of repayment. In order to protect themselves, French elites demanded, purely and simply, control over taxation and government spending, as the cahiers for the Estates General of 1789 make quite clear. During the fiscal crisis of 1787, the Parlement of Paris declared again and again that it had no right to approve taxes and that previous approvals had merely been abuses: "it returned to the first usages of the monarchy and upheld once again the principle that it did not have the right to impose taxes on the people; that this right only belonged to an Estates General or to *the nation assembled by means of deputies.*"[36] In that sense, something like the events of 1789 and their immediate outcome was inevitable. The French government simply had to change to a system in which the propertied elites would have direct say in tax and borrowing policy. Those elites had to put up the money and, without a say on taxation and lawmaking, they were no longer willing to do so.

The fiscal problems of the monarchy had an impact on every aspect of government policy, as the three great diplomatic problems of Louis XVI's reign demonstrated. In the 1770s, still able to borrow money, France could act decisively in foreign affairs, as in its intervention in the American War of Independence. In the 1780s, however, France became a passive observer of diplomatic events because its lack of money made it impossible to project military force. When Catherine the Great of Russia seized the Crimea in 1783, France could do nothing more than encourage Joseph II of Austria to refuse Catherine's deal for dividing up the Balkans. In 1787, the French had to stand idly by when the Prussian army invaded Holland (September), France's erstwhile ally, to restore the deposed House of Orange. France could only look on in dismay at the renewed Russian attack on the Ottoman Empire in that year.

France did take a more aggressive line outside of Europe. The success of the American Colonists gave France hope for new markets in the New World and the alliance with the Dutch (signed 1785) gave France the possibility of using the Dutch colony at the Cape of Good Hope as a springboard to an attack on British India. Throughout the 1780s, the French Council of State debated a variety of plans, some of them truly harebrained, for attacking the British in India and for annexing Egypt.[37]

The End of Royal Sovereignty, 1786–1787

We know that the sovereign alone has the right to make the law, but we also know that this law must be verified, recognized as good, useful, and conforming to the principles of the monarchy. And if the votes are not free in this verification, if the presence of the sovereign prevents this freedom of action, then one no longer finds there a sovereign, but a despot, a tyrant.[38]

Nicolas Ruault, 26 May 1788

THE ODD COUPLE: LOUIS XVI AND MARIE-ANTOINETTE

Louis XVI and Marie Antoinette bear no little responsibility for the unraveling of affairs. Ruault called Louis a king "much beneath his century and his nation. No one can ignore his lack of an interior life, his absolute incapacity in the art of governing and in the control of his wife." In another letter, Ruault suggested that Louis's "unhappiness came from his overly weak and soft character. He is not fit to hold the reins of so great a state; he was born to be an Elector in Germany."[39] Louis faced the humiliation of his public avowal of impotence in the early 1770s; even when an operation enabled him to perform his husbandly duties, street theater (and others) continued to mock him.

Louis was not quick-witted and so cut a dismal figure in "smart" society; his younger brothers, the counts of Provence and Artois, were more socially adept. Ruault constantly reports plots to remove Louis and replace him either with his brother or with a regency in his son's name. Louis disliked Court ritual and detested hunting, an activity critical to the personal relationships of his ancestors and their Court nobility. He preferred to be by himself, hiding in his attic workshop, tinkering with his beloved collection of clocks and spying on the courtiers in the gardens. Maurepas found the new king lacking in royal dignity and rebuked him for his conduct at one royal ball:

> Foreign ambassadors who were present were scandalized; you entered without the captain of your guards and without having yourself announced; your chair was not even there, and you rushed to get in. We are not accustomed to seeing in public our sovereign count for so little.[40]

This rotund, slow-witted, vacillating man made a disastrous king at a time of crisis. Louis did not want for human qualities—he showed himself a man of great physical courage, he was a devoted family man, and he sincerely loved his subjects—but he lacked the ability to be king.

His wife's shortcomings exacerbated his own. Where he hesitated to act, she was impetuous. Where he took seriously the responsibilities of kingship, she was a frivolous, empty-headed, spoiled brat. Where he was a man of blameless personal morality, she led a life of constant scandal. Throughout the 1780s, French public opinion turned against the queen: Necker's publication of the massive pensions to her favorites, like the Polignac family, alienated less favored parts of high society (as well as ordinary taxpayers); the affair of the Diamond Necklace, in which a member of one of the highest French families, the Cardinal of Rohan, had to suffer a public trial for conspiracy to seduce and discredit the queen, dropped her standing even lower. The trial of Rohan demonstrates precisely how far the government had lost control: the Parlement of Paris acquitted him of the charges.

Nor should we underestimate the impact of such actions on the opinions of ordinary people. Shortly after the Rohan trial, the guild of the fishwives of Paris, who had had the immemorial privilege of sending a delegation to present their respects and a gift to the queen of France on her birthday, refused to visit Marie Antoinette, making known their moral disapproval of the queen's behavior. Crowds booed her when she appeared at the palace of Saint-Cloud on the outskirts of the city. The streets of Paris were filled with libels against the queen in the 1780s, often accusing her of infidelity with partners ranging from the king's brothers to her ladies-in-waiting. Her enemies (and his) invented many of these tales, but her personal behavior was far from beyond reproach and her penchant for profligate spending—preserved for posterity in *The Hamlet,* the mock village she had created for she and her friends to play at being milkmaids in the gardens of Versailles—provided a ready target for the monarchy's opponents. This unfortunate royal couple provided the final blows to the legitimacy of the state.

From the eighteenth century to the present day, historians and others have debated the question of whether or not Ancien Régime France could have reformed itself. Had the government reformed, so the argument goes, France could have averted its Revolution. This argument neglects one of the most obvious aspects of French history from the 1760s to the 1780s. The French government tried every sort of reform of which its leaders could conceive. They all failed because they did not address the basic issue facing the state: its loss of legitimacy. A state based on the shared fiction of the king's indivisible sovereignty, a state based on the concept of citizens without sovereignty, could not work.[41] Moreover, elites had begun to shift the focus away from the state and toward the nation. Nicolas Ruault stated the matter unequivocally in a letter to his brother in May 1788: "It is not the king who will charge himself to place limits to his authority. That supposes in him a wisdom, a philosophy, which he does not and cannot have."[42]

France needed sound public finances, which it could get only by obtaining the full confidence of the moneyed elites, who would grant it only if they received some measure of control over fiscal policy, as their counterparts in England possessed. Registration of fiscal edicts in the Parlements provided some measure of control, but the king's regular use of special powers to override Parlementaire objections (including periodic suspensions of the Parlement of Paris, such as the one cited by the archbishop of Narbonne in 1788), and the gradual loss of confidence in the Parlements themselves, made a new controlling body a necessity.

The fundamental conflict revolved around property: its definition and protection. The state, by its essence, could not solve this problem because it rested on three principles that could not survive the changing social, economic, and political reality of the eighteenth century:

1. Everyone was unequal.

2. The king held sovereignty, the ability to make law equally binding on all.

3. Protection of the rights of "citizens," especially their property rights, lay in the realm of contract rather than that of law.

The conflict between the first two of these principles is fairly obvious. Society accepted the principle that everyone was unequal and that unequal treatment of people (for example, by the law) was legitimate precisely because people were unequal, but the king demanded that everyone, of no matter what status, obey laws he promulgated. The conflict between these two views led to two distinct "parties." The ministerial advocates looked to the king's unlimited lawmaking authority as the means by which to reform society. The traditionalists, led by the Parlements, argued that "ministerial despotism" threatened the security of everyone's rights, especially their property. The Parlements' supporters felt that contracts supervised by the courts served as a brake on the authority of the king and his ministers. When the government tried to circumvent the old contracts, the Parlement became the defenders of the public interest. Yet as holders of important privileges, and as defenders primarily of the privileged orders, the Parlements could scarcely be relied upon to reform the abuses of the system. In sharp contrast to the 1760s, when an important segment of public opinion accepted the idea of Parlements as protectors of the commonwealth, in the 1780s, public opinion had come to reject both the ministerial system and the Parlements as means to reform the state.

In the eighteenth century, political discourse returned to the language of the sixteenth century, which stressed the preservation of the "public good" or commonwealth. The French political class had long recognized the distinction between the king's good and that of the public. From the 1760s through the 1780s it moved decisively to reject the government's proposition, defended for almost three hundred years, that the two were coterminous. They thus rejected the proposition's underlying premise, that the state, represented by the king, was the commonwealth. The leading French political thinkers of the eighteenth century harkened back to sixteenth-century ideas to demand a new form of government. Chancellor d'Aguesseau wrote of kingship:

> There has never been and never will be a power that does not come from bosom of God himself. It is He who, having formed men for society, wanted the members of which it is composed to submit to a superior power. . . . In consequence, it is He who is the true author of that power. . . It [the power] can be in the hands of a single person or of many, depending on the constitution of each State. . . . God has even found it good that the manner of this choice depend as well up to a certain point on the will, the genius or the inclination of each of the peoples who form these great societies that one calls a nation or a state.[43]

D'Aguesseau sounds here much like his sixteenth-century predecessors: power comes from God, but men themselves have a degree of choice in who wields it and how it is constituted. Anyone familiar with French legal history, as d'Aguesseau was, could not ignore the historical precedents. The Bourbons, like the Valois, owed their throne to French law, not to God.[44]

The royal ministers had developed a very different idea of government and the people. Charles Gravier, count of Vergennes, Minister of Foreign Affairs of Louis XVI, summarized these views in his response to the demands of the Estates of Brittany to name their own deputies to Court. The Estates cited their "natural rights" in this matter, but Vergennes argued Breton liberties were "simple privilege, founded on a specific concession [of the king]." The Estates argued that their liberties were "rights that the interest of your State did not permit them to forget," whereas Vergennes countered that "the State is the fatherland (*patrie*)."[45] As Vergennes's remark to the Bretons suggests, even in the 1780s, the royal administration continued to propound the view that the state itself could be the repository of the public good. D'Aguesseau's comments, made in the 1740s, show the same ambiguity about the distinction between the "state" and the "nation."

By the 1780s, French elites had clearly formulated an idea of the nation that lay outside, and above, the state. They no longer trusted *either* the state itself or the king to protect the public good. The public wanted a share in the guardianship of the public good, so that neither the programs of ministerial reform nor the ideas of the Parlementaires had any serious chance of success in the long run. Twenty years of discussion on this matter had produced a consensus that the nation was the source of all sovereignty and that its representative body had to share in the lawmaking power. The documents prepared for the Estates General in the spring of 1789 provide irrefutable evidence of massive, indeed nearly universal support for this idea. Unanimity about the sovereignty of the nation, however, did not produce a universal definition of the political nation itself. People could not agree on who constituted the nation, a problem that would bedevil the Revolutionaries, too.

The old, Aristotelian definition of the commonwealth as the collectivity of the citizens did not help much, because it left citizenship undefined. Jean-Jacques Rousseau's *Social Contract,* published in 1762, accepted the principle that all adult men constituted the nation, a definition not likely to find many takers in Parlementaire circles. Earlier, Voltaire had defined the English nation as "the most numerous, even most virtuous, and by consequence the most respectable part of men, composed of those who study the laws and science, of merchants, artisans, in a word, of all that which is not a tyrant."[46] The *cahiers* of 1789 once again make clear the popular preference: their authors had little doubt—all of the citizens called to participate in the drawing up the *cahiers,* together with their families, constituted the nation.

Many looked to England for a model of what to do, but whatever one's attitude toward the English Parliament, all agreed that an institution that gave propertied elites some say in the management of public finance had to exist. The heavy burden of taxation, and the massive abuses within the royal financial system, created a direct connection between the concern of elites about their private property and their concern about the public good. Powerful forces lobbied for change, for movement, and against stability and the old order. The monarchy, the very cornerstone of that old order, was not a likely implementor of the needed changes, however attractive some of the reforming initiatives of certain ministers may have seemed.

The Ancien Régime had fallen apart by the early 1760s, not only in an economic and social sense, but in a political and institutional one as well. The regime had lost its legitimacy. The key demands of elites make obvious the shortcomings of the existing system, and the underlying assumptions of the various parties. The king believed he had custody of the public good, so that only he and his advisors needed to know the workings of the government. The opposition, in contrast, believed the government should reveal its inner workings and make public all information relevant to the stewardship of the commonwealth.

The debate focused on royal financial affairs; it culminated in 1781, when Necker published his famous *Accounting to the King.* In the next six years, others published similar documents, so that informed public opinion for the first time had access to the inner workings of the government's finances. Once this information became public, everyone knew that the king and his ministers had not taken proper care of the *res publica.* The political nation resolved to take it back.

∾ Cultural and Social Change

In changing words, one changes ideas; and in changing ideas, one changes events.

Nicolas Ruault, June 1789

The French Revolution casts an enormous shadow over the second half of the eighteenth century. We know the Revolution took place, so the irresistible tendency is to look for its antecedents in the generation or two before it. In the nineteenth century, French scholars sought out intellectual antecedents in the Enlightenment. By the 1930s, historians had accepted the premise that the ideas of the Enlightenment played a critical role in the coming of the Revolution; some even argued that the changed perspective created by the Enlightenment led directly to the Revolution. Eighteenth-century observers, like the royal minister d'Argenson, argued that the radical changes in "public opinion" would lead to political change, even "revolution," although he would have given that term a less all-encompassing meaning than it took on after 1789.

In recent years, however, this old consensus has fallen apart. While some historians insist that the ideas of the Enlightenment led directly to the Jacobin Terror of 1793–1794, others insist on the uniqueness of the ideas of the Revolution. The latter point out the obvious disjuncture between the political discourse of, say, 1791 or 1792, and that of the early 1780s. Most would accept a clear split between the republicanism of late 1791 and 1792 and the ideas of the early 1780s, but others also insist on a disjuncture between 1789 and 1788. For them, the Revolution created its own political dynamic, one clearly distinct from the discourse of the Ancien Régime. These questions will concern us more in the next chapter, insofar as they relate to the Revolution itself, but they do force us to look carefully at social, intellectual, and cultural developments in the dying days of the Ancien Régime.

French political discourse underwent a fundamental transformation between the Seance of the Scourging (1766) and the calling of the Assembly of Notables in 1787. By 1787, French elites universally accepted the idea that the monarchy needed some sort of representative body to act as a check on the arbitrary behavior of the "six kings." Public opinion rejected the premise that the Parlements could serve this function. People supported the Parlements as the only existing line of defense against ministerial despotism, but also understood that the Parlements were part of the problem, not the solution. How typical Nicolas Ruault must have been in his reaction to the events of 1787, which led to the convocation of the Estates General: "Well, we are witnesses to a strange and rare event. An Estates General at the end of the eighteenth century!" Later, during the debates on how the Estates should meet, he would write: "The previous Estates Generals cannot serve as a model for this one. The spirit of former times is not that of ours: enlightenment has only spread for about a century; we have become a reasoning people."

Ruault reveals the critical factor of change between the 1760s and the 1780s: French elites had broken with tradition, had accepted the idea that reason should serve as the arbiter of the nation's political life. That willingness to accept change—to abandon tradition for tradition's sake—had its roots, as Ruault suggests, in the ideas of Descartes and the philosophers who followed him, but it also had roots in the broader changes in French culture, especially those that took place after 1750. The newly literate population—something like half of the men and a third of the women in northern France could sign their name to a marriage certificate—everywhere bought more books. Literacy brought more people into politics, at least as interested observers.

Women readers demanded more literary texts; production of novels rose markedly. Romantic novels, such as Rousseau's *Julie, or the New Heloise,* were the best sellers among nonreligious books. In the eighteenth century, far more people read Rousseau's fiction than ever read his political philosophy. Despite what we would view as his misogynist ideas, women formed the core of his readership. He and other Romantic authors offered women real benefits: prominent female characters, respect, security. Rousseau's bird-in-a-gilded-cage imagery, and his insistence on the emotionality (and hence nonrationality) of women grate our sensibilities; in a certain way, he denies the full humanity of women.

Looked at from the perspective of many eighteenth-century women, however, his ideas had a different resonance. In much of his writing, he places greater value on emotion than on reason; many of his readers shared that idea. Because women lived in a world of considerable physical insecurity, any man preaching respect for the physical safety of women would find a ready acceptance among women. Ménétra's *Journal,* with its constant tales of rape and sexual assault, makes chillingly clear women's justified concerns about physical security. Rousseau's ideas also blended well with the general cultural acceptance of the value of romantic love; by the late eighteenth century, people increasingly married for love. A literature that stressed that value, in France as in England, had a ready audience.[47]

Late eighteenth-century French literature ran the gamut from devout religious treatises to scandalous novels, like *Dangerous Liaisons* of Laclos, familiar to many today because of the recent films based upon it. People then as now bought mountains of ephemeral books. Most readers were far more familiar with adventure stories, supernatural tales, and romances than they were with Diderot's *Rameau's Nephew* or Rousseau's *Social Contract.* Some great literature had a broad audience: Rousseau's novels or his treatise on education, *Émile;* Voltaire's satires, notably *Candide;* Beaumarchais's plays, the *Marriage of Figaro* and the *Barber of Seville.*

The shift from Voltaire to Beaumarchais tells us much about the evolving nature of French society. *Candide,* published in 1759, assaults a wide array of targets. Voltaire mocks eighteenth-century warfare, implicitly indicts government spending priorities (the government in his fictional El Dorado focuses its resources on the public good, on the amelioration of the lives of its citizens), and preaches the simple life. Above all, however, he indicts the Catholic Church: its priests and friars are invariably villains, guilty of every conceivable sin.

Beaumarchais, writing twenty years later, focuses in another direction. He lampoons social mores, to be sure, but he offers a detailed indictment of the government, particularly of its financial system. The shift in primary target away from the Church and toward the government in these two works offers a fair indicator of the cultural change in the intervening generation. Beaumarchais also offers a much harsher critique of society itself.

From the 1760s to the 1770s, French writers published a wide range of materials, both in France and abroad. The authorities often winked at smuggling of banned texts, many of which made their way directly to Versailles in the government's own diplomatic pouches. People at Court simply had to know what was being said by a Rousseau or a Diderot in order not to appear ridiculous at the Parisian salons. The

FIGARO: THE POLITICAL BARBER

In the *Marriage of Figaro,* in particular, Beaumarchais puts revolutionary social ideas in the mouth of the valet, Figaro.

> No, My Lord Count, you shan't have her! Because you are a great nobleman you think you are a great genius . . . Nobility, fortune, rank, position! How proud they make a man feel! What have *you* done to deserve such advantages? Put yourself to the trouble of being born—nothing more! For the rest—a very ordinary man! Whereas I, lost among the obscure crowd, have had to deploy more knowledge, more calculation and skill merely to survive than has sufficed to rule all the provinces of Spain for a century! And yet you would measure yourself against me! (*Act V, scene 1*)

The original version set the play in France, rather than in Spain, so it is little wonder that Louis XVI banned its performance in 1781. Little wonder, too, given the incessant guerrilla warfare at the Court, that his brother, the Count of Artois, tried to have it staged privately for himself and some friends and that, at first failing to do so, he and others finally got the king to approve (in 1784). Beaumarchais, in the interim, had diplomatically shifted the action to Spain. Artois's action confirms the relative powerlessness of the royal family in the face of cultural change: in order to maintain his image as someone at ease in the "beau monde," Artois had to sponsor a play that must have assaulted his sensibilities, given that he was a raving reactionary.

The Comédie Française put on the first public performance on 27 April 1784. Duchesses, footmen, soldiers—everyone lined up in the foyer of the theater and in the streets outside from early morning to get seats. Beaumarchais made some intemperate remarks about the problems of getting the play to the stage, leading to his arrest and five days in prison. When he was released, he received a hero's welcome at the evening's performance of the play, one attended, so the editors of a recent translation of the play inform us, by the king's ministers. One wonders what they thought of Figaro's lament: "How I would like to have hold of one of those Jacks in office—so indifferent to the evils that they cause."[48]

Beaumarchais's experience demonstrates the loss of governmental control over the cultural life of the country. Elsewhere in the speech cited above, Figaro spells out some of the cultural complaints of Parisian elites. Figaro would have those in office know that "stupidities that appear in print acquire importance only in so far as their circulation is restricted, that unless there is liberty to criticize, praise has no value." Later, released from prison (where he had moldered for offending some foreign potentate with his writings), Figaro decides to

> sharpen my quill again . . . [because] . . . there had been established in Madrid a system of free sale of commodities, which extended even to the products of the press, and that, provided I made no reference in my articles to the authorities or to religion, or to politics, or to morals, or to high officials, or to influential organizations, or to the Opera, or to any theatrical productions, or to anybody of any standing whatsoever, I could freely print anything I liked—subject to the approval of two or three censors!

government, perpetually befuddled by this dilemma, actually stepped up censorship in 1783, despite its obvious unpopularity among elites.[49] Elite political society had a dual attitude toward the government:

1. It held the government in the lowest possible esteem, often seeing the ministers as figures of ridicule.

2. It wanted control of the state for itself, either by naming new ministers or by supporting a minister whose program met with a given group's approval.

Turgot was himself a *philosophe,* and contributed to the *Encyclopédie;* Necker's works met with an overwhelmingly positive response from the Parisian elite. Members of the highest nobility supported some of this dissent: the king's cousin, the duke of Orléans, who owned a private enclave, the Palais Bourbon (now called the Palais Royal) across from the Louvre, allowed the freest possible expression of ideas in his self-policed reserve. Its cafés became hotbeds of political dissent.

Yet the Enlightenment consisted of a mixture of the new and the old. Far too often, we have tried to create false dichotomies, such as the one between the cult of reason, supposedly enshrined in the Enlightenment, and the cult of emotion, represented by Romanticism. Literary criticism, in particular, has grown weary of this distinction. Scholars focusing on eighteenth-century French literature rightly emphasize the symbiotic relationship between reason and emotion in both movements. Focusing on those Enlightenment ideas that we find most amenable conveniently ignores the darker side of the *philosophes:* Voltaire, champion of religious tolerance, was also an anti-Semite.

Nowhere can we see the problem more clearly than in the visual arts. Eighteenth-century French art, especially painting, often jars our sensibilities, yet some of the artists have maintained or even enhanced their reputations. The great sculptors Étienne Falconnet (1716–1791), Jean-Baptiste Pigalle (1714–1785), Claude Michel (Clodion, 1738–1814), and Jean-Antoine Houdon (1741–1828) have left enduring works of art still appreciated. Falconnet's two most famous works could not be more different. In France, his 1742 *Sitting Cupid* provoked endless copies. The second piece, his equestrian statue of *Peter the Great* (1782) in Saint Petersburg, Russia, offers a fitting symbol of French cultural preeminence. Pigalle's fame rests above all on the magnificent funerary monument to marshal de Saxe in the Saint-Thomas church of Strasbourg, although posterity has judged less favorably the many busts he did for royal commissions. Pigalle also headed the Royal Academy of Arts, so he frequently fought with some of the more independent artists of the day. Houdon executed busts of many of the leading figures of the end of the century, such as Thomas Jefferson (1789).

Carle von Loo, the leading painter of the mid-century, has little reputation today. His contemporaries François Boucher and Jean-Baptiste Chardin have endured better. Boucher's utopian peasants, in the *Autumn Pastoral* of 1749, remind us of the rise of pastoralism, just as his *Triumph of Venus* (1740) and *Diana at Rest* (1742) illustrate the great vogue for nudes. Chardin, who received little respect in his own day, is perhaps not surprisingly the most sympathetic of the mid-eighteenth-century painters for our aesthetics. Chardin often painted understated domestic interiors, reminiscent of those of seventeenth-century Dutch artists.

Jean-Baptiste Greuze, who also painted in mid-century, has left an enduring legacy of paintings not at all typical in their subjects, one best symbolized by *A Marriage,* which shows a rich peasant giving the dowry to his son-in-law. The painting shows peasants living in a luxury few farmers could have imagined; it demonstrates as well an important eighteenth-century dichotomy: the active men and the passive women. Boucher offers a rare exception, in his famous portrait of Mme de Pompadour, which treats her with great respect as a *person*. (See Plate.) He shows her half reclining, fully dressed, in front of her bookcase, reading a book. Whatever else may be said against her, Pompadour was perhaps the greatest arts patron of her day, and an individual well versed in the culture of her time. In this, as in so many other things, she mirrored the tastes of the Farmers General, who also actively supported the arts. Most of Boucher's women, and indeed those of most painters, are treated as delicate, beautiful objects or, in some cases, as sentimental observers of male action. Later in the century, women became even more sentimentalized. Jean-Honoré Fragonard, perhaps best known for his four *Progress of Love* (1771–1773) paintings, done for Mme du Barry (who ultimately rejected them), remains the prototype of the painter of Romantic love.

The most famous painter of the late Ancien Régime, Jacques-Louis David, owes his greatest reputation to works done after 1789. Of his works executed under the Ancien Régime, the *Oath of the Horatii* (1785) and the portrait of the Polish noble Count Potocki, stand out as masterpieces. Potocki's portrait presages the later, more famous one of Napoleon crossing the Alps, while the *Horatii*, showing the sons of the Roman patriot Horace swearing an oath to defend the fatherland, offers a remarkable testimony to intellectual trends in the 1780s. David glamorizes the fatherland, and male loyalty to it above all, even to the king. The Romantic sensibilities of the two paintings are evident. David, like so many eighteenth-century painters, puts the women off to one side in the *Horatii*: they weep at the prospect of losing their loved ones. (See Plate 14.) Yet another David painting, *The Lictors Returning Brutus's Son*, shows the complexities of eighteenth-century attitudes toward such women: Brutus appears in the dark foreground, trying to remain Stoic in the face of his loss, while the womenfolk again weep. In this case, however, the illumination of the painting falls squarely on the women, who show that same sensibility so beloved by Rousseau, Richardson, Goethe, or so many other eighteenth-century authors.

Women played a vastly more important role in late eighteenth-century French art than they had in the past. Mme de Pompadour set a style others sought to follow. Women artists finally received some opportunities. Falconnet, mindful of his relatively weak skills as a portraitist, asked Marie-Anne Collot to sculpt the head of his Peter the Great. Diderot praised her skill, demonstrated as well in a bust of him. Two women painters, Adélaide Labille-Guiard and Elisabeth-Louise Vigée-Le Brun, had great success at Court in the 1780s, the latter painting official portraits of the queen (1783) and of the queen and her children (1787). (See Plate.) The Academy accepted both women as full members in 1783. Vigée-Le Brun's self-portrait with child bears testimony to her remarkable abilities, and to the singular esteem in which she has been held by the French artistic establishment: when I visited the Louvre in September 1999, it was the only painting by a woman born before 1800 hanging in the galleries.

Women also played a critical role in the Enlightenment, above all as patrons. They conducted the salons so essential to the development of Enlightenment culture. Women like Julie de l'Espinasse or Mme Geoffrin made of these salons the intellectual center of Paris, indeed one of the great centers of the Western world. One great writer after another read his work to a salon, and the sensibility created within their world, with its emphasis on equality and talent, did much to change political and cultural ideas. These women offered a place of conversation and intellectual inquiry to all of the *philosophes:* Voltaire, Diderot, Helvétius, Rousseau, indeed everyone of any consequence, passed through their doors.[50]

Many resented this newfound female power. Rousseau railed constantly against the salons and their learned women: doubtless he doubly resented his life-long dependence on female patrons. Lesser writers trained their poison pens on powerful political women, from Mme de Pompadour to Marie Antoinette. Pompadour and du Barry differed markedly from Marie Antoinette in that they were, by definition, committing adultery, and thus open to moral rebuke, but a more important distinction should be drawn between du Barry and Marie Antoinette, on one side, and Mme de Pompadour, on the other. Pompadour, unlike the other two, was a highly intelligent, well-educated individual; she intervened in politics as a politician, not as the mindless tool of Court intriguers. Yet even the other two could wield real power on their own. Du Barry commanded (and rejected) some of Fragonard's most famous work, and Marie Antoinette's decision to commission Vigée-Le Brun's official portrait of the royal family must be respected as a courageous, indeed stunning affirmation of women's abilities in a world more than a little reticent to do so.

The Enlightenment reached its peak of production, although not diffusion, between the late 1740s and the early 1760s. Few generations in one country have produced so much literature of so profound an historical significance. The central project of the period was the *Encyclopédie,* a self-described "systematic dictionary" that sought to provide broad definitions of terms both technical and philosophical. Its primary editor, Denis Diderot, wrote well-received novels, art and music criticism, and philosophical tracts. Diderot came from humble provincial origins, a member of the middle class of the small Burgundian town of Langres, educated there in its Jesuit *collège*. His collaborators included a wide range of the upper reaches of society, from nobles such as his co-editor Jean d'Alembert, financiers like Helvétius (one of the Farmers General), to learned doctors. Many of the leaders of this movement, like Diderot, received their education from the Jesuits: the *collège* Louis-le-Grand in Paris alone produced such figures as Voltaire and Helvétius. While in school there, they rubbed elbows with Turgot, both a *philosophe* and a royal minister, as well as the d'Argenson brothers (ministers under Louis XV and classmates of Voltaire) and Chrétien de Lamoignon, son of the chancellor, known to us by the name of one of his estates, Malesherbes.

Chancellor Lamoignon gave his son, Malesherbes, control of government censorship, and thus oversight of the book trade, from 1751–1763. The government's chief censor so much agreed with those he was supposed to regulate that he penned a defense of liberty of the press in 1758–1759, under the title *Memoir on the Book Trade.* Malesherbes had gone even farther in 1752: ordered to seize the second volume of the *Encyclopédie* just before it was to appear, Malesherbes wrote to Diderot to tell him that the book, as well as Diderot's papers, were about to be seized. When Diderot complained that he could not find someone to hide his papers on such short notice, Malesherbes volunteered his own house—an offer Diderot accepted. Thus the government censor's office searched Diderot's house for a manuscript hidden at

Mme Geoffrin's salon. Most of the guests are men, even though a woman runs the salon. Salon culture played a central role in political as well as cultural life, because in the salons the elite society to which the courtiers and ministers belonged passed judgments that could not be ignored.

SOURCE: © Giraudon/Art Resource.

their chief's own house! Malesherbes believed the government could use its resources more wisely by producing literature to justify its action, rather than by wasting resources on suppression of the printed word.

If the official in charge of the book trade held such opinions, how likely was it that the government would be able to control free expression of ideas? Nor was Malesherbes an isolated case. In the county of Burgundy, the intendant, Bourgeois de Boynes, had an arrangement with a local bookseller, Charmet. The bookseller had bribed the appropriate customs officials at an entry point, and backed up his work by providing Bougeois de Boynes with copies of philosophic books theoretically banned from France. After a mix-up at the frontier, when the officials mistakenly seized some books, Charmet provided the intendant with two lavishly bound copies of Raynal's *Philosophical History*; in return, the intendant saw to it that the inspectors burned only those seized books likely to be difficult to sell.

How dramatically did mentalities change in these years? The list of titles tells the story: Montesquieu's *Spirit of the Laws;* Voltaire's *Candide,* his *Century of Louis XIV,* and *Philosophical Dictionary;* Rousseau's *Discourses, Émile, New Heloise,* and *Social Contract;* Quesnay's *Economic Maxims;* Diderot's *Rameau's Nephew;* Buffon's

Natural History; Helvétius's *On the Spirit;* the *Encyclopédie* (volume I appeared in 1751), to mention only a few of them. What country, what time could witness the publication of such texts without undergoing an intellectual revolution? Although historians debate the precise nature of that change, a close textual reading of works from the 1750s demonstrates that authors such as Montesquieu had an immediate impact. Foreign authors, particularly from Great Britain, men such as David Hume in philosophy and Samuel Richardson in literature, also destabilized received wisdom. Diderot and many other *philosophes* accepted English empiricism, yet subscribed wholeheartedly to Richardson's sentimentality. Richardson's *Clarissa* or his *Pamela,* widely praised by Diderot and other French readers, lay the groundwork for Rousseau and Romanticism.

The revolutionary nature of the change led to significant problems of contradiction within the writings of the *philosophes.* Rousseau's ideas on the state of nature appear utterly different in the *First* and *Second Discourses* (1749 and 1755) and *Émile* (1762), as against the *Social Contract* (1762). In the former, Rousseau lauds man in the state of nature and decries the corrupting influence of society, yet in the *Social Contract* he contrasts the superior nature of civil as against natural liberty. Civil liberty, unlike natural liberty, is based on moral choice: "with civil society comes moral liberty, which alone renders man master of himself; because the impulse of appetite alone is slavery, and obedience to a law one has given oneself is freedom." Such contradictions appear everywhere in the work and lives of the *philosophes.* Voltaire railed against despotism, yet believed in enlightened monarchy, typified by his friend Frederick the Great of Prussia (with whom he later fell out). Voltaire, sworn enemy of despotism and abused power, wrote pamphlets for the French government at the time of the Maupeou coup. Diderot detested and denounced the Académie Française, yet his co-editor of the *Encyclopédie,* d'Alembert, became its permanent secretary in 1772.

Diderot believed in a limited education for girls, but provided his own daughter (after some foot dragging) with what was, for a woman of the day, a first-class education, one far in excess of what his own writings suggested. His attitudes toward the people can perhaps sum up the general problem. Here he is writing about the unemployed:

> . . . these lazy men, young and vigorous, who find in our misused charity an easier and more considerable assistance that what they would procure by their labor, fill our streets, our temples, our large roads, our cities and towns, our countryside . . . This vermin could only exist in a State in which the value of men is unknown.[51]

Yet this same Diderot could write to Sophie Volland, on seeing the elaborate gardens of the royal château of Marly:

> . . . in my admiration which I couldn't refuse Le Nôtre [the great landscape architect of Louis XIV]. I called Henri IV and Louis XIV back to life. Louis showed this magnificent edifice to Henri, and Henri said to him: "My son, you're right; it's very beautiful. But I'd like to see the houses of my peasants

in the village of Gonesse." What would he have thought of finding all around these immense and magnificent palaces—of finding, I say, peasants without roofs, without bread, and on straw?[52]

Diderot, in the second passage, is very much the man of modern sensibilities; as Peter Gay suggests, we see in such thoughts the birth of the secular social conscience. In the first passage, however, we see a Diderot who cannot understand that an able-bodied man could be unemployed through no fault of his own. We see him echoing the sentiments of royal ordinances that such people were vermin: one royal administrator of the 1690s, in a commentary on a poor relief edict, called them "garbage."

The distance between the Enlightenment and our own day appears most clearly in their attitudes toward women. Rousseau stands out for his blatant sexism, for his belief that women exist to "serve" men (as he says in *Émile*). Diderot explicitly rejected the notion that men and women are equal, but did admit they should be treated more equally than they were. Others, like the marquis of Condorcet, a key figure of the late Enlightenment, or Helvétius, accepted female equality. Even so hard core a sexist as Rousseau is not so easy to decipher as we might think: he calls the perfect mate for Émile, Sophie (wisdom). Sophie has the natural wisdom of those uncorrupted by society; she has purity of sentiment, a quality far more prized in those days than in ours. We have taken the modern rationalist conceit from the figures of the Enlightenment: the idea that reason provides the answer to all questions. They themselves did not accept that premise, however much they praised the use of reason to destroy the prejudices and ignorance built up over the centuries.

What did their contemporaries actually take from the *philosophes*? What can we say of the evolution of culture in late eighteenth-century France? One can distinguish three levels of reading taste in the country. At the broadest level, people read cheap little books produced by the so-called Blue Library of Troyes (the books had blue covers). These publishers produced for a mass audience. Early in the eighteenth century, they produced above all for the lower classes of the towns; by the second half of the century, most of their production went to the countryside, to the newly literate peasantry. They bought religious books, lives of the saints more than anything else. They bought almanacs: compendia of proverbs, little stories, and advice much like the contemporaneous American best-seller, *Poor Richard's Almanac*. Buyers wanted songbooks, particularly, as the century wore on, of Christmas carols. They purchased primers with a strong religious element, much like those used in New England. Early in the century, they bought chivalric romances, loosely based on medieval epic poems, but later they shifted to fairy tales, which became available only after 1750. One searches in vain for any trace of the *philosophes*.

In provincial towns, people still bought religious literature, especially in areas like Lorraine or Brittany. In southern France, however, buyers sought secular literature. Elites bought "high" literature. In the 1770s and 1780s, the leading authors at the regular booksellers included Voltaire (by far the best-seller), Helvétius, Rousseau, Simon Linguet, baron d'Holbach, Louis-Sebastien Mercier, and abbé Raynal. Side by side with these leading intellectuals, however, one finds the name of writers lost to historical obscurity, like Pidansat de Mairobert, likely author of the scandalous *Anecdotes on*

Mme the countess du Barry. The best-selling forbidden titles ranged from serious works by Voltaire (*Questions on the Encyclopedia*) to pornography (some of it, like the *Maid of Orléans,* also by Voltaire). Legally published books included a range of specialized works on law or medicine, as well as the best-selling novels of the day, like Rousseau's *New Heloise.*

The middle- and upper-class readers of these philosophical works got together to discuss them at academies of arts and sciences, which sprang up in many large provincial cities. These academies recruited most heavily from among royal officers, especially if the town had a Parlement, as at Bordeaux. They also invited a small number of members of the clergy, usually from the cathedral chapters, military nobles, a substantial number of doctors and lawyers, and a smattering of others. One group remained dramatically absent: merchants. Merchants and others excluded from the academies later created their own reading societies, an interesting parallel to the increasing unwillingness of these same merchants to buy royal offices, as their compeers had done in the sixteenth or seventeenth centuries. Reading societies and academies existed side by side with other forms of sociability: provincial salons (more common early in the century) and Masonic lodges, which spread rapidly through France after 1750. All of these venues did much to create a climate of public discussion and to create among public officials and ordinary people alike a sense that public opinion (a phrase first used in its modern sense during these years) had come to be important and legitimate.

Parisian readers provide a much different view. Artisans and servants remained faithful, like their provincial counterparts, to religious works. The middle class, however, turned away from religion. By the 1780s, Parisian publishers scarcely printed religious works. Middle-class Parisian private libraries came to consist overwhelmingly of secular books.[53] Men bought historical works, certainly a reflection of the charged political climate of the times, while women bought novels. The authorities burned banned texts in the public squares, but such activities, as Malesherbes had warned in 1759, merely served to whet the public's appetite. Raynal's *Philosophical History,* which had exhausted its market by 1774, had a remarkable revival seven years later, when the authorities burned it publicly in front of the Parlement of Paris, touching off a renewed demand for the suddenly scandalous text.

Paris had a wide range of texts available to all. These texts ranged from those shouting scandalous stories in the streets and sellers of hastily printed handbills assailing government ministers, public policies or, often by the late 1780s, the queen, to those purveying their wares to the very Parlementaires and royal officials acting to have them banned. Parisians (and others) could also rely on externally published gazettes, the most famous of them the *Gazette of Leiden,* published in French, in the Netherlands, or on journals, such as the scandalous *Mémoires secrets,* issued by Bachaumont, or the more literary *Correspondance,* edited by the German Frederic Grimm. Grimm received letters from many leading figures in Paris, such as Diderot, offering them an outlet for their views. These ideas spread so widely that a Polish policeman confiscating the goods of a Jewish peddler in Galicia in 1788 found a copy of the *Gazette of Leiden* in his sack.

Readers' tastes show us the cultural confusion of the 1770s and 1780s. They clamored for philosophical works, especially in the 1770s, and wanted as well to have more information about contemporary events. Little wonder that they would seek to combine the two, trying to provide some sort of philosophical underpinning for their pet program of reform. As in Eastern Europe under Soviet domination, writers sought often to combine political commentary with sex; in the case of eighteenth-century France, mildly pornographic writings, with obvious political overtones, came from the pens of many great *philosophes*, Voltaire and Diderot among them.

The social mores of the time, too, show its confusion. Fads came and went at a bewildering pace. Some members of high society decided to ape the English: serving afternoon tea (a custom that spread widely among the aristocracy), buying race-horses and betting heavily on them, dressing in English fashion. Gambling became a passion for many, ruining more than one family. The rich went to the Opera, to the Comédie Française, to the street entertainments, to the famous tavern (*guinguette*) of Ramponneau on the outskirts of the city. In Ménétra's *Journal*, again and again we see him rubbing elbows with slumming aristocrats, even playing court tennis with two princes of the blood.

The climate of the 1770s and 1780s seems that of cultural crisis. Robert Darnton's study of forbidden best-sellers reveals Mercier's *The Year 2440* to have been the runaway favorite of the 1780s. Mercier focuses on what this Utopian Paris of the future has eliminated: poverty, prostitution, the standing army, taxes, arbitrary arrest, and slavery. Children read so well that they use the *Encyclopédie* as a grammar school text. Everywhere, people denounce what they view as moral excesses: Mercier's Utopia has abolished coffee, tea, and tobacco as well as the blights noted above.

Pamphleteers issued slanderous libels about the sex lives of Louis XV and Mme du Barry; after Louis XV's death, the same authors soon turned their pens against Marie Antoinette. This seeming societal disgust with sexual promiscuity, however, must be balanced by the widespread acceptance of a culture of male marital infidelity, publicly proclaimed. Rich men flaunted their mistresses, particularly the actresses and singers whom they "sponsored." Courtiers engaged in endless rounds of sexual dalliance, games of love that often overlapped with high Court politics. Diderot could praise effusively the sentimental innocence and purity Richardson portrays in *Pamela*, yet simultaneously write pornography.

What did the Enlightenment leave to posterity? Did its ideas "cause" the French Revolution? Outside of France, we can point to the philosophies of the Scot David Hume and the German Immanuel Kant, to the economic changes of the Industrial Revolution, to the economic principles of Adam Smith, as some of the critical underpinnings of the modern world. To eighteenth-century France, Holland, and England (and its colonies), we owe the creation of modern political culture. The Enlightenment and the French Revolution, with considerable help from movements in other countries, created that political culture. The Enlightenment's emphasis on education, on reason, on equality have largely triumphed in the Western world, and became bedrock principles of modern politics due to the Atlantic Revolutions. Many observers at the time made a direct link between the American Revolution and the changing situation in France. Arthur Young wrote in October 1788: "Nantes is . . . enflammé in the cause of liberty . . . The American revolution has laid the foundations of another in France."[54]

The Enlightenment's curious amalgam of optimism—the belief that mankind can be improved—and pessimism—relying invariably on some higher authority to carry out the improvements—have proved a mixed blessing. Diderot and Voltaire corresponded with, and wrote on behalf of, despots. They wanted these despots to be enlightened, to be philosopher kings or empresses, but they held out little hope for the people themselves, helping themselves. Even Rousseau, supposed apologist of democracy and (male) equality, provided the ideal society of his *Social Contract* with a Lawgiver, who would see what the mass of citizens could not.

Rousseau's works offer the ideal example of the confusing legacies left by the great Enlightenment thinkers. The Rousseau of the *Discourses* (1749 and 1755) emphasized the corrupting influence of society and touted the virtues of "natural" man and woman. These works, and his novel *The New Heloise,* building on the works of his English predecessors (like Richardson), established the foundations of Romanticism. The greatest German Romantic, Goethe, modeled his first novel, *The Sorrows of Young Werther,* directly on *The New Heloise.* Politically, early Romanticism tended to be conservative, yet Rousseau's primary political impact came on the Left, by means of his 1762 treatise, the *Social Contract.* From its stirring opening words—"Man is born free yet he is everywhere in chains"—to its denunciations of power based on force and of slavery, the *Social Contract* offered a devastating rebuke to the existing political and social system. His call for a society based on civil liberty derived from moral (rational) choice echoed loudly in the debates during the Revolution. Little wonder that the Revolutionaries enshrined Rousseau in their Panthéon of heroes or that those most openly claiming to be his heirs—the Jacobins—would have taken up his misogyny, denying women even the most minimal role in the political process.

The Enlightenment left us a split between a thoroughly de-Christianized elite culture, one perhaps best represented in its first generation by the deist Voltaire and in the second by the atheist d'Holbach, and a broader culture still steeped in Judao-Christian beliefs. In January 1788, Ruault summed up elite attitudes remarkably well in a letter to his brother about the Edict of Toleration (allowing Protestants to have some rights): "Never did a book of philosophy or of politics trouble the public order; even a religious book, a work of fanaticism, would only produce today the laughter of disapproval."[55] The leading intellectual circles of most Western countries have remained resolutely antireligious ever since, an attitude that spread eventually to many workers in the cities. At the same time, ordinary people, especially in the countryside, remained religious. The mutually exclusive vocabulary of the two sides has created a permanent and unbridgeable chasm, first made evident during the Revolution.

The story of Nicolas Gérard, a Parisian stonemason/hairdresser convicted of murder in 1783 illustrates just how profoundly ideas could penetrate from one social level to another. Accused of murdering his roommate, Nicolas Kerse, and then stealing Kerse's goods, Gérard proclaimed his innocence throughout the preliminary interrogations, the trial, and even the postconviction torture to which the Parlement subjected him. The bookseller Hardy, who kept a journal of Parisian events in those days, tells us about Gérard's last moments.

> He remained alive on the wheel for about one hour. It is said that this wretch had the audacity to speak with great insolence to his judges . . . Far from manifesting any sign of anguish or repentance at the Châtelet before execution, when the prison chaplain announced to him the arrival of the priest–confessor he said, "Voltaire and Rousseau died without a confessor, and I can do without one just as well as them."[56]

Notes

1. This parody of the Our Father appeared in a libel published in the early 1770s. It is reproduced in R. Darnton, *The Forbidden Best-Sellers of Pre-Revolutionary France* (New York: Norton, 1996), 166.

2. Nicolas Ruault, *Gazette d'un Parisien sous la Révolution. Lettres à son frère, 1783–1796*, ed. A. Vassal and C. Rimbaud (Paris: Librairie Académique, 1976), 73.

3. Ménétra describes himself as one of the leaders in these discussions. Although his description of the general phenomenon of negotiations among the journeymen, the intendant, the Parlement, and the governor rings true, one is less convinced that Ménétra himself played so large a role as he suggests. On his behalf, he says that the group of thirty leaders designated him as the thirty-first because "the council wanted a man who could write"; Ménétra's writing facility, to which the *Journal* itself bears witness, would have made him a useful member of the council.

4. J. Ménétra, *Journal of My Life*, ed. D. Roche, trans. A Goldhammer (New York: Columbia University Press, 1986), 182.

5. The Hôtel de Ville was gutted by fire again during the Paris Commune of 1871; today's structure is a reconstruction of the eighteenth-century one.

6. P. Süskind, *Perfume. The Story of a Murderer*, trans. J. Woods (New York: Washington Square Press, 1986), 3–4.

7. Cited in L. Chevalier, *Laboring Classes and Dangerous Classes in Paris During the First Half of the Nineteenth Century*, trans. F. Jellinek (Princeton: Princeton University Press, 1973), 375.

8. M. Antoine, *Louis XV* (Paris: Fayard, 1989), 405.

9. In this ritual, on Easter Monday, the king touched hundreds of people infected by scrofula. The royal touch supposedly healed those so infected. Louis's confessor refused him Easter communion again in 1740 and 1744.

10. Only those of ancient nobility, in theory going back to 1400, had the right to be presented officially to the king and queen. In reality, anyone whose nobility went back four generations was easily accepted at Court. Most contemporaries believed Pompadour to be the illegitimate daughter of one of the Farmers General, who convinced an underling to marry the pregnant mother.

11. Songs cited in R. Isherwood, *Farce and Fantasy. Popular Entertainment in Eighteenth-Century Paris* (New York: Oxford University Press, 1986), 14–15.

12. Mme de Pompadour's unpopularity stands as testimony to another phenomenon of late eighteenth-century French life, the changing role of women, to which we will return.

13. Story recounted in R. Darnton, *The Forbidden Best-Sellers of Pre-Revolutionary France* (New York: Norton, 1995), 142.

14. E. Le Roy Ladurie, *L'Ancien Régime. L'absolutisme bien tempéré (1715–1770)* (Paris: Hachette, 1991), 158.

15. This quarrel began as a fight between the House of Burgundy (a junior line of the French royal house) and that of France. When Mary of Burgundy married Maximilian of Habsburg in the late fifteenth century, the Habsburgs took up the cudgels in the dispute.

16. The great household positions also possessed considerable patronage power, such as naming the royal pages.

17. Belle-Isle, grandson of Louis XIV's disgraced superintendent of finances, Nicolas Fouquet, would not have qualified for a commission in some regiments; his father, grandfather, and great-grandfather had been nobles (by virtue of offices in the last two cases), but his great-great-grandfather was a draper from Angers.

18. Eighteenth-century intendants married the daughters of other intendants or of high-ranking judges or administrators; their eldest sons became administrators or judges, and they, too, married within the great clan. Military officers who served on the royal councils followed in the footsteps of military fathers (90 percent) and rarely married the daughters of magistrates (10 percent). Their sons married within the group. Mimicking their fathers and grandfathers, 72 percent of the sons pursued a military career and not a single one (among a sample of fifty-one) became a judge or civil administrator. See R. Andrews, *Law, magistracy, and crime in Old Regime Paris, 1735–1789* (Cambridge: Cambridge University Press, 1994), vol. I, Tables 4.1 and 4.3.

19. Some alliances across groups did take place; in the late 1760s, chancellor Maupeou allied with the duke d'Aiguillon. In the 1780s, minister Breteuil descended from high-ranking administrators who had intermarried with the sword nobility and taken on the latter's lifestyle.

20. If we might make a modern American parallel, the secretary of defense protects the interests of the military itself—demanding a certain weapon for purely military reasons—and those of the defense industry—pushing procurement policies that keep large-scale defense contractors in business or convincing the secretary of state that weapon sales abroad are a good foreign policy tool. The controller general had a trickier balancing act, as he often had to mediate the long-standing conflict between the financiers and the bankers.

21. We have long wondered about the exact number of such offices. I use here the figure provided in the most recent (and best) study of venal office holding: W. Doyle, *Venality: The Sale of Offices in Eighteenth-Century France* (Oxford: Clarendon Press, 1996), 60.

22. Provincial Parlements existed in Toulouse, Grenoble, Bordeaux, Dijon, Rouen, Aix, Rennes, Pau, Metz, Besançon, and Douai. Similar courts, often known as superior councils, existed in Colmar (Alsace), Bastia (Corsica, after its annexation in 1768), Arras (later transferred to Douai), Dombes, and Perpignan.

23. Ménétra complains constantly in his *Journal* of his guild wardens abusing their authority in this way.

24. The anticommoner bias had a long history, including edicts barring commoner officers from the infantry and cavalry in 1718 and 1727. The pressures of wars invariably led to the granting of exceptions, merely to keep the army staffed.

25. Gallicanism was the belief in a special status for the French Church. The Parlement supported both royal Gallicanism, the idea that the Crown had effective control of the French Church, and Parlementaire Gallicanism, which insisted on the court's judicial supremacy in legal matters related to the Church.

26. The most obvious manifestations of this principle were the king's inability to remove Crown officers, such as the chancellor, and his inability to sell any part of the royal demesne, of which he had the use but not the ownership.

27. Lawyers could print their court briefs without censorship; many politically minded barristers used this opportunity to urge government reform or to assail the legitimacy of the state. D. Bell's *Lawyers and Citizens* (Princeton: Princeton University Press, 1994), provides an outstanding presentation of this remarkable end run around censorship.

28. Matters of principle aside, La Chalotais was a client of Mme de Pompadour, whose death in 1764 cost him his protector; d'Aiguillon had ties to the rising mistress, du Barry.

29. Here the Parlement of Paris adopted a formula then current in England: the king *in* Parliament held sovereignty.

30. His reforms in this matter merely followed existing rules: as early as the 1750s, landowners had been required to furnish written proof justifying their assessments. The practice lapsed in many regions; Terray merely sought to revive it.

31. N. Ruault, *Gazette*, 78.

32. Adam Smith borrowed heavily from the Physiocrats. They differed from Smith, however, in their emphasis on agriculture, which they felt was the root of all prosperity.

33. Ruault, *Gazette*, 96–97.

34. The rate on annuities guaranteed on two lives, paid as long as either of the people remained alive, reached 9 percent. The government also offered special higher interest to those over sixty: 12 percent a year on life annuities. Necker's friends in the Genevan anks brilliantly manipulated this system. The purchaser did not have to specify his or her own life as the one in question. In 1784, the bankers of Geneva pooled 2 million *livres* to buy annuities guaranteed on the lives of thirty young girls; they then sold shares in the pool. When one of the little girls died young, the entire city attended her funeral.

35. Ruault cites this speech in a letter of 26 May 1788 (*Gazette*, 112).

36. Ruault, *Gazette*, 86, letter of 1 August 1787. Ruault had quoted the councilor Duval-d'Epresmesnil's speech to this effect in a letter of 8 July. Duval-d'Epresmesnil would later be arrested for his radical speeches.

37. The Egyptian plans usually revolved around the idea that Austria and Russia would divide up the Balkans, then ruled by the Ottoman Empire; France would get Egypt, which was a client state of the Ottomans. Joseph II actually proposed this idea to Louis XVI in 1782.

38. Ruault, *Gazette*, 111.

39. Ruault, *Gazette*, letters of 25 August and 19 April 1787.

40. Quoted in J.-F. Solnon, *La Cour de France* (Paris: Fayard, 1987), 433.

41. The phrase comes from Daniel Gordon's recent book, *Citizens without Sovereignty. Equality and Sociability in French Thought, 1670–1789* (Princeton: Princeton University Press, 1994). The implications of this problem, however, are perhaps closer to the heart of another new study: Patricia Wells, *Law and Citizenship in Early Modern France* (Baltimore: Johns Hopkins University Press, 1995), esp. ch. 5.

42. Ruault, *Gazette*, 109.

43. Cited in Antoine, *Louis XV,* 169–70. My translation.

44. French political theory had always held that the king received his power and legitimacy from the French nation, not from God. God sanctified the French choice through the anointing of the king at the coronation, but the source of legitimacy was the people and the law they made. Henry IV, founder of the Bourbon dynasty, offered irrefutable proof of this maxim: French law made him king, even though he was a Protestant.

45. Cited in M. Price, *Preserving the Monarchy. The comte de Vergennes, 1774–1787* (Cambridge: Cambridge University Press, 1995), 140.

46. From his *Philosophical Letters*, cited by J. Grieder, *Anglomania in France, 1740–1789* (Geneva, 1985), 4.

47. Not all eighteenth-century women lionized Rousseau. Mary Wollstonecraft made him her chief target in her *Vindication of the Rights of Woman* (1792).

48. Such is the translation in the Penguin edition, done by J. Wood: *The Barber of Seville and the Marriage of Figaro* (London: Penguin Books, 1964), 200. The French offers a translation problem here: Beaumarchais uses the phrase "ces puissants de quatre jours," literally, "those powerful ones of four days," perhaps colloquially rendered as "those four-day wonders." I would take this phrase as a reference to the incessant changing of royal ministers in the 1770s, when Beaumarchais wrote the play.

49. Ruault, in his letters, several times warns his brother that the postal service can no longer be relied upon for confidential correspondence.

50. France had some women writers: at any given time between the 1750s and the 1780s, about 3 percent of France's published writers were women. These numbers jumped dramatically in 1789.

51. Quotation from the article, "Hôpital," in the *Encyclopédie,* cited in R. Mortier, "Diderot et l'assistance publique, ou la source et les variations de l'article, 'Hôpital', de l'Encyclopédie," in *Le Cœur et la Raison* (Paris, 1990), 224.

52. Letter of 23 September 1763, cited in P. Gay, *The Enlightenment* (New York: Norton, 1969, 1977), vol. II, 39.

53. The poor most often bought their books from wandering peddlers, not from professional book shops.

54. A. Young, *Travels during the years 1787, 1788 and 1789* (London: W. Richardson, 1794), I, 105.

55. Ruault, *Gazette,* 102, letter of 25 January 1788.

56. Andrews, *Law, magistracy, and crime,* 577.

Chapter Twelve

THE DEATH OF THE ANCIEN RÉGIME, 1787–AUGUST 1789

I was enjoying myself and watching my days go by when the French Revolution came suddenly and revived all our spirits. And the word liberty so often repeated had an almost supernatural effect and invigorated us all.

Jacques Ménétra, Parisian glass maker

Charles Paquelin, a winegrower in the tiny Burgundian village of Chassagne, kept a *Notebook of Memories* during the days of the French Revolution. Paquelin's village, slightly south of Beaune, had some connections to the wider world, but it hardly placed him at the geographic center of events in 1789. What does this ordinary Frenchman tell us about his summer of 1789? Let us listen in:

the 29th of July, at around 6 at night, terror is everywhere in the kingdom . . . Everywhere in the region, they have started to ring the alarm . . . all people are in consternation, women and children cry out every place, and try to save themselves by fleeing to the mountains . . . they have sounded the bells to summon the assemblies in all the parishes to stand guard day and night . . . because bands of brigands have formed, who murder, and who bring fire and blood everywhere; because they see no more law there . . . How many men killed, how many brigands hanged; many nobles imprisoned; all the others have fled the kingdom in fear of the anger of the Nation. Many of the bishops in prison; everywhere they [the bishops] hide because they tried to bring famine; they are all grain merchants. Great numbers of châteaux have been burned and razed, great alarms and great repentance. It was during the wheat harvest. Before this great terror, we were greatly menaced by [the prospect of] civil war.[1]

Poor Paquelin. How confusing everything must have been to him and to millions of others. His own testimony shows us that he did not, in fact, write this particularly "memory" on the night of 29 July 1789, but somewhat later. Jean Bart, the leading French specialist on the Revolution in Burgundy, assures us that the village of Chassagne, Paquelin notwithstanding, remained calm in July 1789. Yet Paquelin offers us invaluable testimony about contemporary perceptions of what was taking place.

Paquelin highlights the existence of "terror . . . everywhere in the kingdom." He repeats the widespread rumor of armies of brigands spreading "fire and blood" and claims that village assemblies everywhere sounded the tocsin (alarm bell) to mount guard against these "brigands." He tells us of attacks on châteaux, and of the flight of many nobles. Finally, he suggests that ordinary people viewed bishops as little more than grain traders, partly responsible for the massive increase in bread prices in the spring and early summer of 1789. His memoirs ring true, so long as we use them with care. We now know, and indeed many contemporaries knew, that there were no brigands. Paquelin bears witness rather to the mass hysteria called the Great Fear of 1789: people in many parts of France *believed,* as he did, that such bands of brigands existed. Village assemblies did bring large bands of peasants into being; those bands, and not the brigands, often turned on the local châteaux. Modern research has demonstrated that the peasants rarely burned the châteaux, or killed any nobles. They focused on the seigneur's legal papers, which they burned in the hopes that by destroying the physical evidence of the old titles they could abolish the feudal rights of their owners. Paquelin's accusation against the bishops makes sense: bishops, abbeys, and cathedral chapters held almost all tithes in France, so bishops were "grain merchants." Bands of peasants that summer looted tithe granaries, often burning the emptied barns. What Paquelin does not tell us is that the regions subject to the Great Fear and those in which armed bands of peasants attacked the châteaux were not the same; indeed, we have no surviving evidence of the two events coexisting anywhere.

Paquelin's *Memoirs* bear witness to the astonishingly rapid collapse of the Ancien Régime. The rapidity of its disintegration, not simply in Paris, but *everywhere in France,* alerts us to its fundamentally rotten core. The political system of the Ancien Régime had ceased to serve the function of all states: the regulation of the shared interests of the members of the community. People demanded, and got, a New Regime in a few short months.

The speed of change should not startle us: we have seen a similar collapse in Eastern and Central Europe in 1989. Just as in France in 1789, the political system no longer served the needs of society. A system of seeming great strength thus collapses in a matter of months, with very little violence. People have debated the "inevitability" of the French Revolution since it happened; I am among those who believe it was inevitable. The specific events certainly could not be foretold, but the broader lines of Revolutionary events responded to all the discontinuities between social and economic, and political development in eighteenth-century France. The Ancien Régime tried reform and failed in the 1760s and 1770s. The Ancien Régime, feudal[2] to the core, based on privilege, could not survive. In its place, the French people placed the nation.

We must not, however, confuse the inevitability of political change with the serendipity of political events. The Revolution created its own political dynamic, rapidly moving in directions no one could have predicted. Once underway, its momentum dramatically altered the nature of political discourse. The startling shift in thinking of many of the deputies to the "Estates General" of early May 1789 and the same men as deputies to the "National Assembly" in late June 1789, for example, can only be understood as a response to the events themselves.

The evidence of change could not be more clear, because the political events of 1789 left an unparalleled record of popular political opinions: the *cahiers de doléances,* or lists of grievances, compiled by the inhabitants of every parish in the kingdom. They elected deputies who attended sub-regional assemblies in each of the more than one hundred fifty bailiwicks, where these deputies created a general *cahier* and chose the deputies to the Estates General. In towns, individual guilds wrote *cahiers;* in some guilds, in some cities, the journeymen and the masters wrote two separate *cahiers.* Rural women sometimes played a role in the process: in one sample of twenty-one Burgundian parishes, twelve had women participate in the electoral assembly. How could it have been otherwise in parishes such as Villeberny, in which the two largest taxpayers were the widows Bizot and Guedeney-Mongin? In many towns women's guilds, such as the fishwives or flower sellers of Paris, wrote *cahiers.* Convents, too, had the right to representation: the sisters met to appoint a male representative, often their overseeing priest, to their local assembly and to draw up a *cahier.* In Paris alone, fifty-seven convents sent representatives to the local assembly of the First Estate. Women seem not to have participated at the next level. None of those twelve Burgundian parishes sent a woman as a deputy to the regional assembly and the town-wide assemblies make no mention of them. Within each bailiwick, the clergy and the nobility compiled their own grievances. The vast majority of these documents have survived, providing perhaps the broadest sounding of public opinion in world history.

The Estates General of 1789 touched off a bewilderingly rapid chain of events that led directly to the overthrow of the monarchy (10 August 1792), to the executions of Louis XVI and Marie Antoinette, to a generation of international war, and to the many other remarkable changes we subsume under the name of the French Revolution. These events often must be followed day-by-day, particularly the momentous changes of May–October 1789, which fundamentally and permanently restructured not merely French but European politics. These political changes, themselves partly a response to social, economic, and cultural changes, in turn led to significant social and cultural shifts and, in the long run, to economic ones.

The historian seeking to reconstruct these events does so against a background of supercharged historiographical debate: few periods in human history so violently divide their interpreters. I have tried to synthesize the two most prominent schools, the Classicists and the Revisionists. With modification, I have followed the Classicists in three important ways:

1. I agree with most of them that the Revolution was inevitable because political systems must reflect the underlying economic and social structures of their societies, which the Ancien Régime no longer did by the 1760s.[3]

2. I accept that the Revolution did create in France a unified, modern definition of property.

3. I believe that we can distinguish class differences among the different groups active during the Revolution and that, at certain moments, class differences led to varying political attitudes and action.

The Revisionists reject or would heavily modify these interpretations, particularly the second and third ones. In accepting point one, I am in no way rejecting the arguments of many Revisionists that changes in ideas led to fundamental changes in society.[4] The simplistic argument that noble ideas gave way to "bourgeois" ideas ignores the obvious amalgamation of different sets of values, and misrepresents the complexity of the ideologies of the nobility of Ancien Régime France. Rousseau, the man on whom the most radical Revolutionaries relied for their philosophy, has extremely strong ties to traditional ideas of the provincial French nobility.

The Revisionist argument that the Revolution merely extended pre-existing property relations to all of society and that modern private property existed under the Ancien Régime makes sense, if one makes two caveats. First, the Revolution eliminated other property forms, such as feudal property; second, the Revolution eliminated the private ownership of regulation of many sectors of the commercial economy by abolishing guilds and the venal offices, such as wine broker or inspector of hides, that had owned such rights of regulation. Relationships to property (and to ways of earning one's living) did affect how some people behaved during the Revolution—those involved in manufacturing tended to be far more radical from 1790–1792 than those from the world of law, as we shall see—but the Revisionists rightly renounce any theory that seeks to explain everyone's behavior in this way. In 1789, virtually all of the prominent actors had precisely the same relationship to property: they owned landed estates. Class differences do very little to explain attitudes or actions between April and July 1789, which far more often reflected the fissures of a society of orders. Again and again, we will find profound differences in attitude toward the Revolution expressed by those within the same profession.

As the previous narrative makes clear, I believe the social and economic transformation to the structures of a modern society had taken place well before the Revolution. The Revolution's main positive economic contribution was to bring laws into line with these changed realities.[5] In a direct sense, this change evolved from the modified legal and social structures. State confiscation and resale of property—above all, the property of the Catholic Church (about 10 percent of the land in France)—substantially modified land distribution and eliminated the largest single player in the country's most important market sector, the grain trade. The political process of the Revolution, with its emphasis on male democracy, had profound implications in social and cultural life. At the most basic level of human interaction, the Revolution's foundational principles—liberty, equality, fraternity—encouraged the abolition of traditional barriers of social hierarchy, as in the language of everyday speech. Gone were such honorifics as "monsieur" (my lord) and "madame" (my lady), replaced by "citizen" and "citizeness"; in the long run, the democratization encouraged by the Revolution extended "monsieur" and "madame" to all adult members of society.

This chapter focuses overwhelmingly on political events because I accept wholeheartedly the Revisionist argument that the Revolution was primarily a political event. That event needs to be studied in its political particulars and in the way in which an ever-evolving new world of ideas drove politics in directions all but unimaginable before the Revolution broke out. No document more clearly demonstrates this change than the letter Louis XVI left behind when he tried to run away in June 1791. Although he criticizes the excesses of the Revolutionaries, Louis does so entirely in the political vocabulary created by the Revolution; moreover, he accepts as irrefutable truths ideas he would have hotly contested just three years before. After the events of 1787–1791, even the king himself could no longer think in the same way or even in the same words. Let us turn now to the great events to find out why. In so doing, we must focus first on what happened in Paris, because of the primordial importance of events there; Chapter 13 will provide greater details on what happened in the provinces in 1789.

C H R O N O L O G Y	1787–5 May 1789
Spring 1787	Meeting of first Assembly of Notables
May 1787	Resignation of Calonne; Brienne replaces him
21 May 1787	Lafayette calls for an Estates General
June–July 1787	Court of Peers registers reform edicts— provincial assemblies; revised tax and fiscal system
July 1787	Louis XVI announces he will summon the Estates General by 1792
July 1787	Parlement of Paris exiled
November 1787	Parlement recalled
January 1788	Parlement registers tax reform edicts; limited toleration for Protestants
May 1788	King sends judicial reform edicts to Parlement
7 June 1788	Day of the Tiles in Grenoble
August 1788	King dismisses Brienne; announces Estates General for 1 May 1789; Necker returns to the government
September 1788	Parlement of Paris rules that Estates General will follow rules of 1614
Fall 1788	Second Assembly of Notables
Dec. 1788–Jan. 1789	King issues edicts on rules for the Estates General
March–April 1789	Electoral campaign for the Estates General; redaction of the *cahiers*
April 1789	Reveillon riots in Paris
5 May 1789	Estates General opens at Versailles

∼ The Estates General of 1789 and the *Cahiers de Doléances*

The King has read a great many of the cahiers. *He must have seen with plea-sure that all of France loves him, is devoted to him, and competes with him to reform abuses. Among all those papers written by so many different hands, he will not find a single one that lacks the proper attitude and respect for the royal dignity.*[6]

Nicolas Ruault, 1 April

The government of France staggered from policy to policy, from minister to minister throughout the 1780s. In the early part of the decade, the foreign minister, the count of Vergennes, dominated the government because of the close trust Louis XVI placed in him. After Vergennes's death (1787), Louis turned to successive chief financial of-ficials—Calonne, Brienne, Necker—for key advice. All of these men competed against the king's other ministers for control of state policy; no one individual had Louis XVI's complete confidence, so state policy lacked consistency. The wars of the American Revolution, which ended with the Peace of Paris (1783), brought the French state to the edge of bankruptcy. The new "American" debt, added to the exist-ing debts from the Seven Years' War, created a climate of chaos. By 1786, the royal government did not know where to turn for more money, because its traditional lenders, fearful of an imminent bankruptcy, became unwilling to purchase more government paper.

Desperately seeking an answer to this fiscal crisis, Louis XVI and his chief min-ister of 1787, Charles-Alexandre de Calonne, decided to turn to a device not used since the 1620s: the Assembly of Notables. An Assembly brought together a theoreti-cally handpicked body of the great men of the kingdom. Some people—Princes of the Blood, the great peers, certain archbishops and bishops, first presidents of the Parlements—virtually had to be summoned, so the government actually had far less say in who attended than one might think. These notables heard Calonne describe a government eager to make major reforms in both fiscal and judicial matters. The government wanted to get better control over expenditures and to expand its rev-enues. Calonne told the Assembly that the government took in about 475 million *livres* per year and spent nearly 600 million; he also informed them that France had borrowed over 1.25 billion *livres* in the previous ten years. His figures suggested that the government spent more than half its revenue on interest payments.

He wanted some administrative reforms as well, but there events outran his pro-posals. In the late winter and early spring of 1787, five major disbursement officials de-clared bankruptcy, among them a treasurer of the Navy whose losses amounted to 30 million *livres,* a treasurer of the army, and a receiver general of Rouen, a lynchpin of the syndicate collecting direct tax revenues. The French-language newspaper pub-lished in Holland, the *Gazette of Leiden* reported that royal financial paper declined in value every day; in such a climate, administrative reform became the order of the day. The Assembly of Notables, whose members had been strongly influenced by Necker's *Account Rendered to the King,* recommended a return to some of Necker's ideas, par-ticularly the consolidation of spending authority into fewer hands.

Calonne proposed two basic changes:

1. Greater control over expenses.

2. The elimination of many tax exemptions by creation of a single direct tax.

Calonne proposed a land tax, to be levied *in kind* (i.e., in raw produce), on all landowners. As one might expect of a group whose members made most of their income selling agricultural produce, the prospect of a new, massive seller on the market did not appeal to the Notables; they also raised quite legitimate concerns about the practicality of such a scheme. The Assembly balked at a blanket authorization to tax: they wanted the king to agree to a permanent representative body that would approve all taxes, in return for their acquiescence in the loss of tax exemptions. The king refused. Calonne, faced by an intransigent Assembly and crippled within the government by opposition from other ministers, had to resign. One of the chief spokesmen of the Assembly, Loménie de Brienne, archbishop of Toulouse, a disciple of Necker, took his place. He rapidly sought to put Necker's ideas into practice.

Brienne made a key concession: he accepted the Assembly's position that the king should collect the new land tax in cash, not in kind. The Assembly approved much of Brienne's program: new provincial assemblies, creation of a free market in grain, elimination of the public works *corvée,* and issuance of short-term loans. They agreed in principle with a land tax, but refused to vote for it on the (quite legitimate) legal grounds that they had no right to do so. The lawyers among them knew that no Assembly of Notables had ever approved the creation of a new tax: in the accepted legal view of the time, only an Estates General had such authority.[7] The marquis de Lafayette, one of the members of the Assembly, demanded that the king call the Estates for precisely that reason (21 May 1787).

Brienne and the other ministers quickly drew up the necessary edicts to enact these reforms and sent them to the Parlements for registration. The Parlement of Paris, sitting as the Court of Peers,[8] did register edicts reforming the fiscal administration, cutting expenditures, and, after some debate, even one extending limited civil rights to Protestants. The noble members of the Court of Peers, as well as the leaders of the Parlement, had sat at the Assembly of Notables, so it is little wonder that they took the same positions again. Like the Assembly, they ruled that only an Estates General could vote a new tax. In a self-serving gesture by the Parlementaires, the Court of Peers also opposed the government's plan to reform the judiciary.

Brienne and his chief ally, Keeper of the Seals Lamoignon, persisted. Giving in to the peers, the government announced (July 1787) it would call an Estates General "by 1792." The king sent more reforming edicts to the Parlement of Paris, which refused to register them; he then went to the Parlement, held a *lit de justice,* and forced them to register the acts. The Parlement renounced the forced registration, so Louis exiled them to Troyes. This familiar dance of opposition ended with the recall of Parlement and yet another *lit de justice* (19 November). Once again, Parlement opposed the edicts; the king's cousin, the duke of Orléans, told Louis XVI, "it is illegal." The king replied, in classic absolutist style, "I want it, so it is legal."

The day of such a system had passed: French elites would no longer accept the premise that the will of the prince was law. They now accepted the premise that the law stood above the king, and that the will of the nation, what the eighteenth-century philosophers Denis Diderot and Jean-Jacques Rousseau had called the general will, created the law. Moreover, those elites had turned not only against the king but against the Parlementaire opposition, seeing the Parlements as merely one institution more to be eliminated in the cleansing of the political system. In January 1788, Ruault would write, concerning the Parlement's condemnation of an almanach:

> pendantism, ignorance, prejudice, pretention have long dominated in these sorts of courts; natural reason cannot see the light of day in the Palace of Justice, among all those black robes which fill and darken it. If I were Parlement, one bright morning I would shake off all these ancient villanies and present myself as I ought to be in the midst of the capital of a lively, gay, spirited, and enlightened nation.[9]

Ruault here gives voice to the seismic shift in French politics between the 1760s and the 1780s; whereas in the 1760s elite public opinion had to choose between two parties—that of the ministers and that of the Parlements—by the 1780s, elites had emphatically rejected both of those options, in favor of a third one: the creation of a representative assembly to act as a check on "ministerial despotism." Gabriel-Honoré Riqueti, better known as the count of Mirabeau, who would become the dominant figure of the National Constituent Assembly, summed up the feelings of many in a letter to the royal minister Montmorin (April 1788): "I would never make war against the Parlements, except in the presence of the nation."[10] Once the nation had been assembled, Mirabeau and his allies intended to destroy not only the "absolute" monarchy, but the Parlements, which had been, under the Ancien Régime, the best source of protection from arbitrary governmental behavior.

The government convinced Parlement to go along with a land tax in January 1788. Calonne and Lamoignon introduced their judicial reform program in May. This all but eliminated the jurisdiction of the Parlements, setting up "Grand Bailiwick" courts to hear, without appeal, virtually all cases, creating a Plenary Court for political cases (government edicts, taxation), abolishing torture, and gutting the seigneurial courts. Public opinion favored many of the proposed reforms of local courts, but violently objected to the Plenary Court: Ruault called it "the shameful organ of the oppression of the people."

Brienne simultaneously gutted the existing financial system, going back to Necker's policies. He destroyed the power of the receivers general and other officials with authority to spend the government's money and reduced to five (from several hundred) the number of officials who could authorize spending. The personal credit of the receivers general and of the other powerful financial officers, such as the receiver of the clergy, the treasurers of the Estates of Brittany and Languedoc, and the Farmers General, had underwritten the government's finances for nearly a century.

Brienne's creation of a genuine Central Treasury, with complete authority over government spending, however much sense it made as an administrative measure, greatly upset the capital markets integrated into the old system and made it even more difficult to borrow money. His policies, like Necker's, responded to the desires of the bankers, especially foreign ones, in their ongoing conflict with the financiers, led by the Farmers General.

These reforms put the entire country in an uproar. Provinces like Brittany, in which the nobility had close ties to the Parlement, violently objected to the reduced power of the courts. Towns that had powerful local royal courts, like the presidial-seneschalsy of Vannes, protested. Some towns, those that stood to have Grand Baili-wicks, like Chalon-sur-Saône, just as strongly supported the change. In Brittany, the powerful commoners of Nantes and Rennes formed leagues against the nobles and Parlementaires; in Dauphiné, the population of Grenoble showered with roof tiles the royal troops sent to quell disturbances (7 June 1788). When the troops retired to their barracks, the city's population took control, holding the governor prisoner and forcing the Parlement to lead the resistance to the new edicts.

Brittany and Dauphiné provided diametrically opposed models to the rest of France. In Dauphiné, people from the three orders worked together to oppose "ministerial despotism." Popular resistance successfully faced down the troops and the legal elite then stepped in to provide an ordered structure for resistance. In Brittany, the crisis of 1788 sharply divided the nobility from the Third Estate. Their division grew progressively stronger and more violent; by November 1788, Breton barbers were even refusing to shave or give haircuts to any nobleman. In 1788 and early 1789, most of France reacted to events in a manner similar to Dauphiné, but, once the Revolution gathered momentum, the Breton pattern asserted itself. The fundamental division of May–July 1789 split people by order—nobility versus commoner—because the political system of the Ancien Régime relied on that division. In order to destroy the political system of the Ancien Régime, the Third Estate had no choice but to destroy its two greatest bulwarks: the nobility and the Church hierarchy, itself dominated by the great nobility.

The second Assembly of Notables, called in fall 1788, offered the king no more solace than had the first; indeed, if anything it proved more intransigent on every key demand. From Paris to Rennes, from Grenoble to the villages of Burgundy, traditional authorities crumbled in the face of massive demand for change. In August 1788, acting as a royal coroner, Louis XVI issued the long overdue death certificate of the Ancien Régime: he dismissed Brienne, reappointed Necker, and summoned the Estates General for 1 May 1789.

Some of those close to the king recognized the danger of letting the genie out of the bottle; the Princes of the Blood sent him a *Memoir* on 12 December 1788, cautioning him of the cataclysm to come:

> Sire, the state is in peril; your person is respected, for the virtues of the monarch assure him the homage of the nation; but, Sire, a revolution in the principles of government is being prepared; it is being induced by the fermentation

of minds. Institutions reputed to be sacred, and by means of which this monarchy has prospered for many centuries, are being transformed into problematical questions or even criticized as acts of injustice. . . . Who can say where the recklessness of opinions will stop? The rights of the throne have been questioned; the rights of the two orders of the state divide opinions; soon property rights will be attacked; inequalities of wealth will be presented as an object for reform; already it has been proposed that feudal rights be abolished as a system of oppression, a remnant of barbarism.[11]

Ruault's judgment of this unfortunate document echoed that of all of Paris. The initial sensation gave way to ridicule; he wrote on 8 January 1789 that the princes who had signed the *Memoir* no longer dared showed themselves in public because "the writer of this pitiful rhapsody of feudal rights and privileges has dishonored them in the eyes of the nation in having them sign it."[12]

In Paris, as in the tiniest village, the call for the Estates General generated enormous anticipation. They had not met since 1614, so everyone wondered what they were. How would elections be held? Who could participate in them? How many deputies would come to Paris? What would be the rules governing actions of the Estates? The Parlement of Paris, which had garnered enormous popular support because of its opposition to higher taxes and because it had demanded the king call an Estates General to get new taxes, ruled in September 1788 that the Estates General would meet according to the rules followed in 1614.[13] This ruling made evident to all what leaders of elite public opinion had long recognized: in the new order of things, the Parlement, too, could have no place. Public reaction against the edict led the king, under Necker's influence, to make several key decisions about the rules for the calling of the Estates.

The government decreed that the three estates could meet either separately or together in the bailiwicks; the king further stipulated that each bailiwick would have an equal number of deputies. The king declared that the Third Estate would everywhere represent the countryside, as it had in 1614 in most of the kingdom, and that the Third would have as many deputies as the First and Second Estates combined. He left in abeyance the critical question of whether voting would be by head (individual deputy) or by order (one vote each for the clergy, nobility, and Third Estate). This second method would give each order veto power over all changes, because the immemorial custom of the Estates General was that all three orders had to agree to any binding action.

These rulings created the potential for enormous conflict. First of all, in the *pays d'Etats*, the provision allowing the three orders to sit together left open the possibility that the provincial estates would select the deputies for the Estates General, the practice they had followed in 1614. That situation led to violent conflict in some provinces, above all Brittany. Its dispute between the Second and Third Estates was so bitter that the nobility and the bishops refused to attend the Estates General. The Breton deputies to the Third Estate, once in Paris, created a political club that led the assault against noble privileges. The Breton Club soon attracted members from other provinces; in time, it took the name of the Paris convent in which it met starting in

October 1789: the Jacobins. In the other *pays d'Etats,* by way of contrast, the king intervened directly, ruling that deputies be elected in standard bailiwick assemblies.[14] The provincial estates of Languedoc, Provence, Burgundy, and Dauphiné theoretically lost their right to select the deputies, as their predecessors had done in 1614 (although Dauphiné, in fact, used the old method).

The Deputies

When the deputies arrived in Versailles, the three orders met separately. The First Estate (clergy) differed completely from its 1614 predecessor. Parish priests, perhaps 10 percent of the deputies in 1614, made up two-thirds of the original 295 deputies of the First Estate in 1789.[15] Conversely, bishops, invariably nobles, held only 14 percent of the seats in 1789, as against their 41 percent of 1614. The abbots, so powerful in 1614, obtained only ten seats in 1789. The deputies from the clergy stood out as well by education: over half had a university degree, usually in theology. They also tended to be a little older, a median just over fifty, as against the forty-five of the other two orders.

For the Second Estate, most bailiwicks allowed all nobles to participate in their electoral assemblies. They chose deputies who combined two defining elements of the traditional French nobility: pedigree and military service. Three-quarters of the noble deputies held a title, an extraordinary percentage in a country where fewer than five percent of the nobility could make such a boast. Seventy percent of them could trace their nobility back to 1500 or earlier; that, too, made them stand out in an overall nobility in which 70 percent of the families had been ennobled since 1600. Eighty percent of the noble deputies had served in the military, many of them in combat. The veterans included nineteen men who fought in the wars of the American Revolution, including the marquis de Lafayette. The nobles also stood apart from the other two orders in their lack of education and in the extreme concentration of men from Paris, with about half of them living in the capital. Another one hundred forty-three nobles sat either with the clergy (eighty-five) or the Third Estate (fifty-eight), the latter often recently ennobled men whose views differed from those of the aristocrats.

Allowing for widespread local variations, the Third Estate followed a simple basic pattern. In each parish, the taxpaying heads of households (aged twenty-five or over, resident for a year or more in the parish) met to draw up their grievances and to elect a few representatives to the bailiwick assembly.[16] In the larger towns, people often met by guild or by parish (or both), which sent deputies to the town assembly, which, in turn, sent people to the bailiwick meeting. In the chief town of the bailiwick, the deputies elected by the rural parishes and by the towns met together to elect deputies to go to Paris. They also combined the grievances of the individual parishes into a single, general *cahier.* In Paris itself, a violent dispute between the town government at the Hôtel de Ville and the bailiwick authorities at the Châtelet over who should supervise the elections led to a long delay. In the end, some 11,000 voters in the 60 districts of the city chose electors, who then met at the Hôtel de Ville to select the deputies to the Estates General. Because of the delays related to the procedural dispute, the deputies from Paris had still not been selected when the Estates General opened on 5 May 1789.[17] The deputies from the Third Estate resembled those of the clergy in one important respect: many of them had attended a university and the vast majority had completed secondary studies. Nearly 70 percent of these deputies had legal training.Royal judges or attorneys, usually from the bailiwick courts, held two hundred eighteeen of the six hundred five seats; self-described lawyers occupied another one hundred eighty-one places.

About one-sixth of the deputies to the Estates General lived in Paris; nearly half of them lived in a town of 8,000 or more people, and 75 percent lived in a town of 2,000 or more. Given that 80 percent of French people lived in the countryside, the heavy skewing toward urban elites created the potential for an urban–rural split in response to the actions of the deputies. The electoral procedures—above all those of the Third Estate—favored citizens from the leading town of each bailiwick. Chief judges of bailiwick courts sat as presidents of the electoral assemblies, and one-third of the assemblies chose their presiding officer as a deputy.[18]

Even allowing for this dramatic skewing toward urban interests, however, the deputies to the Estates General had much greater connection to the rural world than the men elected to the Legislative Assembly of 1791. Self-described "farmers" held 46 seats in 1789, but most of the deputies of the Second and Third Estates shared a common economic interest in agriculture because they got the largest share of their income from farm rents, even though they did not live in the countryside. They had only mixed success dealing with rural issues between 1789 and 1791, but their successors, who had even fewer rural ties, proved utterly inept, as we shall see.

The initial call for the Estates also went out to specific corporate groups. Within the Church, abbeys, convents, and cathedral chapters held internal assemblies to draw up *cahiers.* In towns, guilds met separately to draw up their grievances and to name deputies to the town assemblies. The king also wrote to the syndic of the Jews of Alsace to order individual communities of Jews in Alsace and Lorraine to hold meetings, elect representatives, and draw up *cahiers;* the Sephardic Jews of Paris wrote to Necker, protesting that they had not received a similar summons. The Jews of Metz hired the Polish Jew Zalkind Hourwitz to write a pamphlet on their behalf, in which he cited the rights of Jews to be treated the same as others: "The Jews are not foreigners, either by nature or by religion, but are so treated only because others regard them as such and cut them out of society. If they are given the right of Citizenship, then we will see they are French, like the other subjects of the kingdom."[19]

Some French colonies received summonses from the king, while others, such as Saint-Domingue, did not. The population of Saint-Domingue treated the snub as an accidental "oversight" and proceeded to hold elections anyway. The electoral process in Saint-Domingue touched off a multifaceted conflict, pitting white landowners against poor whites, all whites against those of mixed race and blacks (and some of the latter two groups against each other), and slaves against the free. In the end, the rich whites sent one delegation, while a coalition of mulattoes and some whites sent a competing one. This electoral dispute politicized the island and created among its entire population the expectation of important changes. When the political process did not give the people of Saint-Domingue the changes they demanded, they took matters into their own hands, much like the people of France.

The *Cahiers*

At the moment of a general regeneration in the State, all hearts open to flattering hopes; we believe ourselves to live in days as happy for the subjects as they are glorious for the Monarchy, and all Europe already admires the head of a free nation, who shows himself to be the friend of healthy reason and of the truth.[20]

> Preamble to the *cahier* of the clergy of the parish of St-Paul in Paris.

The electoral assemblies also had to draw up general *cahiers,* to present to the king. What did people say? The nobility of the bailiwick of Bruyères, in the duchy of Lorraine, summarized two key points in their first two articles:

the deputy of the nobility of the bailiwick of Bruyères is to be specially charged to vote

1. For liberty of individuals, of citizens, and the suppression of secret letters, as well as the surety of their Estates.
2. To assure properties, such that no one can threaten them or make attempts against them by means of taxes which are not consented by the Estates General.

Everyone wanted protection of their liberty and of their property. In their fourth article, the Bruyères nobility stated the key corollary of these demands: "no new law shall be binding unless it is sanctioned by the Nation." They wanted meetings of the Estates General every three years, at which deputies would vote all taxes. As Gouverneur Morris, an American envoy in Paris wrote in April 1789: "it appears from the Instructions given to the Representatives (called here *les Cahiers*) that certain Points are universally demanded which when granted and secured will render France perfectly free as to the Principles of the Constitution."[21]

Clergy, nobles, Third Estate: everyone demanded that the "Estates General," their name for a representative body, have the authority to vote taxes, to supervise the administration of royal ministers, and, in many cases, to make (jointly with the king) or to approve new laws.[22] The *cahiers* invariably made these demands in a pragmatic, empirical fashion; few of them contained philosophical statements about the nature or locus of sovereignty. They demonstrated profound respect and affection for the king but also gave evidence of changes to come. The nobility of Crépy-en-Valois, for example, swore its allegiance to the nation and the king, in that order. The authors of the *cahiers* supported a constitutional monarchy in which a representative body would have to approve all laws and taxes and the king would be head of the executive branch of government. Morris unequivocally stated the key issue in February: "Your Nation is now in a most important Crisis, and the great Question, shall we hereafter

THE GENERAL *CAHIER* OF THE BAILIWICK OF D'AVAL

The most radical *cahiers* tended to come from the Third Estate, such as that of the bailiwick d'Aval in Franche-Comté. They began with the demand for a "National Constitution," with the exigent provisions:

1. That it be recognized that France is a free nation, that the kingdom is a monarchy governed by the king, following the laws, which cannot be destroyed nor changed without the consent of the nation, legally assembled.

2. That the monarchic power be maintained in all its plenitude and recognize the succession in the august ruling house, hereditary from male to male, by order of primogeniture, to the exclusion of women and their descendants.

3. That the nation cannot be represented except by an Estates General composed of deputies freely elected, of which half shall be chosen from the Third Estate and the others from the first and second orders.

4. That the Estates General shall meet every three years at the least, and votes will be counted there by head, in one and the same chamber.

6. That all laws will be consented to by the Estates General. All taxes, all loans will also be

consented to by the Estates General, who will determine the use of the money.

8. That all privileges or exemptions of any kind, whatever their cause, shall be abolished with respect to taxation levied for public expenses.

9. That individual liberty of all citizens and of their property, civil and political liberty shall be assured; and that *lettres de cachet* (arbitrary orders for arrest) be abolished.

These remarkable deputies went on to a long list of grievances. Under the heading of justice, they demanded abolition of venality of office. They demanded a completely new tax system: creation of a single tax, to be levied on land, with all landholders to be listed on one register; elimination of all interior tolls; creation of a single system of weights and measures; as well as abolition of the existing tax administration. They further insisted on the suppression of censorship and on the liberty of the press. The chapter "On the administration of Communes" had but one article: "Municipal officers in all the kingdom shall be elective, voted triennially, and non-venal."

have a Constitution or shall Will continue to be Law, employs every mind and agitates every heart in France."

The similarity of so many of the general *cahiers* of the Third Estate bore witness both to widespread public agreement on the most serious abuses of the system and to an organized campaign within the Third Estate. Leaders in major towns often sent out "model *cahiers*" or general instructions, so that the less sophisticated rural dwellers would not "mistake" the issues at hand. The Society of Thirty, a group of patriots organized loosely around the duke of Orléans's Palais Royal enclave, and including the duke himself, sought to influence elections and the redaction of the *cahiers*. Men like the young lawyer Antoine Barnave in Dauphiné or the infamous count of Mirabeau in Provence corresponded with each other and with lesser-known patriots, such as the lawyer Jean Navier of Dijon. Navier sent a "Summary of Mandates" to the presidents of Burgundian village assemblies, in which he outlined the program of the patriot party in the Third Estate: voting by head; obligatory consent of the nation, by means of an Estates General, for taxes and laws; periodic and mandatory meetings of the Estates; and tax equality. The Third Estate everywhere, from the Paris suburbs to Burgundian villages, ordered its deputies to refuse to accept all humiliating social distinctions.

Navier, Barnave, Mirabeau, and their allies went beyond these demands, which had broad-based support; they had a more radical agenda. Navier's "Summary" demands support for provincial estates and local tribunals and insists that the primary function of the Estates General is to establish a constitution that would make individual liberty inviolable, respect property, and provide freedom of the press. He wanted the king and the military to take an oath to defend the constitution. Navier's "Summary" even addressed tactical issues. He suggested that if the clergy and nobles refused to vote by head, the deputies of the Third Estate should invite like-minded members of the other two orders to join them in telling the king that they were the Nation, and should then declare themselves the "National Assembly."

Navier's "Summary" makes obvious the political platform of one group within the Third Estate, including its intention to create a National Assembly if the other two orders would not go along with its political ideas. Ruault's letters of the spring of 1789 show that he, too, knew of such plans and reveal that he had great confidence in the Third's ability to carry them out: in February he wrote that "you can believe that the Third will defeat the nobility and the high clergy. If those groups grumble too much about it, we will find a way to get around their votes, which will lead to an even greater revolution."[23] The main leadership of the forthcoming National Assembly—Mirabeau, Brissot, Barnave, Condorcet, and the others—had already begun agitating for a constitutional monarchy in the mid 1780s. When the king announced the calling of an Estates General, these people realized that their opportunity had come; they seized it.

Their radical program faced opposition even within the Third Estate: Navier failed to gain election at Dijon. Yet the opposition failed to see the internal logic of the patriot demands. Most people wanted a representative body to vote laws and taxes; their *cahiers* used the only name they knew for such a body, an "Estates General." That term did *not* mean they wanted *the* Estates General, that is, the actual historical body that had sat most recently in 1614. The most politically sophisticated elements, men such as Navier or Ruault in the Third Estate or the men meeting in the assemblies of the nobility in Paris, understood fully that what they wanted was a "National Assembly": a body elected by the citizens, that is, the men of property. Those who wanted such a "National Assembly" made clear their opposition to the current form of government, but felt that Necker and, to some extent, Louis XVI, supported them.

The patriot party voiced demands widely shared with others, but used a vocabulary most people, even in the Third Estate, were unwilling yet to accept. Two elements helped them convince people to adopt the new vocabulary, and the new thinking it represented. First, the pamphlet literature inundating France during the electoral campaign of 1789 educated people in the new politics. This campaign also greatly heightened tensions between nobles and commoners, making the nobility (the *aristos*) and the bishops into the great enemy of needed reforms. Second, the political developments of May and June 1789 drove those clinging to the old vocabulary and to timid measures of reform into the mentality and reality of revolution.

In the villages, the coalition of legal men who provided virtually all of the presiding officers of electoral assemblies assured the success of the urban middle class program. These "presidents" often did not live in the village; some presided over multiple assemblies. Through these men, the patriot party of Barnave, Mirabeau, Navier, and others out-organized their opponents and elected a solid majority of deputies who were sympathetic to their ideas. The same political process occurred within the nobility. The conservatives, titularly led by the king's brothers, and actually directed by the *parlementaire* Jean-Jacques Duval d'Eprémesnil and the count d'Antraigues, got out their vote. The electoral success of the liberals in the Third Estate and of the conservatives in the Second Estate reduced the prospects of compromise.

The nobility suffered from a critical internal problem in the great political struggle of May–July 1789. Many of its members, such as those who had met in the Paris district assemblies, agreed with the Third Estate that France needed a constitution. They further agreed with the deputies from the Third about almost all of the key elements of that constitution. The conservative nobles, who dominated the elections in the outlying bailiwicks, could not agree on this fundamental point: they hoped to share power with the king, but rejected some of the principles their liberal noble colleagues (and the members of the Third) felt should provide the fundamental underpinnings of that constitution. When the critical moment came, in late June 1789, the liberal nobility sided with the Third Estate.

Parish *cahiers* did not stop with the clauses from the model *cahiers*. Numerically, the peasants dominated these assemblies. They often elected ploughmen to represent them at the bailiwick meetings, and used their village *cahiers* to set out the key demands of rural society. The peasants demanded the elimination of the existing tax system and the creation of a new one based on a fairer system of assessment. The *cahiers* of the clergy tended to fudge a little on how much they would pay, but the nobles and Third Estate almost universally demanded a new system based on a land tax. A majority of the noble *cahiers* even agreed to give up their tax exemptions. One *cahier* after another denounced the salt tax, interior tolls, the absurd proliferation of weights and measures, excessive government spending, venality of office—in short, virtually everything the Ancien Régime stood for. They demanded a permanent "Estates General," which would supervise government ministers, oversee taxation and spending, vote taxes and laws, and "represent" the nation.[24]

Local *cahiers* often mentioned specific grievances or demanded old-fashioned protectionism—like the butchers of Rochefort, who wanted to forbid outside *charcutiers* from bringing cooked meat into the city—but they could also tie broad philosophical principles to local government. We are not surprised to hear the lawyers of Rochefort refer to "this class of citizens [the Third Estate] . . . so long vilified, so often oppressed, which will retake in the national assemblies its rights and the degree of influence that the barbarism of previous centuries has taken from it, that Gothic prejudices still dispute but which reason and equity render unto it." The city's surgeons presaged the attitudes the National Assembly would take when they demanded the abolition of monasteries and convents, which were of "no utility to either religion or the government," and were perpetuated only by "laziness or the caprice of parents." The ordinary inhabitants of the parish of Notre Dame, outside the city walls, gave local voice to the democratic urges so evident at the national level: they demanded the right to elect the local syndic and his assistant, who were to serve two-year terms.[25]

In Paris, the district assemblies of April 1789 immediately put this idea into practice. Their actions demonstrate conclusively that the political nation, particularly the Third Estate, had already determined that they would henceforth have representative, partly democratic government. These people viewed the Estates General as the means to enact such a "revolution." The preamble of the *cahier* of the provosty of Paris, which met in late April, began: "A revolution is being prepared. The most powerful nation in Europe is about to give itself a political Constitution."[26]

The royal convocation letters in Paris had named presidents and secretaries for each district assembly. The voters immediately removed their officers and elected presiding officers, either the old ones, if they were willing to serve because they had been elected, or, if they refused, new ones. Jean-Sylvain Bailly, soon to be mayor of Paris and the first presiding officer of the National Assembly, wrote in his memoirs of his feelings on the glorious twenty-first April, when he attended his local assembly:

> When I found myself in the midst of my district assembly, I felt that I breathed new air; it was the phenomenon of being something in the political order and by the single quality of being a citizen, or rather of being a bourgeois of Paris, because we were still bourgeois and not citizens . . . That assembly, an infinitely small part of the Nation, nonetheless felt both the strength and the rights of all.[27]

The Revolutionary Content of the *Cahiers*[28]

[Before voting any taxes, its deputies] *"must have solemnly declared, recognized, and clearly stated the following rules: 1) That all the French are born free and equal, and that all power must come from the Nation."*

Cahier of the Third Estate of the parish of Filles Saint-Thomas, Paris

We must be absolutely clear on the revolutionary nature of these demands. Many historians, misled by the traditional vocabulary, have suggested that the *cahiers* did not have a "revolutionary" character: not so. If we examine the specific recommendations, and get beyond the rhetorical devices, we can see that the Ancien Régime had virtually no support in France in 1789, save among some a few hidebound aristocrats (both lay and ecclesiastic) and some elements of the poorer provincial nobility. The Estates General—that is, the real institution that had met in 1588 or 1614—had virtually none of the characteristics the men of 1789 attributed to their "Estates General." The *cahiers* demanded a revolution: a complete demolition of the Ancien Régime, root and branch, and the establishment of a constitutional monarchy. They demanded, as Morris rightly said, the substitution of law for will, of liberty and equality for arbitrariness and privilege. Like the Third Estate of d'Aval, they insisted that law derived from "the consent of the nation, legally assembled"; that demand—repeated again and again in the *cahiers,* especially those of the Third Estate but also, let us not forget, in many of those of the nobility and clergy, completely rejected the legitimacy of the Ancien Régime. Moreover, no compromise between this principle and the principle of royal absolutism was possible.

Many *cahiers* demanded local assemblies, also voted by citizens. The idea that people had the right to representation, and that their representatives should control the state, was ubiquitous, as the action of the Parisian districts—electing their presiding officers—made abundantly clear. Oddly enough, the royal government had done much to resuscitate such views, when it created regional assemblies of estates in 1788. Many of the deputies to these local assemblies sought, and obtained, election to the Estates General.

Among the bailiwick *cahiers* of the Third Estate, and even in many noble *cahiers,* such as that of Paris, the principle of a constitution stands out: everyone insisted that the first duty of the new assembly was to write a constitution. The *cahiers* demonstrate the total collapse of the old system. Few spoke up on its behalf. The language shows respect for the king, often referred to as the father of his people, and for monarchic authority, but the specific clauses invariably assault every principle of royal power. The king would keep only executive authority, losing his hold over both the legislative process and the judiciary. The *cahiers* assert the principle of the sovereignty of the nation, even if they do not use the word. For their authors, there could be no doubt: the nation, not the king, made the law. Here the distinction between the more radical *cahiers* of a city such as Paris, and those of outlying areas, became clear. The Parisian *cahiers,* those of the nobles, as well as the ones of the Third Estate, usually specified that the Estates General would make the law, which the king would then sanction.[29] Given that monarchical political theory rested on the principle that the king made the law, their assertions about the role of the Estates in that process are the essence of the revolutionary message. They believed in liberty, for persons and property.

The *cahiers* provide a remarkable road map of what would happen in 1789; the results of May through October 1789 corresponded very closely to what the *cahiers* had demanded. The relative unanimity among the general *cahiers,* that is, in the sentiments of the political elite, led quickly to a set of constitutional principles based directly on those sentiments. The National Constituent Assembly, as it would call itself, made the *nation* the source of sovereignty (lawmaking); gave the Assembly full control over taxation, borrowing, and state administration; established legal equality of individuals, freedom of the press, protection of individual liberty, inviolability of most forms of property, and a judiciary independent of the king's will; and abolished the greatest of the old abuses, such as venality of offices and all forms of privilege. They also agreed on some limitations: many of the *cahiers,* like that of d'Aval, with its insistence on the Salic Law's exclusion of women, demonstrated strong opposition to rights for women. The Assembly took longer to enact legislation over more contentious issues, such as freedom of religion or a "free" market.

"Enlightened" opinion among members of the Third Estate, clergy, and nobility agreed on the fundamental principles. They violently disagreed over other issues, including Church property, compensation for feudal rights, the existence of noble status, and control of the future Assembly. Their two key demands—liberty of people and protection of property—made them look to the king as the executive branch of government, a virtually unanimous clause in the *cahiers*. The *cahiers* of a few radical urban districts, however, revealed a level of hostility and a degree of intolerance for the Ancien Régime that foreboded violent conflicts to come.

The Voiceless

We the inhabitants of the countryside have no deputies in the assembly of the province.

Complaint of the peasantry of Époisses, in Burgundy

During the reading of the cahier, *the least among us were satisfied because we did not reject their complaints.*

Third Estate of parish of Saint-Germain l'Auxerrois in Paris

One little researched aspect of this process deserves mention: the conflict between the opinions expressed in the general *cahiers* and those expressed in the parish assemblies. Everywhere, lawyers or notaries from nearby towns presided over the village assemblies. Within the villages, economic interest usually divided the notables—lawyers or merchants or ploughmen—and the poorer peasants. As noted above, the notables often got the village assembly to enact a "model" *cahier,* adding a few articles about local concerns, or intimidated the poor into silence. Villages in which the seigneurial judges ran the meeting (and the royal letters stipulated that the "local judge" should do so) had particularly divisive meetings. Burgundy, which still had widespread serfdom, was especially fertile ground for "wild" assemblies: those who met after the official assembly and created their own *cahier* (known as the *cahier sauvage,* the "wild" or perhaps "free" *cahier*), the voice of the poor. The *cahiers sauvages* tended to address local issues, such as grievances of tenant farmers against their landlords or of peasants against the local seigneur. In some towns, the poor, usually excluded from the assemblies, likewise protested that their complaints had not been addressed. The self-serving addition of the good citizens of Saint-Germain l'Auxerrois notwithstanding, the Parisian poor in particular felt excluded; self-appointed spokespeople for this group published "*cahiers* of the poor," small pamphlets that set out the grievances of day laborers, porters, water-carriers, and the countless other poor workers of Paris.

At the next level, the bailiwick assembly, the rich ploughmen often provided half or more of the deputies, and many of the wealthy urbanites owned rural estates, so that concerns of rural property holders received a full hearing. The overwhelmingly urban deputies elected by these assemblies took away from the bailiwick meetings a package of important reforms for rural life, yet many deputies often lacked the expertise to understand how such reforms would have to be enacted. They shared with the peasants an abiding interest in destroying the existing taxes and in creating

The Parisian Radicals: Blueprint for Revolution

Reading the *cahiers* of the district assemblies of the Third Estate of Paris reveals the astonishing degree to which the urban radicals had a specific agenda, which they successfully forced upon a country little in sympathy with it. The forty-five voters of the district of Theatins, in the quarter of Saint-Germain-des-Prés, put together a remarkable document, which, in addition to the standard demands, made some far more radical ones. In article 25, they demanded that priests be allowed to marry, "because marriage is in no way incompatible with their functions, nor is it forbidden to them by divine law"; in article 26, they demanded that divorce become legal, "as an indissoluble contract is contrary to the inconstant nature of man"; in article 29, they insisted on religious toleration, because "tolerance is one of the most essential virtues in civil society." Article 30 demanded the abolition of religious orders,

> as contrary to the social will and the good of the fatherland, of which they diminish the population. By this means both simple and gentle, the regular orders of both sexes will be gradually extinguished in France, and their goods, thus acquired by the Nation, will serve for the payment of the public debt and for a multitude of objects of public utility. This article is one of the most important of this *Cahier*.

Just as the citizens of Filles Saint-Thomas predicted the confiscation of Church property and its use for paying off the state debt, so, too, they predicted that the state should divide all ecclesiastical revenues and make sure all parish priests get a salary of 1,200 *livres* (the precise amount the Assembly would later des-

ignate). They even asked the Assembly to finish off the Louvre according to the old plans of the architect Perrault: they wanted the expanded palace to include a library, an art museum, a cabinet of natural history, and a gallery of maps—all to be open to the public every day!

One of their articles (37) asked the Assembly to abolish all "bastilles," a demand echoed in several other Parisian district *cahiers* (and discussed at the general electoral assembly) and one that convincingly suggests that the storming of the Bastille on 14 July was far from an "accidental" incident. The inhabitants of the parish of Saint-Joseph, in the quarter of Les Halles, gave the most eloquent presentation of this demand:

> Article 6: That the Bastille crumble and rot; that this same ground, watered with the tears of victims of arbitrary power, shall henceforth be watered only by tears of relief and thanks; that the locale, condemned by the continued existence of this living sepulcher, shall henceforth be ennobled by a national monument, in honor of our good King, which will recount to posterity the memory of his virtues and his love for the French, of whom he is the father; that the demolished remains of this vast tomb serve as the foundations of a temple to Liberty in honor of the Estates General; and, like the brave Americans, who transformed into defensive weapons the statue of their oppressor, we will transform this abode of tyranny and the tears shed within it into a place of liberty and concord; in a word, let us be French, that is, free, and the support of the Throne and the Fatherland.[30]

a land tax that would be paid by all proprietors, no matter what their status. They also well understood the need to abolish many seigneurial privileges, such as the universally decried hunting monopolies and dovecoats.[31] The village and bailiwick *cahiers* often objected to other seigneurial rights—dues, milling monopolies, courts—but demands for specific changes varied sharply from place to place.

The deputies to the Estates General knew perfectly well that the peasants had expressed their grievances and knew, from reading village *cahiers* or even *cahiers sauvages,* what those grievances were. At the parish and bailiwick meetings, the deputies had heard the peasants voice these complaints. The deputies knew that they themselves had played a critical role in preventing peasant complaints from being sufficiently heard at the national level. All over France it was the same: the farmers who made up the largest segment of the population had few deputies among those sitting in Paris, and those few came from among the wealthiest ploughmen.

Ignoring rural opinion would have profound implications. Historians usually make the modern assumption that the "privileged orders" (clergy and nobles) could only represent themselves, so they take for granted Louis XVI's decision to allow the Third Estate to represent the countryside. These historians forget that the medieval Estates General and most of the provincial estates of France had a different system: the landlords (i.e., the clergy and nobility) represented the countryside.[32] The Estates General of 1560, 1576, 1588, and 1614 used a mixed system: in the areas without provincial estates, the Third Estate represented the countryside; in the *pays d'États,* the nobility and clergy usually did so.

The traditional system made more sense in certain ways. The clergy and nobles often had more common interests with the peasants on tax issues than did the deputies from towns. Urban merchants invariably supported higher direct taxes, levied essentially on landed property; landlords preferred indirect taxes, like duties on wine, because urban dwellers drank more often in taverns than rural ones. Provincial estates, such as those of Brittany and Burgundy, also had many resident rural nobles sitting in their assemblies. The Estates General would have scarcely fifty such men. This rural nobility shared cultural values, above all religious ones, with the peasantry: both groups remained much more closely tied to the Catholic Church than did the urban elites who dominated the Estates General.

On the one hand, by ruling that the "Third Estate" included the rural dwellers, Louis XVI enfranchised the rural mass of the population: about 70 percent of rural men could attend the parish assemblies of 1789. The rural dwellers could count on the Third Estate to support its demands against the nobility. On the other hand, the peasantry's attitudes toward a new tax system and toward the Catholic Church more closely mirrored those of the nobility and clergy, so the Third Estates's actions in those areas were not likely to get much support in the countryside. By ruling in favor of the Third Estate, Louis had recognized a fundamental transformation of French social life: the powerful landowning nobility of late eighteenth-century France no longer lived in the countryside, as its predecessor of 1614 had done. Many of the small-town notaries, lawyers, and judges who sat in the Estates General shared economic interests with the nobles and the peasants because they owned rural estates, but the roots of the rural–urban split that would devastate the Revolution in 1790 and after lay in the creation of an Estates General in which those who actually lived in the countryside had so little voice. When the Legislative Assembly came to power in 1791, the near total absence of rural men exacerbated this initial problem and helped pave the way for counter-revolution.

❧ THE BIRTH OF MODERN FRANCE: 27 APRIL–11 AUGUST 1789

Once the spirit of subordination is lost, the love of independence will start to grow in all hearts.[33]

The Parlement of Paris, remonstration against the Six Acts of 1776

CHRONOLOGY	27 April 1789–11 August 1789
27–28 April	Reveillon Riots in Paris
5 May	Opening of Estates General
7 May	Nobility votes to verify credentials on its own
26 May	Negotiations between Third Estate and nobility break off
4 June	Death of the Dauphin
10 June	Third Estate begins process of constituting itself as the full assembly
13 June	Parish priests begin joining with the assembled Third Estate
17 June	Declaration of the "National Assembly"
19 June	Clergy votes to join the Third in the new Assembly
20 June	Tennis Court Oath
23 June	Royal seance; Assembly refuses king's order to disband
24 June	Clergy disbands, joins the Assembly
25 June	Forty-six nobles join the Assembly
27 June	King orders all deputies to join the National Assembly
11 July	King dismisses Necker
12 July	Royal German regiment attacks crowd in the Tuileries Garden; electors of Paris form the Commune, new city government; customs barriers around Paris destroyed
13 July	Parisian crowds begin to search for grain and arms
14 July	Crowds seize arms at the Invalides, storm the Bastille, murder the Mayor of Paris and the two chief officers at the Bastille
15 July	King appears to the Assembly; vows to work for reform
16 July	Necker reinstated

CHRONOLOGY	(continued)
17 July	King appears at the Hotel de Ville of Paris, accepts the revolutionary cockade; nobles begin fleeing the country
22 July	Murders of Foullon and Bertigny
July–August	Great Fear in the countryside; reorganization of municipal governments
4–5 August	Assembly abolishes "feudalism" and privileges
5–11 August	Assembly debates precise abolition of privileges, issues decree of 11 August "entirely destroying the feudal regime"

The events of the spring of 1789 drove the process ever more in the direction desired by the Society of Thirty and the urban deputies of the Third Estate. The harvest of 1788 had been poor in most of northern France and grain prices rose steadily, peaking in July 1789, just before the new harvest came in. The high price of grain and the climate of political instability led to riots in many cities, such as the Reveillon riots in Paris (April 1789). The government feared precisely such disturbances: Morris and Lafayette discussed potential revolts in Paris as early as 17 April and Morris noted in his diary that the king moved 10,000 troops into the Paris region in anticipation of trouble.[34]

The worst rioting took place shortly after the electoral assemblies held in Paris's districts between 21 and 23 April. The disturbances about bread prices began in earnest on 24 April but worsened sharply on 27 April. At the assembly of the Sainte-Marguerite district, the paper manufacturer Reveillon had publicly stated that the price of bread should be reduced to a level affordable for workers making 15 shillings a day; the saltpeter manufacturer Henriot had said the same in another assembly. Their remarks reached the streets as support for wage reduction, leading crowds of artisans to loot Henriot's house and to destroy utterly Reveillon's house and manufactory (27–28 April). Troops called in to quell the disturbances killed between twenty-five and two hundred people and wounded scores more.[35] Reveillon sought and obtained protective custody in the Bastille, making him one of its last inmates.

Coming on the eve of the opening of the Estates, this riot did not bode well for the political stability of the capital. Contemporaries found these riots particularly suspicious because Reveillon had an outstanding reputation among the workers of Paris; he had spent large sums on relief for his own workers in the winter slowdown of 1788–89 and paid his workers far more than 15 shillings a day. The surviving evidence, such as police arrest records, indicates that none of Reveillon's own workers participated in the riots.[36] Some of those participating in the riots included artisans whose small workshops were threatened by Reveillon's products; these men may have been particularly upset that Reveillon represented the faubourg Saint-Antoine at the city's electoral assembly (which took place the very day of the riot).

Given that one *cahier* after another from the Third Estate had specifically mentioned that their deputies should not suffer any "humiliating distinction" with respect to the other two orders, the physical events of early May greatly strengthened the hand of the hard liners among the Third Estate. One group of deputies of the Third made their displeasure more evident by meeting on the evening of 5 May to destroy immediately the pretense that the group meeting in Versailles was an Estates General. They decided henceforth they would call themselves the "Commons," a term taken from the English; the French word, "communes," had, since the twelfth century, had a frankly revolutionary connotation. The next morning, the Third returned to the great hall, to find that the other two orders had been given separate quarters; the sheer size of the Third dictated that it would meet in the Hall of Menus Plaisirs.

The Estates had a profound political question to answer right at the start: would the Estates vote by order, with one vote each for each order, or by head, with one vote for each deputy? Given that the deputies from the Third Estate outnumbered those of the other two, control of the Estates hinged in the balance.[37] Those who knew the traditional procedures of the Estates General worried that one order could prevent action by its veto: the Estates General had always operated under the principle of consensus—the orders had all to agree for a motion to pass.[38] Given the dominance of the military aristocracy in the Second Estate, they seemed (and were) a formidable barrier to change. Those in the laity who demanded serious reform of the Church and of religious policy worried that the First Estate would use its veto to prevent the creation of religious toleration and to avoid reform within the Church, as had happened in 1560.

At the opening session, the royal spokesmen had proposed to the Estates that some questions might best be settled debating in common and others debating by order. The king would leave the question up to the Estates themselves. This proposal fueled the flames. Throughout the electoral season, pamphlets appeared setting forth the position of the two sides. Pamphlets supporting the position of the Third Estate dominated the field, particularly the incendiary *What is the Third Estate?* of the Abbé Sieyès. In response to his own question, he answered that by all rights the Third Estate was "everything" but that it unjustly had been made to be "nothing." What does it demand to be? "Something." Sieyès argued that the Third Estate *was* the nation, because it represented 95 percent of the people. In May 1789, more and more deputies to the Third Estate came to agree with him. When the nobility voted overwhelmingly (7 May) to verify credentials of nobles on its own and then declared itself duly constituted four days later, the Third Estate hardened its position. The clergy, too, verified independently, but made no declaration. Talks among the three orders dragged on from 7 to 26 May and broke off.

The king tried to get them back together on 29 May, but, as was so often the case, he vacillated. When his oldest son died, on 4 June, his paternal grief overwhelmed any interest in other matters. The Third Estate finally took matters into their own hands on 10 June, passing a motion by Sieyès that it alone was the "national assembly" and inviting the other two orders to join it. Here we do well to remember the "Summary" instructions written by the Dijon lawyer, Navier, which had proposed (in March) precisely this course of action. Given that Navier was in close

5 May 1789

The complications of setting up so unprecedented an occasion led to some delays, so the Estates General did not open until 5 May, at Versailles. The ceremonies themselves introduce us to the critical role of symbolism in the Revolution, and make clear the various currents of opinion. Morris tells us that at the great public procession of 4 May, the crowds shouted "Vive le Roi!" at every opportunity, but that the queen "meets not a single acclamation." His sources at Court told him that the queen and king were greatly offended by the ceremony: the king objected to the duke of Orléans marching with the deputies, rather than as a Prince of the Blood, and to the cold reception granted the queen. When Marie-Antoinette complained to a courtier about "these unworthy French" ("ces indignes Français"), the king's aunt, Madame Adelaide, reportedly replied, you should "say these indignant French, Madame" ("dites indignés, Madame").

At the opening ceremony on 5 May, the clergy and nobility appeared in elegant finery, the Third Estate, by order of the royal master of ceremonies, in simpler black costumes; moreover, in the great Hall of Menus Plaisirs of Versailles, where the opening session took place, a balustrade separated the deputies of the Third Estate from their social superiors. The master of ceremonies, the marquis de Brézé, who tried to regulate the meeting of the Estates using the same criteria he applied at Court, outraged many members of the Third Estate because of the elaborate and, to them, humiliating protocol of the great procession of 4 May 1789. He began the opening ceremony on 5 May by making the Third Estate enter through a side door, rather than the main

one used by the king and the other two orders. Morris, an eyewitness to the session, commented at length on the elaborate finery of the nobility, in their waistcoats and waist-length "lappets" made of "Cloth of Gold, " and contrasted it to the simple black cloth of the Third.

One deputy from the Third, Louis-Marie La Revellière-Lépeaux, "ostentatiously wore brightly colored clothes," while another "old Man who refused to dress in the Costume prescribed for the Tiers and who appears in his Farmer's Habit, receives a long and laud Plaudit." In another break with ceremony, many deputies of the Third, led by Jean-Sylvain Bailly, soon to be mayor of Paris, ostentatiously redonned their hats, despite Brézé's ruling that only the deputies of the first two orders could replace their hats once the king had done so. Morris tells us that "when he [the king] puts it [his hat] on again his Nobles imitate the Example. Some of the Tiers do the same, but by Degrees they one after the other take them off again. The King then takes off his Hat." He we can see a ceremonial confusion on everyone's part: the deputies from the Third know full well they are violating precedent by keeping on their hats, and so slowly acquiesce to old habit. The king, in his turn, perhaps somewhat embarrassed by this situation, responds by removing his hat, which then forced all deputies to do the same. One gets a sense of the general inclination toward reconciliation with the monarchy in another key element of Morris's description: "The Queen rises, and to my great Satisfaction she hears for the first Time in several Months the Sound of *Vive la Reine!* She makes a low Curtesy and this produces a louder Acclamation, and that a lower Curtesy."

contact with those—such as Mirabeau, Barras, Barnave, and the group associated with the Society of Thirty—who led the movement toward a National Assembly from May to June 1789, there is little doubt the premeditated plan of some of the leaders of the Third Estate had been broadly disseminated before the Estates General met. These men planned to accomplish precisely what they did between May and August 1789.

Timothy Tackett suggests that four key factors transformed the middle group favoring compromise into men ready to act unilaterally: "the growing group consciousness of the deputies, the didactic effects of Assembly oratory [especially by the Bretons], the impact of the crowds, and the attitudes and behavior of the Nobility."[39] Moreover, the specific policies recommended by many *cahiers,* even those phrased in the traditional language of the Ancien Régime, in fact supported just such a course of action. The *cahiers* of the Third Estate almost everywhere had insisted on the vote by head. In Paris, the people grew increasingly restive at the unwillingness of the nobility and clergy to turn the Estates General into the first National Assembly. The bookseller Hardy, who kept a diary of events, wrote on 4 June:

> One sees not only with sadness but with much uneasiness that there still exists in the capital as in many other parts of the kingdom, a seed of discord, a germ, a yeast of insurrection, whose flame, hidden and shrouded beneath misleading cinders, can at any moment cause the most considerable fire.[40]

Creating the National Constituent Assembly, 10 June–13 July 1789

If this revolution is fulfilled, it's true, the kings of France will no longer be legislators; they will no longer dispose of that monstrous double power to make the laws and to execute them. But is that losing or is it returning to the principles of reason, equity, and justice that must govern all the world?

Nicolas Ruault, to his brother, 8 July

The clergy and nobles failed to respond, so the Third began its work. On 13 June, three priests joined them, followed by sixteen more in the ensuing days. On 17 June 1789, the group took its most momentous step: on another motion by Sieyès, it adopted the title, "National Assembly" (soon changed to "National Constituent Assembly," to emphasize its primary function of creating a constitution) and further declared all current taxes to be illegal. It covered the government's legal tracks by offering a temporary continuation of existing taxes, but stipulated that the permission would lapse should the National Assembly be dismissed.[41] The letters sent home by individual deputies suggest that all of them feared for the future of their Assembly, and that many of them feared for the security of their persons, indeed for their very lives.

On 19 June, the First Estate voted to join the National Assembly. The next day, when the deputies to the Assembly found their meeting room locked, they adjourned to a nearby tennis court, where they took an oath not to break up until they had established a constitution. The Tennis Court Oath (20 June), immortalized in Jacques David's famous painting,[42] raised the stakes in the political poker game among the royal government, the nobility, and the Third Estate.

Three days later, at a royal sitting of the Estates General, the king sought to mollify all elements, although the nobility expected his statement to support their position: Morris tells us his noble friend the marquis de Boursac "anticipates a World of Triumph to the Noblesse in the Séance of to Morrow. He will I think be mistaken." The king entered to wild enthusiasm from the first two orders, who shouted, as was traditional, "Vive le roi!"; the Third Estate received him in silence. He accepted the principle that the Estates General alone could vote new taxes and loans, promised to abolish the most severe abuses of human rights, such as serfdom and *lettres de cachet,* and agreed to set up provincial estates throughout the kingdom.

Many historians have argued that these promises satisfied the demands of the *cahiers* written just two or three months before, but that they failed because they did not deal with the political events of May and June. In fact, the king did *not* satisfy the most critical demand of the *cahiers*: that the first duty of the Estates General was to draw up a constitution, and thus, that the Estates General, as the representative of the nation, did so on behalf of the principle that the *nation,* not the king, held the sovereignty. The *cahiers* had insisted that the "Estates General" vote both taxes and *laws*; the king had not acceded to this critical second demand. Here we can recall

J.-L. David, The Tennis Court Oath *(1791). David suggests that all three orders participated, whereas only those nobles sitting for one of the other two orders took part. His deliberate falsification gives us some indication of the role of artistic propaganda in creating legitimacy for the new regime.*

SOURCE: The Granger Collection, New York.

Morris's letter of February 1789, which isolated the great question: "shall we have a Constitution or shall Will continue to be Law?" Louis XVI's speech of 23 June left him firmly on the side of Will and so cannot be seen as acceding in any way to the central political demand formulated during the electoral campaign. The deputies of the Third Estate acted in May and June 1789 exactly as their *cahiers* had overwhelmingly instructed them to do: they sought to transform the Estates General into a National Constituent Assembly that would write a constitution, thus establishing the principles that the nation made the law and voted the taxes and that personal liberty and property were inviolable.

The king refused to accept the actions taken by the Third Estate in the previous week, ordered the three estates to continue to meet separately, and gave the privileged *de facto* veto power over any change in their status. He concluded by telling the deputies to disband and suggested openly that:

> If you were to abandon me in this worthy undertaking, then I should continue on my own to act in the interests of my subjects. I command you to disperse immediately and to return tomorrow morning to the rooms set aside for your orders so that you may resume your discussions.

The deputies who had created the National Assembly, bravely ignoring the large number of royal troops surrounding the building, refused. Bailly, who had chaired the meeting taking the Tennis Court Oath, replied to the royal master of ceremonies, "the nation assembled does not have to take orders." Mirabeau was even more direct: "Go tell your master that we are here by the will of the People and that we will not leave unless driven out by bayonets." François Furet has recently reminded us of Victor Hugo's reaction to Mirabeau's words—*Your master!* The king had been declared a foreigner.[43] Mirabeau had taken the final step in the long journey away from a kingdom in which the king could claim to be the personification of the public good, of the nation, and into a state in which the nation, the manifestation of the public good of its citizens, stood apart from and above the king.

The king, for reasons much debated by historians, decided to allow them to stay. Some suggest that he was distracted by the news that Necker had resigned—news passed to him as he left the room (the king dissuaded Necker later that day). Others claim that the king did not dare to resort to force, because of the tumultuous state of nearby Paris. Still others argue that the liberal nobles, led by the marquis de Lafayette, implored the king, who in this version had ordered his bodyguard to dismiss the deputies by force, to act with restraint. Whatever the truth of the matter, Louis did not disperse them. Morris's diary entry for the 23 June is highly instructive. After noting that the aristocrats were "delighted with the King" he makes a more sober assessment: "In the Course of the Conversation they tell me some Anecdotes which convince me that the King and Queen are both confoundedly frightened and I am thence led to conjecture that the Court will still recede."

Events proved Morris right. The people in Paris and Versailles took his interpretation. Everyone, from the man or woman in the street, to the troops, to the deputies to the National Assembly, believed that the Assembly had won a signal victory. In

Paris, large crowds cheered patriot orators and the French Guards refused to act against "fellow citizens" (several Guards ended up in prison for their action). The bookseller Hardy would soon be writing of "an insubordination that spreads progressively, like gangrene." Spectators had been attending the sessions of the Third Estates since late May and they continued to urge on the deputies. Other troops soon followed the example of the French Guards; in early July, minor mutinies broke out among the troops stationed in or near Versailles.

On 24 June, the clergy disbanded as an order and merged with the National Assembly. A day later, forty-six nobles, led by Lafayette and the duke of Orléans, the king's cousin, did the same. The National Assembly received them with wild applause that lasted fifteen minutes. On 27 June, the king invited those deputies from the clergy and nobility who still held out, to join the Assembly. Ruault wrote that "the victory of the Third Estate over the two privileged orders is complete. There are no longer orders in the state." People danced in the streets of Paris. Morris wrote to John Jay: "The King after siding with them [the nobles] was frightened into an Abandonment of them. He acts from Terror only."

As part of a spirit of compromise toward the nobility, the president of the Assembly, Bailly, declared a recess, so the two hundred-odd holdouts could enter with dignity. The Assembly moved quickly to get down to business, establishing thirty working committees, thus creating groups of manageable size; moreover, in a gesture of solidarity, the deputies elected individuals from the two privileged orders to head each work bureau. The most important of these committees was the Constitutional Committee, which, as its name suggests, received the charge of proposing the new constitution. In the main assembly, the deputies arranged themselves in a semi-circle around the president of the Assembly, an office rotated on a regular basis. The more radical deputies began to gather in the seats on the left; the conservatives responded by sitting together on the right: Left and Right, to describe liberals (or radicals, in some cases) and conservatives, have ever since been part of the world's political lexicon.

The king and his supporters bided their time. Public order seemed to be breaking down everywhere. On 30 June, 4,000 people stormed the prison in which the mutinous French Guards were held, releasing them. The king, using the excuse that public order appeared threatened by such disturbances, began to move troops into the vicinity of Versailles: in less than a week, the government moved more than 15,000 soldiers into the environs of Paris, seemingly ready to make a show of force. On 8 July, Mirabeau publicly proclaimed in the Assembly that the king had already brought 35,000 troops to the Paris region and planned to bring 20,000 more, both figures substantial exaggerations, but accurate reflections of public opinion. Many of those around Louis—notably his wife and his brother, the Count of Artois—encouraged him to use these troops to teach the "rabble" a lesson.

Although the king's actual plan remains a matter of debate, contemporaries unanimously agreed with Hardy, who worried about the many troops and artillery flooding into the area around Paris, especially the encampments on the Champs de Mars and the plain of Grenelle, "as if one proposes to undertake the siege of Paris." The Assembly sent the king a delegation on 9 July, asking him to remove the troops and to rely on the loyalty of the nation. The deputy Camusat, from Troyes, wrote that day:

all of the places near Versailles and the capital are filled with soldiers; all of the passages, all means of communication are guarded. Convoys of artillery are arriving from all parts; ten to twelve regiments are expected in eight days, and altogether these different troops will form a body of 50,000 men. . . . Everyone is convinced that the approach of the troops covers some violent design.

Camusat and others did not have long to wait. On 11 July, the king dismissed Necker and created a new ministry. Informed the next morning, Camusat wrote (at 9 A.M.) to his constituents: "It is clear today that they invested Paris and Versailles with cannons and soldiers in order to contain the populace at the moment when they would find out about the disgrace of the only man who still had credit."[44] The Parisians and the deputies particularly feared the foreign regiments that the king had introduced into the area. Their fears proved well founded on 12 July, when the German cavalry set upon a crowd in the Tuileries gardens and its commander sabered to death an old man who dared to offer verbal resistance. All observers agreed that French troops would side with the people: Ruault's letter of 9 July speaks of entire regiments going over to the side of the people in the suburbs of Paris.

Taking the Bastille

On the morning of the 14th, that forever memorable day.

Nicolas Ruault, in his diary

The 14th of July, that day forever memorable.

Bookseller Hardy, in his diary

Yesterday's journée will be forever memorable.

Commune of Paris, 15 July

Parisians organized themselves at four key centers. At the Hôtel de Ville, the roughly four hundred electors of the city of Paris (those who had chosen the deputies to the Estates General) met to deal with two equally disturbing phenomena: the royal offensive against the National Assembly and the decline of civil authority. They took two decisive actions that mirrored those taking place elsewhere. First, they decided to create an urban militia, soon to be called the National Guard, and second, they made themselves into a permanent governing body for the city. They called themselves at first the "permanent community" but ten days later, they became the Commune. Many of the electoral assemblies of the sixty districts of Paris also set up permanent meetings, starting on 12 or 13 July. Some did so on their own initiative, but most at the direct order of the electoral assembly (11 P.M. on 12 July). On the morning of 13 July, the electoral assembly ordered each district assembly to arm two hundred men; later that day, they amended the order to six hundred men per district (48,000 men), to be raised in three days.

Two other centers of action emerged. The cafés of the Palais-Royal hosted large politicized gatherings, doubtless attracted by the protection of the duke of Orléans. He and his fellow members of the so-called Society of Thirty, a group of roughly that size who met regularly in the late 1780s to discuss reform, seem to have had some hand in certain of the demonstrations of July. The final group was the people themselves. In some cases, we can speak of groups of artisans, politicized by the activities at the Hôtel de Ville and at the district assemblies; in a few cases, more dubious elements sought to take advantage of the impending anarchy, but these formed an extreme minority, except in the looting of 12 July.

The long-standing tradition of the French Revolution in July 1789 is that "mobs" formed in the city and sought vengeance on the symbols of royal absolutism. A careful reading of the chronology of events, however, definitively suggests that such was not the case. The crowds who acted on 13 July and 14 July were far from mobs; they were well-organized, usually quite disciplined, and very specific in their goals. Plenty of evidence survives of disorder in the city—of arbitrary arrests, of harassment of the wealthy by the poor, of looting and pillaging by gangs of thieves—but the larger crowds, especially the citizen militia, did not act in this way. In fact, the action of the brigands did as much as anything else to call into being the citizen militia that would carry out the great deeds of 14 July. Even Hardy, whose fear of disorder was such that he refused to leave his house, had to comment on the "good order" of the bourgeois militia that formed on 13 July.

Although we have no surviving written documentation, in terms of direct orders, there can be little doubt that the combined efforts of the district assemblies and the permanent committee (at the Hôtel de Ville) gave considerable direction to the popular movements. The population of Paris did not act blindly or stupidly, nor indeed did they use excessive violence.

The Parisian people took matters into their own hands on 13 and 14 July, seeking to do five things:

1. Maintain order in the city.

2. Find grain to help drive down the price of bread.

3. Obtain arms and ammunition for the new militia.

4. Force the king to restore Necker to power.

5. Carry out some of the demands of the *cahier* of Paris's Third Estate.

The first act in the drama, the looting of forty of the fifty-four gates of the entry duty (*octroi*) barrier (12 July), seems to have been the work of self-interested parties, above all smugglers, wine shop owners, and thieves.[45] Yet the general *cahier* of the Third Estate of Paris had specifically demanded this course of action, as had that of the nobility.

The spectre of such violence encouraged the solid citizens who sat in electoral assemblies to act immediately to restore order. They did so, by calling into being impromptu companies of armed citizens, who then coordinated two efforts already underway: the search for grain and that for arms and ammunition. The effort to find grain did not bear much fruit: the price of bread reached an eighty-year high on 14 July. In this case as in so many others during the Revolution, the high price of bread played a critical role in inciting rebellion or popular action.

The crowds, primarily made up of artisans and shopkeepers, sought next to get their hands on military stores, such as weapons and ammunition. They looted the armorers' shops on 12 July; ominously, the French Guards sent to stop the looting instead fraternized with the crowd. On 13 July, the crowd seized gunpowder from a barge in the Seine and received more succor from royal troops: the two regiments quartered at Saint-Denis sent written word of their commitment to the popular cause. The chief royal official of Paris (the merchants' provost), Jacques de Flesselles, sought to distract these forces by sending them to supposed stores of military goods that proved to be empty. Angry artisans did not forget his "treachery."

On the morning of 14 July, about 8,000 people broke into the military hospital, the Invalides, removing cannons as well as small arms and ammunition. Another large crowd set out for the great royal fortress whose guns overlooked the faubourg Saint-Antoine: the Bastille. Thousands milled around the Bastille, demanding its surrender. A combination of bungling by the garrison and the determination of the radical elements of the crowd led them into the interior courtyard, where the five score defenders, panicked at so vast a throng, opened fire, killing between twenty-five and two hundred, depending on whose estimate one believes.[46] The French Guards joined the crowd and trained five of the Invalides's cannons on the main gate of the Bastille: it surrendered.

Generations of historians have castigated the attackers for what happened next: they murdered seven of the one hundred defenders. Given that those same defenders had just killed or wounded some one hundred fifty to two hundred of their fellows, what seems remarkable is less the murder of the seven than the sparing of the remaining ninety-three. The crowd took out its main fury on the man they held responsible for the deaths of their comrades, the commander of the fortress, de Launay. In a highly traditional gesture, they beheaded him (and his chief lieutenant) and paraded the heads on pikes through the streets. The German officer de Flue, who witnessed close at hand the murder of de Launay, received rough treatment at the hands of the crowd, but "I was astonished that they spared me." They spared his men, too; the Swiss soon enrolled in another regiment.

Another detachment, incensed at what it viewed as the perfidy of Jacques de Flesselles, sought revenge outside the Hôtel de Ville. Many defended de Flesselles as an innocent victim of misinformation, but one discontented artisan put a bullet through the provost's head and the crowd soon afforded de Flesselles the same treatment it had given de Launay. Although some rowdy elements suggested that other heads should join them—one rallying cry reportedly was "all bishops to the lantern post," in fact the city did not witness massive violence. One deputy wrote home on 16 July that "much more was accomplished through fear than through the desire for the good."[47] The English ambassador, the duke of Dorset, wrote that "the regular and resolute conduct of the population surpasses all that can be imagined."

The Storming of the Bastille, *14 July 1789. The artist has embellished the scene, but rightly emphasizes the key role of the cannon taken from the Invalides in the garrison's decision to surrender the Bastille.*

SOURCE: Reproduced from the Collections of the Library of Congress.

Hardy, who deplored the revolutionary crowds, made a stunned exception for the takers of the Bastille. In a classic summary of the events, he wrote:

> One cannot hold back one's astonishment when one reflects on the outcome of events to which we have been witness since the beginning of the week. One can only recall with horror and with trembling the infernal project that existed to introduce into the capital on the 14th or 15th, 30,000 men, seconded by brigands, to run down its citizens and then to clap into irons all those whom the sword had spared. One regards as something absolutely supernatural the taking of the Bastille *in less than three hours,* and as another sort of miracle the calling together and establishment of a bourgeois militia in less than 24 hours.[48]

The crowd in Paris could act with sudden violence: eight days later, they murdered a royal minister, Foullon, and his son, Bertigny, the intendant for Paris. Foullon, who had been the hardliners' choice to replace Necker, had been hiding in the country near Paris. When he tried to run further away, local peasants arrested him, placed him in a cart, his mouth stuffed with straw—a reference to his supposed remark that the starving people could eat grass if they had no grain. Brought back to Paris by a detachment from the new National Guard, the crowd at the Hôtel de Ville pummeled him to death and placed his head on a pike, its mouth again stuffed with straw. Another detachment arrested Bertigny, who suffered the same fate as his father-in-law. These events horrified the solid citizens: letters written home by the deputies themselves suggest that they recoiled far more from this act of violence than from the actions of 13 and 14 July. Morris exclaimed "Gracious God, what a People!" after viewing Foullon's severed head.

This incident aside, however, the great revolutionary days of the summer of 1789 passed with remarkably little violence. George Washington, writing to Morris in early October 1789, correctly stressed the absence of bloodshed in his view that the Revolution was not yet over: "I fear, though it [France] has gone triumphantly through the first paroxysm, it is not the last it has to encounter before matters are finally settled. In a word, the revolution is of too great a magnitude to be effected in so short a space, and with the loss of so little blood."

The Death of "Feudalism," 15 July–11 August 1789

The National Assembly destroys entirely the feudal regime.

Opening words of the National Assembly's decree of 11 August 1789

Louis XVI consulted his ministers and his army commanders; marshal Broglie, head of the army around Paris, assured the king that he could not rely on his troops, especially his French ones. Quite apart from the reliability of the troops, the king also had to consider his ability to borrow money. Capital markets were extremely sensitive to his actions; the government's credit was already feeble by mid-July. A massive military intervention in Paris would have destroyed what little credit France had left. Louis had only to read the *cahiers* to know that. The citizens of the Sorbonne district of Paris had written what was on the minds of all: "it shall be established and recognized as a fundamental maxim, which alone can assure the tranquility and property of citizens, that only the Estates General shall have the right to consent to loans and taxes."[49]

The king took three momentous decisions. First, accompanied by his brothers and a mere handful of soldiers, the king appeared at the Assembly on the morning of 15 July and vowed, in a speech written by the bishop of Autun, Talleyrand (a key leader of the Assembly itself), to work with them to restore the nation. The deputies erupted with joy: several fainted and one "died for joy" from a stroke.[50] Second, on 16 July, Louis recalled Necker, who had fled to Switzerland. Third, the king and the deputies headed to Paris to calm things down. On 17 July, bravely setting forth with a tiny escort, he set out for the Hôtel de Ville, where Bailly gave him "the keys to your good town of Paris, the same ones presented to Henry IV. He reconquered his people;

Bertigny de Sauvigny being led to execution; the head on the pike in front of him is that of his father-in-law, Foullon. This incident shocked contemporaries more than any other in the summer of 1789.

SOURCE: AKG London.

today, the people have reconquered their king." After Bailly's laudatory address, Louis responded, "I will always love my people," and accepted the Revolutionary cockade, an amalgamation of the white of the Bourbons surrounded by the blue and red of the city of Paris.[51] "Then, and not till then, [Louis] received the general shouts of Vive le Roi!" [Morris] from the initially suspicious crowd. All observers recalled how those in the streets shouted this refrain over and over, joined soon by those who had remained indoors; even the sick came to their windows to add their happy voices. Rétif de la Bretonne would later compare the king's presence to "the beneficial sun, seeming to dissipate the thick clouds that covered our horizon," and claim that "the king's arrival gave salve to my wounds."[52]

Once the people of Paris had stormed the Bastille, the Revolution took off in entirely new directions. The symbolic impact of this event is difficult to overestimate. The people had taken, by force, the most universally known (and detested) symbol of "despotism." Reaction throughout France was immediate. Cities, towns, and villages wrote to the Commune of Paris expressing their approval. Châteauroux wrote of "its joy at the happy revolution," while Le Havre spoke of the "Revolution that assures for ever the national liberty." Angers went even further: "A people grown

Louis XVI comes to Paris, 17 July to accept the cheers of the citizens and the keys to the city. On this fateful day, Louis accepted the tricolor flag, created by combining the traditional white of the Bourbons with the colors of Paris, blue and red.

SOURCE: Culver Pictures.

old in slavery, bent down under the yoke of tyrants, has risen up at a stroke, broken its chains, and, on the ruins of despotism, founded the edifice of liberty." The people of Caen, on hearing the news, immediately stormed the enormous medieval castle of the dukes of Normandy, which still overlooks their city. Many of the nobles, among them the king's youngest brother, the Count of Artois, and the clique around Marie-Antoinette, fled the country.

The new order began everywhere. The Commune of Paris took over the maintenance of order in the city, through the means of the National Guard. Immediately, in towns all over France, other urban elites did the same. Urban assemblies like that of Paris sprang into being. Revolutionary committees seized power in sixteen of France's thirty largest towns and shared power in ten others. In the countryside, the Great Fear, the groundless reports of "brigands," led people to organize themselves; entire village communities came together to create a new order. This transition took place with remarkable speed: almost everywhere, a new order was in place by August or September. After some confusing moments in the fall of 1789, the municipal elections of January 1790 established the legal foundation both for new municipal governments and for the principle of elective government.

At the national level, the Assembly went to work on its officially declared new purpose: the creation of a constitution. They had several models before them, most recently that of the new United States of America (1787). Leaders in the Assembly recognized the first key stumbling block: privileges. The Great Fear and the attacks on the châteaux, all luridly described in the popular press of Paris, created an atmosphere of naked fear among urban elites. Ruault's journal of 25 July noted that the Assembly discussed attacks on châteaux: "the country people have pillaged, devastated, some-times even burned a large number of châteaux belonging to nobles, designated 'aris-tocrats,' and have taken, dispersed, and thrown into the fire titles of nobility." In a letter to his brother on 8 August, he made a telling historical comparison:

> We live today in a state of constant alarm created by the large number of evil subjects, by a turbulent, restless population, which wants to burn down half the city so that it can loot the remaining half. *Liberty* is today the catch-word to carry out good on one side and evil on the other. With this single word, one can torch a city, burn châteaux, houses, ravage all the country-side; that's what peasants in various cantons of France are doing today, in hatred of their seigneurs. Liberty can lead to so many evils! This fury re-sembles that abominable madness, the Jacquerie, which covered all of France in mourning after the battle of Poitiers.[53]

He blamed the events on the hatred of the peasants for their seigneurs.

In such an atmosphere, one faction of the Assembly decided it could move deci-sively against the old order. The Breton Club, made up of the radical deputies of the Third Estate from Brittany, plotted to introduce a measure abolishing feudalism on the evening of 4 August, when one of their number, Le Chapelier, would be chairing the meeting. They convinced the duke d'Aiguillon to introduce a motion calling for abolition of serfdom, seigneurial dues, and labor services, in return for compensa-tion. The viscount of Noailles followed him and soon the flood began. In a frenzy of self-sacrifice on the altar of the nation, the deputies denounced or renounced all matter of privileges: hunting, wood gathering, private courts, urban and guild rights, provincial liberties, royal pensions, the tithe, venal offices. As Mirabeau (who actu-ally missed the session), had said in the spring, "privileges are essential as a defense against despotism, but an abomination used against the nation."

Waking up on the morning of 5 August, like a drunkard hung over from a binge, the deputies wondered what they had wrought. Many deputies had spoken cautiously on the night of 4 August, stating that they had to refer back to their constituents to make binding declarations. The deputies from Nantes wrote back to their constituents asking for such authority; in a special assembly held on 14 September, the inhabitants of the city voted to approve the deputies' action and to accord them full powers "in order to cooperate for the well-being of the state." Even the Breton nobility, who were boycotting the Assembly, accepted the actions of 4 and 5 August. In both Nantes and Quimper, local meetings of nobles affirmed the decisions taken by the Assembly. These cautious steps remind us of how weakly many deputies grasped the essence of the changes. The National Assembly had already ruled (2 July) that, as deputies to the National Assembly, its members could not hide behind the traditional obligation of members of an Estates General to refer back to their constituents before taking any action not authorized in their mandates.[54]

The Assembly took a week to sort through the main actions of the night of 4–5 August. They passed a definitive decree on 11 August; Furet rightly calls this decree the death certificate of the Ancien Régime. They abolished various "feudal" [their word] privileges: dovecoats, seigneurial courts, *cens*, hunting monopolies. They also abolished other privileges of the Ancien Régime, such as the tithe of the Church (abolished without compensation) and venal offices (abolished with compensation). They eliminated forever all "pecuniary privileges" of individuals or groups (such as towns, provinces or the Church). Clause 11 made all "citizens without distinction of birth" admissible to all public and ecclesiastical offices and abolished derogation of nobility.

The (male) members of French society agreed that the nation, composed of legally free and equal (male) citizens, would be the new form of political association. As François Furet has written, the decrees of early August

> are among the founding texts of modern France. They destroyed, from top to bottom, aristocratic society and its structure of dependancies and privileges. They substituted for it the modern autonomous individual, free in all that the law does not forbid.[55]

These actions confirmed Morris's judgment of early July, of the "Sovereignty of this Country as being effectually lodged in the Hands of the Assemblée Nationale." Now the Assembly had to use its sovereign authority to create a new constitutional system.

Notes

1. I rely here on the citation of Paquelin available in J. Bart, *La Révolution française en Bourgogne* (Dijon: La Française d'Édition et d'Imprimerie, 1996), 127. My translation.

2. I use feudal in the sense that contemporaries used it: a legal system based on privilege, on private ownership of public authority (seigneurial courts), and on property rights rooted in extra-economic factors. The vast majority of French people in 1789 lived under the judicial authority of a private individual, paid small feudal dues in recognition of such jurisdiction, had to abide by monopolies, such as mills and wine presses, and did not have unrestricted use of their landed property. Eighteenth-century Frenchmen invented the term *féodalité* to describe this system. Some half million people, mostly living in the Burgundies, were still serfs. They lived with great restrictions on their rights to move, to marry, and to inherit property.

3. The date I accept for the disjuncture, the 1760s, well precedes that accepted by most historians from the Classical school, who focus on the 1780s and on change immediately before the Revolution.

4. The philosophical underpinning of the argument here thus accepts only partially the Marxist tenet that social being determines consciousness; I would agree

that such is often the case, for large numbers of people, whose material conditions of life leave them few options. I believe, however, that consciousness, particularly that of individuals, can change for more purely intellectual reasons; furthermore, such change is most likely precisely at moments of extraordinary historical transformation, such as the French Revolution.

5. Its main immediate effect was the devastation of the French economy, on which see Chapter 15.

6. N. Ruault, *Gazette d'un Parisien sous la Révolution. Lettres à son frère.* (Paris: Librairie Académique Perrin, 1976), 129, letter of 1 April 1789.

7. We now know that the Estates General of the fourteenth century did not, in fact, make binding votes about taxation. We also know that the famous vote of a permanent direct tax (*taille*) in 1439 did not take place. In the 1780s, however, all observers believed the Estates General had made binding votes of taxation (those of 1560 actually did do so) and that the royal *taille* dated from the "great meeting" of 1439.

8. The Court of Peers consisted of the regular Parlement, along with the Princes of the Blood and the thirty-five peers of France.

9. Ruault, *Gazette,* letter of 19 January 1788, 102.

10. Cited in F. Furet and M. Ozouf, *Dictionnaire Critique de la Révolution Française* (Paris: Flammarion, 1988), 301.

11. "Memoir of the Princes," in *The French Revolution,* ed. P. Beik (New York: Walker, 1970), 11. Beik attributes the actual memoir to Antoine Auget, an associate of the king's youngest brother, the count of Artois. In addition to Artois, the memoir was signed by his cousins the prince of Condé, the duke of Bourbon, the duke d'Enghien, and the prince of Conti. The third royal brother, the count of Provence, refused to sign it.

12. Ruault, *Gazette,* 121.

13. In fact, the Parlement did allow for some exceptions. In 1614, members of the Parlements had to sit with the Third Estate; in 1789, they would sit with the Second.

14. This ruling applied to all *pays d'États*; it came in response to the turmoil in Brittany, where the two sides had already fought to the finish before the king issued his ruling. In 1614, most of these titular parish priests (curés) did not actually administer their parishes; the actual number of resident parish priests was therefore tiny.

16. As noted above, some parish assemblies allowed women heads of households to participate. Little evidence survives of individual women, living alone, being involved; the heads of households in question were invariably wealthy widows.

17. Many district assemblies in Paris—both of the Third Estate and of the nobility—also protested that the two groups met separately; many nobles insisted that they, too, were citizens of Paris and should meet with the other citizens in a single assembly.

18. This detailed look at the deputies relies on the outstanding recent book of T. Tackett, *Becoming a Revolutionary. The Deputies of the French National Assembly and the Emergence of a Revolutionary Culture (1789–1790)* (Princeton: Princeton University Press, 1996).

19. Ch.-L. Chassin, *Les Élections et les Cahiers de Paris en 1789* (Paris: Jouast et Sigaux, 1888), 4 vols., III, 327.

20. Chassin, *Les Élections,* I, 50-51.

21. Gouverneur Morris to George Washington, 29 April 1789, in *A Diary of the French Revolution,* ed. B. Cary Davenport (Boston: Houghton Mifflin, 1939), two vols., I, 60. Morris was one of the key framers of the American Constitution. All future references to Morris's letters or his diary come from this collection, which is organized chronologically.

22. The *cahiers* of both the nobility and the Third Estate of the Paris districts all contain precisely the same demands in this respect: lawmaking authority rests with the nation, in its Estates General; the state shall respect the freedom of the individual and the inviolability of property; the Estates General shall create laws to guarantee freedom of the press and various other rights; the Estates General alone shall have the right to vote taxes or approve loans. They disagreed on some other issues, notably the vote by head or by order.

23. Ruault, *Gazette,* letter of 24 February 1789, 126. Ruault's bookstore abutted the Palais Royal, chief meeting place of the Society of Thirty. His knowledge of these plans adds further credence to the role of the Society in disseminating this strategy.

24. I say "Estates General" because the traditional Estates General had no right to vote laws. Estates General meeting during a royal minority did have the authority to supervise royal ministers and government spending; those meeting under an adult king, as in 1576, had the right to offer advice about such matters, but no binding authority.

25. Jacques Duguet *et alia, La Révolution Français 1789–1799 à Rochefort* (Projets Editions: Poitiers, 1989). The citation from the lawyers appears on p. 17, that from the surgeons on p. 18, and that from the inhabitants of the parish of Notre Dame on p. 24.

26. Chassin, *Les Élections,* IV (1889), 427.

27. Cited in Chassin, *Les Élections,* I, 307.

28. Some time after I had written this section, a remarkable book by John Markoff and Gilbert Shapiro, *Revolutionary Demands: A Content Analysis of the Cahiers de Doléances of 1789* (Stanford: Stanford University Press, 1998), appeared. Their analysis, as the title suggests, strongly supports the interpretation set forth here.

29. Outlying areas sometimes reversed this wording, making the Estates General approve laws made by the king. A small number of *cahiers,* such as that of the clergy of Paris, insisted that the king alone made the law and upheld the traditional interpretation of the king as absolute but limited. They wrote: "That the French

government is a purely monarchical one; that the sovereign and legislative power resides exclusively in the person of the king. But, in the exercise of his authority, the monarch is bound by fundamental and constitutional laws."

30. Chassin, *Les Élections*, I, 449. Remarkably enough, three days after Parisians had stormed the Bastille, when Louis XVI came to Paris to show his support for the new order, the city government of Paris voted to erect a statue in his honor—on the site of the Bastille.

31. Nobles had the right to keep birds—doves, pigeons—and to prevent anyone from killing them. Peasants everywhere complained that the birds ate the seeds sown in the fields. The *cahier* of the provosty of Paris not only attacked hunting and dovecoats but insisted that all people currently awaiting trial on charges of violating such privileges be released. *Cahiers* often praised the role of seigneurial courts in resolving local disputes between peasants; they insisted on maintenance of similar local courts. They strongly denounced, however, seigneurial courts that resolved disputes between seigneurs and peasants.

32. The Estates General changed format in 1484 in some regions, allowing the Third Estate—formerly just the "communes" (i.e., self-governing towns)—to represent the countryside. These Estates also deliberated in common.

33. Cited in Chassin, *Les Élections*, II, 510. The Six Acts abolished guilds, in the name of the "right to work," possessed by all men. As noted in the previous chapter, opposition to the Six Acts led to their rescission and to Turgot's dismissal.

34. In a letter of the same day, he cited 15,000–20,000 men as the total number of troops recently introduced into and around Paris.

35. Contemporary estimates vary wildly; the likely figure is closer to twenty-five than to two hundred.

36. Nicolas Rétif de la Bretonne, then living in Paris, in his *Les nuits révolutionnaires* (Editions de Paris: Paris, 1989), 28–29, specifically accuses reactionary aristocrats of freeing prisoners from Parisian prisons and encouraging these hoodlums to carry out the riots. Rétif de la Bretonne tends to embellish his stories—the specific accusation lacks proof—but his general point, that forces seeking to destabilize Paris on the eve of the Estates General fomented the disorders, rings true. Morris and other observers had similar suspicions.

37. Deputies straggled into Paris every day, so that on any given day the precise numbers of deputies differed. The best estimates are offered by Tackett, who tells us that by mid-July the Third Estate had six hundred four deputies, the clergy two hundred ninety-five, and the nobility only two hundred seventy-eight (the Breton delegation of nobles refused to participate in the assembly).

38. Modern historians, unaware of the rules of the Estates General, invariably suggest that everyone feared that the two privileged orders would outvote the Third. Not so. During the debates of the nobility of Paris about voting by head or order, some speakers specifically mentioned the desire to avoid one order blocking the will of the other two. When the deputies of the nobility of Paris returned to them

in late June, explaining why they had joined the National Assembly (and agreed to vote by head), they cited the Assembly's fears of single-order veto. Logic would also dictate that the First Estate, dominated by parish priests (whose social origins placed them in the Third), would far more often have combined with the Third than the Second: the events of late June bear out that assessment.

39. Tackett, *Becoming a Revolutionary,* 138.

40. Excerpts of Hardy's diary are reproduced in Chassin, *Les Élections,* III.

41. All of these steps, it should be emphasized, had been recommended by many of the *cahiers,* such as those—both of the Third and of the nobility—of the electoral districts of Paris.

42. David somewhat disingenuously shows the nobles participating; no deputy to the Second Estate was present, although nobles sitting as members of the Third Estate, such as Mirabeau, did take part.

43. Furet and Ozouf, *Dictionnaire,* 301.

44. The tale of Camusat comes from L. Hunt, *Revolution and Urban Politics in Provincial France, Troyes and Reims, 1786–1790* (Stanford: Stanford University Press, 1978), 70–71. Morris's diary entries give credence to a plot to arrest key deputies, dismiss the Assembly, and starve Paris into submission; Ruault, in early July, worried about imminent violence.

45. They did not, however, destroy the gate whose duties ended up in the pockets of the duke of Orléans, one of the leaders of the revolutionary forces, which suggests that even they did not act blindly in their destruction.

46. The German lieutenant de Flue, serving with a small detachment of Swiss at the Bastille, dismissed the common figure of one hundred-sixty killed as too high, because the garrison had fired for so short a time. (Chassin, *Les Élections,* III, 535, n. 2).

47. The deputy Jean-François Gaultier de Biauzat, a lawyer from Clermont-Ferrand, cited in Tackett, *Becoming a Revolutionary,* 166. In note 74 on that page, Tackett suggests other deputies expressed similar sentiments in letters to their families.

48. Chassin, *Les Élections,* III, 575.

49. Chaussin, *Les Élections,* I, 422. Foreign ambassadors gave the same assessment to their governments; Louis had to go along with the Assembly because he lacked the money to do otherwise. Without their help, he could obtain no further funds.

50. Morris, 164.

51. This tricolor of blue-white-red became the symbol of the new France and, in time, the national flag. Dozens of countries, all over the world, have followed France's choice of a tricolored flag. In recent times, we can point to the new Russia flag, with its horizontal stripes of white, blue, and red, and to those of the newly independent states created by the collapse of the Soviet Union and of Yugoslavia.

52. Rétif de la Bretonne, *Nuits,* 45; Ruault, *Gazette,* 438–440; Morris.

53. Ruault, *Gazette,* 447 and 162 (letter). He makes reference to the greatest French peasant rebellion, which took place in 1358, in the aftermath of the English capture of King John at the humiliating defeat of the battle of Poitiers (1356).

54. The cardinal of la Rochefoucauld had made a declaration to the Assembly on 2 July that he could not agree to the deputies meeting together, rather than by order, because his mandate did not authorize such a change, and because the constitutional laws of the monarchy protected his order's right to meet separately. Mirabeau vehemently (and successfully) protested that representatives of the nation could not act in such a manner. Had the Assembly not so ruled, many of the deputies of the nobility and clergy—whose *cahiers* had specified that voting be by order—could have legally claimed the need to refer back to their constituents before agreeing to vote by head. The noble deputies of Paris, who lived close enough to do so easily, actually did take this step.

55. Furet and Ozouf, *Dictionnaire,* 131.

Chapter Thirteen

The Death of the Monarchy

The tumultuous populace of large cities are ever to be dreaded. Their indiscriminate violence prostrates for the time all public authority, and its consequences are sometimes extensive and terrible.[1]

George Washington, to the Marquis de Lafayette, 28 July 1791

The National Constituent Assembly's actions of early August 1789 revealed both the continuity of March through August 1789 and the ruptures to come. The Assembly moved rapidly to enact the program of legislation laid out in the *cahiers*. Virtually everyone agreed the Assembly should make laws, vote taxes and loans, hold ministers accountable, abolish useless and harmful privileges, and create a more responsive and effective government. The Assembly acted to fulfill these goals in July and early August 1789. In so doing, however, it ran up against three fundamental problems that would eventually destroy everything it had built:

1. The extent of the king's power as head of the executive branch of government and in lawmaking.

2. The delicate balance between liberty and property.

3. The role of the Catholic Church.

The decrees of 4–11 August created two precedents whose logical elaboration would prove very damaging. By simply abolishing the tithes, the Assembly eliminated a form of property that had existed for over a thousand years. Did the failure to respect property rights in this form have consequences for other forms of property? Contemporary property owners everywhere expressed such fears and demanded that the state take action to protect their property. Furthermore, by abolishing privileges, did the Assembly make inevitable the abolition not only of nobility but of corporate bodies? (As it turned out, yes.) The plot paranoia that provided a leitmotif to most of the Revolution often stemmed from the fear of mysterious "factions": at first that meant the "aristocrats," but later it came to encompass just about any group of people the writer or speaker wanted to attack.

The popular press—people like Jean-Paul Marat or Camille Desmoulins or Jacques Hébert in the *Père Duchesne*—regularly made ridiculous assertions about one plot or another. In June 1789, Arthur Young expressed "amazement at the ministry permitting such hotbeds of sedition or revolt"; after the fall of the Bastille, these journals became progressively more seditious.[2] The constant drumbeat of attacks against the aristocracy and the queen, in particular, hardened popular opinion against them. Rumors spread everywhere; in Bordeaux, the lawyer Pierre Bernadau reported in October:

> Here, they said that the nobles are assembled to massacre the Third Estate; there, that the count of Artois, with Spanish troops, was at the gates of the city; later, that Bordeaux was entirely mined or that the monks were arming themselves, etc. . . . etc.[3]

Young's journal suggests French people associated Marie Antoinette with a high explosive counterrevolution. In July, at Colmar, people told Young that the queen intended to blow up the National Assembly and massacre the population of Paris; a month later, Auvergnat villagers suspected Young as her agent, sent to blow up their local mine.[4]

People in the provinces swung back and forth. The king's visit to Paris on 17 July sparked many hopes: Bernadau, usually a hostile observer of the Revolution, wrote in his diary on 4 August that "as soon as we learned that calm returned to the capital, our electors wrote a letter of thanks to the Estates General." After a description of Bordeaux's celebrations on that day, with the "brilliant" fireworks, Bernadau warily mused, "Are we now free of danger, so that we can rejoice?" Bernadau's deep breath lasted little more than a week. When he heard of the events of 4–5 August in Paris, and of local reaction to them, he sang a different tune: "We feel every day how much the premature deliberations of the National Assembly expose us to the evils of anarchy."

The 5 October march to Versailles, and the forcible removal of the royal family and National Assembly to Paris, further heightened tensions. Many provincials, such as the nobility of Toulouse, sent off vigorous protests that the king had been made a prisoner and, alone among the French people, did not benefit from the freedom of movement decreed by the Assembly itself in August 1789. The confiscation of Church property in November 1789 added to the unsettled situation, although many worried more about how to get their hands on the land than about the fate of the Church.

The chaos of the summer and early fall of 1789 gave way to a remarkable degree of stability by the start of 1790. Young left Paris on 28 June and spent September to December in Italy. When he returned to France in late December 1789, he found the situation much calmer: no longer did he face arbitrary arrest at every little town. The relatively peaceful municipal elections that began the new year buoyed everyone's hopes. Lafayette wrote hopefully to Washington that "we have come thus far in the Revolution without breaking the ship either on the shoals of aristocracy, or that of factions, and amidst the every reviving efforts of the mourners and the ambitious we are stirring towards a tolerable conclusion."[5] Others took a less sanguine view of events, worried about the lack of an effective executive authority. Once the king and Assembly had been forced to move to Paris (5 October 1789), the king lost any real independence; he became, in effect, a prisoner in his own capital. Yet this prisoner remained the chief executive officer of government, with the authority to name government ministers. He also retained the strong loyalty of the officer corps of the army.

Abolishing tithes and many feudal dues, and the widespread popular perception that people did not have to pay the old taxes anymore, led to economic and political chaos in many regions. The local political climate calmed greatly after the elections of January and February 1790, but the economic problems lingered on. Moreover, the Church, having lost its revenues, could no longer care for the poor. The government, unable to collect taxes, could hardly take its place. Many wealthy families lost their income. Some of them depended on feudal dues for their main support, but far more lost heavily when peasants, no longer forced to go to the lord's mill or wine press, took their business elsewhere. Other peasants simply stopped paying their rent and their taxes. The traditional courts and part of the old tax system still existed in early 1790, but they had lost much of their authority. The inability of the government ministers to provide effective executive leadership hamstrung state action at the national level. When mutinies broke out in the army and the navy, the central government had great difficulty organizing a repression sufficient to restore order without alienating public opinion.

Lafayette would write more tellingly to Washington in March 1790, fleshing out his loose description of the potential shoals the ship of state had to avoid. He worried that the people "mistake licentiousness for freedom" and that "hatred to the ancient system," rather than clear thinking about a new one, dominated the Assembly's agenda. He further noted the continued presence of "two parties, the Aristocratic that is panting for a counter revolution, and the factious which aims at the division of the Empire, and destruction of all authority and perhaps of the lifes of the reigning branch, both of which parties are fomenting troubles."[6]

The apparent success of the Revolution in 1790 did not prove lasting. The events of 1789 and 1790 provided the critical foundation of all that was to come. The precipitant actions of the summer of 1789, which focused on destruction without first considering that something needed to be in place to provide the structures of political society, did much to create the dangerous momentum that led to civil war and the Terror. The inability of leaders in Paris to create an effective national government in 1790 guaranteed that the unstable elements remaining from the compromises of 1789 would overwhelm France. The Assembly could not be both executive and legislative branches, and it would not, perhaps could not, let the king and his officials freely perform executive functions.

George Washington accurately predicted to Gouverneur Morris (13 October 1789) that the discontent of the aristocrats and nobles, the mortification of the royal family (this even before he knew of the October Days), and the "licentiousness of the People" were sources of certain trouble to come. The fundamental splits between the nobility and clergy, and the supporters of the new regime deepened constantly in 1790 and 1791. The Assembly took a progressively harder and harder line against the two former privileged orders: confiscating the property of the Church, abolishing monastic orders, abolishing nobility itself. Little wonder that the local administrations of 1790, which usually contained a broad cross-section of society, including nobles and clergymen, gave way to much more narrowly recruited bodies in 1791. Nobles and clergymen all but disappeared. When the Constituent Assembly gave way to the Legislative Assembly, in September 1791, the same process repeated itself at the national level.

The failure of compromise in 1790 ensured that the carefully constructed Constitution of 1791 had no chance of success. Moreover, the Constitution's chief executive officer, Louis XVI, had already abandoned it before it took effect. The king and his immediate family fled Paris on 20–21 June 1791, forever destroying any chance of compromise among the aristocracy, the Crown, and the people. Some of the left-wing leaders, such as Marat, had been demanding the end to the monarchy long before Louis's flight, which Marat had long predicted. Once Louis had borne out such predictions, the momentum toward a new form of government could not be stopped. In hindsight, we see the republic, established in September 1792, as the sole alternative to the constitutional monarchy set up in 1791, but contemporaries took a different view. Many political leaders sought to create a Regency, usually on behalf of Louis's young son.[7]

The republican position had the overwhelming advantage of internal coherence; many of those who might have been strong supporters of a regency for Louis XVI's son refused to countenance the deposing of the king. The crowd in Paris rallied strongly to the republican side; in August 1792, they stormed the Tuileries Palace and put an end to more than 1,200 years of monarchy in France. The Republic they created lasted only seven years but the change in political culture and social myths survives to our own day.[8]

⌒ The Defeat of the King and the October Days

What a beautiful day, Sire, that Parisians are going possess your Majesty and his family in their city![9]

Mayor Bailly of Paris, to Louis XVI, 6 October 1789

CHRONOLOGY	26 August 1789–21 June 1791
4–11 August 1789	Abolition of Ancien Régime
26 August 1789	Declaration of the Rights of Man and of the Citizen
11 September 1789	Debate on king's veto power; he receives suspensive veto only
5–6 October 1789	Parisian women, followed by the National Guard, march to Versailles; forcibly bring royal family to Paris (Tuileries Palace)
2 November 1789	Confiscation of Church property
3 November 1789	King signs August Decrees

CHRONOLOGY	(continued)
14 December 1789	Reorganization of municipal and local governments
Jan.–Feb. 1790	Municipal elections
17 April 1790	*Assignats* become legal tender
June 1790	*Bagarre de Nîmes*
12 July 1790	Civil Constitution of the Clergy
14 July 1790	Feast of the Federation
31 August 1790	Repression of mutineers at Nancy
February 1791	Second *Camp de Jalès*; municipal elections
2 March 1791	Guilds suppressed
March–April 1791	Pope condemns the Civil Constitution of the Clergy; district elections
2 April 1791	Mirabeau dies
14 June 1791	Le Chapelier Law
20–21 June 1791	Royal family flees Paris; family arrested at Varennes

The Declaration of the Rights of Man and of the Citizen, 26 August 1789

> *Man is born free, and he is everywhere in chains.*
>
> J.-J. Rousseau, *The Social Contract*

The National Constituent Assembly had to determine the foundational principles of the constitution it would write and to enact legislation that would both eliminate the abuses of the old system and put into practice the principles of the new one. The abolition of privileges decreed between 5 August and 11 August paved the way for serious debates about the rule of law. Many deputies demanded a statement of principles to serve as a guideline for their deliberations; the *cahier* of the Third Estate of Paris, like several others, had explicitly demanded "that there be made an explicit declaration of the rights that appertain to all men, and that it declare their liberty, their property, and their security." Lafayette drew up just such a statement and showed it to his friend, Thomas Jefferson, then the American ambassador to France and living in Paris.[10] Various other "patriot" leaders, such as Sieyès, drew up similar documents. The Assembly debated the details and produced one of humankind's most important documents, "The Declaration of the Rights of Man and of the Citizen," passed on 26 August.

They borrowed heavily from Jefferson's *Declaration of Independence* and from George Mason's *Virginia Declaration of Rights*. They began:

> The representatives of the French people, constituted as a National Assembly, and considering that ignorance, neglect or contempt of the rights of man are the sole cause of public misfortunes and governmental corruption, have resolved to set forth in a solemn declaration the natural, inalienable, and sacred rights of man: so that by being constantly present to all the members of the social body this declaration may always remind them of their rights and duties.

The *Declaration* contained remarkably careful language. The Assembly met under the auspices of the "Supreme Being," not of "God," because, to a French person in 1789, the word "God" meant the God of the Catholic Church. The phrase "Supreme Being" not only brought forth memories of the deist principles of Voltaire, it allowed the *Declaration* to be ecumenical in its outreach to members of all religions, even those, such as Judaism, illegal in most of France prior to the Revolution. Once again, as with the abolition of feudalism, principle outran practice for a while: the Jews of eastern France did not get full civil rights until 1791.

Motions of principle were all well and good, but the Assembly had to take specific action. In the wake of the abolition of certain property rights, they quickly moved to protect what we think of as modern property rights. They denounced all "feudal" obligations related to personal status, such as serfdom, as an assault on the basic human right of liberty; the Assembly abolished them without compensation. The deputies ruled, however, that feudal rights based on land were redeemable property: peasants subject to such dues had to pay their owners compensation, later fixed at 25 times the annual payment for the dues in question. Most peasants, hearing that the Assembly had abolished feudal dues, simply stopped paying: "(T)he declarations, conditions and compensations are talked of; but an unruly, ungovernable multitude seize the benefit of the abolition, and laugh at the obligations or recompense."[11] Peasants immediately destroyed dovecoats, weathervanes, and seigneurial bancs in churches, and ostentatiously hunted and fished in forbidden forests and streams. Because seigneurial courts still existed in 1789, seigneurs immediately took their peasants to court to insist on full payment of dues and respect for property. This conflict got out of hand in regions such as Brittany and Guyenne, where large peasant bands burned châteaux and, in some cases, murdered their seigneurs. The large-scale passive resistance of the peasantry paid off in the long run; in 1793, the central legislative body (the Convention, elected in 1792) abolished all seigneurial dues without compensation.

The Assembly also decreed reimbursement for venal offices, hardly surprising in that about 30 percent of its members owned one. The state had no money to pay for these offices; in fact, it had almost no money to pay for anything. Many people refused to pay the old taxes. If we can believe Bernadau, matters got so bad at Bordeaux that the receiver of the old *vingtièmes* on income quartered troops in the

THE DECLARATION OF THE RIGHTS OF MAN
AND OF THE CITIZEN, 26 AUGUST 1789

The *Declaration* begins with a paraphrase from Rousseau's *Social Contract*: "Men are born and remain free and equal in rights," but rapidly abandons Rousseau for the more careful doctrines of John Locke. Clause two shows us the key distinction: "The purpose of all political association is the preservation of the natural and imprescriptible rights of man. These rights are liberty, property, security, and resistance to oppression." Here the Assembly sided with Locke and the Americans, and those who had written the *cahiers*, against Rousseau, who did *not* believe property was a natural right. The deputies stressed the inviolability of property, a matter of great concern to the men of property who dominated assemblies at all levels.

The rest of the *Declaration* brings forth classic principles of modern democratic government: the sovereignty of the people ("nation"), freedom of conscience, freedom of the press, rights to a fair trial, equality before the law, equal obligation to pay taxes, the right to consent to taxes, separation of powers, governmental accountability to "society." The last clause (17) came back to property: "Property being an inviolable and sacred right, no one may be deprived of it except when public ne-

cessity, certified by law, obviously requires it, and on condition of a just compensation in advance." The deputies added this clause, in part, to cover their tracks for the actions taken on 4 and 5 August, when the Assembly had decreed the elimination of so many different forms of property. It needed to reaffirm the principle of property as a natural right and tie that principle directly to confiscations.

The Assembly also made sure, as many contemporaries put it, to protect liberty from license. Clause ten, for example, allowed free expression of opinions, even religious ones, "provided their manifestation does not trouble public order as established by law." Freedom of the press had a similar limitation, because one could print freely only if one accepted "responsibility for any abuse of this liberty in the cases set by the law." In creating these loopholes for future action, the Assembly assured that whoever held the right to make the laws in question would define natural rights. One of their critical mistakes in the coming months would be that they often did so in quite specific terms. They did not learn from the salutary experience of the Americans, that vagueness ("We, the People") has its uses.[12]

houses of the judges of the Parlement of Bordeaux, in order to make them pay their assessments.[13] Desperate for a way to pay off the staggering national debt, the Assembly quickly focused on Church property as the answer.

The clergy were the biggest losers in the new order. The Assembly had abolished the tithes in August 1789, leaving the parish clergy with no means of support. This action alienated many curés who had, up to that point, supported the Revolution, but the Assembly did later vote them a state-paid salary.[14] In November 1789, the Assembly confiscated all the property of the Catholic Church, on behalf of the nation. (See the following text.) The Assembly issued bonds, called *assignats*, secured on the proceeds of the sale of the seized Church property; officers initially obtained reimbursement for their confiscated offices by means of such bonds. This robbing of

Peter's Church to pay for Paul's offices brought together the two greatest conflicts engendered in the fall of 1789: treatment of the Catholic Church and settling of the government's debts.

Provincial Reaction, July–September 1789

> . . . *something was to be done by great folks for such poor ones, but she did not know who nor how, but God send us better, because the* tailles *and dues crush us.*[15]

Unidentified peasant woman, speaking to Arthur Young, 12 July 1789

The greatest events of the summer of 1789 took place in Paris, yet the country did not remain inert. Provincial reaction weighed constantly on the minds of the deputies and the king. The dramatic events of mid-July helped fuel a massive outpouring of disorder in provincial France: local authorities reported more than a 1,000 separate incidents of violence in that month alone. This violence led to a climate of terror, one best symbolized by the Great Fear of late July and early August, which spread through several regions of the kingdom. The decrees of 5–11 August gave the Assembly's response to the disquiet in the provinces.

The storming of the Bastille, and the concomitant creation of the Commune of Paris led to the creation of local Communes in many French towns. Some cities, such as Dijon, changed their governments on their own. Pro-Revolution forces seized power on 15 July, before word of the taking of the Bastille could have reached them. At Caen, on 21 July, the city's population, imitating the action at the Bastille, stormed the great Château of the dukes of Normandy that dominates the city, seizing the arsenal held there; at Strasbourg, the day after they heard the news from Paris, the artisans stormed and looted the Hôtel de Ville. At Orléans, however, the news of the fall of the Bastille prompted no violence, only a special election of 20 men, authorized to be the new government (21 July).

Most towns created new governments; others, like Reims or Montargis, co-opted new men into the old group. At Troyes, a new committee seized power but could not keep control. On 9 September, the old mayor, Claude Huez, and the new committee convened a special hearing on grain supplies. Dissatisfied with the results, a crowd, mainly unemployed textile workers, seized Huez as he stepped down from the platform. When he fled into an adjoining room, they battered down the door and literally tore the old man to pieces. Women and children dragged his corpse through the streets, dumping it in front of the town hall. The crowd then pillaged Huez's house and those of three other leading citizens. In short order, the old royal officials, backed by troops, returned to effective power at Troyes.

Everywhere, the fear of chaos galvanized propertied elites. They sensed that the political order had lost its legitimacy and could no longer be relied upon to protect them or their property. Cities and villages reorganized their local governments in large measure to defend themselves against possible rebellions by the lower classes. The villages affected by the Great Fear invariably met under the auspices of their leading citizens, who took a leadership role in mobilizing them against the dreaded "outsiders."

Both the Great Fear and the actions of the National Assembly in early August had some relationship to real unrest in the countryside. Peasants in Lower Normandy burned twenty-five châteaux in the two weeks prior to 5 August. The 5 August abolition of feudalism led to more violent local action in many regions. Bernadau wrote from Bordeaux that:

> The people, interpreting in its own way the edicts of its representatives, takes the excess of licence for the exercise of liberty. There is not a single country proprietor who dares to count on tomorrow. The peasants permit themselves everything, first against the nobility and the clergy, then against all those whose coat is cut differently from theirs. From every corner of the province, we receive details of the most disastrous scenes: châteaux burned, prisons opened, houses pillaged, citizens insulted, comestibles sold at prices fixed by the buyers.[16]

In July, Arthur Young reported château burnings in the Franche-Comté, lootings in Burgundy; in August and September, he cited widespread resistance to paying dues, rents, and taxes, and witnessed orgies of hunting in Provence.

In Paris and in the provinces, propertied elites, above all members of the legal profession, acted to create a new governing system in the summer and fall of 1789. In town after town, royal officials lost power to a coalition of lawyers, clergy, nobles, merchants, and even, in manufacturing towns like Troyes, richer artisans. The National Assembly's decree of 14 December 1789, creating new local and municipal administrations, provided the framework for the final steps: the municipal, district, and departmental elections of January–February 1790. These fairly democratic[17] elections demonstrated the broad-based support for the Revolution among many groups. Limoges was typical, its voters selecting five lawyers, three nobles, four merchants, a priest, two shopkeepers, and a doctor. Even Troyes elected a new municipal government that included a noble, members of the clergy, former royal officials, lawyers, merchants, and artisans. The largest towns, such as Lille or Paris, had a much greater presence of people from the world of commerce and manufacturing than did smaller ones in 1790; in this matter, they presaged important changes in local governments in 1791 and 1792.

Rural areas, as Young's journal suggests, reacted strongly to the events of the summer of 1789. The peasant *cahiers* of 1789 had demanded abolition of the salt tax and the *taille*; they wanted the Church to use the tithes to pay the local priest and to keep up the poor; many denounced seigneurial obligations. The Assembly abolished feudal dues and tithes and, after the riots and tax strikes of 1790, eliminated the *taille* and the salt tax. Yet they insisted on compensation for many of those dues and often relied on the registers of the *taille* and *vingtième* to determine local assessments for the new land tax. To most peasants, it was just a different name for the hated *taille*. The countless specific local peasant grievances got short shrift from the urban leaders of the Revolution. When the Assembly sided with the landlords in a dispute over whether to call one Breton land tenure arrangement "feudal," the entire region around Vannes revolted. Troops shot more than a score of the rioters; local voters responded by boycotting the

JUST DESSERTS: ARTHUR YOUNG'S SUMMER OF 1789

Arthur Young, the English agronomist, traveled through France and Italy in 1789. He spent June in Paris, recording his precious observations about the great events, but left the city on 28 June. In July and August, he wandered throughout France, and offers us a remarkable view of the variety of local reactions.

Young first heads east, toward Strasbourg. At Château-Thierry on 4 July, he cannot find a single newspaper; in fact, he is shocked to find not a single coffee house! He writes in his journal: "not a newspaper to be seen by a traveller, even in a moment when all ought to be anxiety. What stupidity, poverty, want of circulation! This people hardly deserves to be free." Five days later, Young learns from an army officer that troops were converging on Paris, a rumor confirmed when he reached Metz (14 July). The next day, at the large city of Nancy, Young finds the locals unwilling to act on their own. They cautiously tell him: "We are a provincial town, we must wait to see what is done in Paris."[18]

Reaching Strasbourg on 20 July, Young hears of the storming of the Bastille and witnesses the riot at the Hôtel de Ville. At Colmar, a letter from a local deputy to the Assembly convinces everyone that the queen intends to blow up the Assembly and massacre the Parisians (one wonders if it was the same deputy whose inaccurate letter on the August Decrees touched off riots in the Alsatian countryside). Young comments: "Thus it is in

revolutions, one rascal writes, and an hundred thousand fools believe."

Moving southward toward the Franche-Comté, Young is repeatedly stopped by local militias or National Guard; everywhere, they tell him to wear the cockade of blue-white-red. After one such incident, he admits, "I do not like travelling in such an unquiet and fermenting moment; one is not secure for an hour beforehand." Arriving in Besançon, he reports that

> many châteaus have been burnt, others plundered, the seigneurs hunted down like wild beasts, their wives and daughters ravished, their papers and titles burnt, and all their property destroyed: and these abominations not inflicted on marked persons, who were odious for their former conduct or principles, but an indiscriminating blind rage for the love of plunder. Robbers, galley-slaves, and villains of all denominations, have collected and instigated the peasants to commit all sorts of outrages.[19]

Young here repeats the standard accusations that led to the Great Fear; in fact, we have little evidence of armed bands of evil-doers, nor did many seigneurs lose their lives, nor their wives suffer sexual assault.

Finally, in Besançon, Young again finds newspapers, albeit rather old ones. The countryside around the city, in contrast, remains in nearly complete ignorance of events: "for what the country knows to the contrary, their deputies are in the Bastille, instead of the

elections of 1791, whose local turnout averaged only 5 percent. Little wonder that this region proved to be a hotbed of counter-revolution from 1792–1793. In the southwest, between December 1789 and March 1790, peasant bands from the traditionally radical regions once roamed by the Croquants attacked over 100 châteaux, seeking an end to seigneurial dues. Nor did the rural community care too much about the social origins of landlords they attacked: their assaults targeted nobles (35), clergy (18), and commoners (29) alike.[21]

The peasants had also demanded access to land; the confiscation of Church property gave the government the means of appeasing some of this land hunger by selling high-quality meadows, woods, and arable fields. In some regions, like the

(CONTINUED)

Bastille being razed." Young finds it inconceivable that the nobles do not organize to protect themselves and criticizes the "universal ignorance" of the provinces. At Dijon, on 30 July, he again complains of lack of newspapers and seems astonished that he is the first person to bring news of the riot at Strasbourg. Once again, reports spread everywhere about rural looting (although few murders or burned châteaux). At last Young is able to see if the rumors about brigands—which he had repeated himself—are true: his informant at Dijon, the chemist Morveau, assures him they are not. Young quickly accepts Morveau's proof and conclusions.

At Moulins (7 August), we hear more complaints about the lack of newspapers, but Clermont proves better. There, on 12 August, citizens hear of the great events of 5 August:

> The great news has just arrived from Paris, of the utter abolition of tythes, feudal rights, game, warrens, pidgeons, &c. have been received with the greatest joy by the mass of the people . . . but I have had much conversation with two or three very sensible persons, who complain bitterly of the gross injustice and cruelty of any such declarations of what will be done, but is not effected and regulated at the moment of declaring.

Wandering through the Midi, Young meets up with the same situation he had seen in the east. Everywhere, people lack information: Le Puy, like Moulins, has no newspapers. The lack of information encourages wild rumors and suspicion of all strangers: Young faces arbitrary arrest in a village near Clermont (13 August) and again on both 19 and 20 August, in the countryside of the Vivarais. When he reaches Marseilles (5 September), however, Young finds a quite different situation: "Marseilles is absolutely exempt from the reproaches I have so often cast on others for want of newspapers."

Young's comments, which strongly reinforce other evidence we have about events in provincial France in that summer of 1789, remind us of the stunning changes that overwhelmed society. Provincials often had to act on insufficient information. Individuals, such as the over-zealous Alsatian deputy, could have an enormous impact on local opinion simply because of the scarcity of competing sources of information. Rural people especially relied on rumor; they heard the vague outlines of what had happened (as on 5 August) and reacted to it. Given the agonizingly slow transmission of news from Paris out to many rural areas, and even to some towns, it could not be otherwise. As Young wrote at Besançon on 29 July:

> Thus it may be said, perhaps with truth, that the fall of the King, court, lords, nobles, army, church, and parliaments, proceeds from a want of intelligence being quickly circulated, consequently from the very effects of that thraldom in which they held the people: it is therefore a retribution rather than a punishment."[20]

Cambrésis in the far north, peasants bought an average of 60 percent of the initial properties put up for sale.[22] Yet confiscated rural property in most of France ended up in the hands of the urban middle classes because the state sold most of the land in large blocks. In the regions close to large cities, like Bordeaux or Paris, urbanites often bought 90 percent of the nationalized lands.

The Revolution offered many apparent benefits to peasants, but peasants in many regions of France felt they had been robbed of the full benefits of the new order. They reacted with direct action against landlords, whether it was the peasants of the duke of Liancourt, east of Paris, who simply divided up his wastelands and brought them under their ploughs, or those of the southwest burning châteaux.

These conflicts died down in the fall of 1789—Young spoke of seeing a peasant hanged in Provence for attacking a château—but the evil feelings that underlay them did not go away. Aside from the rich ploughmen, who everywhere bought up confiscated Church property, and those relatively few happy villages in which the peasantry itself, in broad numbers, bought up these lands, most French peasants suffered from unfulfilled expectations by 1790. When the Revolution turned against the Church, the clergy of many regions found ready antigovernment allies among the disillusioned peasantry.

The October Days: The March to Versailles (5–6 October 1789)

The high price of bread was the pretext: the design formed by some since the motion by Saint-Huruge—to have the king and the National Assembly in Paris—was the true motive. It's true that such is the only means to avoid a shortage and to reanimate the commerce of Paris.[23]

Rétif de la Bretonne, speaking of the October Days

The Assembly focused its main efforts on creating a constitution. Should France have a single legislative body or should it, like England and the United States, have a bicameral legislature? Mindful of the potential for the nobility to prevent reform, the Assembly voted (10 September 1789) for a unicameral legislature. After much debate, they also defined the powers of the state executive, that is, the king. He could veto legislation for the duration of a sitting of the new National Assembly but, if a second elected Assembly passed the same law, it took effect over his veto. The king would have no veto over constitutional or financial bills. This debate over the royal veto took place against a restive political climate in Paris. Bread prices rose again, and the king had called in troops once more. Moreover, Louis had not yet signed the decrees of 11 August. Finally, on 5 October, the market women of Paris, incensed by reports that army officers at Versailles had defiled cockades bearing the national colors, and probably egged on by the agents of the duke of Orléans, took matters into their own hands.

Thousands of them marched to Versailles demanding bread and the removal of the king and of the National Assembly to Paris.[24] Lafayette and the National Guard of Paris, some 20,000 strong, soon followed. On the morning of 6 October, the usual misunderstandings led panicky royal guards to fire on the crowd, killing a few; the crowd, in turn, massacred a few of the guards and put their heads on pikes. Some elements of the crowd moved threateningly toward Marie Antoinette's apartments; she fled in her nightgown to the king's room. The royal family had little choice but to join the crowd, now swelled to 60,000, in a procession back to Paris. Led by pikes bearing the severed heads of Louis's guards, the procession slowly wended its way from the great palace of Versailles to the dingy halls of the vacant Tuileries. Henceforth, the royal family lived as prisoners in the Tuileries Palace, right next to one of the most turbulent neighborhoods of Paris. The Assembly, too, moved to the capital. The Paris crowd could now intimidate the government; it was not reticent to do so.

The October Days highlight the critical role of the people in the success of the Revolution. As Morris confided to his diary, "They all suppose, as was supposed in

The March to Versailles, 5 October 1789. Women led this critical popular movement, which brought the royal family and the National Assembly to Paris.

SOURCE: © Giraudon/Art Resource.

the American Revolution, that there are certain Leaders who occasion every Thing; whereas in both Instances it is the great Mass of the People." The March to Versailles completed the triumph of the Parisian radicals. Every step taken from June 1789 (the creation of a National Assembly), through July (storming the Bastille), August (a declaration of rights and abolition of "feudalism"), and October (bringing the king and the Assembly back to Paris) directly responded to articles from the *cahiers* drawn up by the Third Estate of Paris in April 1789. These initial steps, however, left aside the critical question of the new constitution. As Young had written on 20 July, they had two alternatives: a practical constitution (ideally one modeled on that of England!) or "to frame something absolutely speculative. In the former case, they will prove a blessing to their country; in the latter [case], they will probably involve it [France] in inextricable confusions and civil wars, perhaps not in the present period, but certainly at some future one."[25] Young's chauvinism for the English constitution notwithstanding, his larger point rang true, as events would bear out.

As for the man contemporaries viewed as the chief instigator of these events, the duke of Orléans, he quickly lost all credit with the public, as well as with the authorities. The Swiss banker Huber reported that Lafayette had a short conversation with the duke:

> Monseigneur, I am afraid that there will soon be on the scaffold the head of a person bearing your name.[26]

Orléans took the hint: he fled to England, where he remained until July 1790.

⌁ The New Regime Takes Shape

[M. Bellefontaine] *is to be the interpreter of our attachment, of our entire de-*
votion to the Fatherland and to the King, of our sentiments of fidelity to the
new Constitution, of our firm resolution to struggle with all our might, with
all our means, to maintain the laws and the prosperity of the Kingdom, and,
finally, to take, for us and in our name, the oath of the Federation.[27]

The naval workers of Rochefort, naming their representative to the Festival
of the Federation, 1790

The Assembly acted with dispatch and effectiveness on most matters. The deputies
created effective local and regional administrations, particularly in the judicial branch.
They produced a Constitution, sound in most respects. Despite its many successes,
the Assembly ultimately failed because of its inability to deal with four key matters.
First, it hopelessly bungled the creation of a place for the Catholic Church in the new
France. Second, it could not solve the interrelated issues of state debt and taxation.
Third, despite the prominent leadership roles played by many nobles (Lafayette,
Mirabeau, the Lameths), the Assembly could find no place for the nobility in the new
France. Fourth, the deputies failed to create a sound executive branch of government.

The Assembly had encouraged French people to think in new terms by quickly
(December 1789) replacing the provinces with a system of smaller jurisdictions,
called departments (at first, eighty-three, a number since increased). Within the departments, the Assembly created districts, themselves divided into cantons. The new
departments generally took the name of geographic features, such as the name of a
river (Cher) or of mountains (Maritime Alps). The elections of February and March
1790 created new councils at each of these levels of government. Rural landowners
obtained many of the new positions, along with the legal men more often found on
town councils; departmental councils rarely included the merchants, manufacturers,
and artisans found on municipal councils. Individual groups did not monolithically
support or oppose the Revolution. At Toulouse, where barristers obtained election as
mayor, as councilors at the three local levels of government, and as attorneys general
of the district and department, two-thirds of their fellows opposed the New Regime
and some became leaders of the Counter-Revolution. In Paris, barristers provided
one-quarter of the members of the Commune, but most of their brothers refused to
practice law in the new courts.

Municipalities used direct election by all "active" citizens; departmental and district councils used a method of indirect election, in which active citizens chose "electors," who then chose the councils.[28] The restrictive clauses—a minimum
twelve-month residence in the locale and a contribution of three days' wages in
taxes—eliminated few rural men, but disenfranchised almost all of the urban poor.
Something like 70 percent of adult men could vote in the first tier elections and even
the rules about electors, those sitting in the second tier assemblies, left perhaps a
million men eligible.[29] The rules eliminated all women, some of whom, it will be remembered, had voted in 1789. The Assembly's remarkably broad suffrage, far
broader than the existing systems in either Great Britain or the United States, di-

rectly tied the majority of male adults to the political system and gave them a firm and immediate connection to representative government. Just as the broad principles of the *Declaration* suggested, the general will—the male adults—would make and administer the law, either itself or through its representatives, who would merely give voice to the general will.[30]

Here and there, the elections led to problems. The small Burgundian town of Vitteaux provided the extreme case: when Jean Filsjean, lord of Saint-Colombe, a seventy-five-year-old noble, showed up at the electoral assembly, local peasants, outraged at the participation of someone widely believed involved in grain speculation in the 1775 Flour War, took him outside and lynched him. They told the police that he had been a "milord who betrayed the Nation." Elsewhere in Burgundy, where the continued existence of serfdom had poisoned relations between peasants and seigneurs, nobles faced physical attacks.

The two new councils had considerable local power. The district councils had the authority to sell the confiscated Church lands and to apportion taxes among the communes. Municipal governments took over many important functions, such as the maintenance of local order and poor relief. The Assembly, in response to the extensive complaints about the old judicial system, abolished seigneurial courts (1790) and created an entirely new system, based, like the municipalities, on elections. Each canton would have a justice of the peace, elected by the active citizens, for minor cases; each district would have a bureau of peace and reconciliation and a district court of five elected judges, chosen by district or departmental electors.

Civil cases could go to the tribunals only after they passed through the hands of the bureau of peace and the parties had obtained a certificate saying that reconciliation had failed. These new institutions, like the electoral regime itself, reinforced the idea of the nation as a cooperative venture, in which citizens jointly sought the common good, through justice and equity: "the strength and vigor of municipal life constituted one of the most striking characteristics of Revolutionary France."[31] This new local judicial system seems to have worked quickly and cheaply, even in Paris, a notorious hotbed of litigation!

At the national level, the Assembly created an Appeals Court that could rule only on procedural or factual error, and, in time, a High Court of the Nation, for cases involving government misconduct. The delays in creating the High Court proved to be an appalling precedent, because they encouraged the Assembly itself to get involved in such matters, preventing the creation of an immediate, effective judicial process for those accused of crimes against the nation. In the prevailing paranoia of 1789–1794, when opposition to state policy often carried a charge of treason ("*lèse nation*"), political interference in what should have been judicial matters inevitably led to violence.

The Assembly created a judiciary that answered to the people and the Assembly, not to the king. Once again, these actions directly responded to unequivocal demands of the Paris *cahiers*: "The judicial power must be exercised in France, in the name of the King, by tribunals composed of members absolutely independent of all acts of executive power."[32] Alas, that the *cahiers* did not say "independent of the constituted sovereign power," an oversight that soon had tragic consequences.

The provisions about central administration and general constitutional doctrines similarly attacked royal power and previous practice. The Assembly borrowed from the Ancien Régime the rule that the king had to consult with his six ministers (war, Navy, finance, interior, justice, and foreign affairs) and could send the Assembly no proposal that did not have the requisite minister's signature. They radically changed that rule's meaning, however, because the new constitution made ministers directly responsible to the Assembly, not the king, for their conduct. The Assembly circumscribed the king's suspensive veto, barring him from using it on financial bills or constitutional law. They forbade him from declaring war or peace without their consent.

As for the Assembly itself, once it finished writing the Constitution, it would give way to a new body, the Legislative Assembly, which would have seven hundred forty-five deputies. The two-year Legislative Assembly would be chosen by electors selected by the active citizens. The members of the Constituent Assembly, in one of their many unselfish acts, decreed that no one among their number could sit in the upcoming Legislative Assembly. This measure, no matter how nobly conceived, had the unfortunate effect of eliminating from the national legislature the only people in the kingdom with any legislative experience. Many of the deputies of the incoming Legislative Assembly had experience in district and departmental councils, but that did not compensate for their lack of national political experience.

The Constituent Assembly moved cautiously forward but it progressively became more and more radical in its rejection of the Ancien Régime. Having rejected the fundamental basis of that system, privilege, the Assembly began systematically to dismantle every privilege associated with the old system. The Assembly abolished manufacturing monopolies and the monopoly trading companies, and created a free market in grain. True to the grievances their constituents had drawn up, the deputies wanted specific reforms: a fairer tax system, better protection for property rights, a more just legal system, representative government. These pragmatic reform proposals led inexorably to a discussion of philosophical principles that had not appeared in many of the *cahiers*. The more the Assembly debated one change, and the relationship of that change to a given principle, the more it realized it had to make other changes.

The new system, based on law and on the nation, required a new vocabulary: the language of the Ancien Régime clearly could not be used to describe the New Regime. The Assembly, as the *Declaration of the Rights of Man and of the Citizen* makes clear, turned to the one alternate vocabulary then available, that of the Enlightenment. The recent events in the United States of America offered a particularly useful practical application of such a vocabulary. Many leading French intellectuals made that explicit connection. When Young visited Marseille in September 1789, Abbé Raynal told him that "the American revolution had brought the French one in its train." Raynal presciently mused that the constitution being proposed was too "democratical" and would lead to a "species of republic, ridiculous for such a kingdom as France."[33]

The Constitution of 1791 and the laws passed by the National Constituent Assembly created a new France; most of their reforms became permanent. They abolished privilege and put legal equality in its place. They established civil rights for Protestants and Jews (delayed),[34] eliminated the old usages and institutions, instituted uniform weights and measures (the metric system), unified tariffs, and legislated a wide variety of civil rights: freedom of expression, of religion, of assembly, all, of course, somewhat limited by law. They freed the serfs, although not the slaves, abolished internal tolls, tithes, the seigneurial system, the old taxes and privileged tax exemptions, and the temporal holdings of the Catholic Church. They created a new system of courts, relying on elected judges, justices of the peace, and juries. They helped initiate a national citizen militia and popularly elected regional, local, and municipal governments. They legalized divorce, made marriage a civil contract, and extended many civil rights to women, although they did not give women political rights. Before we are too quick to criticize the National Assembly and its Constitution, we must recognize their remarkable achievements.

The Revolution and the Church: Phase One, 1789–1791

> It must be shouted even from the temples: philosophy has resuscitated nature; philosophy has recreated the human spirit and restored heart to society. Humanity died by servitude; it is reborn by thought.[35]

> Abbé Fauchet, funeral oration for those killed in taking the Bastille, 5 August 1789.

Each move forward alienated a different constituency. The confiscation of the property of the Catholic Church (November 1789) naturally upset the clergy, who still possessed enormous influence in many regions, especially rural ones. Their chief spokesman, the Abbé Maury, alerted his fellow deputies to the wider issue raised by the confiscation:

> our possessions serve to guarantee yours. Today it is we who are under attack; but do not deceive yourselves, if we are stripped bare, your turn will come soon. . . . It [the people] will exercise over you all those rights which you exercise over us; it will say that it is the Nation, and that one cannot prescribe against it.[36]

Whatever else may be said about the Church's use of its property, it did provide the material basis for most poor relief in the Ancien Régime. The state's confiscation of Church property implied a nationalization of relief efforts. During the course of the eighteenth century, many royal officials, acting as private individuals, directed local hospitals; the state now took control of them. The roughly fourteen hundred hospitals responding to the initial state inquiry informed the commissioners that their collective income had declined from 21 million *livres* in 1788 to 14 million in 1790. This decline bespoke the disastrous consequences for the poor of the loss of the Church's property and boded ill for their future. Government control of poor relief meant rapid devolution of authority in this matter to local governments, such as municipal authorities. This highly localized organization of relief naturally meant that its quality varied sharply from one town to the next.

The Assembly also abolished religious orders (January 1790), making exceptions only for teaching and charity work. Contemporaries were familiar with stories of "useless" monks and with the age-old tales of lascivious friars and nuns. The utilitarian values of the late eighteenth century had little use for contemplatives, many of whom were, in fact, younger children of wealthy families who had forbidden them to marry so that family property would stay intact. Ordinary people, those a little less affected by the stereotypes of Enlightenment literature, knew the other side of the religious orders: they provided virtually all of the nurses and teachers of eighteenth-century France. People may have detested the wealthy abbots, but they had a much more positive view of the Christian Brothers, who ran schools for poor boys, or of the "grey sisters" who staffed most French hospitals. The Assembly, by abolishing the religious orders, grievously wounded the systems of poor relief and education.[37]

The combined actions against the Church alert us to the greatest gap between the deputies and the rural majority of the French population: the anticlericalism of the deputies. Like Abbé Fauchet, they looked to "philosophy," meaning the great thinkers of the Enlightenment, for answers to moral and political questions. In June 1789, the newly created National Assembly consciously voted not to hang a crucifix in its meeting chamber. Six weeks later, when a priest demanded that mass be celebrated each morning at the Assembly, the deputies burst into laughter. Like the people of Paris, the deputies particularly disliked the monks and the bishops, whose luxurious lifestyle contrasted so sharply with their pious protestations on behalf of the poor. The *cahier* of the Theatins section of Paris had summarized general urban feelings about the religious orders:

> In the future, religious professions must be extinguished and suppressed, as contrary to the social will and to the good of the fatherland, whose population they diminish. . . . (T)heir goods, acquired by the Nation, will serve for the payment of the public debt and for a multitude of objects of general utility.[38]

One of Paris's great cultural successes of the fall of 1789, the play *Charles IX* by Marie-Joseph de Chénier, illustrated the widespread anticlericalism of the capital. In this retelling of the Saint Bartholomew's Day Massacre of 1572, the cardinal of Lorraine urges Charles IX to slaughter the Protestants and blesses the swords of those who will carry out the deed. Chénier costumed the actors in the style of Charles's time and even used the bell of the church of Saint-Germain l'Auxerrois that, legend had it, had rung to signal the start of the massacre, as a prop. Morris commented that "this Piece, if it runs thro the Provinces as it probably will, must give a fatal Blow to the Catholic Religion."

Few deputies of the Third Estate were active Catholics; even many of the nobles, a group generally better disposed toward Catholicism, were not churchgoers. The deputies took a pragmatic attitude toward the religion of the masses: "Like nineteen-twentieths of the Assembly, I believe that religion is useful and that we must therefore allow public worship," wrote one deputy. Another suggested that "religion is the first foundation of the social order."[39] This condescension toward rustic believers had bloody consequences, as we shall see.

The Church had had a mixed reaction to the first stirrings of Revolution. The parish priests largely supported the agenda of the Third Estate in June 1789. They could even see their way to the abolition or modification of tithes; after all, they rarely received the money. The violent split between the church hierarchy and the parish priests in 1789, and between the secular and regular clergy, played into the hands of those who wanted to destroy the power of the Church. On the famous night of 4 August, after a bishop had suggested the abolition of seigneurial rights related to wood gathering, a noble proposed the abolition of tithes. That sort of internal division within the privileged orders carried over into the clergy itself. Abbé Sieyès, after all, had written the most influential and incendiary pamphlet on behalf of the Third Estate in 1789. The bishop of Autun, Charles Talleyrand-Périgord, proposed in October 1789 the confiscation of church property, touching off a violent conflict within the Church.

Mindful of the doubtful loyalty of many ecclesiastics, and possessed itself of a deep anticlericalism, the Assembly sought to ensure the clergy's loyalty by means of a special "Civil Constitution of the Clergy," which spelled out the clergy's rights in the new France. Priests and bishops would become servants of the state, chosen by the departmental or district electors and receiving a state salary. For many parish priests, the 1,200-*livres* salary would have been an improvement over their old income. The Assembly abolished the old bishoprics; each bishop now ruled over a department. The Assembly asked the Pope to approve (literally, to "baptize") these changes in the summer of 1790. He hesitated, both because he detested the principles of the Revolution as blasphemous and because he worried that the Revolutionary government was about to annex his personal enclave within France: Avignon and the Comtat Venaissin.

Four months of futile negotiations led the Assembly to act on its own, demanding that all French ecclesiastics take an oath of loyalty to the Civil Constitution of the Clergy. The bishops almost universally refused: only seven took it. The parish clergy split evenly, primarily along regional lines: priests in the Paris basin and the southeast took the oath, those in the north, the east, and much of the west did not. In some rural areas, the laity demanded that their priest refuse, as a symbol of their unhappiness with the course of the Revolution. Many urban priests, such as those of Dijon, also refused.

The situation worsened in late 1790 and early 1791. The inhabitants of Avignon forcibly annexed Avignon and the Comtat to France. The Pope, further incensed by this action, issued two bulls denouncing the Civil Constitution (spring 1791). The Constituent Assembly, in its last official act (September 1791), ratified Avignon's incorporation into France. Henceforth, the Catholic Church would be an unshakeable enemy of the Revolution. That hostility extended to republicanism everywhere, throughout the nineteenth century. The Catholic Church also associated the Revolution with recognition of the rights of Protestants. In some regions, such as Nîmes, where several hundred Catholics died at the hands of the Protestant National Guard in the *bagarre* (brawl) of April 1790, outright violence could not be controlled.[40] In the summer, 20,000 armed Catholic National Guardsmen responded to the Protestant threat by meeting together at the Camp de Jalès in the Ardeche. When a similar meeting took place in February 1791, thousands of National Guardsmen from an area extending from Marseilles to Lyon converged, only to find the Catholics dispersed. The

National Guard arrested and murdered the Catholic leader, dumping his corpse in the Rhône.[41]

The alienation of many parish clergy greatly exacerbated the rural–urban split. Rural priests were natural leaders of their communities: literate, broadly respected, sharing deep bonds of sympathy with their parishioners. In Breton areas soon to be in open rebellion against the government, the priests refused the oath because of pressure from their congregations. These "refractories" then came full circle, providing a leadership group for those in rural areas who felt betrayed by the Revolution. Other village notables, too, felt increasingly alienated from a Revolution driven more and more by urban concerns. The failure to make a clean abolition of feudal rights provided another serious rural grievance against the Constituent Assembly.

The alienation of the Church from the Revolution was part of a larger process; it did not, in itself, lead to counter-revolution, but helped provide a major piece of its substructure. The great anti-Revolution movements of 1792–1793 often took place in regions in which the local clergy had refused to take the Oath for the Civil Constitution; however, rather than look to those events for causality, we would better understand them as stages in a continuing process. The enormous mental gap in perceptions of the Church between the deputies of the Constituent Assembly and the rural majority illustrates the larger cultural chasm separating the two groups.

Fiscal Madness

> *The deranged state of the finances has obliged them to make a present use of part of the 800 millions, which were intended to pay off so much of the Dette constituée. It having been proved to them that the probable expenses for the three last months of the year will amount to above 230 millions, and that the receipt will be less than 94 millions.*[42]

> Earl Gower, English Ambassador to France, October 1790

Virtually all historians agree that the financial crisis of 1786–1789 precipitated the French Revolution, but few have seriously examined the fiscal system of the Revolutionary government. Two centuries of hindsight have focused on broad philosophical issues, yet the documents of 1789 through 1791 show that the Revolutionaries themselves spent much of their time debating the methods of financing the state, paying off France's enormous state debt, and avoiding bankruptcy. No systematic examination of the portfolios of the deputies to the Constituent Assembly tells us how many of them owned shares in the state debt, but the presence of so many royal officials among the deputies guarantees that a majority of them did so. One member of the Assembly's finance committee estimated the total state debt, including venal offices, to be 4.7 billion *livres.*

Where could the government come up with enough money to pay off these debts and finance the everyday workings of the state? Taxation did not offer an attractive alternative, because the *cahiers* of 1789 had almost universally demanded the abolition of all existing taxes. Although the Assembly voted a temporary continuance of these taxes in 1789, people simply refused to pay. In February 1790, a crowd at Béziers lynched five salt tax collectors. Perhaps responding to the Béziers incident, the Assembly abolished the hated salt tax a month later. In the next eighteen months, it abolished the direct taxes, internal tolls and customs, entry duties, and sales taxes. State revenue plummeted. Necker tried to float a loan (fall 1789); it failed, as did his ludicrous scheme of convincing people to give 25 percent of their income as a "patriotic contribution." His stock with the public fell so far that his dismissal in September 1790 "produced no effect either on the public mind or public funds" (Morris).

The *cahiers* had supported a land tax, levied on all owners; the Assembly enacted one of 400 million *livres* (1791), of which it collected at most 240 million *livres*, spread over parts of two years.[43] Revenues from taxation declined from 180 million *livres* in fiscal year 1790–1791 to 106 million *livres* in fiscal year 1791–1792. Given that the government spent between 600 and 700 million *livres* a year, it had only two choices: increase taxes or generate money from other resources.[44] Moreover, these figures ignore the substantial expenditure that took place at the local level. Writing in September 1790, Jefferson's secretary, William Short, rightly castigated the government for its unwillingness to take the harsh necessary measures: "you will readily believe that a government like this will not adopt the harsh business of forcing taxes so long as they can make use of that gentle means of striking paper to satisfy their demands."[45]

The Assembly quickly proved Short right, by changing the nature of the *assignats*. The Assembly first moved cautiously, retiring some governmental debt by decreeing that the confiscated Church lands would be sold to pay it. They issued *assignats*, large-denomination paper bonds guaranteed by the sale of the confiscated Church property: these bonds bore interest and could be used to buy up the seized land, called the *biens nationaux* (national property). The Assembly then began to use the *assignats* to pay state debts, such as reimbursement of venal offices, a matter of great interest to the many deputies who owned one.

The Assembly's next step eventually proved to be the fatal one. Realizing that the drastically reduced tax revenues could not pay for ongoing state expenses, they made *assignats* into a form of paper currency (September–November 1790). Yet this policy initially had more positive than negative consequences. The initial modest issue bore some relationship to the value of lands backing them, so the *assignats* maintained almost 90 percent of their face value until July 1791.[46] They provided an important respite to the government, putting into circulation about 1.2 billion *livres* by early 1791. The *assignats* provided the only financial solace the state or its creditors got; moreover, as one local official put it, even "the enemies of the Revolution themselves have an interest in this operation [land sales], because it is the only means by which they will be paid the liens they might have on the State." Local commissioners sold millions of *livres* worth of property, and some creditors and officers did get some money back, but both groups lost enormous amounts of capital in the Revolution.

The confused tax situation fitted in closely with major changes in the distribution of rural output. The abolition of the tithe, which removed a charge of about 8 percent on gross production, ended up profiting the landlords; they merely raised rents by a proportional amount. The extinction of seigneurial dues created much more uneven savings, but, once again, landlords kept the savings. Peasants reaped some savings because their direct taxes dropped so sharply in 1791: per capita direct taxation appears to have declined by 55 percent between 1789 and 1791 and to have bottomed out at 9 percent of the 1789 level in 1794.[47] Massive regional disparities in land tax rates continued, because the New Regime often used the tax distribution charts of the old one. Tax policy bore out the fears expressed about insufficient consideration for rural interests: landed interests paid almost all the taxes levied from 1791 to 1794, except for the forced loan of 1793.

The unwillingness of the deputies to vote sufficient taxation and the means to collect it led to three terrible consequences:

1. A loss of public credit, because the state debt could not be repaid.

2. Inadequate funds for departmental administration.

3. A decrease in commercial activity, in part related to the inflation caused by the *assignats.*

The one area in which one can say the Assembly acted with utter irresponsibility is state finance.

◞ THE KING AND THE ASSEMBLY: THE FLIGHT TO VARENNES

I do not know if this [the abolition of nobility] *accords well with the spirit of the Monarchy and if, without thinking about it, we are rapidly heading toward a Republic.*

Nicolas Ruault, to his brother, 22 June 1790

The Revolution maintained enormous reservoirs of support throughout France. People wanted representative government, at local, regional, and national levels. They urgently waited to see what the new constitution would say. In the spring of 1790, in response to the revolutionary events of 1789, peasants all over France organized local festivals, often around the ancient may pole. They festooned the poles with the tri-colored ribbons (cockades) of the Revolution and constructed bonfires of the symbols of seigneurial authority: church pews, weathervanes, and coats of arms. They forced seigneurs to host banquets and to fraternize with them. Soon these *ad hoc* celebrations became more ritualized and codified; they took on the name of federations. The federation celebrations led the Paris authorities to the idea of a great Festival of the Federation, to take place on 14 July 1790, at the Champs de Mars in Paris.

These mixed signals alert us to the extremely tenuous situation of 1790. The economy languished: Young wrote in January 1790 that only the colonial sector remained healthy. Production in one sector after another had fallen off dramatically, a situation that particularly affected the urban workers. The bountiful harvest of 1789 had helped, because bread prices remained low throughout the fall of 1789 and spring of 1790, but massive unemployment left tens of thousands of people on the public dole. Young claimed that over 20,000 Lyonnais, most of them silk weavers, lived off of charity by December 1789. Manufacturing towns like Troyes or Reims, which had already lapsed into recession before the Revolution began, housed thousands of starving workers. The government Committee on Begging's 1791 survey got reports from local officials in 51 of the 83 departments that nearly two million of their 16 million inhabitants (12.5 percent) were beggars. Even allowing for the inclusion of seasonal laborers in this figure, it still suggests a staggering poverty problem.

The titular ruler of this tinderbox of a country, Louis XVI, and his wife, Marie Antoinette, felt increasingly uncomfortable with the course of the Revolution. Louis signed the edicts grudgingly. He did not like the despoiling of Church property or the Civil Constitution. He or the queen personally detested many of the Revolutionary leaders, such as Lafayette. He and his advisors tried to maintain some semblance of control over the process by means of bribery, but the most important leader corrupted by royal money, Mirabeau, died in April 1791. Louis's relatives, above all his brother Artois and his cousins in the Condé family, agitated abroad for the Revolution's defeat. The king and queen corresponded with foreign rulers, first with Marie's brother Joseph, ruler of Austria and the Holy Roman Empire, and then with his successor, her nephew Leopold. The latter proved more sympathetic. He and the king of Prussia, Frederick William II, grew increasingly restive at events in France.

The relationship between the royal government and the Constituent Assembly seemed to be progressing relatively smoothly in early 1790. The king, after several weeks of planning a theatrical gesture, appeared unannounced at the Assembly on 4 February to reassure the deputies that he supported their work. He pledged to support the constitution and to raise his son according to its principles. He concluded, "Let us all, from this day forward, following my example, be moved by one opinion, one interest, one purpose—attachment to the new constitution and ardent desire for the peace, happiness and prosperity of France."[48]

The king's speech prompted the deputies to swear an oath to "be faithful to the nation, the law and the king." Provincial authorities postponed scheduled balloting so that citizens might hear the king's speech read aloud: in Rouen, the assembly voted to illuminate the town that evening and to have the local clergy chant a *Te Deum*, the traditional religious ceremony celebrating great royal victories. The outburst of joy notwithstanding, Morris noted that "I can conceive of no other Effect there [in the provinces] than to encrease Animosity. The Noblesse will consider it as the Effect of Thraldom in which he is held, and the Populace as a Declaration of War against their Superiors."

Louis waxed and waned in his attitude toward events. All observers agreed to his genuine concern for his people and his abhorrence of violence. He believed in some of the reforms of 1789—he often reiterated his willingness to accept consent to taxation—but other aspects of the Assembly's work deeply troubled him. Its anticlericalism, best symbolized by the Civil Constitution of the Clergy, particularly upset the king. His visit on 4 February 1790 and his actions that spring, however, gave hope to many. The great national Festival of the Federation, celebrated at the Champs de Mars (near the present Eiffel Tower) to commemorate the first anniversary of the taking of the Bastille and to signal the birth of the renewed France (official statements focused on the latter), gave

The king and his family walking in the Tuileries garden, without an escort. Louis and his family sought to establish a greater rapport with their subjects by such contact, and by propaganda such as this image. The royal family wears the much simpler modes of dress made popular by the Revolution.

SOURCE: Bibliothèque Nationale, Estampes, c. Hachette.

the king the public opportunity to take an oath of loyalty to the nation and to the constitution.

"Federalists," mainly members of the new National Guard, came from all over France to Paris to join Lafayette and the king in taking such an oath. Some observers felt the king displayed little enthusiasm for the events, but others, such as Earl Gower, thought that "the ceremony of the fourteenth was conducted with astonishing regularity." The nobility was conspicuous by its absence. All of Paris, save the nobles, had helped construct the giant works for the Festival. One group proposed to arrive at the ceremony "behind a hearse decorated with toads, vipers, and rats, intended 'to represent the ruin of the clergy and aristocracy.' "[49] However much the Festival of the Federation, celebrated throughout France on 14 July 1790, emphasized unity, its

The Festival of the Federation 14 July 1790. This massive festival in Paris mirrored those taking place elsewhere in provincial cities, as the entire nation celebrated the anniversary of the fall of the Bastille.

SOURCE: Bibliothèque Nationale, Estampes, coll. De Vinck n. 3761.

underlying message suggested a unity that did not include the aristocracy. Louis, whatever else he may have been, was also one of them.

The happy couple of 14 July 1790 did not last long. Already more radical political groups had begun to organize. The Breton Club, officially renamed (January 1790) the Society of the Friends of the Constitution, but universally known as the Jacobin Club, soon had more than four hundred chapters throughout France. Middle-of-the-road Parisians, like Ruault, feared that the radical club had more real power over events than did the Assembly itself.[50] The Cordeliers Club, led by Parisian radicals such as Jean-Paul Marat and Georges Danton, rallied Lafayette's opponents on the Left, while the monarchical party tried to create a coalition on the Right. Lafayette had reached "the zenith of his influence," as Jefferson's secretary, William Short, put it, "but he made no use of it . . . the time will come when he will repent having not seized that opportunity of giving such a complexion to the revolution as every good citizen ought to desire." Lafayette had many fine qualities, but, as Morris wrote of him in September 1789: "This Man is very much below the Business he has undertaken and if the Sea runs high he will be unable to hold the Helm." In the hurricane swells of 1790–1792, Lafayette, as much as any other individual, helped capsize the ship of state.

The coalition of 1789 suffered from considerable strains in 1790, but it remained strong in many areas. During 1790, many nobles—the Lameth brothers, Mirabeau, Lafayette—continued to play leading roles in national politics, or on departmental councils. The 1791 elections returned very few nobles, indicative of the collapse of the broader coalition of 1790. The Legislative Assembly, also elected in the summer of 1791, contained few nobles or clergymen, a stark contrast to the Constituent Assembly, where they made up about 40 percent of the membership. The Constituent Assembly, in part because of the important presence of nobles and clergymen, had a coalition of monarchists—those who wanted to preserve some power in Louis's hands. The Legislative Assembly had far fewer defenders of the king.

The royal speech of 4 February and the Festival of the Federation provided a somewhat misleading veneer of success. The Constituent Assembly alienated both of the privileged orders by measures such as the Civil Constitution and the legal abolition of nobility (June 1790). In August 1790, provincial events intervened in a critical way: the unpaid troops stationed at Nancy rebelled against their officers. The commander of the nearby garrison at Metz, the marquis de Bouillé, marched on Nancy and stormed the city, leaving 300 dead. After the surrender, Bouillé either hanged or broke on the wheel 33 captured soldiers. The Parisian workers and many middle-class politicians denounced his action, but Lafayette, Bouillé's cousin, defended his relative.[51] The general quickly lost popularity in Paris.

The revolt at Nancy formed part of the nearly universal loss of discipline in the armed forces. Earl Gower reported regularly to his superiors about the inability of the French Navy to find crews to man its ships. The naval base at Brest seems to have been in a state of semi-insurrection for most of 1790 and 1791: "attendance at Constitutional Clubs has occasioned a general disposition among the soldiers to cashier their officers; and, among the many new experiments now making in this country that of an army in which the soldiers are to have the command seems not to be the most promising."[52]

Some of the most important leaders of the Constituent Assembly, men like Antoine Barnave of Dauphiné or Isaac René Le Chapelier of Brittany, sought to create a consensus around the status quo. Barnave and his supporters believed the Revolution had achieved its goals: equality before the law, control of the political process by men of property, elimination of the abuses and "irrationalities" of the Ancien Régime, and a constitution. Most French people from 1790–1791 supported their view, but, as is so often the case in politics, organized groups of dissidents undermined a loosely guarded consensus. The radically revised political order of 1789–1791 created enor-

MIRABEAU

Gabriel Honoré Riqueti, count of Mirabeau, more than any other individual, provided centrist leadership in the National Constituent Assembly. Mirabeau came from a family of old nobility in Provence, but he had been disowned by his family and his order long before the Revolution. He lived the life of a complete wastrel, squandering his wife's fortune (which led to a prison term on the Ile de Ré), running off to Holland with Sophie de Mounier, young wife of an aged president of the *Cour des comptes* of Dôle. The long arm of French justice tracked him down and dragged him back to the prison at Vincennes, where he spent three years (1777–1780). As Furet has remarked, "The count of Mirabeau had taken from the Old Regime an incomparable experience. His future colleagues in the Constituent Assembly were men of law, judges, lawyers. He was a defendant, a prisoner, a litigant."[53]

In the 1780s, Mirabeau became a prominent writer, often working for important politicians, but penning pornography, too. He became friends in Paris with many of the subsequent leaders of the patriot party, such as Brissot; in 1788, he helped found the Society of Friends of Blacks, the French abolitionist organization. Unable to become a deputy of the nobility, he enrolled as a merchant in Marseilles, which elected him to the delegation of the Third Estate. His thundering voice—what Michelet called the "great voice of Paris"—and his imposing presence—Michelet speaks of Mirabeau's huge head, hideous and astounding in its countenance—made him one of the dominant figures of the Assembly.

No man better represented the contrast between deplorable private morality and support for upright public action. At night Mirabeau would carouse and gamble; by day, he argued for the abolition of slavery and the rights of man. He stood forthright against the excesses of royal absolutism—the *lettre de cachet*, which had imprisoned him more than once, was no simple theoretical abuse to Mirabeau—yet he accepted large bribes from the royal Court. The King bought off 200,000 *livres* of his debts, paid him 6,000 *livres* a month (plus 300 more for his copyist!), and promised a further million *livres* at the end of the Assembly. Yet Mirabeau insisted that such payments did not sway him; rather, he felt he led the Court in the direction he wanted to go.

Mirabeau's death, on 2 April 1791, robbed the Assembly of his leadership at a critical moment, and left the king with much less influence in that body. Earl Gower lamented his death because "the Jacobins will no longer be curbed by Mirabeau." All France mourned the loss of the great orator; the Assembly immediately voted to inter his remains at the special shrine for France's heroes, the Panthéon. Gower claimed 28,000 people followed the hearse and that three-fourths of Paris turned out for the procession. After the arrest of Louis XVI, when investigators discovered that Mirabeau had been receiving money from the Court, his remains were ignominiously removed.

---

mous opportunities for organized groups to step into the void and consolidate local, regional or national power. In Paris, Lafayette and several key collaborators cleverly maneuvered to create a hierarchy of professional officers and a core of paid soldiers in a National Guard that would be loyal to its commander, Lafayette. This effort failed: Lafayette once told Morris that the Guard would follow him into battle but that he could not get its members to stand guard duty when it rained.

On the Right, the king and his supporters longed to push the clock backward, to restore some of his power. On the Left, deputies such as Maximilien Robespierre and Jérôme Pétion organized to eliminate all vestiges of monarchical authority. Indeed, by the late spring of 1791 more and more deputies become convinced, like the radical Jacobins whom Young had called enragés in January 1790, that France needed to become a republic.

The king played a critical role in this uncertainty, because he played a double game with everyone. To his most trusted friends, he admitted that he opposed many of the measures in the proposed Constitution, such as the oath for the clergy. By the spring of 1791, he was ready to take critical symbolic actions, such as receiving communion on Palm Sunday from a refractory priest. When the royal family attempted to move from the Tuileries Palace to the château of Saint-Cloud on Paris's outskirts on Easter, the National Guard of Paris surrounded the Tuileries and refused to let the carriages pass. Antiroyal demonstrations in the capital increased; the left-wing press vilified the king, Lafayette, and other "traitors." The king plotted to escape from his *de facto* imprisonment in the capital.

The Revolutionary Press and Radicalization

A single instant will suffice to lead to it [civil war], *if you are sufficiently imbecilic not to prevent the flight of the royal family. . . . bring the king and the dauphin within your walls, guard them well, lock up the Austrian, her brother-in-law and the rest of the family.*[54]

L'Ami du Peuple, 17 December 1790

The revolutionary press played a critical role in the politicization of the people throughout this period. In Paris, the relaxation of censorship in the aftermath of the passage of the *Declaration* accelerated the growth of periodicals: one hundred forty (twenty-seven of them daily newspapers) sprang into being in 1789 alone, and roughly a quarter of these survived for a year or more. In the provinces, the dreary advertising circulars, often called *Affiches* (literally, notices), transformed themselves into real newspapers. First, in May and June, they began to report news from Paris; next, they started to publish major speeches, then political commentaries and summaries of key events in Paris and throughout France. The semi-respectable Parisian press, readily available at cafés throughout the city, ran the gamut from the left-wing *Ami du Peuple* (*Friend of the People*) edited by Jean-Paul Marat to the *Ami du Roi* (*Friend of the King*) of Royou. The less socially acceptable papers included the workers's favorite, *Père Duchesne*, published by the radical Jacques Hébert. The thousands of writers, editors, and illustrators of Paris also published countless pamphlets and broadsheets. These tended to be more radical in their politics (either to Left or Right) and, often, to rely on lewd scandal-mongering. Marie-Antoinette ("The Austrian") provided a particularly popular target for the left-wing publicists, who accused her of a wide range of sexual misdeeds and of political treachery.

The proliferation of published materials led to rapid growth in the printing industry, which boasted over two hundred shops by the late 1790s. The small scale of these printers encouraged radical political thinking, because they had little capital invested in physical plant. The largest printers, like Charles-Joseph Panckoucke (who

Lafayette touches the "res publica" of Marie-Antoinette. This pornographic wood-cut (1790) *is typical of the attacks against the queen. This particular image sullies Lafayette, too, and deliberately ignores the fact that he and the queen detested each other.*

SOURCE: Bibliothèque Nationale.

had twenty-seven presses in his shop), not surprisingly published less incendiary material; his chief newspaper, the *Moniteur*, served as the paper of record for the successive legislative bodies. The leading papers often had circulations of only 3,000 a day, but the total circulation in Paris ran into two or three hundred thousand. Individual issues of certain papers, such as *Père Duchesne*, could, on occasion, sell 60,000–80,000 copies. The audience far exceeded these numbers, because cafés and reading societies subscribed and many subscribers read articles aloud in the cafés and cabarets throughout France.

The limited figures available on subscribers unsurprisingly suggest that right-wing papers had heavily noble and clerical subscriber lists, while left-wing papers went to lawyers, business people, and artisans. A Jacobin paper such as the *Journal de la Montagne* went heavily (in the provinces) to lawyers and business people; the more radical *Ami du Peuple* was read by business people, government officials, and artisans, who subscribed twice as often to it as to the *Journal*. Professionals, largely lawyers, made up 30 percent of the *Journal's* subscribers, but only 8 percent of those of the *Ami du Peuple*.

Here we see another split, this one within the Left. In the early stages of the Revolution, up through 1791, the lawyers dominated the Left; starting in 1792, the readers of the *Ami du Peuple,* those involved in commerce and production, began to take over, especially in Paris and other towns. Although lawyers maintained a strong presence on departmental and district councils through 1792 and 1793, they progressively lost ground on town councils, such as those of Caen or Limoges. They had led sectional assemblies in Paris in 1790 and 1791, but rapidly gave way to small- and medium-scale manufacturers in 1792 and after. The revolutionary commissioners of 1793 in the section of Faubourg-Montmartre, for example, included not one lawyer among the fifteen men; in the section of Gravilliers, in 1792 and 1793, only one of the twenty-six commissioners was a lawyer. Haberdashers, tailors, sawyers, paper manufacturers, and others involved in production led the section.

The Flight to Varennes, 20 June 1791

Stop or I'll fire into the coach.

The postmaster of Ste-Ménéhould

In that case, stop.[55]

Louis XVI

What did these men read in the *Ami du Peuple* and similar publications? Marat tirelessly attacked the king, seeing an aristocratic plot behind every difficulty. Throughout the winter of 1790–1791 and into the spring of 1791, he predicted the king would attempt to flee Paris. On June 20, 1791, in one of the decisive events of the Revolution, Louis proved him right. Louis had well disguised his intentions, even issuing a formal declaration to other European monarchs about his support for the Revolution. He conveniently left behind a manifesto explaining his motives, stressing that the *cahiers* of 1789 had given the deputies a clear mandate: "the making of the laws should be done in concert with the King." He stated, accurately, that "in violation of this clause, the Assembly placed the King entirely outside the constitution."[56] In a long and rambling text, Louis essentially demanded back some of his authority. He accepted the voting of taxes and shared responsibility for the promulgation of laws, but he presented himself as the people's "father, your best friend," who would save them from the factionalism to which the Assembly was prone. Even he used the language of the Revolution to attack it:

> What pleasure will he not take in forgetting all his personal injuries, and in seeing himself again in your midst, when a constitution, which he will have accepted freely, will cause our holy religion to be respected, the government to be established on a firm foundation and to be useful by its actions, the property and position of every person to be disturbed no longer, and laws no longer to be violated with impunity, and, finally, liberty to be established on firm and immovable foundations.

Louis and his family did not get away. Although they slipped neatly through the lines around the palace, a series of little delays made the journey slower than expected. The military escort arranged for the king grew tired of waiting and retired. Finally, the local postmaster of the town of Sainte-Ménéhould recognized the coach and its

The return of the king from Varennes. Surrounded by the National Guard, Louis and his family return to a sullen Paris.

SOURCE: © Gianni Dagli Orti/Corbis.

occupants. He raced ahead to the tiny town of Varennes, where he called out the National Guard, soon joined by the entire population. The Assembly sent deputies and troops to bring them back; four days later, the procession entered a sullen Paris, whose crowds refused to remove their hats as the king passed and who shouted, "Long live the law" and "Long live the nation." On the morning after the flight, thousands of Parisians had entered the unlocked Tuileries, wandering its hall. Ruault, an eyewitness, states that they took only one item: the king's portrait. They tore it to shreds.

Louis claimed that he intended only to go to Montmédy, near the border, to be under the protection of that same marquis de Bouillé who had massacred the mutineers of Nancy. His opponents believed he intended to flee abroad and to organize a monarchist crusade against France. Certainly Marie-Antoinette conducted secret negotiations with her relatives in Austria to do the latter, and the king's brother, the Count of Provence, who did make good on his escape, declared that Louis had intended precisely such a course of action. The king, a traitor to the Nation: what would the Assembly do?

The vast majority of French people in July 1791 believed in a constitutional monarchy. The Assembly created a document that met with widespread approval, but the king's flight greatly exacerbated the split between the moderate mass of citizens and a strident, urban minority of radicals. In most quarters, public respect for

THE LONGEST NIGHT: THE FLIGHT TO VARENNES, 20–21 JUNE 1791

Louise-Elisabeth de Croy-Havré, duchess of Tourzel, was the governess of the royal children during the French Revolution. She miraculously survived the Terror (Gower initially thought her dead in the September Massacres of 1792) and left memoirs of her times of troubles with the royal children. She witnessed firsthand all of the great events, from the March to Versailles through the trials of the king and queen. Let us listen in to some of her reminiscences of the Flight to Varennes, on which she accompanied the royal family.

I was on pins and needles, even though I showed no anxiety, when Madame said to me, "There is M. de La Fayette." I hid Mgr the Dauphin under my skirts, and reassured them both that they could be quite at ease. I was certainly not so . . . Messieurs Bailly and La Fayette had come to attend the king going to bed, and disputed with him; in order not to give them any suspicions, that prince pretended to be in no hurry to go to bed. The king thus had to undress and go to bed; he then had to redo his toilette and put on a wig, to disguise himself. . . . When

he had climbed into the carriage, he held her [the Queen] in his arms, kissed her, and repeated, "How happy I am to see you have arrived!" . . .

We had to put up with several little incidents which prove only too well that the slightest causes influence great events. M. de Fersen, worried that the bodyguards had taken a route other than that indicated to them, was forced to re-cross the barrier to rejoin them, and preferred to take a longer route to avoid inconveniences, which made us lose another half-hour, which, added to the three-quarters of an hour delay in the king's bedchamber, put us an hour and a half behind schedule. . . . To make matters worse, the horses of the king's carriage fell twice between Nintré and Châlons; all of the harnesses broke, and we lost more than an hour repairing this disaster.

[The group changed from the broken-down small carriage to a large one at the barrier of Clichy.] We traveled in a great, commodious berlin carriage, but one that had nothing extraordinary about it . . . I was supposed to be the mistress, under the name of the baroness of Korff; the King passed for my valet, the Queen for my lady's maid, and Madame Elisabeth [the king's aunt] for the nursemaid. . . .

---

the Assembly increased after the king's flight, because they reacted so effectively and so expeditiously to the situation. They suspended the king, required all ministers to report directly to them, and sent a delegation to lead the royal family back to Paris. The urban radicals, such as the Cordeliers Club in Paris, reacted very differently. They denounced the king. The Cordeliers, leading a delegation of 30,000 Parisians, presented the Assembly with a petition demanding a republic or, at least, a plebiscite on the king's position. The Assembly demurred, deciding instead to rule that Louis could be reinstated as king if he agreed to accept the constitution. Departmental councils wrote praising the Assembly's action; in September 1791, they similarly lauded the king's acceptance (13 September) of the constitution. Louis, ever the vacillator, had taken ten days to do so. In Paris, the Left took his ten-day delay as the sign for renewed action.

Events throughout the summer had cast Louis in an ever dimmer light. When the Cordeliers organized a demonstration in favor of a "new organization of the executive power" at the Champs de Mars (17 July), Lafayette's 10,000 National Guardsmen fired on the 50,000 demonstrators, killing fifty, wounding scores, and arresting more than

---

(CONTINUED)

"At last I am out of that city of Paris," said this good prince, "where I have had to drink so much bitterness. Be assured that once I have my butt in the saddle, I will be very different than you have seen me until now." He read to all of us the memoir he had left in Paris to be brought to the Assembly; and he rejoiced in advance of the happiness of which he hoped to give France a taste, of the return of his brothers and his faithful servants, and of the possibility of reestablishing religion and of repairing the evils [done by the Assembly]. . . . Looking at his watch, which marked 8 o'clock, he said, "La Fayette is currently quite personally embarrassed."

. . . Arriving at Pont-de-Sommervel, how great was our sadness and our anxiety when the couriers reported to us that they could find no trace of the troop [awaiting us] nor anyone who could give us any indication about them . . . But our happiness was at an end. The Heavens, which wished to try our August and unhappy sovereigns to the end, allowed the duke of Choiseul to completely lose his head. The enterprise was well beyond his capacities. His heart was pure, and he would have died to save his King, but he did not have that calm courage and

tranquility that allows one cold-bloodedly to judge events and the means to remedy unforeseen circumstances. [The duchess goes on to explain how Choiseul, worried that the King was more than two hours late, decided that the enterprise had been called off and sent home all the troops that were to escort the King on his voyage. The carriage soon reached Ste-Ménéhould.]

M. d'Andouins, captain in Choiseul's regiment, came up to the carriage and whispered to me, "the measures have been badly taken; I will move away so as not to arouse suspicion." These few words pierced our hearts; but there was nothing to do but keep on our route . . .

Evil would have it that the infamous Drouet, son of the Ste-Menehould postmaster, ardent patriot, stood at that moment at the door and, having had the curiosity to look in the carriage, thought that he had recognized the King and positively assured himself of it by comparing the face of that prince with [the portrait on] an *assignat* that he had in his pocket. [Drouet rode ahead to Varennes, where he alerted the local patriots, who stopped the carriage.][57]

---

two hundred fifty people. Public opinion in Paris turned definitely against Lafayette and moved sharply leftward. A little more than a month later, an event outside of France sharply accentuated that trend: the Emperor Leopold (Marie-Antoinette's nephew) and King Frederick William II of Prussia issued the Declaration of Pillnitz, which called on all European powers to restore Louis XVI to his full rights as King of France. The Revolutionaries now could be certain of the hostility of Austria, Prussia, and the Pope. Powerless to do anything against the first two, they legalized the seizure of the French possessions of the latter, Avignon and the Comtat.

THE LEGISLATIVE ASSEMBLY AND THE FALL OF THE MONARCHY

What patriot, what aristocrat could ever write that he who so villainously turned his back on us on June 21st has suddenly become our friend on September 14th?

Nicolas Ruault, to his brother, 20 October 1791

The Constitution of 1791 created a new France, much of which had already taken root before the vote approving the constitution itself (summer 1791). Many of their greatest reforms became permanent: legal equality; the guarantee of such civil rights as freedom of expression, of religion, and of assembly; the abolition of feudalism and legal privilege; the creation of popularly elected regional, local, and municipal governments; the metric system of weights and measures. Some innovations, such as legalized divorce and greater civil rights for women, survived for only a few years. Indeed, many of the civil rights existed more in theory than in practice under later authoritarian rulers, such as Napoleon. In an immediate sense, however, French people strongly supported every major element of the new constitution, save one. The Flight to Varennes had created one intractable constitutional question: how could a king who so violently opposed the new order be trusted with its implementation?

In the last year of its existence, the Constituent Assembly had played an elaborate game with the king. He spent a lot of money to get support from key leaders in the Assembly, above all Mirabeau, and he also dangled control over prospective appointments to ministries in front of key deputies. From July 1790 to April 1791, the king effectively played off Lafayette against Mirabeau, using their great influence over the Assembly to try to preserve some of his own power and to counteract the authority of the radical Jacobins. Already in January 1791, Earl Gower had noted the increasing hostility of the various parties within the Assembly.

> The violence of party is at present so great in the National Assembly that no terms of abuse are omitted by the speakers on either side, and the style of language which used to be confined to the markets, and therefore called *le langage des halles*, is now very frequently adopted in that place.[58]

The rhetorical violence progressively stepped up, especially after the king's flight.

The death of Mirabeau (4/2) meant that the king had to switch to the brothers Alexandre and Charles de Lameth, Adrien Duport, and Antoine Barnave, a quartet whom their contemporaries called "the triumvirate." They belonged to the Jacobin Club, but followed policies to ensure the consolidation of the Revolution's gains. They had strong antimonarchist credentials from the debates of 1789–1790, because they had led the fight to limit the king to a suspensive veto and had also lobbied for a single chamber legislature, to prevent aristocratic influence. By 1791, however, they sought an alliance with some aristocrats and the king, because they wanted to avoid further destabilizing democratization. Barnave summed their view in mid-July: "any new step forward would be a culpable act . . . a further step in the direction of equality would mean the destruction of property."

Inside the Jacobin Club, other elements reacted vigorously against these compromises. The question of rights for people of mixed race in French colonies led to a violent debate in May 1791, in which Barnave and his group supported the whites, while the new Left, led by Robespierre, agitated for the rights of mulattoes.[59] The faction led by Barnave seceded (16 July) from the Jacobins and formed a new political club, named after the convent in which it met, the Feuillants. Lafayette, too, threw his support to this new group.

By September 1791, civil disturbances had broken out in many areas. Catholics and Protestants fought bloody battles in the Midi; anti-noble and anti-urban riots broke out in Quercy and the Auvergne; peasant bands formed in Brittany and the west; parts of Alsace seemed ready to seek the protection of the Emperor. The implementation of the Civil Constitution of the Clergy provided a flash point for this agitation. Supporters of the new order sought to intimidate parish priests into signing the oath of loyalty to the new constitution; they physically drove out priests who refused to sign. The active hostility against non-juring priests soon led to a counterattack against juring ones. Peasants in many regions drove off priests who had taken the oath. Although many non-juring regions, such as the Vannetais, had pre-existing grievances against the Assembly, the implementation of the oath for priests provided an effective rallying point for discontent of all kinds.

The takeover of municipal governments by the commercial and manufacturing interests led to conflicts between those governments and departmental ones, still dominated by lawyers and landowners. Moreover, the commercial and manufacturing group had profound splits within its own ranks. In June, the National Assembly had passed the Le Chapelier Law banning workers' and producers' organizations, which outraged guild members and journeymen, who lost their associations, the *compagnonnages*. Guild members tended to maintain informal bonds in place of the formal ones, and the *compagnonnages* survived, illegally, into the nineteenth century, but the Le Chapelier Law increased the militancy of the *sans-culottes* artisans in every town in France, above all in Paris.

The greater militancy of the Paris *sans-culottes* provided the increasingly mercantile leadership of the sectional assemblies with a large, militant, readily mobilized force. The more moderate legal men, often allied with the Feuillants, had steadily lost ground to the merchants and manufacturers in elected assemblies: in 1791, legal men dropped to a mere 13.6 percent of the electors, less than half the percentage of 1790. In section after section, the average age of those chosen as electors declined from year to year, as did the percentage of those who had been chosen previously, which dropped from just under half in 1791 to less than 20 percent in 1792.

The new national representative body, the Legislative Assembly, also differed markedly from its predecessor. The active citizens had met in June 1791, that is before the king's flight, and chosen electors. The electors met between 29 August and 5 September to choose the new Assembly. Virtually all of the new deputies held positions in local administration. Eighty percent of the deputies from one sample of 17 departments served as local officials, most often on departmental councils.[60] As in the local elections of Paris, the national elections of 1791 highlighted the rise of a new generation to political power. Whereas the average age of the deputies chosen in 1789 was about forty-five, half of the deputies elected in 1791 were under thirty. In the Legislative Assembly, as in local assemblies, men with substantially less stake in the Ancien Régime, those committed to the principles of a new order that rejected everything about the old one, became far more prominent.

The old leaders of the National Assembly continued to hold sway behind the scenes because none of these new deputies had national experience. The Feuillants divided into two groups, one led by the Lameths, Duport, and Barnave, and the other by Lafayette. Together, these groups had the allegiance of three hundred forty-five deputies. The more radical Jacobins, led by Maximilien Robespierre, Jacques-Pierre Brissot de Warville, and Pierre Vergniaud, could claim one hundred thirty-five. Control of the Legislative Assembly thus rested with the uncommitted group of about three hundred deputies.

Many observers in September 1791 believed that the Legislative Assembly would be unable to control the situation because the new state lacked the means for effective action. Unable to collect the new taxes, the Legislative Assembly issued more and more *assignats*, which declined to 63 percent of face value by January 1792. Discipline in the army remained poor; many of its officers, upset at the treatment of the king after his flight, did little to disguise their hostility to the new regime. Between September and December 1791, more than two thousand army officers emigrated from France, bringing the total who left between July 1789 and December 1791 to over 6,000. These desertions left entire units without trained officers.

No money, no army: what was the Legislative Assembly to do? One faction wanted to increase the power of the king. After all, the chaotic situation of the fall of 1791 required strong executive action, and the king was, for good or for ill, the executive branch. This faction gave out feelers to the Court and to the aristocracy. In the climate of the time, any hint of cooperation with the aristocracy created political problems. The second faction believed the king could not be trusted. The most radical among them, such as the leaders of the Cordeliers Club—Danton, Marat, Desmoulins—demanded the deposition of the king and the creation of a republic. The Legislative Assembly sought a middle course, taking a hard line on some issues important to the radicals—thus passing laws demanding that the Counts of Provence and Artois return to France and setting a deadline for all emigrés to return or face confiscation of property and rights—but insinuating Feuillant-backed candidates into the ministries. The king vetoed the two decrees and similarly vetoed a law requiring priests to take an oath to the Constitution of 1791 in place of one to the Civil Constitution of the Clergy. In the midst of this standoff between the king and the Feuillant leadership, the Lameth brothers and Barnave left Paris in disgust, effectively decapitating the Feuillant club. Gower wrote ominously on 2 December 1791:

> An universal expectation of an approaching crisis prevails. Every body acknowledges that France cannot long continue in it's [*sic*] present state; but what the *dénouement* of this tragi-comedy will be remains to be known.

The Revolt on Saint-Domingue

> . . . *this day* [31 March 1792] *15,000 slaves rose up . . . we have abandoned our properties, which are in the power of our slaves, who no longer work; it's the mulattoes who have pushed them to it.*[61]

> M. Clausson to Guittard de Floriban, 23 April 1792

The Feuillant leadership had alienated the Left and the popular classes in Paris by the Le Chapelier Law, by the Champs-de-Mars massacre, and by a brief effort to suppress the political clubs and the radical press (August 1791). The king's veto of the three decrees in the fall of 1791 showed that they did not have support on the Right, either. Events outside France made the situation even more precarious. The critical French colony of Saint-Domingue, wracked for two years by disputes among its white and mulatto elites, erupted in revolt. The whites sent a delegation to the Estates General, using an electoral process that excluded the many free blacks and the mulattoes, who owned one-third of the plantation property, a quarter of the slaves and of the land. Mirabeau strongly objected to seating the white delegation:

> We will demand of them . . . whether they intend to rank their Negroes in the class of men or that of beasts of burden. If the colonies desire that their Negroes be considered men, let them free them, let them permit them to vote, let them allow their Negroes to hold office. In the opposite case, we will ask them to notice that in apportioning the number of deputies to the population of France we have not counted the quantity of our horses and our mules; in the same way, the claim of the colonists [for 20 seats, based on Saint-Domingue's total population] . . . is ridiculous.[62]

Mirabeau's forces won a partial victory: the whites got only six seats.

As for the mulattoes, they, too, sent deputies to France. The Society of Friends of Blacks, an abolitionist group in France that included such important figures as Condorcet and Brissot, led a campaign to seat the mulatto deputies alongside the white ones. Mirabeau and the Abbé Grégoire tried to get them seated in the Assembly, demanding to know how the whites could deny representation to blacks and mulattoes who had met the qualifications for being active citizens. The Assembly tabled the measure.

In response, one of the mulatto leaders, Vincent Ogé, returned to Saint-Domingue and led a revolt. He, his brother, and Jean-Baptiste Chavannes, who had fought in the American Revolution, briefly seized control of the town of Grande-Rivière. The white authorities moved swiftly against them, executed the leaders and displayed their severed heads at major towns (February 1791). Six months later, the slaves took revenge for the murdered men. A revolt in the northern part of the colony burned fourteen hundred sugar and coffee plantations to the ground and wiped out their white population. The revolt spread quickly to the other parts of the colony, laying waste to town and plantation alike. The French government never regained control, although in 1794 one of its commissioners, Léger Sonthonax, legally validated what the slaves's own actions had accomplished: emancipation.[63]

The loss of Saint-Domingue, the riots on Tobago, Martinique, and Guadaloupe—"in truth, it is difficult to say in what part of the French dominions there are not commotions"—crippled the French economy.[64] France had imported something like 180 million pounds of sugar a year in the late 1780s, an amount worth about 75 million *livres*. France re-exported most of this sugar to other parts of Europe (above all Holland and Hamburg). Total trade with the West Indies may have involved as much as 500 million *livres* per year, and the re-export of sugar to the rest of Europe a massive sum as well. The slave, sugar, and coffee trades provided the foundation of prosperity of great ports like Bordeaux (sugar), Nantes (slaves), La

Rochelle, and, to some degree, Marseilles (sugar). Orléans, Bordeaux, La Rochelle, and Marseilles had many refineries. Orléans alone had twenty-seven, which gave employment to six hundred fifty workers. All told, the refineries there poured 1.3 million *livres* into the local economy, either in wages (about 300,000) or in purchasing goods. With the loss of Saint-Domingue's sugar in the fall of 1791, the economic situation in Orléans and Nantes quickly turned desperate. When refiners, shippers, and merchants went bankrupt in these cities or in Bordeaux or Marseilles, they took many other suppliers and backers with them. Thus perished the one sector of the nonagricultural economy that survived intact the cataclysms of 1789.

Agitation on the islands continued from 1791 onward. The white planters of Saint-Domingue, outraged at the Constituent Assembly's mild efforts on behalf of free blacks, stalked out of the Assembly and threatened to declare themselves independent. The initial success of the black rebellion in northern Saint-Domingue led to violent repression, but the seed of rebellion soon spread. French troops and sailors often refused to sail to the West Indies, in part because of the horrifying levels of mortality (due to disease) they suffered there. The mulattoes fought for their political rights, in the name of those principles that motivated the French deputies of 1789. Slaves fought for their freedom, too—fought to make Rousseau's dictum, "man is born free," a living reality. The political climate of 1791 did not bode well for blacks in the West Indies, in part because several leaders of the Assembly owned plantations. The inability to achieve a workable solution in the islands added another element of instability to French politics.

Diplomatic Developments

I find that it is risking a lot: we shall see everything that comes of it.

Guittard de Floriban, reacting to the declaration
of war against Austria, 20 April 1792

Diplomatic developments outside France also affected the course of the Revolution. In eastern Europe, the great powers—Russia, Austria, and Prussia—sought to take advantage of France's weakness. They greedily devoured Poland, partitioned in 1792 and 1795. The Poles initially had the temerity to protest. Their nobility, a far larger group than in the West, constituting perhaps 10 percent of the population, tried to create a new basis for their Commonwealth. In 1791, they promulgated the liberal Constitution of the Third of May, based on the principles of the Declaration of the Rights of Man and of the Citizen, albeit with a different definition of citizenship, which they extended only to nobles and to some town dwellers. When Russia invaded Poland to put a stop to such shenanigans, the other powers, preoccupied with the situation in France, did nothing.

France's example disturbed Western Europe as well. Morris wrote to George Washington in January 1790 that "never perhaps were the Affairs of Europe in a Situation which admits so little of forming any solid Opinion; and this from the spreading of what is called the french disease: Revolt. Hungary, Part of Germany, Italy and

Savoy with France and Flanders are already in different stages of that Disease. Poland is constitutionally afflicted with it." Great Britain looked with trepidation on the sight, worried especially that France would take control of the southern Netherlands. Beginning in 1793, those fears came true. Holland, too, which had had its own abortive revolution in 1787, became less and less stable.

The areas immediately around France faced particular difficulties. The small German states, above all the ecclesiastical electorates of Trier and Mainz, had the special problem of the French émigré communities, whose counterrevolutionary activities had become a major bone of contention by fall 1791. The Legislative Assembly demanded that Louis XVI put pressure on these small states to expel the émigrés, in order to stop their support for counterrevolutionary activity in Alsace and southern France. The Legislative Assembly had to intervene to prevent patriots in Provence from marching on Arles, a center of counterrevolution. This intervention proved to be a temporary respite; in March 1792, a motley volunteer army of 7,000 men laid siege to Arles and captured the city. Parallel peasant rebellions, often focused on anti-noble activity, broke out throughout the region. Peasants in the Midi persecuted refractory priests, grain dealers, and others. Peasants in Brittany and the Vendée, in contrast, turned against juring priests. The first of many Breton rural rebellions began in the winter of 1792.

Louis XVI, under heavy pressure from the Legislative Assembly, sent letters to the Elector–Archbishop of Triers, demanding he expel the emigrés. On 6 January 1792, the Elector legally did so, but his half-hearted action did not mollify the war party in France. Increasingly, Brissot and the leaders of the Assembly demanded war against the German states. Emperor Leopold II massed troops on his side of the border (February 1792). Counterrevolutionary forces everywhere—outside of France, in Brittany and the West, in the Midi—redoubled their efforts. People from all sides wanted war. The patriots believed war would get rid of all the "conspiracies" and would enable them to get firm control of society. The king believed France would lose the war and he would get back his power; the emigrés felt a foreign invasion would restore them to power. Only a few political leaders, Maximilien Robespierre chief among them, spoke out against the war.

In April 1792, the Legislative Assembly declared war on Leopold II. Louis dismissed his Feuillant ministers and brought in members of the Jacobin Club, allies of Brissot. The disorganized French armies immediately suffered defeats; one army lynched its general after a loss. The Austrians waited for the Prussian army to appear. Frederick William II of Prussia declared war only on 21 May. Emigrés soon marched behind the Austrians and Prussians, sure they would control France. The Allied armies, however, dallied near the frontiers. French generals conducted secret negotiations with their Allied counterparts. The king and queen secretly wrote to the Allies, encouraging them to overthrow the Revolution. The Legislative Assembly responded by issuing a new decree exiling non-juring priests and by another to raise 20,000 fresh National Guardsmen to replace the royal guards; the king vetoed both decrees (11 June 1792). Everywhere in France, the situation spun out of control. The value of the *assignats* began to tumble. and unrest spread even more widely in the provinces.

In mid-June, Louis again dismissed his ministers, touching off a march to the Tuileries by the workers of the Saint-Antoine suburb. Seven thousand of them paraded in front of the king, who sat wearing a red cap, symbol of the revolutionary workers. Louis listened to two hours of insults and threats, but never wavered; he even drank a toast to the health of the Nation. The disappointed *sans-culottes* finally went home. Eight days later, Lafayette appeared at the Assembly, seeking a decree against the rioters of 20 June. The Assembly refused. The king and queen distanced themselves from the general, who returned to the front.

Federation Day approached, and with it thousands of provincial National Guardsmen began to appear in Paris for the festivities. Unsure what to do in the crisis, the Legislative Assembly created a new legal device, the official declaration that "the fatherland is in danger," enabling it to institute permanent sessions of all governing bodies and to enlist National Guardsmen into the regular army. These Guardsmen tended to come from the most radical of the cities, such as Brest or Marseilles. The volunteers from the latter arrived in Paris in late July, singing "The Song of the Army of the Rhine." Parisians, much taken by its blood-curdling cries for patriotism, its announcement that "the hour of glory has arrived," and its stirring cadences, rechristened it, "The Marseillaise."

The End of the Monarchy, 10 August 1792

Like the ewe that watches the fight between the dogs and the wolves, I rooted for the former.[65]

> Rétif de la Bretonne, watching the
> storming of the Tuileries, 10 August 1792

The Parisian sectional assemblies, like other government bodies, began to meet on a permanent basis, starting on 25 July. On 20 July, the section of Théâtre-Français on the Left Bank became the first to admit passive citizens to its meetings. Soon, another half dozen radical sections had done the same. The commander of the Allied army marching on Paris, the duke of Brunswick, declared that he would exact "exemplary and forever memorable vengeance" on Paris, if the king were to be harmed.[66] One section after another in Paris now called for the king's removal and the declaration of a republic. In early August, some of the key leaders of the Legislative Assembly spoke up on his behalf; the sections responded by denouncing the Assembly as well. Newspapers openly called for an assault on the Tuileries palace, where the royal family lived.

On 10 August, the assault took place. Thousands of Parisian *sans-culottes*, aided by National Guardsmen from Paris and from the provinces, stormed the palace. Mme de Tourzel claims that Pétion replaced the National Guards on duty at the last minute, with companies on whom he could completely rely. The royal family sought asylum early in the morning at the Legislative Assembly. Some one hundred eighty Guardsmen died in the assault, as did six hundred of the nine hundred Swiss Guards defending the king—many of the latter slaughtered after the king had ordered them to lay down their arms. Vergniaud took the podium to announce the death of the monarchy:

THE MARSEILLAISE

Allons, enfants de la patrie,	Rise up children of the fatherland,
Le jour de gloire est arrivé	The day of glory has arrived!
Contre nous de la tyrannie	Against us the bloody standard
L'étendard sanglant est levé!	Of tyranny has been raised!
Entendez vous dans les campagnes	Do you hear in the countryside
Mugir ces féroces soldats?	Those ferocious soldiers cry out?
Ils viennent jusque dans nos bras	They come right into our midst
Égorger nos fils, nos compagnes	To cut the throats of our sons, our wives.
Aux armes, citoyens,	To arms, citizens,
Formez vos bataillons!	Form your battalions!
Marchons! Marchons!	March! March!
Qu'un sang impur	Let an impure blood
Abreuve nos sillons!	Water our furrows!

English translation adapted from: E. Kennedy, *A Cultural History of the French Revolution* (New Haven: Yale University Press, 1989), 277–278.

The dangers to the fatherland, which are at their worst, come about because of the defiance inspired by the conduct of the head of the executive power in a war undertaken against liberty and our national independence. Addresses from all parts of the empire demand the revocation of the authority granted to Louis XVI; and the Assembly, not wishing to augment its own power by any usurpation of power, proposes that you decree the establishment of a national Convention whose modalities of convocation it will propose; the organization of a new ministry, with the existing ministers provisionally conserving their power until its nomination.[67]

The Legislative Assembly suspended the king, fired his new ministers, and restored the earlier ministry, adding to it the radical leader Georges Danton, the chief architect of the assault of 10 August. So ended the Capetian monarchy founded in 987.

No longer a monarchy, yet still not a republic; a lame duck Legislative Assembly in power; enemy armies poised on the eastern border; peasant rebels in arms in the west: what was France to do? The Legislative Assembly took decisive action. With the king now out of the way, they quickly put into effect the decrees against refractory priests, giving them two weeks to leave the country. The Assembly next accepted Vergniaud's proposal to convoke a convention to draw up a new constitution. Despite the chaos, France held the first round of elections on 27 August, even with the expansion of the electorate by "universal" manhood suffrage, only about 20 percent of the voters turned out for the primary assemblies. The second stage of the process, the electoral assemblies to choose the deputies, took place in early September.

In Paris, workers, on the authority granted by their sectional assemblies, started arresting priests, locking many of them in local convents converted into prisons. The

Prussians invaded France, capturing Longwy and driving toward the capital. The British government informed its French counterpart that it hoped "nothing would happen to the King or his Family because that would escite the Indignation of all Europe." The American ambassador, Morris, took the British note to mean that they "will make War immediately if the Treatment of the King be such to call for or justify Measures of Extremity."

Panic stricken, the government, at Danton's direction, introduced "domiciliary visits," which produced three thousand new detainees in Paris's prisons. Radical papers called for death to traitors and claimed evidence of conspiracies everywhere. When news arrived on 2 September that the Prussians had passed Verdun, the last fortress between them and Paris, the *sans-culottes* took matters into their own hands, executing more than eleven hundred people. They started with about two hundred non-juring priests, moved on to some prominent nobles and the remaining Swiss Guards, and finally to common criminals. The September Massacres had echoes outside of Paris: one crowd butchered the duke of La Rochefoucauld, being taken to Paris for trial, in front of his wife and mother. Crowds at Reims, on the Prussian line of march, massacred non-juring priests. The death of people like La Rochefoucauld, a liberal noble who had distinguished himself in his calls for the abolition of seigneurialism and in his opposition to slavery, signaled the radical triumph. His old friend Lafayette escaped only because he was not in Paris. Sure he was to be arrested and executed, the marquis crossed the lines and was captured by the Prussians.

On 20 and 21 September, two events drew these matters to a close. On 20 September, at Valmy, the French army, led by General Dumouriez, defeated the Prussians, who immediately withdrew back to the Rhine. The next day, in Paris, the new Convention met. Ambassador Morris ironically wrote in his diary: "Nothing new this Day except the Convention has met and declar'd they will have no King in France." George Washington, although farther away, had a better sense of the meaning of the events set in motion on 10 August. He wrote to Morris on 20 October: "We can only repeat the sincere wish that much happiness may arise to the French nation, and to mankind in general, out of the severe evils which are inseparable from so important a revolution." Yet the Revolution, and the evils, had only just begun.

Notes

1. George Washington, *Writings*, ed. John Rhodehamel (New York: Literary Classics of the United States, 1997), 780–781.

2. A. Young, *Travels during the years 1787, 1788 and 1789* (London: W. Richardson, 1794), I, 117–118.

3. M. Lhéritier, ed., *Les débuts de la Révolution à Bordeaux d'aprés les Tablettes manuscrites de Pierre Bernadau* (Paris: Société d'histoire de la Révolution Française, 1919), 101.

4. Young, *Travels*, I, 174–175.

5. *The Letters of Lafayette to Washington, 1777–1799*, ed. L. Gottschalk (Philadelphia: American Philosophical Society, 1976), 346, letter of 12 January 1790. Lafayette wrote these letters in English.

6. *Letters of Lafayette to Washington*, 347, letter of 17 March 1790.

7. In 1789, many had clamored for the duke of Orléans to take Louis XVI's place, but the duke had lost favor by October 1789, as we shall see.

8. Cultural matters are treated in Chapter 15.

9. J. Chalon, ed., *Mémoires de Madame la duchesse de Tourzel, gouvernante des enfants de France de 1789 à 1795* (Paris: Mercure de France, 1969), 33.

10. Interested readers can follow their work in detail in G. Chinard, ed., *The Letters of Lafayette and Jefferson* (Baltimore and Paris: The Johns Hopkins University Press and Les Belles Lettres, 1929), esp. 136–142. Jefferson's official title was minister-in-residence.

11. Young, *Travels*, I, 189.

12. The United States Constitution does not define "people." In twelve of the thirteen original states, it meant "adult white male property owners," but the document did not say that. The U.S. Constitution and its amendments do not say who can vote, but who cannot be denied that right.

13. Bernadau, *La Révolution à Bordeaux*, 100.

14. By 1789, most of parish priests got only a portion of the tithe from its owner, often a bishop or cathedral chapter, but that portion was their main source of income.

15. Young, *Travels*, I, 148.

16. Ibid., 81 and 85.

17. At this stage in French political life, levels of "democracy" refer only to males. All elections banned women as voters and were thus fundamentally undemocratic.

18. Such caution made sense in a conversation with an outsider, to whom they would have been unlikely to reveal any plans they had made.

19. Young, *Travels*, I, 160. Young here uses stereotypical imagery drawn from the memories of the Jacquerie. We have virtually no evidence of peasants raping noble women and very few seigneurs lost their lives. The peasants did burn the papers and, on occasion, the château.

20. Citations are from relevant dates in Young, *Travels*, I, which is organized chronologically.

21. P. Jones, *The Peasantry in the French Revolution* (Cambridge: Cambridge University Press, 1988), 80, table 3. I have combined the totals for nobles (27) and their agents (8).

22. The Church owned 40 percent of the land in the bishopric of Cambrai, as against a nationwide average of about 10 percent.

23. N. Retif de la Bretonne, *Les Nuits Révolutionnaires, 1789–1793*, ed. M. Dorigny (Paris: Les Éditions de Paris, 1989), 55. This work is a selection of texts from Retif's much longer *Les Nuits de Paris*.

24. Some observers, like Rétif de la Bretonne, suggest that prostitutes and criminals (including men disguised as women) played a significant role in the march, but historians generally agree that such people formed a tiny minority of the marchers. Much evidence exists—including police testimony by many of the marchers—to buttress his remarks that the market women (les Dames de la Halle) forced every woman they encountered to join the march.

25. Young, *Travels*, I, 154.

26. P. Burley, *Witness to the Revolution. American and British Commentators in France, 1788–1794* (London: Weidenfeld & Nicolson, 1989), 84.

27. *La Révolution Française à Rochefort*, 94–95.

28. This system directly parallels the American Electoral College and the original indirect election of U.S. Senators.

29. Survey histories of the Revolution, with the notable exceptions of Sutherland and Palmer, typically suggest that the three-days wages restriction eliminated 45 percent of the male population from the voting rolls, and claim that only 50,000 men were eligible to be electors. My research on local tax rolls shows that in 1789, 75 percent of rural taxpayers contributed three days' wages or more. Yet Lille, a town of about 66,000, had only 5,464 eligible voters. Studies of other towns show a similarly limited pool of active citizens. The elections of 1790–1791 actually followed closely the rules of 1789. Malcolm Crook, the leading expert on Revolutionary elections, suggests that more people voted in 1789 than in later elections. He also notes that roughly 50,000 participated in electoral assemblies each year, a figure that led to the second error.

30. Here again, the Assembly departed radically from the ideas of Rousseau, who specifically denounced the use of representatives.

31. A. Soboul, *The French Revolution* (New York, 1974; original French edition 1962), 194–195. Criminal cases proceeded through a separate system, one that had local police courts, district ones, and a departmental Criminal Court. The reforms also created juries, chosen by lot from among a list taken from among the active citizens, although not including them all.

32. Ch.–L. Chassin, *Les Élections et les Cahiers de Paris en 1789* (Paris: Jouast et Sigaux, 1888), 4 vols., III, 333 ff.

33. Young, *Travels*, I, 192–193.

34. Protestants got civil rights in 1789, the Jews of Alsace only in 1791. One manifestation of the extension of civil rights to Jews came with the sale of church property. The Sephardic Jews of Bordeaux made extensive use of their new civil status to buy up such lands.

35. Ruault, letter to his brother, 8 August 1789, 162–163.

36. Cited in F. Aftalion, *The French Revolution, an Economic Interpretation*, trans. M. Thom (Cambridge: Cambridge University Press, 1990), 63.

37. Although the Assembly did not abolish teaching and charitable orders, it did prohibit them from recruiting new members, essentially dooming them to slow extinction.

38. Chassin, *Les Élections*, II, 436.

39. Tackett, *Becoming a Revolutionary*, 71.

40. The *cahiers* of 1789 pointed to future problems over the issue of Protestants. Even relatively liberal *cahiers* from local clergy demanded that Catholicism remain the state church and adopted an intolerant position toward non-Catholics.

41. Sutherland, *Revolution and Counter-Revolution*, 110–113. Sutherland integrates the extensive counter-revolution back into its rightful place in the revolutionary narrative.

42. *The Despatches of Earl Gower*, ed. O. Browning (Cambridge: Cambridge University Press, 1885), 37.

43. The Assembly soon added a tax on moveable property and a commercial licensing fee, the *patente*. Although these taxes eventually (post-1797) became the sound foundation of a new system of state revenue, in the short run, they failed miserably.

44. Earl Gower, the English Ambassador, reported the February 1791 estimate for the current year's spending to be 658 million *livres*. (*Despatches*, 59.)

45. Many areas of France had no land registers, so assessments of the land tax ended up depending on Ancien Régime assessments for the *taille* and the *vingtième*. Taxpayers naturally viewed the "new" land tax as simply the *taille* under a different name.

46. Their value declined sharply after July 1791 (see following text).

47. Once the state established itself on a firmer footing—certainly by 1797, direct tax rates returned to their old levels; in fact, in most parts of France, they seem to have increased by about 20 percent.

48. Cited in M. Fitzsimmons, *The remaking of France. The National Assembly and the Constitution of 1791* (Cambridge: Cambridge University Press, 1994), 94.

49. M. Ozouf, *Festivals and the French Revolution*, trans. A. Sheridan (Cambridge, MA: Harvard University Press, 1988), 47.

50. Arthur Young, who was inducted as a member in January 1790, claimed that the many leaders of the Jacobins were already republicans at that time.

51. Lafayette had, in fact, sent Bouillé a letter urging a harsh repression.

52. Gower, *Despatches*, 94.

53. Furet and Ozouf, *Dictionnaire Critique*, 299.

54. Jean-Paul Marat, *Œuvres Politiques 1789–1793. T. III: Septembre 1790—Décembre 1790*, ed. J. De Cock and C. Goëtz (Brussels: Pole Nord, 1989), 1954.

55. Rétif de la Bretonne, *Nuits*, 74. He surely takes this story from Parisian newspapers.

56. The text of Louis's manifesto can be found in Beik, *French Revolution*, 158–167.

57. Madame de Tourzel, *Mémoires*, 192–200, selections. My translation.

58. Gower, *Despatches*, 53 (28 January 1791).

59. The final compromise gave rights only to mixed-race people born of two free parents.

60. Only three people identified themselves as farmers; in 1789, the provosty of Paris alone had two of them. Two Constitutional bishops (Ariège and Calvados) also can be found in the sample. The only department among the seventeen that sent a priest was the Vendée, which sent two (of nine deputies). Departments of Ain, Aisne, Allier, Basse Alpes, Haute Alpes, Ardeche, Ardennes, Ariège, Aube, Aude, Aveyron, Bouches-du-Rhône, Calvados, Cantal, Charente, Morbihan, and Vendée.

61. Guittard de Floriban, *Journal*, 162.

62. Cited in A. Cooper, *Slavery and the French Revolutionists (1788–1805)*, trans. F. Keller (Lewiston, NY: Edwin Mellen Press, 1988), 58. Letter from Mirabeau to his constituents in Provence. The classic book on the Haitian Revolution remains C.L.R. James, *The Black Jacobins: Toussaint Louverture and the San Domingo Revolution* (London: Allison & Busby, 1936, 1980). C. Fick, *The Making of Haiti: The Saint Domingue Revolution from Below* (Knoxville: The University of Tennessee Press, 1990), contains a precise narrative of events.

63. In Paris, the legislative body serving in February 1794, the Convention, ratified the actions of those who freed the slaves, abolishing both slavery and the slave trade. By then, however, France was at war with Spain and Great Britain, and those two powers had control over much of the island. The sections of the island that those powers did not control, the blacks themselves did.

64. Gower, *Despatches*, 10 (2 July 1790). Gower kept the British government closely informed about events in the West Indies, which were of the greatest interest to them.

65. Rétif de la Bretonne, 92. He rooted for those fighting for the king.

66. Historians often speculate on the impact of the Brunswick Declaration on the Paris crowd, yet Guittard de Floriban only makes mention of it on 3 August, when the government ministers officially announced it to the Legislative Assembly.

67. Mme de Tourzel, *Mémoires*, 369.

Chapter Fourteen

Terror and Triumph, 1792–1794

During this time terror hovered over France and particularly in Paris where everyone lived not only in the greatest penury but also in horror of every kind in (the midst of) murders Everything was in the greatest disorder The French breathed blood They were like cannibals and were real man-eaters Neighbor cold-bloodedly denounced neighbor Blood ties were forgotten I witnessed those days of horror.

Jacques Ménétra—artisan, *sans-culottes,*
national guardsman, section militant, Jacobin—
recounting the Times of Terror, (1792–1793)

Some years after the fact, Ménétra recoils in horror from the deeds in which he himself had played a significant part. His memoirs seek to minimize his own role, yet he served two months as a member of his section's revolutionary committee, or committee of surveillance, which kept an eye out for enemies of the Revolution, accusing and arresting those suspected of insufficient revolutionary ardor. He notes with relief that he lost election to the Paris Commune in that year. His successful opponent and all other members of that body were executed in the aftermath of the fall of Maximilien Robespierre and the Jacobins on 9 Thermidor of the Revolutionary Year II (28 July 1794).[1]

Ménétra and his neighbors, like many Parisian artisans, formed the revolutionary mass of the *sans-culottes:* they stormed the Tuileries on 10 August 1792, participated in the *journées* of 31 May to 2 June 1793 that brought the Jacobins to power, and joined the march against the Convention in April 1795 (the Germinal rising). His section, Bonconseil, intervened to save some local patriots from the September Massacres of 1792, denounced moderates in the fall of 1793, supported the prosecution of the radicals in 1794, and adopted a wait-and-see attitude on 9–10 Thermidor.

Ménétra mentions acquaintances and friends guillotined in those dark days, like his drinking buddy, Barbet Mathieu, a journeyman hosier, and, as the glazier tells us, a man "from Lyons that was a capital sin."[2] These poor unfortunates formed part of the group of about 2,700 people executed in Paris during the Terror (September

1793 to July 1794). Nearly 60 percent of the victims fell in the final three months, during the mindless internecine warfare within the Left or as part of the mass executions of Ancien Régime elites. Tens of thousands more perished in the provinces, above all in cities themselves the center of counterrevolution, such as Lyon, or located near rural insurgencies, like Nantes. Thousands of rebels-in-arms died in the provinces, but the Terror executed many innocents, like Mathieu, denounced for uttering an incautious word at a tavern one night.

Every surviving account of those terrible years stresses the insecurity, disillusionment, and naked fear charactistic of the time. The Terror intimidated citizens everywhere, even in those regions in which few fell as official victims. The region around Paris had not a single official execution, yet these villages, too, suffered. Richard Cobb, in his study of Paris's relationship with its surrounding area between 1792 and 1802, offers one of the most vivid descriptions of the Terror:

> [In Paris] the nights of the Terror, we may suppose, were still and silent ones, unrelieved by the reassuring clatter of the carriages of the gamblers, as they returned from the tables, . . . But the *rural* night was even more silent and potentially more horrific and there was little to allay the panic fears of an isolated peasant family as its adult members tossed, listening to the shrieks of the owls and awaiting the crows of the cocks that would spell the end of the dark tunnel of nocturnal terror.[3]

Throughout the nineteenth century, the fearful remembrance of the Jacobin dictatorship of the Year II served as a rallying cry against democratic change everywhere in Europe. In time, the Left adopted Robespierre and the Jacobins as the precursors of modern revolutionary action; the Right made them into totalitarians. In the late 1980s, a leading French historian touched off a firestorm when he referred to the suppression of the Vendée rebellion by the Jacobins as a "genocide." How did things come to such a pass? What happened in France in the fall of 1792 and spring of 1793 to create the atmosphere conducive to government by Terror? For the answers, let us return to the immediate aftermath of Louis XVI's fall.

⮌ THE BIRTH OF THE REPUBLIC, AUGUST–NOVEMBER 1792

Nothing is more cruel than fear.

Jules Michelet

CHRONOLOGY	August 1792–August 1793
10 August 1792	Storming of the Tuileries; end of the monarchy
August	Decrees establishing new government; mandatory house searches
2–6 September	September Massacres
20 September	Battle of Valmy: French defeat the Prussians

CHRONOLOGY	(continued)
21 September	First meeting of the Convention; declaration of the Republic
6 November	Battle of Jémappes: Dumouriez defeats the Austrians
December 1792	Trial of Louis XVI begins
21 January 1793	Execution of Louis XVI
1 February	Declaration of war against Great Britain and Holland
10–11 March	Massacre at Machecoul, start of Vendée uprising
31 May–2 June	June Days: riots in Paris, collapse of the Girondin government
June	Vendéans capture Saumur and Angers; are repulsed at Nantes; Jacobins gradually take over the government
24 June	Convention approves the Constitution of the Year II
13 July	Assassination of Marat by Charlotte Corday
27 July	Robespierre joins the Committee of Public Safety
23 August	*Levée en masse* (mass conscription)
27 August	British capture Toulon

Jules Michelet, the great nineteenth-century historian, tells a story relayed to him by one of the participants in the attack of 10 August against the Tuileries. The old man recalled a conversation he held with a "rich baker of the Marais" while under fire in the Tuileries courtyard: "Still, it's a great sin thus to kill Christians; but, in the end, that's so many the fewer to open the door to the Austrians." Such sentiments ran high in Paris throughout August and September, because people believed Prussian-led Allied force would soon lay siege to Paris. These fears did not abate until firm news of the withdrawal of the Allied army reached Paris on 2 October.

The sequence of events in late August did little to allay the fears of Parisians. After the *journée* of 10 August, an Insurrectionary Commune, consisting of six men each from the forty-eight sections, replaced the old Commune. This group came overwhelmingly from the world of large-scale artisans, small-scale manufacturers, and merchants. Elections within the forty-eight sections continued throughout August, as one section then another replaced individual deputies. On 24 August, the government required all citizens in Paris to take an oath of civic loyalty, which, for the first time, omitted reference to the king.

The sections and Commune urged decisive action on the Legislative Assembly. That body named an Executive Council to act in place of the king, and took a series of radical steps to reestablish order. They voted to hold elections for a new constitutional Convention, based on "universal"[4] manhood suffrage (although still using a two-tiered system of indirect election), to deport all refractory priests who refused to take a new oath of allegiance, to eliminate even the teaching and hospital religious orders, to ban the wearing of priestly garb in public, to empower municipal governments to arrest "suspects" thought to be enemies of the nation, and to mandate the keeping of civil registers (births, deaths, marriages) by communal authorities, not by the Church. The government actually managed to hold elections amid the chaos of late August and early September. This new legislative body, the Convention, took power on 21 September. Its first official act declared France a republic.

In response to the law of suspects, authorities rounded up refractory priests and other suspected counterrevolutionaries; in Paris alone, they detained nearly a thousand. The Assembly took two other key decisions in late August. First, they created an Extraordinary Criminal Tribunal, to hear cases against traitors. Second, they mandated, and the Commune immediately carried out, a house-to-house search in Paris for arms held by counterrevolutionaries. Two of the most radical sections, Luxembourg and Poissonière, voted, in the words of the latter, "considering the imminent dangers to the Fatherland and the infernal maneuvers of priests, [the section] decides that all priests and suspect persons, held in the prisons of Paris, Orléans and elsewhere, shall be put to death."

The September Massacres, in which Parisians broke into the city's prisons and murdered over one thousand people, followed naturally from the fall of the monarchy. The collapse of the only governmental system France had known for over a millennium destabilized every aspect of society. Developments everywhere boded ill for the new government: General Lafayette surrendered to the Prussians; Longwy surrendered virtually without resistance, allowing the Prussians to surround Verdun, the last fortress on the road to Paris. A massive uprising began in the Vendée. The minister Roland suggested that the government flee Paris.

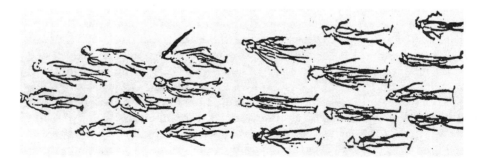

The September Massacres, *1792. The Parisian Guittard de Floriban bears witness to the face of terror, in this sample drawing in his diary.*

Source: C. Guittard de Floriban, *Journal de Célestin Guittard de Floriban, Bourgeois de Paris sous la Révolution,* ed. R. Aubert. (Paris: Éditions France-Empire, 1974).

The Commune of Paris, meeting on the morning of 2 September, voted to sound the tocsin (alarm bell) and to call out the National Guard. Danton, then serving as minister of justice, strongly allied to the Commune, went to the Legislative Assembly to demand measures against traitors. He defended the Commune's sounding of the tocsin, in his most famous speech:

> The tocsin that is being sounded is not an alarm signal; it is the order to charge on the enemies of the Fatherland. To defeat them, messieurs, *il nous faut de l'audace, encore de l'audace, toujours de l'audace* [we will need audacity, still more audacity, always audacity], and France will be saved.

The Assembly dithered in its response, adjourning from 2 P.M. to 6 P.M., that is, precisely when the massacres started. The proposed legislation had demanded the death penalty against those who "refused to serve in person or to give up his arms"; in fact, a second motion went further, demanding the death penalty for all who "directly or indirectly refuse to execute or who in any manner whatsoever interfere with the orders given by and measures taken by the executive power." The Commune voted to arrest Roland, but Danton, whose opposition had prevented the government from leaving, personally tore up the arrest warrant.

The events of July to September 1792 exacerbated a split within the Paris Jacobin Club that had begun in the late spring of 1792. Even in early August, a group around the deposed interior minister Charles-Nicolas Roland and the deputy Jean-Pierre Brissot had sought to compromise with Louis XVI. Historians often call this group the Girondins, because several of its leaders, like Pierre Vergniaud, came from the department of the Gironde (Bordeaux); their contemporaries usually called them the "Rolandins" or the "Brissotins." Roland's wing of the group naturally wanted to increase the powers of the ministers. In the provinces, the Girondins allied strongly with the conservative departmental councils, heavily dominated by large landowners and legal men. These councils remained bastions of constitutional monarchists even after the king's fall.

The Jacobin faction known as the Mountain, led by Maximilien Robespierre, demanded more power for the Convention. Although many leading Jacobins, like Robespierre himself, were men of law, they drew their strongest support from people like Ménétra, the commercial and mercantile interests, and thus had obvious ties to the district and municipal councils, now dominated by those interests.[5] The department of Haute-Vienne offers a good example: 85 percent of the municipal councilors of Limoges were Jacobins, whereas only 42 percent of the departmental councilors belonged to the Club. Outside of the cities, Jacobin clubs spread mainly to rural communes in areas like the Rhône valley that felt threatened by the noble counterrevolution, because people identified the Jacobins with "patriotism," that is, with a policy of vigorous repression of counterrevolutionaries.[6]

In Paris, the Montagnards made common cause with the group focused around the Cordeliers Club, led by Danton, and with the spokesmen of the *sans-culottes*, like the street orators Jacques Roux and Jean Varlet, and the journalists Marat and Jacques-René Hébert, editor of the incendiary *Père Duchesne*. The new Paris Commune, and

THE SEPTEMBER MASSACRES

The inhabitants of the area around the Abbaye prison started the Massacres on 2 September by killing twenty-four priests about to be transferred there; soon, the crowd burst into the Abbaye and massacred its prisoners. The massacres moved from prison to prison for five days: the Carmelite convent, the Maison de Force, the Conciergerie, the Salpetrière, which housed mainly prostitutes, and, finally, Bicêtre, home to the infirm poor, to the syphilitics, and to unwed mothers and their children. The Massacres of 3–6 September often involved hastily convened popular tribunals, which voted life or death for the poor unfortunates in their grasp. In the end, between eleven hundred and fourteen hundred people died, nearly 75 percent of them simple criminals, with no obvious political misdemeanors.

Célestin Guittard, whose diary contains a sketch of bodies lying about to mark the start of the September Massacres (2–6 September 1792), offers the interpretation promulgated by Marat's *Ami du Peuple,* and accepted by many Parisians:

> Today in the prisons they killed all prisoners condemned to death and refractory priests. . . . Necessity required carrying out such executions. Part of Paris was leaving tomorrow and soon after to join the armies: Paris was going to be denuded of armed men, so all of these unfortunates would have been able to slit our throats during the absence of all the citizens. How sad it is to be obliged to come to such extremities, but they say it is better to kill the devil than to have him kill us. . . . Never since the start of the Revolution had Paris found itself in such a crisis as we found ourselves today. The Fatherland finds itself in danger and the enemies are, so to speak, at our door. It is thus the outcome of the battles

that will probably be joined this month, that will decide our fate. Thus they massacred today all afternoon everywhere in Paris.[7]

The September Massacres provide one of the three dominant, lingering, popular images of the Revolution: the storming of the Bastille, the September Massacres, and the Terror. Each carried, and still carries, a specific mneumonic value. The storming of the Bastille is a symbol of the unity of all good citizens in the face of despotism, but carries the overtones of the potential for unchecked violence on the part of the lower classes. The September Massacres stand for the mindless political violence of the lower classes: the French coined the word *septembriseur* to describe those who participated in the massacres, and it soon became an all-purpose invective used against all radicals. The Terror came to represent what happens when the lower classes actually get a share of government.[8] All three share the element of violence and of popular participation. They provided nightmares to the middle class of Europe throughout the nineteenth and into the twentieth century, making them profoundly suspicious of the political participation of the mass of the male population. Those living in Paris hesitated somewhat in their initial reaction, but then the official response became one of approbation for a deed that, if perhaps a little over-enthusiastic, was necessary to save the "Fatherland in danger." Out in the provinces, local elites took a much dimmer view of developments; the September Massacres confirmed all their worst fears about the Parisian masses.

the sections, were their strongholds. As in the provincial cities, so, too, in Paris, the commercial–manufacturing elite now had complete political control. In the aftermath of 10 August, they forced two major reforms of the National Guard: first, its elite formations, bastion of the relatively wealthy (the only ones who could afford the fancy uniforms), had to disband; second, the Parisian Guard broke into forty-eight battalions, one for each section. The merchants, manufacturers, and master artisans thus took from the legal men control of the three levers of power in Paris: the Commune, the sectional assemblies, and the National Guard, whose new commander, the brewer Antoine Santerre, aptly represented the changeover. The Paris elections of August 1792 ratified the changes, and they returned a radical group of men to the Commune and to Paris's seats in the Convention. Almost everywhere in France, with the exception of the departmental councils and the national legislature, the political leadership shifted from the lawyers of 1791 to the mercantile and business elites of 1792.

The two "parties," the Montagnard Jacobins and the Girondins, did not have clear-cut programs in mind, indeed many historians question whether the latter existed at all, other than as a loose coalition. From the perspective of provincial France, the Executive Council ministers had impeccable "patriot" credentials because they had been cashiered by Louis XVI in June and forcibly restored in August. The Parisian radicals mistrusted the ministers, except for their man, Georges Danton, minister of justice. The central factions used every means at their disposal to empower their provincial allies. The Girondin-dominated Executive Council sent its orders to the departmental councils, whereas the Convention relied on the district and municipal councils run by provincial Jacobins.[9] In December 1793, the Montagnard-dominated Convention abolished the departmental councils; when the Girondin group returned to power, in the fall of 1794, they restored the departmental councils and abolished the district ones.

The election (August–September 1792) of the new representative body, the Convention, took place against this rapidly changing political background. The Paris Jacobins sent pamphlets to their associated provincial clubs, urging members to support two hundred fifty deputies from the Legislative Assembly who had "remained faithful to the cause of liberty": one hundred ninety-four of them obtained election. The Feuillant faction, whose policy of constitutional monarchy had been rendered obsolete by the events of 10 August, failed to elect a single deputy. Most of the *conventionnels*, as they were called, belonged to the "Jacobin" clubs, yet aside from exceptions such as the departments of the Loiret or the Orne, where the Girondins manipulated the vote, most provincial electoral assemblies showed little understanding of the Parisian split. In Paris, factional newspapers campaigned openly for their men: the electors supported the Mountain, picking such radicals as Robespierre (the highest vote-getter), Danton, the painter Jacques David, and, in the end, even the paranoid journalist, Marat.[10]

In Paris as in most of the provinces, the elections of 1792, even though conducted under the principle of universal manhood suffrage, suffered from low turnouts. In the Côte d'Or, where 70 percent of those eligible turned out in 1790, only a quarter did so in 1792, exacerbating a trend that started in 1791. The newly enfranchised urban workers generally failed to vote: Paris, political hotbed though it was, had a turnout below 10 percent. In this respect, the election of August to September 1792 followed the standard pattern. Indirect elections for choosing electoral colleges everywhere had substantially lower turnouts than municipal ones, in which the voters actually made the final choice. In Paris, several sections sought to overcome what they viewed as an antidemocratic measure by insisting, in writing, that the electoral assembly refer back to them for approval of the deputies selected. The electoral assembly refused.

The emerging factional split in Paris had close ties to the second and third major political problems of 1792:

> Citizens with little political sophistication easily believed the most absurd possible accusations, but

> France *did* face a staggering array of internal counterrevolutionaries and external opponents.

This general lack of political sophistication extended from the upper classes to the artisans or peasants, as the journals of Guittard, Ménétra, or Young make clear. The lack of an ability to process political information in a sophisticated way had much to do with a political culture formed under a monarchy that revealed as little as possible of why it did what it did. That said, the relatively slow movement of information in the eighteenth century encouraged rumor mongering and paranoia everywhere: in Great Britain or the new United States of America, just as much as in France. Surely the astounding events of the late eighteenth century, which created a climate of nearly unimaginable instability, also encouraged people to look everywhere for deep, dark plots.

French artisans and shopkeepers harbored social and political grievances against the former ruling groups. Ménétra's journal entries for 1789–1790 indicate his hostility to the "nobles with their old parchments and their ancient gallant knights from whom they claim to trace their ancestry when most of them are descended from servants lackeys [and] coachmen" and the clergy, which sought to preserve men in "their ancient Gothic prejudices" and which wanted "to rule by their dogmas and fabulous mysteries." Parisian artisans saw treachery everywhere; they immediately suspected any noble or clergyman of wanting to return to the Ancien Régime, yet, like Ménétra, they would make exceptions for "good" nobles or priests whom they personally knew, and whose conduct since 1789 had not given rise to suspicions.

The lack of experience in open, *public* practical politics, a legacy of the Ancien Régime's limited political culture, combined with the theoretical framework within which the Revolutionaries operated served to create a lethal combination.[11] Robespierre and his supporters relied heavily on the works of Jean-Jacques Rousseau. Men like Barnave, Brissot or Boissy d'Anglas looked to John Locke or to Montesquieu. The former enshrined their ideas in the Constitution of 1793, the latter in the Constitutions of 1791 and 1795. The political actors of France in the 1790s shared their chief failing with their American contemporaries: they could not understand the purpose of political parties. The French carried it to the extreme that there were no declared candidates for election as deputy. Many local elections relied on voice votes. Guittard reports that the approval of the Constitution of 1793 by his section took place by voice roll call vote: "everyone said yes." In cases where they did not, the humiliated minority oftentimes stalked out of such meetings, which then reported a unanimous vote.

The French saw in every coalition or political group a "faction" or a manifestation of what Rousseau called the "corporate will," which he had described, in *The Social Contract* (1762), as the greatest danger to honest government. The unwillingness to accept the legitimacy of group action, particularly action against the group in power, led to an inability to compromise. The Left, in particular, suffered from this malady. Gouverneur Morris correctly foresaw the coming split in September 1792, writing to Jefferson that:

> You will see by the Gazettes that there is the same Enmity between the present Chiefs which prevailed heretofore against those whom they considered as their common Enemies, and if either of the present parties [Jacobins and Girondins] should get the better, they would probably again be divided, for Party, like Matter, is divisible ad infinitum, because things which depend on human opinion can never be tried by any common Standard.

In this way, the situation in France strongly resembled that in the United States of the 1790s: profound suspicion of party/faction yet a need to create parties; a fear of conspiracies yet the existence of real plots; recognition of the need to compromise, as in the U.S. Constitution of 1787 and the French one of 1791, but an inability to accept the legitimacy of opposition.[12]

Politics easily became intensely personal, as Young had written even in January 1790, and major policy disputes overlapped with personal vendettas. In France, this process started to get out of hand in September 1792 and led to riots in the spring of 1793.[13] Both the United States and France also had great difficulty reestablishing legitimacy in the countryside; Shay's Rebellion (1787) and the Whiskey Rebellion (1794) stand as American counterparts to the Chouans and Vendeans of France. One important constant stood out in both countries: the large landowners supported greater powers for regional authorities, states or departments, while the urban merchants, and some lawyers, wanted a stronger central government, often allied with municipalities.

The Mountain and Girondins had divided sharply in the summer of 1792 about the overthrow of the monarchy. They briefly closed ranks on the issue on 10 August but the trial of the king brought out their underlying differences once again. The Girondins, whether a united faction or not, stood for certain policies more in tune with the needs of provincial France. They wanted to try Louis XVI for treason, of which he was certainly guilty, but did not want to execute him. Knowing of the peasants' broad sympathy for the king, many of them wanted his sentence put to a plebiscite. They wanted a separation of Church and state, but did not push for radical action against priests who supported the Revolution. They supported a more federal approach to government, with more power devolved on the departmental councils, so their provincial supporters soon became known as Federalists. The Montagnards wanted to execute Louis, to destroy all vestiges of the Church's power, and to impose the will of the central government on the provinces. Although the first two goals rested on principles as well as practical considerations, the last one, greater authority for the central government, had more to do with the evolving chaos of French society than with any antipathy to local government.

The split between the Montagnards and the Girondins in the late summer of 1792 stemmed, above all, from a dispute about the nature of the new state. The Montagnards, supported firmly by the Parisian populace, rightly believed France needed strong central leadership. Given that civil war had broken out in the west and south, that foreign armies stood perched on France's northern frontier and inside her eastern borders, and that millions of people lived on the edge of starvation, their argument made a lot of sense. The Girondins stood for a federalist France, with more diffuse power and greater local autonomy. Their policy reflected the reality of 1790 and 1791, when some prospect for federalism seemed possible. By the spring of 1793, the foreign war and the massive civil disorder made federalism an essentially untenable option. Little wonder that the conflict between the Girondins and the Montagnards ended in favor of the latter in June 1793.

The Girondins also suffered from an inherent contradiction of their position in the Convention. They supported more authority for the Executive Council, because they dominated it, but that policy weakened their position in the Convention, whose deputies felt it should wield power. That the Montagnards and Girondins acted out of expediency on this issue seems beyond question. At the war ministry, each successive minister systematically purged the bureaucracy of officials from the opposing faction. The first war minister of the post-monarchy era, the Girondin Servan, set the tone for all his successors when he immediately dumped twelve of his thirteen senior officials, setting off howls of protest in Paris. When the Jacobin Pache took over in October 1792, he quickly stacked the ministry with men holding close ties to the Paris sections. No one in Paris protested the accumulation of power in this minister's hands! By the fall of 1792, ministers such as Roland, Clavière, and Servan controlled bureaucracies of between one thousand and two thousand officials, which gave them considerable patronage. In November, Roland used his jurisdiction over elections to issue circulars to local officials; his efforts helped insure the victory of many of his allies to departmental councils.

The precise relationship between the Executive Council and the Convention hamstrung effective governance. Morris summed up the two key problems facing the new government in a letter to Jefferson (23 October 1792):

> whether they can establish an Authority which does not exist, as a Substitute (and always a dangerous Substitute) for that Respect which cannot be restored after so much has been done to destroy it; whether in crying down and even ridiculing Religion they will be able on the tottering and uncertain Base of Metaphisic Philosophy to establish a solid Edifice of Morals; these are the Questions which Time must solve.

The First French Republic, which lasted only seven years, had no such temporal luxury. It failed categorically in its efforts to recreate an executive branch of government to replace the discredited monarchy and in its efforts to root out Catholicism as the moral foundation of ordinary people's lives.

The Death of the King   ∾

History informs us that the Passage of dethron'd Monarchs is short from the Prison to the Grave.

Gouverneur Morris to George Washington, 23 October 1792

The Convention faced a dismal situation. They needed to absorb the authority of the Executive Council and the old Legislative Assembly and, within Paris, to reach a working agreement with the Commune and its allies, the sections, which now met every day. In the provinces, things could hardly have been worse. Peasants in Brittany and the Vendée rebelled against conscription; fighting between republicans and monarchists seemed endemic in the southeast, as peasants in Provence burned one noble château after another in the fall. At Auxerre, a crowd had torn out the heart of a National Guardsman who refused an oath to the new order; at Dijon and Beaune, the municipalities carried out house-to-house searches and arrests; in the countryside, rumors of brigands spread like wildfire. Food shortages appeared in many areas. Serious bread riots broke out in November, starting in the traditionally rich grain lands of the Beauce (near Chartres) and spreading throughout central France.

The defeat of the Prussians at Valmy (20 September)—little more than an artillery duel, but decisive all the same—led to a rapid improvement in the military situation. By the late fall, Revolutionary armies swept to victory in the Low Countries, in Savoy, and in the Rhineland. Drunk with success, the Revolutionaries turned now to their greatest immediate challenge: what to do about "Louis Capet." The political split intensified in the fall of 1792. The Girondin leaders remained members of the Jacobin Club in Paris until October 1792 when, led by Robespierre, the Club expelled Brissot. The other Girondins soon came under attack: the Paris Jacobins expelled Roland on 26 November, and issued circulars attacking Condorcet, Pétion, and other "Brissotins." This approach did not play well in the provinces. Among provincial Jacobin clubs whose attitude we can determine by their written proceedings from the fall of 1792, supporters of Brissot and the Girondins outnumbered those of the Mountain two to one. Clubs in major cities such as Bordeaux, Montpellier, Angers, and Marseille broke off relations with the Paris mother club.

As 1793 began, public opinion, even in the Jacobin clubs, stood firmly in the Girondin camp. When Pétion resigned as mayor of Paris to be a deputy in the Convention, the electors originally chose him again. When he steadfastly refused, the electors turned to the former royal Controller General Lefebvre d'Ormesson, who also refused. Finally, on 30 November, Parisians chose a Girondin mayor, who defeated the Montagnard candidate nearly 2 to 1, but they chose a Jacobin state's attorney, Anaxagoras Chaumette.

The provincial cities, and their Jacobin clubs, largely rejected *sans-culottes* extremism: most of them subscribed to moderate Leftist papers such as Jean-Louis Carra's *Annales patriotiques* rather than to Marat's radical *Ami du Peuple*. The clubs, and other convivial societies (some overtly political, others not) contributed to the enormous demand for Parisian newspapers. Postal inspectors reported that 80,000 of them left Paris for the provinces every day in 1793. This single figure demonstrates the fundamental change that had transpired between 1789, when Young consistently complained about the lack of availability of Parisian newspapers in provincial cities, and 1792, when news poured out of Paris to quench provincial thirsts. That fundamental transformation, to a society with an active, public political process, proved to be the Revolution's most enduring legacy. Henceforth, French citizens, even under authoritarian rulers like Napoleon I, believed that they had a right to know about transpiring political policies and events. The massive information flow of 1792 enabled provincial clubs to make up their own minds about the Parisian events. Virtually without exception, local Jacobins denounced the September Massacres, and reserved their harshest words for Marat. They used the generic term *maratisme* to stigmatize Parisian radicalism.

The international situation, although it improved, still gave cause for concern. Prussia turned away from the French fighting toward Poland, seeking to profit from the upcoming partition of that country, overrun by Russian troops in August. The Austrian army in the southern Netherlands suffered a catastrophic defeat at Jémappes (6 November) at the hands of Dumouriez's army, but the Convention rightly worried about the general's loyalty. After losing the battle of Neerwinden, he went over to the Allies (April 1793). On the Savoy front, much the same thing happened: the victorious general Montesquiou deserted to the enemy (October 1792). The Convention annexed Savoy and Nice (November 1792), and the Rhineland and Belgium (early 1793). The annexation of Belgium, together with the execution of Louis XVI (January 1793), drove the English into the coalition. War against England and Holland became official on 1 February.

Five problems dominated French political life in the fall of 1792 and winter of 1792 to 1793: the government's inability to raise money, the trial of the king, subsistence, conscription, and war. These problems naturally fed on each other. The war required more troops, leading to expanded conscription, and more government spending; falling tax revenues forced the government to issue more *assignats* to pay these higher bills; the greater volume of *assignats* led to inflation, which drove up food prices.[14] Fighting between cities seeking to requisition grain and the surrounding countryside spread from one end of France to another. Peasant hostility to conscription exacerbated hostility between town and country. By late 1792 departments such as Morbihan, on the south coast of Brittany, or the Vendée, had virtually ceased to belong to France. No one voted; no one joined the army or navy; no one paid taxes. The department of Gers, in the Pyrenees, contained not a single tax register. The Convention slowly began to collect arrears for 1791 at the end of 1792, but even in Paris many citizens did not pay their 1792 taxes until the fall of 1793.[15]

Unfortunately for the people, and the government, the harvest of 1792 continued the pattern of spotty production of the major cereals. In the west, local officials claimed farmers harvested only half the usual wheat crops, although they did bring in a normal rye harvest. Shaky harvests combined with the inflationary issuance of new *assignats* (3.5 billion *livres* between April 1792 and September 1793) to double grain prices in 1792. They rose another 60 percent in the first half of 1793. Prices of basic goods such as soap, sugar, and coffee doubled for those who did not have access to hard currency. Although catastrophic for ordinary consumers, *assignats* provided an ingenious remedy for the government's need to buy agriculture produce to feed and move its armies. The large- and medium-scale farmers sold produce for *assignats*, which they used to buy up nationalized land. The government could thus use the nationalized land quite efficiently to pay for its chief operating expense: the army.

That thought hardly comforted urban consumers. In December 1792, the Convention, after a heated debate, decided to create a free trade in grain, abolishing all price controls and hindrances to circulation (except export). Hungry artisans and peasants had different ideas. They forced local authorities to ignore the Convention and impose price controls in almost every town. The Paris Commune spent 500,000 *francs* a day to subsidize the price of grain in the city's markets, yet the city's artisans grew ever more restless. In February 1793, the market women of Paris presented a petition to the Convention demanding price controls; the laundresses demanded the death penalty for soap hoarders. Parisiennes responded to the denial of their petition by breaking into stores and selling sugar, soap, and other goods for "fair" prices. By 26 February, this "popular price setting," had given way in many cases to simple looting. The National Guard had to restore order. Among male politicians, only Jacques Roux, leader of the radical *enragés*, supported the women.

The Trial of the King

People, I die innocent.

Louis XVI, at the scaffold, 21 January 1793

War, grain and sugar riots, breakdowns in local authority—against such a backdrop the Convention had to decide what to do with Louis XVI. After some months of indecision about whether to try Louis, and, if so, how, the Convention decided to try him itself. On 11 December 1792 the king made his way from the Temple prison to the Convention amid sullen, silent crowds. On the floor of the Convention, he insisted on his innocence and demanded the right to legal counsel. The deputies, most of whom were lawyers, agreed to his demand, appointing the famed Enlightenment figure Malesherbes. The deputies had little doubt of Louis's guilt, because an armored box discovered in the Tuileries contained his correspondence with foreign rulers about overthrowing the Revolution. What should they do with him? Should he be condemned to death? Should the people of France vote on his execution?

The Convention's voting took place in an eerie atmosphere. Starting on 13 January, all house lights had to remain on through the night; on 14 January, all public spectacles closed for the day and the government doubled the guards on prisons. On 15 January 1793 the deputies voted 693 to 0 for a verdict of guilty. In the following days, they divided sharply on the question of an appeal to the people: 424 to 283, with the Girondins going down to defeat.[16] Many local clubs that had supported Brissot and Roland in their quarrel with the Paris Jacobins, now turned against the Girondins. Marseille shifted allegiance to the Mountain, bringing the rest of Provence with it.

Indeed, the idea so outraged the Marseille Jacobins that they sent out a circular (1 February) demanding the recall of all deputies who had voted for the appeal to the people.

The deputies divided again on the death penalty: three hundred sixty-one voted for death, seventy-two for death with a delay for clemency, and two hundred eighty-eight against. The next day, another vote tallied three hundred eighty for death and three hundred ten for clemency. Some of the latter, Thomas Paine among them, had no special concern for Louis; they simply opposed the death penalty itself, on principle. Others believed, rightly, that executing Louis would lead to war with England.

All Paris lived uneasily during these January days. On 20 January, the day before the scheduled execution, the Convention, led by the Girondins, voted to seek prosecution of those responsible for the September Massacres. That evening, a monarchist assassinated the Jacobin deputy Le Pelletier de Saint-Fargeau. The Convention doubled the guard at the Temple, fearing that the broadsides plastered through the city proclaiming, "Save the King" "Burn the Guillotine" "Murder the Deputies" might actually lead to an insurrection. The next day, some 80,000 National Guardsmen lined the route from the Temple to the Place de la Concorde. Some witnesses suggest that Louis marched through silent streets, massive crowds struck dumb by a spectacle that would have been unimaginable just months earlier. Louis-Sébastien Mercier, in contrast, denied such reports:

> No alteration could be seen on people's faces, and they lie who printed that stupor reigned in the city. . . . The day of the execution did not make any impression: the shows opened as usual; the cabarets ringing the bloody square emptied their pitchers as usual; cake and paté sellers hawked their wares in sight of the decapitated corpse.

On the square itself, 20,000 men, among them Conquerors of the Bastille, surrounded the guillotine. Louis needed help from his confessor to mount the steep steps; at the top, he spoke to the crowd: "People, I die innocent. I pardon the authors of my death. I pray God that my blood will not fall upon France." Murmurs spread through the crowd, but the drums drowned out the rest of his words. Seconds later, the son of the executioner, Sanson, held up the king's severed head, to cries of "Vive la République!" "Vive la nation!" and "Vive la liberté!" Mercier reports that schoolchildren at the *collège* of the Quatre-Nations tossed their caps in the air at the news. On the scaffold itself, one of the executioners started selling little packets of the king's hair and the crowd surged forward to carry away bloodstained bits of clothing.

∼ The Jacobin Republic, 1793–1794

The monarchy, jealous of its authority, swam in the blood of thirty generations; and you would hesitate to show yourselves severe against a handful of the guilty?[17]

Louis-Antoine de Saint-Just, March 1794

The execution of the king allowed the Convention to focus on its other three problems—local disorder, subsistence, and the war—and to begin serious work on its original purpose: the creation of a new constitution. No specific group had control of the Convention at this time. The Girondins, above all the philosopher Condorcet, completely dominated the Constitutional Committee. They produced a draft of 402 articles by mid-February 1793.[18] Yet the real battle of early 1793 did not take place over constitutional principles. The desperate daily situation required immediate answers based on practical reality, not philosophic niceties. In the gritty political warfare of January through July 1793, the Jacobins took the measure of their Girondin foes.

Given the lack of a directed executive branch of government, the individual ministers often acted as independent executive agents. The Convention sought to rein them in by means of committees. In October 1792, they created a Committee on General Security, which had responsibility for public security, specifically for identifying and arresting enemies of the Republic. Its thirty members came from all political stripes, although it had a strong initial Montagnard contingent. The Girondins reduced the Committee to fifteen and stacked it with their men on 9 January, but the disorder created by the assassination of Saint-Fargeau (20 January) and the death of the king (21 January) led the Convention, on 21 January, to turn again to the hardline Jacobins. Two days later, the radicals forced Roland to resign as minister of the interior, but failed to elect their candidate to replace him. Nor did the Jacobins have much initial success gaining the ministry of justice, vacated on 22 January, or that of war. Two changes of minister of war between January and March led to the appointment of the apparently neutral nonentity Bouchotte. His chief clerk, however, was the Jacobin F.-N. Vincent, who purged the ministry of all Girondins and packed it with Jacobins.

The Convention had created a new committee (1 January 1793) to act as a liaison between the legislature and the Executive Council of Ministers. This arrangement left vague the lines of executive authority. The Convention clarified the matter on 6 April by giving the committee authority over the entire executive branch, except the Ministry of Finances. They gave this new body its cruelly ironic name: the Committee of Public Safety. Six weeks later the Girondins, having shipped more than eighty Jacobin deputies off to the provinces as the Convention's "deputies on mission," used their majority to create yet another commission, the Committee of General Security, which they gave power over the ministries of the interior and of foreign affairs, and the brand new Committee of Public Safety.

The frenzied political infighting took place against a backdrop of instability, counterrevolutionary plots, and mounting hunger. In addition to the various quasi-executive commissions, the Convention created (10 March) a Revolutionary Tribunal to hear cases involving state security and established (21 March) revolutionary committees of surveillance in all communes and large city sections. In Paris, the creation of these committees gave the quasipermanent sectional assemblies, who already possessed an armed force, a powerful new weapon to intimidate their opponents. The mounting price of bread added fuel to the revolutionary flames. The Convention, responding to pressure from the Parisian crowds, mandated a special tax on the rich, to be used to subsidize bread prices, and made *assignats* the sole legal currency. These measures had little immediate effect: on 17 April, Guittard wrote that Paris had had no bread for five days and that armed National Guards stood watch at every bakery in the city. The urban poor everywhere struggled just to eat. A revolutionary explosion could not be far off.

In the countryside, the Convention's February conscription decree for 300,000 men created another explosion.[19] Unlike the "voluntary" military drafts of 1791 and 1792, this one was to resort to force if necessary. Most communes chose their soldiers by the traditional, and universally detested Ancien Régime method: drawing lots. Following in the aftermath of the bungled abolition of feudalism and of the supremely unpopular assault on the clergy, the attempted imposition of a military draft was certain to produce violent opposition. Peasants all over the west shouted "down with the lottery" and took up arms. The revolt in Brittany, the Chouannerie, settled down quickly to a low-level guerrilla warfare, due to prompt and substantial military intervention, but just south of the Loire, in the Vendée, the rebels got the upper hand. In a few weeks, armed bands of 10,000 men roamed the countryside, starting a civil war that would end with tens of thousands of deaths. The government responded to the news of the insurrection by passing a law (19 March) allowing the summary trial and execution of rebels captured in arms. Its initial attempts at suppressing the Vendeans failed miserably; peasant guerrillas bamboozled the government troops, trapped hopelessly in the forbidding hedges of the *bocage* country. By May, the guerrillas had driven out the troops and gone on the offensive.

The Girondins, who had control of the Executive Council of Ministers, naturally received the blame for this disaster, as well as for the other miseries of the spring of 1793. The army's defeats in Belgium, and the treason of the Girondin's favorite general, Dumouriez, further undermined their position. The political debates in the Convention now turned increasingly personal. Robespierre demanded the arrest and trial of Brissot; other radicals demanded the removal of certain deputies as agents of Counterrevolution. Everyone likely agreed with Guittard, who wrote on 13 March: "One cannot be tranquil for a moment!" On 28 March, sections conducted house-to-house searches for arms held by "emigrés, nobles, non-juring priests, servants of nobles, and other suspect persons."

The Montagnards organized their chief allies, the Paris sections, for dramatic action. On 18 April, they circulated a petition in the sections to be sent to all departments, urging the Convention to expel and arrest twenty-two Girondin deputies. The Girondins responded by arresting and trying Marat. When the Convention acquitted him (23 April), he led a triumphal procession through the streets of Paris. A week later, besieged by foreign armies in the north and east and by peasant rebels in the west, the Convention declared the "Fatherland in danger" and ordered all male citizens between the ages of eighteen and fifty to take up arms for the purpose of marching against the western rebels.

Events spun out of control everywhere, especially in Paris. The Girondins tried to use the Committee of General Security to bring the Paris Commune to heel; the Jacobins relied on the Commune and the sections to intimidate the Girondins. The dénouement started in early May. On 1 May, a crowd of 8,000 to 10,000 marched on the Convention, demanding price controls on grain and bread. A delegation of women from Versailles also occupied the Convention itself, refusing to leave without a promise of price controls. The Convention caved in the following day and promulgated the decree on 3 May.

WOMEN AND POLITICS: THE JUNE DAYS

The police reports suggest that women, especially market women, led the opposition to the Girondins. On 13 May, one police agent wrote: "the women persevere in the project of demanding the recall of the twenty-two deputies . . . ; they even have the hope that they will be seconded by the men." Another agent wrote: "evil influences, under the mark of patriotism, have excited these revolutionary heroines to riot and to take up arms so as to dissolve the Convention and cause rivers of blood to flow in Paris." The leading radical women organized a new political club, the Club of Republican Revolutionary Citizenesses on 14 May, perhaps led by Claire Lacombe and Pauline Léon. A Girondin deputy warned the Convention on 25 May of an impending massacre of the Rightist deputies: "the pretext will be a manufactured outbreak of disorder in the Convention; the women will set things going; indeed a regiment of them has already been formed for this iniquitous work."[22]

These events would have enormous long-term implications for the political participation of women in the French Revolution. The Jacobins distrusted women in politics in part because of the important role played by Marie-Jeanne Philippon, wife of the minister Roland. The Convention sought to arrest both she and her husband during the June Days. She actually went to the Convention itself on the night of 31 May to try to convince them of the innocence of her husband. She would be released and re-arrested, finally going the scaffold on 8 November 1793. Her husband committed suicide two days later.

The Jacobins feared, too, the role of the radical women led by Lacombe and Léon. Their alliance with the male radicals, like Hébert, made them potential enemies. Surely the Jacobins also feared the galvanizing role women had played in some of the great Revolutionary days, such as the march to Versailles or the June Days. When they obtained full power, the Jacobins denied women political rights, closed their clubs, and executed or imprisoned their political leaders. The central role of women in the June Days, the very event that brought the Jacobins to power, thus instigated the Jacobins' destruction of women's rights.

On 28 May, a crowd of about three hundred women, in all likelihood organized by the Club of Republican Revolutionary Citizenesses (CRRC), marched on the Convention, demanding the right to bear arms to protect themselves, saying "they wanted to stand guard, like the men."[20] The leaders of the forthcoming insurrection organized in the sections on 29 May, created a central committee for their activities, and then invited the Commune to join them (30 May). The next day, at 4 A.M., the Commune sounded the tocsin. Because Friday 31 May 1793 was a heavy work day, artisans took slowly to the streets.[21] Poor Guittard suspected great things: he spent the day shivering in fright, "wanting to vomit, finding myself all day weak in the legs and with trembling hands." He expressed great relief at the end of the day that nothing had happened, yet recorded 31 May in his diary along with 14 July 1789, 20 June 1791, 10 August 1792, and 21 January 1793 as "four or five truly remarkable days." Saturday, 1 June saw relatively little action until late in the evening, when the workers left their shops and took up arms. Sunday, 2 June, they turned those arms on the Convention. A massive gathering of National Guardsmen and *sans-culottes,* certainly over 75,000 armed men, surrounding the Tuileries Palace and forced the Convention to arrest twenty-nine of its own members, as well as two Girondin ministers. The Mountain had now broken the Girondins, but it took the

TWELVE WHO RULED[23]

The Convention created the twelve-member Committee of Public Safety in April 1793 to provide a liaison with the executive branch ministries; the Committee soon became the *de facto* executive branch of the government. Unlike the ministers, who could not be deputies in the Convention, the Committee of Public Safety consisted of deputies drawn from the Convention, renewed by vote of the assembly every six weeks. Danton and his allies dominated the initial membership, although two of the later Twelve who ruled during the Terror had seats from the beginning: Bernard Barère and Robert Lindet, both lawyers. The Committee added three more of the famous Twelve on the eve of the June Days: Georges Couthon, another lawyer; Louis-Antoine de Saint-Just, a young (twenty-six) former wastrel whom his own mother once imprisoned by *lettre de cachet;* and Marie-Jean Hérault de Séchelles, a member of an ancient noble family and the king's attorney of the Parlement of Paris in the late 1780s. Hérault de Séchelles provided the key leadership for the group during the difficult days of early June 1793, but Couthon, who was confined to a wheelchair because of meningitis, gave several impassioned speeches that deeply affected his colleagues. Hérault de Séchelles maintained close ties with Danton even after the latter's fall from grace. In March and April 1794, he allied with Danton and the Indulgents to try to put a stop to the Terror.

He joined Danton and Desmoulins on the scaffold.

The renewal of the Committee on 10 July led to the removal of Danton and some of his allies. The Convention added two more of the Twelve, André Jeanbon Saint-André, a former Protestant minister; and Pierre-Louis Prieur (called Prieur of the Marne), a lawyer. Seventeen days later, the Convention took the dramatic step of naming the preeminent figure of the Jacobins, Maximilien Robespierre, to the Committee. Soon, the final four members joined: Jean-Nicolas Billaud-Varenne, a lawyer from La Rochelle and failed playwright; Jean-Marie Collot d'Herbois, an actor (and minor playwright) with close ties to Parisian radicals; and two military engineers, Lazare Carnot and Claude-Antoine Prieur-Duverny (called Prieur of the Côte d'Or).[24] Carnot had known Robespierre at Arras, where both belonged to a local literary society: Robespierre had even acted as the lawyer for Carnot's servant in an inheritance lawsuit.

These twelve men well represented the Convention. They came from all over France: three from the Southwest; two each from Burgundy, Picardy, and Paris. Like most of their fellow deputies, eleven of the twelve had had advanced education, eight of them in law. They belonged to the literary public sphere of the late Ancien Régime: eight of them had published a book, pamphlet or play by 1790,

Montagnards until early July to consolidate their position and actually take power themselves.

The Jacobins took over in an atmosphere of utter chaos. In the west, the Vendean rebels swept all before them. They captured town after town in their region. Thouars, Fontenay, and finally, on 9 June, the substantial Loire river city of Saumur fell, defended by none other than the Parisian militia recruited in March, under Santerre. In the south, matters looked just as bad. Factional fighting broke out in Marseille in March, leading local Jacobins to impose new taxes on the rich and enact stern police measures. The local merchants and their workers rose up against the Jacobins, driving the deputies on mission from the city and deposing the Jacobin municipal council. Just up the river, at Lyon, a Jacobin municipality suffered for its failure to control bread prices, a third higher than those of Paris. Once again, discontented workers

(CONTINUED)

and most of them had subscribed to literary societies in their hometown. Like their fellow deputies, they were remarkably young for men asked to take over their country. Nine of them were under forty when they took power. Of the remaining three, Collot d'Herbois was forty-three, Jeanbon Saint-André, forty-four, and Lindet, forty-six.

The Twelve did not have real factions but two clear blocs could be distinguished: the radicals, with strong ties to the *sans-culottes* and the Paris sections—Robespierre, Saint-Just, Couthon, Collot d'Herbois, Billaud-Varenne, and, perhaps, the fickle Barère—and what might be called the functionary wing, Lindet, Carnot, and Prieur of the Côte d'Or. This trio specialized in organization, above all of the military; the public opprobrium that followed 9 Thermidor largely excluded them. Carnot especially kept his reputation. Alone among the Twelve, he remained on the Committee into the fall of 1794 and he became one of the original five Directors of the government created in 1795. The radicals fared less well. Their split in July 1794 led to the execution on 28 July 1794 of Robespierre, Couthon, and Saint-Just. Two of their three chief accusers, Billaud-Varenne and Collot d'Herbois, were later (1795) sentenced to exile in French Guiana, "the dry guillotine," for their part in the Terror. The third member of those who toppled Robespierre, the ever slippery Barère, managed to obtain an acquittal at the 1795 trial.

The streets of Paris bear permanent witness to the historical memory of these figures: only Lindet and Carnot have given their names to streets in the capital.[25] One of the great avenues that flows into the Arc de Triomphe bears Carnot's name, as does a major boulevard. Robespierre's name briefly (1946–1950) graced a small street and the square on which the Jacobin Club formerly met, evidence of the Communist influence in the Paris of 1946. That influence quickly waned. In 1950, the city fathers renamed the square the place du Marché Saint-Honoré and even changed the name of the tiny street, to the rue de la place du Marché Saint-Honoré, perhaps seeking to efface the memory of so controversial a figure. In the great provincial cities, too, major avenues bear Carnot's name and blandly describe him as "the organizer of the victory." His role in the Terror, in which he fully participated (i.e., voting in favor of the execution of Danton and Desmoulins), is conveniently forgotten. As for Robespierre, only Leftist cities, such as Brest, where the main street bears his name, dare to evoke the memory of the soul of the Jacobins.[26] Thus do the avenues and boulevards of every French town become the places of memory for each contemporary political group's version of a mythical French past.

armed themselves and overthrew the municipality. Events in Marseille, Paris, and Lyon had this in common: the party perceived to be in power was attacked by the armed workers of the city, desperate for bread and work. Guittard wrote in his journal that "[the bread shortage] began on July 10th and lasted until September 10th . . . You had to be at the baker's door by 4 A.M. There were those who lined up at midnight." In Paris, workers aimed their hostility at the Girondins who opposed price controls; in Lyon and Marseille, it meant revolt *against* the Jacobins. Word of the Lyon revolt reached Paris in early June, exacerbating tensions there and leading to cries for stern measures against counterrevolutionaries.

Bordeaux, whose deputies headed the Girondins, reacted violently against the actions of 2 June. It declared itself in insurrection against the Convention, sent delegates urging other cities to do the same, and raised troops to march on Paris. Lyon and Marseille joined forces to take Avignon and declared their region in rebellion. Montpellier joined in on 11 June and Toulon, the great Mediterranean naval base, a few days later. In the west, the Breton departments responded with joy and sent troops toward Caen, which had also revolted against the Convention.[27] The Federalist revolt received support in many regions of France, but by no means in a majority of them. The three key centers of Federalist resistance were the west, in an area running from Caen to Upper Brittany; the area around Bordeaux; and the Rhône valley. To that, we must add the Vendée, whose insurrection had nothing to do with Federalism: the Vendeans wanted the return of "their priests and their king." The Federalists wanted neither.

The Montagnards acted quickly on several fronts. They focused immediate attention on the need to draw up a constitution. Rejecting many of the principles brought forward by Condorcet and his committee, the Jacobins hurriedly pushed through a constitution based on a unicameral legislature, directly elected by all male citizens. Their declaration of rights included rights to public assistance, to education, and to resistance of oppression. The Constitution of 1793 also abolished all feudal rights, without compensation, and divided the nationalized property (of the Church and émigrés) into smaller lots, for sale to poor and middling farmers. Amazingly enough, something like 2 million men voted in the constitutional plebiscite of July 1793. Almost all of them voted in favor, but the voting assemblies often held vigorous debates and many of them forwarded proposed amendments to Paris.[28] Turnouts could vary from under 20 percent (17 departments) to over 40 percent (six). Although the Convention ruled that, in the given emergency, it could not enact the Constitution, the plebiscite provided the Convention with desperately needed legitimacy at one of France's most difficult moments.

The Convention turned first to deal with the Federalist rebellion. A small army sent to Caen (August) immediately broke the Federalists there; the rebels of Bordeaux capitulated by October. In both cities, the deputies on mission from the Convention carried out few reprisals. The situation in the southeast, however, was another matter. The anti-Jacobins of Marseille and Lyon had executed local supporters of the Convention, including the deputy on mission in Lyon, Chalier, who quickly became a Revolutionary martyr (all the more so after the publication of his prison memoirs). The Vendeans occupied Angers, a city of 20,000, but the failure of their two-day assault on Nantes led them to return to their *bocages*. The government desperately needed this victory, because Nantes was the only one of France's three greatest ports in its hands.

The war situation deteriorated steadily from March to August. The Austrians captured Condé and Valenciennes; the Savoyards attacked Nice; the Spaniards crossed the Pyrenees, an area which already had a low-level peasant insurgency against the Convention; the Allies recaptured Mainz; and the British sent troops to capture France's West Indian possessions, above all Saint-Domingue. As if defeat in war, treason in the southeast, and rebellion in the west were not enough, on 13 July one of the supporters of the Caen Federalists, Charlotte Corday, assassinated Marat while he was taking a bath. The Convention became more militant in its policies: it removed Danton, now become the symbol of insufficient rigor, from the Committee of Public Safety and replaced him two weeks later with Robespierre, the embodiment of revolutionary vigilance. He led the Convention to its most dramatic move on 11 August: one day after the celebrating the approval of the new Constitution. On Robespierre's motion, the Convention suspended its implementation during the "emergency."

In August 1793, facing continued military threats and runaway inflation, the Convention voted (23 August) the "levée en masse," mass conscription of men aged eighteen to twenty-five, coupled with mobilization of women for work, of nondraft animals for army usage, and of old men to march to public squares, there to proclaim the virtues of patriotism. In early September, in response to the massive *sans-culottes* demonstrations about bread prices and wages, the Convention created "Revolutionary Armies": armed patriots who would seek out traitors and hoarders. They also approved a 40-shilling payment to citizens attending twice weekly meetings of their sections, decided to salary the presidents of revolutionary committees, and agreed to make "terror the order of the day," launching what we know as the Reign of Terror.

THE REIGN OF TERROR

I am without indulgence for the enemies of my country; I know only justice.

Louis-Antoine de Saint-Just, Speech of 8 Ventôse II (26 February 1794)

CHRONOLOGY	September 1793–July 1794
September 1793	Terror made into official government policy; wage and price controls introduced (Law of the General Maximum)
September/October	Curtailment of women's political rights; closing of Club of Republican Revolutionary Citizenesses; arrest of women's leaders
9 October	Convention's forces recapture Lyon
16 October	Execution of Marie-Antoinette
16 October	Jourdan defeats Austrians at Wattignies
17 October	Defeat of Vendéans at Cholet
31 October	Execution of most of the Girondin leaders; others commit suicide
29 November	Execution of Barnave
12 December	Defeat of Vendéans at Le Mans
19 December	Recapture of Toulon; reprisals begin
13–24 March 1794	Hébertists arrested (13 and 14 March) and executed (24 March)

CHRONOLOGY	(continued)
28 March	Condorcet commits suicide
30 March–6 April	Danton, Desmoulins, and "Indulgents" arrested (30 March); tried, and executed (6 April)
April–July	Height of the Paris Terror
8 June	Festival of the Supreme Being
26 June	Jourdan wins battle of Fleurus
27–29 July	Fall and execution of Robespierre, Saint-Just, Couthon, and their allies (9 Thermidor)

Saint-Just's words have the same frightening, implacable coldness today that they bore two hundred years ago. The Jacobins knew only "justice," untempered by mercy; yet they, like political actors from time immemorial, had first to define it. They first focused on the purity of the congregation, weeding out the heretics from their own ranks, purifying the Revolutionary "priesthood." The Leftist newspapers of 1793 and early 1794 mainly attacked each other, casting out the wildest, most hideous accusations. They accused their opponents of hoarding grain amidst a famine; they plotted to restore "Capet's son" (the child of Louis XVI) to the throne; they plotted to marry their leader to Capet's daughter; they plotted to restore the monarchy, with Philip of Orléans as king; they plotted with aristocratic exiles, with peasants rebels, with the British, with the Austrians and Prussians to overthrow the Republic; they plotted to unleash anarchy, by destroying private property and allowing man's basest desires to have unchecked license. Well might Nicolas Ruault lament on 11 June 1793 that "one of the greatest plagues that the Revolution has produced is the frightening license of the newspapers; they pervert public opinion."

From a distance of two hundred years, these accusations seem so ridiculous that we cannot even imagine that people believed them. Yet they did believe some of them and they often acted in direct response to these perceived threats. The accusations focused on people's real and legitimate fears. These included the restoration of the monarchy; the return of the aristocracy; the danger of foreign invasion; the threat of civil war in the Vendée or in the southeast; the shortage of bread; and massive unemployment. These terrible realities had nothing to do with imagination; they were the stuff of everyday life in France in the summer of 1793. People wanted the government to do something to solve these problems. Even Ruault, hardly sympathetic to the Jacobins, would write to his brother on 8 July 1793: "We hope that . . . personal interest will save the Republic and produce the general good, that we will never speak again of Girondins, as if they had never existed."[29] A few weeks later, he would congratulate his brother on the collapse of the Federalists at Evreux and the restoration of "order and obedience to the law."

The Terror can best be understood as three distinct movements:

1. The special case of Paris, tied directly to national politics.

2. The fight against the counterrevolution.

3. An intimidating climate of fear almost everywhere else.

Local officials, invariably directed by a deputy on mission from Paris, did occasionally execute someone. They guillotined non-juring priests, those who aided non-jurors, the odd speculator, some nobles, and a smattering of ordinary people. The authorities used a broader campaign of arrests (70,000+), backed up by the threat of execution, much more than execution. They used intimidation to restore a functioning government: to obtain bread for the starving people of the cities; to collect state revenue; to organize the army; to restore civil order in areas not in rebellion.

Historical memory largely ignores this third Terror; throughout the nineteenth and twentieth centuries, the Terror has meant the grotesque carnival of blood in Paris and, to a lesser degree, the brutal excesses at Lyon, Nantes, and a few other places. The Convention created the legal underpinning of Paris's Terror on 17 September 1793, when it put teeth into the mandate of the Revolutionary Armies by passing a Law of Suspects, allowing the revolutionary committees to arrest Federalists, former nobles, monarchists, and other "enemies of liberty." Twelve days later, the Convention instituted mandatory wage and price controls (the Law of the General Maximum), although it implemented the latter much more quickly than the former. The Convention also struck out at those it viewed as politically suspect. It began a trial of Brissot and the Girondin leaders, arrested the radical Jacques Roux, and closed down the Club of Revolutionary Republican Citizenesses, who had been so instrumental in the May demonstrations and who had been allied with Roux throughout the summer. It simultaneously acted to satisfy the people's need for bread. Guittard tells us on 10 September:

> at last there is bread today in all of the bakers' shops and they have thus dissipated the people who still wanted to gather there. What for, because everyone has as much bread as he wants today. I hope we are finally delivered from this crisis. . . .

The Convention tried and executed the Girondin leaders—Brissot, Vergniaud, and nineteen others went to the guillotine on 31 October. "They were convicted," Guittard writes, "of having plunged themselves into a conspiracy directed against the unity and indivisibility of the Republic, against liberty and the security of the French people." Throughout October and November, the revolutionary tribunals and the Convention sent other notables to the guillotine, among them earlier leaders of the Revolution now fallen from favor, like Barnave, Bailly, Philip of Orléans, and Mme Roland. Many of those who escaped the blade, like Roland or the former mayor of Paris, Pétion, committed suicide. The Convention arrested sixty-five of its own deputies, who had signed a secret denunciation of the events of 2 June, but it did not try them. It tried, convicted, and executed Marie Antoinette (16 October), and several generals suspected of treason.

Generations of historians have recoiled from the "mindless" Terror of 1793–1794, yet the events followed an extremely logical (if deeply perverted) pattern. The Paris Terror began with the fall 1793 assault on the Jacobins's most dangerous political rivals. The country still overwhelmingly wanted something like a constitutional monarchy and the reformed Catholic Church of 1790. The Jacobins thus murdered or drove to suicide all those associated with the compromise solution of 1789–1791—Bailly, Barnave, Philip of Orléans, and many others—and the moderate Girondins, such as Brissot, Roland, and Pétion. Having literally decapitated their most dangerous opponents outside their own movement, Robespierre and his allies moved to consolidate their supremacy on the Left: they naturally murdered all potential rivals, from Danton to Jacques Roux and Hébert.

The Terror, in Paris and in part of the southeast, thus served a partisan political purpose: that of eliminating political threats to Robespierre. The second Terror, the one that killed the most people, formed part of the response to counterrevolution and civil war. Terror by intimidation focused on the subsistence crisis and the creation of a functioning government. The old government structure had completely broken down. Lacking any obvious basis for legitimacy, given the widespread claims by the Convention's opponents that it was illegitimate, the government sought to use brute force and intimidation to establish short-term legitimacy. By January 1794, all three Terrors had succeeded. The Left had destroyed the leadership of the Center and Right; the government had gained the upper hand against counterrevolutionaries; and the state had frightened most French people into obeying their government. These successes, apparent by early 1794, led Danton and others to suggest that the Terror end. Robespierre and his allies disagreed. Desperate to justify continued government by Terror, they made the devastating blunder of turning against their allies on the Left. Once they had killed them (April), they resorted to the old political ploy of persecuting a scapegoated minority. In the France of 1794, the choice of scapegoat was easy: the nobles and the clergy.

The phrase "Reign of Terror" recalls for us the image of the Revolution consuming its own children in Paris. The three phases of the Parisian Terror targeted very distinct groups:

1. The fall 1793 executions of the early leaders of the Revolution and the Girondins, fewer than two hundred people.

2. The internal massacre within the Left, culminating with the death of Danton in early April.

3. A last paroxysm of viciousness, targeted on the scapegoated privileged orders.

Nearly two-thirds of the eleven hundred fifty-eight nobles officially executed during the Terror died between April and July 1794; roughly a third of the clergy executed died in June and July 1794.

While the Convention executed Marie Antoinette, the people of Paris and other major cities stepped up their campaign of organized vandalism against all symbols of the Ancien Régime. They decapitated the royal statues on the portal of Notre

The Last Night of the Girondins

I must tell you of the last night of the Girondins. I have it from Anarcharsis Clootz, who came to see me the night before last. When they were condemned to die at about 11 P.M., they all, minus Valazé, who had stabbed himself in front of the tribunal, met together in a single room to have supper. They had served a very good meal of all that could be obtained at that hour in the Palace quarter: roasts, pastries, delicate wines, liqueurs. They elected a president, it was *la Source* [whom Ruault does not identify], who proposed that

they die right there. 'I feel myself sufficiently courageous, he told them, to kill you all, and myself last, and thus prevent that we should die publicly on the scaffold.' The band of the condemned received this proposition in different ways; they began to eat and drink. In the midst of the meal, they lengthily debated the question of the existence of God and the immortality of the soul. Seventeen of the twenty-one recognized both the one and the other and refused to die at the hand of the president.[30]

Dame and dug up the coffins of France's kings and queens (even good king Dagobert, buried in the seventh century!) at Saint-Denis. Ruault wrote to his brother: "All these monuments to human grandeur and vanity have been destroyed, burned in quicklime last October, at the same time that they tortured the last queen of France and publicly immolated the twenty-one Girondins. Such sad times these are, when the living and the dead are both persecuted for . . . their opinions."[31]

The government's military situation improved in early September 1793, when a French army routed the Austrians at Wattignies, driving them across the frontier. In the south, the newly created Revolutionary Army from Paris joined regular troops and captured Lyon in early October. The Convention demanded vengeance for Lyon's treachery, but the deputy on mission in charge of the repression, Georges Couthon, settled for a few exemplary punishments and for the destruction of the houses of the richest merchants. His replacement, Joseph Fouché, had some seventeen hundred prisoners lined up over hastily dug graves and mowed down with cannon and musket fire. The troops who took Lyon then headed south, to Toulon, where rebels fleeing Marseille had joined local Federalists to invite British intervention. When the French army retook Toulon, in December, seven thousand rebels left with the British. The army shot eight hundred people the next day and guillotined two hundred more in the ensuing month. The Convention mandated that these two cities take new names, Mountain-Port and Ville Affranchie (Freed Town), to efface the shame attached to those of Toulon and Lyon. One minor element of the siege of Toulon is worthy of note. A Corsican artillery captain named Napoleon Bonaparte earned a promotion to brigadier general by directing the bombardment that drove the British fleet from the harbor. Paris celebrated the news of these victories with a mammoth parade in their honor.

The massacres in regions of counterrevolution provide yet another historical example of the brutality of civil war. The cycle of repression–reprisal of the Vendée or the Rhône is, sadly, as old as time. The Terror of Paris, with its blatantly political and social side (the latter in late spring 1794), sprang from the fall of the monarchy

Destroying royal images in Paris: here the crowd demolishes the statue of Louis XIV in the Place des Victories. Today's statue is a later copy of the original.

Source: © Corbis.

and the execution of the king. Killing Louis XVI established the precedent for the elimination of political rivals. The atmosphere in which he was tried, the charges against him—with their emphasis on foreign plots[32]—all led up to the increasingly vituperative, personal, bloody politics of 1793–1794. The Convention took the critical step in June 1793 of arresting its own deputies and charging them with treason. Their execution in October 1793 started the Convention down the slippery slope sure to lead to failure. The foolish executions of the leading deputies of the Left in March and April 1794, carried out *by* deputies from the Left, led to the Left's inevitable collapse in the summer of 1794. Before we get to that episode, however, let us consider the other two elements of the Terror.

The violent Terror took place primarily in four cities: Toulon, Lyon, Nantes, and Paris. Just as the authorities shot hundreds in Lyon or Toulon, so they drowned eighteen hundred at Nantes. The deputy on mission, J.-B. Carrier, and the local authorities began the procedure by tying ninety non-juring priests to a barge, which was then taken to the middle of the Loire and sunk. Local authorities repeated this procedure six times, not only for priests but for Vendéan rebels—men, women, and

children—and even common criminals. Carrier got a hero's welcome when he returned to the Paris Jacobin Club.[33] Nantes had the dubious distinction of executing
the most people during the Terror: almost thirty-five hundred in its department as
a whole.

The *noyades* (drownings) were just part of the repression of the Vendée rebellion. In October, the army defeated the main rebel force at Cholet. The rebels then
marched to Normandy, hoping to link up with the British at Granville. Cut off by
the army, they turned back toward the Loire, suffering the loss of ten thousand
people in fighting near Le Mans and of another three thousand at Savenay. In the
Vendée itself, the "blues" (the royal army) brought fire and sword to every hamlet. In
the words of their commanding general, Turreau, they were to "employ every means
to discover the rebels, everyone will be bayoneted; the villages, farms, woods, wastelands, scrub and generally all which can be burned, will be put to the torch." The
local population dropped by as much as one-third. People abandoned entire towns,
like La Roche-sur-Yonne, which Turreau burned to the ground. Tens of thousands of
people died in the repression, touching off more warfare. The Republic did not gain
full control of the Vendée for another two years, when General Hoche captured and
executed the main rebel leaders.

Terror and counterrevolution went hand-in-hand. The three departments most
affected by the Vendée rebellion accounted for 43 percent of the total executions
during the Terror, and the four most compromised in the southeast for another 18
percent. The majority of "unofficial" executions, certainly more numerous than the
official ones, also came in these two areas. Although the climate created by the Reign
of Terror hung like a pallor over all France, the Terror itself—in the sense of mass executions—took place in a very restrained area. Of the eighty-seven departments in
existence in 1793–1794, thirteen accounted for 89 percent of the executions. Areas
that had extensive counterrevolutionary activity tended to have substantial support
for the Terror. Political opponents fought each other in an intense civil war in places
like the Rhône valley.[34] Places such as Dijon were far more typical: city authorities
arrested five hundred eighty people, a third of them women, but merely confined
many of them to their houses. Only ten locals died under the blade at Dijon, while
seventy more citizens from Dijon's department died in Paris's Terror.

Most of France had a very different experience of the Terror from that of Toulon
or Nantes. Six departments had no executions at all, and sixty-one of them had fifty
or fewer. Even a center of Federalism as important as Calvados was little touched. It
had only seven executions. Most areas used the Terror to enforce specific governmental policies. The committees of surveillance, especially in towns, did not flag in
their efforts to arrest suspects: some seventy thousand people suffered detention.
Once again, there were substantial geographic variances. In some cases, that meant
economic policy—grain requisition or price-fixing—but far more often it meant
enforcement de-Christianization, the Convention's greatest blunder. (See the following text.)

The Terror killed far more people in the Vendée or the southeast than died in
Paris, but the events in the capital captured people's imaginations, then and afterwards. Guittard's journal makes special reference to only a few fall 1793 executions:

the Girondins, Marie-Antoinette, and a few other notables. Although the theme of executions is absent in Guittard's journal, the deaths of the Girondin leaders certainly affected public opinion. Ruault wrote to his brother, in December 1793:

> What would you have me say, my dear friend? What side can I take now in all that is happening? To the sorrows that consume our home [Ruault's son had just died] are joined the horrors, the stupidities, the public follies. . . . Adieu, my dear friend, I cover my eyes so that I do not have to see any more.

Guittard's journal changes dramatically in March 1794, when the violent intra-Left war finally came to a head. The various parties had been slandering each other with ever-increasing vituperation in January and February. The Cordeliers went so far as to drape black crepe around the copy of the Declaration of the Rights of Man hanging in their meeting room. On 4 March, their evening meeting called for an insurrection in Paris, to put an end to the Terror. Robespierre and his allies on the Committee of Public Safety struck back suddenly. In mid-March, the government arrested the Parisian radical leaders, some of whom had only recently been released from prison, and put them on trial.

The fight on the Left had begun in the fall of 1793, when the Montagnards arrested Roux, Varlet, Léon, and Lacombe. This fighting on the Left had created three separate factions: the Jacobin Club, led by Robespierre and his allies; the Cordeliers Club, now the stronghold of the *enragés;* and the Indulgents, consisting primarily of those who had split from the Cordeliers. The Indulgents were led by Danton and by Camille Desmoulins, a journalist who began issuing a new newspaper, the *Vieux Cordelier,* in December 1793. Desmoulins roundly attacked the Committee of Public Safety and Robespierre for their policies, above all for the continuation of a Terror that Danton and Desmoulins believed had outlived its usefulness.

The Jacobins sought, from December 1793 to April 1794, to destroy both of the other factions. They arrested the leaders of the *sans-culottes* in January, released them in February, and then struck again in mid-March. On 24 March, Guittard provides details of the death of the main conspirators: Hébert, Anarchasis Cloots, Rousin (commander of the Revolutionary Army), Momoro (chief administrator of the department of Paris), Vincent (chief administrator of the ministry of war), and thirteen others. He claims that 300,000 spectators watched the guillotine fall. These men, called the *enragés,* had provided the leadership to the *sans-culottes* in Paris, tying together the power of the Paris sections and the Commune. The Convention further cut the power base of this faction by eliminating the Revolutionary Armies, which they had dominated. In May, they even outlawed sectional political clubs.

The Convention had already (January 1794) arrested a prominent former Cordelier, Fabre d'Eglantine, because of his profiteering in the dissolution of the Company of the Indies. On 29 March, they arrested the other leading Indulgents, such as Danton and Desmoulins. Guittard mentions this conspiracy on 5 April, when Desmoulins, Danton, Fabre d'Eglantine, General Westermann, and Hérault de Séchelles, a former member of the Committee of Public Safety, joined ten others on the block. They stood accused of collaborating with the duke of Orléans (and

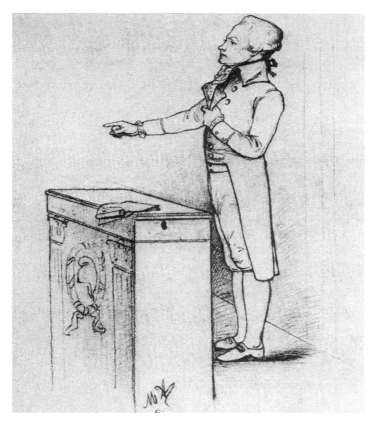

Robespierre giving a speech to the Jacobin Club. The artist provides us with vivid testimony of Robespierre's rigid, almost puritanical demeanor.

SOURCE: Bibliothèque Nationale.

his agent, the traitorous General Dumouriez) to place him on the throne. Another twenty-one people, including the wives of Desmoulins and Hébert, Godot, the archbishop of Paris, and the *procureur syndic* of Paris, Chaumette, went to the block on 13 April. These executions show the Byzantine politics of the time. Fabre d'Eglantine and Hérault de Séchelles had been violent opponents in December 1793; one recent study finds the latter at first an ally of the *enragés* and then an associate of the Indulgents. Desmoulins and Hébert spent much of January and February denouncing each other, yet their wives joined each other in execution. Godel and Chaumette had led the Committee's de-Christianization campaign and had nothing in common with the Indulgents. Robespierre and his allies merely tied them to convenient villains in order to distance themselves from the unpopular excesses of de-Christianization.

THE SINNER AND THE PRINCE OF DARKNESS

Andrzej Wajda's brilliant film, *Danton,* has a dramatic scene in which Danton invites Robespierre to a one-on-one meeting to patch over their differences. Danton, a lover of life and of its many pleasures, has a leading restaurant lay out a sumptuous dinner for the two of them; Robespierre, when he arrives, refuses to eat. He looks with contempt on Danton, who has commanded such a repast in a Paris teeming with the hungry. When Robespierre walks out, Danton trashes the dining room in frustration.

Georges Danton came from the tiny bourg of Arcis-sur-Aube, received a legal education, and took up practice before the Parlement of Paris. In July 1789, he became one of the many street-corner orators inciting the Parisian crowds to militant action. His skills as an orator led to a rapid rise in local politics: he became head of the section of the Cordeliers. Mona Ozouf, noting his imposing physical figure, compares him to a sectional Mirabeau, while Michelet thought him a "lion who descends into a bull, even a wild boar," darkened by his "wild sensuality." Mme Roland (wife of his main enemy) found him "repugnant and atrocious," yet having an "air of great joviality." Ozouf writes that he was "a massacrer without ferocity, a gambler without avidity, a terrorist without maxims, a parvenu without avarice, a frantic lazybones, a tender colossus."[35]

Ruault, whose earlier letters had criticized Danton, wrote more sympathetically about him on the day of his arrest:

Because Danton and Desmoulins wanted to stop the movement of the guillotine, they passed under it themselves; those good sentiments were stifled along with their lives. . . . The misfortune of Danton was to have regained credit with the good patriots and even the men of the world, since he had associated himself with Desmoulins at the *Vieux Cordelier* in an effort to stop the massacres of the Revolutionary Tribunal. These two men, chiefs of a too-famous party, had kept something human and wanted to make others forget their follies, even their

cruelties, by an honorable return to sound principles. The credit of Danton gave umbrage to Robespierre, who is today the king of the revolution, the pontiff of the Eternal, the apostle of that doctrine of the immortality of the soul that he has had pasted up on the pediment of all the churches. . . .

[Danton had told his friends three months ago] 'As long as they say *Robespierre and Danton,* things will go well; I will have nothing to fear; but if they ever say, *Danton and Robespierre,* I am a lost man.' In effect, Danton had begun to be named first. Confidence in him rose each day; tomorrow he will be at the Tribunal; the day after he will be killed with his friends. Such is the fate of patriots enraged and unenraged; such are the effects of anarchy; it devours its own children; it kills its brothers; it eats its own innards; in the end, it is the most horrible and cruelest of all monsters. This frightening monster is today among us in its greatest vigor. None of use can be sure of escaping it, because it strikes wrongly and faultily. Milton forgot to depict it in his hellish scenes."

[Letter of 10 April] "Danton is no more. Robespierre triumphs. The tiger has beaten the lion. But this triumph will be short-lived, if we can believe the prediction of Danton, as he walked to his death; and that man knows about revolution. You are perhaps curious to know of the last minutes of this proud revolutionary. He gaily put up with the interrogation of the Tribunal and mocked his judges and jury throughout; he went to the scaffold laughing at death. He was the only one of the band of the accused to keep a good countenance; when he appeared for the first time before the judges and they asked his name, age, and residence, he replied: 'My name is sufficiently known, you can find it in the Pantheon of history; as for my residence, it will soon be in the void.' . . . [On the way to the scaffold] Danton laughed . . . and argued with Lacroix and Hérault . . . 'that which vexes me is to die six weeks before Robespierre.'

'Danton was the last; when he saw the executioner coming to get him at the bottom of the scaffold, he cried out with a loud voice, *My turn!* and quickly mounted the fatal stairway. . . . Only the head of Danton was shown to the people,

(CONTINUED)

who cried "Vive la République! The eyelids of that head thrashed about, the eyes were lively and full of light, while the executioner promenaded it around the scaffold; the body that the head had just left had been so robust and vigorous, that the head seemed still to look and to breathe, and to hear the cries of the multitude."[36]

Robespierre, born in 1758, came, like Danton, from a provincial town (Arras), where he, too, practiced law. His contemporaries called him the "Incorruptible" for his austere personal life and his inflexible principles. Throughout the Revolution, this leader of the *sans-culottes* continued to wear culottes; in a Paris where Revolutionary manners demanded he remove it, he sported a powdered wig. The German playwright, Büchner, in his work *Danton's Death,* called Robespierre "insupportably honest," while the American historian Robert Palmer suggested that he "had the fault of a self-righteous and introverted man. Disagreement with himself he regarded simply as error . . . He was quick to charge others with the selfish interests of which he felt himself to be free. . . . A lover of mankind, he could not enter with sympathy into the minds of his own

Georges Danton, a sketch by Jan Georg Wille, as Danton made his way to execution.
Source: © Gianni Dagli Orti/Corbis.

(CONTINUED)

neighbors."[37] Michelet rightly called his ascendancy the "Papacy of Robespierre," while Ruault described him as "the prince of revolutionary darkness, who, in dying, saw his party buried with him and the Jacobins defeated, and watched all his projects and friends die with him on the scaffold."

After the imprisonment of Camille Desmoulins, Lucille Desmoulins tried to write to Robespierre, to remind him of his old friendship for her husband:

> Camille saw your pride growing, he felt early on the path you wanted to follow, but he recalled your old friendship, and as far from the insensibilities as from the low jealousies of your Saint-Just, he recoiled from the idea of accusing an old school friend, a fellow artisan of his work. . . . And you, you send him to his death! . . . For you know it yourself, we do not merit the fate that

they prepare for us; and you can change it. If it strikes us, it's you who will have ordered it.[38]

Robespierre had great success as an orator, although his style differed greatly from Danton's. Where the latter overwhelmed the audience with his physical presence and his rolling cadences, with his remarkable knack for the memorable phrase ("l'audace, encore de l'audace, toujours de l'audace"), Robespierre spellbound listeners with his implacable moral intensity and ruthless logic. Where Danton relied on the spontaneous, Robespierre was an inveterate plotter and planner; ironically, his best speeches invariably accused others of precisely these faults.

Robespierre had the good fortune to be consistently ahead of the revolutionary curve: an early and ardent republican and a steadfast

---

An issue of the anti-Hébertiste newspaper, *Le Sappeur Sans-Culotte*, subsidized by the government, gives the general tenor of the propaganda of the time. As he writes, there is "Great Anger of the People against the infamous Père Duchesne and his accomplices, who wanted to free the [royal children in the Temple prison], open the doors to all conspirators held in Paris, cut the throats of the members of the Convention, and proclaim the son of the tyrant Capet (Louis XVI) as king." Guittard, like many others, seems to have bought into these charges. His journal entry for 13 April, the day of the execution of Chaumette *et alia,* reads as follows:

> All eighteen accused of having, in complicity with the infamous Hébert, Clootz, etc. . . . who had their heads cut off on March 24th, conspired against liberty and the security of the French people, in wanting to trouble the state by a civil war, in the aftermath of which the conspirators wanted, in March and April, to dissolve the Convention, assassinate its members and the patriots, destroy the republican Government, make off with the Sovereignty of the people and give a tyrant to the state: little Capet.

Guittard then begins a morbid daily body count. There were thirty-one on 20 April, many of them leaders of the Parlement of Paris; thirteen on 22 April, including such men as Le Chapelier, a leader of the Constituent Assembly; Malesherbes, former censor and counsel for Louis XVI at his trial; and the baron of Châteaubriand, father of the famous nineteenth-century writer. Then on 24 April,

(CONTINUED)

critic of Louis XVI. Louis's flight in June 1791 and the steady move toward republicanism in 1791–1792 seemed to bear out virtually every one of Robespierre's positions. In a February 1794 speech on the principles of the Revolution, he spelled out his view of the new political morality:

> We would wish to substitute in our country morality for egotism, probity for honor, principles for usages, duties for good manners, the empire of reason for the tyranny of fashion, contempt for vice for contempt for misfortune, pride for insolence, grandeur of the soul for vanity, the love of glory for the love of money, good people for good company, merit for éclat, the charm of happiness for the boredom of sensuality, the grandeur of man for the pettiness of the *grands,* a magnanimous, powerful, and happy people for a likeable, frivolous, and mis-

erable one; in a word, all the virtues and miracles of a republic for all the vices and absurdities of a monarchy.[39]

In a political system in which many important leaders had been compromised by efforts to reach some sort of accommodation with the king and the aristocrats—starting with Mirabeau and running up through Barnave and Danton (who had been an ally of Philippe d'Orléans), Robespierre's uncompromising attitude toward the old order gave him tremendous moral authority. Just as Danton's sinning humanity, which so endeared him to his contemporaries and to posterity, gave his enemies the weapons to defeat him, so, too, Robespierre's saintly, uncompromising moralism, which paved the way for his triumphs, in the end led to his death.

there were thirty-five executions and as many again on 28 April; twenty-four on 6 May, including thirteen leaders of the Parlement of Burgundy and eleven former administrators of the department of the Moselle. On 8 May, the executions followed with twenty-eight former Farmers General; and on 10 May, twenty-five people, among them Madame Elisabeth, sister of Louis XVI.[40] On 14 June, it was the turn of the Parlement of Toulouse, twenty-six of whose judges went to the scaffold; on 17 June, sixty-one more, accused of a plot against Robespierre and Collot d'Herbois (who had, in fact, survived an assassination attempt in late May), lost their heads. July's tally included a group of sixteen Carmelites from Compiègne on 17 June and peaked at fifty-five people on 23 June, a group that included the prince of Rohan and the famous Magon brothers, merchant–nobles of Saint-Malo, aged eighty and eighty-one!

Throughout his journal, Guittard dutifully reports the official line about all these executions. The condemned "sought the annihilation of the Republic," or they carried out a "plot against the Republic" or one to "restore the Monarchy" or "against the surety and liberty of the people." He seems never to question the existence of the plots or the guilt of the condemned, although he made a special point of making a drawing of a few of the executions: those of the Girondins, in fall 1793, and of the sixteen Carmelites in July 1794. To read his journal for the months from April to July 1794 is to enter a world gone mad.

Few historical moments have captured the collective imagination so much as the Reign of Terror. Charles Dickens, the great nineteenth-century English novelist,

THE TRIAL

Paris newspapers published the proceedings of some of the famous trials that took place in front of the Revolutionary Tribunal. The English novelist Helen Maria Williams, in Paris for the first half of the 1790s, provides the following translation of the trial of Louis XVI's sister, Madame Elisabeth, who died on 10 May 1794.

President of the Revolutionary Tribunal: When the tyrant, your brother, fled to Varennes, did you not accompany him?

Madame Elizabeth: Every consideration led me to follow my brother; and I made it a duty then, as I should have done on any other occasion.

Court: Did you not appear at the infamous and scandalous orgies of the bodyguard; and did you not walk round the table with Marie Antoinette, to induce each of the guests to repeat the horrid oath which they had sworn to exterminate every patriot . . . ?

Madame Elizabeth: Such orgies I believe never took place; but I declare that I was no manner whatever informed of their having happened, and never had any concern in them.

Court: You do not speak truth and your denial can be of no use to you, when it is contradicted on one side by public notoriety, and on the other by the likelihood which there must be in every sensible man's opinion, that a woman so intimately connected as you were with Marie Antoinette, both by the ties of blood and those of the strictest friendship, could not but be a sharer in her machinations. . . .

[Further accusations and denials]

Court: Were you not yourself anxious in dressing the wounds of the assassins sent to the Champs Elysées by your brother against the brave Marseillais?

[The Court here uses the term assassins to describe the defenders of the Tuileries Palace on 10 August 1792.]

Madame Elizabeth: I never knew that my brother had sent assassins against anyone whatever. If I have ever chanced to assist in dressing the wounded, it was humanity only that could have influenced me; it was not necessary for me to be informed what was the cause of their misfortune to hesitate whether I should afford them relief; and if I make no merit of this, I do not imagine that you can impute it to me as a crime.

Court: It is difficult to reconcile these sentiments of humanity to which you pretend, with that barbarous joy which you discovered, when you saw streams of blood flowing on the 10th of August. Everything leads us to believe you were humane only towards the assassins of the people, and that you have all the savageness of the most bloodthirsty beasts towards the defenders of liberty.[41]

---

captured its terrible dichotomy in the opening lines of *A Tale of Two Cities*: "It was the best of times. It was the worst of times." The Jacobin dictatorship accomplished many extraordinary goals. It organized the first modern army and used it to defeat a coalition of the other European powers in war; it tamed short-term inflation and provided affordable food for France's people; it crushed the Federalist revolt in the south and west and the counterrevolution in the Vendée; it encouraged popular participation in government, particularly by the lower classes; it abolished slavery and the last vestiges of feudalism; it wrote (but did not enact) a constitution that rested on universal manhood suffrage and that enshrined subsistence and public education as human rights. It accomplished these goals in most of France by means of widespread arrests, but with relatively little actual bloodshed. The Jacobins also inspired a remarkable patriotic ardor in their supporters, as even their severest enemies had to admit.

That Terror worked pretty effectively to accomplish its goals. Carnot, as the countless street signs claim, was indeed "the organizer of the victory"; by 1794, the French armies, larger than those of their opponents and now properly armed and supplied, swept all before them. The mobilization of the entire country, a mobilization enforced by Terror but also strongly supported by some elements of the population, worked. The Terror also had short-term success on the economic front. The revolutionary armies forcibly and effectively requisitioned grain from the countryside for the cities. By December, Paris had no more bread lines, using henceforth a system of bread ration cards.[42] Municipalities everywhere subsidized grain for the poor. At Grenoble, by April 1794, nearly ten percent of the city's families received bread directly from the hospital.

These short-term successes notwithstanding, we must not mince words about the Terror. It derailed the French Revolution, debased French political culture, and failed utterly, miserably, and completely as a form of government. Even the short-term successes, like the increased provision of grain, bred long-term failure. Forced requisition of grain supplies in the countryside worked but it inevitably produced resentment and resistance among the peasantry. The horrible grain shortages of 1795 can be traced back directly to the forced requisitions of 1794.

Moreover, in the ten percent of France in which it resorted to violence, the government did so on an unprecedented scale. The Jacobins murdered tens of thousands of their fellow citizens, many of them helpless victims, such as children. They trampled on the legal rights of their opponents by such means as declaring someone "outside the law," and thus subject to immediate arrest, conviction, and execution without normal due process. They removed rights of political participation—in clubs, in sectional assemblies, as petitioners to the Convention—from women. They executed Olympe de Gouges (Marie Gouze), author of the "Declaration of the Rights of Women and the Female Citizen," imprisoned Claire Lacombe and Pauline Léon, and drove the feminist writer Etta Palm d'Aelders into exile. They introduced such odious phrases as "enemies of the people" and "enemies of the Revolution," so grotesquely abused not only in their day but in more recent times.

Leaders such as Saint-Just urged the Convention to confiscate the property of all "enemies of the Revolution," (*Ventôse Decrees,* February–March 1794). They spoke in terms of virtue and justice:

> I do not know how to express my thought by halves. I am without indulgence for the enemies of my country; I know only justice. . . . Those who demand liberty for the aristocrats do not want the Republic, and fear for them. It is a glaring sign of treason, the pity that is shown for crime in a Republic than can be founded only on inflexibility.

They bequeathed to modern political discourse the odious connection between virtue and infallibility. Here they borrowed from Rousseau, who suggested that the general will of the people was sometimes misled, but never wrong. Rousseau never clearly delineates who will articulate the general will, but Saint-Just, Robespierre, and the other Jacobins grew steadily surer: they would. They made sure to silence all other voices who might make similar claims. They therefore executed the radical leaders like Hébert, the feminist leaders like de Gouges, and other major voices of the Left, like Danton and Desmoulins. They saved a special level of rage for those who claimed a similar monopoly on the voice of virtue, the priests.

∼ De-Christianization and Revolution: The War of the Priesthoods

Priests are to morality what charlatans are to medicine.

Robespierre, June 1794

Robespierre, in his speech about "Religious and Moral Ideas and Republican Principles," given in May 1794, as part of his campaign against atheism and on behalf of a new, civil religion dedicated to the Supreme Being and reason, emphasized the one way, the shining path:

> Everything has changed in the physical order; everything must change in the moral and political order. Half the revolution of the world is already accomplished; the other half must be achieved. . . . What conclusion should be drawn from what I have just said? That immorality is the basis of despotism, as virtue is the essence of the republic. . . . Consult only the good of the *patrie* and the interests of mankind. Every institution, every doctrine which consoles and which elevates souls should be welcomed; reject all those which tend to degrade and corrupt them.

He concluded that "the idea of the Supreme Being and the immortality of the soul is a continual recall to justice; it is therefore social and republican." He thus sought to position the Revolution between the excesses of atheism, which he feared would alienate the masses, especially the peasants, and the "darkness," "ignorance," and "superstition" of "fanaticism" (that is, Catholicism). He spoke out especially against the latter:

> Fanatics, expect nothing from us! To recall men to the pure cult of the Supreme Being is to strike a mortal blow at fanaticism. . . . You are your own assassins, and men do not come back to life morally any more than they do physically.[43]

Robespierre's words alert us to one of the Convention's most enduring legacies: de-Christianization. The Republic of the Year II (1793–1794) declared war to the death on religion; ever afterwards, not only in France but in Europe as a whole, republicanism and organized religion—especially, but not exclusively, Catholicism—remained sworn enemies. Each claimed a monopoly on virtue. The republicans claimed virtue emanated from the will of the people, expressed through their elected leaders. The Church claimed virtue emanated from God, revealed to His people by the clergy. The two priesthoods fought, (indeed, still fight), for the souls of the people.

The Jacobin leadership left two related and decisive legacies to nineteenth-century France: the memory of the Terror and aftermath of de-Christianization. The memory of the Terror polarized people's opinions on the political participation of the mass of the working poor and created a severe division between Paris and the provinces. The de-Christianization policy adopted in the fall of 1793 permanently alienated the Catholic Church and its congregations from the revolutionary tradi-tion. The fundamental issue of Left–Right politics in France until the eve of World War I remained the relationship of Church and State. The French republican Left, particularly after 1848, was staunchly anticlerical; the French Catholic Church, well into the twentieth century, identified republicanism with de-Christianization.

The Revolution had had problems with the Catholic Church from the start. The confiscation of Church property in the fall of 1789, the Civil Constitution of the Clergy, and the absorption of the papal properties of Avignon and the Comtat into France (1791) provided a backdrop of hostility to the events of 1793–1801. Non-juring priests did play prominent roles in counterrevolutionary activity, whether among the Chouans in Brittany, the rural rebels in the Midi, or the Vendeans. Thousands of non-juring priests said clandestine masses every Sunday in many parts of France. Through-out the south, excluding the Rhône valley, the main purpose of the Terror was to root out non-juring priests and their allies. In regions outside of the great centers of Terror-ist violence, a quarter of those executed were priests.[44]

De-Christianization added a new dimension to this conflict. It targeted the Con-stitutional church, which had possession of the churches in the fall of 1793, when the campaign began. The Jacobins, by aggressively destroying the Constitutional church, ironically assured that, when the Catholic Church revived, it would be dom-inated by its most conservative element. Little wonder that the Church would be the implacable foe of republicanism for more than century.

The Constitutional church had struggled in 1792 and 1793, particularly in the countryside. The more radical Jacobin deputies and their allies gradually came to see the two churches as one and the same. As one official near Macon wrote:

> Since the beginning of the Revolution, the Catholic cult has been the cause of many troubles. Under the cloak of religion, the progress of civic-mindedness has been much hampered. Disastrous wars have taken place. Would it not be appropriate to authorize only the cult of the Revolution?[45]

The strong impetus toward de-Christianization began in September and October 1793. In part, as Donald Sutherland suggests, it arose because of the immediate con-nection between priests (admittedly non-juring ones) and Counterrevolution. That motivation seems clear in the work of deputies on mission like Couthon and Fouché, each of whom pursued aggressive de-Christianization policies, and in the rhetoric of the Parisian *procureur syndic*, Anaxagoras Chaumette, who gave voice to demands from the *sans-culottes* that the churches be shut down. Ménétra's *Journal* shows how much Parisian artisans had come to view the Church as a bastion of superstition and bigotry before the Revolution. Once the Revolution broke out, they supported ever more vigorous action against the Church:

> these immoral men who constituted a second authority by means of all the chimeras invented by lies and sustained by ignorance backed up by fanaticism and superstition these creatures preferred to see the Nation fall into adversity through decrepitude rather than make the slightest sacrifice.[46]

De-Christianization really began on 5 October 1793, when the Convention changed the calendar. Denouncing the traditional calendar as a testimony to superstition and the Ancien Régime, the Convention decreed that 21 September 1792, the date of the declaration of the French Republic, would henceforth be day one of the Year I. The Convention further decreed that the calendar would have twelve months of thirty days each; each month would have three ten-day weeks; each week would have one day of rest, the *décadi*. Months now took names like Brumaire and Thermidor and days simply took their numerical name (first day, second day).[47] The following day, an unnamed Jacobin leader preached a "republican speech" from the pulpit of Saint-Sulpice. On 11 October, at Saint-Sulpice, the two orders co-existed. In honor of the first *décadi*, the section authorities organized a procession and the planting of an Italian poplar in the square in front of the church; they followed those festivities with a mass in honor of the troops and a brief speech. Two days later, the priests said the normal Sunday masses at Saint-Sulpice, but shops no longer closed. Henceforth, they would close only on the *décadi*. The authorities took the final step the following Tuesday, banning the celebration of the mass.

The climate of hunger and revolutionary fervor in fall 1793 led directly to the stepped-up de-Christianization of November. Under pressure from the Convention, archbishop Godel of Paris tore up his letters of ordination in front of the assembly. The parish priests of Paris followed suit, and those of Saint-Sulpice acted on 10 November. Guittard reports that they made a brief speech to the effect that "theology is to religion as chicanery is to justice, and that they had never believed a word of what they had taught, that they had only done it to fool the people." Two of the three priests had already married. That same day, at Notre Dame, the Commune of Paris organized a festival of Liberty, hiring an actress to portray the goddess of Liberty.

Paris authorities made every parish church turn in its ornaments, to be melted down by the Mint, and demanded all religious books be turned over to them for burning. All priests had to surrender their letters of ordination and abjure Catholicism in favor of the Cult of Reason and Liberty. Every *décadi*, authorities now undertook festivals in honor of Reason and Liberty, complete with moral instruction for the young in republican values. To facilitate this change, the authorities promised to make new instruction books. They took over some of the churches, such as Notre Dame, and made them into Temples of Reason. The more radical elements, like Chaumette, preached atheism.

On the next *décadi*, Guittard's section organized a huge festival, complete with a two-hour procession. The festivities began with a public burning of a pyre made up

De-Christianization. The artisans put on a mock religious procession; French towns had many such processions in 1793 and 1794, as the artisans and others expressed their profound anticlericalism.

SOURCE: Bibliothèque Nationale, Estampes, coll. Hennin n. 11, 702.

of a Papal tiara, a bishop's miter, various religious vestments, and the statue of Saint Peter that had graced the baptistery of Saint-Sulpice, followed by a procession to the church and a ceremony at a new altar. The ceremony had two goddesses (presumably Reason and Liberty, although Guittard does not say so), surrounded by "cavaliers," with the National Guard ranged on one side and ranks of white-clad girls on the other. A "philosopher" gave a speech to the effect that "there was no more religion and no more God, that everything comes from Nature. . . . Thus the new Religion or rather cult is established today in all the churches of Paris." Not long afterward, the inhabitants, led by their school children, marched on the Convention, demanding that it fulfil its promises about new textbooks. All over France, local authorities removed the word "Saint" from place and street names and good republicans began to use names such as Brutus or Bêche (Hoe) or Pissenlit (Dandelion) in place of the discredited saints' names like Pierre or Jean or Marie. The unfortunate daughter of the foreign minister, P.-H. Lebrun, had to go through life known as Civilisation-Jémappes-République.

The Convention backtracked a little in early December, allowing religious ceremonies (Catholic, Protestant, or Jewish) to take place in private; the churches remained closed.[48] Ruault wrote that Robespierre himself "was frightened. He gave a report against this mania which will make of France a country of madmen, atheists, an ungovernable people." Chaumette and Godel played leading roles in the excesses of de-Christianization. Guittard even accused Chaumette of arguing that there "was

STRANGE BEDFELLOWS

Helen Maria Williams offers the following account of the last moments of Chaumette, Godel, and Madame Desmoulins.

It was one of the singular chances of these revolutionary moments that Camille Desmoulins, who with the pointed shafts of his wit had overthrown the idol of the populace, Hébert, perished himself but a fortnight later; and this own wife and the wife of Hébert, seated on the same stone in the Conciergerie, deplored their mutual loss, and were led together to the scaffold. The people, as Madame Desmoulins passed along the streets to execution, could not resist uttering exclamations of pity and admiration:

'How beautiful she is! how mild she looks! what a pity she should perish!' At the foot of the scaffold she embraced the wife of Hébert, bade her companions in the cart farewell, and resigned herself to the executioner with the serenity of an angel. . . . Far different from the meek and placid resignation with which Madame Desmoulins made the sacrifice of life in all its bloom and freshness, was the behaviour of Chaumette the procureur of the commune, and Godel the archbishop of Paris, who perished at the same time. Their aspect testified that death appeared to their perturbed spirits, not in the form he wears to suffering innocence, but armed with all his stings, and clad in all his terrors.[49]

no God and that man has no soul" and forcing priests to preach the same thing. Robespierre and his allies conveniently blamed Chaumette and Godel for the excesses, and sent them to the executioner's block in April 1794. Guittard wrote approvingly: "God discovered their projects and that is always the end of conspirators." By June, Robespierre himself would take part in a Festival of the Supreme Being. The Revolution thus rejected atheism for the deism of such Enlightenment figures as Voltaire.

Outside of Paris, de-Christianization spread slowly. The revolutionary army sent to Lyon in November 1793 carried out iconoclastic destruction along its line of march, which led through such important religious centers as Sens and Auxerre. The soldiers decapitated statues, burned crosses, destroyed ornaments, and looted churches. Such incursions aside, de-Christianization emanated from towns that supported the Jacobins. Areas like Lyon or Marseille in which deputies on mission played an important role in local administration, particularly local repression, had the highest numbers of priests who resigned in response to de-Christianization, but even cities like Limoges came over to the new "faith."

Out in the countryside, de-Christianization was an unmitigated disaster. Everywhere, women led the resistance. The typical chronology can be seen in two villages in the Burgundian department of the Yonne (Auxerre). In Taingy, the district commissioner seized the ornaments in November 1793 and closed the church in March. The following month, the village celebrated a festival of Reason but clandestine Catholic ceremonies took place constantly. In Courgis, the mayor noted that the inhabitants fled into the woods on Easter 1794. Scarcely ten men bothered to listen to the Revolutionary speeches made that day in the church. A crowd of women stoned the men sent to remove the local crosses. In the Yonne, in village after village, the peasants simply broke into the churches on Christmas 1794, to celebrate as they sought fit.

In the department of Haute-Loire, the town of Montpigié gave the authorities a lesson in civil disobedience. Ordered to take an oath to the new government, the local lay religious teachers refused (February 1795). When the mayor sought to arrest the teachers, the rest of the women rioted. He did manage to arrest both the teachers and about one hundred women, but the men soon rioted to get their wives back. The mayor released the married women, who reorganized, returned to the jail, released the teachers, and pummeled the mayor. Another local official, in Saint-Vincent, called upon to lead the celebration on behalf of the Supreme Being in June 1794, had an even more embarrassing failure:

> The unlucky celebrant began his patriotic oration when, at a sign from an old woman, the entire female audience rose, turned their backs on the altar of liberty, and raised their skirts to expose their bare buttocks and to express their feelings to the new deity. Confronted by the spectacle of serried rows of naked female backsides the celebrant was reduced to gibberish.[50]

The fall of Robespierre (July 1794) and the end of the Terror soon afterwards led to a gradual reduction in de-Christianization pressure. By February 1795, the Convention decided to create freedom of religion. Guittard tells us 21 February 1795 was "a remarkable day in the history of France." The decree allowed all religions to have services, provided they did so in specific locales only. The state would furnish neither locales nor salaries for clergy. On Sunday, 8 March 1795, priests openly said mass in Paris for the first time since November 1793; they did so in private homes, rented rooms, and convent chapels, not in the regular churches, which remained closed. Demand was so high that some priests had to say mass continuously from 6 A.M. until midnight. A little over two months later, on 31 May, the Convention returned all churches to the communes and allowed them to be used for religious services. Each commune (or *arrondissement* in large cities) was to have only one church, made equally available to all faiths. As Guittard wrote that day, "it's now a question of knowing if we will observe Sundays and if they will suppress the republican calendar."

In much of France, people organized passive resistance to the republican calendar. They could do little to prevent the changing of market days—the police simply confiscated goods brought to market on the wrong day—but they could subvert the *décadi* and civil marriage ceremonies, and continue to celebrate Sundays and church weddings. The government sought in 1797 to enforce the ban on work on the *décadi,* but that ban extended only to work done in public. Artisans therefore shut their doors and continued to work. Even those who could not work obstinately wore everyday clothes; they turned out in the best clothes only on Sundays, as before. As for weddings, people wore simple clothes to the city hall and elaborate finery to the church. One celebrant, Gabriel Guy, who showed up at a town hall wearing "improper clothing" was asked, given his appearance, if "he wanted the citizeness Marie Forest for his legitimate wife?" He responded "ironically and with insolence, that if he had not wanted her, he would not have presented himself here." His response elicited "immoderate and scandalous laughter."[51]

The Sunday issue had more importance in towns—where municipal governments and section assemblies enforced the new calendar—than in villages, where it
was far more common for the villagers to enforce Sundays and to ignore the *décadi*.
At the end of 1793, the committee of surveillance of the small Burgundian village of
Bèze wrote to their superiors:

> [most of the villagers] like the Republic, or appear to like it. However, we
> must not dissimulate about it, there is one point on which our fellow citi-
> zens are behind the Revolution's course: that of general Reason which it is
> so necessary to substitute for the Empire of superstition because they have
> not abstained from working on a single *décadi*; all of the feasts of the Roman
> cult continue to be celebrated with the same exactitude as before, and per-
> haps this exactitude is the true cause of the neglect of the *décadi,* which
> would be a further reduction of work days if they interwove it with the
> saints days of the old calendar.[52]

They blamed the persistence of such practices on the continued importance of the
clergy in their region. Because of their superior ability to read and write, many local
curés served as the chief civil administrator of their commune. The committee of
surveillance of Bèze suggested that the Convention look into the matter and purge
local administrations. The Convention followed this suggestion, which had echoes
in reports from many deputies on mission.

Here we must remember the centrality of the religious calendar to everyday life.
The Church mandated large numbers of festivals and work-free days, not merely the
fifty-two Sundays, but nearly as many feast days. Eliminating all those days of leisure
and substituting forty-one off days (the thirty-six *décadi* and the five *sans-culottides*
that brought the Revolutionary year up to three hundred sixty-five days) for the
roughly one hundred of the Ancien Régime was not likely to be a popular measure,
for secular as well as religious reasons. Combining the new holidays with the old, as
the committee from Bèze suggested, was similarly impractical.

Two conveniently overlapping objectives motivated the Jacobins in their campaign against the Church. First, as Jean Bart has suggested, the Jacobins desperately
needed to remove rural priests from their role in communal administration. Allowing a Fifth Column to persist within the ranks of the basic level of government made
no political sense. Second, the de-Christianization movement pitted two priesthoods
against one another. The new priesthood, the acolytes of the state, understood the
fundamental need to destroy the Church's hold on the most important elements of
everyday life: birth, marriage, death, subsistence, security, and education (taken in its
broadest possible meaning). The state had long had control of security, but the
Church in France dominated the other five. Its records—copies of which, admittedly, had to be given to state authorities after 1667—registered births, marriages,
and deaths. Its priests performed the rites central to all three. The Church shared
with the state the obligation for poor relief, but it dominated education. The
Jacobins, recognizing the need for the state to take control of real life from the
Church, acted vigorously on each of these fronts. They mandated civil registers of

birth, marriage, and death, as well as the obligation for civil marriage; they secular-
ized poor relief and hospitals; they voted for a national, state-run education system.
The Jacobins believed the state should have control of everyday life, and thus of the
moral system embedded in it. Practical and philosophical considerations thus mandated the elimination of the priests, especially in rural areas.

9–10 Thermidor: The Fall of Robespierre and the Jacobins

*28 July 1794 [10 Thermidor II]: "temperature—29 degrees Centigrade, the
hottest day of the year. In the evening, there was a great thunderstorm." / 29
July "a cooler and more refreshing day."*

Paris weather, 28–29 July 1794, as reported in Guittard's *Journal*

The policy of Terror had made some sense in the crisis situation of the fall of 1793
and winter of 1793 to 1794. The considerable amelioration of the situation everywhere, from the battlefields of Belgium to the killing fields of the Vendée to the bread
markets of Paris, lessened people's sense of urgency. Robespierre and his allies sought,
in part, to maintain a sense of urgency in the spring of 1794 by means of the Terror
itself. The spectacular series of "conspiracies" discovered from February to July gave
them the excuse to step up repression and executions. Few people had a closer identification with the Revolution than Hébert and Danton. Executing them as conspirators and traitors captured the popular imagination as nothing else could have.

The execution of fellow deputies made those sitting in the Convention quite
nervous. Robespierre's constant warnings about new conspiracies and his threats to
root out the traitors disturbed many. He launched a new campaign of this nature in
mid-July 1794, leading his recent allies Collot d'Herbois, Billaud-Varenne, and Barère
to organize the Convention against him. The timing was right for them. The spectacular success of French armies, especially in Belgium, where they defeated the Austrians at Fleurus (26 June) and then occupied Brussels and Antwerp, encouraged
people to think the Terror should end. Given that Robespierre and his allies had just
pushed through the infamous law of 22 Prairial (10 June 1794) that eliminated judicial rights for those accused of treason or conspiracy, and had used that law to implement a massive increase in executions, those opposed to the Terror had reason to
act at once. Robespierre, Saint-Just, and Couthon quarreled sharply with Lindet,
Carnot, Billaud-Varenne, and Collot d'Herbois in late June 1794. On 29 June, Robespierre walked out of the Committee of Public Safety, not to return until 23 July.

Billaud-Varenne and Collot d'Herbois were certainly as well inclined to Terror
as anyone else, but they had personal scores to settle with Robespierre. Carnot, Lindet, and Prieur de la Côte-d'Or, who had the main administrative responsibilities,
seem to have argued for a relaxation of the Terror in order to facilitate their own
work. Many deputies in the Convention echoed the sentiments of Danton's friend,
Thouet, who, after listening to Robespierre's speeches on morality, observed: "It's
not enough for the bugger to be master, he has to be God."[53]

Events moved rapidly in late July. Robespierre had long ago alienated the members of the Committee of General Security, who objected to loss of jurisdiction to the Committee of Public Safety. His enemies were legion: Dantonists, friends of the executed radicals, personal rivals, and the functionary wing. Having purged Paris of the *enragés,* the Cordeliers, and the Indulgents, and having brought the sections to heel by eliminating nightly meetings and making their officers beholden to the Convention, Robespierre had a pretty weak base of support. Even mayor Pache, whose support had been so helpful in March, could no longer be counted upon. When some suggested Pache be arrested with the Hébertistes, the Convention had arrested him in May.

Robespierre turned to the Jacobin Club, denouncing Collot d'Herbois and Billaud-Varenne in an incendiary speech on the night of 26 July. They fled the premises and set to work organizing the deputies at the Convention, many of whom had been terrified by Robespierre's vague calls for more arrests in a speech earlier in the day. On 27 July (9 Thermidor of the Year II, in the Revolutionary calendar), on the floor of the Convention, Billaud-Varenne and his allies called for Robespierre's arrest. When Robespierre sought to speak in reply, the deputies drowned him out with cries of "Down with the tyrant!" and ordered his arrest and that of his supporters: Saint-Just; Couthon, Hanriot, commander of the Paris National Guard; and, on his own demand, Augustin Robespierre, brother of Maximilien.

Robespierre looked to his obvious allies, the Paris Commune. When the prisoners went to the Luxembourg prison, the jailers refused to accept them and sent them on to the Hôtel de Ville. There the Commune, who supported Robespierre, released the prisoners and appealed to the sections for support. Guittard says that Hanriot rode through the city, shouting "close your shops" and ordering his men to turn out. He returned to City Hall and tried to get his cannoneers—roughly two-thirds of the gunners reported for duty—to march on the Convention. They hesitated. Meanwhile, the members of the Commune spread throughout the city, trying to rouse the sections; deputies from the Convention did the same, trying to encourage their supporters. Guittard tells us that by 8 or 9 P.M., everyone in the city was in arms and mustered at the sections. "No one knew which side to take." His journal suggests the situation was touch and go. Robespierre had a strong party but citizens were reluctant to go against the Convention itself.

The Convention acted to place Robespierre and his allies, including the entire Commune, "outside the law." That is, they would, following a law moved by Saint-Just himself, lose all legal rights and be subject to arrest and immediate execution. Ruault's letter of 31 July to his brother strongly emphasizes the critical role of this step in mobilizing public opinion against Robespierre and his allies. The Convention sent deputies and mounted constabulary throughout the city to announce the news; Ruault claims these speeches led the pro-Commune crowds to break up and go home. Guittard reports: "All of the sections decided for the Convention, which was only natural." Detailed studies of the sections show that thirty-nine of the forty-eight did meet that night; of these, thirty-five voted to support the Convention rather than the Commune.

The roughly one-third of the National Guard units who supported Robespierre and the Commune began to lose faith as the night wore on. The workers had a strong

THE ARREST OF CATILINE-ROBESPIERRE [54]

Guittard's journal criticizes Robespierre for being an "ambitious criminal" and suggests, of his death, that it "is where your pride has led you." What ambition had Robespierre had? Here we find out a critical element in Robespierre's failure to gain sufficient support in the city. Guittard tells us what those deputies from the Convention, riding through the city, may have said to their fellow citizens:

> They say he wanted to have himself recognized as king at Lyon and in other departments and to marry the daughter of Capet [i.e., Louis XVI] ... How can a simple individual get such an idea into his head!

This false rumor, as Bronislaw Baczko has suggested, reveals much about Guittard and his fellow Parisians.

> it seems a rumour that deserves to be taken seriously. Not in order to examine its validity; on the contrary, it is because it is so obviously false that it holds our attention. ... a false rumour is a real social fact; in that it conceals a portion of historical truth—not about the news that it spreads, but about the conditions that make its emergence and circulation possible, about the state of mind, the *mentalités* and imagination of those who accepted it as true.[55]

Baczko set out to determine when and how it arose.

He suggests that it spread on the evening of 27 July (9 Thermidor), because none of the documents of earlier in the day, such as the

denunciations of Robespierre at the Convention, mention it. Several of the sectional assemblies of that evening seem to have discussed it, or a version of it. Some of the deputies from the Convention made specific mention of a fleur-de-lis seal found at Robespierre's house and Barère, in his official report to the Convention on 28 July, picked up that tale. The Committee of General Security took seriously the rumored release of the young royals: they sent troops to the Temple prison, to reinforce the guards there. In the Convention's session on the 28 July to discuss the fate of Robespierre, Thuriot, leading the charge, repeated virtually verbatim the claim made by Guittard, that Robespierre had sought to make himself king.[56] Other documents indicate that "workers" lining the route to his execution insulted him with cries of "Isn't he a handsome king?"[57]

Wild rumors, insecurity, extreme fluctuations of political loyalty—such was the madness of Paris in the summer of 1794. Yet these rumors had some relationship to reality. Ruault's letters see Robespierre's death as the revenge of Danton's old friends but he also accuses Robespierre of having sought, on 8 Thermidor, the support of the Jacobins for making himself "the sole head of the Republic." He openly accuses Robespierre of seeking dictatorial powers, an accusation that naturally found public expression as a desire to be "king."

recent grievance against the Commune, which had published a new wage control law on 23 July. The afternoon of 27 July (9 Thermidor), workers had protested the new wage limits in front of the Hôtel de Ville. The evening summons had produced about three thousand men, but their numbers had fallen to a mere two hundred by 1:30 A.M., when the last group left. Thirty minutes later, authorities arrived to arrest Robespierre and his supporters. The two brothers attempted suicide. Maximilien shot himself in the head and Augustin jumped from a window; both survived.

The next day, the Convention executed them all: the Robespierres, Saint-Just, Couthon, Hanriot, and seventeen others. Ruault says that they rode in three carts, draped with the tricolor flag, waved by an executioner as the column proceeded to the place de la Concorde: "It was a holiday, all of high society was at the windows to watch them pass; they applauded and clapped all along the rue Saint-Honoré." He tells us of the victims:

> Only Robespierre showed courage, in thus going to his death, and indignation in hearing these exclamations of joy. His head was wrapped in a cloth, his porcelain eyes, usually so dull, shined with life and animation in these final moments. The other condemned remained motionless; they seemed overcome with shame and sadness. Almost all were covered with blood and mud; Hanriot's eye hung from his head; one would have taken them for a troop of bandits captured in the woods after a violent combat. At 7 in the evening they were dead; an enormous people of men and women had come from all parts of the city to the place Louis XV to watch them be decapitated.[58]

On 29 July, the Convention sent the entire remaining membership of the Commune—seventy-one men—to the scaffold; on 30 July, another dozen lost their heads, all of them former members of the Commune. That same day, Guittard joined the members of his section and marched to the Convention, to offer their congratulations and promises of support: "All of the sections . . . congratulated [the Convention] for having discovered the plot of the criminals who wanted to slit the throat of the Convention and make civil war in Paris." Guittard would later record individual executions, but 30 July is the last day for which he records mass killing.

Robespierre and his allies had followed suicidal tactics. When the Left took power, in June and July 1793, it first purged the deputies of the Center–Left, the Girondins, and then purged itself, killing the Parisian radicals and the Dantonists. Although a further struggle within the radical Left itself led to the immediate events of 9–10 Thermidor, the deaths of the leading Jacobins and of the entire Paris Commune left the remainder of the radical Left without sufficient weight to sustain power. The Revolution's progressive shift to the Left shuddered to a halt; its course shifted back immediately to the Center–Left and then, inexorably, back toward the Right, toward the constitutional monarchy envisioned by the men of 1789. The Jacobins gave democracy a bad name among the middle and upper classes not merely in France but throughout the Europeanized world. Their vision of a Republic based on universal manhood suffrage did not die with them, but three generations would pass before it again became a reality.

Danton died a martyr, punished not for his sins but for his humanity; Robespierre died not only for his sins but for those of Danton and all the others. Where Danton joked in prison, telling the poet Fabre d'Eglantine, one of his fellow victims, "Eh bien, nous deviendrons tous poêtes, nous allons tous faire des vers" ("Well, we are all becoming poets, we are all going to make 'vers,'" the French word both for verses and for worms), Robespierre went glumly to his death, a bullet in his jaw. As Helen Maria Williams put it,

> A proof of the horrible oppression under which we groaned, was, that we lamented the fate of Danton—of Danton, the minister of justice on the 2d

of September, and one of the murderers of liberty on the 31ˢᵗ of May! Yet with all these crimes upon his head, Danton still possessed some human affections; his mind was still awake to some of the sensibilities of our nature; his temper was frank and social, and humanity in despair leant upon him as a sort of refuge from its worst oppressor.[59]

This Danton provided France with a convenient figure to lionize for the positive elements of the Republic of the Year II. Indeed Michelet states openly that the Dantonists created the Republic and tried to create a real justice to sustain it. Every French city has a rue Danton, often one of its most important streets. Paris honors Danton not only with a street but with a prominent statue on the Left Bank, on which are inscribed words from one of his most famous speeches: "After bread, education is the greatest need of the people." In early 1794, Danton was arguing for an end to the Terror: he wanted to stop virtually all of the executions. In later years, he thus became a symbol of what might have been, had not the Jacobins misguidedly descended into Hell in the spring of 1794.

In executing Robespierre, and in expunging his memory from public view whenever possible, France sought, and still seeks, to purify its republican tradition from the evil excesses of its birth. Carnot can stand for the stunning achievements of the republican armies; Danton can represent a republic for all the people, where education is a natural right: let their statues grace public squares and their names adorn the avenues of the chic. Robespierre, as Ruault rightly said, must remain the prince of revolutionary darkness, whose "name will long remain attached to the anarchic terrible splendors of the revolution," and thus dare not be spoken, or acknowledged, in public.[60]

Notes

1. The day of the creation of the Republic, 21 September 1792, was the first day of the Year I. See the following text for details.

2. Lyon, a center of Federalist activity, revolted against the Convention in the spring of 1793. A Revolutionary Army laid siege to the city and captured it in October 1793.

3. R. Cobb, *Paris and its Provinces, 1792–1802* (Oxford: Oxford University Press, 1975), 129.

4. "Universal" manhood suffrage meant all men over twenty-one, who had been domiciled in the same place for a year, and who did not work as servants.

5. The Mountain took its name from the fact that its deputies sat in the upper left hand side of the Salle du Manège in the Tuileries Palace, where the Convention met. Contemporaries called the uncommitted deputies who sat in the lower seats, the Plain. Later, those seeking to polarize the Convention called the uncommitted group the Marais, or Marsh.

6. Here we must distinguish between areas in which the peasants themselves led the counterrevolutionary forces—like the Vendée, in which the Jacobin clubs

did not take root, and those, like part of the Rhône valley, in which the nobility or urban oligarchies led the opposition. The strength of counterrevolutionaries in Arles and Avignon led to extreme politicization of the surrounding countryside: between 50 and 90 percent of the communes in the six departments of the region had Jacobin clubs, a percentage far in excess of that seen anywhere else.

7. *Journal de Célestin Guittard de Floriban, Bourgeois de Paris sous la Révolution,* ed. R. Aubert (Paris: Éditions France-Empire, 1974). Readers can simply refer to the date in question. Guittard was a *rentier,* a man who lived off his investments, such as government annuities. He violently opposed de-Christianization, but the *Journal* suggests he belonged the large uncommitted Center on other political matters.

8. The Left focuses on the birth of liberty (fall of the Bastille) and on the Jacobin rescue of France in its darkest hour; the Right focuses on blood and terror.

9. The district councils—administratively, socially, and politically—stood between the other two. They played a particularly important role in the sale of nationalized lands. I. Guégan, *Inventaire des Enquêtes administratives et statistiques, 1789–1795* (Paris, 1991), shows the Executive Council sent four times as many orders to departmental as against district councils. The Convention sent 70 percent of its requests to districts and municipalities.

10. Their strangest choice was the last man elected, Philippe Égalité, the new name of Philip, duke of Orléans, cousin of Louis XVI.

11. Many historians, following the lead of the great German sociologist Jürgen Habermas, have recently examined the evolving and expanding public sphere that often discussed, in salon conversation or in print, broad policies of reform and even political theory. But these people had very little experience of practical, everyday politics.

12. The Alien and Sedition Acts of 1798 are a classic American example of the equation of party opposition with treason in the 1790s.

13. The United States, of course, offered the unedifying spectacle of the vice-president, Aaron Burr, killing a former secretary of the treasury, Alexander Hamilton, in a duel (1804).

14. One document suggests central government expenses of 3.9 billion *livres,* excluding reimbursements of state debt, between 1 July 1791 and 1 September 1793. Feeding the armies consumed just under 20 percent of total government expenses, and total military costs about two-thirds of all receipts. Taxes produced only 368 million *livres*; the state used *assignats* to cover the rest. Roughly one-third of the *assignats* issued between 1790 and 1795 had been used to buy nationalized lands. When an *assignat* had been used for this purpose, the government burned it.

15. Guittard's journal shows us the state of affairs even in Paris: he did not receive his assessment for the military tax of 1791 until October 1792! He paid promptly (in December) but later tells us he paid one of his 1792 taxes in March 1793 and the other in October.

16. The American ambassador, Morris, wrote to George Washington on 28 December 1792, that he was sure a majority of the deputies would vote to appeal to the people. He informed Washington that Brissot and Roland worked out the details with Tom Paine, who would move in the Convention that Louis and his family be exiled to the United States.

17. Speeches of 8 and 13 Ventôse Year II (26 February and 3 March 1794), reproduced in P. Beik, ed., *The French Revolution* (New York: Walker and Co., 1970), citation on 291.

18. We see again here the close connections of French and American events; the famous Anglo-American pamphleteerist Tom Payne sat on the Convention's Constitutional Committee.

19. This draft did produce 150,000 conscripts.

20. Some historians have been reticent to make this specific connection, but two details in Guittard's testimony suggest its legitimacy. First, the number of women is precisely that organized by the CRRC. Second, Guittard notes that the crowd of two hundred or three hundred women wore "cockades in their bonnets." In September, the leaders of the CRRC got the Convention to decree that all women wear such cockades. I would take the emphasis on cockades in May, and again in September, to the be the calling card of the CRRC.

21. Artisans traditionally operated on a piecework system. They took it easy early in the week—often taking an unofficial holiday on "Holy Monday"—and then worked feverishly to finish their piece quota on Friday and on Saturday morning.

22. The first citation comes from G. Rudé's *The Crowd in the French Revolution* (Oxford, 1959), 121; the second and third are from O. Hufton, *Women and the Limits of Citizenship in the French Revolution* (Toronto, 1992), 30.

23. In homage to R.R. Palmer's indispensable work, published in 1941 by Princeton University Press, reissued in 1965 by Atheneum Publishers in New York.

24. Contemporaries added the names of their home departments to each of the (unrelated) Prieurs who sat on the Committee: Marne is the area around Châlons-sur-Marne, in the old province of Champagne. The Côte d'Or is the department for Dijon, capital of Burgundy.

25. Lindet has a small street named for him.

26. Brest, site of a great navy yard, long had a large working-class electorate, who supported the Communist Party. In the twentieth century, Robespierre has been a hero of the Communists, so they named the main street after him when they got control of the local government. The Paris Métro now has a stop named for him, naturally in one of the suburbs that form part of the "Red Belt" around the city.

27. Caen harbored several of the proscribed twenty-nine, who had fled Paris. The former mayor Pétion, now fallen from grace, was among them.

28. Guittard's journal here offers important evidence that relatively open democracy still operated in the spring and summer of 1793. His entry of 18 April tells us of the Montagnard petition calling for the expulsion of the Girondins that

"anyone who wanted could sign or not sign this petition; they did not force any-one." In July, he records the strong debates over the Constitution in his section. Guittard disliked the Jacobins, so he would have had no reason to gloss over their attempts to stifle democracy.

29. Ruault, *Gazette,* 341.

30. Ruault, *Gazette,* letter of 22 Brumaire, Year II, extract from torn-up letter. 342–343.

31. Ruault, *Gazette,* 343, letter of 1 December 1793.

32. Let us remember, in Louis's case, the foreign plots were quite real.

33. The fall of the Jacobins made Carrier a fine scapegoat; the Convention executed him in December 1794.

34. Among the nine districts of the department of Var (around Toulon) that had twenty or more incidents of revolutionary violence between 1790 and 1793, five had sixteen or more incidents of *counter*revolutionary violence, and three others had more than eleven such incidents each. By way of contrast, twenty of the twenty-two districts that had five or fewer incidents of revolutionary violence, similarly had five or fewer counterrevolutionary incidents.

35. Furet and Ozouf, *Dictionnaire,* 247–248. Ozouf's excellent portrait of Danton appears on pages 247–257.

36. Ruault, *Gazette,* letters of 2 April and 10 April 1794, pp. 347–351.

37. Palmer, *Twelve Who Ruled,* 6–7.

38. *Oeuvres de Camille Desmoulins* (Paris: Ebrard, 1838; reprinted in New York: AMS, 1972), v. II, 217–218. Robespierre never received the letter, which Mme Desmoulins did not finish.

39. Cited in M. Sonenscher, *Work and Wages. Natural law, politics and the eighteenth-century French trades* (Cambridge: Cambridge University Press, 1989), 360. Beik, *French Revolution,* 278, contains a translation, which I have modified slightly.

40. Robespierre opposed her execution but his colleagues on the Committee over-ruled him.

41. J. Fruchtman, Jr., ed., *An Eye-Witness Account of the French Revolution by Helen Maria Williams. Letters Containing a Sketch of the Politics of France* (New York: Peter Lang, 1997), 156–159. The excerpt here contains about half of the tran-script provided by Williams.

42. The Commune based the cards on a house-to-house census conducted in No-vember: all households reported the number of people, their need in bread, and the name of the baker from whom they got bread. They merely brought their card to him and he gave them their ration, at a set price.

43. I have used the translations of Beik, *The French Revolution;* the two speeches are found on pp. 288–312.

44. In contrast, in the three great centers of Terrorist violence, fewer than 7 percent of those killed were priests. By late 1793, non-jurors included two groups: those

who initially refused to swear the oath and those who had initially sworn, but later retracted to protest state policies.

45. Sutherland, *France, 1789–1815,* 211. Sutherland has excellent discussion of these issues on pages 208–217.

46. Ménétra, *Journal of My Life,* 217–218.

47. See appendix for the Revolutionary calendar.

48. Although most places of worship in France were, of course, Catholic churches, there were some Protestant "temples" and Jewish synagogues. The general attitude of the Revolutionaries toward religion is well illustrated by their attitude toward Jews. The Sephardic communities of the western ports (Nantes, Bordeaux), who were quite assimilated and who had had to practice Judaism in secret until 1789, suffered little discrimination. The Ashkenazic communities of the east—Metz and Nancy above all—practiced traditional Judaism in the open. Local communities there attacked religious Jews; the town government of Nancy even sought permission to expel Jews from the city. To their credit, the Paris authorities refused.

49. *An Eye-Witness Account of the French Revolution by Helen Maria Williams,* 150–151. Williams, it should be noted, was herself held prisoner and nearly executed, so she is a strongly anti-Jacobin witness.

50. Hufton, *Women and the Limits of Citizenship in the French Revolution,* 118.

51. A story told by I. Woloch, "'Republican Institutions,' 1797–1799," in *The French Revolution and the Creation of Modern Political Culture. Volume 2: The Political Culture of the French Revolution,* ed. C. Lucas (Oxford, New York, 1988), 378.

52. Bart, *La Révolution en Bourgogne,* 266–267. My translation.

53. Cited in Doyle, *French Revolution,* 277.

54. Helen Maria Williams, who was in prison under sentence of death at the time, claims that she could hear the newspaper hawkers shout this headline on the night of 9 Thermidor. *An Eye-Witness Account,* 187. Catiline was a famous Roman traitor, whose name was often invoked to slur those accused of treason during the French Revolution.

55. B. Baczko, *Ending the Terror. The French Revolution after Robespierre,* trans. M. Petheran. (Cambridge, 1994), 2–3.

56. Guittard may well have repeated in his entry for 27 July what he learned from his newspapers on the 28th or 29th, which would have reported what was said in the Convention. It should be noted that Thuriot made no mention of the marriage.

57. We can note in passing here that Ruault's description of those lining the rue Saint-Honoré as the well-to-do makes much more sense, because the street, then as now, lay in a very fashionable part of town.

58. Ruault, *Gazette,* letter of 30 July 1794 (12 Thermidor), 357–364.

59. *An Eye-Witness Account of the French Revolution by Helen Maria Williams,* 149.

60. Ruault, *Gazette,* 361–362, letter of 12 Thermidor II. In the original, the phrase reads "les fastes anarchiques de la révolution." The word *fastes,* literally "splendors," usually refers to great feasts or balls, such as those given at Versailles. In the context of the letter, I believe Ruault uses it ironically, hence the addition of "terrible."

Chapter Fifteen

REVOLUTIONARY LEGACIES

*There are those who let the dead bury
the dead, and there are those who are forever
digging them up to finish them off.[1]*

J. Baudrillard, *The Illusion of the Dead*

The French Revolution is over.

François Furet, 1978

THE THERMIDORIAN REACTION

CHRONOLOGY	October 1794–October 1795
October 1794	French victories in the German Rhineland
12 November	Convention closes Paris Jacobin Club
8 December	Banned Girondin deputies restored to Convention
24 December	Wage and price controls (General Maximum) relaxed
27 December	Barère, Billaud-Varenne, Collot d'Herbois, and Vadier impeached
January 1795	French troops enter Amsterdam; Dutch renounce the House of Orange and create the Batavian Republic
8 February	Marat's remains removed from Panthéon
8 March	Federalists pardoned; Federalist deputies restored to their seats

CHRONOLOGY	(continued)
1 April	*Sans-culottes* demonstration (Germinal) in Paris; artisans invade the floor of the Convention but movement fails; Billaud-Varenne, Collot d'Herbois, and Vadier sent to French Guiana
5 April	Treaty of Basel: Prussia officially recognizes the French Republic
20–24 May	Prairial uprising in Paris; *sans-culottes* again invade the Convention, again are defeated and disarmed (24 May)
8 June	Death of Louis XVI's son; Count of Provence becomes heir to the throne
22 August	Adoption of Constitution of 1795
1 October	Annexation of Belgium
5 October	Royalist uprising in Paris is crushed; General Bonaparte distinguishes himself in the fighting
16–21 October	Legislative elections under the "two-thirds" decree

The Parisian thunderstorm of 28 July 1794 broke France's fever and created a new political climate. For all intents and purposes, the French Revolution ended that hot July evening, when Robespierre and the Montagnards went to their deaths. The phrase "Thermidorian Reaction" has ever afterward meant a sharp shift rightward in a revolutionary movement and, by implication, an end to the revolution.

> Revolutions age relatively quickly. They age badly, if only because they cannot themselves accept, nor be accepted, except through their symbolism: that of a new departure in History, of a radical rupture in time, of a work scarcely begun, in short, of a perpetual youth. The French Revolution certainly did not age less gracefully than those which succeeded it and were inspired by it. Yet none of them, for good reason, has wished to recognize itself in Thermidor: like a magic mirror, the Thermidorian moment brings back to each newborn revolution the image of usury and of decrepitude that lies in wait for it.[2]

In the revolutionary canon, "Thermidor" ends the youthful love affair with a revolution. That love invariably leads to emotional excesses, to violent swings of mood, to rash actions lamented later in the cool of reasoned reflection. Even those happy to be rid of the violence called forth by strong emotions, however, lament the passing of the ardor that sustains the great deeds of the revolution. The Jacobins, for all their faults, inspired in ordinary Frenchmen, such as the soldiers of the Revolu-

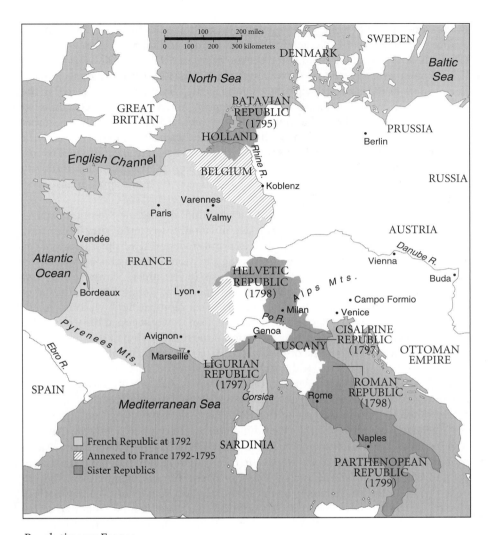

Revolutionary France.

Source: Mortimer Chambers, Raymond Grew, et al., *The Western Experience*, 5th edition (New York: McGraw-Hill, 1991), 844.

tionary armies, an astonishing degree of such Revolutionary ardor. In contrast, the Thermidorians of 1794 initiated a dispiriting period of French history: their contemporaries lamented the moral turpitude of the government and its failure to create a stable political system in France. Their failure led directly to Napoleon Bonaparte's *coup d'état* of 18 Brumaire (9–10 November 1799), which inaugurated nearly seventy-five years of empires and monarchies on French territory.

Yet matters were not so simple; the men who overthrew Robespierre, even aside from the Terrorists like Collot d'Herbois and Billaud-Varenne still sitting as members of the Committee of Public Safety, hardly belonged to the Right in the politics of the France of 1794. Most of the men in the Convention, and many of those in the two Councils of the Directory, had voted for the death of Louis XVI. Those who overthrew Robespierre wanted to preserve much of what the Mountain had done, but also to eliminate its excesses and what they viewed as the tyrannical power vested in the Committee of Public Safety. Indeed, the Convention asked Robert Lindet, a member of the Committee, to draft its annual report for the Year II, presented in September 1794. Lindet stressed the need to avoid revenge and extremism and to recognize the difference between "errors and abuses" and "crimes." His language continued to emphasize the centrality of the sovereign and free "people," a classic Jacobin phrase, and to tie the overthrow of the Girondins (31 May–2 June 1793) to the appropriate course of the Revolution begun in 1789.

Thermidor had started an irresistible momentum toward the Right; Lindet's report marked one of the final spasms of Jacobinism in the rump of the Convention. Having executed Robespierre and his allies primarily because of the excesses of the Terror, the Convention faced the embarrassing situation of having hard-core Terrorists like Billaud-Varenne and Collot d'Herbois in its midst. Many agreed with Ruault, that these men "merited the same recompense" as Robespierre. In the fall of 1794, the Convention gradually came to believe that repudiating the Jacobin ascendancy would preserve the Republic. The Convention slowly stripped the Committee of Public Safety of its power, forcing a quarter of the membership to step down every six weeks. They closed the Jacobin Club of Paris, restored the banned Girondin deputies to the Convention, and expelled the "Terrorists." In 1795, they drew up a new Constitution, creating the government known as the Directory, which brought the Revolution back to a central ground more amenable to most French people. This center failed to hold in the face of the passionate intensity of the Left and Right.

Even after the return of the Girondin deputies (December 1794), the Convention stood well to the left of center in the general French political spectrum. Many *conventionnels,* as the members were called, had supported the Terror; others were comrades in arms of radicals such as Danton. Thermidor did bring the Convention back right of where it had been, but it did not, by any stretch of the imagination, give power to the Right. France's 1794 political spectrum included many counterrevolutionaries, as well as constitutional monarchists. These people, not those who carried out Thermidor, represented the Right. The Thermidorians moved the Convention itself back to a Center–Left position.

The political affiliations of the Thermidorian leaders notwithstanding, the Right benefitted enormously from the changed political climate of 1794–1795. New rules about sales of national land again favored the rich; the Catholic Church returned; Right-wing dandies (the *muscadins*) formed street gangs and terrorized the Left; conservative landowners took over local politics in many regions; the White Terror took bloody revenge on former Jacobins in the southeast. The last days of the Convention (August 1794–October 1795) and the Directory (1795–1799) undid many of the democratic changes wrought between 1789 and 1794, paving the way for the old Montagnard Napoleon Bonaparte to seize power and strangle French democracy after 1799. Revolutionary culture gave way to new outpourings of excess. Ostentation, a lethal vice under the Jacobins, became again the order of the day. Jacques David, the greatest Revolutionary artist, would soon be memorializing Napoleon's self-coronation, an affair whose garish excess equaled Versailles's decadence at its worst.

Settling Scores, 1794

Public opinion now floats uncertainly on many things and many people. Must we love or betray Jacobinism? Was Jacobinism useful or harmful for the establishment of the Republic? There is the timely discussion that ferments all heads from one end of France to the other.[3]

Nicolas Ruault, 8 October 1794

The fall of Robespierre and his allies led inexorably to a shift to the Center. In his journal entry of 31 July 1794, the bourgeois bond holder Célestin Guittard expressed surprise that the Jacobins reopened and continued their meetings. In August, the Convention overturned the law of 22 Prairial (which had stripped legal rights from all accused of treason) and decreed that the Paris sections could meet only once a week, on the *décadi*. The decree also ended the practice of paying citizens 40 shillings to attend: this measure reportedly saved one million *livres* a year.[4]

The political in-fighting hardly ended with the fall of Robespierre. In early September, a deputy denounced Billaud-Varenne, Collot d'Herbois, Barère, Vadier, and David on the floor of the Convention, and called for their arrest. The deputies, after a violent debate, declared his accusations to be calumnious, but he had set the tone for what was to come. Jean-Lambert Tallien and two of his allies, who had led the charge against Robespierre in the Convention, were expelled from the Jacobin Club on 5 September. Four days later, someone attempted to assassinate Tallien. That attempt led to a "tumultuous" meeting of the Convention about the Jacobin Clubs on 10 September. Less than two weeks later, the Convention abolished the forty-eight sectional committees of surveillance, creating twelve new committees in their place, each with jurisdiction over four sections. They kept up the offensive in October, banning popular societies and sectional committees from affiliating or corresponding with each other and mandating that all such societies provide the government with complete lists of membership: names, ages, addresses, professions, places of birth.

Everyone saw these rules for what they were: an attack on the Jacobins. In early November, in response to an attack on the Paris Jacobin Club by some sixty to eighty rock-throwing *muscadins,* the Convention decided to close the Club and seize its papers. Many sections responded ten days later by marching to the Convention to congratulate it for getting rid of an organization that had wished to take its place. The Convention took the final full step on 8 December, recalling the roughly seventy-five deputies expelled by the Mountain. These deputies had opposed the execution of Louis XVI, but they had all voted him guilty of treason; they solidified the Center-Left coalition in charge of the government. In late November and early December, the Convention put Carrier, the butcher of Nantes, on trial: they executed him on 16 December. At the end of the December, in a dramatic demonstration of how much political opinion had shifted since September, the Convention impeached Barère, Billaud-Varenne, and Collot d'Herbois and later placed them under arrest.

The collapse of the Jacobins had immediate repercussions in the provinces. As in Paris, the fall of Robespierre led to an immediate release of thousands of prisoners, most of whom had an understandable hatred of Jacobinism. The Thermidorians quickly eliminated the pro-Jacobin district councils and restored the pro-Girondin departmental councils. They sent out new agents into the communes and departments, to get better control of the actual administration; these agents helped purge countless local officials, from municipalities on up. Such changes took time to implement but their cumulative effect emboldened all enemies of the Jacobins, from the Girondins to the counterrevolutionaries. The deputies on mission soon assaulted the local Jacobin clubs, arresting leaders and purging memberships. Finally, in August 1795, the Convention closed all political clubs and seized their papers.

The worst situation took place in the southeast. In an episode known as the White Terror, local officials purged governing councils and sectional assemblies of all Jacobin sympathizers.[5] In cities such as Marseille and Lyon, where the Jacobins and their enemies had traded power in 1793, this led to more settling of scores. Authorities either encouraged or ignored mobs who assaulted the prisons holding the radicals. At Lyon, the rioters set fire to the prisons "to force the Jacobins on to the roof where they were hacked to death."[6] The mob at Aix, like the one at Lyon, released ordinary criminals and slaughtered the thirty Jacobins in custody. The anti-Jacobins marched an army against Marseille, but it was defeated in battle outside the city. A few weeks later, local anti-Jacobins stormed the prisons of the city and dismembered ninety-seven Jacobins. All over the southeast mobs assaulted local Jacobins. At Avignon, they threw a judge from the local Revolutionary Tribunal into the Rhône river and harpooned him. Many others fell to armed bands in the countryside.

Armed bands of peasants in the Midi and in the west supported a return to the monarchy. The southern bands kept up a low level of guerrilla warfare but those of the Vendée and Brittany posed greater threats. The Bretons sought to link up with a landing of émigré nobles, abetted by the British. An expedition of three thousand debarked on the Rhuys peninsula (June 1795), near Vannes, where it met up with ten thousand Chouans. General Lazare Hoche marched ten thousand regulars to meet them a few days later and, after a brief fight, captured six thousand men. He shot six hundred forty of the émigrés and over one hundred peasants. Three months later, the British tried again, this time sending arms and a fleet to link up with the Vendéan leader Charette, on the coast of Poitou. This expedition carried with it the Count of Artois.

Artois's older brother, the Count of Provence, had become the royal Pretender on 8 June 1795, when Louis XVI's son died in a Paris prison. Provence had issued a foolish proclamation upon becoming the royalist hope, saying that he would restore the Ancien Régime were he to return. His *Proclamation of Verona* (June 1795) made it impossible for all but the most ardent royalists to support his return. Artois and the Vendéans had little luck against Hoche and his regulars. The royal pretender ignominiously left Poitou in November. In the ensuing months Hoche and his men hunted down the main Vendéan leaders, Stofflet and Charette, and executed them (February–March 1796). The Thermidorians, acting first as the Convention (to October 1795) and then as the Directory, decisively defeated the military counter-revolution both in the south and the west. Royalist forces had other avenues of attack, however, and the Directory proved more susceptible to them.

The Constitution of 1795 (Constitution of the Year III)

Civil equality, in fact, is all that a reasonable man can claim. Absolute equality is a chimera; for it to exist, there would have to be absolute equality in intelligence, virtue, physical strength, education, and fortune for all men.[7]

François Antoine Boissy d'Anglas, defending the
Constitution of 1795, 23 June 1795

The Center–Left coalition running the Convention in early August lost power within a month. After the recall of the purged deputies in December 1794, the Convention had a solid Girondin majority. They had a fairly clear idea of what they wanted to do to bring French politics back into line with what they believed the country needed: repudiation of the Terror but salvation of the Revolution. That meant getting rid of those most associated with the Terror, like Billaud-Varenne, and making sure that the urban workers could not effectively influence politics. This first goal naturally led the old Girondins to ally with the Right, many of whom were monarchists.

The deputies clearly set forth their ideas in a new Constitution (1795). The *conventionnels* had three sets of principles on which to draw:

1. Those of the summer of 1789.

2. The Constitution of 1791.

3. The failed Constitution drafted by Condorcet's committee in 1793.

France theoretically lived under the Constitution of 1793, rapidly drafted by Hérault de Sechelles (executed with Danton in April 1794), and adopted by the Convention with scarcely any debate. That Constitution had been suspended before it took effect. The very deputies who had voted for its remarkable principles—universal manhood suffrage, rights of all to education, sustenance, and employment—repudiated their own handiwork. The deputies specifically rejected universal manhood suffrage and its Constitution of 1793. The chief spokesman of the 1795 Constitution, François Boissy d'Anglas, violently attacked the earlier document. In his words, "that constitution, conceived by ambitious men, drafted by schemers, dictated by tyranny, and accepted through terror, is nothing other than the express preservation of all the elements of disorder, the instrument designed to serve the avidity of greedy men, the interest of turbulent men, the pride of the ignorant, and the ambition of usurpers."

The Convention did not completely reject the principle of male democracy, which still had powerful resonance in the France of 1795. They learned from the American experience, borrowing from many American state constitutions the principle that only male property owners would sit in the legislative body. The deputies here harkened back to the mainstream principles of the Enlightenment. As the Physiocrat (and royal minister) Turgot had written:

> Mobile wealth is as fugitive as talent, and unfortunately those who possess no land have a country only through their hearts, through their opinions, through the happy prejudices of childhood. . . . [the ownership of land constitutes] the true and solid link between the proprietor of houses and the fatherland, his true means of providing subsistence for his children, his true citizenship.[8]

The Constitution of 1795 combined many of the principles of the Constitution of 1791 with ideas that had been put forward by the constitutional monarchists in the summer and fall of 1789, only to be rejected. The deputies reversed one of the initial votes taken by the Constituent Assembly when they shifted to a bicameral legislature, with a lower Council of 500 and an upper Council of 250.[9] The new Constitution compromised between the eligibility rules of 1791 and 1793 for the primary elections. Men over twenty-one, paying a given tax, and domiciled in their commune for a full year, could vote. The breadth of this initial suffrage dwarfed the pathetic electorate of Great Britain (well under 50,000) or even of most of the United States.[10] At least 5 million men could vote in the primary process.[11]

Once again, the electoral colleges chosen on the first go-round would meet to select the actual deputies to the Councils. Here the new Constitution reached back to the last-minute, elevated property standard for electors voted, but not enforced, in 1791. Even the elevated standards for electors and deputies left about 500,000 people eligible to serve. Every year, some 30,000 of them were supposed to do so, because the Constitution set a standard of one elector per two hundred eligible voters.[12] Whatever the legal system, local officials seem to have followed established local procedures. How else can we explain the fact that 6.3 percent of the electors of Toulon in 1797 were sailors, who surely did not pay one hundred days' wages in taxes? In the department of the Seine, surrounding Paris, the largest or second largest social group among the electors remained artisans and shopkeepers: about a quarter in 1797 and 1799, and 37 percent in 1798. The most prominent trade was that of grocer (sixteen in 1798, seventeen in 1799); most of the shopkeepers dealt in relative luxury goods (books, jewels, gold), but the 1798 assembly had a large contingent of carpenters (twelve). These men held eligibility, in most cases, because they rented a dwelling/shop assessed at 150 *livres* a year or more. The main group excluded from the electoral assemblies was farmers. Only the richest "cultivators," as they now called themselves, surely less than 5 percent of rural taxpayers, held eligibility.

The Constitution strongly tightened the bonds between land ownership and the offices of elector and deputy. As Ruault put it, in a letter of 28 June 1795,

> According to the spirit of our new Constitution, one must have learned some mechanical craft to be a simple citizen; and to be eligible for certain public functions, one must be an owner of a few morsels of land. One is obliged to have one's ass in the soil, as the peasants of our province would

say, to be something in the new France and to leave the ranks of the vile proletarians.[13]

Boissy d'Anglas put the matter quite bluntly in the final debates:

> . . . We must be governed by the best; the best are those who are best educated and most interested in the maintenance of the laws; now, with few exceptions, you find such men only among those who, owning a piece of property, are devoted to the country that contains it, to the laws that protect it, and to the tranquility that maintains it. . . . A country governed by property owners is an organized society; one governed by the propertyless is in a state of nature.[14]

His reference to the "state of nature" was clear to his fellow deputies. He meant the state of nature of the seventeenth-century English philosopher Thomas Hobbes, which Hobbes defined as a state of war "of every man, against every man." Hobbes went on: "To this war of every man, against every man, this also is consequent; that nothing can be unjust. The notions of right and wrong, justice and injustice, have there no place." Boissy d'Anglas and the other *conventionnels* accepted Hobbes's description as accurate because they believed they had just lived through it. They wanted to enshrine the control of property owners in a new constitution, in the belief that only those with property have a sufficient stake in society to preserve it.[15]

The Last Hurrah of the *Sans-Culottes*

> *Everyone murmurs and is very discontent. . . . when people are hungry and there is no bread, there is no more reason, all the pretty speeches no longer tempt the ear.*
>
> *Journal* of Célestin Guittard, entry of 31 March 1795

The Parisian workers disliked intensely the political evolution of the fall of 1794. Ménétra certainly expressed the sentiments of many artisans in showing relief at the "end of the murders," but he went on: "but people were still unhappy. This National Convention in which everyone had the greatest confidence was and one can say so nothing but a nest of slanderers of vindictive men seeking to slaughter one party so as to replace it with another one."[16] They soon realized that matters had shifted dramatically, when the Convention removed (8 February 1795) Marat's remains from the Panthéon. Several sections demonstrated against this "sacrilege."

Miserable weather and high prices fueled popular discontent. A desperate shortage of firewood intensified a brutal January freeze, which bottomed out on the night of January 22–23, when the lowest temperature in the memory of man (0° F) froze "everything in the houses." The cold snap ended in a thaw so rapid it led to a flash flood on the Seine (29 January). The bread situation alarmed everyone. In March, the government had to ration bread: one pound a day per inhabitant, except for workers, who got a pound-and-a-half. On 20–23 March, the sections called out their companies to stand guard, because the bread rationing had led to "discontentment." Fighting broke out again between the Jacobin supporters and the *muscadins*. On 28 March, a crowd of some five hundred women marched to the Convention demanding bread. The government postponed the elections (putting "water in its [Paris's] wine," as Guittard put it), and banned evening assemblies. On the 31 March, they cut the bread ration to half a pound, and even that amount rarely got to consumers. The next day, ten thousand working poor marched on the Convention, demanding bread, and occupying the assembly hall for four hours. The (unarmed) Germinal Uprising fizzled out in the face of the National Guard. It led to the arrest of sixteen deputies and to the deportation of Billaud-Varenne, Collot d'Herbois, and Vadier, whom the demonstrators had sought to free.

The bread situation worsened, with rations dropping to two ounces a day by early May. This time, the workers arrived armed at the Convention. The Prairial Rising (20 May), was led, Guittard suggests, by women, who demanded "bread and the Constitution of 1793." On the floor of the Convention, the situation got out of hand. The workers murdered a deputy. This time, the deputies from the rump of the old Mountain, who had stood aloof during the Germinal rising, joined the rebels. Under the eyes of armed workers the Convention voted to release Jacobin deputies, to provide bread, and to restore the Constitution of 1793. The initial success did not last, as the loyal National Guard forcibly ejected the demonstrators. The Convention then rescinded its earlier votes and arrested the deputies who had proposed the motions.

The confrontation continued the next day, when a force estimated at forty thousand in support of the Convention faced down a group half its size taken primarily from the *sans-culottes* faubourgs of Saint-Antoine and Saint-Marcel. Many of those supporting the Convention came from National Guard units in Paris; Ménétra, old Jacobin though he was, marched with his section in support of the Convention. On the 23 May, thirty thousand troops surrounded the faubourg Saint-Antoine. Sweeping through it street by street, they disarmed the entire faubourg and arrested between twelve hundred and sixteen hundred. "*Septembriseurs,* massacrers, men of blood," as Guittard called them. The authorities captured those responsible for Féraud's murder and quickly executed them. In the coming weeks, the government arrested another three thousand "suspects," that is, those sympathetic to the Jacobins. In sharp contrast to earlier round-ups and to events going on in the provinces at the same time, these people were not executed. Authorities later released them, although many would be re-arrested during subsequent crackdowns.

Ruault captured the essence of the problem in a letter to his brother on 6 May, in which he described the desperate risings of Germinal and Florial as simple "convulsions of hunger." Yet he did not stop with such an analysis, he continued:

> That which is more unfortunate . . . that which makes the evil almost incurable, is that the government no longer walks with the people. It has against it a frightening majority. Now, a government which walks against and not with the people must necessarily break against that indestructible mass. The former Committee of Public Safety only saw the *sans-culottes,* had eyes only for the poor people; it was more demagogic than democratic. It had all

the rich, all the proprietors against it; it perished. Today, it's the opposite. They only value the proprietors and the rich; they have contempt for the poor, whom they trample under their feet. . . . The great art of founding a Republic in the center of our old Europe is to make the poor and the rich walk together freely, of a common accord.[17]

There would be one more rising in Paris (October 1795), but it was the Right-wing sections that carried it out. Once again, troops stood firm, led by the newly promoted General Napoleon Bonaparte, who turned his cannons on the roughly twenty-five thousand rebels. Ruault told his brother that the troops of the line fired up and down the streets until midnight, when the local prostitutes fanned out to lift the valuables of the fallen. He greatly exaggerates the casualties, estimating the dead at eight thousand (a few hundred would be closer), but his testimony gives us some sense of how seriously contemporaries viewed this uprising.[18]

Some sections, such as that of Bonconseil, sent people to both sides; others supported the Convention. In the end, the troops cleared the bridges over the Seine. The Convention abolished sectional assemblies and the section-dominated National Guard, replacing the latter with a body under its direct control. This rising demonstrated the effectiveness of the measures taken to disarm Paris in May 1795. All the reports suggest that two key factors prevented the rebels, who outnumbered the Convention's supporters by 4 to 1, from winning:

1. They had no cannon.

2. Those who did have firearms, lacked ammunition.

Three weeks later, the Convention officially ended, to be replaced by the new bicameral assembly and an executive consisting of a Directory of five men, who would serve as the executive.

The Directory, 1795–1799

In general, we are finally tired of revolutions and we sigh only for a rest bought by six years of sacrifices, of patience, of calamities, and of glory . . . being as much enemies of anarchy as of despotism, we believe that liberty reposes only in a happy medium.[19]

Vivant Carion, Burgundian journalist, October 1795

C H R O N O L O G Y	November 1795–November 1799
3 November 1795	Directory officially takes power[20]
10 May 1796	Arrest of members of the Conspiracy of the Equals

CHRONOLOGY	(continued)
March–April 1797	Royalist success in legislative elections
26–27 May	Trial of the "Equals" ends; execution of Gracchus Babeuf
15 July	Decrees against refractory clergy repealed
4 September	Elections invalidated, royalist deputies removed from Legislature; local elections overturned, Carnot and Barthélémy removed (18 Fructidor)
5 September	Draconian laws against refractory clergy reinstated
April 1798	Jacobins successful in legislative elections
11 May	Election results again invalidated, new deputies removed
July 1799	Jacobin Club reopens
13 August	Jacobin Club closed again
9–10 November	*Coup d'état* of 18 Brumaire; Napoleon becomes effective ruler of France

What seems clear today is that between the royalists and the terrorists there is a third party which wants one no more than the other and which will combat them both with an equal intrepidity.[21]

L.–S. Mercier, 1795

The repression of the risings of 1795 removed the Parisian masses from their key role in national politics. Power shifted back to the elites who had real economic and social prestige in the country, above all landowners and lawyers. The sales of nationalized land conducted under the Directory auctioned off much larger lots. Guittard mentions that the priory of Evergnicourt (his home village), accounting for 70 percent of the total land sold in the village during the Revolution, went to a society of eleven men in November 1795. The shift from the more balanced land sales of the early 1790s—still dominated by larger buyers, but involving many small ones too—to the large-lot sales of 1796–1799 stands as a clear indication of the nature of the Directory regime and of those who profited from it. The figures for the district of Avallon, in northern Burgundy, tell the tale. The urban middle class bought 80 percent of the land sold there between 1791–1793, only 60 percent of that sold between 1793–1795—when the Jacobins deliberately sold land in smaller plots—and more than 90 percent sold after 1795.

The situation got worse when the Directory eliminated the *assignats* (by then worthless) and replaced them with the *territorial mandates,* in essence, a new form of *assignat.* These notes could be directly redeemed for land, without the formality

The departure of the Thermidorians. This caricature suggests that the deputies leaving office in 1799 had enriched themselves at the public expense.

Source: Bibliothèque Nationale, Estampes, coll. Hennin n. 12516.

of a sale at auction. One recent examination of this mechanism shows that half of the *mandates* issued—1.1 billion *livres*—went to large-scale military suppliers, who immediately turned them into enormous landed holdings. The rich merchant-bankers who supplied the army used this paper money to buy up the land of émigré nobles that came on the market in these years. They obtained bargain prices because the *mandates* depreciated so rapidly in value, becoming worthless by the summer. As the Burgundian farmer Paquelin noted, "people only use paper money to pay their taxes." The government was reduced to the humiliating expedient of collecting taxes partly in kind: even the five Directors received part of their salaries that way.

The Directory suffers in the historiography for its many failures. One might more fairly split its impact into two parts. On the one hand, the Directory failed completely to create a viable political system in France. On the other hand, the Directory supervised the effective creation of what Isser Woloch has called the New Regime, which established the broad outlines of French administration, solidified by Napoleon and calcified by successor regimes in the nineteenth century.[22] The Directory reintroduced bullion coinage (1797), repudiated the government's debt (1797), and put the tax system on a firm footing (1798). Local studies suggest that authorities began systematically to collect the *patente* in 1797; overall records show that receipts from taxation, which had fallen as low as 35 million *livres* in 1794–1795, reached 341 million *livres* in 1798–1799. The Directory even reintroduced excise

TERROR AND TAXES

The government had terrible problems collecting its taxes. Only when the Jacobins introduced draconian controls on a wide range of financial transactions, such as payment of government bond annuities, did things start to get better. In 1791 or 1792, Guittard, the Parisian bond holder, simply collected his bond interest from local government officials and paid no attention to his tax assessments; indeed, it is extremely unclear that he even received proper notice of his obligations. In 1793–1794, however, he found he had to produce tax documents to get his annuity payments: he had to pay the *impôt mobilier* (108 *livres*) and contribute to a forced loan (January 1794, for 237 *livres*) before he could collect what the government owed him. The forced loan proved to be quite effective, producing something like 228 million *livres,* almost all of it actually coming from the rich. Those assessed for 10,000 *livres* or more made up only 7 percent of the taxpayers, but contributed 65 percent of the money.[23]

Guittard gave more money for small special taxes, such as the levy to outfit volunteers for the front (January 1794), monthly payments of from 2 to 6 *livres* to find a substitute for his guard duty or the 44 livres he spent on shirts for two "brothers in arms" going to the front (November 1793). Guittard tells us of the confiscation of all Church ornaments (November 1793), which the government melted down for their gold and silver. The looting of the churches did not enjoy popular support in the countryside but many in the cities, such as the Parisian *sans-culottes,* strongly urged this course of action.

Even after the Jacobins fell from power, Guittard found that the more rigorous procedures they had established lingered on. Under the Directory, these practices became routinized: the government no longer had to rely on raw terror to collect taxes. Written tax rolls and timely collection and disbursement of money became again a normal function of everyday life. In that sense, the Directory provided a New Regime that finally gave France the sort of functional state that people had taken for granted before 1789.

taxes: first on tobacco, then on transit of goods, finally on goods imported into towns—even Paris—in 1798.

The initial steps in the creation of this administration took place in an atmosphere of chaotic dishonesty. Whether it is the letters of Helen Maria Williams or those of Nicolas Ruault, everyone commented upon the appalling corruption. For Ruault, the entire country had been given over to "brigandage, murder, and pillage." He rebuked:

> The agents of the government, which calls itself republican, do not profess any of the principles which must constitute a republican government. Probity, virtue, a certain austerity of mores, which have always existed in infant Republics, and without which they cannot subsist, cannot be found in ours. One does not see in the offices of these men *French* citizens but only corrupt men who sell for *gold* the positions, employments, and functions at the disposition of the ministers; one bargains with them as one would over goods at a market ... The deputies themselves carry out exchange, shamefully trafficking with exchange agents ... This infamous selling corrupts the public spirit at Paris and in all of the departments.[24]

Politically, the Directory lurched from one expedient to the next. No regime born of such blatant moral turpitude could long survive. Mercier wrote, in 1798: "There is not a single day when one does not say: That's immoral!"[25] The August 1795 referendum overwhelmingly approved the new Constitution, yet this support masked underlying discontent with the so-called laws of 5 and 13 Fructidor (August 1795), which mandated that two-thirds of the new deputies had to come from the Convention's ranks. Guittard claimed that his section, which approved the Constitution 1,820 to 6, strongly opposed the Convention's efforts to co-opt its own members into the new body.[26] The available evidence suggests no one else liked them either: the Vendémiaire rebellion was partly a response to the two-thirds decree. Three hundred ninety *conventionnels* obtained seats in the rigged portion of the October 1795 elections, as against only four elected in the open, unrestricted voting.[27] The re-elected deputies selected an additional ninety-four of their fellow *conventionnels* to bring the total returned to five hundred eleven.

The five hundred eleven returning *conventionnels* came overwhelmingly from the old Girondin faction and from the Right wing of the Convention. All of the Girondin deputies outlawed in 1792 who sought re-election were chosen and those who had opposed Louis XVI's execution outnumbered those who had favored it by almost two to one. The overall political make-up of the two Councils leaned much more to the Right than had the Convention. Most estimates suggest three hundred five confirmed republicans, two hundred twenty-six deputies in the middle, and one hundred fifty-eight royalists. The Directory's efforts to maintain a middle-of-the-road approach, however, can be seen in the Councils' choice of the five Directors of the executive council, regicides all: Paul Barras, Louis Marie de La Révellière-Lépreaux, Étienne Letourneur, Jean-François Reubell, and the famous Abbé Sieyès. Sieyès refused to serve, in part because the Convention had rejected some of his ideas about the Constitution. In his place, the Council of 250 chose another regicide, the Montagnard Lazare Carnot. Barras, a former viscount and a firm Jacobin, was the most politically adroit of the group, but the five had no clear direction. The Constitution also required that one of the five be replaced each year, based on a drawing of lots.

The Directory stumbled along in 1796, concerned above all with the foreign war (see the following text), with the subsistence crisis, and with making sure that the radicals did not revive. The Directors had a minor scare in the spring of 1796, the Conspiracy of the Equals. The leader of this group, Gracchus Babeuf, coined its most memorable phrase: "Real equality, the common happiness, or death!" Unfortunately for him and his fellow conspirators, they ended up with the latter. Babeuf proposed a social model that closely resembled modern communism, with social ownership of property. Few of his contemporaries supported such ideas. Even hard-core Jacobins blanched at the abolition of private property. Babeuf's most famous co-defendant, Philippe-Michel Buonarroti, later would become the author of one of the founding texts of modern penal codes. He got off with a jail sentence; Babeuf went to the block in May 1797.

The repression of this comic opera conspiracy formed part of a larger attack on the Jacobins and their allies. Considerable evidence suggests that local authorities deliberately sought to exclude the poor from voting rolls. In some areas, officials arbitrarily set the figure for a day's wages (the minimum tax contribution for a voter) at triple its real level. In others, they manufactured other objections to potential Jacobin voters. The situation varied sharply from department to department. In a sample of eight departments compiled by Malcolm Crook, three had more eligible voters in 1797 than in 1795, three had fewer, and two about the same. The department of Aveyron (Rodez) had the largest increase, up from 18,773 to 32,105, while the Orne (Alençon) had the biggest decline, from 24,435 to 5,154. In the eight departments as a whole, votes cast rose roughly 50 percent. The wild levels of voting volatility between 1795 and 1799 very strongly illustrate the extremely unstable political system. The extremes could range from the department of the Orne, which rose from 5,000 eligibles in 1797 to over 35,000 in 1799; to that of Haute-Garonne (Toulouse, a Jacobin stronghold), where eligibility declined from 32,468 in 1797 to only 12,453 in 1798. Given the obvious chicanery involved in such fluctuations, it is little wonder that French society finally lost respect for the Directory and its elections. Turnouts could be quite respectable in 1798, but this diminished respect became glaringly apparent in 1799, when many departments reported voter turnouts under 10 percent.[28]

The new constitution required elections every year, starting in 1797. The first elections took place in March 1797, immediately after one of the directors, Letourneur, had to step down in favor of François Barthélémy, a member of the Clichy Club, political nexus of the Councils' moderate deputies. These elections accentuated the rightward drift, in part because many potentially Left-leaning voters had not been allowed to cast ballots. Of the two hundred sixty deputies up for replacement, two hundred sixteen were *conventionnels:* only eleven of them won reelection. The royalists won one hundred eighty seats, bringing their contingent in the two councils to about three hundred thirty. General Jean-Charles Pichegru, who had been secretly negotiating with the émigrés, not only became a deputy but was elected president of the Council of 500. Two months of the new assembly proved too much for the more leftist Directors. Barras, Reubell, and La Révellière surrounded Paris with General Hoche's troops, named the general minister of war, and gave the ministry of foreign affairs to Talleyrand, an unscrupulous opportunist.

A few weeks later, on 4 September (18 Fructidor), using troops sent by General Bonaparte, Reubell, La Révellière, and Barras struck again. They had documentary evidence (provided by Bonaparte) of Pichegru's treachery, and used that evidence of conspiracy—and the known royalism of many deputies—to conduct a *coup d'état.* They purged Carnot and Barthélémy and conducted a rump meeting of the Councils to displace one hundred seventy-seven deputies elected in 1797, voting to deport fifty-three of them.[29] Seventeen actually faced deportation, although eight of them, among them Pichegru, escaped. The meeting annulled the elections of forty-nine departments, from the top to the bottom. In the department of the Sarthe, for example, they replaced five hundred ninety-nine of the eight hundred seven elected officials; in the Pas-de-Calais, seventy-three of eighty-seven municipalities were deposed.[30] The Councils closed newspapers, arrested editors, and placed all publications under government supervision for a year. Special military commissions tried and shot one hundred sixty people, and criminal commissions dispatched others. The Councils then enacted new laws against émigré nobles and refractory clergy, demanded that all priests and government officials swear that they "hated monarchy," and arrested thousands of priests.

The following year, the Left revived in the elections, perhaps in part because of the successful efforts of provincial Jacobins to restore the eligibility of low-income voters in places like the Orne.[31] In a broader sense, however, the old Jacobin activists achieved better results because of their revived political activity, in arenas such as the press. Once again, the Directors carried out a purge. This time they eliminated one hundred twenty-seven deputies, eighty-six of them Jacobin sympathizers. The Councils often sided with secessionist electoral assemblies: in nineteen departments, minority groups of electors held separate meetings and chose different deputies, who were then ratified by the Councils. The Councils also invalidated local election results. Predictably, the Councils clamped down on anything that smacked of Jacobinism. In the final elections of the Directory, spring 1799, the government lost again: only sixty-six of its one hundred eighty-seven endorsed candidates won. This time the Councils did follow the law more closely by repudiating twenty-five of the twenty-seven secessionist electoral assemblies. These new elections brought in about fifty Jacobin sympathizers, raising the total to perhaps two hundred fifty in the two Councils.

These election results left the Directory stuck in the middle, year after year. Mercier suggests they sought to create a third "party" (his word), one that rejected monarchy, on the one hand, and "anarchy" (i.e., Jacobinism), on the other. Given that close to two-thirds of the members of the two Councils supported one of these two parties, the Directory had no reasonable chance of survival. The elections of 1797, 1798, and 1799 all demonstrated the overwhelming national rejection of the then-current government. Government candidates lost decisively in 1797 and 1799; they had mixed results in 1798. The electoral campaigns suggest that a significant group of French people wanted to maintain a Republic, but that another large group wanted to return to some elements of pre-republican France. Quite apart from nostalgia for cheaper times (Mercier castigates those who wanted to return to the days of "café au lait" for 6 shillings), a very strong desire to return to the Catholic Church motivated many, especially in the countryside. Given that the urban middle class had obtained most of the land confiscated from the Church, we can have little wonder that they, especially, feared its return.

Many of them certainly wanted a Catholic Church to return, because they believed strongly in the moral usefulness of religion for the masses, but they did not want the Ancien Régime Catholic Church. The devastating impact of de-Christianization on the Constitutional clergy, however, made the return of a compromise Church, one willing to accommodate the Revolution, impossible. In fact, when Napoleon signed the Concordat of 1801 with the Pope, he brought back the non-juring clergy, those most opposed to the republican legacy.

The shift to the Right in 1794–1795 initially gave the Church a chance to come out of hiding. The Paris churches reopened on 21 June 1795, when a bishop led a High Mass at Saint-Germain-l'Auxerrois. Guittard, who claimed that Parisians wanted to take up Sundays and return to the old calendar, says that on 21 June shops were closed and workers idle, even though it was not a *décadi*. Despite the return of the Church, the Constitution of 1795 meant that the new calendar remained the legal one until 1806.[32]

In the countryside, peasants adopted the new calendar only if obliged to do so by overwhelming force. Nor did they turn to Constitutional clergy to restore their services, which had often been conducted clandestinely in any case. They welcomed back the old, "good" priests: those who had refused the Oath. The Councils initially elected in 1797, with their strong contingent of royalists, naturally encouraged the return of the non-juring clergy; they even rescinded the legislation against them (July 1797). The 18 Fructidor coup (September 1797) naturally restored the anticlericals in the Councils. The next day, they overturned the July decree and re-instituted the death penalty for non-juring priests. For the next several months, government officials stepped up persecution of the refractory priests, arresting nearly two thousand of them in France and ten thousand in Belgium. Initial plans to deport them had to be cancelled due to the blockade by the British Navy, so the poor priests had to rot away in prisons on the southwestern coast. The Directory never reached an accommodation with the Church, leaving that task to its successor, the Consulate of Napoleon Bonaparte (Concordat of 1801).

The Economy: Chaos and Renewal

Luxury is like a spirituous liquor that intoxicates the spirit.[33]

L.-S. Mercier, writing of the revival of luxury
in the Paris of the Directory, 1798

The Directory failed utterly in most of its policies. Its initial economic policies, such as the relaxation of price controls, would seem to be another such failure. The end of the Terror accelerated inflation: the *assignats* fell to 20 percent of face value by December 1794. Yet a longer-term view of the Directory's economic and fiscal policies should count them as its greatest success. The post-Thermidor Convention endorsed economic freedom, abolishing wage and price controls in December 1794.[34] The abolition of the Maximum really did little more than recognize what was already happening. Grain prices remained controlled, although forced grain requisition, obviously not a viable long-term solution, gradually ended.

The government could not prevent the catastrophic decline of paper money, first the *assignats* and then the *territorial mandates*. Hyperinflation set in during 1795, when the prices of goods rose from one hour to the next; as Guittard said in April, "one price today, another tomorrow." People like him, who lived on annuities, lost all purchasing power. In February 1796, the government exchanged its old bond for new ones on a 10 to 1 basis, up to 10,000 *livres,* but a month later a 100-*livre assignat* was worth only 40 centimes.

In Paris, a measure of grain that had sold for 15 *livres* in May 1792 cost 5,000 *livres* by October 1795. Bread that sold for 20 *livres* a pound on 12 November cost 50 the next day! A sack of potatoes that had cost 2.5 *livres* in March brought 160 *livres* in November. In town after town, bakers followed the example of those of Rochefort, who made an official declaration of quitting their profession because they could not find sufficient grain to bake their bread. Well might the Burgundian historian Jean Bart call it the "time of empty bellies."

THE HUNGRY BOURGEOIS

The change did not help those seeking to buy bread. Although historians have frequently noted the bad harvest of 1794, Guittard's brother wrote from Champagne that they would have "wine and grain in full beauty" that year. The wine harvest was so full that the "winegrowers did not know what to do with their *assignats*." Guittard's brother Jean, wrote (April 1795) to his unfortunate Parisian sibling that he should come back to their village of Evergnicourt, where they had bread, butter, eggs, a little lard, and wine; he even sent a 12-pound loaf of bread as proof. Guittard's friend M. La Motte, just back from the country, told him the same thing. *Laboureurs* were "the best off, because they have at home milk, butter, cheese, eggs, vegetables, poultry, goats, pigs, fruits, lard." Guittard soon became dependent on the bread from his brother and sister, who continued to send loaves until January 1796. Without these loaves, he would have been in serious difficulty. On August 18, 1795, his cook left him; later in that entry, we perhaps find out why: "Today, for the first time, I had to get bread from the Section" (that is, from the relief committee). His new cook lasted only two weeks.

The Directory made it legal to trade in silverplate for coinage and to use coins again in January 1796; the following month, it abolished the *assignats*—burning the presses in a public demonstration—but markets did not know how to react. The *louis d'or* (an actual gold coin) sold on 23 February for prices ranging from 7,850 to 8,600 *livres*. The madness did not end until 1797, when the government returned to metal currency. Even that took some time, as France did not have enough specie to meet demand. Much of what it did have came from loot sent home by its conquering armies in Italy and the Low Countries. The restoration of a real metal currency began to take effect by the fall of 1797. Stable money, abetted by the good harvests of 1796 to 1798, led to stable prices. The last two years of the Directory did not have the wild fluctuations of earlier times.

The restoration of a real currency in 1797 took place in an economy that lay in shambles. The failure to provide a stable currency, the inability to collect regular taxation, the incessant demands of the national government, the violent requisitions of the Jacobins: all of these policies struck hard blows at every sector. The textile industry had begun its slump in the middle of the 1780s, when overproduction and (after 1786) rising English competition led to widespread decline and to massive unemployment in cities such as Troyes or Reims or in the textile villages of Normandy or Picardy. Production seems to have bottomed out during the Jacobin period and to have started a slow recovery in 1796–1797. Silk cloth production, focused on Lyon, naturally suffered from the Terror and counter-Terror that racked the city for several years.

The coal mines, above all those of Anzin, regained over 80 percent of their Ancien Régime production level (300,000 tons in 1788), after falling as low as 63,000 tons in 1794. As for the colonies, their trade simply disappeared: Saint-Domingue's slave rebellion (see the following text) ended its sugar production, and unrest on Martinique and Guadeloupe undermined their trade, too. In 1793, after the open declaration of war between France and Great Britain, the British seized both Martinique and

Guadeloupe. Although a local insurgency restored the latter to nominal French authority, the British navy's control of the Atlantic eliminated what was left of colonial trade. Many displaced planters fled to New Orleans, where they reinforced that city's French elements. Even that bastion soon gave out: Napoleon sold the city, and the entire Louisiana Territory, to the United States in 1803 for $10 million.

That the Revolutionary period had evil effects on the urban economy is certain: the populations of most major cities declined. Paris lost 100,000 people. The nadir came in 1794–1795, when the death rate rose 50 percent, due largely to malnutrition. Port cities, such as Bordeaux, suffered from the loss of the West Indies and from the British blockade. Bordeaux's population declined from 110,000 in 1790 to only 93,000 in 1801. People left because businesses failed. The forty sugar refineries of 1789 had been reduced to ten by 1800. The local rope and tobacco manufactories that had employed twenty-two hundred people in 1789 gave work to only four hundred in 1801. In France as a whole, industrial output declined by about 40 percent from 1789–1799.

This dismal picture did improve somewhat in the last two years of the Directory. The return to sound money (at least, relatively speaking) and decent grain harvests helped reestablish some economic stability. Farmers with produce to sell did well. Those who supplied the armies did even better. Cotton manufacturing witnessed a sharp upturn in the late Directory period, in part due to army demand. French producers began to introduce new technology, above all the water frame and the new spinning mills, just before 1800. Arms manufacturers did a thriving business, yet the metal sector, which should have prospered in a wartime economy, had its failures. The factories of Le Creusot, for example, lost more than 2 million francs between 1796 and 1801. The islands of economic prosperity, such as certain bankers and investors, stood out in a sea of misery. They helped create the startling disparities of wealth commented upon by all observers in the Paris of the late 1790s.

As Mercier suggests, the luxury trades recovered well under the Directory. The drastic fall-off in production of expensive wines, such as champagne, reversed. Champagne traders like the house of Clicquot began to ship more wine, a precursor to the rapid expansion of the first decade of the nineteenth century. Clicquot shipped 16,000 bottles of champagne in 1790, 32,000 bottles in 1802, and 93,000 bottles a year between 1805–1810. Wigmakers, jewelers, restauranteurs—all those associated with luxury—did well. Mercier tells the amusing story of one such enterprising entrepreneur, who had an unusual path to riches:

> He thought that all the turkeys stuffed with truffles, all the salmons, all the Mayence hams, so many wild boar stews, so many Bologna sausages, so many patés, so many wines, liqueurs, sorbets, ice creams, lemonades had to find there, in the final analysis, their common reservoir, and making it very spacious and above all very commodious for so many people who engage in all manner of voluptuousness, the residue (*caput mortuum*) of the surrounding kitchens would become a gold mine for him. . . .
>
> This man did as the Emperor Vespasian, who leased out the latrines of Rome. His son mockingly reproached him for it, so the Emperor took a

gold coin, put it under the nose of his son, and said to him: "Well, does that smell bad?"

It's in the Palais-Égalité [Palais Royal] that in all ways the gold that comes from that which is most foul, leaves no trace of bad odor.[35]

The Coup of 18 Brumaire

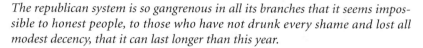

The republican system is so gangrenous in all its branches that it seems impossible to honest people, to those who have not drunk every shame and lost all modest decency, that it can last longer than this year.

Nicolas Ruault, 9 May 1796

War Against Europe: The Rise of Napoleon Bonaparte

Every peasant that I met in the fields, the vineyards or the woods approached me to ask if there were any news of General Bonaparte, and why did he not come back to France; never once did anyone enquire about the Directory.[36]

Joseph Fiévée

CHRONOLOGY	1796–1799
April 1796–July 1797	Bonaparte pummels Austrians and their allies in Italy; creates Cispadane Republic (October 1796), then Cisalpine Republic (July 1797) and Ligurian Republic
December 1796–January 1797	Expedition to Ireland fails; United Irishmen later (spring 1797); crushed by England
18 April 1797	Leoben agreement between Bonaparte and Austrians, ratified as Peace of Campo Formio in October
January 1798	French troops intervene against the Pope; Roman Republic declared; annexation of Mulhouse; *de facto* annexation of left bank of the Rhine[37]
March 1798	Declaration of Helvetian (Swiss) Republic
May–July 1798	Napoleon's victories in Egypt (Battle of the Pyramids, July 1798)
1 August 1798	Admiral Nelson annihilates the French fleet at Aboukir; European war. Fighting in Germany, Italy, and Switzerland; France against the Second Coalition: Great Britain, Austria, Spain, Italian states, and Russia

CHRONOLOGY	(continued)
January 1799	French defeat Neapolitan troops; occupy mainland portion of Kingdom of Naples; declare the Republic of Naples
April 1799	French evacuate Milan; Cisalpine Republic collapses
May 1799	Royalist forces retake Naples; Neapolitan Republic disintegrates
June–August 1799	French defeats in Italy; withdrawal of French troops; end of Roman Republic
23 August 1799	Napoleon abandons his troops in Egypt, secretly sails for France
9 October 1799	Napoleon arrives in France
9–10 November 1799	*Coup d'état* of 18 Brumaire; Napoleon becomes effective ruler of France

The wars of 1794–1799 were a messy business. At the time of Thermidor, France faced a coalition that included Great Britain, Austria, Prussia, and Spain. In 1794, the Revolutionary armies swept to victory in Belgium, where General Jourdan defeated the Austrians (Fleurus, 26 June), and in the Rhineland. Jourdan's victory paved the way for an invasion of the Netherlands (December), where the monarchy, lacking popular support, quickly collapsed. Local "patriots," heirs of the failed revolutionaries of 1787, allied with the French and proclaimed the Batavian Republic. The French soon signed a treaty with this "sister" republic, which left a French force of occupation/protection in place and provided for a huge Dutch indemnity. French forces also occupied the left bank of the Rhine, south and west of Cologne and Luxembourg. Great Britain remained unwavering in its hostility, but France signed peace agreements with Prussia (at Basle, the first European diplomatic recognition of the new government, 1795), Spain (1795), and Austria (1797). Spain even allied with France against Great Britain in 1796, although it would change sides again in 1799.

French military successes relied on three key elements:

1. The sheer size of the armies, which invariably outnumbered their opponents.

2. The revolutionary ardor of the soldiers, a factor commented upon by all observers at the time.

3. The ability of the generals.

The first element derived from France's introduction (1793) of mass conscription, which gave it a substantial advantage over opponents that relied on traditional means of recruitment. The second advantage flowed naturally from the circumstances of the initial fighting. The allies had invaded France, which allowed the French government to rally its people to save "the fatherland in danger." The Jacobin mass conscription of fall 1793 raised about 300,000 men. Each canton received its quota of soldiers, who were usually chosen by lot. The "levée en masse" differed fundamentally from earlier efforts to raise troops in that it fell equally on all men: no longer could the rich buy exemption. Detailed studies of local recruitment show that the well-to-do did, in fact, provide a significant portion of the soldiers, in direct contrast to the situation of earlier conscriptions (1792 and February 1793) that had allowed the rich to buy exemption. Perhaps not coincidentally, those conscriptions had touched off widespread violence (most famously the Vendée rebellion) and led to massive desertions.

Many of the men drafted in 1793 ended up as lifelong soldiers. Men unlucky enough to be of draftable age (eighteen to twenty-five) in the fall of 1793 provided the core of the French armies for the next six years, until the draft of 1799. By late 1794, France had the astounding total of 750,000 men under arms, yet the government raised only 70,000 more soldiers from 1794–1797. This limited recruitment meant that the soldiers inspired by revolutionary ardor in 1793 remained in place as late as 1797 (indeed, many of them even afterward). It also meant that France had a remarkably veteran army in the fighting of 1796–1797.

The failure to recruit sufficient replacements led to a steady decline in the size of the army, which bottomed out at about 325,000 men in 1798. In response to this decline, the Directory instituted the Jourdan Law of 19 Fructidor VI (5 September 1798), the first law of universal conscription in any state. All men aged twenty to twenty-five had to sign up for the draft. In theory, the state would first take the men aged twenty and twenty-one, and then the others, by year, as necessary. In practice, the extraordinary military effort of 1798–1799, which included severe French losses, upset all these careful provisions. The army needed so many replacements that it took men from each of the five classes, which touched off some armed resistance in traditional antidraft regions.

Government officials attached to the armies, often deputies on mission from the Convention, constantly bombarded French troops with propaganda designed to make them committed republicans, yet obedient soldiers. The authorities encouraged the troops to sing Revolutionary songs, like the *Marseillaise* or *Ça ira;* they hosted Revolutionary festivals; they encouraged troops to read pro-government newspapers. French generals believed their men to possess a moral superiority over their opponents, a factor which had something to do with the extensive reliance of the French armies on the bayonet charge.[38]

The third element, the capacity of the generals, can also be tied directly to revolutionary change. In the Ancien Régime, only men from the highest ranks of the aristocracy commanded armies. Sometimes these men could be commanders of talent, like Maurice de Saxe, illegitimate son of the King of Poland; often, they were blundering idiots. The Revolution paved the way for men of moderate social status to rise up in the army. The list of successful generals of 1794–1799—Hoche, Jourdan, Moreau, Bonaparte, and the others—contains not a single member of the great aristocracy. Napoleon liked to say that every soldier in his army carried a marshal's baton in his knapsack, because men rose up due to their bravery and military ability.

Ordinary soldiers, taken from a peasant or artisan family, had little realistic hope of becoming generals, even in the Revolutionary armies, but those from middle-class or petty noble families, like Napoleon himself, proved once again the immemorial advantage of selecting quality leaders from the largest possible pool of candidates. Hoche, who had worked in the royal stables as a boy, and who enlisted as an ordinary soldier in 1783 (he reached the rank of sergeant in 1789), was a rare example of someone rising from the ranks to command.

The French used two different strategies in the areas they conquered. In regions contiguous to France, they usually annexed the territory. France annexed Belgium and the left bank of the Rhine in 1793, lost them in 1794, and re-annexed them in 1795. It later annexed Geneva and Mulhouse, as well as the county of Nice and French Savoy. In the Netherlands and most of Switzerland, however, France encouraged the creation of "sister" republics, which then provided large indemnities to France. In 1796, in the wake of several victories by Napoleon Bonaparte's army, Italian republicans in cities such as Modena created a Cispadane Republic, for which they drew up a constitution. In 1797, Napoleon took more control of this process. He co-opted local Italian republicans at Milan (Cisalpine Republic, 1797) and Genoa (Ligurian Republic, 1797); his successors in Italy followed the same technique at Rome (1798), and Naples (January 1799). Napoleon directly appointed the governments of his two "republics" and left their constitutions in abeyance.

The two different systems of occupation naturally led to distinct fiscal relationships with France. French armies had to pay for themselves. In a place like Belgium, incorporated into France, that meant taxes—over 50 millions francs in 1794 alone. The new "sister" republics, like the Batavians (Dutch), often had to pay indemnities to cover the costs of the French troops stationed on their soil. The Dutch faced an initial payment of 200 million francs, of which they paid three-fourths. The Dutch then had to pay for an army of twenty-five thousand men, although France kept as few as ten thousand men in Holland. French armies became notorious for their systematic looting and pillaging. The duchy of Luxembourg sent deputies to the Convention to complain that "the French remove everything, right down to the doors and windows; they ceaselessly ransom the inhabitants and break everything they cannot carry off."[39] The government sent out artists to select the finest paintings and sculptures of occupied areas: canvases by Rubens and Van Dyck left Belgium in 1794–1795, just as those by great Italian masters made their way from Milan or Venice to Paris in 1797. The Directory even organized a special parade of stolen artworks from Italy on the fourth anniversary of the fall of Robespierre.

In 1796, given the drastic circumstances of the French economy, the armies in the Netherlands and Italy provided the money to keep France afloat. In Italy, the most successful French general was the Corsican Napoleon Bonaparte, who conquered most of north–central Italy in 1796–1797. Bonaparte paid his army in cash and even forwarded some 45 million *livres* worth of coinage back to France in 1796. Bonaparte and the Austrians, without the approval of the Directory government, drew up an agreement that gave Venice to Austria, ending the city's centuries-old independence, and confirmed French gains in the Low Countries, Rhineland, and northern Italy (initial agreement at Leoben, June 1797, confirmed at Campo Formio, October 1797). In separate agreements, Napoleon got the Pope to renounce his rights to Avignon and

YOUNG NAPOLEON

Napoleon Bonaparte seems slowly to be losing his place as a towering figure of the collective imagination, at least in the Anglophone world. Throughout the nineteenth and early twentieth centuries, every successful businessman hoped to be called a "Napoleon of industry," just as every general dreamed of Napoleonic battlefield successes. Wellington, Waterloo, Napoleon, the Old Guard—every school child knew these heroic names and places of memory. Lenin fulminated against the dangers of Bonapartism when he and his colleagues seized power in Russia in 1917. Hitler's empire drew comparisons to that of Napoleon, just as his disaster in Russia in 1941 evoked memories of the ruin of Napoleon's Grand Army of 1812. Orwell called *Animal Farm's* dictator–pig, Napoleon.

Napoleon's image lingers on in France: Paris remains covered in landmarks that sing his praises—the Arc de Triomphe, the column in the place Vendôme—as well as with avenues and streets that bring to mind his great victories or the names of his famous generals. Even French cookbooks contain recipes for the legendary chicken Marengo (his meal before that great victory of 1800) or for the pastries known as "napoleons."

Born in Corsica in 1769, member of a middling noble family, Napoleon grew up speaking Corsican, not French. He went to one of the new royal military schools established for boys from middling noble families and became a lieutenant in the royal artillery. He did little during the first three years of the Revolution, rising to the rank of captain by early 1793. At first uninvolved in Revolutionary politics, he became an avid supporter of the Robespierrist wing of the Jacobins in 1793. His great break came at the siege of Toulon, when his deft placement of cannon and sound tactical advice led to the defeat of the British and the recapture of the city. He earned an immediate promotion to brigadier general.

Robespierre's fall led to Napoleon's brief arrest in the fall of 1794, but he quickly obtained release. Moving to Paris, he became a client of Barras, elected as one of the first five Directors. The Right-wing *vendémiaire* uprising (5 October 1795) gave Bonaparte another chance to show his facility for using cannon. He commanded the artillery, and the troops, who crushed the rebellion. Naturally, such service to a powerful patron like Barras led to military command: Bonaparte took over the army in Italy. His lightning campaign of early 1797 routed the Savoyards; he defeated their Austrian allies in the fall. Master of northern Italy, able to provide the Directory with substantial Italian specie, Bonaparte became, like other leading generals, an important political figure. The death of the most important such rival, Lazare Hoche (19 September 1797), gave Napoleon, scarcely twenty-eight at the time, the hopes of dominating the situation.

The military events of 1798–1799 enhanced Napoleon's standing. His successful campaign in Egypt captured the popular imagination in 1798. His main military rivals—Joubert, Moreau, and Jourdan—suffered defeats in Germany, Italy, and Switzerland between March and August 1799. Joubert conveniently died at the battle of Novi on 15 August. Little wonder that those plotting the overthrow of the Directory looked to Bonaparte for their military support, expecting to use this young general to implement their political agenda.

Yet the young Napoleon had no intention of allowing himself to be used. During his successful first stay in Italy, he reportedly told a friend:[40]

> What I have done so far is nothing. I am only at the debut of the career that I must carry through. Do you think that it is for the glory of the lawyers of the Directory, of Carnot, of Barras, that I triumph in Italy? Do you think it is also to found a Republic? What an idea! A Republic of 30 million men! With our mores, our vices! Where is the possibility of that? It's a chimera that has besotted the French, but which will pass like so many others. They need glory, the satisfactions of vanity. But of liberty, they understand nothing by it.

the Comtat (March 1797) and the king of Sardinia–duke of Savoy to accept French possession of Nice and Savoy (occupied in 1792–1793, and officially ceded in 1797).

With France's Continental opponents all beaten by late 1797, Bonaparte convinced the Directors to allow him to invade Egypt in 1798, to cut off English access to India. He first captured Malta, where he abolished the Crusading order of St. John of Jerusalem that ruled the island. His troops quickly took Alexandria and defeated the Mamelukes at the Battle of the Pyramids (21 July 1798), but his navy was annihilated by the British under Admiral Horatio Nelson, at the Battle of the Nile (1 August). Bonaparte marched an army toward Syria in February 1799 but failed to take Acre (May 1799) and withdrew.

The foolish Egyptian expedition, whose only positive effect was the discovery of the Rosetta Stone (which enabled scholars to decipher ancient Egyptian hieroglyphics), had momentous diplomatic consequences. In the aftermath of Nelson's victory, the Ottoman Empire, to which Egypt owed nominal fealty, declared war on France. The Kingdom of Naples followed suit, sending an army to retake Rome from the French. The Neapolitans succeeded at first but were quickly thrown back by General Championnet, who captured Naples and proclaimed a Republic (December 1798–January 1799). The Republic lasted little more than a month. The Directory cashiered Championnet for exceeding his orders and withdrew most of its troops from Naples. The Neapolitan Republic was quickly overthrown by a peasant rebellion begun in Calabria by Cardinal Ruffo and his "invasion" force of eight men!

Napoleon's Mediterranean adventure had also infuriated Russian Tsar Paul I, who claimed to be the protector of the Knights of Malta. Paul objected as well to his exclusion from the Rastadt talks about the future of the Holy Roman Empire. Soon Russia had allied with Naples against France. The Ottomans allowed the Russians to send a fleet through the Dardanelles and the Austrians permitted Russian troops to winter in their territory. Little wonder that by March 1799 Austria and France were again at war. In the fighting of 1799, Russian armies had great success early in the campaign, driving the French from much of Italy and Switzerland. In the end, poor Allied coordination allowed the French to recover Switzerland, but they were driven from Italy. Meanwhile, Bonaparte abandoned his army of 35,000 in Egypt and secretly returned to France, landing at Fréjus, in southern France, on 9 October.[41]

The Coup

It is a great tragedy for a nation of thirty million inhabitants in the eighteenth century to have to call on bayonets to save the state.

General Napoleon Bonaparte to Foreign Minister Talleyrand,
November 1799

Fighting continued in the north as well. The French suffered losses in the Rhineland and the Low Countries early in 1799, but quickly reversed those trends. By late 1799, they had driven across the Rhine again, and had expelled the invading Anglo–Russian force from the Netherlands. The military problems of the early fall of 1799 exacerbated tensions inside of France. The Directory could not really call upon public support from any group. The *sans-culottes* detested it, both for political and economic reasons; the Jacobin bourgeoisie resented the stolen election of 1798 and the constant measures taken against the Left; the royalist landowners and bourgeoisie felt robbed of their political rights in 1797.

In the summer of 1799, all of these disgruntled groups began to undermine the Directory's authority. The key blow came in late spring 1799, when Reubell had to step down. The Councils replaced him with Sieyès, a vocal opponent of current policies. In short order another director, Treilhard, resigned, to be replaced by an ally of Sieyès, Louis Gohier. Sieyès and Gohier formed an alliance with Barras, and forced out La Révellière and Merlin de Douai. The incoming directors, Roger Ducos (a regicide) and General Jean Moulin, lined up behind Sieyès. The opposition had now taken control of the executive branch of government.

The topsy-turvy world of Parisian politics spun wildly in July 1799. On 6 July, a new political club opened in the Salle de Manège at the Tuileries: the room in which the Convention had met. The Manège Club quickly attracted over three thousand members, among them two hundred fifty of the deputies to the two Councils. Three weeks after it opened, however, the Directory forced the club to move to the Left Bank. On 13 August, the minister of police, the ex-Terrorist Joseph Fouché, closed it entirely. This anti-Jacobin blow, taken by an ex-Jacobin leader, took place at virtually the same moment as some apparently pro-Jacobin moves. On 1 August, the Directory ended press controls, allowed Jacobin papers to reopen, and named Robert Lindet, one of the members of the Committee of Public Safety of the Year II, as finance minister. These various moves made sense, given that the government needed to ally either with elements of the monarchists or of the Jacobins in order to have a working majority in the Councils. The government thus naturally made overtures to each side, yet those overtures often involved repressive measures against the opponents of those being wooed.

Instability in Paris was matched by instability in the provinces. A peasant uprising in the Toulouse region led to a siege of the city—a Jacobin stronghold—and to a battle in which four thousand peasants lost their lives. The Chouans rose again in the west, this time sacking Le Mans (October). Troops quelled the disturbances, but people everywhere feared the rising level of anarchy. In this climate of uncertainty, Napoleon Bonaparte made a triumphant procession from Provence to Paris. In Paris, his brother Lucien, now a member of the Council of 500, held secret negotiations with key political figures such as Sieyès, Roger Ducos, the minister of justice Cambacérès, foreign minister Talleyrand, and some of Bonaparte's old corps commanders. On 9 November, the pro-Bonaparte forces convinced the Councils to pass a motion, made by Lucien himself, to move their meetings to the old palace of Saint-Cloud, on the outskirts of Paris, to forestall action by the Parisian masses. They named Napoleon Bonaparte commander of all troops around Paris. The five Directors then resigned, although Moulin and Gohier did so only under duress.

The next day, 18 Brumaire (10 November 1799), Napoleon Bonaparte came to the chambers of the two Councils. The Elders received him somewhat coldly; the Council of 500 hooted at him, demanded that he be placed outside the law, and finally jostled and cut him. Lucien responded by haranguing the loyal troops outside, telling them the deputies sought to assassinate Napoleon. The troops stormed into the chambers, sweeping aside the small guard, and cleared the hall. A few hours later, rump meetings of the two bodies voted the constitutional changes the Bonapartes had demanded. They excluded sixty-one deputies from their meetings and gave full authority to a new triumvirate of Consuls: Sieyès, Roger Ducos, and Napoleon Bonaparte. So died the Directory and with it the First French Republic.

❧ THE REPUBLICAN LEGACY

> . . . the most persistent ghost of the French Revolution was not the woman of the revolutionary crowds but the counter-revolutionary woman of 1795–1796. . . . she succeeded in becoming the basis of a troubling legend. Her putative control of the family . . . threatened the full flowering of the rational state, the other Eden. Once again, hysterical, perverse, irrational, unreliable Eve was constructed to explain why man was kept from earthly paradise.
>
> Olwen Hufton, Creighton Lecture, 1989

The republican experiment of 1792–1799 revolutionized not merely politics but all of life. The Republic created an expanded France, new law codes, new administrative structures, new cultural mores, and a changed artistic climate. It destroyed the hegemony of Catholicism, rearranged urban–rural relations, established political divisions that would last into the twentieth century, embroiled all of Europe in a series of bloody wars, and provided Europeans with a political vocabulary for their future: some of it perhaps benign, "Right" and "Left," and some of it more sinister, "enemies of the people" and "enemies of the Revolution."

The Revolution, in its all-encompassing magnitude, left a cultural legacy everywhere in the European-influenced world. Just as the Revolution spawned two violently opposed political movements—republicanism and monarchism—so, too, it encouraged two strongly divergent artistic currents—Classicism and Romanticism. The most famous of the Revolutionary artists was Jacques-Louis David, an avowed Jacobin and Robespierrist. Helen Maria Williams even went so far as to call him Robespierre's lackey.

David had achieved considerable fame before the Revolution; his *Oath of the Horatii* (1785) provides an outstanding example of the revival of Classical themes and the cult of the fatherland. His canvases recorded many of the Revolution's highest and lowest moments. Among the most famous of these paintings are his portrayal of the *Tennis Court Oath* (1791), with its deliberately mythologizing techniques; the stark portrait of Marat (1793), lying dead in his bathtub; and a simple sketch of Marie-Antoinette on her way to the guillotine. *The Assassination of Marat,* which, despite its title, does not show the actual deed, presents the viewer with the bleeding martyr clutching his pen, the murder weapon lying beside the tub. It hung in the meeting room of the Convention, to remind all of their Revolutionary duty.

David played a central role in the Jacobin period, not only as a Parisian deputy to the Convention but as the chief decorator of the great Revolutionary festivals. In August 1793, he masterminded a massive festival in honor of the fall of the monarchy.

Its centerpiece was a new figure in the iconography of the Revolution: Hercules, known as the "French people," slaying the Hydra of Federalism. During the Jacobin ascendancy, David spearheaded the movement to replace the previously dominant figure of Revolutionary iconography—Liberty, always presented as a woman (and, as Guittard's journal tells us, often a live woman, rather than a statue)—with the super-masculine one of Hercules.[42] All of David's work for the festivals relied heavily on Classical models and on those of the greatest earlier movement of Classical revival, the Italian Renaissance. The festivities for the June 1794 Festival of the Supreme Being included a statue modeled on Michelangelo's *David,* as well as many Classical allegories. The fall of the Jacobins led to the fall of Hercules. Marianne, the symbol of Liberty, returned to preeminence. David, along with the other leading Terrorists, faced removal from the Convention and arrest in the fall of 1794, but he survived the purge.

David continued to work in accordance with the political dictates of his times. Under the Directory, he went back to historical paintings, offering the *Rape of the Sabine Women* at the exhibition of 1799. He also early tied his star to that of the young Bonaparte, starting (but not finishing) a portrait of him in the late 1790s. Soon, David would provide Bonaparte with great masterpieces to record his triumphs, such as *Napoleon Crossing the Alps,* in which the young and masterful leader, astride a magnificent white horse, leads his troops through the mountains in the most difficult of conditions. (See Plate.) In time, David would record coronations for his new master.

Different approaches flourished in the 1790s in all the arts. Painters such as Greuze and Fragonard continued the traditions of the eighteenth century. The great sculptor Houdon still flourished, doing busts of many of the greatest figures of the day, both French and foreign. Houdon's busts often provide tantalizing clues to the fates of his subjects. The bust of Barnave, now in the Carnavelet Museum in Paris, shows a handsome, proud, indeed haughty young man. (Does the contemptuous glance of the brilliant young lawyer help us to understand why he fell from grace with his colleagues?) A nearby room holds a bust of Mirabeau, his monstrous head dominating the room, his fury warm even in cold stone.

Musicians, too, felt the Revolutionary ferment. In France, composers such as Rouget de Lisle, whose *La Marseillaise* became the anthem of republicanism (and, late in the nineteenth century, under the Third Republic, the national anthem), or Méhul, whose *Chant du départ,* with its words by the poet Marie-Joseph Chénier, rivalled Rouget de Lisle's work in popularity in the 1790s, competed with composers who produced purely traditional operas. Outside of France, whether we look at composers such as Beethoven; writers, such as Schiller; or philosophers, such as Kant, all had to come to terms with the Revolutionary world, even if they rejected it. Here the Revolutionary armies left a fatally mixed legacy. Many intellectuals and artists responded positively to the Revolution. The execution of Louis XVI and the Terror appalled European opinion, but the republican experiment inspired ardor outside of France as well as within. Urban elites agitated for representative, sometimes even republican government. These movements looked to France for an example, and often borrowed French nationalist terminology as a means to oppose ruling monarchs. When the Revolutionary armies began to invade surrounding countries and to impose "republican" governments, however, public opinion began to shift. In Germany especially, but in Italy to some degree as well, nationalism grew as a reaction against the French.

Napoleon, too, elicited such responses. Beethoven first dedicated a symphony to the charismatic republican general, but then angrily rejected the imperial conqueror.

In England, the Revolution touched off a tremendous debate. Opposition focused around the greatest denunciation of the Revolution, Edmund Burke's *Reflections on the Revolution in France* (1790), which ridiculed the idea of a Revolution on behalf of natural rights. Burke had many opponents, most prominent among them Tom Paine, *The Rights of Man* (1791), and Mary Wollstonecraft. She published an attack on Burke, *A Vindication of the Rights of Man,* and then shifted to a broader assault in her most famous book, *A Vindication of the Rights of Woman* (1792). In it, she encouraged men to treat women as equals, and women to act as the reasoned beings they were. She supported equal education for girls and boys and rights for women, based on their capacity to reason. *Vindication* is the foundation text of modern feminism, a classic example of how revolutions have unintended consequences. Wollstonecraft in England, just like Toussaint L'Ouverture in Saint-Domingue, took up the cudgels for liberty for all: in her case for women, in his case for African slaves.

Most of the men who made the French Revolution had no intention of granting greater freedom to either group. The events in France touched off unrest in French West Indian colonies. The complex societies of blacks, mulattos, and whites had great difficulty reaching an agreement about the new political rights. In Saint-Domingue, for example, mulattos owned many plantations and slaves: if political rights were to be based on property, they would get them. Whites, many of whom owned no property, insisted on the primacy of skin color over property. In France, some supported one group, some the other; a few enlightened souls, such as Condorcet, even supported freedom for the slaves. The various legislative bodies went back and forth on this issue. At first blacks and mulattos got no satisfaction, but then the Constituent Assembly decreed (May 1791) that free-born blacks and mulattos should have the same political rights as whites. Later in 1791, blacks took matters into their own hands; one of Guittard's correspondants, a M. Clausson living in Saint-Domingue, wrote him that the rebellion had done 2 billion *livres* of damage.

The Convention abolished slavery (February 1794) but, in reality, the action of the mulattos and slaves themselves had resolved the issue. Led by Toussaint L'Ouverture, the slaves defeated the local whites and mulattos, to say nothing of expeditionary forces sent by the French and the British (1794). All the expeditions of Europeans eventually fell victim to disease. The final French expedition of 1802–1803 actually captured L'Ouverture, but the force soon melted away, its commander among those carried off by yellow fever. L'Ouverture's successor, Jacques Dessalines, then established an independent Haiti. The British captured the other French West Indian islands and held most of them for some time, but these islands reverted to France in the end. The Convention's abolition of slavery, widely praised in France and elsewhere, did not prove permanent. Once he had consolidated power, Bonaparte reestablished both the slave trade and slavery itself on the remaining French islands.

Women fared little better than blacks. The preceding narrative makes clear the important role of women in the great Revolutionary events: the October Days of 1789, the risings of 1793 and 1795. They participated effectively in the ordinary political life of France as well. Individual women, like Madame Roland or Claire

THE CONSERVATIVE RESPONSE: BURKE AND REVOLUTION

No one in the Anglophone world can escape Edmund Burke's views of the French Revolution. Burke's *Reflections on the Revolution in France* (1790) profoundly affected the great Anglophone historian of the Revolution, Thomas Carlisle, just as it influenced Charles Dickens. Dickens's work, in turn, has resonated widely in modern Anglophone culture, not only in such venues as the Hollywood version of *A Tale of Two Cities,* but even in films such as D.W. Griffith's silent classic, *Orphans of the Storm.* Griffith presents us with the entirely fanciful scene of Robespierre and Danton walking the streets of Paris together in spring 1789: the printed descriptions tell us that the sinister, sniveling Robespierre is a "pussy-footer if ever there was one," but that Danton is "the Abraham Lincoln of France"!

Burke, who supported the American Revolutionaries because he believed they fought for their legitimate rights as Englishmen, rejected the French Revolution because of its reliance on abstract principles. Burke's ideas remain Holy Writ for contemporary American conservative writers such as George Will. Let us briefly sample Burke's masterwork.

> I flatter myself that I love a manly, moral, regulated liberty as well as any gentleman of that society [the Revolutionary Society of England, which supported the French Revolution], be he who he will; and perhaps I have given as good proofs of my attachment to that cause, in the whole course of my public conduct. I think I envy liberty as little as they do, to any other nation. But I cannot stand forward, and give praise or blame to any thing which relates to human actions, and human concerns, on a simple view of the object, as it stands stripped of every relation, in all the nakedness and solitude of metaphysical abstraction. Circumstances . . . give in reality to every political principle its distinguishing colour, and discriminating effect. The circumstances are what render every civil and political scheme beneficial or noxious to mankind. Abstractly speaking, government, as well as liberty, is good; yet could I, in common sense, ten years ago have felicitated France on her enjoyment of a government (for she had then a government) without enquiry what the nature of that government was, or how it was administered? Can I now congratulate the same nation upon its freedom? Is it because liberty in the abstract may be classed amongst the blessings of mankind, that I am seriously to felicitate a madman, who has escaped from the protecting restraint and wholesome darkness of his cell, on his restoration to the enjoyment of light and liberty? . . .
>
> I should therefore suspend my congratulations on the new liberty of France, until I was informed how it had been combined with government; with public force; with the discipline and obedience of armies; with the collection of an effective and well-distributed revenue; with morality and religion; with the solidity of property; with peace and order; with civil and social manners. All these (in their way) are good things too; and, without them, liberty is not a benefit whilst it lasts, and is not likely to continue long. The effect of liberty to individuals is, that they may do what they please; We ought to see what it will please them to do, before we risque congratulations, which may be soon turned into complaints. Prudence would dictate this in the case of separate insulated private men; but liberty, when men act in bodies, is *power.* Considerate people, before they declare themselves, will observe the use which is made of *power;* and particularly of so trying a thing as *new* power in *new* persons, of whose principles, tempers, and dispositions, they have little or no experience . . . [43]

Lacombe, provided leadership to political movements of all kinds. The Girondins rallied around Madame Roland, while Lacombe seems to have played a key role in the May 31–June 2, 1793 events that led to their fall. In a speech denouncing female participation in politics, Chaumette, procurator general of Paris, singled out Madame

Equality for blacks. In this 1791 engraving, reason establishes legal equality between whites and blacks. The measure applied to free blacks only; the vast majority of blacks in French colonies legally remained slaves until the Convention abolished slavery on 4 February 1794.

Source: © Giraudon/Art Resource, New York.

Roland and Olympe de Gouges as examples of "denatured women" who wanted to "renounce their sex" in order to be men, that is, in order to participate in public life. In Paris, women attended sectional assemblies and presented petitions to the various legislative bodies. They even voted in certain places. At Laon, for example, they cast their ballots for the Constitution of 1793.

Many French women, such as those in the Roman-law regions of the south, obtained important property rights from the new law codes, fully promulgated by 1793. The law now imposed equal inheritance and forbade favoritism toward one child, such as the oldest male. Married women got greater control of their property and the right to use and enjoy more of the joint family property after the death of their husbands. Under the Ancien Régime, women in some provinces, such as Brittany, had enjoyed extensive property rights, but women in other areas, notably the Roman law regions of the south, suffered from considerable legal discrimination. The new law gave these women a level of legal equality their mothers could never have imagined and contributed mightily to their struggle for greater authority within their families.

The Revolutionaries also legalized divorce (Constitution of 1791). Urban households, in particular, started to take advantage of the new law. Although rural communities had divorce rates of only 1 or 2 percent in the 1790s, large cities such as

Lyon had rates as high as 25 percent (1793; the rate fell to 12 percent the following year). Divorce reform, initially presented as a boon to women either mistreated by their husbands and/or forced into marriages by their families, did not necessarily have its intended consequences. The relaxation of the old ban on divorce made it legally easier for men to abandon their families, a problem that became particularly severe in times of famine, such as 1795. Women's legal gains did not survive the Republic, as Napoleon imbedded profoundly misogynist principles into his legal code.

For most women, the Revolution revolved around the same issues that were critical to men. As women bought and prepared the food, they naturally played key roles in the food riots resulting from subsistence issues. Women artisans, like male ones, also demonstrated about work-related matters: the laundresses who demanded cheaper soap in 1793 provide the best-known but hardly a unique example. Women did not generally act together out of a spirit of cooperation on the basis of gender: the key group opposing the Club of Republican Revolutionary Citizenesses in the fall of 1793 was the market women of Les Halles. The conflict between these two groups of women involved, above all, their relationship to groups of male allies, and to economic grievances (of the market women) not specifically related to gender. That male authorities relished the opportunity to get women out of politics seems beyond question. One Jacobin wrote in September 1793: "It is these counter-revolutionary sluts who cause all the riotous outbreaks, above all over bread. They made a revolution over coffee and sugar, and they will make others if we don't watch out."[44]

The revolutionaries bequeathed to posterity a society built, in theory, around individual rights. They went to great lengths to make sure that the individuals in question were men only, because they (most of them) believed that women lacked reason. In the West Indies, many whites (seconded by allies in France itself) similarly sought to exclude mulatto and black men from full civil rights.

The Revolution also constructed the enduring foundations of the modern French state. Here the Directory deserves some credit. The continuities between 1792 and 1797 are much stronger than we sometimes think. After all, until the elections of 1797, well over half of the men ruling France had been in the legislative body since September 1792. As late as 1799, a third or more of the men in the two Councils had been legislators since the beginning of the Republic. We should not be misled by the political instability of the Directory, because the New Regime took firm root, in virtually every sector, precisely during this period.

To carry out these governmental activities, the bureaucracy expanded constantly in the 1790s. Mercier wrote of these men: "Never has bureaucracy been brought to so exaggerated a point . . . Never has business so languished since the creation of this army of clerks who are to work what valets are to service." He claims this mob of clerks not only "troubled the civic order but demoralized the administration." For him, all these men produced was a mountain of paper:

> An Indian recently come to Paris, whose affairs brought him to a minister's office, struck by these pyramids of circulars which overwhelm the bureaux, did not hesitate to affirm that a single secretary general of the ministry uses more paper in one day than his country uses in an entire year.[45]

THE RIGHTS OF WOMAN

Mary Wollstonecraft's *A Vindication of the Rights of Woman* (1792) laid out the foundation for modern feminism—the belief, as Betty Friedan once put it, that a woman is a human being. Wollstonecraft belonged to radical political circles in England; she had already published an attack on Edmund Burke's *Reflections*, titled *A Vindication of The Rights of Man*. That she took her inspiration from the Revolutionary moment is abundantly clear; *The Rights of Woman* begins with a letter sent to Charles Maurice de Talleyrand, former bishop of Autun, who headed the educational sub-committee of the Constitutional Committee of the Constituent Assembly. Talleyrand had recommended universal state-run education for boys. Wollstonecraft begins by questioning the exclusion of girls from serious education and moves from that opening premise to a ringing avowal of equal rights for women. Before turning to a brief passage from her letter to Talleyrand, it should be noted that several of the male Revolutionary leaders supported rights for women. Condorcet believed women should vote and have full civic rights; Tom Paine, the great Anglo-American pamphleteerist, and a deputy to the Convention, agreed. Even though Condorcet and Paine both sat on the Constitutional Committee of the Convention (the former effectively chaired it), they could not get their principles incorporated into the text they reported out.

To M. Talleyrand-Périgord,

Having read with great pleasure a pamphlet which you have lately published [on compulsory education in France], I dedicate this volume to you, to induce you to reconsider the subject, and maturely weigh what I have advanced respecting the rights of woman and national education: and I call with the firm tone of humanity; for my arguments, Sir, are dictated by a disinterested

---

The Jacobin dictatorship and the Directory combined to make the key innovations. The Jacobins introduced widespread use of centrally appointed agents to help locally elected administrators in their work. The Directory cleared up the confusion in local administration by eliminating the district councils, who had played a key role under the Jacobins, and by standardizing the use of cantonal level municipalities in the countryside. The enormous demands on local administration throughout the 1790s—central governments sent out hundreds of orders for inquests on population, agriculture, poor relief, industry, conscription, etc.—forced people to develop a much more intimate relationship with the central state. The state now knew much more about each French woman or man than it had ever known before. Napoleon would give final form to many of these new institutions—like secondary schools, and departmental prefects (appointed by the central government to administer the department)—but they developed in earnest in the republican years. The negative side of these local reforms, a side grossly exacerbated by Napoleon, was that they vitiated local democracy.[46]

Liberty, Equality, Property: A Cultural Battle

All of us are equal, but some of us are more equal than others.

Napoleon the pig

(CONTINUED)

spirit—I plead for my sex—not for myself. Independence I have long considered as the grand blessing of life, the basis of every virtue—and independence I will ever secure by contracting my wants, though I were to live on a barren heath.

It is then an affection for the whole human race that makes my pen dart rapidly along to support what I believe to be the cause of virtue: and the same motive leads me earnestly to wish to see woman placed in a station in which she would advance, instead of retarding, the progress of those glorious principles that give a substance to morality. My opinion, indeed, respecting the rights and duties of woman, seems to flow so naturally from these simple principles, that I think it scarcely possible, but that some of the enlarged minds who formed your admirable constitution, will coincide with me. . . .

Contending for the rights of woman, my main argument is built on this simple principle, that if she be not prepared by education to become the companion of man, she will stop the progress of knowledge and virtue, for truth must be common to all, or it will be inefficacious with respect to its influence on general practice. . . .

Consider, I address you as a legislator, whether, when men contend for their freedom, and to be allowed to judge for themselves respecting their own happiness, it be not inconsistent and unjust to subjugate women, even though you firmly believe that you are acting in the manner best calculated to promote their happiness? Who made man the exclusive judge, if woman partake with him the gift of reason? . . .

But, if women are to be excluded, without having a voice, from a participation of the natural rights of mankind, prove first, to ward off the charge of injustice and inconsistency, that they want reason—else this flaw in your New Constitution will ever shew that man must, in some shape, act like a tyrant, and tyranny, in whatever part of society it rears its brazen front, will ever undermine morality.[47]

Since the time of the French Revolution, all states of the Europeanized world have struggled with the conflict between liberty and property. For many years the Paris Métro had first- and second-class cars, clear recognition of the Orwellian principle of unequal equality.[48] As Boissy d'Anglas's remarks (cited previously) make clear, those who wrote the Constitution of 1795 would certainly have agreed with Napoleon the pig. Much as we dislike admitting it, our contemporary societies essentially agree. Even today, those with property have effective rights that those without much property lack, as they have had in virtually all human societies.

That sad fact, however, should not hide the remarkable reality of the first half of the statement: that all of us are equal. The French Revolution enshrined that principle forever in the hearts of France's people. As the spread of France's tri-colored flag has subsequently proven, the principle spread eventually throughout the Europeanized world.[49] Even Napoleon, when he wanted to change the constitution of France, held a plebiscite to do so. The Directory repudiated the "anarchic" democracy of the Jacobin ascendancy and restored the severe social divisions of earlier times, but it could not completely destroy the democratic impulse.

The revival of trade led to a revival of many other aspects of Parisian life. People could now seek out luxury goods again. Wigmakers, put out of work by the fashion shift of the radical period, could now get out of politics and get back to work. Jewelers, clothiers—everyone involved in furnishing goods to the upscale population—

had a tremendous revival of business. Even the gambling tables made a comeback in the Palais Royal. Yet they, too, felt the democratic impulse. In sharp contrast to the profile of arrested Ancien Régime gamblers, more than a quarter of those arrested at the gambling dens during the Directory came from the artisan world: shoemakers, coachmen, gardeners, clerks, and many other lower-class men.

One group initially serving only the rich, but soon providing for a more democratic clientele, sparked a revival that has echoes in our own day: restauranteurs. The outbreak of Revolution coincided with the rise of the restaurant in Paris. In the 1780s, *restaurateurs* had begun to shift from their traditional craft—providing restorative soups to customers—to making full meals. Gouverneur Morris's diary speaks constantly of going to the restaurants, and he lists establishments of quite varied quality. The deputies and those with business to do with them provided a steady clientele for the establishments that quickly sprung up around the Palais Royal. Chefs of the great princes, whose patrons had fled France, opened up fashionable restaurants inside the Palais Royal or on adjoining streets. Antoine Beauvilliers, author of *The Art of the Chef* (1814), former chef of the count of Provence (Louis XVI's brother), started the trend before the Revolution. Once it broke out, he was joined in the Palais Royal district by Méot, the ex-chef of the prince of Condé; Robert, who had also worked for Condé; and the so-called Provençal Brothers, who had worked for the prince of Conti. They introduced the cooking of their native Provence to Paris: *brandade* and *bouillabaise* soon became all the rage.[50] If you did not want Provençal fare, then cooking from other regions of France was available. Those inclined to international cuisine could choose from English beefsteak, German sauerkraut, Spanish garbanzos or peppered ham from Xerica, Italian macaroni, polenta, or ices, Russian caviar and smoked eel, Indian rice or curry, American potatoes, chocolate, and pineapples, to cite only a few choices. Mercier describes one of the more outrageous establishments:

> There, one dines Oriental style; but the greedy never enter there. These pleasures are only for the prodigal, but he will find there on certain days all the pomp and bizarreness of the feast of Trimalcion [a Roman hedonist]. At a certain signal, the ceiling opens up and columned floats, guided by a Venus, descend from the sky; sometimes it's Aurora [goddess of the dawn], sometime it's Diana [goddess of the hunt] who comes to seek her dear Endymion. All of them are dressed as goddesses. The connoisseurs make their pick and the divinities, not of Olympus but of the ceiling, join up with their mortals.[51]

Beauvilliers trained the greatest chef of the age, the man who would, more than any other, be responsible for the rise of French *haute cuisine* in the nineteenth century: Antonin Carême. He began as a pastry chef for Beauvilliers but later developed into the most famous chef in the world, working for Tsar Alexander; George IV of England; Talleyrand; and the richest banker of the age, the baron Rothschild.

Carême would later publish several key books of modern cookery; his manuals on pastry became the bible of the new breed of pastrymakers who sprang up in nineteenth-century Paris. He belonged to that world of the Palais Royal under the Directory that reestablished Paris as a luxury capital of the world. The dozen or so famous restaurants of that enclave are all gone, save one. Today, the wealthy tourist can still eat at the Grand Vefour, in the Galerie de Beaujolais of the Palais Royal. With luck, he or she can reserve the table often occupied by a famous eighteenth-century customer, that same Napoleon Bonaparte who brought the Republic, and the Revolution, to a close. The rest of us, like the vast majority of Paris's population under the Directory, have to be satisfied with looking in the window.

New Definitions

The French language has conquered the esteem of Europe and for more than a century has been the classic language there. . . . But that idiom, admitted in political transactions, used in several cities of Germany, Italy, the Low Countries, in a part of the pays of Liège, of Luxembourg, and of Switzerland, even in Canada and on the banks of the Mississippi, by what fate is it still ignored by the great part of the French people?[52]

Report on Public Instruction, made to the Convention (1794)

The French Revolution redefined the meaning of ordinary words and created new words of its own, to describe a world unlike any that had existed before. "Monsieur" and "Madame," once reserved for the nobility, became the property of all urban dwellers, from the humblest artisan to the richest banker. Common names had to be abandoned. Six thousand French towns and villages tried to change their names under the First Republic; Parisians renamed fourteen hundred streets.[53] The more radical militants, such as the *sans-culottes* of Paris, wanted to abolish the use of the polite form of you (*vous*), which traditionally expressed unequal relationships: the powerful addressed the weak as *tu*, the latter responded with *vous*. Even in contemporary France, one's attitude toward the *vous/tu* distinction invariably reflects one's political leanings (the Left prefers *tu*). Most critically, as the *Report on Public Instruction* makes evident, the French language itself became the symbol of freedom. Local languages—dialects, regional variations of French, and distinct languages (Breton, Basque, etc.)—became *de facto* symbols of ignorance, backwardness, and reaction. French republicanism stood for the French language, and its culture. That sense of cultural superiority provided an important impetus both to the homogenization of the cultures of French territory and to later imperialism.

The democratic culture of the Revolution extended into many aspects of daily life. As the modern business suit attests, the clothing of working men (those without culottes) became the model for the clothing of all men at work. Women's fashions rejected the excesses of the final days of Versailles: out went the outrageous wigs, the deeply cut necklines, the wild hoop skirts; in came simple dresses, flattened hairdos, and demure bonnets. The Directory led fashion back in the direction of the scandalous and the excessive, but women's clothing, like men's, gradually became more utilitarian.[54]

Les Tricoteuses Jacobines, ou de Robespierre.
Elles étoient un grand nombre à qui l'on donnoit
40 Sols par jour pour aller dans la tribune des Jacobins
applaudir les motions révolutionnaires.
An 2.

JACOBIN *vociférant une*
Motion à la Tribune.

LE BONET ROUGE.
Beaucoup de Citoyens craignans d'être dénoncés comme
Modérés s'affublent du Bonet rouge!
Les femmes rient de voir leur mari si drôlement coiffés.

Patriotic Jacobin supporters, dressed in the style of 1793 to 1794: simple trousers or dress, and the red bonnet of the Revolution.

SOURCE: Musée Carnavalet.

Women kept other disabilities, too. They did not get real legal equality from the Revolution, although the First Republic treated them far better than Napoleon or his nineteenth-century successors would do. Women bring us back to our original questions: Who are the French? What is France? How did the Revolution change the answers to those questions? No one could deny that a woman, "born and domiciled in France" (to use the constitutional phrase describing male citizens), was "French." She was, after a fashion, a citizen. In many instances, she received the same legal rights and protections as a man. Yet she was not really a citizen, as she had no right to vote or to participate in political life. The state would rely on her to raise good citizens (her sons) and to be a good republican mother, but she had no role in public politics.

As Wollstonecraft suggested, "tyranny, in whatever part of society it rears its brazen front, will ever undermine morality." The Republic, to its credit, never retreated from the Jacobin abolition of slavery, but public opinion still tolerated slavery, which Napoleon reintroduced soon after he took power. The Republic encouraged a tremendous exchange of populations within Europe. Something like 200,000 people fled France. Many nobles, of course, left between 1789 and 1792, but most of the emigrants came from the ordinary mass of the population. Tens of thousands of others moved into France: some of them, like Anarchasis Cloots (from Germany) or Tom Paine or Benjamin Constant (a Swiss), played important roles in French political and intellectual life. Napoleon Bonaparte, soon to be Emperor, came from Corsica, which had been annexed by France only a few years before his birth. Culturally, Corsica, and Bonaparte, had much closer ties to Italy than to France.

The Palais Royal under the Directory. Fashions have not returned to the excesses of the 1780s, but the simple clothing of the Jacobins had given way to much more stylish, and expensive garb. The Palais Royal was filled with restaurants and other forms of entertainment.

Source: Bibliothèque Nationale, Estampes, coll. Destailleur, n. 1012.

Bonaparte offers a superb example of the Revolutionary transformation. He became French, through the schools of the Ancien Régime, because he accepted French culture. The Ancien Régime long followed such a policy, although its application lacked consistency. The Revolution made explicit what had long been implicit: those who accepted French culture could be French citizens. No group better illustrates this principle than the Jews. The Constituent Assembly immediately offered citizenship to the assimilated Jews of Bordeaux and the great ports; they hesitated to allow the Ashkenazic Jews of eastern France, who had not assimilated, the full rights of citizens. In the end, the decoupling of the Church and the State made it possible to allow Alsatian Jews to remain religious Jews, yet to become French citizens. Like all privileged groups, they had merely to "swear the civic oath which will be regarded as a renunciation of all the privileges and exceptions introduced previously in their favor" (Decree of 27 September 1791).

The occupation of areas near France—Belgium, the left bank of the Rhine, parts of Savoy, the county of Nice, Geneva, Mulhouse, Luxembourg—raised thorny questions about what was France and who were the French. The various French governments treated all these regions as part of France: they got their own departments, elected representatives to the legislature, paid regular French taxes. Their citizens were "French." Yet many contemporaries took a dim view of some of the annexations: Carnot strongly opposed the incorporation of the left bank of the Rhine, on the grounds that the German population rejected a direct tie to France. France had already done precisely the same thing in Alsace and the German-speaking parts of Lorraine, but the Revolution changed the meaning of such boundary alteration. The Constituent Assembly had specifically renounced wars of conquest, yet the Convention conveniently circumvented this legality by harkening back to the boundaries of Roman Gaul as the "natural" frontiers of France.

Already in January 1793, Danton declared: "The limits of France are marked out by nature. We shall reach them at their four points: at the Ocean, at the Rhine, at the Alps, at the Pyrenees."[55] Danton's "France" thus brought back the lands of the Salian Franks, around Cologne, the ancient capital of Charlemagne, at Aachen, and even Xanten, which the *Song of Roland* had marked out as the boundary of Francia in the twelfth century. Popular culture had long tied the French to ancient Gaul, and thus adopted the Rhine as France's "natural" frontier. The Revolutionary government, in this as in so many other matters, responded to a genuine public opinion when it annexed these territories and declared their inhabitants "French."

Their inhabitants had other ideas, which the Revolution strengthened. By giving such strong stimulus to the idea of the "nation," the Revolution abetted the resistance of the non-Francophone areas it tried to take over. The citizens of Koblenz or Cologne felt themselves to be German, not French, and no amount of force or French propaganda was likely to change such feelings, so deeply rooted in the local German culture and so watered by the rising tide of German nationalism.

The Revolution, above all the Jacobin government, also created a new strain of French nationalism. Mme de Staël rightly predicted (1798) that the Revolutionaries had proclaimed a Republic "fifty years before the people's minds were ready for it." Even that Republic (founded in the Revolution of 1848) lasted but four years, not to become permanent until 1879. People's minds *were* ready for the French nation forged in the Revolutionary fires. The hottest fire, that of the Jacobins, democratized society to an extent that demolished all preconceptions of the social order, of social identity, and of national identity. Michelet, nationalist and republican, closed his six-volume history of the Revolution (which ends with Thermidor) with a paean to the Jacobins, because these "great hearts, with their blood, made for us the Fatherland."[56]

Just as the Roman world, in collapsing, allowed a new world to take shape, so, too, the end of the Ancien Régime ushered in a new world. The French Revolution did not stand alone in the earth-shattering events of the late eighteenth century. The creation of the American colossus, the unbinding of the industrial Prometheus, the rise of individualism, of which the Revolution was both a cause and an effect: all fundamentally altered the old world. The new world would move much faster. The Revolution, in that sense, was well ahead of its time, because it moved too fast. In French politics, the nineteenth century largely repeated the Revolution, but took one hundred years instead of ten to do its work.

The Revolution transcends French history, has a beginning but no end, because its fundamental goal, the democratization of human society—through liberty, equality, and fraternity—remains unachieved. Furet, rejecting the Marxist interpretation of the Revolution, felt that it had come to an end, that the journey was over. In a certain way, he thus became the heir of Robespierre, for whom the Revolution was a destination, that same shining city on a hill that has inspired so many revolutionaries and which invariably turns from Emerald City into a watered-down version of the London of *1984's* Oceania.

For Danton, the Revolution never ends, because it is a journey. He makes mistakes, repudiates them, becomes the hero of those who want human society bettered, but human. Just as Nicolas Ruault praised Danton's humanity in the days after his death, so, too, the national secretary of the French Socialist Party, Marcel Debarge, recently commented that "I like Danton because I have always had a weakness for people who live, who screw."[57] So, too, do the French, that ever-changing people who name their streets for the old Terrorist. They believe themselves to be the people made by the Revolution: to be those "born and domiciled in France," in whose nation of equal citizens the sovereignty resides; to be those whose fraternal unity grew out of Jacobin democracy; and to be those whose liberty demands the skepticism of Danton, rather than the certainty of Robespierre. They have learned that unified sovereignty, combined with such certainty, provides as great a threat to liberty as the old tyrannies. They have learned that the exclusionist principle, imbedded even in the word "fraternity," with its implicit exclusion of women, invariably destroys the greatness of a nation. Their heroes, like Danton or Henry IV, are lovers of life, in all its messiness, in all its contradictions.

France of the eight hundred-year Capetian monarchy, France of the Revolution, France of human rights and human wrongs, "a hundred, a thousand different Frances of long ago, yesterday or today": all of them live on, their places of memory haunting the human landscape, reminding us that every people, like the French, creates itself, and that the boundaries of every human space, of every France, are a human creation. In defining the "heroes of yesteryear," human societies define their present by means of their past. They name their streets, buildings, public spaces for those heroes, hoping thus, by means of fixing names to seemingly permanent structures, to use the past to define a future when all that will be left of our physical world, as of that of our ancestors, will be such structures.

The Ancien Régime and the Revolution reveal to us the illusion of such thinking. All over France, the physical evidence of the Ancien Régime survives—in churches, palaces, castles, even in place names. The Revolution's legacy lives on in another way, in the hearts and minds of the French people, for whom the revolutionary ideals of liberty, equality, fraternity have become the defining qualities of their human society. They have become, in a word, France.

Notes

1. Cited in M.-H. Huet, *Mourning Glory. The Will of the French Revolution* (Philadelphia: University of Pennsylvania Press, 1997), 149.

2. B. Baczko, "L'expérience thermidorienne," in *The French Revolution and the Creation of Modern Political Culture. V. 2: The Political Culture of the French Revolution,* ed. C. Lucas (Oxford, New York: Permamon Press, 1987), 367. My translation.

3. N. Ruault, *Gazette d'un parisien sous la Révolution. Lettres à son frère. 1783–1796,* ed. A. Vassal and C. Rimbaud (Paris: Librairie Académique Perrin, 1976), 368.

4. This figure, if accurate, suggests that about five thousand people got paid to attend each evening session, if the sessions met (as officially authorized) three times every ten days. The sectional militants, who had met nightly until forbidden to do so in September 1793, often continued relatively permanent sessions in sectional societies, but these had neither government sanction nor subsidy.

5. White was the color of the royalists, hence the name. Let it be noted that the officials who carried out the White Terror were *not* royalists, but republicans, often Girondins.

6. Sutherland, *France 1789–1815,* 266.

7. P. Beik, ed., *The French Revolution* (New York: Walker, 1970), 317–318.

8. Cited in W. Sewell, Jr., *Work and Revolution in France. The language of labor from the Old Regime to 1848* (Cambridge, New York: Cambridge University Press, 1980), 129–130.

9. The Council of 250s members had to be over forty, those of the Council of 500 over thirty. The initial Council of 250 was chosen by lot from among the over-forty deputies elected in 1795.

10. Only one of the original thirteen states had universal manhood suffrage in 1787.

11. Malcolm Crook, *Elections in the French Revolution. An apprenticeship in democracy, 1789–1799* (Cambridge: Cambridge University Press, 1996), estimates that the new rules set the electorate at about 5 million men, perhaps 15 to 20 percent higher than in 1791.

12. D. Woronoff, *The Thermidorian Regime and the Directory 1794–1799,* tr. J. Jackson (Cambridge: Cambridge University Press, 1983; Paris: Editions du Seuil, 1972), and many other surveys suggest a total number of electors of about thirty thousand. Here, as in the earlier discussions on eligible electors in 1791, I am relying on the recent work of two historians, Malcolm Crook and Mel Edelstein, which has conclusively demonstrated that the disenfranchisement clauses eliminated far fewer people than we had thought.

13. Ruault, *Gazette,* 382. Ruault suggests to his brother that they buy a little piece of land and "find a little retreat . . . in this very turbulent Republic."

14. Text of Boissy d'Anglas's speech in Beik, *French Revolution,* 313–324. I have modified his translation of the final phrase.

15. Virtually all members of elite society accepted this principle, whether in France, Great Britain, or the United States. Different systems used different mechanisms to achieve the same end: some American state legislatures, for example, did not give their deputies a salary, making sure that only those of independent means could serve.

16. Ménétra, *Journal of My Life,* 222–223. The translator has here chosen the word "slanderers" where a literal translation would be denunciators.

17. Ruault, *Gazette,* 378–339, letter of 6 May 1795 (16 Floréal) Year III.

18. Ménétra's *Journal* (232–233) recounts his participation, and that of many armed Guardsmen from his section.

19. Cited in J. Bart, *La Révolution française en Bourgogne* (Clermont-Ferrand: La Française d'Édition et d'Imprimerie, 1996), 277.

20. The chronology of military and diplomatic events appears in the following text.

21. Mercier, *Le nouveau Paris,* 467.

22. I. Woloch, *The New Regime. Transformations of the French Civic Order, 1789–1820s* (New York: Norton, 1994).

23. Guittard's contribution of 237 *livres* would place him slightly above the median: roughly 30 percent of those imposed paid 100 *livres* or less, 39 percent between 100 and 999 *livres,* and the final 31 percent more than 1,000 *livres.* The forced loan gave a personal exemption as well as exemptions for each family member, so that the poor rarely had to pay.

24. Ruault, *Gazette,* 395.

25. Mercier, *Le nouveau Paris,* 471.

26. These decrees also made the Convention's deputies eligible to serve again as legislators, except for sixty-five Jacobin deputies, who were banned from re-election. Neither Guittard nor any other source known to me mentions opposition to these clauses.

27. In addition, the government named nineteen *conventionnels* to represent Corsica, then occupied by the English.

28. Crook's statistics suggest remarkable local variations: percentage turnout declined overall, but it ranged from 46 percent in the Doubs down to 6 percent in Charente-Inférieur.

29. The two new Directors were Philippe Merlin de Douai and François de Neufchâteau, who took over primary responsibility for the economy.

30. Here I am relying on the figures cited by Sutherland, *France 1789–1815,* 305.

31. As noted above, these fluctuations varied sharply from area to area: the number of eligibles dropped sharply in the departments around Toulouse and Châlons-sur-Marne.

32. Guittard's pro-Church views, which permeate his *Journal,* make him a somewhat biased witness on this issue, but a majority of French people certainly shared his views on the calendar and the rhythm of everyday life.

33. Mercier, *Le nouveau Paris,* 381.

34. Saint-Just and other Jacobin leaders had supported the free market in 1793.

35. Mercier, *Le nouveau Paris,* 465. He refers both to the latrines and to the prostitution, gambling, and government corruption taking place in the Palais Royal.

36. Cited in F. Furet, *Revolutionary France, 1770–1880,* trans. A. Nevill (Oxford: Basil Blackwell, 1992; Paris: Hachette, 1988), 208.

37. Negotiators from France and the Holy Roman Empire did not create a legal basis for annexation until April 1798, at the Congress of Rastadt, but the French government created four departments in the Rhineland in January 1798 and afterwards treated the area as part of France.

38. Even Napoleon, who began as an artillery officer and usually made effective use of his cannons, believed in the bayonet. This tactical commitment to the bayonet partly explains the extraordinarily high level of casualties in Napoleonic battles.

39. Cited in J. Godechot, "Le 'drainage' des ressources des pays occupés," in *L'État de la France pendant la Révolution (1789–1799),* ed. M. Vovelle (Paris: Éditions la Découverte, 1988), 317.

40. F. Furet, "Bonaparte," in Furet and Ozouf, *Dictionnaire Critique,* 219–220.

41. Bonaparte returned to Italy in 1800, defeating the Austrians at Marengo. Other French successes led to a new treaty, at Lunéville, essentially the same as Campo Formio.

42. Lynn Hunt has dissected the implications of this substitution of Hercules for Marianne within the larger context of Jacobin misogyny. See *Politics, Culture, and Class in the French Revolution* (Berkeley: University of California Press, 1984), esp. Chap. 3.

43. E. Burke and T. Paine, *Reflections on the Revolution in France and The Rights of Man* (Garden City, NY: Anchor Books, 1973), 19–20. This useful paperback, now out of print, contains the full texts of these two fundamental reactions to the French Revolution.

44. Hufton, *Women and Citizenship,* 35.

45. Mercier, *Le Nouveau Paris,* 453 on paper; 469 on *bureaucratie*—a word actually created in 1793 and made widespread by Mercier himself.

46. In that sense, I would argue that they went against a trend already clear at the end of the Ancien Régime. Village communities seem to have revived their own democratic traditions in the eighteenth century, developing powerful village assemblies. Such assemblies existed in late medieval times and in the sixteenth century, but seem to have become disoriented by the transition to the more powerful central state in the seventeenth century. In the eighteenth century, I believe they revived as an effective mechanism mediating village relations with that state. Alas, for the moment such opinions are mere speculation; we lack systematic research on this vital topic that would enable one to offer stronger conclusions.

47. M. Wollstonecraft, *A Vindication of the Rights of Woman,* ed. C. Poston (New York: Norton, 1975, 1988), 3–5, selections.

48. The RER segment of the Métro just abolished this distinction in December 1999. I would see a difference between such means of long-range transportation as trains and planes and mass transit, provided as a public service.

49. The democratic principle, of course, existed in these other regions long before anyone had heard of the French Revolution. The Atlantic Revolutions—in the

United States, the Netherlands, France, Haiti, and Poland, to cite the most prominent—gave new impulse to such principles in many areas.

50. *Brandade* is creamed cod; *bouillabaise* is a fish stew.

51. Mercier, *Le nouveau Paris,* 431. Endymion was the handsome shepherd whom Diana (also goddess of the moon) observed asleep one night. Taken by his beauty, she descended to Earth to kiss him in his sleep. Endymion has been the subject of many poems, perhaps most famously that of John Keats.

52. B. Deloche and J.-M Leniaud, *La Culture des Sans-Culottes* (Paris: Editions de Paris, Presses de Languedoc, 1989), 259–260.

53. Most of these names reverted back later on.

54. Here one must allow for much wider swings of fashion than in men's clothing. Women's clothing, as the annual Paris fashion shows amply attest, still contains significant elements of the extreme, the ridiculous, and the impractical.

55. Doyle, *Oxford History,* 200.

56. Michelet, *Histoire de France,* v. XVII (Lausanne: Editions Rencontre, 1967), 438.

57. Cited in Huet, *Morning Glory,* 163.

A P P E N D I X

Kings of the Franks/Kings of France

Carolingians

Pepin I, the Short	751–768
Carloman and Charlemagne	768–773
Charlemagne	773–814 (Emperor from 800)
Louis I, the Pious	814–840 (Emperor)
Charles II, the Bald	843–877 (Emperor from 875)
Louis II, the Stammerer	877–879
Louis III	879–882
Carloman	882–884 (brother)
Charles the Fat	884–887 (cousin; Emperor)

(*see Capetian line*)

Charles III, the Simple 893–929
(brother of Carloman; effectively king from the death of the Capetian Eudes, in 898, until 922, when he was captured by Raoul, another Capetian king)

(*see Capetian line*)

Louis IV d'Outre Mer	936–954
Lothaire	954–986
Louis V	986–987

Charles of Lorraine, younger brother of Lothaire, received election as king from some barons in 987 but he lost a civil war to Hugh Capet, and is usually not counted among the Kings of France.

Capetians

Beginning with Hugh Capet, the Capetians passed the throne from father to son until Louis X. In those cases in which the throne did not pass to the king's son, I have indicated the relationship in the male line (which alone counted toward inheritance of the throne) between the king and his successor. In the cases of a shift outside the immediate family, I have also indicated the identity of the wife of the new king.

Eudes I 888–898
(*see Carolingian line*)
Robert I 922–923 (brother of Eudes)
Raoul 923–936 (son-in-law of Robert)
(*see Carolingian line*)

Hugh Capet	987–996 (grandson of Robert)
Robert I	996–1031
Henry I	1031–1060
Philip I	1060–1108
Louis VI	1108–1137
Louis VII	1137–1180
Philip II, Augustus	1180–1223
Louis VIII	1223–1226
Louis IX, Saint Louis	1226–1270
Regency: Blanche of Castile	1226–1234 (minority)
	1248–1254 (Crusade)
Philip III	1270–1285
Philip IV, the Fair	1285–1314
Louis X	1314–1316 (brother)
John I	1316 (five days)
Philip V	1316–1322 (brother of Louis X)
Charles IV	1322–1328 (brother)

Valois Branch of Capetians

Philip VI	1328–1350 (grandson of Philip III)
John II	1350–1364
Charles V	1364–1380
Charles VI	1380–1422
Regency: Dukes of Anjou, Berry, Burgundy (uncles)	1380–1382 (minority)
Charles VII	1422–1461
Louis XI	1461–1483
Charles VIII	1483–1498
Regency: Anne of Beaujeu (sister)	1483–1485 (minority)

Orléans Branch of Valois

Louis XII	1498–1514

(cousin; married to Charles VIII's sister; divorced her to marry Charles VIII's widow, Anne of Brittany)

Angoulême Branch of Valois

Francis I	1515–1547

(cousin; married Renée of Brittany, daughter of Louis XII and Anne of Brittany)

Henry II	1547–1559
Francis II	1559–1560
Charles IX	1560–1574 (brother)
Regency: Catherine de Médicis (mother)	1560–1564 (minority)
Henry III	1574–1589 (brother)

Bourbon Branch of Capetians (male descent from Robert of Clermont, son of Louis IX; female descent from Marguerite d'Angoulême, sister of Francis I)

Henry IV	1589–1610
(very distant cousin in male line; married to sister of Henry III, Marguerite de Valois; divorced her and later married Marie de Médicis)	
Louis XIII	1610–1643
Regency: Marie de Médicis (mother)	1610–1614 (minority)
Louis XIV	1643–1715
Regency: Anne of Austria (mother)	1643–1653 (minority)
Louis XV	1715–1774 (great-grandson)
Regency: Philip of Orléans (senior Prince of the Blood; first cousin of king's grandfather)	1715–1723 (minority)
Louis XVI	1774–1792 (grandson)

BIBLIOGRAPHY

A work of this length requires far more reading than one can put down in a bibliography whose aim is to assist readers in getting started with a more detailed look at French history. I have divided the bibliography into three sections: 500 to 1490; 1490 to 1750; and 1750 to 1799. The list focuses on English-language literature. I have cited some of the most important French books, particularly those that treat a subject not adequately discussed in English. I have not listed the archival sources I have used, some of which are cited in the footnotes, because such a list makes no sense in a synthetical book such as this one. I urge readers to look at the bibliographies of these selected works in order to obtain more detailed and specialized lists of books and articles.

Allow me first to cite a few works that treat the general history of France. All synthetic views of French history begin with the works of the great nineteenth-century historians, above all Jules Michelet, *Histoire de France,* published in the middle of the century, and Ernst Lavisse, who edited a fourteen-volume *Histoire de France,* published at the end of the nineteenth and beginning of the twentieth century. I would cite these additional recent syntheses:

J. Marseille, *Nouvelle Histoire de la France.* Paris: Perrin, 1999.

A. Burgière and J. Revel, eds., *Histoire de la France. L'État et les pouvoirs.* Paris: Seuil, 1989.

The five-volume *Histoire de France* originally done for Hachette, now translated into English, the relevant volumes in English are:

G. Duby, *France in the Middle Ages, 987–1460: From Hugh Capet to Joan of Arc,* trans., J. Vale. Oxford and Cambridge, MA: Basil Blackwell, 1991.

E. Le Roy Ladurie, *The French Royal State, 1460–1610,* trans. J. Vale. Oxford and Cambridge, MA: Basil Blackwell, 1994.

E. Le Roy Ladurie, *The Ancien Régime, 1610–1774,* trans. M. Greengrass. Oxford and Cambridge, MA: Basil Blackwell, 1996.

F. Furet, *Revolutionary France, 1770–1880,* trans. A. Nevill. Oxford and Cambridge, MA: Basil Blackwell, 1992.

J. Bart, *Histoire du droit privé: de la chute de l'Empire romain au XIXe siècle.* Paris: Éd. Montchrestion, 1998.

C. Jones, *The Cambridge Illustrated History of France.* Cambridge and New York: Cambridge University Press, 1994.

P. Nora et alia, *Les Lieux de Mémoire.* Paris: Gallimard, 1986, 3 vols. In English as: *Realms of Memory,* trans. A. Goldhammer. New York: Columbia University Press, 1996, 3 vols.

In addition to the general works, we have six important multiauthored collections that deal with specific aspects of French history:

Histoire économique et sociale de la France, ed. F. Braudel and E. Labrousse. Paris: PUF, 1970–1982, 4 vols.

Histoire de la France religieuse, ed. J. Le Goff and R. Rémond. Paris: Seuil, 1988, 4 vols.

Histoire de la France rurale. Multiple editors. Paris: Seuil, 1975–1976, 4 vols.

Histoire de la France urbaine, ed. G. Duby. Paris: Seuil, 1980–1985, 5 vols.

Histoire militaire de la France, ed. A. Blanchard et alia. Paris: PUF, 1992–1994, 4 vols.

A History of Private Life, ed. P. Ariès and G. Duby. Cambridge, MA: Belknap Press of Harvard University Press, 1987–1991, 5 vols.

∾ Section I: 500–1490

Primary Sources

Many of these texts are available in multiple translations and editions. I have listed here the edition most easily available, typically the Penguin paperback edition. I have excluded from this list works of great literature not cited in the footnotes. The best French-language editions of authors such as Corneille or Molière are usually those of Gallimard, the so-called Pléiade editions.

P. Abelard and Heloise, *The Letters of Abelard and Heloise,* trans. B. Radice. London and New York: Penguin Books, 1974.

Anna Comnena, *The Alexiad.* trans. E. R. A. Sewter. Baltimore: Penguin, 1969.

Arab Historians of the Crusades, trans. F. Gabrieli, E. J. Costello. Berkeley: University of California Press, 1969.

Aristotle, *The Politics,* trans. B. Jowett, ed. S. Everson. Cambridge and New York: Cambridge University Press, 1988.

Einhard, *The Life of Charlemagne,* trans. S. Turner, ed. S. Painter. Ann Arbor, MI: University of Michigan Press, 1960, 1972.

J. Froissart, *Chronicles by Froissart,* trans. and ed. G. Brereton. Harmondsworth: Penguin, 1968.

Fulcher of Chartres, *Chronicle of the First Crusade,* trans. M. McGinty. Philadelphia: University of Pennsylvania Press, 1941, 1978.

P. Geary, ed., *Readings in Medieval History.* Peterborough, ONT; Lewiston: Broadview Press, 1989, 1991.

Gesta Francorum et aliorum Hierosolimitanorum: The Deeds of the Franks and the Other Pilgrims to Jerusalem, ed., R. Hill. London: Thomas Nelson and Sons, 1962.

Gregory of Tours, *The History of the Franks,* trans. L. Thorpe. London and New York: Penguin, 1974.

Ibn al-Qal-anis-i, *The Damascus Chronicle of the Crusades.* trans. H. A. R. Gibb. London: Luzac and Co., 1967.

Jerusalem Pilgrimage 1099–1185, ed. J. Wilkinson, J. Hill, and W. Ryan. London: Hakluyt Society, 1988.

Joinville and Villehardouin, *Chronicles of the Crusades,* trans. M. Shaw. Baltimore: Penguin, 1963.

J. Kirshner and K. Morrison, eds., *Readings in Western Civilization, V. 4: Medieval Europe.* Chicago: University of Chicago Press, 1986.

Guillaume de Lorris and Jean de Meun, *Le Roman de la Rose,* ed. F. Lecoy. Paris: Honoré Champion, 1983, 1982, 1973, three vols.

_____, *The Romance of the Rose,* trans. C. Dahlberg. Princeton: Princeton University Press, 1971.

Odo of Deuil, *De profectione Ludovici VII in orientem. The Journey of Louis VII to the East,* trans. V. Berry. New York: Norton, 1965.

A Parisian Journal, 1405–1449, ed. and trans. J. Shirley. Oxford: Clarendon Press, 1968.

Christine de Pisan, *The Book of the Body Politic,* ed. and trans. K. L. Forhan. Cambridge and New York: Cambridge University Press, 1994.

_____, *The Book of the City of Ladies,* trans. E. Richards. New York: Persea Books, 1982.

_____, *The Writings of Christine de Pizan,* ed. C. C. Willard. New York: Persea Books, 1994.

Sidonius Apollinaris, *Poems and Letters,* trans. W. B. Anderson. Cambridge, MA: Harvard University Press, 1936, two vols.

The Song of Roland, trans. G. Burgess. London, New York: Penguin, 1990.

Suger, Abbot of Saint-Denis, *The Deeds of Louis the Fat,* trans. R. Cusimano and J. Moorhead. Washington, DC: Catholic University of America Press, 1992.

Two Lives of Charlemagne, ed. L. Thorpe. Harmondsworth: Penguin, 1969. This text contains both Einhard's life of Charlemagne and that of Notker the Stammerer.

François Villon, *The Poems of François Villon,* trans. G. Kinnell, Hanover: University Press of New England, 1982.

_____, *Œuvres,* ed. J. Dufournet. Paris: Garnier Frères, 1970.

General Works

M. Bloch, *Mélanges historiques.* Paris: EHESS, 1963, 1983.

The Cambridge Medieval History and *The New Cambridge Medieval History.*

R. Dion, *Histoire de la vigne et du vin en France des origins au XIXe siècle.* Paris: Dion, 1959; Flammarion, 1977.

J. Dunbabin, *France in the Making 843–1180.* Oxford and New York: Oxford University Press, 1983.

O. Guillot, A. Rigaudière, and Y. Sassier, *Pouvoirs et Institutions dans la France Médiévale. Des origines à l'époque féodale.* Paris: Armand Colin, 1994, two vols.

E. Hallam, *Capetian France, 987–1328.* London and New York: Longman, 1980.

D. Miller, ed., *The Lewis Mumford Reader.* New York: Pantheon, 1986.

J. Mundy, *Europe in the High Middle Ages, 1150–1309.* New York: Basic Books, 1973.

A. Murray, ed., *After Rome's Fall: Narrators and Sources of Early Medieval History: Essays presented to Walter Goffart.* Toronto: University of Toronto Press, 1998.

Nouvelle histoire de Paris. Paris: Hachette, since 1971. There are twenty volumes in this collection, including two separate ones on Paris during the Revolution.

H. Pirenne, *Histoire de Belgique*, vols. 1–3. Brussels: Maurice Lamertin, 1922.

Chapter 1

W. Davies, *Small Worlds: The Village Community in Early Medieval Brittany.* Berkeley: University of California Press, 1988.

J. Favier, *Charlemagne.* Paris: Fayard, 1999.

P. Fouracre and R. Gerberding, *Late Merovingian France. History and Hagiography, 640–720.* New York and Manchester: Manchester University Press, 1996.

P. Geary, *Before France and Germany: The Creation and Transformation of the Merovingian World.* New York: Oxford University Press, 1988.

R. Gerberding, *The Rise of the Carolingians and the* Liber Historiae Francorum. Oxford: Clarendon Press, 1987.

D. H. Green, *Language and History in the Early Germanic World.* Cambridge: Cambridge University Press, 1998.

J. Heuclin, *Hommes de Dieu et fonctionnaires du roi en Gaule du Nord du Ve au IXe siècle (348–817).* Paris: Presses Universitaires du Septentrion, 1998.

M. Innes, *State and Society in the Early Middle Ages: The Middle Rhine Valley, 400–1000.* Cambridge: Cambridge University Press, 2000.

E. James, *The Origins of France: From Clovis to the Capetians, 500–1000.* New York: St. Martin's Press, 1982.

R. McKitterick, *The Frankish Kingdoms under the Carolingians, 751–987.* London and New York: Longman, 1983. McKitterick has also authored several other important works on the Carolingians, above all on the Carolingian contribution to letters.

R. McKitterick, ed., *Carolingian Culture: Emulation and Innovation.* New York: Cambridge University Press, 1994.

A. Murray, ed., *After Rome's Fall: Narrators and Sources of Early Medieval History: Essays presented to Walter Goffart.* Toronto: University of Toronto Press, 1998.

M. Ruche, *Clovis.* Paris: Fayard, 1996.

J. M. Wallace-Hadrill, *The Frankish Church.* Oxford and New York: The Clarendon Press, 1983.

P. Wells, *The Barbarians Speak: How the Conquered Peoples Shaped Roman Europe.* Princeton: Princeton University Press, 1999.

P. Wolff, *Western Languages, AD 100–1500,* trans. F. Patridge. New York: McGraw-Hill, 1971.

I. Wood, *The Merovingian Kingdoms, 450–751.* London and New York: Longman, 1994.

I. Wood, ed., *Franks and Alamanni in the Merovingian Period: An Ethnographic Perspective.* San Marino: The Boydell Press, 1998.

Chapter 2

D. Barthélemy, *L'an mil et la paix de Dieu: la France chrétienne et féodale, 980–1060.* Paris: Fayard, 1999.

_____, *La société dans le comté de Vendôme, de l'an mil au XIVe siècle.* Paris: Fayard, 1993.

T. Bisson, ed., *Culture of Power: Lordship, Status, and Process in Twelfth-Century Europe.* Philadelphia: University of Pennsylvania Press, 1995.

M. Bloch, *French Rural History: An Essay on Its Basic Characteristics,* trans. J. Sondheimer. Berkeley: University of California Press, 1966; French edition, 1931.

_____, *Feudal Society,* trans. L. Manyon. Chicago: University of Chicago Press, 1961, two vols.

G. Bois, *The Mutation of the Year One Thousand: The Village of Lourmond from Antiquity to Feudalism,* trans. J. Birrell. Manchester and New York: Manchester University Press, 1992.

P. Bonassie, *From Slavery to Freedom in South-Western Europe,* trans. J. Birrell. Cambridge: Cambridge University Press, 1991.

R. Boutruche, *Seigneurie et féodalité.* Paris: Aubier, 1968, 2nd ed.

G. Duby, *The Chivalrous Society,* trans. C. Postan. Berkeley: University of California Press, 1980.

_____, *The Rural Economy and Country Life in the Medieval West,* trans. C. Postan. Columbia, SC, 1968.

_____, *The Three Orders. Feudal Society Imagined,* trans. A. Goldhammer. Chicago: University of Chicago Press, 1980.

_____, *William Marshal, the Flower of Chivalry,* trans. R. Howard. New York: Pantheon, 1985.

T. Evergates, *Feudal Society in the Bailliage of Troyes under the Counts of Champagne, 1152–1284.* Baltimore: Johns Hopkins University Press, 1975.

R. Fossier, *Peasant Life in the Medieval West,* trans. J. Vale. Oxford and New York: Basil Blackwell, 1988. Fossier is the author of other key works, above all his thesis on rural life in medieval Picardy, published in 1968, and the recent *Le travail au Moyen Age*. Paris: Hachette, 2000.

W. Jordan, *From Servitude to Freedom: Manumission in the Sénonais in the Thirteenth Century*. Philadelphia: University of Pennsylvania Press, 1986.

E. Kantorowicz, *The King's Two Bodies: A Study in Mediaeval Political Theology*. Princeton: Princeton University Press, 1957.

S. Reynolds. *Fiefs and Vassals: The Medieval Evidence Reinterpreted*. Oxford: Oxford University Press, 1994.

Y. Sassier, *Hugues Capet: Naissance d'un dynastie*. Paris: Fayard, 1987.

E. Searle, *Predatory Kinship and the Creation of Norman Power, 840–1066*. Berkeley: University of California Press, 1988.

K. F. Werner, *Naissance de la noblesse*. Paris: Fayard, 1998.

Chapters 3–4

J. Baldwin, *The Government of Philip Augustus: Foundations of French Royal Power in the Middle Ages*. Berkeley: University of California Press, 1986.

M. Barber, *The New Knighthood: A History of the Order of the Temple*. Cambridge, New York: Cambridge University Press, 1994.

C. Beaune, *The Birth of an Ideology: Myths and Symbols of Nation in Late-Medieval France,* trans. S. R. Huston; ed. F. L. Chayette. Berkeley: University of California Press, 1991.

M. Bloch, *The Royal Touch: Monarchy and Miracles in France and England,* trans. J. E. Anderson. New York: Dorset Press, 1961, 1989.

G. Bois, *The Crisis of Feudalism: Economy and Society in Eastern Normandy, c. 1300–1550*. Cambridge and New York: Cambridge University Press, 1992; trans. of Paris edition of 1976.

E. A. R. Brown has written many fundamentally important articles that appear in such journals as *Speculum* and *Traditio*.

R. Cazelles, *Étienne Marcel, champion de l'unité française*. Paris: Tallandier, 1984.

_____, *Société politique, noblesse et couronne sous Jean le Bon et Charles V*. Geneva: Droz, 1982. Cazelles's book on political society in the time of Philip of Valois is also insightful.

P. Cole, *The Preaching of the Crusades to the Holy Land, 1095–1270*. Cambridge, MA: Medieval Academy of America, 1991.

P. Contamine, *La noblesse au royaume de France de Philippe le bel a Louis XII*. Paris: PUF, 1997.

_____, *War in the Middle Ages,* trans. M. Jones. Oxford: Basil Blackwell, 1984.

W. Courtenay, *Parisian Scholars in the Early Fourteenth Century: A Social Portrait*. Cambridge: Cambridge University Press, 1999.

G. Duby, *The Age of the Cathedrals: Art and Society, 980–1420,* trans. E. Levieux and B. Thompson. Chicago: University of Chicago Press, 1981, 123.

R. Ellenblum, *Frankish Rural Settlement in the Latin Kingdom of Jerusalem.* Cambridge and New York: Cambridge University Press, 1998.

J. Favier, *François Villon.* Paris: Fayard, 1982. Jean Favier is also the author of many other fine books on French medieval history.

N. Golb, *Les Juifs de Rouen au Moyen Age: Portrait d'une culture oubliée.* Rouen: Publications de l'Université de Rouen, 1985.

J. B. Henneman, *Royal Taxation in Fourteenth Century France: The Development of War Financing, 1322–1356.* Princeton: Princeton University Press, 1971.

Johan Huizinga, *The Autumn of the Middle Ages,* trans. R. Payton and U. Mammitzsch. Chicago: University of Chicago Press, 1996.

W. Jordan, *The French Monarchy and the Jews from Philip Augustus to the Last Capetians.* Philadelphia: University of Pennsylvania Press, 1989.

_____, *Louis IX and the Challenge of the Crusade: A Study in Rulership.* Princeton: Princeton University Press, 1979.

G. Leyte, *Domaine et domanialité publique dans la France médiévale (XIIe–XVe siècles).* Strasbourg: Presses Universitaires de Strasbourg, 1996.

P. Locke, *The Franks in the Aegean.* London and New York: Longman, 1995.

J. Marenbon, *The Philosophy of Peter Abélard.* Cambridge and New York: Cambridge University Press, 1997.

H. Mayer, *The Crusades,* trans. J. Gillingham. Oxford and New York: Oxford University Press, 1988.

J. Mundy, *Men and Women at Toulouse in the Age of the Cathars.* Toronto: Pontifical Institute of Medieval Studies, 1990.

J. Norwich, *Byzantium, The Decline and Fall.* New York: Knopf, 1996.

J. Richard, *Saint Louis: roi d'une France féodale.* Paris: Fayard, 1983.

C. Richter Sherman, *Imaging Aristotle: Verbal and Visual Representation in Fourteenth-Century France.* Berkeley: University of California Press, 1995.

J. Strayer, *The Reign of Philip the Fair.* Princeton: Princeton University Press, 1980. Joseph Strayer has a wide range of books and articles on state building in medieval France; I recommend his other works for anyone interested in the subject.

J. Sumption, *The Albigensian Crusade.* London and Boston: Faber, 1978.

W. TeBrake, *A Plague of Insurrection: Popular Politics and Peasant Revolt in Flanders, 1323–1328.* Philadelphia: University of Pennsylvania Press, 1995.

B. Ketcham Wheaton, *Savoring the Past: The French Kitchen and Table from 1300 to 1789.* Philadelphia: University of Pennsylvania Press, 1983.

SECTION II: 1490–1750

Primary Sources

In addition to the sources listed below, I have made use of the many published volumes of papers and letters of prominent ministers such as Colbert and Mazarin, and the volumes edited by such scholars as P. Boislisle, G. P. Depping, M. Marion, A. Smedley-Weill, and others.

T. Agrippa d'Aubigné, *Œuvres complètes,* ed. E. Réaume de Caussade. Geneva: Slatkine Reprints, 1967.

W. Beik, *Louis XIV and Absolutism: A Brief Study with Documents.* Boston: Bedford/ St. Martin's, 2000.

F. Bertaud (Mme de Motteville), *Memoirs of Madame de Motteville on Anne of Austria and her Court,* ed. C.-A. Saint-Beuve, trans. K. Prescott Wormeley. Boston: Hardy, Pratt & Co., 1901, three vols.

J. Bodin, *Les six livres de la République.* Paris, 1583; reprinted in Geneva, 1967. One should also consult, if possible, the original Paris edition of 1576. The 1606 English translation by Richard Knolles, *The Six Bookes of the Commonweale,* is available in a modern reprint (Harvard, 1962). For a brief taste of Bodin in English, one can turn to Julian Franklin's excellent edition, *On Sovereignty: Four Chapters from Six Books on the Commonwealth* (Cambridge, 1992).

J. Boucher, *La vie de Bayard,* ed. D. Crouzet. Paris: Imprimerie Nationale, 1992.

B. Castiglione, *The Book of the Courtier,* trans G. Bull. Harmandsworth and Baltimore: Penguin Books, 1976

Constitutionalism and Resistance in the Sixteenth Century, ed. J. Franklin. New York: Pegasus, 1969.

R. Descartes, *Discourse on Method and Meditations,* trans. L. Lafleur. Indianapolis, IN: Bobbs Merrill, 1960.

R. Descimon, ed., *Discours pour la majorité de Charles IX et trois autres discours.* Paris: Imprimerie Nationale, 1993.

Elisabeth Charlotte, duchess of Orleans, *A Woman's Life in the Court of the Sun King: The Letters of Liselotte von der Pfalz, 1652–1722,* ed. and trans. E. Forster. Baltimore: Johns Hopkins University Press, 1984.

A. von Harff, *The Pilgrimage of Arnold von Harff,* trans. M. Letts. London and Nendeln: Hakluyt Society, Kraus Reprint Limited, 1946, 1967.

J. Héroard, *Journal de Jean Hérouard,* ed. M. Foisil. Paris: Fayard, 1989, two vols. Héroard was Louis XIII's private physician; this journal is one of our most precious sources of both royal family life and early–modern childhood.

P. Hurault, *Mémoires de Messire Philippe Hurault, comte de Cheverny, Chancelier de France,* in *Collection complète des Mémoires relatifs à l'Histoire de France,* v. XXXVI, ed. M. Petitot. Paris: Foucault, 1819.

L. Labé, *Œuvres complètes,* ed. E. Guidici. Geneva: Droz, 1981.

Louis XIV, *Mémoires for the instruction of the Dauphin,* trans. P. Sonnino. New York: Free Press, 1970.

_____, *Mémoires pour l'instruction du dauphin,* ed., P. Goubert. Paris: Imprimerie Nationale, 1992.

F. de Malherbe, *Œuvres,* ed. A. Adam. Paris: Gallimard, 1971.

M. de Montaigne, *The Complete Works of Montaigne: Essays. Travel Journal. Letters,* trans. D. Frame. Stanford: Stanford University Press, 1958, 1967.

B. de Montluc, *Commentaires.* Paris: Gallimard, 1951.

F. de la Noue, *Mémoires du sieur François de la Noue,* in *Collection complète des mémoires relatifs à l'histoire de France,* v. XXXIV, ed. M. Petitot. Paris: Foucault, 1823.

B. Pascal, *Œuvres Complètes,* ed. L. Lafuma. Paris: Éditions du Seuil, 1963.

F. Platter, *Beloved Son Felix: The Journal of Felix Platter a Medical Student in Montpellier in the Sixteenth Century,* trans. S. Jennett. London: Frederick Muller Limited, 1961.

F. Rabelais, *The Complete Works of François Rabelais,* trans. D. Frame. Berkeley: University of California Press, 1991.

J. Racine, *Œuvres complètes,* ed. L. Estang. Paris: Seuil, 1962.

A. du Plessis, Cardinal Richelieu, *Les papiers de Richelieu,* ed. P. Grillon. Paris: Pedone, 1980–, multiple volumes.

_____, *Testament Politique de Richelieu,* ed. F. Hildesheimer. Paris: Société de l'Histoire de France, 1995. Selections have been translated and edited by H. Hill (Wisconsin, 1961).

P. Ronsard, *Œuvres complètes,* ed. G. Cohen. Paris: Gallimard, 1950.

_____, *Poems of Pierre Ronsard,* trans. N. Kilmer. Berkeley: University of California Press, 1979, bilingual edition.

Le duc de Saint-Simon, *Mémoires,* ed. Y. Coirault. Paris: Gallimard, 1983–88, 8 vols.

Mme. de Sévigné, *Selected Letters,* ed. L. Tancock. London and New York: Penguin, 1982.

G. Tallemant des Réaux, *Les Historiettes,* ed. A. Adam, Paris: Gallimard, 1960–61, two vols.

I have also made extensive use of the many memoirs in the so-called Petitot collection, published in Paris in the early nineteenth century. These editions are not very scholarly and contain many errors, but they are often the only printed version of the memoirs in question. One can see the difference between a modern scholarly edition and the rather loose Petitot approach in the memoirs of the duke of Sully, *Œconomies Royales,* of which all nine volumes are available in the Petitot collection, *Mémoires des sages et royales œconomies d'estat* (Paris, 1819–29), and the first two volumes in the superb modern edition of Bernard Barbiche and Davis Buisseret, *Les œconomies royales de Sully.* Paris: Klincksieck, 1970, 1988.

General Works

The new book of Sharon Kettering, *French Society, 1589–1715* (Harlow: Longman, 2001), reached me as I was putting the finishing touches on the bibliography, so it could not be consulted in the preparation of the text. Interested readers will surely want to read it.

R. Briggs, *Early Modern France, 1560–1715.* Oxford and New York: Oxford University Press, 1977.

R. Chartier, ed., *A History of Private Life, III: Passions of the Renaissance,* trans. A. Goldhammer. Cambridge, MA and London: Belknap Press of Harvard University Press, 1989.

J. Collins, *The State in Early Modern France.* Cambridge: Cambridge University Press, 1995.

A. Croix and J. Quéniart, *Histoire Culturelle de la France, vol. 2. De la Renaissance à l'Aube des Lumières.* Paris: Seuil, 1997.

A. Croix, A. Lespagnol, and G. Provost, eds., *Église, Éducation, Lumières . . . Histoires Culturelles de la France (1500–1830).* Rennes: Presses Universitaires de Rennes, 1999.

J. Delumeau, *Catholicism between Luther and Voltaire.* London: Burns & Oates, 1977; Philadelphia: Westminster Press, 1977; trans. of French edition of 1971. Delumeau has written a wide range of other books examining early–modern religion.

N. Elias, *The Civilizing Process,* trans. E. Jephcott. New York: Urizen, 1978.

_____, *The Court Society,* trans. E. Jephcott. New York: Pantheon, 1983.

M. Foucault, *Discipline and Punish: The Birth of the Prison,* trans. A. Sheridan. New York: Pantheon, 1977.

_____, *Madness and Civilization: A History of Insanity in the Age of Reason,* trans. R. Howard. New York: Pantheon, 1965.

_____, *Les mots et les choses; une archéologie des sciences humaines.* Paris: Gallimard, 1965.

P. Goubert and D. Roche, *Les Français et l'Ancien Régime.* Paris: Armand Colin, 1984, two vols.

J. Habermas, *Structural Transformation of the Public Sphere,* trans. T. Berger. Cambridge, MA: MIT Press, 1989.

P. Haudrère, *L'Empire des Rois, 1500–1789.* Paris: Denail, 1997.

M. Holt, *The French Wars of Religion, 1562–1629.* Cambridge and New York: Cambridge University Press, 1995.

N. Keohane, *Philosophy and the State in France.* Princeton: Princeton University Press, 1980.

R. Jackson, *Vive le Roi!: A History of the French Coronation from Charles V to Charles X.* Chapel Hill, NC: University of North Carolina Press, 1983.

A. Jouanna, *Histoire et dictionnaire des guerres de religion.* Paris: Laffont, 1998.

R. Mandrou, *Des humanistes aux hommes de science (XVIe et XVIIe siècles),* vol. 3 of *Histoire de la pensée européene.* Paris: Seuil, 1973.

B. Quilliet, *La France du Beau XVIe Siècle: 1490–1560.* Paris: Fayard, 1998.

R. and S. Pillorget, *France Baroque, France Classique, 1589–1715.* Paris: R. Laffont, 1995, two vols.

E. Rice, *Foundations of Early–Modern Europe, 1460–1559.* New York: Norton, 1969.

D. van Kley, *The Religious Origins of the French Revolution.* New Haven: Yale University Press, 1996. Van Kley has written several important books on eighteenth-century Jansenism.

Chapters 5–6

Many of the authors listed below have written multiple books; limitations of space make it impossible to list them all, but I would urge readers to use the names provided below as the first step in further bibliographic searches.

D. Lesko Baker, *The Subject of Desire: Petrarchan Poetics and the Female Voice in Louise Labé.* West Lafayette, IN: Purdue University Press, 1996.

F. Baumgartner, *Change and Continuity in the French Episcopate: The Bishops and the Wars of Religion 1547–1610.* Durham: Duke University Press, 1986.

_____, *Henry II.* Durham: Duke University Press, 1988.

B. Bedos-Rezak, *Anne de Montmorency: seigneur de la Renaissance.* Paris: Éditions Publiard, 1990.

P. Benedict, *Rouen during the Wars of Religion.* Cambridge: Cambridge University Press, 1981.

S. Carroll, *Noble Power during the French Wars of Religion.* Cambridge and New York: Cambridge University Press, 1998.

L. Bryant, *The King and the City in Parisian Royal Entry Ceremony.* Geneva: Droz, 1986.

W. Church, *Constitutionalism and Resistance in Sixteenth-Century France.* New York: Octagon, 1941.

D. Crouzet. *Jean Calvin.* Paris: Fayard, 2000.

_____, *Les guerriers de Dieu: la violence au temps des troubles de la réligion, vers 1525–vers 1610.* Seyssel: Champ Vallon, 1990, two vols.

_____, *La nuit de la Saint-Barthélemy: un rêve perdu de la Renaissance.* Paris: Fayard, 1994.

_____, *La sagesse et le malheur: Michel de l'Hôpital, chancelier de France.* Paris: Seyssel, 1998.

N. Z. Davis, *Society and Culture in Early Modern France.* Stanford: Stanford University Press, 1975. Natalie Davis has several other important books and a wide range of articles that are must reading for anyone working on the sixteenth and seventeenth centuries.

R. Descimon and C. Jouhaud, *La France du premier XVIIe siècle, 1594–1661.* Paris: Belin, 1996. Descimon has many fundamental articles, especially on the Catholic League in Paris. They have appeared most often in the journal *Annales E. S. C.*

J. Dewald, *The Formation of a Provincial Nobility: The Magistrates of the Parlement of Rouen, 1499–1610.* Princeton: Princeton University Press, 1980.

B. Diefendorf, *Beneath the Cross: Catholics and Huguenots in Sixteenth-Century Paris.* New York: Oxford University Press, 1991.

J.-F. Dubost, *La France italienne XVIe–XVIIe siècle.* Paris: Aubier, 1997.

J. Franklin, *Jean Bodin and the Rise of Absolutist Theory.* Cambridge: Cambridge University Press, 1973.

R. Giesey, *The Royal Funeral Ceremony in Renaissance France.* Geneva: Droz, 1960.

P. Hamon, *L'argent du roi.* Paris: Comité pour l'histoire économique et financière de la France, 1994. See also his fine book on the financiers, *Messieurs des finances,* published in 1999.

S. Hanley, *The Lit de Justice of the Kings of France.* Princeton: Princeton University Press, 1983.

H. Heller, *Labour, Science and Technology in France, 1500–1620.* Cambridge: Cambridge University Press, 1996.

G. Huppert, *The Style of Paris: Renaissance Origins of the French Enlightenment.* Bloomington, IN: Indiana University Press, 1999.

A. Jouanna, *Le devoir de révolte.* Paris: Fayard, 1988.

S.-H. Kim, *Michel de l'Hôpital: The Vision of a Reformist Chancellor during the French Religious Wars.* Kirksville, MO: Sixteenth Century Journal Publishers, 1997.

R. Kingdon, *Myths about the Saint Bartholomew's Day Massacre.* Cambridge, MA: Harvard University Press, 1988.

R. J. Knecht, *Catherine de' Medici.* New York and London: Longman, 1998.

_____, *Francis I.* Cambridge and New York: Cambridge University Press, 1982.

E. Le Roy Ladurie, *The Beggar and the Professor: A Sixteenth-Century Family Saga,* trans. A. Goldhammer. Chicago and London: University of Chicago Press, 1997.

_____, *Carnival in Romans,* trans. M. Feeney. New York: George Braziller, 1979.

_____, *The Peasants of Languedoc,* trans. J. Day. Urbana, Chicago, London: University of Illinois Press, 1974, 1980. Only the French edition of 1966, *Les paysans de Languedoc,* two vols., contains the full text and the appendices.

J. R. Major, *Representative Government in Early Modern France.* New Haven: Yale University Press, 1980. Major has written a number of other works on the representative institutions of the sixteenth and seventeenth centuries; all are well worth reading.

R. Mandrou, *Introduction to Modern France, 1500–1640. An Essay in Historical Psychology,* trans. R. E. Hallmark. New York: Harper & Row, 1975, 1977.

K. Neuschel, *Word of Honor: Interpreting Noble Culture in Sixteenth-Century France.* Ithaca, NY: Cornell University Press, 1989.

O. Ponçet, *Pomponne de Bellièvre: un homme d'État aux temps des guerres de religion.* Paris: École des Chartes, 1998.

N. Roelker, *One King, One Faith.* Berkeley: University of California Press, 1996.

_____, *Queen of Navarre: Jeanne d'Albret, 1528–1572.* Cambridge, MA: Belknap Press, 1968.

J. M. H. Salmon, *Society in Crisis: France in the Sixteenth Century.* London: Methuen, 1975, 1979. Salmon has edited several other important volumes and published a wide range of books and articles essential to any understanding of early–modern France.

M. Wolfe, *The Conversion of Henri IV.* Cambridge, MA: Harvard University Press, 1993.

J. Wood, *The King's Army.* Cambridge: Cambridge University Press, 1996.

Chapters 7–10

This section, above all chapter ten, relies heavily on local studies done by French and Anglophone scholars. These monographs are highly detailed. In French, one can consult the works of J.-M. Constant (Beauce), P. Bardel (Rouen), G. Cabourdin (Lorraine), P. Deyon (Amiens), G. Frêche (Toulouse), M. Garden (Lyon), P. Goubert (Beauvaisis), J. Meyer (Nantes), M. Morineau (Atlantic trade and many articles on economic history), M. Perrot (Caen), and many others. In English, one has several fine books by Robert Forster, T. Le Goff's excellent study of Vannes, H. Root on Burgundy, F. Ford on Strasbourg, P. Wallace on Colmar, and the specialized works on the criminal justice system by I. Cameron and S. Reinhardt, to cite only a few. The bibliography on the Enlightenment is listed under Section III. Before turning to published work, I would like to acknowledge here the important material I have gleaned from the dissertations of three of my doctoral students: Dr. Sara Chapman, on the Pontchartrain family and clientage under Louis XIV; Dr. Zoë Schneider, on the local court system in Normandy under Louis XIV; and Dr. Karen Taylor, on the school for noble girls at Saint-Cyr. Not only did they provide me with important empirical information about each subject, and with new analytical insights, but their work also led me to important new bibliography.

M. Antoine, *Louis XV.* Paris: Fayard, 1989. Antoine has many other fine books, essential reading for any serious student of eighteenth-century France.

J.-P. Babelon, *Henri IV.* Paris: Fayard, 1982.

B. Barbiche, *Les institutions de la monarchie française à l'époque moderne.* Paris: PUF, 1999.

B. Barbiche and S. Barbiche, *Sully: l'homme et ses fidèles.* Paris: Fayard, 1997.

M.-N. Baudouin-Matuszek, ed., *Marie de Médicis et le Palais du Luxembourg.* Paris: Fondation Septentrion, 1991.

F. Bayard, *Le monde des financiers au XVIIe siècle.* Paris: Flammarion, 1988.

W. Beik, *Absolutism and Society in Seventeenth-Century France.* Cambridge: Cambridge University Press, 1985.

_____, *Urban Protest in Seventeenth Century France.* Cambridge: Cambridge University Press, 1997.

Y.-M. Bercé, *Histoire des Croquants: Étude des soulèvements populaires au XVIIe sièce dans le Sud-Ouest de la France.* Geneva: Droz, 1974, two vols.

J. Bergin, *Cardinal Richelieu: Power and the Pursuit of Wealth.* New Haven: Yale University Press, 1985.

_____, *The Making of the French Episcopate, 1598–1661.* New Haven: Yale University Press, 1996.

P. Bluche, *Louis XIV,* trans. M. Greengrass. Oxford: Basil Blackwell, 1990.

R. Bonney, *Political Change in France under Richelieu and Mazarin.* Oxford: Oxford University Press, 1976. Bonney has written several other important works on state finance.

A. Cabantous, *Les citoyens du large: les identités maritimes en France, XVIIe–XIXe siècle.* Paris: Aubier, 1995.

P. R. Campbell, *Power and Politics in Old Regime France, 1720–1745.* London: Routledge, 1996.

N. Castan, *Justice et répression en Languedoc à l'époque de Lumières.* Paris: Flammarion, 1980.

Y. Castan, *Honnêteté et relations sociales en Languedoc, 1715–1780.* Paris: Plon, 1974.

R. Chartier, *The Cultural Uses of Print in Early Modern France,* trans. L. Cochrane. Princeton: Princeton University Press, 1987.

L. Châtellier, *La religion des pauvres: Les sources du christianisme moderne, XVIe–XIXe siècles.* Paris: Aubier, 1993.

P. Chevalier, *Louis XIII: Roi Cornélien.* Paris: Fayard, 1979.

J. Collins, *Classes, Estates, and Order in Early Modern Brittany.* Cambridge: Cambridge University Press, 1994.

_____, *The Fiscal Limits of Absolutism.* Berkeley: University of California Press, 1988.

A. Corvisier, *Louvois.* Paris: Fayard, 1983.

A. Croix, *La Bretagne aux xviè et xviiè siècles: la vie. la foi. la morte.* Paris: Malouine, 1981, two vols.

J. Dejean, *Ancients against Moderns: Culture Wars and the Making of a Fin de Siècle.* Chicago: University of Chicago Press, 1997.

D. Dessert, *Argent, pouvoir et société au Grand Siècle.* Paris: Fayard, 1984.

_____, *Fouquet.* Paris: Fayard, 1987.

_____, *La Royale: Vaisseaux et marins du Roi-Soleil.* Paris: Fayard, 1996.

J. Dewald, *Aristocratic Experience and the Origins of Modern Culture: France, 1570–1715.* Berkeley: University of California Press, 1993.

_____, *Pont-St-Pierre, 1398–1789: Lordship, Community, and Capitalism in Early–Modern France.* Berkeley: University of California Press, 1987.

A. Farge, *Subversive Words: Public Opinion in Eighteenth-Century France,* trans. R. Morris. University Park, PA: Pennsylvania State University Press, 1995. Farge has written many superb books on eighteenth-century Paris.

J. Farr, *Authority and Sexuality in Early Modern Burgundy* (1550–1730). New York: Oxford University Press, 1995.

_____, *Hands of Glory: Artisans and Their World in Dijon, 1550–1650.* Ithaca, NY: Cornell University Press, 1988.

J.-L. Flandin, *Families in Former Times: Kinship, Household and Sexuality,* trans. R. Southern. Cambridge and New York: Cambridge University Press, 1976.

M. Foisil, *La révolte des Nu-Pieds.* Paris: PUF, 1970.

P. Goubert, *Mazarin.* Paris: Fayard, 1990. Goubert has authored many other essential works, beginning with his magisterial thesis on Beauvais and its region.

H. Hall, *Richelieu's Desmarets and the Century of Louis XIV.* Oxford: Clarendon Press, 1990.

C. Havelange, *De l'œil et du monde: Une histoire du regard au seuil de la modernité.* Paris: Fayard, 1998.

D. Hickey, *The Coming of French Absolutism: The Struggle of Tax Reform in the Province of Dauphiné 1540–1640.* Toronto: University of Toronto Press, 1986.

P. Hoffman, *Growth in a Traditional Society: The French Countryside 1450–1815.* Princeton: Princeton University Press, 1996.

S. Kettering, *Judicial Politics and Urban Revolt in Seventeenth-Century France. The Parlement of Aix, 1629–1659.* Princeton: Princeton University Press, 1978.

_____, *Patrons, Brokers, and Clients in Seventeenth-Century France.* New York and Oxford: Oxford University Press, 1986.

R. Mettam, *Power and Faction in Louis XIV's France.* Oxford and New York: Basil Blackwell, 1988.

P. Minard, *La fortune du colbertisme: État et industrie dans la France des Lumières.* Paris: Fayard, 1998.

L. Moote, *Louis XIII. The Just.* Berkeley and Los Angeles: University of California Press, 1989.

_____, *The Revolt of the Judges.* Princeton: Princeton University Press, 1968.

R. Mousnier, *La Vénalité des offices.* Paris: PUF, 1945, 1970. Mousnier is the author of many books and articles. Although few current historians accept his views on early–modern French society, his model of that society continues to have an important influence on sociologists, and had a great influence both on sociologists and historians from the 1960s through the 1980s.

J.-M. Moriceau, *Les fermiers de l'Île-de-France XVe–XVIIIe siècle.* Paris: Fayard, 1994.

R. Muchembled, *L'invention de l'homme moderne.* Paris: Fayard, 1988.

C. Mukerji, *Territorial Ambitions and the Gardens of Versailles.* Cambridge: Cambridge University Press, 1997.

J.-C. Petitfils, *Le Régent.* Paris: Fayard, 1986.

A. Poitrineau, *Ils travaillaient la France: Métiers et mentalités du XVIe au XIXe siècle.* Paris: Armand Colin, 1992. Poitrineau's other works, above all his thesis on the Auvergne, provide an important contribution to eighteenth-century studies.

B. Porshnev, *Les soulèvements populaires en France avant la Fronde, 1623–1648.* Paris: SEVPEN, 1963.

E. Rapley, *The Dévotes: Women and Church in Seventeenth-Century France.* Montreal: McGill-Queen's University Press, 1990.

O. Ranum, *Artisans of Glory: Writers and Historical Thought in Seventeenth-Century France.* Chapel Hill, NC: University of North Carolina Press, 1980.

_____, *The Fronde: A French Revolution.* New York: Norton, 1993.

P. Sahlins, *Boundaries: The Making of France and Spain in the Pyrenees.* Berkeley: University of California Press, 1989.

T. Schaeper, *The French Council of Commerce, 1700–1715.* Columbus, OH: Ohio State University Press, 1983.

J.-F. Solnon, *La Cour de France.* Paris: Fayard, 1987.

R. Stein, *The French Slave Trade in the Eighteenth Century.* Madison, WI: University of Wisconsin Press, 1979. Stein also has a solid book on the French sugar trade.

P. Wells, *Law and Citizenship in Early Modern France.* Baltimore: Johns Hopkins University Press, 1995.

B. Ketcham Wheaton, *Savoring the Past: The French Kitchen and Table from 1300 to 1789.* Philadelphia: University of Pennsylvania Press, 1983.

Section III: 1750–1799

Primary Sources

The following list of primary sources merely scratches the surface of what is available for the late eighteenth century. Interested readers will want to read the great thinkers of the time, such as Rousseau and Voltaire. I have also listed below only those memoirs that I have used extensively; the list of memoirs available would run on far too long.

P. de Beaumarchais, *The Barber of Seville and the Marriage of Figaro,* trans. J. Wood. Harmondsworth: Penguin Books, 1964.

P. Beik, ed., *The French Revolution.* New York: Walker, 1970.

E. Burke and T. Paine, *Reflections on the Revolution in France and The Rights of Man.* Garden City, NY: Anchor Books, 1973.

Ch.-L. Chassin, *Les Élections et les Cahiers de Paris en 1789.* Paris: Jouast et Sigaux, 1888, four vols., Geneva reprint edition of 1967.

G. Chinard, ed., *The Letters of Lafayette and Jefferson.* Baltimore and Paris: The Johns Hopkins University Press and Les Belles Lettres, 1929.

C. Desmoulins, *Œuvres de Camille Desmoulins.* Paris: Ebrard, 1838; reprinted in New York: AMS, 1972.

The Despatches of Earl Gower, ed. O. Browning. Cambridge: Cambridge University Press, 1885.

O. Equiano, "The Interesting Life of Olaudah Equiano," in *Classic Slave Narratives,* ed. H. L. Gates. New York: Mentor, 1987. A new edition of this classic has just appeared, edited by W. Sollors, *The Interesting Narrative of the Life of Olaudah Equiano.* New York: Norton, 2001.

C. Guittard de Floriban, *Journal de Célestin Guittard de Floriban, Bourgeois de Paris sous la Révolution,* ed. R. Aubert. Paris: Éditions France-Empire, 1974.

L. Gottschalk, ed., *The Letters of Lafayette to Washington, 1777–1799*, ed. Philadelphia: American Philosophical Society, 1976.

M. Lhéritier, ed., *Les débuts de la Révolution à Bordeaux d'après les Tablettes manuscrites de Pierre Bernadau*. Paris: Société d'histoire de la Révolution Française, 1919.

J. de Maistre, *Considerations on France*, trans. and ed. R. Lebrun. Cambridge: Cambridge University Press, 1994.

J.-P. Marat, *Œuvres Politiques*, ed. J. De Cock and C. Goëtz. Brussels: Pole Nord, 1989–1993, 5 vols.

J. Ménétra, *Journal of My Life*, intro. D. Roche, trans. A. Goldhammer. New York: Columbia University Press, 1986.

G. Morris, *A Diary of the French Revolution*, ed. B. Cary Davenport. Boston: Houghton Mifflin, 1939, two vols.

N. Retif de la Bretonne, *Les Nuits Révolutionnaires, 1789–1793*, ed. M. Dorigny. Paris: Les Éditions de Paris, 1989. Excerpts taken from *Les Nuits de Paris*.

N. Ruault, *Gazette d'un Parisien sous la Révolution. Lettres à son frère, 1783–1796*, ed. A. Vassal and C. Rimbaud. Paris: Librairie Académique, 1976.

L. de Tourzel, *Mémoires de Madame la duchesse de Tourzel, gouvernante des enfants de France de 1789 à 1795*, J. Chalon, ed. Paris: Mercure de France, 1969.

G. Washington, *Writings*, ed. John Rhodehamel. New York: Literary Classics of the United States, 1997.

H. M. Williams, *An Eye-Witness Account of the French Revolution by Helen Maria Williams: Letters Containing a Sketch of the Politics of France*, J. Fruchtman, Jr., ed. New York: Peter Lang, 1997.

Witness to the Revolution: American and British Commentators in France, 1788–94. ed. P. Burley. London: Weidenfeld & Nicolson, 1989.

M. Wollstonecraft, *A Vindication of the Rights of Woman*, ed. C. Poston. New York: Norton, 1975, 1988.

A. Young, *Travels during the Years 1787, 1788 and 1789*. London: W. Richardson, 1794, three vols.

General Works

There are many multivolume histories of the Revolution. The classic ones are by Alphonse Aulard, Thomas Carlisle, Jean Jaurès, Georges Lefebvre, and Albert Mathiez. To them one must add Alexis de Tocqueville's *The Old Regime and the French Revolution*, more of an essay than a detailed look at the Revolution, but a book fundamental to any understanding of the historiography of the Revolution.

M. Bouloiseau, *The Jacobin Republic 1792–1794*, trans. J. Mandelbaum. Cambridge: Cambridge University Press, 1983.

A. Cobban, *The Social Interpretation of the French Revolution*. Cambridge: Cambridge University Press, 1964. See also volume I of Cobban's three-volume *History of Modern France*.

W. Doyle, *The Origins of the French Revolution.* Oxford and New York: Oxford University Press, 1980.

_____, *The Oxford History of the French Revolution.* Oxford and New York: Oxford University Press, 1989.

F. Furet, *Revolutionary France, 1770–1880,* trans. A. Nevill. Oxford: Basil Blackwell, 1992; Paris: Hachette, 1988.

F. Furet and M. Ozouf, *Dictionnaire Critique de la Révolution Française.* Paris: Flammarion, 1988.

G. Lefebvre, *The Coming of the French Revolution,* trans. R. R. Palmer. Princeton: Princeton University Press, 1947, 1989.

A. Soboul, *The French Revolution, 1787–1799,* trans. A. Forrest and C. Jones. New York: Random House, 1974.

D. Sutherland, *France 1789–1815, Revolution and Counter-Revolution.* New York: Oxford University Press, 1986.

M. Vovelle, *The Fall of the French Monarchy, 1787–1792,* trans. S. Burke. Cambridge: Cambridge University Press, 1983.

D. Woronoff, *The Thermidorian Regime and the Directory, 1794–1799,* trans. J. Jackson. Cambridge: Cambridge University Press, 1983.

Chapters 11–15

R. Andrews, *Law, Magistracy, and Crime in Old Regime Paris, 1735–1789.* Cambridge: Cambridge University Press, 1994.

K. Baker, *Condorcet, from Natural Philosophy to Social Mathematics.* Chicago: University of Chicago Press, 1975.

_____, ed., *The French Revolution and the Creation of Modern Political Culture.* Oxford and New York: Pergamon Press, 1987–89, four vols.

B. Barry, *Senegambia and the Atlantic Slave Trade,* trans. A. Armah. Cambridge: Cambridge University Press, 1998.

D. Bell, *Lawyers and Citizens: The Making of a Political Elite in Eighteenth-Century France.* Oxford and New York: Oxford University Press, 1994.

L. Berlanstein, *The Barristers of Toulouse in the Eighteenth Century.* Baltimore and London: Johns Hopkins University Press, 1975.

G. Bossenga, *The Politics of Privilege: Old Regime and Revolution in Lille.* Cambridge: Cambridge University Press, 1991.

T. Brennan, *Burgundy to Champagne: The Wine Trade in Early Modern France.* Baltimore: Johns Hopkins University Press, 1997.

_____, *Public Drinking and Popular Culture in Eighteenth Century Paris.* Princeton: Princeton University Press, 1988.

D. Brewer, *The Discourse of Enlightenment in Eighteenth-Century France.* Cambridge: Cambridge University Press, 1993.

R. Brubaker, *Citizenship and Nationhood in France and Germany.* Cambridge, MA: Harvard University Press, 1992.

J. Censer, ed., *The French Revolution and Intellectual History.* Chicago: Dorsey Press, 1989. This work offers a superb collection of articles that summarizes key arguments of such important historians as Furet, Hunt, Lucas, Tackett, and others.

R. Chartier, *The Cultural Origins of the French Revolution,* trans. L. Cochrane. Durham: Duke University Press, 1991.

G. Chaussinand-Nogaret, *The French Nobility in the Eighteenth Century,* trans. W. Doyle. Cambridge and New York: Cambridge University Press, 1985.

L. Chevalier, *Laboring Classes and Dangerous Classes in Paris during the First Half of the Nineteenth Century,* trans. F. Jellinek. Princeton: Princeton University Press, 1973.

R. Cobb, *Paris and Its Provinces, 1792–1802.* Oxford: Oxford University Press, 1975.

_____, *The Police and the People: French Popular Protest, 1789–1820.* Oxford: Clarendon Press, 1970. Cobb wrote many iconoclastic books on the Revolution; his work on the Revolutionary armies of 1793 to 1794 is well worth a look, too.

A. Cooper, *Slavery and the French Revolutionists (1788–1805),* trans. F. Keller. Lewiston, NY: Edwin Mellen Press, 1988.

R. Darnton, *The Forbidden Best-Sellers of Pre-Revolutionary France.* New York: Norton, 1996. Darnton has several other books on Enlightenment publishing and other topics in eighteenth-century cultural history; all are important contributions.

_____, *The Kiss of Lamourette.* New York: Norton, 1990. I particularly recommend the essay, "What was so revolutionary about the French Revolution?" in this collection. It appeared first in the *New York Review of Books.*

B. Deloche and J.-M Leniaud, *La Culture des Sans-Culottes.* Paris: Éditions de Paris, Presses de Languedoc, 1989.

W. Doyle, *Venality: The Sale of Offices in Eighteenth-Century France.* Oxford: Clarendon Press, 1996. Doyle has also authored an important book on the Parlement of Bordeaux.

J. Duguet et alia, *La Révolution Français, 1789–1799 à Rochefort.* Projets Éditions: Poitiers, 1989.

C. Fairchilds, *Domestic Enemies. Servants & Their Masters in Old Regime France.* Baltimore and London: Johns Hopkins University Press, 1984. See also the books by S. Maza and J.-P. Guitton on servants.

C. Fick, *The Making of Haiti: The Saint-Domingue Revolution from Below.* Knoxville, TN: University of Tennessee Press, 1990.

S. Fiette, *La noblesse française des Lumières à la Belle Époque.* Paris: Perrin, 1997.

F. Furet, *Interpreting the French Revolution,* trans. E. Forster. Cambridge and New York: Cambridge University Press, 1981.

D. Garrioch, *Neighbourhood and Community in Paris, 1740–1790.* Cambridge and New York: Cambridge University Press, 1986.

P. Gay, *The Enlightenment.* New York: Norton, 1969, 1977, two vols.

D. Gordon, *Citizens without Sovereignty: Equality and Sociability in French Thought, 1670–1789*. Princeton: Princeton University Press, 1994.

J. Grieder, *Anglomania in France, 1740–1789*. Geneva: Droz, 1985.

N. Hampson, *Danton*. New York: Holmes & Meier, 1978.

O. Hufton, *The Poor of Eighteenth-Century France, 1750–1789*. Oxford: Clarendon Press, 1974.

L. Hunt, *Politics, Culture, and Class in the French Revolution*. Berkeley: University of California Press, 1984.

_____, *Revolution and Urban Politics in Provincial France: Troyes and Reims, 1786–1790*. Stanford: Stanford University Press, 1978.

R. Isherwood, *Farce and Fantasy: Popular Entertainment in Eighteenth-Century Paris*. New York: Oxford University Press, 1986.

C. L. R. James, *The Black Jacobins: Toussaint Louverture and the San Domino Revolution*. London: Allison & Busby, 1936, 1980.

H. C. Johnson, *The Midi in Revolution: A Study of Regional Political Diversity, 1789–1793*. Princeton: Princeton University Press, 1986.

J. H. Johnson, *Listening in Paris: A Cultural History*. Berkeley: University of California Press, 1995.

P. Jones, *The Peasantry in the French Revolution*. Cambridge: Cambridge University Press, 1988.

S. Kaplan, *The Bakers of Paris and the Bread Question, 1700–1775*. Durham: Duke University Press, 1998. Kaplan's earlier works on the grain trade are also must reading for understanding the trade in this most critical of commodities. His delightful work on the historians' quarrel at the time of the Bicentennial (1989), *Farewell Revolution*, offers unmatched insights into the politics of Revolution historiography.

E. Kennedy, *Cultural History of the French Revolution*. New Haven: Yale University Press, 1989.

M. Kennedy, *The Jacobin Club of Marseilles*. Ithaca: Cornell University Press, 1973. Kennedy has also published three books on the history of the Jacobin clubs during the Revolution.

G. Lefebvre, *The Great Fear of 1789*, trans. J. White. New York: Pantheon, 1973. Lefebvre dominated the scholarship of the Revolution from the 1930s through the late 1950s; his thesis on the peasants of northern France during the Revolution, one of the last books he published, is of particular importance. Readers will want to compare his presentation of that issue with the one of Liana Vardi, also listed in this bibliography.

C. Lucas, *The Structure of the Terror: The Example of Javogues and the Loire*. Oxford and London: Oxford University Press, 1973.

F. Lyons, *France under the Directory*. Cambridge: Cambridge University Press, 1975.

F. Malino, *A Jew in the French Revolution: The Life of Zalkind Hourwitz*. Oxford: Blackwell, 1996.

_____, *The Sephardic Jews of Bordeaux: Assimilation and Emancipation in Revolutionary and Napoleonic France*. University, AL: The University of Alabama Press, 1978.

H. Mason, ed., *The Darnton Debate: Books and Revolution in the Eighteenth Century. Studies on Voltaire and the Eighteenth Century, 39.* Oxford: Voltaire Foundation, 1998.

A. Mathiez, *Études sur Robespierre.* Paris: Éditions sociales, 1973. Mathiez wrote many books on the Jacobin period, on topics ranging from famine to Danton.

S. Maza, *Private Lives and Public Affairs.* Berkeley: University of California Press, 1993. See also Maza's fine book on servants (*Domestic Enemies*).

M. Ozouf, *Festivals and the French Revolution,* trans. A. Sheridan. Cambridge, MA: Harvard University Press, 1988.

R. R. Palmer, *Twelve Who Ruled.* Princeton: Princeton University Press, 1941; New York: Atheneum Publishers, 1965. Palmer's study of Alexis de Tocqueville and his father (*The Two Tocquevilles*) makes for an interesting new look at the son.

J.-R. Pitte, *Gastronomie française: Histoire et géographie d'une passion.* Paris: Fayard, 1991.

M. Price, *Preserving the Monarchy: The comte de Vergennes, 1774–1787.* Cambridge: Cambridge University Press, 1995.

D. Roche, *The People of Paris,* trans. M. Evans and G. Lewis. Berkeley: University of California Press, 1987.

G. Rudé, *The Crowd in the French Revolution.* Oxford: Oxford University Press, 1959. Rudé published many fine books on the Revolution, above all on its crowds.

R. Schneider, *The Ceremonial City: Toulouse Observed 1738–1790.* Princeton: Princeton University Press, 1995.

W. Sewell, *Work and Revolution in France: The Language of Labor from the Old Regime to 1848.* Cambridge and New York: Cambridge University Press, 1980. Sewell also has an interesting book on the Abbé Sièyes.

J. Sirich, *The Revolutionary Committees in the Departments of France, 1793–94.* New York: Howard Fertig, 1971; Harvard Historical Studies, 1943.

M. Slavin, *The Hébertistes to the Guillotine: Anatomy of a "Conspiracy" in Revolutionary France.* Baton Rouge, LA: Louisiana State University Press, 1994.

M. Sonenscher, *Work and Wages: Natural Law, Politics and the Eighteenth-Century French Trades.* Cambridge: Cambridge University Press, 1989. Sonenscher's book on the hatters of eighteenth-century France provides a rare in-depth look at one craft.

J. Swann, *Politics and the Parlement of Paris under Louis XV, 1754–1774.* Cambridge: Cambridge University Press, 1995. J. Rogister's book on the same subject offers a directly contrary view to the one set out by Swann.

T. Tackett, *Priest and Parish in Eighteenth-Century France.* Princeton: Princeton University Press, 1977.

_____, *Religion, Revolution, and Regional Culture in Eighteenth-Century France: The Ecclesiastical Oath of 1791.* Princeton: Princeton University Press, 1986.

J. M. Thompson, *Robespierre*. Oxford and New York: Basil Blackwell, 1988. Thompson has also written a one-volume general history of the Revolution.

D. Troyansky, *Old Age in the Old Regime*. Ithaca, NY: Cornell University Press, 1989.

L. Vardi, *The Land and the Loom: Peasants and Profit in Northern France 1680–1800*. Durham: Duke University Press, 1993.

R. Waldinger, P. Dawson, and I. Woloch, eds., *The French Revolution and the Meaning of Citizenship*. Westport: Greenwood Press, 1993.

A. Williams, *The Police of Paris, 1718–1789*. Baton Rouge, LA: Louisiana State University Press, 1979.

The historiographical debates on the French Revolution have moved in new directions since the Bicentennial, so I have created a special sub-section for a selection of the most important recent works that focus directly on the Revolution.

F. Aftalion, *The French Revolution, an Economic Interpretation*, trans. M Thom. Cambridge: Cambridge University Press, 1990.

D. Andress, *Massacre at the Champs de Mars: Popular Dissent and Political Culture in the French Revolution*. Woodbridge, Suffolk: Royal Historical Society, Boydell Press, 2000.

H. Applewhite, *Political Alignment in the French National Assembly, 1789–1791*. Baton Rouge and London: Louisiana State University Press, 1993.

B. Baczko, *Ending the Terror: The French Revolution after Robespierre*, trans. M. Petheran. Cambridge: Cambridge University Press, 1994.

K. Baker, *Inventing the French Revolution*. Cambridge and New York: Cambridge University Press, 1990.

J. Bart, *La Révolution française en Bourgogne*. Dijon: La Française d'Édition et d'Imprimerie, 1996.

S. Bernard-Griffiths, M.-C. Chemin, and J. Ehrard, eds., *Revolution Française et "Vandalisme Revolutionnaire."* Paris: Universitas, 1992.

P. Bourdin, *Le Noir et le Rouge, itinéraire social, culturel et politique d'un prLtre patriote (1736–1799)*. Clermont-Ferrand: Presses Universitaires Blaise-Pascal, 2000.

M. Crook, *Elections in the French Revolution: An Apprenticeship in Democracy, 1789–1799*. Cambridge: Cambridge University Press, 1996.

A. de Baecque, *The Body Politic: Corporeal Metaphor in Revolutionary France, 1770–1800*. Trans. C. Mandell. Stanford: Stanford University Press, 1997.

S. Desan, *Reclaiming the Sacred: Lay Religion and Popular Politics in Revolutionary France*. Ithaca, NY: Cornell University Press, 1990.

A. Forrest, *Soldiers of the French Revolution*. Durham: Duke University Press, 1990. Those interested in military matters will also want to read the works of French scholar J.-P. Bertaud.

M. Fitzsimmons, *The Remaking of France: The National Assembly and the Constitution of 1791*. Cambridge: Cambridge University Press, 1994.

D. Godineau, *The Women of Paris and Their French Revolution,* trans. K. Streip. Berkeley: University of California Press, 1998.

P. Higonnet, *Goodness beyond Virtue: Jacobins during the French Revolution.* Cambridge, MA.: Harvard University Press, 1998.

P. Gueniffey, *La politique de la Terreur.* Paris: Fayard, 2000.

O. Hufton, *Women and the Limits of Citizenship in the French Revolution.* Toronto: University of Toronto Press, 1992.

M.-H. Huet, *Mourning Glory: The Will of the French Revolution.* Philadelphia: University of Pennsylvania Press, 1997.

L. Hunt, *The Family Romance of the French Revolution.* Berkeley: University of California Press, 1992.

J. Markoff, *The Abolition of Feudalism.* University Park, PA: Pennsylvania State University Press, 1996.

J. Markoff and G. Shapiro, *Revolutionary Demands: A Content Analysis of the Cahiers de Doléances of 1789.* Stanford: Stanford University Press, 1998.

A. Mayer, *The Furies: Violence and Terror in the French and Russian Revolutions.* Princeton: Princeton University Press, 2000.

S. E. Melzer and L. Rabine, *Rebel Daughters: Women and the French Rrevolution.* New York and Oxford: Oxford University Press, 1992.

J. Popkin, *Revolutionary News: The Press in France 1789–1799.* Durham: Duke University Press, 1990.

D. Roche, *A History of Everyday Things: The Birth of Consumption in France, 1600–1800,* trans. B. Pearce. Cambridge: Cambridge University Press, 2000. Roche has also written a fine book on the history of clothing in this period.

T. Tackett, *Becoming a Revolutionary: The Deputies of the French National Assembly and the Emergence of a Revolutionary Culture (1789–1790).* Princeton: Princeton University Press, 1996.

J. Tulard, *Les temps des passions. Espérances, Tragédies et Mythes sous la Révolution et l'Empire.* Paris: Bartillat, 1996.

J.-M. Varaut, *La Terreur judiciaire. La Révolution contre les droits de l'homme.* Paris: Perrin, 1993.

M. Vovelle, *Revolution against the Church,* trans. A. José. Columbus, OH: Ohio State University Press, 1991. Vovelle has many other important books on the Revolution and the eighteenth century, above all his writings on the history of *mentalités.*

S. Wahnich, *L'impossible citoyen. L'étranger dans le discours de la Révolution française.* Paris: Albin Michel, 1997.

I. Woloch, *The New Regime: Transformations of the French Civic Order, 1789–1820s.* New York: Norton, 1994. Woloch has written other fine books on the Jacobin clubs after Robespierre and on French veterans.

INDEX